deleted

GOTHIC LITERATURE

A Gale Critical Companion

GOTHIC LITERATURE

A Gale Critical Companion

Volume 2: Authors A-K

Foreword by *Jerrold E. Hogle, Ph.D.*
University of Arizona

Jessica Bomarito, Project Editor

THOMSON

GALE

1043-6183

Detroit • New York • San Francisco • San Diego • New Haven, Conn. • Waterville, Maine • London • Munich

THOMSON
GALE

™

Gothic Literature, Vol. 2

Project Editor
Jessica Bomarito

Editorial
Regan Blinder, Kathy D. Darrow, Jeffrey W. Hunter, Jelena O. Krstović, Julie Landelius, Michelle Lee, Ellen McGeagh, Rachelle Mucha, Thomas J. Schoenberg, Noah Schusterbauer, Lawrence J. Trudeau, Russel Whitaker

Indexing Services
Factiva

Production Services
Zott Solutions, Inc.

Permissions
Margaret Abendroth, Lori Hines, Shalice Shah-Caldwell, Kim Smilay, Andrew Specht

Imaging and Multimedia
Lezlie Light, Daniel Newell, Kelly A. Quin

Product Design
Michael Logusz, Pamela Galbreath

Composition and Electronic Capture
Carolyn Roney

Manufacturing
Rhonda Dover

Product Managers
Marc Cormier, Janet Witalec

LIBRARY OF CONGRESS CATALOGING-IN-PUBLICATION DATA

Gothic literature : a Gale critical companion / foreword by Jerrold E. Hogle ; Jessica Bomarito, project editor.
    p. cm. -- (Gale critical companion collection)
    Includes bibliographical references and index.
    ISBN 0-7876-9470-3 (set hardcover : alk. paper) -- ISBN 0-7876-9471-1 (v. 1 : alk. paper) -- ISBN 0-7876-9472-X (v. 2 : alk. paper) -- ISBN 0-7876-9473-8 (v. 3 : alk. paper)
    1. English literature--History and criticism--Handbooks, manuals, etc. 2. Gothic revival (Literature)--Great Britain--Handbooks, manuals, etc. 3. Gothic revival (Literature)--United States--Handbooks, manuals, etc. 4. Horror tales, American--History and criticism--Handbooks, manuals, etc. 5. Horror tales, English--History and criticism--Handbooks, manuals, etc. 6. American literature--History and criticism--Handbooks, manuals, etc. I. Bomarito, Jessica, 1975- II. Series.
    PR408.G68G675 2006
    820.9'11--dc22
                                                        2005011420

Printed in the United States of America
10 9 8 7 6 5 4 3 2

Contents

CONTENTS

CONTENTS

VOLUME 2

Margaret Atwood 1939-
Canadian novelist, poet, short story writer, essayist, critic, and author of children's books

Jane Austen 1775-1817
English novelist

VOLUME 3

These very useful Critical Companion volumes offer a wide range of historical accounts about, literary excerpts from, and critical interpretations of a long-standing mode of fiction-making that has come to be called "the Gothic." Though this label has most often been attached to "terrifying" or "horrific" pieces of prose fiction ever since Horace Walpole's *The Castle of Otranto* (the founding text of this form, first published in 1764) added the subtitle *A Gothic Story* to its Second British Edition of 1765, the hyperbolic and haunting features of this highly popular, but often controversial, mode have proliferated across the last two-and-a-half centuries in an increasing array of forms: novels, prose "romances," plays, paintings, operas, short stories, narrative and lyric poems, "shilling shocker" tales, newspaper serials and crime-reports, motion pictures, television shows, comic books, "graphic" novels, and even video games. That variety of presentation is what now makes "*the* Gothic" the best phrase for describing this ongoing phenomenon. It has proven to be a set of transportable features more than it has been a single genre. Its variations are not so much similar in compositional form as they are inclined to share certain settings, symbols, situations, psychological states, and emotional effects on readers or audiences, all of which appear at least somewhat in *The Castle of Otranto* but have gone on to vary greatly in their manifestations over time. The incompatible generic ingredients of the

Gothic initially—Walpole saw it as a combination of the supernatural "ancient" and the more realistic "modern" romance—have made it unstable from the start and so have led it to "expatiate" widely and wildly (Walpole's own word in his 1765 Preface) and hence to carry its volatile inconsistency into every form it has assumed, from its beginnings in mid-eighteenth century England to its current profusion throughout the Western world at the dawn of the twenty-first century.

Yet what are the traits that hold "the Gothic" together, if only just barely, as it spreads itself like one of its specters or monstrosities across literary, dramatic, and other audio-visual forms? As the following essays and excerpts show, all truly Gothic stories or stagings take place, at least part of the time, in some sort of antiquated (sometimes falsely antiquated) space, be it a castle, ruin, crumbling abbey, graveyard, old manor house or theater, haunted wilderness or neighborhood, cellar or attic full of artifacts—*or* aging train station, rusted manufacturing plant, or outdated spaceship. This space, reminiscent of *medieval* "Gothic" castles or churches but often existing long after those in more modern recastings of their features, threatens to overwhelm and engulf protagonists (including readers or viewers) in the setting's vastness, darkness, and vaguely threatening, even irrational, depths. That is usually because this space is haunted or invaded by some form of ghost, specter, or monster, a frightening crosser of the supposed boundaries between life and death, natural and supernatural, or "normal" and "abnormal." Usually this figure betokens some hidden "primal crime" buried from sight ages ago or having occurred in the recent past, the truth about which at least seems to lie in the darkest depths, or deepest darkness, of the antiquated space. Gothic protagonists and their readers or viewers, faced with this haunting in such a setting, are thus pulled back and forth (like the Gothic as a mode) between older and newer states of being, longing to escape into the seeming safety of one or the other but kept in a tug-of-war of terrifying suspense between the powers of the past and the present, darkness and daylight, insane incoherence and rational order.

At the same time, the extreme *fictionality* of all these elements is so emphasized in the melodramatic exaggeration of Gothic description and characterizations that the threats in these situations are made to seem both imminent (about to appear) and immanent (sequestered within) *and yet* safely distant, at least for readers or audiences. As in the "scary movies" of more recent times, many of which employ or derive from the Gothic, the spectators of such fictions can experience the thrill of fear that the threats really arouse and at the same time feel entirely safe from those threats because it is all so obviously artificial and unlikely to become real or lead to real consequences. Any fiction that does not have all these basic features to some extent is not really "Gothic" through and through, although many adjacent fictions (such as those of Charles Dickens or Herman Melville or most films directed by Alfred Hitchcock or M. Night Shyamalan) use *pieces* of the Gothic to arouse some of the suggestions and effects associated with it.

Even when fictions are thoroughly Gothic, however, as are the ones most emphasized in these volumes, they can vary widely across a continuum between *terror* and *horror*. Near the end of her life and career, Ann Radcliffe, arguably the most influential British author of Gothic romances in the turbulent 1790s (including *The Mysteries of Udolpho* and *The Italian*), composed a dialogue "On the Supernatural in Poetry" that appeared posthumously with her last novel, *Gaston de Blondeville*, in 1826. There her fictional interlocutors make a clear distinction between devices that invoke "the terrible" (a suspenseful uncertainty about hidden possibilities that *could* be violent or repulsive or supernatural but rarely appear in such extreme forms) and blatant descriptions that

expose "the horrible" (the unambiguously violent, deadly, grotesque, and even horrifically supernatural, so much so that the line between what is "sanctioned" and "forbidden" has been crossed without a doubt). Radcliffe herself, as her novels show, clearly prefers the suggestiveness of terror, to the point where her violence is more potential than actual and the apparently supernatural is always explained away, as is the case with many of her successors in Gothic writing. She thereby places herself and her imitators squarely in the tradition of the "sublime" defined as the safely fearful or awesome by Edmund Burke in his 1757 *A Philosophical Enquiry into the Origin of Our Ideas of the Sublime and Beautiful*.

Gothic "horror," by contrast, became most epitomized in Radcliffe's time by Matthew Lewis's *The Monk* (1796), filled as it is, not just with a vociferous anti-Catholicism that Radcliffe shares, but with explicit sexual intercourse, incestuous rape and murder, the brutal dismembering of a tyrannical nun by a mob, and the physical appearance of Satan himself as homosexually seductive. The blatantly stagey hyperbole of Lewis's style makes all this less immediate than it might otherwise be, but it also defines the "horrible" extreme of the Gothic continuum that locates the mere potentiality of "terror" at its opposite end. It thus helps establish a polarity across which the Gothic has played ever since, as it wafts between, say, Daphne du Maurier's Radcliffean *Rebecca* (1938) and William Peter Blatty's horrific *The Exorcist* (1971) and their ongoing imitators of both types. The Gothic is set off from other forms of fiction by its Walpolean features but also demarcated within itself by its leanings at times towards "terrific" suspense, on the one hand, and graphic "horror," on the other. The two come together mostly in extreme cases such as Stoker's original novel *Dracula* (1897), where suspenseful intimations about the Count's vampiric nature in "sublime" Transylvania give way to his graphic gorging of himself with the blood of a married woman before witnesses in Victorian London, after which he breaks all "normal" gender boundaries by drawing the same woman to *his* breast to suck up his own already vampiric blood. It is this whole range of Gothic possibilities that the following excerpts and accounts explore, since this anamorphic (or self-distorting) and metamorphic (or shape-shifting) form of fiction has been pulled between these extremes, we now see, from its earliest manifestations.

The tension between the terrifying and the horrible in the Gothic, moreover, has developed into another continuum of symbolic possibilities—the "psychological" versus "ontological" or supernatural Gothic—especially since 1800. If Radcliffe's heroines in the 1790s think themselves into states of fear that are finally based on associations of ideas not corroborated by the outside world, it is a small step from there to the projection of a whole state of mind into an external space that is vast, dark, and threatening more because of drives inside the observer than its own separate features. Hence the tormenting Spirits that rise in the Higher Alps at the bidding of the title character in Lord Byron's Gothic verse-drama *Manfred* (1817) are, as he admits, "The mind, the spirit, the Promethean spark, / The lightning of my being" as much as anything else. At about the same time, though, Dr. John Polidori, Byron's personal physician and occasional lover, forecasts the late Victorian coming of Dracula with his Byronic novella *The Vampyre* (1819), in which the predatory Lord Ruthven seems threatening at first only in the suspicious thoughts of the hero (Aubrey) until the latter faces the horror that his own sister "has glutted the thirst of a VAMPYRE," which Ruthven turns out to have been for centuries. In this latter case, Gothic monstrosity is granted the ontological state of being quite outside any observer, a distinct existence confirmed from multiple points of view, as in Stoker's *Dracula*. Throughout the nineteenth century, starting with the Romantic era of Byron and Polidori, the Gothic careens incessantly between the strictly psychological, where ghosts or monsters are more mental than physical, and the unabashedly supernatural in which an other-worldly horror violently invades the space of the self from outside its boundaries. When both are involved, though, the nineteenth century tilts more often towards rooting the supernatural in the psyche. That is certainly the case in Mary Shelley's *Frankenstein* (1818), now the most famous Gothic tale in history, where the half-fantastic creature composed from multiple carcasses is mostly an outsized sewing-together of his creator's most repressed, libidinous, and boundary-crossing impulses.

As supernatural levels of being have become increasingly doubted in the post-Renaissance world of the West, the terrors or horrors generated from within have become a staple of the Gothic and projected onto its haunted settings, just as much as older beliefs in seductive Satan-figures have continued to be in the vein of *The Monk, The Exorcist,* or Anne Rice's *Vampire Chronicles* (1976-2001). The most debated Gothic story in Western history may be Henry James's *The Turn of the Screw* (1898), in which the highly repressed governess of two children in a castellated old estate-house is convinced she sees the ghosts of her predecessor, Miss Jessel, and Jessel's lower-class lover, Peter Quint, but may just as likely be projecting them onto the estate-world she observes as she sublimates her own desires for an absentee Master far above her in social station. Even today, as parts of these volumes show, readers and viewers cannot be sure when they begin Gothic tales or films—though they often find out in "twist" endings (in such pictures as *The Sixth Sense* and *The Others*)—whether the haunting specters they see are the delusions of characters or unambiguously otherworldly, outside any psychological point of view. We sometimes long for the comfort of supernatural visitations but fear how much this longing comes from irrational psychic forces in ourselves and others, and the Gothic plays on and explores these apprehensions, as it has for over two hundred years.

But this last point demands a fuller answer to the most lingering question about the conflicted oddity that is the Gothic as it multiplies into all the forms explored in these volumes: Why do we have this malleable symbolic mode in Anglo-European Western culture and its former colonies, and why does this anamorphic form, torn as it is between extremes (supernatural/realistic, horrible/terrifying, really frightening/merely fictional, ontological/psychological, and others), persist from *The Castle of Otranto* in the 1760s through *Frankenstein* and *Dracula* to films, novels, and video games of today, some of which keep repeatedly adapting some of those older stories for new audiences? Numerous answers are offered in the definitional and interpretive essays that follow, as well as in some Gothic tales themselves, here excerpted at their most indicative moments. But I would like to begin the discussion by suggesting the most overriding reasons why the Gothic has arisen and why it persists as a cultural formation clearly *needed*, as well as wanted, by Western readers and audiences.

To begin with, "the Gothic" comes about at a time in the West when the oldest structures of Christian religiosity (including Roman Catholicism) and social hierarchies seemingly predetermined to the advantage of hereditary aristocrats (symbolized by their castles or estate-houses) are starting to fragment and decay, as in Walpole's principal Ghost (who appears initially in pieces), even as these receding forms hang on as standard grounds of being in the minds of many. At such a time, the older symbols of power seem increasingly hollowed out, like the ruins of medieval Gothic structures, while they also seem locations that vaguely harbor historical foundations for human minds newly liberated by the rational and scientific Enlightenment that is overthrowing the older orders by degrees in the eighteenth century. In this situation, while beliefs about the self-determining (rather than strictly hereditary) individual start to gain ascendancy and give greater weight to personal psychology over predetermined roles, Westerners face an existential anxiety about where they really come from and the orders to which they belong when the best-known external indicators of those groundings are becoming empty repositories, realms filled up with the nostalgic desires projected into them more than the metaphysical and cultural certainties once manifested by them.

As Leslie Fiedler has shown by exposing the basis of the American Gothic in *Love and Death in the American Novel* (1960), this uprooted, yet root-seeking, condition for Westerners around 1765 makes them hover between longings for past securities, though these are also seen as primitively irrational and confining, and longings for rebellion against those patriarchal schemes, which simultaneously produce a sense of guilt about the overthrow of those "fathers," making that revolution a sort of "primal crime." Guilt, after all, is what Walpole's Prince Manfred feels when he finds that his own grandfather once murdered the original founder of Otranto and usurped its birthright from the latter's heirs, the same way as the rising middle class of the eighteenth century (the main readership of the Gothic as time went on) probably felt about gradually decimating the very power-bases it now sought to occupy in place of the aristocracy. In addition, Fiedler writes, this sense of haunted guilt and uncertainties about middle-class entitlement raised "the fear that in destroying the old ego-ideals of Church and State, the West has opened a way for the inruption of darkness: for insanity and the disintegration of the self." The Gothic of Walpole and its acceleration by the 1790s in Radcliffe and Lewis come about, since fictions always respond to the needs of their audiences, to address and symbolize this cultural and psychological condition of early capitalist and pre-industrial modernity. That is why the early Gothic places both desires for lost foundations *and* fears about the irrational darkness lying outside the limits of newly enlightened reason in the same antiquated spaces and their mysterious depths, which Gothic characters from Manfred to Lewis's monk then seek to penetrate

or recover and escape or destroy so as to construct a sense of identity that is somehow both grounded and self-determined. The Gothic is a powerful symbolic indicator, then, of the social and psychic contradictions out of which the modern Western self emerged and keeps emerging, and we need and want it, I would argue, to keep retelling that story that is so basic to our modern sense of ourselves.

The story has kept developing in the West, however, and the Gothic has developed with it. As the ideological belief in personal self-making becomes even more accepted towards the end of the eighteenth and the beginning of the nineteenth centuries, the individual mind comes to be viewed as the dynamic, but also anxious, site of its own "ghosts" and increasing depths. Ann Radcliffe and many of her contemporaries accept the basic premises of empirical psychology, which claims (since John Locke in the 1690s, anyway) that the human mind begins as a near-vacancy and gradually accumulates and organizes the memories it retains (hence the "ghosts") of earlier and more recent sense-perceptions. Adult observations in later life are therefore colored by the associations of previous, and now ghost-like, impressions that are applied to the intake of newer phenomena. Terry Castle can consequently see in *The Female Thermometer* (1995) that the Radcliffean Gothic turns landscapes as well as characters into "spectralized" thoughts within reflective states of mind that make nature seem already painted (and thus filtered by perceivers) and people already colored by older sayings and texts about their "types." To observe at any moment in the Gothic from the 1790s on is to call attention, at least some of the time, to the lenses of perception and the gradually accumulated psychic layers of associated memories that are projected onto any object contemplated or produced by the perceiving self. Ruins and old houses, as well as Frankenstein-ian creatures, are now filled with dark indications of deep past threats because the mind transfers its own layers of developing perceptions, as well as middle-class guilt, into what it sees and thus confronts its own "doubling" there, its deepest internal memories reembodied in perceptions of external depths now haunted by mental ghosts. When Victor Frankenstein first sees the face of his finished creature in Mary Shelley's Gothic book, he falls into a regressive dream in which the mottled visage of his fabrication from dead bodies becomes linked to his longing for his own deceased mother, whose corpse he pre-consciously has seen himself re-embracing while he tries to make life out of death without the biological involvement of a woman. By 1820 at least, the Gothic has become the fictional *locus* where outward quests for self-completion now are seen as mainly inward probings through the archaic layers of the self. Gothic "objects," from antiquated locations to other people to mere things, have thus become manifestations of the perceiver's own growing depths of thought in which the desire for pre-rational foundations is actually pursuing "the mother" conceived of as the initial interplay of self and other that produces the confused beginnings, later repressed, of all thought, sensation, and memory.

It is no wonder, then, that the Gothic comes to be torn constantly between terror and horror, on one level, and the psychological and the clearly supernatural, on another. Terror offers the uneasy comfort that what we fear, being mentally constructed for the most part, could be non-existent in the end (as in Radcliffe's conclusions), except in our own minds. Such solipsism, however, can also be seen as a myopic middle-class or even aristocratic avoidance of the violent upheavals and even greater displacements of older orders brought on by the exploding mercantile and industrial economies—and the racist imperialism that went with them—in the nineteenth century. Consequently, this era's Gothic invasions of the isolated psyche by "horror," the external violence and many forms of non-middle-class "ugliness" that cannot be wished away as mere thought, force this counter-awareness on audiences, albeit through extreme fictionality, increasingly so in the form of the vampire made prominent by Polidori. By the time of the serialized *Varney the Vampire* (1847), usually attributed to Thomas Peckett Prest, and the many stagings of vampire plays in Victorian England, France, and America, this Gothic monster can symbolize many potential invaders of middle-class security simultaneously, from vengeful old aristocrats to foreign and racial "others" to diseases of the blood made more virulent by urban growth, foreign tourism, and the expansion of prostitution. The nineteenth century in the West, we can say, needs the Gothic to carry out and fictively obscure the cultural hesitation at the time between middle-class withdrawal into increasing private spaces, including sheer thought (which thereby confronts its own deep irrationalities), and the need of the same people to face the horrors of growing cities and empires with their illnesses, "unclean" impoverished laborers, exploited women, and enslaved "colored" races.

What the Gothic does in part, among its reaction to these changes, is to increase the struggle between its psychological and supernatural tendencies. First, it becomes the source of many symbols for the concept of the "unconscious" that Sigmund Freud, building on many others, brought into wide prominence by the end of the nineteenth century and the early decades of the twentieth. Especially insofar as the Gothic has gradually become a realm of mental projection and of the mind forced back to the beginnings and hauntings of its own development, it has provided the archaic depths, dim repositories, memory-traces, accumulations of memories layer upon layer, and primal states (including regressions back to "mother" or sheer vacancy) from which Freud and his contemporaries craft their description of the unconscious and its sublimation by pre-conscious and conscious levels of thought. In the early twentieth century, the Gothic therefore comes to be seen as primarily psychological in the sense of *psychoanalytic,* as long having manifested in its haunted spaces and the mental quandaries of its characters the processes of thought described by Freud, even though it is more accurate to say that the Gothic first helped make Freud's schemes conceivable and expressible. Back in Freud's formative period, though, the assertion of the human species's long physical evolution by Charles Darwin and others from the 1850s on challenges the layerings of personal consciousness with a biologically historical progression beyond, yet still working inside, individual people. The Gothic reacts by reinvoking its old invasions of supernatural, or at least trans-individual, forces to show psychological projections running up against pervasive external drives that may really control the psyche after all. Robert Louis Stevenson's *Strange Case of Dr. Jekyll and Mr. Hyde* (1886) may seem to suggest a psychological bifurcation in the Victorian self, with Jekyll as internalized *superego* and Hyde as raging *libido,* but the Doctor's attempts to control this internal split finally cannot prevent the "troglodytic" emergence of all that remains primitively *de*volved in his superficially *e*volved condition. Even more dramatically, Stoker's Count Dracula arouses and enacts unconscious libidinal desires by being a devolved, "child-brain" force supernaturally driving across centuries that invades "civilized" England with all the diseases and the racial and animalistic "others" that the supposedly evolved want to keep distant from themselves and cannot. *The Turn of the Screw* plays out an undecidability between the dominance of the psychological and the power of the supernatural because the nineteenth-century West in its final years needs ways to articulate that it is frantically at odds with itself over what to believe about the deepest foundations of life.

The Gothic from its beginnings and as it evolves with the cultural changes around it, in other words, turns out to be the modern Western world's most striking, if most conflicted, symbolic method for both confronting and disguising its own unresolved struggles with incompatible beliefs about what it means to be human. Walpole's *Castle* starts the tradition by leaving its readers caught where most of them already were: between longings for a fading hierarchical order underwritten by supernatural assurances ("ancient romance") and desires for greater self-determination based on free re-imaginings of uprooted older perceptions ("modern romance"). Radcliffe and Lewis, during the revolutionary 1790s, help readers confront and prevent cultural dissolution by offering reassurances that spectral perceptions of danger to the self can finally control the terror those specters produce *and* shocking revelations *at the same time* that current upheavals are but symptoms of multiple irrationalities that established religion and governments have tried to repress only to force them towards more extreme violence. *Frankenstein* offers a condemnation and a celebration of the scientific and industrial advances puzzled over by its readers, along with symbols for the unsettled debate over whether life is externally infused (by, say, some ultimate Father) or internally generated (primarily within the mother whom Victor both remembers and tries to forget). *Jekyll and Hyde* and *Dracula* both blame individual free will for inviting its underlying depravities into consciousness and point to attacks on the evolved Anglo race by "devolved" levels of humanity from other times and places. In extreme forms of expression that allow us to perceive or avoid such levels in our thinking, the Gothic holds up to us our conflicted conservative *and* progressive tendencies in the full cry of their unresolved tug-of-war in our culture and in ourselves. Our hesitation between psychological and supernatural causes for events *or* between inherited and self-determined foundations of identity *or* between feeling controlled by our pasts and asserting our capacities to alter ourselves decisively in the present: all these still-active antinomies of modern existence are what the Gothic is fundamentally generated to articulate *and* to obscure.

Over one hundred years after Stoker's *Dracula*, of course, the kinds of tendencies we are torn between have changed somewhat, as the more recent Gothic certainly shows. We both want to transcend, even forget, and want to throw ourselves fully into the past (or is it fully past?) condition of slavery and racism that haunts the history of America in William Faulkner's *Absalom, Absalom!* (1936) and Toni Morrison's *Beloved* (1987). We want to preserve childhood innocence and see it as really filled with dark drives to be conquered and controlled in Stephen King's *The Shining* (1977) and Daniel Mann's *Willard* (1982) as well as *The Exorcist* and its "prequels" and sequels on film. We paranoiacally want to find evidence of old conspiracies that explain our current confusions of values and see them as but the imaginings of diseased nostalgic minds in the quite Gothic *X-Files* television series (1993-2002) or the four *Alien* films (1979-97) full of Gothic echoes. Still, the Gothic, as the accounts and excerpts in these volumes will reveal in fuller detail, remains one of the key ways we come to terms, while also avoiding direct confrontation, with the betwixt-and-between, regressive-progressive, seemingly predetermined-hopefully *un*determined nature of modern life. The Gothic is complex and tangled in its proliferations, but fairly simple in its aims: it allows us to play with our inexplicable and haunted modern lives in some fictional safety while concurrently helping us give shape and form to the conflicted beings we really are. I therefore invite our readers to enjoy and ponder the following descents into the Gothic maelstrom of pleasure and fear that reveals so much about modern Western existence.

—*Jerrold E. Hogle, Ph.D.*
University of Arizona

The Gale Critical Companion Collection

In response to a growing demand for relevant criticism and interpretation of perennial topics and important literary movements throughout history, the Gale Critical Companion Collection (GCCC) was designed to meet the research needs of upper high school and undergraduate students. Each edition of GCCC focuses on a different literary movement or topic of broad interest to students of literature, history, multicultural studies, humanities, foreign language studies, and other subject areas. Topics covered are based on feedback from a standing advisory board consisting of reference librarians and subject specialists from public, academic, and school library systems.

The GCCC is designed to complement Gale's existing Literary Criticism Series (LCS), which includes such award-winning and distinguished titles as *Nineteenth-Century Literature Criticism* (*NCLC*), *Twentieth-Century Literary Criticism* (*TCLC*), and *Contemporary Literary Criticism* (*CLC*). Like the LCS titles, the GCCC editions provide selected reprinted essays that offer an inclusive range of critical and scholarly response to authors and topics widely studied in high school and undergraduate classes; however, the GCCC also includes primary source documents, chronologies, sidebars, supplemental photographs, and other material not included in the LCS products. The graphic and supplemental material is designed to extend the usefulness of the critical essays and provide students with historical and cultural context on a topic or author's work. GCCC titles will benefit larger institutions with ongoing subscriptions to Gale's LCS products as well as smaller libraries and school systems with less extensive reference collections. Each edition of the GCCC is created as a stand-alone set providing a wealth of information on the topic or movement. Importantly, the overlap between the GCCC and LCS titles is 15% or less, ensuring that LCS subscribers will not duplicate resources in their collection.

Editions within the GCCC are either single-volume or multi-volume sets, depending on the nature and scope of the topic being covered. Topic entries and author entries are treated separately, with entries on related topics appearing first, followed by author entries in an A-Z arrangement. Each volume is approximately 500 pages in length and includes approximately 50 images and sidebar graphics. These sidebars include summaries of important historical events, newspaper clippings, brief biographies of important figures, complete poems or passages of fiction written by the author, descriptions of events in the related arts (music, visual arts, and dance), and so on.

The reprinted essays in each GCCC edition explicate the major themes and literary techniques of the authors and literary works. It is important to note that approximately 85% of the essays reprinted in GCCC editions are full-text, meaning that they are reprinted in their entirety, including footnotes and lists of abbreviations. Essays are selected based on their coverage of the seminal works and themes of an author, and based on the importance of those essays to an appreciation of the author's contribution to the movement and to literature in general. Gale's editors select those essays of most value to upper high school and undergraduate students, avoiding narrow and highly pedantic interpretations of individual works or of an author's canon.

Scope of Gothic Literature

Gothic Literature, the fourth set in the Gale Critical Companion Collection, consists of three volumes. Each volume includes a detailed table of contents, a foreword on the subject of Gothic literature written by noted scholar Jerrold E. Hogle, and a descriptive chronology of key events throughout the history of the genre. The main-body of volume 1 consists of entries on five topics relevent to Gothic literature and art, including 1) Gothic Literature: An Overview; 2) Society, Culture, and the Gothic; 3) Gothic Themes, Settings, and Figures; 4) Performing Arts and The Gothic; and 5) Visual Arts and the Gothic. Volumes 2 and 3 include entries on thirty-seven authors and literary figures associated with the genre, including such notables as Matthew Gregory Lewis, Stephen King, Edgar Allan Poe, Ann Radcliffe, Mary Wollstonecraft Shelley, and Bram Stoker, as well as entries on individuals who have garnered less attention, but whose contributions to the genre are noteworthy, such as Joanna Baillie, Daphne du Maurier, Washington Irving, Edith Wharton, and Oscar Wilde.

Organization of Gothic Literature

A *Gothic Literature* topic entry consists of the following elements:

- The ***Introduction*** defines the subject of the entry and provides social and historical information important to understanding the criticism.

- The list of ***Representative Works*** identifies writings and works by authors and figures associated with the subject. The list is divided into alphabetical sections by name; works listed under each name appear in chronological order. The genre and publication date of each work is given. Unless otherwise indicated, plays are dated by first performance, not first publication.

- Entries generally begin with a section of ***Primary Sources,*** which includes essays, speeches,

social history, newspaper accounts and other materials that were produced during the time covered.

- Reprinted ***Criticism*** in topic entries is arranged thematically. Topic entries commonly begin with general surveys of the subject or essays providing historical or background information, followed by essays that develop particular aspects of the topic. For example, the Gothic Themes, Settings, and Figures entry in volume 1 of *Gothic Literature* begins with a section providing primary source material that demonstrates gothic themes, settings, and figures. This is followed by a section providing topic overviews, and three other sections: Haunted Dwellings and the Supernatural; Psychology and the Gothic; and Vampires. Each section has a separate title heading and is identified with a page number in the table of contents. The critic's name and the date of composition or publication of the critical work are given at the beginning of each piece of criticism. Unsigned criticism is preceded by the title of the source in which it appeared. Footnotes are reprinted at the end of each essay or excerpt. In the case of excerpted criticism, only those footnotes that pertain to the excerpted texts are included.

- A complete ***Bibliographical Citation*** of the original essay or book precedes each piece of criticism.

- Critical essays are prefaced by brief ***Annotations*** explicating each piece. Unless the descriptor "excerpt" is used in the annotation, the essay is being reprinted in its entirety.

- An annotated bibliography of ***Further Reading*** appears at the end of each entry and suggests resources for additional study. In some cases, significant essays for which the editors could not obtain reprint rights are included here.

A *Gothic Literature* author entry consists of the following elements:

- The ***Author Heading*** cites the name under which the author most commonly wrote, followed by birth and death dates. Also located here are any name variations under which an author wrote. If the author wrote consistently under a pseudonym, the pseudonym will be listed in the author heading and the author's actual name given in parenthesis on the first line of the biographical and critical information. Uncertain birth or death dates are indicated by question marks.

- A *Portrait of the Author* is included when available.

- The **Introduction** contains background information that introduces the reader to the author that is the subject of the entry.

- The list of **Principal Works** is ordered chronologically by date of first publication and lists the most important works by the author. The genre and publication date of each work is given. Unless otherwise indicated, plays are dated by first performance, not first publication.

- Author entries are arranged into three sections: **Primary Sources, General Commentary,** and **Title Commentary.** The Primary Sources section includes letters, poems, short stories, journal entries, and essays written by the featured author. General Commentary includes overviews of the author's career and general studies; Title Commentary includes in-depth analyses of seminal works by the author. Within the Title Commentary section, the reprinted criticism is further organized by title, then by date of publication. The critic's name and the date of composition or publication of the critical work are given at the beginning of each piece of criticism. Unsigned criticism is preceded by the title of the source in which it appeared All titles by the author featured in the text are printed in boldface type. However, not all boldfaced titles are included in the author and subject indexes; only substantial discussions of works are indexed. Footnotes are reprinted at the end of each essay or excerpt. In the case of excerpted criticism, only those footnotes that pertain to the excerpted texts are included.

- A complete **Bibliographical Citation** of the original essay or book precedes each piece of criticism.

- Critical essays are prefaced by brief **Annotations** explicating each piece. Unless the descriptor "excerpt" is used in the annotation, the essay is being reprinted in its entirety.

- An annotated bibliography of **Further Reading** appears at the end of each entry and suggests resources for additional study. In some cases, significant essays for which the editors could not obtain reprint rights are included here. A list of **Other Sources from Thomson Gale** follows the Further Reading section and provides references to other biographical and critical sources on the author in series published by Gale.

Indexes

The **Author Index** lists all of the authors featured in the *Gothic Literature* set, with references to the main author entries in volumes 2 and 3 as well as commentary on the featured author in other author entries and in the topic volumes. Page references to substantial discussions of the authors appear in boldface. Authors featured in sidebars are indexed as well. The Author Index also includes birth and death dates and cross references between pseudonyms and actual names, and cross references to other Gale series in which the authors have appeared. A complete list of these sources is found facing the first page of the Author Index.

The **Title Index** alphabetically lists the titles of works written by the authors featured in volumes 2 and 3 and provides page numbers or page ranges where commentary on these titles can be found. Page references to substantial discussions of the titles appear in boldface. English translations of foreign titles and variations of titles are cross-referenced to the title under which a work was originally published. Titles of novels, plays, nonfiction books, films, and poetry, short story, or essay collections are printed in italics, while individual poems, short stories, and essays are printed in roman type within quotation marks.

The **Subject Index** includes the authors and titles that appear in the Author Index and the Title Index as well as the names of other authors and figures that are discussed in the set. The Subject Index also lists hundreds of literary terms and topics covered in the criticism. The index provides page numbers or page ranges where subjects are discussed and is fully cross referenced.

Citing Gothic Literature

When writing papers, students who quote directly from the *GL* set may use the following general format to footnote reprinted criticism. The first example pertains to material drawn from periodicals, the second to material reprinted from books.

Markley, A. A. "The Godwinian Confessional Narrative and Psychological Terror in *Arthur Gordon Pym.*" *The Edgar Allan Poe Review* 4, no. 1 (spring 2003): 4-16; reprinted in *Gothic Literature: A Gale Critical Companion,* vol. 3, ed. Jessica Bomarito (Farmington Hills, Mich.: Thomson Gale, 2006), 29-42.

Mishra, Vijay. "Theorizing the (Gothic) Sublime," in *The Gothic Sublime* (Albany: State University of New York Press, 1994), 19-43; reprinted in *Gothic Literature: A Gale Critical Companion,* vol. 1, ed. Jessica Bomarito (Farmington Hills, Mich.: Thomson Gale, 2006), 211-17.

Gothic Literature *Advisory Board*

The members of the *Gothic Literature* Advisory Board—reference librarians and subject specialists from public, academic, and school library systems—offered a variety of informed perspectives on both the presentation and content of the *Gothic Literature* set. Advisory board members assessed and defined such quality issues as the relevance, currency, and usefulness of the author coverage, critical content, and topics included in our product; evaluated the layout, presentation, and general quality of our product; provided feedback on the criteria used for selecting authors and topics covered in our product; identified any gaps in our coverage of authors or topics, recommending authors or topics for inclusion; and analyzed the appropriateness of our content and presentation for various user audiences, such as high school students, undergraduates, graduate students, librarians, and educators. We wish to thank the advisors for their advice during the development of *Gothic Literature*

Suggestions are Welcome

Readers who wish to suggest new features, topics, or authors to appear in future volumes of the Gale Critical Companion Collection, or who have other suggestions or comments are cordially invited to call, write, or fax the Product Manager.

Product Manager, Gale Critical Companion
  Collection
Thomson Gale
27500 Drake Road
Farmington Hills, MI 48331-3535
1-800-347-4253 (GALE)
Fax: 248-699-8054

The editors wish to thank the copyright holders of the excerpted criticism included in this volume and the permissions managers of many book and magazine publishing companies for assisting us in securing reproduction rights. We are also grateful to the staffs of the Detroit Public Library, the Library of Congress, the University of Detroit Mercy Library, Wayne State University Purdy/Kresge Library Complex, and the University of Michigan Libraries for making their resources available to us. Following is a list of the copyright holders who have granted us permission to reproduce material in this edition of *Gothic Literature*. Every effort has been made to trace copyright, but if omissions have been made, please let us know.

Copyrighted material in Gothic Literature *was reproduced from the following periodicals:*

Americana: The Journal of American Popular Culture (1900-present), v. 2, spring, 2003. Copyright © 2003 Americana: The Institute for the Study of American Popular Culture. Reproduced by permission.—*American Transcendental Quarterly*, v. 9, March 1, 1995; v. 1, 2001. Copyright © 1995, 2001 by The University of Rhode Island. Both reproduced by permission.—*Arizona Quarterly*, v. 34, 1978 for "The Gothic Formula of 'Bartleby'" by Steven T. Ryan. Copyright © 1978 by Arizona Board of Regents, The University of Arizona, Tucson, AZ. Reproduced by permission of the publisher and author.—*Bucknell Review*, v. XII, May, 1964. Reproduced by permission.—*College English*, v. 27, March 1, 1966 for "Dr. Jekyll and the Emergence of Mr. Hyde" by Masao Miyoshi. Republished in *The Divided Self: A Perspective on the Literature of the Victorians*, New York University Press, 1969, University of London Press, 1969. Copyright © 1966 by the National Council of Teachers of English. Reproduced by permission of the publisher and author.—*Comparative Literature Studies*, v. 24, 1987. Copyright © 1987 by The Pennsylvania State University. Reproduced by permission of the publisher.—*Costerus*, v. I, 1972. Copyright © Editions Rodopi B.V. Reproduced by permission.—*Critical Survey*, v. 15, September, 2003. Copyright © 2003 by Critical Survey. Republished with permission of Critical Survey, conveyed through Copyright Clearance Center, Inc.—*Dalhousie Review*, v. 47, summer, 1967 for "Terror Made Relevant: James's Ghost Stories" by Raymond Thorberg. Reproduced by permission of the publisher and author.—*Deutsche Vierteljahrsschrift für Literaturwissenschaft und Geistesgeschichte*, March 1, 2001 for "The Gothic IMAGINARY: Goethe in Strasbourg" by Kenneth S. Calhoon. Reproduced by permission of the author.—*Dickens Quarterly*, September 1, 1989; v. 16, September 1, 1999. Copyright © 1989, 1999 by the Dickens Society. Both reproduced by permission.—*Dickens Studies Newsletter*, v. VI, September 1, 1975. Copyright © by the Dickens Society. Reproduced by permission.—*Dickensian*, September 1, 1977 for "The Fall of the House of Clennam: Gothic Conventions in Little Dorrit" by

David Jarrett. Reproduced by permission of the author.—*The Edgar Allan Poe Review,* v. IV, spring, 2003 for "The Godwinian Confessional Narrative and Psychological Terror in Arthur Gordon Pym" by A.A. Markley. Copyright © 2003 The Pennsylvania State University. Reproduced by permission of the publisher and author.—*Eighteenth-Century Fiction,* v. 15, January 1, 2003. Copyright © 2003 Eighteenth-Century Fiction, McMaster University. Reproduced by permission.—*ELH,* v. 48, autumn, 1981; v. 59, spring, 1992; v. 70, winter, 2003. Copyright © 1981, 1992, 2003 The Johns Hopkins University Press. All reproduced by permission.—*ESQ: A Journal of the American Renaissance,* v. 18, 1972 for "Poe and the Gothic Tradition" by Maurice Lévy. Translated by Richard Henry Haswell. Reproduced by permission of the publisher and the translator.—*European Romantic Review,* v. 13, June 1, 2002 for "Interracial Sexual Desire in Charlotte Dacre's Zofloya" by Anne K. Mellor. Copyright © 2002 Taylor & Francis Ltd. Reproduced by permission of the publisher and author. http://www.tandf.co.uk/journals—*Faulkner Journal,* v. II, fall, 1986. Copyright © 1987 by Ohio Northern University. Reproduced by permission.—*German Life and Letters,* v. XVIII, 1964-1965. Copyright © 1964-1965 Basil Blackwell Ltd. Reproduced by permission of Blackwell Publishers.—*Gothic. New Series,* v. I, 1986; 1987; v. II, 1987. Copyright © 1986, 1987 by Gary William Crawford. All reproduced by permission of the author.—*Journal of Evolutionary Psychology,* v. X, August 1, 1989. Copyright © 1989 by the Institute for Evolutionary Psychology. Reproduced by permission.—*Journal of Popular Culture,* v. 13, 1979; v. 26, winter, 1992; v. 30, spring, 1997. Copyright © 1979, 1992, 1997 Basil Blackwell Ltd. All reproduced by permission of Blackwell Publishers.—*Literature/Film Quarterly,* v. 21, 1993. Copyright © 1993 Salisbury State College. Reproduced by permission.—*Malahat Review,* 1977 for "Atwood Gothic" by Eli Mandel. Copyright © The Malahat Review, 1977. All rights reserved. Reproduced by permission of the Literary Estate of the author.—*Mississippi Quarterly,* v. XLII, summer, 1989. Copyright © 1989 by Mississippi State University. Reproduced by permission.—*Modern Fiction Studies,* v. XVII, summer, 1971; v. 46, fall, 2000. Copyright © 1971, 2000 The Johns Hopkins University Press. Both reproduced by permission.—*Mosaic,* v. 35, 2002; v. 35, March 1, 2002. Copyright © Mosaic 2002. All acknowledgment of previous publication is herewith made.—*Narrative,* v. 12, January 1, 2004. Copyright © 2004 by the Ohio State University. Reproduced by permission.—*The Nation and The Athenaeum,* v. XXXIII, May 26, 1923. Copyright 1923 New Statesman, Ltd. Reproduced by permission.—*New York Times Book Review,* March 8, 1953 for "The Macabre and the Unexpected" by John Barkham. Copyright 1953, renewed 1981 by The New York Times Company. Reproduced by permission of the Literary Estate of John Barkham.—*Papers on Language and Literature,* v. 20, winter, 1984; v. 37, winter, 2001. Copyright © 1984, 2001 by The Board of Trustees, Southern Illinois University at Edwardsville. Both reproduced by permission.—*Princeton University Library Chronicle,* v. XLIV, spring, 1983 for "A Story Replete with Horror" by Williston R. Benedict. Copyright © 1983 by Princeton University Library. Reproduced by permission of the author.—*Prism(s): Essays in Romanticism,* v. 9, 2001. Copyright © 2001 by the American Conference on Romanticism. Reproduced by permission.—*Review of Contemporary Fiction,* fall, 1994. Copyright © 1994 The Review of Contemporary Fiction. Reproduced by permission.—*Review of English Studies,* v. XIX, 1968. Reproduced by permission of the publisher.—*The Saturday Review of Literature,* v. XVIII, September 24, 1938 for "Sinister House," by Basil Davenport. Copyright © 1938, renewed 1966 Saturday Review Magazine, © 1979 General Media International, Inc. Reproduced by permission of the publisher.—*Studies in American Fiction,* v. 7, spring, 1979. Copyright © 1979 Northeastern University. Reproduced by permission.—*Studies in English Literature 1500-1900,* v. 39, autumn, 1999. Copyright © 1999 The Johns Hopkins University Press. Reproduced by permission.—*Studies in the Literary Imagination,* v. VII, spring, 1974. Copyright © 1974 Department of English, Georgia State University. Reproduced by permission.—*Studies in the Novel,* v. IX, summer, 1977. Copyright © 1977 by North Texas State University. Reproduced by permission.—*Studies in Romanticism,* v. 40, spring, 2001. Copyright 2001 by the Trustees of Boston University. Reproduced by permission.—*Studies in Scottish Literature,* v. XXVIII, 1993. Copyright © G. Ross Roy 1993. Reproduced by permission of the editor.—*Studies in Short Fiction,* v. 21, fall, 1984. Copyright © 1984 by Studies in Short Fiction. Reproduced by permission.—*Studies in Weird Fiction,* spring, 1990; winter, 1994; v. 24, winter, 1999. Copyright © 1990, 1994, 1999 Necronomicon Press. All reproduced by permission of the author.—*Studies on Voltaire and the Eighteenth Century, Transactions of the Eighth International Congress on the Enlightenment III,* v. 305, 1992 for "The Gothic Caleb Williams" by Betty Rizzo. Copyright © 1992 University of Oxford. Reproduced by permission of the publisher and author.—*Victorian Newsletter,* fall, 2002 for "Who Is Heathcliff? The Shadow Knows" by Marilyn Hume. Reproduced by permission of the publisher and author.—*West Virginia University Philological Papers,* v. 42-43, 1997-1998. Reproduced by permission.—*Wordsworth Circle,* v. 31, summer, 2000; v. 34, spring, 2003. Copyright © 2000, 2003 Marilyn Gaull. Both reproduced by permission of the editor.

Copyrighted material in Gothic Literature *was reproduced from the following books:*

Andriano, Joseph. From *Our Ladies of Darkness: Feminine Daemonology in Male Gothic Fiction.* The Pennsylvania State University Press, 1993. Copyright © 1993 by The Pennsylvania State University. Reproduced by permission of the publisher.—Atwood, Margaret. From *The Animals in That Country.* Atlantic-Little Brown Books, 1969. Copyright © 1968 by Oxford University Press (Canadian Branch). All rights reserved. Reproduced by permission of Houghton Mifflin Company, in Canada by Oxford University Press.—Auerbach, Nina. From *Our Vampires, Ourselves.* University of Chicago Press, 1995. Copyright © 1995 by The University of Chicago. All rights reserved. Reproduced by permission of the publisher and the author.—Baldick, Chris. From an Introduction to *Melmoth the Wanderer.* Edited by Douglas Grant. Oxford University Press, 1989. © Oxford University Press 1968, Introduction and Select Biography © Chris Beldick 1989. Reproduced by permission of Oxford University Press.—Bayer-Berenbaum, Linda. From *The Gothic Imagination: Expansion in Gothic Literature and Art.* Fairleigh Dickinson University Press, 1982. Copyright © 1982 by Associated University Presses, Inc. Reproduced by permission.—Bell, Michael Davitt. From *The Development of American Romance: The Sacrifice of Relation.* The University of Chicago Press, 1980. Copyright © 1980 by The University of Chicago. All rights reserved. Reproduced by permission.—Bleiler, E. F. From "Introduction: William Beckford and *Vathek," in Three Gothic Novels:* **The Castle of Otranto, Vathek, The Vampyre.** Edited by E.F. Bleiler. Dover Publications, 1966. Copyright © 1966 by Dover Publications, Inc. Reproduced by permission.—Botting, Fred. From *Gothic.* Routledge, 1996. Copyright © 1996 Fred Botting. Reproduced by permission of the publisher and author.—Botting, Fred. From "Reflections of Excess: Frankenstein, the French Revolution, and Monstrosity," in *Reflections of Excess: Frankenstein, the French Revolution and Monstrosity.* Edited by Allison Yarrington and Kelvin Everest. Routledge, 1993. Reproduced by permission of Taylor & Francis, the editor, and author.—Botting, Fred. From *Gothic.* Routledge, 1996. Copyright © 1996 by Fred Botting. All rights reserved. Reproduced by permission of the pub-

lisher and the author.—Brantly, Susan C. From *Understanding Isak Dinesen.* University of South Carolina Press, 2002. Copyright © 2002 University of South Carolina Press. Reproduced by permission.—Brennan, Matthew C. From *The Gothic Psyche: Disintegration and Growth in Nineteenth-Century English Literature.* Camden House, 1997. Copyright © 1997 by the Editor and Contributors. All rights reserved. Reproduced by permission.—Brown, Jane K. and Marshall Brown. From "Faust and the Gothic Novel," in *Interpreting Goethe's Faust Today.* Edited by Jane K. Brown, Meredith Lee, and Thomas P. Saine. Camden House, 1994. Copyright © 1994 by Camden House, Inc. Reproduced by permission.—Bulwer-Lytton, Edward George. From "Glenallan," in *Gothic Tales of Terror. Volume One: Classic Horror Stories from Great Britain.* Taplinger Publishing Company, Inc., 1972. Copyright © 1972 selection and original material by Peter Haining. Reproduced by permission of the editor.—Burns, Sarah. From *Painting the Dark Side: Art and the Gothic Imagination in Nineteenth-Century America.* University of California Press, 2004. Copyright © 2004 by The Regents of the University of California. Reproduced by permission.—Casebeer, Edwin F. From "Stephen King's Canon: The Art of Balance," in *A Dark Night's Dreaming: Contemporary American Horror Fiction.* Edited by Tony Magistrale and Michael A. Morrison. University of South Carolina Press, 1996. Copyright © 1996 by the University of South Carolina. Reproduced by permission.—Clery, E. J. From "The Politics of the Gothic Heroine in the 1790s," in *Reviewing Romanticism.* Edited by Philip W. Martin and Robin Jarvis. MacMillan Academic and Professional Ltd., 1992. Editorial matter and selection Copyright © Philip W. Martin and Robin Jarvis, 1992. Text Copyrights © Macmillan Academic and Professional Ltd, 1992. Reproduced with permission of Palgrave Macmillan.—Clery, E. J. From *Women's Gothic: From Clara Reeve to Mary Shelley.* Northcote House Publishers, Ltd., 2000, 2004. Copyright © 2000 and 2004 by E. J. Clery. Reproduced by permission.—Clery, Emma. From "Against Gothic," in *Gothick Origins and Innovations.* Edited by Allan Lloyd Smith and Victor Sage. Rodopi, 1994. Copyright © Editions Rodopi B.V. Reproduced by permission.—Conger, Syndy M. From "An Analysis of *The Monk* and Its German Sources," in *Matthew G. Lewis, Charles Robert Maturin and the Germans: An Interpretive Study of the Influence of German Literature on Two Gothic Novels.* Edited by Dr. James Hogg. Institut Fur Englische Sprache Und Literatur, 1977. Copyright © 1976 by Syndy M. Conger. Reproduced by permission.—Conger, Syndy McMillen. From "The Reconstruction of the Gothic Feminine

Ideal in Emily Brontë's *Wuthering Heights*," in **The Female Gothic**. Edited by Juliann E. Fleenor. Eden Press, 1983. Copyright © 1983 Eden Press, Inc. Reproduced by permission of the author.—Davenport-Hines, Richard. From **Gothic**. North Point Press, 1998. Copyright © 1998 by Richard Davenport-Hines. Reprinted by permission of North Point Press, a division of Farrar, Straus and Giroux LLC. In the United Kingdom, Canada and the British Commonwealth by the author.—Dinesen, Isak. From "The Monkey," in **Seven Gothic Tales**. Harrison Smith and Robert Haas, Inc., 1934; The Modern Library 1939. Copyright © 1934 by Harrison Smith and Robert Haas, Inc. Renewed 1961 by Isak Dinesen. Reproduced by permission of the Rungstedlund Foundation. In the United States by Random House, Inc.—du Maurier, Daphne. From **Rebecca**. Doubleday & Company, Inc., 1938. Copyright 1938 Doubleday, Doran and Company, Inc. Renewed 1965 by Daphne du Maurier Browning. Reproduced with permission of Curtis Brown Ltd., London on behalf of The Chichester Partnership.—Duthie, Peter. From **Plays on the Passions**. Broadview Press, Ltd., 2001. Copyright © 2001 Peter Duthie. All rights reserved. Reproduced by permission.—Faulkner, William. From "A Rose for Emily," in **Collected Stories of William Faulkner**. Vintage International, 1995. Copyright 1930, renewed 1958 by William Faulkner. Used by permission of Random House, Inc. In the United Kingdom by the Literary Estate of William Faulkner.—Fedorko, Kathy A. From **Gender and the Gothic in the Fiction of Edith Wharton**. The University of Alabama Press, 1995. Copyright © 1995 The University of Alabama Press. All rights reserved. Reproduced by permission.—Fiedler, Leslie. From **Love and Death in the American Novel. Revised edition.** Stein and Day, 1966. Reproduced by permission of the Estate of Leslie Fiedler.—Fisher, IV, Benjamin F. From "Gothic Possibilities in *Moby-Dick*," in **Gothick Origins and Innovations**. Edited by Allan Lloyd Smith and Victor Sage. Rodopi, 1994. Copyright © Editions Rodopi B.V. Reproduced by permission.—Frank, Frederick S. From "The Gothic *Vathek*: The Problem of Genre Resolved," in **AMS Studies in Eighteenth Century: Vathek and the Escape from Time: Bicentenary Revaluations.** Edited by Kenneth W. Graham. AMS, 1990. Copyright © 1990 by AMS Press, Inc. Reproduced by permission.—Freud, Sigmund. From **The Uncanny**. Translated by David McLintock. Penguin, 2003. Translation and editorial matter Copyright © 2003 by David McLintock. Reproduced by permission of Penguin Books, Ltd. In the United States and the Philippines by the Literary Estate of David McLintock.—Frisch, Shelley L. From "Poetics of the Uncanny: E. T. A. Hoffmann's 'Sand-

man,'" in **The Scope of the Fantastic: Theory, Technique, Major Authors.** Edited by Robert A. Collins and Howard D. Pearce. Greenwood Press, 1985. Copyright © 1985 by The Thomas Burnett Swann Fund. All rights reserved. Reproduced by permission of Greenwood Publishing Group, Inc., Westport, CT.—Gamer, Michael. From an Introduction to **The Castle of Otranto**. Edited, with an Introduction and Notes by Michael Gamer. Penguin Books, 2001. Editorial matter copyright © Michael Gamer, 2001. Reproduced by permission of the author.—Geary, Robert F. From "Carmilla and the Gothic Legacy: Victorian Transformations of Supernatural Horror," in **The Blood Is the Life: Vampires in Literature.** Edited by Leonard G. Heldreth and Mary Pharr. Bowling Green State University Popular Press, 1999. Copyright © 1999 Bowling Green State University Press. Reproduced by permission.—Goddu, Teresa A. From **Gothic America: Narrative, History, and the Nation.** Columbia University Press, 1997. Copyright © 1997 Columbia University Press. Reprinted with permission of the publisher.—Goethe, Johann Wolfgang von. From **Faust: Part One.** Translated by David Luke. Oxford University Press, 1987. Copyright © 1987 by Oxford University Press. Reproduced by permission of Oxford University Press.—Graham, Kenneth W. From "Emily's Demon-Lover: The Gothic Revolution and *The Mysteries of Udolpho*," in **Gothic Fictions: Prohibition/Transgression.** Edited by Kenneth W. Graham. AMS Press, 1989. Copyright © 1989 by AMS Press, Inc. Reproduced by permission.—Griffith, Clark. From "Poe and the Gothic," in **Papers on Poe: Essays in Honor of John Ward Ostrom.** Edited by Richard P. Veler. Chantry Music Press, Inc., 1972. Copyright © 1972 by Chantry Music Press, Inc. Reproduced by permission of the Literary Estate of Clark Griffith.—Gross, Louis S. From **Redefining the American Gothic: From Wieland to Day of the Dead.** UMI Research Press, 1989. Copyright © 1989 Louis Samuel Gross. All rights reserved. Reproduced by permission of the author.—Hannaham, James. From "'Bela Lugosi's Dead and I Don't Feel So Good Either': Goth and the Glorification of Suffering in Rock Music," in **Gothic: Transmutations of Horror in Late Twentieth Century Art.** Edited by Christoph Grunenberg. MIT Press, 1997. Copyright © 1997 The Institute of Contemporary Art, Boston. Reproduced by permission of The MIT Press, Cambridge, MA.—Haslam, Richard. From "Maturin and the 'Calvinist Sublime,'" in **Gothick Origins and Innovations.** Edited by Allan Lloyd Smith and Victor Sage. Rodopi, 1994. Copyright © Editions Rodopi B.V. Reproduced by permission.—Heilman, Robert B. From "Charlotte Brontë's 'New' Gothic," in **From Jane Austen to Joseph Conrad: Essays**

Collected in Memory of James T. Hillhouse. Edited by Robert C. Rathburn and Martin Steinmann, Jr. University of Minnesota Press, 1958. Copyright © 1958 by the University of Minnesota. Renewed 1986 by Robert Charles Rathburn and Martin Steinmann, Jr. All rights reserved. Reproduced by permission.—Heller, Tamar. From *Dead Secrets: Wilkie Collins and the Female Gothic.* Yale University Press, 1992. Copyright © 1992 by Yale University. All rights reserved. Reproduced by permission.—Hoeveler, Diane Long. From "Mary Shelley and Gothic Feminism: The Case of 'The Mortal Immortal,'" in *Iconoclastic Departures: Mary Shelley after Frankenstein: Essays in Honor of the Bicentenary of Mary Shelley's Birth.* Edited by Syndy M. Conger, Frederick S. Frank, and Gregory O'Dea. Fairleigh Dickinson University Press, 1997. Copyright © 1997 by Associated University Presses, Inc. Reproduced by permission.—Hoffmann, E. T. A. From an Introduction to *The Best Tales of Hoffmann.* Edited by E. F. Bleiler. Dover Publications, Inc., 1967. Copyright © 1967 by Dover Publications, Inc. All rights reserved. Reproduced by permission.—Hoffmann, E. T. A. From "The Sand-Man," in *The Best Tales of Hoffmann.* Edited and with an introduction by E. F. Bleiler. Translated by J. T. Bealby. Dover Publications, Inc., 1967. Copyright © 1967 by Dover Publications, Inc. All rights reserved. Reproduced by permission.—Hogle, Jerrold E. From "Stoker's Counterfeit Gothic: *Dracula* and Theatricality at the Dawn of Simulation," in *Bram Stoker: History, Psychoanalysis, and the Gothic.* Edited by William Hughes and Andrew Smith. MacMillan Press Ltd., 1998. Selection and editorial matter Copyright © William Hughes and Andrew Smith, 1998. Text Copyright © Macmillan Press Ltd., 1998. Reproduced with permission of Palgrave Macmillan.—Horner, Sue and Zlosnik, Avril. From "Daphne du Maurier and Gothic Signatures: Rebecca as Vamp(ire)," in *Body Matters: Feminism, Textuality, Corporeality.* Edited by Avril Horner and Angela Keane. Manchester University Press, Manchester, UK, 2000. Copyright © 2000 by Manchester University Press. Reproduced by permission of the publisher and authors.—Howells, Coral Ann. From *Margaret Atwood.* Macmillan Press Ltd., 1996. Copyright © 1996 Coral Ann Howells. All rights reserved. Reproduced with permission of Palgrave Macmillan.—Ingebretsen, Edward J. From "Anne Rice: Raising Holy Hell, Harlequin Style," in *The Gothic World of Anne Rice.* Edited by Gary Hoppenstand and Ray B. Browne. Bowling Green State University Popular Press, 1996. Copyright © 1996 by Bowling Green State University Popular Press. Reproduced by permission.—James, Sibyl. From "Gothic Transformations: Isak Dinesen and the Gothic," in *The Female Gothic.* Edited by Juliann E. Fleenor. Eden Press, 1983. Copyright © 1983 by Eden Press, Inc. Reproduced by permission of the author.—Johnson, Greg. From *Joyce Carol Oates: A Study of the Short Fiction.* Twayne Publishers, 1994. Copyright © 1994 by Twayne Publishers. Reproduced by permission of Thomson Gale.—Keats, John. From "A letter to Richard Woodhouse on September 21, 1819," in *Selected Letters of John Keats, Revised Edition.* Edited by Grant F. Scott. Harvard University Press, 2002. Copyright © 1958 by the President and Fellows of Harvard College. Copyright © renewed 1986 by Herschel C. Baker, the Executor of the author Hyder Edward Rollins. Copyright © 2002 by the President and Fellows of Harvard College. All rights reserved. Reproduced by permission of Harvard University Press.—Kerr, Elizabeth M. From "Otranto to Yoknapatawpha: Faulkner's Gothic Heritage," in *William Faulkner's Gothic Domain.* National University Publications, Kennikat Press, 1979. Copyright © 1979 by Kennikat Press Corp. All rights reserved. Reproduced by permission of the Literary Estate of the author.—King, Stephen. From "The Modern American Horror Movie—Text and Subtext," in *Stephen King's Danse Macabre.* Everest House, 1982, Berkeley Books, 2001. Copyright © 1981 by Stephen King. All other rights expressly reserved. Used by permission of Penguin Group (USA) Inc., 345 Hudson Street, New York, NY 10014. In North America with permission of the author.—King, Stephen. From *Stephen King's Danse Macabre.* Everest Publishing Group, 1982. Copyright © 1981 by Stephen King. All other rights expressly reserved. Used by permission of Penguin Group (USA) Inc., 345 Hudson Street, New York, NY 10014. In North American with permission of the author.—Lamont, Claire. From "Jane Austen's Gothic Architecture," in *Exhibited by Candlelight: Sources and Developments in the Gothic Tradition.* Edited by Valeria Tinkler-Villani and Peter Davidson, with Jane Stevenson. Rodopi, 1995. Copyright © Editions Rodopi B.V. Reproduced by permission.—Lanone, Catherine. From "Verging on the Gothic: Melmoth's Journey to France," in *European Gothic: A Spirited Exchange, 1760-1960.* Edited by Avril Horner. Manchester University Press, Manchetter, UK, 1996. Copyright © 1996 by Manchester University Press. Reproduced by permission of the publisher and the author.—Lawler, Donald. From "The Gothic Wilde," in *Rediscovering Oscar Wilde.* Edited by C. George Sandulescu. Colin Smythe, 1994. Copyright © 1994 by The Princess Grace Irish Library, Monaco. Reproduced by permission.—Le Tellier, Robert Ignatius. From *Sir Walter Scott and the Gothic Novel.* Edwin Mellen Press, 1995. Copyright © 1995 The Edwin Mellen Press.

ing, 1972. Reproduced by permission of the editor.—Railo, Eino. From *The Haunted Castle: A Study of the Elements of English Romanticism.* Routledge, 1927. Reproduced by permission of the publisher.—Ranger, Paul. From *Terror and Pity Reign in Every Breast: Gothic Drama in the London Patent Theatres, 1750-1820.* The Society for Theatre Research, 1991. Copyright © 1991 Paul Ranger. Reproduced by permission.—Rank, Otto. From "The Double as Immortal Self," in *Beyond Psychology.* E, Hauser, 1941. Copyright © 1941 by Estelle B. Rank. Renewed 1969 by Estelle B. Simon. Reproduced by permission of the Literary Estate of the author.—Robertson, Fiona. From *Legitimate Histories: Scott, Gothic, and the Authorities of Fiction.* Clarendon Press, 1994. Copyright © 1994 by Fiona Robertson. Reproduced by permission of Oxford University Press.—Sage, Victor. From *Le Fanu's Gothic: The Rhetoric of Darkness.* Palgrave MacMillan, 2004. Copyright © 2004 by Victor Sage. Reproduced with permission of Palgrave Macmillan.—Savoy, Eric. From "The Face of the Tenant: A Theory of American Gothic," in *American Gothic: New Interventions in a National Narrative.* Edited by Robert K. Martin and Eric Savoy. University of Iowa Press, 1998. Copyright © 1998 by the University of Iowa Press. All rights reserved. Reproduced by permission.—Senf, Carol A. From *The Vampire in Nineteenth-Century English Literature.* Bowling Green University Popular Press, 1988. Copyright © 1988 by Bowling Green State University Popular Press. Reproduced by permission.—Shelley, Percy Bysshe. From "The Assassins," in *Gothic Tales of Terror. Volume One: Classic Horror Stories from Great Britain.* Copyright © 1972 selection and original material copyright by Peter Haining. Reproduced by permission of the editor.—Shetty, Nalini V. From "Melville's Use of the Gothic Tradition," *Studies in American Literature: Essays in Honour of William Mulder.* Edited by Jagdish Chander and Narindar S. Pradhan. Oxford University Press, 1976. Copyright © Oxford University Press 1976. All rights reserved. Reproduced by permission of Oxford University Press India, New Delhi.—Showalter, Elaine. From *Sister's Choice: Tradition and Change in American Women's Writing.* Clarendon Press, 1991. Copyright © 1991 Elaine Showalter. Reproduced by permission of Oxford University Press.—Summers, Montague. From *The Gothic Quest: A History of the Gothic Novel.* The Fortune Press, 1938. Reproduced by permission.—Thomas, Ronald R. From *Dreams of Authority: Freud and the Fictions of the Unconscious.* Cornell University Press, 1990. Copyright © 1990 by Cornell University. Used by permission of the publisher, Cornell University Press.—Tillotson, Marcia. From "'A Forced Solitude': Mary Shelley and the Creation of Frankenstein's Monster," in *The Female Gothic.* Edited by Juliann E. Fleenor. Eden Press, 1983. Copyright © 1983 by Eden Press, Inc. Reproduced by permission of the Literary Estate of Marcia Tillotson.—Valente, Joseph. From *Dracula's Crypt: Bram Stoker, Irishness, and the Question of Blood.* University of Illinois Press, 2002. Copyright © 2001 by the Board of Trustees of the University of Illinois. Used with permission of the University of Illinois Press.—Vincent, Sybil Korff. From "The Mirror and the Cameo: Margaret Atwood's Comic/Gothic Novel, *Lady Oracle,*" in *The Female Gothic.* Edited by Juliann E. Fleenor. Elden Press, 1983. Copyright © 1983 Eden Press, Inc. All rights reserved. Reproduced by permission of the author.—Warfel, Harry R. From *Charles Brockden Brown: American Gothic Novelist.* 1949. University of Florida Press, 1949. Copyright © 1949 University of Florida. Renewed 1977 by Jean Dietze. All rights reserved. Reproduced by permission.—Weissberg, Liliane. From "Gothic Spaces: The Political Aspects of Toni Morrison's *Beloved,*" in *Modern Gothic: A Reader.* Edited by Victor Sage and Allan Lloyd Smith. Manchester University Press, 2004. Copyright © 2004 by Manchester University Press. Reproduced by permission of the publisher and author.—Wharton, Edith. From *The Ghost Stories of Edith Wharton.* Scribner, Simon & Schuster, 1973. Copyright © 1973 by William R. Tyler. Reproduced by permission of Scribner, an imprint of Simon & Schuster Macmillan and the Literary Estate of Edith Wharton and the Watkins/Loomis Agency.—Williams, Anne. From *Art of Darkness: A Poetics of Gothic.* University of Chicago Press, 1995. Copyright © 1995 by The University of Chicago. All rights reserved. Reproduced by permission of the publisher and the author.—Williamson, Paul. From an Introduction to *Gothic Sculpture 1140-1300.* Edited by Nikolaus Pevsner. Yale University Press, Pelican History of Art, 1995. Copyright © 1995 by Paul Williamson. Reproduced by permission.—Wisker, Gina. From "At Home All Was Blood and Feathers: The Werewolf in the Kitchen—Angela Carter and Horror," in *Creepers: British Horror and Fantasy in the Twentieth Century.* Edited by Clive Bloom. Pluto Press, 1993. Copyright © 1993 by Lumiere (Co-operative) Press Ltd. Reproduced by permission.—Wolfreys, Julian. From "'I Wants to Make Your Flesh Creep': Notes toward a Reading of the Comic-Gothic in Dickens," in *Victorian Gothic: Literary and Cultural Manifestations in the Nineteenth Century.* Edited by Ruth Robbins and Julian Wolfreys. Palgrave, 2000. Selection and editorial matter © Ruth Robbins and Julian Wolfreys, 2000. Preface and Chapter 3 © Julian Wolfreys, 2000. Chapter 10 © Ruth Robbins, 2000.

Chapters 1, 2, 4-9, 11, 12 © Palgrave Publishers Ltd, 2000. Reproduced with permission of Palgrave Macmillan.—Womack, Kenneth. From "'Withered, Wrinkled, and Loathsome of Visage': Reading the Ethics of the Soul and the Late-Victorian Gothic in *The Picture of Dorian Gray*," in *Victorian Gothic: Literary and Cultural Manifestations in the Nineteenth Century*. Edited by Ruth Robbins and Julian Wolfreys. Palgrave, 2000. Selection and editorial matter © Ruth Robbins and Julian Wolfreys, 2000. Preface and Chapter 3 © Julian Wolfreys, 2000. Chapter 10 © Ruth Robbins, 2000. Chapters 1, 2, 4-9, 11, 12 © Palgrave Publishers Ltd, 2000. Reproduced with permission of Palgrave Macmillan.—Wood, Martin J. From "New Life for an Old Tradition: Anne Rice and Vampire Literature," in *The Blood Is the Life: Vampires in Literature*. Edited by Leonard G. Heldreth and Mary Pharr. Bowling Green State University Popular Press, 1999. Copyright © 1999 Bowling Green State University Popular Press. Reproduced by permission.—Wood, Robin. From "An Introduction to the American Horror Film," in *American Nightmare: Essays on the Horror Film*. Edited by Robin Wood and Richard Lippe. Festival of Festivals, 1979. Copyright © Robin Wood, Richard Lippe, and Festival of Festivals. All rights reserved. Reproduced by permission of the publisher and the author.—Wright, Angela. From "European Disruptions of the Idealized Woman: Matthew Lewis's *The Monk* and the Marquis de Sade's *La Nouvelle Justine*," in *European Gothic: A Spirited Exchange, 1760-1960*. Edited by Avril Horner. Manchester University Press, Manchester, UK, 2002. Copyright © 2002 by Manchester University Press. Reproduced by permission of the publisher and author.

Photographs and Illustrations in Gothic Literature *were received from the following sources:*

A Description of Strawberry Hill, by Horace Walpole, frontispiece.—Abbotsford, home of Sir Walter Scott, photograph. © Bettmann/Corbis.—Ainsworth, William Harrison, photograph. © Getty Images.—Allston, Washington, photograph. The Library of Congress.—*American Gothic*, painting by Grant Wood, 1930, photograph. Photography © The Art Institute of Chicago. Reproduced by permission.—Atwood, Margaret, photograph by Christopher Felver. Copyright © Christopher Felver/Corbis.—Austen, Jane, engraving.—Baillie, Joanna, photograph. © Hulton-Deutsch/Corbis.—*Balshazzar's Feast*, painting by Washington Allston, ca. 1817-1843. © The Detroit Institute of Arts/Bridgeman Art Library.—Beckford, William, photograph. © Michael Nicholson/Corbis.—Bergman, Ingrid and Heywood Morse in the 1959 film

adaptation of *Turn of the Screw* by Henry James, photograph. © Bettmann/Corbis.—Bierce, Ambrose, drawing by J. J. Newbegin, 1896.—Braddon, Mary Elizabeth, engraving. © Hulton Getty/Liaison Agency.—Brontë, Charlotte, illustration. International Portrait Gallery.—Brontë, Emily, painting by Bramwell Brontë.—Brown, Charles Brockden, print.—Bulwer-Lytton, Edward George, photograph. © Bettmann/Corbis.—Burke, Edmund, photograph. © Bettmann/Corbis.—Capote, Truman, photograph. © Hulton-Deutsch Collection/Corbis.—Carter, Angela, photograph. © Jerry Bauer. Reproduced by permission.—*Castle of Otranto*, by Horace Walpole, c. 1790, illustration.—*Castle of Wolfenbach; a German Story*, by Eliza Parsons, 1793, title page.—*Christine*, movie still, photograph. The Kobal Collection. Reproduced by permission.—Collins, William Wilkie, photograph. The Library of Congress.—Cooper, Alice, performing on the *In Concert* television show on November 24, 1972, photograph. © Bettmann/Corbis.—Dickens, Charles, photograph. Hesketh Pearson.—Dinesen, Isak, photograph. Corbis-Bettmann.—*Dr. Jekyll and Mr. Hyde*, Spencer Tracy as Dr. Jekyll, photograph. © Bettmann/Corbis.—*Dracula*, Helen Chandler, as Mina Seward, with Bela Lugosi, as Count Dracula, photograph. The Kobal Collection. Reproduced by permission.—*Dracula's Guest*, written by Bram Stoker, title page.—du Maurier, Daphne, photograph. © Time Life Pictures/Getty Images.—Faulkner, William, photograph. © Bettmann/Corbis.—*Frankenstein*, by Mary Wollstonecraft Shelley, 1831, illustration. Mary Evans Picture Library. Reproduced by permission.—*Fall of the House of Usher*, by Edgar Allan Poe, illustration. © Bettmann/Corbis.—Gargoyle of 15th Century Spanish Building, photograph. © Manuel Bellver/Corbis.—Gilman, Charlotte Perkins, c. 1890, photograph.—Godwin, William, painting by James Northcote. From *Vindication of the Rights of Women*, by William Godwin, 1802.—*Great Expectations*, by Charles Dickens, illustration. © Corbis.—Hawthorne, Nathaniel, photograph.—Hoffmann, E. T. A., photograph. Mary Evans Picture Library. Reproduced by permission.—Hogg, James, photograph. © Rischgitz/Getty Images.—Irving, Washington, photograph. The National Portrait Gallery, Smithsonian Institution.—James, Henry, photograph.—*Jane Eyre*, Orson Welles as Edward Rochester, with Joan Fontaine as Jane Eyre, photograph. The Kobal Collection. Reproduced by permission.—King, Stephen, photograph. Corbis-Bettmann.—Le Fanu, Joseph Sheridan, photograph.—*Legend of Sleepy Hollow*, by Washington Irving, illustration. © Bettmann/Corbis.—Lewis, Matthew Gregory, photograph by H. W. Pickersgill.—*Varney the Vampire; or, The Feast of Blood*, title page. © Getty

Images.—Lovecraft, H. P., photograph.—Lugosi, Bela, photograph. © Bettmann/Corbis.—Maturin, Charles Robert, photograph. © The Granger Collection, New York.—Melville, Herman, photograph. The Library of Congress.—Morrison, Toni, photograph. Copyright © Nancy Kazerman/ ZUMA/Corbis.—Nave of Basilique de Saint-Denis, June 19, 1996, photograph. © Robert Holmes/ Corbis.—*Nightmare*, painting by Henri Fuseli, 1791. Mary Evans Picture Library. Reproduced by permission.—*Nosferatu*, Max Schreck (Count Orlok) standing on deck of ship, 1922, photograph. © Bettmann/Corbis.—O'Connor, Flannery, photograph. AP/Wide World Photos.—Oates, Joyce Carol, photograph. © Nancy Kaszerman/Corbis.— Peck, Gregory, photograph. The Kobal Collection. Reproduced by permission.—Poe, Edgar Allan, photograph.—Polidori, John William, painting by F. G. Gainsford, c. 1816, photograph. © The Granger Collection, New York.—*Psycho*, Norman Bates (Anthony Perkins) approaching the motel, photograph. © Underwood and Underwood/Corbis.—Reeve, Clara, photograph. © Getty Images.— Rice, Anne, photograph. © Mitchell Gerber/Corbis.—*Roettgen Pieta*, wood carving, c. 1300, photograph. © Erich Lessing/Art Resource, NY.— Schiller, Friedrich von, engraving. The German Information Center.—Scott, Sir Walter, photograph. The Library of Congress.—Shelley, Mary Wollstonecraft, illustration.—*Son of Frankenstein*, with Boris Karloff, Basil Rathbone, and Bela Lugosi, photograph. © Bettmann/Corbis.—Stevenson, Robert Louis, engraving. The Library of Congress.—Stoker, Bram, photograph. © Hulton-Deutsch Collection/Corbis.—*The Castle Spectre*, by Matthew Gregory Lewis, illustration. Mary Evans Picture Library. Reproduced by permission.—*The Fall of the House of Usher*, directed by Roger Corman, photograph. © A.I.P./The Kobal Collection. Reproduced by permission.—*The Haunting*, 1963, movie still. © MGM/The Kobal Collection. Reproduced by permission.—*The Island of Dr. Moreau*, poster. © A.I.P./The Kobal Collection. Reproduced by permission.—*The Italian; or, The Confessional of the Black Penitents,* by Ann Radcliffe, 1797 edition, title page.—*The Mysteries of Udolpho*, frontispieces by Ann Radcliffe.—*The Narrative of Arthur Gordon Pym*, written by Edgar Allan Poe, title page. Special Collections Library, University of Michigan. Reproduced by permission.—*The Old English Baron: A Gothic Story,* by Clara Reeve, 1778, illustration.—*The Recess; or, A Tale of Other Times,* by Sophia Lee, 1786, title page.—*The Shining*, directed by Stanley Kubrick, 1980, photograph. © Warner Bros./The Kobal Collection.—*The Sicilian Romance; or, The Apparition of the Cliffs, an Opera,* by Henry Siddons, 1794, title page.—*The Table of the Seven Deadly Sins*, painting by Hieronymous Bosch, c. 1480-1490, Northern Renaissance, photograph. © Archivo Iconografico, S.A./Corbis.—*The Temptation of Ambrosio*, from Matthew Gregory Lewis's *The Monk*, illustration.—*The Woman in White*, by Wilkie Collins, title page. Special Collections Library, University of Michigan. Reproduced by permission.—*Things as They Are; or, The Adventures of Caleb Williams,* by William Godwin, title page.—*Twin Peaks*, scene from the television series by David Lynch, 1990, photograph. © Corbis Sygma.—Veidt, Conrad and Lil Dagover in the 1920 silent horror film *The Cabinet of Dr. Caligari,* photograph. © John Springer/Corbis.—von Goethe, Johann Wolfgang, photograph. © Bettmann/ Corbis.—Waddy, F., satirical caricature in "Once a Week," 1873. Mary Evans Picture Library. Reproduced by permission.—Walpole, Horace, photograph. © Bettmann/Corbis.—Wharton, Edith, 1905, photograph. The Library of Congress.— *Wieland; or, The Transformation,* by Charles Brockden Brown, Philadelphia, David McKay, Publisher, 1881, title page.—Wilde, Oscar, photograph. The Library of Congress.—*Wuthering Heights*, by Emily Brontë, movie poster, photograph. © Cinema-Photo/Corbis.

1081

- Suger of Saint Denis is born in Saint Denis, France.

1127

- Abbot Suger of Saint Denis begins redesigning the Abbey Church of Saint-Denis in France.

1151

- Abbot Suger of Saint Denis dies on 13 January in St. Denis, France.

C. 1163

- Construction of the current Cathedral of Notre Dame de Paris in France.

C. 1175

- Construction of the current Canterbury Cathedral in England.

C. 1194

- Construction of the current Cathedral of Notre Dame at Chartres (also known as Chartres Cathedral) in France.

C. 1211

- Construction of the current Cathedral of Notre Dame de Rheims (also known as Rheims Cathedral) in France.

1220

- Construction of the Cathedral of Amiens in France.
- Master Elias of Dereham begins designing the Salisbury Cathedral in England.

1245

- Construction of the current Westminster Abbey in London, England.

C. 1329

- Andrea Pisano begins his bronze sculptures for the Baptisery in Florence, Italy.

1485

- Hieronymus Bosch completes the painting *Tabletop of the Seven Deadly Sins*.

C. 1600-01

- William Shakespeare's *Hamlet* is staged.

C. 1606

- William Shakespeare's *Macbeth* is staged.

1717

- Horace Walpole is born on 24 September in London, England.

1727

■ Daniel Defoe's *An Essay on the History and Reality of Apparitions* is published.

1729

● Edmund Burke is born on 12 January in Dublin, Ireland.

● Clara Reeve is born on 23 January in Ipswich, Suffolk, England.

1742

■ Batty and Thomas Langley's *Ancient Architecture Restored and Improved* is published.

1749

● Johann Wolfgang von Goethe is born on 28 August in Frankfurt, Germany.

1750

● Sophia Lee is born in London, England.

■ Horace Walpole and Richard Bentley begin designing Strawberry Hill, Walpole's residence in Twickenham, England.

1753

■ Tobias Smollett's *The Adventures of Ferdinand Count Fathom* is published.

1756

● William Godwin is born on 3 March in Wisbeach, England.

1757

● William Blake is born on 28 November in London, England.

■ Edmund Burke's *A Philosophical Enquiry into the Origin of Our Ideas of the Sublime and Beautiful* is published.

1759

● Johann Christoph Friedrich von Schiller is born on 10 November in Marbach, Germany.

1760

● William Beckford is born on 29 September in London, England.

1762

● James Boaden is born on 23 May at White Haven in Cumberland, England.

● Joanna Baillie is born on 11 September in Bothwell, Lanarkshire, Scotland.

1764

● Ann Radcliffe is born on 9 July in London, England.

■ Horace Walpole's *The Castle of Otranto* is published.

1770

● James Hogg is born in Ettrick, Selkirkshire, Scotland.

1771

● Charles Brockden Brown is born on 17 January in Philadelphia, Pennsylvania.

● Sir Walter Scott is born on 15 August in Edinburgh, Scotland.

1772

● Samuel Taylor Coleridge is born on 21 October in Ottery St. Mary, Devonshire, England.

1773

■ John Aikin and Anna Laetitia (Aikin) Barbauld's *Miscellaneous Pieces in Prose, by J. and A. L. Aikin* is published.

1775

● Matthew Gregory Lewis is born on 9 July in London, England.

● Jane Austen is born on 16 December in Steventon, Hampshire, England.

1776

● Ernst Theodor Wilhelm (later E. T. A.) Hoffmann is born on 24 January in Königsberg, Germany.

1777

■ Clara Reeve's *The Champion of Virtue. A Gothic Story* is published.

1778

- Clara Reeve's *The Champion of Virtue* is published as *The Old English Baron*.

1779

- Washington Allston is born on 5 November in South Carolina.

1780

- Charles Robert Maturin is born on 25 September in Dublin, Ireland.

1781

- Henry Fuseli completes the painting *The Nightmare*.

1783

- Washington Irving is born on 3 April in New York City.
- Sophia Lee's *The Recess; or, A Tale of Other Times* is published.

1786

- The unauthorized translation of William Beckford's *Vathek* is published as *An Arabian Tale*.

1787

- Lewis Nockalls Cottingham is born on 24 October at Laxfield, Suffolk, England.
- William Beckford's *Vathek* is published.

1788

- George Gordon Noel, Lord Byron is born on 22 January in London, England.

1789

- James Cobb's *The Haunted Tower* is produced.
- George Colman the Younger's *The Battle of Hexham* is produced.

1790

- Johann Wolfgang von Goethe's *Faust: Ein Fragment* is published.
- Ann Radcliffe's *A Sicilian Romance* is published.

1791

- Ann Radcliffe's *The Romance of the Forest* is published.

1792

- Percy Bysshe Shelley is born on 4 August in Field Place, Sussex, England.
- Mary Wollstonecraft's *A Vindication of the Rights of Woman: with Strictures on Political and Moral Subjects* is published.

1793

- Mrs. Eliza Parsons's *Castle of Wolfenbach; A German Story* is published.

1794

- James Boaden's *Fontainville Forest* is produced.
- J. C. Cross's *The Apparition* is produced.
- William Godwin's *Things As They Are; or, The Adventures of Caleb Williams* is published.
- Ann Radcliffe's *The Mysteries of Udolpho, A Romance; Interspersed with some pieces of Poetry* is published.
- Henry Siddons's *The Sicilian Romance; or, The Apparition of the Cliff* is produced.

1795

- John William Polidori is born on 7 September in England.

1796

- Marquis von Grosse's *Genius (Horrid Mysteries)* is published.
- Matthew Gregory Lewis's *The Monk: A Romance* is published.

1797

- Horace Walpole dies on 2 March in London, England.
- Edmund Burke dies on 9 July in Beaconsfield, Buckinghamshire, England.
- Mary Wollstonecraft Godwin (later Shelley) is born on 30 August in London, England.
- Matthew Gregory Lewis's *The Castle Spectre: A Drama* is produced.

1798

- Regina Maria Roche's *Children of the Abbey* is published.

- The first volume of Joanna Baillie's *A Series of Plays: In Which it is Attempted to Delineate the Stronger Passions of the Mind—Each Passion Being the Subject of a Tragedy and a Comedy* is published.

- Charles Brockden Brown's *Wieland; or, The Transformation* is published.

1799

- Charles Brockden Brown's *Edgar Huntly; or, Memoirs of a Sleep-Walker* and the first volume of *Arthur Mervyn; or, Memoirs of the Year 1793* are published.

1800

- Washington Allston completes the painting *Tragic Figure in Chains*.

- The second volume of Charles Brockden Brown's *Arthur Mervyn; or, Memoirs of the Year 1793* is published.

1802

- The second volume of Joanna Baillie's *A Series of Plays: In Which it is Attempted to Delineate the Stronger Passions of the Mind—Each Passion Being the Subject of a Tragedy and a Comedy* is published.

1803

- Edward Bulwer-Lytton (Edward George Earle Lytton Bulwer) is born on 25 May in London, England.

- Thomas Lovell Beddoes is born on 30 June in Clifton, Shropshire, England.

- Alexander Jackson Davis is born on 24 July in New York City.

1804

- Nathaniel Hawthorne is born on 4 July in Salem, Massachusetts.

1805

- William Harrison Ainsworth is born on 4 February in Manchester, England.

- Friedrich von Schiller dies on 9 May in Weimar, Germany.

1806

- Charlotte Dacre's *Zofloya; or, The Moor* is published.

1807

- Clara Reeve dies on 3 December in Ipswich, Suffolk, England.

1808

- Johann Wolfgang von Goethe's *Faust—Der Tragödie erster Teil* (*Faust: Part One*) is published.

1809

- Edgar Allan Poe is born on 19 January in Boston, Massachusetts.

1810

- Charles Brockden Brown dies on 22 February in Philadelphia, Pennsylvania.

- Percy Bysshe Shelley's *Zastrozzi, A Romance* is published.

1811

- Percy Bysshe Shelley's *St. Irvyne; or, The Rosicrucian: A Romance* is published.

1812

- Charles Dickens is born on 7 February in Portsmouth, Hampshire, England.

- The third volume of Joanna Baillie's *A Series of Plays: In Which it is Attempted to Delineate the Stronger Passions of the Mind—Each Passion Being the Subject of a Tragedy and a Comedy* is published.

- George Gordon, Lord Byron's *Childe Harold's Pilgrimage: A Romaunt* is published.

1813

- George Gordon, Lord Byron's *The Giaour: A Fragment of a Turkish Tale* is published.

1814

- Joseph Sheridan Le Fanu is born on 28 August in Dublin, Ireland.

- Sir Walter Scott's *Waverly; or, 'Tis Sixty Years Since* is published.

1816

- Charlotte Brontë is born on 21 April in Thornton, Yorkshire, England.

- George Gordon, Lord Byron's *Childe Harold's Pilgrimage: Canto the Third* is published.

- Samuel Taylor Coleridge's *Christabel: Kubla Khan, a Vision; The Pains of Sleep* is published.

- Jane Scott's *The Old Oak Chest* is produced.

1817

- Jane Austen dies on 18 July in Winchester, Hampshire, England.

- Washington Allston begins the painting *Belshazzar's Feast*.

- George Gordon, Lord Byron's *Manfred, A Dramatic Poem* is published.

- E. T. A. Hoffmann's "Der Sandmann" ("The Sandman") is published.

1818

- Matthew Gregory Lewis dies on 16 May during a voyage across the Atlantic Ocean from Jamaica to England.

- Emily Brontë is born on 30 July in Thornton, Yorkshire, England.

- Jane Austen's *Northanger Abbey and Persuasion* is published.

- Mary Wollstonecraft Shelley's *Frankenstein; or, The Modern Prometheus* is published.

1819

- Herman Melville is born on 1 August in New York City.

- Percy Bysshe Shelley's *The Cenci* is produced.

- Washington Irving's *The Sketch Book of Geoffrey Crayon, Gent.* is published.

- John William Polidori's *The Vampyre; a Tale* is published.

1820

- John Keats's *Lamia, Isabella, The Eve of St. Agnes, and Other Poems* is published.

- Charles Robert Maturin's *Melmoth the Wanderer* is published.

1821

- John William Polidori commits suicide on 27 August in London, England.

- Thomas De Quincey's *Confessions of an English Opium Eater* is published.

1822

- E. T. A. Hoffmann dies on 25 June in Berlin, Germany.

- Percy Bysshe Shelley drowns on 8 July in the Gulf of Spezia near Lerici, Italy.

1823

- Ann Radcliffe dies on 7 February in England.

- Richard Brinsley Peake's *Presumption; or, The Fate of Frankenstein* is produced.

1824

- William Wilkie Collins is born on 8 January in London, England.

- Sophia Lee dies on 13 March in Clifton, England.

- Lord Byron dies on 19 April in Cephalonia, Greece.

- Charles Robert Maturin dies on 30 October in Dublin, Ireland.

- Catherine Gore's *The Bond, a Dramatic Poem* is produced.

- James Hogg's *The Private Memoirs and Confessions of a Justified Sinner* is published.

- Washington Irving's *Tales of a Traveller* is published.

1825

- James Fenimore Cooper's *Lionel Lincoln; or, The Leaguer of Boston* is published.

1826

- Edward Bulwer-Lytton's *Glenallan* is published.

1827

- William Blake dies on 12 August in London, England.

- Thomas Moore's *The Epicurean. A Tale* is published.

1830

● Christina Rossetti is born on 5 December in London, England.

1832

● Johann Wolfgang von Goethe dies on 22 March.

● Sir Walter Scott dies on 21 September in Abbotsford, Scotland.

▨ Architect Alexander Jackson Davis completes Glen Ellen, the Baltimore, Maryland residence of Robert Gilmor III.

1834

● Samuel Taylor Coleridge dies on 25 July in England.

1835

● James Hogg dies on 21 November in Scotland.

1836

● William Godwin dies on 7 April in London, England.

▨ Thomas Cole completes the painting *Ruined Tower*.

1837

▨ Charles Dickens's *Posthumous Papers of the Pickwick Club* is published under the pseudonym Boz.

▨ Nathaniel Hawthorne's *Twice Told Tales* is published.

1838

▨ Charles Dickens's *Oliver Twist* is published.

▨ Edgar Allan Poe's *The Narrative of Arthur Gordon Pym* is published.

1839

● James Boaden dies on 16 February in England.

1840

▨ Edgar Allan Poe's *Tales of the Grotesque and Arabesque* is published.

1842

▨ Edward Bulwer-Lytton's *Zanoni* is published.

● Ambrose Bierce is born on 24 June in Horse Cave Creek, Meigs County, Ohio.

1843

● Henry James is born on 15 April in New York City.

● Washington Allston dies on 9 July in Cambridge, Massachusetts.

▨ A. W. N. Pugin's *Apology for the Revival of Christian Architecture in England* is published.

1844

● William Beckford dies on 2 May in England.

1845

▨ Frederick Douglass's *Narrative of the Life of Frederick Douglass, an American Slave* is published.

▨ Edgar Allan Poe's *Tales by Edgar A. Poe* and *The Raven and Other Poems* are published.

1846

▨ Edward Bulwer-Lytton's *Lucretia; or, The Children of Night* is published.

▨ Fyodor Dostoevsky's *Dvoinik: Prikliucheniia gospodina Goliadkina* (*The Double: A Poem of St. Petersburg*) is published.

1847

● L. N. Cottingham dies on 13 October in London, England.

● Bram Stoker is born on 8 November in Clontarf, Ireland.

▨ Charlotte Brontë's *Jane Eyre. An Autobiography* is published under the pseudonym Currer Bell.

▨ Emily Brontë's *Wuthering Heights* is published under the pseudonym Ellis Bell.

▨ *Varney the Vampire; or, The Feast of Blood*, written by either Thomas Peckett Prest or James Malcolm Rymer, is published.

1848

● Emily Brontë dies on 19 December in Haworth, Yorkshire, England.

▨ Charles Dickens's *The Haunted Man, and The Ghost's Bargain* is published.

1849

- Thomas Lovell Beddoes commits suicide on 26 January in Basel, Switzerland.
- Edgar Allan Poe dies on 7 October in Baltimore, Maryland.

1850

- Robert Louis Stevenson is born on 13 November in Edinburgh, Scotland.
- Nathaniel Hawthorne's *The Scarlet Letter: A Romance* is published.

1851

- Mary Wollstonecraft Shelley dies on 1 February in Bournemouth, England.
- Joanna Baillie dies on 23 February in Hampstead, England.
- Nathaniel Hawthorne's *The House of the Seven Gables, a Romance* is published.
- Herman Melville's *Moby-Dick; or, The Whale* is published.

1852

- Harriet Beecher Stowe's *Uncle Tom's Cabin; or, Life among the Lowly* is published.

1853

- Charlotte Brontë's *Villette* is published under the pseudonym Currer Bell.
- Charles Dickens's *Bleak House* is published.

C. 1854

- Oscar Wilde is born on 16 October in Dublin, Ireland.

1855

- Charlotte Brontë dies on 31 March in Haworth, Yorkshire, England.

1856

- Sigismund Solomon Freud (later Sigmund Freud) is born on 6 May in Freiberg, Moravia, Czechoslovakia.
- Herman Melville's *The Piazza Tales* is published.

1857

- Wilkie Collins's *The Dead Secret* is published.
- Charles Dickens's *Little Dorrit* is published.
- G. W. M. Reynolds's *Wagner the Wehr-wolf* is published.

1859

- Washington Irving dies on 28 November in Irvington, New York.

1860

- Charlotte Perkins Gilman is born on 3 July in Hartford, Connecticut.
- Wilkie Collins's *The Woman in White* is published.
- Nathaniel Hawthorne's *The Marble Faun; or, The Romance of Monte Beni* is published.

1861

- Harriet Jacobs's *Incidents in the Life of a Slave Girl, Written by Herself* is published under the pseudonym Linda Brent.

1862

- Edith Wharton is born on 24 January in New York City.
- Edward Bulwer-Lytton's *A Strange Story* is published.

1864

- Nathaniel Hawthorne dies on 19 May in Plymouth, New Hampshire.
- Joseph Sheridan Le Fanu's *Uncle Silas: A Tale of Bartram-Haugh* is published.

1870

- Charles Dickens dies on 9 June in Rochester, Kent, England.

1872

- Joseph Sheridan Le Fanu's *In a Glass Darkly* is published.

1873

- Edward Bulwer-Lytton dies on 18 January in Torquay, Devonshire, England.
- Joseph Sheridan Le Fanu dies on 10 February in Dublin, Ireland.

1882

- William Harrison Ainsworth dies on 3 January.

- Bela Lugosi is born Béla Ferenc Dezsö Blask¢ on 20 October in Lugos, Hungary.

1885

- Karen Christentze Dinesen, who later wrote under the pseudonym Isak Dinesen, is born on 17 April near Copenhagen, Denmark.

1886

- Guy de Maupassant's "La Horla" ("The Horla") is published *Le Gil Blas*.

- Robert Louis Stevenson's *The Strange Case of Dr. Jekyll and Mr. Hyde* is published.

1887

- William Henry Pratt (later Boris Karloff) is born on 23 November in London, England.

1888

- Friedrich Wilhelm Plumpe (later F. W. Murnau) is born on 28 December in Bielefeld, Westphalia, Germany.

1889

- Wilkie Collins dies on 23 September in London, England.

1890

- Howard Phillips Lovecraft is born on 20 August in Providence, Rhode Island.

- Oscar Wilde's *The Picture of Dorian Gray* is published.

1891

- Herman Melville dies on 28 September in New York City.

- Oscar Wilde's *Lord Arthur Savile's Crime, and Other Stories* is published.

1892

- Alexander Jackson Davis dies on 14 January in West Orange, New Jersey.

- Charlotte Perkins Gilman's "The Yellow Wallpaper" is published.

1894

- Robert Louis Stevenson dies on 3 December in Apia, Samoa.

- Christina Rossetti dies on 29 December in London, England.

- Arthur Machen's *The Great God Pan and The Inmost Light* is published.

1896

- H. G. Wells's *The Island of Doctor Moreau: A Possibility* is published.

1897

- William Faulkner is born on 25 September in New Albany, Mississippi.

- Bram Stoker's *Dracula* is published.

1898

- Henry James's *The Two Magics: The Turn of the Screw, Covering End* is published.

1899

- Elizabeth Bowen is born on 7 June in Dublin, Ireland.

- Alfred Hitchcock is born on 13 August in London, England.

1900

- Oscar Wilde dies on 30 November in Paris, France.

1904

- Arthur Machen's "The Garden of Avallaunius" is published.

1906

- Algernon Blackwood's *The Empty House and Other Ghosts* is published.

1907

- Daphne du Maurier is born on 12 May in London, England.

- George Sylvester Viereck's *The House of the Vampire* is published.

1908

- *Dr. Jekyll and Mr. Hyde,* produced by the Selig Polyscope Company, is released.

1909

- *Dr. Jekyll and Mr. Hyde,* produced by the Nordisk Company, is released.

1910

- Gaston Leroux's *Le Fantôme de L'Opéra* (*The Phantom of the Opera*) is published.

- *Frankenstein,* directed by J. Searle Dawley, is released.

1911

- Edith Wharton's *Ethan Frome* is published.

1912

- Bram Stoker dies on 20 April in London, England.

1914

- Ambrose Bierce disappears c. 1 January in Mexico and is presumed dead.

1916

- Henry James dies on 28 February in London, England.

1919

- Shirley Jackson is born on 14 December in San Francisco, California.

- Sigmund Freud's "Das Unheimlich" ("The Uncanny") is published.

1920

- Ray Bradbury is born on 22 August in Waukegan, Illinois.

- *Der Golem, wie er in die Welt kam* (*The Golem: How He Came into the World,* directed by Carl Boese and Paul Wegener, is released.

- *Das Kabinett des Doktor Caligari* (*The Cabinet of Dr. Caligari*), directed by Robert Wiene, is released.

1922

- *Nosferatu, eine Symphonie des Grauens,* directed by F. W. Murnau, is released.

1924

- *Das Wachsfigurenkabinett* (*Waxworks*), directed by Paul Leni and Leo Birinsky, is released.

1925

- Edward Gorey is born on 22 February in Chicago, Illinois.

- (Mary) Flannery O'Connor is born on 25 March in Savannah, Georgia.

1927

- Algernon Blackwood's *The Dance of Death, and Other Tales* is published.

1929

- Ursula K. Le Guin is born on 21 October in Berkeley, California.

1930

- William Faulkner's *As I Lay Dying* and "A Rose for Emily" are published.

1931

- Chloe Ardelia Wofford (later Toni Morrison) is born on 18 February in Lorain, Ohio.

- F. W. Murnau dies on 11 March in Santa Barbara, California.

- *Dracula,* directed by Tod Browning and starring Bela Lugosi in the title role, is released.

- *Frankenstein,* directed by James Whale and starring Boris Karloff as the monster, is released.

- *M,* directed by Fritz Lang, is released.

- William Faulkner's *Sanctuary* is published.

1932

- *Murders in the Rue Morgue,* directed by Robert Florey, is released.

- *White Zombie,* directed by Victor Halperin, is released.

- William Faulkner's *Light in August* is published.

1933

▦ *King Kong,* directed by Merian C. Cooper, is released.

▦ *The Invisible Man,* directed by James Whale, is released.

▦ *Island of Lost Souls,* directed by Erle C. Kenton, is released.

1934

▦ Isak Dinesen's *Seven Gothic Tales* is published.

1935

● Charlotte Perkins Gilman commits suicide on 17 August in Pasadena, California.

▦ *Bride of Frankenstein,* directed by James Whale, is released.

1936

▦ Walter de la Mare's *Ghost Stories* is published.

▦ William Faulkner's *Absalom, Absalom!* is published.

▦ H. P. Lovecraft's "At the Mountains of Madness" is published.

1937

● H. P. Lovecraft dies on 15 March in Providence, Rhode Island.

● Edith Wharton dies on 11 August in St. Brice-sous-Foret, France.

▦ Edith Wharton's *Ghosts* is published.

1938

● Joyce Carol Oates is born on 16 June in Lockport, New York.

▦ Daphne du Maurier's *Rebecca* is published.

1939

● Sigmund Freud dies on 23 September in London, England.

● Margaret Atwood is born on 18 November in Ottawa, Ontario, Canada.

▦ *Son of Frankenstein,* directed by Rowland V. Lee, is released.

1940

● Angela Carter is born on 7 May in London, England.

▦ *Rebecca,* directed by Alfred Hitchcock, is released.

1941

● Howard Allen O'Brien (later Anne Rice) is born on 4 October in New Orleans, Louisiana.

1943

▦ *I Walked with a Zombie, The Leopard Man,* and *The Seventh Victim,* all produced by Val Lewton, are released.

1945

▦ *The Body Snatcher,* directed by Robert Wise, is released.

▦ Elizabeth Bowen's *The Demon Lover, and Other Stories* is published.

▦ H. P. Lovecraft's *Supernatural Horror in Literature* is published.

1947

● Stephen King is born on 21 September in Portland, Maine.

1949

▦ Shirley Jackson's *The Lottery; or, The Adventures of James Harris* is published.

1952

● Clive Barker is born on 5 October in Liverpool, England.

1955

▦ Flannery O'Connor's *A Good Man Is Hard to Find* is published.

1956

● Bela Lugosi dies on 16 August in Los Angeles, California.

▦ *Invasion of the Body Snatchers,* directed by Don Siegel, is released.

1957

- *The Curse of Frankenstein*, directed by Terence Fisher, is released.

1959

- Shirley Jackson's *The Haunting of Hill House* is published.

- *The Mummy*, directed by Terence Fisher, is released.

- *The Twilight Zone* is first televised.

1960

- *The Fall of the House of Usher*, directed by Roger Corman, is released.

- *Psycho*, directed by Alfred Hitchcock, is released.

1962

- William Faulkner dies on 6 July in Byhalia, Mississippi.

- Isak Dinesen dies on 7 September in Rungsted, Denmark.

1963

- Sylvia Plath's *The Bell Jar* is published.

- *The Birds*, directed by Alfred Hitchcock, is released.

- *The Haunting*, directed by Robert Wise, is released.

1964

- Flannery O'Connor dies on 3 August in Milledgeville, Georgia.

- *The Addams Family* is first televised.

- *The Munsters* is first televised.

1965

- Shirley Jackson dies on 8 August in North Bennington, Vermont.

1966

- Frank Zappa and The Mothers of Invention's *Freak Out!* is released.

1968

- Margaret Atwood's *The Animals in That Country* is published.

- *Night of the Living Dead*, directed by George A. Romero, is released.

- *Rosemary's Baby*, directed by Roman Polanski, is released.

1969

- Boris Karloff dies on 2 February at Midhurst in Sussex, England.

- Led Zeppelin's first two self-titled albums are released.

1970

- Black Sabbath's self-titled debut album is released.

- Toni Morrison's *The Bluest Eye* is published.

- *Night Gallery* is first televised.

1971

- Richard Matheson's *Hell House* is published.

- Alice Cooper's *Killer* is released.

- Black Sabbath's *Paranoid* is released.

1972

- Margaret Atwood's *Surfacing* is published.

- Angela Carter's *The Infernal Desire Machines of Doctor Hoffman* is published.

- Alice Cooper's *School's Out* is released.

1973

- Elizabeth Bowen dies on 22 February in London, England.

- *The Exorcist*, directed by William Friedkin, is released.

1974

- Angela Carter's *Fireworks: Nine Profane Pieces* is published.

- *The Texas Chainsaw Massacre*, directed by Tobe Hooper, is released.

- *Young Frankenstein*, directed by Mel Brooks, is released.

1975

- Stephen King's *'Salem's Lot* is published.
- *They Came from Within*, directed by David Cronenberg, is released.

1976

- Margaret Atwood's *Lady Oracle* is published.
- *Carrie*, directed by Brian De Palma, is released.
- *The Omen*, directed by Richard Donner, is released.
- Anne Rice's *Interview with the Vampire* is published.

1977

- Stephen King's *The Shining* is published.
- Joyce Carol Oates's *Night Side: Eighteen Tales* is published.

1978

- *Dawn of the Dead*, directed by George A. Romero, is released.

1979

- Bauhaus's 12-inch single "Bela Lugosi's Dead" is released.
- Angela Carter's *The Bloody Chamber and Other Stories* is published.
- Joy Division's *Unknown Pleasures* is released.
- *'Salem's Lot*, directed by Tobe Hooper, is televised.

1980

- Alfred Hitchcock dies on 29 April in Los Angeles, California.
- Joyce Carol Oates's *Bellefleur* is published.
- *The Shining*, directed by Stanley Kubrick, is released.

1981

- *Stephen King's Danse Macabre* is published.
- Siouxsie and the Banshees's *Juju* is released.

1982

- Joyce Carol Oates's *A Bloodsmoor Romance* is published.

1983

- Stephen King's *Pet Sematary* is published.
- New Order's *Power, Corruption, and Lies* is released.

1984

- Joyce Carol Oates's *Mysteries of Winterthurn* is published.

1986

- Clive Barker's *The Hellbound Heart* is published.
- Siouxsie and the Banshees's *Tinderbox* is released.
- Andrew Lloyd Webber's *The Phantom of the Opera* is produced.

1987

- Toni Morrison's *Beloved* is published.
- The Smiths's *Louder than Bombs* is released.

1988

- Toni Morrison is awarded the Pulitzer Prize for Fiction for *Beloved*.

1989

- Daphne du Maurier dies on 19 April in Cornwall, England.
- *Pet Sematary*, directed by Mary Lambert, is released.

1990

- *Twin Peaks* is first televised.

1992

- Angela Carter dies on 16 February in London, England.
- *Bram Stoker's Dracula*, directed by Francis Ford Coppola, is released.

1993

- Margaret Atwood's *The Robber Bride* is published.

1994

▓ Joyce Carol Oates's *Haunted: Tales of the Grotesque* is published.

▓ *Mary Shelley's Frankenstein,* directed by Kenneth Branagh, is released.

1996

▓ Margaret Atwood's *Alias Grace* is published.

2000

● Edward Gorey dies on 15 April in Cape Cod, Massachusetts.

▓ Margaret Atwood's *The Blind Assassin* is published.

MARGARET ATWOOD

(1939 -)

(Full name Margaret Eleanor Atwood) Canadian novelist, poet, short story writer, essayist, critic, and author of children's books.

Internationally acclaimed as a novelist, poet, and short story writer, Atwood is widely considered a major figure in Canadian letters. Using such devices as irony, symbolism, and self-conscious narrators, she explores the relationship between humanity and nature, unsettling aspects of human behavior, and power as it pertains to gender and political roles. Her authorial voice has sometimes been described as formal and emotionally distant, but her talent for allegory and intense imagery informs an intellectual and sardonic style popular with both literary scholars and the reading public. Atwood has also been instrumental as a critic. She has helped define the identity and goals of contemporary Canadian literature and has earned a distinguished reputation among feminist writers for her exploration of women's issues.

BIOGRAPHICAL INFORMATION

Atwood was born in Ottawa and grew up in suburban Toronto. As a child she spent her summers at her family's cottage in the wilderness of northern Quebec, where her father, a forest entomologist, conducted research. She began to write while in high school, contributing poetry, short stories, and cartoons to the school newspaper. As an undergraduate at the University of Toronto, Atwood was influenced by critic Northrop Frye, who introduced her to the poetry of William Blake. Impressed with Blake's use of mythological imagery, Atwood wrote her first volume of poetry, *Double Persephone*, which was published in 1961. The following year Atwood completed her A.M. degree at Radcliffe College, Harvard University. She returned to Toronto in 1963, where she began collaborating with artist Charles Pachter, who designed and illustrated several volumes of her poetry. In 1964 Atwood moved to Vancouver, where she taught English for a year at the University of British Columbia and completed her first novel, *The Edible Woman* (1969). After a year of teaching literature at Sir George Williams University in Montreal, Atwood moved to Alberta to teach creative writing at the University of Alberta. Her poetry collection *The Circle Game* (1966) won the 1967 Governor General's Award, Canada's highest literary honor. Atwood's public visibility increased significantly with the publication of her poetry collection *Power Politics* in 1971. Seeking an escape from increasing media attention, Atwood left her teaching position at the University of Toronto to move to a farm in Ontario with her husband. In 1986 she again received the Governor General's Award for her novel *The Handmaid's Tale*

(1986) and was later awarded the Booker Prize for her novel *The Blind Assassin* (2000).

MAJOR WORKS

The poems in Atwood's first volume, *Double Persephone* reflect the influence of Blake's contrasting mythological imagery. While this collection demonstrates her penchant for using metaphorical language, Atwood's second volume of poetry, *The Circle Game,* garnered widespread critical recognition. Atwood explores the meaning of art and literature, as well as the Gothic, in the poetry collection *The Animals in That Country* (1968). Presenting the poet as both performer and creator, she questions the authenticity of the writing process and the effects of literature on both the writer and the reader. In *The Journals of Susanna Moodie* (1970) Atwood devotes her attention to what she calls the schizoid, double nature of Canada. Centered on the narratives of a Canadian pioneer woman, *Journals* investigates why Canadians came to develop ambivalent feelings toward their country. Atwood further develops this dichotomy in *Power Politics,* in which she explores the relationship between sexual roles and power structures by focusing on personal relationships and international politics.

The story of an unnamed freelance artist who journeys to the wilderness of Quebec to investigate her father's disappearance, *Surfacing* (1972) focuses on the dichotomous nature of family relationships, cultural heritage, and self-perception. The protagonist of Atwood's novel *Lady Oracle* (1976) is Joan Foster, who writes "costume Gothics" and fakes her own death to avoid the consequences of her past mistakes. The novel depicts relations between mothers and daughters and explores twentieth-century female identity by illustrating the monstrosity of the societal roles created by and for women. Just as Atwood uses monsters (Joan's three-way vanity mirror is a "triple-headed monster" and Joan becomes a "duplicitous monster") to highlight the novel's thematic concerns, so does Joan utilize her own costume Gothic characters and narratives to explore the issues that concern her, and in the end is able to begin writing in a new discipline—science fiction. In her novel *Life before Man* (1979) Atwood dissects the relationships between three characters: Elizabeth, a married woman who mourns the recent death of her lover; Elizabeth's husband, Nate, who is unable to choose between his wife and his lover; and Lesje, Nate's lover, who works with Elizabeth at a museum of natural history. All three characters are emotionally isolated from one another and are unable to take responsibility for their feelings as their relationships deteriorate.

Atwood turned to speculative fiction with her novel *The Handmaid's Tale,* depicting the dystopia of Gilead, a future America in which Fundamentalist Christians have imposed dictatorial rule. Here, in a world polluted by toxic chemicals and nuclear radiation, most women are sterile; those who are able to bear children are forced to become Handmaids, official surrogate mothers who enjoy some privileges yet remain under constant surveillance. Almost all other women have been deemed expendable. While *The Handmaid's Tale* focuses on an imagined future, Atwood's novel *Cat's Eye* (1990) explores how misconceptions about the past can influence people's present lives. The story of Elaine Risley, a prominent artist who returns to her childhood home in Toronto, *Cat's Eye* traces Elaine's discovery that her childhood relationships were often manipulative and that her memories of past events have not always been accurate or honest. Considered by many an allegorical exploration of the realities confronting individuals at the approach of the twenty-first century, this work reveals the implications of evil and redemption in both a personal and social context. In *Cat's Eye,* as in all her works, Atwood forgoes specific political or moral ideologies, concentrating instead on the emotional and psychological complexities that confront individuals in conflict with society.

In *The Robber Bride* (1993) Atwood transforms the Brothers Grimm's grisly fairy tale "The Robber Bridegroom," about a demonic groom who lures three innocent maidens into his lair and then devours them, into a statement about women's treatment of each other. Three middle-aged friends are relieved to reunite at the funeral of the woman who tormented them in college, stealing from them money, time, and men, and threatening their careers and lives. But the villainous Zenia turns up alive, forcing them to relive painful memories and come to terms with the connection between love and destruction. *Alias Grace* (1996) represents Atwood's first venture into historical fiction. Based on a true story Atwood had explored previously in a television script titled *The Servant Girl, Alias Grace* centers on Grace Marks, a servant who was found guilty of murdering her employer and his mistress in northern Canada in 1843. Some people doubt Grace's guilt, however, and she serves out her sentence of life in prison, claiming not to remember the murders. Eventually, reformers begin to agitate for clemency for Grace. In a quest for evidence to support their position, they assign a young doctor, versed in the new science of psychiatry, to evaluate her soundness of mind. Over many meetings, Grace tells the doctor the harrowing story of her life, which has been marked by extreme hardship. Much about Grace, though, remains puzzling; she is haunted by flashbacks of the supposedly forgotten murders and by the presence of a friend who had died from a mishandled abortion. The doctor, Simon Jordan, does not know what to believe in Grace's tales. *The Blind Assassin* involves multiple story lines. It is the memoir of Iris, a dying woman in her eighties who retraces her past with the wealthy and conniving industrialist Richard Griffen and the deaths of her sister Laura, her husband, and her daughter, and it is also a novel-within-a-novel, as interspersed with Iris's wry narrative threads are sections devoted to Laura's novel, *The Blind Assassin*, published after her death.

CRITICAL RECEPTION

The winner of the 1967 Governor General's Award, Canada's highest literary honor, *The Circle Game* established the major themes of Atwood's poetry: the inconsistencies of self-perception, the paradoxical nature of language, Canadian identity, and the conflicts between humankind and nature. In addition to her numerous collections of poetry, Atwood earned widespread attention for *Survival: A Thematic Guide to Canadian Literature* (1972), a seminal critical analysis of Canadian literature that served as a rallying point for the country's cultural nationalists. In *Survival* Atwood argues that Canadians have always viewed themselves as victims, both of the forces of nature that confronted them as they settled in wilderness territory and of the colonialist powers that dominated their culture and politics. She proposes that Canadian writers should cultivate a more positive self-image by embracing indigenous traditions, including those of Native Americans and French Canadians, rather than identifying with Great Britain or the United States.

Several commentators have noted a wide range of Gothic themes, characters, devices, and stylistic elements in Atwood's works. Her poetry collection, *The Animals in That Country*, has been assessed as fitting neatly into the Gothic tradition. This volume contains the poem "Speeches for Dr. Frankenstein," in which Atwood explores dualities, dichotomies, tension between opposites, and doubling. *Surfacing* has been regarded as an example of modern female Gothic for its depiction of an emotionally and socially repressed protagonist who, after learning of her father's disappearance from his cabin, takes a harrowing trip with her lover and another couple to the wilderness. During the journey, she confronts painful memories from her past and, by moving beyond the "surface" of her emotions and allowing herself to truly explore her pain, she is able to free herself from it. *Lady Oracle*, which Sybil Korff Vincent calls "the most Gothic of Gothic novels, a Gothic novel about Gothic novels," has been widely discussed as Atwood's most overtly Gothic work. *Lady Oracle* has been compared to Jane Austen's *Northanger Abbey* for its parodic elements and commentary on the relationship between reality and the representation of it in Gothic literature. Michiko Kakutani (see Further Reading) has asserted that *The Blind Assassin* "showcases Ms. Atwood's narrative powers and her ardent love of the Gothic." This novel, with its parallel narrative structure, twisted, complex plot, murders, mystery, and underlying sense of defeat, has been characterized as closely resembling classic works of Gothic fiction.

PRINCIPAL WORKS

Double Persephone (poetry) 1961

The Circle Game (poetry) 1966

The Animals in That Country (poetry) 1968

The Edible Woman (novel) 1969

The Journals of Susanna Moodie (poetry) 1970

Procedures for Underground (poetry) 1970

Power Politics (poetry) 1971

Surfacing (novel) 1972

Survival: A Thematic Guide to Canadian Literature (criticism) 1972

You Are Happy (poetry) 1974

Lady Oracle (novel) 1976

Selected Poems (poetry) 1976

Dancing Girls, and Other Stories (short stories) 1977

Two-Headed Poems (poetry) 1978

Up in the Tree (juvenilia) 1978

Life before Man (novel) 1979

True Stories (poetry) 1981

Bodily Harm (novel) 1982

Second Words: Selected Critical Prose (criticism) 1982

Bluebeard's Egg (short stories) 1983

PRIMARY SOURCES

MARGARET ATWOOD (POEM DATE 1968)

SOURCE: Atwood, Margaret. "Speeches for Dr. Frankenstein." In *The Animals in That Country,* pp. 42-7. Boston: Atlantic—Little, Brown, 1968.

In the following poem, Atwood comments on the creative process and its effects on both the artist/creator and the work/creation through an imagined dialogue between Dr. Frankenstein and the monster from Mary Shelley's novel Frankenstein.

"Speeches for Dr Frankenstein"

I

I, the performer
in the tense arena, glittered
under the fluorescent moon. Was bent
masked by the table. Saw what focused
my intent: the emptiness

The air filled with an ether of cheers.

My wrist extended a scalpel.

II

The table is a flat void,
barren as total freedom. Though behold

A sharp twist
like taking a jar top off

and it is a living
skeleton, mine, round,
that lies on the plate before me

red as a pomegranate,
every cell a hot light.

III

I circle, confront
my opponent. The thing
refuses to be shaped, it moves
like yeast. I thrust,

the thing fights back.
It dissolves, growls, grows crude claws;

The air is dusty with blood.

It springs. I cut
with delicate precision.

The specimens
ranged on the shelves, applaud.

The thing falls Thud. A cat
anatomized.

O secret
form of the heart, now I have you.

IV

Now I shall ornament you.
What would you like?

Baroque scrolls on your ankles?
A silver navel?

I am the universal weaver;
I have eight fingers.

I complicate you;
I surround you with intricate ropes.

What web shall I wrap you in?
Gradually I pin you down.

What equation shall
I carve and seal in your skull?

What size will I make you?
Where should I put your eyes?

V

I was insane with skill:
I made you perfect.

I should have chosen instead
to curl you small as a seed,

trusted beginnings. Now I wince
before this plateful of results:

core and rind, the flesh between
already turning rotten.

I stand in the presence
of the destroyed god:

a rubble of tendons,
knuckles and raw sinews.

Knowing that the work is mine
how can I love you?

These archives of potential
time exude fear like a smell.

VI

You arise, larval
and shrouded in the flesh I gave you;

I, who have no covering
left but a white cloth skin

escape from you. You are red,
you are human and distorted.

You have been starved,
you are hungry. I have nothing to feed you.

I pull around me, running,
a cape of rain.

What was my ravenous motive?
Why did I make you?

VII

Reflection, you have stolen
everything you needed:

my joy, my ability
to suffer.

You have transmuted
yourself to me: I am
a vestige, I am numb.

Now you accuse me of murder.

Can't you see
I am incapable?

Blood of my brain,
it is you who have killed these people.

VIII

Since I dared
to attempt impious wonders

I must pursue
that animal I once denied
was mine.

Over this vacant winter
plain, the sky is a black shell;
I move within it, a cold
kernel of pain.

I scratch huge rescue messages
on the solid
snow; in vain. My heart's
husk is a stomach. I am its food.

IX

The sparkling monster
gambols there ahead,
his mane electric:
This is his true place.

He dances in spirals on the ice,
his clawed feet
kindling shaggy fires.

His happiness
is now the chase itself:
he traces it in light,
his paths contain it.

I am the gaunt hunter
necessary for his patterns,
lurking, gnawing leather.

X

The creature, his arctic hackles
bristling, spreads
over the dark ceiling,
his paws on the horizons,
rolling the world like a snowball.

He glows and says:

Doctor, my shadow
shivering on the table,
you dangle on the leash
of your own longing;
your need grows teeth.

You sliced me loose

and said it was
Creation. I could feel the knife.
Now you would like to heal
that chasm in your side,
but I recede. I prowl.

I will not come when you call.

GENERAL COMMENTARY

ELI MANDEL (ESSAY DATE 1977)

SOURCE: Mandel, Eli. "Atwood Gothic." *The Malahat Review* 41 (1977): 165-74.

In the following essay, Mandel studies Atwood's utilization of Gothic themes and devices to express and comment upon complex social, political, and psychological issues in her works.

Margaret Atwood's *You Are Happy* offers not only her usual poetic transformations, identifications, witch-woman figures, animal-men, and photograph-poems but also an intriguing set of "Tricks with Mirrors." It is the mirror poems that suggest, more pointedly than usual in her work, questions about duplicity and reflexiveness—concerns quite different from apparently clear and accessible social comment. She writes:

> Don't assume it is passive
> or easy, this clarity
>
> with which I give you yourself,
> Consider what restraint it
>
> takes. . . .
>
> It is not a trick either,
>
> It is a craft:
> mirrors are crafty.
>
> . . . . .
>
> You don't like these metaphors
> All right:
>
> Perhaps I am not a mirror.
> Perhaps I am a pool.
> Think about pools.
>
> (pp. 26-27)

Quite likely the speaker of the poem is meant to be taken as a lover; certainly she speaks to a Narcissus gazing at her as if she were a mirror; and to hear in the voice the artist's warning about craftiness may seem perverse, though the suggestion of allegory is so tempting in Atwood's works it is difficult to resist. In any event, the mirror voice does present ambiguous possibilities that call to mind apparently contradictory qualities in Atwood's writing: clarity and accessibility, certainly, combined with extraordinary deftness in manipulating contemporary modes of speech and image, and a compelling toughmindedness, a ruthless unsentimentality, which is somehow liberating rather than cynically enclosing. These modes and attitudes point to social concerns, but one senses that these surface qualities may be concealing quite different interests. It is not my intention to deny the obvious, that she does handle with force and insight important contemporary social metaphors: the politics of love and self, the mystification of experience, woman as prisoner of the mind police, social institutions as models of the police state, the schizophrenic journey toward health, and so on. But the oracular qualities of her work, no doubt as attractive as social commentary to her readers, deserve more extended commentary than they have received. I am thinking of the gothic elements of her novels,

her consistent and obsessive use of reduplicating images, and her totemic animal imagery.

Margaret Atwood's comment, in a conversation with Graeme Gibson, that *Surfacing* "is a ghost story" provides the point of departure for more than one commentary on her work. Less often noticed is the special form of ghost story Atwood employs, the story in *Journals of Susanna Moodie,* for example. Mrs. Moodie appears to Atwood, we are told, in a dream, later manifesting herself to the poet "as a mad-looking and very elderly lady"; the poems take her "through an estranged old age, into death and beyond." (p. 63) That makes her a ghost in the last poem, "**A Bus Along St. Clair: December,**" where she tells us:

> I am the old woman
> sitting across from you on the bus,
> her shoulders drawn up like a shawl;
> out of her eyes come secret
> hatpins, destroying
> the walls, the ceiling.
>
> (p. 61)

Her earthly life, portrayed in the earlier poems, involves a pattern not unlike the heroine's journey into the backwoods in *Surfacing*: a landing on a seashore apparently occupied by dancing sand-flies, a pathway into a forest, confrontation with a wolfman and other animals, men in masks, deaths of children, including a drowning, sinister plants. Gothic tale is a better name than ghost story for this form, in which the chief element is the threat to a maiden, a young girl, a woman. In a well-known passage, Leslie Fiedler, (allegorizing like mad, incidentally), comments on the chief features of the form, its motifs:

> Chief of the gothic symbols is, of course, the Maiden in flight. . . . Not the violation or death which sets such a flight in motion, but the flight itself figures forth the essential meaning of the anti-bourgeois gothic, for which the girl on the run and her pursuer become only alternate versions of the same plight. Neither can come to rest before the other—for each is the projection of his opposite . . . actors in a drama which depends on both for its significance. Reinforcing the meaning . . . is the haunted countryside, and especially the haunted castle or abbey which rises in its midst, and in whose dark passages and cavernous apartments the chase reaches its climax.[1]

Substitute forest for haunted castle, and think of the ghosts of Mrs. Radcliffe's *The Italian*, and the ghost story or gothic form of an Atwood poem or novel begins to take shape. Obviously, it is richly suggestive of a variety of dark threats, either psychological or hidden in the social structure. Atwood's own political and social commentary on Canadian imagination employs, with superb wit and skill, a victor/victim pattern (the haunted victim, the haunted persecutor, perhaps?) to outline not only an endlessly repeated pattern, but a theory of colonialism, that is, victimization. We see the possibilities: if *Surfacing* presents itself as political and social criticism disguised as ghost story, could it be that *Survival* takes its unusual power precisely from the fact that it is a ghost story disguised as politics and criticism?

A further elaboration is suggested by Ellen Moers' comments in the chapter of *Literary Women* called "The Female Gothic": Gothic, says Moers, is writing that "has to do with fear," writing in which "fantasy predominates over reality, the strange over the commonplace, and the supernatural over the natural, with one definite auctorial intent: to scare. Not, that is, to reach down into the depths of the soul and purge it with pity and terror (as we say tragedy does), but to get to the body itself, its glands, muscles, epidermis, and circulatory system, quickly arousing and quickly allaying the physiological reactions to fear."[2] Moers' emphasis on physiological effect seems appropriate. It points to the kind of imagination found, say, in Michael Ondaatje's work as well as in Atwood's that might appropriately be called a physiological imagination, whose purpose is evident.[3]

Fear. But fear of what? Some say sexuality, especially taboo aspects of sexuality, incest for example: the gothic threat to a young woman carries implications of sado-masochistic fantasy, the victim/victor pattern of *Survival*. Ellen Moers suggests that in Mary Shelley's *Frankenstein*, the real taboo is birth itself; death and birth are hideously mixed in the creation of a monster out of pieces of the human body. (The image involves, as well, the hideousness of duplication and reduplication.) In Atwood's **"Speeches for Dr. Frankenstein,"** her Dr. Frankenstein addresses his creation in unmistakable language about a botched creation, a birth/death confusion:

I was insane with skill:
I made you perfect.

I should have chosen instead
to curl you small as a seed,

trusted beginnings. Now I wince
before this plateful of results:

core and rind, the flesh between
already turning rotten.

I stand in the presence
of the destroyed god:

A rubble of tendons,
knuckles and raw sinews.

Knowing that the work is mine
How can I love you?
(***The Animals in That Country***, p. 44)

If, as he says to his monster, Dr. Frankenstein might have trusted in beginnings, in seed, the narrator of *Surfacing*, it seems, distrusts virtually all births. How much of the haunting proceeds from an abortion? We discern a pattern of mixed birth/death in the book: the baby not born, the baby aborted, the baby about to be born as a furred monster, the drowned brother who didn't drown, the baby peering out of the mother's stomach, the embryo-like frogs, the frog-like embryo, the man-frog father in the waters, hanging from the camera with which he might have photographed the gods.

Who are the ghosts of *Surfacing* then? In *Survival*, which reads like a gloss on *Surfacing*, Atwood tells us that the ghost or death goddess of *The Double Hook* represents fear, but not fear of death, fear of life. And babies? Following a rather horrendous list of miscarriages, cancers, tumours, stillbirths and worse, which she finds in Canadian novels, Atwood remarks laconically, "The Great Canadian Baby is sometimes alarmingly close to the Great Canadian Coffin." (p. 208) Who are the ghosts of *Surfacing*? A mother, a father, a lost child, Indians, the animals: all symbols of vitality, life, our real humanity, that has disappeared and must be brought back. "It does not approve of me or disapprove of me," the narrator says of the creature who is elemental, as she thinks her father has become: "it tells me it has nothing to tell me, only the fact of itself." (p. 187) And she says of her parents after her paroxysm in the woods: "they dwindle, grow, become what they were, human. Something I never gave them credit for." (p. 189) Ghosts: only the human body, repressed, denied; only life denied. All proceeds from the ghosts: a de-realized world: victimization, sexism, deformed sexuality, sado-masochism, tearing away at nature's body, at our own bodies.

But to say this is to accept the *allegory* of gothic that Atwood allows her narrator to spell out for us (it is worth noting that in the best gothic fashion, the daylight world after the horrors of the long night reveals that the ghosts are mechanical or waxwork figures). To say this is also to explain away not only the ghosts but one of the most disturbing and most characteristic of Atwood's qualities, her sense of doubleness, of reduplication, in word and image. Even the victor/

victim pattern recurs and the tale told once in *Surfacing* will be told again. At the end, nothing is resolved.

The ghosts are sexual fears, repressed contents of the imagination, social rigidity. They are also literary images, book reflections, patterns from all those readings in gothic romance, perhaps even the unwritten thesis Atwood proposed for her Ph.D., on gothic romance. Reduplication. Margaret Atwood's first book of poetry bears the title *Double Persephone*. The first poem of *The Circle Game* is called **"This is a photograph of Me,"** and the speaker tells us that if you look closely at the lake, you will discern her image; in parenthesis we are told:

(The photograph was taken
the day after I drowned.

I am in the lake, in the centre
of the picture, just under the surface.

It is difficult to say where
precisely, or to say
how large or small I am:
the effect of water
on light is a distortion

but if you look long enough,
eventually
you will be able to see me.)

(p. 11)

End of brackets. A kind of insane phenomenology takes over that precise meticulous speech; we enter a world of reflections within reflections, totemic duplication (consider the possibilities in the simple four-part structure: man masked; man unmasked; animal masked; animal unmasked) and de-realized experience. Mirror, water and reflection, games like cards and chess, maps or models, eyes and cameras make up the major duplications, though there are more subtle ones in births and ghosts, in movies, photographs, drownings, archeology, astral travel, revenants, echoes, icons, comic books and gardens. The list, I think, could be extended—or duplicated—but its obsessive nature should be clear. It should also be clear that the list points up the literary nature of Atwood's concerns, otherwise fairly successfully disguised by her field of reference, popular and contemporary imagery. In *You Are Happy,* a poem called **"Gothic Letter on a Hot Night"** gives, in a typically wry and throw-away manner, the reflexive pattern of story within story. Presumably this speaker faces a blank page and longs for stories again, but it is not clear whether that is bad (she ought not to live her life in stories) or good (she cannot write and therefore all the bad things the

stories could do will remain undone). Either way, there is a sinister suggestion that the stories (like the poem one writes to drown one's sister, or the things that go on just outside the frame of the picture, the part you cannot see) will in fact, or could in fact, write the lives of the story-teller:

It was the addiction
to stories, every
story about herself or anyone
led to the sabotage of each address
and all those kidnappings

Stories that could be told
on nights like these to account for the losses
litanies of escapes, bad novels, thrillers
deficient in villains;
now there is nothing to write
She would have given almost anything
to have them back,
those destroyed houses, smashed plates,
    calendars.

(p. 15)

An ambiguity, unresolved, is that the poem begins in first person but in the second stanza shifts to third person narrative. The three—the "I" speaking, the "you" addressed, and the "she" who tells stories—remain unidentified. Duplicity, in part, consists in trying to have it both ways. No doubt, Atwood would recoil from my reading backwards to the material from which she begins, and which often seems to form the object of her irony: don't live in stories, you are not literature, if you think you would like it when the gods do reveal themselves try it sometime. So *Surfacing* moves from the world of ghosts back to the place where the narrator can be seen for what she is, a poor naked shivering wretch, scarcely human. But the ambiguity is in the power of the material. *You Are Happy* ends with what looks like a dismissal of "the gods and their static demands," but leaves open the question—again—whether you can only do this if you have been there, have known them. Even in parody and irony (let alone social comments on literary forms) the problem, the puzzle about reduplication remains.

A similar question arises with Robertson Davies' *World of Wonders*; that is, should we read it psychologically, in Jungian terms, as Davies intends, or theatrically, as a series of beautifully structured and terribly inflated poses, or magically, as not only the charlatan's illusions but the magician's powers. This question is somewhere in the background of Michael Ondaatje's *The Collected Works of Billy the Kid* (all the deceit, the obvious lies, as Ondaatje says of another poem) and in Kroetsch's insistent attempt to uninvent the world he wants so desperately to be at home in. Perhaps the disclaimers are essential to the magic of repetition, a kind of Borgesian pretence that the story or poem is really an essay, or that the essay is a story. The problem is, whatever philosophic dilemmas duplication raises about time and cause, psychologically and poetically it seems far more sinister than the writer wishes to admit. Either a fraud or a magician, the crude choice would seem to be. To which we answer (and this involves the reduplication) neither: this is only a story about both.

Psychologically, as Borges points out in *Labyrinths,* the story of a world created by a written version of another world of endless reduplication, of halls of mirrors, is a horror. "Mirrors have something monstrous about them . . . because they increase the number of men."[4] In folklore, the doppleganger motif, in which one meets oneself coming back as one goes forward, signifies either death or the onset of prophetic power. In Jung's commentary on the *I Ching,* synchronicity substitutes chance for cause, a randomness that plays havoc with notions of identity and opens the possibility of occult possession. The vegetable version of this pattern, in its benign form, is sacramental, and in its malign or demonic form, cannibalistic. Atwood's ironic awareness of such patterns pervades her humanized gardens and provides a structural principle for her novel, *The Edible Woman.* But whatever the psychological significance, the literary seems more difficult for her; for in literary terms, as Borges argues, the device of reduplication calls attention to the poem and hence to the fictional nature of the poem's reality. It de-realizes experience:

Why does it disturb us that the map be included in the map and the thousand and one nights in the book of the *Thousand and One Nights*? Why does it disturb us that Don Quixote be a reader of the *Quixote* and Hamlet a spectator of *Hamlet*? . . . The inversions suggest that if the characters of a fictional work can be readers and spectators, we, its readers or spectators, can be fictitious. In 1833, Carlyle observed that the history of the universe is an infinite sacred book that all men write and read and try to understand, and in which they are also written.[5]

Borges remarks that tales of fantasy are not haphazard combinations: "They have a meaning, they make us feel that we are living in a strange world."[6] Focussing on the obvious, the map of Canada in a tourist agency, viewed by a window lady who sees her own reflection containing the mapped country, Atwood gives us a country stranger than we knew:

look, here, Saskatchewan
is a flat lake, some convenient rocks
where two children pose with a father
and the mother is cooking something
in immaculate slacks by a smokeless fire,
her teeth white as detergent.

Whose dream is this, I would like to know:
. . . . .

Unsuspecting
window lady, I ask you:

Do you see nothing
watching from under the water?

Was the sky ever that blue?

Who really lives there?
("**At the Tourist Centre in Boston**")

Borges' temptation is solipsism (think of your life as a dream). But Atwood's poem characteristically questions the dream. No matter that this is the American dream of Canada, "A manufactured hallucination"; the Unsuspecting Reflection, water and sky in her own head, doesn't surface, lives with her unanswered questions.

It would be possible, I suppose, to read Atwood's career as a search for techniques to answer those questions honestly, resolve the reflecting/reflector dilemma by demystifying experience. Certainly by the time of *Power Politics* she attained an impressive command of deflating ironies; a poem like "**They Eat Out**" sets up opposing stereotypes of magical thinking in an atmosphere of fried rice and pop culture:

I raise the magic fork
over the plate of beef fried rice

and plunge it into your heart.
There is a faint pop, a sizzle

and through your own split head
you rise up glowing;

the ceiling opens
a voice sings Love is a Many

Splendoured Thing
you hang suspended above the city

in blue tights and red cape,
your eyes flashing in unison.
. . . . .

As for me, I continue eating;
I liked you better the way you were
but you were always ambitious.

But writing has its own power, its metaphors, like mirrors in the language. No one knows what word the heroine of *Surfacing* will speak first. It is possible that she will say nothing. Silence can be the strategy of those who have endured. But if there is any sense to my argument that Atwood's obsessive concern with mirror and reflection is an attempt to resolve an impossible dilemma about writing and experience, or about fiction and wisdom; and at the same time, a sort of playing about with the fires of magical possession, then I would guess that tormented girl would turn toward us and say:

> You don't like these metaphors
> All right
> Think about pools.

Notes

1. *Love and Death in The American Novel,* Meridian Books, (New York, 1962), 111-112.

2. *Literary Women,* Doubleday and Company (New York, 1976), 90.

3. Like Atwood, Ondaatje, especially in *The Collected Works of Billy the Kid,* and Robert Kroetsch in *The Studhorse Man* and *Badlands,* tend to bring together images of sexuality, dismemberment, and poetics, poetic and sexual obsessions leading to anatomies.

4. "Tlön Uqbar, Orbïs Tertius," *Labyrinths,* New Directions (New York, 1962), 3.

5. Partial Magic in the Quixote," *Labyrinths,* 196.

6. "Tales of the Fantastic" in *Prism international,* Volume Eight, Number One, (Summer, 1968), p. 15.

CORAL ANN HOWELLS (ESSAY DATE 1996)

SOURCE: Howells, Coral Ann. "Atwoodian Gothic: From *Lady Oracle* to *The Robber Bride.*" In *Margaret Atwood,* pp. 62-85. New York: St. Martin's Press, 1996.

In the following excerpt, Howells examines Atwood's unique manipulation of Gothic themes, imagery, and narrative techniques.

Atwoodian Gothic is both sinister and jokey, rather like the scary game which Atwood describes in **Murder in the Dark,** a game about murderers, victims and detectives played with the lights off. The only other thing the reader needs to know is that the victim is always silent and that the murderer always lies:

> In any case, that's me in the dark. I have designs on you, I'm plotting my sinister crime, my hands are reaching for your neck or perhaps, by mistake, your thigh. You can hear my footsteps approaching, I wear boots and carry a knife, or maybe it's a pearl-handled revolver, in any case I wear boots with very soft soles, you can see the cinematic glow of my cigarette, waxing and waning in the fog of the room, the street, the room, even though I don't smoke. Just remember this, when the scream at last has ended and you've turned on the lights: by the rules of the game, I must always lie.[1]

This game is emblematic of Atwoodian Gothic; its aim is to scare, yet it is a sort of fabricated fright; there are rules and conventions and we enter into a kind of complicity because we want to be frightened. Atwood suggests, 'You can say: the murderer is the writer' and then either the book or the reader would be the victim, which makes an interesting identification between Gothic storyteller and murderer, trickster, liar. We could take that one stage further with Atwood's female Gothic storytellers, Joan Foster in **Lady Oracle,** Zenia in **The Robber Bride** and Atwood herself, identified as sybils, witches, supreme plotters all ('I have designs on you').

So, what is Gothic? At the core of the Gothic sensibility is fear—fear of ghosts, women's fear of men, fear of the dark, fear of what is hidden but might leap out unexpectedly, fear of something floating around loose which lurks behind the everyday. The emblematic fear within Gothic fantasy is that something that seemed to be dead and buried might not be dead at all. Hence the Gothic outbreaks of terror and violence as things cross forbidden barriers between dream and waking, life and death. It is easy to recognise a Gothic novel for it is characterised by a specific collection of motifs and themes, many of which come through folklore, fairytale, myth and nightmare. One of the most succinct accounts of the Gothic as a literary genre is Eve Kosofsky Sedgwick's critical study *The Coherence of Gothic Conventions,* which identifies two key terms to define the Gothic: the Unspeakable and Live Burial.[2] Arguably those terms might be seen as different images for the same thing for they both relate to what is hidden, secret, repressed, and which is threatening precisely because it is still alive and blocked off from consciousness though ready to spring out, transformed into some monstrous shape—like Freud's *unheimlich,* both familiar and alien to us.[3] It is this uncanny quality of Gothic which is embodied in its obsession with the transgression of boundaries and with transformations—'change from one state into another, change from one thing into another'.[4] On the level of the supernatural, there is the phenomenon of ghosts transgressing boundaries between life and death, while on the psychological level there is the erosion of boundaries between the self and the monstrous Other. (What does a Gothic protagonist see or fear to see when she looks in the mirror?) In the borderline territory between conscious and unconscious, a space is opened up for doubles and split selves, which are not total opposites but dependent on each other and linked by a kind of unacknowledged complicity, like Dr Frankenstein and his monster. To return to that game in *Murder in the Dark*: Atwood reminds players that they may take turns to be murderer or victim, for one role does not preclude the other. Gothic finds a language for representing areas of the self (like fears, anxieties, forbidden desires) which are unassimilable in terms of social conventions. In relation to fiction, the major point to consider is how these transgressions are expressed through narrative, most obviously in the shifts from realism to fantasy signalled in dreams and hallucinations, when frequently the working out of dreams is crucial to the plot. There is also the difficulty any Gothic story has in getting itself told at all: Gothic plots are characterised by enigmas, multiple stories embedded in the main story, multiple narrators and shifting points of view, and mixed genres, where fairy tale may blur into history or autobiography. At all times the Gothic narrative suggests the co-existence of the everyday alongside a shadowy nightmarish world.[5]

Not surprisingly, the Gothic romance has traditionally been a favourite genre for women writers, from Ann Radcliffe's *The Mysteries of Udolpho (1794)*, Mary Shelley's *Frankenstein* (1818), the Brontës' *Wuthering Heights* and *Jane Eyre* (1840s), through to Daphne Du Maurier's *Rebecca* (1938), Jean Rhys's *Wide Sargasso Sea* (1966), and the contemporary fiction of Margaret Atwood, Angela Carter, Beryl Bainbridge, Alice Munro. It is a devious literature through which to express female desires and dreads, and in Atwood it is easy to see the traditional forms surviving, updated but still retaining their original charge of menace and mystery, while balancing women's urge toward self-discovery and self-assertiveness with self-doubts, between celebration of new social freedoms and women's sense of not being free of traditional assumptions and myths about femininity. It is to this territory of Gothic romance that Atwood returns again and again, using its images and motifs and its narratives of transgression. To glance briefly at the pervasiveness of Gothic in Atwood, one would need to start with her early watercolours from the late 1960s where sinister knights in armour with hidden faces peer at damsels dressed in red, or dark male figures hold unconscious purple female bodies in their giant arms.[6] *Surfacing* might be construed as a ghost story in the Canadian wilderness, a reading suggested by Atwood in an early interview when she explained that she was writing in the tradition of the psychological ghost story:

You can have the Henry James kind, in which the ghost that one sees is in fact a fragment of one's own self which has split off, and that to me is the most interesting kind and that is obviously the tradition I'm working in.[7]

The motifs of haunted wilderness and the split self are still there 20 years later in the story 'Death by Landscape' in *Wilderness Tips*, just as the werewolf image which was there in *The Journals of Susanna Moodie* recurs in 'Age of Lead' in that same collection. The title story in *Bluebeard's Egg* (1983) is a modern revision of fairy tale,[8] while *Bodily Harm* (1981) and *The Handmaid's Tale* (1985) exploit traditional Gothic motifs in their representation of classic female fears of sexual violence or imprisonment. In *Cat's Eye* (1988) the protagonist is haunted by the past and by her doppelganger Cordelia ('Lie down, you're dead!') who represents the other half of herself, her dark mad twin. There is also a poem 'The Robber Bridegroom' in *Interlunar* (1984), and it is interesting to note that 'The Robber Bridegroom' was considered by Atwood as a possible title for *Bodily Harm.* In this recirculation of images and themes, we note very repetitive patterns which are the identifying marks of a literary genre. The same stories are being retold, as the reader is constantly reminded through intertextual allusions to fairy tales and old Gothic romances, so that versions that might look contemporary and new circle around old enigmas. It is from this Gothic continuum that I wish to single out *Lady Oracle* (1976) and *The Robber Bride* (1993) in order to examine what transformations of Gothic conventions Atwood has managed in novels that are nearly 20 years apart; to see how her changing use of Gothic conventions reflects her responses to shifts in cultural mythology, especially in her thinking about women. What we find is the reworking of traditional Gothic motifs within the frames of realistic fiction, for unlike her protagonist Joan Foster in *Lady Oracle,* Atwood does not 'write with her eyes closed'. On the contrary, Atwood is an attentive and often satirical critic of contemporary Canada, exposing popular myths and social ideologies for Atwood has designs on us. But then, of course, so did Joan Foster, and so did Zenia, the Robber Bride.

Atwood described *Lady Oracle* as 'a realistic comic novel colliding with Gothic conventions—I give you *Northanger Abbey*', as she explained for a lecture in 1982.[9] It is also a fictive autobiography, told by a woman who is a novelist and a poet, suggesting shadowy parallels with Atwood herself in her early days of fame when she was becoming a cultural ikon in Canada. More to the point because this novel is not autobiography but an autobiographical fiction, there are strong parallels with *Cat's Eye* told by that other successful woman artist, Elaine Risley the painter. In both cases a woman struggles to find her voice, to define her identity through telling her life story in different versions. *Lady Oracle* and *Cat's Eye* are curiously similar autobiographical projects because the stories the protagonists tell offer multiple versions of their lives which never quite fit together to form the image of a unified and coherent self. Who is Joan Foster, who writes popular Gothic romances under the pseudonym Louisa K. Delacourt? What is the significance of Lady Oracle, Joan's other pseudonym when she writes poetry? The one thing the reader can be sure about with Joan is that she is a fantasist, and a trickster: 'All my life I'd been hooked on plots'.[10]

Lady Oracle is a story about storytelling, both the stories themselves and the writing process, for Joan offers us multiple narratives figuring and refiguring herself through different narrative conventions. The novel is structured through a series of interlocking frames. First, there is the story of Joan's real life in the present, set in Italy where she has escaped after her fake suicide in Toronto, Canada. Enclosed within this is her private memory narrative of a traumatic childhood filled with shame, pain and defiance centring on her relationship with her neurotic mother, of an adolescence when she escapes to London and becomes a writer of popular Gothics, her marriage to a Canadian, her celebrity as a poet, to be followed by the threat of blackmail and her second escape from Canada to Italy. Embedded within this narrative are snippets from Joan's Gothic romances ('Bodice Rippers' as she calls them), which provide more glamorous and dangerous plots than everyday life in Toronto, or even in Italy, during the late 1960s and early 1970s. Then there is a fourth narrative thread, the curiously mythic 'Lady Oracle' poems, produced as Joan believes by Automatic Writing when she looks into a dark mirror in her bedroom in Toronto. These shifting frames generate a series of comic collisions, confrontations and escape attempts, but there are no clear boundaries between them as borders blur between present and past, art and life. Joan's fantasies of escape and transformation are always duplicitous and riddled with holes, so that one story infiltrates another and fantasy is under continual barrage from the claims of real life. Joan may adopt multiple disguises in the form of fancy costumes, wigs, different names and different personas, but 'it was no good; I

couldn't stop time, I could shut nothing out' (p. 277). Through this shimmer of different figures, the reader wonders if there is any chance of getting beyond the veils to the centre of the plot or to the enigma of Joan Foster herself. Do we ever get beyond the distorting funhouse mirrors? Joan is nothing if not a self-caricaturist as well as a parodist of Gothic romance conventions, as she switches between real life and fantasy roles in a continual process of double coding. All these fantasies are arguably distorted versions of herself, a process described by Paul de Man in his essay, 'Autobiography as Defacement': 'Autobiography deals with the giving and taking away of faces, with face and deface, figure, figurations and disfiguration' in images of the self endlessly displaced and doubled.[11]

It is arguable that Joan constructs the Gothic plots in her own life. From her point of view even her life story could be seen as a tale told by a ghost, speaking from beyond her watery grave in Lake Ontario: 'I planned my death carefully; unlike my life, which meandered along from one thing to another, despite my feeble attempts to control it' (p. 7). Of course this 'death' is another of her contrived plots for Joan is not dead at all. One of the things that frightens her most in Italy is that people at home in Canada will think that she is really dead, and not even miss her. Having escaped from her husband Arthur in Toronto, Joan realises that the other side of her escape fantasy is isolation:

> The Other Side was no paradise, it was only a limbo. Now I knew why the dead came back to watch over the living: the Other Side was boring. There was no one to talk to and nothing to do.
>
> (p. 309)

Such reflection is a result of Joan's rueful recognition of the gap between real life and fantasy, for she is haunted by memories of her visit to this same Italian village the previous year with her husband and is now filled with the longing that he will come to rescue her from her own perfect plot which begins to look 'less like a Fellini movie than that Walt Disney film I saw when I was eight, about a whale who wanted to sing at the Metropolitan Opera . . . but the sailors harpooned him' (p. 9). Critics have been rather fond of saying that Joan's real-life narrative and the Gothic novel she is writing in Italy start off separate and gradually become entwined till at the end of the narrative borders blur and Joan enters the Gothic maze in *Stalked by Love*.[12] That observation is true as far as it goes, but that is not far enough. Borders between realism and fantasy are blurred from the beginning as Joan continually slides from the embarrassments of the present into fantasy scenarios and back again, for she is an escape artist who is beset by one inconvenient insight, 'Why did every one of my fantasies turn into a trap?' (p. 334).

. . . . .

The Robber Bride could be classified as a mutant form of female Gothic romance with the return of a 'demonic woman' from the dead in a story about transgressions, magic mirrors, shape changers and dark doubles, betrayals and omens of disaster, until the final defeat of the demon by three women friends when her body is burned up and its ashes scattered over the deepest part of Lake Ontario. There is also a multiple homecoming and the restoration of social and family order at the end. Here we find the key Gothic elements of the unspeakable and the buried life, together with a whole range of traditional motifs like vampires, spells, soul stealing and body snatching. It could also be argued here that the traditional Gothic plot is 'upside-down somehow', for though there are female victims there are no rescuing heroes, just as there are no tombs, mazes or haunted houses; in this story the blood belongs to history and to metaphor. All of which highlights the fact that *The Robber Bride* is a postmodernist fiction which exploits the shock effects that occur when Gothic fairy tale migrates into totally different genres like the failed family romance, the detective thriller, and documentary history. Tony, the professional historian among the three friends, knows this technique and how it might be used to engage the interest of listeners and readers:

> She likes the faint shock on the faces of her listeners. It's the mix of domestic image and mass bloodshed that does it to them.[13]

The novel is both like a fairy tale as its title indicates and like history, which—as Tony explains—is always 'a construct' (p. 6), being the combination of different kinds of textual evidence: social documentary, private memory narrative and imaginative reconstruction. History is a discontinuous text with crucial gaps, so that different interpretations of the facts are always possible. Tony's words recall those of the American historiographer Hayden White, who suggests that the narratives of history always reconstruct the available facts of the past for readers in the present according to congenial ideological perspectives and identifiable literary patterns like the quest of the hero or fables of decline and fall.[14]

The Robber Bride is the story of Zenia, another of Atwood's missing persons like Offred in *The Handmaid's Tale* or Cordelia in *Cat's Eye*, told through the multiple narratives of her three friends, Antonia Fremont (Tony), Roz Andrews, and Charis. As each of the three tells her own life story, different overlapping frames of reference are set up through which Zenia's character and significance are given meaning, though Zenia never exists independently of the stories of others. It is through her relationships that Zenia's identity is constructed, but it is also transformed as it is refigured through the perspectives of a military historian (Tony), a successful businesswoman (Roz) and a New Age mystic (Charis). These women are all living in Toronto on 23 October 1990, a crucial date for the narrative as on that day they are having lunch together at a fashionable Toronto restaurant called the Toxique and 'Zenia returns from the dead' (p. 4). Through the swirl of contemporary history which Atwood sketches as a globalised scene of disasters the novel focuses on this one particular event, the kind of 'definitive moment' so useful to historians—and to novelists—after which 'things were never the same again. They provide beginnings for us, and endings too' (p. 4). The postmodern self-reflexivity of the narrative is signalled in the first and last sections, entitled 'Onset' and 'Outcome', told by Tony who has a 'historian's belief in the salutary power of explanations' while realising the 'impossibility of accurate reconstruction.' Yet for all its enigmas and secrets and dark doubles—traditional Gothic elements which we are reminded are also the features of historical and psychological narratives—the novel is structured quite schematically, moving out from the crisis of Zenia's Gothic reappearance in the restaurant five years after her memorial service, then scrolling back through the life stories of all three in an attempt to track Zenia down, only to return to the Toxique again about a week later where the final crisis occurs. Though the three friends have met to exchange stories of their confrontation with Zenia, whom they have all tracked down on the same day and to celebrate their resistance and her defeat, they discover something even more startling has happened: Zenia is dead, really dead this time. As Tony's husband West says, 'Again? I'm really sorry' (p. 449), and there is a second memorial service for Zenia a year later which is a replay of the earlier one, when the friends scatter her ashes and return to Charis's house to tell stories about Zenia all over again.

Within that contemporary frame the memory narratives of Tony, Charis and Roz all occur in chronological sequence charting the history of changing cultural fashions in Toronto over the past 30 years. Tony's section ('Black Enamel') recounts her memories of meeting Zenia as a student in the 1960s as it tracks back through Tony's unhappy childhood, and recounts Zenia's many attempts to rob Tony of her money, her professional reputation, and her beloved West. Charis's section ('Weasel Nights') focuses on her memories of Zenia in the 1970s, the era of hippies and draft dodgers, her American lover Billy and their daughter August, with flashbacks to her childhood as a victim of sexual abuse; it ends with Zenia's seduction of Billy and his disappearance. Roz's section ('The Robber Bride') recounts her meetings with Zenia in the 1980s and follows a similar pattern of recall: childhood memories, marriage, motherhood and a successful business career, up to Zenia's seduction of Roz's husband Mitch and his eventual suicide. Only Tony survives with her man, and it is left to her to give a narrative shape to the fragments of Zenia which exist in the multiple anecdotes of these women: 'She will only be history if Tony chooses to shape her into history' (p. 461).

For all three Zenia is the 'Other Woman', and her existence challenges the optimistic assertion of the early 1970s feminists which Roz recalls with some scepticism in 1990:

> 'The Other Woman will soon be with *us*', the feminists used to say. But how long will it take, thinks Roz, and why hasn't it happened yet?'
>
> (p. 392)[15]

Zenia represents a powerfully transgressive element which continues to threaten feminist attempts to transform gender relations and concepts of sexual power politics. It is the otherness of Zenia which is figured in her three avatars in this novel, identified in the different life stories told by the three friends. One avatar is from fairy tale: *The Robber Bridegroom* by the Brothers Grimm, which is here feminised by Roz's twin daughters and savagely glossed by her through the parodic mode of double-coding:

> **The Robber Bride,** thinks Roz. Well, why not? Let the grooms take it in the neck for once. The Robber Bride, lurking in her mansion in the dark forest . . . The Rubber Broad is more like it—her and those pneumatic tits.
>
> (p. 295)

A second avatar is from the Bible, the figure of Jezebel in the Old Testament (1 Judges: 21). This is prefigured in Charis's childhood when with her grandmother she used to choose revelatory passages from the Bible at random and once lit on the death of Jezebel; that 'message' is confirmed

on the very day of her last confrontation with Zenia by her morning Bible reading:

> She realized it as soon as she got up, as soon as she stuck her daily pin into the Bible. It picked out Revelations Seventeen, the chapter about the Great Whore.
>
> (p. 420)

There is a third avatar advanced by Tony near the end, that of the medieval French Cathar woman warrior, Dame Giraude, who in the thirteenth century defended her castle against the Catholic forces of Simon de Montfort. She was finally defeated and thrown down a well. This is the most unsettling of Zenia's avatars because it introduces a new perspective on her otherness which extends beyond the demonic. Just as Tony very much admires the reckless courage of Dame Giraude fighting for a lost cause so too she has a sneaking admiration for Zenia as a guerrilla fighter, despite her own humiliations at her hands:

> Zenia is dead, and although she was many other things, she was also courageous. What side she was on doesn't matter; not to Tony, not any more. There may not even have been a side. She may have been alone.
>
> (pp. 469-70)

This is a recognition of the 'otherness' of Zenia, which cannot be accommodated within the parameters of the friends' stories. Tony has always associated Zenia with war—or 'Raw' in terms of her own subjective life. As a result of having known Zenia, Tony contemplates writing a book about female military commanders: '*Iron Hands, Velvet Gloves*, she could call it. But there isn't much material' (p. 464). It is also Tony who wishes to give Zenia's ashes a sort of military burial on Armistice Day: 'An ending, then. November 11, 1991, at eleven o'clock in the morning, the eleventh hour of the eleventh day of the eleventh month' (p. 465).

Whichever way we look at it, the most interesting figure in the novel is Zenia, the 'demonic woman'; she is there in the title and it is her story which defines and focuses the narrative. How is it that this traditionally Gothic figure survives as such a powerful force in Atwood's novel about contemporary social reality in 1990s Toronto? I wish to suggest that Atwood herself has done a Dr Frankenstein performance here, reassembling parts of old legends and fairy tales in order to create her female monster who strides through three Canadian women's stories from the 1960s to the 1990s haunting their lives and wreaking havoc. However, Atwood revises the *Frankenstein* ending for it is the monster who destroys herself and it is the three friends who survive, though their memories of Zenia will live on. This is perhaps putting it rather melodramatically, but what Zenia represents will always exceed the bounds of decorum. Her power is the power of female sexuality, and the figure of Zenia relates directly to contemporary social myths about femininity; it also relates to male (and female) fantasies about the feminine; and in addition it challenges feminist thinking about gender relations. In her reading from **The Robber Bride** at the National Theatre in London in 1993 Atwood offered an important clue to an interpretation of her new novel when she said, 'It's a book about illusion: now you see it, now you don't.' Through Zenia's story Atwood confronts the ideology of traditional female romance where 'getting the power means getting the man, for the man *is* the power' (a statement made by Atwood in Wales in 1982). In this novel Atwood is investigating the extent to which that old proposition about power still holds true in the feminist—or post-feminist—1990s. In answer to a question asked at the National Theatre, 'Why should women now mind much about having men taken away from them by other women?', Atwood replied, 'This is not ideology; it's real life.' I would add that **The Robber Bride** is also fantasy, for this is a fantastic tale which examines once again the fantasies that underpin real life as well as fiction. Female sexuality has always been a problem for real women and real men, just as it is a problem for feminism: 'Male fantasies, male fantasies, is everything run by male fantasies?' (p. 392). Have women internalised these fantasies to such an extent that as Roz fears, 'You are a woman with a man inside watching a woman'? Atwood answers Roz's rhetorical questions by investigating the effects of fantasies of desirable femininity on women themselves. Zenia inhabits that fantasy territory:

> The Zenias of this world . . . have slipped sideways into dreams; the dreams of women too, because women are fantasies for other women, just as they are for men. But fantasies of a different kind.
>
> (p. 392)

Who is Zenia? And what kind of fantasy is she for her three contemporaries? Zenia seems to be real but she has a double existence for she belongs to two different fictional discourses, that of realism and of fantasy. She is a very transgressive figure who exists both as a character in the realistic fiction and also as the projection of three women's imaginations. As the Other Woman, her identity is fabricated through their stories about her, which are all stories of seduction, betrayal

and humiliation. She herself is an enigma. Indeed she derives meaning only within the signifying structures of other people's stories and then always retrospectively. Zenia is a liar, a floating signifier, possibly a void and certainly a fraud. There is no indication that she has any independent subjective life, unless it is her 'aura' which is savagely at variance with her glamorous appearance; it is according to Charis, 'a turbulent muddy green . . . a deadly aureole, a visible infection' (p. 66). At least this is how Zenia appears to one of her victims, always on the loose and ready to rob them of whatever is most precious to them. Zenia is everything they want most and everything they fear, for she represents their unfulfilled desires just as she represents their repressed pain-filled childhood selves. She is the dark double of them all, having multiple identities but no fixed identity. As Tony discovers after systematic research:

> Even the name Zenia may not exist . . . As for the truth about her, it lies out of reach, because—according to the records, at any rate—she was never even born.
>
> (p. 461)

Indeed, there are three different versions of Zenia's life story which have been tailored to fit the lives of Tony, Charis, Roz. She is what they most desire and dread to be. They all think occasionally that they would like to be someone other than the persons they are; most of the time they would like to be Zenia. It is no wonder that Tony reaches this conclusion:

> As with any magician, you saw what she wanted you to see; or else you saw what you yourself wanted to see. She did it with mirrors. The mirror was whoever was watching, but there was nothing behind the two-dimensional image but a thin layer of mercury.
>
> (p. 461)

Why cannot the three women let Zenia go, when they believe she is dead and when they have been to her memorial service five years earlier? Having been tricked and robbed by Zenia of men, money and self confidence, they keep on meeting once a month for lunch because of her. The positive outcome is that they become fast friends, and it is worth noting that this is the first time such a group of loyal female friends has appeared in Atwood's fiction. However, the fact remains that they meet to tell stories about Zenia, and actually it is their collective need of her which brings her back from the dead—or would do so, if she were really dead. When she commits suicide the three friends stand looking at her, still needing to believe that she is looking at them:

Zenia revolves slowly, and looks straight at them with her white mermaid eyes.

She isn't really looking at them though, because she can't. Her eyes are rolled back into her head.

(pp. 446-7)

The switch in narrative perspective reminds readers of whose is the active needy gaze and it is not Zenia's. Even when they have scattered her ashes in Lake Ontario at the end, their stories will still be about Zenia. They need her, or their stories about her, in order to define themselves, for the 'good' women are shown to be as dependent on the 'Other Woman' as she is on them. Zenia is inside each one, for she represents their unfulfilled shadow selves: 'Was she in any way like us? thinks Tony. Or, to put it the other way around: Are we in any way like her?' (p. 470). The dark reflection in the magic mirror is still there, in that 'infinitely receding headspace where Zenia continues to exist' (p. 464).

As Alison Light wrote of Daphne du Maurier's *Rebecca,* that story of another 'demonic' woman:

It demarcates a feminine subjectivity which is hopelessly split within bourgeois gendered relations . . . [it] makes visible the tensions within the social construction of femininity whose definitions are never sufficient and are always reminders of what is missing, what could be.[16]

Light's remark about a woman's novel of the late 1930s needs very little updating in relation to **The Robber Bride** written nearly 60 years later where the concept of split feminine subjectivity is shared by all three of Atwood's protagonists. Signalled in their doubled or tripled names (Tony/ Antonia Fremont/Tnomerf Ynot; Roz Andrews/ Rosalind Greenwood/Roz Grunwald; and Charis, formerly known as Karen), it is commented on explicitly in all three. Since childhood Tony has always been able to write and spell backwards: 'It's her seam, it's where she's sewn together; it's where she could split apart' (p. 19). Similar comments are offered about Charis, who was 'split in two' as a sexually abused child (p. 263) and about Roz, whose life was 'cut in two' when her Jewish father returned to Toronto after the Second World War (p. 332). All three have a seam, a split, which is the space of repression occupied by their 'dark twins' and Zenia operates on this edge of desire and lack which is the borderline territory of the marauding Gothic Other.

Zenia is a threat because of her flaunting sexuality, her deceptions and betrayals, her ruthless contempt for others and her random destructiveness. With her siren song she seduces men and pulls them inside out and then abandons them, though as Tony realises there is nothing gender-specific about this with Zenia:

How well she did it, thinks Tony. How completely she took us in. In the war of the sexes, which is nothing like a real war but is instead a kind of confused scrimmage in which people change allegiances at a moment's notice, Zenia was a double agent.

(p. 185)

The otherness which Zenia represents has to be construed as deviant, dangerous and threatening, and it has to be annihilated again and again. Her punishment is very like Rebecca's in the earlier novel when Rebecca suffered murder, vilification and cancer of the womb; Zenia commits suicide—or was she murdered?—she is discredited through the revelation that she was a drug dealer and possibly an arms smuggler, and she is reputed to be suffering from ovarian cancer. As Tony repeats, 'Zenia is history', which does not necessarily mean that she is dead and out of the way but that her story will continue to be retold in different versions and endlessly speculated upon. It is symptomatic that even her funeral urn splits in two and her ashes blow about all over her three mourners. In this Gothic fairy tale retold from a feminist perspective, Zenia is a very disruptive figure for she is the spectacle of desirable femininity, a beautiful façade which hides whatever is behind it. (Is it neurotic insecurity? or nothingness? or frigidity? or is it ruthless egoism?) The final image of Zenia is given by Tony in her ambiguous elegy:

She's like an ancient statuette dug up from a Minoan palace: there are the large breasts, the tiny waist, the dark eyes, the snaky hair. Tony picks her up and turns her over, probes and questions, but the woman with her glazed pottery face does nothing but smile.

(p. 470)

Always an enigma, Zenia is still present or as present as she ever was within her shifting figurations. During the narrative she has taken on all the pains of the twentieth century as the Jewish victim of Nazi persecution and of European wars, as displaced person, as victim of violence and sexual abuse, as suffering from cancer, AIDS and drug addition—just as she has been the ikon of desirable femininity, Robber Bride, Whore of Babylon, and woman warrior. She remains un-dead, a vampiric figure desiring 'a bowl of blood, a bowl of pain, some death' (p. 13) for she derives her life from the insecurities and desires of the living.

The ending of **The Robber Bride** is not an ending but merely 'a lie in which we all agree to conspire' (p. 465). We are reminded of Atwood's voice in **Murder in the Dark** whispering, 'I have designs on you . . . by the rules of the game, I must always lie.' Atwood takes Gothic conventions and turns them inside out, weaving her illusions 'like any magician making us see what she wants us to see', as she transgresses the boundaries between realism and fantasy, between what is acceptable and what is forbidden. Of course these are fictions; **Lady Oracle** and **The Robber Bride** are illusions created by Atwood's narrative art, but they speak to readers in the present as they challenge us to confront our own desires and fears. Atwood, like the old Gothic novelists, like Joan Foster and like Zenia, 'does it with mirrors'.

Notes

1. Margaret Atwood, *Murder in the Dark* (1984) (London: Virago, 1994) pp. 49-50.

2. Eve Kosofsky Sedgwick, *The Coherence of Gothic Conventions* (New York and London: Methuen, 1986) pp. 4-5.

3. For a succinct discussion of the uncanny, see Rosemary Jackson, *Fantasy: The Literature of Subversion* (London: Methuen, 1981) pp. 63-72.

4. Earl Ingersoll (ed.) *Margaret Atwood: Conversations* (London: Virago, 1992) p. 45.

5. See also C A Howells, *Love, Mystery and Misery: Feeling in Goltic Fiction* (London: Athlone Press, 1978); William Patrick Day, *In the Circles of Fear and Desire: A Study of Gothic Fantasy* (Chicago and London: University of Chicago Press, 1985) and Michelle A. Massé, *In the Name of Love: Women, Masochism and the Gothic* (Ithaca, N.Y., and London: Cornell University Press, 1992).

6. Sharon R. Wilson, 'Sexual Politics in Margaret Atwood's Visual Art (With an Eight-Page Color Supplement)', in K. van Spanckeren and J. Garden Castro (eds) *Margaret Atwood: Vision and Forms* (Carbondale: Southern Illinois University Press, 1988) pp. 215-232.

7. *Conversations*, p. 18.

8. C. A. Howells, 'A Question of Inheritance: Canadian Women's Short Stories', in J. Birkett and E. Harvey (eds.), *Determined Women: Studies in the Construction of the Female Subject, 1900-90* (London: Macmillan, 1991) pp. 108-20.

9. Quoted from Atwood's address delivered at a conference 'Imagined Realities in Contemporary Women's Writing', Dyffryn House, Cardiff, October 1982.

10. Margaret Atwood, *Lady Oracle* (1976) (London: Virago, 1993) p. 310.

11. Paul de Man, 'Autobiography as Defacement', *MLN*, vol. 94 (1979) pp. 931-55.

12. For a full account of criticism of *Lady Oracle,* see Margery Fee, *The Fat Lady Dances: Margaret Atwood's Lady Oracle* (Toronto: ECW, 1993).

13. Margaret Atwood, *The Robber Bride* (1993) (London: Virago, 1994) p. 3.

14. Hayden White, 'The Historical Text as Literary Artefact', in *Tropics of Discourse: Essays in Cultural Criticism* (Baltimore, Md, and London: Johns Hopkins University Press, 1978) pp. 81-100.

15. As an interesting historical note which shows how attentive Atwood is to precision of contemporary detail, from 1972-77 there was a Toronto-based feminist collective newspaper called *The Other Woman*. This information is from M. Fulford (ed.), *The Canadian Women's Movement, 1960-1990: A Guide to Archival Resources* (Toronto: ECW, 1992) p. 53.

16. Alison Light, 'Returning to Manderley—Romance Fiction, Sexuality and Class', *Feminist Review*, vol. 16 (1984) pp. 7-25.

TITLE COMMENTARY

Lady Oracle

SYBIL KORFF VINCENT (ESSAY DATE 1983)

SOURCE: Vincent, Sybil Korff. "The Mirror and the Cameo: Margaret Atwood's Comic/Gothic Novel, *Lady Oracle*." In *The Female Gothic*, edited by Julian E. Fleenor, pp. 153-63. Montreal, Quebec, and London: Eden Press, 1983.

In the following essay, Vincent illustrates how, with Lady Oracle, *Atwood invents "a new sub-genre—the comic/ Gothic," that conforms to the sensibilities of the Female Gothic tradition without the expected elements of terror and resolution, and with an updated representation of the psyche of the contemporary woman.*

Atwood has created a new sub-genre—the comic/Gothic—which more accurately depicts the psychological condition of the modern woman than does the traditional Gothic novel. In **Lady Oracle,** we find the Female Gothic novel explored from virtually every angle. It is not a true Gothic in that it does not, at any time, arouse feelings of terror and it does not leave the reader with any satisfactory sense of relief. Rather, Atwood gives us an anatomy of both the Female Gothic and the Gothic sensibility. She explores a number of possible explanations for the development of such a sensibility and demonstrates that it may find expression in various literary forms. She also shows that the familiar trappings of the Gothic— the pursuits and escapes, the sense of isolation, the cruelty, the ambivalent, persecuting/protecting males, the hostile females, the elaborate details of costume, the hints of supernatural influences—are not sufficient to guarantee a Gothic novel.

What constitutes a Gothic novel is not so much those elements as the attitude—the feeling

FROM THE AUTHOR

AN EXCERPT FROM *LADY ORACLE*

Arthur never found out that I wrote Costume Gothics. . . .

He wouldn't have understood. He wouldn't have been able to understand in the least the desire, the pure quintessential need of my readers for escape, a thing I myself understood only too well. Life had been hard on them and they had not fought back, they'd collapsed like soufflés in a high wind. Escape wasn't a luxury for them, it was a necessity. They had to get it somehow. And when they were too tired to invent escapes of their own, mine were available for them at the corner drugstore, neatly packaged like the other painkillers. They could be taken in capsule form, quickly and discreetly, during those moments when the hair-dryer was stiffening the curls around their plastic rollers or the bath oil in the bath was turning their skins to pink velvet, leaving a ring in the tub to be removed later with Ajax Cleanser, which would make their hands smell like a hospital and cause their husbands to remark that they were about as sexy as a dishcloth. Then they would mourn their lack of beauty, their departing youth. . . . I knew all about escape, I was brought up on it.

SOURCE: Atwood, Margaret. "Chapter 4." In *Lady Oracle*, 1976. Reprint, pp. 31-2. New York: Anchor Books, 1998.

of fear, the concept of multiple selves or no self, the search not for a "they" but for an "I." With the same elements and the same attitude, but in different proportions, and with a gift for the unexpected simile, Atwood produces a comic novel instead. The reader is too busy laughing at the predicaments and observations of the heroine to feel anything like terror, but she can certainly identify with her feelings and experience a distinct unease.

This new sub-genre, comic/Gothic, has a sound psychological basis. Freud noted long ago that the comic situation reassures us that the victim is stronger than she appears. She will triumph over her adversity, perhaps merely by her resignation and acceptance, or by her absurd defiance. Enjoyment is derived from the saving of psychic energy which would otherwise be expended on pity or fear. When the heroine derides herself and depicts her tribulations as comical she is saving both herself and the audience the energy needed for grief and compassion. She is also forestalling the pain which would ensue if the story were told seriously and the audience were *not* sympathetic. With each joke she demonstrates to the world and to herself that she has mastered her anxiety over her pain. At the same time she punishes the originator of the pain—parent, lover, the world in general, or part of her own psyche—by degrading the originator.[1]

Humor releases suppressed emotions and eases frustrations. Humorists "choose grim laughter as a homeopathic protection against total disintegration."[2] The function of humor is "the expression and release of the nervous, muscular and, at base, psychic reflexes of aggression."[3] The critical detachment of the comic speaker dispels anxiety, while the energy of the unexpressible emotion is released in harmless laughter at something trivial or absurd. In a situation where there is no apparent resolution and hence no restorative catharsis, humor helps to ease the anger and pain of both speaker and reader.

Atwood's humor in *Lady Oracle* tends to be female humor in that it presupposes a female audience. The heroine, Joan, also uses "courting humor," which is the humor women use towards men, and consists of adopting a childlike, "dumb Dora" posture, or teasing and thus offering a challenge which provokes a libidinous response and a desire to overpower the female. The exercise of wit requires a certain "distancing" of the audience. It is an intellectual exercise and is antithetical to the sensual and emotive relationship which the courting woman hopes will prevail. When she does use wit it is an anti-courting device, signalling that she does not want or expect an emotional relationship and that she is not to be regarded as a female.

Atwood, through her narrator/heroine, Joan, more often employs female-to-female humor. She exhibits hostility towards men, anger at the female condition, personal anecdotes about the body and its functions, sexual experiences, and, of course, allusions to the Gothic novels which are being satirized. The comic devices most often employed are absurd similes and imagery, ironic understatement, and caricature or exaggeration. Such humor acts as a tension-relieving mechanism, and establishes rapport between author and audience through common interests and problems. As the teller of a humorous tale, Joan gains a sense of power. She deliberately manipulates her audience and experiences a sense of control lacking in her actual life.

Joan's self-deprecating humor also indicates her terrible ambivalence about being female, which is the heart of the traditional Gothic novel. Her body is seen as a traitor leading her into painful situations. By joking about her body she exerts control. The humor which Joan directs towards her mother further underscores the hostility about being female. The usual psychodynamics of comedy are a reversed oedipal situation; a father figure is turned into an impotent clown while the child is free and victorious. Joan's humor debases the all-powerful mother with whom she is competing, hopelessly and fearfully, for the love of the father, and her self-deprecating humor represents a self-imposed punishment for those longings.

Atwood's comic/Gothic novel thus carries out in a somewhat different way the functions of the traditional Gothic. The Gothic novel is a literary representation of our innermost fears. What we fear so much is ourselves. Using Pogo's words to describe the Gothic we see that "we have met the enemy and she is us." Or perhaps more accurately, the Gothic depicts multiple selves engaged in some endless psychic basketball game wherein the team members frequently foul each other in their anxiety to score. Those selves within us which seem to dominate our waking lives are often the victims in our dreams. The pleasure-seeking self, resenting the suppression which the conscious, achieving self has enforced in the waking hours, punishes the self in the dream. The achieving self recognizes that there is that within her that can destroy her, and the person as a whole recognizes that conflicts within are threatening her over-all well being.

The Gothic novel, and the dream of pursuit and escape which it articulates, is an expression of our fears of those enemies within us. We are our own harshest critics and most severe task-masters; we are also our own mermaids who will wreathe our limbs with seaweed and draw us down into the waters of madness.

These conflicts, especially prevalent in societies where considerable emphasis is placed on personal achievement and self-denial, are common to both women and men, and Gothic novels are certainly not the exclusive property of female writers and readers. The Female Gothic, however, is a category within the genre which specifically deals with female anxieties and conflicts from a female perspective. In addition to possessing the general characteristics of pursuit and escape, loneliness, elements of the supernatural, sadism, and a sense of antiquity, it relates particularly to the female condition.

For a woman, achievement has historically and universally depended upon being beautiful, desirable and fertile. Through her sexuality, every girl is taught, she will acquire the male who will protect her, provide for her, and give her an identity. At the same time, her sexuality entails the discomfort and mysterious terror of the menstrual flow, the threat of ravishment or penetration, the discomfort and innate repugnance of bearing within one's own body an alien being, and the pain and danger of childbirth.

So, while the practical daytime girl bends every effort towards enhancing her desirability and securing a mate, the nighttime girls longs to remain child or neuter. In dreams she threatens and punishes the daytime girl. Virtually every Female Gothic portrays the same dream image: the young, lovely girl fleeing through the night, bare branches tearing at her flimsy clothing, a shadowy male figure nearby, and a huge old house looming behind her. The heroine is being pursued and tormented for no very clear reason by no very clear enemy. The author may supply some superficial rationale for the pursuit, but it is apparent that it is her sexual desirability that makes the heroine a victim.

The male is often both persecutor and rescuer, reflecting the ambivalent position which males occupy in relation to females, as well as the woman's mixed emotions toward sexual intercourse. Other females also frequently menace the heroine. They are expressions of her own libidinous longings which will lead her into the perilous entrapments of marriage and childbearing. But they are also expressions of the stern conscience which exacts morality, purity, duty and self-sacrifice. Nature—the branches of the image—conspires to strip the heroine of her protection. The vast structure of knowledge, custom and order (the old house of the image) is no shelter; it is a prison, a madhouse, a charnelhouse, haunted with memories of pain, helplessness and failure. The message is as subtle as a billboard: it is not safe to be a woman.

The Gothic brings the dream to consciousness and resolves its terror. Unlike a nightmare, in the novel the heroine does elude and outwit her pursuers. Eventually, through a happy combination of beauty, brains, and character, she makes the passage into womanhood, is loved and respected, and achieves status and security. The reader is permitted to live out her own terrors and desires vicariously, always secure in the knowledge that the author is in control. The author will wake her from the nightmare in time and make certain that her daytime perception of herself and her place in the world is reaffirmed. The highly formulaic and predictable structure, trite symbolism, and stereotyped characterization of most Gothics assure the reader that it is safe to proceed and enables the reader to relax her ego-protecting barriers so that her thwarted, secret selves may for a time find some conscious expression.

The peculiarly female perspective of the Female Gothic is demonstrated by its setting and attention to detail. The setting is usually indoors, not merely because women generally spend most of their time indoors, but also because most of their perils are internal—within the family, within their bodies, within their souls. Attention to details of costume, furnishings and customs, one of the more delightful esthetic pleasures of the Female Gothic, reflects female perception first of all because within the restricted female milieu such details are more noticeable. Furthermore, female achievement often depends on a mastery of such details. A successful woman is identified by her clothes, furniture, etc. An elaborate delineation of small details gives an illusion of power. As a little girl delights in dressing and undressing her dolls, a woman delights in decorating her home, because here she has dominion. The careful furnishing of the novel, which Atwood so ably satirizes in her novel-within-a-novel, demonstrates mastery of the situation.

As well, an emphasis on concrete objects assures us of reality. Women in particular are often isolated from contact with others and have comparatively few opportunities to assure themselves of their own reality through sports, say, or to gain fame and recognition through achievements. Identity is gained through things: "I am my china, my pictures, my perfume. I know I exist because I cleaned this cup." At times this dependency on things creates an illusion that the things dominate the person. The special horror of things is a common element in Gothic novels. They seem to take on a perverse life of their own, a horror well depicted by the surrealist painters. An image familiar to all movie-goers is the hero, driven to distraction, smashing a mirror. This is an assertion of one's mastery over the world of things, an

insistence on an autonomous identity apart from any image. For who among us has not at some time grasped the goblet, felt it cold and hard against our fingers, and felt ourselves somehow weak, soft, fluid—not quite *there?*

In the Gothic those prosaic things assume an air of menace. Why are the jewels glittering, the candelabra gleaming, the curtains rustling? Are they really there, or do I imagine them? Am I really here or do they imagine me? Through a scrupulous attention to minor details, the author causes the novel to affect the reader on many levels at once, from an ordinary interest in the environment of the fiction providing credibility and verisimilitude, to the striking of sympathetic vibrations of horror within the reader.

The Female Gothic, then, expresses conflicts within the female regarding her own sexuality and identity, and uses a highly stylized form and elaborate detail to effect psychic catharsis. Whereas the psychological novel analyzes the roots of anxiety and its effects realistically and conquers anxiety through reason, the Gothic dramatizes anxiety and through exaggeration—playfulness, even, in the case of *Lady Oracle*—renders it harmless. It permits us to experiment, to play at terror, to become familiar with it and recognize it as a fact of life. *Lady Oracle*'s emphasis on playfulness renders it more compatible with the contemporary woman's condition as it dramatizes and externalizes her inner conflicts.

Unlike the traditional Gothic, which has no humor, this novel abounds in ludicrous images and metaphors. For example, "I felt through my brain for whatever scraps of political lore might be lodged there inadvertently, like bits of spinach among my front teeth."[4] However, it follows the typical Gothic plot development, leading the reader through the suspense of trying to discover who or what is persecuting the heroine.

Although the novel begins at a chronological point where the heroine has apparently achieved safety from her supposed enemies, she is, in fact, in the most critical danger from her true inner enemies. As she recalls her life, we are introduced to the various possibilities which might account for her terror—her mother, her uncertain sense of identity, the pressures of society, her sexual conflicts, her experiences with men, her fear of death, and her own warring selves.

To make obvious that this is an analysis of the Gothic form, *Lady Oracle* is a novel-within-a-novel. Joan, the heroine, writes "costume Gothics." We are invited to compare her personal narrative with her works in progress, which represent a sub-text to what she tells us about herself. As she works through her own inner mazes, the personal narrative and the work-in-progress begin to merge, and her various selves achieve some sort of synthesis. As readers we are often more caught up in the work-in-progress than the "true" narrative, just as Joan lives more fully in her fantasy life than in her real life.

A comparison of the openings of the true and fictive narratives provides an insight both into Joan's nature and the Gothic sensibility. She begins her confession with "I planned my death carefully." She has lost control of her life and must destroy her former self by making her death an artistic creation, thus gaining control of her life and mastering her fear of death. She is "feeble," her life "flabby" and convoluted, "scrolling and festooning like the frame of a baroque mirror"—an image revealing a surrealistic and dreamlike synaesthesia which perceives a mirror frame as a living vine. Death is definite and hard, depicted through images of a Quaker church and a severe black dress. She longs for order, silence, simplicity, wishing to escape a tawdry, confusing circus world of trumpets, megaphones and spangles. She speaks of a "shadow," of a "corpse"—Gothic symbols representing spiritual threat and material corruption. Believing the shadow will be mistaken for the reality, she will play a hoax on death. She will create her self by herself. But her image of herself as a bungler insures that she will fail, will remain the persecuted heroine of her own romances.

Comparing this to the opening of the work-in-progress, we find the heroine, Charlotte, is also thinking about death—the death of her mother. There is a similar concern with clothing, allusions to neatness and purity through a Quaker reference, a similar palette of black, white and gray, and reference to a frame, symbolizing entrapment. But there is also sunshine and emotion. Key words are *tears, sad, darling, heart,* and *hopeful.* The vine-like characteristics of Joan's mirror-frame are actually the "curling tendrils" of Charlotte's mother's hair, like spider webs. The vine-like mirror-frame of Joan's confession is an actual frame on a cameo brooch which is Charlotte's only legacy from her dead mother. Joan's life, which seems to her an empty, shifting, imageless mirror, in her novel is concentrated into the cameo—a precise, perfect, unchanging image derived from the mother, which she can wear as she chooses and hence control. What is more, Charlotte is by trade a jeweler and can refashion the cameo as she likes.

We learn from these two versions of a Female Gothic within a Gothic, contemporary vs. traditional, that the Gothic sensibility both fears and longs for death as an end to fear. It prefers a world of fantasy which it can control. It has an uncertain sense of identity, fears its own wild impulses, and has a concomitant passion for control.

Bearing in mind that storytelling is a means of survival for Joan, if we can trust her confession, her problems originated with her uncertain sense of identity beginning with her own name. She was named "Joan" after Joan Crawford (whose real name was Lucille). She does not feel adequate to the movie-star image and suspects she was really named for the martyred Joan of Arc.

In a seminal episode, chubby little Joan is denied the opportunity to perform as a butterfly in a ballet recital because of her appearance. She is cast as a mothball, comic relief, instead. The mothball is an instrument of death for the butterflies, and for her own fragile ego. Disguised as the mothball, Joan expresses her rage and frustration in a socially approved way, as a comedian. This dramatizes Joan's survival techniques—disguise, comedy, and death. She symbolically destroyes her enemies, including those within her who longed to be butterflies and rebelled at her humiliation. The mothball is also a preservative, and with disguise, comedy and symbolic death, she preserves what is left of her ego.

To defy her mother and the society which pressures her into being beautiful and punishes any deviation, Joan overeats and becomes grossly fat. But, more than from defiance, she "ate from panic. Sometimes I was afraid I wasn't really there, I was an accident. . . . Did I want to become solid as a stone, so she wouldn't be able to get rid of me. . . . What had I done?" Her tenuous sense of reality is buttressed by the material—the food she consumes and her own obvious and solid flesh.

Overeating also renders Joan safe from the sexual advances which she fears. "It is not sexually titillating to observe the torture of a fat person," she observes. Ambivalence towards sexuality is demonstrated in another passage wherein she is accosted in the park by a man who first exposes himself and then hands her a bunch of daffodils. Subsequently her female companions from her Brownie troupe blindfold her and leave her tied to a tree. A man whom she suspects is the exhibitionist rescues her. In her dreams the fleetingly glimpsed penis turns into menacing tentacles, and then into glorious flowers. Here is the mingled terror and desirability of the pending sexuality of the prepubescent girl. She longs for the forbidden sexual act which will deliver her from her helpless childhood state, but also feels fear, guilt, shame, and a need for punishment. Desire for sexual maturity is a desire to gain the secret knowledge and power that her mother has, and which the mother both forbids to and demands of her. Through a male she can conquer the internalized mother figure who denies her her true identity.

Ambivalence towards sexuality is emphasized by the contrasts between the erotic passages of Joan's confession and her fiction. In the latter, words such as *fiery* and *wild animal* abound: it is serious, dangerous and thrilling. In the former, erotic scenes are ludicrous. A middle-aged lover in striped pajamas seduces Joan, who has a sprained ankle. She surrenders her virginity because she is too embarrassed to admit she didn't know he was making advances. A lover called the Royal Porcupine advances on Joan, growling softly. She protests he hasn't washed his hands. Joan imagines making love with the produce-vendor, "surging together on a wave of plums and tangerines," mingling her romantic nature and her earthy perceptions.

Joan's identity confusion is demonstrated by the two images of her self—a ballerina and a circus fat lady. These meld into a fat lady dressed in a ballerina costume walking a high wire over a crowd. Although Joan longs for achievement and adulation, she fears it and so invents other selves. She becomes thin and beautiful, takes an alias, and flees to England to create her own life. "I'd spent all my life learning to be one person and now I was a different one. I had been an exception, with the limitations that imposed; now I was average and I was far from used to it." She lies about her past and denies her former self. The old photograph of herself on her bureau is identified as a fictitious aunt who "was always trying to tell me how to run my life." But just as within the overweight body of the teenager there was a slender ballerina, so surrounding the beautiful adult woman is the wraith of the circus fat lady she still feels she is.

Joan establishes a truly separate identity as Louisa Delacorte, author of Costume Gothics, successful, independent, self-sufficient—and through her writing can play out all her fantasies. Her "good" heroines can be punished and persecuted, and also achieve success. Her "bad" heroines (who resemble Joan physically) indulge in all sorts of wanton and lascivious behavior, humiliate the

"good" heroine, and then are destroyed. Sin, guilt, shame, expiation are all worked out in the fantasy world. "As long as I could spend a certain amount of time each week as Louisa I was all right, I was patient and forbearing, warm, a sympathetic listener. But if I was cut off, if I couldn't work at my current Costume Gothic, I would become mean and irritable, drink too much, and start to cry."

Louisa gratified Joan's superego. As a bumbling, absent-minded housewife, Joan gratifies her id. She marries Arthur, a high-minded young man who looks "Byronic" and reminds her of the hero of her current novel. He loves her for her earnest, energetic failures in the kitchen and her obvious female attractions. She is careful to keep hidden both her success as a writer and her past as an overweight Brownie.

Joan experiments with automatic writing, develops her psychic powers, and discovers still more selves. The automatic writings are published as a volume of poetry, called "Lady Oracle." It seems to Joan an "upside-down Gothic" with all the right elements but no true love and happy ending. The poems are filled with images of pain and death, and describe a tri-partite woman— dark, redgold and blank—who must be obeyed. As she stares into her mirror and transcribes, Joan glimpses the ghost of her mother. Her mother had owned a triplicate mirror, and always appeared to the child as having three heads. The adult Joan owns a triplicate mirror, too.

The poems are a huge success and still another self appears—Joan the celebrity. "My dark twin, my funhouse mirror reflection. She was taller than I, more beautiful, more threatening. She wanted to kill me and take my place."

Even for as skillful a dissembler as Joan, it becomes increasingly difficult to keep separate the strands of her real life and keep distinct the realms of fantasy and reality. She takes a lover, the Royal Porcupine, and with him lives out her fantasies. He is the romantic, dangerous hero of her novels, willing to be her playmate, to dress up in absurd costumes, and to waltz through an empty loft clad only in a lace tablecloth. But this purely libidinous life cannot last. He wants to marry her and read the morning paper together, and Joan fears the merging of the real and the phantom. She knows that every woman longs for a dashing hero in a cape who will rescue her from a balcony but she really wants a husband to help her with the dishes. She dare not lose the distinction between the two worlds, for then she will lose control. Her novels enable her to satisfy both needs, for herself as well as for her readers. Joan is always sympathetic to her reader's needs; unlike Austen's *Northanger Abbey*, a comic novel satirizing the readers of Gothic novels, Atwood's comic novel satirizes the Gothic but understands its function.

Joan's fictions begin to take on some of her real-life traits. Humor seeps in, as for example "Redmond's eye slid like a roving oyster over her blushing countenance." At the same time her life becomes more like one of her fictions. She becomes involved in a terrorist plot, is blackmailed, and receives ominous threats from a never-revealed enemy. These are the external signs of her inner conflict: "There was always that shadowy twin, thin when I was fat, fat when I was thin, myself in silvery negative. . . . It was never-never land she wanted, that reckless twin. But not twin even, I was more than double. I was triple, multiple, and now I could see that there was more than one life to come, there were many."

To regain control, Joan fakes her own death. "Maybe I really did want to die, or I wouldn't have pretended to do it. But that was wrong; I pretended to die so I could live, so I could have another life." By killing her old selves, Joan punishes them for the wicked deeds she has enjoyed, and atones. But the past she has tried to bury, the old selves she has tried to destroy, rise up in her imagination as a huge featureless fat lady—". . . my ghost, my angel, then she settled and I was absorbed into her. Within my former body I gasped for air."

She protests against the female nature which engulfs her. She knows that she does not want to spend her life in a cage as a "fat whore, a captive Earth Mother." She wants to be female and yet create, control, take responsibility for her own life, dare to want glory for her own achievements— and this is as difficult as a fat lady crossing a high wire. "You could dance, or you could have the love of a good man. But you were afraid to dance, because you had this unnatural fear they'd cut your feet off."

At the extreme of a terror which she ascribes to male domination, Joan attacks the next man she encounters, a harmless reporter. Subsequently she aids his recovery and confesses her true story to him. Presumably the "new Joan" has found her true identity, resolved her internal conflicts, and henceforth will be brave, honest, aggressive and responsible. That she has defended herself, albeit mistakenly—after all, this is a comic novel— presupposes she has found a self worth defending.

By drawing blood from the male, rendering him helpless (she hits him over the head with a bottle) and then reviving him, Joan turns the male into the ravished and rescued, and herself into persecutor and protector. Like her father, who had been both a doctor and an assassin during the war, she can give and take life. She need no longer fear her own femaleness, nor the males who forbid her an identity. Joan decides she will no longer write Gothics; she will write a novel about real people—"less capes and more holes in stockings." The novel thus shows the "characteristic comic movement from a lesser to a greater awareness of worldly reality."[5]

Atwood's conclusion is too reassuring to be reassuring. We suspect that Joan is once again adopting a disguise to elude the realities of her psychic conflicts—this time the militant female. It may be that the condition of women in the modern world is not so grave anymore, and such "new Joans" can indeed create themselves. In today's more open environment, with more opportunities for personal achievement and independence, and hence less dependence on sexuality for survival, with more comradeship between the sexes, with medical advancements and better sex education, women need not suffer the terrors and conflicts which the traditional Gothic novel psychologically dramatizes. The choices and possibilities are not so hard and fixed as a cameo; they are fluid, changeable, like the shifting images in a funhouse mirror.

But this multiplicity and uncertainty produces its own psychic state. Instead of terror there is anxiety and confusion. We all know laughter is as much a response to tension as are screaming or crying, but it is a more socially acceptable response. As women move out into the crowded streets of contemporary life, the piercing scream of the terrified Gothic heroine seems to be giving way to the nervous giggle of the uncertain comic/Gothic heroine. Insofar as the ancient fears and restrictions of women persist, the inner conflicts of women persist and the genre remains viable.

Notes

1. Martin Grotjahn, M.D., *Beyond Laughter: Humor and the Sub-Conscious,* (New York: McGraw-Hill, 1957), p. 257.

2. Jesse Bier, *The Rise and Fall of American Humor* (New York: Holt, Rinehart & Winston, 1968), p. 307.

3. Ibid., p. 456.

4. Margaret Atwood, *Lady Oracle* (New York: Simon & Schuster, 1976).

5. Robert Heilman, *The New Ways of the World: Comedy and Society* (Seattle: Univ. of Washington Press, 1978), p. 182.

FURTHER READING

Criticism

Barzilai, Shuli. "'Say That I Had a Lovely Face': The Grimms' 'Rapunzel,' Tennyson's 'Lady of Shalott,' and Atwood's *Lady Oracle*." *Tulsa Studies in Women's Literature* 19, no. 2 (fall 2000): 231-54.

Views Lady Oracle *as a künstlerroman, with sources from works by the Brothers Grimm and Tennyson.*

Becker, Susanne. "Exceeding Even Gothic Texture: Margaret Atwood and *Lady Oracle*." In *Gothic Forms of Feminine Fictions*, pp. 151-98. Manchester, England: Manchester University Press, 1999.

Delineates the various elements of the Gothic tradition within Lady Oracle.

Grace, Sherill. "More than A Very Double Life." In *Violent Duality: A Study of Margaret Atwood*, edited by Ken Norris, pp. 111-28. Montreal, Quebec: Véhicule Press, 1980.

Asserts that Lady Oracle *is "an amusing parody of Gothic romance and realist conventions, a satiric commentary on Atwood's own experiences as a writer and upon aspects of contemporary society, and a portrayal of 'the perils of Gothic thinking.'"*

Ingersoll, Earl G. and Philip Howard, editors. *Margaret Atwood: Conversations* Princeton, N.J.: Ontario Review Press, 1978, 265 p.

Collection of interviews with Atwood from the 1970s.

Kakutani, Michiko. A review of *The Blind Assassin*, by Margaret Atwood. *The New York Times* (8 September 2000): 43.

Laudatory assessment of The Blind Assassin.

McCombs, Judith. "'Up in the Air So Blue': Vampire and Victims, Great Mother Myth and Gothic Allegory in Margaret Atwood's First, Unpublished Novel." *Centennial Review* 33, no. 3 (summer 1989): 251-57.

Examines the gothicism present in Atwood's treatment of motherhood in her first, unpublished novel.

McKinstry, Susan Jaret. "Living Literally by the Pen: The Self-Conceived and Self-Deceiving Heroine-Author in Margaret Atwood's *Lady Oracle*." In *Margaret Atwood: Reflection and Reality*, edited by Beatrice Mendez-Egle and James M. Haule, pp. 58-70. Edinburgh: Pan American University, 1987.

Assesses Atwood's treatment of Joan Foster as the heroine of Lady Oracle *as it compares to the conventional depiction of heroines in classic Gothic fiction.*

McMillan, Ann. "The Transforming Eye: *Lady Oracle* and Gothic Tradition." In *Margaret Atwood: Vision and Forms*, edited and with an introduction by Kathryn VanSpanckeren, edited by Jan Garden Castro, pp. 48-64. Carbondale: Southern Illinois University Press, 1988.

Compares Atwood's treatment of chastity and the victimization of women to Jane Austen's treatment of the same subjects in Northanger Abbey, *and explores the authors' sources in the Gothic tradition.*

Northey, Margot. "Sociological Gothic: Wild Geese and *Surfacing*." In *The Haunted Wilderness: The Gothic and Grotesque in Canadian Fiction*, pp. 62-9. Toronto, Ontario and Buffalo, N.Y.: University of Toronto Press, 1976.

Asserts that Atwood's novel Surfacing *utilizes the Gothic mode to comment on conditions in society, and is an example of what Northey terms "sociological Gothic" literature.*

Poznar, Susan. "The Totemic Image and the 'Bodies' of the Gothic in Margaret Atwood's *Cat's Eye*." *Yearbook of Comparative and General Literature* 47 (1999): 81-107.

Treats Cat's Eye *as a künstlerroman and compares it to Horace Walpole's* The Castle of Otranto.

Rosowski, Susan J. "Margaret Atwood's *Lady Oracle*: Social Mythology and the Gothic Novel." *Research Studies* 49, no. 2 (June 1981): 87-98.

Surveys the Gothic elements in Lady Oracle.

OTHER SOURCES FROM GALE:

Additional coverage of Atwood's life and career is contained in the following sources published by Thomson Gale: *American Writers Supplement*, Vol. 13; *Authors and Artists for Young Adults*, Vols. 12, 47; *Beacham's Encyclopedia of Popular Fiction: Biography & Resources*, Vol. 1; *Bestsellers*, Vol. 89:2; *Contemporary Authors*, Vols. 49-52; *Contemporary Authors New Revision Series*, Vols. 3, 24, 33, 59, 95, 133; *Contemporary Literary Criticism*, Vols. 2, 3, 4, 8, 13, 15, 25, 44, 84, 135; *Contemporary Novelists*, Ed. 7; *Contemporary Poets*, Ed. 7; *Contemporary Popular Writers*; *Contemporary Women Poets*; *Dictionary of Literary Biography*, Vols. 53, 251; *DISCovering Authors*; *DISCovering Authors: British*; *DISCovering Authors: Canadian*; *DISCovering Authors: Modules, Most-studied Authors, Poets, and Novelists*; *DISCovering Authors 3.0*; *Encyclopedia of World Literature in the 20th Century*, Ed. 3; *Exploring Novels*; *Feminism in Literature: A Gale Critical Companion*; *Feminist Writers*; *Literature and Its Times*, Vol. 5; *Literature Resource Center*; *Major 20th-Century Writers*, Eds. 1, 2; *Major 21st-Century Writers*; *Novels for Students*, Vols. 1, 14, 18, 20; *Poetry Criticism*, Vol. 8; *Poetry for Students*, Vol. 7; *Reference Guide to Short Fiction*, Ed. 2; *St. James Guide to Young Adult Writers*; *Short Stories for Students*, Vols. 3, 13; *Short Story Criticism*, Vols. 2, 46; *Something about the Author*, Vol. 50; *Twayne's Companion to Contemporary Literature in English*, Ed. 1; *Twayne's World Authors*; *World Literature Criticism*; and *World Writers in English*, Vol. 1.

JANE AUSTEN

(1775 - 1817)

English novelist.

Originally written between 1798 and 1799, but not published until 1818, *Northanger Abbey* is considered Jane Austen's first significant work of fiction, and is her only work to be widely studied as part of the Gothic literary tradition. The novel is in part a burlesque of the Gothic and sentimental fiction that was popular in the late eighteenth and early nineteenth centuries particularly of Ann Radcliffe's novels, such as *The Mysteries of Udolpho*. In addition to its parodic elements, *Northanger Abbey* also follows the maturation of Catherine Morland, a naive eighteen-year-old, ignorant of the workings of English society and prone to self-deception. Influenced by her reading of novels rife with the overblown qualities of horror fiction, Catherine concocts a skewed version of reality by infusing real people, things, and events with terrible significance. However, Catherine's impressions, though clouded by Gothic sentiment, often hint at an insightful, if unconscious, judgment of character that cuts through the social pretensions of those around her. In this respect Austen's novel carries on an ironic discourse which makes it not only a satire, but also a sophisticated novel of social education.

BIOGRAPHICAL INFORMATION

Austen began writing while she was still living at her childhood home at Steventon Rectory in Hampshire, England. Her life at Steventon, though sheltered from the world at large, gave her an intimate knowledge of a segment of English society—the landed gentry—that was to provide the material for most of her fiction, and by 1787 Austen had already begun to produce stories, dramas, and short novels. In 1795 she commenced writing *Elinor and Marianne*, an early version of her first published novel, *Sense and Sensibility* (1811). One year later, she started *First Impressions*, the work that eventually evolved into *Pride and Prejudice* (1813). When Austen finished *First Impressions* in 1797, her father submitted it to a London publisher. Although rejected, the story remained a popular favorite among the circle of relations and acquaintances with whom Austen shared her writings. In 1798 and 1799 Austen wrote most of a novel that was later revised, bought by the publisher Richard Crosby, and advertised in 1803 as "In the Press, SUSAN; a novel, in 2 vols." It remained unpublished, however, and was later revised again and published in 1818, after Austen's death, as *Northanger Abbey*, along with the novel *Persuasion*.

MAJOR WORKS

Austen's career is generally divided into an early and a late period, the former encompassing the juvenilia, as well as *Sense and Sensibility, Pride and Prejudice,* and *Northanger Abbey,* the latter including *Emma* (1816), *Mansfield Park* (1814), and *Persuasion.* They are separated by a hiatus of eight years. There is a remarkable consistency in the work of the early and late periods, marked by a certain mellowing of tone in the later works. The plots of Austen's novels revolve around the intricacies of courtship and marriage between members of the upper class. Austen's detractors in more egalitarian eras find fault with what they perceive to be a rigid adherence to a repressive class system. Also, in commenting on the narrowness of her literary world and vision, some critics wonder if novels of such small scope can truly reflect the human condition. However, Austen's talents are uniquely suited to her chosen subject. Her realm is comedy, and her sense of the comedic in human nature informs her technique, which is judged as superb for its delineation of character, control of point of view, and ironic tone. Although Austen chose as her subject the people she knew best, she illuminated in their characters the follies and failings of men and women of all times and classes.

While ostensibly a burlesque of the conventional modes of Gothic horror fiction, *Northanger Abbey* is also a novel of education that focuses on the theme of self-deception. Austen portrays Catherine as an inversion of the typical Gothic heroine, making her neither beautiful, talented, nor particularly intelligent, but rather ordinary in most respects. In contrast, several other characters in the novel are presented as pastiches of stock Gothic characters—Isabella and General Tilney, for example, are parodies of the damsel and the domestic tyrant. These individuals seem to fit into Catherine's deluded perspective of the world which, in the tradition of Miguel de Cervantes's *Don Quixote,* leaves her unable to distinguish between reality and the romanticized version of life she finds in popular novels. Other characters in the novel serve to balance the work. Henry Tilney is often regarded by critics as Austen's mouthpiece—though he, too, is occasionally an object of irony and ridicule. For example, he fails to realize that Catherine's delusions, though excessive, hint at the true nature of people and events. Thus, Catherine is the first to understand that General Tilney, although not a murderer, is cruel and mercenary. This ironic aspect of the novel alludes to a larger theme in the work, that of the moral significance of social conventions and conduct—a subject that Austen explored in greater detail in later novels.

Catherine's introduction into society begins when Mr. and Mrs. Allen, her neighbors in Fullerton, invite her to vacation with them in the English town of Bath. There she meets the somewhat pedantic clergyman Henry Tilney and the dramatic Isabella Thorpe, who encourages Catherine in her reading of Gothic fiction. Her circle of acquaintances widens with the arrival of James Morland, Catherine's brother and a love interest for Isabella, and John Thorpe, Isabella's rude, conniving brother. The setting shifts from Bath to Northanger Abbey, the ancestral home of the Tilneys, when John deceives General Tilney, Henry's father, into believing that Catherine is an heiress. Austen's satire of Gothic horror novel conventions begins as Henry and Catherine drive up to the Abbey and the former plays on the heroine's romantic expectations of the estate. When Catherine reaches her destination she is disappointed to find a thoroughly modern building, completely lacking in hidden passageways, concealed dungeons, and the like. Later, Austen allows Catherine's imagination to run amok, only to reveal the objects of her fears as ordinary and mundane. At the climax of the novel, General Tilney—whom Catherine suspects of having murdered or shut up his wife somewhere in the abbey—turns the heroine out after learning that she does not come from a wealthy family. At the close of the novel, the outraged Henry proposes marriage to Catherine, now divested of her delusions by Henry and his sister Eleanor. General Tilney, who proves to be not a murderer, but rather an individual of questionable moral and social character, eventually gives his consent to the marriage after learning that his daughter Eleanor is also engaged—to a wealthy Viscount.

CRITICAL RECEPTION

Critics have generally regarded *Northanger Abbey* to be of lesser literary quality than Austen's other mature works. Some scholars have observed occasional lapses in her narrative technique of a sort that do not appear in later novels. By far the greatest debate surrounding *Northanger Abbey,* however, is the question of its aesthetic unity. Critics have traditionally seen the work as part novel of society, part satire of popular Gothic fiction, and therefore not a coherent whole. Detractors, focusing on the work as a parody, have found its plot weak, its characters unimaginative and superficial, and its comedy anticlimactic due to its reliance on an outmoded style of fiction. Others, while conceding the lack of an easily discernible organizing principle, argue that the work is unified on the thematic level as not merely a satire of popular fiction, but also an ironic presentation of a self-deceived imagination that is quixotically wrong about reality but right about human morality. In addition, critics have considered *Northanger Abbey* a transitional work, one that moves away from the burlesque mode of juvenilia and toward the stylistic control of such masterpieces as *Mansfield Park* and *Emma*.

PRINCIPAL WORKS

Sense and Sensibility (novel) 1811

Pride and Prejudice (novel) 1813

Mansfield Park (novel) 1814

Emma (novel) 1816

Northanger Abbey and Persuasion. 4 vols. (novels) 1818

Lady Susan (novel) 1871

The Watsons (unfinished novel) 1871

Love and Friendship and Other Early Works (juvenilia) 1922

[Sanditon] Fragments of a Novel (unfinished novel) 1925

Jane Austen's Letters to her Sister Cassandra and Others (letters) 1932

Volume the First (juvenilia) 1933

Volume the Third (juvenilia) 1951

Volume the Second (juvenilia) 1963

PRIMARY SOURCES

JANE AUSTEN (NOVEL DATE 1818)

SOURCE: Austen, Jane. "Chapter 14." In *Northanger Abbey.* 1818. Reprint edition, pp. 107-16. New York: Signet, 1996.

In the following excerpt from Northanger Abbey, *first published in 1818, Catherine discusses the pleasure she derives from reading Gothic fiction—Ann Radcliffe's* Mysteries of Udolpho, *in particular—versus what she perceives as the drudgery of reading nonfiction works, such as histories.*

The next morning was fair, and Catherine almost expected another attack from the assembled party. With Mr. Allen to support her, she felt no dread of the event: but she would gladly be spared a contest, where victory itself was painful, and was heartily rejoiced therefore at neither seeing nor hearing anything of them. The Tilneys called for her at the appointed time; and no new difficulty arising, no sudden recollection, no unexpected summons, no impertinent intrusion to disconcert their measures, my heroine was most unnaturally able to fulfil her engagement, though it was made with the hero himself. They determined on walking around Beechen Cliff, that noble hill whose beautiful verdure and hanging coppice render it so striking an object from almost every opening in Bath.

"I never look at it," said Catherine, as they walked along the side of the river, "without thinking of the south of France."

"You have been abroad then?" said Henry, a little surprised.

"Oh! No, I only mean what I have read about. It always puts me in mind of the country that Emily and her father travelled through, in *The Mysteries of Udolpho.* But you never read novels, I dare say?"

"Why not?"

"Because they are not clever enough for you—gentlemen read better books."

"The person, be it gentleman or lady, who has not pleasure in a good novel, must be intolerably stupid. I have read all Mrs. Radcliffe's works, and most of them with great pleasure. *The Mysteries of Udolpho,* when I had once begun it, I could not lay down again; I remember finishing it in two days—my hair standing on end the whole time."

"Yes," added Miss Tilney, "and I remember that you undertook to read it aloud to me, and that when I was called away for only five minutes to answer a note, instead of waiting for me, you took the volume into the Hermitage Walk, and I was obliged to stay till you had finished it."

"Thank you, Eleanor—a most honourable testimony. You see, Miss Morland, the injustice of your suspicions. Here was I, in my eagerness to get on, refusing to wait only five minutes for my sister, breaking the promise I had made of reading it aloud, and keeping her in suspense at a most interesting part, by running away with the volume, which, you are to observe, was her own, particularly her own. I am proud when I reflect on it, and I think it must establish me in your good opinion."

"I am very glad to hear it indeed, and now I shall never be ashamed of liking *Udolpho* myself. But I really thought before, young men despised novels amazingly."

"It is *amazingly;* it may well suggest *amazement* if they do—for they read nearly as many as women. I myself have read hundreds and hundreds. Do not imagine that you can cope with me in a knowledge of Julias and Louisas. If we proceed to particulars, and engage in the never-ceasing inquiry of 'Have you read this?' and 'Have you read that?' I shall soon leave you as far behind me as—what shall I say?—I want an appropriate simile.—as far as your friend Emily herself left poor Valancourt when she went with her aunt into Italy. Consider how many years I have had the start of you. I had entered on my studies at Oxford, while you were a good little girl working your sampler at home!"

"Not very good, I am afraid. But now really, do not you think *Udolpho* the nicest book in the world?"

"The nicest—by which I suppose you mean the neatest. That must depend upon the binding."

"Henry," said Miss Tilney, "you are very impertinent. Miss Morland, he is treating you exactly as he does his sister. He is forever finding fault with me, for some incorrectness of language, and now he is taking the same liberty with you. The word 'nicest,' as you used it, did not suit him; and you had better change it as soon as you can, or we shall be overpowered with Johnson and Blair all the rest of the way."

"I am sure," cried Catherine, "I did not mean to say anything wrong; but it *is* a nice book, and why should not I call it so?"

"Very true," said Henry, "and this is a very nice day, and we are taking a very nice walk, and you are two very nice young ladies. Oh! It is a very nice word indeed! It does for everything. Originally perhaps it was applied only to express neatness, propriety, delicacy, or refinement—people were nice in their dress, in their sentiments, or their choice. But now every commendation on every subject is comprised in that one word."

"While, in fact," cried his sister, "it ought only to be applied to you, without any commendation at all. You are more nice than wise. Come, Miss Morland, let us leave him to meditate over our faults in the utmost propriety of diction, while we praise *Udolpho* in whatever terms we like best. It is a most interesting work. You are fond of that kind of reading?"

"To say the truth, I do not much like any other."

"Indeed!"

"That is, I can read poetry and plays, and things of that sort, and do not dislike travels. But history, real solemn history, I cannot be interested in. Can you?"

"Yes, I am fond of history."

"I wish I were too. I read it a little as a duty, but it tells me nothing that does not either vex or weary me. The quarrels of popes and kings, with wars and pestilences, in every page; the men all so good for nothing, and hardly any women at all—it is very tiresome; and yet I often think it odd that it should be so dull, for a great deal of it must be invention. The speeches that are put into the heroes' mouths, their thoughts and designs—the chief of all this must be invention, and invention is what delights me in other books."

"Historians, you think," said Miss Tilney, "are not happy in their flights of fancy. They display imagination without raising interest. I am fond of history—and am very well contented to take the false with the true. In the principal facts they have sources of intelligence in former histories and records, which may be as much depended on, I conclude, as anything that does not actually pass under one's own observation; and as for the little embellishments you speak of, they are embellishments, and I like them as such. If a speech be well drawn up, I read it with pleasure, by whomsoever it may be made—and probably with much greater, if the production of Mr. Hume or Mr. Robertson, than if the genuine words of Caractacus, Agricola, or Alfred the Great."

"You are fond of history! And so are Mr. Allen and my father; and I have two brothers who do not dislike it. So many instances within my small circle of friends is remarkable! At this rate, I shall not pity the writers of history any longer. If people like to read their books, it is all very well, but to be at so much trouble in filling great volumes, which, as I used to think, nobody would willingly ever look into, to be labouring only for the torment of little boys and girls, always struck me as a hard fate; and though I know it is all very right and necessary, I have often wondered at the person's courage that could sit down on purpose to do it."

"That little boys and girls should be tormented," said Henry, "is what no one at all acquainted with human nature in a civilized state can deny; but in behalf of our most distinguished historians, I must observe that they might well be offended at being supposed to have no higher aim, and that by their method and style, they are perfectly well qualified to torment readers of the most advanced reason and mature time of life. I use the verb 'to torment,' as I observed to be your own method, instead of 'to instruct,' supposing them to be now admitted as synonymous."

"You think me foolish to call instruction a torment, but if you had been as much used as myself to hear poor little children first learning their letters and then learning to spell, if you had ever seen how stupid they can be for a whole morning together, and how tired my poor mother is at the end of it, as I am in the habit of seeing almost every day of my life at home, you would allow that 'to torment' and 'to instruct' might sometimes be used as synonymous words."

"Very probably. But historians are not accountable for the difficulty of learning to read; and even you yourself, who do not altogether seem particularly friendly to very severe, very intense application, may perhaps be brought to acknowledge that it is very well worth-while to be tormented for two or three years of one's life, for the sake of being able to read all the rest of it. Consider—if reading had not been taught, Mrs. Radcliffe would have written in vain—or perhaps might not have written at all."

Catherine assented—and a very warm panegyric from her on that lady's merits closed the subject. The Tilneys were soon engaged in another on which she had nothing to say. They were viewing the country with the eyes of persons accustomed to drawing, and decided on its capability of being formed into pictures, with all the eagerness of real taste. Here Catherine was quite lost. She knew nothing of drawing—nothing of taste: and she listened to them with an attention which brought her little profit, for they talked in phrases which conveyed scarcely any idea to her. The little which she could understand, however, appeared to contradict the very few notions she had entertained on the matter before. It seemed as if a good view were no longer to be taken from the top of an high hill, and that a clear blue sky was no longer a proof of a fine day. She was heartily ashamed of her ignorance. A misplaced shame. Where people wish to attach, they should always be ignorant. To come with a well-informed mind is to come with an inability of administering to the vanity of others, which a sensible person would always wish to avoid. A woman especially, if she have the misfortune of knowing anything, should conceal it as well as she can.

The advantages of natural folly in a beautiful girl have been already set forth by the capital pen of a sister author; and to her treatment of the subject I will only add, in justice to men, that though to the larger and more trifling part of the sex, imbecility in females is a great enhancement of their personal charms, there is a portion of them too reasonable and too well informed themselves to desire anything more in woman than ignorance. But Catherine did not know her own advantages—did not know that a good-looking girl, with an affectionate heart and a very ignorant mind, cannot fail of attracting a clever young man, unless circumstances are particularly untoward. In the present instance, she confessed and lamented her want of knowledge, declared that she would give anything in the world to be able to draw; and a lecture on the picturesque immediately followed, in which his instructions were so clear that she soon began to see beauty in everything admired by him, and her attention was so earnest that he became perfectly satisfied of her having a great deal of natural taste. He talked of foregrounds, distances, and second distances—side-screens and perspectives—lights and shades; and Catherine was so hopeful a scholar that when they gained the top of Beechen Cliff, she voluntarily rejected the whole city of Bath as unworthy to make part of a landscape. Delighted with her progress, and fearful of wearying her with too much wisdom at once, Henry suffered the subject to decline, and by an easy transition from a piece of rocky fragment and the withered oak which he had placed near its summit, to oaks in general, to forests, the enclosure of them, waste lands, crown lands and government, he shortly found himself arrived at politics; and from politics, it was an easy step to silence. The general pause which succeeded his short disquisition on the state of the nation was put an end to by Catherine, who, in rather a solemn tone of voice, uttered these words, "I have heard that something very shocking indeed will soon come out in London."

Miss Tilney, to whom this was chiefly addressed, was startled, and hastily replied, "Indeed! And of what nature?"

"That I do not know, nor who is the author. I have only heard that it is to be more horrible than anything we have met with yet."

"Good heaven! Where could you hear of such a thing?"

"A particular friend of mine had an account of it in a letter from London yesterday. It is to be uncommonly dreadful. I shall expect murder and everything of the kind."

"You speak with astonishing composure! But I hope your friend's accounts have been exaggerated; and if such a design is known beforehand, proper measures will undoubtedly be taken by government to prevent its coming to effect."

"Government," said Henry, endeavouring not to smile, "neither desires nor dares to interfere in such matters. There must be murder; and government cares not how much."

The ladies stared. He laughed, and added, "Come, shall I make you understand each other, or leave you to puzzle out an explanation as you can? No—I will be noble. I will prove myself a man, no less by the generosity of my soul than the clearness of my head. I have no patience with such of my sex as disdain to let themselves sometimes down to the comprehension of yours. Perhaps the abilities of women are neither sound nor acute—neither vigorous nor keen. Perhaps they may want observation, discernment, judgment, fire, genius, and wit."

"Miss Morland, do not mind what he says; but have the goodness to satisfy me as to this dreadful riot."

"Riot! What riot?"

"My dear Eleanor, the riot is only in your own brain. The confusion there is scandalous. Miss Morland has been talking of nothing more dreadful than a new publication which is shortly to come out, in three duodecimo volumes, two hundred and seventy-six pages in each, with a frontispiece to the first, of two tombstones and a lantern—do you understand? And you, Miss Morland—my stupid sister has mistaken all your clearest expressions. You talked of expected horrors in London—and instead of instantly conceiving, as any rational creature would have done, that such words could relate only to a circulating library,

she immediately pictured to herself a mob of three thousand men assembling in St. George's Fields, the Bank attacked, the Tower threatened, the streets of London flowing with blood, a detachment of the Twelfth Light Dragoons (the hopes of the nation) called up from Northampton to quell the insurgents, and the gallant Captain Frederick Tilney, in the moment of charging at the head of his troop, knocked off his horse by a brickbat from an upper window. Forgive her stupidity. The fears of the sister have added to the weakness of the woman; but she is by no means a simpleton in general."

Catherine looked grave. "And now, Henry," said Miss Tilney, "that you have made us understand each other, you may as well make Miss Morland understand yourself—unless you mean to have her think you intolerably rude to your sister, and a great brute in your opinion of women in general. Miss Morland is not used to your odd ways."

"I shall be most happy to make her better acquainted with them."

"No doubt; but that is no explanation of the present."

"What am I to do?"

"You know what you ought to do. Clear your character handsomely before her. Tell her that you think very highly of the understanding of women."

"Miss Morland, I think very highly of the understanding of all the women in the world—especially of those—whoever they may be—with whom I happen to be in company."

"That is not enough. Be more serious."

"Miss Morland, no one can think more highly of the understanding of women than I do. In my opinion, nature has given them so much that they never find it necessary to use more than half."

"We shall get nothing more serious from him now, Miss Morland. He is not in a sober mood. But I do assure you that he must be entirely misunderstood, if he can ever appear to say an unjust thing of any woman at all, or an unkind one of me."

It was no effect to Catherine to believe that Henry Tilney could never be wrong. His manner might sometimes surprise, but his meaning must always be just: and what she did not understand, she was almost as ready to admire, as what she did. The whole walk was delightful, and though it ended too soon, its conclusion was delightful too; her friends attended her into the house, and Miss Tilney, before they parted, addressing herself with respectful form, as much to Mrs. Allen as to Catherine, petitioned for the pleasure of her company to dinner on the day after the next. No difficulty was made on Mrs. Allen's side, and the only difficulty on Catherine's was in concealing the excess of her pleasure.

The morning had passed away so charmingly as to banish all her friendship and natural affection, for no thought of Isabella or James had crossed her during their walk. When the Tilneys were gone, she became amiable again, but she was amiable for some time to little effect; Mrs. Allen had no intelligence to give that could relieve her anxiety; she had heard nothing of any of them. Towards the end of the morning, however, Catherine, having occasion for some indispensable yard of ribbon which must be bought without a moment's delay, walked out into the town, and in Bond Street overtook the second Miss Thorpe as she was loitering towards Edgar's Buildings between two of the sweetest girls in the world, who had been her dear friends all the morning. From her, she soon learned that the party to Clifton had taken place. "They set off at eight this morning," said Miss Anne, "and I am sure I do not envy them their drive. I think you and I are very well off to be out of the scrape. It must be the dullest thing in the world, for there is not a soul at Clifton at this time of year. Belle went with your brother, and John drove Maria."

Catherine spoke the pleasure she really felt on hearing this part of the arrangement.

"Oh! yes," rejoined the other, "Maria is gone. She was quite wild to go. She thought it would be something very fine. I cannot say I admire her taste; and for my part, I was determined from the first not to go, if they pressed me ever so much."

Catherine, a little doubtful of this, could not help answering, "I wish you could have gone too. It is a pity you could not go all go."

"Thank you; but it is quite a matter of indifference to me. Indeed, I would not have gone on any account. I was saying so to Emily and Sophia when you overtook us."

Catherine was still unconvinced; but glad that Anne should have the friendship of an Emily and a Sophia to console her, she bade her adieu without much uneasiness, and returned home, pleased that the party had not been prevented by her refusing to join it, and very heartily wishing that it might be too pleasant to allow either James or Isabella to resent her resistance any longer.

TITLE COMMENTARY

Northanger Abbey

CECIL S. EMDEN (ESSAY DATE 1968)

SOURCE: Emden, Cecil S. "The Composition of *Northanger Abbey*." *Review of English Studies* 19 (1968): 279-87.

In the following essay, Emden offers evidence to support his theory that portions of Northanger Abbey *that parody Gothic literature were added—sometime around 1798—to a narrative that had been completed sometime around 1794.*

The first three novels of Jane Austen were a long time on the stocks for a variety of reasons, such as conscientious authorship and discouragement from publishers. It naturally followed that all three were subjected to sundry revisions. Much can be learnt about her craftsmanship and her development as a novelist by investigating the circumstances in which these novels were amended. *Northanger Abbey*[1] is specially worth this kind of study because it was, as I shall argue here, the object of a major revision, as well as minor revisions spread over a number of years. Attempts to establish the dates of the first version and of the major revision can be facilitated by noting variations in the author's tone and manner, which are often attributable to her changing attitudes of mind. Clear evidence is to be found of similarities between features in her juvenilia and features in those portions of the book which include satire of the silly sentimental novel and of contemporary manners. Contrariwise, there is little, if any, sign of the influence of her juvenilia on those parts, about a quarter of the whole, which aim at burlesquing the horror-novel. Moreover, the behaviour of the heroine in the burlesque passages and that in the light satire of the main portion are often incompatible. I intend, therefore, in this article to elaborate the arguments I advanced in 1950[2] to the effect that the main body of the novel was written in about 1794, and that the sections burlesquing horror-novels, and Mrs.

Radcliffe's *The Mysteries of Udolpho* in particular, were added some four years later.

As early as 1913, William Austen-Leigh and R. A. Austen-Leigh pointed out, in their *Life and Letters,*[3] that there is considerable weakness in the structure of *NA*, namely, the unsatisfactoriness of the Gothic episodes in relation to the rest of the story. They remarked on the evident superiority of interest and lightness of touch in the Bath episodes; and they added that, though this disparity was doubtless inherent in the scheme of the story, the author would hardly have tolerated such a defect at a later stage in her career. This kind of point was taken up again in 1939 by Miss Mary Lascelles, in her *Jane Austen and her Art* (Oxford, 1939), where she notices that the skit on the Gothic sensational novel is 'not . . . well woven into the rest of the fabric', and, furthermore, that there is but

> slight connexion between Catherine's fancied adventures and her actual adventures at the climax of the story. . . . And not all the light, gay references to her heroineship at the end can draw these two together.
>
> (p. 64)

After this, little, if anything, was written about such problems until I published my suggestions with a view to developing the comments made by the Austen-Leighs and Miss Lascelles. Since 1950, a few literary critics have made close studies of *NA,* and they, too, have found difficulties in the disharmony between the Bath and the Gothic episodes. As I have, since 1950, been able to augment and, I hope, strengthen the arguments in favour of my theory, it will be best if I mention some of the views expressed by other people in the last fifteen years or so before expounding my contentions afresh.

Some of the comments of recent critics, though illuminating and valuable, do not reach the point of asserting that the Gothic passages are incongruous with the non-Gothic. Professor Mudrick recognizes that Jane Austen provided herself with a problem when she wrote a novel which was to be at the same time realistic and burlesque.[4] Mr. A. D. McKillop regards the 'playful anti-Gothic satire' as subordinate to the satire on the sentimental novel, and to be a rather crude intrusion on the story.[5]

Two quite recent comments refer expressly to my theory. Mr. B. C. Southam deals with it sympathetically:

> In *Northanger Abbey* the patterns of burlesque are elaborate and ingenious, but they are not always exactly related to the course of the hero-

ine's experiences and adventures, and there is a good case for Mr. Emden's theory: that Jane Austen added the Gothic element to a story which was originally concerned with a young girl's entry into society, not unlike the adventures of Catharine Percival [in *Catharine, or the Bower,* one of Jane Austen's juvenilia].[6]

Professor Litz regards my argument as 'in some ways an attractive hypothesis' and surmises that 'the specifically Gothic extensions of her burlesque occurred to Jane Austen while she was at work on *Northanger Abbey,* and that they were painlessly inserted during the drafting of the first version'. The word 'painlessly' presumably refers to his impression that the interpolations can be readily identified, a point which I shall discuss later. Professor Litz, however, considers that there seems to be no warrant for postulating an early satire on the sentimental novel.[7]

Several critics have been minded to attribute an early date for *NA,* but have felt inhibited from doing so in view of the particulars given in a memorandum prepared by Jane Austen's sister, Cassandra, probably soon after Jane's death in 1817. The memorandum was written on two leaves of paper. The first includes the dates of composition of 'First Impressions', *Sense and Sensibility, Mansfield Park, Emma,* and *Persuasion.* She stated on the second leaf: 'North-hanger Abbey was written about the years 98 & 99.' It looks as if she had been asked if she could add a date for *NA.* She may, perhaps, have been referring to the date of its completion, for it was to all intents finished in 1798, although some small improvements were doubtless made in 1803, and even in 1816. The entry for *NA* is vague, whereas the entries on the first leaf mostly include detailed dates, and may well have been based on written evidence rather than mere recollection.

In formulating my case for the separate dating of the non-Gothic and the Gothic passages, I must first try to substantiate that the composition of the non-Gothic passages was undertaken about 1794. Those parts of *NA* which consist of satire of the silly sentimental novel and of contemporary manners disclose some obvious resemblances to her satire in the whimsical and often extravagantly phrased diction to be found in much of her juvenilia (written in 1790-3). Anyone who has studied these youthful expressions of exuberance will agree that it is not necessary to go beyond the first chapters of *NA* for illustrations of this link. On the first page the author includes an Austen family joke about the name 'Richard', of just the type that we can discern here and there in the juvenilia. We soon learn, too, that Catherine's father 'was not in the least addicted to locking up his daughters', a piece of high-spirited waggishness. Then Catherine's role as a heroine is portrayed in fanciful terms, reminiscent of the prentice satires of the sentimental novel: 'But when a young lady is to be a heroine the perverseness of forty surrounding families cannot prevent her.' Her falling in love, however, was not without mishaps; and her pillow is 'strewed with thorns and wet with tears'. 'And lucky may she think herself if she get another good night's rest in the course of the next three months.'[8] Similar exaggerative sentences are to be found near the end of the book:

> A heroine returning, at the close of her career, to her native village, in all the triumph of recovered reputation, and all the dignity of a countess, with a long train of noble relations in their several phaetons, and three waiting-maids in a travelling chaise-and-four behind her is an event on which the pen of the contriver may well delight to dwell. . . .[9]

These passages have just the farcical quality to be found in many of her youthful experiments in authorship, where her satire is freakish and effervescent. There can be little doubt that, by 1798, she had ceased to portray preposterous situations with irrepressible whimsicality.

One or two specific similarities between characters in the juvenilia and those in *NA* are worth quoting so as to reinforce the point made in the preceding paragraph. In *Catharine, or the Bower* (1792) there is a heroine who in several respects anticipates Catherine in *NA.* Both these characters, as Miss Lascelles has pointed out,[10] have similar 'romantic notions, aptitude for friendship, appetite for pleasure, and readiness to be pleased'. But the likenesses between the two boon companions of these two heroines are more definite, and more striking. Isabella, in *NA,* is in a number of ways a close parallel to Camilla in *Catharine, or the Bower.* They were both superficial, and in the same ways. They both set immoderate store by the effect they could make by their personal appearance, especially their dress. They were both apt to indulge in extravagant statements; and, soon afterwards, they asserted the opposite with equal zest and assurance, and without the least sign of embarrassment or consciousness of the absurdity of their behaviour. They both used the same kind of affected and *outré* language, doting on people, and calling a man, for instance, 'a horrid creature', and a girl 'the sweetest creature in the world'.[11] They both, in fact, provided strong contrasts with the heroines, for they were both worthless butterflies. It is much more likely that the author would have reused such characters as

Catharine and Camilla within two years of their creation than after six years, by which time her technique and the subjects which interested her had changed radically. Again, General Tilney, in *NA,* with his prodigious irascibility, combined with his insufferable behaviour as the tyrannical father and his barbarous treatment of Catherine as his guest, becomes so ogre-like that he is easily related to one or two farcical villains in the juvenilia. Jane Austen would hardly have introduced so impossible a person into a novel in 1798.

About the end of 1816, she composed an Advertisement, or what we might today call a prefatory note, for *NA,* at a time when, having bought back her manuscript from the publisher to whom she had sold it some years earlier, she was again considering publication. Some expressions in this note, which I have italicized in the extracts quoted below, may support the view that the book was begun about 1794 rather than 1798. She wrote:

> This little work was finished in the year 1803, and intended for immediate publication. . . . Some observation is necessary upon *those parts of the work* which thirteen years have made comparatively obsolete [chiefly no doubt the Gothic portions]. The public are entreated to bear in mind that thirteen years have passed since it was finished, *many more since it was begun,* and that during that period, places, manners, books and opinions have undergone considerable changes.

It is reasonable to suppose that 'many' years means more than the five years between 1798 and 1803. Changes of the kind she mentioned would have been more likely to have taken nine years than five years.

In so far as we are able to draw up a programme of her literary activities during the 1790s, it would seem that she had but little free time between 1794 and the autumn of 1798. 'Lady Susan', a short sketch in the form of a novel-in-letters, about a third of the length of *NA,* was probably written early in 1795, and 'Elinor and Marianne' in late 1795 and early 1796. 'First Impressions' occupied the autumn of 1796 and up to August 1797; and she must have been busy on *Sense and Sensibility* in November and December 1797 and until the end of the summer of 1798. Thus we see that, between the end of 1794 and the autumn of 1798, there were only brief intervals in her writing activities, mere breathing spaces, or time to think about the next task. If, as we have assumed, it is more than unlikely that she could have written in the strain of her juvenilia as late as 1798, we may conclude that the only period in which the original *NA* could have been written is in about 1794.

I recognize that there are two objections which might be made to the dating of the non-Gothic portions of *NA* as early as 1794. Dr. R. W. Chapman, in his edition of the novels, has pointed out that this novel, like others of hers, seems to have been based on a calendar; and he suggested that the calendar for 1798 would meet the case. This, however, does not necessarily fix that year as the date of original composition. It will be found that other years will fit equally well, 1795 for instance. It might also be alleged that Jane Austen did not have adequate knowledge of Bath as early as 1794 to be able to write the Bath episodes at that stage. But her nephew, James Edward Austen-Leigh, who knew her well, wrote, in the *Memoir*, which he published in 1870, that he believed that she sometimes visited her relations, the Coopers, in Bath 'long before she resided there herself', from 1801 to 1806. Furthermore, the authors of the *Life and Letters* state that she was supposed to have visited her uncle, Dr. Cooper, in Bath before he died in 1792. It has also been suggested that she stayed in Bath with her relations, the Leigh Perrots, at some stage in the period 1790-4.

I must now try to make my arguments acceptable from another point of view. Having put forward reasons why the non-Gothic portions were written about 1794, I think it is desirable to give reasons why the Gothic passages were inserted about 1798. As *Udolpho* was not published until 1794, it is not likely that any considerable skit on it would be both written and published until sufficient time had elapsed for a widespread impression to be made, not only by *Udolpho*, but by the other horror-novels mentioned in the Gothic interpolations, some of which were not published until 1797 and 1798.[12] We know that Jane Austen was at work on *NA* in 1798, so that this provides an initial ground for assuming that the Gothic passages were introduced then. The situation was propitious. The original *NA* had doubtless proved too short for a novel; and she would have been glad to seize on any opportunity to enlarge it. Moreover, it is likely that she would exploit the stir created among the novel-reading public over *Udolpho* in order to improve the prospects of the publication and success of *NA*. If she could introduce a longish burlesque, she could achieve both ends at the same time.

The two Catherines, that of the main story and that of the story within a story, are inconsistent. The steady, sensible, and essentially unmelodramatic Catherine of the non-Gothic passages does not match at all well with the sensational, irresponsible Catherine in the Gothic passages, where, for instance, she remarks to Isabella, as a result of her early reading of *Udolpho*: 'Oh! I am delighted with the book! I should like to spend my whole life reading it' (p. 40). There is too much affectation about this for Catherine.

A little later: 'Catherine was then left to the luxury of a raised, restless and frightened imagination over the pages of *Udolpho*, lost from all worldly concerns of dressing and dinner, incapable of soothing Mrs. Allen's fears on the delay of an expected dressmaker . . .' (p. 51). She could doubtless be thoroughly intrigued by a horror-novel, but not to the extent of neglecting her obligations to Mrs. Allen, to whom she always behaved with studious solicitude, even under provocation. When she was being shown over Northanger Abbey by her host, 'Catherine could have raved at the hand which had swept away what must have been beyond the value of all the rest, for the purposes of mere domestic economy . . .' (p. 184). The real Catherine would certainly have never 'raved' about any such subject, or indeed at all.

After Henry had caught her spying in his late mother's bedroom (an exploit she would never have undertaken), and gently indicated to her how foolish, and even ill-mannered she had been in her suspicions and actions, she realized that 'it had all been a voluntary, self-created delusion, each trifling circumstance receiving importance from an imagination resolved on alarm, and every thing forced to bend to one purpose by a mind which, before she entered the Abbey, had been craving to be frightened' (pp. 199-200). The Catherine of the non-Gothic passages could never have allowed herself to be caught up in such crack-brained flights of fancy; nor could she have departed so far from her strict code of good manners; nor, indeed, would she have preferred the lure of sensationalism to the good opinion of the young Tilneys. It is impossible to believe that any of the above-quoted passages were written at the same time as the Bath episodes.

Sometimes the Gothic passages interrupt topics of conversation, or have the appearance of clumsy digressions. Two passages, in volume i, chapter 6 (passages which relate to Catherine's pleasure in reading *Udolpho*), were evidently introduced into the Bath episodes to prepare the way for her exercising the role of investigator of suspected villainy when she reached the Abbey. The first of these interpolations interferes with the sequence of a discussion between her and Isabella on the subject of dress; and the second involves an abrupt break in a conversation between the two girls about behaviour to young men. And, in volume i, chapter 11, there are four brief interpolations, one comprising remarks about *Udolpho*, made quite inappropriately to Mrs. Allen, and three about Blaize Castle, which are introduced, more adroitly, into conversations about a proposed drive towards Bristol, and during the drive itself. Their intention is obviously to demonstrate Catherine's increasing curiosity about the kinds of scenery and ancient buildings pictured by Mrs. Radcliffe. The intense interest she displayed in the antiquity of Northanger Abbey as soon as she arrived there would not have been convincing without this preparation.

The main, and much the largest Gothic section, covering some thirty pages, and including the account of Catherine's terrifying experiences, and eventually embarrassing encounter with Henry, at the Abbey, is introduced in volume ii, chapters 5-9,[13] though parts of the original *NA* still have their place here and there. The first four paragraphs of chapter 10 continue the main Gothic section, after which there is an interpolated sentence designed to ease the transition back to the basic story: 'The anxieties of common life began soon to succeed to the alarms of romance.' Jane Austen seldom handled her structural problems as palpably as this.

Three short passages describing Catherine's recollections of being enthralled by sensationalism when at the Abbey (the first at the end of her visit there, the second on her way home, and the third when she had reached home), are inserted in volume ii, chapters 13, 14, and 16 respectively. No doubt they were introduced so as to help sustain the illusion that the *Udolpho* theme is inherent in the plot of the novel.

The readiness with which the Gothic passages can be identified is proof that scarcely any rewriting of the surrounding text was undertaken. Miss Lascelles evidently noticed this, and she has already been quoted as saying that these passages are 'not . . . well woven into the rest of the fabric'. We can, moreover, notice marked contrasts in readability between the sprightliness of the satire in the Bath episodes and the rather laborious description of Catherine's distressing apprehensions of bogies at the Abbey. The Gothic passages tend, in fact, to be heavy-going, barely deserving the name of burlesque, for they often fail to be ludicrous; and the only occasion on which they can be said to be amusing is in a passage in volume ii, chapter 5, where, on the way to the Abbey, Henry Tilney, in a sportive mood, describes to Catherine the horrific situations in which a sensational heroine might find herself.

It is generally admitted that the Gothic passages do not harmonize satisfactorily with the main story; and it can even be alleged that they are detrimental to its merits as a work of art. If I have succeeded in establishing the probability that these easily identifiable passages were added some years after the date of the first draft, this might well tend to a heightened recognition of the author's skill. Any experimenter who adopts the bold, but simple expedient of deleting the interpolations (in a spare copy) will find that he has not only eliminated the incongruities but has also restored the story to its original symmetry. And he will have done something more valuable still: he will have revealed that Catherine, the most entrancing *ingénue* in English fiction, can by this means be truly appreciated, exempt from features quite unsuited to her, and with all her lovable qualities unimpaired.

Notes

1. In this article abbreviated *NA*. The references to this novel are to the Oxford Illustrated Edition, ed. R. W. Chapman (London, 1933).

2. *N. & Q.*, cxcv (1950), 407-10.

3. p. 97.

4. M. Mudrick, *Jane Austen, Irony as Defense and Discovery* (Princeton, 1952), p. 39.

5. 'Critical Realism in *Northanger Abbey*', in *Jane Austen, A Collection of Critical Essays*, ed. I. Watt (Englewood Cliffs, N.J., 1963), pp. 52-61.

6. B. C. Southam, *Jane Austen's Literary Manuscripts* (Oxford, 1964), p. 62.

7. A. W. Litz, *Jane Austen, A Study of her Artistic Development* (London, 1965), p. 175.

8. *NA*, pp. 13, 16, 90.

9. Ibid., p. 232.

10. *R.E.S.* N.S., iii (1952), 184.

11. Jane Austen, *Minor Works*, ed. R. W. Chapman (London, 1954), pp. 202, 207. Cf. *NA*, pp. 40, 62, 118.

12. *NA*, pp. 40, 48.

13. In modern one-volume editions, chapters 1-16 of volume ii of the original two-volume edition become chapters 16-31.

SYNDY MCMILLEN CONGER (ESSAY DATE 1987)

SOURCE: Conger, Syndy McMillen. "Austen's Sense and Radcliffe's Sensibility." *Gothic*, n.s., 2 (1987): 16-24.

In the following essay, Conger argues that rather than denouncing Ann Radcliffe's Gothic "sensibility" in

Northanger Abbey, Austen affirms its essence and expands upon its utility as both a heroic virtue and a means of achieving growth.

The intrinsic value of **Northanger Abbey** is still disputed, but its significance in literary history generally is not: it is viewed as a key moment in the history of the novel. Here Ann Radcliffe's Female Gothic, the last representative of a century of literary emotionalism, is parodied to death by the novel of social realism: here Louis Bredvold's "natural history of sensibility"[1] comes to an end. Recent revisionists[2] see Austen as more indebted to her predecessor but still believe that she resists Radcliffe's endorsement of the heart. Marilyn Butler insists that Austen's heroines "are rebuked for letting interiority guide them" (140, 145), and Sandra M. Gilbert and Susan Gubar also argue that Catherine Morland, foreshadowing Austen's later heroines, must "relinquish" her "subjectivity" to save herself (121, 129, 144).[3] This vision of Austen sacrificing Radcliffe's subjectivity on the altar of realism or propriety or common sense wants some revision itself, for it rests on cursory assumptions about Radcliffe's achievement. The two authors are not poles apart at all on the question of sensibility; they are, on the contrary, two of the most prominent of many women writers involved in a late-century enterprise best briefly described as "saving sensibility."[4]

By the time Radcliffe completed *The Italian,* she had also reformed the English Gothic novel, divorcing it from sensation and wedding it to sentiment. She focuses her fictions not on the supernatural and irrational forces that drive forward Horace Walpole's *Castle of Otranto* but rather on the sensitive human psyche responding to such forces; and the effect is to establish that special form of eighteenth-century sensitivity, sensibility, as the behavioral norm. In Radcliffe's world sensibility is not confined to a few amiable eccentrics: all her good characters have it; conversely, all her wicked characters are without it, are, instead, slaves to the brute passions. Yet she never recommends sensibility blindly. First she reconstructs it,[5] then tests it for viability in the laboratory of Gothic terrors.

This rehabilitation of sensibility[6] was no small undertaking. A cult term that emerged mid-century but eluded precise definition, at first it referred to a bundle of loosely compatible but positive ideas: "delicate sensitiveness of taste" or "the capacity for refined emotion"; most specifically the "readiness to feel compassion for suffering," to forgive, and to be charitable (OED, cf. Hagstrum 5-9). Especially after the appearance of

The Sorrows of Young Werter in England in 1779, however, it began to seem suspect, to raise a number of troubling questions. Was its cultivation more apt to lead to emotional refinement or excess, sensitivity to others or egotism, morality or pathological behavior? It declined in status, mocked and abandoned by leading authors and rendered lugubrious by minor ones. Radcliffe's guarded endorsement of it in *The Mysteries of Udolpho* suggests that she was well aware of this tarnished reputation.

Mr. St. Aubert, the heroine's father, is willing to defend sensibility only as the lesser of two evils: "Whatever may be the evils resulting from a too susceptible heart, nothing can be hoped from an insensible one" (1.20). For St. Aubert, sensibility is a central, even an indispensable human attribute, but not a sufficient virtue unto itself. "Sentiment is a disgrace," says the dying man to his daughter, "instead of an ornament, unless it lead us to good actions" (1.80). Since it too easily invites self-indulgence or "the pride of fine feeling" (1.79), both of these being obstacles to fellow-feeling, its necessary companions are self-control and moderation: "I would not annihilate your feelings, my child, I would only teach you to command them"; "All excess is vicious" (1.20). Actually, his praise of sensibility, when compared to the successes of its avatars in *Udolpho* and *The Italian,* is unnecessarily faint. These characters do occasionally succumb to excessive emotionality; but, more often, the special gifts of sensibility serve them well, helping them to survive in a hostile world.

First, they are acutely perceptive. They use their senses: visual, common, moral. They combine an awareness of their own hearts with a scrutiny of others' faces to gain an intuitive knowledge or "emotional consciousness" (OED) of their situations. When left alone, they tend to scan their minds, sorting out and, if necessary, challenging their feelings or their ideas; they tend to set their inner lives in order. At other times, the same sensitivity and capacity for fine discernment turns outward—they are all skilled physiognomists: they scan eyes, study gestures, and draw accurate inferences about the emotional or moral state of persons around them (Ellena de Rosalba's study of her jailor Spalatro's face, for instance, saves her life). This special consciousness of inside and outside, coupled with their capacity for intense concentration, often grants them the advantage in self-control.[7] They are conversant with their own hearts and this habitual rational attention to emotion sets them free from passion's tyranny. Under stress their minds are nearly always clear, agile and strong. Witness Emily talking to Count Morano just as he has decided to abduct her by force: "Calm, Intreat you, these transports, and listen to reason, if you will not to pity. You have equally misplaced your love, and your hatred" (2.264).

These characters of sensibility are clearly designed to be stronger than the creations of mid-century ironists Mackenzie and Sterne, Harleys and Yoricks who were frequently immobilized by their own or others' emotions. Radcliffe's sensibility is much more than passive capacity for refined emotions, even for compassion. It energizes the whole mind, heightening its ordinary powers of perception, communication, concentration, and self-control. It is a new normative, moderate, rational subjectivity; and it is worth saving because it is a saving grace. The startling fact about recent Radcliffe criticism, seen in this light, is that it sees her fictions as hypocritical and deeply subjective. Radcliffe indulges in "every excess of sensibility which she explicitly warns against" (Kahane 52); her fictions "might virtuously proclaim the merits of self-control," but what they show is a "world governed by subjectivity." They are pure "exploration of her heroines' inner state of being at various levels of consciousness," one such level being "'inner rage and unspecified . . . guilt'" (Butler 133).

This preoccupation with Radcliffe's supposed covert message at the expense of her overt one focuses attention on a single but essential fact about Gothic fiction, one amply discussed by students of the genre from Eino Railo to Tzvetan Todorov—its subrational appeal. But Gothic fiction appeals to us, such students are quick to add, because it brings some order to the chaotic subrational realm.[8] The Gothic objectifies fears and desires in specific events, characters, and objects and then rationalizes them, making the latent manifest and, at the same time, usually less threatening. This objectifying process leads Todorov to suggest that Gothic fiction is ersatz psychoanalysis; and recent studies of the Female Gothic support his claim. Tania Modleski argues that the Female Gothic enables women readers to "work through profound psychic conflicts," that it legitimizes a temporary paranoia in readers by allowing them to identify with guiltless heroines placed in a hostile environment (83). These fictions give vent to terror and hostility but without finally recommending such attitudes (Fleenor 17).

Political persuasion may determine whether critics view this textual doubleness as therapeutic or repressive, but I doubt if it justifies their refus-

ing to see the doubleness at all, of insisting that Radcliffe, for Austen saw that doubleness, even if she responded to it with characteristic tact. She worried about Radcliffe's affective appeal but without condemning it; and she did not let it undermine her admiration for the ethic of sensibility that Radcliffe's texts manifestly defend. In fact, *Northanger Abbey* moves towards a subtle endorsement of that ethic, while Catherine acts out a confrontation with the problem of the Gothic's special subjective appeal.

Catherine's misreadings and misadventures have been much discussed, but a few points need to be made about them for present purposes.

Catherine is a naive reader, consuming *Udolpho* without ever activating her analytical faculty: she reads for plot and for thrills (1.25). Moreover, she allows Mrs. Radcliffe to activate her dream-making process; and that leads her to confuse fiction and reality as had her cervantick predecessor and, also as she had, to imitate the heroines of her idol. In this case, by practicing physiognomy, by reading a man's character in his face: General Tilney's "silent thoughtfulness," "downcast eyes," and "contracted brow" add up in her roused imagination to the "air and attitude of a Montoni!" (2.150).

Catherine's muddle reflects clear recognition on Austen's part of the danger of Gothic fiction—its activation of passive-agressive fantasies and volatile emotions; but her response to that danger is neither to condemn the reader nor the author, but simply to insist on the separateness of fiction and reality (Glock 44-45) and, even more important, on the inapplicability of emotions depicted and elicited in fiction to life. As Catherine sadly notes to herself after Henry's astonished lecture—"Dearest Miss Morland, what ideas have you been admitting?" (2.159)—we had best confine our "craving to be frightened" (2.160) to the aesthetic realm.

Northanger Abbey does not limit its evaluation of Radcliffe's subjective appeal, however, to these few negative moments. On the contrary, it contains many suggestions that *Udolpho* presents Catherine with psychological benefits as well as dangers. It may not enhance her power of self-control, but it nevertheless does increase her abilities to see and to converse. While she views Bath from the hills with the Tilneys, Catherine is able to compare the new scene to Radcliffe's "the south of France" and to chat, as a result, more easily with Henry; and if it guides her aesthetic appreciation of landscape in Bath, it intensifies her moral awareness at the Abbey. On the one hand, this results in a mistaken inference about the General, but, on the other, it also provides a helpful bridge in Catherine's education between the moral idyll of her childhood and the crasser actual world outside her home.

Catherine notices herself that she feels somehow protected by *Udolpho*—a neglected insight of hers that anticipates Modleski's thesis by 200 years: "While I have Udolpho to read," she assures Isabella Thorpe, "I feel as if nobody could make me miserable" (1.25). The reviewers of Austen's day might have insisted that such an attitude endangered Catherine's virtue; Austen's text, however, demonstrates that Catherine is right,

that *Udolpho* shields her from graver actual dangers, a delightful reversal of the reviewers' favorite cliche. At the Allens', Catherine's "raised, restless, and frightened imagination" busies itself with *Udolpho* while her adult chaperone worries about dressmakers (1.34). In town Catherine ponders the mystery of the black veil whenever Isabella chatters to her mindlessly about clothes or men or her brother John rattles about carriages and women's faces (1.22-23). Upon arrival at the Tilney abbey, Catherine views the spotless well-lit, modernized interior with the eye of a disappointed Gothic addict, oblivious to the General's struggle to impress her with his riches (1.128). *Udolpho* may burden Catherine temporarily with a few embarrassing fantasies, but it is often the best of the offered leisure pursuits and a positive preventive to vanity, frivolity, or materialism—a position on novel reading, incidentally, also taken by Mr. Rambler and another of his admirers, Mary Wollstonecraft.[9]

Implicit in Catherine's story is at least one other tribute to *Udolpho*: a subtle endorsement of Radcliffe's ethic of sensibility. Those who persist in seeing Catherine as progressing away from such an ethic may be dazzled by the parody into believing that its presence somehow magically banishes everything Radcliffe stood for from Austen's fictive world. If *Northanger Abbey* moves its heroine away from one kind of subjectivity, however, it is only to move her towards another. It is not so much a progress as a process of refinement, one in which the heroine is gradually divested (Moler 36) of certain excessive traits and certain false friends until she stands before us, at the end, as an approximation of Radcliffe's ideal (granted, that in Austen's fiction there are only approximations of ideals) of rational sensibility (Duckworth 8).

Catherine begins her story as a tomboy, a reluctant scholar, and a naif, still "ignorant and uninformed as the female mind at seventeen usually is" (1.5). She is also burdened, however, by excessive sensibility; she is indiscriminately good-natured and the difficulties she has at Bath stem as much from her "too susceptible heart" as they do from her inexperience. She thinks well of nearly everyone, and refuses to pass judgment on her brother James's new friends, the Thorpes. It seems harsh to infer from this, however, as Stuart Tave has done, that Catherine is an "amiable idiot" (60); for even in the brisk round of mindless activity she is caught up in at Bath, she shows signs of awakening sensitivity, discernment, and self-control. She doubts Henry's playful assertions, she worries about the impropriety of riding in carriages and missing appointments, and she finally sees that she must, for the sake of her own and her friends' feelings, sometimes say no to the whims of others. Her sensibility, even if it renders her gullible, at the same time makes her teachable and flexible, two valuable assets in the complex moral world of Austen's novels.

Isabella presents a particular danger to Catherine in her still malleable condition, that of tempting her to become a heroine of false sensibility. Isabella's mode of discourse, which Catherine begins to echo during her Bath period, is exaggerated and insincere, the vocabulary of sentiment without the substance to back it up that St. Aubert deplores. The Tilneys are a better influence on Catherine. Eleanor Tilney is presented as Isabella's foil, the genuine version of what Isabella professes to be: all decorum, sensitivity, and fellow-feeling. She is very much like her analogue Emily St. Aubert, but with one important exception: she does not wear her heart on her face. Her sensibility is concealed by a quiet reserve (1.38).

In contrast, Henry enters the novel in the role of a talkative antic commentator. He mocks the Bath society's attention to surfaces so much that Catherine concludes, shortly after meeting him, that he indulges "himself a little too much with the foibles of others" (1.15). Gilbert and Gubar agree, pegging him as "his father's son," opinionated, condescending, even insensitive and misogynistic to a degree (140); but the fact remains that he is by far the more sympathetic of Catherine's two suitors. John Thorpe's remarks begina and end with himself and his own concerns; he remains blind to his weaknesses and essentially unaware of the needs of others. In contrast, Henry, even if his discerning mind is sometimes "more nice than wise" (1.84), knows himself and attends to others. He is his sister's counterpart: a complete man of sensibility disguised in motley. He has moral sense, common sense, a keen capacity for empathy, acuteness of apprehension, refined taste, and a capacity for forgiveness too, even of a young woman who sees his father as a murderer! Henry generally keeps this sensibility under cover of his wit; but when he is pressed by his father to abandon Catherine and to consider a financially more advantageous marriage, his sentimental values emerge. He rejects the advice of his father and hastens to Catherine's house to bring about a visibly sentimental unraveling: "He felt himself bound as much in honour as in affection to Miss Morland" (2.202).[10]

At Northanger Abbey, then, Catherine is taught to distinguish sentimental fiction from reality, but, as might be surmised by the company she keeps, she is not stripped of her sensibility. Her abbey experiences rather refine her character than revolutionize it. Much that is affected and adolescent falls away at the abbey—the extravagance of diction, imagination, and curiosity. What remains is essentially Radcliffe's ideal: the well-regulated, yet sensitive and charitable, mind. After the General has peremptorily ordered Catherine to leave, even though she is stunned and deeply shamed, she checks her own grief to minister to Eleanor's. When Eleanor begs her, with a "look of sorrow," to write her despite her father's interdict, Catherine's pride melts "in a moment" and she instantly says "Oh, Eleanor, I will write to you indeed" (2.185). Eleanor is equally generous in these last moments, pressing her pocket money on Catherine for the unexpected journey. Not just their tears and words on this occasion, but their acute consciousness of the moral and emotional dimensions of the crisis, their giving and forgiving natures, and their self-control for each others' sakes, mark them as heroines of sensibility in Radcliffe's sense.

Radcliffe's special subjectivity does not seem to me to be sacrificed in this scene or elsewhere in *Northanger Abbey*. What has been sacrificed, if anything, is the assumption that sensibility is necessarily on the face or in the self-consciousness of the characters. Sensibility here and elsewhere in Austen's works has become so quiet that it is often overlooked. It has no unmistakable surface characteristics.[11] It can underlie Henry's teasing conversation as well as the sweet, serious discourse of his sister; Mrs. Allen's absent-minded permissiveness but also Mrs. Morland's gentle scrutiny and periodic lectures. In this context, it should be fairly obvious why Austen seems skeptical of the Gothic frame that Radcliffe had given to sensibility. Austen needed to divest it of the Gothic atmosphere of exaggeration to save it for her own more subtle fictional reality, one where faces more often serve as masks than as windows to the heart.

One can only be sure that someone else has sensibility in an Austen novel after a lapse of time and events: only if a professed concern for others has been translated, as St. Aubert recommends, into actions, tested by adversity, and remains unshaken, is it true sensibility. Three characters in *Northanger Abbey* clearly fail this test of time, even though they imagine themselves in firm possession of aesthetic and moral sense: both the Thorpes' and the General's attentiveness to Catherine melt away with their misconceptions of the Morland fortune. In contrast, there is no special awareness in Eleanor, Henry, Mrs. Morland, or Catherine that their actions can be identified with a code called sensibility, yet they obviously can. It is as if, to survive, sensibility has gone underground. Radcliffe had declared it to be normative; Austen rather clearly but unobtrusively assumes it to be, mentioning it less often than Radcliffe but nevertheless granting it a central position in *Northanger Abbey* that it never after relinquishes. People with it in her novels—Catherine, Marianne Dashwood, Colonel Brandon, Anne Elliott, and Fanny Price—need never be given up for lost; and those without it (just as St. Aubert had assured Emily)—the Thorpes, the Misses Steele or Bertram—are seldom to be saved. For Austen not only is sensibility, as it is for Radcliffe, a measure of moral excellence and the key to true propriety; it has also become the leaven for growth, the secret ingredient of her Bildungsroman. Clearly, *Northanger Abbey* does not mark the death of Radcliffe's sensibility but rather its fruitful transfiguration.

Notes

1. Stuart M. Tave argues persuasively for this keen distinction between Radcliffe and Austen. Others who do so include Frank W. Bradbrook, Waldo S. Glock, Kenneth Moler, and Mary Lascelles.

2. They base their arguments on Harold Bloom's assumptions about authors and their predecessors and the "anxiety of influence." Judith Wilt offers a similar reading but her focus is not so conspicuously feminist. My own revisionist reading is closest to Jean Hagstrum's, who sees Austen's novels as contemplative reconsiderations of the values of sensibility. I draw on Hans-Robert Jauss's reception theory; particularly, on his convictions that texts are best considered in contexts, in relationship to analogous works in their time (synchronic study) and in the past (diachronic study), and that these relationships are nearly always complex ones.

3. Cf. the similar readings of David Levine, of Judith Wilt, who sees Austen's heroines trying to "cut . . . destructive emotion down to size" (135), and of Coral Ann Howells, who emphasizes Austen's greater attention to "balance" in matters of feeling.

4. Katharine Rogers has suggested that eighteenth-century English women writers felt, to some degree, liberated by the literary mode of sensibility, even though they were often ambivalent about it. It authorized the expression of emotions which the culture-at-large (and their conduct books) did not. Sensibility may have appealed to women on a number of other levels as well: linguistic, social, ethical. Women at the time were encouraged to be silent, or if allowed to speak, were untrained to speak the language of pure logic. Sensibility valued the non-verbal forms of communication fostered by silence—sympathy, facial expression, gesture—and it spoke characteristi-

cally in a language that was alogical, that blended together thought and emotion. They faced poverty, even disgrace, if they were ever judged harshly by parents or husbands. The literature of sensibility emphasized suitors, husbands, and fathers who forgave. The fascination of women writers and readers of fiction with sensibility in the eighteenth century received attention early in our century from J. M. S. Tompkins. More recently, their interest in foreign literature of sensibility has been under investigation by Grieder and Conger.

5. Gary Kelly (51) sees the importance of sensibility for Radcliffe but believes that reason constitutes for her an opposing set of values. Howells does, too, discussing feeling in various Gothic novelists, including Radcliffe, in a much more general sense.

6. Useful critics on sensibility besides Louis Bredvold are Ronald S. Crane, Jean Hagstrum, John K. Sheriff, and Ian Watt. For special attention to women, see also Carol Gilligan, Katharine Rogers, and Patricia M. Spacks.

7. Nina da Vinci Nichols (205) has recently made an important distinction between Radcliffe's and Matthew G. Lewis's Gothic fiction. Radcliffe's characters are concerned about identity and "power over the self"; Lewis's Ambrosio is motivated by a desire for "power over others."

8. Theodore Ziolkowski reiterates the necessity of reason in the making of Gothic literature in *Disenchanted Images*.

9. See Samuel Johnson's Rambler No. 4 and Mary Wollstoncraft's *Vindication* (18.2). See also the works by Robert Scholes on Johnson and Austen and by Lloyd W. Brown and Margaret Kirkham on Austen and Feminism.

10. The conclusion of *Northanger Abbey* is a visibly sentimental unraveling. Radcliffe could hardly have done better. The heroine sits over her needlework, "sunk again, without knowing it herself, into languor and listlessness." The hero suddenly arrives and is introduced by a "conscious daughter" to her mother; and he is doing his best to apologize for the lack of propriety in his sudden appearance "with the embarrassment of real sensibility." The mother, too, manages a good-natured response: "He did not address himself to an uncandid judge or a resentful heart. Far from comprehending him or his sister in their father's misconduct, Mrs. Morland . . . received him with the simple professions of unaffected benevolence . . ." (2.196).

11. Spacks sheds valuable light on Austen's interest in concealment.

Works Cited

Austen, Jane. *Northanger Abbey* Ed. John Davie. New York: Oxford UP, 1980.

Bloom Harold. *The Anxiety of Influence.* New York: Oxford UP, 1973.

Bradbrook, Frank W. *Jane Austen and Her Predecessors.* Cambridge: Cambridge UP, 1966.

Bredvold, Louis I. *The Natural History of Sensibility.* Detroit: Wayne State UP, 1962.

Brown, Lloyd W. "Jane Austen and the Feminist Tradition." *Nineteenth-Century Fiction* 28 (1973): 321-38.

Butler, Marilyn. "The Woman at the Window: Ann Radcliffe in the Novels of Mary Wollstonecraft and Jane Austen." *Women and Literature* 1 (1980): 128-48.

Conger, Syndy M. "Fellow Travellers: Englishwomen and German Literature." *Studies in Eighteenth-Century Culture* 14 (1984): 143-71.

Crane, Ronald S. "Suggestions towards a Genealogy of the 'Man of Feeling.'" *English Literary History* 1 (1934): 205-30.

Duckworth, Alistair. *The Improvement of the Estate.* Baltimore: Johns Hopkins UP, 1971.

Fleenor, Julian E. Ed. "Introduction," *The Female Gothic.* Montreal, Quebec: Eden, 1983. 3-28.

Gilbert, Sandra M. and Susan Gubar. *The Madwoman in the Attic: The Woman Writer and the Nineteenth-Century Literary Imagination.* New Haven: Yale UP, 1979.

Gilligan, Carol. *In a Different Voice.* Cambridge: Harvard UP, 1982.

Glock, Waldo. "Catherine Morland's Gothic Illusions: A Defense of *Northanger Abbey*." *Rocky Mountain Review of Language and Literature* 32.1 (1978): 33-46.

Goethe, Johann Wolfgang von. *The Sorrows of Young Werter: A German Story.* Trans. Richard Graves. London: Dodsley, 1779.

Grieder, Josephine. *Translations of French Sentimental Prose Fiction in Late Eighteenth-Century England: The History of a Literary Vogue.* Durham: Duke UP, 1975.

Hagstrum, Jean. *Sex and Sensibility: Ideal and Erotic Love from Milton to Mozart.* Chicago: U of Chicago P, 1980.

Howells, Coral Ann. *Love, Mystery, and Misery: Feeling in Gothic Fiction.* London: Athlone, 1978.

Jauss, Hans-Robert. *Literaturgeschichte Als Provokation Der Literaturwissenschaft.* Muenchen (Munich): Wilhelm Fink, 1979.

Kahane, Claire. "Gothic Mirrors and Feminine Identity." *The Centennial Review* (Winter 1980): 43-64.

Kelly, Gary. "'The Constant Vicissitude of Interesting Passions' Ann Radcliffe's Perplexed Narratives." *Ariel-E* 10 (1979): 45-64.

Kirkham, Margaret. *Jane Austen: Feminism and Fiction.* Totowa, NJ: Barnes and Noble, 1983.

Lascelles, Mary. *Jane Austen and Her Art.* New York: Oxford UP, 1939.

Modleski, Tania. *Loving with a Vengeance: Mass-Produced Fantasies for Women.* Hamden, CT: Archon, 1982.

Moler, Kenneth. *Jane Austen's Art of Allusion.* Lincoln: U of Nebraska P, 1968.

Nichols, Nina da Vinci. "Place and Eros in Radcliffe, Lewis, and Brontë." In *The Female Gothic* see under Fleenor).

Radcliffe, Ann. *The Italian.* Ed. Frederick Garber. London: Oxford UP, 1968. *The Mysteries of Udolpho.* Ed. Bonomy Dobree. New York: Oxford UP, 1970.

Railo, Eino. *The Haunted Castle.* New York: Humanities, 1964.

Rogers, Katharine M. "The Liberating Effect of Sentimentalism." Ch. 4 in *Feminism in Eighteenth-Century England.* Urbana: U of Illinois P, 1982.

Scholes, Robert. "Dr. Johnson and Jane Austen." *Philological Quarterly* 54 (1975): 380-90.

Sheriff, John K. *The Good-Natured Man: The Evolution of a Moral Ideal, 1660-1800.* University: U of Alabama P, 1982.

Spacks, Patricia M. "Taking Care." Ch. 3 of *The Female Imagination.* London: Allen and Unwin, 1976.

Tave, Stuart M. *Some Words of Jane Austen.* Chicago: U of Chicago P, 1973.

Todorov, Tzvetan. *The Fantastic: A Structural Approach to a Literary Genre.* Trans. Richard Howard. Ithaca, NY: Cornell UP, 1973.

Tompkins, J.M.S. *The Popular Novel in England, 1770-1800.* Lincoln: U of Nebraska P, 1961.

Watt, Ian. "Sense Triumphantly Introduced to Sensibility." In *Jane Austen: "Sense and Sensibility," "Pride and Prejudice," and "Mansfield Park"*: A Casebook. Ed. B. C. Southam. New York: Macmillan, 1976. 119-29.

Wilt, Judith. *Ghosts of the Gothic: Austen, Eliot, and Lawrence.* Princeton: Princeton UP, 1980.

Wollstonecraft, Mary. A Vindication of the Rights of Women. Ed. Charles W. Hagelman, Jr. New York: Norton, 1967.

Ziolkowski, Theodore. *Disenchanted Images: A Literary Iconology.* Princeton: Princeton UP, 1977.

CLAIRE LAMONT (ESSAY DATE 1995)

SOURCE: Lamont, Claire. "Jane Austen's Gothic Architecture." In *Exhibited by Candlelight: Sources and Developments in the Gothic Tradition,* edited by Valeria Tinkler-Villani, Peter Davidson, and Jane Stevenson, pp. 107-15. Atlanta, Ga. and Amsterdam: Rodopi, 1995.

In the following essay, Lamont discusses the significance and symbolic use of Gothic architecture in Northanger Abbey.

When Catherine Morland is invited to visit the Tilneys at Northanger Abbey these are her reflections:

> She was to be their chosen visitor, she was to be for weeks under the same roof with the person whose society she mostly prized—and, in addition to all the rest, this roof was to be the roof of an abbey!—Her passion for ancient edifices was next in degree to her passion for Henry Tilney—and castles and abbies made usually the charm of those reveries which his image did not fill. To see and explore either the ramparts and keep of the one, or the cloisters of the other, had been for many weeks a darling wish, though to be more than the visitor of an hour, had seemed too nearly impossible for desire. And yet, this was to happen. With all the chances against her of house, hall, place, park, court, and cottage, Northanger turned up an abbey, and she was to be its inhabitant. Its long, damp passages, its narrow cells and ruined chapel, were to be within her daily reach, and she could not entirely subdue the hope of some traditional legends, some awful memorials of an injured and ill-fated nun.[1]

This paper is about Jane Austen's Gothic architecture. I have started with a quotation which expresses Catherine Morland's view of Gothic architecture, that it is a matter of "castles and abbies". The Gothic novels of the late-eighteenth century make frequent use of these two types of medieval building, the castle and the monastery, both of which had a domestic function but were not primarily defined by that function. As these two settings figure repeatedly in Gothic novels they come to take on features of two opposing signifying systems. The castle is associated with aggression, extroversion and the male; it dominates its landscape. The monastery is associated with repression, introversion and the female, and lies half-hidden in a valley. It is typical of early Gothic novels to be set in remote parts of continental Europe, and in an earlier century. However vestigial the historical sense of the novelists they set their novels in some sort of medieval world. In *Northanger Abbey,* however, the setting is in the south-west of England in Jane Austen's present, the late eighteenth and early nineteenth centuries. Medieval castles and monasteries were visible in her world but both would have lost their *raison d'être,* military or spiritual. They would be visible as ruined, restored or imitated.

In *Northanger Abbey* the heroine makes her first visit from home to Bath, apparently one of the least Gothic of settings. Having been originally a Roman settlement, it was rebuilt in the eighteenth century with neo-classical architecture as the medicinal properties of its waters were exploited. From Bath Catherine Morland makes two Gothic excursions. The first is the abortive trip to Blaize Castle; the second is the visit to Northanger Abbey. Catherine imagines Blaize Castle to be "an edifice like Udolpho" (102), and before agreeing to go on the trip asks "may we go all over it? may we go up every staircase, and into every suite of rooms?" (102) She anticipates "the happiness of a progress through a long suite of lofty rooms" or "along narrow, winding vaults" (104). The party never reaches Blaize Castle, and it is never actually pointed out in the novel that it was it was not, as John Thorpe had asserted, an old castle, "the oldest in the kingdom" (101), but an eighteenth-century Gothic imitation.[2]

There is no doubt about the age of Northanger Abbey. Catherine learns its history from Eleanor Tilney:

Many were the inquiries she was eager to make of Miss Tilney; but so active were her thoughts, that when these inquiries were answered, she was hardly more assured than before, of Northanger

Abbey having been a richly-endowed convent at the time of the Reformation, of its having fallen into the hands of an ancestor of the Tilneys on its dissolution, of a large portion of the ancient building still making a part of the present dwelling although the rest was decayed, or of its standing low in a valley, sheltered from the north and east by rising woods of oak.

Critics of the Gothic motif of the monastery usually stress imprisonment rather than the spiritual role of such a building. A monastic building in the Gothic novel is a place where someone is kept either against their will or at least in denial of the full range of their passions. Catherine Morland shares this view; she expects to find evidence of "an injured and ill-fated nun" (150). Eleanor Tilney's account of the history of Northanger Abbey, however, does not appear to invite that interpretation. Northanger had been "a well-endowed convent at the Reformation" which had "fallen into the hands of an ancestor of the Tilneys on its dissolution" ("fallen" implies either coming down, or chance). The word "convent" was in the late eighteenth century just acquiring its specific modern meaning of a religious house for women.[3] We may read the convent as a safe and spiritual retreat for women, which has now become the personal property of one man. What was endowed as a convent has become a private house where women are oppressed by one man, and a man significantly called *General* Tilney. His name indicates that he would be more at home in a castle. Catherine Morland, who is not interested in history, and particularly not the "quarrels of popes and kings" (123), does not meditate on this paradox. For her a castle or an abbey would do. She does not detect that although castles may have lost their original purpose with the cessation of fighting, it is a question whether the same can be said of a convent. One thing that the English Reformation has achieved is to give the powerful male, whose attributes are reflected in the castle, ownership also of the convent.

General Tilney exercises his ownership of Northanger Abbey in a way that no other man does in Jane Austen's novels. In her other novels a woman is mistress of the house and is in charge of the domestic arrangements. This is still the case when the mistress is not a wife but an unmarried daughter. Even Sir Walter Elliot in *Persuasion* does not deny his daughter her rights as mistress of the house. General Tilney issues invitations on behalf of his daughter and orders meals, overriding his daughter in each case (148, 171, 186). Catherine expects the domestic arrangements at Northanger to be in Eleanor's hands: after Henry Tilney's frightening account of a Gothic bedroom she takes comfort from the belief that "Miss Tilney, she was sure, would never put her into such a chamber as he had described!" (167) (She does not say that the Abbey would not have such a chamber.)

Jane Austen's norm of village Anglicanism does not imply that society is any the better for the dissolution of a convent. Catherine Morland's progress in the novel is from her parsonage home at Fullerton to the vicarage she will share with Henry Tilney at Woodston. Between these two havens of integrity she visits Bath and Northanger. Both of these, built as places of healing, have lost their proper function and are now given over to fashion and materialism.

Catherine's Gothic reveries are filled with "castles and abbies": "To see and explore either the ramparts and keep of the one, or the cloisters of the other, had been for many weeks a darling wish . . ." (150). For Catherine a Gothic castle should contain, besides its defining architectural features of ramparts and keep, towers and long galleries, suites of lofty rooms, many staircases, and narrow, winding vaults (101-102, 104). An abbey should have cloisters, long, damp passages, narrow cells and a ruined chapel (150). That much she has gathered from her reading of Gothic novels, before her conversation with Henry Tilney in the curricle on the way to Northanger. He confirms her view that a Gothic house has staircases, gloomy passages and lofty rooms, not to mention "a secret subterraneous communication between your apartment and the chapel of St Anthony, scarcely two miles off" (164, 166).

How are these expectations fulfilled at Northanger Abbey? Jane Austen does not usually spend much time describing a house from the outside. She is more interested in a house as a living space, and with its interior dynamics. However, the approach to a Gothic building is an important descriptive moment in the Gothic novel, and Catherine's first sight of Northanger Abbey cannot be passed over:

> every bend in the road was expected with solemn awe to afford a glimpse of its massy walls of grey stone, rising amidst a grove of ancient oaks, with the last beams of the sun playing in beautiful splendour on its high Gothic windows. But so low did the building stand, that she found herself passing through the great gates of the lodge into the very grounds of Northanger, without having discerned even an antique chimney.
>
> (167)

In the Gothic that draws on architecture the façade is frequently presented as the face in front

of the labyrinthine brain behind (Poe's House of Usher is perhaps the most famous example). Northanger Abbey will not be read from the outside, and the heroine enters with no guidance.[4]

Once inside, Catherine is first shown into "the common drawing-room". The architectural feature mentioned in that room is the Gothic window:

> The windows, to which she looked with peculiar dependence, from having heard the General talk of his preserving them in their Gothic form with reverential care, were yet less what her fancy had portrayed. To be sure the pointed arch was preserved—the form of them was Gothic—they might be even casements—but every pane was so large, so clear, so light! To an imagination which had hoped for the smallest divisions, and the heaviest stone-work, for painted glass, dirt and cobwebs, the difference was very distressing.
>
> (168)

Catherine is obviously in a house which has undergone modern restoration. The General has preserved the pointed arches of the windows, but has made a compromise with history in not restoring painted glass, small divisions in the panes, dirt, and cobwebs. He has picked on a characteristic feature, the pointed arch, for preservation and discreetly modernized the rest. The Gothic here appears to be optional; it is not structurally necessary. Catherine may criticize this compromise, but then she has no clear sense of the implications of what she is asking for. She wants not only the original windows, but also the dirt derived, presumably, from many years of subsequent neglect. As her mother was to remark of her, "Catherine would make a sad heedless young house-keeper to be sure . . ." (245).

Of all Jane Austen's novels, **Northanger Abbey** gives the most detailed description of a domestic interior. It is the only one of her novels to make serious use of architecture in its plot. The Gothic house with its complicated interior, its subterranean vaults, or, especially in later novels, its attics, lends itself to interpretation which sees these architectural features as representing aspects of life which have been frustrated or repressed. For all Henry Tilney's terrifying description of the subterranean passage that leads from the heroine's bedroom to the ruined chapel of St Anthony (166) Northanger Abbey is not described as having any subterranean passages, not even a decent cellar. Nor is it described as having an attic. The architecture, and any psychological reading of it, is not based on a vertical view of the house with "normal life" on one or two floors and the suppressed abnormal in basement or attic below or above. The important architectural feature of Northanger

Abbey is not its vertical dimensions, but its horizontal ones. Catherine expected an abbey to have cloisters; Northanger Abbey does; it is based on a quadrangle.

On her first evening Catherine sees that the house is built on a quadrangle (168). The next day she is given a tour. The house surrounds a court (181), and it has two floors. On the ground floor are the public rooms and offices, and on the upper floor the bedrooms. The rooms on the ground floor are tall, which is why the "broad staircase of shining oak" required "many flights and many landing-places" to reach the upper floor (168). Catherine is first taken round the building on the ground floor. She is taken through a suite of rooms: the "common drawing-room", which led into "a useless anti-chamber" which led in turn into "the real-drawing-room" which led into the library (186). Catherine had expected a Gothic building to offer "suites of rooms", that is rooms leading off each other, rather than each going off a hall or corridor. Northanger Abbey offers such a suite, though not quite up to Catherine's wishes (186). As she is taken round the quadrangle she is told that three sides retain the original Gothic architecture, and that of these one was more Gothic than the other two in that it retained elements of its convent origin in the remains of a cloister and cells (187). The fourth side of the building was modern. After being shown round the ground floor, Catherine is taken upstairs. There, the organization of the rooms was different. The rooms did not open off one another in a suite, but there was on the inner side of the quadrangle a corridor or gallery, whose windows looked across the quadrangle, and off this gallery were the bedrooms whose windows therefore looked outwards (168). Eleanor Tilney shows Catherine round the upper floor, but she is twice interrupted by an imperious request from her father before they can get right round. On both occasions they are stopped at a folding door, on the far side of which is the room which Eleanor's mother had occupied (189, 194). The consequence is that Catherine has been taken round the house on the ground floor; but only round part of it on the upper floor.

Catherine had glimpsed beyond the folding door on the upper floor "a narrower passage, more numerous openings, and symptoms of a winding stair-case" (189). She deduced that this was the side of the house where the remains of the original abbey were most preserved (191). She had seen that it had a staircase, and her Gothic imagination had speculated that Mrs Tilney could have

been taken down it "in a state of well-prepared insensibility" (191). On the third attempt to see Mrs Tilney's room Catherine goes alone.[5] She walks round the gallery, through the folding door, and enters Mrs Tilney's room (196). She is disappointed. It is a pleasant modern room, with sash windows, through which the western sun was shining. Gothic rooms, as had been established earlier, have casement windows (168). It was usually the east wing in a Gothic novel that was the most ruinous.[6] Catherine had wanted to visit a Gothic house; she has done so, and has been muddled by its architecture. She realizes her mistake in interpreting the upper floor of Northanger Abbey in terms of her Gothic expectations rather than in the light of her knowledge of the ground floor. She knew that the fourth side of the quadrangle was modern; but she had not supposed Mrs Tilney's room to be at one end of that side (196).

I have suggested that an important feature of the Gothic interior is the suite of rooms, one room leading off another. In the Gothic building the room does not have have certain bounds. This is true on the ground floor of Northanger Abbey, where one room leads off another in wealthy show. It is of more threatening significance in the Gothic bedroom. As Henry Tilney points out, a Gothic heroine hoping to have safety at last in a bedroom finds that the room has no lock, or that some hidden door opens off it (165-66). The Gothic bedroom is not a place of security because its bounds are not secure; there might be a hidden opening within it leading to a succession of vaulted chambers containing who knows what horrors, most of which are not at first noticed.[7] This is the parodic version of the splendid suite of rooms. The two versions of the suite of rooms may be thought of as representing public show and private neurosis. At Northanger Abbey Catherine was relieved to find that her room was decorated with wallpaper (169). The Gothic bedroom would be hung with tapestry, and there would be no knowing, until some storm of wind revealed an irregularity in the wall behind, what sort of hidden entrance it might conceal. It is an indication of the all-revealing nature of modern architecture, and the speedy collapse of her Gothic fantasies, that Catherine was so sure that the doors that she observed in Mrs Tilney's modern room led only to dressing-closets that she did not even bother to check that that was so: "she had no inclination to open either" (196).

It is a feature of recent criticism of **Northanger Abbey** to acknowledge but not stress Catherine's

Gothic disappointments. Feminist critics in particular have drawn attention to the fact that while Catherine may have been mistaken in thinking that Mrs Tilney had been either murdered or imprisoned, no one believes that she had been a happy woman. The patriarchal power of General Tilney over the women in his household is the modern equivalent of the authoritarian power of the Gothic hero.[8] The fact that Catherine's three disappointments (over the chest, the ebony cabinet and Mrs Tilney's room) all involve her expectations of Gothic evidence being followed by an extremely domestic reality (the folded counterpane, the laundry list, and the well-kept bedroom) can be read as a reproof to Catherine for her failure to realize the progress of society which has allowed a comfortable home to supersede the discomforts of the Gothic. Or, following Katherine Ferguson Ellis, her discoveries can be read as representing the tyranny of the home-as-haven ideal on the woman who inhabits it.[9] In such readings *Northanger Abbey* is a Gothic novel in spite of itself.

Northanger Abbey is a Gothic novel which uses architecture as a way of exploring unacknowledged areas of human psychology. If one such area is patriarchal power, another is the nature of the attraction which Catherine feels for Henry Tilney. Repeatedly, Catherine's interest in Gothic architecture is matched by her interest in Henry Tilney: "Her passion for ancient edifices was next in degree to her passion for Henry Tilney" (149). On the way to Blaize Castle she had "meditated, by turns, on broken promises and broken arches, phaetons and false hangings, Tilneys and trap-doors" (103). On the road to Northanger she had "an abbey before, and a curricle behind" (162). In deciding to explore Mrs Tilney's room on her own she chooses a day when Henry Tilney is away. But he returns before he is expected. Catherine has just let herself out of the bedroom and closed the door:

> At that instant a door underneath was hastily opened; some one seemed with swift steps to ascend the stairs, by the head of which she had yet to pass before she could gain the gallery. She had no power to move. With a feeling of terror not very definable, she fixed her eyes on the staircase, and in a few moments it gave Henry to her view.

> "Mr Tilney!" she exclaimed in a voice of more than common astonishment. He looked astonished too. "Good God!" she continued, not attending to his address, "how came you here?—how came you up that staircase?"

> "How came I up that staircase!" he replied, greatly surprised. "Because it is my nearest way from the stable-yard to my own chamber; and why should I not come up it?"
>
> (196-97)

Catherine had not experienced Gothic terror in the bedroom; she was feeling it now. Catherine knew that Gothic buildings had staircases, and she knew of the existence of this one. She is surprised because the only function she had had for that staircase was for Mrs Tilney to be brought down it "in a state of well-prepared insensibility". The staircase had not delivered an unconscious woman, however, but a lover come back before he was expected.

Northanger Abbey is the only novel by Jane Austen in which the heroine goes to stay in the hero's home, and there is sexual tension in her use of its architecture. Catherine's love of Henry Tilney and her love of the Gothic had always been confused. In her search for Mrs Tilney's room she manages to put herself in the direct route between the stables and Henry's bedroom. As Henry points out where she stands is in his space rather than in hers:

> "This passage is at least as extraordinary a road from the breakfast-parlour to your apartment, as that staircase can be from the stables to mine."
>
> (197)

There seems to be sexual adventure in Catherine's Gothic enquiries. Her conscious mind is exploring a Gothic bedroom; but in so doing she is suppressing knowledge she had about the house. Henry Tilney rushing up the staircase while she is frozen at the top of it is a powerful image. Her astonished question, "how came you here?" is a statement of her failure to understand the architecture which had so engrossed her imagination.

Notes

1. Jane Austen, *Northanger Abbey* (1818), ed. Anne Henry Ehrenpreis, Penguin, 1972, 149-50.

2. Andor Gomme, Michael Jenner and Bryan Little, *Bristol: An Architectural History,* London, 1979, 174-75.

3. *The Oxford English Dictionary*, 2nd edn, 1989, convent, sb., 6.

4. In contrast, Emma remarks of the other abbey in Jane Austen's novels, Donwell Abbey, home of Mr Knightley, "It was just what it ought to be, and it looked what it was" (*Emma* [1816], ed. Ronald Blythe, Penguin, 1966, 353).

5. Catherine's solitary exploration of Northanger may draw on Blanche's exploration of Chateau-le-Blanc in Ann Radcliffe, *The Mysteries of Udolpho* (1794), ed. Bonamy Dobrée, Oxford, 1966, 479-80.

6. For instance in *The Mysteries of Udolpho*, 377. This detail was picked up by Walter Scott in a humorous account of the types of novel popular in his day, ". . . must not every novel-reader have anticipated a castle scarce less than that of Udolpho, of which the eastern wing had long been uninhabited . . ." (*Waverley* [1814], ed. Claire Lamont, Oxford, 1981, 3).

7. This is true of Emily's bedroom at Udolpho (*The Mysteries of Udolpho*, 235) and Adeline's in Ann Radcliffe's *The Romance of the Forest* (1791), ed. Chloe Chard, Oxford, 1986, 144.

8. Sandra M. Gilbert and Susan Gubar, *The Madwoman in the Attic*, New Haven and London, 1979, 135.

9. Kate Ferguson Ellis, *The Contested Castle: Gothic Novels and the Subversion of Domestic Ideology*, 1989, x-xii.

FURTHER READING

Bibliographies

Handley, Graham. *Jane Austen: A Guide Through the Critical Maze*. New York: St. Martin's Press, 1992, 139 p.

Provides a guide to Austen criticism from early reviews through the 1980s.

Roth, Barry. *An Annotated Bibliography of Jane Austen Studies, 1984-94*, Athens: Ohio University Press, 1996, 438 p.

Offers a bibliography of studies on Jane Austen.

Biographies

Austen-Leigh, James. *A Memoir of Jane Austen*. London: R. Bentley, 1870, 364 p.

Presents an affectionate biography of Austen by her nephew.

Chapman, R. W. *Jane Austen: Facts and Problems*. Oxford: Oxford University Press, 1948, 224 p.

Provides an early biography by one of Austen's twentieth-century critics.

Halperin, John. *The Life of Jane Austen*. Baltimore: Johns Hopkins University Press, 1984, 399 p.

Links Austen's life to her works.

Jenkins, Elizabeth. *Jane Austen: A Biography*. New York: Grosset and Dunlap, 1948, 286 p.

Offers a detailed treatment of Austen's life and works.

Nokes, David. *Jane Austen: A Life*. New York: Farrar, Straus & Giroux, 1997, 512 p.

Attempts to correct the portrait of the sweet maiden aunt painted by Austen's family; considered by critics to be somewhat speculative in its alternative interpretation of Austen's life.

Tomalin, Claire. *Jane Austen: A Life*. New York: Knopf, 1997, 352 p.

Offers a popular biography focusing on Austen's family.

Criticism

Auerbach, Nina. "Jane Austen and Romantic Imprisonment." In *Jane Austen in a Social Context*, edited by David Monaghan, pp. 9-27. Totowa, N.J.: Barnes & Noble, 1981.

Discusses tone, satire, and Gothic elements in Northanger Abbey.

Clarke, Stephen. "Abbeys Real and Imagined: Northanger, Fonthill, and Aspects of the Gothic Revival." *Persuasions* 20 (1998): 93-105.

Compares Austen's depiction of Gothic architecture and the monastery to Gothic conventions, within the context of Gothic Revival architecture.

Derry, Stephen. "Freud, the Gothic, and Coat Symbolism in *Northanger Abbey*." *Persuasions* 18 (December 1996): 49-53.

Theories of Sigmund Freud inform this assessment of the use of the coat as a symbol of Catherine Morland's sexuality in Northanger Abbey.

Dussinger, John A. "Parents against Children: General Tilney as Gothic Monster." *Persuasions* 20 (1998): 165-74.

Explores Austen's gothicism in her representation of General Tilney as an example of cruelty in parent-child relations in Northanger Abbey.

Gay, Penny. "In the Gothic Theatre." *Persuasions* 20 (1998): 175-84.

Offers parallels between the handling of anxiety and fear in Northanger Abbey and in Ann Radcliffe's The Romance of the Forest.

Hermansson, Casie. "Neither Northanger Abbey: The Reader Presupposes." *Papers on Language and Literature: A Journal for Scholars and Critics of Language and Literature* 36, no. 4 (fall 2000): 337-56.

Assesses Northanger Abbey as a parody of a Gothic novel.

Hoeveler, Diane. "Vindicating Northanger Abbey: Mary Wollstonecraft, Jane Austen, and Gothic Feminism." In *Jane Austen and Discourses of Feminism*, edited by Devoney Looser, pp. 117-35. New York: St. Martin's, 1995.

Studies correlations between the feminist ideals expressed in Northanger Abbey and in Mary Wollstonecraft's A Vindication of the Rights of Woman.

Jerinic, Maria. "In Defense of the Gothic: Rereading *Northanger Abbey*." In *Jane Austen and Discourses of Feminism*, edited by Devoney Looser, pp. 137-49. New York: St. Martin's, 1995.

Rejects the classification of Northanger Abbey as a parody of the Gothic novel and argues that it is "an imitation, and not a complete rejection, of Ann Radcliffe's The Mysteries of Udolpho."

Levine, George. "Translating the Monstrous: *Northanger Abbey*." *Nineteenth-Century Fiction* 30, no. 3 (December 1975): 335-50.

Maintains that General Tilney's "monstrousness is part of Jane Austen's literary imagination," and argues that the fact that Northanger Abbey is "to a certain extent trapped by the materials of literary gimmickry it rejects" is an intentional, integral part of parodic style and is evocative of Austen's later novels.

Mudrick, Marvin. "The Literary Pretext Continued: Irony versus Gothicism: *Northanger Abbey*." In *Jane Austen: Irony as Defense and Discovery*, pp. 37-49. Princeton, N.J.: Princeton University Press, 1952.

Regards Austen's juxtaposition of the "Gothic and bourgeois worlds" in "ironic contrast" in Northanger Abbey as the author's method of "invalidat[ing]" the Gothic narrative form.

Roberts, Bette B. "The Horrid Novels: The Mysteries of Udolpho and Northanger Abbey." In *Gothic Fictions:
Prohibition/Transgression*, edited and with an afterword
by Kenneth W. Graham, pp. 89-111. New York: AMS,
1989.

Compares Ann Radcliffe's Mysteries of Udolpho *to*
Northanger Abbey, *identifying elements in the latter
work as parody of the former.*

Sears, Albert C. "Male Novel Reading of the 1790s, Gothic
Literature and *Northanger Abbey*." *Persuasions* 21 (1999):
106-12.

Views Northanger Abbey *in terms of its perspective on
male readers of Gothic fiction at the end of the eighteenth
century.*

Tandrup, Birthe. "Free Indirect Style and the Critique of the
Gothic in *Northanger Abbey*." In *Romantic Heritage: A
Collection of Critical Essays*, pp. 81-92. Copenhagen:
University of Copenhagen, 1983.

*Highlights Austen's use of free indirect discourse to
denounce Gothic literature in* Northanger Abbey.

Wallace, Tara Ghoshal. "*Northanger Abbey* and the Limits of
Parody." *Studies in the Novel* 20 (1988): 262-73.

*Remarks on the roles of the narrator and the reader in the
parodic discourse in* Northanger Abbey.

Wilt, Judith. *Ghosts of the Gothic: Austen, Eliot, and Lawrence.*
Princeton, N.J.: Princeton University Press, 1980, 307 p.

*Full-length analysis of gothicism in the works of Jane
Austen, T. S. Eliot, and D. H. Lawrence.*

OTHER SOURCES FROM GALE:

Additional coverage of Austen's life and career is contained
in the following sources published by Thomson Gale: *Au-
thors and Artists for Young Adults*, Vol. 19; *Beacham's Guide to
Literature for Young Adults*, Vol. 3; *British Writers*, Vol. 4; *Brit-
ish Writers: The Classics*, Vol. 1; *British Writers Retrospective
Supplement*, Vol. 2; *Concise Dictionary of British Literary
Biography, 1789-1832; Dictionary of Literary Biography*, Vol.
116; *DISCovering Authors; DISCovering Authors: British; DIS-
Covering Authors: Canadian; DISCovering Authors: Modules,
Most-studied Authors and Novelists; DISCovering Authors 3.0;
Exploring Novels; Feminism in Literature: A Gale Critical Com-
panion; Literary Movements for Students*, Vol. 1; *Literature and
Its Times*, Vol. 2; *Literature and Its Times Supplement*, Vol. 1;
*Literature Resource Center; Nineteenth-Century Literature Criti-
cism*, Vols. 1, 13, 19, 33, 51, 81, 95, 119, 150; *Novels for
Students*, Vols. 1, 14, 18, 20; *Twayne's English Authors; World
Literature and Its Times*, Vol. 3; *World Literature Criticism*; and
Writers for Young Adults Supplement, Vol. 1.

JOANNA BAILLIE

(1762 - 1851)

Scottish poet, playwright, editor, and critic.

Although Baillie was well recognized and respected among the literati during her lifetime, her works fell into neglect soon after her death and have only resurfaced in literary scholarship within the last several decades. She is now recognized for her significant influence on such writers as William Wordsworth, Lord Byron, and Percy Bysshe Shelley, and is considered by many critics to have served as a model for later women writers. Baillie's works, which include twenty-six plays and several volumes of poetry, provide insight into the history of dramatic theory and criticism as well as into the history of women's roles in theatre.

BIOGRAPHICAL INFORMATION

Baillie was born in 1762 in Bothwell, Lanarkshire, Scotland to James Baillie, a pastor, and his wife, Dorothea Hunter. Baillie was born a premature twin; her unnamed sister died within hours of delivery. Her parents already had two children, Agnes and Matthew. In the late 1760s, Baillie's father was promoted to a higher position at the collegiate church at Hamilton, a country setting that allowed Baillie the opportunity to enjoy outdoor activities. Though her brother attended school, Baillie did not, relying instead on her father for her education. James Baillie, as was typical for the time, stressed to his daughter the importance of developing her moral faculties over her intellectual skills, and emphasized that one should not give into one's emotions. Baillie was not fond of her studies and did not learn to read until, as she stated, she was nine years old. In the early 1770s, both Baillie sisters were sent to a Glasgow boarding school, and it was there that Joanna first developed an interest in books, writing and adapting stories to entertain her classmates. Baillie also became interested and quite proficient in the study of mathematics, abstract theorizing, problem solving, and philosophy. In 1778, when James Baillie died, the family became dependent on Dorothea's brother, William Hunter, a well-known anatomist who provided them with financial security as well as residence at his estate in Long Calderwood. Upon Hunter's death in 1783, Matthew inherited his uncle's medical school and London home, and the Baillie family moved to London to manage the new household. In 1790, while living in this London home, Baillie anonymously published *Poems: Wherein It Is Attempted to Describe Certain Views of Nature and of Rustic Manners.* The small volume did not receive sufficient notice or circulation to satisfy Baillie, and she reprinted much of it, along with other poems written while she was in her seventies, in an expanded version entitled *Fugitive Verses,* in 1840. Upon Matthew's marriage, the Baillie women moved to Hampstead, where they remained for the rest of their lives. In 1798, Baillie published, again anonymously, the first of what would eventually be three volumes of plays (the second and third volumes were published in 1802 and 1812, respectively). These volumes were entitled *A Series of Plays: In Which It Is Attempted to Delineate the Stronger Passions of the Mind—Each Passion Being the Subject of a Tragedy and a Comedy,* but were more commonly known as *Plays on the Passions.* The first volume contained, among others, *Basil,* a tragedy on love; *The Tryal,* a comedy on love; and possibly Baillie's most famous play, *De Monfort,* a tragedy on hatred. Baillie died in 1851.

MAJOR WORKS

Baillie's first publication, *Poems: Wherein It Is Attempted to Describe Certain Views of Nature and of Rustic Manners,* received little attention until after she had established a literary career. The first volume of *Plays on the Passions,* however, which Baillie published anonymously, quickly became the focus for discussion in literary circles, making this her first critically acclaimed work. Previously, success on the stage had been a prerequisite for the publication of a drama, but Baillie's publication of plays that had never been performed piqued the interest of many readers. In the preface, Baillie revealed her intent to trace the passions "in their rise and progress in the heart." She stated further that "a complete exhibition of passion, with its varieties and progress in the breast of man, has, I believe, scarcely ever been attempted in Comedy." The prevailing assumption of critics was that the anonymous author of *Plays on the Passions* was a man, until it was pointed out that there were more heroines in the dramas than heroes, and speculation began that the writer might be a woman. Baillie's authorship of the work was not revealed until 1800, when the third edition was published with her name on the title page. Sir Walter Scott, who some critics suspected had authored *Plays on the Passions,* became friends with Baillie and encouraged her to write more dramas. The second volume of *Plays on the Passions,* published in 1802, was well received by the public. Another collection entitled *Miscellaneous Plays* was published in 1804. In 1812, Baillie's last volume of *Plays on the Passions* was published, and was assessed as representing a departure from her earlier theories. Baillie noted that the second and last volume of the series had not received as much

praise as had the first, and she retired from active publishing for a number of years.

Many of Baillie's tragedies, *De Monfort* and *Orra* (1812; included in Volume 3 of *Plays on the Passions*) in particular, have been discussed as examples of Gothic fiction. The plays' eerie settings have been compared to those of Ann Radcliffe's novels, but Baillie's haunting plots and tortured characters are often regarded as more direct than Radcliffe's. In addition, her plays are noted for their strong female characters and social commentary. *De Monfort* centers on a love triangle devoid of romantic intentions, which leads to a murder, while *Orra* tells the tale of a young, independent heiress who refuses to wed and ultimately is driven mad by a fake haunting designed to trick her into marriage. The title character in *Count Basil* struggles to reconcile his desire for love and honor. *The Tryal* offers opposing perspectives on love, and *Witchcraft* (1836; included in *Dramas*) focuses on three women identified as witches, one of whom narrowly escapes being burned at the stake.

CRITICAL RECEPTION

Critics comment on the depiction of the effects of the intense emotions expressed by many of Baillie's characters, an approach that E. J. Clery refers to as "interiorized Gothic." Clery credits Baillie's style with inspiring later Gothic writers such as Charlotte Dacre, Charles Brockden Brown, Mary Shelley, and Edgar Allan Poe. Several critics point to Baillie's use of the Gothic to critique the morals and values of her time, especially with regard to traditional views of women. Peter Duthis asserts that several of Baillie's plays, *Count Basil* and *De Monfort* in particular, portray the tension wrought by upheavals in aristocratic society and the threat such upheavals posed to traditional gender roles. After Baillie's death, her works were gradually forgotten, and it was not until the late twentieth century that Baillie's writings again garnered scholarly interest. Drama historians and feminist commentators in particular recognize the historical importance of Baillie's complex and pyschologically insightful portrayals and her commentary on gender dynamics and social mores.

PRINCIPAL WORKS

Poems: Wherein It Is Attempted to Describe Certain Views of Nature and of Rustic Manners [anonymous] (poetry) 1790

A Series of Plays: In Which it is Attempted to Delineate the Stronger Passions of the Mind—Each Passion Being the Subject of a Tragedy and a Comedy. 3 vols. (plays) 1798, 1802, and 1812

Miscellaneous Plays (plays) 1804

Rayner (play) 1804

The Family Legend: A Tragedy (play) 1810

Metrical Legends of Exalted Characters (poetry) 1821

A Collection of Poems. Chiefly Manuscript, and from Living Authors [editor] (poetry) 1823

A View of the General Tenour of the New Testament Regarding the Nature and Dignity of Jesus Christ: Including a Collection of the Various Passages in the Gospels, Acts of the Apostles, and the Epistles Which Relate to That Subject (essay) 1831

†*Dramas.* 3 vols. (plays) 1836

Fugitive Verses (poetry) 1840

Ahalya Baee: A Poem (poetry) 1849

Lines to Agnes Baillie on Her Birthday (poetry) 1849

* The first volume was published anonymously in 1798, with the author identifying herself for the second and third volumes, in 1802 and 1812, respectively. Volume 1 includes *De Monfort, Basil,* and *The Tryal.* Volume 3 includes *Orra: A Tragedy, in Five Acts.*

† This collection includes the plays *Witchcraft, The Separation,* and *Henriquez,* among others.

PRIMARY SOURCES

JOANNA BAILLIE (ESSAY DATE 1798)

SOURCE: Baillie, Joanna. "Introductory Discourse." In *A Series of Plays: In Which it is Attempted to Delineate the Stronger Passions of the Mind—Each Passion Being the Subject of a Tragedy and a Comedy.* Vol. 1, 1798. Second edition, pp. 1-11. London, 1799.

In the following excerpt from her "Introductory Discourse" to Volume 1 of her Plays on the Passions, *first published in 1798, Baillie comments upon the universal human preoccupation with emotion, the spiritual, and the unknown.*

It is natural for a writer, who is about to submit his works to the Publick, to feel a strong inclination, by some Preliminary Address, to conciliate the favour of his reader, and dispose him, if possible, to peruse them with a favourable eye. I am well aware, however, that his endeavours are generally fruitless: in his situation our hearts revolt from all appearance of confidence, and we consider his diffidence as hypocrisy. Our own word is frequently taken for what we say of

ourselves, but very rarely for what we say of our works. Were these three plays, which this small volume contains, detached pieces only, and unconnected with others that do not yet appear, I should have suppressed this inclination altogether; and have allowed my reader to begin what is before him, and to form what opinion of it his taste or his humour might direct, without any previous trespass upon his time or his patience. But they are part of an extensive design: of one which, as far as my information goes, has nothing exactly similar to it in any language: of one which a whole life's time will be limited enough to accomplish; and which has, therefore, a considerable chance of being cut short by that hand which nothing can resist.

Before I explain the plan of this work, I must make a demand upon the patience of my reader, whilst I endeavour to communicate to him those ideas regarding human nature, as they in some degree affect almost every species of moral writings, but particularly the Dramatic, that induced me to attempt it; and, as far as my judgment enabled me to apply them, has directed me in the execution of it.

From that strong sympathy which most creatures, but the human above all, feel for others of their kind, nothing has become so much an object of man's curiosity as man himself. We are all conscious of this within ourselves, and so constantly do we meet with it in others, that like every circumstance of continually repeated occurrence, it thereby escapes observation. Every person who is not deficient in intellect, is more or less occupied in tracing amongst the individuals he converses with, the varieties of understanding and temper which constitute the characters of men; and receives great pleasure from every stroke of nature that points out to him those varieties. This is, much more than we are aware of, the occupation of children, and of grown people also, whose penetration is but lightly esteemed; and that conversation which degenerates with them into trivial and mischievous tattling, takes its rise not unfrequently from the same source that supplies the rich vein of the satirist and the wit. That eagerness so universally shewn for the conversation of the latter, plainly enough indicates how many people have been occupied in the same way with themselves. Let any one, in a large company, do or say what is strongly expressive of his peculiar character, or of some passion or humour of the moment, and it will be detected by almost every person present. How often may we see a very stupid countenance animated with a smile, when the learned and the wise have betrayed some native feature of their own minds! and how often will this be the case when they have supposed it to be concealed under a very sufficient disguise! From this constant employment of their minds, most people, I believe, without being conscious of it, have stored up in idea the greater part of those strong marked varieties of human character, which may be said to divide it into classes; and in one of those classes they involuntarily place every new person they become acquainted with.

I will readily allow that the dress and the manners of men, rather than their characters and disposition are the subjects of our common conversation, and seem chiefly to occupy the multitude. But let it be remembered that it is much easier to express our observations upon these. It is easier to communicate to another how a man wears his wig and cane, what kind of house he inhabits, and what kind of table he keeps, than from what slight traits in his words and actions we have been led to conceive certain impressions of his character: traits that will often escape the memory, when the opinions that were founded upon them remain. Besides, in communicating our ideas of the characters of others, we are often called upon to support them with more expence of reasoning than we can well afford, but our observations on the dress and appearance of men, seldom involve us in such difficulties. For these, and other reasons too tedious to mention, the generality of people appear to us more trifling than they are: and I may venture to say that, but for this sympathetick curiosity towards others of our kind, which is so strongly implanted within us, the attention we pay to the dress and the manners of men would dwindle into an employment as insipid, as examining the varieties of plants and minerals, is to one who understands not natural history.

In our ordinary intercourse with society, this sympathetick propensity of our minds is exercised upon men, under the common occurrences of life, in which we have often observed them. Here vanity and weakness put themselves forward to view, more conspicuously than the virtues: here men encounter those smaller trials, from which they are not apt to come of victorious, and here, consequently, that which is marked with the whimsical and ludicrous will strike us most forcibly, and make the strongest impression on our memory. To this sympathetick propensity of our minds, so exercised, the genuine and pure comick of every composition, whether drama, fable, story, or satire is addressed.

If man is an object of so much attention to man, engaged in the ordinary occurrences of life, how much more does he excite his curiosity and interest when placed in extraordinary situations of difficulty and distress? It cannot be any pleasure we receive from the sufferings of a fellow-creature which attracts such multitudes of people to a publick execution, though it is the horrour we conceive for such a spectacle that keeps so many more away. To see a human being bearing himself up under such circumstances, or struggling with the terrible apprehensions which such a situation impresses, must be the powerful incentive, which makes us press forward to behold what we shrink from, and wait with trembling expectation for what we dread.[1] For though few at such a spectacle can get near enough to distinguish the expression of face, or the minuter parts of a criminal's behaviour, yet from a considerable distance will they eagerly mark whether he steps firmly; whether the motions of his body denote agitation or calmness; and if the wind does but ruffle his garment, they will, even from that change upon the outline of his distant figure, read some expression connected with his dreadful situation. Though there is a greater proportion of people in whom this strong curiosity will be overcome by other dispositions and motives; though there are many more who will stay away from such a sight than will go to it; yet there are very few who will not be eager to converse with a person who has beheld it; and to learn, very minutely, every circumstance connected with it, except the very act itself of inflicting death. To lift up the roof of his dungeon, like the *Diable boiteux*, and look upon a criminal the night before he suffers, in his still hours of privacy, when all that disguise, which respect for the opinion of others, the strong motive by which even the lowest and wickedest of men still continue to be moved, would present an object to the mind of every person, not withheld from it by great timidity of character, more powerfully attractive than almost any other.

Revenge, no doubt, first began amongst the savages of America that dreadful custom of sacrificing their prisoners of war. But the perpetration of such hideous cruelty could never have become a permanent national custom, but for this universal desire in the human mind to behold man in every situation, putting forth his strength against the current of adversity, scorning all bodily anguish, or struggling with those feelings of nature, which, like a beating stream, will oft'times burst through the artificial barriers of pride. Before they began those terrible rites they treat their prisoners kindly; and it cannot be supposed that men, alternately enemies and friends to so many neighbouring tribes, in manners and appearance like themselves, should so strongly be actuated by a spirit of publick revenge. This custom, therefore, must be considered as a grand and terrible game, which every tribe plays against another; where they try not the strength of the arm, the swiftness of the feet, nor the acuteness of the eye, but the fortitude of the soul. Considered in this light, the excess of cruelty exercised upon their miserable victim, in which every hand is described as ready to inflict its portion of pain, and every head ingenious in the contrivance of it, is no longer to be wondered at. To put into his measure of misery one agony less, would be, in some degree, betraying the honour of their nation, would be doing a species of injustice to every hero of their own tribe who had already sustained it, and to those who might be called upon to do so; amongst whom each of these savage tormentors has his chance of being one, and has prepared himself for it from his childhood. Nay, it would be a species of injustice to the haughty victim himself, who would scorn to purchase his place amongst the heroes of his nation, at an easier price than his undaunted predecessors.

Amongst the many trials to which the human mind is subjected, that of holding intercourse, real or imaginary, with the world of spirits: of finding itself alone with a being terrifick and awful, whose nature and power are unknown, has been justly considered as one of the most severe. The workings of nature in this situation, we all know, have ever been the object of our most eager inquiry. No man wishes to see the Ghost himself, which would certainly procure him the best information on the subject, but every man wishes to see one who believes that he sees it, in all the agitation and wildness of that species of terrour. To gratify this curiosity how many people have dressed up hideous apparitions to frighten the timid and superstitious! and have done it at the risk of destroying their happiness or understanding for ever. For the instances of intellect being destroyed by this kind of trial are more numerous, perhaps, in proportion to the few who have undergone it, than by any other.

How sensible are we of this strong propensity within us, when we behold any person under the pressure of great and uncommon calamity! Delicacy and respect for the afflicted will, indeed, make us turn ourselves aside from observing him, and cast down our eyes in his presence; but the first glance we direct to him will involuntarily be one of the keenest observation, how hastily soever it may be checked; and often will a returning look of inquiry mix itself by stealth with our sympathy and reserve.

But it is not in situations of difficulty and distress alone, that man becomes the object of this sympathetick curiosity; he is no less so when the evil he contends with arises in his own breast, and no outward circumstance connected with him either awakens our attention or our pity. What human creature is there, who can behold a being like himself under the violent agitation of those passions which all have, in some degree, experienced, without feeling himself most powerfully excited by the sight? I say, all have experienced; for the bravest man on earth knows what fear is as well as the coward; and will not refuse to be interested for one under the dominion of this passion, provided there be nothing in the circumstances attending it to create contempt. Anger is a passion that attracts less sympathy than any other, yet the unpleasing and distorted features of an angry man will be more eagerly gazed upon, by those who are no wise concerned with his fury or the objects of it, than the most amiable placid countenance in the world. Every eye is directed to him; every voice hushed to silence in his presence; even children will leave off their gambols as he passes, and gaze after him more eagerly than the gaudiest equipage. The wild tossings of despair; the gnashing of hatred and revenge; the yearnings of affection, and the softened mien of love; all the language of the agitated soul, which every age and nation understands, is never addressed to the dull nor inattentive.

It is not merely under the violent agitations of passion, that man so rouses and interests us; even the smallest indications of an unquiet mind, the restless eye, the muttering lip, the half-checked exclamation, and the hasty start, will set our attention as anxiously upon the watch, as the first distant flashes of a gathering storm. When some great explosion of passion bursts forth, and some consequent catastrophe happens, if we are at all acquainted with the unhappy perpetrator, how minutely will we endeavour to remember every circumstance of his past behaviour! and with what avidity will we seize upon every recollected word or gesture, that is in the smallest degree indicative of the supposed state of his mind, at the time when they took place. If we are not acquainted with him, how eagerly will we listen to similar recollections from another! Let us understand, from observation or report, that any person harbours in his breast, concealed from the world's eye, some powerful rankling passion of what kind soever it may be, we will observe every word, every motion, every look, even the distant gait of such a man, with a constancy and attention bestowed upon no other. Nay, should we meet him unexpectedly on our way, a feeling will pass across our minds as though we found ourselves in the neighbourhood of some secret and fearful thing. If invisible, would we not follow him into his lonely haunts, into his closet, into the midnight silence of his chamber? There is, perhaps, no employment which the human mind will with so much avidity pursue, as the discovery of concealed passion, as the tracing the varieties and progress of a perturbed soul.

It is to this sympathetick curiosity of our nature, exercised upon mankind in great and trying occasions, and under the influence of the stronger passions, when the grand, the generous, and the terrible attract our attention far more than the base and depraved, that the high and powerfully tragick, of every composition, is addressed.

Note

1. In confirmation of this opinion I may venture to say, that of the great numbers who go to see a publick execution, there are but very few who would not run away from, and avoid it, if they happened to meet with it unexpectedly. We find people stopping to look at a procession, or any other uncommon sight, they may have fallen in with accidentally, but almost never an execution. No one goes there who has not made up his mind for the occasion; which would not be the case, if any natural love of cruelty were the cause of such assemblies.

GENERAL COMMENTARY

E. J. CLERY (ESSAY DATE 2000)

SOURCE: Clery, E. J. "Joanna Baillie and Charlotte Dacre." In *Women's Gothic: From Clara Reeve to Mary Shelley*, pp. 85-116. Devon, United Kingdom: Northcote House in Association with the British Council, 2000.

In the following excerpt, Clery surveys Baillie's Gothic dramas, particularly De Monfort *and* Orra.

In 1798, the year after Radcliffe bowed out of the literary scene, a volume was published anonymously with the arresting title *A Series of Plays: In Which It Is Attempted to Delineate the Stronger Passions of the Mind.* The contents did not disappoint. There was an '**Introductory Discourse**' outlining not only a grandiose scheme for the analysis of each passion in a paired tragedy and comedy, but also a radical theory for regenerating dramatic writing. The three plays themselves

were judged to be masterly; particularly the tragedies, *De Monfort* and *Basil*, focused respectively on the antithetical passions of hate and love (those posited by the philosopher Malebranche as the root passions). The plots had a simplicity and the language a poetic resonance that had long been missing from British drama.

The volume soon aroused intense interest and speculation. Who was the author? The first reviews, in the *New Monthly Magazine* and the *Critical Review,* praised the strength and originality of the writing while assuming that the author was a man. Some thought it might be Walter Scott. Back in Bath, Hester Piozzi recorded that 'a knot of Literary Characters [including Sarah Siddons] met at Miss [Sophia] Lee's House . . . deciding—contrary to my own judgment—that a *learned man* must have been the author; and I, chiefly to put the Company in a good humour, maintained it was a woman. Merely, said I, because the heroines are *Dames Passées*, and a man has no notion of mentioning a female after she is five and twenty.'[1] The dramatist Mary Berry had received the book incognito from the author, and had stayed up all night reading it, noting in her diary the following year that 'The first question on every one's lips is, "Have you read the series of plays?" Every body talks in the raptures I always thought they deserved of the tragedies, and of the introduction as of a new and admirable piece of criticism'.[2] She too was of the opinion that the author was a woman, 'only because, no man could or would draw such noble and dignified representations of the female mind as Countess Albini and Jane de Monfort. They often make us clever, captivating, heroic, but never rationally superior.'[3] The opinion grew that Ann Radcliffe was the author, trying her powers in a new genre. Mrs Piozzi reported it as fact to one correspondent. A Mrs Jackson spread the rumour, with a detailed list of stylistic evidence; Radcliffe apparently tried and failed to contact her and put a stop to it.

The play *De Monfort* went into production at Drury Lane, with Sarah Siddons and her brother John Philip Kemble in the lead parts, and still the author did not come forward to claim credit and payment. The playbills were silent on the matter. But some time before its theatrical unveiling, Joanna Baillie disclosed her name, and on opening night, 29 April 1800, she attended with a party of friends and relations. One critic described in retrospect the astonishment caused by the revelation of her authorship:

The curiosity excited in the literary circle, which was then much more narrow and concentrated than at present; the incredulity, with which the first rumour that these vigorous and original compositions came from a female hand, was received; and the astonishment, when, after all the ladies who then enjoyed any literary celebrity had been tried and found totally wanting in the splendid faculties developed in those dramas, they were acknowledged by a gentle, quiet and retiring young woman, whose most intimate friends, we believe, had never suspected her extraordinary powers.[4]

It is a literary Cinderella story, in which the heroine goes to the ball and lives happily ever after. In spite of recent misguided attempts by some feminist critics to represent Baillie as an oppressed and marginal writer, the fact is that she went on to a highly productive publishing career, a career met with continuous acclaim, and crowned by the appearance of her collected poems and plays in 1851, just before her death aged 88.[5] She had a large circle of friends including some of the most prominent cultural figures of the day. Maria Edgeworth, Anna Laetitia Barbauld, Walter Scott, Lord and Lady Byron, Wordsworth, and Southey, were among her ardent admirers. If her work came under attack from the notoriously severe pen of Francis Jeffrey at the *Edinburgh Review,* assassin of *Lyrical Ballads,* then it has to be said she was in excellent company.[6] Her sex was neither a barrier to success and celebrity, nor a shield against serious criticism. Her exceptional literary status, transcending conventions of gender, rested on a tradition which by now included the outstanding examples of Siddons and Radcliffe: women who displayed genius through rule-breaking and the imaginative flights characteristic of Gothic.

Joanna Baillie was born in 1762. Her father was a Presbyterian minister who became professor of divinity at the University of Glasgow before dying in 1783. The Baillies were descendants of the Scottish patriot Sir William Wallace. Her mother was the sister of the famous surgeon Dr William Hunter, who at his death left his London practice and property to Joanna's brother, Matthew. In 1784 Joanna travelled south to join him with her mother and elder sister Agnes. When Matthew married, the Baillie women set up independently in Hampstead, where Joanna and Agnes were to remain until the end of their long lives.

As a child at boarding school Joanna had excelled in music, drawing, mathematics and theatrical improvisations. A birthday poem addressed to Agnes recalls how she discovered her skill for story-telling through the pleasure of evoking fear and wonder in her sister, an eager auditor:

ABOUT THE AUTHOR

AN EXCERPT FROM A DEATH NOTICE IN
HARPER'S NEW MONTHLY MAGAZINE

Joanna Baillie, the most illustrious of the female poets of England, unless that place be assigned to Elizabeth Barrett Browning, notwithstanding her many affectations and great inequalities, died at Hampstead, on the 23d of February, at the age of 90 years, within a few weeks. She is best known by her *Plays on the Passions,* in which she made a bold and successful attempt to delineate the stronger passions of the mind by making each of them the subject of a tragedy and a comedy. . . . Her dramas are wrought wholly out from her own conceptions, and exhibit great originality and invention. Her power of portraying the darker and sterner passions of the human heart has rarely been surpassed. Scott eulogized "Basil's love and Montfort's hate" as a revival of something of the old Shaksperean strain in our later and more prosaic days. But her dramas have little in common with those of Shakspeare, so full of life, action, and vivacity. Their spirit is more akin to the stern and solemn repose of the Greek dramas. They have little of the form and pressure of real life. The catastrophe springs rather from the characters themselves than from the action of the drama. The end is seen from the beginning. Over all broods a fate as gloomy as that which overhung the doomed House of Atreus. Her female characters are delineated with great elevation and purity. Jane de Montfort—with her stately form which seems gigantic, till nearer approach shows that it scarcely exceeds middle stature; her queenly bearing, and calm, solemn smile; her "weeds of high habitual state"—is one of the noblest conceptions of poetry.

SOURCE: "Monthly Record of Current Events." *Harper's New Monthly Magazine* 2, no. 11 (April 1851): 709.

Thy love of tale and story was the stroke
At which my dormant fancy first awoke,
And ghosts and witches in my busy brain

Arose in sombre show, and motley train.
This new-found path attempting, proud was I,
Lurking approval on thy face to spy,
Or hear thee say, as grew thy roused attention,
'What! is this story all thine own invention?'[7]

Her first publication was a book of poetry which appeared in 1790 but went almost unnoticed. Already, though, it showed her interest in the study of human nature and the influence on the mind of contrasting passions. The subtitle explains that the poems will illustrate 'the Different Influence Which the Same Circumstances Produce on Different Characters' and there is a series of 'Addresses to the Night' by 'A Fearful Mind', 'A Discontented Mind', 'A Sorrowful Mind' and 'A Joyful Mind'.[8]

Passion in the Present Tense

Baillie's tragedies, particularly *De Monfort* and *Orra,* have been discussed as examples of Gothic writing in a number of critical studies.[9] Some of the settings are indeed strongly reminiscent of Radcliffe: the woods by night in *De Monfort,* with a requiem sounding faintly from an isolated convent; the castle in *Orra,* the haunt of outlaws under cover of strange legends, riddled with secret passages, its chambers furnished with locks on the outside. But in terms of plot, they represent an inversion of Reeve and Radcliffe's technique of encrypting homicidal passion in the distant past, and a decisive rejection of the tragicomic structure which permitted the redemption of evil. The contrast should perhaps even be understood as polemical. The trappings of Radcliffe-romance are included by Baillie only to emphasize their essential irrelevance: the real drama is all in the mind. Baillie refuses to buffer the tortured scenes she represents. This is passion in the present tense, as it had also appeared in Lee's *The Recess,* but in Baillie it is simplified and refined to achieve the transparency of a theorum. The remarks of Joseph Donohue regarding Baillie's conception of dramatic character are especially resonant: 'Gothic drama, beginning with Home's *Douglas,* placed special emphasis on an event that took place years before and continues to exert its effects thereafter. *De Monfort* internalizes this convention by redefining it as a mental process in which an evil passion inexplicably takes root in the fallow soul of man and slowly chokes away his life force.'[10]

This experiment bears some relation to Lewis's *The Monk,* as an illustration of the corrosive effect of lust on the character of Ambrosio. The *Plays on the Passions,* as they are generally called, made an important contribution towards the opening up of new possibilities within Gothic writing, as a now-familiarized audience looked for ever-stronger sensations. Future Gothic writers— Charlotte Dacre, Charles Brockden Brown, Mary Shelley, Edgar Allan Poe—would follow this direction of interiorized Gothic.

Baillie's 'Introductory Discourse' from the 1798 volume of plays provides a theoretical basis for the externalized spectacle of inner passions. Wittily, she frames the discussion in terms of the ruling passion of the reader. We are all, she claims, driven to poetry and fiction by curiosity about human nature. We want to go beyond the official accounts of history writing, penetrate the private space of the home and, further, to enter into the minds of others and rummage among their secret desires and motives. We can be diverted for a while by images of the marvellous in romance, or the artifices of sentimental fiction, or the pleasures of epic and pastoral verse, but the 'great master-propensity' for authentic pictures of nature will always reassert itself. Our curiosity about 'beings like ourselves' must be fed if we are to lend a work of literature our 'sympathetick interest'. Nowhere is this rule more applicable than in drama: pared down as it is to dialogue, if the characters do not speak from nature, then the author can offer no compensating distractions. The study of human nature and the persuasive depiction of character— which Baillie terms 'characteristick truth'—are crucial to the dramatist's art.

Baillie represents the taste for tragedy as something universal and primitive. Tragedy is the 'first-born' of dramatic genres, for a number of reasons. In addition to catering to the 'natural inclination' for 'scenes of horrour and distress, of passion and heroick exertion', tragedy permits the maximum exercise of curiosity and sympathy. In tragedy we are permitted behind the scenes into the lives and minds of 'heroes and great men', normally only glimpsed from afar. And in tragedy we see those extremes of conflict and suffering which most powerfully engage our feelings. At this point Baillie introduces the ultimate purpose of tragedy (now personified as a female muse), which doubles as a sketch of her own innovative theatrical practice:

> to her only it belongs to unveil to us the human mind under the dominion of those strong and fixed passions, which seemingly unprovoked by outward circumstances, will from small beginnings brood within the breast, till all the better dispositions, all the fair gifts of nature are borne down before them. Those passions which conceal themselves even to the dearest friend; and can, often times, only give their fulness vent in the

lonely desert, or in the darkness of midnight. For who hath followed the great man into his secret closet, or stood by the side of his nightly couch, and heard those exclamations of the soul which heaven alone may hear, that the historian should be able to inform us? and what form of story, what mode of rehearsed speech will communicate to us those feelings whose irregular bursts, abrupt transitions, sudden pauses, and half-uttered suggestions, scorn all harmony of measured verse, all method and order of relation?

No wonder Baillie's contemporaries were riveted by her vision. It is both alluring and intensely sinister. The passions are constructed as an inexplicable fatality, divorced from social context, unfolding with an irresistible autonomous force, pent up within an individual life which it will parasitically devour. And the audience is to be made privy to this horrible spectacle of a soul eaten alive, will eavesdrop on exclamations of isolated torture which only heaven should hear,[11] will be initiated into the language of the unspeakable. The workings of the soul are represented as absolutely private and secret, precisely in order to enhance the pleasure of violation and absolute public exposure in the name of 'sympathy' and knowledge.

In a study of this length, it is not possible to explore very far the social resonances of Baillie's poetics, though it is easy enough to identify certain ideological affinities. Baillie brilliantly refashions tragedy along Gothic lines for an age of possessive individualism and state surveillance. Her theatre most closely resembles Jeremy Bentham's panopticon, the ideal prison, in which the perfect visibility of the prisoners by an unseen eye stands, according to Michel Foucault's well-known account, as a general model for relations of power in the modern liberal state. But the baleful cast of her ideas has been obscured in recent criticism, by a determination to take the stress on sympathetic identification as a cosy, feminine alternative to 'patriarchal' tragic practice. Attempting to set up Baillie as a feminist sacred cow does her no favours. There is nothing cosy about her tragedies nor the response to them demanded of the viewer. Like the other writers discussed in this book, she was determined above all to make her mark in the literary world, and was willing to use the most powerful—the most ideologically arresting—means to do so. Issues of gender play a part in this ambition. But Baillie was intent on demonstrating her ability as a woman to rival men in the display of genius, not on defining an alternative feminine aesthetic. Harriet Martineau spoke of

cherishing Baillie's memory for the 'invulnerable justification which she set up for intellectual superiority in women'.[12]

In the **'Introductory Discourse'**, there is an interesting shift in the gender of personal pronouns relating to dramatic writing. At first, when Baillie discusses the primary concerns of the dramatist, she refers to 'him' and 'his' works. At a later stage, as she warms to her argument, tragedy (it has already been noted) is personified as a 'she', who puts into effect 'her' various techniques, including the innovations cited above. Personification is a common enough device in aesthetic discussion of the time, but here, given the sex of the author which would be revealed in the third edition of 1800, there is a fortuitous merging of art and artist, equivalent to Sarah Siddons's representation as the Tragic Muse. There is a subliminal message asserting women's capacity for representing and embodying tragic passion, reinforced by a statement in a footnote:

> I have said nothing here with regard to female character, though in many tragedies it is brought forward as the principal one of the piece, because what I have said of the above characters is likewise applicable to it. I believe there is no man that ever lived, who has behaved in a certain manner, on a certain occasion, who has not had amongst women some corresponding spirit, who on the like occasion, and every way similarly circumstanced, would have behaved in the like manner.

But Baillie goes much further than simply claiming her place among tragedians. The overall purpose of the **'Discourse'** is a critique of the entire dramatic inheritance in tragedy and comedy, condemnation of tired imitation in contemporary practice, and a call for bards possessing 'strong original genius' to point the way back to truth and nature. It goes without saying that the author herself must be numbered among this elite. While she is appropriately modest as a neophyte, she also has the courage of her convictions: 'I am emboldened by the confidence I feel in that candour and indulgence, with which the good and enlightened do ever regard the *experimental efforts* of those, who wish in any degree to enlarge the sources of pleasure and instruction amongst men'. Innovation is her *raison d'être*. Her manifesto is not bolstered by didacticism. Indeed, she rebukes tragic poets who have been led away from analysis of the passions by 'a desire to communicate more perfect moral instruction'. The benefit of tragedy should derive from 'the enlargement of our ideas in regard to human nature': a knowledge of the self, which may indirectly lead to moral improvement.

The project Baillie outlined publicly at the age of 36 lasted almost a lifetime. In the course of her prolific career she produced three volumes of *Plays on the Passions*—ten plays in all—and thirteen other plays, not to mention numerous poems. Bertrand Evans has proposed that ten of the tragedies can be categorized as Gothic drama: *Orra, The Dream, Henriquez, Romiero, Ethwald* (in two parts), *De Monfort, Rayner, The Family Legend, The Separation,* and *Witchcraft*.[13] I will be discussing only two of them, already mentioned: *De Monfort* (1798), by far the best known of her works then and now, and *Orra* (1812), which Evans claims best illustrates 'Miss Baillie's "Gothicity"'.[14]

Kemble's rapid determination to bring *De Monfort* to the stage of Drury Lane, in spite of the play's anonymity, has already been mentioned. It is unsurprising, given the fact that the play might have been written as a vehicle for himself and Siddons. Baillie's nephew suggested that the characters of De Monfort and his elder sister Jane were indeed intended as portraits of the two actors.[15] For Kemble, the role of a man of fine qualities driven to murder by an irrational hatred presumably reflected his talents as an interpreter rather than his actual personality. But in the case of Jane De Monfort, a woman who has nobly sacrificed her life to the duty of caring for her orphaned siblings, but who is still capable of enthralling every man she meets with her beauty and bearing, the terms in which she is praised in the play unquestionably echo descriptions of Siddons.[16] She is 'A noble dame, who should have been a queen' (*DM* I. i. 5); 'So stately and so graceful is her form', comments a servant, 'I thought at first her stature was gigantic' (*DM* II. i. 10-11): the awe she inspires is almost supernatural, as is her ability to turn all around her into willing slaves. It is understandable that Siddons requested Baillie to 'write me more Jane De Monforts'. The production only lasted for eleven performances and there are mixed reports of its reception,[17] but Siddons chose it for her benefit on 5 May 1800, acted the role again in Edinburgh in 1810 with her son Henry as De Monfort, and continued to use the play in recitations.[18]

The plot takes the novel form of a perverse love triangle, without romantic love. De Monfort is monomaniacally attached to Rezenfelt through his hatred, and there are homoerotic undercurrents in their interaction. Jane, De Monfort's sister, who raised him after the death of their mother, attempts to draw him away from this hate by appealing to their mutual love, which itself has a focused intensity verging on the incestuous. The addition of a third current, an unfounded rumour mentioned in passing that Rezenfelt and Jane are secretly in love, produces a short-circuit in De Monfort's mind that leads to murder. He waylays Rezenfelt in the woods outside the town and savagely stabs him to death.

The context for the drama is deliberately vague. The initial stage direction sets the scene as simply 'a town in Germany'. At the outset we learn that De Monfort has left his home to return to the town where he once lived. He is moody and irascible, yet his servants are loyal, and a friend, Count Freberg, who hurries to greet him, bears witness to his previously amiable nature. A first aside from De Monfort to the audience, however, signals a radical disaffection from his surroundings. The second scene develops suspense, as indications of De Monfort's pathology emerge, through symptom (he wrecks a room at the very mention of Rezenvelt), and the image of an incommunicable interiority. He taunts Freberg for his attachment to social surfaces and inability to penetrate the depths of human nature:

> That man was never born whose secret soul,
> With all its motley treasure of dark thoughts,
> Foul fantasies, vain musings, and wild dreams,
> Was ever open'd to another's scan.
>
> (*DM* I. ii. 96-8)

The play's concern with the distance between workable social conduct and the tangled depths of selfhood is shown thematically through numerous references to clothing and masks. Flimsy, changeable garments, often inappropriately worn, metaphorize the thin layer of public seeming, a fragile membrane that if severed, would enable the passions to pass freely from subjective confinement into violent reality. The anxiety provoked by this idea finds relief only in the figure of Jane, who represents an ideal of transparent meaning, a seamless union of nature and apperance. And yet Jane is chiefly responsible for the disastrous release of De Monfort's hatred.

In a key episode in the second scene of Act II, Jane forces her brother to confess his feelings. Impervious to his attempted defence of his 'secret troubles', his 'secret weakness', she applies every weapon of emotional blackmail. De Monfort agrees at last to 'tell thee all—but, oh! thou wilt despise me. / For in my breast a raging passion burns, / To which thy soul no sympathy will own—' (*DM* II. ii. 8-10). And so it transpires: Jane is horrified and uncomprehending. Threatened with rejection, De Monfort agrees to meet Rezenfelt and be reconciled with him, an action which will only result in an escalation of their animosity. The problem is that De Monfort did not—could not—'tell all'. The intensity of his hatred is not proportionate to the identifiable cause: Rezenfelt's habit of covertly goading him while pretending friendship. It is the nature of a ruling passion to be monstrous, autogenic, incommunicable. In De Monfort's case it grows to overpower one of his other prime characteristics, pity.

The audience is called upon to wonder as they witness the hero's deterioration, rather than to understand it in logical terms. As a bridge, there is the more homely yet comparable spectacle of the Countess Freberg's envy of Jane, exacerbated by the latter's kindly condescension. But from the final scene of Act IV through the final Act, as the drama grows wilder it is shifted to the appropriate setting of a wood where 'Foul murders have been done, and ravens scream; / And things unearthly, stalking through the night, / Have scar'd the lonely trav'ller from his wits' (IV. ii. 223-5), and to a lonely convent which stands in it. The 'thickly-tangled boughs' provide the obvious correlative for De Monfort's state of mind as he stalks his victim, and the old Gothic convent where he is brought, frozen with horror, after committing the act, is a monument to isolation. Jane arrives, once again shattering his solitude, and endeavouring to fix his mind on prayer and redemption. But the failure of communication—Jane: 'What means this heavy groan?' De Monfort: 'It has a meaning'—sums up the strange confusion of the scene as he, shackled by officers of justice, quickly expires of an internal haemorrhage. In Baillie's original version the peculiar non-event of De Monfort's death occurs off-stage, as if this reverse of a *coup de théâtre* were designed to taunt the audience, with its penchant for predictable shock-tactics. When Edmund Kean restaged the play in 1821, at the urgent request of Byron,[19] at least two important revisions were introduced. De Monfort's hatred was motivated by a love rivalry with Rezenfelt, and De Monfort was brought on-stage to die. These changes help to indicate the originality, the troubling strangeness, of the original version.[20]

'A Midnight in the Breast'

De Monfort's collapse and death are brought about partly by remorse, partly by sheer horror at the nature of the act he has committed, and specifically, superstitious fear at being left alone with the corpse of his victim. An early poem, 'The Ghost of Edward', dealt with the fanciful horrors that attack the mind. There is 'a midnight in the breast': in this instance also, fear is exacerbated by guilt.[21] Fear of the supernatural—in isolation from any causal factors—was the passion Baillie determined to explore at full length in a tragedy from her last volume of *Plays on the Passions* published in 1812, *Orra.* Set in the late fourteenth century in Switzerland, it concerns the machinations in the household of Count Hughobert, where his ward, the heiress Orra, is being pressured to marry Hughobert's son, Glottenbal, while also being wooed by a young nobleman of reduced fortunes, Theobald. The plot may sound conventional but the heroine is not. She wants to marry no one and live independently (there is some slight mention of charitable works), and manages to persuade Theobold to be her friend rather than her lover. She is not especially beautiful (Theobold: 'to speak honestly, / I've fairer seen', I. i. 129-30), and her character is a composite of mirth and dread, as if Annette, Emily's servant from *The Mysteries of Udolpho,* had usurped the lead role. Romantic love is displaced, as it was in *De Monfort* and in many of Baillie's other plays, with the result that expectations are disrupted and it becomes possible to create more interesting and varied parts for women.

Orra adores ghost stories, and this is her downfall. She is not only highly susceptible to fear but also addicted to the sensation:

> Yea, when the cold blood shoots through every
>   vein:
> When every pore upon my shrunken skin
> A knotted knoll becomes, and to mine ears
> Strange inward sounds awake, and to mine eyes
> Rush stranger tears, there is a joy in fear.
>
>   (II. i. 170-75)

Her chief resource to feed her passion is Cathrina, one of her attendants, who has an inexhaustible supply of supernatural legends. But Cathrina is in the power of Rudigere, an illegitimate relation of the count's who plots to marry Orra in order to improve his fortunes. Cathrina has been his mistress and borne his child, and, to save her reputation, she enters into Rudigere's plot to have Orra removed to an ancient castle rumoured to be haunted. There he will use Orra's fear to blackmail her into a union with Glottenbal (he tells the count), but in fact with himself. Theobald learns of the conspiracy, and plans to rescue her by impersonating the spirit of the place, a spectre huntsman. But a message forewarning her goes astray, and terror at his ghostly appearance drives her into a state of derangement, from which, it seems, she will not recover. A repentant Hughobert arrives on the scene with his family, and the villainous Rudigere kills both himself and his rival, the obtuse Glottenbal.

As in the case of **De Monfort,** the relation of **Orra** to an emergent Gothic genre is not straightforward. The play is a medley of familiar tropes: the haunted castle with a story of murder attached to it, riddled with secret passages (cf. almost any Gothic novel from *Castle of Otranto* onwards); the band of outlaws who use the castle as a hide-out under cover of supernatural rumour (cf. *The Mysteries of Udolpho,* Charlotte Smith's *The Old Manor House,* and many others); the noble outlaw chief (a childhood friend of Theobald, who lends his assistance; cf. Schiller, and Dacre's *Zofloya*); the heroine kept in a bedchamber with locks on the outside only (*Mysteries of Udolpho* etc.); the ballad tradition of elopement with a phantom lover (Bürger's 'Lenore', and its variants); the rescue involving impersonation of a phantom lover which ends in disaster (cf. the Bleeding Nun episode from *The Monk*). Indeed, the play's generic knowingness might lead one to imagine that its purpose was solely critical, even satirical. It is worth bearing in mind that two of the best-known burlesques of Gothic were published soon after: E. Stannard Barrett's *The Heroine* in 1813 and Jane Austen's *Northanger Abbey* in 1818. Certainly it is true to say that the devices included by Baillie are more or less stripped of affect: the supernatural is explained so far in advance that the audience is in no danger of falling in with Orra's delusions. But on the other hand, neither is the viewer permitted the security of detached criticism. Baillie maintains sympathetic identification with the heroine throughout the play by showing her insight into her own situation, her courageous resistance to oppression, and her inner struggle against fear. The catharsis of terror for the audience comes with the final scene, and the pitiful spectacle of Orra surrounded by mind-forged monsters.

Orra's passion for fear is not blamed. Like De Monfort's hatred it is something inexplicable and irresistible, an inner sublime. Baillie clearly indicates in her characterizations that possession of a powerful ruling passion is an index of greatness of soul; but it also creates an imbalance which is ultimately self-destructive. It opens De Monfort to criminality, and Orra to victimage. The audience is not called upon to judge and condemn, but rather to lend their understanding and, at the same time, to wonder at these human meteors and derive a vicarious thrill from their disastrous fates. As in all Gothic writing, the purpose of instruction is a fig-leaf; the fundamental pleasure is amoral. Baillie's methods reflected and faciliated the shift of Gothic away from the conventions which had been associated with the earlier phase of experimental supernaturalism and were thus becoming redundant, to the surer foundations of an inner landscape. Passion itself becomes the plot, but unmotivated, reified, an object of fascination in its own right. It would be inappropriate as well as anachronistic to call this *psychological* drama. The diseases of the mind are not submitted to logic. The increase of knowledge may be Baillie's expressed aim, but it is knowledge of an unabashedly corrupt and disingenuous kind, combining the pleasure of unveiling with the retention of some ultimate mystery.

Discussion of Baillie's drama has almost always excluded mention of her poetry, but she was a well-regarded and frequently anthologized poet as well. Her choice of subject matter and form was wide-ranging, but includes a number of supernatural ballads which Orra would have appreciated. Her **Metrical Legends of Exalted Characters** was said to have brought her £1,000 from the publishers Longman,[22] and went through two editions in the year of publication, 1821. 'The Ghost of Fadon', from this volume, is based on a legend concerning William Wallace, a distant ancestor of Baillie.[23] Here, in contrast to the plays, the supernatural is manifestly public. Not only does the ghost appear to a whole company of soldiers, but he challenges Wallace to a duel, and physically blocks him when he tries to escape, eventually presiding over the burning of the castle where the company had attempted to find shelter after military defeat by the English. He is public, too, in his historical significance. He is the spectre of Fadon, a follower killed by Wallace under suspicion of spying. The haunting suggests that he was wrongfully killed, an omen of bad luck for the nation.

> Day rose; but silent, sad, and pale,
>   Stood the bravest of the Scottish race;
> And each warrior's heart began to quail,
>   When he look'd in his leader's face.

There were a variety of Gothic modes current—several forms of fiction, tragic drama, ballads, odes, prose poems in the manner of Ossian—and Baillie felt no inhibition about testing her powers in more than one. In this poem she flaunts her ability to play on the superstition of her readers, while also signalling her personal investment in nationalist politics.

Notes

1. Cit. Margaret S. Carhart, *The Life and Works of Joanna Baillie*, Yale Studies in English, 64 (New Haven: Yale University Press, 1923), 15. See also Norton, *Mistress of Udolpho*, 185-7.

2. Cit. Carhart, *Joanna Baillie*, 17.

3. Cit. Carhart, *Joanna Baillie*, 15.

4. *Quarterly Review*, cit. Carhart, *Joanna Baillie*, 17.

5. Ellen Donkin's chapter on Baillie in *Getting Into the Act* (London: Routledge, 1995) is the prime example; she lays great emphasis on Piozzi's statements that by revealing her identity and therefore her sex Baillie opened herself to spiteful criticism, but fails to provide any persuasive evidence. The current dominant reading of Baillie by critics such as Anne Mellor and Catherine Burroughs suggests that she was self-marginalized, that is, writing from a position of conscious subordination and gendered critique; with this interpretation, too, I would disagree. Gender politics is not the beginning and end of Baillie's audacious challenge to theatrical orthodoxy. She was simply the most visionary and influential dramatist of her day.

6. See Carhart, *Joanna Baillie*, 47-52, which counters Donkin's very partial version.

7. 'Lines to Agnes Baillie on Her Birthday', *The Dramatic and Poetical Works of Joanna Baillie* (London: Longman, Brown, Green and Longmans, 1851), 811.

8. Some of the poems were later included in revised form in *Fugitive Verses* (1740). See Roger Lonsdale's remarks in *Eighteenth-Century Women Poets: An Oxford Anthology* (Oxford and New York: Oxford University Press, 1989), 429-30.

9. Notably Bertrand Evans, *Gothic Drama from Walpole to Shelley* (Berkeley and Los Angeles: University of California Press, 1947); Paul Ranger, *Terror and Pity*; and Jeffrey N. Cox (ed.), *Seven Gothic Dramas, 1789-1825* (Athens: Ohio University Press, 1992), which contains the text of *De Monfort*.

10. Joseph W. Donohue, *Dramatic Character in the English Romantic Age* (Princeton: Princeton University Press, 1970), 81.

11. A formulation repeated by Baillie in *De Monfort*, IV. ii. 26-7.

12. Cit. Carhart, *Joanna Baillie*, 64-5; Harriet Martineau, *Autobiography*, ed. M. W. Chapman (Beston, 1877), vol. I, p. 270.

13. Evans, *Gothic Drama*, 201.

14. Evans, *Gothic Drama*, 201.

15. Cit. Carhart, *Joanna Baillie*, 116.

16. See Campbell, *Mrs Siddons*: 'Joanna Baillie has left a perfect picture of Mrs Siddons, in her description of *Jane de Monfort*' (p. 303).

17. See Carhart, *Joanna Baillie*, 121-2.

18. See Carhart, *Joanna Baillie* (pp. 128-42), on the stage history of De Monfort after the original Drury Lane production. Cox, *Seven Gothic Dramas* (pp. 55-7), has an interesting discussion of Siddons as a dramatic interpreter of Gothic, but sees her acting style as typically passive, in contrast to Paula Backscheider, and

19. At the time, Byron was a member of the management committee at Drury Lane.

20. Another strategy of containment in the first performed version was the Epilogue, written by the Duchess of Devonshire. In the most conventional terms, it urges the audience to 'bid the scene's dread horror cease / And hail the blessing of domestic peace'. It is included in Cox, *Seven Gothic Dramas*, 313-14.

21. From *Poems* (1790), reproduced in Lonsdale, *Eighteenth-Century Women Poets*.

22. Carhart, *Joanna Baillie*, 29.

23. The poem is included in Jerome M. McGann (ed.), *The New Oxford Book of Romantic Period Verse*, (Oxford and New York: Oxford University Press, 1993).

Abbreviations

DM Joanna Baillie, *De Monfort: A Tragedy*, in *Seven Gothic Dramas 1789-1825*, ed. Jeffrey N. Cox (Athens, OH: Ohio University Press, 1992).

TITLE COMMENTARY

Plays on the Passions

PETER DUTHIE (ESSAY DATE 2001)

SOURCE: Duthie, Peter. Introduction to *Plays on the Passions*, by Joanna Baillie, pp. 11-57. Peterborough, Ontario: Broadview Press, Ltd., 2001.

In the following excerpt from his introduction to Plays on the Passions, *a modern edition of Volume 1 of the plays published in 1798, Duthie studies the plays' socially progressive message and surveys critical reaction to the plays throughout history.*

The 1798 edition as a text of social reform

Elizabeth Barrett Browning passionately declared Joanna Baillie to be "the first female poet in all senses in England."[1] Catherine Burroughs, a modern critic, though not as expansive in her praise, honours Baillie as Romantic drama's "mother" (*Closet Stages* 14). On the surface, Baillie's work certainly encapsulated the new Romantic spirit. The passions are foremost in her work, not as ornament but as her central source of creativity and explorations of aberrant psychology. We see her unwavering dedication to nature and a more natural use of language. Though it was contrary to the contemporary bourgeois optimism of the happy ending, we also see her steadfast adherence to a tragic vision. Her frequent introduction of exotic, gothic elements into the settings and action of her plays moved toward the absolute darkness of suicide and suggestive relationships bordering on incest. And we see her intense interest in Shakespeare's creative genius and in improving the sense of three-dimensional realism in the theatre. So strong are the trappings of Romanticism in Baillie's work that modern proponents of her literary contributions to early nineteenth-century and Victorian literature (Brewer 44) have explored potential connections between the 1798 **"Introductory Discourse"** and Wordsworth's 1800 "Preface" to the *Lyrical Ballads*.[2] At issue here, though, is both Baillie and Wordsworth's powerful debt to the eighteenth-century moralist thinkers. For instance, Wordsworth's famous definition of good poetry as "the spontaneous overflow of powerful feelings" is really a poetic meditation on the idea of the association of feelings. As we have seen, Baillie's debt is no lighter.

Productive comparisons of Baillie's work to the Romantic movement and nineteenth-century Gothic drama, however, such as Jeffrey Cox's introduction to *Seven Gothic Dramas: 1789-1825,* focus not on the superficial, but rather on Baillie's connections to clandestine reform. Cox writes:

> Gothic drama is the most subtle theatrical attempt of the 1790's to resolve the ideological, generic, and institutional problems facing playwrights of the day. At least for a moment, the Gothic drama offered a way to overcome the strains placed upon theatrical representation—essentially through a new aesthetic of sensationalism. It seemed to resolve the tensions within the hierarchy of genres—essentially by discovering a new ground of high tragedy in the tactics of popular drama. And the Gothic provided the means to represent the ideological struggles of the day in a way that would not arouse the wrath and thus the censorship of the Lord Chamberlain's Examiner of Plays, John Larpent.[3] The Gothic is *the* theatrical form in the 1790's because it could contain all of pressures placed upon the drama.
>
> (12)

As Ellen Donkin notes, "playwriting, as a profession for women, was an overt violation of all the rules of social conduct. It conferred on women a public voice. It gave them some control over how women were presented on stage" (Donkin 18). As we have seen, Baillie wrote from a domestic centre with strong political impulses. This pattern is repeated throughout the plays in this edition. Central to each play is a woman who withdraws into the privacy of the "closet" in search of solutions to the problems of the world

at large. This is the very arena in which we have previously failed to appreciate Baillie. Daniel Watkins writes in his "Class, Gender, and Social Motion in Joanna Baillie's *De Monfort*" that the fate of Joanna Baillie specifically and eighteenth-century drama more generally is "attributable to the inability—or unwillingness—of scholarship to probe the deeper structures of a work whose significance is barely glimpsed on its surface" (116). Watkins, though writing exclusively about *De Monfort,* describes the entire contents of Baillie's 1798 volume when he explains that:

> . . . despite [Baillie's] awareness of the limitations of theater in her day, she chooses drama to reveal, in ways that lyric poetry cannot, the ideological conflicts disturbing and shaping the passions that constitute her primary thematic and psychological interest. As a genre in decline, drama in the Romantic age is at once weighted with nostalgia and desire for the once-powerful and stable social world that had brought it to prominence, and, at the same time, pressured by the confidence, individualism and sheer defiance of the social energies struggling to assert . . . their new-found power and authority.
>
> (109)

The source of the thinking behind this statement is Fredric Jameson, author of *The Political Unconscious* (1981), who believes any text is a "utopian moment" (55), a point at which the contradictions of the real world are symbolically resolved. Since history has a nasty habit of preserving only one voice from any confrontation, it behooves us as readers and critics to read for the other voices which were "stifled and reduced to silence" (85).

Using Jameson's model, the reader's role becomes one of mediation, "to demonstrate what is not evident in the appearance of things, but rather in their underlying reality" (39). This mediation must embrace the inherent structural contradictions and oppositions in the text; it must, in Jameson's words, "register its capacity for differentiation and for revealing structural oppositions and contradictions" (42) in order to bridge these ideological gaps to reach moments of symbolic unification. Through Jameson's method we are finding transhistorical vehicles "for our experience of the real" (48) which, when employed, will direct our attention to the "informing power of forces or contradictions which the text seeks in vain wholly to control or master . . ." (49). Examining Baillie's work in this way, across social contradictions of class and gender, we can begin to see that she has compiled in the 1798 edition alone what appears to be a more cohesive collection than originally thought, one that develops a utopian solution to the social situation facing women at the end of the eighteenth century in England.

The anxiety that marks all three plays is expressed by a pervasive confusion in male-dominated social settings. The all-consuming love portrayed in *Count Basil* marks the struggle between a growing individualism and a sense of duty to the social collective. Though Basil can admit his status as part of the military collective—he tells the Duke "Were I indeed free master of myself, / Strong inclination would detain me here . . ." (2.1.30-31)—yet in the next scene countering his friend Count Rosinberg's accusations that he is "weaker than a child" (2.2.101), he declares that he feels "a new-born pow'r" within himself that will make him "twenty-fold" the man he was "before this fated day." *The Tryal*, by contrast, seeks more a resolution to the insecurity between the genders in a declining aristocratic society. Amidst the superficiality of one soirée after the next and the social posturing, deceit and invasion of the values of commerce, Agnes conducts a test of Harwood's masculine integrity. Harwood's values are challenged by men of the establishment like Colonel Hardy who, on hearing that Agnes—at least to his understanding—is not an heiress, gives Harwood some equivocal advice: "That is a great mistake, to be sure" he tells Harwood, "yet many a man has not advanced the less rapidly in his profession, for having had a portionless wife to begin the world with. It is a spur to industry." And finally, *De Monfort* examines a threatened and decaying aristocracy in a world now driven by a robust yet rough, rising middle class. The traditional social hierarchy, upon which his identity relied, is being turned on its head; the old definitions of class and nobility no longer apply. De Monfort's deep-seated hatred for Rezenvelt seems to come from the relative ease with which his unwelcome peer rises from compromised beginnings to full status with De Monfort. Rezenvelt's impressive ascent through his class must certainly suggest to a disoriented De Monfort a corresponding fall. De Monfort's social position is now tenuous, and Rezenvelt exemplifies the new energy and brash confidence of a middle class that threatens to depose him.

Faced with these contradictions, Baillie constructs three utopian resolutions, restoring the woman's voice to each. In *Count Basil*, posed at the point of imminent battle between clashing male forces and caught within Victoria's gaze, Basil neglects his masculine duties. In an act of male solidarity, Rosinberg struggles to help Basil

maintain his sense of himself, while Geoffry stands as a haunting, battle-worn, yet noble emblem of service to the state. On the other hand, the Duke and his minister, Gauriecio, are men, in Geoffrey's words, of "narrow policy" (3.1.98) who, in their Machiavellian ways, know how to turn the nobility of others' service into gain for themselves. Gauriecio particularly, who pretends to be the "tool and servant" (2.3.170) of the Duke, understands how to manipulate a social collective aroused with "warm heroic feelings" (3.2.15). Ironically, in manipulating a collaborator to incite dissension amongst Basil's troops, he provokes him to smash the collective of the army by inducing the troops to think. "And he who teaches men to think, though nobly," counsels Gauriecio, "Doth raise within their minds a busy judge / To scan [Basil's] actions" (3.2.25).

Amid this confusion is the Countess of Albini, who functions here as a momentary fantasy of how this male-dominated ideological struggle might be resolved. Magically, the link between the play's debate and its feminist resolution is the long-deceased mother of Victoria, a woman whom both Geoffry and Albini knew and admired. Her memory carries vestiges of a less confusing morality, but Geoffry can only "trace some semblance of her mother" (1.1.51) in Victoria. We become particularly aware of Albini in the second act, when she is seen attending to her young female charges, they playing chess and she "sitting by them reading to herself" (2.4.1sd). Though there is no concrete evidence of any connection between Baillie and Mary Wollstonecraft (1759-97), author of *A Vindication of the Rights of Woman* (1792)—indeed, middle-class women were not particularly disposed to liking Wollstonecraft (Donkin 28)—*Count Basil* can be seen as a skilful blending of Baillie's interests in human psychology with Wollstonecraft's political notions of tyranny. Baillie's descriptive and ideological connections to Wollstonecraft are extensive and meticulously patterned. Of primary importance, however, is how Albini, living in a society in which women enslave themselves through their tyranny of sensuality over men, comes to stand as a voice of educated reason amid this social degeneration. She argues, as does Wollstonecraft, that the debate between collective responsibilities and the urges of an independent self is empty; in fact, the two poles find synthesis in the union of educated, aware women and men. After a discussion between Albini and her young charges, who have been extolling the virtues of "the triumphs of all-powerful beauty" (2.4.27), Albini questions their argument: "And is, indeed, a plain domestic dame, / Who fills the duties of an useful state, / A being of less dignity than she, / Who vainly on her transient beauty builds / A little poor ideal tyranny?" (2.4.33-37). Strong collectives are constructed on strong individuals. To reinforce the complexity and importance of the figure of Albini, Baillie links her ideologically with Rosinberg, who regards her with "profound respect" (3.3.128). He is, to Baillie's mind, the closest one might find to an ideal man—should we choose to accept this possibility—because of his intelligence, his inner respectability, his capacity for compromise and change, and his inclination to meet women on common ground.

With the typical bombast of an eighteenth-century comedy, *The Tryal* presents its case in its first lines. Just as Mr. Withrington's house stands as a monument to a confusing blend of conservative aristocratic and progressive bourgeois social conduct in Bath, then known for its frivolous, vacationing, aristocratic clientele, so does Withrington. To Withrington's opening line to Agnes and Mariane: "Pooh, pooh, get along, young gipsies, and don't tease me any more" (1.1.1), Agnes, immediately seizing her function in the play with language replete with legal connotations, replies: "So we will, my good sir, when you have granted our suit." Agnes becomes a comic fusion of Jane De Monfort in *De Monfort* and Countess of Albini in *Count Basil*. Though she seeks marriage, as young women of that time were expected to do, she reverses the roles of marital control. Her early catalogue of aristocratic men, and those who aspire to be so, and her critique of the accepted social mechanisms of marriage align her philosophically with Albini. Protesting to Withrington, Agnes does not speak like a compliant female of the eighteenth century (see 1.1.28-41). And Withrington does not chastise or correct her, as men of his station in other contemporary forms of sentimental fiction most certainly would have. Instead, he complies with his niece's wishes, partly in respect of her rationality but mainly from the pressure of Agnes's powerful sense of self. Baillie constructs Agnes from male Shakespearean roles; she is more of a Benedick than a Beatrice. With the will and manipulative powers of a female Petrucio, she taunts Harwood with a ruse of ill-tempered behaviour (3.2.83-124).

And so Agnes pushes him to the brink with her contrary behaviour, but it is in her transformation as a Hamlet, determined to prove Harwood's ultimate worth, that she engineers a final trial—a play, of sorts, within a play. Using some of the same devices that might be employed by contemporary writers of courtroom fiction, she strips away Harwood's conventional social trappings of to prove that he is, indeed, one of those distant men of sense. But when Harwood in effect collapses on the stand, he reveals his worth, not his guilt. Baillie has constructed, in comic form, a woman metaphorically seizing control of a male-dominated justice system and elevating it to an institution that discerns moral innocence from guilt. As well, in a resounding vote of support and a full test and transformation of the traditional use of the feminine pronoun, Withrington taunts the conniving Mr. Opal, a man of little substance, in his own pantomime of outrage over Opal's empty vows to Mariane, "I will not see my niece wronged. The law shall do *her* [my italics] justice, whatever expense it may cost me" (5.2.304-05).

De Monfort clearly represents the most dramatic display of masculine angst the 1798 edition has to offer, driven by elemental class rivalry. Daniel Watkins suggests that Jane De Monfort has "changed through the course of the drama in ways that keep a bourgeois sensibility alive" (115). After the deaths of Rezenvelt and De Monfort, "Jane's character gradually begins to represent, in idealized form, an individualism and subjectivity over against aristocratic and religious structures of value—to display, that is, bourgeois sensibilities shorn of the ugliness associated with Rezenvelt's character." Watkins views Jane De Montfort in her final entrance—a true Gothic scene set in the gloom of a convent chapel—as a "Roman matron" (114). Indeed, some of her speeches reflect this image; however, though Jane initially weeps in grief for her dead brother—as a reader of sentimental fiction might expect—she quickly "shakes off the weakness of grief, and . . . steps forward with dignity" (5.4.113sd). This scene of Jane, surrounded by friends, servants, and clerics, becomes reminiscent of an early painting of Christ before the crucifixion. Baillie fuses the "Roman matron" with the image of a "feminized Christ," a figure beyond the fallible laws of the world. In her stage directions, Baillie writes: "*Here they all hang about her:* FREBURG *supporting her tenderly,* MANUEL *embracing her knees, and old* JEROME *catching hold of her robe affectionately.* BERNARD, *abbess, monks, and nuns likewise gather her, with looks of sympathy*" (5.4.104sd). When two officers of the law enter to determine De Monfort's cause of death, one "simple word" from Jane ends their investigation.

Baillie's women in the 1798 edition form a female triumvirate that infiltrates the key foundations of their culture. The Countess of Albini is a woman with a unified vision. For her, education is the powerful altering force in society, offering future solutions for a stronger social collective, a collective built on the strengths of both independent men and women. Agnes seeks control in legal models, forcing broader, more ideal notions of justice down into the social realm. And Jane De Monfort's speeches of final religious blessings shine as a spiritual and moral beacon above them all. It is no wonder that Mrs. Sarah Siddons reportedly demanded of Baillie, "Make me some more Jane De Monforts" (*Works* xi).

Contemporary Criticism of the 1798 edition

Some insight into the difficulties Baillie faced in the literary community is provided by a brief survey of the contemporary reviews (Appendix E) in response to the publishing phenomenon of the *Plays on the Passions*. She must have been greatly encouraged by the early reviews supportive of her design. The *Analytical Review* (May 1798) wrote approvingly of the plays as a "task of such extremely difficult execution" and of Baillie as a talented playwright who had a "complete . . . knowledge of the springs of human action" and a "familiarity with every emotion of the heart . . ." (524). While the reviewer of the *Critical Review* (September 1798) was at first "inclined to smile at a plan so methodical and so arduous" (13), he later appraised the preface as a product of "good sense and modesty" and the edition as a whole as a "work which . . . will not only be honourable to the writer, but to the literature of our country." His sense of the 1798 edition was that though it was a "small part of the projected plan," the plays were enough to determine not only that the design was "excellent" but also that the author was "equal to the task of properly executing it" (21).

These reviewers also sensed great promise in the individual plays. The *Monthly Review* (September 1798), written by a friend of Baillie's[4] who was unaware of the identity of the author, sensed a "rugged and inharmonious" quality to the verse and an "antientry of phrase which often savours of affectation." But he felt Baillie's characters were "in general strongly discriminated" and the scenes filled with "beautiful passages" (66). The *Critical Review* (September 1798) declared **Count Basil** an "admirable tragedy" (17) written by someone who had "studied nature deeply" and evocative of England's "old and excellent dramatic writers." Though **The Tryal** was seen as inferior to the tragedies, **De Monfort** was felt to reveal the

"same genius, and the same knowledge of the human heart" (19) as **Count Basil.** The *Eclectic Review* (August 1813), in response to Longman and Co.'s three-volume edition, declares Baillie's work unlike other drama of the day. Her "personages are not always ranting or whining, in the extasies of love, or the agonies of despair, or the madness of rage: they really do talk . . . like men and women of this world,—men and women who have some other bond of connection with the reader besides speaking the same language, and acknowledging the same rules of prosody" (168). Her characters are "strongly marked, and yet highly poetical, frail and infirm, and yet very interesting" (170). De Monfort, to this reviewer, is "brave and generous and manly, struggling with an infernal passion, bearing up and making head against it, and at length finally borne down by it, and brought to the perpetration of a deed cowardly, ungenerous, and unmanly," but it is the character of Rezenvelt he most admires. "There is a carelessness in the delineation of this character, a flowing freedom in the outline" which he feels is "seldom to be met with in Miss Baillie, and which puts us more in mind of Shakespeare than any thing in the volumes." The complex mix of "hatred" and "gibing gaiety" of Rezenvelt's character, exposed with a "carelessness that seems to mock the uneasiness it occasions," prompts the reviewer not to hesitate "in pronouncing De Monfort the most original tragedy of the present age, and Rezenvelt a character the most her own of any she has produced" (171).

But as early as January 1799, reviewers, perhaps not as vociferously, voiced Francis Jeffrey's concern that Baillie's plan was a problematic vehicle to advance her dramatic theories. Even though in 1811 he included Baillie amongst the greatest poets of the age, including Robert Southey, William Wordsworth, and Samuel Taylor Coleridge, eight years earlier, in *Edinburgh Review* (July 1803), Jeffrey bluntly attacked not only the plan of Baillie's dramatic project but also her key purpose as a playwright—to write plays of moral import. The *New London Review* declared the plan "more philosophical than dramatic" (72) and felt it capable of producing interesting plays, though neither a "practicable method" nor a "desireable one." This reviewer viewed Baillie's system of delineation as "too tedious and circumstantial for a species of composition of which the effect, whatever regard it may be necessary to pay to character and to passion, depends, in an equal degree, upon ACTION. . . ." Baillie's delineations of character were too "languid and uninteresting in representation." Audiences, in this reviewer's estimation, do not have the "time, inclination, or capacity to enter minutely into discriminations of character." For this reason most "dramatists . . . have generally hurried into the heart of a passion" (72-73). The *British Critic* (March 1799) expressed concerns that seldom will "one passion be found unconnected with others" (285). Conceding that though he felt Baillie capable of executing her plan, as Jeffrey had, this reviewer expressed his aesthetic and moral concerns that "To separate and individualize the passions, therefore, is to leave the path of Nature; and to make the possessor of one bad propensity in all other respects virtuous, is to apologize for vice, and to make us pity rather than abhor it" (185). The *Imperial Review* (March 1804) concurs that the passions mingle "promiscuously" (226) rather than adhere to botanical classifications. And the *Edinburgh Magazine* (June 1818) reviewer is concerned that the characters and the incidents in Baillie's plays are "merely a mirror in which to contemplate the passions, or rather a microscope, by means of which she seems to think that she has brought within the sphere of our vision things too minute for the naked intellectual eye" (517). This he feels is the "radical defect of her plays, and casts an air of restraint and formality over the whole of her performances," and it is because of her persistence in "fettering herself by a false system" (519) that her plays are not "added to the stock of the English Stage" (517).

In reading these reviewers, we must remain aware of their confirmed gender and cultural biases that challenged Baillie's belief in a "corresponding spirit" between men and women. Francis Jeffrey predicted that Baillie just might well produce some unforgettable work in the future with the "proper management" (277). Contemplating the existence of "a sex in soul" (517), the *Edinburgh Magazine* (June 1818), in what was meant as a compliment,[5] discovered in Baillie's plays the merging of masculine "energy" and feminine "purity." These assumptions about gender spilled over into the reviewers' comments on the plays themselves. One finds it preposterous that Harwood, "a young man bred up in London, and on a companionable footing with fops of fashion," is able to fall in love instantaneously "with a girl, whose appearance is by no means seducing" (340). In the same vein, another, the *Imperial Review* (March 1804), struggles with Rezenvelt's interest in Jane De Monfort who, in its words, is represented as "verging into autumnal virginity" (343). Though conceding the potential

for error here, the reviewer ventures that "we are not quite convinced that we should have been so industriously prohibited from imaging Jane of a more lovely age; which would have added probability to the suspicion her brother conceives of an attachment between her and Rezenvell [sic]." This reviewer comments, as well, on a pronoun agreement problem in *The Tryal*, a "grammatical inaccuracy" he notes, "not unfrequent in female conversation" (340).[6]

Just as their sexist perspective prevented them from hearing the voices of Baillie's heroines, the cultural myopia of these reviewers makes it impossible for them to see the social implications of her work. For instance, the critic of *Imperial Review* (March 1804) also struggled to reconcile the "different parts" (342) of *De Monfort*. Blind to the potential hatred between established and emerging classes, he guesses a "puerile lust after universal estimation, and a spiteful envy of his antagonist" as the cause of De Monfort's emotional distemper. Later the *Edinburgh Magazine* isolates the source of this inability to comprehend De Monfort's character. This reviewer accepts Othello's jealousy, for instance, as an accurate delineation of passion nurtured in the hot and passionate lands of the Moors. Of De Monfort's festering hatred, "it is the want of a proper soil in which to plant such a passion, and the culture necessary to its growth" (517) that he finds inconceivable.

Baillie bore the criticism and the resistance to her project bravely. In the preface to the second volume of *Plays on the Passions* (1802) she stoically describes the earlier response to her work as the "best calculated to make a work go on well—praise mixed with a considerable portion of censure" (**Works** 104).

This new edition of *Plays on the Passions* is not intended to force a false sense of totality upon the 1798 edition; rather, the intent is to offer it to a new reading public as something more than simply a fragment of a larger project. As interest in Baillie's writing slowly but surely grows, the 1798 edition deserves to be explored as a text unto itself. Indeed, it was Baillie's wish not to publish her work in large volumes in which the plays would "crowd, and jostle, and tread upon one another's heel" (**Works** 288). Here in one volume is an opportunity to re-think the character of the eighteenth century in all its dynamic diversity, to reconsider the role women played in the artistic communities of those times, and to review our place at the end of over two hundred years of profound social change. Baillie offers us all of this and more, along with an enjoyable reading experience and an eternal reminder of the joys of a constructive life dedicated to simple, creative expression. As Baillie humbly writes in her "**An Address to the Muses**":

> But O, such sense of matter bring!
> As they who feel and never sing
> Wear on their heart; it will avail
> With simple words to tell my tale;
> And still contented will I be,
> Though greater inspirations never fall to me.
>   (Lonsdale, *Women Poets* 441)

Notes

1. Quoted in Kerry McSweeney's introduction to *Aurora Leigh* (Oxford: Oxford University Press, 1993) xvii.

2. See Donald Reiman "Introduction" and Marlon B. Ross *The Contours of Masculine Desire*.

3. John Larpent (1741-1824) was Examiner of Plays from 1737 to 1824.

4. Samuel B. Rogers (1763-1855), author of *The Pleasures of Memory* (1792), wrote this review (see *Works* x and Carhart 42-43).

5. Byron is famous for two sexist compliments to Baillie. The first, he wrote in a letter (1815): that "Women (saving Joanna Baillie) cannot write tragedy. They haven't experienced the life for it." The second (1817) more boldly professed that "Voltaire was asked why no woman has ever written even a tolerable tragedy, 'Ah (Said the Patriarch) the composition of a tragedy requires testicles.' If this be true, Lord knows what Joanna Baillie does—I suppose she borrows them" (qtd. in Donkin 78).

6. See note to *The Tryal* 4.1.37 on Baillie's education.

Works Cited/Recommended Reading

Baillie, Joanna. *A view of the General Tenour of the New Testament Regarding the Nature and Dignity of Jesus Christ.* London: Longman, 1831.

———. *The Dramatic and Poetical Works.* 1851. Hildesheim and New York: Georg Olms Verlag, 1976. Facsimile edition.

———. *Joanna Baillie: A Series of Plays.* 3 vols. 1798, 1802, 1812. Ed. Donald H. Reiman. New York and London: Garland Press, 1977.

———. *A Series of Plays.* Ed. Jonathan Wordsworth. Oxford and New York: Woodstock Books, 1990.

Brewer, William D. "Joanna Baillie and Lord Byron." *Keats-Shelley Journal* 44 (1995): 165-81.

———. "The Prefaces of Joanna Baillie and William Wordsworth." *The Friend: Comments on Romanticism* 1.2 (1991): 34-47.

Burroughs, Catherine B. *Closet Stages.* Philadelphia: U of Pennsylvania P, 1997.

Cox, Jeffrey N., ed. *Seven Gothic Dramas 1789-1825.* Athens: Ohio UP, 1992.

Donkin, Ellen. *Getting Into The Act: Women Playwrights in London, 1776-1829.* London: Routledge, 1995.

Jameson, Fredric. *The Political Unconscious: Narrative as a Socially Symbolic Act.* Ithaca: Cornell UP, 1981.

Lonsdale, Roger, ed. *Eighteenth-Century Women Poets: An Oxford Anthology.* Oxford: Oxford UP, 1989.

Watkins, Daniel P. "Class, Gender, and Social Motion in Joanna Baillie's *De Monfort.*" *The Wordsworth Circle* 23-2 (Spring 1992): 109-17.

Contemporary Reviews

British Critic 13 (Mar. 1799): 284-90.

Critical Review ns 24 (Sept. 1798): 13-22.

Eclectic Review 10 (July 1813): 21-32; (Aug. 1813): 167-86.

Edinburgh Magazine (*Scots Magazine*) ns 2 (June 1818): 517-20.

Edinburgh Review 2 (July 1803): 269-86.

Imperial Review 1 (Mar. 1804), 335-44; 2 (May 1804): 89-97.

Monthly Review ns v27 (Sept. 1798): 66-69.

New London Review 1 (Jan. 1799): 72-74.

Witchcraft

MARJEAN D. PURINTON (ESSAY DATE 2001)

SOURCE: Purinton, Marjean D. "Socialized and Medicalized Hysteria in Joanna Baillie's *Witchcraft.*" *Prism(s): Essays in Romanticism* 9 (2001): 139-56.

In the following essay, Purinton analyzes Baillie's portrayal of what was often medically and scientifically sanctioned persecution of women in her drama Witchcraft.

Because many Romantic-period dramas are engaged with political frenzy following the French Revolution and are shaped by psychosocial issues associated with the Gothic, it is not unusual for us to see "madness," in various manifestations, playing a significant part on the stage. The physiology of excessive emotions had also become, by the end of the eighteenth century, a significant focus of scientific inquiry and discourse. By the early nineteenth-century, the prevailing medical opinion had gendered emotions so that women who exhibited excessive feelings and unconventional behaviors were "hysterical," a physiological effect of their inferior biology, the symptom of their anatomical reproductive capacity.[1]

As I have argued elsewhere, the intertextuality of science and medicine in Romantic drama may explain the predominance of gothic and melodrama during the late eighteenth and early nineteenth centuries.[2] Numerous Romantic dramas stage physicality in gothic forms that are significantly redefined by discursive and cultural inter-

ABOUT THE AUTHOR

In the "Introductory Discourse," which abounds in imagery, the author has exhibited much knowledge of the human mind, and has displayed his information and discernment in such a style, as convinces the reader, at the outset, that he is not incompetent to the arduous task he has undertaken. He treats at great length, and with much ingenuity, on the construction of the drama; in which, . . . he has not adhered to his own rules. He expresses his approbation of those styles of writing which apply more forcibly to the heart than to the fancy, and thinks the drama the most approved vehicle. . . .

The Tragedy of *De Monfort* is still superior to *Basil*. The hero is a more original character, and more forcibly drawn; but it is too diffuse. The last act might be omitted altogether with advantage, adding a little only at the end of the fourth. With these improvements it would make an excellent play, and one which, we have no doubt, would be received with the greatest pleasure by an English audience. . . .

It is with great pleasure that we notice a publication, in which so much original genius for dramatic poetry is evidently displayed. May we not hope that, in the unknown author of these Dramas, exists the long wished-for talent, which is to remove the present opprobrium of our theatres, and supply them with productions of native growth, calculated not for the destruction of idle time, but, for the amusement of ages? We are willing, in some degree, to cherish the expectation.

SOURCE: A review of *A Series of Plays In Which It Is Attempted to Delineate the Stronger Passions of the Mind*, Vol. 1, by Joanna Baillie. *The British Critic and Quarterly Theological Review* 13 (March 1799): 284-90.

ests in science. Science did, in fact, take form in the theatre, where production strategies were shaped by the machinery of staging and dramatic content was manifestly and latently concerned with medical discoveries and practices.[3] Conversely, the theatre was appropriated by science as the actual site for staging its experiments. Since the seventeenth century, Robert Boyle's demonstrations for students were staged as anatomical theatres of medicine with formalized and regularized performances.[4] Staged dissections functioned in spectacularly pedagogical ways in science's institutional training. Scientific and medical interests were theatricalized in other public but non-dramatic forms, such as traveling shows, itinerant lectures with demonstrations, extravagant displays or exhibitions, and forums at the Royal College of Surgeons.[5] Social controversies connected to medical sciences were also frequently staged for public display in non-dramatic settings such as courtrooms and executions.[6]

Seemingly natural elements associated with science and medicine were staged as gothic and technologically designed and manipulated to create a world of illusions and phantasmagoria.[7] Both gothic and science were discursive fields upon which anxieties about social identity and physicality could be displaced, and the gothic conventions of drama were particularly convenient for playwrights' use in negotiating the influences of science and medicine upon culture. The strategy for performing the discourses of science and practices of medicine, I call the "techno-gothic," an ideologically charged and melodramatic structure in which disturbing issues and forbidden topics are recontextualized by the intersecting fields of the supernatural and science—or gothic and technology. The techno-gothic relies upon a set of readily available and easily recognized dramatic conventions (gothic) that function as interpretation of scientific discourses (technology) within theatricalized contexts of social critiques and cultural changes. Techno-gothic drama is, in fact, a product of the Romantic revolution in science, as its forms mediate post-Enlightenment dualisms such as biochemistry and magic, romance and gothic, medicine and quackery, bodies and spirits. The techno-gothic came to be expressed in two popular and powerful performance modes: grotesques and ghosts.

Techno-gothic grotesques embody discursively constructed and spectacularly displayed monsters or aberrations. Historically, monsters had been exhibited in public places, but it is the beginning of the nineteenth-century when teratology began to decipher in scientific terms the grotesque bodies theatrically displayed.[8] Physicality offered a way of performing scientific preoccupations with the body, its anatomy, is physiology, its potential for disease and deformity, its propensity for physical disabilities and socio-sexual transgressions. The techno-gothic grotesque makes visible the threatening "other," simultaneously disturbing and appealing, terrifying and pleasurable.[9] Science and stage engendered new perceptions of physicality, transforming the body into a text that could be read and interpreted by both the trained medical gaze and the curious theatergoer. Physiognomy and phrenology comprised scientific disciplines intent on reading the body, but reading a performing body, and one that was physically grotesque, was especially tricky as it was legitimately artificial and fictive, disguised and costumed.[10] While the malformed, hybrid, and at times carnivalesque, monstrous, and sick body of the techno-gothic grotesque excited contradictory responses of sympathy and abomination, it also destabilized cultural norms.[11] Its physical physicality was, on the one hand, a spectacular body of gothic terror and curiosity; and, on the other hand, a politicized text placed on display at the anatomical "clinic" where theatergoers or readers could participate in the culture's scientific interpretations and medical diagnoses.

If the techno-gothic grotesque created a performing body that could not be easily read, the techno-gothic ghost challenged legibility in its performance of disembodiment. In their unstable and myriad forms, techno-gothic ghosts resist spatial limitations and discernable significations. Technologically designed special effects of the stage and the culture's preoccupation with hysteria stimulated the imagination to contemplate the absence of substance, religious and pagan spirits, inchoate psychology and neurology—areas which science sought to explain with empirical evidence. By manipulating the ways light bounced from a polished and curved plane, for example, production managers could create optical effects. Spectators looking into a mirror could be terrified by the appearance floating upon its surface, a phantom signifying fictions generated by both superstition and science.[12] By manipulating characters' responses and plot developments, playwrights could create discursive and dramatic phantasmagoria that pricked spectators' and readers' imaginative participation in the culture's craze over mental and physical matters. Ghosts were, of course, a gothic convention at the beginning of the nineteenth century, but they were also the way in which Romantic-period playwrights could theatricalize the scientific scrutiny and speculation of

mental disorders—hallucinations, hysteria, deliria, madness, mania—that were charged with new medical significations.

For women playwrights, especially, techno-gothic grotesques and ghosts provided a way for them to participate in the scientific revolution of the early nineteenth century in a speaking position rather than as an object. For women writers, it was particularly complicated to portray a body scientifically sexed as female and culturally gendered as feminine, for, by some medical accounts, female bodies were already grotesque. It was similarly tricky for women playwrights to portray "mad" or hysterical women in their dramas, characters that seemed to confirm scientific interpretations of women as victims of their own bodies, always with the propensity for excessive and uncontrollable emotions. One way for women to challenge the biological limits placed on them by science was to stage madness as a deliberate and calculated strategy used by female characters, a "staged" guise or costume put on to deceive male characters who assume that they are truly mad. We see this strategy, for example in Sophia Lee's 1794 tragedy *Almeyda; Queen of Granada.* Joanna Baillie's drama **Witchcraft** (1836), however, exposes the theoretical and fictive nature of medical science in characterizing male but especially female characters as techno-gothic grotesques possessed by techno-gothic ghosts. At a metadramtic level, furthermore, **Witchcraft** stages a society haunted by a techno-gothic ghost in its depiction of sixteenth- and seventeenth-century witch hunts as conceptual analogues to early nineteenth-century medical practices intent on dominating, controlling and persecuting women by naming them as techno-gothic grotesques, witches marginalized as "others" whose diseased presence must be purged from the social body.[13]

Baillie writes her play at the apex of literary and scientific discussions about monstrosity and phantasmagoria, and these discourses, no doubt, informed her thinking about women persecuted by social conventions based on superstition and fiction but legitimized by religion and medicine. Even by the middle of the nineteenth century and following prolific scientific activity, the unknown, superstition, and spectral still created fear and terror. Charles Lamb asserts in "Witches and Other Night-Fears" (1823) that the most cruel, tormenting devil to humankind is "the simple idea of a spirit unembodied" (80). In *Letters on Demonology and Witchcraft* (1830), Walter Scott diagnoses those who claimed to see apparitions as "mad," pathologically unbalanced, deceived by a "lively dream, a waking reverie, the excitation of a powerful imagination, or the misrepresentation of a diseased organ of sight" (344). It was also in 1830 that John Herschel offers a scientific explanation for seemingly intangible phenomena by identifying the optical necessity of something between the eye and the thing seen. What the "thing" is, he concedes, has been variously conjectured. Some imagine that "all visible objects are constantly throwing out from them, in all directions, some sort of resemblances or spectral forms of themselves, when received by the eyes, produce an impression of objects" (249-50). One of the definitions of "spectral," Anne Williams reminds us, is "produced merely by the action of light on the eye or on a sensitive medium" (114). Optical illusions, whether reflected by the human eye, the magic lantern shows, or the theatre's curved mirrors, generated medical and popular interest.[14]

Baillie explicitly acknowledges in her note to **Witchcraft** that the subject of the drama was suggested to her by her reading of Scott's *The Bride of Lammermoor* (1819) and its concern with witchcraft trials that she found curious but unsatisfactorily developed. In a journal entry dated 22 July 1827, Walter Scott notes Baillie's tragedy and ponders: "Will it be real Witch craft—the *Ipsissimus Diabolus* [the very devil himself]—or an imposter—or the half crazed being who believes herself an ally of condemned spirits and desires to be so? That last is a sublime subject" (*Journal* 331). Baillie's note to her drama reveals how the suspicion of being a witch powerfully convinces the accused that she is a witch. Baillie's reading public would have been familiar with the powerful and electrifying influence of staged science as itinerant lecturers and "doctors" performed electrocutions of torpedo fish, intoxications by nitrous oxide as well as extravagant displays of magneticism and galvanization. At the end of the eighteenth century, Franz Anton Mesmer had made famous showy and popular demonstrations in magnetic healing, hypnosis, and somnambulism.[15] Surgeons, such as John Hunter, maintained anatomical collections that included skulls, feral children, dissected appendages, and colonized specimens, all with a variety of physical deformities. More commercialized "freak" shows featured giants, midgets, bearded ladies, hermaphrodites, and mad women.[16] These variously displayed techno-gothic grotesques constituted Romantic-period analogues to public trials and executions of seventeenth-century witches—monsters, dehumanized "others" displayed and purged from a "normative" social body.

Baillie's thinking about witchcraft might have been influenced by a specific seventeenth-century witchcraft case involving a Scottish midwife, Margaret Lang, whose dangerous mixture of medical skill and spiritual gifts made her the perfect target of a witch hunt in Erskine, near Paisley, the setting of Baillie's play, and whose plight was chronicled in *A History of the Witches of Renfrewshire*. In 1696, Christian Shaw, the eleven-year old daughter of a Scottish lord, accused Margaret and two dozen others of bewitching her and conspiring with the devil to kill her. Once "Pinched Maggie," as she came to be called, was named, others came forward with accusations of having seen her at nocturnal "witch" gatherings at Kilmalcolm at which magic was practiced. Margaret was sentenced to be hanged and then burned.[17] Baillie would have probably recognized the theatricality of accused witches public examinations, trials, and executions during the seventeenth century as well as the spectacle such a re-staging of witchcraft would create for early nineteenth-century spectators. In an 1827 letter to Walter Scott, Baillie proclaims: "Renfrew Witches upon a polite stage! Will such a thing ever be endorsed!" (**Letters** 1.441). Witch-hunts in Scotland, as Baillie's reading would have revealed, endorsed beliefs in diabolical conspiracies—a notion dramatized in Baillie's play—and amassed over 1,337 executions plus additional deaths from suicides, torture, and neglect. The Presbyterian Church ordered its Calvinist ministers to seek out witches, and all women, especially those who challenged patriarchal society, were potential witches.[18]

Ecclesiastical condemnation of independent women had, during the course of the late eighteenth and early nineteenth centuries, been replaced with an equally powerful check on female liberation—scientific and medical "discoveries" that pronounced women inferior in anatomy and in mind. Baillie, of course, grew up in a household of physicians; her uncle, Dr. William Hunter, and her brother, Dr. Matthew Baillie, were renowned anatomists whose medical theatres were, in fact, the sites of medical instruction.[19] Baillie's medical knowledge would have recognized the historical associations of female healers and midwives with witchery—a connection that reclassified "wise" women as "evil" and "melancholic" and helped to legitimize the male medical profession of the late eighteenth and early nineteenth centuries.[20] It was during this time that uterine theories of hysteria were reintroduced into medical discourses. Inspired by botanical and zoological taxonomies of naturalists Carolus Linnaeus and the Comte de Buffon, physicians linked hysteria causally to female sexuality.[21] With shadows of the earlier religious theories about witchcraft still lingering in the social unconscious, medical discourses re-eroticized madness as a distinctly female disorder and recontextualized witches as neurotic, hysterical, psychotic, and emotionally disturbed women. What had been attributed to witchcraft was now attributed to the weaker female constitution. In short, women who did not perform the roles assigned by patriarchal culture were diagnosed as mad—techno-gothic grotesques outside the boundaries of "normative" society as classified by the period's scientific revolution.

It is in the context of these cultural changes that Baillie's drama portrays male figures of legal and ecclesiastical authority in collusion against any woman, regardless of class or circumstances, believed to be involved in witchery.[22] From the beginning of the play, Grizeld Bane, Mary Macmurren, and Elspy Low are reputed witches whose nocturnal activities on the moor and economic hardships cast suspicion on them. The Sheriff reifies these local stereotypes in his question: "Are not witches always old and poor?" (3.2.630). These three hags routinely meet at "Warlock's Den," a deserted cave in the woods; during a stormy night, they have been seen dancing with a man presumed dead for three years, a techno-gothic ghost that figures significantly in rendering the women techno-gothic grotesques. Furthermore, Mary Macmurren's son Wilkin is an idiot, a mental derangement popularly believed to be the result of her intercourse with the devil. By all accounts of the play's characters, these women are techno-gothic grotesques, monsters and human aberrations to be feared and avoided or eliminated. Of course, any contact with them makes even healthy innocents guilty by association.

All three witches have cleverly eluded arrest until Mary Macmurren is found in the custody of constables in Act Four, but she is saved from being burned at the stake by a decree from the King and Parliament declaring that "the law punishing what has been called the crime of witchcraft as a felonious offense be repealed. . . . Henceforth there shall no person be prosecuted at law as a wizard or witch, throughout these realms" (5.2.641). While Mary is not proven innocent of witchcraft, the law that would condemn her is unmasked as unjust. Other means of marginalizing threatening women are nonetheless devised, and the revelation about Grizeld Bane at the end of the play points to the ways in which post-

Enlightenment medicine names women insane, a techno-gothic grotesque, a strategy for containing women that will not be declared unlawful.

We learn that Grizeld is "a miserable woman whose husband was hanged for murder, at Inverness, some years ago, and who thereupon became distracted . . . [and] was . . . kept in close custody. But she has, no doubt," Fatheringham reports, "escaped from her keepers, who may not be very anxious to reclaim her" (5.2.642). Ironically, it is not witchcraft but mental illness that afflicts Grizeld, a nineteenth-century diagnosis of female behavior when it does not conform to social standards. Matthew Baillie's own account in his third Gulstonian Lecture of 1794 medically explains Grizeld's abilities to overpower her keepers and how her various actions throughout the play might be attributable to her nerves' excitement of her muscles into motion: "Muscles are capable of being thrown into a much greater degree of contraction by emotions of the mind than perhaps by any other cause; and it is this circumstance which gives the astonishing strength sometimes exerted by maniacs" (147). Here physiological interpretations make legitimate observations of behaviors attributed to those with mental and emotional disorders—techno-gothic grotesques termed "witches" by the culture depicted in Baillie's drama.

While these techno-gothic grotesques have done no harm to anyone, the drama unmasks the dangerous techno-gothic grotesque of Refrewshire, a woman whose appearances and economic station betray her monstrous heart and the witchery she attempts to effect in order to realize personal revenge for unrequited love. Annablla Gordon seizes upon the cultural disposition in which suspicion of women breeds unreasonable, hysterical responses and repression. Eleven-year-old Jessie Dungarren has not been well, and the prevailing church and medical interpretation of her infirmity of sleeplessness, fever, erratic behavior—babbling and convulsions—is that she has been bewitched. Her nervous disease, as Thomas Trotter characterizes it in his 1807 A View of the Nervous Temperament, arises from the mind that, under the influence of this malady, can conjure up "blue devils, ghosts, hobgoblins" (185). While Trotter attributes nervous temperament to various female mental and bodily functions, in Baillie's drama, it is suspected that Grizeld Bane, Mary Macmurren, and Elspy Low are somehow involved. This situation is perfect for Annabella's own little drama of witchcraft to implicate Violet Murrey as a witch. Violet is in love with Robert Dungarren, the man

Annabella believes she would have if Violet were not in her way, a fictive situation that modifies the 1696 Margaret Lang witch-hunt with elements of gothic romance.

An additional ingredient to Annabella's brew is the reporting of Rutherford, the parish minister, of having seen, or at least of having believed to have seen, Violet with the ghost of a dead man on the moor. Violet has already been discredited as a healthy member of society through the actions of her father, a man who had been convicted of murder and who was believed to have died following his escape from prison. We know that the techno-gothic ghost she meets on the moor during the stormy night is none other than her father, very much alive but in hiding until he can prove his innocence. Violet is unwilling to betray her father, who must remain apparitional to everyone else. With Violet's character already tainted, Annabella realizes that it will not take much contrived evidence to cast her as a witch, and with the help of Black Bawldy, a gullible herdboy, Annabella seals Violet's fate. During one of Jessie's fits, she reportedly tears the garment of the witch with whom she wrestles. Annabella pays Bawldy to secure one of Violet's gowns so that she may tear it, matching the tear with that Jessie has snatched from her ghostly visitor. This is the evidence that convinces even the skeptical citizens that Violet is guilty of witchcraft. Annabella has convinced herself that Violet will not be allowed to be executed, for as she assures Bawldy, "Mary Macmurren will be burnt, for an example to all other witches and warlocks, but a respite and pardon will be given to Violet Murrey; it is only her disgrace, not her death, that is intended" (4.2.633). She is, however, playing with the fire of societal ignorance and fear.

We come to realize that Annabella is delusional, a state of mind, along with delirium, that was of immense interest to the medical professionals of the Romantic period. In *An Inquiry into the Nature and Origin of Mental Derangement* (1798), Alexander Crichton maintains: "All delirious people, no matter whether they be maniacs or hypochondriacs, or people in the delirium of fever, or of hysteria, differ from those of a sound mind in this respect, that they have certain diseased perceptions and notions in the reality of which they firmly believe, and which consequently become motives of many actions and expressions which appear unreasonable to the rest of mankind" (1.137-38). Annabella suffers from what Crichton refers to as one kind of diseased notion entertained by delirious people: "They are

diseased abstract notions, referable to the qualities and conditions of persons and things, and [her] relation to them; as when [she] imagines that [her] friends have conspired to kill [her]" (1.141), or in Annabella's case, imagines that Violet will rob her of the man she loves. As we have seen, however, Annabella has to persuade herself that "revenge is sweet; revenge is noble; revenge is nature" (5.1.637), as she is tormented by conflicted mental commotions.

Grizeld accurately assesses Annabella's character when she tells her that she is the "best" of Satan's queens and princesses, for "there is both wit and wickedness in thee to perfection" (4.2.633). Grizeld alarms Annabella with a rhetoric that would brand her the very techno-gothic grotesque that Annabella would declare of others, and Grizeld emphasizes: "There is not a cloven foot, nor a horned head of them all wicked and bolder than thou art" (5.1.638). Annabella scornfully dismisses Grizeld's accusations: "She is but raving: the fumes of her posset have been working in her brain" (4.2.634). Although each woman characterizes the other as a techno-gothic grotesque, it is only Grizeld that is marked by religion and medicine as witch, as hysterical who must, therefore, be extracted from society. These dramatically enhanced character analyses direct our attention to the importance of perspective in perception. Just as Annabella cannot see the techno-gothic ghost to which Grizeld points in the corner of the room as the "Master" they both serve, the good people of Renfrewshire cannot see Annabella for the techno-gothic grotesque she is. It is only when Anabella's strangled corpse is laid before the crowd gathered for the witches' execution that she is unmasked as techno-gothic grotesque. Like the crowd in Baillie's drama, we read the spectacular body of Annabella differently; we come to see her as a woman complicit in using the fear of witchcraft to serve her own selfish goals and to deflect attention from her own neurotic behaviors.

Madness serves post-Enlightenment medicine in a similar way to that of seventeenth-century religion's deployment of witch-hunting—as a check on female power and independence. Baillie's play explores the roots of early nineteenth-century's psycho-medical treatment of women and its continued perversion of the magic-healer-witch into the hysteric by male physicians who linked hysteria causally with female sexuality. Medical science is exposed as interpretative and inexact as "witchcraft" itself, as the bewitching effects of cultural hysteria are staged. Metadramatically, witchcraft functions as a metaphor and commentary on madness as a cultural signifier and as a kind of cultural ghost haunting the medical and scientific practices of Baillie's day. In *Madness and Civilization*, Michel Foucault describes a pedagogical technique used to treat mad patients during the Romantic period that replicates the metadramatic cure for social madness staged in Baillie's **Witchcraft**. According to Foucault, "the cure by theatrical representation" was often successful with patients who had come to see illusion as reality (187). Staged illusions and images presented an alternative reality to that created by patients, and they sometimes came to recognize that their perceptions of reality were fictions of their own making. The patients, like Baillie's readers, are forced to confront what Foucault describes as "a crisis which is, in a very ambiguous manner, both medical and theatrical" (180).

Witchcraft offers us a theatrical illusion of social reality, a pedagogical strategy adopted from medical practices, encouraging us to reevaluate medical perceptions of hysteria offered in the scientific revolution of her day that continue to inform our perspectives on madness. In this way, Baillie's **Witchcraft** anticipates twentieth-century arguments by American psychological feminists like those of Juliet Mitchell and Phyllis Chesler, who point out that female behavior is termed "mad" by a social and medical culture that requires repressed female sexuality and rejects attempts to reconnect mind and body from its post-Enlightenment divisive taxonomies and as well as twentieth-century positions by American feminist spiritualists like those of Starhawk and Carol Christ who seek to reclaim witchcraft and goddess religions as enabling discourses and practices for female identity.[23]

Notes

1. In *Madness and Civilization*, Michel Foucault notes that until the end of the eighteenth century "the uterus and the womb remained present in the pathology of hysteria" (144), informing notions at the beginning of the nineteenth century identifying "hysteria and hypochondria as mental diseases" (158). Laurinda S. Dixon explains that the ancient notion of the capricious womb, capable of extensive sympathy with the rest of the body, remained a fixture of eighteenth-century medical theory, and by the beginning of the nineteenth century, women's susceptibility to illness was based on their "proper" function in society and their "peculiar" anatomy. According to Dixon, medical theorists used "the authority of biology to justify maintaining the cultural and political differences between the sexes that were thought to be crucial to social stability" (*Perilous Chastity* 236). Mark S. Micale points out that nineteenth-century notions of hysteria were defined by a set of highly negative character traits

in women: "eccentricity, impulsiveness, emotionality, coquettishness, deceitfulness, and hypersexuality" (*Approaching Hysteria* 24). Peter Melville Logan discusses the transition of female hysteria from a physical to a psychological ailment (*Nerves and Narratives* 93-107).

2. See my essays "Science Fiction and Techno-Gothic Drama: Romantic Playwrights Joanna Baillie and Jane Scott," *Romanticism on the Net* 21 (February 2001); "Byron's Disability and the Techno-Gothic Grotesque" in *The Deformed Transformed, European Romantic Review*, forthcoming; "Theatricalized Bodies and Spirits: Techno-Gothic as Performance in Romantic Drama," *Gothic Studies*, forthcoming.

3. Barbara Marie Stafford (*Body Criticism* 366-75) and Paul Ranger ("*Terror and Pity Reign in Every Breast*" 70-119) delineate various scientific and stage devices popular during the Romantic period.

4. See Roy S. Porter ("Medical Science and Human Science in the Enlightenment" 64-66) for a discussion of Thomas Beddoes's and Humphry Davy's experiments in pneumatic medicine and their lectures on chemistry in theatres built specifically for scientific studies. According to Margaret S. Carhart, Joanna Baillie's uncle, William Hunter, maintained the Hunter School of Anatomy on Windmill Street in London. The medical school included an anatomical theatre and museum, and Joanna's brother, Matthew Baillie, inherited it in 1783 (*The Life and Work of Joanna Baillie* 9-11). Matthew Baillie was named Physician Extraordinary to King George III in 1810.

5. See Cathy Cobb and Harold Goldwhite (*Creations of Fire* 151-211); Edwin Clarke and L. S. Jacyna (*Nineteenth-Century Orgins of Neuroscientific Concepts* 160-211); Gloria Flaherty ("The Non-Normal Sciences: Survivals of Renaissance Thought in the Eighteenth Century" 71-91); Lindsay Wilson (*Women and Medicine in the French Enlightenment* 104-24); Ludmilla Jordanova ("Gender, Generation and Science: William Hunter's Obstetrical Atlas" 385-412); Christopher Fox ("Introduction: How to Prepare a Noble Savage: The Spectacle of Human Science" 11-12); Robert Bogdan (*Freak Show* 106-11 and "The Social Construction of Freaks" 23-37); Elizabeth Grosz ("Intolerable Ambiguity: Freaks as/at the Limit" 55-66) for discussions of various non-dramatic shows and displays featuring aberrant bodies.

6. In *Romantic Theatricality*, Judith Pascoe characterizes the theatricality of the 1794 Treason Trials and the public spectacle of Marie Antoinette, for example (33-67 and 95-129). My essay "Women's Sovereignty on Trial: Joanna Baillie's Comedy 'The Tryal' as Metatheatrics" analyzes the public's fascination with theatricalized litigation and ritualized courtship/marriage staged in Baillie's 1798 comedy as a pedagogical strategy for women (132-57). In her Introductory Discourse to the 1798 *Plays on the Passions*, Baillie points out the pedagogical function of public processions and hangings that, like drama, can generate "sympathetic curiosity" between actor and spectator (2). Foucault notes how, in the nineteenth century, madness was a public spectacle with organized performances in which madmen sometimes played the roles of actors and sometimes played the role of spectators (*Madness and Civilization* 68-70). Madness was a thing to be looked at, Foucault explains, and "madmen remained monsters—that is, etymologically, beings or things to be shown" (70).

7. See Paul Ranger ("*Terror and Pity Reign in Every Breast*" 19-41), Richard Leacroft (*The Development of the English Playhouse* 119-238), and Terry Castle (*The Female Thermometer* 140-67) for explanations about how science affected theatrical staging devices and special effects.

8. Robert Bogdan's describes exotic exhibitions of "freaks" accompanied by scientific discourses and teratological taxonomies. According to Bogdan, showmen often asked scientists to authenticate monsters, for "linking freak exhibits with science made the attractions more interesting, more believable, and less frivolous . . ." ("The Social Construction of Freaks" 29; see also *Freak Show* 1-21).

9. Mariana Warner has shown how the grotesque paradoxically presents terror and mockery in its "parodic harshness, sick humour, shivery manipulation of fear and pleasure in the monstrous" (*No Go the Bogeyman* 67). See also Lucie Armitt's distinction between grotesque and caricature (*Theorising the Fantastic* 68-70).

10. Deidre Lynch points out that a performer's face provided spectacular evidence of how passions "stamped" the muscles of the face. Spectators were expected to look at the sentiment written across the performer's body ("Overloaded Portraits: The Excess of Character and Countenance" 137). According to E. J. Clery, David Garrick's technique of acting was dependent on the audience's knowledge of the body, a taxonomy of the passions registered by facial expressions and bodily gestures (*The Rise of Supernatural Fiction, 1762-1800* 42-49).

11. Freddie Rokem acknowledges that a staged body functions as a "sign" of "cultural and aesthetic codes of bodily behavior" for audiences ("Slapping Women: Ibsen's Nora, Strindberg's Julie, and Freud's Dora" 222). Veronica Kelly and Dorothea von Mucke maintain that the body stands in a multiple complex relations to culturally produced meanings. In the production of dominant cultural codes, the body "regulate[s] the excesses of signifying practice and define[s] the subjectivity of agents in the semiotic transaction" ("Introduction: Body and Text in the Eighteenth Century" 9).

12. Terry Castle points to the ways in which non-dramatic but staged science excited audiences to question the reality of optical illusions in magic lantern shows, which "developed as mock exercises in scientific demystification, complete with preliminary lectures on the fallacy of ghost-belief" ("Phantasmagoria: Spectral Technology and the Metaphorics of Modern Reverie" 30). See also Terry Castle (*The Female Thermometer* 168-89) and Barbara Marie Stafford (*Body Criticism* 366-75).

13. Foucault describes how the social fear, a fear formulated in medical terms but animated by a moral myth, arose throughout the Romantic period that madness was a mysterious disease, contagious and corrupting (*Madness and Civilization* 199-220).

14. In the Introductory Discourse to the 1798 *Plays on the Passions*, Baillie remarks about the compelling nature of the world of spirits, our interest in finding ourselves "alone with a being terrific and awful, whose nature and power are unknown." Baillie adds that we prefer vicarious explorations of the supernatural as an object of inquiry: "No man wishes to see the Ghost himself, which would certainly procure him the best information on the subject; but every man wishes to see one who believes that he sees it, in all the agitation and wildness of that species of terror" (3).

15. Interestingly, Franz Anton Mesmer argued that medicine had ignored a majority of chronic illnesses, including epilepsy, mania, melancholy, so-called "illnesses of the nerves," often confusing crisis with disease ("Dissertation by F. A. Mesmer, Doctor of Medicine, on His Discoveries" 105).

16. Dennis Todd details the celebrated case of Mary Toft, the illiterate wife of a poor journeyman cloth-worker, who purportedly gave birth to her first rabbit in October 1726, an incident that excited medical and public attention (*Imaginary Monsters* 1-37). Rosi Braidotti notes that the medical profession benefited by examining human exhibits in raree shows (*Nomadic Subjects* 91-92). Scientists who examined "freaks," explains Bogdan, frequently presented their commentaries in newspapers and pamphlets, and some exhibits were presented to medical societies (*Freak Show* 106-111). See Also Richard D. Altick (*The Shows of London* 217-20).

17. *A History of the Witches of Renfrewshire* 151-52. The Renfrew Witches incident is discussed by Anne Llewellyn Barstow (*Witchcraze* 124-25).

18. Christina Larner (*Enemies of God* 63). Mary Daly notes that a 1563 Scottish witch-law dropped the distinction between "good" and "bad" witch (*Gyn/Ecology* 193), and so in the case Renfrew Witches, any witchcraft would have been persecuted. The English Parliament made accusations of witchcraft and sorcery illegal in 1736.

19. "Life of Joanna Baillie" ix. See also Margaret Carhart (*Life and Work of Joanna Baillie* 9-11).

20. See, for example, Barbara Ehrenreich and Deidre English (*Witches, Midwives, and Nurses* 6-20); Mary Daly (*Gyn/Ecology* 183-213).

21. Mark S. Micale (*Approaching Hysteria* 22-23). For a developed analysis of the causal links of hysteria to female sexuality, see Ilza Veith's *Hysteria: The History of a Disease*.

22. Elizabeth A. Fay includes a brief mention of Baillie's *Witchcraft*, which, she maintains, "explores how real social restrictions on women's behavior or their imaginations can lead them literally into life-threatening situations that are historically plausible, such as accusations of witchcraft" (*A Feminist Introduction to Romanticism* 117).

23. See, for example, Juliet Mitchell's *Psychoanalysis and Feminism*, Phyllis Chesler's *Women and Madness*, Starhawk's "Witchcraft as Goddess Religion" (394-400), and Carol P. Christ's "Why Women Need the Goddess: Phenomenological, Psychological, and Political Reflections" (345-58).

Works Cited

Altick, Richard D. *The Shows of London*. Cambridge, MA: Harvard UP, 1978.

Armitt, Lucie. *Theorising the Fantastic*. London: Arnold, 1996.

Baillie, Joanna. *The Collected Letters of Joanna Baillie.* Vol. 1. Ed. Judith Bailey Slagle. Madison, NJ: Fairleigh Dickinson UP, 1991.

———. Introductory Discourse to *Plays on the Passions.* 1798. *The Dramatic and Poetical Works of Joanna Baillie, Complete in One Volume.* 2nd ed. London: Longman, 1851. 1-18.

———. *Witchcraft: A Tragedy in Prose, in Five Acts* in *Miscellaneous Plays.* 1836. *The Dramatic and Poetical Works of Joanna Baillie, Complete in One Volume.* 2nd ed. London: Longman, 1851. 613-43.

Baillie, Matthew. "The Gulstonian Lectures, Read at the College of Physicians, May 1794: Lecture III." *Lectures and Observations on Medicine.* London: Taylor, 1825. 140-60.

Barstow, Anne Llewellyn. *Witchcraze: A New History of the European Witch Hunts.* London: Pandora, 1994.

Bogdan, Robert. *Freak Show: Presenting Human Oddities for Amusement and Profit.* Chicago: U of Chicago P, 1988.

———. "The Social Construction of Freaks." *Freakery: Cultural Spectacles of the Extraordinary Body.* Ed. Rosemarie Garland Thomson. New York: New York UP, 1996.

Braidotti, Rosi. *Nomadic Subjects: Embodiment and Sexual Difference in Contemporary Feminist Theory.* New York: Columbia UP, 1994.

Carhart, Margaret S. *The Life and Work of Joanna Baillie.* New Haven: Yale UP, 1923; rpt. Archon Books, 1970.

Castle, Terry. *The Female Thermometer: 18th-Century Culture and the Invention of the Uncanny.* New York: Oxford UP, 1995.

———. "Phantasmagoria: Spectral Technology and the Metaphorics of Modern Reverie." *Critical Inquiry* 15.1 (1988): 26-61.

Chesler, Phyllis. *Women and Madness.* New York: Doubleday, 1972.

Christ, Carol P. "Why Women Need the Goddess: Phenomenological, Psychological, and Political Reflections." *All American Women: Lives that Divide, Ties that Bind.* New York: Macmillan, 1986. 345-58.

Clarke, Edwin, and L. S. Jacyna. *Nineteenth-Century Origins of Neuroscientific Concepts.* Berkeley: U of California P, 1987.

Clery, E. J. *The Rise of Supernatural Fiction, 1762-1800.* Cambridge: Cambridge UP, 1995.

Cobb, Cathy, and Harold Goldwhite. *Creations of Fire: Chemistry's Lively History from Alchemy to the Atomic Age.* New York: Plenum Press, 1995.

Crichton, Alexander. *An Inquiry into the Nature and Origin of Mental Derangement: Comprehending a Concise System of the Physiology and Pathology of the Human Mind, and a History of the Passions and Their Effects.* 2 vols. London: Cadell and W. Davies, 1798.

Daly, Mary. *Gyn/Ecology: The Metaethics of Radical Feminism.* Boston: Beacon, 1978.

Dixon, Laurinda S. *Perilous Chastity.* Ithaca: Cornell UP, 1995.

Ehrenreich, Barbara, and Deidre English. *Witches, Midwives, and Nurses: A History of Women Healers.* New York: Feminist Press, 1973.

Fay, Elizabeth A. *A Feminist Introduction to Romanticism.* Malden, MA: Blackwell, 1998.

Flaherty, Gloria. "The Non-Normal Sciences: Survivals of Renaissance Thought in the Eighteenth Century." *Inventing Human Science: Eighteenth-Century Domains.* Ed. Christopher Fox, Roy S. Porter, and Robert Wokler. Berkeley: U of California P, 1995. 271-91.

Foucault, Michel. *Madness and Civilization: A History of Insanity in the Age of Reason.* 1965. Trans. Richard Howard. New York: Vintage, 1988.

Fox, Christopher. "Introduction: How to Prepare a Nobel Savage: The Spectacle of Human Science." *Inventing Human Science: Eighteenth-Century Domains.* Ed. Christopher Fox, Roy S. Porter, and Robert Wokler. Berkeley: U of California P, 1995. 1-30.

Grosz, Elizabeth. "Intolerable Ambiguity: Freaks as/at the Limit." *Freakery: Cultural Spectacles of the Extraordinary Body.* Ed. Rosemarie Garland Thomson. New York: New York UP, 1996. 55-66.

Herschel, John Frederick William. *A Preliminary Discourse on the Study of Natural Philosophy.* 1830. New York: Johnson Reprint, 1996.

A History of the Witches of Renfrewshire. 1698. New ed. Paisley: Alexander Gardner, 1877.

Jordanova, Ludmilla. "Gender, Generation and Science: William Hunter's Obstetrical Atlas." *William Hunter and the 18th-Century Medical World.* Ed. William F. Bynum and Roy S. Porter. Cambridge: Cambridge UP, 1985. 385-412.

Kelly, Veronica, and Dorothea von Mucke. "Introduction: Body and Text in the Eighteenth Century." *Body and Text in the Eighteenth Century.* Ed. Veronica Kelly and Dorothea von Mucke. Stanford: Stanford UP, 1994. 1-20.

Lamb, Charles. "Witches, and Other Night-Fears." 1823. *Essays of Elia and Last Essays of Elia.* New York: Dutton, 1978. 76-82.

Larner, Christina. *Enemies of God: The Witch-hunts in Scotland.* London: Chatto & Windus, 1981.

Leacroft, Richard. *The Development of the English Playhouse.* Ithaca: Cornell UP, 1988. "Life of Joanna Baillie." *The Dramatic and Poetical Works of Joanna Baillie, in One Complete Volume.* 2nd ed. London: Longman, 1851. v-xx.

Logan, Peter Melville. *Nerves and Narratives: A Cultural History of Hysteria in 19th-Century Prose.* Berkeley: U of California P, 1997.

Lynch, Deidre. "Overloaded Portraits: The Excess of Character and Countenance." *Body and Text in the Eighteenth Century.* Ed. Veronica Kelly and Dorothea von Mucke. Stanford: Stanford UP, 1994. 112-43.

Mesmer, Franz Anton. "Dissertation by F. A. Mesmer, Doctor of Medicine, on His Discoveries." 1799. *Mesmerism: A Translation of the Original Scientific and Medical Writings of F. A. Mesmer.* Trans. and compiled by George Bloch. Los Altos, CA: William Kaufmann, 1980. 89-130.

Micale, Mark S. *Approaching Hysteria: Disease and Its Interpretations.* Princeton: Princeton UP, 1995.

Mitchell, Juliet. *Psychoanalysis and Feminism.* Harmondsworth: Penguin, 1974.

Pascoe, Judith. *Romantic Theatricality: Gender, Poetry, and Spectatorship.* Ithaca: Cornell UP, 1997.

Porter, Roy S. "Medical Science and Human Science in the Enlightenment." *Inventing Human Science: Eighteenth-Century Domains.* Ed. Christopher Fox, Roy S. Porter, and Robert Wokler. Berkeley: U of California P, 1995. 53-87.

Purinton, Marjean D. "Bryon's Disability and the Techno-Gothic Grotesque in *The Deformed Transformed.*" *European Romantic Review,* forthcoming.

———. "Science Fiction and Techno-Gothic Drama: Romantic Playwrights Joanna Baillie and Jane Scott." *Romanticism on the Net* 21 (Feb. 2001). http: www.sul.stanford .edu/mirrors/romnet.

———. "Theatricalized Bodies and Spirits: Techno-Gothic as Performance in Romantic Drama." *Gothic Studies,* forthcoming.

———. "Women's Sovereignty on Trial: Joanna Baillie's Comedy *The Tryal* as Metatheatrics." *Women in British Romantic Theatre: Drama, Performance, and Society, 1790-1840.* Ed. Catherine Burroughs. Cambridge: Cambridge UP, 2000. 132-57.

Ranger, Paul. *"Terror and Pity Reign in Every Breast": Gothic Drama in the London Patent Theatres, 1750-1820.* London: Society for Theatre Research, 1991.

Rockem, Freddie. "Slapping Women: Ibsen's Nora, Strindberg's Julie, and Freud's Dora." *Textual Bodies: Changing Boundaries of Literary Representation.* Ed. Lori Hope Lefkovitz. Albany: SUNY P, 1997. 221-43.

Scott, Walter, Sir. *The Journal of Sir Walter Scott.* Ed. W.E.K. Anderson. Oxford: Clarendon, 1972.

———. *Letters on Demonology and Witchcraft, Addressed to J. G. Lockhart, Esq.* 1830. 2nd ed. London, 1831.

Stafford, Barbara Marie. *Body Criticism: Imaging the Unseen in Enlightenment Art and Medicine.* Cambridge: Massachusetts Institute of Technology Press, 1991.

Starhawk. "Witchcraft as Goddess Religion." *Women in Culture.* Ed. Lucinda Joy Peach. Malden, MA: Blackwell, 1998. 394-400.

Todd, Dennis. *Imaging Monsters: Miscreations of the Self in Eighteenth-Century England.* Chicago: U of Chicago P, 1995.

Trotter, Thomas. *A View of the Nervous Temperament; being a Practical Enquiry into the Increasing Prevalence, Prevention, and Treatment of those Diseases Commonly Called Nervous, Bilious, Stomach and Liver Complaints; Indigestion, Low Spirits, Gout, & c.* London: Longman, 1807.

Veith, Ilza. *Hysteria: The History of a Disease.* Chicago: U of Chicago P, 1965.

Warner, Mariana. *No Go the Bogeyman: Scaring, Lulling, and Making Mock.* New York: Farrar, Straus & Giroux, 1998, 1999.

Williams, Anne. *Art of Darkness: A Poetics of Gothic.* Chicago: U of Chicago P, 1995.

Wilson, Lindsay. *Women and Medicine in the French Enlightment: The Debate over Maladies des Femmes.* Baltimore: The Johns Hopkins UP, 1993.

FURTHER READING

Biography

Carhart, Margaret Sprague. *The Life and Work of Joanna Baillie.* New Haven, Conn.: Yale University Press, 1923, 215 p.

Comprehensive, authoritative biography and overview of Baillie's works.

Criticism

Brigham, Linda. "Aristocratic Monstrosity and Sublime Femininity in *De Monfort.*" *SEL: Studies in English Literature, 1500-1900* 43, no. 3 (summer 2003): 701-18.

Examines Baillie's theories regarding the emotions, as stated in her "Introductory Discourse" to the first volume of Plays on the Passions, *and compares them to the theories of Edmund Burke to illustrate how "they relate to political and feminist topics in the 1790s and early nineteenth century."*

Burroughs, Catherine B. "English Romantic Women Writers and Theatre Theory: Joanna Baillie's Prefaces to the *Plays on the Passions.*" In *Re-Visioning Romanticism: British Women Writers, 1776-1837,* edited by Carol Shiner Wilson and Joel Haefner, pp. 274-96. Philadelphia: University of Pennsylvania Press, 1994.

Studies Baillie's prefaces to her Plays on the Passions *as examples of "theatre theory" and "locates them within a tradition of women writing about the stage."*

———. "'Out of the Pale of Social Kindred Cast': Conflicted Performance Styles in Joanna Baillie's *De Monfort.*" In *Romantic Women Writers: Voices and Countervoices,* edited by Paula R. Feldman and Theresa M. Kelley, pp. 223-35. Hanover, N.H.: University Press of New England, 1995.

Argues that the "dramaturgical tension that results from" De Monfort's *"conflicting acting modes" ("statuesque stasis" vs. "emotive school") indicates that Baillie was ambivalent "about prescribing a particular style of performance for characters navigating her fictionalized social settings."*

Dowd, Maureen A. "'By the Delicate Hand of a Female': Melodramatic Mania and Johanna Baillie's Spectacular Tragedies." *European Romantic Review* 9, no. 4 (fall 1998): 469-500.

Compares Baillie's dramatic works to those of Friedrich von Schiller and maintains that "the gaps between Baillie's prefatory rhetoric and her dramatic productions operate as a cultural performance that usefully illuminates the intersection of commercial concerns, national interest, and gender issues in late eighteenth- and early nineteenth-century British theater."

Forbes, Aileen. "'Sympathetic Curiosity' in Joanna Baillie's Theater of the Passions." *European Romantic Review* 14, no. 1 (March 2003): 31-48.

Discusses Baillie's theory of "sympathetic curiosity," as evidenced in her plays, and asserts that "Baillie innova-

tively combines the two concepts [of 'sympathy' and 'curiosity'] in a dramatic tension that aims to delineate the human passions."

Gamer, Michael. "National Supernaturalism: Joanna Baillie, Germany, and the Gothic Drama." *Theatre Survey* 38, no. 2 (November 1997): 49-88.

Discusses the debate over Gothic drama's legitimacy and examines how Baillie produced engaging plays which managed to avoid the stigma afforded other Gothic works.

Harness, William. "Celebrated Female Writers: Joanna Baillie." *Blackwood's Edinburgh Magazine* 16, no. 91 (August 1824): 162-78.

Highly laudatory overview of Baillie's career.

Jeffrey, Francis. A review of *A Series of Plays In Which It Is Attempted to Delineate the Stronger Passions of the Mind*, Vol. II, by Joanna Baillie. *The Edinburgh Review* 11, no. 4 (July 1803): 269-86.

Mixed review of the second volume of Plays on the Passions.

———. A review of *A Series of Plays: In Which It Is Attempted to Delineate the Stronger Passions of the Mind*, Vol. III, by Joanna Baillie. *The Edinburgh Review* 19, no. 38 (February 1812): 261-90.

Assesses the third volume of Plays on the Passions *as "decidedly inferior to any of her former volumes" but declares that "at the same time . . . it contains indications of talent that ought not to be overlooked, and specimens of excellence, which make it a duty to examine into the causes of its general failure."*

Meyers, Victoria. "Joanna Baillie's Theatre of Cruelty." In *Joanna Baillie, Romantic Dramatist: Critical Essays*, compiled by Thomas C. Crochunis, pp. 87-107. New York and London: Routledge, 2004.

Examines Baillie's treatment of human psychology and morality in Plays on the Passions, *particularly in terms of her presentation of violence and cruelty.*

Purinton, Marjean D. "Joanna Baillie's *Count Basil* and *De Monfort*: The Unveiling of Gender Issues." In *Romantic Ideology Unmasked: The Mentally Constructed Tyrannies in Dramas of William Wordsworth, Lord Byron, Percy Shelley, and Joanna Baillie*, pp. 125-62. Newark, Del.: University of Delaware Press, 1994.

Places Baillie's works within the context of works by other women writers of her time and examines the overlap of political and gender issues in Count Basil *and* De Monfort.

Watkins, Daniel P. "Class, Gender, and Social Motion in Joanna Baillie's *De Monfort*." *Wordsworth Circle* 23, no. 2 (spring 1992): 109-17.

Stresses the historical value of De Monfort*'s depictions of social conditions and class conflicts.*

OTHER SOURCES FROM GALE:

Additional coverage of Baillie's life and career is contained in the following sources published by Thomson Gale: *Dictionary of Literary Biography*, Vol. 93; *Literature Resource Center*; *Nineteenth-Century Literature Criticism*, Vols. 71, 151; and *Reference Guide to English Literature*, Ed. 2.

WILLIAM BECKFORD

(1760 - 1844)

(Also wrote under the pseudonyms Lady Harnet Marlow and Jacquetta Agneta Manana Jenks) English novelist and travel writer.

Beckford is primarily remembered for his novel *Vathek* (1787), which has been consistently hailed as a seminal contribution to the genre of oriental romance, and less consistently as part of the Gothic tradition. The story of an evil caliph's journey to the underworld in pursuit of forbidden knowledge, *Vathek* is noted for its captivating plot and unique narrative style.

BIOGRAPHICAL INFORMATION

Beckford was born into one of the richest and most prominent families in England. His father, William Beckford, formerly lord mayor of London, had accumulated great wealth from investments in Jamaican sugar plantations and his mother, Maria Hamilton, was of noble ancestry. As the only child of a late marriage, Beckford was pampered by both parents, but he received a rigorous education in preparation for a political career and could speak French fluently at age four. When he was nine, "England's wealthiest son," as Lord Byron called Beckford, inherited his father's estate. Afterwards, he continued to follow a rigid program of classical studies under the strict guidance of his mother, amid a succession of tutors. Despite their efforts, an interest in oriental literature, thought to have been brought on by his reading of *The Arabian Nights*, became Beckford's passionate obsession. In 1777, he left with a tutor for Geneva, Switzerland, to complete his education. There Beckford met a number of notable figures, including Voltaire, and began his first literary work, an autobiographical narrative entitled *The Long Story* that was never completed and remained unknown until a portion of it was published in 1930 as *The Vision*.

Following his return from Switzerland in 1778, Beckford entered into a tumultuous period of his life. While touring England in 1779, he developed what he called a "strange wayward passion" for William Courtenay, the eleven-year-old son of Lord Courtenay of Powderham Castle. Beckford also became romantically involved with Louisa Beckford, the unhappily married wife of one of his cousins. Despite the emotional distress he suffered as a result of these relationships, Beckford published his first work in 1780, a burlesque of then-popular sketches of painters' lives entitled *Biographical Memoirs of Extraordinary Painters*. Later in 1780, the restless Beckford began a European tour that his family hoped would help solve his emotional problems and prepare him for public life. Though it failed to alleviate his mental anguish, his journey resulted in *Dreams, Waking Thoughts, and Incidents* (1783), an epistolary travel book composed from notes kept during his trip. After this work had been printed, however, Beckford suppressed its distribution and burned all but a few copies; biographers have speculated that his family thought the content of *Dreams, Waking Thoughts, and Incidents* might damage his political prospects or add to rumors circulating about his friendship with Courtenay.

In 1781, Beckford hosted a sumptuous Christmas party that he later credited with directly inspiring his exotic oriental novel, *Vathek*. For three days, Courtenay, Louisa Beckford, and other guests wandered through Beckford's country home surrounded by music, dancers, and theatrical lighting effects. Shortly after this fantastical celebration, Beckford wrote the initial French-language draft of *Vathek* in one sitting, though scholars believe that he revised and expanded the novel many times before its publication four years later. In this work, the caliph Vathek travels to the underworld domain ruled by Eblis, a satanic figure. There, Vathek seeks forbidden wisdom, only to face eternal damnation in the Palace of Subterranean Fire. Beckford based many of his characters upon historical figures and provided a wealth of oriental detail, including descriptions of Eastern costumes, customs, and plant and animal life. He intended to add to this story four episodic tales narrated by sufferers in the Palace of Subterranean Fire, and while composing them, he arranged for the Reverend Samuel Henley, an oriental enthusiast and former professor, to translate the entire work into English and add footnotes explaining the oriental allusions. Beckford's completion of the episodes, however, was hindered by misfortune. At his family's insistence, he married Lady Margaret Gordon in 1783, a match they hoped would quell rumors concerning his homosexuality. In June 1784 the couple's first child was stillborn. Later that same year Beckford was publicly accused of sexual misconduct with Courtenay, and the resulting scandal forced Beckford and his wife to flee to Switzerland, where Margaret Beckford died in May 1786 after giving birth to their second daughter. Throughout these ordeals, Beckford instructed Henley to withhold his English translation of *Vathek* until the companion episodes were finished. In a betrayal of trust, however, Henley released an anonymous English translation of *Vathek* in June 1786. Beckford subsequently published a French edition of *Vathek* in order to claim authorship, and the uncompleted episodes remained unpublished until 1912.

For the next ten years, Beckford spent the majority of his time abroad, traveling throughout Switzerland, France, Italy, Spain, and Portugal. In 1796, he returned permanently to England. Ostracized from society, he spent much of the remainder of his life collecting books, paintings, and rare objects of art and building Fonthill Abbey, an extravagant Gothic structure. Beckford grew notorious as the creator of the increasingly popular *Vathek*, which had been reissued numerous times since its publication, and as the eccentric owner of Fonthill, where he lived until financial difficulties forced him to sell the estate in 1822 and move to Landsdown Crescent, Bath. Beckford's literary output during this period was scant. In the late 1790s, he wrote two minor novels burlesquing the sentimentalism of contemporary novelists, *Modern Novel Writing; or, The Elegant Enthusiast* (1796) and *Azemia* (1797). In 1834, he published *Italy: With Sketches of Spain and Portugal*, a two-volume work that consists of extensive revision of *Dreams, Waking Thoughts, and Incidents* as the first volume and an account of his journeys through Spain and Portugal as the second. His final travel book, *Recollections of an Excursion to the Monasteries of Alcobaça Batalha*, appeared in 1835. After living his last years in relative seclusion, Beckford died at Landsdown in 1844.

MAJOR WORKS

Apart from *Vathek*, Beckford's works fall loosely into two categories: travel sketches and satirical writings. His travel sketches, including *Dreams, Waking Thoughts, and Incidents, Italy: With Sketches of Spain and Portugal*, and *Recollections of an Excursion to the Monasteries of Alcobaça and Batalha*, are generally commended for their balanced prose and descriptive artistry. Of Beckford's satiric writings, *Biographical Memoirs of Extraordinary Painters* is praised as a witty burlesque, while *Modern Novel Writing* and *Azemia* are usually dismissed as minor works.

CRITICAL RECEPTION

Though most of his writings met with favorable receptions and have continued to be praised by scholars, Beckford's lasting critical acclaim rests upon *Vathek*. In discussing *Vathek*, critics have focused on its style, autobiographical overtones, and historical significance. While acknowledging *Vathek's* popular appeal, commentators have consistently been troubled by what early reviewer William Hazlitt (see Further Reading) termed its "mixed style." Critics have noted a tonal shift from the initially comic account of Vathek's journey to the tragic depiction of, in the words of Jorge Luis Borges (see Further Reading), "the first truly atrocious Hell in literature." Reviewers have ascribed this variance to authorial attributes ranging from artistic coarseness, to moral ambivalence, to a genius for irony. Beckford's unusual life and his treatment of aberrant sexual themes, puerile innocence, and domineering mothers have also led to a profusion of biographical interpretations of *Vathek*, particularly during the nineteenth and early twentieth centuries. Later twentieth-century commentators, however, generally avoided biographical critiques, emphasizing instead Beckford's anticipation of the orientalism of such nineteenth-century poets as Lord Byron, Thomas Moore, and Robert Southey. Critics generally note that unlike the works of earlier English authors who employed oriental elements to embellish philosophical musings or to serve moralistic purposes, *Vathek* exhibits a fascination with exoticism for its own sake, with Beckford placing greater emphasis than previous writers upon producing an accurate depiction of the East. Commentators also point out that in *Vathek* Beckford combined polished Augustan prose with such characteristically Romantic concerns as human aspiration, loss of innocence, and the mysterious, thus reflecting the incipient transition in English literature from Neoclassicism to Romanticism. For its historical significance, as well as its continuing fascination for readers, *Vathek* is regarded as a minor masterpiece. Furthermore, as critics such as Frederick S. Frank have argued, the novel's structure, themes, and symbolism place *Vathek* firmly in the tradition of Gothic fiction.

PRINCIPAL WORKS

Biographical Memoirs of Extraordinary Painters (fictional memoirs) 1780

Dreams, Waking Thoughts, and Incidents (travel sketches) 1783

*Vathek (novel) 1787

Modern Novel Writing; or, The Elegant Enthusiast, and Interesting Emotions of Arabella Bloomville [as Lady Harriet Marlow] (novel) 1796

Azemia [as Jacquetta Agenta Mariana Jenks] (novel) 1797

Italy: With Sketches of Spain and Portugal. 2 vols. (travel sketches) 1834

Recollections of an Excursion to the Monasteries of Al-cobaça and Batalha (travel sketches) 1835

†The Episodes of Vathek (novel fragment) 1912

‡The Vision (novel fragment) 1930; published in *The Vision. Liber Veritatis*

*   The unauthorized translation of *Vathek* was published as *An Arabian Tale*, 1786.

†   This work consists of Beckford's original French-language episodes, dated 1783-86, and an English translation of them.

‡   *The Vision* is part of Beckford's unfinished narrative, known as *The Long Story*, written in 1777.

PRIMARY SOURCES

WILLIAM BECKFORD (NOVEL DATE 1786)

SOURCE: Beckford, William. *"The History of the Caliph Vathek."* In *An Arabian Tale, from an Unpublished Manuscript: With Notes Critical and Explanatory*, pp. 1-10. London, 1786.

In the following excerpt from the unauthorized 1786 translation of Vathek, *the title character is introduced and the setting for the narrative is established.*

Vathek, ninth *Caliph* of the race of the Abassides, was the son of Motassem, and the grandson of Haroun Al Raschid. From an early accession to the throne, and the talents he possessed to adorn it; his subjects were induced to expect, that his reign would be long, and happy. His figure was pleasing, and majestick; but when he was angry, one of his eyes became so terrible, that no person could bear to behold it; and the wretch upon whom it was fixed, instantly fell backward; and, sometimes, expired. For fear, however, of depopulating his dominions, and making his palace desolate; he, but rarely, gave way to his anger.

Being much addicted to women, and the pleasures of the table; he sought, by his affability, to procure agreeable companions; and he succeeded the better, as his generosity was unbounded; and his indulgences, unrestrained: for, he was, by no means, scrupulous: nor did he think, with the Caliph, Omar Ben Abdalaziz; that it was necessary to make a hell of this world, to injoy Paradise in the next.

He surpassed in magnificence all his predecessors. The palace of Alkoremmi, which his father Motassem had erected, on the hill of Pied Horses; and which commanded the whole city of Samarah; was, in his idea, far too scanty: he added, therefore, five wings; or rather, other palaces: which he destined for the particular gratification of each of his senses.

In the first of these, were tables continually covered, with the most exquisite dainties; which were supplied, both by night and by day, according to their constant consumption; whilst the most delicious wines, and the choicest cordials, flowed forth from a hundred fountains, that were never exhausted. This Palace was called THE ETERNAL OR UNSATIATING BANQUET.

The second, was stiled THE TEMPLE OF MELODY, OR THE NECTAR OF THE SOUL. It was inhabited by the most skilful musicians, and admired poets of the time; who not only displayed their talents within, but, dispersing in bands without, caused every surrounding scene to reverberate their songs; which were continually varied in the most delightful succession.

The palace named THE DELIGHT OF THE EYES, OR THE SUPPORT OF MEMORY; was one entire enchantment. Rarities collected from every corner of the earth, were there found in such profusion, as to dazzle and confound, but for the order in which they were arranged. One gallery exhibited the pictures of the celebrated Mani; and statues, that seemed to be alive. Here, a well-managed perspective attracted the fight; there, the magick of opticks agreeably deceived it: whilst the Naturalist, on his part, exhibited, in their several classes, the various gifts that Heaven had bestowed on our globe. In a word, Vathek omitted nothing, in this palace, that might gratify the curiosity of those who resorted to it; although he was not able to satisfy his own; for, he was, of all men, the most curious.

THE PALACE OF PERFUMES, which was termed likewise, THE INCENTIVE TO PLEASURE, consisted of various halls, where the different perfumes which the earth produces, were kept perpetually burning in censers of gold. Flambeaus and aromatick lamps were here lighted, in open day. But, the too powerful effects of this agreeable delirium might be avoided, by descending into an immense garden; where an assemblage of every fragrant flower diffused through the air the purest odours.

The fifth palace, denominated THE RETREAT OF JOY, OR THE DANGEROUS; was frequented by troops of young females, beautiful as the Houris, and not less seducing; who never failed to receive, with caresses, all whom the Caliph allowed to approach them: for, he was by no means disposed to be jealous, as his own women were secluded, within the palace he inhabited, himself.

Notwithstanding the sensuality in which Vathek indulged, he experienced no abatement in the love of his people; who thought, that a sovereign immersed in pleasure was not less tolerable to his subjects, than one that employed himself in creating them foes. But, the unquiet and impetuous disposition of the Caliph, would not allow him to rest there. He had studied so much for his amusement, in the life-time of his father, as to acquire a great deal of knowledge; though not a sufficiency to satisfy himself: for, he wished to know every thing; even, sciences that did not exist. He was fond of engaging in disputes with the learned, but liked them not to push their opposition with warmth. He stopped the mouths of those, with presents, whose mouths could be stopped; whilst others, whom his liberality was unable to subdue, he sent to prison, to cool their blood: a remedy that often succeeded.

Vathek discovered also a predilection for theological controversy; but, it was not with the orthodox that he usually held. By this means he induced the zealots to oppose him, and then persecuted them in return; for, he resolved, at any rate, to have reason on his side.

The great prophet Mahomet, whose Vicars the Caliphs are, beheld with indignation, from his abode in the seventh heaven, the irreligious conduct of such a vicegerent. "Let us leave him to himself," said he to the Genii, who are always ready to receive his commands: "let us see to what lengths his folly and impiety will carry him: if he run into excess, we shall know how to chastise him. Assist him, therefore, to complete the tower, which, in imitation of Nimrod, he hath begun; not, like that great warriour, to escape being drowned; but from the insolent curiosity of penetrating the secrets of Heaven:—he will not divine the fate that awaits him."

The Genii obeyed; and when the workmen had raised their structure a cubit, in the day-time; two cubits more were added, in the night. The expedition with which the fabrick arose, was not a little flattering to the vanity of Vathek. He fancied, that even insensible matter shewed a forwardness to subserve his designs; not considering that the successes of the foolish and wicked form the first rod of their chastisement.

His pride arrived at its height, when having ascended, for the first time, the eleven thousand stairs of his tower, he cast his eyes below, and beheld men not larger than pismires; mountains, than shells; and cities, than bee-hives. The idea, which such an elevation inspired, of his own grandeur, completely bewildered him; he was almost ready, to adore himself; till, lifting his eyes upward, he saw the stars, as high above him, as they appeared, when he stood on the surface of the earth. He consoled himself, however, for this transient perception of his littleness, with the thought of being great in the eyes of others; and flattered himself, that the light of his mind would extend, beyond the reach of his sight; and transfer to the stars the decrees of his destiny.

With this view, the inquisitive Prince passed most of his nights on the summit of his tower: till he became an adept in the mysteries of astrology; and imagined that the planets had disclosed to him the most marvellous adventures, which were to be accomplished by an extraordinary person-age, from a country altogether unknown. Prompted by motives of curiosity, he had always been courteous to strangers; but, from this instant, he redoubled his attention; and ordered it to be announced by sound of trumpet, through all the streets of Samarah, that no one of his subjects, on peril of his displeasure, should either lodge or detain a traveller; but, forthwith, bring him to the palace.

Not long after this proclamation, there arrived in his metropolis, a man so hideous, that the very guards who arrested him, were forced to shut their eyes, as they led him along. The Caliph himself appeared startled at so horrible a visage; but, joy succeeded to this emotion of terror, when the stranger displayed to his view, such rarities as he had never before seen; and of which he had no conception.

In reality, nothing was ever so extraordinary as the merchandize this stranger produced. Most of his curiosities, which were not less admirable for their workmanship, than splendor, had be-sides, their several virtues; described on a parch-ment fastened to each. There were slippers, which enabled the feet to walk; knives that cut without the motion of a hand; sabres, which dealt the blow, at the person they were wished to strike: and the whole, enriched with gems, that were, hitherto, unknown.

The sabres, especially, whose blades emitted a dazzling radiance; fixed more than all, the Caliph's attention; who promised himself to decypher, at his leisure, the uncouth characters engraven on their sides. Without, therefore, demanding their price; he ordered all the coined gold to be brought from his treasury, and commanded the merchant to take what he pleased. The stranger complied, with modesty and silence.

Vathek, imagining that the merchant's tacitur-nity was occasioned by the awe which his pres-ence inspired; incouraged him to advance, and asked him, with an air of condescension: "Who

he was? whence he came? and where he obtained such beautiful commodities?" The man, or rather, monster, instead of making a reply, thrice rubbed his forehead, which, as well as his body, was blacker than ebony; four times clapped his paunch, the projection of which was enormous; opened wide his huge eyes, which glowed like firebrands; began to laugh with a hideous noise, and discovered his long, amber-coloured teeth, bestreaked with green.

WILLIAM BECKFORD (LETTER DATE 9 DECEMBER 1838)

SOURCE: Beckford, William. "Extract from a note ap-pended to a letter on December 9, 1838." In *The Life of William Beckford,* edited by John Walter Oliver, pp. 89-91. London: Oxford University Press, 1932.

In the following excerpt from a note appended to a letter dated December 9, 1838, Beckford recounts the circum-stances that inspired him to write Vathek.

Immured we were 'au pied de la lettre' for three days following—doors and windows so strictly closed that neither common day light nor common place visitors could get in or even peep in—care worn visages were ordered to keep aloof—no sunk-in mouths or furroughed fore-heads were permitted to meet our eye. Our société was extremely youthful and lovely to look upon—for not only Louisa in all her gracefulness, but her intimate friend—the Sophia often mentioned in some of these letters—and perhaps the most beautiful woman in England, threw over it a fascinating charm. Throughout the arched Halls and vast apartments we ranged in, prevailed a soft and tempered radiance—distributed with much skill under the direction of Loutherbourg himself a mystagogue. The great mansion at Fonthill which I demolished to rear up a still more extraor-dinary edifice was admirably calculated for the celebration of the mysteries. The solid Egyptian Hall looked as if hewn out of a living rock—the line of apartments and apparently endless pas-sages extending from it on either side were all vaulted—an interminable stair case, which when you looked down it—appeared as deep as the well in the pyramid—and when you looked up—was lost in vapour, led to suites of stately apartments gleaming with marble pavements—as polished as glass—and gawdy ceilings—painted by Casali with all the profligacy of pencil—for which in that evil day for the arts he was so admired. From these princely rooms—a broad flight of richly carpeted comfortable steps led to another world of deco-rated chambers and a gallery designed by Soane,—still above which—approached by winding stairs—

FROM THE AUTHOR

AN EXCERPT FROM "NYMPH OF THE FOUNTAIN," WRITTEN C. 1791

Meanwhile the Count's servants were exerting their utmost efforts to revive the extinguished fire. They thought they could hear the sound of human voices within, whence they concluded that the Countess was still alive. But all their stirring and blowing were ineffectual. The wood would no more take fire than if they had put on a charge of snowballs. Not long afterwards Count Conrad rode up full speed, and eagerly inquired how it fared with his lady. The servants informed him that they had heated the room right hot, but that the fire went suddenly out, and they supposed that the Countess was yet alive. This intelligence rejoiced his heart. He dismounted, knocked at the door, and called out through the keyhole, 'Art thou alive, Matilda?' And the Countess, hearing her husband's voice, replied, 'Yes, my dear lord, I am alive, and my children are also alive.' Overjoyed at this answer, the impatient Count bade his servants break open the door, the key not being at hand, he rushing into the bathing-room, fell down at the feet of his injured lady, bedewed her unpolluted hands with the tears of repentance, led her and the charming pledges of her innocence and love out of the dreary place of execution to her own apartment, and heard from her own mouth the true account of these transactions. Enraged at the foul calumny and the shameful sacrifice of his infants, he issued orders to apprehend and shut up the treacherous nurse in the bath—The fire now burned kindly,— the chimney roared,—the flames played aloft in the air,—and soon stewed out the diabolical woman's black soul.

SOURCE: Beckford, William. "Nymph of the Fountain." In *Gothic Tales of Terror, Volume One: Classic Horror Stories from Great Britain*, edited by Peter Haining. 1972. Reprint edition, pp. 138-75. Baltimore, Md.: Penguin Books Inc., 1973.

you entered another gallery,—filled with curious works of art and precious cabinets. Through all these suites—through all these galleries—did we roam and wander—too often hand in hand— strains of music swelling forth at intervals— sometimes the organ—sometimes concerted pieces—in which three of the greatest singers then in Europe—Pacchierotti, Tenducci, and Rauzzini— for a wonder of wonders—most amicably joined. Sometimes a chaunt was heard—issuing, no one could devine from whence—innocent affecting sounds—that stole into the heart with a bewitching languour and melted the most beloved the most susceptible of my fair companions into tears. Delightful indeed were these romantic wanderings—delightful the straying about this little interior world of exclusive happiness surrounded by lovely beings, in all the freshness of their early bloom, so fitted to enjoy it. Here, nothing was dull or vapid—here, nothing ressembled in the least the common forms and usages, the 'train-train' and routine of fashionable existence—all was essence—the slightest approach to sameness was here untolerated—monotony of every kind was banished. Even the uniform splendour of gilded roofs—was partially obscured by the vapour of wood aloes ascending in wreaths from cassolettes placed low on the silken carpets in porcelain salvers of the richest japan. The delirium of delight into which our young and fervid bosoms were cast by such a combination of seductive influences may be conceived but too easily. Even at this long, sad distance from these days and nights of exquisite refinements, chilled by age, still more by the coarse unpoetic tenor of the present disenchanting period—I still feel warmed and irradiated by the recollections of that strange, necromantic light which Loutherbourg had thrown over what absolutely appeared a realm of Fairy, or rather, perhaps, a Demon Temple deep beneath the earth set apart for tremendous mysteries—and yet how soft, how genial was this quiet light. Whilst the wretched world without lay dark, and bleak, and howling, whilst the storm was raging against our massive walls and the snow drifting in clouds, the very air of summer seemed playing around us—the choir of low-toned melodious voices continued to sooth our ear, and that every sense might in turn receive its blandishment tables covered with delicious viands and fragrant flowers—glided forth, by the aid of mechanism at stated intervals, from the richly draped, and amply curtained recesses of the enchanted precincts. The glowing haze investing every object, the mystic look, the vastness, the intricacy of this vaulted labyrinth occasioned so bewildering an effect that it became impossible for any one to define—at the moment—where he stood, where he had been, or to whither he was wandering—such was the confusion—the perplexity so many illuminated storys of infinitely varied apartments gave rise to. It was, in short, the realization of romance in its most extravagant intensity. No wonder such scenery inspired the description of the Halls of Eblis. I composed *Vathek* immediately upon my return to town thoroughly embued with all that passed at Fonthill during this voluptuous festival.

It will be seen that the Khalifeh's adventures were written down, not at the age of seventeen as Lord Byron has chosen to fancy, but at the age of twenty and two.

TITLE COMMENTARY

Vathek

THE ENGLISH REVIEW (REVIEW DATE SEPTEMBER 1786)

SOURCE: A review of *The History of Caliph Vathek: An Arabian Tale,* by William Beckford. *The English Review* 8 (September 1786): 180-84.

In the following excerpt, the critic offers a negative assessment of Vathek, *faulting principally its morality.*

We are told in the preface to [*Vathek*], "that it is translated from a manuscript, which, with some others of a similar kind, was collected in the East by a man of letters, and communicated to the editor above three years ago." In an age that has abounded so much with literary impostures, we confess that we cannot see the propriety of such a palpable fiction. The general strain of the work, and the many allusions to modern authors, indicate the author to be an European.

As an imitation of Arabian tales, this work possesses no in considerable merit. The characters are strongly marked, though carried beyond nature; the incidents are sufficiently wild and improbable; the magic is solemn and awful, though sometimes horrid; anachronisms and inconsistencies frequently appear; and the catastrophe is bold and shocking. The chief defect of the work arises from the moral, which is the foundation of the tale, and tinctures the whole. Indolence and childishness are represented as the source of happiness; while ambition and the desire of knowledge, so laudable and meritorious when properly directed, are painted in odious colours, and punished as crimes. The most formidable foes of princes, especially oriental princes, are indolence and the love of pleasure; and those passions that put the powers of the soul in motion, and lead to brilliant actions, though sometimes misapplied, are always respectable. . . .

The moral which is here conveyed, that ignorance, childishness, and the want of ambition, are the sources of human happiness, though agreeable to the strain of eastern fiction, is inconsistent with true philosophy, and with the nature of man. The punishments of vice, and the pains of gratified curiosity, ought never to be confounded. Although the *tree of knowledge* was once forbidden, in the present condition of humanity it is the *tree of life*.

The notes which are subjoined to this history contain much oriental learning, and merit the attention of the curious reader.

E. F. BLEILER (ESSAY DATE 1966)

SOURCE: Bleiler, E. F. "William Beckford and *Vathek.*" In *Three Gothic Novels*: The Castle of Otranto, Vathek, The Vampyre, edited by E. F. Bleiler, pp. xix-xxx. New York: Dover Publications, Inc., 1966.

In the following excerpt, Bleiler provides details from Beckford's life and on the composition and publication of Vathek.

In October 1817, Samuel Rogers the poet happened to be not too far from Salisbury, when he received an invitation to visit Fonthill Abbey, the home of the eccentric millionaire and author William Beckford. Fonthill Abbey was surely the most remarkable building in England at the time, and a contemporary letter by Lady Bessborough describes Rogers's impressions:

> He was received [at the thirty-eight-foot-high doors, which were opened] by a dwarf, who, like a crowd of servants thro' whom he passed, was covered with gold and embroidery. Mr. Beckford received him very courteously, and led him thro' numberless apartments all fitted up most splendidly, one with Minerals, including precious stones; another the finest pictures; another Italian bronzes, china, etc. etc., till they came to a Gallery that surpass'd all the rest from the richness and variety of its ornaments. It seem'd clos'd by a crimson drapery held by a bronze statue, but on Mr. B.'s stamping and saying, 'Open!' the Statue flew back, and the Gallery was seen, extending 350 feet long. At the end an open Arch with a massive balustrade opened to a vast Octagon Hall, from which a window shew'd a fine view of the Park. On approaching this it proved to be the entrance of the famous tower—higher than Salisbury Cathedral [over 285 feet]; this is not finish'd, but great part is done. The doors, of which there are many, are violet velvet covered over with

ABOUT THE AUTHOR

AN EARLY REVIEW OF *VATHEK*

The editor in the Preface to [*Vathek*] informs us, that it is translated from an unpublished Arabian Manuscript, which was put into his hands about three years ago, with some more of the same kind, by a gentleman who had collected them during his travels in the East. How far the above assertion is founded in truth, it may not be easy, nor is it material, to determine. If it be not a translation, the author has, at least, shewn himself, generally speaking, well acquainted with the customs of the East, and has introduced a sufficient quantity of the marvellous, an absolutely necessary ingredient to enable the work to pass muster as an Arabian Tale. It however differs from the generality of them, in this, that it inculcates a moral of the greatest importance, viz. That the pursuit of unlawful pleasures, and such as are repugnant to the principles of religion and morality, unavoidably leads us to misfortunes in this life, and misery in the next; and that the enjoyment resulting from them is at best but precarious and nugatory. . . .

Such is the scope of this tale, which, whether it be the produce of Arabia, or of the fertile banks of the Seine, (which a variety of circumstances induces us to believe it is) from the eagerness of mankind to admire whatever o'ersteps the limits of nature, and hurries us into the regions of fancy, bids fair to acquire that popularity which the moral it inculcates well deserves.

SOURCE: A review of *The History of Caliph Vathek: An Arabian Tale*, by William Beckford. *European Magazine and London Review* 10 (August 1786): 102-04.

purple and gold embroidery. They pass'd from hence to a Chapel, where on the alter were heaped Golden Candlesticks, Vases, and Chalices studded over with jewels; and from there into a great musick room, where Mr. Beckford begg'd Mr. Rogers to rest till refreshments were ready, and began playing with such *unearthly* power. . . . They went on to what is called the refectory, a large room built on the model of Henry 7 Chapel, only the ornaments gilt, where a Verdantique table was loaded with gilt plate fill'd with every luxury invention could collect. They next went into the Park with a numerous Cortege, and Horses and Servants, etc., which he described as equally wonderful, from the beauty of the trees and shrubs, and manner of arranging them, thro' a ride of five miles . . . and came to a beautiful Romantick lake, transparent *as liquid Chrysolite* (this is Mr. Rogers's, not my expression), covered with wildfowl. . . . [On the next day Mr. Rogers] was shewn thro' another suite of apartments fill'd with fine medals, gems, enamell'd miniatures, drawings, old and modern, curios, prints and Manuscripts, and last a fine and well-furnish'd library, all the books richly bound and the best editions, etc. etc. An Old Abbe, the Librarian, and Mr. Smith, the water-colour painter, who were there, told him there were 60 fires always kept burning, except in the hottest weather. Near every chimney in the sitting rooms there were large Gilt fillagree baskets fill'd with perfum'd coals that produc'd the brightest flame.

The creator and ruler of this almost unbelievable Gothic empire of some six thousand landscaped acres, a huge cathedral-like building with the highest tower in England, to say nothing of a fifteen-mile-long outer wall, twelve feet high and topped with spikes, was of course William Beckford (1760-1844), the author of ***Vathek***.

Beckford was the only legitimate son of William Beckford the Elder, an important political and mercantile figure of the day. Pitt's lieutenant and John Wilkes's friend, the elder Beckford had been Lord Mayor of London twice. Licentious, colorful, shrewd yet reckless, he was the firebrand of the Whig opposition. He was also probably the richest man in England, with a family cloth business, extensive property holdings in England, and a fortune in government bonds. A West Indian by birth, he was also one of the largest land and slave owners in Jamaica. As later events proved during the lifetime of his son, this wealth was not all honestly gained. He died in 1770, when his son was ten years old.

The Lord Mayor obviously planned to mould his son into an empire builder. Young William was brought up bilingually on English and French, started Latin at six, and Greek and philosophy at ten. Italian, Spanish, Portuguese, law, physics, and other sciences were added at seventeen. His tutors were selected from the best practitioners in various fields. Foremost among them was young Wolfgang Mozart, who gave him piano lessons while in England. In his old age Beckford claimed to have given the tune "Non più andrai" to Mozart in their childhood; he also claimed that Mozart had written him telling him that he planned to use it in *The Marriage of Figaro*. Unfortunately, since no trace of this correspondence has survived, the whole story is very suspect.

The senior Beckford's plans did not work out. It was true that young William was precociously intelligent, very gifted verbally, musically and artistically, and a handsome and appealing child. He certainly had many qualities which might have carried out his father's hopes. But he was also emotionally unbalanced, passionate, haughty, vindictive, and a thoroughgoing hedonist. He did not care about manipulating men in his father's way; he simply bought them, as needed, with his enormous fortune. Politics meant little to him, and in later life he became an M.P. mostly to protect his own interests at Fonthill. Worst of all, from his father's point of view, he was either not interested in business or had no aptitude at all for it; money to him was simply something that flowed in and could be used to buy pleasures.

Another facet of his personality that emerged when he was very young was an escapism focused on the Near East. He devoured *The Arabian Nights* and its imitations, and gathered together everything that he could about the Moslem world. All through his later life, no matter where he travelled, no matter what he was doing, the magic world of medieval Islam encompassed him. While this interest may have been fostered by his Orientalist art tutor, Alexander Cozens, perhaps a deeper reason lay within his own personality; Beckford often referred to himself as a Caliph, and where better than in the whimsical, irresponsible world of the fictional Harun al-Rashid could he find his dreams made real?

Beckford's early life was scandalous, even by eighteenth-century standards. His early maturity followed a pattern: he could remain in England for only short periods of time, for scandal soon would mount so high that his family would be forced to ship "the fool of Fonthill" to the Continent until things could cool off. During this period he took his cousin's wife as a mistress. This caused a family schism, but the situation was made worse when it was discovered that this was mostly a tactic to establish a homosexual relationship with young "Kitty" Courtenay. On the Continent, he travelled with such magnificence (including musicians and artists) that his entourage was at times taken for the Austrian Emperor's. Such ostentation he could well afford, for during the 1780's he had a fortune of about a million pounds and a yearly income of one hundred and fifty thousand pounds, both of which figures should be multiplied by twelve, in most areas, to indicate their present purchasing power. Attracted by the wealth, the worst adventurers from the stews of Venice became his intimates, and the shadiest circles of Paris and Naples knew him well.

Around the end of 1781 Beckford became acquainted with Samuel Henley, who was to be his collaborator on *Vathek*. Henley, who was currently tutoring cousins of Beckford's at Harrow, had been professor of moral philosophy at William and Mary in Virginia, but as a Tory had returned to England at the Revolution. Although his personal life was not the most reputable, he was in orders, was a very competent scholar, and had some pretensions to being an Orientalist. Beckford first employed him to edit *Dreams, Waking Thoughts and Incidents,* which was based on Beckford's travels in Spain and Portugal. The book was prepared for the press, was printed, and ready to be distributed in 1783 when Beckford's family forced the book to be suppressed. It is not known why the family took such violent measures, since the book is harmless enough, but it has been suggested that it was too frivolous for a future ruler of empire. Just what Henley contributed is also not exactly known.

Some time early in 1782 Beckford began to work on his Arabian tale, *Vathek.* In his old age, he claimed to have written it in three days and two nights, but references in his letters indicate that the book took considerably longer, perhaps three or four months. On April 25th he referred to it as "going on prodigiously," and by the end of May it was finished.

Beckford wrote his novel in French, and then decided to translate it. He was dissatisfied with his own translation, however, considering it too Gallic. He then recruited Henley to help him. For the next couple of years, while Beckford flitted back and forth between England and the Continent, the two men worked on it desultorily.

In 1783 the scandal with "Kitty" Courtenay was on the point of breaking disastrously. Beckford's family seems to have feared a criminal prosecution, and persuaded him to marry and beget a couple of children. In this year he married Lady Margaret Gordon, by whom he had two children before her death in May 1786. In 1784 he returned to Paris, where in addition to moving in high social circles he became involved in the shabby occultism that surrounded the court. In the same year, back in England, he became a Member of Parliament, was proposed for a baronage, but was rejected, presumably because of his personal life.

By the spring of 1785 *Vathek* was basically finished, except for notes which Henley was to provide, and four nouvelles (the Episodes) which Beckford planned to insert in the framework of the story. These were still incomplete. In June 1785 Beckford left for Switzerland, leaving both the French and English manuscripts of *Vathek* with Henley, who wanted to continue work on them. In February 1786 Beckford may have begun to suspect that Henley was moving too fast, for he baldly ordered him not to publish: "The Publication of *Vathec* must be suspended at least another year. I would not have him on any account precede the French edition . . . the Episodes to *Vathec* are nearly finished, and the whole thing will be completed in eleven to twelve months."

In the first week of June 1786, however, *The History of the Caliph Vathek, An Arabian Tale from an Unpublished Manuscript, with Notes Critical and Explanatory* appeared on the London bookstalls. Henley had broken faith. Beckford did not learn of publication for several months, but was understandably furious at Henley's breach of confidence. He raged at Henley, who replied disingenuously that he thought Beckford wanted the book published. He also referred adroitly to the scandal that had caused Beckford's marriage, and hinted that his association with Beckford was really an attestation of faith in him.

Henley unquestionably acted badly, but it is difficult to understand why he risked alienating a wealthy and powerful patron. Greed for money may have motivated him, or perhaps (since it is known that he felt proprietary toward the English *Vathek*) he feared that *Vathek* would follow the way of *Dreams, Waking Thoughts and Incidents* and never see publication. Needless to say, his actions led to a breach with Beckford, who never forgave him. Henley spent the rest of his life in poverty, making a poor living at teaching, hack writing, and editing. Beckford even had the satisfaction of rejecting an appeal for financial help. Henley died in 1815.

The further history of *Vathek* is confused, since soon after Henley's English translation appeared, two French language editions were published, one at Lausanne, the other at Paris. It used to be believed that Beckford had rushed the Lausanne edition into print from his original manuscript, and then, recognizing that it needed improvement, had corrected his text and reissued it at Paris. Now, however, the situation is believed to have been more complex. According to the modern reconstruction of events, Beckford had no copy of his French manuscript, which may

have been lost in the mails or retained by Henley. Beckford thereupon obtained a copy of the English book and hired Jean-David Levade, a hack translator, to turn it back into French. This version of *Vathek* was published at Lausanne; Beckford apparently did not see it until it was printed. When he saw it, he recognized that it was unworthy of him. He invoked the help of French literary friends, and set about retranslating it himself. This translation was then published at Paris. In 1815 Beckford prepared a third, revised French edition, which also appeared in Paris.

The text of *Vathek,* too, has presented problems. Four stories, told by denizens of Hell whom Vathek met in the halls of Iblis, were to have been inserted in the framework. Beckford spoke of working on them, but after the appearance of Henley's translation, he seems to have put them aside. They remained a legend during Beckford's lifetime, and as the novel rose in critical estimation, many persons asked to see them, including Lord Byron. But Beckford would not show them to anyone, and after a time it came to be believed that they had never existed at all.

At the turn of the present century, however, three French manuscripts were found in a document chest in the possession of one of Beckford's collateral descendants, the Duke of Hamilton. These manuscripts turned out to be the two long stories, **"The Story of Prince Alasi and the Princess Firouzkah"** and **"The Story of Prince Barkiarokh,"** as well as a fragment entitled **"The Story of the Princess Zulkaïs and the Prince Kalilah."** These three stories, which are in the same vein as *Vathek,* were published in French and in Sir Frank Marzials's English translation from 1909 to 1912.

. . . . .

III

Beckford's *Vathek* is almost universally recognized as a minor work of genius and as the best Oriental tale in English, but paradoxically there is strong doubt whether *Vathek* really should be placed in the stream of English literature. It was written in French, and all its major predecessors and sources were French. In English literature it stands isolated; it had no real forerunners and no worthy successors.[1]

The development of the Oriental tale in the eighteenth century was overwhelmingly a French phenomenon. Its manifestations in other languages, such as in the work of Gozzi and Wieland, are obviously derivative and of secondary importance. The genre began with Galland's French translation of *The Thousand and One Nights* (1704-1712), which was received with delight and enthusiasm. There had been earlier Oriental material in Italian and French, it is true, but none of this had the overwhelming power that *The Thousand and One Nights* demonstrated. These stories appealed strongly to the Rococo mind, what with the wide range of opportunities they offered: delicacies of style, elaboracies of construction, adventure, eroticism, moralism, sensibility, fantasy, philosophy and irony.

Many great authors contributed to the development of the Oriental tale in France. There were Voltaire's *contes philosophiques* (*Zadig, La Princesse de Babylone,* etc.), Montesquieu's satire on French institutions (*Lettres persanes*), and the humorous half-parodies of Caylus (*Contes orientales*) and Count Anthony Hamilton (*Les quatre Facardins,* etc.). There were also many collections of less distinguished stories imitating *The Arabian Nights,* but which were simply more or less successful thrillers. T. S. Gueullette, for example, wrote collections of Chinese tales, Moghul tales, Tartarian tales, and even Peruvian tales, all of which provided dreary imitations of Galland's spirited translation. At one time, during the last part of the eighteenth century, a compilation of such "Arabian" material was published; entitled *Cabinet des fées,* it runs to several hundred volumes.

In English literature the Oriental tale is far less important. It remained a half-subliminal form, sometimes used as a vehicle for criticism; sometimes as an embodiment for a moral sentiment or an allegory; sometimes as a frame for an essay, as with Addison; and sometimes even as a story for its own sake. Goldsmith's *Citizen of the World* and Johnson's *Rasselas* are the only members of the form that survive at all (except *Vathek*), and there seems little else that deserves to live, with the possible exception of certain of Dr. Hawkesworth's stories. Most Oriental material is poverty-stricken in both idea and execution.

Beckford's contribution lies in the imagination that he brought to a basically dull genre. He was successful in regaining the sense of wonder that permeated the original Islamic stories. His was a recreation of the Gothicism of Islam, a cultural milieu as medieval as the European Gothicism of Walpole and his contemporaries. Beckford created afresh the Magic culture in its most delightful as well as its most horrific form.

Vathek is a skilfully plotted, amusing story, pervaded with a strong feeling for irony and a sense of the ludicrous that emerges from even the sinister activities of the mad caliph and his frenzied companions. The story is original with Beckford, for no Islamic sources have ever been found, although there does seem to have been a Caliph Watik. What parallels exist between *Vathek* and other works of literature are mostly of French origin. Yet part of his story he found very close at hand. Carathis, as his contemporaries recognized, is the image of his mother; Nouronihar is probably based on his mistress and cousin, Mrs. Peter Beckford, who shared impiety, lust and stupidity with Nouronihar; and Vathek is obviously and admittedly Beckford himself in his headlong quest for new sensation, new beauty, and peace. A forewarning of Vathek is to be found in one of the dreams reported in Beckford's *Dreams, Waking Thoughts and Incidents*: "I hurried to bed, and was soon lulled asleep by the storm. A dream bore me off to Persepolis; and led me thro' vast subterraneous treasures to a hall, where Solomon, methought, was holding forth on their vanity." Equally, the domains of Vathek came to be represented in Fonthill, and just as Walpole's *Castle of Otranto* is the embodiment of a building, *Vathek* is a man, a building, and a mode of thought all remarkably hypostatized as a novel.

Note

1. M. G. Lewis, who shared with Beckford the characteristics of great wealth, West Indian possessions, moral turpitude, and a taste for the marvelous, and the young George Meredith are the only authors who seem to have produced even entertaining work in this tradition immediately after Beckford. The Oriental ethnographic novel of Thomas Hope, James Morier and Meadows Taylor was a different phenomenon, with roots in both the picaresque novel and Sir Walter Scott.

FREDERICK S. FRANK (ESSAY DATE 1990)

SOURCE: Frank, Frederick S. "The Gothic *Vathek*: The Problem of Genre Resolved." In Vathek *and the Escape from Time: Bicentenary Revaluations,* edited by Kenneth W. Graham, pp. 152-72. New York: AMS, 1990.

In the following essay, Frank argues for the placement of Vathek *within the Gothic tradition.*

This short essay investigates the problem of genre or genres in Beckford's *Vathek.*[1] The paper develops an argument for a Gothic *Vathek*, a work that is structurally, thematically, and symbolically in harmony with the central motifs of an emergent Gothic tradition. The critical argument is built upon four propositions about the generic characteristics of Beckford's orientalized Gothic novel, those features of form and theme which *Vathek* shares in common with other Gothic examples taken from the period. The four Gothic aspects that I want to examine are: first, the pattern of the demonic quest or perverse pilgrimage, a Gothic version of the long and dark voyage of the hero; second, the physical and psychological nature of the protagonist, since I want to argue that Vathek himself is an early manifestation of the heroic villainy so characteristic of the Gothic novel's tormented tormentor, those towering and terrifying beings who have risked all for evil or those "grand, ungodly, godlike"[2] men who can slay with the eye or paralyze with the voice or immobilize their victims in other unusual ways; third, the preference of the characters for diminishing enclosures and similar forms of architectural sequestration as denoted by such Gothic locales as towers, grottos, caverns, contracting corridors, and subterranean theatres of hellish anguish; and finally, the evocation of a hypothetically malignant cosmos, an ontologically unreliable and ambiguously deceiving Gothic universe in which all moral norms are inverted or twisted, where disorder is far more likely than order, and where universal darkness can bury all without warning and at any moment.

If we take the metaphoric aspects of *Vathek* seriously, the novel makes its statement about God, the self, and the world in a speculative manner similar to other models of high Gothic fiction. Like other Gothic writers active at the end of the eighteenth century, Beckford uses his own Gothic novel to confront the moral ambiguities of an inexplicable universe; nor can we overlook the fact that Beckford ends *Vathek* with an austere moral concerning nothing less than "the condition of man upon earth."[3] *Vathek's* Gothic, like other varieties of Gothic within the genre, certainly does amuse and entertain us, and no one would want to overlook the role of the ludicrous in Beckford's Gothic text. But the risible diversion of the reader is not always its sole aim or end. Gothics such as *Vathek* are also concerned with matters of first and final causation as well as fundamental issues of existence. Furthermore, Gothics such as *Vathek* project a disquieting *Weltanschauung* and by so doing, they engage us in final questions by displaying for the reader a world in which evil is stronger than good, instability more probable than stability, and unnatural passions closer to the true core of human behavior than the calm control of the intellect. Inquisitive characters in Gothic fiction (the inordinately curious caliph Vathek is a prime example) are forced to ask their questions and seek their answers in a sort of intellectual vacuum without the support of stable value systems to affirm any answers their quest might lead them to. Symbolically speaking, they must move through a landscape of collapsed ego-ideals wherein the older symbols of authority, secular and divine, lie everywhere in ruin. Beckford's characters, like the entrapped casts of other Gothic novels, are never free, although they may delude themselves with the dream of freedom by their sensual and sadistic conduct. At issue throughout *Vathek,* as one pro-Gothic reader of the novel has stated it, is the "contradiction between the illusion of man's freedom and the reality of his imprisonment in a necessitarian universe."[4]

From the advantageous retrospective of literary history, *Vathek* can be studied as a prototype of the subjective and subversive Gothic tendencies in the late eighteenth century which were beginning to challenge and displace an exhausted classicism and a moribund rationalism in the arts. The Gothic novel attained its astounding preeminence (in the form of literally thousands of horrid titles) in the late 1790s in the maiden-centered romances of Mrs. Radcliffe and the outrageous supernaturalism of Lewis's *The Monk*. Nearly four decades separate *Vathek* from the masterworks of Gothicism, Mary Shelley's *Frankenstein* (1818), Maturin's *Melmoth the Wanderer* (1820), and James Hogg's *Confessions of a Justified Sinner* (1824). But at the beginnings of the Gothic movement, Beckford's *Vathek* enjoyed the unique status of being a model for the emergent energies of the Gothic. Yet, the *Vathek* of 1786 has no close literary equivalent, unless the irrational itself be denominated a genre. Preceding *Vathek* were several narrative experiments important to recognize in summarizing the rise of the Gothic genre: Thomas Leland's *Longsword, Earl of Salisbury* (1762); Horace Walpole's *Castle of Otranto* (1764); Clara Reeve's *Old English Baron* (1777). Leland's *Longsword,* an elaborately plotted romance of chivalry set in an imaginary Middle Ages, contained both the quest and a panorama of grandly gloomy architectural settings. Walpole's *Otranto* supernaturalized the sinister properties of Gothic architecture and added the pursuing hero-villain and the fleeing maiden as they performed their violent minuet in "the long labyrinth of darkness,"[5] the basement of the haunted castle. Clara Reeve relaxed and normalized the irrational atmosphere already associated with the new genre, but she also cleverly installed a forbidden chamber within the castle, thus donating a mandatory fixture to the Gothic interior. At the climax of *Vathek,* we have an enlarged version of Clara Reeve's chamber of horrors. These romances were the only available Gothic models when Beckford sat down to compose his *Vathek.* Beckford was very much aware of these Gothic contemporaries and conscious too of the rational malaise that had generated their Gothic endeavors. The Gothics of Leland, Walpole, and Reeve had challenged the efficacy of rationalism both as an outlook and a response to existence. In its abhorrence of limits and its repudiation of a meaningful universe, the Gothic *Vathek* of Beckford is an extension of the darkening vision of these first Gothics.

The first reviewers of *Vathek* found no difficulty in assigning Gothic traits to the work. *The English Review* for 1786, to choose just one instance, discussed *Vathek* in terms of vigorous extremes and grotesque energy. "The characters," noted the reviewer, "are strongly marked though carried beyond nature; the incidents are sufficiently wild and improbable; the magic is solemn and awful, though sometimes horrid; anachronisms and inconsistencies frequently appear; and the catastrophe is bold and shocking."[6] The sadistic absurdities and diabolical climax aroused the moral fury of the reviewer of the 1834 edition. Writing in *The Southern Literary Messenger,* the reviewer denounced the novel's Gothic qualities as "obscene and blasphemous in the highest degree. . . . We should pronounce it, without knowing anything of Mr. Beckford's character, to be the production of a sensualist and an infidel—one who could riot in the most abhorred and depraved conceptions—and whose prolific fancy preferred as its repast all that was diabolical and monstrous, rather than what was beautiful and good."[7]

Modern criticism of *Vathek,* however, has tended to dismiss or ignore the novel's affinities with "the monstrous and diabolical" currents of Gothicism in order to stress Beckford's predisposition to irony and his cynical undercutting of *Vathek*'s carefully built moods of terror. With the exception of the conclusion of the quest far down within the fiery Hall of Eblis, *Vathek,* is viewed as a work which shows so much vacillation between hilarity and horror that to call it Gothic in any sense is to misrepresent its literary essence and its generic category. The anti-Gothic view is expressed by one of the best twentieth-century editors of *Vathek,* who believes that any concession to Gothic responses would deny Beckford's comic purposes. "There was nothing in *Vathek,*" Roger Lonsdale assures us, "which obliged reviewers to connect it with contemporary 'Gothic' tendencies in the novel. It is not easy to see that *Vathek* sets out to exploit the imaginative terror, the suspense of psychological shock tactics which were entering the English novel about this time."[8] The case against a Gothic *Vathek* gathers additional impetus from the opinions of R. D. Hume and Frederick Garber, two sympathetic and perceptive interpreters of Gothic fiction. Garber, who has edited Mrs. Radcliffe's *The Italian* (1797) and written many incisive commentaries on the place of the Gothic in literary history, nevertheless can find no place for *Vathek* in the annals of Gothicism. Writes Garber: "*Vathek* has been called a counterpart of the Gothic but it shows none of that calculated fuzziness through which the Gothic exposed the uncertainty of our daily perceptions of experience."[9] And R. D. Hume, whose 1969 *PMLA* essay, "Gothic Versus Romantic: A Revaluation of the Gothic Novel," is something of a landmark in the debate over the Gothic genre's crucial importance and its growing scholarly respectability, finds *Vathek* to be too flippant, ironic, and burlesque in tone to merit a Gothic classification. Writes Hume: "*Vathek* is often treated as a Gothic novel on the grounds that it exploits horror and magic scenery in *Schauer-Romantik* fashion. Yet I must agree with the work's recent editor that *Vathek* is not centrally of the Gothic type. Its horrors reach the point of burlesque, and its continual return to a detached and even comic tone set it apart."[10] For Hume, and his position may be regarded as the orthodox position on *Vathek*'s Gothicism, the work is best comprehended within the subgenres of comedy such as farce, burlesque, and harlequinade, "a dark-tinged but high spirited comedy" and "an existential crisis defused by comic exaggeration."[11]

Beckford shares with other early Gothic writers a paradoxical sense of the chaotic whereby images of former order are demonically reversed. Thus, it is Satan (or Eblis, as the archfiend is called in the Muhammadan tradition) who is the prime mover and highest authority in *Vathek*'s anarchic and nihilistic universe; the unspeakably repulsive becomes the attractive or the hilarious blurs into the hideous; the infernal replaces the celestial as the objective of the quester's journey; and the desire for damnation supplants salvation as the pilgrim soul's sharpest desire. These bizarre inversions directly connect *Vathek* with some major Gothic themes found in other specimens of Gothicism from Walpole's *Otranto* to Maturin's *Melmoth.* After consciously choosing evil, Beckford's Satanic hero makes a first voyage of no return in his profane quest for an infernal Xanadu. In the dark voyage of the hero may be seen a composite of Gothic motifs: a displacement of soul and loss of self which the hero attempts to counter by a descent to the lower depths; the hero's mounting awareness of the futility of spiritual values and the pointlessness of human wisdom and intelligence; realization of a universe controlled by a fiendish deity devoted to man's confusion and despair; the Faustian problem of the overreacher's limitless desire in a limited cosmos; and the ridiculousness of suffering as symbolized by the proximity of pleasure and pain in many of Vathek's adventures en route to hell.

The mythic and philosophic elements of the Gothic outlook first converge in the physical and psychological aspects of Vathek himself, a model Gothic protagonist. Whether he be a debauched monk, rapist nobleman, cruel count, ferocious brigand, or malicious caliph, the Gothic villain is a two-sided personality, a figure of great power and latent virtue whose chosen career of evil is the result of a clash between his passionate nature and the unnatural restraints of conventions, orthodoxy, and tradition. Moreover, Vathek is the first Gothic villain whose moral and physical features are given in detail. Vathek's predecessor, Manfred, in *The Castle of Otranto*, is barely described at all and one looks in vain for any lavish description of the hideous Gothic face and frame, always a landmark passage in later varieties of the Gothic. But in the makeup of Beckford's caliph, we find the progenitor of almost every single later Gothic villain, for Vathek's Satanic personality is inscribed in his face and single overwhelming eye. The lethal optic, like Vathek's private tower, is an image of absolute and pernicious power. It connotes his contempt for rational and mortal limits and functions as it will in later Gothic figures as a weapon of visionary penetration. Vathek is first introduced to the reader by way of the awesome eye: "His figure was pleasing and majestic; but when he was angry, one of his eyes became so terrible, that no person could bear to behold it; and the wretch upon whom it was fixed, instantly fell backward, and sometimes expired."[12] Vathek's deadly glance, the single eye that can maim or slay, is almost immediately transplanted to the Gothic features of Mrs. Radcliffe's Montoni and Schedoni, Lewis's Ambrosio, and attains its demonic zenith first in the blazing eyes of Melmoth the Wanderer and eventually in the ocular stimulus to madness in the "vulture eye" of the prostrate old man in Poe's "The Tell-Tale Heart." The Gothic eye which is frequently used to immobilize a reluctant maiden or to paralyze a rival heir to the castle originates with Beckford's caliph.

Complementing the ferocious and supernatural eye in the personage of Vathek is the character's passionate commitment to evil, the final stage of Faustian curiosity and ungratified sensuality. Vathek's passion for the supreme climb culminated by a haughty seclusion within a tower, or its reverse, the ultimate descent to the Palace of Subterranean Fire, are two images of perverted aspiration which give *Vathek* its model Gothic structure. Vathek's toweromania, or compulsion to elevate and isolate himself in contemptuous pride at some supreme pinnacle is counterpointed throughout the narrative by his excessive grottophilia, the impulse to descend to an ultimate darkness there to dwell eternally within a fiery abyss presided over by demons. Inspired by "an insolent curiosity of penetrating the secrets of heaven,"[13] Vathek transmits to the Gothic villains who come after him in the genre a powerful longing for absolutes in a universe devoid of such finalities. Atop one of his flaming towers, Vathek amuses himself with the mass strangulation of his subjects. In the depths of the earth at the opposite end of the novel's axis of Gothic action he joins the vast congregation of the damned upon seeing his breast become "transparent as crystal, his heart enveloped in flames."[14] The Gothic *Vathek* is the genre's first full-length portrait of a tormented tormentor, a metaphysical isolate and a monomaniac who thirsts to realize himself in evil.

Various examples of the Vathekian traits of future Gothic villains might be cited to demonstrate Beckford's major contribution to the making of the Gothic hero. Here, for example, is Count Rudiger of Frankheim, the hero of Monk Lewis's little known Gothic novella, *Mistrust: or, Blanche and Osbright*. When we first see this titanic villain, he is standing in an open grave glaring defiantly upward in a posture of mortal defiance. Note that Count Rudiger derives both the death-dealing eye and the fatal passion from *Vathek*. Those powerful emotions which would certainly prove fatal to any ordinary human being become a source of malignant strength for the Vathekian character who denounces life even as he seeks to triumph over it:

> His heart was the seat of agony; a thousand scorpions seemed every moment to pierce it with their poisonous stings; but not one tear forced itself into his bloodshot eyeballs; not the slightest convulsion of his gigantic limbs betrayed the silent tortures of his bosom. A gloom settled and profound reigned upon his dark and high-arched eyebrows. Count Rudiger's stature was colossal;

the grave in which he stood, scarcely rose above his knees. His eyes blazed; his mouth foamed; his coal-black hair stood erect, in which he twisted his hands, and tearing out whole handsful by the roots, he strewed them on the coffin, which stood beside his feet.[15]

If the character of the protagonist helps to identify the genre of *Vathek*, the hero's destination and his progressively frustrated experiences as he approaches his journey's end further define just how deeply Gothic the work is. Vathek's Gothic grail is nothing less than damnation for himself and those who accompany him in the voyage downward and inward to hell. The quest is demonic because it begins in torment, proceeds through heightened degrees of self-destruction, and climaxes in the hopeless horror of body and of soul for the disappointed quester. Unlike a traditional epic hero whose descent into the underworld takes him to his heroic limits and yields him a transcendent or victorious release from the darkness of self-doubt, Vathek's descending voyage ends in perplexity, guilt, and despair. Gifted with the power of perpendicular imagination, a necessary angle of vision for realizing the upper and lower limits of Gothic fantasy, Beckford conveys his hero along a vertical axis of exotic anguish and blue fire effects. Enroute to hell, Vathek and Nouronihar traverse an insular landscape rich in diabolical spectacle. Indeed, it is almost as if we were hearing descriptions of Dante's inferno as Laurence Sterne might have written them. The algolagnic terrain offers stairways spiraling downward to black depths of no return, Gothic pits containing chuckling ghouls who must be fed on live children, a pyramid of skulls nearly as high as the Gizeh monument, reptiles with human faces, toxic delicacies and idolatrous banquets consisting of "roasted wolf" vultures à la daube . . . rotten truffles; boiled thistles: and such other wild plants, as must ulcerate the throat and parch up the tongue,"[16] odd lights and bizarre beasts including an omnipresent squadron of vultures, flaming towers, and a kaleidoscopic subterranean amphitheatre in which Vathek's sorceress mother, Carathis, performs obscene rites amidst an ornate charnel decor to the accompaniment of a shrieking chorus of one-eyed negresses and burning mummies. Across quivering plains of black sand, through swarms of curious insects, past batallions of howling cripples and cubit-high dwarfs, into blizzards of burning snowflakes Vathek makes the Gothic's downward voyage of no return.

Vathek's precursor, the European Faust had sold his soul out of a desire for power and pleasure, but Beckford's Islamic Faust already possesses these and willingly renounces them to seek pain and damnation. One of the deepest and most enduring patterns of the Gothic quest which brings the ambitious character to the horror of horrors in an underground of no return is to be observed in Vathek's perverse pilgrimage. The Gothic hero's abhorrence for limits stimulates his Satanic vanity; his vanity expresses itself in a destructive pursuit of an ideal of horrid beauty typically depicted elsewhere throughout Gothic fiction by the maiden and villain performing their deadly duet of flight and pursuit through the subterranean passageways of a haunted building. The destructive pursuit of beauty culminates in spiritual and metaphysical frustration for Vathek thus implying an irrationally determined universe in which man is fixed as an eternal victim condemned to occupy forever some chamber of horrors. In Vathek's case, the destination is an "immense hall . . . where a vast multitude is incessantly passing"[17] in a never-ending parade of anguish.

The transcendental or epic hero often climaxes his quest by arriving at some vision of totality, but when Gothic heroes venture into the heart of darkness their experiences at the dead center often invert the conventional romance's pattern of achievement and self-fulfillment. From Beckford's Vathek to Melville's Captain Ahab, the Gothic hero is a frustrated quester whose pursuit of the absolute ends by condemning him to endless circuits '"round perdition's flame."[18] Gothic novels after *Vathek* adhere to the pattern of the ironic quest, a destructive version of the hero's long journey to a dark place which the Gothic hero makes not in order to rescue the maiden but to rape her.

The pro-Gothic reading of Beckford's strange novel enables us to recognize the motif of the dark, inward voyage as a characteristic of the genre at large. Gothic romances like *Vathek* mock the very form they feed on for they "retain the structure of romance, but invert the hero's progress. The result is a linear descent: aesthetically, from the Hill of the Pied Horses to the Hall of Eblis; psychologically, from wishfulfillment to frustration; and metaphysically, from a vision of humanity as unlimited potentiality to humanity as finite actuality in an alien world."[19] Other characters throughout the Gothic genre who decide to risk all for evil suffer the fate of Vathek in similar gruesome confinements of body and soul. In Gothic terms, the Eblis episode means a permanent condition of disunity between the self and nature, the self and society, and the self and God. At the end of the novel, we have entered the zone of ultimate cosmic discord intensified by the dreadful apprehension that the world is under the control of a demon and that there is "no exit." The imagery of death-in-life or life-in-death which typifies the high Gothic through such situations as premature burial, cadaverous enclosure, and lingering impalement attains its first full development in the descriptions of Vathek and company in the Hall of Eblis.

The final point to be made for a Gothic *Vathek* involves the way in which the work's atmosphere goes beyond comedy, irony, and wild disorder to evoke the theme of a malignant universe in which the imagination, always striving to be free of rational bounds, is repeatedly denied its goals. Freedom of mind is perpetually at issue throughout Gothic fiction, the physical flight and pursuit through avenues of darkness and the other forms of dreadful entrapment all indicating symbolically the imagination's containment by finite ideas and restrictive ideological structure. Beyond the buffoonery of *Vathek,* the theme of freedom is powerfully stated through Vathek's continuous contact with a world that continuously disappoints his suprarational desire to liberate himself from all mortal restraints. Each of his Gothic ordeals is a perverse universe's reminder to him of an invincible and limited reality impeding every effort of the imagination to break through rational defenses. This menace of limits which a malignant cosmos fixes upon its creatures of aspiring imagination is at the very core of *Vathek*'s Gothicism as well as a trait of the Gothic tradition at large, where characters constantly strive to be free but exist in bondage to some grotesque enclosure, be it a haunted castle or an arabesque Hades thronged with the damned in flaming heart postures. In her important treatise, "On the Pleasure Derived from Objects of Terror," (1792) Beckford's contemporary, the Gothic theorist Ann Letitia Aikin Barbauld, describes the degree of terror experienced when a character is confronted and overwhelmed by an unholy or perverse "otherness," as Vathek is each time he attempts to overreach the limits of self. Higher Gothic horror of the sort we encounter in the climactic scenes in the Hall of Eblis places *Vathek* in the highest category of the Gothic genre, the region of total ontological distress, where the mythology of the imaginative self as an agent of control gives way to the nightmare of a supreme and malignant "otherness" which cannot be escaped or transcended. The conditions of such an otherness are expressed by Mrs. Barbauld

as "Solitude, darkness, low-whispered sounds, obscure glimpses of objects, flitting forms [which] tend to raise in the mind that thrilling, mysterious terror which has for its object the 'powers unseen and mightier than we,'"[20] precisely the conditions which prevail at the frustrated terminus of Vathek's imaginative quest.

G. R. Thompson has written that "the Gothic romance is a genre that in its historical development, as well as in individual texts, moves from a stable modality of clearly defined conventions and forms toward an unstable and deliberately indeterminate modality. Frequently, the Gothic veers toward the grotesque, a mode of inherent instability that plays on the dissolution of norms— ontological, epistemological and aesthetic."[21] The Gothic *Vathek* is just such an apocalyptic narrative where the problem of genre can only be resolved by viewing the work as part of the energetic revolt against reason spearheaded by the dominance of the tale of terror during the closing decades of the eighteenth century. In the chaotic landscape of the Gothic tradition it stands like one of Beckford's infernal towers deep within the zone of ultimate Gothic fantasy where we find not just a destabilization of the norms cited by Thompson, but the dark universe's mockery of all human striving.

Notes

1. William Beckford, *Vathek*, ed. Roger Lonsdale (London: Oxford Univ. Press, 1970).

2. Herman Melville, *Moby Dick*, chapter 16 ("The Ship").

3. Beckford, *Vathek*, p. 120.

4. Kenneth W. Graham, "Beckford's 'Vathek': A Study in Ironic Dissonance," *Criticism*, 14 (1972), 252.

5. Horace Walpole, *The Castle of Otranto: A Gothic Story*, in *Three Gothic Novels*, ed. E. F. Bleiler, p. 36.

6. *English Review*, 8 (1786), 180-184.

7. *Southern Literary Messenger*, 1 (1834), 188-189.

8. Roger Lonsdale, Introduction to *Vathek* by William Beckford, pp. vii-xxxi.

9. Frederick Garber, "Beckford, Delacroix, and Byronic Orientalism," *Comparative Literature Studies*, 18 (1981), 321-332.

10. R. D. Hume, "Exuberant Gloom, Existential Agony, and Heroic Despair: Three Varieties of Negative Romanticism," in *The Gothic Imagination: Essays in Dark Romanticism*, ed. G. R. Thompson, pp. 109-117.

11. R. D. Hume, "Exuberant Gloom," p. 117.

12. Beckford, *Vathek*, p. 1.

13. Beckford, *Vathek*, p. 4.

14. Beckford, *Vathek*, p. 114.

15. Matthew G. Lewis, *Mistrust: or, Blanche and Osbright,* in *Seven Masterpieces of Gothic Horror,* ed. R. D. Spector, pp. 237-330.

16. Beckford, *Vathek,* p. 49.

17. Beckford, *Vathek,* p. 109.

18. Melville, *Moby Dick,* Chapter 36 ("The Quarter-Deck").

19. Randall Craig, "Beckford's Inversion of Romance in *Vathek,*" *Orbis Litterarum,* 39 (1984), 95-106.

20. Ann Letitia Aiken Barbauld, "On the Pleasure Derived from Objects of Terror," in *The Evil Image,* eds. Patricia L. Skarda and Nora Crow Jaffe, pp. 10-13.

21. G. R. Thompson, "The Form of Gothic Romance," a paper delivered at the Modern Language Association Meeting, Washington, DC, December 1984, pp. 1-26.

R. B. GILL (ESSAY DATE JANUARY 2003)

SOURCE: Gill, R. B. "The Author in the Novel: Creating Beckford in *Vathek.*" *Eighteenth-Century Fiction* 15, no. 2 (January 2003): 241-54.

In the following essay, Gill examines the authentic authorial persona in Vathek.

According to David Hume, "The mind is a kind of theatre where several perceptions successively make their appearance; pass, re-pass, glide away, and mingle in an infinite variety of postures and situations."[1] Hume's well-known account of personal identity aptly describes William Beckford—petulant heir to great wealth, a member of Parliament, connoisseur, architectural dilettante, fugitive from sexual scandal, and author of **Vathek,** one of the most enjoyable and intriguing of the eighteenth-century Oriental tales. Across the pages of **Vathek** and, indeed, of Beckford's whole life pass and mingle the successive actors of his disjointed identity.

Hume's caution to the reader is especially relevant in Beckford's case: "the comparison with theatre must not mislead us. They are the successive perceptions only, that constitute the mind; nor have we the most distant notion of the place, where these scenes are represented, or of the materials, of which it is compos'd." The spectators of Beckford's life and the readers of his tale have wished to know the materials of which his inner self was composed in order to explain his theatrics, but they have never agreed on what they found. And Beckford himself, complaining of the mask he wore, yet intent on preserving a gentlemanly image, a man unwillingly hastened by his family and his wealth from one performance to the next, seems never to have found that inner being with which he could be at peace. The result is that there are many Beckfords, some he himself created and many created by his various critics.

But these created selves are, to use Hume's terms for personal identity, "merely verbal" (p. 262). These verbal Beckfords are plots without a story, the texts he and we write in lieu of an anchoring identity. The problem in Beckford's case lies not so much in this textuality as in our desire (and his) to find the originating self of that text. The ambiguities surrounding Beckford prompt a search for biographical explanations. Yet

Beckford's personae within *Vathek* and his life are clearly created ones, even though they are offered as biographical fact. In this respect, Beckford's presence in the novel is typical of other authorial personae, artistic creations that paradoxically function properly only when taken as factual biography. But when that paradox tempts critics into the impossible task of locating the true self of the author, they find only what Hume notes is a mysterious and inexplicable fiction. *Vathek* is a clear case of a novel especially in need of a biographical centre to resolve its ambiguities.[2] Not finding that centre or authorial identity, critics (and Beckford himself) have created a number of identities to satisfy their own perceptions of the needs of the novel.

A straightforward Oriental tale whose quick narrative and polished style cover no depths of complex psychological characterization, *Vathek* would not seem to offer special problems of interpretation. Yet critical views of this novel vary widely. It has been seen as both Gothic and non-Gothic, satiric and non-satiric, realistic and fantastic, neoclassic and romantic, socially conventional and anti-bourgeois, metaphysical and messageless, as well as both unified and split in its sensibility. *Vathek* has been valued for its "correctness of costume," criticized for its elaborate explanatory notes, and, notably, regarded as moral, immoral, amoral, and "anti-moral."[3]

The diverse critical opinions arise in part from the intriguing mixture of opposites in Beckford's style. Whether we consider it Oriental or Gothic or whatever, *Vathek* is essentially the sort of fabular parable that the eighteenth-century reader enjoyed. It is thus outside the realistic mainstream that has come to represent for us the novel's most characteristic mode of addressing moral issues. And yet, on its surface at least, it is an explicitly moral parable. Consequently, there is difficulty for us, as there was for Beckford's contemporaries, in reconciling the fabular, Eastern exoticism of *Vathek* with its moral elements. Further, we cannot say of *Vathek,* as we can of *Candide* and *Rasselas,* that its imaginative centre lies in the moral message, for our interest in the perverse actions of the characters frequently jars with the conventional morals, particularly the closing moral that "the condition of man upon earth is to be— humble and ignorant."

There is an additional mixing of opposites in the self-conscious playfulness of Beckford's style. Like Sterne, Beckford watches himself write and is intrigued by the possibilities of expressing himself in guises—now moral, now perverse, now coy,

now sublime. He cannot resist indulging himself momentarily in some ludicrous or incongruous aspect of his material. The storks, for instance, that join the morning prayers of Nouronihar and Gulchenrouz by the lake are a poke at the solemnity of religious greybeards, but their incongruity as members of the worshipping congregation is so striking that it distracts attention from the narrative, an indulgence we enjoy as part of a highly self-referential style. Beckford is not willing to suppress these moments of self-conscious fun; *Vathek* smiles at its sardonic incongruities from the first paragraph to its closing moralisms.

Beckford uses authorial self-consciousness in the text of *Vathek* to remove himself from his occult material and thus to preserve, or create, an aura of sophistication and control. Here is no romantic subordination or merging of author with his outré creation, as we find in the works of Poe. Rather, *Vathek* is an eighteenth-century amalgam of Pope's proud epic notes in the *Dunciad* (a similarity Beckford recognized) and Sterne's sophisticated and intensely self-aware metafiction. Beckford wants us to observe him laughing at his subject, manipulating it: a gentleman engaged with compromising material but, nevertheless, in thorough control of it and able to smile knowingly at his own folly. In this mixture of opposites, *Vathek,* like many other neoclassical works, has a civilized sophistication that acknowledges its own role-playing.

In fact, Beckford cared greatly about the image of himself created in *Vathek.* In this respect the novel is a literary counterpart of Fonthill, the Gothic abbey on which he later lavished his efforts and money. On occasion he claimed, somewhat misleadingly, to have written the novel in several days in a fit of inspiration, and he romanticized about the "most extravagant intensity" of the Christmas celebration at Fonthill that formed part of the inspiration of the novel. Beckford's letters reveal that he was very much aware of the effect of his image on others—and that he enjoyed the thought. *Vathek* is "the only production of mine which I am not ashamed of" he wrote to Samuel Henley; and in a different letter he spoke of the "honours" with which he expected *Vathek* to be received. To another correspondent he wrote of "ma vanité" of the Caliph, and in the journal of his stay in Portugal he noted that he was "extremely impatient" to receive "the last monthly reviews in which I expect to read a critique on *Vathek.*" Cyrus Redding, his first biographer, recalled, "To abuse *Vathek* he deemed a personal insult. His pride took the alarm and he could scarcely restrain his anger, so fierce when aroused, though evanescent."[4]

The references in his letters to shame, honour, and pride reveal his characteristic concern with the relationship between his work and his reputation. Biographers often note the changes that Beckford made in his papers and letters in order that they appear most advantageous. Contemporaries of Beckford such as Mrs Thrale, William Hazlitt, and Byron understood the degree to which public appearance was involved in Beckford's effects and enjoyed the scandal that attended his reputation. A continuing motif in the Portuguese journal, written shortly after publication of *Vathek,* is Beckford's awareness that others are watching his carefully contrived self-image: "I hear there is no conversation in Lisbon but of my poetry." "My reputation as a devotee spreads prodigiously." Although he notes, "I am sick of forming the chief subject of conversation at all the card tables," he also takes care to record the surprise with which "the whole herd of precentors, priests, musicians and fencing masters" listen to his playing and singing. Again, "my singing, playing and capering subdues every Portuguese that approaches me." In preparation for a trip to a convent, he writes, "I am furbishing up a string of highly polished saintly speeches for the occasion." And later, "for flippery in crossing myself and goosishness in poking out my head I will turn my back to no one." Beckford, then, works carefully to create a persona; he attentively watches people react to that image; and he self-consciously distances himself from his creation through self-abnegating humour with such references as "flippery," "goosishness," and "capering."[5]

It is true that he grew restive with his public self. In one entry, after worrying about a possible scrape with a "young friend," he continues with the complaint often quoted by critics, "How tired I am of keeping a mask on my countenance. How tight it sticks—it makes me sore." Significantly, he immediately follows this complaint with self-conscious observation upon it: "There's a metaphor for you. I have all the fancies and levity of a child."[6] The ingredients of Beckford's dilemma are here—the concern with image, the restiveness, and the recurrent self-consciousness that flickers over his thoughts and actions. He does not remove his mask but worries, instead, about getting into a scrape. For all the restiveness, the image of himself that Beckford contrived to project was exterior: he was concerned with his public reputation, with the appurtenances of a gentlemanly and leisured class, with his adeptness in Oriental matters, and

with the skill of his style and of the "magnificence" with which *Vathek* concludes.

Yet that exterior image has never seemed sufficient or trustworthy, a circumstance that accounts for the central critical dilemma of *Vathek.* The novel's puzzling mixture of opposites invites the reader to seek an inner author, the "real" Beckford accessible through psychological examination. Behind the varying judgments of Beckford's novel lie critical assessments of his inner person. There are explanations that he was impotent, homosexual, bisexual, dominated by a Calvinist mother, grieving for his dead wife, a leisurely country gentleman, bitter, mad, vile, sadistic, a "barely socialized psychopath," and so on.[7] Without question, the novel is a document in Beckford's life, as biographically relevant as, say, his construction of Fonthill. Nor is Beckford the type of artist whose work rises self-contained and impersonal above its historical contingencies. *Vathek* is a minor novel, interesting in itself certainly, but also of legitimate interest as a record of the tastes of its author and age.

Nevertheless, for all the care and intelligence expended on it, the search for the inner, unifying Beckford has not been successful. Mme de Staël, to whom Beckford had given a copy of his travelogue *Dreams, Waking Thoughts and Incidents,* wrote to him, "You dream when you have nothing to describe. Imagination, which invents or represents objects, has never been given more freedom." Likewise, André Parreaux has noted that seeing "le vrai visage" of Beckford behind his mask is a matter of great difficulty. V.S. Pritchett claimed that "everything Beckford writes is suspect, for truth and fiction are hard to separate in this incessantly revising and play-acting autobiographer."[8] And that is the dilemma. The search for the interior Beckford seems a necessary step to reconciling the opposites in his life and work, but that search cannot lead us past the contrived and public mask it was Beckford's fate to wear.

For both practical and theoretical reasons, the inner Beckford cannot be found. First, it is important to bear in mind the well-known dangers of moving back and forth between biography and art. One need not be unduly afraid of the Intentional Fallacy or of its reverse, biography based on interpretation of the artist's works, to recognize the difficulties and dangers and, therefore, the need of great caution. Is Fielding the compassionate observer of the ambiguities of mercy in *Tom Jones* or the sterner remembrancer of justice in *Amelia*? And to what extent can we move from his actual experience as magistrate of the Bow Street police court to the more sombre judicial tone of that later novel?

But no matter how receptive we are to the intermingling of biography and art, we must allow for the great practical difficulties that interfere with our understanding of the relevant facts of Beckford's life. Beckford was born to a public family with the expectation and the means of creating and protecting an appropriate public image. There is evidence that the suppression of *Dreams, Waking Thoughts and Incidents* came as a result of family fears that its injudicious subjectivity might endanger a public career. "Neither Orlando nor Brandimart," he wrote of the matter, "were ever more tormented by Daemons and Spectres in an enchanted Castle than Wm. Bd. in his own Hall by his nearest relations."[9]

His marriage to Lady Margaret Gordon again seems the result of a family strategy, as was his short stay in Parliament. Lady Hamilton's vivid letter to Beckford in 1780 attempting to dissuade him from a scandalous liaison in Venice stresses the public image that Beckford's relations valued above all. What is the struggle against temptation for, she asks. "No less than *honor, reputation* and all that an honest and noble Soul holds most dear, while Infamy, eternal infamy (my soul freezes while I write the word), attends the giving way to the soft alluring of a criminal passion."[10] For most of his life Beckford seems to have resented and struggled against these impositions on his private self, but he did not throw them off. The private Beckford remained cloistered. Unlike Byron, Parreaux notes, Beckford would not play the role of outcast but tried to maintain the fiction of having a privileged place in the society of his time.[11] In fact, much of the pathos of Beckford's life results from the disparity between his compromised reputation and his expectations of an aristocratic, privileged position. Beckford chose an unhappy role to play, but the important point here is that he chose the public and proper role urged on him by his family.

Beckford's sexuality has been a key concern of critics looking for the inner explanation of *Vathek*'s opposites. In 1785 Beckford left England temporarily in the wake of a scandal over his relationship with the young William Courtenay. The opprobrium remaining from this incident together with continuing rumours plagued him throughout his life. But our understanding of this matter is enormously complicated by the practical difficulties of determining the facts, by the differ-

ent theoretical models used to explain the facts, by the limitations of any sort of psychological explanation, and by the divergent uses that critics make of their conclusions even when they agree on the facts. We know that Beckford was married with two daughters, that his wife maintained her faith in him, and that he grieved her death. What lies behind the protective public face must be surmised. Beckford's letters and papers contain helpful information, but, as noted, they were revised in places with the intention of portraying a desirable image; they are often oblique, and, as Boyd Alexander observes, Beckford "dramatises and exaggerates his moods and feelings." Beckford himself lamented in his *Journal,* "I have more profligacy of tongue than of character and often do my utmost to make myself appear worse than I am in reality."[12]

Further, even where the facts seem clear, there is the theoretical difficulty of knowing how to interpret them. What do we want to say—that he was homosexual, bisexual, merely self-indulgent without a strongly marked sexual orientation? Do we want to psychoanalyse him as a case of "narcissistic paederasty"? This last diagnosis is informative, a perceptive use of psychological criticism to explain the tensions in Beckford's style, but at bottom it illustrates the limitations of attempts to explain what lurks behind the scenes of the mind. Its diagnosis, "narcissistic paederasty,"[13] is not defined precisely enough for use as the key to a complex man's very difficult personality. It includes childishness as well as child-love; it is metaphorical ("a self-devouring child wishing to rape his own image"); and it is governed by the need to find a psychological unity beneath the behavioural data. Like so many explanations of sexuality, it is an imposition of a unifying concept on separate facets of behaviour. This interpretation, then, leaves us in the biographical dilemma. It is meaningful precisely because it creates a unifying matrix for separate and heterogeneous elements in Beckford's actions. As we have seen, we need interpretation imposed on the discrete items of Beckford's life in order to understand them in relationship with each other. Yet, equally clearly, there is no justification for believing that whatever interpretation we may impose is historically verifiable truth.

What indeed does it mean to "understand" the sources of a person's acts and ideas? One's actions stem from the intricate causal network that is one's whole being; therefore, no explanation can be complete. Any attempt at explanation must be an abstraction, a grouping or a simplification of a myriad causes. It represents the critic's decision about where to draw the line between significance and insignificance. And that decision must necessarily be personal and subjective. What shall we make, for instance, of an opinion that *Vathek* may embody Beckford's complex reaction to his "possessive and autocratic mother"?[14] Again, I find the suggestion reasonable but am not certain that any array of biographical facts, no matter how extensive, would persuade another reader less convinced of the importance of parental influence than I am. What then of his equally dominating father, Alderman Beckford, twice Lord Mayor of London, robust heterosexual and extrovert, who seems to have been both amused and impatient with the whims of his wilful child? Do our own explanatory models hold that fathers are not as influential as mothers?[15] Or do we see a malign conjunction in their mutual influences? The point, of course, is that each of us will delineate the boundaries between significance and insignificance in different ways, ways owing as much to our explanatory models of child development as to objectively demonstrable facts about William Beckford.

Critics whose thinking is determined by one explanatory model will regard another as lacking in the requisite rigour of method and verifiability. Many types of explanations have only practical justification and, therefore, offer no *a priori* reasons why their results may not be duplicated by another type of explanation. Thus, psychoanalysis may in practice accomplish in contemporary society what advice from village elders or purification rituals accomplished in other ages. Because these explanatory models enable a person better to function in his or her environment and a critic to unite disparate facts under a common hypothesis, we value them highly. A model or system of beliefs with explanatory powers will come to seem self-evident, its underlying assumptions justified by the results they produce. In Beckford's case, some sort of sexual hypothesis may unite his behaviour patterns with the ambivalent closing moral of *Vathek* and with what we know of human behaviour from our own experiences and studies. These are significant results. They may lead us to accept the critic's interpretation, but they leave unanswered such questions as whether we understand Beckford's behaviour patterns as they really were and whether the psychological aspects of the hypothesis (for instance, "narcissistic paederasty") are empirically verifiable concepts.

Further, even satisfying explanations leave undetermined the extent to which the critic's own interpretations are mediated by personal and social codes.[16] The subtleties of George Haggerty's account of Beckford's search for a "true heart's friend"[17] are an advance over earlier stereotypes or what he calls "essentialist" categorizations, but his views so clearly originate in a personal thesis concerning "love" that one accepts them with the same caution necessary in reading Timothy Mowl's more commonsensical portrait of Beckford as robust bisexual horseman. The openness with which we now discuss sexual behaviour allows honest explorations, but falls easy prey to the temptations of biographical creation, which it is the purpose of this paper to delineate. Sex is far too interesting a matter to approach dispassionately. Self-congratulation on exposing the equivocations of past critics, the wrinkled pleasure of rehearsing Beckford's perfervid letters, and the rivalries of competing models of Beckford's desires all increase the risks that personal zest rather than objectivity accounts for our explanations.

What in the end are the truth-value and the verification procedure of a claim that Beckford died "at the age of eighty-four—unrepentant, unreformed, and immature"?[18] I choose this remark because it comes from a respected critic of Beckford; it is both adroit and compelling. Yet its virtues are dexterity of statement (entirely a verbal virtue) and ability to bring a number of biographical strands into a single formulation (a literary and logical virtue). Neat summation is appealing in a linear, logical mode such as biography, but life itself is confused, contradictory, and illogical. What counts as a literary virtue may be in fact a liability in the search for truth. As we have seen, such a claim has its own sort of meaningfulness, but we who understand ourselves only with difficulty may remain sceptical of the biographer's ability to reduce another human's inner being to clear patterns.[19]

Hume's point was similar and adds to the theoretical obstacles we face in finding a "real" Beckford. Although we have a great "propension . . . to imagine something unknown and mysterious, connecting the parts" of our personal identity, that mysterious something is a feigned support and centre rather than a "true" entity. We know only the perceptions of others and ourselves rather than their causes. Instead of the "nice and subtle questions concerning personal identity [which] can never possibly be decided," Hume notes that the mind "gives rise to some fiction or imaginary principle of union." Our personal identity is a "grammatical" matter, a syntax of the self created from discrete parts (pp. 254, 262-63).

Hume's scepticism springs from philosophical analysis and properly concerns the existence of personal identity rather than its characteristics, which I claim Beckford and his critics are searching for. Back of Hume's analysis, however, lies an English—and especially an eighteenth-century English—emphasis on the social bases of personality, the self as acted role. As Lord Chesterfield writes (notoriously but not atypically) to his son, "Manner is all, in everything; it is by manner only that you can please, and consequently rise."[20] And in his account of himself, Hume stresses his own manners and sociability: "I was a man of mild dispositions, of command of temper, of an open, social, and cheerful humour. . . . Even my love of literary fame, my ruling passion, never soured my temper."[21] An eighteenth-century gentleman might well doubt the inner self, for the class and the age place their interests in mannerly, social roles. For Hume, Chesterfield, and Beckford, one's identity was created, a composed grammar or syntax of the self rather than a deep structure.

We can return now to Beckford with some sympathy and understanding for his lot, that of replacing personal identity with a public face. In *Vathek* we have a work whose mixture of opposites seems to demand an author's personality to give it unity. Yet the very prominent personality that Beckford interjects into *Vathek* stands aloof from his material, for Beckford is eager that we see him laughing and manipulating the diverse attitudes of *Vathek* without being compromised by naïve commitment to them. That public, mannered Beckford is all we have—but not all we need if we are to depart satisfied with a unified impression of *Vathek.* And so we create for Beckford an inner, unifying personality, *aware now that it is our own creation.* We do for the novel what Beckford did for it: we write an imaginatively embellished biography of the Caliph of Fonthill just as he wrote of *Vathek* Billah, ninth Caliph of the Abassides.[22]

We end up with creations—an aristocratic Beckford defying middle-class morality in *Vathek,* or an infantile, sexually insecure Beckford projecting his interests on the novel, or a "nervous, self-conscious, shoulder-shrugging" littérateur, or even the impersonal artist whose work "might not be due so much to [his] own neuroses as to certain conventions" within an artistic tradition.[23] Our Beckford may or may not be the "true" Beckford,

but this construction renders the novel more meaningful. Where conflicting opposites have deconstructed author and novel, the interpretive critic has reconstructed them. Thus, we find the many different Beckfords in the critical literature. To some extent these critics are creating their own selves in the person of Beckford, shaping the work so it will pass through the network of their own adaptive and defensive strategies, as Norman Holland has put it. To some extent, no doubt, their work is a more literary attempt to supply an orderly grammar of logical relationships to their perceptions of *Vathek.*[24]

In each of these cases lies the reality, now often noted in biographical as well as critical studies, that every subject is changed by the discourse that embodies it. William Epstein has observed that "the decline of faith in the unmediated, ontological status of 'events'" must influence all but the most unexamined approaches to biography.[25] Any Beckford that we (and he) perceive is a product of the interpretive codes that govern our cognitive being. What sort of man lies behind or transcends these codes is, as Hume would put it, a "nice and subtle question" (p. 262). For, indeed, whether we take our cue from Hume or Derrida, the absolute origin of perception is inseparable from the activity that records it. Whether we look at the issue practically, theoretically, or (to use eighteenth-century terms) in the clear light of reason, the Beckford we find is a creation of cultural and interpretive codes. The insights of Enlightenment English empiricism, the twists of postmodern criticism, and the reticence of polite and experienced observers of human nature can go no further than the public Beckford.

There is no alternative to accepting the dilemma of the desirability and impossibility of biographical interpretation. A critic must put together a unified interpretation of the data, knowing all along that interpreted data is meaningful creation rather than fact independent of its expression. That is the dilemma of all biography; Beckford's case only makes it especially clear. In the end, we come to something very close to Hume's sceptical reflections on personal identity. We (and Beckford himself) know the "successive perceptions" (p. 253) of the novel and the life but lack the most distant notion of their underlying causes or, for that matter, of their basic unity. Yet we see Beckford struggling unsuccessfully to find himself and critics struggling to create narratives to bind together their perceptions. The effort in each case must be unsuccessful, but, paradoxically, it is also understandable and necessary.

Notes

1. David Hume, *A Treatise of Human Nature*, ed. L.A. Selby-Bigg (Oxford: Oxford University Press, 1965), p. 253. References are to this edition.

2. Roger Lonsdale writes: the "difficulty of attaching any clear meaning or satiric purpose to *Vathek* has also tended to force its readers back on the author itself for enlightenment." See introduction, William Beckford, *Vathek* (Oxford: World's Classics, 1983), p. viii.

3. Summaries of critical reactions can be found in Lonsdale, pp. xix-xxii; Dan J. McNutt, *The Eighteenth-Century Gothic Novel: An Annotated Bibliography of Criticism and Selected Texts* (New York: Garland, 1985), pp. 265-310; and Brian Fothergill, *Beckford of Fonthill* (London: Faber and Faber, 1978), pp. 128-35.

4. Fothergill, p. 134. See also Lonsdale, pp. x-xiv; and *The Journal of William Beckford in Portugal and Spain 1787-1788*, ed. Boyd Alexander (New York: John Day, 1955), p. 139.

5. Beckford, *Journal*, pp. 38, 41, 44, 76, 86, 92, and 225. For discussion of Beckford's revisions and his reputation, see Guy Chapman, *Beckford* (New York: Scribner's, 1937), p. 323; Timothy Mowl, *William Beckford: Composing for Mozart* (London: John Murray, 1998), passim; James Lees-Milne, *William Beckford* (Montclair, NJ: Allanheld, Osmun, 1979), p. 107; and McNutt, pp. 288, 301-4.

6. Beckford, *Journal*, p. 41. See also André Parreaux, *William Beckford: Auteur de "Vathek"* (Paris: Nizet, 1960), p. 76.

7. See John T. Farrell, "A Reinterpretation of the Major Literary Works of William Beckford," *Dissertation Abstracts* 45 (1984), 1758A (University of Delaware); George E. Haggerty, *Men in Love: Masculinity and Sexuality in the Eighteenth Century* (New York: Columbia University Press, 1999), pp. 136-51; and Mowl, p. 111.

8. Mme de Staël is quoted in William Beckford, *Dreams, Waking Thoughts and Incidents*, ed. Robert J. Gemmett (Rutherford, NJ: Fairleigh Dickinson University Press, 1971), p. 26; Parreaux, p. 78; V.S. Pritchett, "Vile Body," *New Statesman* 63 (1962), 265-66.

9. Chapman, p. 168.

10. Beckford, *Dreams, Waking Thoughts and Incidents*, pp. 16-17.

11. Parreaux, p. 77.

12. Quoted in Boyd Alexander, *Life at Fonthill, 1807-1822* (London: Rupert Hart Davies, 1957), p. 26.

13. See Magdi Wahba, "Beckford, Portugal and 'Childish Error,'" *William Beckford of Fonthill, 1760-1844: Bicentary Essays*, ed. Fatma Moussa Mahmoud (Port Washington, NY: Kennikat, 1960), p. 58.

14. Lonsdale, introduction to *Vathek*, p. viii.

15. For differing ideas of parental influence, see Lonsdale, introduction to *Vathek*, p. viii; and Mowl, p. 31.

16. For discussions of limitations imposed by "conceptual paradigms" and hypotheses, see David E. Swalm, "Locating Belief in Biography," *Biography* 3 (1980), 23; and Ira Bruce Nadel, *Biography: Fiction, Fact and Form* (New York: St Martin's Press, 1984), pp. 10, 209.

17. Haggerty, p. 151.

18. Alexander, p. 15.

19. See Noel Chabani Manganyi, "Psychobiography and the Truth of the Subject," *Biography* 6 (1983), 44-45, 50.

20. Earl of Chesterfield, *Letters to His Son by the Earl of Chesterfield* (Washington: M. Walter Dunne, 1901), 2:395.

21. Ernest Campbell Mossner, "My Own Life," *The Life of David Hume* (Austin: University of Texas Press, 1954), p. 615.

22. See Kenneth W. Graham, "Implications of the Grotesque: Beckford's *Vathek* and the Boundaries of Fictional Reality," *Tennessee Studies in Literature* 23 (1978), 64.

23. James Henry Rieger, "Au Pied de la Lettre: Stylistic Uncertainty in *Vathek*," *Criticism* 4 (1962), 310; James K. Folsom, "Beckford's *Vathek* and the Tradition of Oriental Satire," *Criticism* 6 (1964), 53.

24. Norman Holland, "Unity Identity Text Self," *PMLA* 90 (1975), 816-17; Peter Nagourney, "The Basic Assumptions of Literary Biography," *Biography* 1 (1978), 93.

25. William Epstein, *Recognizing Biography* (Philadelphia: University of Pennsylvania Press, 1987), p. 36.

FURTHER READING

Biographies

Alexander, Boyd. *England's Wealthiest Son: A Study of William Beckford*. London: Centaur Press, 1962, 308 p.

A highly regarded study of Beckford's character that incorporates material from unpublished documents.

Brockman, H. A. N. *The Caliph of Fonthill*. London: Werner Laurie, 1956, 219 p.

A study of Beckford that focuses on his life at Fonthill Abbey.

Fothergill, Brian. *Beckford of Fonthill*. London: Faber and Faber, 1979, 387 p.

A detailed examination of Beckford's life.

Oliver, J. W. *The Life of William Beckford*. London: Oxford University Press, 1932, 343 p.

Full-length biography of Beckford.

Criticism

Borges, Jorge Luis. "About William Beckford's *Vathek*." In *Other Inquisitions: 1937-1952*, translated by Ruth L. C. Simms, pp. 137-40. Austin: University of Texas Press, 1943.

Offers his assessment of the Palace of Subterranean Fire in Vathek, *maintaining that the novel is an early example of the "uncanny."*

Conant, Martha Pike. "The Imaginative Group." In *The Oriental Tale in England in the Eighteenth Century*, pp. 1-72. New York: Columbia University Press, 1908.

Explores Vathek's *unique qualities as well as its place in the history of the oriental tale in eighteenth-century England.*

Garrett, John. "Ending in Infinity: William Beckford's *Arabian Tale.*" *Eighteenth-Century Fiction* 5, no. 1 (October 1992): 15-34.

Attempts "to chart the terrain of Vathek *from the dual perspective of East and West, which is how Beckford himself viewed it.*"

Gemmett, Robert James. *William Beckford.* Boston: Twayne Publishers, 1977, 189 p.

A full-length survey of Beckford's life and works.

Graham, Kenneth W. "Beckford's *Vathek:* A Study in Ironic Dissonance." *Criticism* 14, no. 3 (summer 1972): 243-52.

Maintains that Beckford's adept use of ironic dissonance in Vathek *enabled him to "achieve a successful blending of the improbable and the true."*

Haggerty, George E. "Literature and Homosexuality in the Late Eighteenth Century: Walpole, Beckford, and Lewis." In *Homosexual Themes in Literary Studies,* edited by Wayne R. Dynes and Stephen Donaldson, pp. 167-78. New York: Garland, 1992.

A comparative study that focuses on recurring homosexual themes in the works of Beckford, Horace Walpole, and Matthew Gregory Lewis.

Hazlitt, William. "Mr. Beckford's *Vathek,*" *The Complete Works of William Hazlitt: Literary And Political Criticism,* Vol. 19, edited by P. P. Howe, pp. 98-104. London: J. M. Dent and Sons, Ltd., 1933.

Originally published in the Morning Chronicle *on October 20, 1823. Praises* Vathek *as a moral work, claiming that because of Beckford's balanced use of irony and dispassionate depiction of evil, readers "take the virtuous side in self-defence, and are invited into a sense of humanity."*

Hume, Robert D. "Exuberant Gloom, Existential Agony, and Heroic Despair: Three Varieties of Negative Romanticism." In *The Gothic Imagination: Essays in Dark Romanticism,* edited by G. R. Thompson, pp. 109-27. Pullman: Washington State University Press, 1974.

Uses the term "Negative Romanticism" to classify writers who "are possessed by the Romantic discontents, but entirely lack the Romantic faith in man's ability to transcend his condition or transform it" and who often exhibit a resultant attraction to dark forces, and considers the extent to which Vathek *is a Negative Romantic novel.*

Keegan, P. Q. "Gleanings from Anglo-Oriental Literature." *The New Monthly Magazine,* no. 66 (June 1877): 674-87.

Focuses on Vathek *as a study of the results of extreme selfishness and excess.*

More, Paul Elmer. "William Beckford." In *The Drift of Romanticism: Shelburne Essays.* Eighth series, pp. 1-36. New York: Houghton Mifflin Company, 1913.

Evaluates Beckford's symbolic representation of Romantic egotism in Vathek.

OTHER SOURCES FROM GALE:

Additional coverage of Beckford's life and career is contained in the following sources published by Thomson Gale: *British Writers,* Vol. 3; *Dictionary of Literary Biography,* Vols. 39, 213; *Literary Movements for Students,* Vol. 1; *Literature Resource Center; Nineteenth-Century Literature Criticism,* Vol. 16; *St. James Guide to Horror, Ghost & Gothic Writers;* and *Supernatural Fiction Writers.*

CHARLOTTE BRONTË

(1816 - 1855)

(Also wrote under the pseudonym Currer Bell) English novelist and poet.

The author of vivid, skillfully constructed novels, Brontë created female characters who broke the traditional, nineteenth-century fictional stereotype of a woman as submissive and dependent, beautiful but ignorant. Her highly acclaimed *Jane Eyre* (1847) best demonstrates these attitudes: its heroine is a plain woman who displays intelligence, self-confidence, a will of her own, and moral righteousness. With an oeuvre consisting of four novels, some poems, and other writings from her youth, Brontë is hailed as a precursor of feminist novelists, and her works, often depicting the struggles and minor victories of everyday life, are considered early examples of literary realism. Her novels, particularly *Jane Eyre* and *Villette* (1853), have been discussed as part of the Gothic literary tradition, and contain elements of mystery, heightened passions, and the supernatural.

BIOGRAPHICAL INFORMATION

The eldest surviving daughter in a motherless family of six, Brontë helped to raise her remaining brother, Branwell, and two sisters, Emily and Anne. Her father, a strict Yorkshire clergyman,

believed firmly in the values of self-education and forbade his family from socializing with other children. Intellectual growth was encouraged, however, and he introduced his family to the Bible and to the works of William Shakespeare, William Wordsworth, Lord Byron, and Sir Walter Scott. In their youths, the Brontë siblings collaborated on a series of imaginative stories, plays, and poems set in the fictional land of Angria. Charlotte's contribution to these tales, which were collected and published posthumously as *Legends of Angria* (1933), served as a catalyst for her mature works and marked the beginning of her interest in writing.

For many years Brontë concealed her writing from her family. After the accidental discovery that Emily, too, secretly wrote verse, and that Anne shared their interest, the three published, at their own expense, *Poems by Currer, Ellis and Acton Bell* (1846). The sisters assumed masculine pseudonyms both to preserve their privacy and to avoid the patronizing treatment they believed critics accorded women writers. *Poems* sold only two copies, but Charlotte was undeterred and continued to write. Her first novel, *The Professor* (1857), was rejected by six publishers, but her next work, *Jane Eyre*, was accepted immediately. The work received lavish attention, was praised by Queen Victoria and George Eliot, and brought Brontë into popular literary circles, where she met William Makepeace

Thackeray (to whom she dedicated the second edition of *Jane Eyre*), Matthew Arnold, and Harriet Martineau.

Brontë went on to publish two more novels, *Shirley* (1849) and *Villette*. During the writing of *Shirley*, Brontë experienced a series of personal tragedies that marked the beginning of a time of intense sorrow and loneliness. Within a period of about nine months, Brontë lost her three remaining siblings, first Branwell, then Emily, and finally Anne in the spring of 1849. After their deaths, Brontë found it very trying to write in solitude. She eventually began work on her final novel, *Villette*, basing its plot and characters on her unpublished *The Professor*. The year after *Villette*'s publication, in 1854, Brontë married Arthur Bell Nicholls. She became pregnant early in 1855, dying in March of that year from complications related to her pregnancy. *The Professor* was published after her death, in 1857.

MAJOR WORKS

Many who have studied Brontë's life and works have noted connections between the two, with each of her novels reflecting autobiographical details. In *Jane Eyre*, the young heroine spends many years as a student, and later a teacher, at a strict girls' boarding school, Lowood. This fictional school bears a resemblance to the Clergy Daughters' School at Cowan Bridge, the harsh institution where Brontë and her sisters were sent during their youths. As an adult Jane Eyre becomes a governess, a job also held by Brontë. The somber tone of Brontë's second published novel, *Shirley*, reflects her grief following the deaths of her brother and two sisters. The heroine of the book, modeled after Emily, is a stoic figure whose courage serves as both a tribute to Brontë's sister and a lesson to the reader. *Shirley* depicts the friendship of two women, Caroline Helstone and Shirley Keeldar, in the midst of conflict and upheaval in the industrial region of Yorkshire, England. Brontë's travels to Brussels and her passionate attachment to Constantin Héger, a married schoolmaster in whose home she lived, are recreated in the student-teacher relationships and in the male characters of *The Professor* and *Villette*.

CRITICAL RECEPTION

While *Jane Eyre* was immediately popular, initial critical reception of the novel varied. Several commentators admired the power and freshness of Brontë's prose; others, however, termed the novel superficial and vulgar. Perhaps the best known early review, by Elizabeth Rigby (see Further Reading), flatly condemned *Jane Eyre* as "an anti-Christian composition." Still other critics questioned the authorship of the novel. Some doubted that a woman was capable of writing such a work, while E. P. Whipple of the *North American Review* contended that the book was coauthored by a man and a woman. In succeeding generations, the critical assessment of *Jane Eyre* improved considerably, and for many years, Charlotte was considered the outstanding literary figure of the Brontë family. However, David Cecil's essay (see Further Reading), published in the early 1930s, proclaimed Emily the greater writer and marked a temporary end of Charlotte's critical superiority in the eyes of some critics. Influenced by Cecil's article, these critics compared Charlotte's works to those of Emily, disputing the originality and intellectual quality of Charlotte's novels. Many studies of Brontë's works are focused more on her life than on her writing. During the nineteenth century, reviewers often addressed the nature of Jane's character; by the turn of the century, critics tended to assess Jane as a person of courage and integrity. Critical interpretations during the twentieth and twenty-first century have tended to be more specific in their approach. The characters of Jane, Rochester, and Bertha have been the subjects of detailed analyses, and reviewers have also debated the nature and import of Rochester's disability. Critics frequently discuss the novel's structure, its symbolism, and its autobiographical elements. Feminist literary criticism has given new impetus to a revaluation of the significance of Brontë's attempts to depict through her fiction some of the struggles of women in the nineteenth century. While twentieth- and twenty-first-century discussions of the novel's single theme vary, most scholars agree that in *Jane Eyre* Brontë wished to stress the possibility of equality in marriage.

In terms of Brontë's novels as examples of Gothic literature, many critics have posited that Brontë broadened the definition of Gothic. While not adhering strictly to the model of traditional Gothic literature, Brontë did borrow liberally from the genre, incorporating dark, mysterious, and supernatural elements into the plots of her novels. In his influential 1958 essay, Robert B. Heilman described Brontë's works as "new Gothic" novels that expand the Gothic tradition by exploring the place of heightened passions in routine, daily life. Her use of Gothic literary elements, Heilman wrote, "released her from the patterns of the novel of society and therefore permitted the flowering of her real talent—the talent for finding and giving dramatic form to impulses and feelings which . . . increase wonderfully the sense of reality in the novel." A number of critics have suggested that Brontë expanded Gothic conventions through her unconventional female characters. In her 1999 essay, for example, Toni Wein categorized *Villette* as a departure from traditional Gothic literature because the female characters, with their manipulations and survival mechanisms, are portrayed as heroic rather than evil. In a 1979 essay, Caesarea Abartis examined the ways in which Brontë both adhered to and deviated from Gothic convention, suggesting that *Jane Eyre* is a precursor to the modern romance novel.

PRINCIPAL WORKS

Poems by Currer, Ellis and Acton Bell [as Currer Bell, with Ellis and Acton Bell (pseudonyms of Emily and Anne Brontë)] (poems) 1846

Jane Eyre. An Autobiography [as Currer Bell] (novel) 1847

Shirley: A Tale [as Currer Bell] (novel) 1849

Villette [as Currer Bell] (novel) 1853

The Professor: A Tale [as Currer Bell] 1857

Emma (unfinished novel) 1860

*The Brontës' Life and Letters (letters) 1908

Legends of Angria (juvenilia) 1933

Five Novelettes: Passing Events, Julia, Mina Laury, Henry Hastings, Caroline Vernon (novellas) 1971

* This work includes letters written by Charlotte, Emily, and Anne Brontë.

PRIMARY SOURCES

CHARLOTTE BRONTË (STORY DATE 1833)

SOURCE: Brontë, Charlotte. "Napoleon and the Spectre." In *Great Ghost Stories: 34 Classic Tales of the Supernatural,* compiled by Robin Brockman, pp. 415-20. New York: Gramercy Books, 2002.

The following short story originally appeared in a manuscript titled "The Green Dwarf" (dated 10 July 1833-2 September 1833) and was first published in 1919.

Well, as I was saying, the Emperor got into bed.

'Chevalier,' says he to his valet, 'let down those window-curtains, and shut the casement before you leave the room.'

Chevalier did as he was told, and then, taking up his candlestick, departed.

In a few minutes the Emperor felt his pillow becoming rather hard, and he got up to shake it. As he did so a slight rushing noise was heard near the bed-head. His Majesty listened, but all was silent as he lay down again.

Scarcely had he settled into a peaceful attitude of repose, when he was disturbed by a sensation of thirst. Lifting himself on his elbow, he took a glass of lemonade from the small stand which was placed beside him. He refreshed himself by a deep draught. As he returned the goblet to its station a deep groan burst from a kind of closet in one corner of the apartment.

'Who's there?' cried the Emperor, seizing his pistols. 'Speak, or I'll blow your brains out.'

This threat produced no other effect than a short, sharp laugh, and a dead silence followed.

The Emperor started from his couch, and, hastily throwing on a *robe-de-chambre* which hung over the back of a chair, stepped courageously to the haunted closet. As he opened the door something rustled. He sprang forward sword in hand. No soul or even substance appeared, and the rustling, it was evident, proceeded from the falling of a cloak, which had been suspended by a peg from the door.

Half ashamed of himself he returned to bed.

Just as he was about once more to close his eyes, the light of the three wax tapers, which burned in a silver branch over the mantelpiece, was suddenly darkened. He looked up. A black, opaque shadow obscured it. Sweating with terror, the Emperor put out his hand to seize the bell-rope, but some invisible being snatched it rudely from his grasp, and at the same instant the ominous shade vanished.

'Pooh!' exclaimed Napoleon, 'it was but an ocular delusion.'

'Was it?' whispered a hollow voice, in deep mysterious tones, close to his ear. Was it a delusion, Emperor of France? No! all thou hast heard and seen is sad forewarning reality. Rise, lifter of the Eagle Standard! Awake, slayer of the Lily Sceptre! Follow me, Napoleon, and thou shalt see more.'

As the voice ceased, a form dawned on his astonished sight. It was that of a tall, thin man, dressed in a blue surtout edged with gold lace. It wore a black cravat very tightly round its neck, and confined by two little sticks placed behind each ear. The countenance was livid; the tongue protruded from between the teeth, and the eyes all glazed and bloodshot started with frightful prominence from their sockets.

'*Mon Dieu!*' exclaimed the Emperor, 'what do I see? Spectre, whence cometh thou?'

The apparition spoke not, but gliding forward beckoned Napoleon with uplifted finger to follow.

Controlled by a mysterious influence, which deprived him of the capability of either thinking or acting for himself, he obeyed in silence.

The solid wall of the apartment fell open as they approached, and, when both had passed through, it closed behind them with a noise like thunder.

They would now have been in total darkness had it not been for a dim light which shone round the ghost and revealed the damp walls of a long, vaulted passage. Down this they proceeded with mute rapidity. Ere long a cool, refreshing breeze, which rushed wailing up the vault and caused the Emperor to wrap his loose nightdress closer round, announced their approach to the open air.

This they soon reached, and Nap found himself in one of the principal streets of Paris.

'Worthy Spirit,' said he, shivering in the chill night air, 'permit me to return and put on some additional clothing. I will be with you again presently.'

'Forward,' replied his companion sternly.

He felt compelled, in spite of the rising indignation which almost choked him, to obey.

On they went through the deserted streets till they arrived at a lofty house built on the banks of the Seine. Here the Spectre stopped, the gates rolled back to receive them, and they entered a large marble hall which was part concealed by a curtain drawn across, through the half transparent folds of which a bright light might be seen burning with dazzling lustre. A row of fine female figures, richly attired, stood before this screen. They wore on their heads garlands of the most beautiful flowers, but their faces were concealed by ghastly masks representing death's-heads.

'What is all this mummery?' cried the Emperor, making an effort to shake off the mental

shackles by which he was so unwillingly restrained, 'Where am I, and why have I been brought here?'

'Silence,' said the guide, lolling out still further his black and bloody tongue. 'Silence, if thou wouldst escape instant death.'

The Emperor would have replied, his natural courage overcoming the temporary awe to which he had at first been subjected, but just then a strain of wild, supernatural music swelled behind the huge curtain, which waved to and fro, and bellied slowly out as if agitated by some internal commotion or battle of waving winds. At the same moment an overpowering mixture of the scents of moral corruption, blent with the richest Eastern odours, stole through the haunted hall.

A murmur of many voices was now heard at a distance, and something grasped his arm eagerly from behind.

He turned hastily round. His eyes met the well-known countenance of Marie Louise.

'What! are you in this infernal place, too?' said he. 'What has brought you here?'

'Will your Majesty permit me to ask the same question of yourself?' said the Empress, smiling.

He made no reply; astonishment prevented him.

No curtain now intervened between him and the light. It had been removed as if by magic, and a splendid chandelier appeared suspended over his head. Throngs of ladies, richly dressed, but without death's-head masks, stood round, and a due proportion of gay cavaliers was mingled with them. Music was still sounding, but it was seen to proceed from a band of mortal musicians stationed in an orchestra near at hand. The air was yet redolent of incense, but it was incense unblended with stench.

'*Mon Dieu!*' cried the Emperor, 'how is all this come about? Where in the world is Piche?'

'Piche?' replied the Empress. 'What does your Majesty mean? Had you not better leave the apartment and retire to rest?'

'Leave the apartment? Why, where am I?'

'In my private drawing-room, surrounded by a few particular persons of the Court whom I had invited this evening to a ball. You entered a few minutes since in your nightdress with your eyes fixed and wide open. I suppose from the astonishment you now testify that you were walking in your sleep.'

The Emperor immediately fell into a fit of catalepsy, in which he continued during the whole of that night and the greater part of the next day.

GENERAL COMMENTARY

ROBERT B. HEILMAN (ESSAY DATE 1958)

SOURCE: Heilman, Robert B. "Charlotte Brontë's 'New' Gothic." In *From Jane Austen to Joseph Conrad: Essays Collected in Memory of James T. Hillhouse,* edited by R. C. Rathburn and Martin Steinman, pp. 118-32. Minneapolis: University of Minnesota Press, 1958.

In the following essay, Heilman illustrates how Brontë added depth and complexity to the Gothic heroines of her works.

In that characteristic flight from cliché that may plunge him into the recherché the critic might well start from *The Professor* and discover in it much more than is implied by the usual dismissal of it as Charlotte Brontë's poorest work. He might speculate about Charlotte's singular choice of a male narrator—the value of it, or even the need of it, for her. For through William Crimsworth she lives in Héger, making love to herself as Frances Henri: in this there is a kind of ravenousness, inturning, splitting, and doubling back of feeling. Through Crimsworth she experiences a sudden, vivid, often graceless mastery. But these notes on the possible psychology of the author are critically useful only as a way into the strange tremors of feeling that are present in a formally defective story. Pelet identifies "a fathomless spring of sensibility in thy breast, Crimsworth." If Crimsworth is not a successful character, he is the channel of emotional surges that splash over a conventional tale of love: the author's disquieting presence in the character lends a nervous, off-center vitality. The pathos of liberty is all but excessive (as it is later in Shirley Keeldar and Lucy Snowe): Crimsworth sneers, ". . . I sprang from my bed with other slaves," and rejoices, "Liberty I clasped in my arms . . . her smile and embrace revived my life." The Puritan sentiment (to be exploited partially in Jane Eyre and heavily in Lucy Snowe) becomes tense, rhetorical, fiercely censorious; the self-righteousness punitive and even faintly paranoid. Through the frenetically Protestant Crimsworth and his flair for rebuke Charlotte notes the little sensualities of girl students ("parting her lips, as full as those of a hot-blooded Maroon") and the coquettish yet urgent sexuality of Zoraide Reuter perversely

responding to Crimsworth's ostensible yet not total unresponsiveness to her: "When she stole about me with the soft step of a slave, I felt at once barbarous and sensual as a pasha."

Charlotte looks beyond familiar surfaces. In Yorke Hunsden she notes the "incompatibilities of the 'physique' with the 'morale.'" The explosive Byronic castigator has lineaments "small, and even feminine" and "now the mien of a morose bull, and anon that of an arch and mischievous girl." In this version of the popular archetype, "rough exterior but heart of gold," Charlotte brilliantly finds a paradoxical union of love and hate; she sees generosity of spirit sometimes appearing directly but most often translated into antithetical terms that also accommodate opposite motives—into god-like self-indulgence in truth-telling; almost Mephistophelian cynicism; sadism and even murderousness in words.

Charlotte's story is conventional; formally she is for "reason" and "real life"; but her characters keep escaping to glorify "feeling" and "Imagination." Feeling is there in the story—evading repression, in author or in character; ranging from nervous excitement to emotional absorption; often tense and peremptory; sexuality, hate, irrational impulse, grasped, given life, not merely named and pigeonholed. This is Charlotte's version of Gothic: in her later novels an extraordinary thing. In that incredibly eccentric history, *The Gothic Quest,* Montague Summers asserts that the "Gothic novel of sensibility . . . draws its emotionalism and psychology . . . from the work of Samuel Richardson." When this line of descent continues in the Brontës, the vital feeling moves toward an intensity, a freedom, and even an abandon virtually non-existent in historical Gothic and rarely approached in Richardson. From Angria on, Charlotte's women vibrate with passions that the fictional conventions only partly constrict or gloss over—in the center an almost violent devotedness that has in it at once a fire of independence, a spiritual energy, a vivid sexual responsiveness, and, along with this, self-righteousness, a sense of power, sometimes self-pity and envious competitiveness. To an extent the heroines are "unheroined," unsweetened. Into them there has come a new sense of the dark side of feeling and personality.

The Professor ventures a little into the psychic darkness on which *Villette* draws heavily. One night Crimsworth, a victim of hypochondria, hears a voice saying, "In the midst of life we are in death," and he feels "a horror of great darkness." In his boyhood this same "sorceress" drew him "to the very brink of a black, sullen river" and managed to "lure me to her vaulted home of horrors." Charlotte draws on sex images that recall the note of sexuality subtly present in other episodes: ". . . I had entertained her at bed and board . . . she lay with me, . . . taking me entirely to her death-cold bosom, and holding me with arms of bone." The climax is: "I repulsed her as one would a dreaded and ghastly concubine coming to embitter a husband's heart toward his young bride; . . ." This is Gothic, yet there is an integrity of feeling that greatly deepens the convention.

From childhood terrors to all those mysteriously threatening sights, sounds, and injurious acts that reveal the presence of some malevolent force and that anticipate the holocaust at Thornfield, the traditional Gothic in *Jane Eyre* has often been noted, and as often disparaged. It need not be argued that Charlotte Brontë did not reach the heights while using hand-me-down devices, though a tendency to work through the conventions of fictional art was a strong element in her make-up. This is true of all her novels, but it is no more true than her counter-tendency to modify, most interestingly, these conventions. In both *Villette* and *Jane Eyre* Gothic is used but characteristically is undercut.

Jane Eyre hears a "tragic . . . preternatural . . . laugh," but this is at "high noon" and there is "no circumstance of ghostliness"; Grace Poole, the supposed laugher, is a plain person, than whom no "apparition less romantic or less ghostly could . . . be conceived"; Charlotte apologizes ironically to the "romantic reader" for telling "the plain truth" that Grace generally bears a "pot of porter." Charlotte almost habitually revises "old Gothic," the relatively crude mechanisms of fear, with an infusion of the anti-Gothic. When Mrs. Rochester first tried to destroy Rochester by fire, Jane "baptized" Rochester's bed and heard Rochester "fulminating strange anathemas at finding himself lying in a pool of water." The introduction of comedy as a palliative of straight Gothic occurs on a large scale when almost seventy-five pages are given to the visit of the Ingram-Eshton party to mysterious Thornfield; here Charlotte, as often in her novels, falls into the manner of the Jane Austen whom she despised. When Mrs. Rochester breaks loose again and attacks Mason, the presence of guests lets Charlotte play the nocturnal alarum for at least a touch of comedy: Rochester orders the frantic women not to "pull me down or strangle me"; and "the two dowagers, in vast white wrappers, were bearing down on him like ships in full sail."

The symbolic also modifies the Gothic, for it demands of the reader a more mature and complicated response than the relatively simple thrill or momentary intensity of feeling sought by primitive Gothic. When mad Mrs. Rochester, seen only as "the foul German spectre—the Vampyre," spreads terror at night, that is one thing; when, with the malicious insight that is the paradox of her madness, she tears the wedding veil in two and thus symbolically destroys the planned marriage, that is another thing, far less elementary as art. The midnight blaze that ruins Thornfield becomes more than a shock when it is seen also as the fire of purgation; the grim, almost roadless forest surrounding Ferndean is more than a harrowing stage-set when it is also felt as a symbol of Rochester's closed-in life.

The point is that in various ways Charlotte manages to make the patently Gothic more than a stereotype. But more important is that she instinctively finds new ways to achieve the ends served by old Gothic—the discovery and release of new patterns of feeling, the intensification of feeling. Though only partly unconventional, Jane is nevertheless so portrayed as to evoke new feelings rather than merely exercise old ones. As a girl she is lonely, "passionate," "strange," "like nobody there"; she feels superior, rejects poverty, talks back precociously, tells truths bluntly, enjoys "the strangest sense of freedom," tastes "vengeance"; she experiences a nervous shock which is said to have a lifelong effect, and the doctor says "nerves not in a good state"; she can be "reckless and feverish," "bitter and truculent"; at Thornfield she is restless, given to "bright visions," letting "imagination" picture an existence full of "life, fire, feeling." Thus Charlotte leads away from standardized characterization toward new levels of human reality, and hence from stock responses toward a new kind of passionate engagement.

Charlotte moves toward depth in various ways that have an immediate impact like that of Gothic. Jane's strange, fearful symbolic dreams are not mere thrillers but reflect the tensions of the engagement period, the stress of the wedding-day debate with Rochester, and the longing for Rochester after she has left him. The final Thornfield dream, with its vivid image of a hand coming through a cloud in place of the expected moon, is in the surrealistic vein that appears most sharply in the extraordinary pictures that Jane draws at Thornfield: here Charlotte is plumbing the psyche, not inventing a weird *décor*. Likewise in the telepathy scene, which Charlotte, unlike Defoe in dealing with a similar episode, does her utmost to actualize: "The feeling was not like an electric shock; but it was quite as sharp, as strange, as startling: . . . that inward sensation . . . with all its unspeakable strangeness . . . like an inspiration . . . wondrous shock of feeling. . . ." In her flair for the surreal, in her plunging into feeling that is without status in the ordinary world of the novel, Charlotte discovers a new dimension of Gothic.

She does this most thoroughly in her portrayal of characters and of the relations between them. If in Rochester we see only an Angrian-Byronic hero and a Charlotte wish-fulfillment figure (the two identifications which to some readers seem entirely to place him), we miss what is more significant, the exploration of personality that opens up new areas of feeling in intersexual relationships. Beyond the "grim," the "harsh," the eccentric, the almost histrionically cynical that superficially distinguish Rochester from conventional heroes, there is something almost Lawrentian: Rochester is "neither tall nor graceful"; his eyes can be "dark, irate, and piercing"; his strong features "took my feelings from my own power and fettered them in his." Without using the vocabulary common to us, Charlotte is presenting maleness and physicality, to which Jane responds directly. She is "assimilated" to him by "something in my brain and heart, in my blood and nerves"; she "must love" and "could not unlove" him; the thought of parting from him is "agony." Rochester's oblique amatory maneuvers become almost punitive in the Walter-to-Griselda style and once reduce her to sobbing "convulsively"; at times the love-game borders on a power-game. Jane, who prefers "rudeness" to "flattery," is an instinctive evoker of passion: she learns "the pleasure of vexing and soothing him by turns" and pursues a "system" of working him up "to considerable irritation" and coolly leaving him; when, as a result, his caresses become grimaces, pinches, and tweaks, she records that, sometimes at least, she "decidedly preferred these fierce favors." She reports, "I crushed his hand . . . red with the passionate pressure"; she "could not . . . see God for his creature," and in her devotion Rochester senses "an earnest, religious energy."

Charlotte's remolding of stock feeling reaches a height when she sympathetically portrays Rochester's efforts to make Jane his mistress; here the stereotyped seducer becomes a kind of lost nobleman of passion, and of specifically physical passion: "Every atom of your flesh is as dear to me as my own. . . ." The intensity of the pressure which he puts upon her is matched, not by the fear and revulsion of the popular heroine, but by a responsiveness which she barely masters: "The crisis was perilous; but not without its charm . . ." She is "tortured by a sense of remorse at thus hurting his feelings"; at the moment of decision "a hand of fiery iron grasped my vitals . . . blackness, burning! . . . my intolerable duty"; she leaves in "despair"; and after she has left, "I longed to be his; I panted to return . . ."—and for the victory of principle "I abhorred myself . . . I was hateful in my own eyes." This extraordinary openness to feeling, this escape from the bondage of the trite, continues in the Rivers relationship, which is a structural parallel to the Rochester affair: as in Rochester the old sex villain is seen in a new perspective, so in Rivers the clerical hero is radically refashioned; and Jane's almost accepting a would-be husband is given the aesthetic status of a regrettable yielding to a seducer. Without a remarkable liberation from conventional feeling Charlotte could not fathom the complexity of Rivers—the earnest and dutiful clergyman distraught by a profound inner turmoil of conflicting "drives": sexuality, restlessness, hardness, pride, ambition ("fever in his vitals," "inexorable as death"); the hypnotic, almost inhuman potency of his influence on Jane, who feels "a freezing spell," "an awful charm," an "iron shroud"; the relentlessness, almost the unscrupulousness, of his wooing, the resultant fierce struggle (like that with Rochester), Jane's brilliantly perceptive accusation, ". . . you almost hate me . . . you would kill me. You are killing me now"; and yet her mysterious near-surrender: "I was tempted to cease struggling with him—to rush down the torrent of his will into the gulf of his existence, and there lose my own."

Aside from partial sterilization of banal Gothic by dry factuality and humor, Charlotte goes on to make a much more important—indeed, a radical—revision of the mode: in *Jane Eyre* and in the other novels, as we shall see, that discovery of passion, that rehabilitation of the extra-rational, which is the historical office of Gothic, is no longer oriented in marvelous circumstance but moves deeply into the lesser known realities of human life. This change I describe as the change from "old Gothic" to "new Gothic." The kind of appeal is the same; the fictional method is utterly different.

When Charlotte went on from *Jane Eyre* to *Shirley*, she produced a book that for the student of the Gothic theme is interesting precisely because on the face of things it would be expected to be a barren field. It is the result of Charlotte's one deliberate venture from private intensities into public extensities: Orders in Council, the Luddites, technological unemployment in 1811 and 1812, a social portraiture which develops Charlotte's largest cast of characters. Yet Charlotte cannot keep it a social novel. Unlike Warren, who in the somewhat similar *Night Rider* chose to reflect the historical economic crisis in the private crisis of the hero, Miss Brontë loses interest in the public and slides over into the private.

The formal irregularities of **Shirley**—the stop-and-start, zig-zag movement, plunging periodically into different perspectives—light up the divergent impulses in Charlotte herself: the desire to make a story from observed outer life, and the inability to escape from inner urgencies that with centrifugal force unwind outward into story almost autonomously. Passion alters plan: the story of industrial crisis is repeatedly swarmed over by the love stories. But the ultimate complication is that Charlotte's duality of impulse is reflected not only in the narrative material but in two different ways of telling each part of the story. On the one hand she tells a rather conventional, open, predictable tale; on the other she lets go with a highly charged private sentiency that may subvert the former or at least surround it with an atmosphere of unfamiliarity or positive strangeness: the Gothic impulse.

For Charlotte it is typically the "pattern" versus the "strange." She describes "two pattern young ladies, in pattern attire, with pattern deportment"—a "respectable society" in which "Shirley had the air of a black swan, or a white crow. . . ." When, in singing, Shirley "poured round the passion, force," the young ladies thought this "strange" and concluded: "What was *strange* must be *wrong*; . . ." True, Charlotte's characters live within the established "patterns" of life; but their impulse is to vitalize forms with unpatterned feeling, and Charlotte's to give play to unpatterned feeling in all its forms. She detects the warrior in the Reverend Matthew Helstone; reports that Malone the curate "had energy enough in hate"; describes Shirley weeping without apparent reason; recounts Mrs. Yorke's paranoid "brooding, eternal, immitigable suspicion of all men, things, creeds, and parties"; portrays Hiram Yorke as scornful, stubborn, intolerant of superiors, independent, truculent, benevolent toward inferiors, his virtues surrounding an aggressive *amour propre*.

Shirley is given a vehement, sweeping, uninhibited criticalness of mind; in her highly articulate formulations of incisive thought is released a furious rush of emotional energy. Within the framework of moral principles her ideas and feelings are untrammeled. She vigorously debunks clichés against charity, but against the mob she will defend her property "like a tigress"; to Yorke's face she does a corrosive analysis of his personality; she attacks Milton in a fiery sweeping paean to Eve, the "mother" of "Titans"; in an almost explosive defense of love she attacks ignorant, chilly, refined, embarrassed people who "blaspheme living fire, seraph-brought from a divine altar"; when she insists that she must *"love"* before she marries, her "worldly" Uncle Sympson retorts, "Preposterous stuff!—indecorous—unwomanly!"

Beside the adults who in ways are precocious are the precocious children—the Yorkes who have their parents' free-swinging, uninhibited style of talk; Henry Sympson, having for his older cousin Shirley an attachment that borders on sexual feeling; and most of all Martin Yorke, aged fifteen, to whose excited pursuit of Caroline, almost irrelevant to plot or theme, Charlotte devotes two and a half zestful chapters. Martin is willing to help Caroline see Robert Moore, "her confounded sweetheart," to be near her himself, and he plans to claim a reward "displeasing to Moore"; he thinks of her physical beauties. Once he gets between Robert and Caroline at goodbye time; "he half carried Caroline down the stairs," "wrapped her shawl round her," and wanted to claim a kiss. At the same time he feels "power over her," he wants her to coax him, and he would like "to put her in a passion—to make her cry." Charlotte subtly conveys the sexuality of his quest—a rare feat in the nineteenth-century novel.

In Robert Moore, the unpopular mill-owner, Charlotte finds less social rightness or wrongness than his strength, his masculine appeal; her sympathy, so to speak, is for the underside of his personality. It "agreed with Moore's temperament . . . to be generally hated"; "he liked a silent, sombre, unsafe solitude"; against the vandals his "hate is still running in such a strong current" that he has none left for other objects; he shows "a terrible half" of himself in pursuing rioters with "indefatigable, . . . relentless assiduity"; this "excitement" pleases him; sadistically he likes to "force" magistrates to "betray a certain fear." He is the great lover of the story; he almost breaks Caroline's heart before he marries her, and he even has a subtle impact on Shirley, teasingly communicated, though officially denied, by Charlotte.

What Caroline yields to is his "secret power," which affects her "like a spell." Here again Charlotte records, as directly as she can, simple sexual attractiveness. From the problem novel she veers off into "new Gothic"; in old Gothic, her hero would have been a villain.

True to convention, the love stories end happily. But special feelings, a new pathos of love, come through. Louis Moore demands in a woman something "to endure, . . . to reprimand"; love must involve "prickly peril," "a sting now and then"; for him the "young lioness or leopardess" is better than the lamb. There is that peculiarly tense vivacity of talk between lovers (the Jane-Rochester style), who discover a heightened, at times stagey, yet highly communicative rhetoric, drawing now on fantasy, now on moral conviction, verging now on titillating revelation, now on battle; a crafty game of love, flirting with an undefined risk, betraying a withheld avowal, savoring the approach to consummation, as if the erotic energy which in another social order might find a physical outlet were forcing itself into an electric language that is decorous but intimately exploratory. Between Louis Moore, who has "a thirst for freedom," and Shirley, to whom finding love is the Quest for the Bridle (for "a *master* [whom it is] impossible not to love, and very possible to fear"), there is an almost disturbingly taut struggle, a fierce intensification of the duel between Mirabel and Millamant, complex feelings translated into wit, sheer debate, abusiveness of manner, and a variety of skirmishings; Louis, the lover, adopting the stance of power and consciously playing to fright; the pursuit of an elusive prey ending in a virtual parody of "one calling, Child! / And I replied, My Lord"; over all of this a singular air of strained excitement, of the working of underlying emotional forces that at the climax leads to a new frenetic intensification of style in Louis's notebook:

> "Will you let me breathe, and not bewilder me? You must not smile at present. The world swims and changes round me. The sun is a dizzying scarlet blaze, the sky a violet vortex whirling over me."

> I am a strong man, but I staggered as I spoke. All creation was exaggerated: colour grew more vivid: motion more rapid; life itself more vital. I hardly saw her for a moment; but I heard her voice—pitilessly sweet. . . . Blent with torment, I experienced rapture.

Nor does Charlotte's flair for "unpatterned feeling" stop here: Shirley, the forceful leader who has already been called "a gentleman" and "captain," languishes under the found bridle of the masterful lover, whom she treats chillily and subjects to "exquisitely provoking" postponements of marriage; he calls her a "pantheress" who "gnaws her chain"; she tells him, "I don't know myself," as if engagement had opened to her eyes a previously undetected facet of her nature. Though "these freaks" continue, she is "fettered" at last; but not before the reader is radically stirred by the felt mysteries of personality. Before Charlotte, no love story tapped such strange depths, no consummation was so like a defeat.

Here Charlotte is probing psychic disturbance and is on the edge of psychosomatic illness. The theme draws her repeatedly. When Caroline thinks Robert doesn't love her, she suffers a long physical decline, described with painful fullness. She "wasted," had a "broken spirit," suffered "intolerable despair," felt the "utter sickness of longing and disappointment," at night found "my mind darker than my hiding-place," had "melancholy dreams," became "what is called nervous," had "fears I never used to have," "an inexpressible weight on my mind," and "strange sufferings," believed at times "that God had turned His face from her" and sank "into the gulf of religious despair." Charlotte divines this: "People never die of love or grief alone; though some die of inherent maladies which the tortures of those passions prematurely force into destructive action." Caroline lingers in illness, has fancies "inscrutable to ordinary attendants," has a hallucination of talking to Robert in the garden. Shirley, having been bitten by a dog which she believes to be mad, becomes seriously ill; psychosomatic illness springs directly from Charlotte's special sensitivity to the neurotic potential in human nature. A complementary awareness, that of the impact of the physical on the psychic, appears when she observes the "terrible depression," the "inexpressible—dark, barren, impotent" state of mind of Robert when he is recovering from a gunshot wound.

To give so much space to a lesser work is justifiable only because some of its contents are of high historico-critical significance. Though *Shirley* is not pulled together formally as well as *Jane Eyre* or even the more sprawling *Villette,* and though the characters are as wholes less fully realized, still it accommodates the widest ranging of an extraordinarily free sensibility. Constantly, in many different directions, it is in flight from the ordinary rational surface of things against which old Gothic was the first rebel in fiction; it abundantly contains and evokes, to adapt Charlotte's own metaphor, "unpatterned feeling." It turns up unexpected elements in personality: resentfulness, malice, love of power; precocities and perversities of response; the multiple tensions of love between highly individualized lovers; psychic disturbances. And in accepting a dark magnetic energy as a central virtue in personality, Charlotte simply reverses the status of men who were the villains in the sentimental and old Gothic modes.

Of the four novels, **Villette** is most heavily saturated with Gothic—with certain of its traditional manifestations (old Gothic), with the undercutting of these that is for Charlotte no less instinctive than the use of them (anti-Gothic), and with an original, intense exploration of feeling that increases the range and depth of fiction (new Gothic).

As in **Jane Eyre,** Charlotte can be skillful in anti-Gothic. When Madame Beck, pussyfooting in espionage, "materializes" in shocking suddenness, Lucy is made matter-of-fact or indignant rather than thrilled with fright. "No ghost stood beside me . . ." is her characteristic response to a Beck surprise. Once the spy, having "stolen" upon her victims, betrays her unseen presence by a sneeze: Gothic yields to farce. Technically more complex is Charlotte's use of the legend of the nun supposedly buried alive and of the appearances of a visitant taken to be the ghost of the nun: Charlotte coolly distances herself from this by having Lucy dismiss the legend as "romantic rubbish" and by explaining the apparitions as the playful inventions of a giddy lover. True, she keeps the secret long enough to get a few old Gothic thrills from the "ghost," but what she is really up to is using the apparitions in an entirely new way; that is, for responses that lie beyond the simplicities of terror.

First, the apparitions are explained as a product of Lucy's own psychic state, the product, Dr. John suggests, of "long-continued mental conflict." In the history of Gothic this is an important spot, for here we first see the shift from stock explanations and responses to the inner human reality: fiction is slowly discovering the psychic depths known to drama for centuries.

Then, when Lucy next sees the nun, she responds in a way that lies entirely outside fictional convention: "I neither fled nor shrieked . . . I spoke . . . I stretched out my hand, for I meant to touch her." Not that Lucy is not afraid, but that she is testing herself—an immense change from the expectable elementary response: the *frisson* disappears before the complexer action that betokens a maturing of personality.

Finally, Paul and Lucy both see the spectre and are thus brought closer together: they have had what they call "impressions," and through sharing the ghost they assume a shared sensibility. Paul says, "I was conscious of rapport between you and myself." The rapport is real, though the proof of it is false; the irony of this is a subtle sophistication of Gothic.

The responsiveness, the sensitivity, is the thing; many passages place "feeling" above "seeing" as an avenue of knowledge. Reason must be respected, for it is "vindictive," but at times imagination must be yielded to, like a sexual passion at once feared and desired. There is the summer night when the sedative given by Madame Beck has a strange effect:

> Imagination was roused from her rest, and she came forth impetuous and venturous. With scorn she looked on Matter, her mate—
>
> "Rise!" she said; "Sluggard! this night I will have *my* will; nor shalt thou prevail."
>
> "Look forth and view the night!" was her cry; and when I lifted the heavy blind from the casement close at hand—with her own royal gesture, she showed me a moon supreme, in an element deep and splendid.
>
> . . . She lured me to leave this den and follow her forth into dew, coolness, and glory.

There follows the most magnificent of all Charlotte's nocturnes: that vision of the "moonlit, midnight park," the brilliance of the fete, the strange charm of places and people, recounted in a rhythmical, enchanted style (the "Kubla Khan" mode) which at first reading gives the air of a dream mistaken for reality to what is in fact reality made like a dream. This is a surrealistic, trance-like episode which makes available to fiction a vast new territory and idiom. The surrealistic is, despite Montague Summers, one of the new phases of Gothic, which in its role of liberator of feeling characteristically explores the non-naturalistic: to come up, as here, with a profounder nature, or a nature freshly, even disturbingly, seen.

The surrealism of Lucy's evening is possible only to a special sensitivity, and it is really the creation of this sensitivity, in part pathological, that is at the apex of Charlotte's Gothic. In **The Professor** the tensions in the author's contemplation of her own experience come into play; in **Shirley** various undercurrents of personality push up into the social surfaces of life; in **Jane Eyre** moral feeling is subjected to the remolding pressures of a newly vivid consciousness of the diverse impulses of sexuality; and in **Villette** the feeling responses to existence are pursued into sufferings that edge over into disorder. The psychology of rejection and alienation, first applied to Polly, becomes the key to Lucy, who, finding no catharsis for a sense of desolation, generates a serious inner turmoil. She suffers from "a terrible oppression" and then from "anxiety lying in wait on enjoyment, like a tiger crouched in a jungle . . . his fierce heart panted close against mine; . . . I knew he waited only for sun-down to bound ravenous from his ambush." Depression is fed by the conflict between a loveless routine of life and her longings, which she tried to put down like "Jael to Sisera, driving a nail through their temples"; but this only "transiently stunned" them and "at intervals [they] would turn on the nail with a rebellious wrench: then did the temples bleed, and the brain thrill to its core."

These strains prepare us for the high point in Charlotte's new Gothic—the study of Lucy's emotional collapse and near breakdown when vacation comes and she is left alone at the school with "a poor deformed and imbecile pupil." "My heart almost died within me; . . . My spirits had long been gradually sinking; now that the prop of employment was withdrawn, they went down fast." After three weeks, storms bring on "a deadlier paralysis"; and "my nervous system could hardly support" the daily strain. She wanders in the street: "A goad thrust me on, a fever forbade me to rest; . . ." She observes a "growing illusion" and says, ". . . my nerves are getting overstretched; . . ." She feels that "a malady is growing upon" her mind, and she asks herself, "How shall I keep well?" Then come "a peculiarly agonizing depression"; a nine-days storm: "a strange fever of the nerves and blood"; continuing insomnia, broken only by a terrifying nightmare of alienation. She flees the house, and then comes the climactic event of her going to a church and despite the intensity of her Protestant spirit entering the confessional to find relief.

From now on, overtly or implicitly, hypochondria and anxiety keep coming into the story—the enemies from whose grip Lucy must gradually free herself. At a concert she spotted the King as a fellow-victim of "that strangest spectre, Hypochondria," for on his face she saw its marks, whose meaning, "if I did not *know*, at least I *felt*, . . ." When, after her return to Beck's on a rainy night, things are not going well, a letter from Dr. John is "the ransom from my terror," and its loss drives her almost to frenzy. She describes night as "an unkindly time" when she has strange fancies,

doubts, the "horror of calamity." She is aware of her "easily-deranged temperament." Beyond this area of her own self-understanding we see conflicts finding dramatic expression in her almost wild acceptance of Rachel's passionate acting of Phèdre ("a spectacle low, horrible, immoral"), which counterbalances her vehement condemnation of a fleshy nude by Rubens (one of the "materialists"). Paul identifies her, in a figure whose innocence for him is betrayed by the deep, if not wholly conscious, understanding that leads Charlotte to write it: "a young she wild creature, new caught, untamed, viewing with a mixture of fire and fear the first entrance of the breaker in."

There is not room to trace Lucy's recovery, especially in the important phase, the love affair with Paul which is related to our theme by compelling, as do the Jane-Rochester and Louis Moore-Shirley relationships in quite different ways, a radical revision of the feelings exacted by stereotyped romance. What is finally noteworthy is that Charlotte, having chosen in Lucy a heroine with the least durable emotional equipment, with the most conspicuous neurotic element in her temperament, goes on through the history of Lucy's emotional maturing to surmount the need for romantic fulfillment and to develop the aesthetic courage for a final disaster—the only one in her four novels.

Some years ago Edmund Wilson complained of writers of Gothic who "fail to lay hold on the terrors that lie deep in the human soul and that cause man to fear himself" and proposed an anthology of horror stories that probe "psychological caverns" and find "disquieting obsessions." This is precisely the direction in which Charlotte Brontë moved, especially in Lucy Snowe and somewhat also in Caroline Helstone and Shirley Keeldar; this was one aspect of her following human emotions where they took her, into many depths and intensities that as yet hardly had a place in the novel. This was the finest achievement of Gothic.

Gothic is variously defined. In a recent book review Leslie Fiedler implies that Gothic is shoddy mystery-mongering, whereas F. Cudworth Flint defines the Gothic tradition, which he considers "nearly central in American literature," as "a literary exploration of the avenues to death." For Montague Summers, on the other hand, Gothic was the essence of romanticism, and romanticism was the literary expression of supernaturalism. Both these latter definitions, though they are impractically inclusive, have suggestive value. For originally Gothic was one of a number of aesthetic developments which served to breach the "classical" and "rational" order of life and to make possible a kind of response, and a response to a kind of thing, that among the knowing had long been taboo. In the novel it was the function of Gothic to open horizons beyond social patterns, rational decisions, and institutionally approved emotions; in a word, to enlarge the sense of reality and its impact on the human being. It became then a great liberator of feeling. It acknowledged the non-rational—in the world of things and events, occasionally in the realm of the transcendental, ultimately and most persistently in the depths of the human being. (Richardson might have started this, but his sense of inner forces was so overlaid by the moralistic that his followers all ran after him only when he ran the wrong way.) The first Gothic writers took the easy way: the excitement of mysterious scene and happening, which I call old Gothic. Of this Charlotte Brontë made some direct use, while at the same time tending toward humorous modifications (anti-Gothic); but what really counts is its indirect usefulness to her: it released her from the patterns of the novel of society and therefore permitted the flowering of her real talent—the talent for finding and giving dramatic form to impulses and feelings which, because of their depth or mysteriousness or intensity or ambiguity, or of their ignoring or transcending everyday norms of propriety or reason, increase wonderfully the sense of reality in the novel. To note the emergence of this "new Gothic" in Charlotte Brontë is not, I think, to pursue an old mode into dusty corners but rather to identify historically the distinguishing, and distinguished, element in her work.

TITLE COMMENTARY

Jane Eyre

E. P. WHIPPLE (ESSAY DATE OCTOBER 1848)

SOURCE: Whipple, E. P. "Novels of the Season." *The North American Review* 67, no. 141 (October 1848): 354-70.

In the following excerpt from a review of Jane Eyre, *Whipple presumes the novel was written largely by Patrick Branwell Brontë—due to the novel's "masculine tone"—with additional material supplied by the Brontë sisters. Whipple also asserts that the Brontës' portrayal of the darker side of humanity is not representative of most people, but rather of "a sense of the depravity of human nature peculiarly their own."*

Not many months ago, the New England States were visited by a distressing mental epidemic, passing under the name of the "*Jane Eyre* fever," which defied all the usual nostrums of the established doctors of criticism. Its effects varied with different constitutions, in some producing a soft ethical sentimentality, which relaxed all the fibres of conscience, and in others exciting a general fever of moral and religious indignation. It was to no purpose that the public were solemnly assured, through the intelligent press, that the malady was not likely to have any permanent effect either on the intellectual or moral constitution. The book which caused the distemper would probably have been inoffensive, had not some sly manufacturer of mischief hinted that it was a book which no respectable man should bring into his family circle. Of course, every family soon had a copy of it, and one edition after another found eager purchasers. The hero, Mr. Rochester, (not the same person who comes to so edifying an end in the pages of Dr. Gilbert Burnet,) became a great favorite in the boarding-schools and in the worshipful society of governesses. That portion of Young America known as ladies' men began to swagger and swear in the presence of the gentler sex, and to allude darkly to events in their lives which excused impudence and profanity.

While fathers and mothers were much distressed at this strange conduct of their innocents, and with a pardonable despair were looking for the dissolution of all the bonds of society, the publishers of *Jane Eyre* announced *Wuthering Heights,* by the same author. When it came, it was purchased and read with universal eagerness; but, alas! it created disappointment almost as universal. It was a panacea for all the sufferers under the epidemic. Society returned to its old condition, parents were blessed in hearing once more their children talk common sense, and rakes and battered profligates of high and low degree fell instantly to their proper level. Thus ended the last desperate attempt to corrupt the virtue of the sturdy descendants of the Puritans.

The novel of *Jane Eyre,* which caused this great excitement, purports to have been edited by Currer Bell, and the said Currer divides the authorship, if we are not misinformed, with a brother and sister. The work bears the marks of more than one mind and one sex, and has more variety than either of the novels which claim to have been written by Acton Bell. The family mind is strikingly peculiar, giving a strong impression of unity, but it is still male and female. From the masculine tone of *Jane Eyre,* it might pass altogether as the composition of a man, were it not for some unconscious feminine peculiarities, which the strongest-minded woman that ever aspired after manhood cannot suppress. These peculiarities refer not only to elaborate descriptions of dress, and the minutiæ of the sick-chamber, but to various superficial refinements of feeling in regard to the external relations of the sex. It is true that the noblest and best representations of female character have been produced by men; but there are niceties of thought and emotion in a woman's mind which no man can delineate, but which often escape unawares from a female writer. There are numerous examples of these in *Jane Eyre.* The leading characteristic of the novel, however, and the secret of its charm, is the clear, distinct, decisive style of its representation of character, manners, and scenery; and this continually suggests a male mind. In the earlier chapters, there is little, perhaps, to break the impression that we are reading the autobiography of a powerful and peculiar female intellect; but when the admirable Mr. Rochester appears, and the profanity, brutality, and slang of the misanthropic profligate give their torpedo shocks to the nervous system,—and especially when we are favored with more than one scene given to the exhibition of mere animal appetite, and to courtship after the manner of kangaroos and the heroes of Dryden's plays,—we are gallant enough to detect the hand of a gentleman in the composition. There are also scenes of passion, so hot, emphatic, and condensed in expression, and so sternly masculine in feeling, that we are almost sure we observe the mind of the author of *Wuthering Heights* at work in the text.

The popularity of *Jane Eyre* was doubtless due in part to the freshness, raciness, and vigor of mind it evinced; but it was obtained not so much by these qualities as by frequent dealings in moral paradox, and by the hardihood of its assaults upon the prejudices of proper people. Nothing causes more delight, at least to one third of every community, than a successful attempt to wound the delicacy of their scrupulous neighbours, and a daring peep into regions which acknowledge the authority of no conventional rules. The authors of *Jane Eyre* have not accomplished this end without an occasional violation of probability and considerable confusion of plot and character, and they have made the capital mistake of supposing that an artistic representation of character and manners is a literal imitation of individual life. The consequence is, that in dealing with vicious personages they confound vulgarity with truth,

and awaken too often a feeling of unmitigated disgust. The writer who colors too warmly the degrading scenes through which his immaculate hero passes is rightly held as an equivocal teacher of purity; it is not by the bold expression of blasphemy and ribaldry that a great novelist conveys the most truthful idea of the misanthropic and the dissolute. The truth is, that the whole firm of Bell & Co. seem to have a sense of the depravity of human nature peculiarly their own. It is the yahoo, not the demon, that they select for representation; their Pandemonium is of mud rather than fire.

CAESAREA ABARTIS (ESSAY DATE 1979)

SOURCE: Abartis, Caesarea. "The Ugly-Pretty, Dull-Bright, Weak-Strong Girl in the Gothic Mansion." *Journal of Popular Culture* 13 (1979): 257-63.

In the following essay, Abartis illustrates how Jane Eyre *serves as "the prototype for the modern Gothic" or romance novel in which a female protagonist overcomes personal challenges and escapes peril to win the love of a man to whom she will remain "subordinate economically and socially."*

If you ask a reader of modern Gothic novels to describe the heroine, you are liable to get an impossible portrait: the Gothic heroine is passive, weak and virginal, but simultaneously, or under another name and in another novel, she is passionate, strong and independent. How do these apparently paradoxical types function in the Gothic formula? In the former type of plot someone else—usually the hero—wins; in the latter type she loses. These types can be seen clearly in four novels: Charlotte Brontë's *Jane Eyre* (1847), Daphne du Maurier's *Rebecca* (1938), Victoria Holt's *Kirkland Revels* (1962) and Claudette Nicole's *House at Hawk's End* (1971).[1]

If I may be permitted to judge a book by its cover, I can derive some of the chief elements of the Gothic novel from the artist's cover painting. Always there is a young and beautiful woman facing front, with a high wind scattering her hair about. Often she is wearing a nightgown. Invariably she is running away from a gloomy castle or Victorian mansion which has a light in only one window. Less often there is a second figure on the cover—a man—strong, handsome, with the symbols of wealth and power. He may be riding a horse in pursuit of the heroine, or perhaps standing some distance behind her, watching her. The composition of the cover depicts, in short, the character, plot and setting of the Gothic novel: in

ABOUT THE AUTHOR

WILLIAM DEAN HOWELLS LAUDS THE TITLE CHARACTER OF *JANE EYRE*

[No] heroine of Thackeray's except Becky Sharp seems to me quite so alive as the Jane Eyre of Charlotte Brontë, whom I do not class with him intellectually, any more than I class her artistically with the great novelists. . . . She was the first English novelist to present the impassioned heroine; impassioned not in man's sense but woman's sense, in which love purifies itself of sensuousness without losing fervor. . . .

Old-fashioned, I have suggested; but now, after reading [the scene in which Rochester's mad wife makes her first appearance], I find that hardly the word. It is old-fashioned only in the sense of being very simple, and of a quaint sincerity. The fact is presented, the tremendous means are used, with almost childlike artlessness; but the result is of high novelty. Few would have had the courage to deal so frankly with the situation, to chance its turning ludicrous, or would have had the skill to unfold its fine implications of tenderness, and keep them undamaged by the matter-of-fact details. But Charlotte Brontë did all this, and did it out of the resources of her own unique experience of life, which never presented itself in the light of common day, but came to her through strange glooms, and in alternations of native solitude and alien multitude, at Haworth and in Brussels. The whole story, so deeply of nature, is steeped in the supernatural; and just as paradoxically the character of Jane Eyre lacks that final projection from the author which is the supreme effect of art, only because she feels it so intensely that she cannot detach it from herself.

SOURCE: Howells, William Dean. "Heroines of Nineteenth-Century Fiction." *Harper's Bazaar* 33, no. 50 (15 December 1900): 2094-100.

The modern Gothic has its roots in the eighteenth- and nineteenth century thrillers like Walpole's *The Castle of Otranto* (1764), Ann Radcliffe's *The Mysteries of Udolpho* (1794), Matthew Lewis' *The Monk* (1796), Charles Brockden Brown's *Wieland* (1798) and Mary Shelley's *Frankenstein* (1818). The purpose of these novels is presumably to elicit and purge feelings of fear and horror in the reader. This purgation is achieved by setting the story in castles appointed with secret passages, ghosts, corpses, spooky sounds and A Dark Secret. In the modern Gothic the supernatural has been pretty much suppressed and rationalized, while the heroine and her romantic interests have assumed the center of the novel. Thus in *Kirkland Revels*, what seems to be an apparition is ultimately explained logically; in *House at Hawk's End*, just as important as the solution to the mystery is the choice of a lover from the three men who present themselves to the heroine. The Gothic novel has moved from ghostly horrors to love fantasies and this shift has sociological implications. This category of popular fiction is written almost, or perhaps exclusively, for women, about women and by women (the pseudonyms are nearly always female even though some of the writers are male). In the past, it has been dismissed from serious study because it is subliterary, but it is an immensely popular form, as I have discovered from casual inquiries of women and from examining bookracks in supermarkets, drugstores and bookstores.[2] The Gothic novel gains significance, if not from its artistry then from its overwhelming popularity.

The prototype for the modern Gothic is Charlotte Brontë's *Jane Eyre*. Brontë exploits all the motifs and themes of the Gothic novel, but in an ambiguous way. Jane is an impoverished orphan who is neglected and abused by her aunt. Jane eventually becomes a governess to a child at Thornfield Hall where the master is Edward Rochester, a moody, brusque, older man. She almost marries Rochester before the secret of the third floor is made known: Rochester has a wife—demented and bestial. Ultimately, of course, Jane and Rochester marry, but only after his first wife has died in the fire which destroys the manor and cripples and blinds Rochester in a poetic punishment for his bigamous desires.

Jane is the picture of an outsider. She is an orphan; more, she is a poor orphan; more than that, a homely, unloved, poor orphan. Almost obsessively and from the first page, Jane emphasizes what she calls her "physical inferiority" (ch. 1, 5), that is, her unattractive face and slight

a rich and exotic setting the lovely heroine meets with some vague danger from which she must escape.

figure. Years later, after Jane has grown up, she meets her nursemaid Bessie, who agrees in that evaluation, "You were no beauty as a child." Jane reponds with a rueful smile: "I felt that it was correct, but I confess I was not quite indifferent to its import: at eighteen most people wish to please, and the conviction that they have not an exterior likely to second that desire brings anything but gratification" (ch. 10, 80). On her first day as governess, she dresses herself carefully:

> It was not my habit to be disregardful of appearance, or careless of the impression I made: on the contrary, I ever wished to look as well as I could, and to please as much as my want of beauty would permit. I sometimes regretted that I was not handsomer. I sometimes wished to have rosy cheeks, a straight nose, and small cherry mouth; I desired to be tall, stately, and finely developed in figure; I felt it a misfortune that I was so little, so pale, and had features so irregular and marked.
>
> (ch. 11, 86)

Jane's description of her physical appearance is a key to her personality; she has irregular features and irregular views, but she longs for "regularity." Jane sees herself as different by temperament and education from many of the people with whom she associates. Thus, she looks down on uneducated vulgar servants like Sophie, Grace Poole and even Mrs. Fairfax, none of whom can be a companion to her soul, but Jane is also alienated from the rich and beautiful people because she is poor and homely.

From childhood she has been strong, passionate and independent—when she strikes back at John Reed who is bullying her, when she rebels and denounces Mrs. Reed for her coldness, when she decides to leave Lowood to look for a position as governess, when she leaves Rochester because she cannot live with him unmarried, when she resists St. John's proposal despite his almost hypnotic power over her. She is a restless and curious woman. At Thornfield she occasionally separates herself from the household to go to the roof of the house and to look toward the horizon and imagine the variety and adventure of the world that she can never see:

> . . . then I longed for a power of vision which might overpass that limit; which might reach the busy world, towns, regions full of life I had heard of but never seen: that then I desired more of practical experience than I possessed; more of intercourse with my kind, of acquaintance with variety of character, than was here within my reach. I valued what was good in Mrs. Fairfax, and was good in Adele; but I believed in the existence of other and more vivid kinds of goodness, and what I believed in and wished to behold. . . . It is

in vain to say human beings ought to be satisfied with tranquillity: they must have action; and they will make it if they cannot find it. Millions are condemned to a stiller doom than mine, and millions are in silent revolt against their lot. Nobody knows how many rebellions are in silent revolt against their lot. Nobody knows how many rebellions ferment in the masses of life which people earth. Women are supposed to be very calm generally: but women feel just as men feel; they need exercise for their faculties and a field for their efforts as much as their brothers do; they suffer from too rigid a restraint, too absolute a stagnation, precisely as men would suffer; and it is narrow-minded in their more privileged fellow-creatures to say that they ought to confine themselves to making puddings and knitting stockings, to playing on the piano and embroidering bags. It is thoughtless to condemn them, or laugh at them, if they seek to do more or learn more than custom has pronounced necessary for their sex.

> (ch. 12, 96-7)

This strong feminist statement is, however, undermined by the plot. Jane exhibits heroic discontent and eccentricity—traits that the readers of the novel identify with and admit to themselves only in their fantasies where wealth and status are bequeathed upon them so that their discontent can be relieved and their eccentricity redeemed. It is ironic that even Jane, original and passionate as she avows herself, is subdued to a conventional ending. She does not travel to faraway cities and meet with vital and various people. The closest she gets to attaining this dream is to marry a well-traveled man.

The master of Thornfield, Edward Rochester, falls in love with her despite the fact that she is "poor and obscure, small and plain" (ch. 23, 224). He admires her sincerity, intelligence, passion and strength and promises to be true to her:

> "To women who please me only by their faces, I am the very devil when I find out they have neither souls nor hearts—when they open to me a perspective of flatness, triviality, and perhaps imbecility, coarseness, and ill-temper: but to the clear eye and eloquent tongue, to the soul made of fire, and the character that bends but does not break—at once supple and stable, tractable and consistent—I am ever tender and true."
>
> (ch. 24, 228-9)

When Rochester proposes to Jane, he says she is his "equal" and his "likeness" (ch. 23, 223).

Rochester perceives their relationship in terms of power. When they at last reveal their love to each other, after having held back the admission out of mingled pride and humility, Rochester says to her: "Jane, you please me, and you master me—

you seem to submit, and I like the sense of pliancy you impart" (ch. 24, 229). Jane is also aware of her power over him:

It little mattered whether my curiosity irritated him; I knew the pleasure of vexing and soothing him by turns; it was one I chiefly delighted in, and a sure instinct always prevented me from going too far: beyond the verge of provocation I never ventured; on the extreme brink I like to try my skill

(ch. 26, 138)

She is his subordinate economically and socially, but emotionally she enjoys power over him.

Jane is an active principle in the novel, not a damsel in distress. She even performs the function of the savior—almost always reserved to the male protagonist in more recent examples of the Gothic novel. She saves Rochester's life at least once and helps him twice. The first time she meets him, he falls off his horse and he must lean on her because he has sprained his ankle. She saves his life when she wakes in the night to smell smoke and puts out the fire that Bertha had started in Rochester's bedroom. At the end, Jane returns to a Rochester who has been crippled and blinded in the fire that burns down Thornfield Hall. Her return lifts him out of his depression. In a sense, she is no longer physically inferior to him (because he has lost a hand and an eye), nor is she financially dependent on him (because of her inheritance). She says to him, "I love you better now, when I can really be useful to you, than I did in your state of proud independence, when you disdained every part but that of the giver and protector" (ch. 37, 392).

The ending is not the ending of a typical Gothic novel. Paradoxically it is Jane's Victorian scruples that save her from being a conventional Gothic heroine. It is not a ghost or murderer that chases Jane from Thornfield Hall but the revelation of the existence of Rochester's first wife. The Gothic machinery grinds to a halt; what propels the rest of the book is Jane's struggle with the immorality of her love. If the questions of guilt and religion were removed, the book could conceivably end earlier with, for example, a fire on the day after Rochester's confession. The conflagration could remove the inconvenient first wife, but not harm Rochester. He could save Jane and thereby prove his love. This would be a more typical modern Gothic ending. Apparently, however, Rochester's payment of a hand and an eye is essential to the scheme of retribution. When she returns to him at the end, it is not, however, as his equal. Implicit in the final chapter is the

reversal of their roles: whereas before he was the powerful father-figure and she the child, at the end she is the mother-figure and he the helpless child.

Another Gothic novel in which the heroine "saves" the hero but still submits to convention and domestic joys is *Rebecca*. The narrator is, like Jane Eyre, a shy and sensitive orphan. She is not a governess but she performs an analogous service— she is a companion to a wealthy woman. Like Jane, she is considerably younger than her husband—she is twenty-one, he is in his forties and very much a father-figure to her.[3] The heroine is throughout the novel known only as the second Mrs. de Winter. We never learn her maiden name, nor her given name. There is a story in that omission, for it is her function to become completely the second Mrs. de Winter and to assume control of Manderley, the centuries-old ancestral home. The Great Old House is the indispensable setting of the Gothic novel and the symbol of what the Gothic heroine, typically lower class but well-educated and "different," aspires to and deserves. As in this novel, the house is often important enough to be named, and it is symbolic of the wealth and states that the reader yearns for and the heroine achieves. The Great House is not, however, associate with political power and not the symbol of what a Lady Macbeth aspires to. It is a glorified domestic dwelling—that which will make the little woman of the house into the lady; it is a middle-class housewife's dream. Once the heroine has possession of the house, the emphasis is on conspicuous consumption—on the magnificent parties, the dinners, the furnishings, the repartee of the guests. (We will never find a Gothic novel set in an efficiency apartment.) When Maximilian de Winter brings his young bride to Manderley, she tries to accustom herself to the elegance of the estate:

I leant back in my chair, glancing about the room, trying to instil into myself some measure of confidence, some genuine realisation that I was here, at Manderly, the house of the picture postcard, the Manderley that was famous. I had to teach myself that all this was mine now, mine as much as his, the deep chair I was sitting in, that mass of books stretching to the ceiling, the pictures on the walls, the gardens, the woods, the Manderley I had read about, all of this was mine now because I was married to Maxim.

(ch. 7, 69)

That is her struggle throughout the book—to achieve the true possession of Manderley, to assume her rightful place as Mrs. de Winter, lady of leisure.

Out of her insecurity, the second Mrs. de Winter suspects that everyone, the servants and friends, admired the first Mrs. de Winter, Rebecca, and she believes that Maxim still loves his first wife. The heroine's problems consist of getting society and the servants to accept her. Maxim finally confides to his wife that he killed Rebecca, that she was debauched and wanted to ruin him. The last fourth of the book, after the dark secret is revealed, is about the coroner's inquest into the death of Rebecca and the magistrate's investigation. Now the roles of hero and heroine are reversed. Like Jane Eyre, the second Mrs. de Winter must comfort her husband:

> Maxim came over to me where I was standing by the fireplace. I held out my arms to him and he came to me like a child. I put my arms around him and held him. We did not say anthing for a long time. I held him and comforted him as though he were Jasper [their pet dog]
>
> (ch. 25, 352)

In the course of their ordeal, she demonstrates her loyalty and love. When Maxim is finally free of the murder charge, she is determined to take control of the house. She has grown up, she says, and this is what she has grown into:

> I would go and interview the cook in the kitchen. They would like me, respect me. . . . I would learn more about the estate, too. . . . I might take to gardening myself, and in time have one or two things altered. . . . There were heaps of things that I could do, little by little. People would come and stay and I should not mind. There would be the interest of seeing to their rooms, having flowers and books put, arranging the food
>
> (ch. 27, 376)

Exactly what Jane Eyre was protesting against: making puddings and knitting stockings. She becomes the lady of the manor in this realization, the domestic achiever *par excellence*. At the end, the second Mrs. de Winter, like Jane Eyre, is deprived of the Great House, which in both cases burns down, but she is not deprived of the respectability that the Great House represents. Almost anthropormorphized, the house becomes the scapegoat for the sins committed in it. The death of the house allows the heroine to be preserved in spite of her dallying with a naughty man. The heroine is mildly punished; the evil past is purified by fire; wealth and love remain as the heroine's reward.

In these novels the heroine "saves" the hero and thereby demonstrates her worthiness to be the lady of the house. She is, in effect, the frog princess who becomes transformed by the love of a good-bad man, and inherits the rewards. But

Orson Welles as Edward Rochester, and Joan Fontaine as Jane Eyre, in a scene from Robert Stevenson's 1944 film adaptation of *Jane Eyre*.

there is another pattern frequently found in Gothic novels in which it is the heroine who is saved by the hero, in such novels as *Kirkland Revels* and *House at Hawk's End*.

In *Kirkland Revels*, the heroine, Catherine Corder, will eventually marry Simon Redvers, who, in this case, is not much older, nor richer, nor classier than she is. Catherine has greater wealth and higher status than Simon—but this is a result of her first marriage to Simon's cousin. She is spirited, sensible, charming and courageous, and despite, or perhaps, because of these qualities she must be rescued at the end by the hero. While she is not an orphan and not impoverished she does feel alienated and unloved. She meets and marries Gabriel Rockwell, heir to Kirkland Revels, a three-hundred year old mansion. One week after he has taken her to the estate, he is found dead and the family assumes he committed suicide by jumping from a parapet. Catherine learns that she is pregnant and Gothic events transpire: she awakens and sees a person at the foot of her bed; an item is missing from her room; she sees a hooded figure. Catherine assumes that her husband was killed because he was heir to the estate; if her child is a boy, he will be heir and will also be killed. Catherine, spunky and nosey, keeps searching for the killer of her husband. At the end the villain chloroforms Catherine and takes her to a mental institution. The hero, like "a knight of old," saves her at the last minute (ch. 7, 250). Perhaps this is as liberated as the genre can get. Even though the heroine is active, logical and self-possessed, she must be in the grip of the villain for a thrilling climax so that she can be saved by the hero—not a girl friend or a brother, but a lover. Every spirited heroine needs a lover—if only to save her at the end. Certainly one of the implications of such a plot is that in a husband and in love there is safety.

Jean Burroughs, the heroine of *House at Hawk's End,* is the most "liberated" and the most in need of saving. She is a sophisticated city-girl, a buyer for a large dress house, who comes to Nova Scotia to forget the swingers and to forget the suicide of an old boy friend. Gothic events begin to happen: she hears noises; she sees a red glow on the sea; there is a rock slide that almost kills her; someone tries to sink her boat when she is sailing. In the last two chapters she is saved twice by her hometown boy friend—once from a mob that wants to burn down her house and a second time from the villains who want to drown her. This is the simplest, barest example of the Gothic formula that emphasizes the union of love and danger. When Jean comes to the town, two men court her. One is a good guy and one is a bad guy, but she is not able to sort out the good from the evil until the very end. A mistake in her love life could be fatal. The true lover proves his love by saving the heroine, but there is another implication for the heroine. Love is what the Gothic heroine lives for, what fulfills her, what saves her in the end.

The rewards and goals are the same for both kinds of heroines, for the strong and the weak, the unlovely and the lovely, the naive and the sophisticated, the proud and the humble, the saving and the saved. After a trial by danger there will be a husband, and often wealth. Historically, the Gothic novel was a way of purging horror and fear, a way of explicating and integrating the supernatural and irrational. In more recent Gothic novels the central character is female and love becomes a major interest: love solves the mystery and love is the reward for the heroine.

These books are an index to the dreams of many women readers and their fantasies of adventure and love. The heroine is an underdog who finds, in her man, the Prince Charming who can make a Cinderella out of her, who validates her hidden beauty and worth. The heroine is never the shopgirl who marries the clerk. She is never a

doctor; never the woman who seeks adventure and is able to deal with it entirely by herself. If literature is, as Kenneth Burke says, "equipment for living," the contemporary Gothic novel equips the reader to be passive and to hanker after mansions.

Notes

1. Charlotte Brontë, *Jane Eyre,* ed. Richard J. Dunn (New York: Norton & Co. 1971), Daphne du Maurier, *Rebecca* (New York: Avon, 1938), Victoria Holt, *Kirkland Revels* (New York: Fawcett World Library, 1962), Claudette Nicole, *House at Hawk's end* (Greenwich Conn.: Fawcett, 1971), Chapter and page citations will be given in the text.

2. I was able to find only four studies of contemporary Gothic novels, all of which I recommend: Joanna Russ, "Somebody's Trying to Kill Me and I Think It's My Husband: The Modern Gothic," *Journal of Popular Culture,* 6 (Spring, 1973), 666-691; Kay J. Mussell, "Beautiful and Damned: The Sexual Woman in Gothic Fiction," *Journal of Popular Culture,* 9 (Summer, 1975), 84-89; John G. Cawelti, *Adventure, Mystery, and Romance: Formula Stories as Art and Popular Culture* (Chicago: Univ. of Chicago Press, 1976); Ellen Moers, *Literary Women* (Garden City, N.Y.: Doubleday, 1976).

3. Maximilian responds to his wife's questions in this way, "Well, then. A husband is not so very different from a father after all. There is a certain type of knowledge I prefer you not to have. It's better kept under lock and key. So that's that. And now eat up your peaches, and don't ask me any more questions, or I shall put you in a corner" (ch. 16, 202).

Villette

W. R. GREG (ESSAY DATE APRIL 1853)

SOURCE: Greg, W. R. "Recent Novels: *Villette.*" *The Edinburgh Review* 97, no. 198 (April 1853): 387-90.

In the following excerpt, Greg offers a laudatory assessment of Villette.

Villette, by the author of *Jane Eyre,* is a most remarkable work—a production altogether *sui generis.* Fulness and vigour of thought mark almost every sentence, and there is a sort of easy power pervading the whole narrative, such as we have rarely met. There is little of plot or incident in the story; nearly the whole of it is confined to the four walls of a *Pensionnat* at Brussels; but the characters introduced are sketched with a bold and free pencil, and their individuality is sustained with a degree of consistency, which marks a master's hand. The descriptions, too, whether the subjects of them be solemn, ludicrous, or pathetic, are wonderfully graphic and pictorial. It is clear at a glance that the groundwork and many of the details of the story are autobiographic; and we never read a literary production which so betrays at every line the individual character of the writer. Her life has evidently been irradiated by but scanty sunshine, and she is besides disposed to look rather pertinaciously on the shady side of every landscape. With an almost painful and unceasing consciousness of possessing few personal or circumstantial advantages; with spirits naturally the reverse of buoyant; with feelings the reverse of demonstrative; with affections strong rather than warm, and injured by too habitual repression; a keen, shrewd, sagacious, sarcastic, observer of life, rather than a genial partaker in its interests; gifted with intuitive insight into character, and reading it often with too cold and critical an eye; full of sympathy where love and admiration call it forth, but able by long discipline to dispense with it herself; always somewhat too rigidly strung up for the hard struggle of life, but fighting sternly and gallantly its gloomy battle,—the character which Lucy Snowe has here drawn of herself presents rather an interesting study than an attraction or a charm.

TONI WEIN (ESSAY DATE AUTUMN 1999)

SOURCE: Wein, Toni. "Gothic Desire in Charlotte Brontë's *Villette*." *SEL: Studies in English Literature, 1500-1900* 39, no. 4 (autumn 1999): 733-46.

In the following essay, Wein examines Brontë's re-working of earlier Gothic devices and imagery in Villette, *particularly in terms of how she used them to depict gender roles and sexual desire.*

A letter of 16 June 1854 reads as follows: "My dear Ellen, Can you come next Wednesday or Thursday? I am afraid circumstances will compel me to agree to an earlier day than I wished. I sadly wished to defer it till the 2nd week in July, but I fear it must be sooner, the 1st week in July, possibly the last week in June . . . This gives rise to much trouble and many difficulties as you may imagine, and papa's whole anxiety now is to get the business over. Mr. Nicholls with his usual trustworthiness takes all the trouble of providing substitutes on his own shoulders."[1]

Despite the language of reluctance and regret, Charlotte Brontë was facing neither surgery nor the firing squad. Rather, the "it" she refers to in this letter to her friend, Ellen Nussey, is her long-deferred marriage. Admittedly, this letter carries biographical and psychological interest. But I am more interested in the way her characterization of Arthur Nicholls as "providing substitutes" announces a theme and dominant trope crucial to

understanding Brontë's literary maneuverings.[2] Like her future husband, Brontë works a series of substitutions in her novels.

Much light has been shed by critics who have focused on these doublings, displacements, repressions, and subversions.[3] Despite their varying theoretical backgrounds, consensus that Brontë employed these strategies as a critique of Victorian culture has gradually coalesced. To that end, identities, bodies, gender, and genre have all been said to migrate; and, indeed, all of these emigrants wash up on the shores of Belgium's Villette. Yet less attention has been paid to an even more significant aspect of Brontë's work: her reterritorialization of migratory texts. Pondering Brontë's substitutions for possible relocations yields insights about her professionalism as well as her literary products.

After all, *Villette* is Brontë's reworking of her first novel, *The Professor.* Her initial efforts to publish it had provoked continual rebuffs from publishers; after the encouragement of George Smith had produced the success of *Jane Eyre,* Brontë's repeated suggestions that he next publish *The Professor* prompted gentle rebukes. Part of the objection to *The Professor* was its size, two volumes, a distinctly anomalous commodity.[4] Charlotte wrote Smith on 5 February 1851, withdrawing her offer of her "martyrized M.S." to one "who might 'use it to light an occasional cigar.'" In her letter, Charlotte ironically suggests that she should be locked up in prison for twelve months, at the end of which time she would come out either "with a 3 vol. M.S. in my hand, or else with a condition of intellect that would exempt me ever after from literary efforts and expectations."[5] In September, Smith placed additional pressure on her by repeating the firm's post-*Jane Eyre* suggestion that she write a novel in serial form. Charlotte refused.[6]

Although little credit is given to Charlotte as a business-woman, we can see her awareness of literary marketing from the very beginnings of her career as a novelist, a transition motivated by financial pragmatics after the failure of the sisters' volume of poems, for whose publication they had been forced to pay.[7] When she finally revised *The Professor,* her remodeling entailed more than a narrative elaboration and a narratorial shift from the third into the first person. Brontë also carved emphatically Gothic features onto what had been principally a double *bildungsroman.* Those Gothic features bear a canny resemblance to one of the most scandalous Gothic texts of the previous century, Matthew Lewis's *The Monk* (1796).

A tale of substitutions and possession, *The Monk*'s relics in *Villette* speak to Brontë's struggle to gain possession of herself as a woman, as an author, and as an heir to literary conventions. As Luce Irigaray imagines the dilemma: "How find a voice, make a choice, strong enough to cut through these layers of ornamental style, that decorative sepulchre, where even her breath is lost. Stifled under all those airs."[8] But the voice that Charlotte Brontë finds by tunneling out from within the tomb of the Gothic novel does more than keen a "female Gothic" or lament the "feminine carceral" of domestic space.[9] In *Villette,* that voice cries out against institutional forces of education, of art, and of religion, a message also contained in *The Monk.*[10] She thereby sounds a second alarm: that possession can be barred as effectively by business conventions of literature as by literary conventions of style or voice. At the same time that the word possession points to ownership, it also means a haunting. To form the self, whether as a private individual or as a professional author, one must strive to ensure that the self one possesses is not formed or possessed by others.

Brontë's possession by Gothic in general may have provided her with models to substitute a different structural logic of desire from that fostered by serialization,[11] as Linda K. Hughes and Michael Lund have described it: "[its] intrinsic form more closely approximates female than male models of pleasure. Rather than inviting sustained arousal of attention until the narrative climax is reached, spending the driving energy of narrative and sundering the readers from the textual experience, the installment novel offers itself as a site of pleasure that is taken up and discharged only to be taken up again (some days or weeks later), and again, and again."[12] Yet I do not thereby mean to imply that Brontë resorts to a male structure of desire. Instead, in true Gothic tradition, she hybridizes: she encloses her structurally deferred climaxes in a three-volume tomb, at the same time that she thwarts the serial's (and autobiography's) construction of intimacy between readers and characters through her (and Lucy's) refusal to provide closure.

Brontë's structural Gothicizing reads as evidence that she consciously engaged in rewriting gender codes.[13] But by limiting our attention to examples of so-called "female Gothic," and by seeing Ann Radcliffe as the only precursor for Brontë, we miss seeing how her reworking of gender codes also serves her professionalism.[14] Narratively and thematically, Brontë redefines desire. In mapping the traces of *The Monk* in *Villette,* then, I will contend that Brontë draws on *The Monk* because in that novel she finds an analysis of substitution's dangers and delights. For Lewis, both dangers and delights lie in substitution's resemblance to a pornographic economy of exchange. Lewis sees women as counters in that system of barter. Forced to enter into an economy of exchange that demanded she relinquish autonomy while it promised her some range of mobility beyond the confines of the home, Brontë responds by making the nun the figure through which erotic desire becomes buoyantly disembodied and endlessly deferred, the possession of the self through substitution.[15]

Even more than *Jane Eyre,* with its "madwoman in the attic," *Villette* is a haunted text. Brontë possesses her literary heritage by creating a surrogate Gothic. Critics usually point to the haunting figure of the nun as the key Gothic element, although they seldom agree about its significance. To Sandra Gilbert and Susan Gubar, the nun is a projection of Lucy's need for nullity;[16] for Eve Sedgwick, the nun dramatizes Lucy's constitutive need for doubleness. Christina Crosby detects the nun as mirroring the narcissistic Lacanian Imaginary Other.[17] To some, the nun represents Brontë's anticlericalism;[18] while Q. D. Leavis, who saw the nun as nothing more than a plot device for maintaining suspense and for generating sales, is not far removed from Brontë's contemporary, the reviewer of the *Literary Gazette,* who recognized a Byronic prototype when identifying the nun as "a phantom of the Fitz-fulke kind."[19] But a covey of nuns broods over more characters than Lucy. Paul's history with Justine-Marie forms the most obvious analogue. The prehistory of the pensionnat also suggests whole generations subject to ecclesiastic visitations whose terror—diurnal or nocturnal—may have been equal. These nuns form a sisterhood that extends beyond the borders of Villette, back to the Gothic novels half a century old.

Of all the possible precursors, Lewis's *The Monk* looms the largest in Brontë's text. Our first introduction to the legend of Brontë's nun reveals its close bonds with the story of Lewis's Agnes. Like the pensionnat's nun, Agnes is immured alive in the vaults of her convent "for some sin against her vow."[20] Agnes's sin is fecund concupiscence; we never learn what the Belgian nun had done, although a sexual aura attaches to her by association, both because wanton nuns and monks were a cliché by that time, and because Ginevra confiscates the nun's identity to cover her own escapades.[21] Confiscation of identity lies at the core of Lewis's tale as well: Agnes lands in the convent only after she has attempted to elope with her lover, Don Raymond, by assuming the guise of a bleeding nun, said to haunt the castle of her aunt.

If any figure can be said to haunt the pages of *Villette,* it is this last unwilling nun, Beatrice de

las Cisternas. Raymond and Agnes's concerted plan fails when the real ghostly nun appears in Agnes's stead. Raymond cannot tell the difference; instead, he rapturously clasps the phantom to his breast and exclaims: "Agnes! Agnes! Thou art mine / Agnes! Agnes! I am thine! / In my veins while blood shall roll, / Thou art mine! / I am thine! / thine my body! thine my soul!" (p. 166). This jubilant crowing of patriarchal possession soon sticks in Raymond's craw, however. The Bleeding Nun nightly visits Raymond's bedchamber, not to glut him with the pleasures of the flesh, since she has none, but to rewrite his poetic will by reversing the possessive pronouns: "Mine thy body! Mine thy soul" (p. 170). Beatrice's haunting of Raymond's bedchamber, at the precise moment when his desire was to be realized, resembles the nun's appearances to Lucy at moments when she, too, seems poised to find happiness beyond the walls of her confinement, especially through her growing intimacy with Dr. John. Given the resemblance, it is doubly surprising that critics of Brontë read the scene as revealing Lucy's psychological inability to cathect with another human being or her anxieties about sex, or that critics of Lewis fail to so read his scene. Rather than evenly distribute a unilinear reading of this nature to either scene, however, we should recognize the similarity of their underlying logic. Like Lucy, Raymond has his desire stimulated by the encounter, setting off a chain reaction through which he will learn to love precisely the same kind of emaciated nun, as though the nun carries a contagion which purges the fleshly from both Raymond and Agnes.

Raymond escapes the nun's possession when the Wandering Jew miraculously arrives to shrieve her soul. Raymond, too, is enjoined to penitence: he must lay Beatrice's bones to rest in her ancestral grave, much as Lucy can only free herself from her obsession with Dr. John by burying his letters to her. In fact, Lucy creates a second tomb, sealing her letters under a slab of slate and mortar right beside that of the Belgian nun. And she acquires the casket in which those letters will rest by journeying into the "old historical quarter of the town," and purchasing a used glass jar from the "old Jew broker" who owns the pawn shop, as though *Villette,* the book, had metaphorically domesticated and domiciled the Wandering Jew in Villette, the town.[22]

This scene does not exhaust the presence of resemblances between *The Monk* and *Villette.*[23] Nevertheless, the burial in the garden marks an apotheosis. Raymond's scene of burial may stage his penitence, but that repentance permits him to substitute new objects of desire. The same interpretation applies to Brontë's reenactment of Lewis's scenes. Like Lucy and Raymond, Brontë has her desire pointed by her Gothic encounters. Like theirs, this desire substitutes a new outlet for its original source. We can read these resemblances as a metanarrative about Brontë's authoring of her own literary self, for, while she exhumes ancestral texts, she also buries the spirit of their letters.

Brontë rejects and rewrites the perverted representations of women and/or of values that rustle through these earlier Gothic letters. It is not so much the logic of substitution to which she objects. This logic governs male Gothic from the time of Horace Walpole's *The Castle of Otranto*, where Theodore is rewarded with another bride to replace the innocent female destroyed by Gothic ambition.[24] Brontë targets the locus of this substitution in Lewis. With the exception of Beatrice, women are either bartered brides, functioning to consolidate wealth and status, or battered virgins, servicing a similar passion for power now figured as sexual dominance.

At first glance, Lewis may seem to critique such an instrumental attitude toward sexuality by revealing the pornographic outlook underlying it through his portrait of Ambrosio. Ambrosio, "drunk with desire," consummates his apostasy and his ecstasy in Matilda's arms, muttering "Thine, ever thine" (Lewis, p. 109). But just as Ambrosio's reference to his liaison as his "commerce with Matilda" reveals the economics of desire, so his swift revulsion betrays the tendency of consummation to consume the consumer, making any such lasting fidelity impossible (pp. 230, 236-7). Both Matilda and Ambrosio are victims of a gendered double bind. The more time Matilda spends with Ambrosio, the more she wants him: the more she wants him, the less he wants her. But Lewis here seems to want to have it both ways: he first blames Matilda for having caused Ambrosio's disgust, then delineates how such generosity inaugurates an increasingly selfish reaction.

The ambiguity of Lewis's position could arise from his attempt to analyze the way Ambrosio's entrapment in this situation, like his incarceration in the monastery, teaches him progressively to devalue other lives. Lewis shows how such induration causes Ambrosio to split Matilda in two. When Ambrosio mentally divorces Matilda from her body, emotionally discarding all but her physical shell which he refers to as "it," Lewis brilliantly conveys the magnitude of such objectification of the feminine (p. 241). Offended, Lewis's censors made him substitute the conventional pronoun

"she" in the fourth and fifth editions for the blatant disregard suggested by the indefinite pronoun. But their tiny sentimentalizing gesture seems impotent against the onslaught of Ambrosio's dehumanization of Antonia. Ambrosio may at first *think* that he loves Antonia chastely, but appreciation of her beauty rapidly transforms itself into appetite (p. 243): "Grown used to her modesty, it no longer commanded the same respect and awe: he still admired it, but it only made him more anxious to deprive her of that quality which formed her principal charm" (p. 255). When Ambrosio finally captures Antonia in the charnel vaults of the monastery, even his gaze can no longer hold her in a fixed image. Instead, her identity migrates, mingling first with the corrupt bodies surrounding her, then dissolving into that of her dead mother, killed by Ambrosio (p. 364).

However, Lewis's delight in describing these scenes supplements and cancels the analysis of danger. Although Ambrosio's desire for Antonia vanishes with her rape, he still cannot let her go free; he imagines keeping her a prisoner of his new desire for an endless succession of penitent nights (p. 371). Only Matilda's arrival, and the warning that they are surrounded by archers come to rescue Antonia, breaks the spell of irresolution in which Ambrosio seeks to hold Antonia. He takes her in the same position in which he had earlier raped her, both times prostrate with supplicating prayers, now using his poniard as the weapon of penetration.

Beyond the pornographic violence of the scene lies a still more pernicious implication, one that mitigates his seeming sympathy with Matilda and Antonia's plight. Women are trapped in a double bind. As vestal females, they are vulnerable to appropriation. But Lewis also implies that sexual desire in women unleashes in them a potential masculinity that provokes Ambrosio's distaste: "Now [Matilda] assumed a sort of courage and manliness in her manners and discourse, but ill calculated to please him. She spoke no longer to insinuate, but command . . . *Pity is a sentiment so natural, so appropriate to the female character, that it is scarcely a merit for a woman to possess it, but to be without it is a grievous crime*" (pp. 233-4, my emphasis). The final words of the passage collapse the values of the omniscient narrator with those of Ambrosio. So, too, does the portrait of Beatrice, who like Matilda momentarily rises above her gendered fate and receives in consequence a narrative punishment all the more severe.

Only women who mask their masculine intelligence with feminine modesty receive approbation. The reward to women for such complicitous compliance is to become commodified and hence substitutable. With Antonia conveniently dead, it does not take Lorenzo long to substitute Virginia. Once again, the narrator foreshadows his approval of Lorenzo's decision, placing "not unwisely" into the mouth of Lorenzo's uncle the maxim that "'men have died, and worms have ate them, but not for love!'"—a proverb that failed to disturb the censors (p. 381). This unacknowledged quotation from William Shakespeare's *As You Like It* also disguises the potential feminism of its original utterance. Rosalind speaks those words to Orlando while playing Ganymede playing Rosalind, in order to cure Orlando of his idealism and to incite his appreciation for her self, rather than for some Petrarchan fiction. By surreptitiously relocating those words into the mouth of the duke, Lewis makes the maxim part of the "old boy" network of truth, which is further validated by the authority of the omniscient narrator who boldly declares his status as M.P. in the third edition. In contrast to the protean authority of the men, the women are unidimensional clichés, fixated in their affections and transfixed accordingly by their circumstances.

If Lewis's novel collapses the authorial and characterological perspectives, its message also merges with that articulated by Brontë's father and Robert Southey. They warned her that women had no right to possess a literary career. Later in life, Charlotte wrote that her father had always instilled in her the view of writing and literary desires as a rebellion from her female duties.[25] She heard the same strictures from Southey, whom she wrote for advice about how to become a professional poet. Despite his protestation of impropriety, Southey must certainly have known how many women had successfully made literature the "business" of their lives at that juncture.

Brontë's novel, then, is "new Gothic" insofar as it makes women's authorization of substitution, demonic in Lewis, heroic.[26] Each of the women in *Villette*—Madames Beck and Walravens, Mrs. Bretton, Ginevra, Lucy, and Polly—survives by a strategy of substitution. Ginevra stands as the most obvious entry here. Madame Beck fails to obtain a youthful lover, but she gains voyeuristic satisfaction from her role as *surveillante*. Mrs. Bretton lives in John (Brontë, p. 267); Madame Walravens becomes a death-like ringer for her granddaughter, stealing in the process the house, affection, and jewels that might otherwise have been Justine-Marie's.[27]

Perhaps the most astute pupil of substitution is little Polly, who early learns to corral her desire precisely by displacing it. The first example of her mastery of this technique, which she will employ to such great effect with John, occurs when she is merely seven. Knowing she is about to leave the household and return to her papa, Polly longs to rush to Graham and tell him the news, hoping that his despair will match her own. Instead, she fondles Lucy Snowe: "In the evening, at the moment Graham's entrance was heard below, I found her at my side. She began to arrange a locket-ribbon around my neck, she displaced and replaced the comb in my hair; while thus busied, Graham entered" (p. 40). Polly then gets Lucy to deliver the news, freeing herself to observe Graham's reaction.

In fact, alone of all the women in *Villette*, Lucy at first seems to be innately passive. Peter Brooks may see desire as the very spark necessary for all narrative, but Lucy seems curiously devoid of passion or need at the start of hers.[28] But, of course, the novel reveals that calm to be fictive, the result of a momentary translation, a fact that the mature Lucy knows and signals to the reader by prefacing her momentary poise in language that underscores its artificiality: "In the autumn of the year _____, I was staying at Bretton; my godmother having come in person to claim me of the kinsfolk with whom was at that time fixed my permanent residence" (p. 6). The unnamed "kinsfolk" from whom Lucy so strenuously distances herself can be none other than the parents she loses. Although we never learn what happens, the shadow of those events and the subsequent vagrancy of Lucy's life cast doubt on the "fixity" and "permanence" of all existence, as does the passive construction of her temporary placement there. What Lucy learns in the course of her life is to seize control of her translations. Without that lesson, her fate would have resembled that of Miss Marchmont, frozen into place by events. And it is through Polly that Lucy will first learn to activate her desires.

Lucy feels compelled to intervene in Polly's actions, to exercise vicarious restraint over the child's emotions (p. 13); Polly's emotions, however, seem to exercise more power over Lucy than the reverse. Stoic Lucy, "guiltless" of the "curse" of "an overheated and discursive imagination," nonetheless imagines rooms to be "haunted" by Polly's presence (p. 15). Polly's proposed absence causes Lucy to break through her normal reserve. She invites Polly into her bed "wishing, yet scarcely hoping, she would comply"; when Polly comes, "gliding like a small ghost over the carpet," she is "warmed . . . soothed . . . tranquillized and cherished" in Lucy's arms (p. 44).

Moreover, as far as we know, Polly is the only person ever to share Lucy's bed. Gilbert and Gubar are right to follow Leavis in seeing Polly as Lucy's other self. But they miss the fact that, from the beginning, Polly is described in imagery that connects her to the full-grown nuns Lucy will later encounter. If Polly is a "demure little person in a mourning frock and white chemisette," a frock that Lucy pointedly tells us is black three pages earlier, her costume merges with her actions to turn her into a type of the bleeding nun (p. 20): doggedly hemming a handkerchief for her father, the needle "almost a skewer, pricking herself ever and anon, marking the cambric with a track of minute red dots; occasionally starting when the perverse weapon—swerving from her control—inflicted a deeper stab than usual; but still silent, diligent, womanly, absorbed" (p. 20). Far from representing a type that must be feared or renounced, the nun in **Villette** represents Lucy Snowe's embrace of her provisional status.[29] The nun blends into Lucy's persona so that she, too, becomes a "silence artist," defying mystery by adopting it (pp. 680-2).[30] How fitting, then, that Ginevra bequeaths the costume of the nun to Lucy.

Once so metaphorically habited, the swelled presence of desire takes on a religious cast.[31] For both Lucy and Polly, the handwritten word of John supplants the word of God and becomes a physical revelation (pp. 254, 326-7, 342-3). Each performs a similar ritual of dilation, going so far as to pray before she revels in the letter. But Paul's letters do more than refresh or sustain (p. 713); they enable Lucy to incorporate her lover, so that his absence marks the summit of their love: "I thought I loved him when he went away; I love him now in another degree; he is more my own" (p. 714). Paul's fate when clasped to Lucy's heart must mirror Lucy's when cradled in the "bosom of my kindred": both types of love can be safely possessed only in the reflection of memory, while the actual bodies must endure the clammy embrace of the engulfing sea. Immured in the convent of knowledge Paul had created for her, Lucy's life becomes one of singular, not serial, devotion. Her conventual existence appears most strongly in the collapse of her narrative into the histories of the three Catholics who had seemed her nemeses, in a final act of substitution (p. 715). She may not count her beads in a Carmelite convent,

but she does tell her story, her metaphorical habit of black and white a fitting emblem of the printed page.

The unspoken fact of Paul's fate signals how heretical Brontë's narrator and narrative truly are.[32] Charlotte had originally planned to end the book with a clear announcement of Paul's death. Her father objected strenuously, declaring his dislike for books that "left a melancholy impression on the mind."[33] Unable or unwilling to defer completely to his wish for a "happy ending," Charlotte left her story open, thus resigning it to the pornographic imagination that her father, Patrick Brontë, had always identified with the novelistic. In his book, *The Cottage in the Wood,* he had written: "The sensual novelist and his admirer, are beings of depraved appetites and sickly imaginations, who having learnt the art of *self-tormenting,* are diligently and zealously employed in creating an imaginary world, which they can never inhabit, only to make the real world, with which they must necessarily be conversant, gloomy and insupportable."[34] Literary endeavor becomes masturbation in Patrick's barely-coded epithet of "self-tormenting"; the hothouse secrecy surrounding such employment accounts for its resultant depravity and sickliness.

Southey had warned her of such danger: "The day dreams in which you habitually indulge are likely to induce a distempered state of mind; and, in proportion as all the ordinary uses of the world seem to you flat and unprofitable, you will be unfitted for them without becoming fitted for anything else. Literature cannot be the business of a woman's life, and it ought not to be."[35] Southey's reference to Charlotte's "habitual indulgence" also characterizes her ambition as a "distempered," diseased fixation for which the only prescription is healthy, self-abnegating work. The patronizing chauvinism of his attitude resonates through the uncredited allusion to Shakespeare. Here Southey, a male poet wielding masculine privilege through the words of another male poet, simultaneously implies that Charlotte has fallen into Hamlet's state, and invokes Hamlet's injunctions to Ophelia to "get thee [to] a nunn'ry."[36] **Villette** demonstrates Brontë's acceptance of Southey's implicit advice, as well as the perverse spin she put on it.

While the pseudonymical "Currer Bell" occupied a high niche in literary opinion, her reviews harp on her "depravities" even as they praise her "Passion and Power."[37] The *Christian Remembrancer* admits that Brontë has tempered "the outrages on decorum, the moral perversity, the toleration of, nay, indifference to vice" which had "deform[ed]" her *Jane Eyre,* but it joins numerous other critics of Lucy who decry her for her willingness to fall in love and her ability to be in love with two men at the same time or for her "masculine" style.[38] Even reviewers who found *Villette* "pleasant" criticized Lucy Snowe's morbidity and her "tormenting self-regard."[39] While all uniformly praised the abundance of well-drawn characters, they nonetheless bemoaned the lack of "breathless suspense, more thrilling incidents, and a more moving story."[40] Conversely, the story is said to move too much: the narrative jumps and the focus wavers.[41] Reviewers' desires seem to be piqued and frustrated at the same time.[42] Their complaints ironically vindicate the triumph with which Charlotte Brontë pursued her anomalous path. Eschewing simultaneously the need for closure and for the embodiment of desire in a female body, a containment that in Lewis enforces female powerlessness, Brontë frees the hallmark of the pornographic, the desire *for* desire,[43] into the space of literary contingency, as generations of readers and critics who have been teased by Lucy Snowe can testify.

Notes

1. Clement Shorter, *The Brontës: Life and Letters,* 2 vols. (New York: Haskell House Publishers, 1969), 2:362.

2. Nicholls had to find a substitute curate for Patrick Brontë's congregation and a priest to preside at the wedding. On the marriage day, Patrick Brontë suddenly refused to attend, and Nicholls had to find a substitute to give Charlotte away. Her friend, Miss Wooler, performed that function. On Charlotte Brontë's arrogation of fact to fancy in *Villette,* see Juliet Barker, *The Brontës* (New York: St. Martin's Press, 1995), pp. 668, 704-5, 708, 713, 715. Cf. Claudia Klaver, "Homely Aesthetics: *Villette*'s Canny Narrator," *Genre* 26, 4 (Winter 1993): 409-29.

3. A brief listing would include Robyn R. Warhol, "Double Gender, Double Genre in *Jane Eyre* and *Villette.*" *SEL* 36, 4 (Autumn 1996): 857-75; Patricia E. Johnson, "'This Heretic Narrative': The Strategy of the Split Narrative in Charlotte Brontë's *Villette,*" *SEL* 30, 4 (Autumn 1990): 617-31; John Kucich, *Repression in Victorian Fiction: Charlotte Brontë, George Eliot, and Charles Dickens* (Berkeley, Los Angeles, and London: Univ. of California Press, 1987); Nina Auerbach, *Woman and the Demon: The Life of a Victorian Myth* (Cambridge MA and London: Harvard Univ. Press, 1982), pp. 127-8; Sandra Gilbert and Susan Gubar, *The Madwoman in the Attic: The Woman Writer and the Nineteenth-Century Literary Imagination* (New Haven and London: Yale Univ. Press, 1979); Eve Sedgwick, *The Coherence of Gothic Conventions* (New York: Arno Press, 1980), especially chap. 3, "Immediacy, Doubleness, and the Unspeakable: *Wuthering Heights* and *Villette,*" pp. 104-53.

4. On the importance of length, see Shorter, 1:382, and Herbert Rosengarten and Margaret Smith, introduc-

tion to *Villette* by Brontë, ed. Rosengarten and Smith (Oxford: Clarendon Press, 1984), pp. xi-xlix, xv.

5. Qtd. in Rosengarten and Smith, p. xv.

6. Rosengarten and Smith, p. xviii. Brontë's claim that "she was unwilling to release her work for publication before it had been completed" flies in the face of other evidence. According to Elizabeth Gaskell, Brontë contemplated "tales which might be published in numbers" (*The Life of Charlotte Brontë,* ed. Alan Shelstone [New York: Penguin, 1975], p. 293). I owe this information to Catherine A. Judd's "Male Pseudonyms and Female Authority in Victorian England," in *Literature in the Marketplace: Nineteenth-Century British Publishing and Reading Practices,* ed. John O. Jordan and Robert L. Pattern (Cambridge: Cambridge Univ. Press, 1995), pp. 250-68, 264-5 n. 20. Barker records in *The Brontës* that Brontë had originally planned "three distinct and unconnected tales which may be published either together as a work of three volumes of the ordinary novel-size, or separately as single volumes" (p. 499).

7. Judd forms one recent exception, drawing on the healthy precedent of Gaskell's treatment of Charlotte Brontë in *The Life.*

8. Luce Irigaray, "Any Theory of the 'Subject' Has Always Been Appropriated by the 'Masculine,'" in *Speculum of the Other Woman,* trans. Gillian C. Gill (Ithaca: Cornell Univ. Press, 1985), pp. 133-46, 143.

9. See Ellen Moers, *Literary Women* (New York: Doubleday, 1976); Tamar Heller, "*Jane Eyre,* Bertha, and the Female Gothic," in *Approaches to Teaching Brontë's "Jane Eyre,"* ed. Diane Long Hoeveler and Beth Lau (New York: Modern Language Association of America, 1993), pp. 49-55. Klaver aligns the Gothic elements, especially the nun, with "typically Radcliffean devices to create suspense and speculation in her narrative, but then [Lucy], also like [Ann] Radcliffe, dismisses them all with the most banal of rational explanations" (p. 418). On the distinction between male and female Gothic, from which I wish to distance myself, see Robert Miles, *Gothic Writing, 1750-1820: A Genealogy* (London and New York: Routledge, 1993), especially pp. 88, 98, 103-4; and Anne Williams, *Art of Darkness: A Poetics of Gothic* (Chicago and London: Univ. of Chicago Press, 1995), pp. 18-24. She calls *The Monk* a pornographic narrative because sexuality is shown as the "prime motive" of all action (p. 116). Yet to her, Ambrosio's carnality lines him up with the feminine.

10. By comparison, Bretton Hall and La Terrasse seem almost the only nonconfining spaces.

11. See Barker, pp. 160-1, 191, 500.

12. Linda K. Hughes and Michael Lund, "Textual/sexual pleasure and serial publication," in Jordan and Patten, pp. 143-64, 143.

13. A position shared by Warhol, p. 858.

14. Rather than being suffocated by the present's contradictory attitude to female authorship, Charlotte cleared space for herself by preserving the male pseudonym and simultaneously creating a very private female persona as the source for her literary output. See Judd's very persuasive discussion, especially pp. 252-3, 257-8.

15. This essay both draws on and modulates the work of Kucich. I find Kucich's discussion extremely attractive, especially his attention to the place of desire in

Brontë's work, but he defines her desire as repressed (pp. 38-9); see p. 30 for his definition of repression. Cf. Steven Marcus, *The Other Victorians: A Study of Sexuality and Pornography in Mid-Nineteenth-Century England* (New York: Basic Books, 1964), especially p. 195. Marcus's attention to the pornographic fantasy of endless seminal fluid finds an interesting counterpart in Brontë's text, which increasingly spews out water imagery inextricably intertwined with eruptions of desire, whether frustrated or realized. For a small sample, see pp. 6, 152, 218-9, 221, 223, 258, 420-1 of *Villette*. The "lecture pieuse" of Catholic martyrs incites the same pornographic response: "it made me so burning hot, and my temples and my heart and my wrist throbbed so fast, and my sleep afterwards was so broken with excitement, that I could sit no longer" (p. 162).

Obviously, *The Monk* fixed much of its pornographic gaze on the explicit sexuality of religious figures. Perhaps another telling resemblance between the two novels lies in *The Monk*'s greatest provocation to scandal: its censure of the Bible as pornographic. Though considerations of length prevent me from detailing Brontë's biblical allusions, she heretically rewrites the Bible as much as she piously cites it. Cf. Susan VanZanten Gallagher, "*Jane Eyre* and Christianity," in Hoeveler and Lau, pp. 62-8; and Keith A. Jenkins, "*Jane Eyre*: Charlotte Brontë's New Bible," in Hoeveler and Lau, pp. 69-75. Many of *Villette*'s citations are perverse applications of water, fountain, and thirst imagery originally found in the two books of "Johns"—the Gospel according to John and Revelation; see John 4:13-5, 6:35, and 7:37 and Rev. 7:16, 14:7, and 22:17. I would suggest that, in this imbricated relationship, we find Brontë's greatest heresy, her incorporation of and twist on the pornographic imagination.

16. Gilbert and Gubar, p. 425.

17. Christina Crosby, "Charlotte Brontë's Haunted Text," *SEL* 24, 4 (Autumn 1984): 701-15. LuAnn McCracken Fletcher articulates a similar position when she claims the nun emphasizes the fictionality of identity ("Manufactured Marvels, Heretic Narratives, and the Process of Interpretation in *Villette*," *SEL* 32, 4 [Autumn 1992]: 723-46).

18. See Robert Heilman, "Charlotte Brontë, Reason, and the Moon," in *Critical Essays on Charlotte Brontë*, ed. Barbara Timm Gates (Boston: G. K. Hall, 1990), pp. 34-49, 36; and Harriet Martineau, "Review of *Villette* by Currer Bell," in Gates, pp. 253-6, 255. Janice Carlisle considers the nun a figure of repressed desire in "The Face in the Mirror: *Villette* and the Conventions of Autobiography," in Gates, pp. 264-87, 282-3, while E. D. H. Johnson sees her as equal to the unreason Lucy must renounce ("'Daring the Dread Glance': Charlotte Brontë's Treatment of the Supernatural in *Villette*," *NCF* 20, 4 [March 1966]: 325-36).

19. Q. D. Leavis, introduction to *Villette* (New York: Harper Colophon, 1972), p. xxiii, cited by Gilbert and Gubar, p. 683 n. 13. Review of *Villette* in *The Literary Gazette* (5 February 1853), rprt. in *The Brontës: The Critical Heritage*, ed. Miriam Allott (London and Boston: Routledge and Kegan Paul, 1974), pp. 178-81, 180.

20. Matthew Lewis, *The Monk*, ed. Louis Peck (New York: Grove Press, 1952), p. 148. Citations will come from this edition and henceforth will be cited parenthetically.

21. See Max Byrd, "The Madhouse, the Whorehouse, and the Convent," *PR* 44, 2 (Summer 1977): 268-78.

22. Brontë, *Villette*, ed. Rosengarten and Smith, p. 423. All references to *Villette* will be to this edition and henceforth will be cited parenthetically in the text.

23. Cf. the descriptions of Baroness Lindenburg and Madame Beck in character (Brontë, pp. 95, 98, 100-2, 695-7; Lewis, pp. 123, 145); in habits of spying (Brontë, pp. 100, 421-2, 647; Lewis, p. 155); and in a taste for young men (Brontë, pp. 140-5; Lewis, pp. 147-50). Paul's history after the death of Justine-Marie reads like Raymond's fate had he not been freed from the Bleeding Nun. More importantly, when Lucy describes Paul as monitor of mores and as the human heart, he suddenly resembles Satan (Brontë, pp. 486-7; Lewis, pp. 416-7).

24. As the Gothic novel reaches the end of its first phase with Charles Robert Maturin's *Melmoth the Wanderer*, the structural logic of substitution dominates the sexual logic.

25. Barker, p. 243. Thus, Carol Christ sees Brontë steeling herself to prefer a realist aesthetic, especially in *Villette*, as a means of subduing this mutinous attraction ("Imaginative Constraint, Feminine Duty, and the Form of Charlotte Brontë's Fiction," *WS* 6, 3 [1979]: 287-96).

26. The phrase is Heilman's; see his "Charlotte Brontë's 'New' Gothic," in *From Jane Austen to Joseph Conrad: Essays Collected in Memory of James T. Hillhouse*, ed. Robert Rathburn and Martin Steinmann Jr. (Minneapolis: Univ. of Minnesota Press, 1958), pp. 118-32. I interpret her "newness" very differently.

27. When the old woman emerges from the stone walls of the Rue des Mages, behind the portrait of her granddaughter, "the portrait seemed to give way" (Brontë, p. 562).

28. Peter Brooks, *Reading for the Plot: Design and Intention in Narrative* (Oxford: Clarendon Press, 1984). Brooks's strictly male notion of desire and its accompaniments deforms his definition of women's plots as resistance and endurance: "a waiting (and suffering) until the woman's desire can be a permitted response to the expression of male desire" (p. 330).

29. Lucy is not unique among Brontë's women in this respect: Eliza Reed in *Jane Eyre* and Sylvie in *The Professor* both enter convents. See Kucich, p. 92. Kate Millett has Lucy trying on and rejecting all of the alternative female role models (*Sexual Politics* [New York: Doubleday, 1970], pp. 140-7, rprt. in Gates, pp. 256-64). Joseph P. Boone calls the nun the "false mirror of [Lucy's] sexuality" ("Depolicing *Villette*: Surveillance, Invisibility, and the Female Erotics of 'Heretic Narrative,'" [*Novel* 26. 1 (Fall 1992)]: 20-42).

30. On Lucy as a "silence artist," see Sedgwick, pp. 130-1. Ultimately Sedgwick sees the nun as corresponding to the letters. Cf. Gilbert and Gubar's suggestion that "Lucy is the nun who is *immobilized* by this internal conflict" (p. 412, my emphasis).

31. Cf. Kucich, p. 109.

32. Anne Mozley's unsigned review for the *Christian Remembrancer* (April 1853) shows that the narratorial and characterological heresy fused in the public's mind (rprt. in Allott, pp. 202-8, 202).

33. Barker, p. 723.

34. Qtd. in Barker, p. 243.

35. Barker, p. 262.

36. William Shakespeare. *The Tragedy of Hamlet, Prince of Denmark.* in *The Riverside Shakespeare,* 2d edn., ed. G. Blakemore Evans (Boston and New York: Houghton Mifflin, 1997), pp. 1183-1245, III.i.120.

37. G. H. Lewes in the *Leader* (12 February 1853), rprt. in Allott, pp. 184-6, 184.

38. Mozley, p. 203. See esp. William Makepeace Thackeray's letters of March and April 1853, rprt. in Allott, pp. 197-8.

39. Review of *Villette* in *The Spectator* (12 February 1853), rprt. in Allott, pp. 181-4, 181.

40. Lewes, p. 184.

41. Mozley, p. 204; review of *Villette* in the *Athenaeum* (12 February 1853), rprt. in Allott, pp. 187-90, 188; and review of *Villette* in *Revue Des Deux Mondes* (15 March 1853), rprt. in Allott, p. 199-200, 199.

42. Review of *Villette* in *Putnam's Monthly Magazine* (May 1853), rprt. in Allott, pp. 212-5, 214.

43. On the link between the specularized female body and female powerlessness, see Elaine Scarry. *The Body in Pain* (Oxford: Oxford Univ. Press, 1992), pp. 207, 361 n. 20. Susan Faludie's article on the Hollywood porn industry shows male porn stars in suffering acknowledgment that the "desire *for* desire" rules pornographic producers and consumers alike ("The Money Shot," *New Yorker* [30 October 1995]. pp. 64-87).

FURTHER READING

Bibliographies

Crump, Rebecca W. *Charlotte and Emily Brontë: A Reference Guide.* 3 vols. Boston: G. K. Hall, 1982-1986, 194 p.

Provides an annotated compilation of secondary sources from 1846 to 1983.

Passel, Anne. *Charlotte and Emily Brontë: An Annotated Bibliography.* New York: Garland Publishing, 1979, 359 p.

Organizes criticism by text.

Biographies

Gaskell, Elizabeth. *The Life of Charlotte Brontë.* London: E. P. Dutton, 1908, 411 p.

Offers a biography by one of Brontë's contemporaries; includes large extracts from Brontë's correspondence.

Gérin, Winifred. *Charlotte Brontë: The Evolution of Genius.* London: Oxford University Press, 1967, 617 p.

Biography focusing on Charlotte Brontë's development as an author.

Gordon, Lyndall. *Charlotte Brontë: A Passionate Life.* New York: W. W. Norton, 1996, 418 p.

Provides revisionist insights into Brontë's life.

Miller, Lucasta. *The Brontë Myth.* New York: Knopf, 2004, 351 p.

Offers a biography that retraces myth surrounding the Brontë sisters, particularly Charlotte.

Criticism

Alexander, Christine. "'That Kingdom of Gloom': Charlotte Brontë, the Annuals, and the Gothic." *Nineteenth-Century Literature* 47, no. 4 (March 1993): 409-36.

Examines the influence on Brontë's writings of the Gothic tales included in popular nineteenth-century periodicals and annuals, gift books containing poetry, prose fiction, and illustrations.

Avery, Simon. "'Some Strange and Spectral Dream': The Brontës' Manipulation of the Gothic Mode." *Brontë Society Transactions* 23, no. 2 (October 1998): 120-35.

Explores the ways in which the Brontës each utilized and modified the traditional Gothic.

Cecil, David. "Charlotte Brontë." In *Early Victorian Novelists: Essays in Revaluation,* pp. 119-54. New York: Bobbs-Merrill, 1935.

Delineates Brontë's flaws as a novelist while at the same time averring that she is a creative genius and that even her weakest passages are "pulsing with her intensity, fresh with her charm."

Chen, Chih-Ping. "'Am I a Monster?': *Jane Eyre* among the Shadows of Freaks." *Studies in the Novel* 34, no. 4 (winter 2002): 367-84.

Relates Brontë's presentation of Bertha Mason in Jane Eyre *to the freak shows popular during the nineteenth century, suggesting parallels between Bertha's "enfreakment" and Jane's search for her own identity.*

Chesterton, G. K. "Charlotte Brontë as a Romantic." In *Charlotte Brontë, 1816-1916: A Centenary Memorial,* pp. 49-54. London: T. Fisher Unwin, 1917.

Discusses the coexistence of romance and realism in the novels of Charlotte Brontë.

Crosby, Christina. "Charlotte Brontë's Haunted Text." *SEL: Studies in English Literature, 1500-1900* 24, no. 4 (autumn 1984): 701-15.

A feminist interpretation that examines the impact of Gothic elements on Villette, *a work often categorized as a realist novel.*

DeLamotte, Eugenia C. "Gothic Romance and Women's Reality in *Jane Eyre.*" In *Perils of the Night: A Feminist Study of Nineteenth-Century Gothic,* pp. 193-228. New York: Oxford University Press, 1990.

Explores the combination of Gothic elements and realism in Jane Eyre *and the impact of that combination on Jane's quest for her identity.*

Gubar, Susan. "The Buried Life of Lucy Snowe: *Villette.*" In *The Madwoman in the Attic: The Woman Writer and the Nineteenth-Century Literary Imagination,* by Sandra M. Gilbert and Susan M. Gubar, pp. 399-440. New Haven, Conn.: Yale University Press, 1979.

Suggests that Villette, *with a protagonist cut off from society, family, money, and confidence, "is perhaps the most moving and terrifying account of female deprivation ever written."*

Martin, Robert Bernard. "*Jane Eyre.*" In *Accents of Persuasion: Charlotte Brontë's Novels,* pp. 57-108. London: Faber & Faber, 1966.

An interpretation of Jane Eyre *as a novel that seeks a balance between reason and passion.*

Milbank, Alison. "'Handling the Veil': Charlotte Brontë." In *Daughters of the House: Modes of the Gothic in Victorian Fiction*, pp. 140-57. New York: St. Martin's, 1992.

Delineates Brontë's expansion of the traditional women's role in Gothic literature.

Nicoll, W. Robertson. "Charlotte Brontë and One of Her Critics." *The Bookman* 10 (January 1900): 441-43.

Presents a review of Villette *from the* Christian Remembrancer *and a response by Brontë in which she protests the reviewer's judgments of her character.*

Rai, Amit S. "The Black Spectre of Sympathy: The 'Occult' Relation in *Jane Eyre*." *Lit: Literature Interpretation Theory* 14, no. 3 (July-September 2003): 243-68.

Asserts the importance of sympathy in Jane Eyre *as a "paradoxical mode of power."*

Rigby, Elizabeth. "*Vanity Fair*—and *Jane Eyre*." *The London Quarterly Review*, no. 167 (December 1948): 82-99.

An unsigned review attributed to Rigby. Describes Jane Eyre *as a "remarkable" work, but criticizes the author for a combination of "total ignorance of the habits of society, a great coarseness of taste, and a heathenish doctrine of religion."*

Woolf, Virginia. "*Jane Eyre* and *Wuthering Heights*." In her *Collected Essays*, pp. 185-90. London: The Hogarth Press, 1966.

Compares Jane Eyre *with* Wuthering Heights, *praising the former as a vivid, absorbing, passionate, and poetic novel.*

OTHER SOURCES FROM GALE:

Additional coverage of Brontë's life and career is contained in the following sources published by Thomson Gale: *Authors and Artists for Young Adults*, Vol. 17; *Beacham's Guide to Literature for Young Adults*, Vol. 2; *British Writers*, Vol. 5; *British Writers: The Classics*, Vol. 2; *British Writers Retrospective Supplement*, Vol. 1; *Concise Dictionary of British Literary Biography, 1832-1890*; *Dictionary of Literary Biography*, Vols. 21, 159, 199; *DISCovering Authors*; *DISCovering Authors: British*; *DISCovering Authors: Canadian*; *DISCovering Authors Modules: Most-studied Authors* and *Novelists*; *DISCovering Authors 3.0*; *Exploring Novels*; *Feminism in Literature: A Gale Critical Companion*; *Literature and Its Times*, Vol. 2; *Literature Resource Center*; *Nineteenth-Century Literature Criticism*, Vols. 3, 8, 33, 58, 105, 155; *Novels for Students*, Vol. 4; *Twayne's English Authors*; *World Literature and Its Times*, Vol. 4; and *World Literature Criticism*.

EMILY BRONTË

(1818 - 1848)

(Full name Emily Jane Brontë; also wrote under the pseudonym Ellis Bell) English novelist and poet.

Brontë is considered an important yet elusive figure in nineteenth-century English literature. Although she led a brief and circumscribed life, spent in relative isolation in a parsonage on the Yorkshire moors, she left behind a literary legacy that includes some of the most passionate and inspired writing in Victorian literature. Today, Brontë's poems are well regarded by critics, but they receive little attention, and her overall reputation rests primarily on her only novel, *Wuthering Heights* (1847). While Brontë incorporated into that work the horror and mystery of a Gothic novel, the remote setting and passionate characters of a Romantic novel, and the social criticism of a Victorian novel, she transformed all of these traditions. In this story of extraordinary love and revenge, Brontë demonstrated the conflict between elemental passions and civilized society, resulting in a compelling work that has been elevated to the status of a literary classic. At the same time, Brontë's writings have raised many questions about their author's intent. Unable to reach a consensus concerning the ultimate meaning of her works and reluctant to assign them a definitive place in the English literary tradition, critics continue to regard Brontë as a fascinating enigma in English letters.

BIOGRAPHICAL INFORMATION

Although Brontë's life was outwardly uneventful, the unusual circumstances of her upbringing have prompted considerable scrutiny. One of six children born to Maria Branwell Brontë and the Reverend Patrick Brontë, she was raised in the parsonage at Haworth by her father and maternal aunt following her mother's death in 1821. In 1825 she was sent to the Clergy Daughters' School at Cowan Bridge, but returned to Haworth when her sisters Maria and Elizabeth became ill at the institution and died. A significant event in Brontë's creative life occurred in 1826 when Patrick Brontë bought a set of wooden toy soldiers for his children. The toys opened up a rich fantasy world for Emily and her siblings Charlotte, Branwell, and Anne: Charlotte and Branwell created an imaginary African land called Angria, for which they invented characters, scenes, stories, and poems, and Emily and Anne later conceived a romantic legend centered upon the imaginary Pacific Ocean island of Gondal. The realm of Gondal became a lifelong interest for Brontë and, according to many scholars, a major imaginative source for her writings. In addition to composing prose works (now lost) concerning the history of Gondal, she wrote numerous poems that were evidently directly inspired by Gondal-related themes, characters, and situations. While Brontë was intellectually precocious and began writing poetry at an early age, she failed to establish social contacts outside of her family. She briefly attended a school in East Yorkshire in 1835 and worked as an assistant teacher at the Law Hill School near Halifax in about 1838, but these excursions from home were unsuccessful, ending in Brontë's early return to Haworth. She stayed at the parsonage, continuing to write poetry and attending to household duties, until 1842, when she and Charlotte, hoping to acquire the language skills needed to establish a school of their own, took positions at a school in Brussels. Her aunt's death later that year, however, forced Brontë to return to Haworth, where she resided for the rest of her life.

In 1845, Charlotte discovered one of Emily's private poetry notebooks. At Charlotte's urging Emily reluctantly agreed to publish some of her poems in a volume that also included writings by her sisters. *Poems by Currer, Ellis, and Acton Bell,* reflecting the masculine pseudonyms adopted by Charlotte, Emily, and Anne, respectively, was published in May 1846. While only two copies of the book were sold, at least one commentator, Sydney Dobell, praised Emily's poems, singling her out in the *Athenaeum* as a promising writer and the best poet among the "Bell" family. Meanwhile, Brontë had been working on *Wuthering Heights,* which was published in 1847 in an edition that also included Anne's first novel, *Agnes Grey.* Brontë's masterpiece was poorly received by contemporary critics who, repelled by the vivid portrayal of malice and brutality in the book, objected to the "degrading" nature of her subject. Brontë worked on revising her poetry after publishing *Wuthering Heights,* but her efforts were soon interrupted. Branwell Brontë died in September 1848, and Emily's health began to decline shortly afterwards. In accordance with what Charlotte described as her sister's strong-willed and inflexible nature, Brontë apparently refused medical attention and died of tuberculosis in December 1848.

MAJOR WORKS

Although Brontë is more distinguished as a novelist than as a poet, scholars regard her poetry as a significant part of her oeuvre. In particular, lacking first-hand information concerning her life and opinions, commentators have looked to the poems as a source of insight into Brontë's personality, philosophy, and imagination. Critics have attempted to reconstruct a coherent Gondal "epic" from Brontë's poems and journal entries. In addition to identifying Gondal's queen, commonly referred to as Augusta Geraldine Almeda, and her lover Julius Brenzaida as key characters in the Gondal story, scholars have underscored the presence of wars, assassination, treachery, and infanticide in Brontë's fantasy realm. Critics have consequently noted many similarities between the passionate characters and violent motifs of Gondal and *Wuthering Heights,* and today a generous body of criticism exists supporting the contention that the Gondal poems served as a creative forerunner of the novel.

In *Wuthering Heights,* Brontë chronicles the attachment between Heathcliff, a rough orphan taken in by the Earnshaw family of Wuthering Heights, and the family's daughter, Catherine. The two characters are joined by a spiritual bond of preternatural strength, yet Catherine elects to marry her more refined neighbor, Edgar Linton of Thrushcross Grange; ultimately, this decision leads to Catherine's madness and death and prompts Heathcliff to take revenge upon both the Lintons and the Earnshaws. Heathcliff eventually dies, consoled by the thought of uniting with Catherine's spirit, and the novel ends with the suggestion that Hareton Earnshaw, the last descendant of the Earnshaw family, will marry Catherine's daughter, Catherine Linton, and abandon Wuthering Heights for Thrushcross Grange.

CRITICAL RECEPTION

Initially, critics failed to appreciate Brontë's literary significance. While commentators acknowledged the emotional power of *Wuthering Heights,* they also rejected the malignant and coarse side of life that it depicted. Charlotte Brontë responded to this latter objection in 1850, defending the rough language and manners in her sister's novel as realistic. At the same time, however, she acknowledged the dark vision of life in the book, which she attributed to Emily's reclusive habits. This focus on Brontë's aloofness, combined with the mystical aspects of her poetry and the supernatural overtones of *Wuthering Heights,* fostered an image of the writer as a reclusive mystic that dominated Brontë criticism into the twentieth century. During that century, however, a number of modern studies brought Brontë's craftsmanship to light. Recognition of her artistry increased dramatically as scholars discovered the sophistication and complexity of her images, characterizations, themes, and techniques in *Wuthering Heights.* Interest in her poetry has also grown, primarily due to investigations into its Gondal background, so that today Brontë is the focus of considerable scholarly attention as both a novelist and poet.

Many critics have noted the Gothic elements in Brontë's novel, particularly the distinct architecture of Wuthering Heights, the characterization of Heathcliff as a dark, brooding hero, and ghostly wanderings on the moors. Syndy McMillen Conger wrote that *Wuthering Heights* arouses emotions "central to the Gothic experience: melancholy, desire, and terror." Commentators observe that Brontë heightened her story as well with fierce animal imagery and scenes of raw violence. Dream motifs figure prominently in *Wuthering Heights,* and critics also stress the importance of windows as symbolic vehicles for spiritual entrance and escape in the novel. While the Gothic tradition influenced Brontë, she also deviated from that tradition in significant ways, notably in her characterization of Catherine Earnshaw. The typical Gothic heroine is petite, naïve, and morally virtuous, but Catherine, as Conger wrote, is "complicated, analytical, and uninhibited." The subject of wide-ranging critical debate for generations, *Wuthering Heights* continues to defy categorization and endures as a literary classic.

PRINCIPAL WORKS

Poems by Currer, Ellis, and Acton Bell [as Ellis Bell, with Currer and Acton Bell (pseudonyms of Charlotte and Anne Brontë)] (poems) 1846

**Wuthering Heights* [as Ellis Bell] (novel) 1847

†*Life and Works of the Sisters Brontë*. 7 vols. [with Charlotte and Anne] (novels and poetry) 1899-1903

The Shakespeare Head Brontë. 19 vols. (novels, poetry, and letters) 1931-38

Gondal Poems (poetry) 1938

The Complete Poems of Emily Jane Brontë (poetry) 1941

*   This edition of *Wuthering Heights* was published with Anne Brontë's novel *Agnes Grey.*

†   This work includes letters written by Charlotte, Emily, and Anne Brontë.

PRIMARY SOURCES

EMILY BRONTË (NOVEL DATE 1847)

SOURCE: Brontë, Emily. "Chapter 1." In *Wuthering Heights*. 1847. Reprint edition, pp. 1-6. New York: Bantam Dell, 2003.

The following excerpt comprises Chapter 1 of Wuthering Heights, *which was first published in 1847.*

1801—I have just returned from a visit to my landlord—the solitary neighbour that I shall be troubled with. This is certainly a beautiful country! In all England, I do not believe that I could have fixed on a situation so completely removed from the stir of society. A perfect misanthropist's Heaven: and Mr. Heathcliff and I are such a suitable pair to divide the desolation between us. A capital fellow! He little imagined how my heart warmed towards him when I beheld his black eyes withdraw so suspiciously under their brows, as I rode up, and when his fingers sheltered themselves, with a jealous resolution, still further in his waistcoat, as I announced my name.

'Mr. Heathcliff?' I said.

A nod was the answer.

'Mr. Lockwood, your new tenant, sir. I do myself the honour of calling as soon as possible after my arrival, to express the hope that I have not inconvenienced you by my perseverance in soliciting the occupation of Thrushcross Grange: I heard yesterday you had had some thoughts—'

'Thrushcross Grange is my own, sir,' he interrupted, wincing. 'I should not allow any one to inconvenience me, if I could hinder it—walk in!'

The 'walk in' was uttered with closed teeth, and expressed the sentiment, 'Go to the Deuce': even the gate over which he leant manifested no sympathizing movement to the words; and I think that circumstance determined me to accept the invitation: I felt interested in a man who seemed more exaggeratedly reserved than myself.

When he saw my horse's breast fairly pushing the barrier, he did pull out his hand to unchain it, and then suddenly preceded me up the causeway, calling, as we entered the court,—

'Joseph, take Mr. Lockwood's horse; and bring up some wine.'

'Here we have the whole establishment of domestics, I suppose,' was the reflection, suggested by this compound order. 'No wonder the grass grows up between the flags, and cattle are the only hedge-cutters.'

Joseph was an elderly, nay, an old man: very old, perhaps, though hale and sinewy.

'The Lord help us!' he soliloquised in an undertone of peevish displeasure, while relieving me of my horse: looking, meantime, in my face so sourly that I charitably conjectured he must have need of divine aid to digest his dinner, and his pious ejaculation had no reference to my unexpected advent.

Wuthering Heights is the name of Mr. Heathcliff's dwelling. 'Wuthering' being a significant provincial adjective, descriptive of the atmospheric tumult to which its station is exposed in stormy weather. Pure, bracing ventilation they must have up there at all times, indeed: one may guess the power of the north wind blowing over the edge, by the excessive slant of a few stunted firs at the end of the house; and by a range of gaunt thorns all stretching their limbs one way, as if craving alms of the sun. Happily, the architect had foresight to build it strong: the narrow windows are deeply set in the wall, and the corners defended with large jutting stones.

Before passing the threshold, I paused to admire a quantity of grotesque carving lavished over the front, and especially about the principal door; above which, among a wilderness of crumbling griffins and shameless little boys, I detected the date '1500,' and the name 'Hareton Earnshaw.' I would have made a few comments, and requested a short history of the place from the surly owner; but his attitude at the door appeared to demand my speedy entrance, or complete departure, and I had no desire to aggravate his impatience previous to inspecting the penetralium.

One step brought us into the family sitting-room, without any introductory lobby or passage: they call it here 'the house' preeminently. It includes kitchen and parlour, generally; but I believe at Wuthering Heights the kitchen is forced to retreat altogether into another quarter: at least I distinguished a chatter of tongues, and a clatter of culinary utensils, deep within; and I observed no signs of roasting, boiling, or baking, about the huge fire-place; nor any glitter of copper saucepans and tin cullenders on the walls. One end, indeed, reflected splendidly both light and heat from ranks of immense pewter dishes, interspersed with silver jugs and tankards, towering row after row, on a vast oak dresser, to the very roof. The latter had never been underdrawn: its entire anatomy lay bare to an inquiring eye, except where a frame of wood laden with oatcakes and clusters of legs of beef, mutton, and ham, concealed it. Above the chimney were sundry villanous old guns, and a couple of horse-pistols: and, by way of ornament, three gaudily painted canisters disposed along its ledge. The floor was of smooth, white stone; the chairs, high-backed, primitive structures, painted green: one or two heavy black ones lurking in the shade. In an arch under the dresser, reposed a huge, liver-coloured bitch pointer, surrounded by a swarm of squealing puppies; and other dogs haunted other recesses.

The apartment and furniture would have been nothing extraordinary as belonging to a homely, northern farmer, with a stubborn countenance, and stalwart limbs set out to advantage in knee-breeches and gaiters. Such an individual seated in his armchair, his mug of ale frothing on the round table before him, is to be seen in any circuit of five or six miles among these hills, if you go at the right time after dinner. But Mr. Heathcliff forms a singular contrast to his abode and style of living. He is a dark-skinned gipsy in aspect, in dress and manners a gentleman: that is, as much a gentleman as many a country squire: rather slovenly, perhaps, yet not looking amiss with his negligence, because he has an erect and handsome figure; and rather morose. Possibly, some people might suspect him of a degree of underbred pride; I have a sympathetic chord within that tells me it is nothing of the sort: I know by instinct, his reserve springs from an aversion to showy displays of feeling—to manifestations of mutual kindliness. He'll love and hate equally under cover, and esteem it a species of impertinence to be loved or hated again. No. I'm running on too fast: I bestow my own attributes over liberally on him. Mr. Heathcliff may have entirely dissimilar reasons for keeping his hand out of the way when he meets a would-be acquaintance, to those which actuate me. Let me hope my constitution is almost peculiar: my dear mother used to say I should never have a comfortable home; and only last summer I proved myself perfectly unworthy of one.

While enjoying a month of fine weather at the seacoast, I was thrown into the company of a most fascinating creature: a real goddess in my eyes, as long as she took no notice of me. I 'never told my love' vocally; still, if looks have language, the merest idiot might have guessed I was over head and ears: she understood me at last, and looked a return—the sweetest of all imaginable looks. And what did I do? I confess it with shame—shrunk icily into myself, like a snail; at every glance retired colder and farther; till finally the poor innocent was led to doubt her own senses, and, overwhelmed with confusion at her supposed mistake, persuaded her mamma to decamp.

By this curious turn of disposition I have gained the reputation of deliberate heartlessness; how undeserved, I alone can appreciate.

I took a seat at the end of the hearthstone opposite that towards which my landlord advanced, and filled up an interval of silence by attempting to caress the canine mother, who had left her nursery, and was sneaking wolfishly to the back of my legs, her lip curled up, and her white teeth watering for a snatch.

My caress provoked a long, guttural gnarl.

'You'd better let the dog alone,' growled Mr. Heathcliff in unison, checking fiercer demonstrations with a punch of his foot. 'She's not accustomed to be spoiled—not kept for a pet.'

Then, striding to a side door, he shouted again—'Joseph!'—

Joseph mumbled indistinctly in the depths of the cellar, but gave no intimation of ascending; so his master dived down to him, leaving me *vis-à-vis* the ruffianly bitch and a pair of grim shaggy sheep-dogs, who shared with her a jealous guardianship over all my movements.

Not anxious to come in contact with their fangs, I sat still; but, imagining they would scarcely understand tacit insults, I unfortunately indulged in winking and making faces at the trio, and some turn of my physiognomy so irritated madam, that she suddenly broke into a fury, and leapt on my knees. I flung her back, and hastened to interpose the table between us. This proceeding roused the whole hive. Half-a-dozen four-footed fiends, of various sizes and ages, issued from hidden dens to the common centre. I felt my heels and coat-laps peculiar subjects of assault; and, parrying off the larger combatants as effectually as I could with the poker, I was constrained to demand, aloud, assistance from some of the household in reestablishing peace.

Mr. Heathcliff and his man climbed the cellar steps with vexatious phlegm: I don't think they moved one second faster than usual, though the hearth was an absolute tempest of worrying and yelping.

Happily, an inhabitant of the kitchen made more dispatch: a lusty dame, with tucked-up gown, bare arms, and fire-flushed cheeks, rushed into the midst of us flourishing a frying-pan: and used that weapon, and her tongue, to such purpose, that the storm subsided magically, and she only remained, heaving like a sea after a high wind, when her master entered on the scene.

'What the devil is the matter?' he asked, eyeing me in a manner I could ill endure after this inhospitable treatment.

'What the devil, indeed!' I muttered. 'The herd of possessed swine could have had no worse spirits in them than those animals of yours, sir. You might as well leave a stranger with a brood of tigers!'

'They won't meddle with persons who touch nothing,' he remarked, putting the bottle before me, and restoring the displaced table. 'The dogs do right to be vigilant. Take a glass of wine?'

'No, thank you.'

'Not bitten, are you?'

'If I had been, I would have set my signet on the biter.'

Heathcliff's countenance relaxed into a grin.

'Come, come,' he said, 'you are flurried, Mr. Lockwood. Here, take a little wine. Guests are so exceedingly rare in this house that I and my dogs, I am willing to own, hardly know how to receive them. Your health, sir!'

I bowed and returned the pledge; beginning to perceive that it would be foolish to sit sulking for the misbehaviour of a pack of curs: besides, I felt loath to yield the fellow further amusement at my expense; since his humour took that turn.

He—probably swayed by prudential considerations of the folly of offending a good tenant—relaxed a little in the laconic style of chipping off his pronouns and auxiliary verbs, and introduced what he supposed would be a subject of interest to me,—a discourse on the advantages and disadvantages of my present place of retirement.

I found him very intelligent on the topics we touched; and before I went home, I was encouraged so far as to volunteer another visit tomorrow.

He evidently wished no repetition of my intrusion. I shall go, notwithstanding. It is astonishing how sociable I feel myself compared with him.

TITLE COMMENTARY

Wuthering Heights

E. P. WHIPPLE (ESSAY DATE OCTOBER 1848)

SOURCE: Whipple, E. P. "Novels of the Season." *The North American Review* 67, no. 141 (October 1848): 354-70.

In the following excerpt, Whipple presumes that the author of Wuthering Heights *is male and faults the novel as amoral and offensive.*

Acton Bell, the author of **Wuthering Heights,** . . . when left altogether to his own imaginations, seems to take a morose satisfaction in developing a full and complete science of human brutality. In *Wuthering Heights* he has succeeded in reaching the summit of this laudable ambition. He appears to think that spiritual wickedness is a combination of animal ferocities, and has accordingly made a compendium of the most striking qualities of tiger, wolf, cur, and wild-cat, in the hope of framing out of such elements a suitable brute-demon to serve as the hero of his novel. Compared with Heathcliff, Squeers is considerate and Quilp humane. He is a deformed monster, whom the Mephistopheles of Goethe would have nothing to say to, whom the Satan of Milton would consider as an object of simple disgust, and to whom Dante would hesitate in awarding the honor of a place among those whom he has consigned to the burning pitch. This epitome of brutality, disavowed by man and devil, Mr. Acton Bell attempts in two whole volumes to delineate, and certainly he is to be congratulated on his success. As he is a man of uncommon talents, it is needless to say that it is to his subject and his dogged manner of handling it that we are to refer the burst of dislike with which the novel was received. His mode of delineating a bad character is to narrate every offensive act and repeat every vile expression which are characteristic. Hence, in *Wuthering Heights,* he details all the ingenuities of animal malignity, and exhausts the whole rhetoric of stupid blasphemy, in order that there may be no mistake as to the kind of person he intends to hold up to the popular gaze. Like all spendthrifts of malice and profanity, however, he overdoes the business. Though he scatters oaths as plentifully as sentimental writers do interjections, the comparative parsimony of the great novelists in this respect is productive of infinitely more effect. It must be confessed that this coarseness, though the prominent, is not the only characteristic of the writer. His attempt at originality does not stop with the conception of Heathcliff, but he aims further to exhibit the action of the sentiment of love on the nature of the being whom his morbid imagination has created. This is by far the ablest and most subtle portion of his labors, and indicates that strong hold upon the elements of character, and that decision of touch in the delineation of the most evanescent qualities of emotion, which distinguish the mind of the whole family. For all practical purposes, however, the power evinced in *Wuthering Heights* is power thrown away. Nightmares and dreams, through which devils dance and wolves howl, make bad novels.

SYNDY MCMILLEN CONGER (ESSAY DATE 1983)

SOURCE: Conger, Syndy McMillen. "The Reconstruction of the Gothic Feminine Ideal in Emily Brontë's *Wuthering Heights.*" In *The Female Gothic,* edited by Julian Fleenor, pp. 91-106. Montreal, Quebec: Eden Press, 1983.

In the following essay, Conger studies the influence of the traditional Gothic genre on Wuthering Heights *as well as Brontë's innovations within and upon the Gothic tradition, particularly in terms of her portrayal of the heroine.*

In the first chapter of *Wuthering Heights,* Emily Brontë invites her readers to expect a Gothic thriller, an eighteenth-century form bound by a set of narrative conventions long established and easily recognized by 1847. She opens her tale by sketching the outline of a dwelling on a hill, which, like the Gothic castle in its age, disrepair, and isolation, is a monument to the fragility of human constructs. Next she fills in details designed to elicit the emotions central to the Gothic experience: melancholy, desire, and terror. The hilltop is bleak with the only vegetation being "a few stunted firs" and "a range of gaunt thorns."[1] Grass grows between the flagstones leading to the door, over which the narrator sees Gothic ornamentation: "grotesque carving," "a wilderness of crumbling griffins and shameless little boys," and a barely visible ancient date "1500" and name. Like the narrator's name, "Lockwood," which has the unsettling connotation of something or someone being shut out, and the name above the door, "Hareton Earnshaw," which suggests nature's mockery of woman's birthright or wages (*hare + earn + shaw,* 'a clump of bushes or trees; thicket; copse'), other names also evoke that sense of vague threat so pervasive in the Gothic world: "Wuthering Heights" for a house constantly buffeted by "atmospheric tumult" and "Heathcliff" for the abruptly inhospitable landlord. While Lockwood quickly recognizes the morose, dark-skinned gypsy as an isolato and a misanthrope, the reader is very apt to assume, in this context, that he is a Gothic villain.

Critics often take note of these Gothic characteristics but rarely linger on them, perhaps assuming that Gothic details are mere "trappings" (a favorite word, after all, of early students of the Gothic novel),[2] decorative devices which could in no way touch the essence of *Wuthering Heights.* Such an assumption can handicap readers, condemning them to unnecessary historical short-sightedness in their interpretation of Brontë's masterpiece. The rather obvious fact that *Wuthering Heights* is much more than a re-creation of Gothic formulae should not deter us from asking ourselves what Brontë did for the Gothic tradition and what the Gothic tradition did for Brontë. Her contribution to the tradition was to give it aesthetic respectability and also to introduce liberating modifications into what had become an overly rigid plot form. The tradition provided her with a unique opportunity to define for herself and for her readers a new kind of Gothic heroine.

From the protagonist's perspective, the traditional Gothic plot can be briefly described as fearful periods of pursuit and flight or confinement, persecution, and escape; brief interludes of reconciliation with loved ones; and a final, advantageous marriage and the restoration of tranquillity. Brontë's first modification in this traditional formula is to introduce her heroine not as a marriageable young woman but as a child. Catherine will also be wooed, terrorized and pursued, and married, but Brontë first develops her into a complex and individualized character. Her second innovation is to reverse the significance attached to marital and extramarital love. Brontë's heroine is married early in the novel, but this marriage is no resolution as it is in the traditional Gothic. It does not settle conflicts but exacerbates them, and in Brontë's structure, replaces the period of fearful confinement found in the middle of the traditional Gothic novel. Whether or not Nelly believes the perception valid, for Catherine marriage has seemed a dungeon: "Oh! I'm burning! I wish I were out of doors—I wish I were a girl again, half savage, and hardy, and free. . . ." This second change signals nothing less than a redefinition of freedom. In the early Gothic novel freedom is associated with escape from the dark usurper into marriage. In **Wuthering Heights,** however, in a way which underlines Brontë's adherence to the romantic inversion of eighteenth-century values,[3] freedom is inextricably bound to a social outcast and to the lawless—even incestuous—relationship he offers her.

This redefinition of freedom is rather too radical to have grown simply from Brontë's discontent with the traditional strictures of a genre. At the hub of both structural changes stands the heroine, and this suggests that underlying Brontë's urge to modify Gothic conventions is a dissatisfaction with contemporary fictional definitions of femininity and feminine happiness. Indeed, the portrait of the heroine which emerges from the novel makes such a conclusion ineluctable; for Catherine is a Gothic heroine quite free from the social and literary proscriptions of her forerunners. For this reason with Emily Brontë the term Female Gothic may be said to take on special significance.

ABOUT THE AUTHOR

H. F. CHORLEY'S NEGATIVE RESPONSE TO
WUTHERING HEIGHTS
Here are two tales [*Agnes Gray* and *Wuthering Heights*] so nearly related to *Jane Eyre* in cast of thought, incident, and language as to excite some curiosity. All three might be the work of one hand,—but the first issued remains the best. In spite of much power and cleverness; in spite of its truth to life in the remote nooks and corners of England, *Wuthering Heights* is a disagreeable story. The Bells seem to affect painful and exceptional subjects:—the misdeeds and oppressions of tyranny—the eccentricities of "woman's fantasy." They do not turn away from dwelling upon those physical acts of cruelty which we know to have their warrant in the real annals of crime and suffering,—but the contemplation of which true taste rejects. The brutal master of the lonely house on "Wuthering Heights"—a prison which might be pictured from life—has doubtless had his prototype in those ungenial and remote districts where human beings, like the trees, grow gnarled and dwarfed and distorted by the inclement climate; but he might have been indicated with far fewer touches, in place of so entirely filling the canvas that there is hardly a scene untainted by his presence. . . . Enough of what is mean and bitterly painful and degrading gathers round every one of us during the course of his pilgrimage through this vale of tears to absolve the Artist from choosing his incidents and characters out of such a dismal catalogue; and if the Bells, singly or collectively, are contemplating future or frequent utterances in Fiction, let us hope that they will spare us further interiors so gloomy as the one here elaborated with such dismal minuteness.

SOURCE: Chorley, H. F. "Our Library Table." *The Athenaeum,* no. 1052 (25 December 1847): 1324-25.

It no longer simply means Gothic novels written by females for females, imitative of male forms and attitudes. With Brontë it means literature which deliberately reorders the Gothic experience in order to speak to women about themselves in a new way. Brontë's departures from the conventional Gothic heroine—and the implications of those departures for her readers—will be the focus of the remainder of this essay. It begins with a review of Catherine's foremothers.

The picture of ideal femininity which emerges from early novels in the Gothic tradition is at once reductive and fragmented, a negative fictional construct born of a repressive society. The eighteenth-century Gothic heroine is made exemplary more for what she lacks than for what she has. Antonia wins praise from Lewis in *The Monk* (1796), for example, for lacking fullness of figure, for being "rather below than above the middle size" and "light and airy."[4] She also wins praise for lacking any distinctive physical qualities: "her eyes were not very large, nor their lashes particularly long." Hers is not an awesome physical beauty, Lewis explains, but a beauty of temperament—of the submissive personality: "not so lovely from regularity of features, as from sweetness and sensibility of countenance. . . ."

Submissiveness is a key personality trait of the persecuted Gothic maiden well into the nineteenth century.[5] Insofar as it is humanly possible, she obeys the dicta of parents and society, given perhaps their most uncompromising articulation by Isabella's mother in Maturin's *Melmoth the Wanderer* (1820): "perfect obedience . . . and unbroken silence."[6] Only when the Gothic heroine is confronted by dastardly behavior does she offer positive resistance, but it typically takes the puerile form of empty threats, unanswered prayers, or unheard shrieks. In less life-threatening circumstances, she frets and waits but rarely makes an independent attempt to change the questionable values or behavior of those around her. Isabella's response to Manfred's indignities in *The Castle of Otranto* (1764) is paradigmatic: she flees the secular world without any attempt to expose his outrageous desires. True, Radcliffe's Ellena Rosalba (*The Italian*, 1797) once refuses to accept unpleasant alternatives offered her by an unjust abbess, and Emily St. Aubert (*The Mysteries of Udolpho*, 1792) similarly refuses to sign away her property rights despite Montoni's threats. But this is a passive resistance, the last resort of those convinced they are powerless. Active, constructive resistance lies outside the ken or the capability of the early Gothic heroine. Submissiveness, this time coupled with total self-abnegation, is even held up as ideal by Mary Wollstonecraft's daughter in her *Frankenstein* (1817). Mary Shelley grants her heroine

Elizabeth intelligence, but Victor prizes her most for her "light and airy" figure and her yielding nature: "No one could better enjoy liberty, yet no one could submit with more grace than she did to constraint and caprice."[7] She is to him most "enchanting" when she is "continually endeavouring to contribute to the happiness of others, entirely forgetful of herself."

As the above examples may already have suggested, the early Gothic heroine was not only weak-willed but also sometimes weak-minded, although in this respect she grows in stature as the nineteenth century approaches. Isabella's mind is never assessed by Walpole and Lewis' Antonia is not even allowed to read an unexpurgated Bible for fear her mind will be tainted. Radcliffe's heroines, although they seem schooled most in the useful and fine arts of sewing, drawing, versifying, painting, and singing, sometimes also receive more rigorous intellectual training. Emily St. Aubert's father insists that she study Latin, English, and science: "'A well-informed mind,' he would say, 'is the best security against the contagion of folly and vice.'"[8] Maturin's Immalee-Isidora has the most formidable mind of all; her thoughts are often intelligent and boldly heterodox. She bewilders her Roman Catholic mother, for instance, by insisting on the precedence of piety over ceremony. Nor does Isidora easily accept the suppression of her naturally exuberant emotions by her mother, who brands them "violent" and "unmannerly."

Such signs of intellect, however, most not be overrated. The scanty training these girls receive cannot give them sufficient strength to cope independently with the perplexities they encounter without and within, and they are easy prey not only for fortune hunters but for themselves. Lacking constructive ways of occupying their minds, they frequently suffer from excess sensibility, a painfully exaggerated state of emotional awareness, bringing with it acute sensitivity to external stimuli and a tendency to fall victim to the paralyzing, diffuse emotions of sentiment and anxiety. Just as nameless wishes and fears will invade the idle mind, so dark imaginings often usurp the ill-informed mind. These heroines have overly vivid imaginations, a propensity to invent dangers where none exist. Emily is repeatedly warned by her father about the dangers of overly fine feelings, but when Montoni shuts her in his remote castle, she is much more the victim of the terrors she invents than she is of him. Even if these heroines survive the tests of sensibility and fancy, they are sure to capitulate intellectually during the ordeal of love. The minds of Emily and Immalee, both relatively perceptive young women, turn to butter when they are with their lovers. They lose all ability to think or act on their own.

Physically slight, emotionally passive, and intellectually ill-trained—wherein lies such a heroine's stature? Primarily in her moral impeccability. The Gothic heroine is morally flawless; hers is a purity of mind which becomes more pronounced as the turn of the century approaches. She never has a vindictive thought, even in the wake of abuses. She never dreams an unacceptable dream. Her innocence is so thorough in some cases that she has virtually no knowledge at all of evil. Antonia must learn only too late what the special glint in the friar Ambrosio's eye means. Immalee listens incredulously to Melmoth's tales of man's cruelty to his fellow creatures: "'In the world that thinks!' repeated Immalee, 'Impossible!'" These heroines are Eves before the fall, invested with mythical perfection which first becomes explicit in Maturin's portrayal of Immalee. Of sexuality and physical passion these mythical creatures are equally ignorant, a clue to us that their creators equated passion with evil. Antonia "knows not in what consists the difference of Man and Woman." "Of passion," Immalee said "she knew nothing, and could propose no remedy for an evil she was unconscious of"

Balancing the frail, submissive paragon in early Gothic fiction is the dark, imperious, passion-ridden one, the femme fatale. She has the independence of spirit, the emotional vibrancy, the ingenuity, and the moral fallibility the heroine often lacks, but she pays a price for these strengths. She is their victim. In her youth, the dark woman is often loving but of a "warm and voluptuous character" as was Beatrice de las Cisternas in The Monk. As she ages, if her wishes are in any way thwarted, and they invariably are, she grows insatiable, ungovernable, and even deliberately wicked. She becomes then an exacting and jealous competitor for a young man's affections, as is the Baroness Lindenberg in The Monk; or a "vindictive, yet crafty and deceitful" mother, as is the Marchesa de Vivaldi in The Italian;[9] or a mercilessly punitive Mother Superior as are the abbesses in The Italian and The Monk. Her last days and her death may be unquiet. Her conscience may weigh heavily enough with crimes to drive her into temporary insanity and delirium, as it does Signora Laurentini in The Mysteries of Udolpho; and just as she is a conscience-plagued woman in life, so she may be transformed after death into a restless ghost, as Beatrice becomes the "Bleeding Nun" of The Monk.; At her most extreme, the femme fatale has struck an alliance with the devil, as has Matilda in The Monk in this case her kiss damns as well as fires the soul of her lover, Ambrosio.

The woman reading this fiction in the eighteenth century is hardly to be envied. The price she paid for the privilege of emotional release was high; she was most cruelly reduced and divided against herself. She might temporarily enjoy reading of the villain's lust or the hero's sentimental adoration, but she was quietly being instructed at the same time to choose between two equally impossible feminine models. Did she yearn only to be virtuous? Then she must strive for a body "light and airy" and a mind equally so; she must be utterly compliant, selfless, dependent, and pure. Did she pine instead for an all-subsuming, passionate love affair? Then she must expect to be soundly punished, even damned, or become vicious, subject to criminal impulses and madness. The choice is rather obviously unsatisfactory, at the very least encouraging the female reader to repress any urges to express or please herself, and—perhaps even more dangerously in the long run—perpetuating the myth that she was fated, whether good or bad, to be a victim of passions beyond her control, if not of her own, then those of others. Little wonder that Mary Wollstonecraft repudiated such fiction in Maria, or, The Wrongs of Women (1798) and such feminine models in A Vindication of the Rights of Women (1792): "I wish to persuade women to endeavor to acquire strength, both of mind and body."[10] In such fiction the bounds of femininity were painfully narrow.

In the first few episodes of **Wuthering Heights,** Emily Brontë studiously avoids recreating such stereotyped Gothic heroines. The reader meets no gentle maiden or femme fatale in these early scenes; instead Brontë offers two Catherines, one far too sullen to qualify as the angelically compliant Gothic heroine, and the other far too complex. The younger Catherine is fair and pretty but unpardonably rude to Lockwood when he comes to tea, a rudeness which is easily traceable in the personality of her mother, the elder Catherine, as it emerges from her childish scrawl and Lockwood's dream. This elder Catherine as a child is at once naughty and loving, disobedient and loyal, and a childish specter both terrifying and pitiful. From the outset, then, she is clearly a new composite heroine, combining positive and negative attributes of earlier feminine characters of the Gothic tradition.

This is not to deny a family resemblance between Catherine and the Gothic heroines before her. She is, for example, as easily tyrannized by emotions and unrealistic fantasies as Emily St. Aubert. She grieves at Heathcliff's disappearance until she makes herself physically ill, even as a strong young woman. Then, when a second bout of illness proves fatal during her first pregnancy, violent emotions are again the primary underlying cause, something Nelly recognizes but cannot understand or help. Her fantasies, though a comforting refuge against a hostile environment for Catherine the child (the fantasy of her father in heaven, for example), are sadly self-defeating and delusive for Catherine the adult. She should see that her marriage to Edgar cannot "aid Heathcliff to rise" when the two men despise each other. She should see that even if her wealth could in some way aid Heathcliff, she could still never marry him so long as Edgar remained alive. She should, after Isabella's elopement, work to reconcile herself to the inevitable rift between Edgar and Heathcliff instead of withdrawing to a world of unrecoverable childhood fantasies: "Oh, if I were but in my own bed in the old house!" Sometimes the fantasies cause positive harm. Her delusory accusations of Nelly only harden her nurse against her; and her fantasy-inspired wish to catch a breath of night air from the moors does little to cure her fever.

The family resemblance is strongest between Radcliffe's and Maturin's heroines and Catherine. Like them, she is drawn to nature, though for her it is not an emblematic reminder of God's Providence, as they believe, but rather is itself divine. Catherine's heaven is the heath: ". . . heaven did not seem to be my home," Catherine admits to Nelly as she shares a dream she's had of dying, "and I broke my heart with weeping to come back to earth; and the angels were so angry that they flung me out, into the middle of the heath on the top of Wuthering Heights; where I woke sobbing for joy." Catherine also shares with Emily, Ellena, and Immalee a propensity to almost deify her lovers, to over-idealize love bonds. The passages which illustrate this are often quoted, but they are so central to this point and a number of others to follow that they are included here in their entirety:

> I've no more business to marry Edgar Linton than I have to be in heaven; and if the wicked man in there had not brought Heathcliff so low, I shouldn't have thought of it. It would degrade me to marry Heathcliff now; so he shall never know how I love him; and that, not because he's handsome, Nelly, but because he's more myself than I am. Whatever our souls are made of, his and mine are the same, and Linton's is as different as a moonbeam from lightning, or frost from fire. . . . I cannot express it; but surely you and everybody have a notion that there is, or should be, an existence of yours beyond you. What were the use of my creation if I were entirely contained here? My great miseries in this world have been Heathcliff's miseries, and I watched and felt each from the beginning; my great thought in living is himself. If all else perished, and *he* remained, I should still continue to be; and, if all else remained, and he were annihilated, the Universe would turn to a mighty stranger. I should not seem a part of it. My love for Linton is like the foliage in the woods. Time will change it, I'm well aware, as winter changes the trees. My love for Heathcliff resembles the eternal rocks beneath—a source of little visible delight, but necessary. Nelly, I *am* Heathcliff—he's always, always in my mind. . . .

> (pp. 100-02)

This speech has been heralded as the articulation of a new love ethos, one with metaphysical dimensions: the identification of love as a natural, hence amoral, impulse which cannot be judged by sublunary standards.[11] Such assumptions, viewed from the perspective of the Gothic tradition, however, are actually not new at all. Catherine's words echo sentimental love declarations in the pages of Radcliffe and Maturin. Strikingly similar in diction and tone to the words above, for example, are Immalee's words mourning and idealizing her love for the absent Melmoth: "The lightnings are glancing round. . . . I lived but in the light of his presence—why should I not die when that light is withdrawn?" Immalee even reaches out for the same metaphors and absolute expressions in her attempt to express what seems to her inexpressible: "Roar on, terrible ocean! thy waves . . . can never wash his image from my soul,—thou dashest a thousand waves against a rock, but the rock is unmoved—and so would be my heart." Catherine's uniqueness, critical opinion to the contrary, does not reside in how she loves.

Catherine and Immalee have in common not only how they love but whom they love. Both prefer their demon lovers, rebels against the human and the divine, a preference which at first seems to identify both heroines as notably nonconformist. Yet *Melmoth the Wanderer* and **Wuthering Heights** exist on very different levels of abstraction, and parallels between the two must be drawn carefully. Melmoth's rebellion is one of mind and soul; he himself is a preternatural Faustian character whose function in the novel is mythical—repeated reenactment of Satan's temptation. The story of his temptation of Immalee, consequently, has few social implications; it is primarily spiritual allegory.[12] Heathcliff, on the other hand, is a flesh and blood landlord whose crimes are primarily social ones—alienation of a father's affections, usurpation, seduction, tyranny over wife and child—and the story of Catherine's love for him abounds in social and psychological implications. Seen in these terms, Catherine is by far the more radical of the two heroines, for she chooses a social outcast, one who pits himself against economic and conjugal privilege and one whose implicit democratic and romantic values could alter the fabric of society.[13]

Still another important distinction between Immalee and Catherine should be drawn. Although Immalee loves a damned soul, her love for him is conventional, in terms of Gothic fiction, insofar as it is faultlessly pure. She loves him for awakening her emotionally and intellectually, and she is blinded until the very end of her life to the malicious side of his nature. Catherine's love for Heathcliff is far less immaculate. Far from being blind to his fiendish qualities, she sees them with unerring clarity: ". . . he's a fierce, pitiless, wolfish man." Catherine's attachment to this "wolfish man," although sometimes expressing itself in terms of compassion or affection, is more often disturbing in its admixture of antagonism, pathological loyalty, arrogance, monomania, narcissism, and incest. In fact, there is a touch of the pathological about Catherine in other attitudes she shares with her prototypes: she is not simply the occasional victim of whim or imagined terror but her passions' willing slave; she is not simply appreciative of nature but a nature worshipper, a near pagan; and she is not simply the unwitting prey of a rebel lover but embraces her lover's anarchic values. In depicting such a rebel heroine as Catherine, Brontë not only goes beyond Gothic conventions, she hovers visibly close to the limits of the socially acceptable. Nevertheless, her readers are not quite free to reject Catherine, as they could villains like Manfred or Ambrosio, unless they are willing to reject a heroine. Instead, they must entertain the possibility that a woman need not be angelically pure to be worthy of attention. Clearly, even when Catherine seems most like her prototypes, she is very different from them. It is time to examine those differences.

What distinguishes Catherine above all is the unique complexity and energy of her personality. Catherine's mind is complicated, analytical, and uninhibited, all qualities never before granted a Gothic heroine. Catherine's complexity is more than amply illustrated by her central conflict, the seeds of which lie buried in her childhood memo- ries of a benevolent father, a fire and brimstone servant, and a selfish, tyrannical brother. These adult models produce in Catherine a love of gentle kindness, a well-informed aversion to cruelty, and a keen sense of injustice. At the same time they encourage in her a sympathetic admiration and love for her stoic fellow sufferer, the gypsy child Heathcliff—her father inspires her to it, Hindley drives her to it. Heathcliff becomes increasingly cruel himself as a young man, but Catherine's love for him persists, eventually, according to Nelly, growing immoderate.

Catherine's conflict first takes form after she unexpectedly finds herself a guest in the home of the Lintons after a midnight ramble with Heathcliff on the moors. Although she at first expresses disdain for the spoiled, rich children, she returns home from her stay metamorphosed. Now Heathcliff's angry and uncouth appearance repels her and she rebukes him. Subsequently she suffers acutely when he is banished for a fight with the haughty Edgar, and she finds her feelings reversed. She becomes impatient with the whining Edgar and longs for Heathcliff. Her unresolved feelings for the two young men cause a crisis, of course, when Edgar proposes. She isn't certain—should she bow to the love-hate she feels for the savage but oppressed Heathcliff, or should she acquiesce to Edgar, refined and gentle like her father, but somewhat distant and cowardly? Which one does she admire the most and dislike the least? When Catherine tries to explain her indecision to the exasperated Nelly, she represents it not as a battle between head and heart but as a disturbance of soul. In reply to Nelly's question, "Where is the obstacle?" Catherine replies "'Here! and here!' . . . striking one hand on her forehead, and the other on her breast. 'In whichever place the soul lives.'" This is a conflict which engages, in a manner unprecedented in Gothic heroines, ambiguous desire against ambiguous desire, complex against complex, ego against alter-ego ("Nelly, I *am* Heathcliff").

Gothic heroines were traditionally placed in a conflict situation between a dark seducer and a fair lover, but theirs was an external conflict;[14] they never felt—or admitted they felt—a pull in two directions. Catherine is the first important exception to that pattern, for she internalizes her conflict completely. She is not simply placed between two lovers; she feels divided between two lovers. From this Brontë's story derives at least two important advantages. First, the symbolic resonance of the traditional Gothic triad of characters is enhanced. Now both villain and lover

Advertisement for William Wyler's 1939 film adaptation of *Wuthering Heights*.

can be seen as extensions of the heroine's mind and can represent her own conflicting social and emotional needs. Catherine wishes to marry wisely, to enhance her uncertain social status, but she has also contemplated marrying unwisely—for love alone—and living a beggarly existence with Heathcliff. She needs an environment which can shield her from emotions of ravaging intensity, and yet she isn't content without the childhood companion who is most apt to inspire such emotions. She longs for the near pathological attachment of Heathcliff as much as for the gentle, more rational adoration of Edgar. Second, this internalization, since it obviously increases the psychological complexity of the Gothic heroine, broadens immeasurably the bounds within which femininity may move. A heroine's mind, Brontë is insisting here, need not be a blank tablet. It may sometimes be plagued by contradictory or self-defeating desires.

Nor is Catherine's mind passive, dependent, or inhibited. She seems to have been born with an energetic need to analyze, articulate, and conquer what she sees around and within herself.

This is plain from the very beginning of the novel in her Testament diary (which covers, as Lockwood reports, "every morsel of blank that the printer had left." She compares and judges Hindley incisively as a father figure: "Hindley is a detestable substitute." Notice that she is keenly aware of injustice and expresses that insight by artfully juxtaposing the self-indulgent comfort Hindley allows himself and the pain he inflicts on others: "While Hindley and his wife basked downstairs before a comfortable fire . . . we were . . . groaning and shivering . . . ," or, "Frances pulled his [Heathcliff's] hair heartily; and then went and seated herself on her husband's knee, and there they were, like two babies, kissing and talking nonsense by the hour. . . ."

Catherine is also willing to subject herself publicly to unflinching analysis, although she is not entirely free of subtle self-deceptions. As a young woman, she convinces herself mistakenly that Heathcliff will not care if she marries Edgar. Later she nearly convinces herself that Edgar and Heathcliff have killed her when, as Heathcliff reminds her, she has actually broken her own heart. Despite such delusions, Catherine is vastly superior in self-understanding to the previous Gothic heroines who were, for the most part, passive and impassive receptors; and she shares her understanding without affectation or scruple. Earlier heroines had internalized the laws of propriety too fully ever to air the contents of their minds publicly, nor did they always fully know their own minds. Ellena's response to Vivaldi's urgent pleas to marry him rather than seek retirement is all too typical. The situation begs for honest emotional response and an intelligent reassessment of plans, but Ellena refuses to change her answer. She "gently reproached him for doubting the continuance of her regard . . . but would not listen. . . . She represented . . . that respect to the memory of her aunt demanded it." After Vivaldi departs, Ellena is left to disperse encroaching depression, a sign of unexamined and unresolved concerns.

In contrast, Catherine rarely hides or fails to scrutinize her own thoughts, sometimes with breathtaking honesty. Her character gains breadth and depth and credibility as she shares not only surface responses, but unrecoverable dreams of the past, impossible dreams for the future, sentiments from the dark, not so respectable corners of her mind, and misgivings about those sentiments. "I want to cheat my uncomfortable conscience . . ."; "Nelly, I see now, you think me a selfish wretch . . ."; "What did I say, Nelly? I've forgotten. Was he vexed at my bad humour this afternoon?"; "Why am I so changed? Why does my blood rush into a hell of tumult at a few words? I'm sure I should be myself were I once among the heather." Catherine may seem narcissistic and unrestrained, but she is nonetheless a valuable corrective to unreflective and unresponsive Gothic heroines that preceded her. The same concerns which impel Walpole's heroine to flight, Lewis' to prayer, Radcliffe's to diversions, and Maturin's to daydreams, compel Catherine to examine her own heart. She is the first fully introspective Gothic heroine.

These strengths, however much they may win Catherine grudging admiration, do not make her easier to live with. Her list of human imperfections is so long one wonders that she is a heroine at all. It should come as no surprise that Brontë has created in Catherine a heroine whose faults often closely resemble those of the traditional femme fatale of Gothic fiction. She is sometimes a raving fury; and, before her, such fury is displayed only by the scheming, ambitious Signora Laurentini, Beatrice, and the Baroness Lindenberg. Also like these wicked women, Catherine is often proud, self-centered, imperious, manipulative, and cruel. She coerces those around her into obedience by command, humiliation or self-punishment (Brontë's depiction of the little Catherine as a girl whose heart's desire is a riding whip is far from gratuitous). Her love is literally fatal both to her and to Heathcliff. Most important and emblematic of all these darker characteristics, however, is Catherine's introduction into the story as a ghost. Despite her appearance as a defenseless child-specter who has lost her way on the moors, Lockwood's response to her in his nightmare is horror, and rightly so. The experience has the earmarks of the classic ghost story: the scratching sound on the windowpane, the ice-cold hand, the melancholy voice, the seductive pleading, and the bleeding. This scene firmly allies *Wuthering Heights* with the Gothic tradition, of course. However, another more important alliance is also struck here—an intimate alliance between the Gothic heroine and the demonic or supernatural realm.

In earlier novels, the heroine moves apart from this world, terrorized or occasionally helped by it, and indeed sometimes helping to create it in her own frightened imagination, but never actively participating in it. She is a creature of the diurnal sphere, estranged from nocturnal desires and terrors, perceiving them as outside threats, as totally "other," and as uncanny. Only the villain-

esses ally themselves with the dark powers. Catherine, by contrast, is introduced by Brontë as an uncanny, nocturnal creature, an identity she never completely sheds. For a short time she has a promisingly happy life as Edgar's wife in the "sunshine" at Thrushcross Grange, but she emerges from and returns to a nightmare world of "wuthering" self-destructive passions: greed, revenge, lovehate. In a most telling moment during her final illness, Catherine feels herself haunted and Nelly forces her to realize that the ghost she thinks she sees is her own mirrored reflection: "'Myself,' she gasped, 'and the clock is striking twelve! It's true, then; that's dreadful!'" This poignant scene at once recalls the earlier scene in which Catherine is a child-ghost and refines the sense in which we should see her as an adult. She is self-tortured, haunted by her own unfulfillable, child-like desires. Since Heathcliff is equally plagued by such hopeless desires, it is only too appropriate that she should haunt him, too, after her death. Brontë has naturalized the supernatural in a most convincing way through Catherine, but beyond that she has also given her readers a heroine more complete and more truly pitiful than earlier ones. Catherine finally experiences what is the most somber insight a Gothic character can have or inspire: that the demonic springs from her own imagination. Catherine is the first Gothic heroine to acknowledge the dark side of her soul.

Catherine's dark side and her recognition of that dark side represent a change of major importance in the depiction of heroines in the Gothic. Such self-recognition—that "of the enlightened person feeling haunted by some demonic self"—is believed by Francis Russell Hart to lie at the center of the Gothic experience. His description of that experience reads like a commentary on Catherine's mirror scene:

> What gives the point its full and terrifying truth in an enlightenment context is that the demonic is no myth, no superstition, but a reality in human character or relationship, a novelistic reality. . . . Are there really ghosts? asks Carlyle-Teufelsdröckh. *We* are ghosts.[15]

What Hart says is particularly true for male characters in the Gothic, who are granted some degree of imperfection and self-awareness from the beginning. Manfred is made to see fully the wickedness of his lust for power; Ambrosio finally recognizes himself as a willing devil's accomplice; and after William Frankenstein's murder, Victor admits his own complicity in this diabolic deed: "Sleep fled from my eyes; I wandered like an evil spirit." Not until Brontë, however, does the Gothic heroine come to a comparable level of wholeness and self-awareness. Catherine's self-recognition is not without pain, but it is a pain that heals, one which allows sympathetic readers to cease utterly denying their own negative impulses. The split in the feminine psyche implicitly encouraged by earlier Gothic fiction is, through Catherine, questioned. Further, the Gothic heroine has been freed from what was always the worst of the tyrannies inflicted on her: that of the ideal of moral perfection.

Although it would be an overstatement to say that Brontë has given us a completely mature heroine, it can certainly be said that she has offered us a more mature vision of woman's character than did authors from Walpole to Maturin, one much more integrated and less restricted physically, emotionally, and intellectually.[16] By way of final illustration and summary, I would like to focus briefly on heroines' death scenes, partly because they have been slighted, but mostly because Catherine's death scene is pivotal in the realigning of reader sympathies. Only if Brontë allows Catherine to face death admirably can we be sure that she is being recommended to us as a heroine.

Walpole's Matilda dies a perfectly exemplary death. Killed by her father in their chapel, she is selfless, pious, and forgiving as her life ebbs slowly away. Her only thoughts are for her parents: ". . . as soon as Hippolita was brought to herself, she [Matilda] asked for her father . . . seizing his hand and her mother's, locked them in her own, and then clasped them to her heart. Manfred could not support this . . . pathetic piety."[17] Radcliffe consistently paints two pictures of female death, both in the exemplary mode, one offering a positive, the other a negative, model. Emily's mother dies with perfect composure born of lifelong self-control and piety, and she is surrounded by solicitous loved ones when she dies. Signora Laurentini and Madame Cheron, on the other hand, die disquieted and abandoned, the one tortured by memories of her wickedness, the other by the greed of her hastily-chosen husband. The final hours of Lewis' heroine are horrific, yet she dies with as much serentiy as Emily's mother. Antonia is drugged, then entombed, and finally raped and stabbed to death by Ambrosio in a corpse-filled vault; she nevertheless surrenders her life with gentle resignation, selflessly spending her last minutes convincing Lorenzo that he should not despair. Maturin's angelic Isidora also dies in a dungeon, a prison of the Inquisition where she has been placed because of her liaison with Mel-

moth, but she nonetheless dies without resentment and with his name on her lips: "Paradise! . . . *Will he be there!*"

Catherine's death is not nearly so exemplary and edifying. Death and suffering are not really the result of someone else's malice but of her own headstrong refusal to relinquish Heathcliff's friendship to save her marriage. She throws a tantrum after Edgar requires her to choose between him and Heathcliff. Then she lives for a week on nothing, in the words of Nelly, but "cold water and ill-temper," a form of self-abuse which weakens her already fragile constitution. Nor does Catherine have much composure during the last months of her life. Rather, she suffers agonies as extreme as those of the most wicked femme fatale: melancholy, regression, temporary disorientation, helpless fury, self-pity, and the terrors of paranoia and delusion. Like other heroines, Catherine is allowed the comfort of having her loved one with her during her last conscious moments, but again these moments are markedly different from those of Matilda's, Antonia's or Isidora's. Her concern is not to comfort Heathcliff but to punish him for what she believes is his heartlessness. She refuses to pity him, accuses him of being the death of her, and expresses the vindictive wish that he could be made to suffer as much as she has: "I wish I could hold you . . . till we were both dead! I shouldn't care what you suffered. I care nothing for your sufferings. Why shouldn't you suffer? I do!" His own frenzy at being thus accused checks her anger, however, and she suddenly modifies her wish: "I only wish us never to be parted. . . ." Then she relents even more, asking him to embrace and forgive her as she has forgiven him, and his embrace conveys the love he cannot articulate.

In death, as in life, Brontë allows Catherine to be a whole and credible person, one with negative and positive characteristics. The noble martyr-like stances of Matilda, Antonia, and Immalee on the edge of the grave are not to be scoffed at; but from the reader's perspective, these saintly images are apt to create anxiety or guilt. The authors have made idols of their heroines, unattainable ideals to emulate. Women are to die selflessly, sweetly, obediently, and without any regrets or anger, even in death to be denied the privilege of swerving for a moment from the path of perfection. Catherine's death, in contrast, is not one to recommend for imitation; much of the time Catherine is at her vindictive worse. Still, despite her childish behavior, she manages in her last moments to achieve forgiveness and an open expression of her love. Nor should we forget the "unearthly beauty"

Brontë gives her dying heroine. Brontë's implicit lesson to her female readers was clearly that they could, even if they were overwhelmed momentarily by cruel or selfish thoughts, hope to die with some dignity and some small measure of comfort.

As no attempt was made here to prove a direct influence of specific Gothic novels on *Wuthering Heights,* no time was spent on works identified as important in molding either Brontë's mind or her work. Of all the literary influences on the Brontës—and those include the works of Shakespeare, Milton, Richardson, Radcliffe, E. T. A. Hoffmann, Scott, Wordsworth, Tennyson, and George Sand[18]—Helene Moglen believes the single most important figure was Lord Byron. The rebellion that was Byron's life, including his flagrant violations of propriety in matters of love, and especially his scandalous affair with his half-sister, apparently left a deep impression on the young Brontës. Their juvenalia include transparently Byronic values and characters.[19] Moglen's emphasis on Byron serves well as a reminder that a literary event just as crucial to the making of *Wuthering Heights* as the Gothic novel was the Romantic revolution. Its spirited affirmation of the value of individual subjective experience, and its tentative dream of woman as intellectual companion as well as lover, no doubt encouraged Brontë in her efforts to create a new, intelligent, imaginative, and passionate heroine. Brontë could also draw inspiration from the turn-of-the-century Wollstonecraft who, in fact, was more the radical, pleading for the outright rejection of the myth of romantic passion in her *Vindication.*[20] Like her sister Charlotte, Emily could never quite give up this myth,[21] but this very refusal may finally account for the extraordinary success of *Wuthering Heights.* Brontë was finally a more successful iconoclast than Wollstonecraft. With none of the self-conscious irritation of Jane Austen in *Northanger Abbey* (1818) but with just as much persuasiveness, Brontë deconstructed Walpole's feminine ideal and replaced it with her own. The alluring surface romance of *Wuthering Heights* and its initial evocation of Gothic convention are the sugar coating which apparently made the feminist pill quite palatable. At least for the duration of Brontë's "Gothic thriller," readers tacitly accept a number of irreverently non-Victorian notions about women: a woman should be assumed to have physical and intellectual as well as emotional needs and strengths; a woman has the right to physical, emotional, and intellectual autonomy both before and after marriage; a woman has the right to be imperfect—to be mistaken, passionate,

inquisitive, angry, confused, and even selfish or cruel, and still command respect as a human being; a woman has the right to be outstanding, to be openly intelligent and complex, and still command affection.

These ideas are tempered in the latter half of the novel, but the statement Brontë makes through Catherine and Heathcliff, as so many modern readers continue to acknowledge, is the one that haunts the mind. Although there are disgruntled censors of the ilk of John Beversluis, who insists that Catherine is simply a petulant, indecisive woman,[22] the admirers drown them out. Catherine is named Brontë's "supreme and original creation,"[23] and her love for Heathcliff is "what . . . D. H. Lawrence called true humanity."[24] Through it Brontë is "positing . . . natural human values, especially, love and integrity, against a corrupt and deadened society"[25] and "affirming . . . man and woman's more primary needs."[26] Part of this praise no doubt springs from our own continuing reluctance to relinquish the myth of romantic love unto death which Brontë dramatizes, but it nevertheless demonstrates the power Catherine continues to exert on the modern imagination. Brontë's rescue of the languishing maiden from the Gothic bastille began no revolutions; but it has unquestionably helped to save both heroine and genre from oblivion and to free the woman from the persistent fetters of the eighteenth-century ideal, which were, according to Wollstonecraft, "worse than Egyptian bondage."[27]

Notes

1. Emily Brontë, *Wuthering Heights,* ed. Hilda Marsden and Ian Jack (Oxford: Clarendon Press, 1976).

2. Early discussion of the Gothic novel by Ernest Baker, Edith Birkhead, K.K. Mehrota, Eino Railo, Montague Summers, and Devendra Varma tend to dwell on Gothic "devices" and their sources and to slight important questions about the structure and psychological function of the novels. In the last fifteen years, however, new theoretical ground has been broken on these questions by such studies as: Gerhard Bierwirth, "Die Problematik des englischen Schauerromans: Ein kritisches Modell zur Behandlung diskriminierter Literatur," Diss. Frankfurt/M., 1970; Peter Brooks, "Virtue and Terror: *The Monk,*" *ELH,* 40, 2 (1973), 249-63; Francis Russel Hart, "The Experience of Character in the English Gothic Novel," in *Experience in the Novel,* Selected Papers from the English Institute, ed. Roy Harvey Pearce (New York: Columbia Univ. Press, 1968); Robert D. Hume, "Gothic Versus Romantic: A Revaluation of the Gothic Novel," *PMLA,* 84 (1969), 282-90; Ellen Moers, "Female Gothic," in *Literary Women* (New York: Doubleday & Co., 1963); and Tzvetan Todorov, *The Fantastic: A Structural Approach to a*

Literary Genre, tr. Richard Howard (Ithaca, N.Y.: Cornell Univ. Press, 1975). Moers' study is the best available discussion of Brontë in the context of the Female Gothic tradition.

3. I am indebted to Helene Moglen's most lucid discussion of the Brontës and Romanticism in *Charlotte Brontë: The Self Conceived* (New York: W.W. Norton & Co., 1976), pp. 19-78, 230-42, and also to her interpretation of *Wuthering Heights* as an "account of the development of a human personality, the specifically female personality," in "The Double Vision of *Wuthering Heights*: A Clarifying View of Female Development," *The Centennial Review of Arts and Sciences,* 15 (1971), 391-405.

4. Matthew Lewis, *The Monk: A Romance,* ed. Howard Anderson (New York: Oxford Univ. Press, 1973), p. 9.

5. Patricia Meyer Spacks, "The Dangerous Age," *Eighteenth-Century Studies,* 11, 4 (Summer, 1978), 417-38, emphasizes the importance of submissiveness (p. 432) as does Katharine M. Rogers, *The Troublesome Helpmate: A History of Misogyny in Literature* (Seattle: Univ. of Washington Press, 1966).

6. Charles Robert Maturin, *Melmoth the Wanderer,* ed. William F. Axton (Lincoln: Univ. of Nebraska Press, 1961), p. 253.

7. Mary Wollstonecraft Shelley, *Frankenstein, or The Modern Prometheus* (The 1818 Text), ed. with variant readings, James Rieger (Indianapolis: The Bobbs-Merrill Co., 1974), p. 30.

8. Ann Radcliffe, *The Mysteries of Udolpho: A Romance Interspersed with some Pieces of Poetry,* eds. Bonamy Dobrée and Frederick Garber (New York: Oxford Univ. Press, 1970), p. 6.

9. Ann Radcliffe, *The Italian, or the Confessional of the Black Penitents: A Romance,* ed. Frederick Garber (New York: Oxford Univ. Press, 1968), p. 7.

10. Mary Wollstonecraft, "An Introduction to the First Edition," of *A Vindication of the Rights of Women with Strictures on Political and Moral Subjects,* ed. Charles W. Hagelman, Jr. (New York: W.W. Norton & Co., 1967), p. 34. Helen Mews, *Frail Vessels: Woman's Role in Women's Novels from Fanny Burney to George Eliot* (Univ. of London: The Athlone Press, 1969), believes that "society's two different images of women, inherited from the long past," caused "perplexity" and "tension" for women between 1750 and 1850 (p. 5).

11. Two recent reaffirmations of this romantic interpretation are H.P. Sucksmith's "The Theme of *Wuthering Heights* Reconsidered," *Dalhousie Review,* 54, 3 (Autumn, 1974), 418-28; and Peter Widdowson's "Emily Brontë: The Romantic Novelist," *Moderna Sprak,* 56, 1 (1972), 1-19.

12. ". . . a tragic allegory of Christian history," Axton's introduction to *Melmoth the Wanderer,* p. xvii. Contrasting *Melmoth* and *Wuthering Heights* reveals the weakness in Mews' contention that Brontë's message is "poetic," not "social" (p. 80).

13. See Arnold Kettle, "Emily Brontë: *Wuthering Heights,*" in Vol. I of *An Introduction to the English Novel* (Evanston: Harper & Row, 1960).

14. An insightful Freudian analysis of the Gothic heroine's situational conflict has been done by Cynthia Griffin Wolff entitled "The Gothic Hero-Villain: An Attractive Nuisance." (See Wolff's essay in this anthology.)

15. Hart, pp. 94, 99.

16. Moglen, "The Double Vision," pp. 391-93.

17. Horace Walpole, *The Castle of Otranto: A Gothic Story,* ed. W.S. Lewis (New York: Oxford Univ. Press, 1964), p. 106.

18. For discussion of Brontë's possible sources, see Mary Visick, *The Genesis of Wuthering Heights* (London: Oxford Univ. Press, 1958); Ruth M. Mackay, "Irish Heaths and German Cliffs: A Study of the Foreign Sources of *Wuthering Heights,*" *Brigham Young University Studies,* 7 (1965), 28-39; Leicester Bradner, "The Growth of 'Wuthering Heights,'" in *Wuthering Heights: An Anthology of Criticism,* ed. Alastair Everitt (New York: Barnes & Noble, 1967), pp. 14-38; J.V. Arnold, "George Sand's *Mauprat* and Emily Brontë's *Wuthering Heights,*" *Revue de la littérature comparée,* 46 (1972), 209-18; Rolf R. Nicolai, "'Wuthering Heights': Emily Brontë's Kleistian Novel," *South Atlantic Bulletin,* 38, 2 (1973), 23-32; and Patrick Diskin, "Some Sources of 'Wuthering Heights,'" *NQ* (July/August, 1977), 354-61.

19. Moglen, *Charlotte Brontë,* esp. pp. 26-33.

20. Wollstonecraft, "that grand passion not proportioned to the puny enjoyments of life, is only true to the sentiment, and feeds on itself," p. 66. Cf. pp. 121-122.

21. Moglen speaks convincingly in concluding *Charlotte Brontë* of "her continuing inability to break free of that circle of romantic idealism which had bound her to life," p. 226.

22. John Beversluis, "Love and Self Knowledge: A Study of *Wuthering Heights,*" *English,* 24, 120 (Autumn, 1975), 77-82.

23. Leicester Bradner, p. 38.

24. F.H. Langman, "Thoughts on *Wuthering Heights,*" in Everitt, p. 76.

25. Widdowson, p. 17.

26. Sucksmith, p. 422.

27. Wollstonecraft, p. 179.

MARILYN HUME (ESSAY DATE FALL 2002)

SOURCE: Hume, Marilyn. "Who Is Heathcliff? The Shadow Knows." *Victorian Newsletter* 102 (fall 2002): 15-18.

In the following essay, Hume explores how Brontë uses the character of Heathcliff to reveal and represent the will of the unconscious or "shadow" side of humanity.

Charlotte Brontë asks in the preface to the 1850 edition of **Wuthering Heights,** "Whether it is right or advisable to create things like Heathcliff," and goes on to say that she scarcely thinks it is. She also suggests that the author has little control over this creative process once it has been set in motion, claiming that it has a life of its own (xxxvi). What is it in Heathcliff that so concerns Charlotte Brontë that she feels a need to question the wisdom of his existence? Is it pure evil in some demonic form? Is it wild unbridled passion, part of the nature of the moors? Is he more simply a tyrant, a cruel sadistic despot? Is he a romantic lover, slave to his own passions and victim of circumstance? In Heathcliff Emily Brontë gives us all of these characters and phenonena. He is not one to the exclusion of the others: he is all. In Heathcliff we have a man to stir our feelings, a man to enrage our senses, engage our passions and walk over our graves. He disturbs us so because he reflects our unconscious minds. He plays out our fantasies and our nightmares. Heathcliff is a man formed by the unconscious projections of the characters in the novel—the projection of all they find unacceptable in themselves. He is a man formed, particularly, by the unconscious projections of the narrators and Catherine Earnshaw. Everything rejected by the conscious sensibilities of Lockwood, Nelly Dean and Catherine finds unlimited freedom of expression in Heathcliff, where it surfaces to taunt and confuse its creators. These unconscious projections of unacceptable traits take the form of "The Shadow" as described by Carl G. Jung.

C. G. Jung sees shadow as manifesting in his own dreams and in the dreams of his analysands. Aspects of the shadow are also projected on to others:

> The shadow personifies everything that the subject refuses to acknowledge about himself and yet is always thrusting itself upon him directly or indirectly—for instance, inferior traits of character and other incompatible tendencies. . . . The shadow is that hidden, repressed, for the most part inferior and guilt laden personality whose ultimate ramifications reach back into the realm of our animal ancestors and so comprise the whole historical aspect of the unconscious. If it has been believed hitherto that the human shadow was the source of all evil, it can now be ascertained on closer investigation that the unconscious man, that is, his shadow, does not consist only of morally reprehensible tendencies, but also displays a number of good qualities, such as normal instincts, appropriate reactions, realistic insights, creative impulses, etc.
>
> (399)

Shadow is encountered either in our dreams or projected onto the world. In *Wuthering Heights,* others project their shadow side on to Heathcliff. In this essay we look specifically at how that occurs with the characters of Lockwood, Nelly Dean and Cathy.

Wuthering Heights is written with a framed narrative. The first narrator is Mr. Lockwood and the second is Nelly Dean. These two narrators see Heathcliff differently. Their perception of him is

ABOUT THE AUTHOR

CHARLOTTE BRONTË'S PREFACE TO THE 1850 EDITION OF *WUTHERING HEIGHTS*
Wuthering Heights was hewn in a wild workshop, with simple tools, out of homely materials. The statuary found a granite block on a solitary moor; gazing thereon, he saw how from the crag might be elicited a head, savage, swart, sinister; a form moulded with at least one element of grandeur—power. He wrought with a rude chisel, and from no model but the vision of his meditations. With time and labour, the crag took human shape; and there it stands colossal, dark, and frowning, half statue, half rock: in the former sense, terrible and goblin-like; in the latter, almost beautiful, for its colouring is of mellow grey, and moorland moss clothes it; and heath, with its blooming bells and balmy fragrance, grows faithfully close to the giant's foot.

SOURCE: Bell, Currer (psuedonym of Charlotte Brontë). "Preface to Wuthering Heights." In *The Life and Works of the Sisters Brontë*: Wuthering Heights *by Emily Brontë and* Agnes Grey *by Anne Brontë.* Vol. 5, 1903. Reprint edition, pp. liii-lviii. AMS Press, Inc., 1973.

influenced by their own perception of themselves. In the case of Lockwood, he at first sees Heathcliff as similar to himself. This view is expressed by Lockwood in the following excerpt and is from the start a little hard for the reader to accept:

> "Thrushcross Grange is my own, sir," he interrupted, wincing, "I should not allow anyone to inconvenience me, if I could hinder it—walk in!" The "walk in" was uttered with closed teeth and expressed the sentiment, "Go to the Deuce!" Even the gate over which he leant manifested no sympathising movement to the words, and I think that circumstances determined me to accept the invitation; I felt interested in a man who seemed more exaggeratedly reserved than myself.
>
> (3)

Lockwood wants to see in Heathcliff a man who is reserved, and more so than himself. He wants to see this level of reservation as admirable in Heathcliff and therefore fine in him too:

I know, by instinct, his reserve springs from an aversion to showy displays of feeling—to manifestations of mutual kindness. He'll love and hate equally under cover, and esteem it a species of impertinence to be loved or hated again—No, I'm running on too fast—I bestow my own attributes over liberally on him.

(5)

By Lockwood's own admission, he consciously bestows his attributes on Heathcliff. Consciously he sees himself as reserved and finds this acceptable. Consciously he bestows that attribute on Heathcliff. The shadow, however, personifies everything the subject refuses to acknowledge about himself. What is it that Lockwood refuses to acknowledge about himself that he unconsciously projects onto Heathcliff? Emily Brontë soon gives us an example of Lockwood's unconscious self. Lockwood tells of an incident in which he met a young woman to whom he was attracted. He makes it plain to her that he is attracted to her but when she responds he shuns her. She is so overwhelmed with confusion at her supposed mistake that she leaves. He confesses that because of this he has gained the reputation of deliberate heartlessness, a reputation he cannot accept (6). He cannot see himself as heartless, yet clearly he is.

Emily Brontë gives us another look at this true aspect of Lockwood's character in the episode when he sees Cathy's ghost:

The intense horror of nightmare came over me; I tried to draw back my arm, but, the hand clung to it, and a most melancholy voice sobbed,

"Let me in-let me in!"

"Who are you?" I asked, struggling, meanwhile, to disengage myself.

"Catherine Linton," it replied, shiveringly. . . . "I'm come home, I'd lost my way on the moor!"

As it spoke, I discerned, obscurely, a child's face looking through the window—Terror made me cruel; and finding it useless to attempt shaking the creature off, I pulled its wrist on to the broken pane, and rubbed it to and fro until the blood ran down and soaked the bed clothes.

(25)

Lockwood admits that in his dream he is cruel and deliberately heartless but these are aspects of his personality that he does not consciously accept. Lockwood cannot integrate cruelty as part of who he is, so he relegates cruelty to his shadow side. He projects this shadow onto Heathcliff. He is attracted to Heathcliff not for the reasons of his conscious mind but because Heathcliff personifies his forbidden self. Heathcliff is cruel and deliberately heartless.

Lockwood also has a strange Biblical dream which serves to illuminate his shadow. He dreams he is travelling with Joseph to hear the famous James Branderham preach from the text "Seventy Times Seven" (22). He dreams that Joseph, the preacher or himself has committed the "First of the Seventy First," and is to be publicly exposed and excommunicated. This refers to the story in Matthew known as "The Parable of the Unforgiving Servant." The sin referred to is that of unforgiveness: "Then Peter came to Jesus and asked, 'Lord, if my brother keeps on sinning against me, how many times do I have to forgive him? Seven times?' 'No, not seven times,' answered Jesus, 'but seventy times seven'" (Matt. 18: 21-22). In the dream Lockwood fights with the whole assembly. He has no weapon to use in self defense. Joseph and the others all have staves. In the language of symbols, the stave used as a weapon has punitive meaning (Tresidder 191). In Jungian psychology it is generally believed that when a person is in conflict with someone else in a dream that other person is a shadow figure representing qualities the dreamer refuses to admit as part of his personality (Robertson 130). Lockwood, not suprisingly, offers us no interpretation of this dream, other than to blame it on bad tea and bad temper. We are given no interpretation from any other source in the text and yet it would seem to have some meaning. Using the Jungian model, one may reasonably propose that Lockwood is repressing his desire to punish others and his inability to forgive them. In the dream he is going to be exposed and punished by the whole assembly and by Joseph, whom he refers to as his most ferocious assailant, and by Branderham. These figures all represent the repressed side of Lockwood in his dream. In his waking life Heathcliff represents this shadow side of Lockwood. Lockwood's repressed punitive side finds free expression in Heathcliff: Heathcliff is punitive, ferocious and unforgiving.

The second narrator, Nelly Dean, has a different part to play in forming Heathcliff. We have no dreams to give us a glimpse of Nelly's unconscious mind. Nelly does, however, fantasize about Heathcliff, particularly about the circumstances of his birth:

"You're fit for a prince in disguise. Who knows, but your father was Emperor of China, and your mother an Indian queen, each of them able to buy up, with one week's income, Wuthering Heights and Thrushcross Grange together? And you were kidnapped by wicked sailors, and brought to England. Were I in your place, I would

frame high notions of my birth; and the thoughts
of what I was should give me courage and dignity
to support the oppressions of a little farmer."

(57)

Heathcliff as far as we can learn from the text
does not fantasize about his parentage. Nelly
fantasizes about Heathcliff's parentage. Nelly, it
appears, is not content with her own humble station in life, a station determined by parentage.
Nelly is a servant, but she does not like to be
treated as one. When she is treated as a servant
she objects. When Catherine, for example, treats
her as a servant she refers to Catherine as haughty
and says, "she ceased to hold any communica-
tions with me except as a mere servant" (87). Nelly
finds this form of communication unacceptable.
Nelly has no mysterious background to fantasize
about for herself. Indeed, such fantasies on her
own behalf would be incompatible with Nelly's
view of herself as, "a steady, reasonable kind of
body" (62). Romantic thoughts and fancies are
not part of Nelly's conscious thinking. It would
not be acceptable for a country girl to be so fanciful. She must find some other outlet for these
desirable but forbidden fantasies. Nelly relegates
these desires and fantasies to her unconscious
mind where they manifest in the romantic persona of Heathcliff.

Cathy, though not a narrator, is clearly crucial
to the development of Heathcliff. Emily Brontë
uses Cathy as the one character who understands
Heathcliff, the only one who knows his true
character. She knows him so well because he is,
indeed, part of her. He is her shadow side.

Heathcliff comes into Cathy's life when they
are children. They quickly become very close,
recognizing in each other a common wildness,
lack of convention and love of the moors:

> But it was one of their chief amusements to run
> away to the moors in the morning and remain
> there all day, and the after punishment grew a
> mere thing to laugh at. The curate might set as
> many chapters as he pleased for Catherine to get
> by heart, and Joseph might thrash Heathcliff till
> his arm ached; they forgot every thing the minute
> they were together again, at least the minute they
> had contrived some naughty plan of revenge; and
> many a time I've cried to myself to watch them
> growing more reckless daily, and I not daring to
> speak a syllable for fear of losing the small power I
> still retained over the unfriendly creatures.

(46)

Nelly describes two equally truculent children.
Wild and defiant of any convention or guidance,
they are described by her as "unfriendly" and as
"creatures." As children they are a pair. Then,

beginning with her visit to the Lintons, Cathy
starts to repress this side of her nature. She
consigns it to her unconscious shadow and lives
it, as projection, through Heathcliff. From this
point on the boundary between Cathy and Heathcliff blurs. When she returns from Thrushcross
Grange she is dressed like a lady. She adopts the
airs and graces of a lady and consciously cultivates
her relationship with Edgar Linton. She decides
over a very short period of time that she will
marry him. Cathy feels that she is repressing part
of herself but is powerless to stop. She cannot accept her own wild nature as an integral part of her
personality and conform to the dictates of her
society to be a lady. She chooses the latter. She
rejects the wild part of herself in the form of
Heathcliff. She tells Nelly that it would degrade
her to marry Heathcliff now that he is so low.
Cathy's inability to be true to her feelings and
marry Heathcliff also serves as metaphor for her
rejection of "the hatless little savage" (52) she can
no longer allow herself to be. Cathy's savage
nature is relegated to her unconscious shadow side
where it immediately manifests in Heathcliff.
Cathy, to comfirm this, dramatically declares that
she is Heathcliff:

> My love for Linton is like the foliage in the woods.
> Time will change it, I'm well aware, as winter
> changes the trees—my love for Heathcliff re-
> sembles the eternal rocks beneath—a source of
> little visible delight, but necessary. Nelly, I am
> Heathcliff—he's always, always in my mind—not
> as a pleasure, any more than I am always a pleasure
> to myself—but as my own being—so, don't talk of
> our separation again—it is impracticable.

(82)

From this moment on, Heathcliff fully embodies Cathy's rejected self.

When Cathy returns from Thrushcross
Grange, Heathcliff is at first nowhere to be found.
He continues to hide from Cathy and to sulk.
Then, still at this point seeing himself as Cathy's
partner, he starts to question his role. He hangs
around Nelly for awhile and finally summons up
the courage to say, "Nelly, make me decent, I'm
going to be good" (55). Nelly takes this on as her
project. She washes Heathcliff and dresses him up.
She encourages him to frame high notions of his
birth, suggesting that perhaps he may be a prince
from some foreign land. She tells him that all he
needs to be handsome as he wishes is to have a
good heart. Heathcliff as a young boy wants to be
fair and handsome and have a chance at being
rich like Edgar Linton. In fact, he wants the same
things Cathy wants, and at this point is willing to
try to get them by following Cathy's lead and

conforming. He is ready to be amiable. An amiable Heathcliff, however, is not acceptable to anyone. The Lintons are perfectly content to be amiable themselves. They don't need and won't accept that from Heathcliff. Hindley is determined to keep Heathcliff down and together they thwart Heathcliff's attempt to "be good." From Heathcliff's first appearance at Wuthering Heights as "a dirty, ragged, black-haired child" (36), he has a disruptive effect on all those around him. Cathy and Hindley are upset because the gifts their father has for them are broken. The household is thrown into confusion by his arrival. They refer to him as "it" and they reject him:

> They entirely refused to have it in bed with them, or even in their room, and I had no more sense, so I put it on the landing of the stairs, hoping it might be gone by the morrow. By chance, or else attracted by hearing his voice, it crept to Mr Earnshaw's door and there he found it on quitting his chamber. Inquiries were made as to how it got there; I was obliged to confess, and in recompense for my cowardice and inhumanity was sent out of the house.
>
> (37)

Heathcliff has spent only one night at Wuthering Heights at this point and already there is confusion and conflict. Not only is there external conflict between the children and Heathcliff, and the children and their father, and Mr. Earnshaw and Nelly, but there is also internal conflict in Nelly. Nelly refers to her actions as cowardly and inhuman. A peaceful domestic scene becomes one of confusion, chaos and conflict. Throughout the novel, Heathcliff causes chaos, confusion and conflict among others. He also causes the same emotions within others. It is fair to say that where Heathcliff is, there is no peace. What is it in Heathcliff that so disrupts others?

It is an aphorism that whatever most attracts or repels us in another is generated by something in ourselves: something of ourselves we see reflected back to us by the recipient of our attention. It is our unconscious shadow side that so disturbs and attracts us. It is this shadow that we find reflected back to us that so upsets our psyche. The characters in **Wuthering Heights**, especially, but not exclusively, Lockwood, Nelly Dean and Catherine, face their shadow in Heathcliff. In Heathcliff they are brought face to face with everything they refuse to acknowledge in themselves. When they are faced with this embodiment of their shadow, it is no wonder that chaos, confusion and conflict ensue. And when she is faced with this embodiment, it is no wonder that

Charlotte Brontë questions the wisdom of the creation of Heathcliff. Heathcliff is, after all, unacceptable.

Works Cited

Brontë. Emily. *Wuthering Heights*. 1847. New York: Penguin Classics, 1995.

Good News Bible: Today's English Version. New York: American Bible Society, 1976.

Jung, C. G. *Memories, Dreams, Reflections*. Ed. Aniela Jaffe; trans. Richard and Clara Winston. New York: Vintage Books, 1989.

Robertson, Robin. *Beginners Guide to Jungian Psychology*. York Bach, ME: Nicholas Hays, Inc., 1992.

Tresidder, Jack. *Dictionary of Symbols*. San Fransisco: Chronicle Books, 1998.

FURTHER READING

Bibliographies

Barclay, Janet M. *Emily Brontë Criticism 1900-1982: An Annotated Checklist*. Westport, Conn.: Meckler, 1984, 162 p.

Provides an annotated list of writings on Emily Brontë.

Crump, Rebecca W. *Charlotte and Emily Brontë: A Reference Guide*. 3 vols. Boston: G. K. Hall, 1982.

Provides critical sources from 1846-1983.

Biography

Grin, Winifred. *Emily Brontë*. Oxford: Oxford University Press, 1971, 290 p.

Offers a scholarly biography that attempts to clarify the myths about Brontë's personality.

Criticism

Apter, T. E. "Romanticism and Romantic Love in *Wuthering Heights*." In *The Art of Emily Brontë*, edited by Anne Smith, pp. 205-22. London: Vision Press, 1976.

Discusses Brontë's treatment of Romantic love in Wuthering Heights, *noting that Catherine and Heathcliff's relationship is presented as "suffering love," whereas Cathy and Hareton's bond serves as "an alternative to that destructive, Romantic love."*

Brennan, Matthew C. "Emily Brontë's *Wuthering Heights*." In *The Gothic Psyche: Disintegration and Growth in Nineteenth-Century English Literature*, pp. 77-96. Columbia, S.C.: Camden House, 1997.

Examines the impact of Gothic convention on Wuthering Heights.

Cottom, Daniel. "I Think; Therefore, I Am Heathcliff." *ELH* 70, no. 4 (winter 2003): 1067-88.

Examines Gothic novels, including Wuthering Heights, *in light of the writings of philosopher René Descartes.*

Davies, Cecil W. "A Reading of *Wuthering Heights*." *Essays in Criticism* 19, no. 3 (July 1969): 254-72.

Refers to Brontë's poetry and the Gondal stories in an examination of the mysticism of Wuthering Heights.

Dobell, Sydney. "Sydney Dobell's Article on Currer Bell, Contributed to the *Palladium* in 1850." *Brontë Society Transactions* 5, no. 28 (1918): 210-36.

> Assumes that Wuthering Heights *was written by Currer Bell (pseudonym of Charlotte Brontë) and approaches it as that author's first work, deeming it a novel of extraordinary power but uneven form.*

"*Wuthering Heights* and *Agnes Grey*." *The Eclectic Review* 1 (February 1851): 222-27.

> Praises Brontë's depiction of scenery in *Wuthering Heights, but asserts that the novel's characters are exaggerated and unsympathetic, and the situations unbelievable.*

Haggerty, George E. "The Gothic Form of *Wuthering Heights*." *Victorian Newsletter* 74 (fall 1988): 1-6.

> Argues that in Wuthering Heights *Brontë "looks into the heart of Gothic fiction, . . . uncovers the most deeply rooted formal problems which Gothic novelists themselves were never able to resolve, and forges a solution to those problems out of the literary smithy of her own soul."*

Knoepflmacher, U. C. *Wuthering Heights: A Study.* Athens: Ohio University Press, 1994, 138 p.

> An in-depth examination of Wuthering Heights *that analyzes the novel's context, structure, meaning, and critical reception.*

Lewes, George Henry. A review of *Wuthering Heights,* by Emily Brontë. *The Leader* 1, no. 30 (28 December 1850): 953.

> Provides a qualified endorsement of Wuthering Heights, *pronouncing it a powerful but coarse work.*

Pykett, Lyn. "Gender and Genre in *Wuthering Heights*: Gothic Plot and Domestic Fiction." In *Wuthering Heights: Emily Brontë,* edited by Patsy Stoneman, pp. 86-99. New York: St. Martin's Press, 1989.

> Examines Wuthering Heights *in the context of late eighteenth- and early nineteenth-century literature, studying in particular "the relationship of the woman writer to the history and tradition of fiction."*

Sedgwick, Eve Kosofsky. "Immediacy, Doubleness, and the Unspeakable: *Wuthering Heights* and *Villette*." In *The Coherence of Gothic Conventions.* 1976. Reprint edition, pp. 97-139. New York: Methuen, 1986.

> Discusses both the direct and indirect modes of narration and communication in Wuthering Heights.

Stoneman, Patsy, ed. *Emily Brontë*: Wuthering Heights. New York: Columbia University Press, 1998, 208 p.

> Selected commentary on Wuthering Heights, *including essays by Q. D. Leavis, Terry Eagleton, and Sandra Gilbert.*

Swinburne, Algernon Charles. "Emily Brontë." *The Athenaeum,* no. 2903 (16 June 1883): 762-63.

> Addresses several controversial aspects of Wuthering Heights, *including the novel's unusual structure and depiction of cruelty and brutality.*

Symons, Arthur. "Emily Brontë." *The Nation* 23, no. 21 (24 August 1918): 546-47.

> Lauds the passion and intensity of Wuthering Heights, *deeming it an unforgettable work.*

Thomas, Ronald R. "Dreams and Disorders in *Wuthering Heights*." In *Dreams of Authority: Freud and the Fictions of the Unconscious,* pp. 112-35. Ithaca, N.Y.: Cornell University Press, 1990.

> Explores the role of dreams in Wuthering Heights *using the theories of Sigmund Freud.*

Twitchell, James. "Heathcliff as Vampire." *Southern Humanities Review* 11 (1977): 355-62.

> Surveys critical reactions to Heathcliff in Wuthering Heights, *suggesting that the character is metaphorically akin to a vampire.*

Vitte, Paulette. "Emily Brontë, Rimbaud, Poe and the Gothic." *Brontë Society Transactions* 24, no. 2 (October 1999): 182-85.

> Traces the treatment and manipulation of the Gothic tradition in poetry by Brontë, Edgar Allan Poe, and Arthur Rimbaud.

OTHER SOURCES FROM GALE:

Additional coverage of Brontë's life and career is contained in the following sources published by Thomson Gale: *Authors and Artists for Young Adults,* Vol. 17; *Beacham's Encyclopedia of Popular Fiction: Biography & Resources,* Vol. 1; *Beacham's Guide to Literature for Young Adults,* Vol. 3; *British Writers,* Vol. 5; *British Writers: The Classics,* Vol. 1; *British Writers Retrospective Supplement,* Vol. 1; *Concise Dictionary of British Literary Biography, 1832-1890; Dictionary of Literary Biography,* Vols. 21, 32, 199; *DISCovering Authors; DISCovering Authors: British; DISCovering Authors: Canadian; DISCovering Authors Modules: Most-studied Authors, Novelists,* and *Poets; DISCovering Authors 3.0; Exploring Novels; Feminism in Literature: A Gale Critical Companion; Literature and Its Times,* Vol. 1; *Literature Resource Center; Nineteenth-Century Literature Criticism,* Vols. 16, 35; *Poetry Criticism,* Vol. 8; *Twayne's English Authors; World Literature and Its Times,* Vol. 3; and *World Literature Criticism.*

CHARLES BROCKDEN BROWN

(1771 - 1810)

American novelist, essayist, and short story writer.

B rown is remembered as the author of the first Gothic novel produced by an American. *Wieland; or, The Transformation* (1798), which draws on the traditions of both Gothic and sentimental novels, explores such issues as suicide, murder, seduction, and insanity. He also wrote three other novels dealing with horror and the supernatural, all with a peculiarly American flavor, replacing the expected tropes of European Gothic with American images, including the frontier, forests, caves, and cliffs. Many critics fault Brown's work for what are perceived as serious stylistic and structural deficiencies, but they also express admiration for his intense artistic vision and his struggle to reconcile his Romantic imagination with the Enlightenment ideals of reason and realism. Brown is also recognized as one of the first Americans to gain a significant audience abroad and to attempt to support himself through his literary endeavors; for this reason he has been called the first professional writer in the United States. His work also reflects an interest—radical for his time—in the rights and roles of women. Hailed as a central figure in the literature of horror and the supernatural, Brown has been seen as an important influence on the masters of Ameri

can Gothic writing, including Edgar Allan Poe, Nathaniel Hawthorne, William Faulkner, and Stephen King.

BIOGRAPHICAL INFORMATION

Brown was born to a Quaker family in Philadelphia in 1771. The Quakers' disdain for formal higher education resulted in the sixteen-year-old Brown's being apprenticed to a lawyer. While employed at the law office, Brown pursued his literary interests and joined the Belles Lettres Club, where he participated in philosophical and political discussions. In 1789 he published a series of essays as "The Rhapsodist," in which he analyzes the effectiveness of the government created after the American Revolution. His interest in radical social and political ideas was furthered by his reading of Mary Wollstonecraft's *A Vindication of the Rights of Women* (1792) and William Godwin's *An Enquiry concerning Political Justice* (1793). Many critics have maintained that these two works heavily influenced Brown's later thinking and writing. After abandoning his legal career in 1792, Brown completed his first novel, the now-lost *Sky-Walk*, in 1797. During the next several years, Brown embarked upon a period of extraordinary literary activity, publishing *Alcuin* (1798), a fictional dialogue on women's rights, and his first significant novel, *Wieland*, in 1798. *Ormond*, the first part of *Arthur Mervyn,* and *Edgar Huntly* all appeared during 1799. The proceeds from these works, however, were not sufficient for Brown to support himself, and as he grew increasingly interested in marrying and having a family, Brown joined his family's mercantile business in 1800. During his courtship of Elizabeth Linn in the early 1800s, Brown wrote the second part of *Arthur Mervyn* and his last two novels, *Clara Howard* and *Jane Talbot,* which were published in 1801. At this point, Brown turned to journalistic endeavors, producing political pamphlets and essays, and editing a journal. He married in 1804 and supported his wife and children on his editorial work after the family business dissolved in 1806. Brown died in 1810, of tuberculosis.

MAJOR WORKS

Brown wrote essays, short stories, and political pamphlets, and translated a work of nonfiction about the United States from the French, but modern critics have given little attention to these works, except as a means of elucidating aspects of Brown's major novels. The dialogue *Alcuin,* although considered a minor work, is studied by modern critics in an effort to dissect Brown's feminism. In this fictional exchange between a man and a woman, arguments both for and against political and educational equality of the sexes are presented. Brown continued to explore such issues in his novels, which all contain strong female characters. Like Brown's minor works, the sentimental novels *Clara Howard* and *Jane Talbot* generate relatively little critical interest and are regarded as exhibiting Brown's shift from radical to more conservative views.

The plots of Brown's four major novels, which combine elements of the Gothic and the sentimental novel, are often considered convoluted and episodic, though highly imaginative. What unites the novels is Brown's focus on psychological aberrations and the reactions and development of his characters. The epistolary novel *Wieland,* Brown's best-known work, is about an archetypal Gothic heroine, Clara Wieland, whose peaceful life with her brother, Theodore, and his family is destroyed by the appearance of a mysterious stranger, Carwin. Theodore begins to hear a disembodied voice, which he takes to be God's, and thereafter he hurls himself into an obsessive religious melancholy. He hears the voice command him to kill his wife and children, which he

does. He is about to murder his sister and the man she loves when Carwin confesses he has been responsible for the voices. But, shockingly, he was not responsible for the voice that commanded Theodore to murder his family. *Wieland* has been seen variously as a cautionary tale on the dangers of religious fervor, an indictment of patriarchal institutions, a critique of Puritanism, and a self-referential allegory of the writing process itself.

Edgar Huntly also explores the problems of humans' inability to trust their sense perceptions. In the novel, the narrator follows the sleepwalking Huntly, whom he suspects is his best friend's murderer, through a labyrinthine frontier. His journey symbolizes the moral dilemma at the core of the novel: whether criminology can begin to fathom a mind in nightmarish conflict. *Ormond* focuses on Brown's ideas regarding the necessity of educational equality for women. The villainous Ormond terrorizes the beautiful Constantina Dudley after having had her father killed, holding her captive and threatening to rape her. But she defeats him (and the oppression he symbolizes) by stabbing him. In *Arthur Mervyn,* as a plague of yellow fever ravages Philadelphia, the narrator rescues the young waif Mervyn, whose true nature remains ambiguous to the very end. The story has been interpreted as Brown's argument for civic responsibility toward the impoverished, the ill, and the downtrodden. Brown examines, by way of the apparently innocent narrator's adventures, the theme of appearance versus reality. The narrator becomes implicated in several crimes, but his declarations of benevolent intentions contradict his actions.

CRITICAL RECEPTION

Brown is known as being the first professional fiction writer in the United States, but he struggled to support himself through his literary efforts, turning toward journalism and editorial work in his later years to make a living. However, Brown's writing was well received by some contemporary critics, who praised his clear and forceful style and knowledge of the human heart while maintaining that his stories were improbable and that his use of detail and his narrative technique interfered with plot movement. Many important nineteenth-century writers admired Brown's works, including Poe, Hawthorne, John Keats, Sir Walter Scott, and Mary Shelley, who counted Brown's four Gothic novels among her six favorite books.

In the late nineteenth and early twentieth centuries, critics focused on the importance of Brown's contribution to American letters. For his use of realistic details of American life, particularly his portrayal of Native Americans and the frontier, and for his role in initiating the American literary preoccupation with psychological horror, Brown was acclaimed as a pioneer in fiction and the father of American Gothic literature. Critics who viewed his contribution as mainly historical, however, censured his overblown style, illogical plots, and unrealistic characters. From the mid-twentieth century on, critics have generally acknowledged the weaknesses in Brown's style but praised his attempts at reconciling eighteenth-century Enlightenment ideals with nineteenth-century Romantic principles; his exploration of the conflict between rationalism and the irrational power of the imagination; and his creation of the particularly American brand of Gothic fiction. Some critics have argued that Brown's novels cannot be truly classified as Gothic but rather as romances of mystery and terror that are only "superficially" Gothic, using Gothic trappings to delve into the psychology of the characters. Other commentators consider Brown's use of the Gothic as similar to that of William Godwin in its focus on the psychological and the revolutionary, while yet others have regarded Brown's gothicism as based more on German sources and works by English authors. As the interest in the genre of Gothic literature grows, so does interest in and admiration of Brown's works, which are widely viewed as innovations in American gothicism and the literature of psychological horror.

PRINCIPAL WORKS

Alcuin: A Dialogue (fictional dialogue) 1798

Wieland; or, The Transformation (novel) 1798

Arthur Mervyn; or, Memoirs of the Year 1793. 2 vols. (novel) 1799-1800

Edgar Huntly; or, Memoirs of a Sleep-Walker. 3 vols. (novel) 1799

Ormond; or, The Secret Witness (novel) 1799

Clara Howard (novel) 1801; also published as *Philip Stanley; or, The Enthusiasm of Love,* 1807

Jane Talbot, a Novel (novel) 1801

*Carwin, the Biloquist, and Other American Tales and Pieces. 3 vols. (unfinished novel and short stories) 1822

The Novels of Charles Brockden Brown. 7 vols. (novels) 1827

The Rhapsodist, and Other Uncollected Writings (essays and novel fragment) 1943

The Novels and Related Works of Charles Brockden Brown. 6 vols. (novels and unfinished novels) 1977-87

*Memoirs of Stephen Calvert (unfinished novel) 1978

* *Carwin, the Biloquist* and *Memoirs of Stephen Calvert* were published earlier in William Dunlap's *The Life of Charles Brockden Brown: Together with Selections from the Rarest of His Printed Works, from His Original Letters, and from His Manuscripts before Unpublished,* 1815.

PRIMARY SOURCES

CHARLES BROCKDEN BROWN (ESSAY DATE 1798)

SOURCE: Brown, Charles Brockden. "Advertisement." In *Wieland: or, The Transformation: An American Tale,* n.p. New York: T & J Swords, 1798.

In the following introduction to Wieland, *Brown urges the reader to consider the artistic merits of his work.*

The following Work is delivered to the world as the first of a series of performances, which the favorable reception of this will induce the Writer to publish. His purpose is neither selfish nor temporary, but aims at the illustration of some important branches of the moral constitution of man. Whether this tale will be classed with the ordinary or frivolous sources of amusement, or be ranked with the few productions whose usefulness secures to them a lasting reputation, the reader must be permitted to decide.

The incidents related are extraordinary and rare. Some of them, perhaps, approach as nearly to the nature of miracles as can be done by that which is not truly miraculous. It is hoped that intelligent readers will not disapprove of the manner in which appearances are solved, but that the solution will be found to correspond with the known principles of human nature. The power which the principal person is said to possess can scarcely be denied to be real. It must be acknowledged to be extremely rare; but no fact, equally uncommon, is supported by the same strength of historical evidence.

Some readers may think the conduct of the younger Wieland impossible. In support of its possibility the Writer must appeal to Physicians and to men conversant with the latent springs and occasional perversions of the human mind. It will not be objected that the instances of similar delusion are rare, because it is the business of moral painters to exhibit their subject in its most instructive and memorable forms. If history furnishes one parallel fact, it is a sufficient vindication of the Writer; but most readers will probably recollect an authentic case, remarkably similar to that of Wieland.

It will be necessary to add, that this narrative is addressed, in an epistolary form, by the Lady whose story it contains, to a small number of friends, whose curiosity, with regard to it, had been greatly awakened. It may likewise be mentioned, that these events took place between the conclusion of the French and the beginning of the revolutionary war. The memoirs of Carwin, alluded to at the conclusion of the work, will be published or suppressed according to the reception which is given to the present attempt.

CHARLES BROCKDEN BROWN (NOVEL DATE 1798)

SOURCE: Brown, Charles Brockden. "Chapter 1." In *Wieland: or, The Transformation: An American Tale*, pp. 1-11. New York: T & J Swords, 1798.

In the following excerpt from the first chapter of Wieland, *the protagonist addresses the reader.*

I feel little reluctance in complying with your request. You know not fully the cause of my sorrows. You are a stranger to the depth of my distresses. Hence your efforts at consolation must necessarily fail. Yet the tale that I am going to tell is not intended as a claim upon your sympathy. In the midst of my despair, I do not disdain to contribute what little I can to the benefit of mankind. I acknowledge your right to be informed of the events that have lately happened in my family. Make what use of the tale you shall think proper. If it be communicated to the world, it will inculcate the duty of avoiding deceit. It will exemplify the force of early impressions, and show, the immeasurable evils that flow from an erroneous or imperfect discipline.

My state is not destitute of tranquillity. The sentiment that dictates my feelings is not hope. Futurity has no power over my thoughts. To all that is to come I am perfectly indifferent. With regard to myself, I have nothing more to fear. Fate has done its worst. Henceforth, I am callous to misfortune.

I address no supplication to the Deity. The power that governs the course of human affairs has chosen his path. The decree that ascertained the condition of my life, admits of no recal. No doubt it squares with the maxims of eternal equity. That is neither to be questioned nor denied by me. It suffices that the past is exempt from mutation. The storm that tore up our happiness, and changed into dreariness and desert the blooming scene of our existence, is lulled into grim repose; but not until the victim was transfixed and mangled; till every obstacle was dissipated by its rage; till every remnant of good was wrested from our grasp and exterminated.

How will your wonder, and that of your companions, be excited by my story! Every sentiment will yield to your amazement. If my testimony were without corroborations, you would reject it as incredible. The experience of no human being can furnish a parallel: That I, beyond the rest of mankind, should be reserved for a destiny without alleviation, and without example! Listen to my narrative, and then say what it is that has made me deserve to be placed on this dreadful eminence, if, indeed, every faculty be not suspended in wonder that I am still alive, and am able to relate it.

GENERAL COMMENTARY

LESLIE FIEDLER (ESSAY DATE 1960)

SOURCE: Fiedler, Leslie. "Charles Brockden Brown and the Invention of the American Gothic." In *Love and Death in the American Novel*, pp. 126-61. New York: Criterion Books, 1960.

In the following excerpt from his influential analysis of American novelists, Fiedler emphasizes Brown's importance as an innovator in the American Gothic tradition.

A dream of innocence had sent Europeans across the ocean to build a new society immune to the compounded evil of the past from which no one in Europe could ever feel himself free. But the slaughter of the Indians, who would not yield their lands to the carriers of utopia, and the abominations of the slave trade, in which the black man, rum, and money were inextricably entwined in a knot of guilt, provided new evidence that evil did not remain with the world that had been left behind—but stayed alive in the human heart, which had come the long way to America only to confront the horrifying image of itself. Finally, there was the myth of Faust and of the diabolic bargain, which, though not yet isolated from gothic themes of lesser importance (that isolation was to be the work of American writers!), came quite soon to seem identical with the American myth itself.

How could one tell where the American dream ended and the Faustian nightmare began; they held in common the hope of breaking through all limits and restraints, of reaching a place of total freedom where one could with impunity deny the Fall, live as if innocence rather than guilt were the birthright of all men. In Huck's blithe assertion, "All right, I'll *go* to Hell," is betrayed a significant undermeaning of the Faustian *amor fati,* at least in its "boyish" American form: the secret belief that damnation is not all it is cracked up to be. In a strange way, the naturalized Faust legend becomes in the United States a way of denying hell in the act of seeming to accept it, of suggesting that it is merely a scary word, a bugaboo, a forbidding description of freedom itself! At any rate, Americans from the beginning responded passionately to the myth itself; even in the 1680's, before the invention of the main tradition of the novel, one Boston bookseller sold in the Colonies sixty-six copies of *The History of the Damnable Life and Deserved Death of Dr. John Faustus.* It was, needless to say, a record unapproached in those times by any other "light literature."

When the gothic novel appeared, then, it was greeted with great enthusiasm by Americans, who passed quite quickly from importing and reading its prototypes to attempting to emulate them. In this case, only ten years elapsed between the publication of the novels of Mrs. Radcliffe and Lewis and the first American gothic romances. Yet the gothic mode—though appealing enough for various reasons—proved difficult to adapt to the demands of the American audience and the deeper meanings of American experience. By the time our own first attempts were being made, there was everywhere in the United States (aware of itself as a product of the Enlightenment) an uneasiness with darkness of all kinds, a feeling that the obsession with evil was an outgrown vice of Calvinism. Certainly the generation of Jefferson was pledged to be done with ghosts and shadows, committed to live a life of yea-saying in a sunlit, neo-classical world. From the bourgeois ladies to the Deist intellectuals, the country was united in a disavowal of the "morbid" and the "nasty." No wonder the American pioneer in gothic fiction, despite the acclaim he won abroad, was driven first to abandon the gothic for the sentimental, then to give up novel writing completely.

If it had been only a matter of finding a reading public for the gothic, the situation would not have been really critical—only unprofitable; but there were other problems. The gothic, after all, had been invented to deal with the past and with history from a typically Protestant and enlightened point of view; but what could one do with the form in a country which, however Protestant and enlightened, had (certainly at the turn of the eighteenth century!) neither a proper past nor a history? It was easy enough for the American writer to borrow certain elements, both of cast and setting, from the tale of terror; the Maiden in flight, for instance, was readily adaptable, and the hero-villain viable at least as a visual image—his burning eyes and furrowed brow transplanted themselves without difficulty. But what was to be done about the social status of such hero-villains? With what native classes or groups could they be identified? Traditionally aristocrats, monks, servants of the Inquisition, members of secret societies like the Illuminati, how could they be convincingly introduced on the American scene?

Similarly, it was not hard to provide the American equivalents of the moors, hills, and forests through which the bedeviled maidens of the gothic romances were accustomed to flee. But what of the haunted castle, the ruined abbey, the dungeons of the Inquisition? In America, such crumbling piles, architecturally and symbolically so satisfying to the eighteenth-century reader and writer, are more than a little improbable. Yet on them, not only the atmosphere, but an important part of the meaning of the tale of terror depended; what political or social implications the form possessed were inextricably bound up with such images. An early American gothicist like the I. Mitchell who published in 1811 *The Asylum; or, Alonzo and Melissa* was able to imagine a gothic country house on Long Island; but such a structure in such a place remains not merely unconvincing but meaningless. The haunted castle of the European gothic is an apt symbol for a particular body of attitudes toward the past which was a chief concern of the genre. The counterpart of such a castle fifty miles from New York City has lost all point.

The problem of the gothic romance in this regard is analogous to that of the sentimental novel. Both had arisen out of a need of the bourgeoisie, fighting for cultural autonomy in a class society, to find archetypal characters and situations to embody their conflict with the older ruling classes. Just as the sentimental archetype had projected the struggle of the middle classes with established secular power, portrayed as a menace to their purity, so the gothic projected the struggle of those classes with ecclesiastical authority, portrayed as a threat to their freedom. In America, which possesses neither inherited aristocratic privilege nor an established Church, the anti-aristocratic impulse of the seduction theme is, as we have said, translated into feminism and anti-intellectualism; while the impatience with the past implicit in the gothic fable undergoes an even more complex metamorphosis. Charles Brockden Brown, single-handed and almost unsustained, solved the key problems of adaptation, and though by no means a popular success, determined, through his influence on Poe and Hawthorne, the future of the gothic novel in America.

There is a sense in which the American novel had begun before the appearance on the literary scene of Charles Brockden Brown, and another in which it had yet to begin after his death; yet he represents the beginning of a serious tradition of fiction in the United States, at once establishing the gothic form and (it is an illuminating conjunction) founding the highbrow novel. The best-seller had been invented before any of his books appeared, and the more serious, though ill-fated, attempt of William Hill Brown had been made when Brockden Brown was only eighteen; but before him certainly, no writer of prose fiction had tried to live by his work. Brown himself was conscious of the audacity of his project, about which his friend and first biographer Dunlap commented later: "To become exclusively an author was at that time a novelty in the United States, and . . . no one had relied solely upon the support of his talents, and deliberately chosen this station in society."

If Brown deserved no other credit, he should be remembered at least as the inventor of the American writer, for he not only lived that role but turned it into a myth, later developed by almost everyone who wrote about his career. That he tried the impossible and that he failed; that he had disavowed his own art before his untimely death of tuberculosis at the age of thirty-nine; that he hardened from a wild disciple of the Enlightenment, a flagrant Godwinian ("Godwin came and all was light!") into a pious conservative; that he drew his inspiration from loneliness and male companionship, and that he ceased to be a creative writer when he married; that over his whole frantic, doomed career, the blight of melancholy presides. In a sense, Brown invented Edgar Allan Poe—all, that is to say, that the American writer came to seem to the mind of Europe and the sensibility of Romanticism—before Poe had ever

written a line. Actually the latter poet was one year old when Brown died.

From the beginning, at any rate, it has been hard to describe Charles Brockden Brown without seeming to compose a poem on a symbolic subject. The portrait painter Sully, who saw him just before his death, has left the following account:

> It was in the month of November,—our Indian summer,—when the air is full of smoke. Passing a window one day I was caught by the sight of a man, with remarkable physiognomy, writing at a table in a dark room. The sun shone directly upon his head. I shall never forget it. The dead leaves were falling then. It was Charles Brockden Brown.

If this seems less the product of observation than of Romantic fancy, it is no more fanciful than Brown's own description of himself to his dearest friend, Elihu Hubbard Smith, as "The child of passion and inconstancy, the slave of desires that cannot be justified . . ."; and it is considerably more restrained and faithful to fact than the account of his death, wracked by poverty and disease, imagined half a century later by his fellow Philadelphian and gothic heir, George Lippard. "The Heart Broken" is the title of Lippard's piece, by which he hoped, apparently, to do for Brown what Baudelaire was to do for Poe; but Lippard was unable to preserve the image of Brown as the victim of American philistinism after he had ceased to seem a figure of first literary importance.

To this very day, however, it is hard to rescue the man from the myth, to discover, for instance, even so simple a matter of record (one would assume) as what Brown looked like. According to one standard biography his hair was straight and "black as death," his complexion pale, sallow, and strange, accented by the "melancholy, broken-hearted look of his eyes." Another account describes him as "short and dumpy, with light eyes and hair inclining to be sandy, while the expression on his face reflected ill health rather than intellect. . . . Yet vividly in his countenance glowed the light of benevolence." Which is the truer portrait, the legendary delineation of what he hoped to seem or the more scholarly account with its overtone of debunking? Which is the *real* Charles Brockden Brown, the Brown who proved capable of bringing the American novel to birth?

The established facts of his brief career give some clues to the answer. He was born in Philadelphia in 1771 (the year in which Goethe published *Götz von Berlichingen*), and lived all his life in that city and in New York. He came from Quaker stock, which may have had some influence on his meditative habits, otherwise encouraged by his frail constitution and life-long sickliness. He is reported to have been a prodigy and to have received from the start a schooling worthy of his talents; but he was, despite the praise that later came to his work, much of it from the best qualified sources, irremediably melancholy. Intellectual energy and gloom complemented each other in his personality. Though he never ceased proposing to himself the most ambitious cultural schemes, he complained (or boasted—the tone is ambiguous) that he was incapable not only of real happiness but even of the "lively apprehension of misfortune."

What especially plagued him at the start was a conflict between the commitment to a career in the law, into which his family had urged him, and his own literary schemes, which he dreamed would distinguish both him and his country. At the age of sixteen, for example, he had already laid out plans for glorifying America (and Charles Brockden Brown!) with three epics, on Columbus, Pizzaro, and Cortez. New and radical ideas, derived ultimately from the Encyclopedists and more directly from Godwin and Mary Wollstonecraft, tilted the balance against his proposed career as a lawyer; and put him into even sharper opposition to the society in which he lived. To promulgate notions of social justice and to write novels, to revolutionize American life and to achieve literary fame: this double ambition he came to feel as a single impulse, not unlike certain young radical writers in the United States of the 1930's. The literary form which eminently suited both such political allegiances and such literary aspirations was at the moment he began to write (the 1790's were almost gone) the "new novel," which is to say, the gothic romance in its doctrinaire Godwinian form. "To equal *Caleb Williams*" was the best Brown could hope for himself.

If there was a contradiction between the dream of a rational Commonwealth and the hectic exploitation of horror in the gothic, Brown did not feel it. His friend Smith, more consistent advocate of the Enlightenment, might admonish him, "The man of Truth, Charles, the pupil of Reason has no mysteries," but Brown could turn with equanimity from the works of Diderot to *The Horrid Mysteries* of the Marquis of Grosse. As a writer, he proposed both to produce books with a "moral tendency" (enlightened, of course) and to "ravish the souls" of his readers with "roaring passions." The essential human passion to which he hoped to appeal in his examination of society, as well as by his exploration of terror, was curiosity: that curiosity of the sentimentalizing eighteenth century for which the proper study of mankind was the heart of man, "*l'étude profonde du coeur de l'homme, véritable dédale de la nature*"—clues to which the Marquis de Sade was convinced he had discovered in Richardson. "If you tell me," Brockden Brown once wrote, "that you are one of those who would rather travel into the mind of a ploughman than the interior of Africa, I confess myself of your way of thinking." It is a sentiment which linked Richardson and Pope, de Sade and Diderot, and which joined them in a common enterprise with Mrs. Radcliffe, the Marquis von Grosse, and Brown himself.

After publishing a dialogue on woman's rights called *Alcuin*—a preliminary concession to his doctrinal commitments, Brown plunged into a feverish bout of creative activity which saw the publication within two years (from September of 1798 to November of 1799) of his four best novels, *Wieland, Ormond, Arthur Mervyn* (Part I), and *Edgar Huntly;* and which left him with the uncompleted fragments of as many more. *Wieland,* which many readers value above all the rest, he completed within a month. This frantic outburst of energy seems to have been cued by two events, one internal, one external: first, his abandonment of the law and his decision to stake everything on his talent as a writer; and second, the death of his friend Elihu Hubbard Smith, who fell victim to yellow fever just as *Wieland* was coming off the press.

Brown had already lived through one epidemic in Philadelphia in 1793, but it was his second experience with the pestilence in the New York epidemic of 1798 that took possession of his imagination. Images of this disaster crept into the pages of *Ormond* and *Arthur Mervyn,* becoming for Brown symbols of all that is monstrous and inexplicable in life. Like Defoe before him and Manzoni and Camus afterward, he found in the plight of the city under a plague an archetypal representation of man's fate. For Brown, moreover, the general calamity was given added poignancy by the death of his friend, who, being a doctor, had not been able to flee its ravages. Despite the fact that he stayed with Smith throughout, actually falling ill himself though not critically, Brown apparently felt guilt as well as dismay at his friend's early death. He may even have suspected (who knows?) that he had infected Smith, carried the principle of infection which destroyed him.

It is possible that the character of Sarsefield, who appears first in *Ormond,* then in *Edgar Huntly,* with no explanation of the duplication, and who represents in each case the protagonist's closest friend, may play in the dreamlike plots of those two books the role of Smith. In *Ormond*, Sarsefield is slain by Turks, and is revenged in the best Achilles-Patroclus fashion by Ormond, who gallops from the field, five bloody heads of his opponents dangling from his saddle. In *Edgar Huntly,* the fantasy becomes even more ambiguously sinister, with Edgar shooting once at Sarsefield, Sarsefield once at him, though they are bound to each other by mutual love and the special bond between protector and protégé.

Brown's first four completed novels, combining as they do the appeals of the gothic and the sentimental, and written with a vigor unprecedented in American fiction, might have been expected to win a substantial audience for their author; but though they were critically well received, they didn't sell. The records show much praise, but no second editions. Partly in despair at not achieving popular success, partly out of a loss of faith in the radical principles which had been his motive force, Brown began to disengage himself from his commitment to fiction. As early as 1799, he had become the editor of a new magazine, and gradually the journalist, the man of letters took over from the poet, the mythopoeic writer. The process passed through two stages: first, a disavowal of the tale of terror, with its melancholy and pursuit of the outrageous; then a total rejection of the novel. The year 1800 saw the completion of the second part of *Arthur Mervyn* and the exhaustion of Brown's first spasm of creative energy. At this point he made a public pledge to abandon "the doleful tone and assume a cheery one," to substitute "moral causes and daily incidents in the place of the prodigious and the singular"—that is, to leave the gothic and take up the domestic sentimental.

But there had already been an undeclared shift in his attitudes between *Wieland* and *Ormond* on the one hand and *Edgar Huntly* and *Arthur Mervyn* on the other. The character of Carwin in *Wieland* (further developed in an unfinished work called *Carwin the Biloquist*) combines, in the style of Goethe, qualities of Don Juan and Faust. Carwin at one point declares to Clara, the suffering heroine of *Wieland* whom he stalks with Lovelace-like single-mindedness through the novel, "Even if I execute my purpose, what injury is done. Your prejudices will call it by that name, but it merits it not." He is the Richardsonian seducer, refusing even to grant that the dishonor which he threatens is real; all his formidable talents, even the mysterious gift of ventriloquism (which Brown calls "biloquism") are devoted to separating Clara from her true lover, maneuvering her into a position where she will have no protection against his assault.

Carwin, however, does not *look* like Don Juan: "His cheeks were pallid and lank, his eyes sunken, his forehead overshadowed by coarse, straggling hairs . . . his chin discoloured by a tetter. . . . And yet his forehead . . . his eyes lustrously black, and possessing, in the midst of haggardness, a radiance inexpressibly serene and potent . . . served to betoken a mind of the highest order. . . ." It is the face, of course, of the gothic hero-villain, of Mrs. Radcliffe's Schedoni or M. G. Lewis' Ambrosio: the ravaged aspect and hypnotic eye of one driven by a Faustian "thirst of knowledge," which was "augmented as it was supplied with gratification." "Curiosity," a Godwinian term, is the name Brown prefers for the Faustian lust to know; and Carwin even pleads in self-defense, after his activities have helped push Wieland, the brother of Clara, over the edge of religious insanity, that his "only crime was curiosity."

On this plea, Brown seems quite willing to acquit his hero-villain of any final guilt; for "curiosity" was his own reigning passion and Carwin is the projection of himself: insatiable seeker and man of many voices. "To excite and baffle curiosity," Brown once wrote about his own purpose as a novelist, "without shocking belief, is the end to be contemplated." In the end, Carwin is permitted to leave the pages of *Wieland* unpunished, though without any rewards—to take up once more his role of Wandering Jew, a tabooed figure incapable of finding rest or love. The true villain of the piece is not the doctrinaire revolutionary, the skeptical Carwin, but the religious fanatic, the believing Christian, Wieland, who ends by murdering his wife and threatening the life of his sister.

Through Wieland, Brown manages to project at once his distrust of religiosity and his obsession with the destructive aspects of the brother-sister relationship. *Geschwisterinzest* is everywhere in our literature (from William Hill Brown to Hawthorne, from Poe to William Faulkner) associated with death; only Brockden Brown, however, is willing to portray it as naked aggression. The tender alliance of brother and sister, so beloved of the Romantics, becomes in his works a brutal conflict; his brothers rob, cheat, and harry their sisters, yet are bound to them so closely that (as in *Edgar Huntly*) each feels his own life and death mysteriously linked to the fate of the other. At the climax of *Wieland,* Clara, threatened with death by her now maniacal brother, seems forced to choose between her own life and his. Brown relents a little, however, managing (through the intervention, this time beneficent, of Carwin) to contrive a resolution in which Wieland, taking up the knife Clara has dropped, stabs himself. The weapon is the sister's, but the hand which wields it the brother's own.

In *Ormond,* to whose sentimental aspects we have alluded earlier, the deed that is only threatened in the earlier book occurs. The Persecuted Maiden strikes back in self-defense; Constantia, Brown's second version of the Clarissa character he first sketched as Clara, kills her attacker, Ormond. Constantia, however, is not the sister of Ormond; and he is, therefore, permitted—the censor taken off guard—to approach her not in madness but in simple lust. Nevertheless, a point is made of Constantia's extraordinary resemblance to the actual sister of Ormond, as if to alert us to the fact that we are being presented with a case of attempted incest and fratricide once removed, though neither of these crimes, of course, could be proved in court. It is an extraordinary piece of duplicity. Brown does not dare openly imagine even murder between characters of one blood— only the approach to it; and to portray sexual passion between them goes far beyond the limits of his audacity. Nevertheless, he manages to suggest atrocities by using the dream device of splitting a single protagonist into two apparently unrelated actors.

There is, however, another significance to the murder of Ormond by Constantia, and this meaning Brown establishes with satisfactory clarity. By permitting his new Clarissa (however churchless he makes her out of respect to Godwin or Mary Wollstonecraft) to stab Lovelace-Faust, he symbolically disowns whatever in himself corresponds to the "curiosity," dedication to passion, and contempt for ordinary morality symbolized by the latter figure. After this, neither the Seducer nor the Faustian man is permitted to occupy the center of Brown's fiction; and even the love-combat of brother and sister is pushed to the periphery. He abandoned *Carwin the Biloquist* in mid-course and turned to *Arthur Mervyn* with its new kind of hero.

The yellow fever epidemic determines this unconfessed dividing line in his work: on the one hand, breaking up the group of New York intellectuals of which Smith had been the leading figure; and on the other hand, suggesting a new image for human misery, which cast doubt on man's ability to cope with it successfully. "The evils of pestilence by which this city has lately been afflicted will probably form an era in its history," Brown writes in the preface to *Arthur Mervyn.* "The schemes of reformation and improvement to which they will give birth, or, if no efforts of human wisdom can avail to avert the periodical calamity, the change in manners and population . . . will be, in the highest degree, memorable." The key phrase, of course, is "if no efforts of human wisdom can avail," reflecting the first shadow of the doubt which will eventually black out in the heart of Brown his youthful faith in "schemes of reformation and improvement."

From this point forward, at any rate, Brown's protagonists are dependent boys in search of motherly wives, rather than phallic aggressors in quest of virgins to sully. Victimized by cruel masters, images of the Bad Father, such protagonists wander about the world buffeted and misunderstood, until some understanding female, rich and mature and sexually experienced, provides them a haven. In them, "curiosity" still prevails, but it is no longer the fanatic passion of a Faust to know everything, only the nagging need of an ignorant boy to discover the adult secrets of the locked chamber, the forbidden room, the sealed chest. The Bluebeard myth replaces that of the Satanic bargain; and "curiosity" leads not to selling one's soul to the Devil, but to braving the taboo imposed by a cruel and irrational master. Having peeped through the keyhole at the forbidden mysteries, the curious boy is thenceforth persecuted, not for his guilt, but because of his knowledge of another's.

This Bluebeard mythos Brown had discovered in his reading of Godwin, for whom it embodied a theory of the eternal guiltlessness of the exploited (the apprentice blacklisted and bullied), the inevitable guilt of the exploiter (the conscience-wracked master taking out his self-hatred and fear on the boy who knows too much). Not the apparent criminal, Godwin's *Caleb Williams* suggested, but the system of social control which made criminals—which drove the best to seem, if not to become, the worst—was to blame! In the Bluebeard legend, however, the breaker of the taboo is the woman, the recalcitrant wife bucking the limitations of a male-controlled society; and though she lives through a moment of daring, she is portrayed finally as passive and weak—her chief weapon hope. Similarly, the later heroes of Brown seem almost feminine in their passivity and their proneness to flee rather than fight; in some ways, they seem closer to the Persecuted Maiden than to any of the traditional prototypes of the hero.

Yet even more than they seem women, perhaps, Brown's frightened young men seem children, little boys prowling the corridors of a nighttime house, where behind closed doors adults perform unimaginable acts of darkness. Certainly, like motherless children, those young men are adopted into marriage at the happy ending of their adventures. So Arthur Mervyn is taken in hand by Mrs. Achsa Fielding ("she is six years older than you . . . she has been a wife and a mother already"), after a final nightmare in which he imagines the dead husband-father arising to shoot him through the heart. "My heart had nothing in it but reverence and admiration," he cries, protesting the innocence of his affection; but some guilt (some buried sense of the incest taboo broken) haunts him all the same. "Was she not the substitute of my lost mama? Would I not have clasped that beloved shade?"

The fact that Arthur Mervyn finally prefers the maternal widow, Mrs. Fielding, to Eliza Hadwin, a girl of fifteen, just the "age of delicate fervor, of inartificial love," infuriated Shelley, who, for all his admiration of Brown, could never forgive him for marrying off his hero to a sedate and wealthy Jewess instead of a poor "peasant-girl." There is, indeed, something symbolic in the choice at which Shelley, granted his point of view, had a right to rebel. For as surely as the death of Ormond had signified Brown's rejection of the demonic, his abandonment of Eliza represented his turning away from a Romantic commitment to art to an acceptance of the responsibilities of bourgeois life.

Clara Howard and *Jane Talbot,* those attempts at creating a sentimental novel without seduction, mark (as we have noticed) an effort at winning the great female audience; but more than that, they are further steps toward silence. In them, even the Bluebeard archetype has been surrendered and with it all desire to titillate curiosity or stir the darker passions. Brown is ready for the final disavowals, the surrender of his remaining liberal views ("From visionary schemes of Utopian systems of government and manners," his first biographer wrote, "Mr. Brown, like many others, became a sober recorder of things as they are") and of his career as an author ("Book-making, as you observe," Brown commented to his brother in 1800, "is the dullest of all trades, and the

utmost any American can look for, in his native country, is to be reimbursed his unavoidable expenses").

With this brother and another, he went into the commission-merchant business; and, to set a final seal upon his capitulation, in 1804 married. But failure dogged his business efforts, compelling him at one point to sell "pots and pans over the counter," and tuberculosis brought suffering to his private life. What creative energies he had left, he devoted in these final years to *The Literary Magazine and American Register,* a periodical pledged always to keep in mind that "Christian piety is the highest excellence of human beings" and committed to printing material "free from sensuality and voluptuousness," which, "whether seconded or not by genius and knowledge, will . . . aim at the promotion of public and private virtues." Of his fiction, which came to seem to him as much an error as his early political activity, he wrote in 1803:

> I am far from wishing, however, that my reader should judge of my exertions by my former ones. I have written much, but take much blame to myself . . . and . . . no praise for any thing. I should enjoy a larger share of my own respect, at the present moment, if nothing had ever flowed from my pen, the production of which could be traced to me.

Myth (perhaps acted out by Brown himself as fact) has it that his last attempt at a tragedy he burned, keeping the ashes in a snuff-box on his desk until his death of tuberculosis in 1810.

TITLE COMMENTARY

Wieland; or, The Transformation

AMERICAN REVIEW AND LITERARY JOURNAL (REVIEW DATE JANUARY-MARCH 1802)

SOURCE: A review of *Wieland; or, The Transformation,* by Charles Brockden Brown. *American Review and Literary Journal* 2, no. 1 (January-March 1802): 28-38.

In the following excerpt from a mixed review of Wieland, *the critic asserts that narrative style, technique, and characterization in the novel present challenges for the reader.*

It will imply some commendation of the author's powers of narration, when we say, that having begun the persual of [*Wieland*], we were irresistibly led on to the conclusion of the tale.

The style is clear, forcible and correct. Passages of great elegance might be selected, and others which breathe a strain of lively and impassioned eloquence.

It is impossible not to sympathize in the terror and distress of the sister of Wieland. Persons of lively sensibility and active imaginations may, probably, think that some of the scenes are too shocking and painful to be endured even in fiction.

The soliloquies of some of the characters are unreasonably long, and the attention is wearied in listening to the conjectures, the reasonings, the hopes and fears which are successively formed and rejected, at a moment when expectation is already strained to its highest pitch. These intellectual conflicts and processes of the imagination show fertility of conception, and the art of the narrator; but this art is too often exercised in suspending the course of action so as to render the reader restless and impatient. The generality of readers love rather to be borne along by a rapid narrative, and to be roused to attention by the quick succession of new and unexpected incidents.

The characters which are introduced are not numerous; nor are they such as may be easily found in the walks of common life. Carwin is an extraordinary being, and, in some degree, incomprehensible. If his prototype is not in nature, he must be acknowledged the creature of a vigorous fancy, fitted to excite curiosity and expectation. The author seems to have intended to exhibit him more fully to view; but not having finished the portrait, or doubtful of the effect of the exhibition, has reserved him for some future occasion, when he may be made the hero of his own story. The consequences produced by the exercise of the powers imputed to him were not foreseen, and were beyond the reach of his control. Their exertion was from the impulse of caprice, or for a momentary self-gratification. He is the author of the most dreadful calamities, without any malicious or evil intention.—The reader sees the misery and ruin of an amiable family, by ignorant and deluded beings, undeserving the severity of punishment.—The endowments of such a being as Carwin, if they can possibly exist to the extent here imagined, are without advantage to the possessor, and can be of no benefit to mankind. This seems to be the principal lesson taught by the delineation of such a character.

Wieland and his family, in retirement, devoted to contemplation and study, and mixing little in the varied scenes of enlarged society, furnish few

of those instructive facts and situations which may be supposed to occur in the usual progress of life. The even tenor of their existence is not broken by the stronger impulses of social feeling, or agitated by the conflict of violent passions. Their repose is disturbed, and their imaginations excited, by unknown and invisible agents. Comparisons, therefore, with the actual or probable situation of the reader, are not often suggested, nor are many precepts of instruction to be derived from examples too rare for general application. Against the freaks of a *ventriloquist*, or the illusions of a madman, no rules can be prescribed for our protection. No prudence or foresight can guard us against evils which are to flow from such causes. The example of Wieland may teach us, indeed, the necessity of placing due restraints on the imagination; the folly of that presumptuous desire which seeks for gratifications inconsistent with the laws of existence and the ordinary course of nature; and to be content with the light which is set before us in the path of our moral and religious duties, without seeking for new illuminations. From the exhibition, however, of an infatuated being, deluded by the suggestions of a disturbed intellect, into the commission of acts the most unnatural and horrid, it is doubtful whether any real good is to be derived. But whether benefit or harm, or how much of either is to be received from tales of this kind, we are not prepared to decide, and they are questions not easily solved. The good or ill effect of a book, in most cases, depends on the previous disposition and character of the reader.

The author has certainly contrived a narration deeply interesting; and whatever may be its faults, and some we have ventured to remark, **Wieland,** as a work of imagination, may be ranked high among the productions of the age.

HARRY R. WARFEL (ESSAY DATE 1949)

SOURCE: Warfel, Harry R. "*Wieland; or, The Transformation.*" In *Charles Brockden Brown: American Gothic Novelist,* pp. 96-115. Gainesville: University of Florida Press, 1949.

In the following essay, Warfel surveys the context surrounding the compilation and critical reception of Wieland.

During the autumn and winter of 1797-1798 Brown fell in love with Miss Susan A. Potts, a young Philadelphian about whom no information survives. On March 29, 1798, Smith showed Dunlap a letter in which Brown described himself as assiduously writing novels and in love. Late in April Miss Potts visited New York City. After calling to pay his respects, Smith reported: "Without being beautiful, she is very interesting. Our talk was on common topics, as there was a third person present, but it evinced good sense. All that I see is in her favor." Parental objection to their marriage, possibly because Miss Potts was not a Quaker, caused relations to be broken off forcibly. On occasion the novelist made light of his lovelorn state, but without doubt his feelings had been rudely shocked by the attitude of his family, particularly that of his mother whose intervention finally forced the issue.

On July 3, 1798, Brown arrived in New York City for another of his extended visits. His health was pretty well restored, although his spirits flagged at thoughts of the unkind tactics of his family. For nine days he resided with Dunlap; then on July 12 he moved into the quarters of Smith and Johnson at 45 Pine Street.

Johnson's law practice had increased extensively because of the rage for speculation in Western lands, the purchase of foreign notes, and litigation relating to contracts. Smith's medical practice had grown, partly because of connections made at the hospital and partly because of favorable public interest in the *Medical Repository.* Physicians recognized his attainments by calling him as a consultant. Brown, alone during much of the day, was free to concentrate upon the completion of his projects. At leisurely breakfasts and dinners the three men ran over the ground of their many interests; each day brought new schemes for doing good. They worried over Seth and Horace Johnson, whose business was on the verge of bankruptcy. In Philadelphia, Joseph Bringhurst, Jr., had suffered imprisonment for debt as a result of unfortunate business commitments. Knowing the integrity of these friends, the three roommates worried less about them than about laws which permitted egregious wrongs. The ground of their religious beliefs was retraced, but Johnson refused to go the whole road in renouncing orthodox Christianity. Brown was testing theological ideas in **Wieland**; the more he wrote the less certain he was of the attainment of a simple solution of complicated psychological and social problems.

The triumvirate moved about the city as a unit in social visits to the homes of Roulet, Seth and Horace Johnson, the two Millers, Dr. Mitchill, Boyd, Templeton, Riley, Lovegrove, Charles Adams, Moses Rogers, General Hughes, and William and Gurdon Woolsey. Almost daily the three friends visited Dunlap or he visited them. At these houses as guests were some of the most distinguished men of the day. Timothy Dwight, Yale's president, stopped by frequently. General Bloomfield crossed the river from New Jersey to meet New York friends. Albert Gallatin occasionally came to the city to look after political interests as well as to complete business matters concerned with his manufacturing activities in the Monongahela River Valley. Noah Webster on a research tour requested critical comments upon the first chapter of *A Brief History of Epidemic Diseases.* Jedidiah Morse, preacher and geographer, was carrying on a crusade against the Illuminati, a European subversive order with some few adherents in

America. Hints for **Ormond** were derived from this pugnacious fundamentalist. Statesmen from New England lingered a day or two in New York in passing to and from the capitol in Philadelphia; Senator Uriah Tracy of Connecticut had been especially friendly in introducing political leaders. Yet no other event seemed quite so notable this summer as the appearance, on July 27, of President John Adams. A military company paraded its maneuvers from early morning until his arrival at five P.M. The three friends waited at the Battery all day to meet the national leader who was the father of their intimate companion.

Into one other organization Brown was drawn on July 16, 1798. In company with Smith, William Johnson, and Samuel Miles Hopkins, he went to Dr. Samuel Latham Mitchill's rooms at Columbia College, where, in addition to the host, they found Dr. Edward Miller and the Reverend Samuel Miller. After some discussion the group founded the American Mineralogical Society. In addition to those present at the meeting, the following were admitted as charter members: William Dunlap; Solomon Simpson, a Jewish merchant; and George J. Warner, a watchmaker.

At breakfast on August 7, Smith, Johnson, Dunlap, and Brown talked over the project of bringing out through T. and J. Swords a weekly magazine. The success of the *Medical Repository,* issued by the same printers, augured well for a literary paper, especially if the novelist were to take charge. Before active work could be begun, yellow fever again terrified the city, and the dynamic leader of the group had fallen victim.

The Friendly Club had discontinued meeting after the normal attendance in May dwindled to one or two members besides the three roommates. In a sense the American Mineralogical Society replaced the earlier club, although Mitchill held the new group quite rigorously to a discussion of scientific matters. Brown trailed Smith to these meetings; there is no evidence that the busy novelist devoted himself seriously to a study of the classification or chemical analysis of rocks. Recognizing the need for companionship, Brown merely went along with Smith and Johnson; at this time he did not strike out for himself to create friends of his own.

Brown brought to New York, as evidence of enthusiasm for novel writing, the first pages of a new book. In Philadelphia on April 12, 1798, he had read to Dunlap "the beginning to a novel undertaken since *Sky-Walk;* he calls it **Wieland; or, The Transformation.** This must make a very fine book." On July 3 Dunlap noted further: "C. B. Brown arrives from Philadelphia—last from Princeton—and takes up his abode with me. He has brought his second novel but not completed." The little circle of intimates passed the manuscript around. Smith found it "no way inferior to *Sky-Walk.*" By July 10 eighty-four pages of manuscript had been completed. Smith took this packet to Hocquet Caritat, bookseller and owner of New York's fashionable circulating library, who purchased the rights to the novel. On July 23 copy was sent to the printer, T. and J. Swords. Having received fifty dollars as an initial payment, Brown hurried to a conclusion to keep pace with the typesetters. On August 5 the novel was completely written, although some additions and alterations in the proof were made as late as August 24. The book was published on September 14, 1798, and put on sale at a dollar a copy.

Wieland; or, The Transformation is a terror story in which the narrator, the beautiful Clara Wieland, is driven toward madness by a series of shivering experiences, is rescued at the end, and is allowed to complete her gloom-clouded life in marriage. She is the daughter of a German-born religious fanatic who has come to America as a missionary and who has foretold his death by strange, unannounced means of retribution for supposed lax service to God. With trembling joints and chattering teeth he goes one sultry August midnight, in customary solitude, to worship in a private chapel on his estate. Half an hour later his wife notices a gleam of light in the chapel. There follows a loud report like the explosion of an undersea bomb. Piercing shrieks seem to be a call for help. The blaze resembles a cloud impregnated with light, but the building is not on fire. Brought to his bed, the fanatic states that while engaged in silent prayers he was disturbed by a faint gleam of light in the chapel as if someone carried a lamp. On turning to look at the supposed intruder, he was struck on the right arm by a club. A bright spark fell on him, and in a moment his clothes were burned to ashes. Wieland dies by spontaneous combustion, exactly in the manner of the priest Don G. Maria Bertholi, as described in the London *Literary Magazine* of May, 1790. But the question is raised by Clara whether this event is "fresh proof that the Divine Ruler interferes in human affairs" or is the natural consequence of "the irregular expansion of the fluid that imparts warmth to our heart and blood, caused by the fatigue of the preceding day, or flowing by established laws from the condition of his thoughts."

It is against this background of religious mania and of imagined supernatural intervention in the affairs of men that the main story is related. Clara and her brother Theodore, who are about seven and ten years old, respectively, when their father dies, are reared by a maiden aunt under circumstances of affluence. Wieland's studious habits and musical interests arise from a humorless, melancholy disposition. The history of religion and the textual accuracy of Cicero are his favorite studies. Neither child has been able to forget the terrifying childhood experience, and almost every significant incident clangs the bell of memory to renew the indelible impact of that tragic occurrence. The story proper begins six years after Theodore has married Catharine Pleyel and after four children have been born to this union.

Like his father, Theodore is a religious enthusiast who imagines that he can have direct communication with God. The ardent Clara sees in almost every unmarried man a potential suitor; secretly she has nourished affection for Henry Pleyel, Catharine's brother, a rationalist engaged to the German baroness Theresa von Stolberg. One evening, as the four are conversing, Wieland goes to his father's chapel, now converted to a study and music hall, to find a letter. A mysterious voice warns him to return to the house. Seven times in the course of a few weeks the voice is heard under varying and increasingly mystifying circumstances. Wieland is certain of the supernatural origin of the voice, Clara thinks the voice is supernatural but not malevolent in intention, and Pleyel, who has been told of the death of his sweetheart in one of the voice's statements, wavers momentarily until his rationalistic tendency reasserts itself.

A stranger named Carwin, an escaped convict from Ireland with eyes and voice suggesting powers of witchcraft, comes into the family circle. On one occasion he appears in Clara's bedroom at midnight after the voice has been heard. He assures her that but for the supernatural protection afforded by the voice he would have seduced her. Pleyel, whose affection has centered on Clara, witnesses Carwin's departure from her room and turns angrily against her because of her seemingly profligate conduct.

Wieland goes mad under the strain of the circumstances and, because he thinks he hears a divine command, strangles his wife and children and bashes in the head of Louisa Stuart, a young girl living with the Wielands. His attempt on Pleyel's life fails. Carwin suddenly appears and explains his ventriloquial powers just as Wieland

menaces Clara. Aware of his error, Wieland grasps her penknife, with which she intended to slay him, and plunges the blade to the hilt in his own neck.

Three years later Clara resumes the narrative. Theresa is dead in childbirth. Pleyel, having learned the truth about Clara's innocence, marries her. The story of Louisa Stuart's parents is briefly concluded as a parallel narrative leading to an identical moralized conclusion. Stuart had wounded Maxwell in a duel, and in revenge Maxwell had seduced Stuart's wife. When Stuart learns of his wife's self-exile in shame, he pursues Maxwell to secure revenge. A challenge is issued, but at night Stuart is murdered by an unknown swarthy assassin. This briefly narrated secondary story is designed to give point to the lesson that "the evils of which Carwin and Maxwell were the authors owed their existence to the errors of the sufferers." If Mrs. Stuart had crushed her disastrous passion, and if Stuart had not sought an "absurd revenge," the catastrophe would not have occurred. If Wieland had framed juster notions of moral duty and if Clara had been gifted with ordinary equanimity or foresight, the double-tongued Carwin would not have ensnared them.

This conclusion has an anticlimactic force, since the scene shifts from the Wieland family to the Stuart family. Though esthetically the episode cannot be justified today, to the story-telling moralist in 1798 it helped to give a ring of truth, for dueling and seduction were frowned upon. The parallel between common and uncommon experiences heightens the necessity for a rationalistic examination of evidence before one draws conclusions or engages in actions likely to destroy life or happiness.

The novel has other defects. Conversation occurs too seldom, and then chiefly in Wieland's confession. Most of the episodes are summarized too briefly. Description tends to be general and expository rather than pictorial. Opportunities for magnificent scenes are not exploited; a notable example is the comment following the discovery of the bodies of the five murdered children: "Why should I protract a tale which I already begin to feel is too long?" This episode of a religious maniac's murder of his family expands an account, as related in the New York *Weekly Magazine* of July 20, 1796, of James Yates' murder of his whole family in Tomhanick, New York, in December, 1791.

The virtues of the novel are numerous. The main story moves with steady crescendo to a powerful climax. It is, as Thomas Love Peacock said, "one of the few tales in which the final explanation of the apparently supernatural does not destroy or diminish the original effect." The reader is so engrossed in the plight of the narrator, Clara, since she is under threat throughout, that the explanation by Carwin of his cunning serves but to increase the danger to Clara's mental balance and life. Brown organized his story, unlike most Gothic tales, around the theme of mental balance and the ease with which that balance is destroyed. The pseudo-supernatural materials, spontaneous combustion and ventriloquism, serve to make credible Theodore's insanity. Clara is prostrated at two periods, and in the presence of Carwin she faints twice. She possesses a hereditary dread of water. Her education, she says, did not fit her for perils such as she encounters. In the moralizing conclusion, therefore, she advises the necessity for maintaining one's balance through a rationalistic attitude towards all phenomena.

The plot unfolds skillfully. The initial chapters set the somber, tragic mood of the tale; ever present in the minds of Clara and Theodore, and used advantageously by Carwin, are the events of the elder Wieland's fiery death; that episode chimes in the memory like a knell, horrifyingly symbolical of a dread, inevitable catastrophe. The small cast of characters, closely interknit through marriage and affection, as well as through the proximity of their residences to each other and to the city of Philadelphia, makes plausible each turn of the action. Clara's penknife appears early as a weapon of defense, and at last serves its tragic purpose in Theodore's hand. Every detail of the main story is adequately motivated.

The unfolding of the tale from three angles evinces masterly command of plot structure. After Clara has narrated the events from her point of view, Theodore confesses to the court, and finally Carwin unravels the mystery. Each flickering light and each of the seven appearances of the ventriloquial voice is accounted for. If Brown managed the dovetailing of these three reports less artfully than recent writers of detective fiction have done, it should be remembered that he was pioneering in a field where Poe, thirty years later, is credited with originality. Brown anticipated Hawthorne in the use of multiple explanation of seemingly supernatural events.

It is often erroneously assumed that Theodore is the central character in the novel. The story revolves about the narrator, Clara, a young woman of exceptional mentality, fortitude, loyalty, and frankness. She begins by asking attention to her

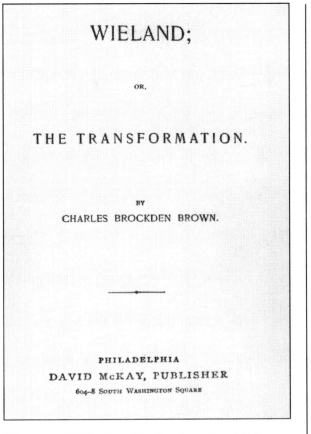

WIELAND;

OR,

THE TRANSFORMATION.

BY

CHARLES BROCKDEN BROWN.

PHILADELPHIA
DAVID McKAY, PUBLISHER
604-8 South Washington Square

Title page of *Weiland; or, The Transformation*, 1798.

own plight, "a destiny without alleviation." She worries over the supernatural agency of the voices; she sighs for a lover and unhesitatingly reveals her hopes; she who had spurned Dashwood on an earlier occasion feels the menace of a practiced seducer in a series of midnight actions, the unhappy result of which is the temporary loss of her hoped-for husband, Pleyel; she dreams of threats to her life and meditates upon their meaning; she stumbles upon the murdered Catharine and children; Theodore twice is within an inch of murdering her; and in the end she becomes the bride of Pleyel.

The subtitle of the novel, "The Transformation," occurs thrice in the text. It first describes Carwin's alteration from an Englishman into an Irishman. Clara next uses the term in relation to herself: "Was I not likewise transformed from rational and human into a creature of nameless and fearless attributes?" Finally it describes Theodore: "Wieland was transformed at once into a *man of sorrows.*" Although the word is not used directly about Pleyel, the description of his ineffable anguish on berating Clara for her alleged lapse from virtue indicates a similar "transformation." At the very beginning of the novel, in the third paragraph, Clara describes the transformation of the status of the whole family: "The storm that tore up our happiness and changed into dreariness and desert the blooming scene of our existence is lulled into grim repose, but not until the victim was transfixed and mangled, till every obstacle was dissipated by its rage, till every remnant of good was wrested from our grasp and exterminated." The title, which refers as much to the family as to Theodore, certainly must not be interpreted as excluding Clara from the central position.

Brown endowed his main characters with a sufficient variety of traits to make their friendship plausible and their actions credible. Although he drew his incidents and persons as much from books as from life, his emphasis upon psychopathic traits adds depth to characters whose range of action is narrow in the physical world. This intense intellectuality in *Wieland* gives it precedence in importance over almost all other early American novels. Quite apparent is Brown's indebtedness to contemporary sensationalist psychology, to Erasmus Darwin's chapter on "Mania Mutabilis" in *Zoönomia,* and to other writings on insanity. Dr. Cambridge's lecture to Clara echoes Dr. Benjamin Rush. Not until the advent of Poe and Hawthorne does another fictionist create characters tormented by brooding minds.

Not only in the psychological passages is *Wieland* a vehicle of intellectuality. Everywhere are evidences of learning. There has been research in religion, in old books, in encyclopedias. A problem in emending Cicero occupies some time of Theodore, who is an accomplished Latin textual scholar and a student of the history of religion. These characters are children of the Enlightenment. Each possesses utopian dreams. Clara muses on methods to end the alliance between the practice of agriculture and ignorance; she hopes that "this trade might be made conducive to or at least consistent with acquisition of wisdom and eloquence." Her heart is readily "touched with sympathy for the children of misfortune." Pleyel, a possessor of a skeptical mind in most matters, urges Theodore to claim estates in Germany because wealth would "afford so large a field for benevolence." Theodore refuses, however, on the ground that wealth and power are two great sources of depravity.

Brown's style emphasizes the intellectuality of the novel. The vocabulary is large; the words are not notably learned; although the tendency to employ polysyllables of Latin derivation is appar-

ent: "My calmness was the torpor of despair, and not the tranquillity of fortitude." Circumlocution replaces direct description: "he fell in love" becomes "he had not escaped the amorous contagion." The uniqueness of Brown's style lies in the short, rapid-fire sentences which cannonade the reader's mind with ideas faster than they can be absorbed. Fiction should proceed pictorially; Brown's story marches steadily forward under sententious garb as if he were vying with Rochefoucauld or Pascal in the writing of the following aphorisms:

> As a consolation in calamity religion is dear.
>
> Some agitation and concussion is requisite to the due exercise of human understanding.
>
> This scene of existence is, in all its parts, calamitous.
>
> Ideas exist in our minds that can be accounted for by no established laws.
>
> Surprise is an emotion that enfeebles, not invigorates.
>
> Mankind are more easily enticed to virtue by example than by precept.
>
> Terror enables us to perform incredible feats.
>
> Time will obliterate the deepest impressions.

These sentences parallel similar ones in William Godwin's *Caleb Williams* and *An Enquiry into Political Justice.* But they also parallel statements in Robert Bage's *Hermsprong* and in other fiction of a liberal tendency. Although Brown had been reading Godwin and had despaired of surpassing this master in the first pages of *Arthur Mervyn,* he was not merely copying plot or ideas or style in *Wieland.* There are more similarities with Bage's novel than with Godwin's, for in Bage are the German characters, an octagonal pleasure house, a thirty-thousand-acre plantation of the type mentioned by Ludloe and Carwin, a nature-setting with a perpendicular descent, and a generally radical intellectual tendency. Brown also was familiar with Anne Radcliffe's novels of suspense wherein seemingly supernatural occurrences were explained away as natural phenomena. His descriptions and his use of the sex motif follow the pattern of her novels.

Of considerable interest in the history of fiction are the references to German characters and the use of German Gothic formulæ. The end of the eighteenth century saw a shift of British intellectual interests away from France because of the declaration of war in 1793. German exiles and men like Matthew Lewis and Henry MacKenzie turned attention to the hitherto unexploited literary production of Prussia. Christoph Martin Wieland (1773-1813) was being mentioned in the magazines with fulsome praise for his epic *Oberon* (1780), a work which Brown read in 1793. Here in the public eye was a man whose sensitivity gave plausibility to Theodore's possession of religious mania. Dunlap had translated Schiller's and Kotzebue's dramas, and the New York *Weekly Magazine* had serialized Schiller's *The Ghostseer* and Cajetan Tschink's *The Victim of Magical Delusion*. Brown had read these two novels, and possibly the initial creative impulse and rationalistic theme of *Wieland* came from the latter. Other German and English novels doubtless influenced Brown, but by and large *Wieland* is an original work in subject, theme, plot, and execution.

Despite its publication at the very height of the plague on September 15, 1798, the book received favorable attention. With the resumption of normal city life, the New York *Spectator* of November 10, 1798, extolled the book in a review nearly a column in length: "The style is correct and energetic, and we may venture to assert the writer has established his reputation as a man of genius." The reviewer called upon his fellow citizens to support the author: "On the reception of this volume depends the future exertions of this ingenious man. Shall it be said that America, whose citizens have been famed for their superior knowledge and love of letters, is so destitute of liberality as to refuse or neglect patronizing an attempt like the present? And shall this stigma in a particular manner rest upon our city? . . . Forbid it, patriotism; forbid it, all that has any connection with science [that is, learning] and the *Amor Patriæ*."

On January 2, 1799, another reviewer in the same newspaper stated: "*Wieland; or, The Transformation* . . . is certainly the best novel this country has produced. It is a work which no one can read with inattention, and is peculiarly engaging to well-cultivated and refined understandings. Every person, however well informed he may be, must find his curiosity gratified and his mind enlarged after a candid and judicious perusal of this ingenious performance. This is not the flimsy production of a wretched hireling or a mercenary garreteer, but the well-finished composition of one who may be truly called 'a man of genius.' In a word, I think we may with propriety assert that the writer of *Wieland* was desirous of producing a work from the perusal of which no one could rise without being strengthened in habits of sincerity, fortitude, and justice." In *The American Review and Literary Journal* of July-September, 1801, this state-ment was made: "The author of *Wieland* is almost the first American who has adventured in this path of literature, and this production is the first of the kind which has attracted much public attention." Caritat took copies with him to England, and brief critiques there were favorable.

Evidently the sale was not sufficient to call for a second edition immediately. Samuel Griswold Goodrich reprinted it in 1829 in a collected edition of the novels, and in 1841 W. Coquebert issued a French translation, *Wieland, ou la voix mystérieux*. Meantime, Hawthorne, Poe, and other critics praised Brown and *Wieland*; and since its first publication the book has been acclaimed a minor classic in American literature.

Something of Brown's tremulous concern over the fate of *Wieland* appears in a letter of December 25, 1798, to Thomas Jefferson: "In thus transmitting my book to you, I tacitly acknowledge my belief that it is capable of affording you pleasure and of entitling the writer to some portion of your good opinion. I . . . hope that an artful display of incidents, the powerful delineation of characters and the train of eloquent and judicious reasoning which may be combined in a fictitious work will be regarded by Thomas Jefferson with as much respect as they are regarded by me."

As soon as *Wieland* was completed, Brown resumed work on *Carwin, The Biloquist* which, he had announced in his preface to *Wieland*, would "be published or suppressed according to the reception which is given to the present attempt." *Carwin* never was completed; the surviving fragment was first printed in *The Literary Magazine and American Register* between 1803 and 1805.

Carwin, The Biloquist forms a preliminary volume to *Wieland*, much as the first part of Godwin's *Caleb Williams* describes the villain's career before the hero is introduced. Carwin, son of a western Pennsylvania farmer, possesses a curiosity like Caleb Williams'. At fourteen he becomes interested in ventriloquism through the operation of a five-fold echo in a glen. He succeeds in mimicking every species of sound, human and animal. Sent to live with an aunt in Philadelphia, he meets Ludloe, a wealthy Irishman and agrees to go to Europe.

Ludloe enunciates a strange code of conduct: he seems to be an anarchist; his talk savors of the subversive ideas of the Illuminati. He echoes Alcuin on the subject of the perverting nature of all professions, on the evils of cohabitation, and on the misguided thinking of women as a result of false principles of education. He believes that "the absurd and unequal distribution of property gave birth to poverty and riches" and that the evils which infest society are caused by the errors of opinion. A perfectionist, he believes further "that man is the creature of circumstances; that he is capable of endless improvement; that his progress has been stopped by the artificial impediment of government; that by the removal of this, the fondest dreams of imagination will be realized." Ludloe also has "a scheme of utopian felicity, where the empire of reason should supplant that of force; where justice should be universally understood and practiced; where the interest of the whole and of the individual should be seen by all to be the same; where the public good should be the scope of all activity; where the tasks of all should be the same, and the means of subsistence equally distributed."

Carwin while studying in Spain embraces Roman Catholicism. His correspondence with Ludloe leads to the exposition of a plan for a new nation to be established on the colonization principle of the manumission societies; he believes that men persist in retaining error because they are creatures of habit, and that in a new land "a new race, tutored in truth, may in a few centuries overflow the habitable world." Not until he arrives in Dublin does Carwin discover Ludloe's secret, but the novel breaks off before the two men come to open conflict. The sequel in *Wieland* accuses Carwin of murdering Lady Jane Conway and of robbing Ludloe—charges which Carwin claims are false.

Brown felt that his narrative was following too closely the pattern of *Caleb Williams* and of the beginning of *Arthur Mervyn,* already published in the Philadelphia *Weekly Magazine.* In abandoning his plan, he laid aside a swift-paced tale involving only a single strand of action. Carwin possesses little distinctiveness in character, and the conflict between him and Ludloe would have been difficult to manage on ideological or psychological grounds because both have similar utopian notions. No ideas are in conflict, and *Carwin* develops no theme of importance equal to that of *Wieland.* But where *Wieland* is almost wholly original, *Carwin* seems wholly derivative in pattern and character from Godwin. Though the verbal power remains, Brown correctly diagnosed the chief weakness of the novel when he wrote in 1805 that "the narrative [is] of too grave and argumentative a cast."

On September 4, 1798, Brown wrote to Dunlap: "I have written something in the history of

Carwin, which I will send. I have deserted for the present from the prosecution of this plan, and betook myself to another which I mean to extend to the size of *Wieland* and to finish by the end of this month, provided no yellow fever disconcerts my plan." On the 24th, while he and Dunlap were together in Perth Amboy to escape the ravages of yellow fever, Dunlap noted in his diary: "Read the beginning of Charles' last novel called *Calvert* (proposed to be changed to *Caillemour*) or *The Lost Brothers.*" This work, the first volume of an uncompleted pentalogy, was entitled **Memoirs of Stephen Calvert** and was first published serially in Brown's *Monthly Magazine and American Review* from June, 1799, to June, 1800; Dunlap reprinted it in his biography of Brown.

MICHAEL T. GILMORE (ESSAY DATE SUMMER 1977)

SOURCE: Gilmore, Michael T. "Calvinism and Gothicism: The Example of Brown's *Wieland*." *Studies in the Novel* 9, no. 2 (summer 1977): 107-18.

In the following essay, Gilmore analyzes the influence of Milton's Biblical epic Paradise Lost *on* Wieland.

Charles Brockden Brown's "Gothic" novel **Wieland; or The Transformation** (1798) was long read as an expression of Enlightenment rationality. The author's purpose, according to this view, was to caution readers "against credulity and religious fanaticism."[1] But the rationalist interpretation has come under spirited attack in recent years, partly as a result of a reassessment of *le genre noir* in general, and the Calvinist underpinning of Brown's tale has begun to gain the recognition it deserves.[2] Nevertheless, the misreadings persist in one form or another, and even Larzer Ziff, who properly insists that "Brown ends his journey through the mind by approaching the outskirts of Edwards' camp," misconstrues the novel's denouement as a conventional happy ending. Further, Ziff's analysis of the sentimental seduction theme is a source of confusion, the effect of which is to trivialize Brown's principal concern.[3] For the Carwin-Clara-Pleyel triangle has little to do with sentimental love: rather it is Brown's version of the temptation in the garden, and **Wieland** itself is his retelling of the biblical fable of the Fall of Man.

It is well known that William Godwin's *Caleb Williams* had a major impact on Brown and that its publication in 1794 prompted the American to turn to the writing of fiction. Much stressed by critics, the Godwinian influence is usually cited as proof of Brown's radicalism and hostility to religion. As Joel Porte has recently shown, however, *Caleb Williams* possesses an "exacerbated Calvinist framework" and breathes the spirit of *Paradise Lost.* With Falkland in the role of the harsh Divinity and Caleb as the sinful Adam, it charts a course of guilt, suffering, and relentless persecution, ending with a reversal in which the eponymous hero, having succeeded in vindicating himself in a court of law, is overcome by remorse and acknowledges that "he is precisely the 'monster of depravity' whom he had been represented as being all along." In the ruined Gothic world of *Caleb Williams,* argues Porte, there is no hope, no prospect of grace or redemption.[4]

And yet the conclusion of Godwin's novel would seem to suggest that the author did in fact have a scheme of salvation, a scheme which is unmistakably Calvinist and may even have derived from his reading of Jonathan Edwards.[5] *Caleb Williams,* which Godwin wrote, as he claimed in the preface, in order to expose "Things as They Are," is profoundly antilaw in outlook and expounds the view that the English legal system is a tool of class oppression. On a different or deeper level, however, the book is addressed to the issue of salvation by works or faith. Mr. Raymond, captain of a band of thieves patterned after Robin Hood's mythical crew, declares to Caleb that "either . . . we all of us deserve the vengeance of the law, or law is not the proper instrument of correcting the misdeeds of mankind." As Old Testament God, Falkland uses the "remorseless fangs of the law" to hound Caleb with the threat of extinction; but once the wretched victim is imprisoned and arraigned for judgment, the pursuer declines to appear to press charges. Jehovah becomes Christ in an unexpected *volte-face;* and Caleb, who has doggedly protested his innocence, thereby denying his need for grace, is transformed into Cain or the Wandering Jew. In the novel's postscript, he goes to a magistrate and turns the law against Falkland himself, who is convicted and dies after three days. He will not rise again for Caleb Williams. For the latter, having figuratively slain Christ—"A nobler spirit lived not among the sons of men," he now says of Falkland—awakens too late to his corrupt nature and participation in the primal crime. He might have secured himself from damnation, he realizes, if "I had opened my heart to Mr. Falkland, if I had told to him privately the tale I have now been telling . . ."—if, in short, he had thrown himself upon the mercy of the Redeemer and made a confession of sin.[6] What Godwin's residual Calvinism reduces down to is the conviction that only

through Christ and the covenant of grace can mankind be saved; given human depravity, there is no salvation through law or good works.

Crane Brinton, in his work on the French Revolution, has commented on the resemblance between Protestant and Robespierrean theology, arguing that "the men who made the Terror were compeers of the first Crusaders, of Savonarola, of Calvin."[7] Brinton's thesis is perfectly illustrated by Godwin, whose radicalism bears the indelible stamp of his orthodox upbringing. In the case of Brown, who was raised as a Quaker, the Calvinist mood informing both *Wieland* and the fragment *Memoirs of Carwin the Biloquist* probably stems as much from the eighteenth-century American background as from his immersion in Enlightenment literature. The *Memoirs of Carwin,* which was composed at roughly the same time as *Wieland* but not published until 1803, strongly evinces the traces of both Godwin and native religious thought. Brown's closest friend, Elihu Hubbard Smith, was a graduate of Yale who introduced the novelist to Timothy Dwight, the grandson of Jonathan Edwards; and it is not impossible that Brown was familiar with the great theologian's writings. But Brown himself hinted at another source of influence, a source conned by Edwards and Godwin alike: John Milton. While Carwin perfects his ventriloquism, for example, he peruses Milton's *Comus* (p. 281);[8] and although *Paradise Lost* is not actually mentioned by name in the fragment, its theme is crucial and pervasive. Carwin is consumed by a perverse lust for knowledge which his father denounces as "incorrigible depravity" (pp. 275-76). After an almost supernatural fire that burns down his father's barn—a reminder, perhaps, of the fiery sword that the Angel Michael waved behind Adam and Eve as he drove them from Paradise—Carwin leaves the pastoral setting where he was born, wanders to the city, and catches the eye of the mysterious Ludloe, who proposes to finance him on a voyage to Europe. A Utopian schemer and apparent Illuminatus, Ludloe plays Falkland to Carwin's Caleb Williams. He seems to possess preternatural powers of which his protégé stands in awe. Like Milton's God, he projects a new Eden, and like Edwards's Christ, he demands a full and sincere confession from those seeking membership in the exalted order to which he belongs. "Perdition or felicity will hang upon that moment" (p. 344), says Ludloe in reference to the confession, adding that "concealment is impossible" and that every secret must be divulged (p. 350). Carwin, however, resolves to withhold the knowledge of his biloquism from his confessor; and shortly thereafter Brown abandoned the manuscript, leaving unanswered the question of his protagonist's fate.

It is in **Wieland,** of course, that he furnishes the answer, an answer that has been foreshadowed by Carwin's insatiable curiosity, his unwillingness to confess all, and his transformation into a Spanish Catholic: This last detail is especially significant in light of the conventional Gothic technique of displacing the action to a Catholic setting, with its ubiquitous decaying abbeys, monasteries, and catacombs. To embrace Catholicism, as Protestant authors indoctrinated with the theology of John Calvin knew in their bones, was to ensure perdition, since Catholics clung to the misguided belief that salvation could be won by spurning the world or performing good works within it. This was to deny the need for divine election and to gloss over the universal depravity of mankind, which rendered truly virtuous actions impossible without an infusion of the Holy Spirit. On the issue of salvation by works Catholics and Protestant Armenians locked arms, and what has passed as the anticlericalism of the Gothic school might more properly be viewed as a veiled protest against the waning of Calvinist dogma around the turn of the eighteenth century. That the Gothicists themselves frequently shared in the general disquietude of the age is true, but at the same time they were too thoroughly steeped in Puritanism to find the Catholic or Armenian alternative a meaningful

one. William Godwin, after all, went from Calvinism to atheism but was never tempted by the Church of England, and his hunger for innerworldly sainthood surely accounts at least in part for his attraction to the French Revolution. Carwin's adoption of Catholicism, to which Brown alluded again in **Wieland,** is not, therefore, simply a convenient device for endowing the villain with an aura of exoticism. Instead it is an outgrowth of the explicitly Calvinistic bias of the Gothic school and stamps Carwin as one of the damned, an unrepentant sinner who counts upon the false security of the legal covenant to preserve him from the vengeance of a righteous God. It is altogether consistent with his repudiation of Christ-Ludloe and his subsequent protests of innocence throughout the novel. Despite having set in motion the train of events that culminates in the younger Wieland's suicide, he will defend himself against Clara's accusations of depravity, allowing that his morals are "far from rigid" but insisting that he is not the "desperate or sordid criminal" that she charges him with being (p. 230).

And yet the almost oppressive theological temper of Brown's tale is barely sensed at the outset, the participants themselves confidently consigning it to the past. Although Clara concedes that the history of her father's strange death, which she recounts in the introductory chapters, has left an impression on her that "can never be effaced" (p. 21), the idyllic middle-class landscape inhabited by herself, her brother, Catherine, and Pleyel retains few traces of the morbid spirituality to which the elder Wieland fell prey. Brown's subtitle "An American Tale" suggests that he saw in his central foursome a microcosm of the bourgeois American society that by 1798 stood in defiant opposition to the Puritan past. Surely it is no coincidence that at one point in the narrative Pleyel refers to a Ciceronian oration that makes "the picture of a single family a model from which to sketch the condition of a nation" (p. 34). Unruffled rationality, moderation, and middle-class ease are the distinguishing marks of the Mettingen setting; the temple that the senior Wieland kept bare—"without seat, table, or ornament of any kind" (p. 12)—and consecrated to the worship of the Deity has been cluttered with a harpsichord, pedestal, and bust of Cicero, Enlightenment trappings that symbolize a rejection of the austere Protestantism of an earlier day. The God-charged universe of Cotton Mather and Jonathan Edwards has narrowed to a common sense world that would have gladdened the heart of Benjamin

Franklin. Even the childhood environment of the younger Wielands has been scrupulously based on enlightened principles, with special emphasis on the golden mean: "our education," comments Clara, "had been modeled by no religious standard" (p. 24), the aunt who raised her and her brother seldom deviating "into either extreme of rigor or lenity" (p. 22). Once a guide for personal conduct, religion has become merely a subject for casual debate, and assembled at their "fane" on the Schuylkill, the circle of intimates whiles away the hours in aimless cultural pursuits.

If the Wielands have renounced the past, however, Theodore has not succeeded in exorcising the ghost of his father, which continues to haunt him in the form of an inchoate longing for what the Puritans would have called a conversion experience. "Moral necessity, and calvinistic inspiration," according to Clara, "were the props on which my brother thought proper to repose" (p. 28). She further describes him as grave, thoughtful, and given to melancholy. But Brown has taken pains to distinguish Wieland from authentic Calvinists and to spell out the dangers inherent in his background and sensibility. While apprenticed to a merchant in England, the senior Wieland had come into contact with the doctrines of the Camissards, a Huguenot sect notorious for its antinomian excesses. Having emigrated to America with the intention of preaching to the Indians, he had connected himself to no established church and abjured all forms of social worship. A separatist and enthusiast, he had lived in daily expectation of a direct message from the Almighty. Even the mother of Clara and Theodore, although not a fanatic like their father, did not belong to any congregation and was a devout disciple of the mystical Count von Zinzendorf, whose separatist impulses were a thorn in the side of Gilbert Tennent. The aunt who reared the younger Wielands was a separatist of a different order, but a separatist nonetheless. She preserved her charges, in Clara's words, "from the corruption and tyranny of colleges and boarding-schools" (p. 22); and Theodore and his sister have carried on the family tradition in their own enlightened fashion. Fortunate enough to find their temperaments duplicated in Catherine and Pleyel, they have gradually withdrawn from "the society of others, and found every moment irksome that was not devoted to each other" (p. 23).

Thus Brown has carefully sketched in the flaws of upbringing and character that will eventually issue in Wieland's antinomian mania and Clara's fits of madness. Whereupon he introduces into the narrative the figure of Carwin, and his implicit criticism of American life begins to move in the direction of epic, as it becomes increasingly clear that the fable underlying his novel is Milton's *Paradise Lost.* Clara is utterly captivated by the appearance of Carwin, who begs at her door for water dressed in virtual rags. That a stranger who reminds her of a rustic clown should exert so powerful a hold on her imagination would seem absurd were it not for the fact that her portrait of him so strikingly resembles the fallen Angel Lucifer or the Wandering Jew Ahasuerus:

> yet his forehead, so far as shaggy locks would allow it to be seen, his eyes lustrously black, and possessing, in the midst of haggardness, a radiance inexpressibly serene and potent, and something in the rest of his features, which it would be vain to describe, but which betoken a mind of the highest order, were essential ingredients in the portrait.
>
> (p. 61)

The faded grandeur that Clara detects in Carwin's countenance plunges her into a maze of mournful associations which call into question the Edenic bliss of her present life, and for the first time since the tragedy of her father she is troubled by intimations of mortality: "Death must happen to all" (pp. 62-63). Although she argues that her infatuation with the mysterious wanderer should not be mistaken for love, there is good reason to believe that Clara is sexually drawn to him, and that the storm which rages outside her window while she studies his picture is both an omen of future disaster and an emblem of the tumultuous passions aroused by his presence. Indeed, it is a Miltonic storm such as accompanied the transgression in Eden, a circumstance which is entirely appropriate in view of the fact that Carwin will bring death and sin into the garden of *Wieland.* For he is Brown's Gothic tempter, and Clara has become the novelist's American Eve.

It is worth noting, for example, that the biloquist has but a single name. The absence of a surname or Christian name—for the reader never knows which one it is that Carwin lacks—implies an estrangement from society that brands him as an outcast and misfit. In spite of the apparent ease with which he insinuates himself into the Mettingen setting, Carwin's ultimate failure to shed his solitude places him in the company of archetypes such as Lucifer, Cain, and Ahasuerus. Bumbler that he proves to be, the biloquist is nevertheless modeled on Milton's conception of Satan. So extensive, in fact, are the parallels between *Wieland* and *Paradise Lost* that it is hard to imagine how they have been overlooked. Carwin's eloquence is an obvious case in point. Overhearing him converse with her servant, Clara is forcibly struck by the sweetness of his voice; and his uncanny powers of speech occasion the numerous misunderstandings that shatter the novel's surface tranquillity. Repeatedly Clara is under the misapprehension that he is speaking directly into her ear; in Milton's classic, Satan is discovered squatting like a toad, "close at the ear of Eve" (4.800). Envious of Eve's love for Adam, the Arch-Fiend is filled with wonder when he first beholds the primal parents, and the sight of their beauty, refulgent with the image of God, almost swerves him from his sinister purpose. Similarly, Carwin is jealous of Clara's passion for Pleyel, although he also expresses admiration for the latter's "exquisite sagacity" (p. 236), and he hesitates to employ his verbal skills against them. Clara in particular captures his fancy, Judith having told him that her mistress's "perfections were little less than divine" (p. 227). In *Paradise Lost,* Satan addresses Eve as scarcely inferior to the angels, and entering the sleeping form of the serpent, he literally licks the ground on which she treads (9.526).

There are, moreover, striking affinities between the dream in which Lucifer appears to Eve and entices her to the tree of knowledge, and that in which Wieland beckons Clara to the edge of an abyss. Clara's dream has generated a host of conflicting interpretations. To critics who favor the sentimental seduction reading, for example, the chasm evokes a latent fear of incest; to William H. Manly, it stands for the insanity that runs in the Wieland family.[9] Another interpretation, one based on Brown's indebtedness to Milton, seems more probable, however. In both the novel and the epic, the dreams eventually come true; beguiled by Satan, Eve eats of the forbidden fruit, and Clara is physically menaced by Theodore, who believes himself under a divine injunction to slay her. But the physical threat is less important, ultimately, than the fact that her brother compels Clara to confront the evil within herself. We will return later to this decisive turning point in her narrative; for the present, it is enough to suggest that the pit toward which she hastens is hell—the hell that awaits those who taste of the fruit of the tree of knowledge of good and evil. There are several hints to this effect. Clara is stopped short in her progress by a voice crying "Hold," by which Brown may have wished to recall the heavenly prohibition imposed on Adam and Eve. Further, the mysterious voice summons Clara to "Remember your father, and be faithful"; and she shud-

ders with fright, as if she beheld "suspended over me, the exterminating sword" (pp. 72-73).

But the portent of the dream is temporarily lost sight of, even by Clara herself, after the scene in which she approaches the closet door and is again arrested by the command to "Hold!" Imagining because of her dream that Theodore is her enemy, she leaps to the conclusion that he is the person hiding within the closet and calls to him to come out, exclaiming "I know you well." But the person who steals forth is Carwin, not Theodore, and the focus of danger is thus shifted to the biloquist (pp. 96-102). The brother becomes the other in a dramatic turnabout which has the effect of seeming to isolate evil in an external agent. The importance of this scene for Clara's development cannot be overstressed, since she will continue almost to the end of her narrative to regard the intruder as the sole cause of the sufferings that destroy her family's happiness. As Milton's God was careful to explain to the angels, however, He created man able to withstand temptation, thereby rendering him inexcusable for having sinned. Clara will only grasp this truth at the last.

This is not to say, of course, that Carwin is guiltless. Although her brother will eventually undermine Clara's conviction of her own innocence, it is the "double-tongued" wanderer who brings about her fall in the eyes of Pleyel. This is what the controversial seduction episode is really about: deceived by Carwin's ventriloquism, and convinced that Clara has succumbed to the villain's wiles, Pleyel charges her—in accents unmistakably Miltonic—with having committed the primal sin: "O wretch!—thus exquisitely fashioned—on whom nature seemed to have exhausted all her graces; with charms so awful and pure! how art thou fallen! From what height fallen! A ruin so complete—so unheard of!" (p. 117). Pleyel goes on to accuse Clara of consummate depravity, despairing that "In thy ruin, how will the felicity and honor of multitudes be involved" (pp. 117-18). He describes Carwin as the blackest of criminals, a Satanic schemer whose devices "no human intelligence is able to unravel" and who has leagued with infernal spirits in order to wage "a perpetual war against the happiness of mankind" (pp. 148-49). Clara herself now says of the biloquist that "this a foe from whose grasp no power of divinity can save me" (p. 126). As her words indicate, Carwin has completely replaced her brother as the source of her fears. And indeed Pleyel pictures Clara, in what appears to be a deliberate allusion to her dream, as "rushing to the verge of a dizzy precipice," led on by the cunning seducer (p. 147). The denunciations that he hurls at her, and her indignant protests of purity, recall the bickering between Adam and Eve after the Fall:

Thus they in mutual accusation spent
The fruitless hours, but neither self-condemning,
And of their vain contest appeared no end.
[9. 1187-89]

"Neither self-condemning"—Milton's words go to the core of the novel's concern, and underline the mutual failure of Clara and Pleyel to assume responsibility for their transgressions. What is more, as the confrontation at Pleyel's house demonstrates, both are unwilling to go beyond reliance on the legal covenant. Pleyel takes upon himself the office of unforgiving judge—Clara calls him "inexorable" (p. 129)—and he denies her the Christian charity that might have repaired the misunderstandings engendered by Carwin's duplicity. He holds her to the relentless letter of the law:

An inscrutable providence has fashioned thee for some end. Thou wilt live, no doubt, to fulfil the purposes of thy maker, if he repent not of his workmanship, and send not his vengeance to exterminate thee, ere the measure of thy days be full. Surely nothing in the shape of man can vie with thee!

(p. 135)

Clara likewise spurns the message of Christ and demands justice instead of mercy. "I come hither not to confess," she informs her accuser, "but to vindicate" (p. 133). Here the Godwinian aspect of Brown's tale comes to the fore, and here too the true meaning of the secrecy theme is cast into bold relief. The issue for Brown is manifestly the reluctance of sinful man to lay bare his heart—an ordeal that Poe, for one, considered impossible, and that Edwards regarded as essential for salvation. Although Clara hears out Pleyel in silence and persists in believing herself blameless, she has been guilty of concealing her true feelings from him, and her concealment has contributed to their estrangement as much as Carwin's officiousness. She has also kept secret the interview with the would-be murderer whose summons interrupted her dream at the summerhouse—an interview, as Pleyel rightly surmises, that took place with the Satanic biloquist, albeit that Clara was then ignorant of his identity. The reader knows, however, from Clara's own words, words written after the fact but inserted into her narrative prior to the climactic scene with Pleyel, that her "scruples were preposterous and criminal. . . . My errors have taught me thus much wisdom;

that those sentiments which we ought not to disclose, it is criminal to harbour" (p. 90).

Clara's fall, like that of the primal couple, ushers sin and death into the Edenic world of **Wieland.** Having left Pleyel's house—significantly, he has announced his intention of setting out on a long journey—she returns to a Mettingen despoiled by her brother's murderous rampage. Overcome by what she sees, she casts the entire burden of guilt on Carwin. She assumes that he is the murderer of her brother's family; and even Theodore's confession does not shake her belief that the author of woe is the biloquist, to whom she attributes supernatural powers. This is to deny man's complicity in the Fall and to reject—in Edwards's words—"The Great Christian Doctrine of Original Sin." To Clara's disordered mind, evil is extrinsic, not integral to human nature:

O brother! spare me, spare thyself: There is thy betrayer. He counterfeited the voice and face of an angel, for the purpose of destroying thee and me. He has this moment confessed it. He is able to speak where he is not. He is leagued with hell, but will not avow it; yet he confesses that the agency was his

(p. 245)

In this speech, Clara is implicitly proclaiming her own innocence as well as Theodore's and taking refuge in the legal covenant—the covenant predicated on the mistaken notion that fallen man is essentially unfallen, and that Lucifer alone is responsible for sin. Moments later, however, she is brought up sharply by the discovery that she is prepared to defend herself against Wieland's attack by plunging her penknife into his heart, a weapon that she has all along insisted that she will use only against herself. This realization sets off a reversal of sentiment that recalls Caleb Williams's despair after the trial of Falkland:

I estimate my own deserving; a hatred, immortal and inexorable, is my due, I listen to my own pleas, and find them empty and false: yes, I acknowledge that my guilt surpasses that of all mankind: I confess that the curses of a world, and the frowns of a deity, are inadequate to my demerits. Is there a thing in the world worthy of infinite abhorrence? It is I

(pp. 249-50)

Admittedly, the act that Clara contemplates is one of self-defense—but that is precisely Brown's point. For although any court of law would deliver a verdict of justifiable homicide (just as Caleb Williams is vindicated in a court of law), Clara—finding herself capable of slaying her own brother—has ceased to think in terms of the law. She has finally accepted the fact of human corruption: the "adders" of sin are now lodged in her own breast (p. 256).

Clara is prostrated with grief and self-loathing after the death of her brother. Much like Milton's Eve, she craves "quick deliverance from life and all the ills that attend it" (p. 261), and she revolts against the inevitable decree that she must quit the scene of her former bliss:

> O unexpected stroke, worse than of Death!
> Must I thus leave thee, Paradise: thus leave
> Thee, native soil, these happy walks and shades,
> Fit haunt of gods?
>
> [9.268-71]

Clara has accepted her culpability, but she still shrinks from its consequences. It is not until her home is consumed by flames—as in the **Memoirs of Carwin,** the conflagration recalls Michael's fiery sword—that she resigns herself to banishment from the garden and agrees to accompany her uncle on a voyage to Europe. The last chapter of the novel is therefore dated at Montpellier in France, and is written, significantly enough, three years after the narrative proper. It finds Clara chastened but "not destitute of happiness" (p. 262), for her sanity has been restored and she has been reunited with her American Adam. She now admits that "no human virtue is secure from degeneracy" (p. 270), and she has made a full confession of her former sentiments to Pleyel. Inevitably one is reminded of Eve's moving speech to Adam in *Paradise Lost*: "Living or dying, from thee I will not hide / What thoughts in my unquiet breast are risen . . ." (9.974-75). In Calvinist terms, Clara has been reborn through the agency of Christ: she has bared her soul and given her assent to the doctrine of original sin. "It will not escape your notice," she writes, "that the evils of which Carwin and Maxwell were the authors, owed their existence to the errors of the sufferers" (p. 273). Man is partner with Satan in the Fall.

In the last book of *Paradise Lost,* Adam almost rejoices over his sin because of Michael's prophecy of the coming of Christ; by the concluding pages of Brown's novel, Clara has grown to a measure of self-awareness that was beyond her when she dwelt in the Mettingen Eden. The transformation of Brown's title refers, then, both to the Fall and the promise of redemption; and it is altogether fitting that Hawthorne's *Marble Faun* (1860) was published in England under the title *Transformation,* its subject being the Fortunate Fall. As for Carwin, the ventriloquist acknowledges his misconduct, but, as he correctly insists, he has committed no crime punishable by human law. "I cannot justify my conduct," he tells Clara, "yet my only crime was curiosity" (p. 231). Caleb Williams's crime was no different: curiosity, after all, is the primal sin. Escaping the clutches of Ludloe, Carwin makes his way into a remote district of Pennsylvania, where he engages "in the harmless pursuits of agriculture" (p. 268). Blind to his own depravity, ignorant of his need for grace, the villain returns to the garden from which Clara and Pleyel have been expelled and becomes an "innocent" American yeoman. This is Brown's devastating judgment on Franklin's America: it no longer has any place for those who penetrate to the truth of the human heart. Clara is doomed to permanent exile from a land which has lost the sense of sin.

The apologetic tone of Brown's "advertisement," and his apprehensions concerning his tale's reception, are reminiscent of the somewhat defensive posture adopted by Edwards in the preface to *The Great Christian Doctrine of Original Sin Defended* (1757). Barely forty years separate the publication of the two works, both of which deal, as Brown announced in his "advertisement," with "the moral constitution of man" (p. 3). Edwards, writing in the aftermath of the Great Awakening, still retained some hope of restoring his countrymen to "the principles and scheme of religion maintained by our pious and excellent forefathers."[10] No such hope animates Brown's "veiled sermon," as Fred Lewis Pattee once called it.[11] And so it is fitting that **Wieland** is built on the fable of *Paradise Lost*. For in going back to Milton for his inspiration, Brown was doing more than paying tribute to the greatest of Puritan authors. He was also addressing a theme that was to engage a host of later American novelists: the promise of America, he strongly suggests, is the "paradise lost" in **Wieland.**

Notes

1. David Lee Clark, *Charles Brockden Brown: Pioneer Voice of America* (Durham: Duke Univ. Press, 1952), pp. 168-69. See also Harry R. Warfel, *Charles Brockden Brown: American Gothic Novelist* (Gainesville, Fla.: Univ. of Florida Press, 1949), pp. 104-5.

2. For important reassessments of the Gothic novel, see Lowry Nelson, Jr., "Night Thoughts on the Gothic Novel," *The Yale Review,* 52 (Winter 1963), 236-57; Robert D. Hume, "Gothic Versus Romantic: A Revaluation of the Gothic Novel," *PMLA,* 84 (1969), 282-90: and the essays in G. R. Thompson, ed., *The Gothic Imagination: Essays in Dark Romanticism* (Pullman, Wash.: Washington State Univ. Press, 1974), particularly Joel Porte's "In the Hands of an Angry God: Religious Terror in Gothic Fiction," pp. 42-64. The religious theme in Brown has been noted by Larzer

Ziff, "A Reading of *Wieland*," *PMLA*, 67 (1962), 51-57; and Donald A. Ringe, *Charles Brockden Brown* (New York: Twayne Publishers, 1966), pp. 25-48.

3. See Ziff, pp. 51-57.

4. Porte, pp. 52-55.

5. On Edwards's influence on Godwin, see Alfred Owen Aldridge, "Jonathan Edwards and William Godwin on Virtue," *American Literature*, 18 (1947), 308-18.

6. William Godwin, *Caleb Williams*, ed. David Mc-Cracken (New York: Oxford Univ. Press, 1970), pp. 233, 273, 278-79, 296, 323, 325-26.

7. Crane Brinton, *A Decade of Revolution: 1789-1799* (New York: Harper Torchbooks, 1963), pp. 158-61. The similarity between the Puritan and French Revolutions has been examined in detail by Michael Walzer, *The Revolution of the Saints: A Study in the Origins of Radical Politics* (Cambridge, Mass.: Harvard Univ. Press, 1965).

8. I will be referring to Fred Lewis Pattee's edition of *Wieland; or The Transformation*, which includes the fragment *Memoirs of Carwin the Biloquist* (New York: Harcourt, Brace & World, 1926). Page references will appear in the text.

9. Ziff, p. 54; also see Leslie A. Fiedler, *Love and Death in the American Novel*, rev. ed. (New York: Dell, 1966), pp. 74-104, 126-61; and William M. Manly, "The Importance of Point of View in Brockden Brown's *Wieland*," *American Literature*, 35 (1963), 317-18.

10. Jonathan Edwards, *The Great Christian Doctrine of Original Sin Defended*, ed. Clyde C. Holbrook (New Haven: Yale Univ. Press, 1970), p. 102.

11. Introduction to *Wieland*, p. xxviii.

FURTHER READING

Bibliography

Witherington, Paul. "Charles Brockden Brown: A Bibliographical Essay." *Early American Literature* 9 (1974): 164-87.

Bibliography of critical assessments of Brown's works, arranged chronologically.

Biography

Clark, David Lee. *Charles Brockden Brown: Pioneer Voice of America*, Durham: Duke University Press, 1952, 363 p.

Important critical biography emphasizing Brown's radical political and social thought.

Criticism

Baym, Nina. "A Minority Reading of *Wieland*." In *Critical Essays on Charles Brockden Brown*, edited by Bernard Rosenthal, pp. 87-103. Boston: G. K. Hall, 1981.

Takes issue with other scholars' opinions of Brown's writing, and praises Brown's literary achievements and genius; focuses on Wieland.

Bradshaw, Charles C. "The New England Illuminati: Conspiracy and Causality in Charles Brockden Brown's *Wieland*." *The New England Quarterly* 76, no. 3 (September 2003): 356-77.

Examines Brown's depiction of contemporary events and circumstances in late-eighteenth-century New England in Wieland.

Christophersen, Bill. "Picking Up the Knife: A Psycho-Historical Reading of *Wieland*." *American Studies* 27, no. 1 (spring 1986): 115-26.

Focuses on Clara's transformation as a metaphor for the transformation of America from British colony to young nation.

Goddu, Teresa A. "Diseased Discourse: Charles Brockden Brown's *Arthur Mervyn*." In *Gothic America: Narrative, History, and the Nation*, pp. 31-51. New York: Columbia University Press, 1997.

Delineates how Brown utilizes the Gothic to depict both the causes of and possible solutions to societal ills in Arthur Mervyn.

Grabo, Norman S. *The Coincidental Art of Charles Brockden Brown.* Chapel Hill: University of North Carolina Press, 1981, 209 p.

Maintains that coincidental occurrences in Brown's fiction are part of a conscious, discernible artistic pattern.

Krause, Sydney J. "Penn's Elm and Edgar Huntly: 'Dark Instruction to the Heart.'" *American Literature* 66, no. 3 (September 1994): 463-84.

Analyzes some of the historical details in Edgar Huntly and comments on Brown's appropriation of history in his gloomy fictional depiction of the American experience.

Lee, A. Robert. "A Darkness Visible: The Case of Charles Brockden Brown." In *American Horror Fiction: From Brockden Brown to Stephen King*, pp. 13-32. London: Macmillan, 1990.

Examines the characteristics of Brown's novels that contain elements of the genre of horror.

Levine, Paul. "The American Novel Begins." *American Scholar* 35 (1966): 134-48.

Postulates that Brown's works anticipate rather than begin the tradition of the American novel.

Loshe, Lillie Deming. "The Gothic and the Revolutionary." In *The Early American Novel*, pp. 29-58. New York: Columbia University Press, 1907.

Claims that the importance of the Gothic novel in early American fiction evidences Brown's importance as an author.

Pattee, Fred Lewis. Introduction to *Wieland; or, The Transformation*, by Charles Brockden Brown, pp. ix-xlvi. New York: Harcourt Brace Jovanovich, 1926.

Identifies rational, sentimental, and Gothic strains in Wieland.

Pribek, Thomas. "A Note on Depravity in *Wieland*." *Philological Quarterly* 64, no. 2 (spring 1985): 273-79.

Refutes the notion that the characters in Wieland *are inherently evil, suggesting instead that they should be read as rational characters who are undone by the villainy of an outsider.*

Ringe, Donald A. "Charles Brockden Brown." In *American Gothic: Imagination and Reason in Nineteenth-Century Fiction*, pp. 36-57. Lexington: University Press of Kentucky, 1982.

Discusses how Brown developed the Gothic in his writing by adapting a European mode of fiction to the very different conditions of American life.

——. *Charles Brockden Brown.* Revised edition. New York: Twayne Publishers, 1991, 141 p.

Provides a detailed analysis and critical evaluation of Brown's life and works.

Rombes, Nicholas, Jr. "'All Was Lonely, Darksome, and Waste': *Wieland* and the Construction of the New Republic." *Studies in American Fiction* 22 (1994): 37-46.

Asserts that through the characters of Carwin and Clara, Brown was recommending that America embrace a democracy that would allow different viewpoints to be heard.

Scheiber, Andrew J. "'The Arm Lifted Against Me': Love, Terror, and the Construction of Gender in *Wieland*." *Early American Literature* 26, no. 2 (1991): 173-94.

Explores the ambiguity of Clara's characterization, attributing it to her status within masculine and patriarchal institutions of the time.

Schneck, Peter. "*Wieland*'s Testimony: Charles Brockden Brown and the Rhetoric of Evidence." *REAL: The Yearbook of Research in English and American Literature* 18 (2002): 167-213.

Discusses the treatment of evidence and testimony and their relationship to rhetoric and moral judgment in Wieland.

Sickels, Eleanor. "Shelley and Charles Brockden Brown." *PMLA: Publications of the Modern Language Association of America* 45, no. 4 (December 1930): 1116-28.

Attempts to define the extent to which Percy Shelley was influenced by Brown.

Vilas, Martin S. *Charles Brockden Brown; A Study of Early American Fiction.* Burlington, Vt.: Free Press Association, 1904, 66 p.

Examines Brown's life and works and evaluates his lasting influence on American literature.

OTHER SOURCES FROM GALE:

Additional coverage of Brown's life and career is contained in the following sources published by Thomson Gale: *American Writers Supplement*, Vol. 1; *Concise Dictionary of American Literary Biography 1640-1865*; *Dictionary of Literary Biography*, Vols. 37, 59, 73; *Feminist Writers*; *Literary Movements for Students*, Vol. 1; *Literature Resource Center*; *Nineteenth-Century Literature Criticism*, Vols. 22, 74, 122; *Reference Guide to American Literature*, Ed. 4; *St. James Guide to Horror, Ghost & Gothic Writers*; and *Twayne's United States Authors*.

ANGELA CARTER

(1940 - 1992)

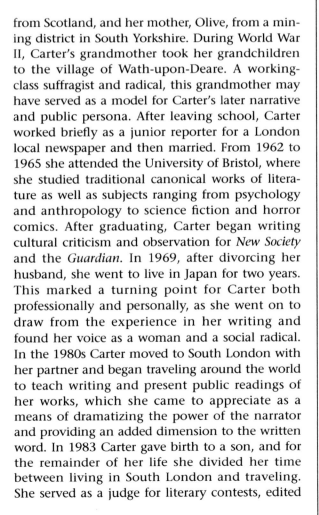

(Full name Angela Olive Carter) English novelist, short story writer, nonfiction writer, scriptwriter, and author of children's books.

Carter is best remembered for her science fiction and fantasy writings in which she undertakes a feminist critique of Western history and culture. Combining components of Gothicism, surrealism, eroticism, pornography, myth, and fairy tales, Carter explores such themes as violence, the distribution of power in contemporary society, and female sexuality. Carter's work is distinguished by its display of unrestrained imagination, colorful imagery, and sensuous prose. Equally notable are the Dickensian eccentricities of her characters and her talent, as one critic has noted, for seamlessly infusing realistic narratives with elements of the macabre and fantastic. Although alternately praised and faulted for her extravagant Gothic approach, Carter is highly regarded as a writer of unique and imaginative fiction and sharply political and insightful feminist nonfiction.

BIOGRAPHICAL INFORMATION

Carter was born in London, England, on May 7, 1940. Her journalist father, Hugh Stalker, came from Scotland, and her mother, Olive, from a mining district in South Yorkshire. During World War II, Carter's grandmother took her grandchildren to the village of Wath-upon-Deare. A working-class suffragist and radical, this grandmother may have served as a model for Carter's later narrative and public persona. After leaving school, Carter worked briefly as a junior reporter for a London local newspaper and then married. From 1962 to 1965 she attended the University of Bristol, where she studied traditional canonical works of literature as well as subjects ranging from psychology and anthropology to science fiction and horror comics. After graduating, Carter began writing cultural criticism and observation for *New Society* and the *Guardian*. In 1969, after divorcing her husband, she went to live in Japan for two years. This marked a turning point for Carter both professionally and personally, as she went on to draw from the experience in her writing and found her voice as a woman and a social radical. In the 1980s Carter moved to South London with her partner and began traveling around the world to teach writing and present public readings of her works, which she came to appreciate as a means of dramatizing the power of the narrator and providing an added dimension to the written word. In 1983 Carter gave birth to a son, and for the remainder of her life she divided her time between living in South London and traveling. She served as a judge for literary contests, edited collections, compiled anthologies, and wrote introductions and essays. Carter died of cancer on February 16, 1992.

MAJOR WORKS

Carter described herself as a Gothic writer, and early on in her works she displayed a fondness for decadent opulence, squalor, darkness, and sexual violence, elements that she intertwined with feminist and philosophical concerns. Carter's vivid descriptions of Britain's counterculture create a surreal atmosphere in which strange incidents are commonplace. The protagonist of *Shadow Dance* (1966) is portrayed as the embodiment of the apathy and amorality of his generation. Acting on impulse, he disfigures his beautiful girlfriend and eventually commits murder. *The Magic Toyshop* (1967) depicts the sexual coming-of-age of a young woman who loses her parents and must live in a household of eccentric relatives. *Several Perceptions* (1968) concerns a suicidal young man and his encounters with various strange individuals. *Heroes and Villains* (1969) is a futuristic tale of Earth a century after atomic devastation has splintered its population into antagonistic factions. *Love* (1971), a bleak story of the obsessive nature of love, centers on a young man whose suicidal wife and drug-abusing brother are dependent upon him. *The Infernal Desire Machines of Doctor Hoffman* (1972) recounts the efforts of the protagonist to restore reality in a world where machines give unconscious images concrete form. In *The Passion of New Eve* (1977), a fervent denunciation of sexism and machismo, a man experiences rape and other brutalizations after being surgically transformed into a beautiful woman. A number of the characters in *Nights at the Circus* (1984), winner of the James Tait Black Memorial Prize, are archetypes of female oppression and liberation. In this novel Carter offers a symbolic portrait of the female condition, populating her story with the bizarre characters of a traveling circus and focusing on the personal liberation of a six-foot-tall winged woman.

Carter's numerous stories, which, like her novels, are derived from fables, fairy tales, and mythology, have been collected in three volumes: *Fireworks: Nine Profane Pieces* (1974), *The Bloody Chamber and Other Stories* (1979), and *Black Venus* (1985). In the oft-cited "Afterword" from *Fireworks*, which many critics have cited as her literary manifesto, Carter argued that the tale, unlike the short story, "interprets everyday experience through a system of imagery derived from subter-

ranean areas behind everyday experience." In that essay, Carter also defines the gothicism that informs her work, stating that the tradition "grandly ignores the value systems of our institutions; it deals entirely with the profane." She notes too its themes of cannibalism and incest, its exaggeration of reality, its ornate and unnatural style, and black humor—all of which seek to provoke unease. The sense of unease in Carter's tales is derived from her use of violence and eroticism and the startling images she presents of female sexuality. The image of blood, for example, as a symbol of female menstruation and defloration is featured prominently in her short fiction. In a story from *The Bloody Chamber and Other Stories*, Carter describes a necklace as a "bloody bandage of rubies," thus emphasizing the violence of sexual intercourse and the loss of virginity through the image of a slit throat while at the same time pointing out the economic value society attaches to chastity. Carter also wrote a fictionalized reconstruction of parts of the life of Edgar Allan Poe, entitled "The Cabinet of Edgar Allan Poe," which was published in the magazine *Interzone* in 1982.

In her most often discussed nonfiction work, *The Sadeian Woman: An Exercise in Cultural History* (1979), Carter examines the two feminine stereotypes of pornographic literature: the dangerous temptress and the innocent victim. Carter argues that the writing of the Marquis de Sade, whose characters Justine and Juliette embodied these stereotypes, can be read as feminist satire of the sexual roles men create for women. Ultimately, however, Carter finds de Sade's quest for the limits of acceptable behavior a failure, believing that he succumbed to an acceptance of traditional sexual roles. *Nothing Sacred* (1982) is an anthology of Carter's feminist and political articles. Carter's nonfiction illuminates many of the themes and ideas about the dark side of human nature and society that she sets forth in her fiction.

CRITICAL RECEPTION

While writers as diverse as Anthony Burgess, Salman Rushdie, and John Hawkes have expressed great admiration for Carter's writing, other reviewers have responded with incomprehension or revulsion. The elements of the fantastic upon which Carter focuses her narratives have been assessed as confusing and unbelievable by many critics. Her extravagant Gothic approach has been alternately praised and faulted by commentators. Additionally, while Carter's revisions of traditional fairy tales have been lauded overall, some commentators have lamented the absence of concrete alternatives for her heroines. Such critics argue that because Carter rewrote the tales within their original structures, she robbed her protagonists of any real sense of choice and actually perpetuated patriarchal precepts. Feminist critics, however, have embraced what they characterize as Carter's unwavering honesty and commitment to her social and political standards in her works.

Today Carter's stories are widely anthologized and she is studied in schools and universities as the most important English fantasist of her generation. Those who admire her works point to their humor, wit, and pathos even in presentations of horrific situations and depictions of disturbing characters. Carter is regarded too as the most subversive and radical proponent of a modern neo-Gothic movement, as she celebrates the imminent collapse of traditional notions of order. Carter uses gothicism to provoke unease in the hopes that misguided patriarchal assumptions about women and sexuality might be overturned. Thus she uses horror, violence, pornography, surrealism, and dark humor to criticize and dismantle patriarchal cultural conventions, offering a uniquely vivid feminist critique of Western history and culture.

PRINCIPAL WORKS

Shadow Dance (novel) 1966; also published as *Honeybuzzard*, 1967

Unicorn (poetry) 1966

The Magic Toyshop (novel) 1967

Several Perceptions (novel) 1968

Heroes and Villains (novel) 1969

The Donkey Prince (juvenilia) 1970

Miss Z, the Dark Young Lady (juvenilia) 1970

Love (novel) 1971; revised edition, 1987

The Infernal Desire Machines of Doctor Hoffman (novel) 1972; also published as *The War of Dreams*, 1974

Fireworks: Nine Profane Pieces (short stories) 1974; revised as *Fireworks: Nine Stories in Various Disguises*, 1981

The Passion of New Eve (novel) 1977

The Bloody Chamber and Other Stories (short stories) 1979

The Sadeian Woman: An Exercise in Cultural History (nonfiction) 1979; also published as *The Sadeian Woman and the Ideology of Pornography*, 1979

Nothing Sacred: Selected Writings (essays) 1982; revised edition, 1992

Nights at the Circus (novel) 1984

Black Venus (short stories) 1985; also published as *Saints and Strangers*, 1986

Come unto These Yellow Sands: Four Radio Plays (broadcasts) 1985

The Virago Book of Fairy Tales [editor] (fairy tales) 1990; also published as *The Old Wives' Tale Book*, 1990

Wise Children (novel) 1991

Expletives Deleted: Selected Writings (essays) 1992

The Second Virago Book of Fairy Tales [editor] (fairy tales) 1992; also published as *Sometimes Strange Things Still Happen*, 1993

American Ghosts and Old World Wonders (short stories) 1993

Burning Your Boats: Collected Short Stories (short stories) 1995

The Curious Room: Plays, Film Scripts and an Opera (plays, scripts, and libretto) 1996

Shaking a Leg: Collected Journalism and Writings (nonfiction) 1997

PRIMARY SOURCES

ANGELA CARTER AND ANNA KATSAVOS (INTERVIEW DATE 1988)

SOURCE: Carter, Angela, and Anna Katsavos. "An Interview with Angela Carter." *Review of Contemporary Fiction* 14, no. 3 (fall 1994): 11-18.

In the following excerpt from an interview conducted in New York City in 1988, Carter comments on some of her works.

The stories in **The Bloody Chamber** are very firmly grounded in the Indo-European popular tradition, even in the way they look. A friend of mine has just done a collection of literary fairy tales from seventeenth- and eighteenth-century France, things like the original "Beauty and the Beast," which is in fact from the oral tradition. There's this long history in Europe of taking elements from the oral tradition and making them into very elaborate literary conventions, but all the elements in that particular piece, *The Bloody Chamber,* are very lush.

I was looking at it again last week. I read from it for the first time in ages the other night, and I thought, this is pretty cholesterol-rich because of the fact that they all take place in invented landscapes. Some of the landscapes are reinvented ones. **"The Bloody Chamber"** story itself is set quite firmly in the Mont Saint Michel, which is this castle on an island off the coast of Brittany; and a lot of the most exotic landscapes in it, the Italian landscapes, were quite legit. **"The Tiger's Bride"** landscape, admittedly, is touristic, but it's one of the palaces in Mantua that has the most wonderful jewels, and that city is set in the Po Valley, which is very flat and very far out, so in the summer you can imagine the mist rolling over. The landscapes there [*The Bloody Chamber*] are quite real. Even the werewolf stories are set in some horror-filled invented landscapes, but there's more a kind of down-to-earthness in those stories.

. . . . .

I was reading **"The Company of Wolves"** the other day, and there are a whole lot of verbal games in that that I really enjoy doing, "the deer departed," for example. . . . There was one thing in the movie *The Company of Wolves,* when the werewolf-husband says he's just going out to answer a call of nature, and one of the critics wrote to me and said, "I didn't even notice this the first time." That's the sort of thing I like doing. These are sort of private jokes with myself and with whoever notices, and I used to enjoy doing that very much. There are lots of them in *Nights at the Circus,* which was intended as a comic novel.

I've always thought that my stories were quite loaded with jokes, but the first story that I wrote that was supposed to be really funny, out and out funny, was a **"Puss-in-Boots"** story in *The Bloody Chamber.* I mailed that to a radio place, and they censored it. (It was done on what we call Radio Three, an art channel, which uses a lot of material from BBC Radio and World Service that you don't get here.) They cut it! They removed, according to the producer, about half a spool of bed springs!

. . . . .

There's a story in *The Bloody Chamber* called **"The Lady and the House of Love,"** part of which derives from a movie version that I saw of a story by Dostoyevsky. And in the movie, which is very good, the woman, who is a very passive person and is very much in distress, asks herself

the question, "Can a bird sing only the song it knows, or can it learn a new song?" Have we got the capacity at all of singing new songs? It's very important that if we haven't, we might as well stop now. Can the marionette in that story behave in a way that she's not programmed to behave? Is it possible?

GENERAL COMMENTARY

GINA WISKER (ESSAY DATE 1993)

SOURCE: Wisker, Gina. "At Home All Was Blood and Feathers: The Werewolf in the Kitchen—Angela Carter and Horror." In *Creepers: British Horror and Fantasy in the Twentieth Century,* edited by Clive Bloom, pp. 161-75. Boulder, Colo.: Pluto Press, 1993.

In the following essay, Wisker surveys Carter's use of horror, fantasy, and the Gothic.

A house full of locked doors that open only into other rooms with other locked doors, for, upstairs and downstairs, all the rooms lead in and out of one another like a maze in a bad dream.
'The Fall River Axe Murders'[1]

Angela Carter's sense of horror is based on the grotesque, the bizarre and excessive, a kind of baroquely overlaid nightmare which has uneasy echoes for us. She investigates the stuff of myth and dreams and in doing so unearths rather unpleasant, perverse sexual fantasies, digging further behind the suburban mind to identify the interest in the werewolf tale, the fairytales of Bluebeard and his wives and Beauty and the Beast. In investigating our subconscious horrors, Carter brings a chill to the domestic and the everyday. Opening a kitchen drawer in the Carter kitchens of our minds, we are always like Melanie in *The Magic Toyshop* likely to meet something horrid:

Melanie hummed to herself as she hung cups from their hooks and propped the plates. She opened the dresser drawer to put away the knives and spoons. In the dresser drawer was a freshly severed hand, all bloody at the roots.

The details are domestic and realistic, the episode and object monstrous, inexplicable, though Uncle Philip is a sort of urban Bluebeard in his own way, and Melanie has been thinking of Poe. In Carter's horror, the mazes of the ordinary mind in the ordinary house are entered to reveal gothic torture chambers and spiral staircases leading down to dungeons.

In **'The Fall River Axe Murders'** Carter looks at the catalysts, the events and moments which made murder inevitable in the claustrophobic middle-class normality of the Fall River, Massachusetts Borden household. She does not linger on the blood. Threat permeates the descriptions: of ties which 'garotte' their virtuous wearers and the oppressive constricting clothes the women wear in this sweating, constrained household. Carter investigates. Her probing of details reveals gaps and silences, 'what the girls do on their own is unimaginable to me' and of Emma, Lizzie's sister that, 'she is a blank space'. (**Black Venus**) The iron-backed, capital-accumulating father, the repressed, stifled sisters, the air of suppurating normality; these permeate Carter's descriptions of this fated family, our knowledge of whose violent fate lurks and drips over every restrained comment, calm as the clichéd 'still waters' of Lizzie's nature as she drives hatpins into her hat or weighs the axe which slaughtered her pigeons to make a pie for her stepmother.

Horror in much of Angela Carter's writing captures a sense of a potion containing the monstrous and the everyday. Lizzie Borden is a figure for this, and we are reminded that given the right circumstances and the appropriate kind of suburban claustrophobia, we might all erupt and give our family 40 whacks with an axe.

Carter explores those locked rooms. The mazes and corridors and doors of conformity and normality which we use to confuse and hide away our destructive drives, and our nightmares are replicated in the twists and turns of the fiction's realistic artifice, while networks of imagery hint, suggest and occasionally dramatically reveal the sources of the terror, the disgust and the horror. There are blood, feathers and much worse, in all of Angela Carter's kitchens. 'The structure of fantastic narratives is one founded upon contradictions.'[2] There are many recognisable realistic details, dates, times, typical clothing and furniture in the text. The places are familiar, and at the same time the surreal and the symbolic provide another layer of meaning. Metaphor combines with metonymy and the oxymoronic mixture is the fabric of her language.

Carter's fiction disinters and utilises the stuff of dreams. The fiction proves dreams palpably 'real', and so shows itself as psychologically based horror which owes much to Freud, Jung and to Melanie Klein. Her dream—and magic-based landscapes are rendered tangible because, she insists, dreams are part of our lives, and related to the myths we use to describe and direct our lives, 'There is certainly confusion about the nature of dreams which are in fact perfectly real: they are real as dreams and they're full of *real* meaning as dreams.'[3]

Like Bruno Bettelheim, whose work influenced **The Bloody Chamber**, Carter uses dream and fantasy material to reflect inner experiences and processes, ways of rendering and coping with the palpable conscious world and the reactions of the unconscious.

The break with the notion of a straightjacket of the real releases energies leading to a fuller understanding of how meanings are created, values constructed and versions of worth and of reality validated over other versions. Fantasy is a useful mode 'Because it is a narrative structured upon contraries, fantasy tells of limits, and it is particularly revealing in pointing to the edge of the "real".'[4] And as Jackson says, 'breaking single, reductive "truths", the fantastic traces a space within a society's cognitive frame. It introduces multiple, contradictory "truths": it becomes polysemic.'[5]

Horror, gothic and the use of fantasy combine in Carter's work. The collapse of boundaries and divisions, between the animate and the inanimate is a regular element of fantasy, while one chief tool of terror is the reduction of man to an object, a machine, a doll or an automaton. This is a frequent characteristic in an Angela Carter story or novel. In her examination of sexual politics and their psychological motivation and their social representations, she repeatedly presents scenarios where women are manipulated as marionettes (**The Magic Toyshop**), or preferred as tableaux vivants: disempowered objects of desire, as in the hideous living-sex museum of Madame Schreck in **Nights at the Circus,** or preferred dead and kept as mementoes in Bluebeard's castle. She allies her examination of the basis of terror and horror with an interest in sexual power and perversion, and so it is that the ones rendered immobile and automated are usually women in the hands of men, manipulated by power or for money; it is a logical enactment of the 'living doll' image.

The most consistently developed example of the recurring automaton, puppet or doll image in Carter's fiction can be found in the early '**The Loves of the Lady Purple**' (**Fireworks**) where the doll who enacts the quiet circus professor's violent erotic fantasies, comes to life and finally repeats them in reality, draining him in an act of vampirism.

The Asiatic professor reminds us of Carter the author.

> The puppet master is always dusted with a little darkness. In direct relation to his skill he propagates the most bewildering enigmas for, the more lifelike his marionettes, the more godlike his marionettes and the more radical the symbiosis between inarticulate doll and articulating fingers.

He acts as intermediary between audience and the dolls, the 'undead', here deliberately described in the language used to describe vampires. The puppet master's dolls are a mixture of magic and realism; the stories they enact speak to the audience of a certain repressed and unspeakable reality and the more extreme, bizarre or perverse the incidents in which they are involved, the closer the recognition of those selves and secrets the readership keep behind their own locked doors.

The professor has no language which can be understood and his apprentice is deaf, his other foundling helper dumb, but the Lady Purple blazons her messages in her actions accompanied by the appropriately weird but untranslatable stories of the professor. As Queen of the Night, the Lady Purple, object of all the professor's sexual fantasies, is 'filled with necromantic vigour' with the vitality of the professor passing directly through into her, draining him while she embodies that traditional perverse twinning of sex and pain, the erotic and power. She is 'a distillation of those of a born woman . . . the quintessence of eroticism'. Nightly she acts out the story invented of her life, lusts and eventual reduction to a marionette. The stylised, symbolic puppet characters and sexual scenarios are equally figures 'in a rhetoric' where the abstract essence of erotic woman can be bought, used, manipulated and later shelved. The constant oscillation between the language of artifice and the language of the real, tells the story Lady Purple enacts, as if it were a true record.

Ironically her power is emphasised as one who encourages the acting out of fantasies which then reduce her lovers to objects. 'She, the sole perpetrator of desire, proliferated malign fantasies all around her and used her lovers as the canvas on which she executed boudoir masterpieces of destruction. Skins melted in the electricity she generated.' For those watching the show she embodies the object of their desire as well as their fears, rendering them ultimately safe because of the awareness of artifice. This mimics the activity of horror fiction: embodiment, audience enjoyment, and a sense of release and security. The

interest, the drive, the fears do not disappear. Indeed, Carter suggests they return nightly.

Modern horror tales emerged as a genre with the secularisation of society and the leaking away of religious explanations of the odd and inexplicable.[6] Science also could not explain all that was unusual and strange, so a space for these expressions was found in the genre of horror which itself was enabled to ask questions about the power of religious controls as well as the dangers of science. Things 'out of control' and objects 'come to life' emerge as the main example of these expressions. As Martin Barker puts it looking at the lobby surrounding the horror comic censorship of the 1950s in *A Haunt of Fears*.

> It is the sense of helplessness in the face of unpredictable objects and processes that make such narratives work as horror. In this . . . they come closest to film horror, where the classic motifs—dark nights, unknown threats, and ritual incantations to control the forces of evil—are just what leave us deliciously shuddering when they are well manipulated.[7]

Lady Purple is a thing come to life, and a thing out of control. She is more than that though, for she is the embodiment of the perverse and lustful thoughts and dreams both of her creator the professor and the audiences who enjoy watching a doll act out sado-masochistic fantasies. Her coming to life is ironically the downfall of those who have thus positioned her (the professor and future male victims in the brothel). She also embodies the frighteningly circular and inevitable re-enactment of myth. Lady Purple is a vengeful fetishistic object, sado-masochistic and horror fantasy combined.

Fetishism is the stuff on which pornography thrives and Carter takes further into social critique her manipulation of fantasy and horror's technique of confusing the boundaries between animate and inanimate, objects of desire and object to be controlled and destroyed. In **The Magic Toyshop** is a palimpsest of popular fictional forms, fairytales, myths, girls' own paper stories. Through examination of Melanie's adolescent construction of herself in the semi-pornographic art modes in which woman is represented by great painters and writers, Carter examines how the myths of our femininity, our sexual being come to be fashioned upon us and come to be that part of us with which we willingly collude, blind to their reifying implications. These implications: rape, violation, pregnancy, are indicated in the positioning of Edward Bear 'swollen stomach concealing striped pyjamas' and Lorna Doone, 'splayed out, face down in the dust under the bed'—remnants of childhood. Moreover, we are also presented with the sacrificial tone of the virginally white bridal pictures of Melanie's mother.

> Her mother exploded in a pyrotechnic display of satin and lace, dressed as for a medieval banquet. . . . A wreath of artificial roses was pressed low down on her forehead. . . . She carried a bunch of white roses in her arms, cradled like a baby.

She is a meal to be devoured, a firework display, and when Melanie tries on her mother's dress it acts as a malevolent object, drowning and capturing her.

Bunty, Judy, Schoolfriend and *Girl* stories often concentrate on the 'little mother' who stands as a surrogate for her siblings when their parents are, as are Melanie's, killed in a plane crash. Plucky tomboys also abound. Melanie pictures herself in all these roles, and rejects them, but still awaits the kiss of a prince charming to awaken her from herself into a role he designs. In the working-class East London toyshop there is a wicked uncle, no stepmother or wicked aunt, and it is his designs on Melanie which cast her in the role of the traditional female victim, manipulated into a rape victim through his control. Uncle Philip is a child's nightmare figure, a character from a fairytale by the Brothers Grimm.

> Uncle Philip never talked to his wife except to bark brusque commands. He gave her a necklace that choked her. He beat her younger brother. He chilled the air through which he moved. His towering, blank-eyed presence at the head of the table drew the savour from the good food she cooked.

His menace is both physical and psychological and the spell he casts over the household renders them mute and powerless.

The moment in which Melanie, reified by her role as Leda in Uncle Philip's puppet version of that high art pornographic favourtte, Leda and the Swan, is overwhelmed by the monstrous wooden and feathered swan, which is both horror and pure farce. In her mixture of the horrific and the humorous, Carter resembles Roald Dahl, whose short stories have similar twists to hers, and who similarly re-writes 'Little Red Riding Hood'. Dahl comments, 'What's horrible is basically funny . . . in fiction I mean.'[8] Angela Carter's delicate mixture of slapstick, irony and the machinations of Sadeian horror typifies her stylistic strategies; an ornate overlay of Western myths and representations, funny, fantastic and frightening. It is deeply revelatory about the forms

and intentions of Western art from the National Gallery and Sadlers Wells to the toyshop. Melanie last recalls 'Swan Lake' when her father took her to see it. The embrace of the plywood and feathered swan is a mock up of the many languorous godlike embraces between a loving Leda and an elegant swan found in the world's great art galleries, celebrated in hauntingly beautiful tones by Yeats in 'Leda and the Swan' where phrases such as 'terrified vague fingers' and 'feathered glory' suggest that the aesthetic enjoyment overcomes the sense of the strange and horrific; a version of a grotesque, power myth rape many women readers find bizarre.

Carter's version emphasises the otherness, the disempowering and the horror.

> All her laughter was snuffed out. She was hallucinated. She felt herself not herself, wrenched from her own personality, watching this whole fantasy from another place; and in this staged fantasy, anything was possible. Even that the swan, mocked up swan, might assume reality itself and rape this girl in a blizzard of white feathers.

Horror here is a direct effect of the dramatic embodiment of despotic patriarchal power writ large and backed up by the collusion of that other patriarchal power base—high art. Carter's debunking of this high art, patriarchy's dubiously intellectually tarted up sadistic power games, empowers us all to reveal the unpleasantnesses, the potential sick violence, underlying everyday mythic representations of sexual relations.

The dangers are no less real despite the slapstick rendering of events, but Carter's irony and slapstick humour provide themselves with a liberating vehicle to expose and defuse such powers. 'Like fate or the clock, on came the swan, its feet going splat, splat, splat.'

In *Nights at the Circus,* male fear, horror and fascination at female sexual parts are figured in the geography of Madame Schreck's brothel, where the girls work in the basement.

> Madame Schreck organised her museum, thus: downstairs, in what had used to be the wine cellar, she'd had a sort of vault or crypt constructed, with wormy beams overhead and nasty damp flagstones underfoot, and this place was known as 'Down Below', or else, 'The Abyss'. The girls was all made to stand in stone niches cut out of the slimy walls, except for the Sleeping Beauty, who remained prone, since proneness was her speciality. And there were little curtains in front and, in front of the curtains, a little lamp burning. These were her 'profane altars' as she used to call them.

The offhand, everyday Cockney tones of the winged, iconic aerialiste Fevvers renders these traditionally gothic horrors almost domestic, but visions of a visiting judge who ejaculates when black hooded and when a noose is placed round his neck, and of clients who revel in the gothic nightmare of clanking chains, who are turned on only by recumbent, seemingly dead women, and all the trappings of a mixture of Poe and de Sade illuminate the dubious interrelationship between a love of horror and a perverse sexuality: a desire to brutalise women. Women, of course, collude in their own dehumanisation. Fevvers's avarice leads her into the clutches of the determinedly male, sadistic Duke, whose own brand of mastery consists of reducing his objects of desire to just that, a miniaturised, gilded objet d'art. The Grand Duke represents sterile power.

> His house was the realm of minerals, of metals of vitrification—of gold, marble and crystal; pale halls and endless mirrors and glittering chandeliers that clanged like wind-bells In the draught from the front door . . . and a sense of frigidity, of sterility, almost palpable.

It is a gothic horror threat of potential disempowerment and reification since all therein is artifice and glitter.

Murderous histories, sexual mutilations of women, and the *frisson* of total control of the human by rendering it entirely useless, pure art ornament and entertainment: the Duke's collection embodies his vile proclivities.

Fevvers's earlier encounter with Christian Rosencreutz, whose sexual perversity was related to his wish to gain new powers by sacrificing what he feared, is an echo of a familiar gothic encounter with Rosicrucianism. Carter replicates the seductive powers, the *frissons* of horror, and exposes a basis of horror in desires to dehumanise, to control, to fix, pin, collect and, perhaps, destroy the adored object. Humour, irony and slapstick undercut and disempower the perpetrators of torture, terror and death in her work and female victims soar above what could destroy them, using for their own ends the very images and forms which could otherwise represent them in a constrained sense.

Fevvers's own canny common sense enables her to turn the Duke's lust against him and she escapes into the Fabergé model of the transSiberian railway: a celebratory moment when magic and realism confusingly and amusingly unite. Fevvers escapes, a feathered intacta, icon of dreams, 'bird' woman and yet her own person. The last laugh is on the loving journalist Walser who wishes to pin her down with facts, and on the readers who want her metaphors explained, but who are left instead realising that the best thing to do with myths and metaphors is to reclaim them for our own variety of interpretations, rather than accepting any fobbed off on us by a patriarchal culture.

Reclamation is the key also for Rosaleen, the Red Riding Hood figure in '**Company of Wolves.**' The grotesque horror of being eaten alive by a lascivious wolf is replaced by the turning of the tables, as she celebrates her own sexual powers, burns her own clothing, becomes a werewolf herself and so tames the beast, thus proving her mother's comment, 'if there's a beast in man it meets its match in women too'. It might seem trite, or even dangerous as some have suggested that Carter merely repeats much of the sexist psychology of eroticism, but it is a way of suggesting reversal, using irony and the technique of 'the pulling of the plug' on a socially constructed version of horror based on a pornography which always renders the woman as victim.

Slow mental and physical torture, claustrophobia, a living death . . . this is the stuff of her horror and recalls Poe as it does the Jacobean. But her vision is more ironic and amused. Her aims are related to reversal, there is a consistent drive towards celebration and carnival. In the midst of being almost eaten by the big bad wolf, Red Riding Hood/Rosaleen is empowered by her awareness of the strength of her own virginity, as well as that of her emergent sexuality. This is a reclamation of the body as a site for woman's empowerment. Virginity in myth 'normally' renders a woman both magically safe and ideally fitted to be a sacrificial victim, in a system which sees virginity as a commodity. Here Rosaleen celebrates, her clothes burned by choice in her granny's fire, a werewolf herself?

Fires such as that in *The Magic Toyshop* are purgatorial: the evil die, the good are doubtless rescued. This is in the true tone of Shakespearean late Romance which suggests tragedy and horror but ultimately avoids or overcomes it. There are hints of death by drowning, of tragedy entering our living rooms when Tiffany, the Ophelia-like spurned innocent stripper in *Wise Children* disappears, but she escapes and lives again. Twins are produced from pockets, dead uncles reappear twice as large and filled with largesse. Reunions and unifications replace the open endings of some of the earlier works. Carnival towards which all Carter's work has long leant, triumphs over horror in her most recent work *Wise Children*.

Carter's best horror writing is more suited to the art of the short story than to longer fiction. Like Poe she goes for 'unity of effect', telling individual, perfectly controlled tales which retell and often revalue a myth or legend, which develop and embody a particular lurking perversity or nightmare, and which explore the horrific sources of real events. As in traditional gothic tales, we are terrified because the atmosphere threatens us, the familiar is our familiar nightmare. Beautifully, fatally, realistic, encyclopedic details combine with the immediate, mythic, nightmarish and surreal. In '**The Company of Wolves,**' we are told that,

> at night, the eyes of wolves shine like candle flames yellowish, reddish, but that is because the pupils of their eyes fatten on darkness and catch the light from your lantern and flash it back at you—red for danger; if a wolf's eyes reflect only moonlight, then they gleam a cold and unnatural green, a mineral, a piercing colour.

The movement of nightmare is enacted with a rich mixture of visual and psychologically threatening imagery:

> If the benighted traveller spies those luminous, terrible sequins stitched suddenly on the black thickets, then he knows he must run, if fear has not struck him stock still.

> But those eyes are all you will be able to glimpse of the forest assassins as they cluster inevitably around your smell of meat.

And her language draws the reader in and implicates them as it reproduces a fascinating and compelling mixture of terror and the *frisson* of joy at such terror.

The title story of **The Bloody Chamber** is one such perfect gothic tale in which we are seduced and drawn in as slowly as the victim, the virginal wife of this art collecting Bluebeard. The language of food consumption, aesthetic pleasure and avaricious cruelty dominates her descriptions of him, his wooing and her collusion. Threat drips slowly from every crevice. His is 'possessed of that strange, ominous calm of a sentient vegetable life, like one of those cobra-headed funereal lilies whose white sheaths are curled out of a flesh as thick and tensely yielding to the touch as vellum.' His desire she perceives but does not understand though the 'choker of rubies, two inches wide, like an extraordinarily slit throat' presages the total ownership he has in mind while his 'sheer carnal avarice' watching her in gilded mirrors positions her both as consumable meat, and art object. Mirrors, billowing gauze curtains, indecipherable imprecations from (traditional, gothic) menials,

huge beds and lilies: these gothic familiars draw in and thrill the reader, who wants yet to cry out a warning.

Carter's intertextuality provides a smile of recognition, 'All the better to see you' says the lupine, leonine, vampirish, art/wife collecting descendant of Browning's Duke who keeps pictures and relics of previously, mysteriously, dead wives. The ravishment is surreal, particularly as he removes all her clothes except the choker, and mirrors reflect every move:

> Rapt, he intoned: 'Of her apparel she retains/Only her sonorous jewellery'.

> A dozen husbands impaled a dozen brides while the mewing gulls swung on invisible trapezes in the empty air outside.

Carter investigates also the notion of the 'pleasures of the flesh' and here reveals a link between pornography and horror: man as flesh, skin covering meat, the source of the horror of cannibal tales and movies like *The Silence of the Lambs*. 'The strong abuse, exploit and meatify the weak, says Sade' (**The Sadeian Woman**). 'She knew she was nobody's meat' is a challenge Rosaleen holds up to the wolf, though necrophagy (exposition of the meatiness of human flesh) and cannibalism lurk behind Bluebeard's delights at his new wife. 'I saw him watching me in the gilded mirrors with the assessing eye of a connoisseur inspecting horseflesh, or even of a housewife in the market, inspecting cuts on the slab.' This terrifies but attracts her, as she recognises her own potential for corruption. His sexual 'appetite' and then his 'taste' for her she mistakenly feels will protect her when she investigates the locked rooms of his house in his absence. We know versions of the story, know she will find the remains of dead ex wives. As with many gothic horror tales of castles, locked doors, horrid secrets, threatening husbands and marital violence, walled up wives, spiders, jewelled daggers and necklaces, the very familiarity produces a *frisson* for the reader, and the familiarity here of the old tale captures and captivates us. Languoroushess, inevitability, these entrap the reader as they entrap the bride about to be turned into a 'meal' for her murderous husband who swings a cruel sword, and forces her to dress in white as the sacrificial victim, to his lustful power. The warrior mother rescues the bride with the aid of the new servant. The story becomes a romp, but its horror has a sexual and social basis we won't forget, and which returns in many another of her tales.

In **The Sadeian Woman** Carter notes, 'Sexuality, stripped of the idea of free exchange, is not in any way humane; it is nothing but pure cruelty. Carnal knowledge is the infernal knowledge of the flesh as meat.' The potential of devouring lurks behind **'The Tiger's Bride'** but the proud voyeuristic beast is tamed with the girl's love and her recognition of her own tigerishness. In 'The Lady of the House of Love', a female vampire strikes a familiar terror, her necessary plan involving the capture of male morsels. Her room is funerary, pungent with smoke and elaborate, and in true vampire fashion her seemingly virginal beauty is evidence of her desires as, 'In her white lace negligee stained a little with blood, the Countess climbs up on her catafalque at dawn each morning and lies down in an open coffin.' Metamorphosis takes place as she turns into a nocturnal creature sniffing out lesser prey. Change and the question of what it means to be human, that fearsome ingredient of Victorian horror of the *Dr Jekyll and Mr Hyde* type, but with its roots further back in the Jacobean horror of wolfish brothers carrying legs of corpses over their shoulders in *The Duchess of Malfi*—these crowd many of Carter's short stories. Here the rococo strangely juxtaposes images and descriptions which conjure up a night world of horror.

> the voracious margin of huntress's nights in the gloomy garden, crouch and pounce, surrounds her habitual tortured somnambulism, her life or imitation of life. The eyes of this nocturnal creature enlarge and glow. All claws and teeth, she strokes, she gorges; but nothing can console her for the ghastliness of her condition, nothing.

Employing what David Punter calls 'the dialectic of persecution', Carter's gothic investigates the extremes of terror, leading the audience gradually into realms which are nightmarish and horribly familiar.[9]

* * *

Influences on Carter's work include Isak Dinesen, who continued gothic interest in decayed aristocracy, and as a feminist writer, filtered society's problems 'through a pervading and ironic self-consciousness' much as does Fevvers, and the protagonist of **The Bloody Chamber.**[10] Another main influence is in the nightmarish, surrealist and psychologically fired night wanderings of transvestite characters in Djuna Barnes, particularly the highly Jacobean *Nightwood* (1937). *Nightwood* belongs to a tradition of lesbian gothic writing, which highlights the sexuality implicit in such horror figures as vampires, werewolves and zombies. Richard Dyer comments that,

> a number of . . . writers on the horror film have suggested, adapting Freudian ideas, that all

'monsters' in some measure represent the hideous and terrifying form that sexual energies take when they 'return' from being socially and culturally repressed. Yet the vampire seems especially to represent sexuality . . . s/he bites them, with a bite that is just as often described as a kiss.[11]

Werewolves are favourites in **The Bloody Chamber** collection, their sexuality emphasised as handsome young men who leap in front of girls, men with eyebrows meeting suspiciously in the middle; men who want to eat you up and devour you sexually. The main vampire is a woman in **'The Lady of the House of Love'** who lures in wandering men who, 'led by the hand to her bedroom . . . can scarcely believe their luck'.

Investigating her relationship to other postmodernist writers we find many parallels with the American gothic of Purdy, Pynchon and Coover. Recognition of this appears in her epigraph to **Heroes and Villains** which comes from Leslie Fiedler's exploration of the American gothic, *Love and Death in the American Novel.*[12] The epigraph runs: 'The Gothic mode is essentially a form of parody, a way of assailing clichés by exaggerating them to the limit of grotesqueness.'[13]

One of Carter's main stated aims is demythologising, unpicking and unpacking the myths and legends (those fictions) which shape and control our lives, whether safely contained in a fairytale or shaped around us in newspaper articles, adverts or television stereotypes. The human mind forces experience into familiar shapes so that it can comprehend it, but in so doing it simplifies into stereotype and myth, which themselves seem then to us to have safely embodied the less pleasant of those experiences, mental or physical, by objectifying and fictionalising them in this way. Stereotypes, myths and fictions are shorthand, but they exercise a control on the expressions and forms of the everyday world. Carter particularly intends to demythologise the fictions related to sexuality, and horror is one of her means. She exposes the relationship between sex and power, the erotic, the perverse; she digs behind the ostensibly comfortable and safe surfaces and shows up oppressions, reification, torture and dehumanisation lurking in the everyday. One way she does this is by re-examining and rewriting fairytales and myths, and another is to explore incidents in which the everyday explodes, revealing the horrors which lurk behind it.

Violence against women has long been a characteristic of much horror writing, as well as pornography. The essential powerlessness of the virginal, entrapped, victimised girl is a stock feature of pornography as it is of gothic horror which deals with taboos: 'Incest, rape, various kinds of transgressions of the boundaries between the natural and the human'.[14] Angela Carter is a clever manipulator of the techniques of horror, terror and the gothic. She takes the impetus and the structure of gothic-based romance tales for women and reappropriates them for a sexual politics which demythologises myths of the sexual powerlessness and victim role for women. She uses their structure to turn their usual denouements on their heads. As Tania Modleski argues in *Loving with a Vengeance*, gothics are 'expressions of the "normal" feminine paranoid personality' which incorporates guilt and fear, 'the paranoid individual faces physical persecution (as in dreams of being attacked by murderous figures)'.[15]

Moral and more importantly physical persecution predominate, and the reader is encouraged to wallow in the guilt and fear, and to imagine themselves as a victim, while in romantic developments of gothic fiction, persecution is 'experienced as half-pleasurable'. Romantic heroines turn their 'victimization into a triumph'. If we explore the novels which combine the gothic and the romantic there is a (for a feminist reader) tremendous disempowering celebration of this victimisation as satisfying and ultimately productive of reward. Paulina Palmer, examining Margaret Atwood's **Bodily Harm** makes comments as appropriate for Carter as for Atwood, about the reappropriation of a genre, the gothic romantic, designed very much for women,

> the Gothic genre, traditionally noted for its representation of woman as victim, becomes in Atwood's hands the perfect medium for depicting contemporary woman caught unaware in the 'rape culture' which pervades society. Motifs associated with the genre . . . include: the ingenuous heroine as the victim of male manipulation and attack; an intrigue plot in which the male protagonists compete for power; the collapsing of conventional boundaries between external/internal and animate/inanimate; and the reference to certain socially taboo topics—in this case cancer, and sado-masochistic sexual practice.[16]

The resurgence in interest in horror writing by women which has produced *The Virago Book of Ghost Stories*[17] and the fiercer, more radical *Skin of Our Soul*[18] enables us to ask questions about where Angela Carter relates to other women horror writers and what might be said to be any specifically female characteristics in the horror genre. The very latest of the popular fictional forms to be reclaimed by feminist critics, investigating the operation of popular fictional characteristics in the work of women writers within the genre, hor-

ror writing might very properly be said to have originated with women, with the work of Ann Radcliffe's *Mysteries of Udolpho* or with Mary Shelley's *Frankenstein*. Great women writers throughout the centuries have produced ghost stories and horror stories, but perhaps one of the problems of reclaiming horror as a genre for women is this very equation of the female victim, the edge of the pornographic, with horror.

Lisa Tuttle argues that men and women's perceptions of fear are to some extent similar, but in others different because of their social positioning:

> Territory which to a man is emotionally neutral may for a woman be mined with fear, and vice-versa, for example: the short walk home from the bus-stop of an evening. And how to understand the awesome depths of loathing some men feel for the ordinary (female) body? We all understand the language of fear, but men and women are raised speaking different dialects of that language.[19]

Women's contemporary horror fiction explores sexual license, alternative sexual relationships, and the power in 'normal' relationships. There are many tales which feature fear of Incest, of patriarchal rape, of life-draining mother, hatred of devious, bitchy, beautiful women. There are hidden cruelties in what are 'normally' perceived as loving or nurturing relationships, and there are forbidden fantasies of lesbian partnerships or incestuous partnerships. Taboos are explored.

Angela Carter's gothic horror reappropriates women's powers. The thrills and spills of the romantic gothics are there, but the terroriser turned faithful lover is not. The main gains are self respect, liberty and equal relationships. Red Riding Hood ends up happy with the wolf, Bluebeard's wife is liberated, Fevvers settles for Walser, and retains her secret, her magic. Glittering, contradictory, intertextually familiar and playful, Angela Carter's horror brings into the clear light of the semirealistic domestic kitchen, the nasty thoughts, fears and nightmares lurking in the cellars of our minds. And she gives us something magical too. Hers is not the horror of the abyss: it is not ultimately a black vision, it's too Rabelaisian for that, too funny and celebratory.

Notes

1. Books by Angela Carter referred to in the text: *The Magic Toyshop* (London 1967); *Heroes and Villains* (London: 1969); *Fireworks* (London: 1974); *The Bloody Chamber* (London: 1979); *The Sadeian Woman* (London: 1979); *Nights at the Circus* (London: 1984); *Black Venus* (London: 1985); *Wise Children* (1991).

2. Rosemary Jackson, *Fantasy: the Literature of Subversion* (London: 1981) p. 41.

3. Angela Carter in conversation with John Haffenden, *The Literary Review* no. v (1984) p. 37.

4. Iris le Bessiere, *Le Récit Fantastique: La Poétique de l'Incertain* (Paris: 1974) p. 62.

5. Jackson, p. 23.

6. Lee Daniells, *Fear: a History of Horror in the Mass Media* (London: 1977).

7. Martin Barker, *A Haunt of Fears: the Strange History of the British Horror Comics Campaign* (London: 1984) p. 129.

8. Roald Dahl interviewed in *Twilight Zone* (Jan-Feb. 1983).

9. David Punter, *The Literature of Terror: a History of Gothic Fictions from 1765 to the Present Day* (London: 1980) p. 130.

10. Ibid., p. 379.

11. Richard Dyer, 'Children of the Night. Vampirism as Homosexuality, Homosexuality as Vampirism' in Susanna Radstone ed., *Sweet Dreams: Sexuality, Gender and Popular Fiction* (London: 1988) p. 54.

12. Leslie Fiedler, *Love and Death in the American Novel* (New York: 1960).

13. Angela Carter, *Heroes and Villains* (London: 1981).

14. Punter, p. 19.

15. Tania Modleski, *Loving with a Vengeance* (New York: 1984) pp. 81 and 83.

16. Paulina Palmer, *Contemporary Women's Fiction* (Brighton: 1989) p. 91.

17. Richard Dalby ed., *The Virago Book of Ghost Stories* (London: 1990).

18. Lisa Tuttle ed., *The Skin of Our Soul: New Horror Stories by Women* (London: 1990) Introduction.

19. Ibid., p. 5.

HEATHER JOHNSON (ESSAY DATE 1994)

SOURCE: Johnson, Heather. "Textualising the Double-Gendered Body: Forms of the Grotesque in *The Passion of New Eve*." In *Angela Carter*, edited by Alison Easton, pp. 127-35. New York: St. Martin's Press, 1994.

In the following essay, originally published in Contemporary Review *in 1994, Johnson examines Carter's treatment of "two characters of compound identity in* The Passion of New Eve" *to illuminate the nature of the grotesque.*

The world of Angela Carter's fiction is inhabited by fabulous, monstrous creations: she-wolves, bird women, drag queens. The composite nature of these mythic figures often becomes the point of textual fascination in several of her novels and short stories. In order to examine the treatment of such composite images more closely, this article will focus on two characters of compound identity in *The Passion of New Eve*: Eve(lyn) and Tristessa. Specifically, I wish to argue that Carter's text reclaims the figure of the double-gendered body through the shifting values of the term *grotesque* that can be charted in the development of the narrative. This use of the grotesque also intersects and informs the parody of gender norms in the novel. In a reading of these figures as grotesque, one can discover here the two distinctive forms of this term as proposed by Bakhtin and the corresponding values generally associated with the term itself. It is possible to recognise one of these as positive and the other as negative.

A definition of the term *grotesque realism* is located in Bakhtin's reading of Rabelais and is dependent on a set of images that describe a transgressive body—one which emphasises the lower stratum, which takes pleasure in bodily functions, and which embraces an interrelation of death and birth. He describes this grotesque body as open, protruding, secreting, a body of becoming: 'In grotesque realism . . . the bodily element is deeply positive.' The material body is shown to be 'festive' and 'utopian'.[1] Bakhtin also delineates a second meaning of the term *grotesque* as 'post-Romantic'. This refers to the grotesque in its modern sense as it furnishes descriptions of alienation, hostility, and inhumanity. To this form it is possible to assign a negative value since its meaning is preoccupied with issues of rejection and revulsion. Its use in common speech is clearly derogatory.

Both these forms of the grotesque are inscribed in the bodies of the two central figures. Carter's protagonist begins the novel as the male Evelyn but is transformed physically and then mentally into a woman—Eve. Captured in the desert by the women of Beulah, Evelyn is taken to meet the self-designed goddess 'Mother', whose body seems to fill the captive's visual frame: 'She was so big she seemed, almost, to fill the round, red-painted, over-heated, red-lit cell.'[2] Her arms are 'like girders', her vagina is 'like the crater of a volcano', and Evelyn imagines 'the sun in her mouth' (p. 64). In the manner of Artemis, Mother has required the sacrifice of one breast from each of her followers and has 'flung a patchwork quilt stitched from her daughters' breasts over the cathedral of her interior' (p. 60). Thus she presents an imposing figure of physical amplitude and abundant fertility. Here we can see some aspects of the Rabelaisian grotesque—the bodily form exaggerated to excess, the symbol of fertility, and the focus on the lower stratum. This focus is obviously emphasised further by the subsequent construction of Eve's womb and the location of Beulah's uterine rooms beneath the desert floor. The image is not without humour, of course—'Her nipples leaped about like the bobbles on the fringe of an old-fashioned, red plush curtain' (p. 64)—and here it coincides, in its celebration of excess, with the notion of carnivalesque laughter, a significant feature of the Rabelaisian mode.

Carter uses the figure of Mother to disrupt patriarchal conceptions of the female body, as the grotesque body irrupts into the conventional presentation of that body. The description of Mother is filtered through the male sensibility of Evelyn as narrator and as such enacts a parody of the conventional maternal image through physical exaggeration, excess, and distortion. Evelyn responds to Mother as a monster: 'the bull-like pillar of her neck, . . . false beard of crisp, black curls', and the obvious result of the programme of grafting fill him with 'squeamish horror' (p. 59). In the context of Carter's novel this reaction is significant since Evelyn is responding as a male to an exaggerated female body. The figure of Mother can be regarded as pivotal here in accounting for the shift in meaning of the grotesque. Evelyn's interpretation of her body as disgusting rather than life-affirming is soon transferred onto his own new body. Evelyn is castrated and then transformed by two months of plastic surgery into a biological woman. Once completed, the new Eve finds that she is 'as mythic and monstrous as Mother herself' (p. 83). This neatly illustrates Mary Russo's criticism of Bakhtin's definition of the bodily grotesque. Russo notes that he 'fails to acknowledge or incorporate the social relations of gender in his semiotic model of the body politic, and thus his notion of the Female Grotesque remains . . . repressed and undeveloped'.[3] Her point is that the female body is already displaced and marginalised within social relations since it is often a body which must either conform to a set of regulated norms or be dismissed as Other. Therefore, the body which is female and grotesque must be recovered from a place of double exile. The post-Romantic definition of the grotesque as the described experience of alienation, isolation, and marginalised irregularity corresponds to the kind of physical difference featured in Carter's novel.[4] This difference is dependent on the composite nature of Eve and her counterpart, Tristessa—both acquire the identity of the hermaphrodite. A hint of Evelyn's future shape comes early in the novel, when he is browsing through the attic of his neighbour the alchemist: 'There was a

ABOUT THE AUTHOR

JAMES BROCKWAY ON CARTER'S "GOTHIC PYROTECHNICS" IN *FIREWORKS*

It would be possible almost to give an account of the contents and nature of *Fireworks* by quoting from Angela Carter's own words in these tales. From the magnificent story "The Loves of Lady Purple," to my taste the finest in the book and one which harps back happily to the puppets in "The Magic Toyshop," one could take 'freedom from actuality' and 'immune to the drab world of here and now' and 'bewildering entertainment' and 'Here the grotesque is the order of the day' and 'Everything in the play was entirely exotic' and, best of all, I think: 'a thick, lascivious murmur like fur soaked in honey which sent unwilling shudders of pleasure down the spines of the watchers', except that I also think Angela Carter will find plenty of readers who shudder most willingly.

One could also quote some of her idiosyncratic adjectives to say all: appalling, ghastly, violet, violent, perverse, torrid, desolate, vicious, viscous, cavernous, sub-aqueous, indecent, lewd, fernal, leprous, lycanthropic, stagnant, demented. But this would be to suggest a gothic orgy, whereas for all the highly deliberate, deliberately ornamental embroidery of this laden prose, it is the intelligence at work beneath it all which raises almost everything here to the level of art. For intelligence is another attribute of genuine art, and intelligence here is both active and unusual.

SOURCE: Brockway, James. "Gothic Pyrotechnics." *Books and Bookmen* (February 1975): 55-6.

seventeenth century print, tinted by hand, of a hermaphrodite carrying a golden egg that exercised a curious fascination upon me' (p. 13). Any sense of fascination that might have been occasioned by a real androgynous body is expressed as revulsion and derision when the hermaphroditic nature of Tristessa is brutally revealed. The reclusive film star's glamour is world renowned and based on the construction of her femininity. So when it is discovered that under her gowns and fragile appearance she is actually a man, the very basis of the constitution of femininity is brought into question. The group which captures Tristessa subjects her to various forms of torture, treating her as a grotesque because of her dual nature: 'They made ropes from twisted strips of his own négligé and tied him by his wrists from a steel beam, so there he dangled, naked, revealed' (p. 129). The image of Tristessa's exposed body suggests a reading of the grotesque as wholly negative—this androgyne is a 'freak' to its captors and is spared no form of ridicule or humiliation. When Eve is seen to be sympathetic towards their victim, she is treated with the same cruelty.

This interpretation of the grotesque body is also confirmed by the experience of the abject, which we can read across the bodies of Eve(lyn) and Tristessa. Kristeva's category of the abject locates the source of alienation in the subject's body and in the moment when one being emerges from or merges into another. This corresponds to Evelyn's repulsion at the sight of Mother whose likeness is then stamped onto his own body. In Kristeva's definition of the abject it is possible to comprehend fully its traumatic effects: it is 'what disturbs identity, system, order. What does not respect borders, positions, rules. The in-between, the ambiguous, the composite.'[5] In Carter's novel experience of the abject occurs when each body is forced to transgress socially established boundaries of gender as written on the body. We have seen that Evelyn reacts with horror at the moment of her biological transformation, the form of her own body provoking a sense of disgust. When his own transformation into a biological woman is complete, the sense of disgust is articulated through a direct comparison to Mother's: 'I would wince a little at such gross modulation of a flesh that had once been the . . . twin of my new flesh' (p. 77). The rearrangement of the body's borders means that Evelyn responds to himself as if he had been modelled after a monster as hideously devised as Frankenstein's.

Similarly, a transgressive act is inscribed in the removal of Tristessa's gown. This marks a significant textual shift in meaning that is enacted in the violently forced reconsideration of her sexual status. Made to acknowledge the presence of her hidden genitalia, Tristessa experiences a shift in identity to which he responds with 'wailing [which] echoed round the gallery of glass' (p. 128). Both characters are forced to recognise their own formation, and it is at the moment of change in

ontological certainty that they too participate in the abjection of their bodies. Beyond this subjective view of the grotesque body, the image of a composite being, unnatural and constructed out of seemingly disparate parts, is clearly the body experienced as grotesque by the other characters. The Gothic setting of Tristessa's glass house, where she is abused by the intruders, contains bodily images that further accentuate the theme of self-invention and physical reconstitution. In Tristessa's waxwork mausoleum, 'The Hall of the Immortals', exquisitely fashioned corpses are dismembered by Tristessa's attackers, and when they decide that a mock wedding is to take place between Eve and Tristessa, they gather the scattered limbs together in order to construct witnesses for the event. Yet in doing this, 'they put the figures together haphazardly, so Ramon Navarro's head was perched on Jean Harlow's torso and had one arm from John Barrymore Junior, the other from Marilyn Monroe and legs from yet other donors—all assembled in haste, so they looked like picture-puzzles' (p. 134).

This simile of the picture-puzzle brings us to the heart of our understanding of the modern or post-Romantic grotesque. This composite image has the appearance of something that is unresolved and provokes a reaction in the viewer that strives to unify the obvious disparities, thereby rescuing it for the realm of the normal, the familiar. Through ridicule and objectification of the Other, people attempt to reassure themselves of their own normality, their regularity. In his introduction to the memoirs of a nineteenth-century French hermaphrodite, Michel Foucault has shown that from the Middle Ages through to the last century, anyone whose sexual status was open to question was required to choose one sexual identity for life and usually it was a doctor's task to decipher which was the 'true' sex of the body. And now, in the twentieth century, the idea of one sex being close to 'the truth' has not been completely dispelled. It is still widely believed that homosexuality and the swapping of gender characteristics are somehow 'errors'—that is, Foucault says, 'a manner of acting that is not adequate to reality' and, further, that 'sexual irregularity is seen as belonging more or less to the realm of chimera'.[6]

As we have seen, the image of the chimera, that fabulous mythical creature of mixed forms, is at the centre of Carter's novel. The fantastic element in her fiction is often treated by the narrative voice with the banal tone of acceptance characteristic of writing in the vein of magical realism. And here, any scenario or person that might at first seem unusual, including the figures of Eve, Tristessa, and even Mother, are treated in the text as factual, not as frightening aberrations. And so it is that the central figure of this novel sets out on a journey of discovery and, through the reading of his/her own body, embraces the full spectrum of gender identities, some of which were once alien to him—most notably those of the female. Evelyn, then, begins his trip with this intent:

> I would go to the desert, to the waste heart of that vast country, the desert on which they turned their backs for fear it would remind them of emptiness—the desert, the arid zone, there to find, chimera of chimeras, there, in the ocean of sand, among the bleached rocks of the untenanted part of the world, I thought I might find that most elusive of all chimeras, myself.
>
> (p. 38)

In our reading of the bodies of this central character and its companion, it is possible to discover more than one meaning of the grotesque. When Eve and Tristeassa embrace, once they are alone, Eve is aware that 'we had made the great Platonic hermaphrodite together' (p. 148). In Plato the hermaphrodite is the original human form which was then split into two, thus accounting for the two sexes and the human desire to rejoin with an original mate. In *The Passion of New Eve,* the reaction to the hermaphroditic subject first appears to belong to a reading of the grotesque similar to the image of the grotesque often found in southern American writing—Carson McCullers, for example, has used this image to explore the lives of those regarded as freakish and marginalised by society. However, if we return to Rabelais, we may discover an interesting connection between that bodily grotesque of carnival, which Bakhtin finds in his work, and the post-Romantic grotesque in which the irregular body reflects a modern condition of alienation. These two possible renderings of the grotesque meet in the central character of Rabelais's *Gargantua and Pantagruel.* For here is the description of the emblem on the hat that Gargantua wears: 'Against a base of gold weighing over forty pounds was an enamel figure very much in keeping. It portrayed a man's body with two heads facing one another, four arms, four feet, a pair of arses and a brace of sexual organs male and female. Such, according to Plato's *Symposium,* was human nature in its mystical origins' (qtd in Bakhtin, p. 323).

So what do we make of this image of the epitomic form of the positive grotesque wearing an emblem of the negative grotesque? They are both situated outside the official culture, but the first is celebratory, disruptive, redemptive. The grotesque of the modern period, as our use of the word as a term of derision attests, represents rejection, exile, and abnormality. When Gargantua champions the hermaphrodite as the symbol of the grotesque, he celebrates the fact that all humans once had that form, that we all share the origins of the grotesque. The fact that the hermaphroditic figure is rejected as alien in modern times suggests a denial of this condition, not out of respect for scientific fact but due to the social pressures towards visual conformity. And this sense of denial is applied to any body which displays chimerical characteristics.

Thus it is significant that New Eve is ultimately reconciled to her changed body. New Eve's body has been designed by Mother to reflect an ideal of perfect femininity as determined by social norms. Yet it is clear that Eve herself regards the process by which this appearance of normality has been achieved as grotesque in itself. She cannot forget that her present body is a manufactured one: 'I had been born out of discarded flesh, induced to a new life by means of cunning hypodermics, . . . my pretty face had been constructed out of a painful fabric of skin from my old inner thighs' (p. 143). When Eve looks into the face of Tristessa she is instantly reminded that they are 'mysteriously twinned by [their] synthetic life' (p. 125).

In transcending this view of her body, overcoming the resistant feelings about her condition, Eve(lyn) participates in a celebration of her chimerical nature when she is united with Tristessa after the destruction of the glass house. The moment of sexual congress between the two hermaphroditic figures may be dismissed by some as a heterosexual fantasy of recaptured unity. Yet the celebration of the body and its transgression of gender boundaries is, I think, intended to espouse a positive reading of this image.

The relocation of the chimerical, the hermaphroditic, within the realm of possibility, as a source of origin and a site for pleasure, is written in the bodies of these two characters. Carter playfully recentres the figure of chimerical form in this novel. In her use of the grotesque Carter parodies those characters, such as Mother and Zero, who impose a myopic perspective on the constitution of gender identity, while challenging traditional perspectives on gender and its boundaries. As Eve(lyn) and Tristessa embrace, they form a single bodily image in which these boundaries are temporarily lost. It is tempting to read this image as an example of Bakhtin's positive grotesque in which the death of one and the birth of another can be seen in the one body: 'two bodies in one, the budding and the division of the cell' (Bakhtin, p. 52). As Eve begins to grow into her newly grafted identity and Tristessa enters into the final hours of his life, they share this climactic dissolution of identity, making the shape of this one fabulous, mythic creature together.

Notes

[Heather Johnson's essay is the first of three essays included in this collection (*Angela Carter*, edited by Alison Easton. New York: St. Martin's Press, 1994) which draw on aspects of Mikhail Bakhtin's work on carnival and the grotesque to explore relations of social power and their historical contexts in Carter's work. (Carter herself did not read Bakhtin's work until after the publication of *Nights at the Circus*, a novel for which his ideas also provide a useful lens.) *The Passion of New Eve*, the subject of Johnson's essay, charts the journey of the male, English narrator, Evelyn, through a futuristic United States where by surgical means he is forced to become female (his/her body made the patriarchal idealisation of woman). Renamed Eve, she eventually meets with and makes love with the ageing film star, Tristessa, revealed to be biologically male. These two transgressive bodies thus demonstrate, indeed recognise the constructiveness of the gendered body; normality in Eve is made to seem grotesque. Bakhtin's ideas of the grotesque, based on his reading on Rabelais, are central to an understanding of the literature of the body in political terms—the grotesque body is excessive, monstrous and revolting, with the power to disrupt limits fixed by present powers. Mary Russo reads the grotesque specifically as a female form—woman's existence, and in particular her body, as monstrous in patriarchal eyes. Johnson also refers to Foucault (whose work on sexuality and the power of social institutions was important to Carter) to establish how normality and abnormality in gender roles are constructed by those who police sexuality in society. Kristeva's psychoanalytic but politically charged ideas of abjection—a horror at and attempted expulsion of things which disturb established identity, system, order—are also used to describe the characters' subjectivity in recognising their own formation. The essay finally asks whether the grotesque can still be read positively. Ed.]

1. Mikhail Bakhtin, *Rabelais and His World* (Bloomington, 1984), p. 19; hereafter cited parenthetically.

2. Angela Carter, *The Passion of New Eve* (London, 1986), p. 63; hereafter cited parenthetically.

3. Mary Russo, 'Female Grotesques: Carnival and Theory', in *Feminist Studies/Critical Studies*, ed. Teresa de Lauretis (Basingstoke, 1988), p. 219.

4. My use of the term *post-Romantic* is taken from Bakhtin who has chosen it to distinguish between a modern understanding of the term *grotesque* and the much earlier meaning grounded in the social reality of the Middle Ages. I realise that this distinction is by no means an absolute one and exceptions do exist in the post-Romantic period.

5. Julia Kristeva, *Powers of Horror: An Essay on Abjection* (New York, 1982), p. 4.

6. *Herculine Barbin: Being the Recently Discovered Memoirs of a Nineteenth-Century French Hermaphrodite*, trans. Richard McDougall, introd. Michel Foucault (Brighton, 1980), p. x.

BEATE NEUMEIER (ESSAY DATE 1996)

SOURCE: Neumeier, Beate. "Postmodern Gothic: Desire and Reality in Angela Carter's Writing." In *Modern Gothic: A Reader,* edited and with an introduction by Victor Sage and Allan Lloyd Smith, pp. 141-51. Manchester: Manchester University Press, 1996.

In the following essay, Neumeier explains how Carter employs the Gothic in her fiction to explore "the nature of desire and of reality."

According to Angela Carter 'we live in Gothic times',[1] where the marginalised subgenres of the past have necessarily become the appropriate and dominant modes of our present discourse. This view corresponds with the more general recent discussions of the development of the literary fantastic from the emergence of the Gothic mode in the eighteenth century to the contemporary practice of postmodernism. Neil Cornwell, among others, claims that 'the fantastic has itself become the dominant mode in the modern novel'. It is part of what he terms the '"portmanteau novel" . . . to designate the complex, multi-levelled or multi-layered novel', characterised by irony, parody, intertextuality, and metafiction.[2] Leslie Fiedler, quoted by Angela Carter in an epigraph to her novel *Heroes and Villains*, sees the Gothic mode as 'a form of parody, assailing clichés by exaggerating them to the limit of grotesqueness'.[3] Emphasising the importance of this tradition for her own writing, Angela Carter characterises Gothicism as a genre ignoring 'the value systems of our institutions', and dealing 'entirely with the profane'. Its 'characters and events are exaggerated beyond reality, to become symbols, ideas, passions . . . style will tend to be ornate, unnatural—and thus operate against the perennial human desire to believe the word as fact . . . [The Gothic] retains a singular moral function—that of provoking unease.'[4] Gothicism in this sense is placed in opposition to mimetic art, to realism, and situated within the realm of non-mimetic art, of fantasy and the fantastic, areas which have always been associated with imagination and desire.

Images and symbols of 'infernal desire' which trace the forbidden paths of cultural taboos are the particular domain of fantastic literature, the acknowledged literature of the unreal, in which the questions discussed in this essay by necessity arise: namely the questions of the nature of desire and of reality. Angela Carter's novels and tales provide superb examples of a literary and theoretical exploration of these features.[5]

Eros and Thanatos: the subject as battle-ground

In her novel *The Infernal Desire Machines of Dr Hoffman*, Angela Carter engages the hero/narrator and her readers in what she makes him call a veritable 'Reality War' (27). In this war reality is linked to order, reason, and rationality as opposed to fantasy, imagination, chaos, and desire. The unnamed Minister of State and Dr Hoffman respectively figure as representatives of Super Ego and Id, reality principle and pleasure principle, as the narrator informs us. So we are presented with what seems to be a paradigmatic Freudian drama by its own definition, a text which writes its own interpretation as it goes along. Whereas earlier Gothic/fantastic texts had to be interpreted in psychoanalytic terms by readers and critics, this text provides its own reading.

But, of course, there is more to it than meets the eye/I of the hero/narrator whose vision is questioned and whose I-dentity is at stake. First of all, the figurehead of reality and rationality, the Minister, remains conspicuously absent throughout the novel (apart from a recorded conversation between the Minister and Dr Hoffman's ambassador at the outset of the novel). Likewise, his counterpart Dr Hoffman, the representative of infernal desire, appears only at the very end, although he (and possibly the Minister?) seems to have been present throughout the novel in various disguises (e.g. as peep show proprietor, as Sadeian Count). Hence Carter's 'Reality War' seems to be displaced onto the level of actions involving the narrator/hero, Desiderio, and Hoffman's daughter, Albertina. Desiderio, working for the Minister, is sent on a quest to save mankind, a mission which can only be accomplished by destroying Dr Hoffman. Appointed to the position of an 'Inspector of Veracity' (40) Desiderio visits a town fair, meets a peep show proprietor in

whose tent he is supposed to marvel at wax models of the 'Seven Wonders of the World' (42)—a veritable catalogue of the fragmented human body (womb, eyes, breasts, head, penis, mutilated body, culminating in the representation of copulating bodies) and its interpretation in images of desire (and fear). Another tent reveals a series of pictures of 'A Young Girl's Most Significant Experience' (58), which turns out to be the proverbial Sleeping Beauty being kissed by a Prince who is transformed into Death. These images (wax models, pictures) bear strange resemblances to persons and events in Desiderio's past and future: one of the women depicted in the 'Seven Wonders of the World' resembles the beautiful and enigmatic Albertina, who had earlier appeared in the shapes of a black swan and that of Dr Hoffman's male ambassador. The castle represented inside the wax model womb reappears at the end of the novel as Hoffman's Gothic abode. The paintings of the Sleeping Beauty resemble Desiderio's past amorous encounter with the town mayor's daughter Mary Anne (the night before) and her future death (the next morning). After this fatal event Desiderio has to flee from the Police who charge him with seduction, murder, and necrophily performed on a minor as well as with impersonation of a government inspector (62). During the course of the novel he lives as an Indian among the River People, travels as nephew of the peep show proprietor from fair to fair, accompanies a Sadeian Count to the perversions of the 'House of Anonymity' (128), falls into the hands of a cannibalistic tribe, is received in the land of the Centaurs, until he finally reaches the castle of his opponent Dr Hoffman.

The dialectic and reversibility of the pattern of flight and persecution, of the figures of victim and persecutor as known from classical Gothic/fantastic novels like *Frankenstein* and *Dracula* is thematised throughout in association with the quest motif. Desiderio's mission is death: the destruction of Dr Hoffman. Yet almost from the start this mortal mission is accompanied and sometimes replaced by the quest for love of Albertina, Hoffman's daughter, an unmistakable hint at the Freudian tenet of the inseparability of Eros and Thanatos. Desiderio pursues and saves Albertina who in turn rescues him and in fact is his constant companion, most significantly in the disguise of Lafleur, the servant of the notorious Sadeian Count. Here the link between the ambivalence of the structural pattern and the figural pattern in Gothic/fantastic literature is made obvious. The technique of using various disguises, of changing identities, of splitting/multiplying personalities is taken to an ironic extreme. It seems only logical that after having been presented consecutively as a government inspector, an Indian, a nephew of a peepshow proprietor, and a guest of a Sadeian count, Desiderio finally realises himself in a mirror in Hoffman's castle as 'entirely Albertina in the male aspect' (199). If Albertina, as she claims, has been 'maintained in [her] various appearances only by the power of [Desiderio's] desire' (204), then the identification of the Minister and Dr Hoffman with rationality and desire respectively, also has to be questioned. All 'the roles are interchangeable' (39), as the doctor's ambassador explicitly points out. The neat borderline between reality and pleasure principle has become more and more blurred.

The described pattern of similarities between the images presented at the travelling fair and the experiences of the hero recurs throughout the novel. Image and experience constantly reflect each other, or rather appear as inseparable. Aptly, the peep show proprietor lectures the hero that the models and slides shown at the fair once belonged to Hoffman's museum of 'symbolic constituents of representations of the basic constituents of the universe' from which all possible situations of the world can be deduced. Consequently the symbols can be interpreted as 'patterns from which real events may be evolved' (95). So the novel identifies this set of samples as what could be called the constituents of a grammar of desire 'derived from Freud' (108). Furthermore, the constituents of this grammar, as they are translated into Desiderio's experiences, can be directly connected to Todorov's distinction between themes of perception (e.g. metamorphoses) and themes of discourse (desire) in fantastic literature: in Carter's novel themes of perception appear as metamorphoses between the human and the animal aspect (Centaurs), between animate and inanimate (animal furniture in the 'House of Anonymity'), between object and subject (acrobats dissolving, transformations of personalities). Among the catalogue of themes of desire figure allusions to necrophily (Sleeping Beauty, embalmed Mrs Hoffman) and incest (River People), homosexual rape (Acrobats of Desire), rape by Centaurs (Albertina), torture (tattooing), sadism and blasphemy ('House of Anonymity'), and cannibalism (River people, Black tribe, Centaurs). Moreover the ancestry of the Doctor himself is firmly rooted in the Gothic tradition of Dracula, whereas the Count is explicitly linked to de Sade: names representing perceptions of the world governed by infernal desires.

Throughout the novel Desiderio is confronted with Gothic transformations of self and desire without ever reaching the consummation of his own single desire, Albertina. When their union finally is about to take place, he kills her in order to escape from being literally reduced to a—in Deleuze's and Guattari's terms—'desiring machine'.[6] For the fate prepared for him and Albertina by the Doctor is to permanently become part of 'a pictorial lexicon of all the things a man and a woman might do together within the confines of a bed of wire six feet long by three feet wide' (214). In recent criticism this murder has received diverse readings. On the one hand, David Punter reads it as an example of 'the defeat of the political aspirations of the 1960s, and in particular of the father-figures of liberation, Reich and Marcuse' as well as a result of Desiderio's having been 'formed by the Minister's society, by the society of apparent institutional order and totalitarian conformism'.[7] On the other hand, Ricarda Schmidt sees it as a result of Carter's attempt to show 'that the absolute rule of desire would make life just as repressive, sterile and static as the absolute rule of reason', and argues that the author supposedly 'examines the promise of desire completely and always fulfilled and finds that it does not guarantee happiness and freedom'.[8] Both readings seem to presuppose the attainability of a realm of desire without its vocabulary and grammar, presenting desire mostly in the Gothic forms of the return of the repressed, mixed with pain. The course of the whole novel, however, reveals the inseparability of desire from the projectionist's sample of images. Images, symbols, and myths are structuring the unconscious as much as the conscious. Pleasure principle and reality principle cannot be kept apart. In this sense Carter's novel can also be read as a parody on psychoanalytic attempts to pen 'desire in a cage' (208), to define it as the Other of rationality and reason. Carter's Dr Hoffman thus aptly appears to combine aspects of the father-figures of psychoanalysis (Freud) and of Gothicism (namely E. T. A. Hoffmann, E. A. Poe, and de Sade) respectively, thus reminding the reader in various ways of the inseparability of the fantastic and its Freudian interpretations: first, the reader, of course, remembers the fact that Freud developed his theory of the uncanny in relation to a story by E. T. A. Hoffmann. Secondly, the appearance of the doctor in the novel is presented as a mock analytic situation, where the doctor is sitting on a stool holding the hand of a woman on a couch, who, however, in a Poe-like Gothic twist of the scene, turns out to be the embalmed corpse of the doctor's dead wife. Desire remains a zero unit, a pure absence like death. So Desiderio's erotic quest necessarily implies at the same time an entropic pull. Desire as a vacant term, defined as a lack, has to be given an object and thereby filled with meaning. Death by necessity remains an imaginary space, a space of non-reality, which gains its meaning solely in relation to reality as difference, as other, as realm after life. In that respect the (nondescript) space of death and the (non-directional) movement of desire both point towards a void or an absolute zero point. But because absence cannot be represented, we are ironically left with embalmed corpses and the futile killing of desire (as represented by Albertina's death) and its inevitable return as a narrative of memory—in yet another kind of representation.

Reality and fantasy: the confusion of image and object

This notion of the inseparability of desire (and death) from its representations, its cultural constructions (images, symbols, myths), has decisive consequences for the notions of reality and fantasy/the fantastic with regard to their fictional representations. Most definitions of the fantastic and its related areas have centred on its correlative opposition to the real. This implies a definition of the real as governed by the principles of order and rationality. The fantastic then—as its counterpart—is viewed as an expression of reality's constraints, giving space to the unreal, the unseen, and unsaid. The representational forms of the fantastic are by necessity historically bound and thus vary according to the changing value systems (and thus reality concepts) of the society to which they relate. Following Todorov's familiar and often applied terminology,[9] the unreal or the Other is explained as supernatural within religious societies and is thus contained within the realm of the marvellous, the unhistoric; within secular societies the unreal is naturalised, e.g. in terms of a subjective perception, and thus can be contained as uncanny within the realm of the mimetic. The historical development of naming the unaccountable other as evil has consequently been traced as a gradual process of internalisation ranging from the devil (Lewis, *The Monk;* Maturin, *Melmoth*), to demons (villain/heroes of Ann Radcliffe and the Brontës) to the self as Other (Stevenson, *Dr Jekyll and Mr Hyde;* Hitchcock, *Psycho*). Today, critics like Rosemary Jackson see the fantastic as 'confound-ing the marvellous and the mimetic', as an aspect of instability and uncertainty, as that which lies beyond interpretation. Thus the fantastic in her words fundamentally 'traces the limits of [culture's] epistemological and ontological frame' by problematising vision (eye) and language (I) as reliable constituents of reality.[10] The fantastic, Rosemary Jackson goes on to explain, 'plays upon difficulties of interpreting events/things as objects or as images, thus disorienting the reader's categorisation of the "real" to such an extent that reason and reality appear as arbitrary shifting constructs'.[11] Applying these ideas to the tradition of Gothic literature, the decisive difference between earlier examples and contemporary texts of the fantastic becomes clear. While Frankenstein's monster and Stoker's vampires materialise as product of self and invasion of self respectively and become real, Angela Carter's creatures never become real in that sense. Angela Carter actualises images as objects and events, just as Mary Shelley and Bram Stoker did in the nineteenth century, but she insists on the process of actualisation rather than on the actualisation itself, creating a constant limbo between object as image, and image as object. Her fictions express Rosemary Jackson's theoretical persuasion that 'things slide away from the powerful eye/I which seeks to possess them'.[12] The travelling heroes of several of her novels, particularly those of *The Infernal Desire Machines of Dr Hoffman* and *Nights at the Circus,* are confronted with recurring clusters of images commonly identified as representations of the relational/oppositional other: namely, the unknown country, the travelling fair or circus, and—of course—the Gothic mansion and its inhabitants.

The unknown country recalls the fictional tradition of *Robinson Crusoe* and *Gulliver's Travels* respectively as two complementary ways of naturalisation (familiarisation as appropriation) of the unknown on the one hand and estrangement (defamiliarisation as satire) of the known on the other hand. Carter explicitly and ironically takes up both traditions by referring to Yahoos and Houyhnhnms in *The Infernal Desire Machines of Dr Hoffman* and in *Nights at the Circus,* and to Friday in the story '**Master**' in *Fireworks.* Her heroes' experiences in unknown countries among unknown people provide ample opportunities to ridicule Western civilisation and its attempts at defining the Other in its own terms. Thus their wonder at the absurd nature of unknown mores, magic rituals, and languages only refers back to their/our own societies: in *Nights at the Circus*

Jack Walser's explanation of the way the Siberian natives deal with foreigners can thus be related directly to the above-mentioned explanation of the history of Gothic/fantastic literature: 'Since they did not have a word for "foreigner", they used the word for "devil" instead and began to get used to it' (253). Similarly Walser's observation of the natives' tendency to confound object and image only reflects his and our own: 'The Siberian natives cannot distinguish between a bear as a household pet and as a "minor deity," "a transcendental kind of meta-bear" in the narrator's diction' (257). Furthermore, Walser himself (and the reader) cannot distinguish between the heroine Fevvers as a bird woman and Fevvers as a symbol of Victory, Death, Freedom or whatever other associations are evoked throughout the novel. In comparison and contrast to Swiftian satire Angela Carter not only uses the motif of the unknown country to criticise contemporary society, but eventually rather to represent ironically the process of signification and its arbitrariness and thus unreliability, a process which is all-encompassing and thus without conceivable alternative.

The travelling fair and the circus recall literary traditions associated with aspects of inversion and/or imitation of the known world. The world of the fair and the circus is the everyday world upside down: the abnormal becomes the norm within its confines, yet it always remains exotic with regard to the outside world. Angela Carter is interested in precisely this ambivalence: the other as a norm and as a monstrosity on display. In *The Infernal Desire Machines of Dr Hoffman* the observer/hero is tempted to explain the art of the Acrobats of Desire, such as juggling their own eyes or dismembering themselves, as that of tricksters who play with the human perception (perhaps using mirrors to create their effects). But this reassuring interpretation of the unreal as real (uncanny) is destroyed later on: the acrobats clearly do transcend the possible; (thus they seem to belong to the realm of the marvellous). But at the same time, the narrator reminds us of the fact that 'often, the whole fair seemed only another kind of set of samples' (110), of images displayed in the tent of the peep show proprietor. The fantastic double vision or rather oscillation between the different interpretations remains unresolved. In *Nights at the Circus* the heroine Fevvers, the bird woman, is celebrated as the world's 'Greatest Aerialiste'. But eventually her admirer and biographer Walser hits upon the paradox of meaning when he ponders: 'if she were indeed a

lusus naturae, a prodigy, then—she was no longer a wonder . . . but—a freak . . . As a symbolic woman, she has a meaning, as an anomaly, none' (161). This not only applies to the attitude of others towards her, but also to her vision of self. The threat of being 'no Venus, or Helen, or Angel of the Apocalypse, not Izrael or Isfahel . . . [but] only a poor freak', throws her into a crisis which, however, is prevented by the gaze of her onlookers: 'the eyes fixed upon her with astonishment, with awe, the eyes that told her who she was' (290). In order to signify the birdwoman has to believe in herself as an image and a symbol. Meaning and representation are by necessity symbolic constructions, artefacts.

The issue of gender: ontology v. iconography

The analysis so far has shown that Angela Carter's fictional exercises in Gothicism are very effective renditions of her theoretical statements on the nature of the genre which deals in exaggeration, distortion, in cliché images and symbols. An additional attraction of the Gothic genre for Carter is its potential of integration insofar as it allows her to link fairy tale and pornography in her novels and many of her short stories. Since, according to Carter, both are derived from myth, both exhibit 'a fantasy relation to reality', depicting wo/man as 'invariable' and denying his/her 'social context'.[13] Thus in *The Infernal Desire Machines of Dr Hoffman* the vampiric Sadeian Count is described in utterly theatrical terms as 'connoisseur of catastrophe' (122) whose 'rigorous discipline of stylisation' (123) forces him to remain 'iconoclast, even when the icons were already cast down': 'As if from habit he pissed on the altar [of a ruined chapel] while the valet set out the meal' (125). During their visit to the 'House of Anonymity' the Count and Desiderio change into hooded costumes which according to the narrator 'were unaesthetic, priapic and totally obliterated our faces and our self-respect; the garb grossly emphasised our manhoods while utterly denying our humanity. And the costumes were of no time or place' (130). Consequently they are confronted not with women, but with variations of 'ideational femaleness', which turn out to be 'sinister, abominable, inverted mutations, part clockwork, part vegetable and part brute' (132). In a climactic scene the Count as 'the Pope of the Profane, officiating at an ultimate sacrament . . . snatched a candle . . . and used it to ignite the rosy plumage of a winged girl' (133), who, however,—as the reader is informed subsequently—far from being real 'had only been a life-like construction of papier mâché on a wicker frame' (134). In *Nights at the Circus* the winged girl has materialised, and after having been displayed in Mme Schreck's museum of woman monsters, has to escape first from being bled to death by the quasi-vampiric Christian Rosencreutz and later from being diminished to a miniature artefact by a demonic collector of toys and other rarities. The airs of omnipotence displayed by these Gothic villains are, however, counteracted not only by their theatricality, but also by their 'quivering pusillanimity' (*Infernal Desire Machines,* 145) which shows itself as soon as they are faced with resistance.

The artificiality of Gothicism and its machinery is further revealed in Angela Carter's short story '**The Lady of the House of Love**' (from her collection *The Bloody Chamber*),[14] where the vampire queen is likened by the hero to a doll, to a clockwork wound up years ago, to an automaton (102), and her mythical midnight mansion is stripped of all horror and fascination by the morning light: 'now you could see how tawdry it all was, how thin and cheap the satin, the catafalque not ebony at all but blackpainted paper stretched on ruts of wood, as in the theatre' (106). Similarly, when Desiderio reaches Dr Hoffman's castle, he realises: 'I was not in the domain of the marvellous at all. I had gone far beyond that and at last I had reached the power house of the marvellous, where all its clanking, dull, stage machinery was kept' (*Infernal Desire Machines,* 201).

A final twist in Carter's use of Gothicism is thus related to the idea of gender. Whereas earlier Gothic fiction shows the materialisation of ideas (Frankenstein's monster, Dracula), Angela Carter uses Gothicism to reveal the process of transformation of human beings, particularly women into symbols and ideas by the process of gender construction. Gothicism as a blend of fairy tale and pornography most obviously shows the replacement of the ontological by the iconographic. In her analysis of de Sade, *The Sadeian Woman,* Angela Carter links pornography to the stylisation of graffiti:

> In the stylisation of graffiti, the prick is always presented as erect, in an alert attitude of enquiry or curiosity or affirmation; it points upwards, it asserts. The hole is open, an inert space, like a mouth waiting to be filled. From this elementary iconography may be derived the whole metaphysic of sexual differences—man aspires; woman has no other function but to exist, waiting. The male is positive, an exclamation mark. Woman is

negative. Between her legs lies nothing but zero, the sign for nothing, that only becomes something when the male principle fills it with meaning.[15]

In her novel *The Passion of New Eve* Angela Carter uses Gothicism (among other genres) in this sense to reveal the process of gender construction as a process which places the hero turned heroine Eve/lyn 'outside history' (125), because it is a process of being transformed by 'the false universals of myth' (136). But how can wo/man be situated in history, in the real world, if this world, too, is a symbolic construction? The answer to this question given by the narrator/hero(ine) of the novel, 'a critique of these symbols is a critique of our lives' (6), indicates that Carter intends to move from the symbolic level of her texts to the symbolic representation of our reality.

Conclusion

As pointed out above, Angela Carter's fantastic creatures never become real in the way Frankenstein's monster or Dracula do. They necessarily must stop short, because the real only exists as absence, as vanishing zero point in a world constructed by images, symbols, and myths. If the fantastic is defined as tracing the limits of our cultural frame, as that which lies beyond interpretation, then the real as that which cannot be represented has become the 'real' topic of the postmodern fantastic. Yet this topic can never be grasped but can only be encircled (via parody, intertextuality, metafiction, and irony) in an endless process of de-mystification which, however, always acknowledges its own futility. The fantastic has not been replaced by Freud's psychoanalysis, as Todorov suggested, but has rather been reinvigorated by Lacan's revision of Freud. Rather than rendering the reader/critic unnecessary, Angela Carter provides him with the concrete textual illustrations of current literary theory.

Notes

1. A. Carter, Afterword to *Fireworks: Nine Profane Pieces* (London: Quartet Books, 1974), p. 122.

2. N. Cornwell, *The Literary Fantastic: From Gothic to Postmodernism* (Hempstead: Harvester, 1990), pp. 145, 154.

3. A. Carter, *Heroes and Villains* (Harmondsworth: Penguin Books (1969) 1981).

4. Afterword to *Fireworks.*

5. The following texts are used: *The Infernal Desire Machines of Dr Hoffman* (Harmondsworth: Penguin Books (1972) 1982); *Nights at the Circus* (London: Picador (1984) 1984); *The Bloody Chamber* (Harmondsworth: Penguin Books (1979) 1987); *The Passion of New Eve* (London: Virago Press (1977) 1982).

6. G. Deleuze and F. Guattari, *Anti-Oedipus* (New York: Viking, (1972) 1977), Chapter 1.

7. D. Punter, 'Angela Carter: Supersessions of the Masculine', *Critique* 25:4 (1984), pp. 209-22; 211, 213.

8. R. Schmidt, 'The Journey of the Subject in Angela Carter's Fiction', *Textual Practice* 3:1 (1989), pp. 56-7; 61.

9. See Tzvetan Todorov, *The Fantastic: A Structural Approach to a Literary Genre*, trans. Richard Howard (Ittace, NY: Cronell University Press (1970) 1973).

10. R. Jackson, *Fantasy: The Literature of Subversion* (London: Methuen, 1981), pp. 12, 30.

11. *Ibid.*, pp. 20, 21.

12. *Ibid.*, p. 46.

13. A. Carter, *The Sadeian Woman: An Exercise in Cultural History* (London: Virago Press, 1979), pp. 6, 16.

14. On Gothicism in Angela Carter's tales see Patricia Duncker, 'Re-Imagining the Fairy Tales: Angela Carter's Bloody Chambers', *Literature and History* 10:1 (spring 1984), pp. 3-14.

15. *The Sadeian Woman*, p. 4.

FURTHER READING

Criticism

Ducornet, Rikki. "A Scatological and Cannibal Clock: Angela Carter's 'The Fall River Axe Murders.'" *Review of Contemporary Fiction* 14, no. 3 (fall 1994): 37-43.

Shows how Carter uses the symbolism of clocks and time to transform the story of Lizzie Borden's murder of her father and stepmother into what the critic sees as an overblown representation of human tragedy in her novel The Fall River Axe Murders.

Duncker, Patricia. "Queer Gothic: Angela Carter and the Lost Narratives of Sexual Subversion." *Critical Survey* 8, no. 1 (January 1996): 58-68.

Examines gothicism, homosexuality, and heterosexuality in Carter's fiction.

Fowl, Melinda G. "Angela Carter's *The Bloody Chamber* Revisited." *Critical Survey* 3, no. 1 (January 1991): 71-9.

Traces the sources of tales in The Bloody Chamber.

Lee, Alison. *Angela Carter*. New York: Twayne, 1997, 146 p.

Book-length study of Carter's life and works.

Lokke, Kari E. "*Bluebeard* and *The Bloody Chamber*: The Grotesque of Self-Parody and Self-Assertion." *Frontiers* 10, no. 1 (1988): 7-12.

Compares Carter's version of the Bluebeard legend with Max Frisch's, noting that both authors use the grotesque as a method for exposing the brutality that informs traditional patriarchal views of women.

McLaughlin, Becky. "Perverse Pleasure and Fetishized Text: The Deathly Erotics of Carter's 'The Bloody Chamber.'" *Style* 29, no. 3 (1995): 404-22.

Shows how Carter's story "The Bloody Chamber" explores the connection between the eroticism of life and the sensuality of death.

Peach, Linden. "Euro-American Gothic and the 1960s: *Shadow Dance* (1966), *Several Perceptions* (1968) and *Love* (1970)." In *Angela Carter*, pp. 26-70. New York: St. Martin's Press, 1998.

Traces Carter's indebtedness to the Euro-American Gothic tradition; notes how through a combination of Gothic and psychological fantasy Carter pursues themes and motifs from nineteenth-century American writers, notably Edgar Allan Poe and Herman Melville.

Sceats, Sarah. "Oral Sex: Vampiric Transgression and the Writing of Angela Carter." *Tulsa Studies in Women's Literature* 20, no. 1 (2001): 107-21.

Examines Carter's use of vampire tropes to explore gendered behavior and heterosexual power relations.

Stoddart, Helen. "*The Passion of New Eve* and the Cinema: Hysteria, Spectacle, Masquerade." In *The Gothic*, edited by Fred Botting, pp. 111-31. Suffolk, England, and Rochester, N.Y.: D. S. Brewer, 2001.

Discusses questions about the depiction—in Gothic terms—of Tristessa in The Passion of New Eve and explores notions of spectacle, gender identity, and psychoanalysis.

OTHER SOURCES FROM GALE:

Additional coverage of Carter's life and career is contained in the following sources published by Thomson Gale: *British Writers Supplement*, Vol. 3; *Contemporary Authors*, Vols. 53-56, 136; *Contemporary Authors New Revision Series*, Vols. 12, 36, 61, 106; *Contemporary Literary Criticism*, Vols. 5, 41, 76; *Dictionary of Literary Biography*, Vols. 14, 207, 261; *DISCovering Authors 3.0*; *Exploring Short Stories*; *Feminist Writers*; *Literature Resource Center*; *Major 20th-Century Writers*, Eds. 1, 2; *Major 21st-Century Writers*; *Reference Guide to Short Fiction*, Ed. 2; *St. James Guide to Fantasy Writers*; *St. James Guide to Science Fiction Writers*, Ed. 4; *Short Stories for Students*, Vols. 4, 12; *Short Story Criticism*, Vol. 13; *Something about the Author*, Vols. 66, 70; *Supernatural Fiction Writers*; *Twentieth-Century Literary Criticism*, Vol. 139; and *World Literature and Its Times*.

WILKIE COLLINS

(1824 - 1889)

(Full name William Wilkie Collins) English novelist, short story writer, travel writer, and playwright.

Considered a skillful manipulator of intricate plots, Collins is remembered as a principal founder of English detective fiction. His novels of intrigue and suspense, although as popular in Collins's day as the works of such Victorian luminaries as Charles Dickens, Anthony Trollope, and William Thackeray, were frequently dismissed by critics as sensationalist fiction. By the twentieth century, Collins began to receive recognition for his innovations in the detective genre, for his unconventional representation of female characters, and for his emphasis on careful plotting and revision, a practice that foreshadowed modern methods.

BIOGRAPHICAL INFORMATION

Collins was named for his father, William, a landscape painter, and his godfather, the artist Sir David Wilkie. Raised among artists and writers in England, Collins rebelled against the routine at the tea-broker's firm where, at the age of seventeen, he'd been placed by his father. He subsequently studied at Lincoln's Inn and was called to the Bar in 1851, but was to use his legal expertise only when writing fiction. After his father's death in 1847, Collins wrote *Memoirs of the Life of William Collins, Esq., R. A.* (1848) and two years later a lengthy novel, *Antonina; or, The Fall of Rome* (1850). Soon after the publication of his first novel, Collins made the acquaintance of Charles Dickens, and the two became close friends, working together on Dickens's magazines, traveling together, and occasionally collaborating on stories. He achieved immense popularity after the publication of his sensation novel *The Woman in White* in 1860, which spawned a literary vogue for such fiction that peaked in 1868 with the appearance of his highly successful *The Moonstone.* Always a frustrated playwright, Collins made dramatic adaptations of these and several of his other works of fiction, which were produced in England and the United States with fair success. After rising to fame, Collins became the subject of considerable scrutiny due to his unconventional personal life. Collins lived with his mistress—said to have been the model for the "woman in white"—and supported, in addition, another woman by whom he had three illegitimate children. Although Collins was accepted by literary friends, he was often ostracized by society at large for his unorthodox way of life. His rage at hypocritical morals and perhaps his desire to emulate Dickens inspired Collins to compose the didactic novels of his later years. He died in London in September of 1889.

MAJOR WORKS

Collins's first novel, *Antonina* was an imitative, historical romance in the style of Edward Bulwer-Lytton's *The Last Days of Pompeii*. It focuses on the siege of patriarchal Rome by a Gothic army. At the center of the tale is Antonina, a young girl who, after being wrongly cast out of her home by her father, falls in love with a Gothic soldier. Featuring an intricate plot and told through a series of monologues, *The Woman in White* is framed as a Gothic romance and offers two very different heroines: the strong and passionate Marian Holcombe and her half-sister, the beautiful and passive Laura Fairlie. The latter is manipulated by the novel's villain, Count Fosco, agrees to marry Fosco's henchman, and is subsequently robbed of her identity and forced into an asylum. Aided by her half-sister. she escapes and, along the way, uncovers numerous family secrets, including the story of the ghostly "woman in white" whom she has encountered in the past. Mysterious characters and vestiges like those used in *The Woman in White* also appear in "The Yellow Mask" (1856) and *The Black Robe* (1881).

CRITICAL RECEPTION

Although Collins has been called "the father of the English detective novel," critics have begun to give his Gothic tales increased attention. In *Antonina*, several critics note that he provides a strong portrayal of the "female Gothic" through the title character and her nemesis (and, some commentators argue, double), Goisvintha. Critics have also noted Collins's use of the Gothic to recast history in this tale. Collins turned to social criticsm in *The Woman in White*, again utilizing the Gothic to frame his commentary on certain behaviors. Although this tale also introduced a less traditional, soon-to-be much-emulated character, the amateur detective, Fred Botting has noted that Collins cast this personage against a classicly passive Gothic heroine who represents loss and suffering. In addition, Botting notes Collins's introduction of the spectral title character as well as his employment of doubling and family secrets. Susan M. Griffin has posited that the Gothic elements of *The Woman in White*, as well as those in "The Yellow Mask" and *The Black Robe*, convey a particularly anti-Catholic sentiment. Critics have also noted in Collins's Gothic works a departure from the traditions of popular fiction to create an insightful and subtly critical portrait of Victorian society.

PRINCIPAL WORKS

Memoirs of the Life of William Collins, Esq., R. A. (biography) 1848

Antonina; or, The Fall of Rome (novel) 1850

Rambles Beyond Railways (travelogue) 1851

Basil: A Story of Modern Life (novel) 1852

Hide and Seek (novel) 1854

After Dark (short stories) 1856

The Dead Secret (novel) 1857

*The New Magdalen (novel) 1857

The Queen of Hearts (short stories) 1859

The Woman in White (novel) 1860

No Name (novel) 1862

Armadale (novel) 1866

The Moonstone (novel) 1868

Man and Wife (novel) 1870

Poor Miss Finch (novel) 1872

The Frozen Deep and Other Stories (short stories) 1874

The Law and the Lady (novel) 1875

The Two Destinies (novel) 1876

The Fallen Leaves (novel) 1879

The Haunted Hotel: A Mystery of Modern Venice (novella) 1879

A Rogue's Life: From His Birth to His Marriage (novel) 1879

Jezebel's Daughter (novel) 1880

The Black Robe (novel) 1881

Heart and Science (novel) 1883

I Say No (novel) 1884

The Evil Genius (novel) 1886

The Guilty River (novel) 1886

Little Novels (novellas) 1887

The Legacy of Cain (novel) 1889

Blind Love (unfinished novel) 1890

*   This novel was rewritten as a play, *The New Magdalen*, in 1873.

COLLINS

WILKIE COLLINS (STORY DATE AUGUST-SEPTEMBER 1875)

SOURCE: Collins, Wilkie. "Miss Jéromette and the Clergyman." In *Great Ghost Stories: 34 Classic Tales of the Supernatural*, compiled by Robin Brockman, pp. 351-74. New York: Gramercy Books, 2002.

The following excerpt is from a short story originally published as "The Clergyman's Confession" in the 1875 August-September issue of The Canadian Monthly; *it was retitled "Miss Jéromette and the Clergyman" and collected in* Little Novels *in 1887.*

IX

I had sent the housekeeper out of my study. I was alone, with the photograph of the French-woman on my desk.

There could surely be little doubt about the discovery that had burst upon me. The man who had stolen his way into my house, driven by the terror of a temptation that he dared not reveal, and the man who had been my unknown rival in the by-gone time, were one and the same!

Recovering self-possession enough to realize this plain truth, the inferences that followed forced their way into my mind as a matter of course. The unnamed person who was the obstacle to my pupil's prospects in life, the unnamed person in whose company he was assailed by temptations which made him tremble for himself, stood revealed to me now as being, in all human probability, no other than Jéromette. Had she bound him in the fetters of the marriage which he had himself proposed? Had she discovered his place of refuge in my house? And was the letter that had been delivered to him of her writing? Assuming these questions to be answered in the affirmative, what, in that case, was his 'business in London'? I remembered how he had spoken to me of his temptations, I recalled the expression that had crossed his face when he recognized the handwriting on the letter—and the conclusion that followed literally shook me to the soul. Ordering my horse to be saddled, I rode instantly to the railway-station.

The train by which he had travelled to London had reached the terminus nearly an hour since. The one useful course that I could take, by way of quieting the dreadful misgivings crowding one after another on my mind, was to telegraph to Jéromette at the address at which I had last seen her. I sent the subjoined message—prepaying the reply:

'If you are in any trouble, telegraph to me. I will be with you by the first train. Answer, in any case.'

There was nothing in the way of the immediate dispatch of my message. And yet the hours passed, and no answer was received. By the advice of the clerk, I sent a second telegram to the London office, requesting an explanation. The reply came back in these terms:

'Improvements in street. House pulled down. No trace of person named in telegram.'

I mounted my horse, and rode back slowly to the rectory.

'The day of his return to me will bring with it the darkest days of my life.' . . . 'I shall die young, and die miserably. Have you interest enough still left in me to wish to hear of it?' . . . 'You shall hear of it.' Those words were in my memory while I rode home in the cloudless moonlight night. They were so vividly present to me that I could hear again her pretty foreign accent, her quiet clear tones, as she spoke them. For the rest, the emotion of that memorable day had worn me out. The answer from the telegraph-office had struck me with a strange and stony despair. My mind was a blank. I had no thoughts. I had no tears.

I was about half-way on my road home, and I had just heard the clock of a village church strike ten, when I became conscious, little by little, of a chilly sensation slowly creeping through and through me to the bones. The warm balmy air of a summer night was abroad. It was the month of July. In the month of July, was it possible that any living creature (in good health) could feel cold? It was not possible—and yet, the chilly sensation still crept through and through me to the bones.

I looked up. I looked all round me.

My horse was walking along an open high-road. Neither trees nor waters were near me. On either side, the flat fields stretched away bright and broad in the moonlight.

I stopped my horse, and looked round me again.

Yes: I saw it. With my own eyes I saw it. A pillar of white mist—between five and six feet high, as well as I could judge—was moving beside me at the edge of the road, on my left hand. When I stopped, the white mist stopped. When I went on, the white mist went on. I pushed my horse to a trot—the pillar of mist was with me. I urged him to a gallop—the pillar of mist was with me. I stopped him again—the pillar of mist stood still.

The white colour of it was the white colour of the fog which I had seen over the river—on the night when I had gone to bid her farewell. And the chill which had then crept through me to the bones was the chill that was creeping through me now.

I went on again slowly. The white mist went on again slowly—with the clear bright night all round it.

I was awed rather than frightened. There was one moment, and one only, when the fear came to me that my reason might be shaken. I caught myself keeping time to the slow tramp of the horse's feet with the slow utterance of these words, repeated over and over again: 'Jéromette is dead. Jéromette is dead.' But my will was still my own: I was able to control myself, to impose silence on my own muttering lips. And I rode on quietly. And the pillar of mist went quietly with me.

My groom was waiting for my return at the rectory gate. I pointed to the mist, passing through the gate with me.

'Do you see anything there?' I said.

The man looked at me in astonishment.

I entered the rectory. The housekeeper met me in the hall. I pointed to the mist, entering with me.

'Do you see anything at my side?' I asked.

The housekeeper looked at me as the groom had looked at me.

'I am afraid you are not well, sir,' she said. 'Your colour is all gone—you are shivering. Let me get you a glass of wine.'

I went into my study, on the ground-floor, and took the chair at my desk. The photograph still lay where I had left it. The pillar of mist floated round the table, and stopped opposite to me, behind the photograph.

The housekeeper brought in the wine. I put the glass to my lips, and sat it down again. The chill of the mist was in the wine. There was no taste, no reviving spirit in it. The presence of the housekeeper oppressed me. My dog had followed her into the room. The presence of the animal oppressed me. I said to the woman, 'Leave me by myself, and take the dog with you.'

They went out, and left me alone in the room.

I sat looking at the pillar of mist, hovering opposite to me.

It lengthened slowly, until it reached to the ceiling. As it lengthened, it grew bright and luminous. A time passed, and a shadowy appearance showed itself in the centre of the light. Little by little, the shadowy appearance took the outline of a human form. Soft brown eyes, tender and melancholy, looked at me through the unearthly light in the mist. The head and the rest of the face broke next slowly on my view. Then the figure gradually revealed itself, moment by moment, downward and downward to the feet. She stood before me as I had last seen her, in her purple-merino dress, with the black-silk apron, with the white handkerchief tied loosely round her neck. She stood before me, in the gentle beauty that I remembered so well; and looked at me as she had looked when she gave me her last kiss—when her tears had dropped on my cheek.

I fell on my knees at the table. I stretched out my hands to her imploringly. I said, 'Speak to me—O, once again speak to me, Jéromette.'

Her eyes rested on me with a divine compassion in them. She lifted her hand, and pointed to the photograph on my desk, with a gesture which bade me turn the card. I turned it. The name of the man who had left my house that morning was inscribed on it, in her own handwriting.

I looked up at her again, when I had read it. She lifted her hand once more, and pointed to the handkerchief round her neck. As I looked at it, the fair white silk changed horribly in colour—the fair white silk became darkened and drenched in blood.

A moment more—and the vision of her began to grow dim. By slow degrees, the figure, then the face, faded back into the shadowy appearance that I had first seen. The luminous inner light died out in the white mist. The mist itself dropped slowly downwards—floated a moment in airy circles on the floor—vanished. Nothing was before me but the familiar wall of the room, and the photograph lying face downwards on my desk.

X

The next day, the newspapers reported the discovery of a murder in London. A Frenchwoman was the victim. She had been killed by a wound in the throat. The crime had been discovered between ten and eleven o'clock on the previous night.

GENERAL COMMENTARY

TAMAR HELLER (ESSAY DATE 1992)

SOURCE: Heller, Tamar. "Becoming an Author in 1848: History and the Gothic in the Early Works of Wilkie Collins." In *Dead Secrets: Wilkie Collins and the Female Gothic*, pp. 38-57. New Haven, Conn.: Yale University Press, 1992.

In the following excerpt, Heller asserts that Collins developed his later Gothic style in his earlier, non-Gothic, works.

Wilkie Collins' first work, published in 1848 when he was twenty-four, was a biography of his father, the respected painter and Royal Academician William Collins. In contrast to the matrilineal tradition of the female Gothic, *Memoirs of the Life of William Collins* is a monument to the male artist that celebrates the bond between father and son. Chronicling William's Franklinesque rise from poverty to prosperity through unrelenting industry, Collins eulogizes his father as an exemplary family man and, above all, an empowering predecessor. The *Memoirs* were, however, an anomaly in the career their publication launched. Not only was Collins to turn from writing biography to writing fiction, but the filial piety of the *Memoirs* was to be replaced by a melodramatic Gothicism that would have shocked the father who reportedly avoided in his painting all that was "coarse, violent, revolting, fearful"[1]— everything, in other words, that came to be associated with his son's art.

The *Memoirs*, then, can be seen as a generic dead end for Collins, as can his first novel, *Antonina* (1850), a bustling historical epic in the style of Scott and Bulwer-Lytton. Yet these often neglected early works have an important place in Collins' oeuvre as fictions of origins in which he interrogates the sources of his art and experiments with representational strategies. Most significant, the *Memoirs* and *Antonina* draft the kind of plot that was to become characteristic of Collins' later and more mature work from *Basil* onward, in which a narrative about literary authority is cast as a story about gender and, in particular, as a family romance in which the father is invested with the social and artistic power from which the mother is excluded.

In *Basil*, the son who is the figure for the emergent bourgeois artist defies the authority of his father and is subsequently disinherited. The plot concerning rebellion against the father is already embedded in the early works that are the focus of this chapter, but it is complicated by a nostalgia for the patriarchal power beginning to decline in the *Memoirs* and dramatically waning in the novel about the Fall of Rome, home of the paterfamilias. As I suggested above, the figure of William Collins looms large in the *Memoirs* as an image for masculine authority and as the Romantic predecessor, since he not only was a friend of Wordsworth and Coleridge, but also practiced in his landscapes a Romantic fidelity to Nature. Yet the father's Romanticism (like that of Wordsworth and Coleridge in their later years) was of a conservative variety that eschewed political radicalism in favor of "Toryism" (II, 55). If the *Memoirs* were a dead end for Collins, it was because the work suggested the end of the (paternal) line for this Romanticism as a form of art worthy of the son's emulation, not only because he was more liberal than his father but also because William's conservative philosophy no longer had validity in the politically stormy world of the 1830s and 1840s. Collins declared in a brief autobiographical sketch written in the early 1860s, "An author I became in the year 1848,"[2] and his early works are about what it meant to launch an artistic career in the period culminating in the European revolutions of that year, but beginning in England with the movement for Chartist reform that Collins refers to in the *Memoirs* and represents in his historical narrative in *Antonina*.

Becoming an author in 1848 suggests an oedipal narrative in which the son can produce only once he has acknowledged, through the publication of the *Memoirs*, the death of his Tory father. Yet even as the *Memoirs*, and particularly *Antonina*, which is more explicitly about defying the father's rules, show how Collins departs from William's example, they are also pervaded by a sense of the newfound absence of paternal authority—a loss figured in his first novel as a crisis of male power that will become pronounced rather than diminished in the later fictions. This narrative about a crisis of male power is really about a crisis of definition, in which the post-Romantic and bourgeois male writer attempts to define his own authority in the absence of the father's. The fall of the father's authority is connected in turn with the rise of a hitherto repressed maternal or feminine power that, in a way similar to the fictions discussed in [chapter one of *Dead Secrets*] is associated both with revolution and with the Gothic. It is in fact Collins' uneasy relation to the Gothic, which comes to inspire his art, that forms the major generic and ideological tension of *Antonina*, a novel in which patriarchal Rome is besieged by the Gothic army that is embodied in

2a monstrous female figure of ressentiment. In this narrative, as would become more evident in such later novels as *Basil* and *The Woman in White,* Collins is simultaneously attracted to the rebellion associated with the feminine and repulsed by it, as he seeks to constitute an aesthetic authority structured by the ideology of bourgeois manliness.

. . . . .

Antonina: *The Invasion of the Gothic*

After he had finished eulogizing his father as patriarch and predecessor, Collins returned to the "classical romance"[3] he had interrupted to write the *Memoirs.* In doing so, he turned from a narrative in praise of the father to one about rebellion against fathers. In *Antonina; or, The Fall of Rome,* published in 1850, the Roman paterfamilias Numerian, an ascetic bent on reforming the corruptions of the early Church, discovers his daughter Antonina hiding a lute, which she has been playing despite his commands that she avoid sensual pleasures. Smashing the instrument to pieces, he orders her to her room, where she is visited that night by Vetranio, the dissolute young aristocrat who gave her the lute and who forces this clandestine entrance in order to seduce her. In the midst of this scene, Antonina is again discovered by her puritanical father, who incorrectly assumes that she has been succumbing to temptation rather than virtuously resisting it. Dramatically disinheriting her, he exiles her from his house, thus thrusting her into the events surrounding the Fall of Rome and, figuratively, into the tumultuous history that lurks behind the stately facade of the *Memoirs.*

Collins himself drew the parallel between the events of antiquity in *Antonina* and the type of contemporary "fierce political contention" he alludes to at the end of the *Memoirs.* In a letter to Richard Bentley, the editor who accepted *Antonina,* he referred to the revolutionary events of 1848, and especially to the siege of Rome that followed: "I have thought it probable that such a work might not inappropriately be offered for your inspection, while recent occurrences continue to direct public attention particularly on Roman affairs."[4] In making such analogies between his own world and that of the past, Collins had many antecedents. The nineteenth-century historical novel, developed most influentially by Scott, was often a vehicle for encoding responses to contemporary events. Moreover, the subgenre of historical fiction to which *Antonina* belongs—the novel about the decline of empire—was a

particularly popular way of representing, as Lee Sterrenburg argues, "anatomies of failed revolutions" in the aftermath of the French Revolution and the Napoleonic Wars.[5]

The details of the siege of Rome in *Antonina* could have been influenced by accounts of the events of 1848-49, but the novel is more generally inspired by the idea of revolution itself, since Collins had started it prior to 1848. In particular, the portrait of Roman society in *Antonina* recalls how the class-stratified British society of the 1830s was startled by the emergence of the Chartist movement, which suggested the possibility of a new English revolution. The setting of the novel, indeed, illustrates the scene Collins described in the *Memoirs* where, during the "social and political convulsions" accompanying Reform Bill agitation in the 1830s, the "noble and wealthy," threatened by the "popular revolution" symbolically mirrored by the "mysterious pestilence" of cholera, had "little time . . . to attend to the remoter importance of the progress of national Art" (I, 344-45). *Antonina* begins with the Roman aristocracy, an Epicurean and "effeminate" lot,[6] reluctantly but rapidly engulfed by the famine and plague overwhelming the city during the blockade of Rome by the Goths. The artist-figure Vetranio, the brilliant but debauched poet who gives Antonina her lute, is an image for the artistic and social decadence precipitating the Fall of Rome. Collins' diagnosis of the excesses of the Roman elite is reminiscent of the portraits in such other Victorian narratives of the corrupt ancien régime before the French Revolution as Carlyle's *The French Revolution* (1837) and Dickens' *A Tale of Two Cities* (1859). The Goths at the gate in *Antonina* externalize the forces within Roman society that resist the venal tyranny of rulers called "the oppressors of the world" (375). Upper-class luxury and cruelty are juxtaposed with hints of covert lower-class mutiny and ressentiment, and the narrator claims that the "dangerous and artificial" position of the "poorer classes" was "one of the most important of the internal causes of the downfall of Rome" (76).

In the context of this political allegory, Collins' portrayal of the Fall of Rome tells a different story from the *Memoirs* of what it means to become an author in 1848. The biography clings to the image of the father as predecessor, even as it suggests that his art is no longer viable in 1848. *Antonina,* however, is a novel about how, amid a "world-wide revolution" (341), the power of fathers has come to lack meaning for the emergent artist, who is now aligned with the forces of rebellion against established hierarchies. The expulsion of Antonina from her father's house for insubordination (her presumed sexual fall figures her fall into art) is the darker narrative of familial conflict that the filial piety of the **Memoirs** papers over. With Numerian recalling, as Nuel Pharr Davis points out, the harsher and more intolerant qualities of William Collins,[7] **Antonina** spells out the oedipal narrative, hinted at in the father's biography, in which the transgressive child becomes an artist by being thrust out of the father's house into an atmosphere of turbulent historical change. Such a narrative associates the father with the outmoded aristocracy the revolution replaces, not inappropriately since, although William Collins is portrayed as the heroic bourgeois in the **Memoirs,** his patrons were largely aristocratic.

This oedipal narrative, however, is complicated by the sex change that transforms the portrait of the artist as a young man into the portrait of the artist as a young girl. Making the artist into a daughter revises the patrilineal plot of the **Memoirs,** in which the son inherits the father's artistic power. To feminize the figure for the son, in fact, hyperbolically underscores his alienation from the father's art; when Antonina is expelled from her father's house, she is cast out from the entire patriarchal tradition represented by the Fathers of the early Church who are Numerian's inspiration. In the absence of a masculine tradition, the artist is aligned with a feminine one that resurrects the figure of the mother repressed in the **Memoirs,** even if only to associate her with illegitimacy and exclusion from authority. By playing the lute, Antonina becomes connected in her father's eyes with her dead mother (a Spaniard, a foreigner), whom she dimly remembers singing to her "hour after hour, in her cradle" (122). Since Antonina's mother was unfaithful to her father, this feminine tradition is linked not only to art but also to adultery; as Numerian says when he discovers Vetranio in his daughter's room, "her mother was a harlot before her!" (195).

This association of feminine art with actual or presumed sexual fall implies that the feminine tradition is a renegade one that represents rebellion against the father's law. Such feminine rebellion, although it switches the sex of the child protagonist in the oedipal plot, retains that plot's emphasis on a struggle with the father. Still, Antonina's rebellion, unlike her mother's, is of the most mild-mannered kind, since she is neither a harlot nor defiant after her brutal treatment by her father; her greatest desire, in fact, is to be reconciled with him. In this case, then, femininity

represents not so much an alternative form of artistic power to the father's as it does powerlessness and vulnerability. Not only does Antonina become an icon of terrified passivity (she spends vast portions of the novel either frightened or asleep), but she soon ceases to be a figure for the artist, preserving a fragment of her smashed lute but never again playing it.

In this sense, transforming the artist into a daughter minimizes the extent of the rebellion against the father, since she leaves his house only to be immediately transferred to the protection of another male figure. Wandering accidentally into the Gothic camp, Antonina is shielded by Hermanric, a young warrior, who swiftly falls in love with her. Antonina and "Her Man" are then exemplars of an embryonic domesticity that provides a private haven in a heartless world: "While a world-wide revolution was concentrating its hurricane forces around them . . . they could . . . completely forget the stormy outward world, in themselves" (341). This domestic ideal represents the new bourgeois ideology that rises, phoenix-like, from the fall of the aristocracy.[8]

Hermanric in particular emerges as a figure for the bourgeois manhood who, by controlling women within domesticity, is an alternative to the other classes, which are either too emasculated (the effeminate aristocracy) or too emasculating (the lower classes who revolt against those above them). Early in the novel, Collins ecstatically prophesies the rise of the middle classes following a vignette in which a stalwart Roman farmer vehemently denounces the aristocratic "tyrants" whose "rank had triumphed over my industry" (83):

> By this time he had lashed himself into fury. His eyes glared, his cheeks flushed, his voice rose. Could he then have seen the faintest vision of the destiny that future ages had in store for the posterity of the race that now suffered throughout civilized Europe, like him—could he have imagined how, in after years, the "middle class," despised in his day, was to rise to privilege and power; to hold in its just hands the balance of the prosperity of nations; to crush oppression and regulate rule; to soar in its mighty flight above thrones, and principalities, and ranks and riches, apparently obedient, but really commanding—could he but have foreboded this, what a light must have burst upon his gloom, what a hope must have soothed him in his despair!
>
> (83-84)

This paean to the messianic middle class accumulates clauses with a rhetorical feverishness that echoes the farmer's outburst. The bourgeois man thus seems to be allowed the rebellion against the ancien régime ("apparently obedient, but really commanding") denied to both the daughter Antonina and the insolent lower classes. Yet Hermanric, the novel's principal figure for this emergent bourgeois manhood, is rendered singularly powerless. Although in the passage following the farmer's speech Collins synecdochically compares the bourgeoisie to "just hands," Hermanric's hands become immobilized. To punish him for his transgression in protecting his Roman enemy Antonina rather than killing her, Hermanric's angry sister Goisvintha severs the tendons in his hand with a knife. That he is shortly afterward slain as a deserter by a posse of vengeful Huns adds an appropriate finale to this symbolic castration.

The eruption of the sister into the scene of proto-domesticity between Antonina and Hermanric points both to Goisvintha's importance in the novel and to the energy with which she disrupts its conventions. Literally female Gothic, she also figuratively signals the invasion of the Gothic genre into Collins' art. In the most obvious sense, her crazed desire to revenge her family, massacred by the Romans, recalls the obsessed melodramatic figures in the Gothic tradition. Goisvintha evokes Gothic conventions in a general way, but through her the genre also is associated more specifically with images of feminine power and violence. To explain her "mysterious and powerful influence" over her brother (217), Collins emphasizes how Gothic culture is structured around women's position as priests and seers, a "remarkable ascendency of the woman over the man" (215). In her first scene with Hermanric in the novel, indeed, it appears as if she had "changed sexes" (20) with her brother; the phallic woman, she seizes the knives and swords he will not wield against Antonina in an attempt to use them herself. Throughout the novel, the narrative voice disapprovingly comments on Goisvintha's usurpation of the male role: she is "harsh and unwomanly" (213), the "unappeasable and unwomanly Goisvintha" (381), who speaks in a "broken, hoarse, and unfeminine" voice (23).

This emphasis on Goisvintha's rebellion against gender roles links her to her Roman enemy Antonina (whom at one point she stabs with her ever-ready knife) as an embodiment of the daughter's covert rebellion against her father. In this position as doppelgänger, Goisvintha recalls the prominence of such doubles in the Gothic tradition, while also, more importantly, evoking the genre's representation of revolution. In *Antonina*, the Gothic gives Collins a language for figuring revolution, even as it aligns that language with the feminine. Goisvintha is the novel's figure for revolution; an early version of Dickens' Madame Defarge (for whom she may have been a model),[9] she seethes with ressentiment against Roman tyrants. Her iconic embodiment of the monstrous mother (it is the death of her children that fuels her outrage) recalls Carlyle's image of the "insurrection of women" during the French Revolution as an uprising of mothers, "Judiths" and "Menads" defined by their power to mutilate and disempower men, as Goisvintha does to Hermanric.[10]

Goisvintha's feminine "insurrection" again ties her to Antonina, for if the female Goth is a rebellious mother, Antonina is connected through her mother with a tradition of feminine revolt against the father's law. Whereas the rise of the feminine rebellious energy that Goisvintha represents precipitates the waning of patriarchal power—during the course of the novel the rigidly ascetic Numerian becomes weak and senile—it poses an even more significant threat to the new bourgeois order signified by the domesticity of Hermanric and Antonina. In this bourgeois ideology, woman is not a rebellious but a submissive partner, a solace amid the storms of history (surely it is appropriate that Goisvintha stabs Antonina in the throat, as if to emblematize this type of silencing). Goisvintha, however, is sacrificed—quite literally—to restore domesticity. Captured by the demented Ulpius, who is obsessed with reviving the cult of the pagan gods, she is offered to them, as if in parody of her own phallic energy, by being impaled on a large sword. Yet Goisvintha's violent chastisement, which excises both feminine power and the Gothic energy that figures it, ultimately excludes history itself from the novel. After the deaths of both the female Goth and her crazed assailant, the energy of the historical narrative dissipates, allowing for the reconciliation of Antonina with her repentant father and the reestablishment of domesticity, albeit (since Hermanric is dead) in an impotent and desexualized form.

This exclusion of history has the paradoxical effect of making the novel subtitled "The Fall of Rome" elide that event. Concluding the story after the first blockade of Rome by the Goths, the narrator turns from the image of Antonina and her father mourning over Hermanric's grave to ask:

> Shall we longer delay in the farmhouse garden? No! For us, as for Vetranio, it is now time to depart! While peace still watches round the walls of Rome; while the hearts of the father and daughter still repose together in security after the trials that have wrung them, let us quit the scene! Here, at last, the narrative that we have followed over a dark and stormy tract, reposes on a tranquil field; and here let us cease to pursue it!
>
> So the traveler who traces the course of a river, wanders through the day among the rocks and precipices that lead onward from its troubled source; and, when the evening is at hand, pauses and rests where the banks are grassy and the stream is smooth.
>
> (656)

The transitory nature of this final scene ("while peace still watches round the walls of Rome") reminds the reader that this domestic sunniness is soon to be interrupted, and perhaps destroyed, by the "dark and stormy" history it holds only imperfectly at bay.

In terms of *Antonina*'s representation of 1848, such an ending is in one sense appropriate. By concluding the novel after the Goths' first blockade, the "world-wide revolution" of Rome's fall is still in the process of happening, just as, presumably, social conditions were ripe for revolutionary movements, even though the 1848 revolution did not travel to England. Still, the narrator's "No!" after he asks if he should linger in Rome recalls what Georg Lukács referred to as the "denial of history" in bourgeois literature following 1848. Surveying the historical novel after Scott, Lukács examines how the bourgeoisie, who had portrayed themselves prior to 1848 as revolutionary heroes in a drama of historical "progress," react to the threat of proletarian uprisings that contest their power as much as that of the upper classes. The form that this bourgeois reaction takes after 1848, Lukács argues, is to elide the representation of history as a type of rebellion of one class against another, dwelling instead on narratives that suggest the inevitability of bourgeois hegemony.[11]

Some recent critics have adopted and elaborated on Lukács' theory to trace how literature uses domestic ideology as a particularly powerful means of naturalizing bourgeois authority in the 1848 period. In his study of the English historical novel, Nicholas Rance locates 1848 as the moment of a shift from the historical fiction of Scott and Bulwer-Lytton to domestic fiction that normalizes bourgeois ideology.[12] A more detailed history of this shift is provided by Nancy Armstrong, who underscores the separation between political themes and domestic ones that became pronounced in English fiction by the 1840s. As Armstrong argues, novels of the 1840s imply that the world of politics should be isolated from domesticity, even as they suggest that struggles between classes can be regulated in the same way as rebellions within families.[13]

By moving, at the end of *Antonina*, beyond history to take refuge in a patently fragile domesticity, Collins both participates in this narrative economy and points to its inherent weakness. Although *Antonina* embodies the energy of revolution and rebellion in female characters and then silences them, this maneuver does not restore male authority over the family, history, or the narrative itself: Numerian is senescent and powerless, and Hermanric is dead. Moreover, the conclusion of *Antonina* does not solve the problem of Collins' own literary authority, of his becoming an author in 1848. The novel that rejects the law of the father imagines art and rebellion as the provenance of female figures, who are in turn contained and circumscribed. In this novel about the invasion of the Gothic, the power concentrated in the figure of Goisvintha represents the narrative energy of the Gothic that invades Collins' art even as, in this revolutionary moment, he turns farther away from the father's example. The attempt to exorcise the Gothic or to hold it at bay anticipates the narrative pattern that would become more pronounced in the novels that follow *Antonina*, in which a crisis of power for the male artist is linked with the rise of a female power associated with or figured by the Gothic. The male artist's efforts to ally himself with or to contain the power of these female and Gothic figures form the major narrative tension of Collins' later fictions. In *Antonina*, however, these tensions are resolved only by an evasion of closure that suggests an inability to tell the narrative of 1848. Although the novel figures the waning of the patriarchal power eulogized in the *Memoirs*, at this early moment in his career Collins could not imagine an alternative image of either male or female authority.

Notes

1. W. Wilkie Collins, *Memoirs of the Life of William Collins, Esq., R.A., With Selections from His Journals and Correspondence* (1848; reprint, Wakefield, W. Yorkshire: EP Publishing, 1978), II, 311. All references will be to this edition, a facsimile of the original two-volume edition, and are cited by both volume and page. Since Collins dropped the initial "W." in most of the books he published after the *Memoirs*, I refer to him in all subsequent citations of his works as Wilkie Collins.

2. Wilkie Collins, "Memorandum, Relating to the Life and Writings of Wilkie Collins" (1862), in Morris L. Parrish and Elizabeth V. Miller, *Wilkie Collins and Charles Reade: First Editions (with a Few Exceptions) in the Library at Dormy House, Pine Valley, New Jersey* (London, 1940; reprint, New York; Franklin, 1968), 4. This brief autobiographical sketch is printed in its entirety on pp. 4-5.

3. The phrase is Collins', from his "Memorandum," in Parrish and Miller, *Wilkie Collins and Charles Reade*, 4.

4. Wilkie Collins to Richard Bentley, 30 August 1849, quoted in Sue Lonoff, *Wilkie Collins and His Victorian Readers: A Study in the Rhetoric of Authorship* (New York: AMS Press, 1982), 68-69.

5. See Lee Sterrenburg, "Mary Shelley's *The Last Man*: Anatomies of Failed Revolutions," in *The Endurance of Frankenstein: Essays on Mary Shelley's Monster*, ed. George Levine and U. C. Knoepflmacher (Berkeley: University of California Press, 1979), 326-27, where he discusses the numerous "post-Napoleonic works of literature and painting which shared analogous themes of the end of the race or the end of empire." An early pre-Napoleonic example of this type of work is Volney's *Ruins of Empire* (1791), which the monster hears Felix and Safie reading in *Frankenstein;* a later example is Bulwer-Lytton's *The Last Days of Pompeii* (1834), probably a source for *Antonina*.

6. Wilkie Collins, *Antonina; or, The Fall of Rome*, vol. 17 of *The Works of Wilkie Collins* (New York: Peter Fenelon Collier, [1900]), 38. All references will be to this edition and are cited by page in the text.

7. Davis, *Life of Wilkie Collins*, 44.

8. There is one quite bizarre scene that underscores the importance of domestic ideology in *Antonina* while simultaneously pushing it into the realm of Gothic horror. When the decadent Vetranio holds his "Banquet of Famine," during which selected aristocrats and their lackies propose to commit mass suicide by drinking themselves to death, he places in a curtained alcove the body of a woman he found on the street, "propped up on a high black throne" with her arms "artifically supported" and "stretched out as if in denunciation over the banqueting-table" (501). This black humor is meant to emphasize, with Vetranio's characteristic cynical satire, the presence of mortality and the Roman's impending doom. When one of the plebeian guests, the hunchbacked and sinister Reburrus, rises to toast the figure Vetranio calls the "mighty mother" of "mystic revelations" (501), he realizes with horror that she is in fact his mother, whom he had spurned when she reproached him for his neglect. Overwhelmed with repentance, Reburrus collapses, repeating hypnotically "MY MOTHER! MY MOTHER!" (504). Thus although the figure of the mother here is indeed "mighty," an icon of violated domesticity that enforces that ideology, she is also a Gothic image that terrorizes men, much as does that emasculating female Goth, Goisvintha, whose role I discuss later in this chapter.

9. Dickens' portrait of Madame Defarge in *A Tale of Two Cities* may have been influenced by Collins' Goisvintha, since he could have read *Antonina* either when it first appeared (he had subscribed to the *Memoirs* on their publication) or later, when he and Collins were more closely associated. Although Dickens' portrait of the revolutionary woman, like Collins', was surely also influenced by Carlyle's revision of Burke in *The French Revolution*, there are many specific similarities between Madame Defarge and Goisvintha. Both women are consumed by the desire to revenge their families (Madame Defarge even comes with her own sidekick, the Vengeance), and both egg on vacillating men (Hermanric, Ernest Defarge) who shrink from killing their female enemies.

10. See Thomas Carlyle, *The French Revolution*, in *Works* (Boston: Centennial Memorial Edition, [1904]), vol. I, chap. 4 ("The Menads"), 243: "descend, O mothers; descend, ye Judiths, to food and revenge!"

11. See Georg Lukács, *The Historical Novel* (1937), trans. Hannah and Stanley Mitchell, with an introduction by Fredric Jameson (1963; reprint, Lincoln: University of Nebraska Press, 1983), especially 171-250.

12. See Rance, *The Historical Novel and Popular Politics* (New York: Barnes, 1975), chap. 1, "The Historical Novel after Scott," 37-62.

13. In general, her *Desire and Domestic Fiction: A Political History of the Novel* (Oxford: Oxford University Press, 1987) charts the rise of this representational strategy; see in particular the chapter "History in the House of Culture," 161-202.

DUBLIN UNIVERSITY MAGAZINE (REVIEW DATE FEBRUARY 1861)

SOURCE: "Recent Popular Novels: *The Woman in White.*" *Dublin University Magazine* 57, no. 338 (February 1861): 200-04.

In the following excerpt, the critic offers a negative assessment of The Woman in White.

[In **The Woman in White**] the spirit of modern realism has woven a tissue of scenes more wildly improbable than the fancy of an average idealist would have ventured to inflict on readers beyond their teens. Mr. W. Collins has for some years been favourably known to the general reader as a painstaking manufacturer of stories, short or long, whose chief merit lies in the skilful elaboration of a startling mystery traceable to some natural cause, but baffling all attempts to solve it until the author himself has given us the right clue. Some praise is also due to him for the care with which these literary puzzles are set off by a correct if not very natural style, a pleasing purity of moral tone, and a certain knack of hitting the more superficial traits of character. When we have said all we can for him, we have said nothing that would entitle him to a higher place among English novelists, than the compiler of an average school-history would enjoy among English historians. . . .

[Take the plot away from **The Woman in White**,] and there is nothing left to examine. There is not one lifelike character: not one natural dialogue in the whole book. Both hero and heroine are wooden, commonplace, uninteresting in any way apart from the story itself. . . .

What character his personages have, the author prides himself on bringing out in a way which other novelists will do well not to imitate. If they neither say nor do aught characteristic on their own account, yet in connexion with the story most of them have a good deal to write about themselves or about each other. This, indeed, forms the main peculiarity of the book. . . . [As Collins claims in his preface:] "The story of the book is told throughout by the characters of the book," each of them in turn taking up the wondrous tale at the point where his or her shadow falls most invitingly across the scene. . . . What movement the story has could have been imparted by much simpler means; and

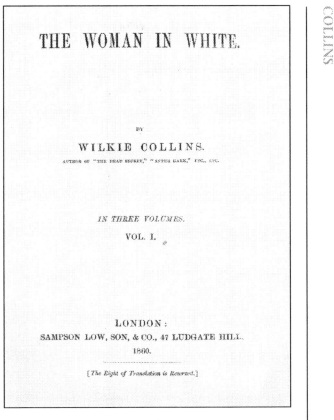

Title page of *The Woman in White*, 1860.

we would rather have seen the characters developed in the usual way, than by a process about as credible and straightforward as that employed by the spirits who are supposed to move our drawing-groom tables. . . .

But the attempt to combine newness of form and substance with reality of treatment has led to failure of a still more glaring kind. Throughout the book circumstances grotesque or improbable meet you at every turn. You are bidden to look at scenes of real modern life, described by the very persons who figured therein, and you find yourself, instead, wandering in a world as mythical as that portrayed on the boards of a penny theatre or in the pages of a nursery tale.

MARGARET OLIPHANT (ESSAY DATE MAY 1862)

SOURCE: Oliphant, Margaret. "Sensation Novels." *Blackwood's Edinburgh Magazine* 91, no. 559 (May 1862): 564-84.

In the following excerpt, Oliphant discusses sensation novels and praises The Woman in White *as an outstanding effort in the genre.*

Ten years ago the world in general had come to a singular crisis in its existence. The age was lost in self-admiration. We had done so many things that nobody could have expected a century before—we were on the way to do so many more, if common report was to be trusted. We were about inaugurating the reign of universal peace in a world too deeply connected by links of universal interest ever to commit the folly of war again—we had invented everything that was most unlikely, and had nothing before us but to go on perfecting our inventions, and, securing all the powers of nature in harness, to do all manner of peaceable work for us like the giants in the children's story. What a wonderful difference in ten years! Instead of linking peaceful hands, and vowing to study war no more, we have turned Industry away from her vaunted work of putting a girdle round the world, and set her to forge thunderbolts in volcanic din and passion. In that momentous interval great wars have begun and ended, and fighting has come into fashion throughout the palpitating earth. We who once did, and made, and declared ourselves masters of all things, have relapsed into the natural size of humanity before the great events which have given a new character to the age. Though we return with characteristic obstinacy and iteration to the grand display of wealth and skill which in 1851 was a Festival of Peace, we repeat the celebration with very different thoughts. It is a changed world in which we are now standing. If no distant sound of guns echoes across seas and continents upon our ears as we wander under the South Kensington domes, the lack of the familiar sound will be rather disappointing than satisfactory. That distant roar has come to form a thrilling accompaniment to the safe life we lead at home. On the other side of the Atlantic, a race *blasée* and lost in universal *ennui* has bethought itself of the grandest expedient for procuring a new sensation; and albeit we follow at a humble distance, we too begin to feel the need of a supply of new shocks and wonders. Those fell Merrimacs and Monitors, stealing forth with a certain devilish invulnerability and composure upon the human ships and men to be made fire and carnage of, are excitement too high pitched for comfort; but it is only natural that art and literature should, in an age which has turned to be one of events, attempt a kindred depth of effect and shock of incident. In the little reflected worlds of the novel and the drama the stimulant has acted strongly, and the result in both has been a significant and remarkable quickening of public interest. Shakespeare, even in the excitement of a

new interpretation, has not crowded the waning playhouse, as has the sensation drama with its mock catastrophes; and Sir Walter himself never deprived his readers of their lawful rest to a greater extent with one novel than Mr Wilkie Collins has succeeded in doing with his **Woman in White**. We will not attempt to decide whether the distance between the two novelists is less than that which separates the skirts of Shakespeare's regal mantle from the loftiest stretch of Mr Bourcicault. But it is a fact that the well-known old stories of readers sitting up all night over a novel had begun to grow faint in the public recollection. Domestic histories, however virtuous and charming, do not often attain that result—nor, indeed, would an occurrence so irregular and destructive of all domestic proprieties be at all a fitting homage to the virtuous chronicles which have lately furnished the larger part of our light literature. Now a new fashion has been set to English novel-writers. Whether it can be followed extensively, or whether it would be well if that were possible, are very distinct questions; but it cannot be denied that a most striking and original effort, sufficiently individual to be capable of originating a new school in fiction, has been made, and that the universal verdict has crowned it with success.

Mr Wilkie Collins is not the first man who has produced a sensation novel. By fierce expedients of crime and violence, by *diablerie* of divers kinds, and by the wild devices of a romance which smiled at probabilities, the thing has been done before now. The higher class of American fiction, as represented by Hawthorne, attempts little else. In that strange hybrid between French excitement and New England homeliness, we recognise the influence of a social system which has paralysed all the wholesome wonders and nobler mysteries of human existence. Hectic rebellion against nature—frantic attempts by any kind of black art or mad psychology to get some grandeur and sacredness restored to life—or if not sacredness and grandeur, at least horror and mystery, there being nothing better in earth or heaven; Mesmerism possibly for a make-shift, or Socialism, if perhaps it might be more worth while to turn ploughmen and milkmaids than ladies and gentlemen; or, if none of these would do, best to undermine life altogether, and find what creeping honours might be underground: here a Scarlet Letter and impish child of shame, there a snake-girl, horrible junction of reptile and woman. The result is no doubt a class of books abounding in sensation; but the effect is invariably attained by violent and illegitimate means, as fantastic in themselves as they are contradictory to actual life. The Master of English fiction, Sir E. B. Lytton, has accomplished the same end, by magic and supernaturalism, as in the wild and beautiful romance of *Zanoni*. We will not attempt to discuss his last wonderful effort of this class, which is a species by itself, and to be judged only by special rules, which space debars us from considering. Of all the productions of the supernatural school, there is none more perfect in its power of sensation, or more entirely effective in its working out, than the short story of the 'Haunted House,' most thrilling of ghostly tales; but we cannot enter upon this school of fiction, which is distinct from our present subject. Mr Dickens rarely writes a book without an attempt at a similar effect by means of some utterly fantastic creation, set before his readers with all that detail of circumstance in which he is so successful. Amid all these predecessors in the field, Mr Wilkie Collins takes up an entirely original position. Not so much as a single occult agency is employed in the structure of his tale. Its power arises from no overstraining of nature:—the artist shows no love of mystery for mystery's sake; he wastes neither wickedness nor passion. His plot is astute and deeply-laid, but never weird or ghastly; he shows no desire to tinge the daylight with any morbid shadows. His effects are produced by common human acts, performed by recognisable human agents, whose motives are never inscrutable, and whose line of conduct is always more or less consistent. The moderation and reserve which he exhibits; his avoidance of extremes; his determination, in conducting the mysterious struggle, to trust to the reasonable resources of the combatants, who have consciously set all upon the stake for which they play, but whom he assists with no weapons save those of quick wit, craft, courage, patience, and villany—tools common to all men—make the lights and shadows of the picture doubly effective. The more we perceive the perfectly legitimate nature of the means used to produce the sensation, the more striking does that sensation become. The machinery of miracle, on the contrary, is troublesome and expensive, and never satisfactory; a miraculous issue ought to come out of it to justify the miraculous means; and miraculous issues are at war with all the economy of nature, not to say that they are difficult of invention and hard to get credit for. A writer who boldly takes in hand the common mechanism of life, and by means of persons who might all be living in society for anything we can tell to the contrary, thrills us into wonder, terror, and breathless interest, with posi-

tive personal shocks of surprise and excitement, has accomplished a far greater success than he who effects the same result through supernatural agencies, or by means of the fantastic creations of lawless genius or violent horrors of crime. When we are to see a murder visibly done before our eyes, the performers must be feeble indeed if some shudder of natural feeling does not give force to their exertions; and the same thing is still more emphatically the case when the spiritual and invisible powers, to which we all more or less do secret and unwilling homage, are actors in the drama. The distinguishing feature of Mr Wilkie Collins' success is, that he ignores all these arbitrary sensations, and has boldly undertaken to produce effects as startling by the simplest expedients of life. It is this which gives to his book the qualities of a new beginning in fiction. There is neither murder, nor seduction, nor despair—neither startling eccentrics nor fantastic monsters in this remarkable story. A much more delicate and subtle power inspires its action. We cannot object to the means by which he startles and thrills his readers; everything is legitimate, natural, and possible; all the exaggerations of excitement are carefully eschewed, and there is almost as little that is objectionable in this highly-wrought sensation-novel, as if it had been a domestic history of the most gentle and unexciting kind. . . .

The ordinary belief of the public, backed by recent experience, seems to be that there are few trades more easy than the writing of novels. Any man who entertains this opinion, would do well to take a backward glance over the early works of Mr Wilkie Collins. These productions, all of which have come into existence with elaborate prefaces, and expositions of a "purpose," will prove to the reader that the **Woman in White** is not a chance success or caprice of genius, but that the author has been long engaged in preparatory studies, and that the work in question is really the elaborate result of years of labour. Academical sketches and studies from the life are not always interesting to the general spectator; nor are painters apt to exhibit them, by way of showing how much pains were necessary before the picture could be composed, and the figures duly set and draped; yet when the great work is complete, there is an unquestionable interest in the fragments of suggestion from which, one by one, the perfect composition grew. We will not inquire whether the **Woman in White** is a sufficiently great work to merit such an exposition; but every reader who thinks so has it in his power to study the portfolio of sketches by which the author measured his strength. We confess that it has, up to a recent time, been a marvel to us what possible interest any human creature could be supposed to take in the motives which induced a rational man and tolerable writer to weave such a dreary web as the *Dead Secret,* or to commit to print and publicity such a revolting story as *Basil.* It appears, however, that the author knew what he was about; his last successful work has thrown a gleam of intelligibility even upon his prefaces, and it is with the respect due to persevering labour and difficulties overcome that we approach the book which shows how much he has profited by his probation. Let us not neglect such an opportunity for a moral. To judge this author by the portfolio of imperfect sketches which he liberally confided to the world before uncovering the picture for which they were made, nobody would have concluded him likely to open a new path for himself, or to produce a remarkable and thrilling effect by the most modest and subtle means. The sketches are often diffuse and washy—sometimes coarsely horrible—scarcely at all betraying that fine faculty of perception which can divine and seize upon the critical instant, neither too early nor too late, in which lies the whole pictorial force and interest of a lengthened scene. Mr Wilkie Collins has profited in the very highest degree by his preparatory labours. He has improved upon all his early works to an extent which proves in only too edifying and complete a way the benefits of perseverance and painstaking. The very excellence of the result tempts us to an ungracious regret. Would that those memoranda by which future generations may trace "the steps by which he did ascend," had but been less confidingly intrusted to the public! Such a disclosure of all the beginnings and early essays of a successful career is possible only to literature. Other crafts keep their experiments out of sight. Authors alone have that ingenuous confidence in the world, and belief in its candour and kindness, which emboldens them to submit the first utterances of the muse to its great ear, and confide to it all the particulars of their progress. Fortunately, the confidence is rarely misplaced. When the hour arrives, and the man becomes famous, the indulgent world applauds his success without pausing to remind him of his failures. Let us follow the charitable example. Mr Wilkie Collins has made many a stumble on the laborious ascent; his progress upward has been jolting and unharmonious by time; but now that he has reached a height upon which he can pause and receive the congratulations of his friends, let not ours be the hand to throw his earlier imperfec-

tions in his face. If he makes as much progress in time to come as he has done in the past, there is no predicting what future altitude may await the author of the *Woman in White.*

The novel itself is too well known to call for anything like a critical review at our hands. We need not discuss over again so familiar a tale, or dwell upon the characters which are, all but Fosco, undeniably subordinate to the story, and to the delicate succession of sensations by which that story is set forth. Mr Wilkie Collins insists upon the fact that readers have written to him expressing their interest in "Laura," and "Miss Halcombe," and "Anne Catherick;" a fact, indeed, which it is very easy to account for, seeing that there could be no story but by means of these figures. But in reality the truth is, that one cares very little for these characters on their own account, and that Mr Hartright and Sir Percival Glyde and the rest are persons whom we regard with but the mildest interest so far as themselves are concerned. The distinguishing characteristic of the book (always excepting Fosco) is the power and delicacy of its sensation incidents; the simple manner in which they are brought out; generally the perfect naturalness of the fact, and always the extremely effective manner in which the critical moment and event strike into the tale, giving it a precision and distinctness which no other expedient could supply so well.

HENRY JAMES (ESSAY DATE 9 NOVEMBER 1865)

SOURCE: James, Henry. "Miss Braddon." *The Nation* 1, no. 19 (9 November 1865): 593-94.

In the following excerpt, James lauds the realism in The Woman in White *and maintains that Collins's skill as an author sets the novel apart from ordinary sensation fiction.*

[*The Woman in White,*] with its diaries and letters and its general ponderosity, was a kind of nineteenth century version of *Clarissa Harlowe.* Mind, we say a nineteenth century version. To Mr. Collins belongs the credit of having introduced into fiction those most mysterious of mysteries, the mysteries which are at our own doors. This innovation gave a new impetus to the literature of horrors. . . . A good ghost-story, to be half as terrible as a good murder-story, must be connected at a hundred points with the common objects of life. . . . Less delicately terrible, perhaps, than the vagaries of departed spirits, but to the full as *interesting,* as the modern novel reader understands the word, are the numberless possible forms of human malignity. Crime, indeed, has always been a theme for dramatic poets; but with the old poets its dramatic interest lay in the fact that it compromised the criminal's moral repose. Whence else is the interest of *Orestes* and *Macbeth*? With Mr. Collins . . . the interest of crime is in the fact that it compromises the criminal's personal safety. The play is a tragedy, not in virtue of an avenging deity, but in virtue of a preventive system of law; not through the presence of a company of fairies, but through that of an admirable organization of police detectives. Of course, the nearer the criminal and the detective are brought home to the reader, the more lively his "sensation." They are brought home to the reader by a happy choice of probable circumstances; and it is through [his] skill in the choice of these circumstances—[his] thoroughgoing realism—that Mr. Collins . . . [has] become famous. . . .

Mr. Collins's productions deserve a more respectable name [than sensation novel]. They are massive and elaborate constructions—monuments of mosaic work, for the proper mastery of which it would seem, at first, that an index and notebook were required. They are not so much works of art as works of science.

FRED BOTTING (ESSAY DATE 1996)

SOURCE: Botting, Fred. "Homely Gothic." In *Gothic*, pp. 113-34. London and New York: Routledge, 1996.

In the following excerpt, Botting discusses the Gothic conventions in The Woman in White.

In **The Woman in White** the transgressions of individual desire threaten family and society from within. Wilkie Collins was preeminent among the sensation novelists of the 1860s. Sensational effects, however, owe much to Gothic, particularly Radcliffean, styles of evoking terror, mystery and superstitious expectation. The plot, figures and narrative form of **The Woman in White** also structurally resemble Radcliffe's Gothic, though transposed into shapes more appropriate to the nineteenth century. Henry James, in the *Nation* (1865), credits Collins with 'having introduced into fiction those most mysterious of mysteries, the mysteries which are at our own door'. 'Instead of the terrors of "Udolpho"', James goes on, 'we were treated to the terrors of the cheerful countryhouse and the busy London lodgings. And there is no doubt that these were infinitely the more terrible' (p. 742). None the less, Gothic patterns pervade Collins's novel. The Gothic heroine, passive and persecuted, is presented as an image of

loss and suffering, especially when seen through the eyes of that new Victorian hero, the amateur detective. Anne Catherick, the woman of the title, is scarcely present in the novel, her spectral appearances in dark city streets, deserted graveyards and garden retreats gesturing towards the mysteries and terrors the narrative resolves. As a ghostly figure pointing to the past crimes of an illegitimate aristocrat and the sufferings and persecutions which he inflicts on her, Anne Catherick's appearances also anticipate the trials of the novel's Gothic heroine who, as a half-sister, is both literally and narratively her double. As a reminder of older Gothic family romance patterns, the double is also used to present a more terrible possibility as a figure that threatens the loss of identity.

The novel, indeed, is framed quite self-consciously as a Gothic romance. Towards the end, the hero, Hartright, reviews the story:

'The sins of the father shall be visited on the children.' But for the fatal resemblance between the two daughters of one father, the conspiracy of which Anne had been the innocent instrument and Laura the innocent victim, could never have been planned. With what unerring and terrible directness the long chain of circumstances led down from the thoughtless wrong committed by the father to the heartless injury inflicted on the child!

(p. 514)

Echoing Walpole's partial justification for *The Castle of Otranto*, the oldest Gothic plot of all is re-enacted in the story of the consequences of secret paternal crime. The self-consciousness and the duplicity of the Gothic is presented in the text's doubles: Anne and Laura, mirror images of female oppression, fortitude, passivity and sacrifice, within and in the name of the family, are not the only Gothic pairing. The role of villain is also doubled. One is Sir Percival Glyde, who persecutes Anne to keep his own dark family secret and marries Laura in the hope of dispossessing her of her inheritance. He is the selfish, brutish example of economic and oppressive villainy. The other, Count Fosco, is a figure of aesthetic and imaginative villainy. His diabolical cunning and creative intelligence are combined with a vain, self-indulgent and cruel character that, in a corpulent body, signal him to be the real and ambivalent object of horror. He devises the most callous schemes with the same delight that he exhibits playing games. His intellectual vanity and aesthetic self-consciousness are displayed with a flourish when, in the confession he is forced to write at the end, he recommends his idea of abducting and substituting Laura for Anne as a model plot for English romance writers (p. 568).

As in the Radcliffean romance, the mysteries surrounding the spectral appearance of Anne Catherick are finally furnished with a rational explanation. Through the investigative efforts of Walter Hartright and Marian Halcombe, Laura's relation, the aura of mystery and terror is disclosed as an intricate but material plot. Unlike earlier Gothic narratives, the interwoven narratives composing the novel—lawyers' reports, domestics' statements and villain's confession—are presented as extended legal documents. The legalistic form is central to re-establishing a proper narrative against the webs of deceit woven by the villains. Law, reason and identity are thus linked as narrative forms. The careful comparison of narrative clues and temporal consistency regarding events, in the analysis of dates, times and timetables, provides the means to rescue the abducted Laura. The secret of Glyde's illegitimacy is found in a text. Moreover, it is the manipulation of stories that enables the substitution of Laura for Anne, while a properly legal account of events proves her identity and establishes her rights to her inheritance and property.

A rational explanation of criminal mysteries by means of detection and law rather than the hand of Providence situates Gothic patterns in a thoroughly Victorian context. It is an amateur detective who comes to the rescue of a persecuted wife. Female persecution and imprisonment are of a more modern cast with the asylum replacing the convent and the country house the castle. The dark labyrinth of terror is located in the city, a 'house-forest' populated by spies and conspirators (p. 379). Fosco, an adept chemist, especially when it comes to drugs, embodies the villainous potential of scientific intelligence. As a refugee from a Europe that, in 1848, was wracked by revolutionary upheavals and subversive conspiracies, he is also associated with dangerous, and imported, political ideas. The superiority of English values of law, liberty and domesticity is reaffirmed only after the terrors of losing one's identity, freedom and life have been encountered. Happy domesticity is restored in the marriage of Hartright and Laura, but only at the price of the sacrifice of her double. It is, moreover, a displaced sense of closure since, at the beginning of the novel, it was the spectral, mysterious and helpless appearance of Anne that excited Hartright's interest and became his object of desire. Sacrificed, she became a sacred and impossible object, her ghostly distance and her death a sign of the fragility of a social order caught between the duplicitous power or impotence of fathers and husbands.

Closure is partial, a sense of loss remains. Threats to law, domestic relations and cultural and sexual identity are only temporarily rebuffed. In Victorian culture, too, a loss, increasingly irreparable by reason or law alone and articulated in terms of spiritualism and horror, governs perceptions of science, nature, crime, and social degeneration. Later in the century the threats to cultural identity reappear, to be presented, in a different combination of scientific rationality and sacred horror, as distinctly sexual in nature.

Works Cited

Collins, Wilkie, *The Woman in White* (1860), ed. Harvey Peter Sucksmith, Oxford, Oxford University Press, 1980.

James, Henry, 'Mary Elizabeth Braddon' (1865), *Literary Criticism*, ed. Leon Edel, New York, The Library of America, 1984.

SUSAN M. GRIFFIN (ESSAY DATE JANUARY 2004)

SOURCE: Griffin, Susan M. "The Yellow Mask, the Black Robe, and the Woman in White: Wilkie Collins, Anti-Catholic Discourse, and the Sensation Novel." *Narrative* 12, no. 1 (January 2004): 55-73.

In the following essay, Griffin analyzes Collins's anti-Catholic discourse in "The Yellow Mask" and The Black Robe, *and argues that Collins transforms this pattern of rhetoric into sensational Gothic narrative in* The Woman in White.

Summarizing the Gothic history of sensationalism, Patrick Brantlinger traces a movement from the religious to the secular: "By a kind of metaphoric sleight of hand, the Gothic romance has managed to make secular mystery seem like a version of religious mystery." By the time of sensationalism, Brantlinger argues, there is "not even a quasi-religious content" (32). Without claiming that sensation novels are, as such, religious, I nonetheless want to suggest that anti-Catholicism can provide those masks, cloaks, and mysteries, ready-made, as it were.[1] One way to achieve the sleight of hand by which the secular takes on a religious aura is by brandishing the narrative vestments and vestiges inherited from the Gothic.

The secularized mysteries of sensationalism replaced religion in another sense as well. In an 1863 *Quarterly Review* article deploring sensationalism, John Murray complained that "A class of literature has grown up around us, usurping in many respects, intentionally or unintentionally, a portion of the preacher's office, playing no inconsiderable part in moulding the minds and forming the habits and tastes of its generation; and doing so principally, we had almost said exclusively, by 'preaching to the nerves'" instead of to judgment, as preachers should do (252). "To think of pointing a moral by stimulants of this kind," Murray pronounces, "is like holding a religious service in a gin-palace" (262). While Murray mentions a few sensation novels that deal directly with religious subjects (e.g., Charles Maurice Davies's *Philip Paternoster: A Tractarian Love Story*), his larger

point is that religious discourse informs the sensation novel less as content and more as form. The rhetorical persuasions of the pulpit are now displaced onto the pages of the sensation novel, and, counterintuitively, reading is more bodily than listening. These sensational sermons are exercises in repeated—eventually habitual— stimulation, "moulding minds, forming tastes and habits."

The phrase "preaching to the nerves" not only captures sensationalism's secularizing of religious rhetorical forms, but also indicates how sensationalism physicalizes ideology. Ann Cvetkovich has argued persuasively that sensationalism's embodiment of social structures, its naturalizing of representations and their meanings, is importantly political (25).[2] The techniques of sensationalism underscore narrative's intimate and intricate dependence upon readerly affect. ("Think of her as you thought of the first woman who quickened your pulses within you that the rest of her sex has no art to stir. Let the kind, candid blue eyes meet yours, as they met mine, with the one matchless look that we both remember so well. . . . Take as her as the visionary nursling of your own fancy, and she will grow upon you, all the more clearly, as the living woman who dwells in mine," Walter Hartright famously asserts, instructing Collins's readers in the uses of sensory memory and association [50].) Individual Victorian reading experiences were, of course, diverse,[3] but the majority of those readers who consumed Collins's narratives would have shared a history of experience with anti-Catholic discourse. Reinforcing a set of polemical Protestant prejudices in their audience and presenting the Papacy as a cultural, political, and economic force in nineteenth-century Britain, fictions that borrow from anti-Catholic discourse play on readers' fears, arousing their suspense and subsequent speculation. My argument, then, is not simply that the motifs of no-Popery found their way into sensation fiction (although they did), but that sensationalism's narrative structures, forming and formed by the learned associations of its audience, are borrowed in part from anti-Catholicism.

Wilkie Collins, that most secular and sensational of nineteenth-century writers, is rarely thought of as a novelist of religious polemic. Yet in 1855 and again in 1881, Collins published two fictions that conform closely to the patterns of anti-Catholic narrative: "**The Yellow Mask**" (appearing first in Dickens's *Household Words* and then in the 1856 collection *After Dark*) and ***The Black Robe*** (serialized in the *Sheffield Independent* in England, *Frank Leslie's Magazine* in the United States, and *Canadian Monthly* in Canada; published in three volumes by Chatto & Windus). Collins's other writings on religion are sparse: a piece on the Carmelite convent in Cornwall titled "**The Nuns of Magwan**," in *Rambles Beyond Railways*; "**A Plea for Sunday Reform**" for the left-wing *Leader*; a translation of Balzac's story of priests and nuns, "**The Midnight Mass**," published in *Bentley's Miscellany*; and comments on Rome and "Romanism" in his letters. William Collins, Wilkie's father, was a Tractarian who despised the Italian Catholicism that he encountered in Rome. He had hoped that Wilkie would attend Oxford and enter the Church—an astonishing instance of misplaced parental ambitions given the relentless unconventionality of his son. Yet, I want to argue that the conventions of religious polemic are at work in what we now perceive as Collins's fictional innovations, particularly in his strategies for readerly engagement.

Anti-Catholicism, which had been allied to the novel from its eighteenth-century beginnings in the work of Ann Radcliffe and other Gothic writers,[4] persisted throughout most of the nineteenth century and manifested itself in characteristic fictional form.[5] Its rhetoric, plots, imagery, and characters would have been familiar to Collins's popular readership. Harriet Martineau, for one, recognized the formulae: she stopped writing for *Household Words* because of what she perceived as its anti-Catholic bias, manifested specifically in "**The Yellow Mask**." In a letter to Charles Dickens, Martineau indignantly quoted from an advertisement for an American magazine's reprint of the story: "'the story is ingenious and fraught with considerable interest. The despicable course of "Father Rocco" pursued so stealthily for the pecuniary benefit of "holy mother church"; shows what stuff priestcraft is made.'" Martineau, like the American audience at which the advertisement was aimed, recognized standardized language of Protestant polemic—the quotation marks around "holy mother church," the term "priestcraft." She expostulated, "The last thing I am likely to do is to write for an anti-catholic publication; and least of all when it is anti-catholic on the sly" (422).[6] *Punch,* always astute at spotting genres and types, identifies Collins as the writer of a "No-Popery" in a cartoon from January 1882: Collins is portrayed in Linley Sambourne's caricature "As the Man in White doing Ink-and-Penance for Having Written **The Black Robe**." What both the American advertisement and the *Punch* cartoon assume is precisely what Collins himself counted

on: a set of audience expectations and recognitions regarding Roman Catholicism.

Such trained audience reactions would have been particularly useful to a writer of sensation fiction, so named in part because of its insistent manipulation of readerly emotions. This essay looks at the functions of anti-Catholicism in two little-known Collins fictions and describes briefly the way that he reworks its standard elements in his most-read novel, **The Woman in White**. I suggest that in creating the genre of sensation fiction, Collins turns to what are already well-worn formulae. Tamar Heller's *Dead Secrets* has shown how much Collins's major works owe to the "female gothic" tradition that he draws on and distances himself from. Building on that insight, my study reads these three fictions as participating in and revising genres of anti-Catholicism. The yellow masks and black robes—the clichéd images that Henry James characterizes elsewhere as a "Scarlet Woman" who is "dressed out terribly in a table-cloth, and holds in her hands the drawing-room candlesticks" (*Essays* 862)[7]—are transformed in Collins's brilliant creation of a woman in white.

Woman in white, black robe, yellow mask. With the exception of *The Wreck of the Golden Mary*, a Dickens Christmas tale to which Collins contributed, Collins never again used a color in a title. Primarily what the colors point to is that these texts are in some sense costume dramas. All three garments—dress, robe, and mask—serve as identifying covers: signals that the figure is both in disguise and playing a standard role. For example, "black robe" stands for "Jesuit"; the book's first edition stressed the narrative's use of associative iconography by filling the cover frame with a stylized black robe marked with the words "The Black Robe." Two *Punch* cartoons for 1850 and 1851 display the polemical uses of costume, showing as well how the character types of anti-Catholic discourse had become near-folkloric. Foregrounded in Collins's titles, then, is his debt to generic plots and characters.

In his 1863 critique Murray explains (and complains about) how such visual cues position sensation novels as interchangeable commodities.[8] In the railway stalls, consumers are enticed by book covers showing

> A pale young lady in a white dress, with a dagger in her hand, evidently prepared for some desperate deed; or a couple of ruffians engaged in a deadly struggle; or a Red Indian in his war-paint; or, if the plot turns on smooth instead of violent villainy, *a priest persuading a dying man to sign a*

paper; or a disappointed heir burning a will; or a treacherous lover telling his flattering tale to some deluded maid or wife. The exigencies of railway traveling do not allow much time for examining the merits of a book before purchasing it; and the keepers of bookstalls as well as refreshment-rooms, find an advantage in offering their customers something hot and strong, something that may catch the eye of the hurried passenger, and promise temporary excitement to relieve the dulness of the journey.

(253 emphasis mine)

In other words, the packaging of these goods relies on a now-familiar mechanism of consumer commodification: immediately recognizable "branding," here by means of genre-specific depictions (think of the studies of dime novels by Bill Brown and romance fiction by Janice Radway). Genre is made visible. The reader knows what she is buying. At the same time, of course, variation must ensure that this is not a product previously purchased. (In the preface to the 1860 edition of **The Woman in White,** Collins himself maintained that the "two main elements in the attraction of all stories" are "the interest of curiosity, and the excitement of surprise" [646].) The secular sermon that is the sensation novel is, finally, a matter of economics; as Murray puts it, "No divine influence can be imagined as presiding over the birth of his [the sensation novelist's] world, beyond the market-law of demand and supply" (252).

The specific market uses of anti-Catholic discourse are suggested by the way it informs Collins's travel piece **"The Nuns of Magwan." Rambles from Railways** is, as its title implies, a trip back in time, away from modern technology and timetables, exploring "one of the remotest and most interesting corners of our old English soil" (2). Cornwall, with its "primitive population" and ancient legends, is at once an exoticized destination and the space of England's past. Collins begins his visit to Magwan among the churchyard graves, proceeding to the "ancient" manor house, now converted to a convent, in which a group of twenty Carmelite nuns are immured. Cloistered nuns, and in particular the Carmelite order, held a particular fascination for nineteenth-century Protestants. Paintings like Charles Allston Collins's *Convent Thoughts* and John Everett Millais's *The Vale of Rest* portrayed the cloistered nun cryptically as a figure of sublimated passion, claustration, and death (Casteras). And in both Benjamin Disraeli's *Lothair* and Henry James's *The American,* the female character who turns away from life and marriage to the death-in-life of the convent does so by joining the Carmelites.

HE WROTE THE 'WOMAN IN WHITE.'

Caricature published in *Once a Week* in 1873, of Wilkie Collins erecting a poster advertising his *The Woman in White.*

For Wilkie Collins, the Carmelite convent provides "a romance which we may still study, of a mystery which is of our own time" (144). Sounding like Nathaniel Hawthorne in the preface to *The Marble Faun* ("Romance and poetry, ivy, lichens, and wall-flowers need Ruin to make them grow" [3]), Collins seeks a means of infusing the present with mystery and finds it in the aura of ancient Rome: "Even to this little hidden nook, even to this quiet bower of Nature's building, that vigilant and indestructible Papal religion, which defies alike hidden conspiracy and open persecution, has stretched its stealthy and far-spreading influence. Even in this remote corner of the remote west of England, among the homely cottages of a few Cornish peasants, the imperial Christianity of Rome has set up its sanctuary in triumph—a sanctuary not thrown open to dazzle and awe the beholder, but veiled in deep mystery behind gates that only open, like the fatal gates of the grace, to receive, but never to dismiss again to the world without" (144). This brief characterization of Roman Catholicism indicates its usefulness for sensationalism. With the phrase "Papal religion," Collins seeks to trigger the British Protestant paranoia that sees Catholic conspiracies everywhere.[9]

Like the Italian secret society that tracks Count Fosco across England and France, the Papacy represents an international power that is, importantly for Collins's writerly strategies, both omnipresent *and* secret, thus inviting investigation. The sanctuary at Magwan, like the convent and the confessional in anti-Catholic polemic, provides a space for the audience's "knowing" projection, allowing for the participatory reading that was to become so essential to sensation fiction, especially in its serial form. Collins's emphasis throughout **"The Nuns of Magwan"** is on the nuns' hidden status, on how their faces, forms, and even voices are concealed from the outside world. Dwelling on the nuns' burial grounds and funeral rites, Collins analogizes the secrecy of convent life to that of the grave: "This is all—all of the lives, all of the deaths of the sisterhood at Lanhearne that we can ever know! The remainder must be conjecture. We have but the bare stern outline that has been already drawn—who shall venture, even in imagination, to colour and complete the picture which it darkly, yet plainly, indicates?" (149). Although Collins continues to argue that we should not attempt to imagine, and consequently to judge, the emotions of the nuns, his repeated use of rhetorical questions invites just such speculation. That is, his audience's familiarity with the forms of anti-Catholicism allows it to "colour and complete" the picture that the dark outlines of Roman Catholicism "plainly indicat[e]."

"The Yellow Mask" also depends upon Collins's audience's recognition of standard formulae: "of what stuff priestcraft is made," as the story's American publishers promised. **"The Yellow Mask"** tells of a poor, virtuous Italian maid, Nanina, who is accompanied through the streets of Pisa by her big, ugly, mongrel dog, the comically named Scarammuccia. Nanina becomes the beloved of a wealthy Pisan nobleman, Fabio d'Ascoli. Interfering with their love is Father Rocco, a priest convinced that a large part of the d'Ascoli fortune rightfully belongs to the Church. When we first meet Father Rocco, he is using a mirror to spy on Nanina and Fabio; later he manages to separate the lovers, secreting the young girl in a house where she is watched continually. Father Rocco's power comes not just from his secret network of operatives but also from the fact that he has trained his young parishioners in obedience. As part of his plan to enrich the Church, the priest manages to marry Fabio off to his niece. When she dies unexpectedly, Father Rocco's plotting becomes more elaborate: among his machinations are the manufacture of the ghostly "Yellow Mask," a figure dressed in the yellow fabric that decorated Fabio's first wife's apartments and whose mask conceals what looks to be the face of her corpse. In short, the priest attempts to scare the superstitious Fabio into submission to his will. The scheme fails, Father Rocco disappears, and Nanina and Fabio happily marry.

The standard features of this story—the priest who plots to "return" riches to the Church through a combination of trickery and guilt, a Catholic system of spies, religious training in unquestioning obedience, the beloved young woman held incommunicado, the living corpse, the alliance of Roman Catholicism and superstition—are mitigated here by the relative mildness of Catholicism's crimes. Unlike the sinister Jesuits who glide throughout much anti-Catholic fiction, this Italian priest is presented as generally virtuous and fair-minded, though willing to practice deception, not to mention enlisting the aid of a scheming, mercenary female prostitute in what he sees as the Church's best interests.

While Collins relies on Protestant preconceptions in this story, he is not yet "preaching to the nerves" of his audience. If, in Margaret Oliphant's famous characterization of the woman in white's hand, "Few readers will be able to resist the mysterious thrill of this sudden touch. The sensation is distinct and indisputable. The silent woman lays her hand upon our shoulder as well as upon that of Mr Walter Hartright" (118), the sight of the yellow mask raises scarcely a shudder.[10] **"The Yellow Mask,"** set "about a century ago" in "the ancient city of Pisa" and narrated with an arch irony, positions its readers at a historical and cultural distance. The comic tone that Collins flirts with throughout the narrative can be seen in the lengthy description of the nearly insurmountable problem of finding thirty virtuous young women to serve as shepherdesses at the fancy-dress ball at which the Yellow Mask eventually appears. And that terrifying vision is, we should remember, clad, not unlike Henry James's tablecloth-shrouded Scarlet Woman, in the bedroom curtains (setting the style for Margaret Mitchell's Scarlett O'Hara). Indeed, when he republished the story in *After Dark*, a collection in which each tale is introduced by a framing story of origination, Collins attributed it to a wizened Italian professor who is writing, Casaubon-like, an unfinished multivolume work on "The Vital Principle." Amidst the papers and books that overflow the professor's study, is a mangy stuffed dog—Scarammuccia had been lovingly preserved by his mistress, and it is his history that turns out to be the tale of **"The**

Yellow Mask." With this frame, Collins glances slyly at the hoary props that sustain his tale. Like the character from *commedia del arte* for whom he is named, Scarammuccia is a stock comic character whose exploits are knowingly expected by his audience.

Unlike the half-mocking Gothic tale of "**The Yellow Mask**," *The Black Robe* is both an astute psychological study and Collins's most sustained attack on the Catholic Church. Like *After Dark* and *The Woman in White*, *The Black Robe* is a documentary narrative, incorporating manuscripts (diaries, letters, etc.) supposedly by several hands. The good and evil sides of "**The Yellow Mask**"'s Father Rocco are divided in this later novel. We get not one but two Jesuits—two Black Robes: the sincere young Father Penrose (who nonetheless falsely presents himself as the layman "Arthur Penrose") and the cynical older Father Benwell, both of whom disguise their affiliations and intentions, a combination familiar to Victorian readers from, among other sources, Frances Trollope's anti-Catholic *Father Eustace, a Tale of the Jesuits*. Collins's narrative revolves around the conflict between Stella Eyrecourt and Father Benwell for, in her case, the love and, in his, the fortune of Lewis Romayne—the characters' names hinting at their stereotypical narrative functions. "Would the priest or the woman win the day?" Collins's narrator asks (124). Would Romayne be a faithful husband and father or would he "restore" his riches to the Catholic Church? Finally, at the behest of the Jesuit Superior, Romayne renounces his wife and enters the Catholic clergy. He becomes a powerful, indeed "fanatical," preacher and an ambitious rising star in the Church hierarchy—a favorite of the Pope and selected for a cardinalship. However, he falls ill and, dying, realizes the wrongness of his retreat into the Catholic priesthood. He speaks three last "sacred" words: "Wife and Child" (446)—Collins countering Christ's last words of renunciation and what Protestants saw as Catholic preoccupation with the Four Last Things (Death, Judgment, Heaven, and Hell).[11] Deathbed scenes in anti-Catholic fiction inevitably stage struggles over inheritance (church or family?) and test the truth of religion (the Protestant confident acceptance of death or terrified Catholic uncertainty?).[12] Recognizing at last the "unnatural" wasted life of celibacy, Romayne affirms normative Victorian domesticity.

The Black Robe can, in fact, be read as one of a specific group of sensational fictions published during the 1860s-1880s that depicted a triangulated relationship between husband, wife, and priest. Writers like Eliza Lynn Linton, Robert Buchanan, and Emma Worboise describe Anglican clergymen who have become so entranced with High Church Ritualism that they are in danger of crossing over, with their spellbound flocks, to Rome. These novels become a site for discussion of the contemporary state of marriage in Britain.[13] Like these fictions, *The Black Robe* attacks Catholic celibacy as deeply misogynist, as antipathetic to domesticity and family. Father Benwell cynically remarks that he has learned all about women in the confessional, a claim that would have resonated for Collins's readers. The British public, clergy, and Parliament had reacted vociferously to the attempted reintroduction of auricular confession as a Church of England practice in the 1860s and 1870s, a scandal that peaked with the publication of a secret manual for confessors, *The Priest in Absolution*, in 1866 and 1870. In her study of Victorian women as "confessional subjects," Susan Bernstein quotes W. J. Brockman's mid-nineteenth-century *Letter to the Women of England on the Confessional*: "I know not another reptile in all animal nature so filthy, so much to be shunned and loathed, and *dreaded by females*, both married and single, as a Roman Catholic priest or bishop who practices the degrading and demoralizing office of Auricular Confession" (41). Father Benwell's disgust for women marks him as just such a reptile: "I felt grateful to the famous Council which definitely forbade the priests of the Catholic Church to marry," Father Benwell muses. "*We* might otherwise have been morally enervated by the weakness which *degrades* Romayne—and priests might have become instruments in the hands of women" (133-34 emphasis mine).

Operative in what Collins sees as Catholic misogyny is also what he depicts as the homosocial, indeed, at times homoerotic, relations between men that comprise the Church hierarchy. The traditional Protestant critique of Catholic celibacy as fostering "unnatural" sexual attachments was intensified in nineteenth-century Britain by the seemingly "Papist" Oxford movement in the 1840s and Ritualism in the 1860s and 1870s—both of which proved attractive to the nation's elite young men. "UnEnglish and unmanly," these religious practices were thought to foster a hothouse homosexuality foreign to real Englishmen.[14] What Collins represents in *The Black Robe* is the Jesuit Provincial's cynical manipulation of such a system—his scheme to have the innocent but desirable Penrose attach Romayne to himself and thus Catholicism. "Why do you want him so much—when you have got

Me?" Stella asks vainly regarding Penrose (260), the intimate who addresses Romayne as "my more than friend—my brother in love—!" (312).

"UnEnglish" too is the "Retreat" to which Father Benwell sends Romayne to separate him from his wife. Like the convent at Magwan, the Retreat is represented as a foreign enclave hidden in Protestant England. Entering this deliberately unassuming building, protected by a "high brick wall," "The convert privileged to pass the gate left Protestant England outside, and found himself, as it were, in a new country" (335). Again, Collins echoes the polemical rhetoric of the day. In 1870, a Parliamentary Inquiry into Catholic "Conventual and Monastic Institutions" was instituted. Charles Newdegate, the inquiry's primary sponsor, argued that inspections of these Catholic clerical enclaves were necessary because "There is a growing feeling that the Conventual and Monastic Institutions are being treated by the House of Commons as if they were exempt jurisdictions, subject to Papal Authority, but . . . exempt from the authority of Parliament" (qtd. in Arnstein 146). Newdegate had proposed such an inquiry repeatedly in the past, arguing that, by making themselves not only immune but actually invisible to English law, convents constituted foreign sovereign territories situated within Great Britain. By 1870, his colleagues agreed that these imported, extrajuridical institutions needed to come under government control.

If **The Black Robe** reflects the religious and political controversies of its time, it also reveals how far Collins had come as a writer since "**The Yellow Mask**."[15] The haunting of Fabio by his wife's ghost in the earlier fiction is reworked in **The Black Robe** into Romayne's persecution by a mysterious voice blaming him as an "assassin" for his killing of a man in a duel. Collins moves beyond the crude, preliminary manipulation of Fabio's guilt in "**The Yellow Mask**" and depicts the slow breaking down and remaking of Romayne's sanity: Father Benwell "wound his way deeper and deeper into Romayne's mind, with the delicate ingenuity of penetration, of which the practice of years had made him master" (351).[16] The Jesuit's infamous ability to control minds, depicted in novels ranging from Trollope's *Father Eustace* to Eugene Sue's *Wandering Jew*, is detailed step by step, helping to structure Collins's plot. Here Collins's personal interest in the mesmerism that finds its way into novels like **The Woman in White** and **The Moonstone** is expressed through the machinations of "the Catholic system [that] . . . showed to perfection its masterly knowledge

of the weakness of human nature, and its inexhaustible dexterity in adapting the means to the end" (336-37).[17] In an 1854 letter regarding the Immaculate Conception, Collins describes what he saw as the readiness of Catholics to abandon their individual judgment and give themselves over to priestly control: "Does any Papist make use of his reason when he lets his Church give him his religion? Does not his Church expressly tell him he must give up his reason, and accept mysteries which outrage it, implicitly as matters of faith. Does not every good Papist who will not let his butcher, baker, wife, or children, rob him of one particle of his common sense if he can help it, voluntarily hand that common sense over altogether to the keeping of his Priest whenever his Priest asks for it?" (1:130).

The Collins character who most intrigued his nineteenth-century readers wields just such a priestly power[18]—**The Woman in White**'s Count Fosco, whose wife obeys him unquestioningly, who overrides Percival's every personal judgment, and who mesmerizes even the independent Marion: "They are the most unfathomable gray eyes I ever saw: and they have at times a cold, clear, beautiful, irresistible glitter in them, which forces me to look at him, and yet causes me sensations, when I do look, which I would rather not feel" (221). Margaret Oliphant's description of Fosco underscores the racial and nationalist assumptions that Collins's readership brought to the tale: "No villain of the century, so far as we are aware, comes within a hundred miles of him: he is more real, more genuine, more *Italian* even, in his fatness and size, in his love of pets and pastry, than the whole array of conventional Italian villains, elegant and subtle, whom we are accustomed to meet in literature" (566-67). Fosco spells out those assumptions to Marion, "You know the character which is given to my countrymen by the English? We Italians are all wily and suspicious by nature, in the estimation of the good John Bull" (245). Written in 1859, when Neapolitan exiles were flocking to London, and set in 1851, when the Great Exhibition seemed to have provided the perfect pretext for spies to enter the country, **The Woman in White** was guaranteed an audience who knew what to except from such foreigners (Peters 215; Sutherland ix).

Fosco himself lightly suggests, "I am a Jesuit, if you please to think so—a splitter of straws—a man of trifles and crotchets and scruples" (246), but the catalogue of Jesuitical characteristics that Collins's audience would recognize is less benign: a learned member of a secret society, clever at disguise, part of an international system of spies based in Rome, confessor-like in his knowledge of others' secret sins and failings, engaged in a voluminous foreign correspondence even as he intercepts others' missives, an Italian with ties to France. Fosco walks with the Jesuit's silent tread, and looks with his penetrating, mesmerizing stare. He even shares a trait commonly attributed to Catholic priests and nuns—a childlike greed for sweets—a trope that typically points to thwarted sexuality. And of course there is the eminently jesuitical plot he concocts: a marriage triangle, a contested inheritance, a kidnapping, blackmail, a deathbed defrauding of a fortune. Laura's warning about the man who has come between her and her husband—"Do not make an enemy of Count Fosco!"—reverberates with the frightened cries of heroines whose homes and marriages are invaded by priests: "God help me!" Stella Eyrecourt cries, "the priest has gotten between us already!" (274).

The story of Anne Catherick's and then Laura Fairlie's enforced immurement in and subsequent escape from an institution echoed popular nineteenth-century tales of escaped nuns, especially given the resemblance between their white clothing and a nun's habit and veil, and the frequent analogy that Protestant polemicists made between convents and lunatic asylums. ("If lunatic asylums are bound to admit a Government inspector, why should a nunnery, which is but another sort of lunatic asylum, be left altogether uncared for and unwatched?" asked a *Morning Advertiser* editorial [qtd. in Arnstein 135].) Escaped nuns were much on the English mind in the 1860s, a period in which seventy-one convents were founded in Great Britain, which saw hundreds of petitions calling for government inspection of convents, and, in 1869, a spectacular legal case regarding convent life, *Saurin* v. *Star*. All of these events led to Newdegate's success in finally passing the Convent Inspections Act.[19]

If convent stories are echoed in *The Woman in White*'s confinement plot, they may also provide a less obvious structural model for the novel's sensationalism. From the beginning, what has most compelled *The Woman in White*'s audience is its narrative construction: "As the Judge might once have heard it, so the Reader shall hear it now," Walter Hartright announces (5). Collins claimed to be the first to write a novel in which the narrative is presented by a series of documents by diverse hands from which the reader constructs the full story. Victorian critics, however, were quick to point out precedents (*Wuthering Heights* is a favorite example), and later scholars have fol-

lowed suit, tracing the sensation novel's architectonics to trial records and newspaper reports. Anti-Catholic literature, specifically the renegades' tales told by escaped nuns and former priests that proliferated in Victorian America and Great Britain, suggests another compelling model. The most famous of these narratives was Maria Monk's *Awful Disclosures of the Hotel Dieu Nunnery*, an international bestseller first published in 1836 and never since out of print, but Monk's is only one of many such tales. These "factual" accounts are narratively constructed so as to confirm their status as evidence. The renegade is granted a privileged position as participatory witness—"I alone am escaped to tell you"—in books that stress the incontrovertibility of first-person experience and narration, claims to truth-telling echoed in Walter Hartright's insistence that "No circumstance of importance, from the beginning to the end of the disclosure, shall be related on hearsay evidence" (5). Escaped nuns' narratives are framed by and interspersed with authenticating documentation of multiple kinds and by diverse hands: affidavits, signed letters of introduction, confirmatory accounts, excerpts from newspaper reports, footnotes, maps, drawings.[20] The publishers of Rebecca Reed's *Six Months in a Convent* assert that "the labor of seeing so many individuals, collecting such a mass of facts and testimony, and putting it together *correctly* . . . mak[e this narrative] . . . complete and unanswerable" (264). (Visible in these structures is, of course, the interpenetration of the Gothic—sensation fiction's other point of origin—and the anti-Catholic.) When Wilkie Collins includes "The Narrative of the Doctor" and "The Narrative of the Tombstone" in **The Woman in White** (indeed, when he frames the story of **The Black Robe** with an "eye-witness" account, an unfinished diary, and an order for a wedding dress), he draws on the popular generic forms of anti-Catholic discourse and on a readership who had learned from them how to assemble and judge a story.

The cultural training in anti-Catholic characters, plots, and narrative structures shared by **The Woman in White**'s audience had been heightened by specific historical events at mid-century. Yet the patterns of anti-Catholic polemic that undergird **The Woman in White** do not make it an anti-Catholic fiction. Unlike **The Black Robe** or even the playful **"Yellow Mask,"** Collins's greatest sensation novel is markedly secular. Symptomatic is the fact that, while a church contains the novel's long-kept secret and serves as the primary scene of violence and punishment, it is only the vestry that is of importance; the mystery uncovered there is legal and moral rather than religious. (Henry James alluded to such secularism when, after calling Collins and Mary Elizabeth Braddon "our modern Euripides and Shakespeare," he explained that in the sensation novel "The play is a tragedy, not in virtue of an avenging deity, but in virtue of a preventive system of law" ["Miss Braddon" 123]). In neither visit to the church does

Walter Hartright encounter a clergyman, only the lay clerk along with a row of empty vestments, described in the *All-the-Year-Round* and three-volume versions of the novel as a "bundle of limp drapery and wanting nothing but legs under them to suggest the idea of a cluster of neglected curates who had committed suicide, by companionably hanging themselves all together" (695).[21] Like these priestly shrouds, the church itself, "an ancient, weather-beaten building, with heavy buttresses at its sides"—dating back, no doubt, to pre-Reformation England—figures the role of "Romanism" in the novel (506). Surrounded by an abandoned village, "worm-eaten" and "crumbling," littered with scraps of "old wood carvings from the pulpit, and panels from the chancel, and images from the organ loft," the building is, in effect, a ruin (508-509). In contrast to the organic cultural meaning that John Ruskin read in ancient Catholic cathedrals, this shrine is reduced to fragments that foster associative affect, not theology.

My point is not that the Catholic Church serves as a mere setting—**The Woman in White** is not, like Charles Kingsley's *Hypatia, Or Old Foes with New Faces*, an allegory for contemporary society set in antiquity. Instead, as in Collins's ruined church, the structures of anti-Catholicism allow sensationalism to intermix ancient forms and contemporary scandals. It is precisely this mixture that readers of sensation novels have, from the beginning, seen as constitutive of the genre, faulting or praising these fictions' claim to reveal the dark truths behind the facade of the ordinary. As the archbishop of York complained, "They want to persuade people that in almost every one of the well-ordered houses of their neighbours there [is] a skeleton shut up in some cupboard." Murray defined "proximity" as "one great element of sensation" (255). Describing what is "sensational" about the "sensation novel," Brantlinger states, "peace masks violence; innocent appearances cloak evil intentions; reality itself functions as a mystery until the sudden revelation of guilt which is always lurking in the shadows" (41).

The discourse of anti-Catholic polemic readily served the sensation novelist's technique of balancing the known and the unknown, inviting the reader's forward plot projection, providing recognizable figures of mystery, clothing them in typifying disguises. Jenny Bourne Taylor contends that:

Sensation fiction certainly shared a common pool of narrative tropes, but these were not stable, they drew on and broke down distinct methods of generating strangeness within familiarity, of creating the sense of a weird and different world within the ordinary, everyday one. . . . And it was through these intricate interactions that its appeal to sensation, to "nerves," had both such psychological resonance and social complexity, providing it with the means that enabled it to explore "those most mysterious of mysteries, the mysteries that are at our own doors" by bringing into play the possibilities offered by its central narrative feature—*secrecy* and *disguise*.

(7)

Summarizing Collins's career for *Temple Bar* in 1890, Edmund Yates captures the balancing act between the expected and the unexpected, the realistic and the outrageous, that is sensationalism. Characterizing Collins as a "manufacturer of plots," Yates explains, "Nobody imagines the misfortunes of **Poor Miss Finch,** and her blue-complexioned lover, the masquerades of Magdalen Vanstone, the machinations of the Romish Church in **The Black Robe,** the remarkable coincidences of **Hide and Seek,** or the melodramatic farrago of **The Frozen Deep,** to be precisely scenes from real life. But, truth being stranger than fiction, possibly they might be" (274-75).

Known and unknown, *heimlich* and *unheimlich.* Understanding the nature of anti-Catholic rhetoric allows us to recognize how this productive tension is both central to sensationalism's marketing success and generative of the epistemological uncertainty that Brantlinger, among others, sees as foundational to the genre. For modern, nineteenth-century Protestants in Britain and America, the Catholic Church was positioned as the uncanny.[22] The teleology of Protestant history meant that "Romanism" was the primitivism that Protestantism left behind. But, maddeningly, the Church of Rome refused to be bypassed, refused to die. Within nineteenth-century polemical narrative, the Catholic is often analogized to the Jew—stubborn and unregenerate. What makes this (failed) story of religious progress particularly problematic is the fact that Protestantism needs to be able to trace its authority and authenticity back to Catholicism. This imperfectly repressed scene of origination makes Romanists what Catherine Sinclair, in her virulently anti-Catholic novel of 1852 *Beatrice,* calls "the unknown relative."

Winifred Hughes's comment on the role of masks in sensation fiction is suggestive here: "In sensation fiction masks are rarely stripped off to reveal an inner truth, for the mask is both the transformed expression of the 'true' self and the means of disclosing its incoherence. In the process, identity itself emerges as a set of elements that are

actively constructed within a dominant framework of social interests, perceptions, and values. These novels thus focused on the ambiguity of social and psychological codes to insinuate that seeming, too, is not always what it seems to be" (8).[23] Behind the yellow mask lies another—in this case a death mask. Wearing that death mask is the woman, once known as Teresa, now calling herself Brigida, with a hidden, disreputable past about which we never learn the details. Father Benwell presents himself as a lowly clergyman, "elderly, fat, and cheerful" (42), rather than revealing his true rank as the provincial of the Society of Jesus. He instructs Father Penrose, a Jesuit of lower rank, to appear as the layman Arthur Penrose. "Arthur Penrose"'s secular clothing covers his black robe, which itself cloaks the fundamentally decent man who is Arthur Penrose. Marion suspects Fosco of wearing a wig, and it turns out that his most distinctive—and unsettling—physical attribute, his size, is itself a mask, a fat suit.[24] Even when he is displayed naked at the novel's end, he remains disguised: viewed through "a glass screen," Fosco has the costume of "a French artisan" hung above him, and the mark of the Brotherhood that he bears has been "obliterated" by a covering wound (the letter "T" for traitor)—this writing on the body vividly figuring Collins's authorial work (640). Epistemological ambiguity is imaged in these visible layers of "seeming."

But is the fact that the Woman in White and Count Fosco have secret identities ever really a secret? Recognizing that these two creations wear, among their other costumes, those of the stock polemical characters of nun and priest helps us to go a step further than Taylor. It is a *signaled* secrecy, an *advertised* disguise that are operative in sensationalism's readerly engagement, as when Count Fosco teases, "I am a Jesuit if you choose to think so" (246). Writing in the *North British Review* in February 1863, Alexander Smith characterized the experience of reading Collins: "If a young lady goes into the garden a moment before dinner, you know that some one is waiting for her behind the laurels. If two people talk together in a room in a hot summer day, and one raises the window a little, you know that a third is crouching on the gravel below, listening to every word, and who will be prepared to act upon it at the proper time" (141). Smith deplored the feverish excitement, "the passion of curiosity," that Collins, "the master of mystery," incites in his audience, but his description of the charged engagement of readers who rapidly turned the pages of **The Woman in White** is relevant here. Like the lurid covers that entice purchasers at railway stalls, robes and masks, *when recognized as such,* awake audience expectations—expectations based on prior experience—and direct reading modes. The figures and stories of anti-Catholic discourse, easily discerned by experienced Victorian readers, serve Collins well in developing his sensationalist style.

As so often, *Punch* gets it right in Sambourne's depiction of Collins in a *transparent* disguise, costumed absurdly for a role in a way that signals precisely that he is costumed. He is, ludicrously, a man (beard pointedly intact) dressed up in a bedsheet and a woman's bowed cap, adopting a distinctly feminine stance (notice the little-girl position of his slipper-shod feet). Surrounded by emblems of his fictions (the moonstone, the athlete and supplicant female of *Man and Wife,* stacked books and floor covering marked with other titles), Collins holds a "Roman candle." His penitent's robe, along with his abashed stance, are clearly put on for the occasion. Is he being put to bed early for his naughtiness? Is his guise a corrective humiliation meted out by an angry Catholic confessor? Is he ineptly veiling his identity to escape punishment? In any case, Collins's repentance is nothing if not superficial (not even "skin deep"), for we are told that he does "Ink-And-Penance" for writing *The Black Robe*—that is, his penance for writing is writing. The implication is that he will give *Punch*'s readership more of the same, that he will add to the stacks of books that surround him.

The caricature models as well the workings of anti-Catholic discourse in Collins's sensational writing. Caricature is an art form intimately tied to its audience's knowledge—a fact well-known to anyone who has ever shown *Punch* to a group of bewildered college freshman or, for that matter, puzzled over a Victorian political cartoon herself. Sambourne's wit is wholly dependent upon its viewers' history as experienced readers not only of *Punch* but also of Collins's own narratives.[25]

In fact, Wilkie Collins did not again take up the props and plots of anti-Catholic polemic, a tradition that was considerably weakened by the end of the century. Nonetheless, in a formulaic early fiction, a genre-defining novel at the height of his career, and one of his late didactic fictions, Collins made pragmatic use of habits both clerical and readerly. Anti-Catholic discourse offered Collins narrative forms (the multiple, evidentiary narratives of the renegade's tale), plot patterns (female escape from an institution), recognizable character types (the Jesuit), and iconography (a woman in white). It afforded him as well an audi-

ence already schooled in the participatory reading strategies so definitive of sensationalism. The open secrets of "Romanism" provided a configuration conducive to the play between known and unknown that mark both sensation fiction's epistemology and its marketability. Part of what made this new mode of writing and reading so "hot and strong" was that it borrowed from an old recipe in brewing the latest news. Sensation fiction was, as Murray says, "refreshment"—a reanimation of both traditional forms and the well-trained palates of its consumers.

Notes

1. While religious content is obviously not a generic requirement of sensationalism, there are sensation novels that center on religion; for example, Charles Reade's *Griffith Gaunt,* as well as those by Buchanan, Linton, and Worboise mentioned below. Although they are not speaking about polemical anti-Catholic literature, Helsinger, Sheets, and Veeder interestingly suggest that "America's most shocking fiction may in fact be women's *religious* novels" (123).

2. See also Loesberg and Miller for important discussions of the ideologies of sensationalism.

3. For example, see Altick's (in *Common Reader*), Brantlinger's, and Flint's explorations of the differences that class and gender make in reading.

4. On the anti-Catholicism of the eighteenth-century Gothic, see Tarr.

5. On anti-Catholicism and nineteenth-century fiction, see Franchot, Griffin, Maison, and Wolff.

6. Martineau's indignation was further fueled by the fact that she had had a story of her own, "The Missionary," turned down by Dickens for *Household Words* on the grounds that it presented a Jesuit priest positively. "I have had little hope of 'Household Words' since the proprietors refused to print a historical fact (otherwise approved of) on the ground that the hero was a Jesuit: and now that they follow up this suppression of an honourable truth by the insertion of a dishonouring fiction (or fact,—no matter which) they can expect no support from advocates of religious liberty or lovers of fair-play: and so fond are English people of fair-play, that if they knew this fact, you would soon find your course in this matter ruinous to your publication" (422). Martineau's 1861-1862 novella "Sister Anna's Probation" depicts Catholicism less positively. Perhaps Martineau's most famous statement on Roman Catholicism was her critique of Charlotte Brontë's *Villette* as anti-Catholic.

7. James's quip comes from a review of Benjamin Disraeli's *Lothair.* Given Disraeli's positive depictions of Roman Catholicism in his earlier novels, *Lothair* provides another surprising example of anti-Catholic fiction's pervasiveness.

8. On sensation novels themselves, and the sensations associated with them, as constructed commodities, see Cvetkovich.

9. On nineteenth-century British anti-Catholicism, see Arnstein, Best, Griffin, Norman, Paz, and Wolffe.

10. Swinburne, however, found "The Yellow Mask" an "admirable story" (263).

11. For another depiction of this Catholic meditative practice as a rejection of life, love, and domesticity, see Mary Ward's *Helbeck of Bannisdale.*

12. See, for example, Catherine Sinclair's *Beatrice.*

13. I am referring to Linton's *Under Which Lord?,* Buchanan's *Foxglove Manor,* and Worboise's *Overdale; or, The Story of a Pervert: A Tale for the Times.* See Griffin, *Anti-Catholicism.*

14. On the perceived connection between Romanism and homosexuality, see Hanson and Hilliard.

15. In making this statement, I dispute the standard chronology that sees Collins's writing as going only downhill after *The Moonstone.* Swinburne is probably the first and the most famous critic to make this claim: "What brought good Wilkie's genius nigh perdition? / Some demon whispered—'Wilkie! Have a mission'" (qtd. in Peters 313). While *The Black Robe* cannot be ranked with the masterpieces of the 1860s, it is an interesting psychological study that sold well in three countries (Peters 398).

16. There are other aspects to this novel that I slight here, including an earlier secret marriage on Stella's part and her eventual marriage to her first love, a missionary exile and rescue for Penrose, etc.

17. On Collins and mesmerism, see especially Taylor.

18. For nineteenth-century reactions to Fosco, see the reviews of *The Woman in White* collected in Page.

19. For the fullest discussion of these events, see Arnstein.

20. See Griffin, "Awful"; and Franchot.

21. On Dickens's revisions, see John Sutherland's note to the Oxford edition of *The Woman in White* (Collins 695). He notes that Kathleen Tillotson argued that Collins revised to avoid the similarity to Dickens's *Martin Chuzzlewit.*

22. On the role of the uncanny in sensationalism, see Taylor.

23. See also Peters on "The Yellow Mask": "The characteristic device of a mask concealing a face which is in fact another mask, behind which lurks the face of the wrong woman, has the suggestive quality of layered deceit which intrigued him, and which was to be more fully developed in the novels he wrote in the 1860s" (150). For the *Dublin University Magazine,* this layering of masks and types represented a weakness in Collins's writing: "Sir Percival Glyde is made up of, at least, two utterly different beings: a two-fronted mask on top of a stage-cloak" (Review 105).

24. The clergy are not the only ones who conceal their pasts in Collins's novel: everyone from Stella's mother, who paints over her age and illness in order to sustain her social position, to Stella herself, who conceals a prior marriage.

25. On *Punch* and anti-Catholicism, see Altick's *Punch.*

Works Cited

Altick, Richard. *The English Common Reader.* Chicago: Univ. of Chicago Press, 1957.

———. *Punch: The Lively Youth of a British Institution, 1841-1851.* Columbus: The Ohio State Univ. Press, 1997.

Arnstein, Walter. *Protestant versus Catholic in Mid-Victorian England: Mr. Newdegate and the Nuns.* Columbia: Univ. of Missouri Press, 1982.

Bernstein, Susan David. *Confessional Subjects: Revelations of Gender and Power in Victorian Literature and Culture.* Chapel Hill: Univ. of North Carolina Press, 1997.

Best, G. F. A. "Popular Protestantism in Victorian Britain." In *Ideas and Institutions of Victorian Britain,* edited by Robert Robson, 115-42. London: Bell, 1967.

Brantlinger, Patrick. "What is 'Sensational' about the 'Sensational Novel'?" *Nineteenth Century Fiction* 37 (1982): 1-28.

Brown, Bill. *Reading the West: An Anthology of Dime Westerns.* Boston: Bedford, 1997.

Buchanan, Robert. *Foxgolove Manor.* 1884. New York: Garland, 1975.

Casteras, Susan P. "Virgin Vows: the Early Victorian Artists' Portrayal of Nuns and Novices." *Victorian Studies* 24 (1981): 157-84.

Collins, Wilkie. *After Dark.* 1856. Freeport: Books for Libraries, 1973.

———. *The Black Robe.* New York: Fenelon Collier, 1881.

———. *The Letters of Wilkie Collins.* Edited by William Baker and William M. Clarke. 2 vols. New York: St. Martin's Press, 1999.

———. *Rambles from Railways.* 1851. London: Westaway Books, 1948.

———. *The Woman in White.* 1860. Edited by John Sutherland. New York: Oxford Univ. Press, 1996.

———. *The Yellow Mask.* New York: Lupton, n.d.

Cvetkovich, Ann. *Mixed Feelings: Feminism, Mass Culture, and Victorian Sensationalism.* New Brunswick: Rutgers Univ. Press, 1992.

Flint, Kate. *The Woman Reader, 1837-1914.* New York: Oxford Univ. Press, 1993.

Franchot, Jenny. *Roads to Rome: The Antebellum Encounter with Catholicism.* Berkeley: Univ. of California Press, 1994.

Griffin, Susan M. *Anti-Catholicism and Nineteenth-Century Fiction.* Cambridge: Cambridge Univ. Press, in press.

———. "Awful Disclosures: Female Evidence in the Escaped Nun's Tale." *PMLA* 111 (1996): 93-107.

Hanson, Ellis. *Decadence and Catholicism.* Cambridge: Harvard Univ. Press, 1997.

Hawthorne, Nathaniel. *The Marble Faun; Or, the Romance of Monte Beni.* Vol. 4, *The Centenary Edition of the Works of Nathaniel Hawthorne.* Edited by William Charvat et al. Columbus: The Ohio State Univ. Press, 1968.

Heller, Tamar. *Dead Secrets: Wilkie Collins and the Female Gothic.* New Haven: Yale Univ. Press, 1992.

Helsinger, Elizabeth, Robin Lauterbach Sheets, and William Veeder. *The Woman Question.* Chicago: Univ. of Chicago Press, 1989.

Hilliard, David. "UnEnglish and Unmanly: Anglo-Catholicism and Homosexuality." *Victorian Studies* 25 (1982): 181-210.

James, Henry. *Essays on Literature, American Writers, English Writers.* New York: Library of America, 1984.

———. "Miss Braddon." In *Wilkie Collins: The Critical Heritage,* edited by Norman Page, 122-24. London: Routledge, 1974. First published in *The Nation,* 9 November 1865, 593-95.

Kingsley, Charles. *Hypatia, Or Old Foes with New Faces.* London: Parker, 1853.

Linton, Eliza Lynn. *Under Which Lord?* 1879. New York: Garland, 1976.

Loesberg, Jonathan. "The Ideology of Narrative Form in Sensation Fiction." *Representations* 13 (Winter 1986): 115-37.

Maison, Margaret. *Search Your Soul, Eustace: A Survey of the Religious Novel in the Victorian Age.* London: Sheed and Ward, 1961.

Mansel, Henry. "Sensation Novels." *Quarterly Review* 113 (April 1863): 252-68.

Martineau, Harriet. *Harriet Martineau's Autobiography.* Vol. 2. London: Smith, 1877.

Miller, D. A. *The Novel and the Police.* Berkeley: Univ. of California Press, 1988.

Monk, Maria. *Awful Disclosures of The Hotel Dieu Nunnery of Montreal, Revised, with an Appendix.* 1836. New York: Arno, 1977.

Norman, E. R. *Anti-Catholicism in Victorian England.* New York: Barnes and Noble, 1968.

Oliphant, Margaret. "Sensation Novels." *Blackwood's* 91 (May 1862): 564-84.

Page, Norman, ed. *Wilkie Collins: The Critical Heritage.* London: Routledge, 1974.

Paz, D. G. *Popular Anti-Catholicism in Mid-Victorian England.* Stanford: Stanford Univ. Press, 1992.

Peters, Catherine. *The King of Inventors: A Life of Wilkie Collins.* Princeton: Princeton Univ. Press, 1991.

Radway, Janice A. *Reading the Romance: Women, Patriarchy, and Popular Literature.* Chapel Hill: Univ. of North Carolina Press, 1984.

Reade, Charles. *Griffith Gaunt, or, Jealousy.* Boston: Ticknor and Fields, 1866.

Reed, Rebecca Theresa. *Six Months in a Convent, or, The Narrative of Rebecca Theresa Reed, Who was Under the Influence of the Roman Catholics about Two Years, and an Inmate of the Ursuline Convent on Mount Benedict, Charlestown, Mass., Nearly Six Months, in the Years 1831-32 With Some Preliminary Suggestions by the Committee of Publication.* 1835. New York: Arno, 1977.

Review of *The Woman in White,* by Wilkie Collins. In *Wilkie Collins: The Critical Heritage,* edited by Norman Page, 104-108. London: Routledge, 1974. First published in *Dublin University Magazine,* February 1861, 200-203.

Sinclair, Catherine. *Beatrice; or, the Unknown Relatives.* 1852. New York: Garland, 1975.

Smith, Alexander. Review of *No Name,* by Wilkie Collins. In *Wilkie Collins: The Critical Heritage,* edited by Norman Page, 136-38. London: Routledge, 1974. First published in *Saturday Review,* 17 January 1863, 84-85.

Sue, Eugene. *The Wandering Jew.* [London]: Chapman & Hall, 1844-45.

Swinburne, A. C. "Wilkie Collins." In *Wilkie Collins: The Critical Heritage,* edited by Norman Page, 253-64. London: Routledge, 1974. First published in *Fortnightly Review,* 1 November 1889, 589-99.

Tarr, Sister Mary Muriel. *Catholicism in Gothic Fiction.* New York: Garland, 1979.

Taylor, Jenny Bourne. *In the Secret Theater of the Home.* New York: Routledge, 1998.

Trollope, Frances Milton. *Father Eustace: A Tale of the Jesuits.* 3 vols. 1847. London: Garland, 1975.

Ward, Mary. *Helbeck of Bannisdale.* 1898. New York: Penguin, 1983.

Wolff, Robert Lee. *Gains and Losses: Novels of Faith and Doubt in Victorian England.* New York: Garland, 1977.

Wolffe, John. *The Protestant Crusade in Great Britain, 1829-1860.* Oxford: Clarendon-Oxford Univ. Press, 1991.

Worboise, Emma Jane. *Overdale: or, the Story of a Pervert: A Tale for the Times.* London: Clack, 1869.

Yates, Edmund. "The Novels of Wilkie Collins." In *Wilkie Collins: The Critical Heritage,* edited by Norman Page, 273-77. London: Routledge, 1974.

FURTHER READING

Biographies

Peters, Catherine. *The King of Inventors: A Life of Wilkie Collins.* Princeton: Princeton University Press, 1991, 500 p.

Provides a portrait of Collins's life.

Criticism

Bernstein, Stephen. "Reading Blackwater Park: Gothicism, Narrative, and Ideology in *The Woman in White.*" *Studies in the Novel* 25, no. 3 (fall 1993): 291-305.

Considers the relationship between the Gothic setting of The Woman in White *and representations of class, gender, and genre in the novel.*

Booth, Bradford A. "Wilkie Collins and the Art of Fiction." *Nineteenth-Century Fiction* 6, no. 2 (September 1951): 131-43.

Discusses the effect of Collins's love of melodrama on his novels.

Cvetkovich, Ann. "Ghostlier Determinations: The Economy of Sensation and *The Woman in White.*" In *Wilkie Collins,* edited and with an introduction by Lyn Pykett, pp. 109-35. New York: St. Martin's Press, 1998.

Argues that the most sensational moments in The Woman in White *enable the character Walter Hartwright's ascent to power to appear to be the result of chance occurrences.*

OTHER SOURCES FROM GALE:

Additional coverage of Collins's life and career is contained in the following sources published by Thomson Gale: *British Writers Supplement,* Vol. 6; *Concise Dictionary of British Literary Biography, 1832-1890*; *Dictionary of Literary Biography,* Vols. 18, 70, 159; *Literature Resource Center*; *Mystery and Suspense Writers*; *Nineteenth-Century Literature Criticism,* Vols. 1, 18, 93; *Reference Guide to English Literature,* Ed. 2; *Reference Guide to Short Fiction,* Ed. 2; *St. James Guide to Crime and Mystery Writers,* Vol. 4; *Supernatural Fiction Writers,* Vol. 1; and *World Literature and Its Times,* Vol. 4.

CHARLES DICKENS

(1812 - 1870)

(Also wrote under the pseudonym of Boz) English novelist, short story writer, playwright, poet, and essayist.

Since the publication of his first novel, *The Posthumous Papers of the Pickwick Club* (1837; better known as *The Pickwick Papers*), Dickens has achieved popular and critical recognition of a level rarely equaled in English letters. Almost all of his novels display, to varying degrees, his comic gift, his deep social concerns, and his extraordinary talent for creating unforgettable characters. Many of his creations, most notably Scrooge from the ghost story *A Christmas Carol* (1843), have become familiar English literary stereotypes. Some of his characters are grotesques; Dickens loved the style of eighteenth-century Gothic romance, even though the popularity of those novels was on the wane, and his fiction features many elements of that genre. Dickens was thus a late contributor to the development of Gothic English literature. However, he played a major role in establishing the "Christmas ghost story" as an institution, and many eminent Victorian writers dabbled in the production of ghost stories only because he championed the form. Novels by Dickens that owe a debt to the Gothic tradition include *The Old Curiosity Shop* (1841), *Bleak House* (1853), *Little Dorrit* (1857), *Great Expectations* (1861), and *Our Mutual Friend* (1865). In these works Dickens combines social realism with exaggeration, surrealism, fantasy, and the picaresque to tackle important questions about the poor and disadvantaged in English society and to dramatize the consequences of rapid industrialization on its victims. He used the devices of literary horror to arouse public consciousness about terrible social conditions and to explore themes of greed, corruption, individual and institutional evil, reality versus unreality, imprisonment, and death. Although Dickens's Gothic-inspired fiction is highly entertaining, he also used it as a vehicle to express his moral outrage at the state of the social order and as a platform to reform what he saw as the worst excesses and injustices in English society.

BIOGRAPHICAL INFORMATION

Dickens was the son of John Dickens, a minor government official who constantly lived beyond his means and was eventually sent to debtor's prison. This humiliation deeply troubled young Dickens, and even as an adult he was rarely able to speak of it. As a boy, he was forced to work in a factory for meager wages until his father was released from prison. Although he was an excellent student, he left school at fifteen, as was the norm, and did not attend university. What he lacked in formal education, however, he made up for by spending long hours at the British Museum Library, reading works of English history and literature, especially Shakespeare. Late in his teens, Dickens learned shorthand and became a court reporter, which introduced him to journalism and aroused his contempt for politics. His early short stories and sketches, first published in newspapers and magazines, were later collected as *Sketches by Boz* (1836). The book sold well and received generally favorable notices. That year he married Catherine Hogarth, the daughter of his friend George Hogarth, who edited the newly established *Evening Chronicle*; Dickens was to have ten children with her. His next literary venture was *The Pickwick Papers*. By the time the fourth monthly installment was published, Dickens was the most popular author in England. His fame soon spread throughout the rest of the English-speaking world, and eventually to the Continent.

Success followed upon success for Dickens, and the number of his readers continued to grow. In 1842 he traveled to the United States, hoping to find an embodiment of his liberal political ideals. He returned to England deeply disappointed, dismayed by America's lack of support for an international copyright law, acceptance of the inhumane practice of slavery, and what he judged as the vulgarity of the American people. He then spent much time traveling and campaigning against social evils with his pamphlets and other writings. He also founded and edited several periodicals and wrote scores of essays. From 1844 to 1845 Dickens lived in Italy, Switzerland, and Paris. He continued to publish prolifically and became an extremely wealthy man. In 1858 Dickens separated from his wife and formed a close relationship with the actress Ellen Ternan. He also gave a great number of public readings from his works in both England and America, which left him exhausted. Many believe that increasing physical and mental strain led to the stroke Dickens suffered while working on *The Mystery of Edwin Drood* (1870), left unfinished at his death. When he died in 1870, England mourned the death of one of its favorite authors. His tombstone reads: "He was a sympathiser with the poor, the suffering, and the oppressed; and by his death, one of England's greatest writers is lost to the world."

MAJOR WORKS

Many of Dickens's novels are clearly inspired by the Gothic tradition: *Pickwick Papers, Oliver Twist* (1838), *Nicholas Nickleby* (1839), *Hard Times* (1854), *The Old Curiosity Shop, Great Expectations, Bleak House, Little Dorrit, Dombey and Son* (1848), *A Tale of Two Cities* (1859), *Our Mutual Friend* and *The Mystery of Edwin Drood* all contain Gothic elements within their humorous, picaresque structure, employing melodrama, hyperbole, and horror to drive home their themes. Of the novels, only *Edwin Drood*—a whodunit in which the prime suspect is John Jasper, uncle of the missing Edwin, who frequents opium dens and conceals a secret passion beneath his seeming respectability— has a plot that one traditionally associates with Gothic literature. The rest, from *Oliver Twist*, about the life of an orphan who escapes from a workhouse only to endure the horrors of life on the London streets, to *A Tale of Two Cities*, which chronicles the lives of the aristocracy and lower classes through the times leading up to and during the French Revolution, use Gothic-inspired characters, atmosphere, melodramatic moments, and sensational situations within a more conventional frame to underscore the horrors of modern industrial life as the author saw them.

Dickens's ghost stories are mostly light comedies sharpened with a spice of terror. *A Christmas Carol* is the most famous of all nineteenth-century ghost stories. It is about the transformation of Ebenezer Scrooge from a miser to a generous being, and is a moral allegory as well, but one that makes judicious use of horror. Dickens's other Christmas ghost tales include *The Chimes* (1844), *The Cricket on the Hearth* (1846), and *The Haunted Man and the Ghost's Bargain* (1848). His two best non-Christmas ghost stories are considered "The Trial for Murder," in which the ghost of a murdered man becomes a thirteenth juror in order to make certain that justice is done, and "The Signalman," a tale of premonitory apparitions in which a luckless signalman fails to make advantageous use of his warnings and their ultimate betrayal of his confidence.

CRITICAL RECEPTION

Few authors have achieved the critical and popular success Dickens enjoyed both during his lifetime and after. Before he was thirty he had become one of the most successful writers England had known, and by the time he was forty he was an international celebrity. Dickens's critical and popular appeal continues unabated to this day; his works have been made into motion pictures and have generated more critical commentary than any other English author save Shakespeare. Scholarship on Dickens's writing is extensive, but those interested in the Gothic elements of his fiction have concentrated on several areas. They have noted how Dickens modifies the devices found in Gothic romance for his own purposes, using elements of surrealism and humor to paint portraits of darkly comic characters who become representatives of moral decay, corruption, greed, and evil in the modern world. Critics have also discussed Dickens's Gothic settings, attempted to trace the Gothic influences on his work, explored the use of Gothic touches in various works, and admired his skillful use of horror to offer sharp social critiques. They acknowledge, though, that Dickens's ultimate interest was not in the supernatural and thus he was not a pioneer or key figure in Gothic fiction. Rather, the general consensus is that Dickens used the Gothic in his own work as a genre that he enjoyed in order to entertain as well as edify, modifying and reworking the Gothic mode to make it his own and to create a fictional universe that would highlight for his readers what Dickens viewed as many of the most pressing social issues of his time.

PRINCIPAL WORKS

Sketches by Boz, Illustrative of Every-Day Life and Every-Day People [as Boz] (sketches and short stories) 1836

*Posthumous Papers of the Pickwick Club [as Boz] (novel) 1837

Oliver Twist (novel) 1838

The Life and Adventures of Nicholas Nickleby (novel) 1839

Barnaby Rudge (novel) 1841

The Old Curiosity Shop (novel) 1841

American Notes for General Circulation (travel essay) 1842

A Christmas Carol in Prose (short story) 1843

The Chimes (short story) 1844

The Life and Adventures of Martin Chuzzlewit (novel) 1844

The Cricket on the Hearth (short story) 1846

Pictures from Italy (travel essay) 1846

Dealings with the Firm of Dombey and Son (novel) 1848

The Haunted Man, and The Ghost's Bargain (short stories) 1848

The Personal History of David Copperfield (novel) 1850

Bleak House (novel) 1853

Hard Times for These Times (novel) 1854

Little Dorrit (novel) 1857

A Tale of Two Cities (novel) 1859

Great Expectations (novel) 1861

The Uncommercial Traveller (sketches and short stories) 1861

Our Mutual Friend (novel) 1865

No Thoroughfare [with Wilkie Collins] (play) 1867

The Mystery of Edwin Drood (unfinished novel) 1870

*   All of Dickens's novels were originally published serially in magazines, usually over periods of one to two years.

PRIMARY SOURCES

CHARLES DICKENS (STORY DATE 1836-1837)

SOURCE: Dickens, Charles. "The Goblins Who Stole a Sexton." In *Great Ghost Stories: 34 Classic Tales of the Supernatural,* compiled by Robin Brockman, pp. 251-61. New York: Gramercy Books, 2002.

The following excerpt is from a short story originally published in The Pickwick Papers, *1836-1837.*

Gabriel started up, and stood rooted to the spot with astonishment and terror; for his eyes rested on a form that made his blood run cold.

Seated on an upright tombstone, close to him, was a strange unearthly figure, whom Gabriel felt at once, was no being of this world. His long fantastic legs which might have reached the ground, were cocked up, and crossed after a quaint, fantastic fashion; his sinewy arms were bare; and his hands rested on his knees. On his short round body, he wore a close covering, ornamented with small slashes; a short cloak dangled at his back; the collar was cut into curious peaks, which served the goblin in lieu of ruff or neckerchief; and his shoes curled at his toes into long points. On his head, he wore a broad-rimmed sugar-loaf hat, garnished with a single feather. The hat was covered with the white frost; and the goblin looked as if he had sat on the same tombstone very comfortably, for two or three hundred years. He was sitting perfectly still; his tongue was put out, as if in derision; and he was grinning at Gabriel Grub with such a grin as only a goblin could call up.

'It was *not* the echoes,' said the goblin.

Gabriel Grub was paralysed, and could make no reply.

'What do you do here on Christmas Eve?' said the goblin sternly.

'I came to dig a grave, sir,' stammered Gabriel Grub.

'What man wanders among graves and churchyards on such a night as this?' cried the goblin.

'Gabriel Grub! Gabriel Grub!' screamed a wild chorus of voices that seemed to fill the churchyard. Gabriel looked fearfully round—nothing was to be seen.

'What have you got in that bottle?' said the goblin.

'Hollands, sir,' replied the sexton, trembling more than ever; for he had bought it of the smugglers, and he thought that perhaps his questioner might be in the excise department of the goblins.

'Who drinks Hollands alone, and in a churchyard, on such a night as this?' said the goblin.

'Gabriel Grub! Gabriel Grub!' exclaimed the wild voices again.

The goblin leered maliciously at the terrified sexton, and then raising his voice, exclaimed: 'And who, then, is our fair and lawful prize?'

To this inquiry the invisible chorus replied, in a strain that sounded like the voices of many choristers singing to the mighty swell of the old church organ—a strain that seemed borne to the sexton's ears upon a wild wind, and to die away as it passed onward; but the burden of the reply was still the same, 'Gabriel Grub! Gabriel Grub!'

The goblin grinned a broader grin than before, as he said, 'Well Gabriel, what do you say to this?'

The sexton gasped for breath.

'What do you think of this, Gabriel?' said the goblin, kicking up his feet in the air on either side of the tombstone, and looking at the turned-up points with as much complacency as if he had been contemplating the most fashionable pair of Wellingtons in all Bond Street.

'It's—it's—very curious sir,' replied the sexton, half dead with fright; 'very curious, and very pretty, but I think I'll go back and finish my work, sir, if you please.'

'Work!' said the goblin, 'what work?'

'The grave, sir; making the grave,' stammered the sexton.

'Oh, the grave, eh?' said the goblin. 'Who makes graves at a time when all other men are merry, and takes a pleasure in it?' Again the mysterious voices replied, 'Gabriel Grub! Gabriel Grub!'

'I'm afraid my friends want you Gabriel,' said the goblin, thrusting his tongue further into his cheek than ever—and a most astonishing tongue it was—'I'm afraid my friends want you, Gabriel,' said the goblin.

'Under favour, sir,' replied the horror-stricken sexton, 'I don't think they can, sir; they don't know me, sir; I don't think the gentlemen have ever seen me, sir.'

'Oh yes they have,' replied the goblin; 'we know the man with the sulky face and grim scowl, that came down the street tonight, throwing his evil looks at the children, and grasping his burying spade the tighter. We know the man who struck the boy in the envious malice of his heart, because the boy could be merry, and he could not. We know him, we know him.'

Here, the goblin gave a loud shrill laugh, which the echoes returned twenty-fold: and throwing his legs up in the air, stood upon his head, or rather upon the very point of his sugar-loaf hat, on the narrow edge of the tombstone: whence he threw a somerset with extraordinary agility, right to the sexton's feet, at which he planted himself in the attitude in which tailors generally sit upon the shop-board.

'I—I—am afraid I must leave you, sir,' said the sexton, making an effort to move.

'Leave us!' said the goblin, 'Gabriel Grub going to leave us. Ho! ho! ho!'

As the goblin laughed, the sexton observed, for one instant, a brilliant illumination within the windows of the church, as if the whole building were lighted up; it disappeared, the organ pealed forth a lively air, and whole troops of goblins, the very counterpart of the first one, poured into the churchyard, and began playing at leap-frog with the tombstones: never stopping for an instant to take break, but 'overing' the highest among them, one after the other, with the most marvellous dexterity. The first goblin was a most astonishing leaper, and none of the others could come near him; even in the extremity of his terror the sexton could not help observing, that while his friends were content to leap over the common-sized gravestones, the first one took the family vaults, iron railing and all, with as much ease as if they had been so many street-posts.

At last the game reached to a most exciting pitch; the organ played quicker and quicker; and the goblins leaped faster and faster: coiling themselves up, rolling head over heels upon the ground, and bounding over the tombstones like footballs. The sexton's brain whirled round with the rapidity of the motion he beheld, and his legs reeled beneath him, as the spirits flew before his eyes: when the goblin king, suddenly darting towards him, laid his hand upon his collar, and sank with him through the earth.

When Gabriel Grub had had time to fetch his breath, which the rapidity of his descent had for the moment taken away, he found himself in what appeared to be a large cavern, surrounded on all sides by crowds of goblins, ugly and grim; in the centre of the room, on an elevated seat, was stationed his friend of the churchyard; and close beside him stood Gabriel Grub himself, without power of motion.

'Cold tonight,' said the king of the goblins, 'very cold. A glass of something warm, here!'

At this command, half a dozen officious goblins, with a perpetual smile upon their faces, whom Gabriel Grub imagined to be courtiers, on that account, hastily disappeared, and presently returned with a goblet of liquid fire, which they presented to the king.

'Ah!' cried the goblin, whose cheeks and throat were transparent, as he tossed down the flame, 'This warms one, indeed! Bring a bumper of the same, for Mr Grub.'

It was in vain for the unfortunate sexton to protest that he was not in the habit of taking anything warm at night; one of the goblins held him while another poured the blazing liquid down his throat; the whole assembled screeched with laughter as he coughed and choked, and wiped away the tears which gushed plentifully from his eyes, after swallowing the burning draught.

'And now,' said the king, fantastically poking the taper corner of his sugar-loaf hat into the sexton's eye, and thereby occasioning him the most exquisite pain: 'And now, show the man of misery and gloom, a few of the pictures from our own great storehouse!'

As the goblin said this, a thick cloud which obscured the remoter end of the cavern, rolled gradually away, and disclosed, apparently at a great distance, a small and scantily furnished, but neat and clean apartment. A crowd of little children were gathered round a bright fire, cling-ing to their mother's gown, and gambolling around her chair. The mother occasionally rose, and drew aside the window-curtain, as if to look for some expected object: a frugal meal was placed near the fire. A knock was heard at the door: the mother opened it, and the children crowded round her, and clapped their hands for joy, as their father entered. He was wet and weary, and shook the snow from his garments, as the children crowded round him, and seizing his cloak, hat, stick and gloves, with busy zeal, ran with them from the room. Then, as he sat down to his meal before the fire, the children climbed about his knee, and the mother sat by his side, and all seemed happiness and comfort.

But a change came upon the view, almost imperceptibly. The scene was altered to a small bedroom, where the fairest and youngest child lay dying; the roses had fled from his cheek, and the light from his eye; and even as the sexton looked upon him with an interest he had never felt or known before, he died. His young brothers and sisters crowded round his little bed, and seized his tiny hand, so cold and heavy; but they shrunk back from its touch, and looked with awe on his infant face; for calm and tranquil as it was, and sleeping in rest and peace as the beautiful child seemed to be, they saw that he was dead, and they knew that he was an Angel looking down upon, and blessing them, from a bright and happy Heaven.

Again the light cloud passed across the picture, and again the subject changed. The father and mother were old and helpless now, and the number of those about them was diminished more than half; but content and cheerfulness sat on every face, and beamed in every eye, as they crowded round the fireside, and told and listened to old stories of earlier and bygone days. Slowly and peacefully, the father sank into the grave, and soon after, the sharer of all his cares and troubles followed him to a place of rest. The few, who yet survived them, knelt by their tomb, and watered the green turf which covered it, with their tears; then rose, and turned away; sadly and mournfully, but not with bitter cries, or despairing lamentations, for they knew that they should one day meet again; and once more they mixed with the busy world, and their content and cheerfulness was restored. The cloud settled upon the picture and concealed it from the sexton's view.

'What do you think of *that*?' said the goblin, turning his large face towards Gabriel Grub.

Gabriel murmured out something about its being very pretty, and looked somewhat ashamed, as the goblin bent his fiery eyes upon him.

'*You* a miserable man!' said the goblin, in a tone of excessive contempt. 'You!' He appeared disposed to add more, but indignation choked his utterance, so he lifted up one of his very pliable legs, and flourishing it above his head a little, to insure his aim, administered a good sound kick to Gabriel Grub; immediately after which, all the goblins in waiting crowded round the wretched sexton, and kicked him without mercy: according to the established and invariable custom of courtiers upon earth, who kick whom royalty kicks, and hug whom royalty hugs.

GENERAL COMMENTARY

JULIAN WOLFREYS (ESSAY DATE 2000)

SOURCE: Wolfreys, Julian. "'I Wants to Make Your Flesh Creep': Notes toward a Reading of the Comic-Gothic in Dickens." In *Victorian Gothic: Literary and Cultural Manifestations in the Nineteenth Century*, edited by Ruth Robbins and Julian Wolfreys, pp. 31-59. New York: Palgrave, 2000.

In the following excerpt, Wolfreys examines the complementary use of comedy and the Gothic in Dickens's works.

It is the fear one *needs*: the price one pays for coming contentedly to terms with a social body based on irrationality and menace.

Franco Moretti

Gothic novels are technologies that produce the monster as a remarkably mobile, permeable, and infinitely interpretable body.

Judith Halberstam

A baby savage, a young monster, a child who had never been a child, a creature who might live to take the outward form of a man, but who, within, would live and perish a mere beast.

Charles Dickens, *The Haunted Man*

Love your other

The gothic is always with us. Certainly, it was always with the Victorians. All that black, all that crêpe. All that jet. All that swirling fog. If there is a transition in the nature of the gothic from the end of the eighteenth century to the middle years of the nineteenth century, it is marked by an inward turn perhaps. There is an internalization to be considered not so much as a denial of the gothic as it is a form of intimacy. In writing of the nineteenth century which manifests a gothic turn, there is an embrace of the uncanny within ourselves rather than a displacement or projection on to some foreign or distant other. In part, the turn inward and the interest in the otherness within is signalled in part during what is termed the high Victorian period by the intense fascination, obsession even, with English manners, with Englishness and all that is the most alien to the definition of Englishness, not in some foreign field, but in England, the heart of darkness itself. It is through what James Twitchell describes as the sober English concern with darkness, mesmerism and Satanism (1981, 33), that the gothic aspect of Englishness is revealed. Far from disappearing, it may be argued, the gothic, ingested and consumed, becomes appropriate, 'a legitimate subject of literature', to employ Twitchell's phrase (1981, 33). It is not so much that the vampire is sought out. Rather, vampiric feeding on otherness constitutes a significant aspect of English letters. In particular, that which is fed on are images of children and the idea(l) of the feminine.

The mid-nineteenth century interest in children, adolescents and women represents a transitional moment in the gothic, for, as is well known, the gothic of the latter years of the eighteenth century focused its terror of the other on foreigners, on Catholics, on distant lands and long-ago days, on creepy castles and even creepier foreigners, most of whom were explicitly Mediterranean 'of a certain sort', if not out-and-out 'Oriental', in the well-known sense given that word by Edward Said. After the moment to which I refer—a moment admittedly forty years or so in length—the Victorian gothic turned once again to the foreigner, to the outsider, to the otherness of colonized lands and imperial subjectivities, as essays at the close of this volume discuss.[1] But for that double moment traced, as it were, parabolically, from the moment at which Victoria came to the throne to that other moment when many of the Victorian writers thought of specifically as Victorian were either dead, dying, or consigned to writing mostly poor poetry on the Isle of Wight, the gothic mode of representation was turned on the British by the British. If there is, as James Kincaid says in Chapter 1 of [*Victorian Gothic: Literary and Cultural Manifestations in the Nineteenth Century*], a turn from the castle to the nursery, there is also a turn from some foreign field that is most decidedly not forever England, to the playing fields and private gardens of the English, to domestic interiors and to the streets of England's capital.

The gothic is thus found among the hedgerows, in the rosebushes, along country lanes. It is to be found on the Yorkshire moors and throughout the exotic Babylon of the Empire's capital, London, particularly in the back passages of the metropolis. It is to be found equally in boarding houses and amongst the houses of quiet squares. This is true at least of the literary, between the years 1840 and 1870. Most especially and insistently, the gothic is always to be found in the texts of Charles Dickens, from **The Pickwick Papers** in 1836-37, to **The Mystery of Edwin Drood,** in 1870. That escape from the uncanny is impossible, we acknowledge, at least since Freud. That the return of the repressed is inescapable and inevitable, we acknowledge equally. These qualities are our own, they inhabit our being in its most intimate recesses, even, and especially, when we project them as though they were being projected from elsewhere, from some *other* place, other than the other within. But what if we seek to embrace this alterity? What if we revel in its haunting quality, as, I argue, did the Victorians? What if we play Oprah Winfrey, Sally Jesse Raphael, Montel Williams or even—nightmare of nightmares—Jerry Springer, to that gothic aspect of ourselves, always already lurking in the moments of anxiety and the fearful perception of imminent terror which our daytime selves simultaneously deny, yet secretly anticipate? As all good, or even mediocre therapists will tell you, you'll never get rid of the uncanny, the other. So give it a good hug, love your other as you loathe yourself. Perhaps even tickle it, solicit a little laughter. Like a visitor who has overstayed their welcome, the uncanny may not take the hint when you begin to clear the coffee table, but at least you can amuse yourself at its expense.

"The Fat Boy"

The title of this essay is well known. It comes from that most famous of narcoleptics (literary or otherwise), the 'Fat Boy', AKA 'young opium eater' (1988, 345)—no doubt in deference to Thomas De Quincey—from **The Pickwick Papers.** The scene is equally well-known, but no less comical and worth repeating for all that.

It was the old lady's habit on the fine summer mornings to repair to the arbour in which Mr. Tupman had already signalised himself, in form and manner following:—first, the fat boy fetched from a peg behind the old lady's bed-room door, a close black satin bonnet, a warm cotton shawl, and a thick stick with a capacious handle; and the old lady having put on the bonnet and shawl at her leisure, would lean one hand on the stick and the other on the fat boy's shoulder, and walk leisurely to the arbour, where the fat boy would leave her to enjoy the fresh air for the space of half an hour; at the expiration of which time he would return and reconduct her back to the house.

The old lady was very precise and very particular; and as this ceremony had been observed for three successive summers without the slightest deviation from the accustomed form, she was not a little surprised on this particular morning, to see the fat boy, instead of leaving the arbour, walk a few paces out of it, look carefully around him in every direction, and return towards her with great stealth and an air of the most profound mystery.

The old lady was timorous—most old ladies are—and her first impression was that the bloated lad was about to do her some grievous bodily harm with the view of possessing himself of her loose coin. She would have cried for assistance, but age and infirmity had long ago deprived her of the power of screaming; she, therefore, watched his motions with feelings of intense terror, which were in no degree diminished by his coming up close to her, and shouting in her ear in an agitated, and as it seemed to her, a threatening tone,—

'Missus!'

Now it so happened that Mr. Jingle was walking in the garden close to the arbour at this moment. He too heard the shout of 'Missus,' and stopped to hear more. There were three reasons for his doing so. In the first place, he was idle and curious; secondly, he was by no means scrupulous, thirdly, and lastly, he was concealed from view by some flowering shrubs. So there he stood, and there he listened.

'Missus', shouted the fat boy.

'Well Joe', said the trembling old lady. 'I'm sure I have been a very good mistress to you Joe. You have invariably been treated very kindly. You have never had too much to do; and you have always had enough to eat.'

This last was an appeal to the fat boy's most sensitive feelings. He seemed touched as he replied, emphatically,—

'I knows I has.'

'Then what do you want now?' said the old lady, gaining courage.

'I wants to make your flesh creep', replied the boy.

This sounded like a very blood-thirsty mode of showing one's gratitude; and as the old lady did not precisely understand the process by which such a result was to be attained, all her former horrors returned.

(Dickens 1988, 92-3)

The scene is stage-comic, and, in its stage management, provides the would-be gothic writer—or scourge of timid old ladies everywhere—with a textbook example of how to bring a scene off that is at once both gothic, potentially terrifying in its eventual outcome, as all good scenes of gothic tension should be, and, simultaneously, unremittingly comic. Although all is soon revealed after the last moment described above, as is usually the case in the novels of, for example,

Anne Radcliffe, when the rational explanation arrives to calm down the unbearable agitation of being (for both the reader and the principal subject), nonetheless, Dickens works the scene in at least two different directions at once. The scene relies for both its gothic tension and its knowing comic solicitation of that tension on producing the simultaneity of feeling, while, also, providing the reader with a Hitchcock-like view from above down onto the terror-stricken old lady, rather similar to the elevation permitted the reader over Catherine Morland by Jane Austen, in *Northanger Abbey*. We know, because we have been told repeatedly, that the old lady is deaf. This is why the Fat Boy bellows. Nonetheless, this does nothing to allay the old lady's fears. If anything, they are increased. Furthermore, his bellowing in anticipation of the revelation of a secret goes directly contrary to the laws of gothic. He shouts when he should be whispering, and it is a summer's day at a country cottage, and not the dead of night or dead of winter in some far-off chateau, castle or monastery. We might even suggest that the scene is knowingly anti-gothic, that Dickens is just having a laugh at the expense of tired form, a form he loved as a child and continues to embrace throughout his career, were it not for the fact that the deaf old lady is genuinely terrified. She is made even more an abject figure by her being unable to scream. The comedy of the scene only works because there is such a departure from routine, as Dickens makes quite clear, and because the force of the old lady's emotions is not to be denied. It is in part the cruelty of this scene which makes us laugh, whether or not we choose to admit it.

The moment in the garden is, then, exemplary of the comic-gothic. The reader works—and is expected to work—in a number of ways at once here, not least in accommodating the ludic oscillation between comedy and cruelty, the latter as the necessity for the former, the former the outcome of what happens when you get close enough to the gothic to see how the special effects work (which is precisely what Dickens does). At the same time, the scene sets for us all sorts of normal patterns of behaviour, which we are asked to take for granted, solely for the purpose of departing from them so excessively. Yet something remains unsettling in this scene, two things to be precise, moments when the gothic never quite resolves itself away. The first is the Fat Boy's own agitation, that nervousness of demeanour as he prepares himself for his greatest performance (walking in and out of the arbour is merely for the purposes of warming up). The second is the

Fat Boy's outburst, which serves as the title for this essay: 'I wants to make your flesh creep'. Why the Fat Boy should wish to do this is a mystery, unless he is merely relishing the effect, like all good stage villains. Also, the news he has to impart is hardly the sort to make the flesh creep. The gothic is quite exploded, though the uncanny remains, thereby intimating the return, if not of the repressed, then, at least, of that which cannot be described. Quite.

To make someone's flesh creep is, we might say, Young Opium Eater's desire. Anyone less like Thomas De Quincey, the man who made even Wordsworth gothic, is hard to imagine. But the desire of the Fat Boy's finds its target in the terrified old lady. The Fat Boy understands that creeping flesh is a necessity if the narrative he wishes to unfold is to be deemed successful. He relishes his role, his performative status in the whole event. It is participation that is important. The Fat Boy is thus exemplary of the domestic gothic. He no longer is content, like so many good British subjects, with sitting back and enjoying being scared. He wants to take part. The English, no longer afraid—temporarily—of Catholics and foreigners (the Irish of course are always an exception, but that has to with proximity to home, as all good cultural historians will acknowledge) need to scare themselves, to cut a caper at home, put on a sheet and run around going 'hoo, hoo', for their own delight and terror. There are no bogeymen abroad, so why not pretend to be a little spooky in one's own back yard? As Sam Weller's knowing sobriquet for the Fat Boy attests, the other is within us, in this case in the form of the drug possible addict. And of course, it doesn't really matter if the Fat Boy is addicted, what matters is that he might be. The perceived drug addict as the most gothic of figures, then, haunted from within, tremulous without. Right in our own gardens. This is what we are witness to, and the Fat Boy plays it up unmercifully. As James Kincaid notes in his essay in [*Victorian Gothic: Literary and Cultural Manifestations in the Nineteenth Century*], the Fat Boy is double, both 'harmless toy and raging demon'. Doubleness is, of course, a feature of the uncanny, as Freud acknowledged (1953-1974 v.17, 233). It is this doubleness which Dickens remarks through the ambivalence of the comic-gothic.

Kincaid also raises the issue of the boy's appetite, his constant desire to consume flesh, and to turn whatever he consumes into flesh. It is interesting to speculate, in the light of Kincaid's remarks, on a possible connection between the

Fat Boy and the contemporary concern with cannibalism, in relation to the distrust of medical science's advocacy of anatomy, as H.L. Malchow discusses (1996, 110ff).[2] As Malchow suggests, there were growing worries about 'domestic, if metaphoric, cannibalism' as a manifestation of the gothic in the form of anatomical dissections in the 1830s, given voice in places both high and low, in *The Lancet* and in popular songs of the day (Malchow 1996, 110). Perhaps from a fear of the anatomist's knife and its implied relation to 'barbaric' practices, a grim humour, a '[d]issection-room humor' arose during the period, and 'Dickens made much use of this kind of humor' from **Pickwick** to **Our Mutual Friend,** as Malchow acknowledges (114-15). Malchow cites the dinner scene between the medical students Bob Sawyer and Ben Allen, who joke about the 'source' of their meat (a child's leg), terrifying Mr Pickwick. He also recalls the meal consumed by Wegg and Mr Venus in **Our Mutual Friend,** in the taxidermist's shop, where the two men are surrounded by jars containing the pickled remains of 'Indian and African infants', along with scenes from **Bleak House** (1996, 115). Harry Stone also notes the frequency of the 'comic mode' in relation to the theme of cannibalism, citing the example of the Fat Boy (1994, 77-9). As Stone makes clear, Young Opium Eater makes little if any distinction between animal and human flesh (78). Such comedic business succeeds, argues Stone, in banishing the gothic quality of such moments. However, I would argue that the gothic element remains potent precisely because it is never banished absolutely. Instead, it operates as gothic because of its immanence and its promise, laying below the surface and getting under our skins, waiting suggestively to make our flesh creep. As with many instances of alterity, the comic-gothic operates through proximity and intimacy.

The scenes with the Fat Boy and other scenes in Dickens' writing clearly revel in the comic-gothic as it pertains particularly to children, where the young become the source of sustenance and comedy. There is the grimly comic moment in **Great Expectations** when Magwitch begins to eye hungrily Pip's fat cheeks, saying 'Darn Me if I couldn't eat 'em . . . and if I han't half a mind to't!' (1994, 5). Eating young boys is much on Magwitch's mind, for he conjures the spectral young man who, Pip is promised, will find a way to Pip's heart and liver, in order that they may be torn out and roasted (1994, 6). As fascinating as such moments of potential cannibalism are, and departing from Malchow's study, Dickens is, we

would suggest, not so much interested in bringing the foreign, gothic other home, as finding it already at home, at the dinner table, locating the gothic *within* English humour. The grotesque is a necessary component of such comedy. In turn, comedy devours, it feeds off the other, often to hilariously ghoulish effect. The Fat Boy is, in a figurative, if not literal sense, the embodiment of comic cannibalism (again, see Stone's argument). Consuming flesh and fowl, he also has digested the gothic sensibility, to regurgitate it in a particularly stagey and English manner.

Written on the Body

The Fat Boy impresses us, of course, because, not to put it too coyly, he is *fat*.[3] His excessive, grotesque, quivering corporeality names him. This mountain of flesh, who consumes more flesh and sleeps, is known by his body, by the excessiveness he embodies. Were he not fat, could we laugh at him, could he provide us with comic and gothic moments? Probably not. The flesh is everything, it makes the act believable, and it is his size, as well as his creepy proximity, which terrifies the old lady. Dickens knows this, no doubt, and relishes the blubbery monstrousness of the boy, seeing in it not only a good turn but also a sure-fire commercial winner, guaranteed to keep us coming back for more. It is almost as if one can imagine Dickens advertising the Fat Boy in the words reserved for Mr Whackford Squeers, speaking of his son: '"Here's flesh!" cried Squeers, turning the boy about, and indenting the plumpest parts of his figure with divers pokes and punches. . . . "Here's firmness, here's solidness"' (1986, 517). There is a slight difference between the boys however, it should be noted. While the Fat Boy provides comedy by inflicting (metaphorical and psychological) pain, here it is the almost equally rotund Master Squeers who feels the pain while being part of the comedy. Fatness is not the bodily articulation of comic pain and gothic, grotesque excess so much as it is the medium through which such discourses may be expressed, and onto which they may be inscribed. What we as readers comprehend from one fat boy to another is the use to which the child's corpulence may be put, the abuse which it endures for the sake of the joke, at a moment where pain and pleasure are inextricably linked. The experience of both and their simultaneity is, for the reader, of the flesh made word and the word fleshed out, embodied. It is, as with so many gothic narratives, an 'experience rooted in the body', as Steven Bruhm puts it (1994, xv). And for all the comedy, both the Fat Boy and young Whackford perform for us as gothic bodies, in Bruhm's definition of this corporeal and textual phenomenon, for it is principally their bodies which are 'put on display' in all their 'violent, vulnerable immediacy' (1994, xvii).

It is through the figure of the figure that Dickens, by such examples, draws upon the discourse of the gothic, a form of writing which 'needs to be regarded', as Robert Miles argues, 'as a series of contemporaneously understood forms, devices, codes, figurations, for the expression of the "fragmented subject"' (1993, 3). Young Opium Eater and Young Whackford overflow their limits, their identities breaking down to become excessive and grotesque articulations. They are exploited and made to work. Dickens understands therefore, in the words of José Gil, that the body 'carries the symbolic exchanges and correspondences between the different codes that are in play'. He continues: '[t]he body is the exchanger of codes . . . on its own the body signifies nothing, says nothing. It always speaks only the language of the other (codes) that comes and inscribe themselves on it' (1998, 99). This seems particularly true of the Fat Boy, who, despite his corpulence, his idleness and gluttony, is, as James

Kincaid puts it, hollow, this hollowness in all its gothic splendour being 'the mysterious hollowness of fascinating caverns' (1992, 95). Dickens writes the boy as hollow in order to fill him from other places; he writes him as fat in order to write large the conjunction of the comic and gothic discourses which find their meeting place in the particular scene already considered. It is not that the Fat Boy is always in gothic mode, although, arguably, his constant state of being-narcoleptic is suggestive of zombies or the undead, albeit of a carnivalesque order. We might even suggest, given his often death-like state—extending the performative aspect further—that the Fat Boy's performance is analogous to an act of mesmerism on Dickens' part,[4] as well as an act of ventriloquism through the mesmerized boy by the author. Dickens puts on a theatrical turn by having the Fat Boy adopt a gothic mode of discourse, arriving with the promise of a tale to harrow the old woman, in a low, comic parody of Hamlet's father (both, after all, involve gardens in one way or another).

But is it possible to find the conjunction of the comic and the gothic in bodies which are decidedly not obese? One possible example of this is worked through in the scene leading up to Oliver asking for more food, as Harry Stone discusses (1994, 81; for more concerning Stone's discussion, see below). Another example comes from *The Uncommercial Traveller.* In the article entitled **'Wapping Workhouse'**, the narrator, on his way to that institution, encounters a rather strange boy who is referred to four times in two pages as an *apparition* (1987, 19-20). The ghastly and grotesquely comic come together in the bodily form and voice, whose most noticeable features are 'a ghastly grin and a [voice] like gurgling water' (1987, 19). The unnerved narrator remarks of the locks by which they are standing '"A common place for suicide"', to which the uncanny figure, returns in a possible jest (which may just be a misheard response), '"Sue?" returned the ghost with a stare' (19). With music-hall timing, not missing a beat, the proper name of one of the dead comes back, with that gallows humour to be found everywhere in Dickens' writing. Yet it is not merely the pun which is important, the joke at the expense of self-slaughter. Importantly, the scene is set up through the body of this ghostly creature, especially in that humorous *rictus* and in the voice of the drowned. The body of the apparition is, once more, expressly written as an empty figure on which are traced the comic and the uncanny. Everything about the young man is uncanny, uncomfortable, especially his wit, which insists on disrupting the meaning of words.

Thus Dickens, again, abusing identity in order to entertain, raising a laugh as well as raising the dead.

. . . . .

Scaring children is fun

If children are, from certain perspectives, constructed socially and through various cultural narratives as different from adult, rational human beings, this is no doubt a self-sustaining process which, in fearing the otherness of the child, the adolescent, the teenager, rewrites the narrative of childhood being in order to maintain its alterity, precisely for the purpose of punishment. The child's world is, as James Kincaid says, 'unnecessary, useless'; strictly speaking, it is a made-up world, creative rather than mimetic (Kincaid 1992, 221). In recognizing this, the adult may recognize a certain lost world, and seek to punish its other for the loss of that which we failed to keep within our grasp. So, we might say, what we want is facts, not fantasy. And what better way at getting back at the childlike delight in the gothic—that which scares us because we have grown ever so sensible, rational—than to punish it with that mode of representation by which the child can create laughter? Even while children may triumph occasionally in the text of Dickens, it remains a fact nonetheless that, at some point, they are punished in some fashion for their difference. All too frequently, the writing of punishment in Dickens' novels takes a gothic turn (which is never comical), as in the process of 'education' at Dotheboys Hall, in the death of Paul Dombey, or in the manifestation of a school master named Bradley Headstone.

There are, however, other ways of punishing the child whereby the gothic mode may be maintained and in which Dickens indulges, while comedy is reintroduced for the amusement of the (no doubt) adult reader, who may, like any number of Dickens' adult characters, tend to understand children as 'naturally wicious'. Because at some level the child, adolescent or teenager is perceived in all his or her (frequently gothic) otherness, so fun may be made through the gothic mode. Not all children get to have the last laugh, as does Bailey Jr.[5]

Oliver Twist provides one example of comedy—albeit of a very dark variety—at the expense of the child, as Oliver progresses from the workhouse, to the undertaker's, to Fagin's den (all

gothic structures), where other children enjoy themselves but not Oliver. (No doubt there is something of the morality tale here; all children, being naturally wicious, have criminal propensities, Oliver's plight is a warning to us all, my dears, concerning the inevitable recidivism of childhood.) Harry Stone offers a fascinating discussion of the well-known moment when Oliver asks for more (Stone 1994, 79-81). This moment, argues Stone, is equally laughable and fearful:

> the scene in which Oliver asks for more . . . is generated by a bizarre and laughable fear. Everyone is familiar with the scene itself, but how many remember the fear that generates the scene? That fear flows directly from a terrifying cannibalistic threat, but this threat—a threat made by one workhouse boy that he will devour another—is cauterized by its outlandishness and its humour: we chuckle rather than shudder, and we dismiss the threat as a bit of humorous Dickensian grotesquerie; the threat, we feel, has no abiding importance. But Dickens does not dismiss the threat, nor does he discount it or forget it.
>
> (1994, 81)

This is an admirable reading of the comic-gothic event, though I would argue that it is not a question of dismissing the threat so much as seeking to domesticate it, making it manageable through emphasizing the comic register. This is a precarious moment for, in the potential effect of making manageable, the economy of the workhouse—that which seeks to make children manageable—may become reproduced in and by the textual satire. Dickens will not let us do this, however, for his text maintains the fearful and the comic, the gothic and the humorous, in a precarious balance where the seemingly opposing discursive and psychic poles in question here open between them an uncanny *aporia* into which either mode threatens constantly to overflow and commingle.

The other well-known Dickensian scared child is Pip who, like Oliver, spends much of his early life in gothic surroundings—whether the marshes, his parents' gravestones, or Miss Havisham's—or in proximity to gothic moments, such as that of the soldiers' arrival at Joe's door, in search of Magwitch, described as an 'apparition' (1994, 30). Of such moments, the most comical for the reader, though not for Pip, is the following:

> It was a rimy morning, and very damp. I had seen the damp lying on the outside of my little window, as if some goblin had been crying there all night, and using the window for a pocket-handkerchief. Now, I saw the damp lying on the bare hedges and spare grass, like a coarser sort of spiders'

webs. . . . The marsh-mist was so thick, that the wooden finger on the post . . . was invisible to me until I was quite close under it. Then, as I looked up at it, while it dripped, it seemed to my oppressed conscience like a phantom devoting me to the Hulks.

The mist was heavier yet when I got out upon the marshes, so that instead of my running at everything, everything seemed to run at me. This was very disagreeable to a guilty mind. The gates and dykes and banks came bursting at me through the mist, as if they cried as plainly as could be, 'A boy with Somebody-else's pork pie! Stop him!' The cattle came upon me with a suddenness, staring out of their eyes, and steaming out of their nostrils, 'Holloa, young thief!' One black ox, with a white cravat on—who had to my awakened conscience something of a clerical air—fixed me so obstinately with his eyes, and moved his blunt head round in such an accusatory manner that I blubbered out to him, 'I couldn't help it sir! It wasn't for myself I took it!' Upon which he put down his head, blew a cloud of smoke out of his nose, and vanished with a kick-up of his hind legs and a flourish of his tail.

(1994, 16-17)

Between the pie and the cattle, there is more of gravy than of grave about this scene,[6] even if, despite its clerical air, the black ox bears more than a passing resemblance to the devil rather than any clergyman, while Pip's behaviour recalls in parodic fashion Hamlet's words concerning the reaction of guilty creatures, given certain stimuli. There is a subtle distance between Pip's older, narrating self, and his younger, other identity. While the elder Pip may well be able to construct the narrative comically at his other's expense, his younger self clearly is not in on the joke, and is terrified by the spectral cattle and the animated features of the landscape. The goblins, spiders' webs and the dripping phantom finger-post operate within a gothic mode, as the supernatural scene displaces the real world in leading to the comedy of frightened childhood.

That there is a discernible gap between the older and the younger Pip suggests to what extent the child as other has to be punished by its older manifestation. There is a double movement here, in imagination and memory, for while the elder Pip remembers the scene, he is also shaping its narration in a particular gothic fashion. His younger self's terror is transformed into a medium for entertainment. And this is not the only example of Pip's comic-gothic abilities at the expense of the young. His manipulation of gothic discourse is presented when, in London, he hires a 'boy in boots' (1994, 216). Invoking *Frankenstein*, Pip remarks that he makes a '*monster*' of the boy, who has 'little to do and a great deal to eat' (notice

once more the obsession with children eating), these being the '*horrible* requirements' with which 'he *haunted* my existence' (1994, 216; emphases added). Furthermore, Pip refers to the boy as an 'avenging phantom'. Whether or not Pip intends to be humorous, his description of the boy in boots is comical even while it is indebted to gothic discourse; more to the point, we can read that the gothic child is inescapable. It is always present, and always hungry—for something.

. . . . .

Gothic narrative at the end of the eighteenth and, again, at the end of the nineteenth century sought to assert a sense of national identity in response to fears of the foreign. Such irrational fears sought to identify and marginalize the other and all that was not-English, as is well known. Perhaps closest to home in the nineteenth century is the equally well-known representation of the Irish as monstrous.[7] What we may come to understand from Dickens, however, is that the gothic, the monstrous, the other, is a lot closer than we are comfortable in acknowledging. Taking the gothic and exploring it comically is one method of assuming proximity, if not intimacy, with the subject. Comic discourse and performance brings down the defences of the psyche. It allows the connection to be made between high and low, self and other. In so doing, it seeks to make us face the 'monstrous' within ourselves, so to make our flesh creep, making us tremble, simultaneously with laughter *and* fear, just enough so as to allow us a view of ourselves we had always striven to deny and to project onto others.

Notes

1. On gothic images of race, see H.L. Malchow (1996), who discusses the literary representation of the foreign as gothic other from the Napoleonic period to the fin-de-siècle, addressing usefully questions of monstrosity, cannibalism, vampirism and homoeroticism to the figure of 'half-breed' as a gothic form.

2. See also Chris Baldick (1987, 106-20), on the monstrous and Dickens' gallows humour. Baldick discusses the comic references to galvanism, from Sawyer and Allen forward, and to the 'animation of the apparently inanimate' (107). He also considers how the comedic effect is achieved through a dark exuberance on the author's part, discussing as well the question of dismemberment and dissection. Baldick argues that there is 'more to all this ghoulishness than a gratuitous *frisson;* it is of a piece with Dickens' synecdochal, Carlylean representation of character and of the fragmented body' (110). Furthermore, for Baldick, Dickens maps monstrosity onto the body as a product of 'crushing social pressures' (112). This may be true in part, but there is a certain distortion in Baldick's argument inasmuch as he takes the issue of fragmentation as directly Carlylean—Dickens' productions being a manifestation akin to the anxiety of influence per-

haps—rather than seeing Carlyle's writing as similarly produced, and not the original source as Baldick seems to assume implicitly. Arguably, the 'contamination' of fictive discourse with traces of scientific, anatomical and gothic textuality, speaks of the general historicity and materiality of Dickens' text, in which materiality Carlyle is also enfolded. The gothic as genre provides Dickens with a recognizable form of bourgeois entertainment which misshapes and in turn is distorted by contemporaneous discourses of the period.

3. On flesh, fatness, and their carnivalesque relation to the erotic in *Pickwick*, with particular attention to the Fat Boy, see James R. Kincaid's essay 'Fattening up on Pickwick' (1995, 21-35). Elsewhere, Kincaid argues that the stories we tell today concerning child abuse are, in their structures and circuitry, essentially gothic narratives, filled with so much terror that we become paralysed by them, unable to act (1998, 10-13). From this perspective, what is perhaps particularly terrifying in Dickens' gothic reinventions is that he is able to invest the gothic with humour. Of course, there are many children in Dickens who are neither fat nor funny, who inhabit the realm of the gothic and who are systematically abused, as is the case of the children of the workhouse in *Oliver Twist* or the boys of that other gothic pile, Dotheboys Hall, in *Nicholas Nickleby* as mentioned in the essay. Dickens' sense of the gothic in his depiction of such institutions works on the reader to appal at the recurring institutional abuse which occurs through the lack of nourishment, whether literal or metaphorical. Where children are comical in Dickens, and not merely the subjects of humour (and this is the distinction between the Fat Boy and Whackford, between Bailey Jr. and Oliver Twist; see the section 'Scaring children is fun', above) the gothic mode can be read as being put to use as a revenge, rather than a return of the repressed. Precariously enough, the comic-gothic, coming from some other place within, promises to effect destabilization of normative social relations and the circuitry of power which such relations maintain.

4. On questions of mesmeric agency, see Chapter 6 by Alison Chapman and Chapter 8 by Roger Luckhurst [, both in *Victorian Gothic: Literary and Cultural Manifestations in the Nineteenth Century*]. For a full-length study of mesmerism and its popularity as a form of entertainment, see Alison Winter's excellent study, *Mesmerized: Powers of Mind in Victorian Britain* (1998).

5. If the difference between the child who causes laughter and who is laughed at in Dickens can be described briefly, perhaps the question is one of class, and of the child's class position. Both Bailey and the Fat Boy are working class, their 'low' position indicated through their speech, through non-standard spelling and the emphasis by Dickens on idiomatic expression. Neither boy speaks the standard English of the middle-classes or of the narrator. Oliver Twist and Pip on the other hand, always speak standard English, without the trace of idiom or accent peculiar to the working class. They are thus implicitly given 'universal' voices. Within the narrative logic of *Great Expectations* Pip's 'voice' may of course be explained away: he is the adult narrator, recalling his own boyhood, and he has undergone education which has erased any signs of local accent which he may have had as a child. Oliver, on the other hand, always speaks English 'correctly', thereby signalling that, even as a child, in the workhouse or in Fagin's hideout, he has always already transcended both class and locale. It would seem then,

as a provisional thesis by which to explain the difference between those who generate humour and those who are its objects, that the comic-gothic is, for Dickens, a working class mode of articulation, which shares certain proletarian affinities with the grotesque, the carnivalesque, the melodramatic, and the music hall; in short, with all forms of popular entertainment.

6. The words are of course those of Ebenezer Scrooge in response to Marley's ghost (1988, 19). Although not a child, Dickens has Scrooge respond in a manner which is instructive with regard to the comic-gothic. Following the well-known retort, Dickens remarks, 'Scrooge was not much in the habit of cracking jokes, nor did he feel, in his heart, by any means waggish then. The truth is, that he tried to be smart, as a means of distracting his own attention, and keeping down his terror; for the spectre's voice disturbed the very marrow in his bones' (19). Despite Dickens' protestations, the line is, of course, funny, whether it was intended or not. However, the inadvertent recourse to humour in opposition to terror provides the reader with one more comic-gothic moment, which is, again, connected to consumption, to what is inside us. This is expressed both in Scrooge's remark, and those preceding the gravy pun, but also, importantly in Dickens' own expression of spectral disturbance in 'the very marrow in [Scrooge's] bones'. The ghost makes Scrooge's flesh creep, while the text moves spectrally across the boundary of the character's remarks to those of the narrator.

7. See, for example, the well-known cartoon by John Tenniel, 'The Irish Frankenstein', published in *Punch* (20 May 1882), where in a typical conflation between the name of the creator and his creature, the Irish are represented as a monstrous, bloodthirsty, masked creature. H.L. Malchow's *Gothic Images of Race in Nineteenth-Century Britain* (1996), provides what is to date the most sustained consideration of the relation between the aesthetics and politics of representation, from *Frankenstein* to the *fin-de-siècle*. On related matters of race and the connections made between 'foreigners' and women, see Meyer (1996); also on the issue of race and degeneration, see Greenslade (1994).

Bibliography

Baldick, Chris. *In Frankenstein's Shadow: Myth, Monstrosity, and Nineteenth-Century Writing*. Oxford: Clarendon Press, 1987.

Bruhm, Steven. *Gothic Bodies: the Politics of Pain in Romantic Fiction*. Philadelphia: University of Pennsylvania Press, 1994.

Dickens, Charles. 'A Christmas Carol'. In *Christmas Books*. Ed. Ruth Glancy. Oxford: Oxford University Press, 1988. 1-90.

Dickens, Charles. *Bleak House*. Eds George Ford and Sylvere Monod. New York: W.W. Norton & Company, 1977.

Dickens, Charles. *Great Expectations*. Ed. Margaret Cardwell. Int. Kate Flint. Oxford: Oxford University Press, 1994.

Dickens, Charles. *Martin Chuzzlewit*. Ed. P.N. Furbank. London: Penguin, 1986.

Dickens, Charles. *Nicholas Nickleby*. Ed. Michael Slater. Harmondsworth: Penguin, 1986.

Dickens, Charles. *Our Mutual Friend*. Ed. Adrian Poole. London: Penguin, 1997.

Dickens, Charles. *Our Mutual Friend*. Ed. Michael Costell. Oxford: Oxford University Press, 1989.

Dickens, Charles. *The Pickwick Papers*. Ed. James Kinsley. Oxford: Oxford University Press, 1988.

Dickens, Charles. *The Uncommercial Traveller and Reprinted Pieces*. Int. Leslie C. Staples. Oxford: Oxford University Press, 1987.

Freud, Sigmund. 'On the Uncanny'. In *The Standard Edition of the Works of Sigmund Freud*. Vol. 17. Ed. and Trans. James Strachey. London: Hogarth Press and the Institute for Psychoanalysis, 1953-1974. 233-8.

Gil, José. *Metamorphoses of the Body*. Trans. Stephen Muecke. Minneapolis: University of Minnesota Press, 1998.

Greenslade, William. *Degeneration, Culture, and the Novel, 1880-1940*. Cambridge: Cambridge University Press, 1994.

Hurley, Kelly. *The Gothic Body: Sexuality, Materialism, and Degeneration at the Fin de Siècle*. Cambridge: Cambridge University Press, 1996.

Kincaid, James R. *Annoying the Victorians*. New York: Routledge, 1995.

Kincaid, James R. *Child-Loving: the Erotic Child and Victorian Culture*. New York: Routledge, 1992.

Kincaid, James R. *Erotic Innocence: the Culture of Child Molesting*. Durham: Duke University Press, 1998.

Malchow, H.L. *Gothic Images of Race in Nineteenth-Century Britain*. Stanford: Stanford University Press, 1996.

Meyer, Susan. *Imperialism at Home: Race and Victorian Women's Fiction*. Ithaca: Cornell, 1996.

Miles, Robert. *Gothic Writing 1750-1820: a Genealogy*. London: Routledge, 1993.

Stone, Harry. *The Night Side of Dickens: Cannibalism, Passion, Necessity*. Columbus: Ohio State University Press, 1994.

Twitchell, James B. *The Living Dead: a Study of the Vampire in Romantic Literature*. Durham: Duke University Press, 1981.

Winter, Alison. *Mesmerized: Powers of Mind in Victorian Britain*. Chicago: The University of Chicago Press, 1998.

Wolfreys, Julian. *Writing London: the Trace of the Urban Text from Blake to Dickens*. Basingstoke: Macmillan, 1998.

TITLE COMMENTARY

Bleak House

ANN RONALD (ESSAY DATE SEPTEMBER 1975)

SOURCE: Ronald, Ann. "Dickens' Gloomiest Gothic Castle." *Dickens Studies Newsletter* 6, no. 3 (September 1975): 71-5.

In the following essay, Ronald traces Dickens's use of the Gothic in Bleak House.

In most eighteenth-century Gothic novels the physical setting was key. The enormous, often ruined medieval castle, filled with gloomy, mysterious interiors, internally connected by labyrinthine passageways and externally obscured by mists and fog, fascinated readers of Mrs. Radcliffe's age. When following generations lost interest in the Gothic novel, the Gothic castle *per se* began disappearing, but the imagery used to describe such buildings remained useful. Nineteenth-century novelists often borrowed the ruined building, the twisting passages, the darkened interiors, the obscuring powers of fog, and transformed them to suit their own purposes. In **Bleak House** particularly, Charles Dickens incorporated the structural imagery of the Gothic castle in important and original ways.

He hardly intended us to picture Bleak House itself as a Gothic castle. Yet before John Jarndyce took possession it looked ruined—"dilapidated, the wind whistled through the cracked walls, the rain fell through the broken roof, the weeds choked the passage to the rotting door" (viii)—almost Gothic. In her descriptions of Bleak House refurbished, Esther communicates little sense of ruin but conveys an impression of Gothic intricacy by noting the "bountiful provision of halls and passages" and "cottage-rooms in unexpected places, with lattice windows and green growth pressing through them" (vi). Surely, though, Dickens envisioned the building more complexly than the slightly-Gothic piece of eccentric stage setting seen by Esther.

Alice van Buren Kelly, in her essay in *NCF* [*Nineteenth-Century Fiction*] (December 1970), "The Bleak Houses of **Bleak House**," correctly calls the Jarndyce residence a metaphor for the entire novel. Bleak House possesses a labyrinthine structure that echoes the twisting complexity of the plot and innumerable rooms that suggest the multiplicity of settings found throughout the book, while the fog "everywhere" swirls around both. Bleak House is **Bleak House.** But Kelley does not see Bleak House as a pseudo-semi-Gothic castle, and as a result she interprets the Jarndyce home as a somewhat positive symbol—and the final Woodcourt residence, similarly named, as even sunnier. If we accept the fact that Dickens is working from the Gothic mode, we cannot agree with her conclusions. Certain negative psychological states—fear, terror, horror—traditionally arise from Gothicism, and Gothic castles appear in novels to help evoke those moods. I view Bleak House, then, as but an emblem for the kind of transformation Dickens makes throughout the book. If it is an emblem rather than a symbol, it serves principally to intimate the richer atmospheric and deeper psychological constructs communicated by his more vivid transformations. For example, his technique in presenting Bleak House simply foreshadows the more powerfully-Gothic drawing of Chesney Wold.

The Dedlock mansion in Lincolnshire more closely resembles the conventional castle, although Esther sees it first as only "a picturesque old house." She naively tells the reader that "on everything, house, garden, terrace, green slopes, water, old oaks, fern, moss, woods again, and far away across the openings in the prospect, to the distance lying wide before us with a purple bloom upon it, there seemed to be such undisturbed repose" (xviii). But after she learns the identity of her mother, Esther's perceptions change. Then Chesney Wold becomes "the obdurate and unpitying watcher" of Lady Dedlock's misery, and, terrified, Esther rushes past "long lines of dark windows, diversified by turreted towers, and porches, of eccentric shapes, where old stone lions and grotesque monsters bristled outside dens of shadow, and snarled at the evening gloom over the escutcheons they helt in their grip" (xxxvi). Dickens heightens her imagination momentarily to perceive Chesney Wold in terms of evil, but has her, quite characteristically, drop the subject before it becomes to intense. The omniscient narrator, the voice speaking in the historical present with a sense of continuing and relentless action, conveys more of the real Gothic horror of Chesney Wold. He describes the decayed country estate, surrounded by "a general smell and taste of the ancient Dedlocks in their graves" (ii), like a ruin. And sometimes, in true Gothic fashion, that ruin is haunted: "Mists hide in the avenues, veil the points of view, and move in funeral-wise across the rising grounds. On all the house there is a cold, blank smell, like the smell of a little church, though something dryer: suggesting that the dead and buried Dedlocks walk there, in the long nights, and leave the flavour of their graves behind them" (xxxix).

It seems to me that with these two views of Chesney Wold—Esther's and the omniscient narrator's—Dickens echoes the two points of view conventionally found in Gothic novels.[1] Terror-Gothic—Esther's brand—titillates and then closes the reader's mind to further perceptions while horror-Gothic—the omniscient narrator's—opens and expands it toward new horizons. Of course the reader responds more intensely and more intelligently to the latter. But Dickens is not

through with the Dedlock estate yet; he has only been preparing us for an even more complex reaction. He wants to terrify us not with grotesque statues, not with aristocratic ghosts, not with Gothic trappings, but with reality.

His ultimate presentation of Chesney Wold occurs in the turret-room during the moonlit conversation between Lady Dedlock and Mr. Tulkinghorn. There the setting, an almost-Gothic tower with mysterious footsteps sounding on the nearby Ghost's Walk, recedes into the background while the characters talk. Since the reader already has assimilated a total awareness of Chesney Wold from Esther and the omniscient narrator, Dickens need not describe the turret-room in more detail. For background he can expect the previous Gothic connotations of fear and horror to merge with the present, very real, horror and fear. Together, the psychological and the real fuse into an intellectual environment for the terrible conversation. We cannot help but shift uncomfortably in our chairs while we read more quickly to reach the climax of the scene because Mr. Tulkinghorn, *in that* place, terrifies us just as much as he terrifies Lady Dedlock. And our response to what we are reading, far more intense than we would ever have to something by Mrs. Radcliffe of Monk Lewis, has been triggered by fairly conventional Gothic imagery.

But there is an even more important way that Dickens uses those conventions, a way that is at once more creative and more terrifying. He borrows the elements of a Gothic castle to describe not a single building but an entire city, London itself. Of course the fog is "everywhere," obscuring the city both literally and figuratively from the very beginning, and those mists intertwine among an extraordinary number of buildings and streets that the author has chosen to picture in terms of their Gothic components. The result is a Gothic-inspired but Dickens-created terror even more gripping than that imposed by Chesney Wold. Before we examine that final result, however, we need to look specifically at certain descriptions of Dickens' London, for he achieves a subsidiary end along the way.

Many of Dickens' London-dwellers live in gloomy, mysterious buildings or rooms. Mr. Tulkinghorn's permanent residence sets the tone, for he lives in a large house, once a house of state, with a variety of "roomy staircases, passages, and ante-chambers," in whose "shrunken fragments" of greatness "lawyers lie like maggots in nuts" (x). Guarded by the pointing figure of Allegory on his ceiling—suggesting the terror of mute pursuit—Mr. Tulkinghorn lives in a place that intimates ruin, just as he himself embodies ruin wherever he goes. Mr. Vholes, another creature of prey, also frightens the reader with his continual blackness and his powerful hold over Richard Carstone, and Mr. Vholes operates from an office that is almost a replica of himself. The omiscient narrator explains that "three feet of knotty floored dark passage brings the client to [his] jet black door, in an angle profoundly dark on the brightest midsummer morning, and encumbered by a black bulk-head of cellarage staircase," and then shows us the interior, with its "smell of must and dust" blended with that "of unwholesome sheep" and its greasy and gloomy corners, "last painted or whitewashed beyond the memory of man" (xxxix). Richard, Mr. Vholes's victim, lives in "a dull room, fadedly furnished" (li). Their abodes, described in terms of Gothic imagery, reflect and reinforce our perceptions of the characters, just as they do when Dickens shows us the residence of Mrs. Jellyby, or of Harold Skimpole, or even the country estate of Lady Dedlock. Thus we see that Dickens uses his images in still another specialized way—to aid characterization.

Several times throughout the novel he overtly states that this is his intention. As Mr. Tulking-horn "is to look at, so is his apartment" (x) in the afternoon dusk. The inhabitants of the Smallweed apartment dwell "in a little narrow street, always solitary, shady, and sad, closely bricked in on all sides like a tomb" (xxi). The dark little parlour itself stands "certain feet below the level of the street—a grim, hard, uncouth parlour, only orna-mented with the coarsest of baize table-covers, and the hardest of sheet-iron tea-trays, and offer-ing in its decorative character no bad allegorical representation of Grandfather Smallweed's mind" (xxi). Such an apartment reminds us of a dungeon in the depths of an abandoned castle, and the Gothic mysteriousness of the interior reinforces the puzzling uneasiness we feel whenever Grand-father Smallweed is present. Many of the charac-ters in **Bleak House**—Grandfather Smallweed, Mr. Tulkinghorn, Mr. Vholes, for example—substanti-ate the reader's sense of terror at unknown pursuit, and their complementary residences emphasize that feeling.

Our overwhelming sense of London, though, is one of ruin, particularly when we react to the slum of Tom-all-Alone's, with its "crazy houses" and tumbling tenements" and "ruined shelters" on "a black, dilapidated street" (xvi), or when we look into "the room with the dark door" at Mr. Krook's: "a sad and desolate place it was; a gloomy, sorrowful place, that gave . . . a strange sensation of mournfulness and even dread" (xiv). Dickens underscores that sense of ruin by describing the streets on which these shells sit. Tom-all-Alone's "is a street of perishing blind houses, with their eyes stoned out; without a pane of glass, without so much as a window-frame, with the bare blank shutters tumbling from their hinges and falling asunder; the iron rails peeling away in flakes of rust; the chimneys sinking in; the stone steps to every door (and every door might be Death's Door) turning stagnant green; the very crutches on which the ruins are propped, decaying" (viii). And such a description is only one of many.

Sometimes the author chooses to emphasize the labyrinthine windings of the streets connect-ing those grim, stark ruins. When Esther first ar-rives in the city, she comments on "the dirtiest and darkest streets that ever were seen in the world" (iii), and at one point she comes to "a nar-row street of high houses, like an oblong cistern to hold the fog" (vi). The omniscient narrator also remarks "the great wilderness of London" (xlviii). In particular, when Esther joins Inspector Bucket in the search for Lady Dedlock, our sense of the mysterious complexity of the city is reinforced. Esther tells us: "We rattled with great rapidity through such a labyrinth of streets, that I soon lost all idea where we were; except that we had crossed and re-crossed the river, and still seemed to be traversing a low-lying, water-side, dense neighbourhood of narrow throughfares, che-quered by docks and basins, high piles of ware-houses, swing-bridges, and masts of ships" (lvii). Dickens further emphasizes the impression of a maze after the two searchers turn to descend "into a deeper complication of such Streets" (lix). Finally, Esther describes the last few blocks of her journey to the gloomy burial ground; her impres-sions are confused, a haze of street-lamps, of dark, of dawn, of driving sleet. She recollects "the wet house-tops, the clogged and bursting gutters and water-spouts, the mounds of blackened ice and snow over which we passed, the narrowness of the courts by which we went" (lix). And then she stands "under a dark and miserable covered way, where one lamp was burning over an iron gate, and where the morning faintly struggled in. The gate was closed. Beyond it, was a burial ground—a dreadful spot in which the night was very slowly stirring; but where I could dimly see heaps of dis-honoured graves and stones, hemmed in by filthy houses, with a few dull lights in their windows, and on whose walls a thick humidity broke out like a disease" (lix). What eighteenth-century Gothic novel possesses a more chilling pursuit through its castle?

However, the real intellectual terror of Dickens' London again comes through the words of the omniscient narrator. He expresses, not the superficial terror of the malleable Esther, but the terror of an expanding mind, one who sees the reality of a nineteenth-century English city with its murky industrialization and grim complexity leading into a maze of anonymity. Pherhaps the reader's emotions extend even beyond the range of terror; perhaps he begins to feel a sense of horror at modernity, as Dickens indeed did. This is not a horror caused by supernatural devices, a horror that circumscribes the souls of fictional heroines and closes their minds, but a horror caused by an expansion of man's view of reality. And even Esther can learn to see, as we do, the awesome horror of the modern city:

> It was a cold, wild night, and the trees shuddered in the wind. The rain had been thick and heavy all day, and with little intermission for many days. None was falling just then, however. The sky had partly cleared, but was very gloomy—even above us, where a few stars were shining. In the north and north-west, where the sun had set three hours before, there was a pale dead light both beautiful and awful; and into it long sullen lines of cloud waved up, like a sea stricken immovable as it was heaving. Towards London, a lurid glare overhung the whole dark waste: and the contrast between these two lights, and the fancy which the redder light engendered of an unearthly fire, gleaming on all the unseen buildings of the city, and on all the faces of its many thousands of wondering inhabitants, was as solemn as might be.
>
> (xxxi)

London, an environment of horror burning in the fires of Hell, stands as the central structure in **Bleak House.** Its multitude of streets, winding between shadowy dwelling places, parallel the passageways of an old abandoned ruin, while its great number of murky, dingy, darkened interiors suggest the multiple suites and chambers of a Gothic castle, each with its own mysterious and shadowy corners. Ultimately, then, obscured by fog and portrayed in terms of ruin, London becomes Dickens' Gothic castle. As such it conveys a total sense of mystery, terror, and even horror, not found in previous novels of Gothic heritage, and as such it opens the mind of the reader to a new perception of reality. The ruined eyeless buildings of Tom-all-Alone's, the dirty dark interiors of Mr. Vholes and Grandfather Smallweed, the twisting maze of London streets, and the grim fog of Chancery all combine into a single Gothic image to promote the reader's involvement with the horror of an urban environment. It is this involvement that is new; no longer can the reader sit back and enjoy the flighty fancies of a mechanical heroine. Instead, he himself must participate in the emotions suggested by otherwise rather conventional Gothic imagery. Dickens' London in **Bleak House** is indeed a Gothic ruin, but it is a Gothic ruin of a new generation, and as such it functions to open the mind of perceptions never imagined by novelists of the previous century.

Note

1. See Robert D. Hume, "Gothic versus Romantic: A Revaluation of the Gothic Novel," PMLA 84 (March 1969) 292-90, for a full discussion of the distinctions between terror-Gothic and horror-Gothic.

Great Expectations

THOMAS LOE (ESSAY DATE SEPTEMBER 1989)

SOURCE: Loe, Thomas. "Gothic Plot in *Great Expectations.*" *Dickens Quarterly* 6, no. 3 (September 1989): 102-10.

In the following essay, Loe explores the origins of the Gothic plot devices used in Great Expectations.

In spite of the enormous amount of critical attention the plot of **Great Expectations** has received in the last two decades, there has been a reluctance on the part of critics to identify its structure in terms of traditional genres. The novel's length, number of characters, and elaborate texture make plot identification a subtle issue, especially since the sense of progression of the story is skillfully interwoven with the development of Pip's character. With few exceptions, critics looking at structure tend to synthesize all these elements into one main plot. Such syntheses demonstrate that **Great Expectations** is probably the most unified of Dickens's novels, but in unraveling the elaborate tissue of its unifying elements they invariably fail to account for its diversity of action.

My thesis is that there are three main lines to the concrete experiences and literal actions of **Great Expectations,** and that these can be described by using traditional genre designations: the *Bildungsroman,* the novel of manners, and the Gothic novel. My primary concern is with the Gothic plot because its particular structural significance has been virtually ignored. One could argue that this is only because *Great Expectations* is such a successful work: its generally acknowledged superior plot construction conceals the overlapping patterns of its different genres in a way that one would expect in a work of deeply resonant unity. K. J. Fielding, for example, claims that in *Great Expectations* Dickens "completely mastered the skill of construction" (221), and Lionel Stevenson says that it "was his masterpiece of form and structure" (351). Yet Dickens's own ambivalence about the conclusion and the ongoing critical debate about the meaning and appropriateness of the two endings suggest that the various plots do not coalesce as neatly at the end of the novel as they are synthesized during its development. Examining the plot lines through the terms afforded by genre may not resolve interpretive debate, but it will allow insight into the structures that knit the book together, help reveal what the interpretive issues are, and establish parallels for comparing novels.

Viewing *Great Expectations* as *Bildungsroman* is the most popular approach through genre. George Worth's invaluable *Great Expectations: An Annotated Bibliography* published in 1986 reveals about two dozen studies that employ the concept as a significant way of reading the novel. G. B. Tennyson, for example, writes "To my mind the most complete expression of the Bildungsroman is *Great Expectations*" (143). Critics who view the novel as a *Bildungsroman* tend to find the same patterns and reveal that there is nothing particularly sequential to those patterns because they consist more of thematic elements than structural ones. G. Robert Strange's remark, "*Great Expectations* is not more profound than other development-novels, but it is more mysterious" (111) locates its chief distinction. The reason it is more mysterious is that the *Bildungsroman* plot in *Great Expectations,* unlike most other novels of the genre, is given a sense of sequential progression and heightened action through a combination with other plots. My contention is that the story of Pip's story of psychological and moral formation and his social progress is supported and directed by the simpler and more tightly knit plot derived from the Gothic novel.

The fictional biographical or autobiographical impulses of the nineteenth-century novel could easily become the "large loose and baggy monsters" Henry James describes without a more definite shaping force (84). Students of the *Bildungsroman* generally agree that it was left to Marcel Proust, James Joyce, and Virginia Woolf to perfect the techniques of point of view and pat-

terned motifs necessary to structure that complex genre. In terms of his *Bildungsroman* plot, Pip's journey is the metaphor of his development, and Joe is emblematic of the standard which Pip has left and to which he must eventually return in order to make accurate judgments about himself. Joe does not change, although he progresses in time, and the *Bildungsroman* plot he represents is not so much static as circular for Pip, which Meyer Abrams suggests is typical of the genre which has a "dialectical organization—it must have reached the *Wissenschaft* at the end of its journey before it can set out upon that journey from its beginning" (235). Any remaining questions about the suitability of the term as applied to *Great Expectations* are answered by Marianne Hirsch's conclusive "The Novel of Formation as Genre: Between *Great Expectations* and Lost Illusions." Pip's maturation progress, which includes his mistakes, may be judged against that standard to which he repeatedly returns from London, a circling progress of the coming together of younger and older self (Halperin 110): "ostensibly to make reparation to the neglected Joe, an intention never realized" (Brooks 125).

Most critics are naturally interested in describing the development of Pip's character, for it is in Pip's personality and the evolution of that personality that the salient literary merit of the book resides. The movement is a process in which Pip's ability to perceive his fall becomes an essential part of the discovery of self, as well as providing a venue for him to discover what he must do to redeem himself. In this way *Great Expectations* can move from rudimentary meanings to more complex ones in its powerfully harmonious fashion. But these are not systematic or casual movements, and they reflect meaning, not action; theme, not structure. Even with modern techniques for interior dramatization, the shape of the *Bildungsroman* plot generally described by critics remains a loosely chronological one, a fluid movement of gradually increasing self-consciousness punctuated by epiphanies.

A sharper sense of progression is provided for *Great Expectations* by its novel of manners plot. An enormously popular genre in the latter part of the eighteenth century and the early part of the nineteenth century, the novel of manners had expended much of its raison d'être by mid-century. Although it had provided a guide for the newly emerging middle class into the mysteries of an increasingly complex bourgeois society, it was soon too limited by its subject to meet the demands of a better educated and more sophisticated audience. Distinguished by its focus on piloting an individual through the nuances of society's rituals, the novel of manner plot does have a more orderly structure than the *Bildungsroman*, but because its concern is primarily with social practice rather than with growth of an individual, it generally lacks any substantial development in depicting its protagonists. In fact, the novel of manners could be regarded as the obverse of the *Bildungsroman*: instead of offering the teasing subtleties of growing self-knowledge, it offers situations where an individual must compromise or give up claims to individuality in order to succeed. Although many important *Bildungsromane* stop short of the protagonist's "accommodation to the modern world" (Buckley 18), this same "accommodation" is one of the distinguishing features of the novel of manners.

The plot of this genre is best exemplified by the basic situation of Jane Austen's novels: a female protected by her unmarried domestic situation becomes involved in a romance which leads her away from her family and toward an integration with society. Part of the appeal of these actions has been that they are unremittingly realistic; its courtships were treated in the mimetic manner of the novel rather than that of the romance. Marriage, as a confirmation of society's values, usually takes place, but whether it does or not, marriage provides closure. The mainspring for the pacing of the events in the story, however, is the love story itself, a major difference between the novel of manners and the *Bildungsroman*. If Pip were female, the importance of the romance to his story and the effect it has on the development of his character would be much more evident since his situation is a typical one for many eighteenth and nineteenth-century novel-of-manners heroines. The romance provides a reasonably casual sequence with a logical progressive series of developing successes and failures and separations and reunions. It has, then, a greater fixed pattern to its actions than the *Bildungsroman*.

The waning interest in the novel of manners had much to do with the evolution of a confidence by middle-class Victorians in their social practices. Yet the novel of manners still proved to be a powerful source for satire: by exposing the hypocrisy and self-interest of upwardly mobile aspirations, the novel of manners could offer an amusing corrective. This latent power is a potent force in all established genres. The generally acknowledged expectations of Pip consist of his aspirations to fulfill a superficial and limited no-

Illustration from *Great Expectations*.

tion of what it meant to become a "gentleman"; the novel of manners plot which structures these expectations inverts the progress of events and the obligatory romance included with them, so that they become a parody for revealing humbler expectations characterized by the work ethic so central to the Victorian middle class. Dickens thereby afforded his readers some luxury of seeing Pip's middle-class aspirations distinct from their own and disarmed much of the threat of an uncomfortable identification with Pip's aspirations. Yet, the plot of social progress orders events as it deconstructs and mocks them; like most parodies it depends upon the original plot of a work while mocking its theme.

Much of the vitality provided by the novel of manners plot derives from its familiar situations and simple casual progress; it is easy to trace the distinct logic of Pip's social movements even though they coalesce with formation of his character: Pip is motivated to leave his apprenticeship to Joe because of his infatuation with Estella. He accepts the opportunity to go to London in order to become a gentleman so that he might win her favor. In London he accepts the unsavory lodgings, friendships, and cultural opportunities as those appropriate to the style of a gentleman when they are, in fact, parodies of real culture. His comic experiences with fashionable education at the hands of the Pockets or his travails with the Finches of the Grove provide only caricatures of what should be available to him, yet Pip feels these experiences promote his desirability. His feeling for Estella is ridiculed by her and by her eventual acceptance of his rival, Bentley Drummle, who possesses the veneer of social accomplishment Pip is striving to attain for himself. His increasing talent for wasting time and money, going "from bad to worse" (309; ch. 36) is documented by the cycle of his visits to Jaggers and his returns to his marsh village. His lack of industry is countered by Herbert's energy when the latter eventually begins to plan for his own life. While we are shown that Pip is not "naterally vicious" (33; ch. 4) by the parallel with Orlick who seems to be, we also know his accomplishments are limited to those superficial attainments that define a gentleman for Magwitch and Jaggers. We know that Pip reads, attends plays, and can speak foreign languages, but these never become dramatized as an integral part of his personality. His social attainments are, apparently, only for show. Eventually Pip's fashionable accomplishments are revealed to him in all their essential hollowness, and his actions turn to rebuilding his values on a secure personal basis. He realizes he is as much a monster as Frankenstein's (363; ch. 40). "Pip's acquired 'culture' was an entirely bourgeois thing;" writes Humphry House, "it came to little more than accent, table manners, and clothes" (159).

If Joe can be regarded as the emblem of the *Bildungsroman* plot, Estella can be regarded as the emblem of the novel of manners plot and marriage or the possibility of marriage as its metaphor. The romance involving Estella also gives an initial motivation and a continuing rationale for Pip's actions in the social world, even though the scenes from that social world often resemble parodies or exposés. Significant changes in Pip's social behavior are demarcated by his reaction to Estella, like his decision to ask Biddy, who is in many ways Estella's counter, to marry him. At least partially because the novel of manners plot in *Great Expectations* is essentially a satiric inversion of the genre, Dickens is prevented from concluding the novel with Pip's unequivocal union with Estella, which would thereby appear to embrace the very mode of plot he has been caricaturing. Nevertheless, this frequently interrupted but uncomplicated plot provides a solid medium for carrying the novel's convincing social texture. Even so, compared to the plots of other popular mid-nineteenth century novels that could be regarded as candidates for the novel of manners genre, *Great Expectations'* structural rhythms are much more logically tightened than simple romance and social situation allow, especially in its final stage. The plot that combines with the novel of manners plot and the *Bildungsroman* plot to accomplish this tightness derives from the Gothic novel.

The resurgence of critical interest in the Gothic novel and its influence on the English novel from the 1970s onward parallels the interest in the *Bildungsroman*. A connection between the two genres in *Great Expectations* has been observed by several literary historians such as Walter Reed who sees them as "counterfictions": "a novel of *Bildung* unable to free itself from Gothic *schauer*" (171-2). Even though the presence of the general effect of the Gothic novel has been observed in Dickens's novel, little has been written about the Gothic plot of *Great Expectations,* perhaps because the greatest obvious effect of the Gothic novel is its affective atmosphere. Extended studies of such Gothic qualities range from Walter Phillips's early *Dickens, Reade, and Collins: Sensation Novelists* of 1917 to ones like A. C. Coolidge Jr.'s which have shown how Dickens utilized Gothic techniques to establish pacing and arouse heightened responses. Above all else, it is a genre dominated by its setting. The major effect of this setting is to establish a sense of isolation for its protagonists and create situations beyond the social norms of generally accepted practices and behavior. Since the Gothic novel offers experiences that call ordinary modes of perception into question, it seems ideal as a medium for developing the *Bildungsroman*'s emerging self-consciousness. Yet the Gothic novel also possesses an equally distinct plot. In *Great Expectations* this plot has usually been identified as its "mystery" plot, and its presence has been decribed or praised by critics from the time of its publication to the present. The Gothic plot is the highest energy plot of all three plots. Its deliberate causal progress, excitement, and suspense are so evident, in fact, that it is usually seen only as another element of sensationalism. In the hands of a skilled novelist like Dickens, however, the clear-cut pacing and causality become a vehicle for structuring the much less energetic plots of character development and social progress in *Great Expectations.* Barbara Hardy writes that "Pip's progress in *Great Expectations* is probably the only instance of a moral action where the events precipitate change and growth as they do in George Eliot or Henry James" (51). *Great Expectations* need only be compared to the very similar "biographical" story of *David Copperfield,* or to the dominance of melodrama and sensationalism in *Oliver Twist,* in order to recognize the thoroughly synergetic relationship of the plots that involve Pip.

What distinguishes the Gothic novel plot from a simple mystery plot and what are the dynamics of such a plot? The "suspense" plots or plot sequences identified by Phillip Marcus appear to have strong Gothic plot characteristics. Peter Wolfe also is surely writing about Gothic plot as well when he asserts that the ". . . melodrama ignores complexity and subtlety. It simplifies reality into ready categories of good and evil, and it aims at evoking a simple response—like horror, sympathy, or loathing" (337). Yet the actual terms of the Gothic plot could be defined more specifically, and its relationship with the other plots clarified. It is perhaps best seen in terms of the structure perfected by Ann Radcliffe and still a puissant force for structuring types of popular narrative today. The essential ingredient of this plot derives from an element defined by Edmund Burke's *Philosophical Enquiry into the Origin of Our Ideas of the Sublime and Beautiful* published about 1757. Burke's *Enquiry* became a virtual handbook of narrative principles for novelists and painters trying to achieve the sublime effect. The preeminent quality Burke locates that can be successfully applied to plot is that of obscurity. In Anne Radcliffe's most accomplished novel, *The Italian,* and in many of the novels that follow it, this principle takes the form of "layering" mystery upon mystery within a powerfully affective atmosphere so that the original motivation for the novel's action is greatly obscured. The original motivation is most often a crime, frequently involving an inheritance and heir, and its effects are visited upon a subsequent generation—usually represented by the character of an innocent and passive young female—who must seek assistance from a more powerful and experienced donor in order to resolve the mysteries of her origin and thereby reestablish a sense of order. In this type of natural or "explained" Gothic novel, what seems to be supernatural forces acting for a pervasive threatening evil always have some eventual rational explanation. A romance is present in such novels as well, but its story is made up of a series of separations and reunions which are distinctly secondary to the action precipitated by the persecutions of an unidentified villain, just as the romance plot is secondary in the *Bildungsroman.* Above all else, the Gothic plot provides a logic for the actions of the story which seem to have no apparent connections, and they need to be followed backwards in order to recreate the primal crime. In this regard the Gothic novel is the

forerunner of the detective story; it is no accident that Dickens introduced the first detective, Inspector Bucket of *Bleak House,* to the English novel and that Dickens himself was a friend, colleague, and sometime collaborator of Wilkie Collins, who wrote the first English detective novel, *The Moonstone.*

The Gothic novel plot of *The Italian* fits the literal circumstances of the action of *Great Expectations* very closely, and, even though subdued by the *Bildungsroman* and novel of manners plots that dominate the first two stages of Pip's story, this plot initiates the action of the novel and emerges in the final stage to unify and conclude the novel. Some specific parallels could even be argued to exist between the two novels if not pressed too far: Pip resembles both the persecuted Ellena and Vivaldi in his passivity and innocence; Miss Havisham, in her dedication to revenge, resembles the plotting Marchesa; Magwitch and Schedoni have similar roles as accomplices to Compeyson and Nicola, and their ultimate exposures of one another and their deaths are also similar; both books have henchmen like Orlick and Spalatro, who figure in the final explanations about the suspicions of persecution that permeate the novels; and Estella's relationship as daughter to Magwitch is very much like the father-daughter relationship thought to exist between Ellena and Schedoni. The most important structural similarity, though, is the way crime and two shadowy criminals, Nicola and Compeyson, lurk in the backgrounds of the plots in both novels. In *Great Expectations* these archvillains function as they do for the Gothic novel in general: they provide memorable, smoothly coherent actions by allowing the malignant effect of an original evil to be traced through cliff-hanging interruptions. Crime, the manifestation of this evil, is the major metaphor of this plot for all Gothic novels. "That evil genius" (437; ch. 50) Compeyson, despite his only occasional, furtive presence, is the emblematic character for crime and the prime mover of the Gothic plot which eventually ties together all the major lines of action in *Great Expectations.*

So, although Compeyson and his crimes have been taken to task by critics because they are obscure in the first two thirds of the novel and then blatant and melodramatic, it is from their very obscurity that they derive their forcefulness and eventual dominance in the structure of the novel. Dickens begins the action with the intrusion of Magwitch and Compeyson into the formative starting point of Pip's life, his "first most vivid and broad impression of the identity of things"

(9; ch. 1), which becomes interwoven with the images of crime, convicts, guilt, and terror which characterize his narrative. Magwitch and Miss Havisham, as well as Estella, Pip, and Jaggers, are important participants in this hidden Gothic plot, and even Orlick's mysterious behind-the-scenes actions are enveloped in his associations of Compeyson. The effect of Pip's imagination working on the associations he has with Orlick, for example, heighten his reaction to the glimpses and reports of a "lurker" he gets (352; ch. 40; 384; ch. 43) prowling around his lodgings. This response parallels and presages the move awful "terror" generated later by the presence of Compeyson, who is revealed by Mr. Wopsle to have sat behind Pip in the theater: "I cannot exaggerate the enhanced disquiet into which this conversation threw me, or the special and peculiar terror I felt as Compeyson's having been behind me 'like a ghost'" (414; ch. 47). The "special and peculiar" effect is created largely because it is a secret and internalized one. It is an interior effect, a psychological one, created by an imaginative reaction to events, rather than the actual events themselves. Robert Heilman has shown how the similar Gothic accoutrements of *Jane Eyre* create an internalized heightened response in that novel. This same principle of obscurity, so skillfully utilized by Ann Radcliffe, employs Pip's internatlized fears to create links between the various plots in *Great Expectations*. Compeyson's crimes against Miss Havisham and Magwich are created before the time that the novel opens (Notes 321), and the consequences that are visited upon Pip and Estella by their distorted donors are greatly removed from the times and scenes of the crime itself. It is these removed actions that have to be sorted out retrospectively, making the gothic plot resemble a detective plot.

From a retrospective perspective the Gothic plot appears straight-forward, like the evil behind it. It consists of Pip's initial help to Magwitch and Magwitch's subsequent attempt to play patron to Pip. Magwitch tries to revenge himself against the society he feels is responsible for his criminal fall and subsequent prosecution, linked in his mind with Compeyson. The parallel plot for Estella is created by Miss Havisham in revenge against men for being deserted by Compeyson. Both plot motivations are bound tightly with Compeyson's evil. Although overlaid in the first two thirds of the novel by the *Bildungsroman* plot and the novel of manners plot, the Gothic plot is kept active by interspersed, brief, but important, reminders of its presence, such as the man stirring his rum-and-

water with a file (89; ch. 10) or the later indirect encounter with this same emissary on a stage coach (246; ch. 28). Fear-inspiring Gothic imagery connected with death, decay, violence, and mental distortions support such actions, and foreshadow the eruption of the Gothic plot with Magwitch's appearance in Chapter Thirty-nine, in what Pip calls "the turning point of my life" (324; ch. 37). Locating the stories and motivations and sorting out the connections between Compeyson, Magwitch, Miss Havisham, Arthur Havisham, and Jaggers make up the rest of the Gothic plot. These correspond generally with the separate plot lines that are played off against one another by creating expectations for the reader, and then interrupted with another story. Even though the plotting and actions leading up to the final river flight and its aftermath are often regarded as "one of the highest achievements of the sensation novel" (Stevenson 352), they are integrally bound with the deliberate obscurity of the main Gothic plot that flows, subdued or dominant, throughout the novel. What has been deliberately concealed is finally revealed for maximum effect. This third type of plot is also bound closely with the change of heart that Pip has towards Magwitch, the last important development of his *Bildungsroman* plot, and with the concurrent collapse of his social aspirations inspired by his idealization of Estella, the motivation behind the novel of manners plot.

Seeing the variety of plots that makes up the actions and series of intricate connections between characters in *Great Expectations* leads one to conclude with Peter Brooks that the novel's "central meanings depend on the workingsout of its plot" (114). With the revelations that come about through the manipulation his life and the deliberate withholding of information that has let him misconstrue events so that he fails to plot his own life knowingly, Pip does indeed seem "cured" (138) of plot, or very nearly so, as Brooks asserts. The subdued Pip at the end of the novel accepts a plot option he unwittingly created for himself earlier in the action when he generously bought Herbert a partnership in Clarriker & Co., and he joins Herbert and Clara where, by dint of hard work over a long period, he moves from clerk to partner. Pip's secretly playing patron to Herbert was, as Dickens himself wrote, "The one good thing he did in his prosperity; the only thing that endures and bears good fruit" (Notes 323). Pip's eleven years' work in Cairo is recounted in two short paragraphs and seems far removed from his earlier energetic plots. The confirmation of the work ethic in this final plot would be endorsed by Victorians, but it does not make a story worth telling.

Yet the continuing appeal of the plots we do get in *Great Expectations* is in understanding the general truth of all their selfishness, guilt, misinterpretations, extravagent feelings, egotism, and violent actions. Sorting out the three main plots that carry these truths helps to do this, even though the net result of the mixture of plots in *Great Expectations* is clearly greater than the mere sum of its separate parts, and such sorting must necessarily ignore other essential ingredients. What the identification of various plots reveals especially well, however, is the authentic drama of nightmarish quality of an individual's life when others have manipulated it, and the consequent need for moral self-determination. The amalgam of plots in *Great Expectations* created by Dickens's mature, resourceful, and highly imaginative understanding of reality resembles the mixed texture of life itself, and the reader of *Great Expectations* must understand and actively reconstruct its plots and their relative importance, just as life's patterns must be understood and evaluated in the constant process of reappraising our own versions of reality.

Works Cited

Abrams, M. H. *Natural Supernaturalism*. London: Oxford UP, 1971.

Buckley, Jerome H. *Season of Youth: The Bildungsroman from Dickens to Golding*. Cambridge: Harvard UP, 1974.

Brooks, Peter. *Reading for the Plot: Design and Intention in Narrative*. New York: Vintage-Random, 1985.

Coolidge, A. C. *Charles Dickens as Serial Novelist*. Ames, IA: Iowa State UP, 1967.

Dickens, Charles. *Great Expectations*. New York: Signet-NAL, 1963.

———. *Dickens' Working Notes for His Novels*. Ed. Harry Stone. Chicago: U of Chicago P, 1987.

Fielding, K. J. *Charles Dickens: A Critical Introduction*. 2nd Ed. Enlarged. London: Longmans, 1965.

Hardy, Barbara. "The Change of Heart in Dickens' Novels." *Victorian Studies* 5 (1961-2), 49-67. Rpt. in *Dickens: A Collection of Critical Essays*. Ed. Martin Price. Englewood Cliffs, NJ: Prentice, 1967. 39-57.

Halperin, John. *Egoism and Self-Discovery in the Victorian Novel: Studies in the Ordeal of Knowledge in the Nineteenth Century*. New York: Burt Franklin, 1974.

Heilman, Robert B. "Charlotte Brontë's 'New' Gothic." *From Jane Austen to Joseph Conrad*. Ed. Robert C. Rathburn and Martin Steinmann, Jr. Minneapolis: U of Minnesota P, 1958. 71-85. Rpt. in *The Victorian Novel: Modern Essays in Criticism*. Ed. Ian Watt. London: Oxford UP, 1971. 165-80.

Hirsch, Marianne. "The Novel of Formation as Genre: Between Great Expectations and Lost Illusions." *Genre* 12 (1979): 293-311.

House, Humphry. *The Dickens World*. 2nd. Ed. 1942. Oxford: Oxford UP, 1979.

James, Henry. "Preface to the Tragic Muse." *The Art of the Novel*. Ed. R. P. Blackmur. New York: Scribners, 1934. 79-97.

Marcus, Phillip. "Theme and Suspense in the Plot of *Great Expectations*." *Dickens Studies* 2 (1966): 57-73.

Phillips, Walter C. *Dickens, Reade, and Collins: Sensation Novelists*. New York: Columbia UP, 1917.

Radcliffe, Ann. *The Italian, or The Confessional of the Black Penitents: a Romance*. Oxford: Oxford UP, 1968.

Reed, Walter. *An Exemplary History of the Novel: The Quixotic Versus the Picaresque*. Chicago: U of Chicago P, 1981.

Stange, G. Robert. "Expectations Well Lost: Dickens' Fable for His Time." *College English* 16 (1954-5): 9-17. Rpt in *The Victorian Novel: Modern Essays in Criticism*. Ed. Ian Watt. London: Oxford UP, 1971. 110-22.

Stevenson, Lionel. *The English Novel: A Panorama*. Boston: Houghton, 1960.

Tennyson, G. B. "The *Bildungsroman* in Nineteenth-Century English Literature." *Medieval Epic to the 'Epic Theatre' of Brecht: Essays in Comparative Literature*. Ed. Rosario P. Armato and John M. Spalek. Los Angeles: U of Southern California Press, 1968. 135-46.

Wolfe, Peter. "The Fictional Crux and the Double Structure of *Great Expectations*." *South Atlantic Quarterly* 73 (Summer 1974): 335-47.

Little Dorrit

DAVID JARRETT (ESSAY DATE SEPTEMBER 1977)

SOURCE: Jarrett, David. "The Fall of the House of Clennam: Gothic Conventions in *Little Dorrit*." *Dickensian* 73, no. 383 (September 1977): 155-61.

In the following essay, Jarrett analyzes Dickens's use of the Gothic in Little Dorrit.

Charles Dickens had no time for the kind of romance of history celebrated by the garish Mrs Skewton in *Dombey and Son* (1847-8). 'Those darling bygone times,' she exclaims to Mr Carker in Warwick Castle, 'with their delicious fortresses, and their dear old dungeons, and their delightful places of torture, and their romantic vengeances, and their picturesque assaults and sieges, and everything that makes life truly charming! How dreadfully we have degenerated!'[1]

To write a Gothic romance would be as foreign to Dickens as to idealise the Middle Ages, and Mrs Skewton herself supplies a suitable image to represent his attitude towards some aspects of the

ABOUT THE AUTHOR

MICHAEL HOLLINGTON ON "DICKENSIAN GOTHIC"

Judging by some of the allusions to Gothic writing in *Sketches by Boz* and other early works, readers can readily conclude that Dickens carved out for himself at an early stage a clear program for its transformation and modernization. Dickensian Gothic, his early writings seem to announce, will be contemporary and urban rather than medieval and exotic, its wonders and horrors presented through paradoxical, plural combinations and juxtapositions of tragedy and comedy rather than through conventional melodramatic formulae aimed at achieving single, concentrated terror effects. The apparent common purpose, for instance, of three references to Mrs. Radcliffe and one to Sir Walter Scott, authors whom Dickens as a young man clearly sought to emulate, seems to be to suggest that such 'real' horrors may rank with or indeed surpass the imaginary horrors for which his predecessors had become famous. Their related rhetorical strategies, in fact, can be seen as a sequence of progressive humorous 'turns of the screw,' a ratcheting up of more and more hyperbolic claims on behalf of a 'new Gothic' against an old.

SOURCE: Hollington, Michael. "Boz's Gothic Gargoyles." *Dickens Quarterly* 16, no. 3 (September 1999): 160-77.

Gothic mode. He was certainly familiar with the Gothic conventions, not least from his experience of the theatre, where Gothic melodrama, deriving directly from Gothic romance, 'flowered on the English stage in the 1790's, [and] bloomed luxuriantly for fifty years or so'.[2] And the Gothic has made a positive contribution to Dickens's novels, so that it is commonplace to talk of the Gothicism of *The Old Curiosity Shop* (1841), *Barnaby Rudge* (1841), and *Great Expectations* (1860-1).[3] The use of Gothic elements in *Little Dorrit* (1855-7), however, has not been treated, and it is to this novel that I shall turn after brief reference to the relevant Gothic conventions.

In Gothic fiction the central element is always the gloomy Gothic building which is inextricably associated with the villain, usually a persecuting and usurping parent-figure. The symbolic significance of the building can vary as much as the visible shape of its various transformations which we encounter in Gothic Otranto, in Miss Havisham's decayed Satis House, and in Randolph's uncanny house in Truman Capote's *Other Voices, Other Rooms* (1948). It generally appears endued with a sinister life of its own, is in a ruinous state, and is often destroyed at the climax. There are many stock devices in Gothic fiction, including the animated portrait of *The Castle of Otranto* (1764), but perhaps the most important after the castle are the dream and the old manuscript. They are as versatile as the archetype of the Gothic castle, though they can be best observed in their most straightforward form in Clara Reeve's *The Old English Baron* (1778) and Ann Radcliffe's *The Romance of the Forest* (1791). The hero or heroine in Gothic fiction confronts the Gothic castle and descends into it as into a dream; in this deathly enclosure comes a revelation, which may be accomplished through an old manuscript, a prophetic dream, or some equivalent, and which probably concerns the hero's search for the secret of his birth and the necessity of setting right the wrongs passed from one generation to another.

In chapter three of *Little Dorrit* Arthur Clennam, returning to London on a Sunday evening, sees the city in the grip of an archaic oppressive religious tyranny which centres, for him, on his mother and her house. The Clennam house is the grim architectural core of the novel, containing a guilty secret and offering a vague parental threat. Arthur

> . . . came at last to the house he sought. An old brick house, so dingy as to be all but black, standing by itself within a gateway. Before it, a square court-yard where a shrub or two and a patch of grass were as rank (which is saying much) as the iron railings enclosing them were rusty; behind it, a jumble of roots. It was a double house, with long, narrow, heavily-framed windows. Many years ago, it had had it in its mind to slide down sideways; it had been propped up, however, and was leaning on some half-dozen gigantic crutches: which gymnasium for the neighbouring cats, weather-stained, smoke-blackened, and overgrown with weeds, appeared in these latter days to be no very sure reliance.[4]

Though reduced in scale and not literally Gothic in architectural style, Mrs Clennam's house is the equivalent of the castle of Gothic romance, for it has an antique gloomy life of its own ('it had had it in its mind to slide down sideways'), and in its decay and mystery it matches its inhabitants. And, of course, as Arthur suspects, it contains the secret of a guilty deed which the heir must identify and expose before he can be given his true heritage. Dickens himself likens the house ironically to 'a castle of romance', wretched and hopeless (I, iii, 40).

In the chapter which follows our introduction to the Clennam house there is a frightening variation of the prophetic or revelatory dream of Gothic fiction:

> When Mrs Flintwinch dreamed, she usually dreamed, unlike the son of her old mistress, with her eyes shut. She had a curiously vivid dream that night, and before she had left the son of her old mistress many hours. In fact it was not at all like a dream, it was so real in every respect.
>
> (I, iv, 41)

Indeed, what is so horrible about Affery's dream is that it is no dream at all. Affery in her 'dream' sees the unaccountable multiplication of her husband, 'Mr Flintwinch awake . . . watching Mr Flintwinch asleep' (I, ii, 42), and she almost witnesses a murder too. It is a dangerous knowledge that she is beginning to acquire, in best Gothic fashion, through 'dream'. By bringing the Gothic archetype of the ruin, inhabited by a threatening parental or ancestral power, from the forest of romance and into the world of the novel and nineteenth century London, Dickens brings the horror of what was to him an unreal romantic world into the real, and thus makes it more affecting. Similarly, by removing from the dream device of Gothic romance the actual dream, and yet still describing the events witnessed by the befuddled Affery in terms of dream, he renders the device more truly haunting and powerful than it had been in, say, *The Old English Baron.*

When Affery determines at length to tell her dreams (II, xxx, 763-786) her contribution to revealing the guilt concealed in the Clennam house works in conjunction with Dickens's equivalent to the Gothic old manuscript device. For it is here that Blandois recounts his ugly 'history of this house', a 'history of strange marriage, and a strange mother, and a revenge, and a suppression' (II, xxx, 771). His story is drawn from old papers—a codicil to Gilbert Clennam's will and the letters of Arthur's barbarously treated real mother—which Flintwinch had double-locked in an iron box and given to his twin brother, witnessed by Affery in her 'dream'. These papers, of course, reveal the secret of the hero's birth and show what restitution must be made in this generation.

Mrs Clennam's religion is characterised through an architectural metaphor when Dickens attributes to her the following religious sentiments:

> Smite Thou my debtors, Lord, wither them, crush them; do Thou as I would do, and Thou shalt have my worship: this was the impious tower of stone she built up to scale Heaven.
>
> (I, iv, 47)

And though the image primarily suggests the tower of Babel, yet, because of the way in which Dickens has been using the conventions of Gothic romance in *Little Dorrit,* it merges with that of the central archetype of Gothic fiction. For there is no doubt that in some ways Mrs Clennam belongs to the grisly romance of history represented by Mrs Skewton's sentiments in Warwick Castle quoted above. When Flintwinch leads Arthur to his mother it is a progress as to the ancestral tomb that belongs to 'those darling bygone times' of torture and tyranny:

> Arthur followed him up the staircase, which was panelled off into spaces, like so many mourning tablets, into a dim bed-chamber, the floor of which had gradually so sunk and settled, that the fireplace was in a dell. On a black bier-like sofa in this hollow, propped up behind with one great angular black bolster, like the block at a state execution in *the good old times* [italics mine], sat his mother in a widow's dress.
>
> (I, iii, 33)

At the core of the decaying family house is the heavy atmosphere of mortality, guilt, and threat. As Arthur quickly perceives, it is Little Dorrit who is obscurely threatened, and she, in her modesty, her vulnerability, her quiet generosity, and, of course, in her littleness, is clearly a re-working of the 'orphan-of-the-castle' Gothic heroine. She even has a choice of castles to contain her quietness in their gloom—Mrs Clennam's house and the Marshalsea.

Dickens, even if somewhat ironically, early suggests the violent possibilities implied in the Clennam household's menacing of the orphan Little Dorrit. For what he could learn about Little Dorrit in the first instance

> . . . Arthur was indebted in the course of the day to his own eyes and to Mrs Affery's tongue. If Mrs Affery had had any will or way of her own, it would probably have been unfavourable to Little Dorrit. But as 'them two clever ones'—Mrs Affery's perpetual reference, in whom her personality was swallowed up—were agreed to accept Little Dorrit as a matter of course, she had nothing for it but to follow suit. Similarly, if the two cleaver ones had agreed to murder Little Dorrit by candle-light,

Mrs Affery, being required to hold the candle, would no doubt have done it.

(I, v, 53)

An edge of ironic humour there might be to this, but we have already seen Flintwinch on the brink of murdering his own brother by candle-light, and the sinister power of the 'two clever ones' over Affery is made clear by the enormity of the crime in which she would 'no doubt' have participated.

When Arthur Clennam talks to his mother of 'our House' he means neither the building in which the mother has shut herself away, nor a line of titled ancestors in a family vault. But we have seen Dickens suggesting such a vault when describing Mrs Clennam in her room. In the awkward interview with his mother in which he refuses to take over the family business Arthur is leading up to the enquiry about the possibility of his dead father's secret guilt: 'If reparation can be made to any one, if restitution can be made to any one, let us know it and make it' (I, v, 49), he says. A little before, he has said:

'Mother, our House has done less and less for some years past, and our dealings have been progressively on the decline. We have never shown much confidence, or invited much; we have attached no people to us; the track we have kept is not the track of time; and we have been left far behind.'

(I, v, 46)

Although it is a House of Business that is the subject of this speech the emotional atmosphere would equally suit an old, run-down aristocratic line retreating into Gothic obscurity. And it is plain, when a little later Arthur visits his father's room of business, that we are meant to see this suggestion in the above passage.

The room Arthur Clennam's deceased father had occupied for business purposes . . . was so unaltered that he might have been imagined still to keep it invisibly, as his visible relict kept her room up-stairs. . . . His picture, dark and gloomy, earnestly speechless on the wall, with the eyes intently looking at his son as they had looked when life departed from them, seemed to urge him awfully to the task he had attempted. . . .

(I, v, 54)

The portrait does not quite step out of its frame, like that in *The Castle of Otranto*, or as Charles Maturin seems to make the seventeenth century depiction of Melmoth in *Melmoth the Wanderer* (1820).[5] But Dickens does animate the portrait for Arthur and it does seem to be having a significant effect in prompting him to do something about the mysterious wrong that its subject

perpetrated or knew. If one were to say that the father's portrait 'speaks' to Arthur in the 'haunted' house, this would not misrepresent Dickens's meaning. For Arthur it is a house haunted by memories and guilty secrets, and, right up until its destruction, there is the possibility that it is more literally haunted by ghostly persons unseen. Affery, driven to the fringes of insanity, is conscious of noises that are not 'rats, cats, water, drains', of 'a rustle and a sort of trembling touch behind' her (I, xiv, 185). It is only the prediction of her becoming otherwise 'sensible of a rustle and touch that'll send [her] . . . flying to the other end of the kitchen' that stops Affery pursuing the matter. But for the reader there remains the possibility that a mysterious Flintwinch twin is secreted somewhere about the house.

If he had imitated Mrs Radcliffe's *A Sicilian Romance* (1790) Dickens would have immured the true mother of Arthur for years in the seemingly haunted Clennam house. He avoids this romantic cliché, but develops a nonetheless sensational situation. The guilty secret of the Clennam household turns out to be the suppression of the circumstances of his birth, and its unfolding reveals to him his true parentage. And such a revelation forms part of much Gothic fiction, where the search for the parent or the secret of birth amounts to an obsession. It is not simply that the true identity of Arthur's mother has been kept from him; she had been put in the nightmare situation of being given to the charge of a lunatic-keeper—a situation such as Maturin frenziedly portrays in *Melmoth the Wanderer*.[6] The horror of her plight is grotesquely understated and implied by Flintwinch's remark: 'My brother, Ephraim, the lunatic-keeper . . . speculated unsuccessfully in lunatics, he got into difficulty about over-roasting a patient to bring him to reason' (II, xx, 783).

The pretended translator of the first edition of *The Castle of Otranto* apologises in his preface for what becomes an obsessive fear in Gothic fiction, the passing on of the family curse, usually bound up with the passing on of the ancestral castle. In his translator *persona* Walpole says:

. . . I am not blind to my author's defects. I could wish he had grounded his plan on a more useful moral than this; that *the sins of the fathers are visited on their children to the third and fourth generation.*[7]

Mrs Clennam belongs to the world of Gothic horror in this matter of inherited punishment. When she finally unbends before Little Dorrit and offers some justification of her past life Mrs Clennam says of her behavior toward Arthur:

'I kept over him in the days of his first remembrance, my restraining and correcting hand. I was stern with him, knowing that the transgressions of the parents are visited on their offspring, and that there was an angry mark upon him at his birth.'

(II, xxix, 754)

It is no accident that Dickens uses in **Little Dorrit** the climactic destruction of the building that *Otranto* had established as the Gothic convention.[8] When Mrs Clennam is returning to her house with Little Dorrit, after her all-important experience of being 'broken by emotion', they hear 'a sudden noise like thunder':

In one swift instant, the old house was before them, with the man [Blandois] lying smoking in the window; another thundering sound, and it heaved, surged outward, opened asunder in fifty places, collapsed, and fell. Deafened by the noise, stifled, choked, and blinded by the dust, they hid their faces and stood rooted to the spot. The dust storm, driving between them and the placid sky, parted for a moment and showed them the stars. As they looked up, wildly crying for help, the great pile of chimneys which was then alone left standing, like a tower in a whirlwind, rocked, broke, and hailed itself down upon the heap of ruin, as if every tumbling fragment were intent on burying the crushed wretch deeper.

(II, xxxi, 793-4)

Again the house is endued with life: it seems to will the extermination of Blandois. And again we see how close is the connection between house and owner. The house completes a victory over Blandois which Mrs Clennam had begun, and, after she has been 'broken by emotion as unfamiliar to her eyes as action to her frozen limbs' (II, xxxi, 790), then the house itself is broken. Further, with the destruction of the house Mrs Clennam's life is effectively over, for afterwards, 'except that she could move her eyes and faintly express a negative and affirmative with her head, she lived and died a statue' (II, xxi, 794).

After the fall of the house of Dorrit the 'mystery of the noises' is explained; they were the groans of a failing structure. 'Affrey, like greater people, had always been right in her facts, and always wrong in the theories she deduced from them' (II, xxxi, 794). So we have a rational explanation of the apparently ghostly noises, and its ingenuity rivals that of Ann Radcliffe, a past master at such eventual explanations of seemingly supernatural terrors.

In relation to his presentation of the Clennam household Dickens, then, appears to adapt the following Gothic conventions: the sinister old castle that harbours mystery, gloom and guilty secrets; the hero's search for the secret of his birth; the setting right of wrongs passed from one generation to another; the use of dreams; the ancestral portrait motif; the old manuscript; and the climactic destruction of the castle. Of course, not all these features would seem Gothic-inspired if they occurred in isolation, and there are further possibilities. For example, Blandois has many of the features of the Gothic villain, and the view of Little Dorrit as an 'orphan-of-the-castle' Gothic heroine might bear development. But enough has been said to indicate that Dickens was able to adapt Gothic conventions not to undermine, but to intensify his portrayal of reality.

Notes

1. Dickens, *Dealings with the Firm of Dombey and Son, Wholesale, Retail, and for Exportation*, New Oxford Illustrated Dickens, 1950, p. 387.

2. Michael Booth, *English Melodrama*, 1965, p. 67.

3. See e.g. the reference to *Great Expectations* under 'Gothic Novel' in S. Barnet *et al.*, *A Dictionary of Literary Terms* (1964), p. 78; also Anthony O'Brien, 'Benevolence and Insurrection: The Conflicts of Form and Purpose in *Barnaby Rudge*', *Dickens Studies*, v (May 1969), 29.

4. Dickens, *Little Dorrit*, New Oxford Illustrated Dickens, 1953, Bk.I, ch.iii, 31.

5. Maturin, *Melmoth the Wanderer*, ed. Douglas Grant, 1953, I,i,20.

6. *Melmoth* I, iii, 28-60.

7. Walpole, Preface to the First Edition, *The Castle of Otranto*, ed. W. S. Lewis, 1964, p. 5.

8. For confirmation that 'the catastrophe of [*Little Dorrit*] . . . formed part of his original plan, and was not suggested by a contemporary occurrence', see the Introduction of Charles Dickens the Younger to *Little Dorrit* (Macmillan, 1953), pp. xxvii-xx; it is not included in the Oxford Illustrated edition.

FURTHER READING

Criticism

Cordery, Gareth. "The Cathedral as Setting and Symbol in *The Mystery of Edwin Drood*." *Dickens Studies Newsletter* 10, no. 4 (December 1979): 97-103.

Explores the symbolic function of the cathedral in Edwin Drood *as it functions as a backdrop to the story.*

Duncan, Ian. *Modern Romance and Transformations of the Novel: The Gothic, Scott, Dickens.* Cambridge: Cambridge University Press, 1992, 295 p.

Examines the relationship between the revival of the romance form and the ascendancy of the novel in British literary culture, from 1760 to 1850; begins with the first identification of modern prose fiction in the late-eighteenth-century Gothic novel before discussing the work of Sir Walter Scott and Dickens.

Frank, Lawrence. "News From the Dead: Archaeology, Detection, and *The Mystery of Edwin Drood.*" *Dickens Studies Annual* 28 (1999): 65-102.

Argues that The Mystery of Edwin Drood *is a meditation on the nature of historical knowledge as well as the act of knowing or detection.*

Harris, Jean. "'But He Was His Father': The Gothic and the Impostorious in Dickens's *The Pickwick Papers.*" In *Psychoanalytic Approaches to Literature and Film,* edited by Maurice Charney and Joseph Reppen, pp. 69-79. Rutherford, N.J.: Fairleigh Dickinson University Press, 1987.

Shows how Dickens modifies the Gothic convention in The Pickwick Papers.

Hodgell, Pat. "Charles Dickens' *Old Curiosity Shop*: The Gothic Novel in Transition." *Riverside Quarterly* 8, no. 3 (July 1990): 152-69.

Contends that Dickens's use of Gothic elements even after the genre's heyday freed gothicism from its stereotypes, enabled it to be adapted to address new social pressures, and affirmed the potential of its motifs in psychological terms.

Jackson, Rosemary. "The Silenced Text: Shades of Gothic in Victorian Fiction." *Minnesota Review* 13 (1979): 98-112.

Includes a detailed analysis of Dickens's appropriation of the Gothic for his own thematic purposes.

Kirkpatrick, Larry. "The Gothic Flame of Charles Dickens." *Victorian Newsletter* 31 (1967): 20-4.

Illustrates how The Old Curiosity Shop, Little Dorrit, *and* Our Mutual Friend *are related to the Gothic literary tradition.*

Kostelnick, Charles. "Dickens's Quarrel with the Gothic: Ruskin, Durdles and *Edwin Drood.*" *Dickens Studies Newsletter* 8 (1977): 104-9.

Claims that the character of Durdles in The Mystery of Edwin Drood *is a caricature of John Ruskin's Gothic workman.*

McMaster, R. D. "Dickens and the Horrific." *Dalhousie Review* 38 (1958): 18-28.

Discusses Dickens's reading of pulp horror fiction and its influence on his work.

Pritchard, Allan. "The Urban Gothic of *Bleak House.*" *Nineteenth-Century Literature* 45, no. 4 (March 1991): 432-52.

Maintains that Bleak House *is Dickens's supreme achievement in the Gothic mode and a crucially important novel for the nineteenth-century transformation of Gothic fiction.*

Ragussis, Michael. "The Ghostly Signs of *Bleak House.*" *Nineteenth-Century Fiction* 34, no. 3 (December 1979): 253-80.

Examines the motif of nomenclature and the mystery of language in Bleak House.

Robson, John M. "Crime in *Our Mutual Friend.*" In *Rough Justice: Essays on Crime in Literature,* pp. 114-40. Toronto, Ontario: University of Toronto Press, 1991.

Studies the many and various instances of criminal activity and violent acts in Our Mutual Friend.

Showalter, Elaine. "Guilt, Authority, and the Shadows of *Little Dorrit.*" In *Rough Justice: Essays on Crime in Literature,* pp. 114-40. Toronto, Ontario: University of Toronto Press, 1991.

Characterizes the shadow motif in Little Dorrit *as emblematic of the spiritual darkness of Victorian society.*

Sucksmith, Harvey P. "The Secret of Immediacy: Dickens's Debt to the Tale of Terror in *Blackwood's.*" *Nineteenth-Century Fiction* 26, no. 2 (September 1971): 145-57.

Analyzes the influence of the realistic tales of terror that Dickens read in Blackwood's *magazine on his development as a writer.*

Thiele, David. "The 'Transcendent and Immortal . . . HEEP!': Class Consciousness, Narrative Authority and the Gothic in *David Copperfield.*" *Texas Studies in Literature and Language* 42, no. 3 (fall 2000): 201-22.

Discusses the characterization of the dastardly Uriah Heep in David Copperfield *and explores the significance of the Gothic on the novel's narrative mode.*

Tracy, Robert. "Clock Work: *The Old Curiosity Shop* and *Barnaby Rudge.*" *Dickens Studies Annual* 30 (2001): 23-43.

Examines the antique settings and other elements that invoke the atmosphere of Gothic fiction in The Old Curiosity Shop *and* Barnaby Rudge.

OTHER SOURCES FROM GALE:

Additional coverage of Dickens's life and career is contained in the following sources published by Thomson Gale: *Authors and Artists for Young Adults,* Vol. 23; *Beacham's Guide to Literature for Young Adults,* Vols. 1, 2, 3, 13, 14; *British Writers,* Vol. 5; *British Writers: The Classics,* Vols. 1, 2; *Children's Literature Review,* Vol. 95; *Concise Dictionary of British Literary Biography, 1832-1890; Dictionary of Literary Biography,* Vols. 21, 55, 70, 159, 166; *DISCovering Authors; DISCovering Authors: British; DISCovering Authors: Canadian; DISCovering Authors Modules: Most-studied Authors* and *Novelists; DISCovering Authors 3.0; Exploring Novels; Junior DISCovering Authors; Literary Movements for Students,* Vol. 1; *Literature and Its Times,* Vols. 1, 2; *Literature and Its Times Supplement,* Vol. 1; *Literature Resource Center; Major Authors and Illustrators for Children and Young Adults,* Eds. 1, 2; *Nineteenth-Century Literature Criticism,* Vols. 3, 8, 18, 26, 37, 50, 86, 105, 113; *Novels for Students,* Vols. 4, 5, 10, 14, 20; *Reference Guide to English Literature,* Ed. 2; *Reference Guide to Short Fiction,* Ed. 2; *St. James Guide to Crime and Mystery Writers; St. James Guide to Horror, Ghost & Gothic Writers; Short Story Criticism,* Vols. 17, 49; *Something about the Author,* Vol. 15; *Supernatural Fiction Writers,* Vol. 1; *Twayne's English Authors; World Literature and Its Times,* Vol. 4; *World Literature Criticism; Writers for Children;* and *Writers for Young Adults.*

ISAK DINESEN

(1885 - 1962)

(Born Karen Christentze Dinesen; also known by her married name Karen Blixen; also wrote under the pseudonyms Tania Blixen, Osceola, and Pierre Andrézel) Danish short story writer, autobiographer, novelist, playwright, and translator.

Dinesen is best known for *Seven Gothic Tales* (1934) and the autobiographical novel *Out of Africa* (1937; *Den afrikanske farm*). Acclaimed for her poetic prose style, complex characters, and intricate plots, Dinesen explored such themes as the lives and values of aristocrats, the nature of fate and destiny, God and the supernatural, the artist, and the place of women in society. Her works defy easy categorization, though she incorporated elements of Gothic and horror as well as humor in her stories. Hailed as a proto-feminist by some critics, scorned as a colonialist by others, Dinesen is chiefly regarded as a masterful story-teller. Ernest Hemingway remarked that the Nobel Prize for Literature he received in 1954 should have been awarded to her.

BIOGRAPHICAL INFORMATION

Born in Rungsted, Denmark, Dinesen was the daughter of an army officer who was a friend of Hans Christian Andersen and who wrote a book about his experiences as a fur trapper among the Indians of the northern United States. Dinesen studied English at Oxford University and painting at the Royal Academies in Copenhagen, Paris, and Rome. Following her marriage to her cousin Baron Bror Blixen-Finecke in 1914, Dinesen moved to East Africa as the owner and manager of a coffee plantation near present-day Nairobi, Kenya. Following the death of her lover Denys Finch-Hatton and the eventual sale of her farm in 1931—events that are dramatized in *Out of Africa*—Dinesen returned to Denmark, where she completed her first book, *Seven Gothic Tales*. Subsequent works included several more short story collections and numerous essays and novels in both Danish and English. Although she suffered from chronic spinal syphilis, emaciation, and the physical frailty attendant to these conditions, Dinesen continued to lecture and give interviews in her final years. She became a founding member of the Danish Academy in 1960 and died in Rungsted in 1962.

MAJOR WORKS

Seven Gothic Tales is a collection of short stories written in a romantic style, employing fantasy to explore aristocratic sensibilities and values. In "The Deluge at Norderney," a Cardinal directs his high-born companions to give up their places on a boat to save peasants during a flood. "The Dreamers," one of Dinesen's most traditionally Gothic stories, tells of a mysterious, beautiful singer who lost her voice due to an accident. Devastated by her loss, she travels through Europe, constantly changing her identity and taking on a series of lovers. *Out of Africa* presents Dinesen's experiences as a British coffee plantation owner in East Africa, documenting her relationship with the Africans who lived and worked on and around her plantation, her divorce from Baron Blixen, her affair with Denys Finch-Hatton, and the failure of her coffee enterprise. The short stories in *Winter's Tales* (1942), with their simpler narrative style and attention to landscape, history, and life of Denmark, solidified Dinesen's standing in the Danish literary community. "Sorrow-Acre" is based on a medieval Danish folktale and is set in eighteenth-century Denmark. The story examines the inevitable social consequences of the master-servant relationship: how aristocratic values and traditions govern the attitudes and actions of a landlord toward a thieving serf and his mother. During the Nazi occupation of Denmark, Dinesen wrote *The Angelic Avengers* (1946), a mystery-thriller about two orphaned girls. The manuscript was smuggled out of Denmark and published under the pseudonym Pierre Andrézel. Dinesen continually denied authorship of the book, however, because she was unsatisfied with its literary quality. *Last Tales* (1957) is a collection of short stories divided into three sections—New Gothic Tales, New Winter's Tales, and Tales from *Albondocani*. These works represent a return to her earlier literary style, themes, and characters. In "Echoes," for instance, Pellegrina Leoni, who first appears in *Seven Gothic Tales*, is an ex-opera star, devastated by the loss of her voice. Consequently, a disgruntled Pellegrina uses elaborate disguises to ensure her anonymity. She remarks that when it comes to fate and life, God can be both a charlatan and "jokester" with his human creations. *Skygger paa Græsset* (1960; *Shadows on the Grass*) recalls Dinesen's African experiences. In this nonfiction work she focuses on the lives of several of the African servants and friends about whom she first wrote in *Out of Africa*. The novel *Ehrengard* (1963) was published posthumously and was Dinesen's last work. Its themes include the notion of the artist as creator and interpreter of life. The story follows the artist Cazotte's lust for Ehrengard, while she sits for a portrait. Cazotte's objective is to humiliate her and in the process diabolically usurp God's role as the defining artist of creation and master of life.

Among Dinesen's other posthumously published works are *Carnival: Entertainments and Posthumous Tales* (1977); *Breve fra Afrika 1914-31* (1978; *Letters from Africa: 1914-1931*), which contains her correspondence with family and friends during her years in Africa; and *Daguerreotypes, and Other Essays* (1979), containing the well-known "Bonfire Speech," which presents her thoughts on many feminist issues.

CRITICAL RECEPTION

Dinesen's writings have been widely praised and enthusiastically received. *Seven Gothic Tales*, her first collection, was released in the United States during the Great Depression, and audiences gravitated to Dinesen's mysterious, exotic, fantastical stories as a pleasurable escape from the dreariness of everyday life. In addition to noting her vivid imagination, critics have applauded her prose style, her facility with complicated plots and characters, and her natural gift for storytelling. While many scholars have claimed that her picture of Africa in *Out of Africa* is romanticized, they note that the story is engaging, well-structured, and presents a detailed picture of life among British expatriates in Africa. Several commentators have noted similarities between Dinesen's views on identity, spirituality, and meaning and those of Danish philosopher Søren Kierkegaard; others have detected the influence of Aldous Huxley and Sigmund Freud on the development of Dinesen's themes and characters, particularly in such works as "Carnival."

Critics have noted that a number of Dinesen's stories reflect her admiration of the Gothic literature of the late eighteenth and early nineteenth centuries. Dinesen borrowed several elements of the Gothic tradition, writing fanciful tales of mysterious, suspenseful, supernatural happenings. Writing a century after the height of Gothic literature's popularity, she also modified Gothic conventions, informing her stories with a more liberal moral code than the earlier works. Critics have also noted a feminist sensibility in Dinesen's tales that was not evident in Gothic works of preceding centuries. Another difference between traditional Gothic literature and the works of Dinesen is the earlier authors' intent to frighten readers; Susan C. Brantly pointed out that "the supernatural for Dinesen simply represents freedom of the imagination."

PRINCIPAL WORKS

Seven Gothic Tales (short stories) 1934

Sanhedens Haevn [*The Revenge of Truth*] (play) 1936

Out of Africa [*Den afrikanske farm*] (autobiography) 1937

Winter's Tales (short stories) 1942

Farah (novel) 1950

En Baaltale med 14 Aars Forsinkelse [*Bonfire Speech Fourteen Years Delayed*] (essay) 1953

Last Tales [*Sidste Fortaellinger*] (short stories) 1957

Anecdotes of Destiny [*Skaebne-Anekdoter*] (short stories) 1958

Skygger paa Græsset [*Shadows on the Grass*] (autobiography) 1960

Osceola (short stories and poetry) 1962

Ehrengard (novel) 1963

Essays (essays) 1965; enlarged edition published as *Mit livs mottoer og andre essays*, 1978

Carnival: Entertainments and Posthumous Tales (short stories) 1977

Breve fra Afrika 1914-31 [*Letters from Africa: 1914-1931*] (letters) 1978

Daguerreotypes, and Other Essays (essays) 1979

Samlede (essays) 1985

PRIMARY SOURCES

ISAK DINESEN (STORY DATE 1934)

SOURCE: Dinesen, Isak. "The Monkey." In *Seven Gothic Tales*, pp. 109-63. New York: Modern Library, 1934.

The following excerpt comprises the first section of one of the most popular of Dinesen's Seven Gothic Tales.

I

In a few of the Lutheran countries of northern Europe there are still in existence places which make use of the name convent, and are governed by a prioress or chanoiness, although they are of no religious nature. They are retreats for unmarried ladies and widows of noble birth who here pass the autumn and winter days of their lives in a dignified and comfortable routine, according to the traditions of the houses. Many of these institutions are extremely wealthy, own great stretches of land, and have had, during the centuries, inheritances and legacies bequested to them. A proud and kindly spirit of past feudal times seems to dwell in the stately buildings and to guide the existence of the communities.

The Virgin Prioress of Closter Seven, under whose hands the convent prospered from the year 1818 to that of 1845, had a little gray monkey which had been given her by her cousin, Admiral von Schreckenstein, on his return from Zanzibar, and of which she was very fond. When she was at her card table, a place where she spent some of her happiest hours, the monkey was wont to sit on the back of her chair, and to follow with its glittering eyes the course of the cards as they were dealt out and taken in. At other times it would be found, in the early mornings, on top of the step-ladder in the library, pulling out brittle folios a hundred years old, and scattering over the black-and-white marble floor browned leaves dealing with strategy, princely marriage contracts, and witches' trials.

In a different society the monkey might not have been popular. But the convent of Closter Seven held, coördinately with its estimable female population, a whole world of pets of all sorts, and was well aware of the order of precedence therein. There were here parrots and cockatoos, small dogs, graceful cats from all parts of the world, a white Angora goat, like that of Esmeralda, and a purple-eyed young fallow deer. There was even a tortoise which was supposed to be more than a hundred years old. The old ladies therefore showed a forbearance with the whims of the Prioress's favorite, much like that which courtiers of a petticoat-governed court of the old days, conscious of their own frailty, might have shown toward the caprices of a royal *maîtresse-en-titre*.

From time to time, particularly in the autumn, when nuts were ripening in the hedges along the roads and in the large forests that surrounded the convent, it happened that the Prioress's monkey would feel the call of a freer life and would disappear for a few weeks or a month, to come back of its own accord when the night frosts set in. The children of the villages belonging to Closter Seven would then come upon it running across the road or sitting in a tree, from where it watched them attentively. But when they gathered around it and started to bombard it with chestnuts from their pockets, it would roll its eyes and grind its teeth at them, and finish by swiftly mounting the branches to disappear in the crowns of the forest.

It was the general opinion, or a standing joke amongst the ladies of the convent, that the Prioress, during these periods, would become silent and the victim of a particular restlessness, and would seem loth to act in the affairs of the house, in which at ordinary times she showed great vigor. Amongst themselves they called the monkey her *Geheimrat,* and they rejoiced when it was to be seen again in her drawing-room, a little chilled after its stay in the woods.

Upon a fine October day, when the monkey had in this way been missing for some weeks, the Prioress's young nephew and godson, who was a lieutenant in the Royal Guards, arrived unexpectedly at the convent.

The Prioress was held in high respect by all her relations, and had in her time presented at the font many babies of her own noble blood, but this young man was her favorite amongst them. He was a graceful boy of twenty-two, with dark hair and blue eyes. Although he was a younger son, he was fortunately situated in life. He was the preferred child of his mother, who had come from Russia and had been an heiress; he had made a fine career. He had friends, not everywhere in the world, but everywhere in that world, that is of any significance.

On his arrival at the convent he did not, however, look like a young man under a lucky star. He came, as already said, in headlong hurry and unannounced, and the ladies with whom he exchanged a few words while waiting for admission to his aunt, and who were all fond of him, noticed that he was pale and looked deadly tired, as if under some great agitation of mind.

They were not unaware, either, that he might have reason to be so. Although Closter Seven was a small world of its own, and moved in a particular atmosphere of peace and immutability, news of the greater world outside reached it with surprising quickness, for each of the ladies had her own watchful and zealous correspondents there. Thus these cloistered women knew, just as well as the people in the center of things, that during the last month clouds of strange and sinister nature had been gathering over the heads of that very regiment and circle of friends to which the boy belonged. A sanctimonious clique of the capital, led by the Court-Chaplain, of all people, who had the ear of high personages, had, under pretense of moral indignation, lifted their voices against these young flowers of the land, and nobody knew for certain, or could even imagine, what might come out of that.

The ladies had not discussed these happenings much amongst themselves, but the librarian of the convent, who was a theologian and a scholar, had been dragged away into more than one tête-à-tête, and encouraged to give his opinion on the problem. From him they had learnt to connect it somehow with those romantic and sacred shores of ancient Greece which they had till now held in high esteem. Remembering their young days, when everything Greek had been *le dernier cri,* and frocks and coiffures had been named *à la grecque,* they wondered—Could the expression be used also to designate anything so little related to their young ladies' dreams of refinement? They had loved those frocks, they had waltzed with princes in them; now they thought of them with uneasiness.

Few things could have stirred their natures more deeply. It was not only the impudence of the heroes of the pulpit and the quill attacking warriors which revolted the old daughters of a fighting race, or the presentiment of trouble and much woe that worried them, but something in the matter which went deeper than that. To all of them it had been a fundamental article of faith that woman's loveliness and charm, which they themselves represented in their own sphere and according to their gifts, must constitute the highest inspiration and prize of life. In their own individual cases the world might have spread snares in order to capture this prize of their being at less cost than they meant it to, or there might have been a strange misunderstanding, a lack of appreciation, on the part of the world, but still the dogma held good. To hear it disputed now meant to them what it would mean to a miser to be told that gold no longer had absolute value, or to a mystic to have it asserted that the Lord was not present in the Eucharist. Had they known that it might ever be called into question, all these lives, which were now so nearly finished, might have come to look very different. To a few proud old maids, who had the strategic instincts of their breed developed to the full, these new conceptions came very hard. So might have come, to a gallant and faithful old general who through a long campaign, in loyalty to higher orders, had stood strictly upon the defensive, the information that an offensive would have been the right, and approved, move.

Still in the midst of their inquietude every one of the old women would have liked to have heard more of this strange heresy, as if, after all, the tender and dangerous emotions of the human heart were, even within their own safe reclusion, by right their domain. It was as if the tall bouquets of dried flowers in front of the convents' pier glasses had stirred and claimed authority when a question of floriculture was being raised.

They gave the pale boy an unsure welcome, as if he might have been either one of Herod's child martyrs, or a young priest of black magic, still within hope of conversion, and when he walked up the broad stair which led to the Prioress's rooms, they evaded one another's eyes.

The Prioress received her nephew within her lofty parlor. Its three tall windows looked out, between heavy curtains which had on them borders of flower garlands done in cross-stitch, over the lawns and avenues of the autumnal garden. From the damask-clad walls her long-departed father and mother gazed down, out of broad gilt frames, with military gravity and youthful grace, powdered and laced for some great court occasion. Those two had been the young man's friends since he was a baby, yet today he was struck and surprised by a puzzled, even a worried, look upon their faces. It seemed to him also, for a moment, that there was a certain strange and disquieting smell in the room, mixed with that of the incense sticks, which were being burned more amply than usual. Was this, he thought, a new aspect of the catastrophal tendencies of his existence?

The boy, while taking in the whole well-known and harmonious atmosphere, did not want or dare to waste time. After he had kissed his aunt's hand, inquired after her health and the monkey and given her the news of his own people in town, he came straight to the matter which had brought him to Closter Seven.

"Aunt Cathinka," he said, "I have come to you because you have always been so good to me. I should like"—here he swallowed to keep his rebellious heart in place, knowing how little indeed it would like it—"to marry, and I hope that you will give me your advice and help."

TITLE COMMENTARY

Seven Gothic Tales

SIBYL JAMES (ESSAY DATE 1983)

SOURCE: James, Sibyl. "Gothic Transformations: Isak Dinesen and the Gothic." In *The Female Gothic,* edited by Julian E. Fleenor, pp. 138-52. Montreal, Quebec: Eden Press, 1983.

In the following essay, James studies Dinesen's unique approach to writing in the Gothic tradition.

In *Women Artists,* Karen Petersen and J. J. Wilson suggest that in their struggle to work as artists women have sometimes adopted an off-the-mainstream style which keeps them out of competition with the men in their field. Petersen and Wilson point to Marie Laurencin's choice of painting style as an example of this tactic, and note the reaction to women artists who opt for such a solution:

> One wonders if she would have painted in a quite so determinedly pastel and "feminine" style if she had not felt pushed into it by the need to differentiate herself from such strong influences as Pablo Picasso and Braque. She made a place for herself by her very separateness and received that approval that seems to come to those women who do not try to compete with male artists on their own ground.[1]

Isak Dinesen, entering the literary scene with a book called *Seven Gothic Tales,* may at first glance appear to have opted for a minor and even out-moded genre by choosing, in the midst of the twentieth century, to write tales that draw on the Gothic tradition. Indeed, Dinesen did not believe in competition between women and men, feeling that the sexes should be equal but different. However, there was no element of evasion in her decision to work in a minor fictional form. There was nothing humble or self-effacing about either her choice or her handling of this genre; there was, in fact, as Howard Green notes, a quality of arrogant confidence:

> Now to take such a musty and flyblown genre, to transform it into an elegant embodiment of her own philosophical convictions, and to make of it a popular success as well as a *succès d'estime*—that was literary daring of a high order. And there was arrogance to match it both in the substance of those convictions, so antagonistic to our own, and in the way she inveigled us into swallowing them under the guise of innocent entertainment.[2]

Dinesen's treatment of the Gothic is, like her treatment of everything in her tales, particularly Dinesenian, treading a twisty line, reaching back to transform certain aspects of the past that she considers valuable into modes operable in the present. Among those philosophic convictions of which Green speaks is a particular insistence on an aristocratic, artistic, and most importantly, imaginative understanding of one's self and the world. The Gothic provided her with a useful tool in the illustration of this belief:

> "When I used the word 'Gothic,'" she told *The Atlantic Monthly* editor Curtis Cate, "I didn't mean the real Gothic, but the imitation of the Gothic, the Romantic age of Byron, the age of that man—what was his name?—who built Strawberry Hill, the age of the Gothic revival."[3]

That imitation, of course, is what we generally think of as *the* Gothic. It was particularly suited to Dinesen's purposes since part of the original impetus behind the earlier Gothic revival was the need for an outlet for the imagination in an age of reason, and an allied interest in the oriental tale and stories of imaginary voyages, to which the popularity of the *Arabian Nights,* first translated into English in the early eighteenth century, testified.[4] For Dinesen the imagination is all important, not just as an aesthetic dictum, but as a philosophical tenet and psychological necessity—indeed, as a moral/spiritual guide. She was seen as, and saw herself as, a modern Scheherezade; like Scheherezade, the magic of her tales deters the listeners from action until they have understood, through the tales, the larger pattern of the universe and can act within it wisely. Dinesen described herself thus:

> I belong to an ancient, idle, wild and useless tribe, perhaps I am even one of the last members of it, who, for many thousands of years, in all countries and parts of the world, has, now and again, stayed for a time among the hard-working honest people in real life, and sometimes has thus been fortunate enough to create another sort of reality for them, which in some way or another, has satisfied them. I am a storyteller.[5]

In part, her work was directed at satisfying the need for magic which she felt "the little man, the simple man" [sic] experienced in the same way as the natives on her African farm "who could never get enough of her telling of fanciful tales."[6] Ultimately, it was the world's need for magic which she addressed. Her tales were meant not only to fulfill a yen for the fantastical, but to affect the reader's understanding of reality itself.

Dinesen had turned to writing to put her own life in perspective, to explain her personal tragedies to herself.[7] What that writing most often dealt with was the understanding of life by means of the imagination. As Robert Langbaum puts it:

> The point is that you don't get at the truth about the world or yourself by going straight to it. You get at it by seeming to move away to an esthetic distance. You get at it through artifice and tradition—by assimilating your particular event to a recurring pattern, your particular self to an archetype.
>
> (p. 20)

Dinesen advocated imaginative truth over the sort of plain truth that, as one of her characters says, tailors and shoemakers need. This was not meant as an escape from reality, but as something to be kept in a proper relation with reality. That is, we are not to get lost in dreams, not to live only in the imaginative world or try to play the artist in life with too heavy a hand (in which case, because our imaginations are not great enough, things will always get out of control). Instead, the imagination serves as a way into the reality of things, a reality we can grasp only through an imaginative apprehension. At its extreme, says Donald Hannah, the imagination functions in Dinesen's work as a kind of aesthetic equivalent for an abandoned Christian tradition. Dinesen, he maintains, believes that Job's questioning of God's purpose stems from a failure of imagination. The kind of answer Job gets from God demands an imaginative response, and it is only by this that we can "comprehend the design, understand the purpose of our existence—and be reconciled to our lot."[8]

Given Dinesen's attitude toward the imagination, it is not surprising to find that she replaces the Gothic emphasis on moral sentiment—that which enables us to "distinguish right from wrong" and propels us "toward a realization of the good, the beautiful, and the true"[9]—with an emphasis on the imagination which works for her as a kind of moral sentiment. She also replaces the direct authorial Gothic preachiness, the self-important solemnity that we find, for example, in Radcliffe's passages on St. Aubert's efforts to train Emily in the proper brand and degree of sensibility. Instead, Dinesen makes a more indirect presentation of her message through in-set tales; through a more symbolic use of events; and, in most typically Dinesenian fashion, through witty conversation. This last method relates to her speaking of the Gothic she drew on as imitation or artificial Gothic. The very modernness of her treatment lies to a great extent in just this awareness of the artificiality of the Gothic trappings, in a self-consciousness that is part of the wit yet does not mock or parody the Gothic. Within, Dinesen often "creates an intensity . . . sets the story in the atmosphere of the imagination where life can be explored in depth."[10] Her use of wit operates like her use of the fantastic tale, the *Arabian Nights,* a form which Glenway Wescott refers to as "so primitive a type of fiction—intended to amuse, to amaze, and to allure the imagination"—much like the Gothic itself. He suggests she found support for her approach in certain tenets of the ancients: "Aristotle said: 'Impossibilities are justified if they serve the purpose of the poetry.' Longinus said: 'The effect of genius is not to persuade or to convince but rather to transport the audience out of its usual frame of mind.'"[11] Dinesen translates Longinus' concept of the sublime into the powers of wit, the fantastic and the imaginative that take us out of more ordinary states of mind.

These same considerations extend to her treatment of the supernatural—the scare element of the Gothic: "In Gothic writings fantasy predominates over reality, the strange over the commonplace, and the supernatural over the natural, with one definite auctorial intent: to scare."[12] This intent certainly was and is a primary factor in the general appeal of the Gothic. However, the thrill of being frightened is not enough to account for our constant interest in this genre. Gothic writers also had serious purposes, as Ellen Moers points out in her discussion of female Gothic writers, indicating the relevance of their work to so much of women's situation.[13] Rather than scariness itself, it is the satisfaction of the need for imagination and the component of psychological reality (on which the best of the Gothic writers such as Radcliffe based their scariness) which accounts for the continuing power and popularity of the form. Lionel Stevenson describes the process:

> In departing from realism Mrs. Radcliffe stumbled upon the whole realm of the unconscious. The standard situations in her stories are those which recur in everyone's nightmares. . . . [S]he had the knack of stimulating the reader's own dream-making function, which then took over and supplied the private horrors of each individual imagination.[14]

Radcliffe, says Andrew Wright, supplied us with a means by which every one of her mysteries was "ultimately explicable as natural rather than supernatural phenomena"[15] and gave us, if not an explanation, at least a basis in psychological reality.

Dinesen's tales are fantastical, but never scary. She had a poor opinion of Poe's tales: "'He scares you but that's all.'"[16] Like Radcliffe, the supernaturalism in her tales is grounded in psychological reality; but unlike Radcliffe, she is not concerned with providing rational explanations in natural terms. The supernatural elements are viewed almost matter-of-factly, with a willing suspension of belief or with that extraordinary state of mind which the imaginative tale creates for us. Robert Langbaum notes that in some of her tales:

> . . . the supernatural situation is so embedded in a symbolic framework as to leave little of the un-rationalized aura that gives the effect of weirdness. . . . Her stories are fantastic in the way wit is—in the jubilant freedom with which possibilities are stretched and ideas combined.
>
> (p. 89)

Dinesen moves beyond the psychological into explanations founded on symbolic and mythic reality. Her tales teach us wisdom through an imaginative apprehension. The Gothic supplies the imaginative landscape, atmosphere, and episodes. The form also gives her the necessary distance to lead us into a state of mind in which we can make that imaginative realization. Her use of the Gothic is like her use of so many other older values and myth systems, bringing out what is important in them while transforming them into a mode workable in the twentieth century. She does not suggest, says Langbaum, that we return to these old values, but that we find modern equivalents for them. We can do this as she does, by creating new values and myths, by returning to an even earlier time in which they were manifest in a better spirit, or by translating them, arriving at "traditional values only through the most strikingly modern transvaluations."[17]

Dinesen's most traditionally Gothic story in terms of its characterizations and psychological atmosphere is *The Angelic Avengers.* However, this novel is not typical, either of her work or of her general handling of the Gothic, and must be regarded as she herself categorized it, an illegitimate child, published under another pseudonym. More typical of her work and, in that category, the most Gothic of her tales, is "**The Monkey**" which appeared in her first volume, *Seven Gothic Tales.* "The Monkey" is filled with Gothic elements: a convent, a ruined castle, an interminable lawsuit, a magic potion, strange forebodings, the good and tyrannical parents, seduction threats, monsters, and of course, heroines and villains. But most of these acquire special twists. The convent is a secular retreat "for unmarried ladies and widows of noble birth who here pass the autumn and winter days of their lives in a dignified and comfortable routine. . . ."[18] Although it is secluded from the world, the place is far from otherworldly; the women may be out of the game, but they are extremely interested in its goings on. The lawsuit has a happy outcome, but this plays no real part in the events of the plot and functions primarily in a psychological sense, illustrating in the Count's manner of accepting his good fortune one aspect of behaving in a properly aristocratic spirit.

The ruined castle is not frightening in a properly Gothic sense; it is a place of love, spiritual aristocracy, and a certain freedom. Langbaum places it in the realm of the pastoral: ". . . [it] is removed from time, and thus contrasts with that other retreat, Cloister Seven, which by its very pretension to be a convent, shows its worldliness and involvement in time."[19] Its chaos contrasts with the convent's routine and duty. Unlike the closeness to nature and animals that life at the castle represents, at the convent even the animals are domesticated—all except the Prioress' monkey, which plays a major role in the story's resolution.

The tale has a marriage plot at its heart, but it is one that arises from rather unique motives. Boris, about whom some scandal has arisen concerning alleged homosexual activities, decides to marry in order to squelch the rumors. He journeys to the convent to ask his aunt, the Prioress, to name a suitable bride. She chooses Athena Hopballehus, Boris' childhood friend, who lives in the neighboring ruined castle. Athena will be the pawn in this game of convention and duty; she will clear his honor.

Athena leads us into Dinesen's transformation of a truly major Gothic element—the heroine. Radcliffe, says Moers, ". . . firmly set the Gothic in one of the ways it would go ever after: a novel in which the central figure is a young woman who is simultaneously persecuted victim and courageous heroine."[20] Now this is certainly true of Athena, but in Dinesen's presentation we see how far the type has advanced beyond Radcliffe's Emily. Athena is one of a long line of women characters in Dinesen whom we might call the militant innocent or young warrior woman. A more mundane or less insightful writer than Dinesen might have referred to her as a "tomboy," and she follows that stereotype in much of her behavior, fierceness and independence. She may even harbor a wish to be a boy, since she can see that the things she values in life seem to be reserved for the male roles. But, and here is where Dinesen really departs from the conventional stereotype, she does not really wish to be a boy; she desires to be a girl and still retain her freedom of action. As "tomboy" she relates to that tradition of tomboys in women's literature which Moers attributes to the prohibitions on outdoor activities for females: "For in every age, whatever the social rules, there has always been one time of a woman's life, the years before puberty, when walking, running, climbing, battling, and tumbling are as normal female as they are male activities."[21] As a tomboy who wants to retain her powers and freedom, while still being female, she connects with the tradition of Gothic heroines who "in the power of villains . . . are forced to do what they could never do alone, whatever their ambitions: scurry up the top of pasteboard Alps, spy out exotic vistas, penetrate bandit-infested forests."[22] While remaining extremely "feminine" and within the

"proprieties," says Moers, they prove themselves through courage and self-control in the face of physical danger.

All that taken into consideration, a simple descriptive comparison of Emily with Athena shows immediately how far Dinesen has extended the definition of Gothic heroine:

> In person, Emily resembled her mother; having the same elegant symmetry of form, the same delicacy of features, and the same blue eyes, full of tender sweetness. But, lovely as was her person, it was the varied expression of her countenance, as conversation awakened the nicer emotions of her mind, that threw such a captivating grace around her.[23]

Emily, says Andrew Wright, is a "credible heroine of sensibility" and a Gothic heroine *par excellence* who has education in the sciences and "elegant literature," who plays the flute and writes poetry, and who is an only child with an undying affection for her father.[24]

Athena is also an innocent and a motherless only child who prefers to remain with her father. There the similarities end. Athena is a strong young woman, "six feet high and broad in proportion," whose beauty has nothing to do with delicacy or elegant symmetry: "Beneath her flaming hair her noble forehead was white as milk; lower down her face was, like her broad wrists, covered with freckles. Still she was so fair and clear of skin that she seemed to lighten up the hall on entering it. . . ." Like most of Dinesen's women, she is surrounded by bird imagery; she is also symbolically linked to a great she-bear who killed five men and she embodies both the peaceful and the dangerous aspects of wild animals. She may not be so well-read as Emily, at least not in the same subjects, but she has read much about the French revolution; she is a revolutionary who wishes she had met Danton and who would like to see where the guillotine stood and wear the Phrygian bonnet.

Athena is in some ways close to Catherine of *Wuthering Heights* who represents clearly the young woman's desire to retain her freedom, a desire Moers notes in Catherine's delirious outcry against her adult state as Mrs. Linton: "'I wish I were a girl again, half savage and hardy, and free. . . .'" Dinesen's young warrior women harbor the not particularly unrealistic belief that in losing their innocence and becoming adult women, especially wives and mothers, they will lose their freedom; consequently they fight against entering the experience. Childerique in **"The Caryatids"** typifies this female warrior innocent:

She had no desire to be desired, and her woman's kingdom of longing, rapture and jealousy seemed to her all too vast; she did not want to take up the scepter at all. Like a young stork which considers that it runs very well, and does not care to fly, she had to be lured into her element.[25]

Luring such a young woman into "her element" can be an arduous struggle and at times the forces trying to make her enter experience find themselves curiously defeated in the very attainment of their goal. The Gothic heroines created by female writers have often put up just such resistance with just these results; in Dinesen the process becomes even more graphic.

The Prioress does not doubt that Athena will accept Boris' proposal, for she has lived an isolated life with her father in his castle, has heard the women of the convent speak of other brilliant marriages in society, and has never before had a proposal of marriage. She is the supreme innocent whom Boris doubts has ever heard of love or even looked at herself in the mirror. During a conversation at the castle, Athena, according to Langbaum:

. . . demonstrates her innocence by the question she asks regarding the old Wendish idol of the goddess of love, which "had the face and façade of a beautiful woman" but "presented at the back the image of a monkey." How did they know, she asks, "which was the front and which the back?"

(p. 83)

The Prioress considers her easy prey; Boris sets off for her castle.

Athena's father is delighted with the proposed marriage and prospects look good for a conventional "happy ending." But no one has realized that Athena is as fiercely independent and virginal as her name, that she loves her solitude and has chosen to spend her life unmarried, caring for her aging father, and that she is prepared to fight for this choice. The Prioress will not be so easily denied and thus invites Athena to a seduction supper at the convent. During this scene the whys of Athena's refusal become clearer and we see how Dinesen has also transformed the idea of Gothic villainy. Here the threat lies not in forced marriage to the wrong man or even, at this point, in seduction, but in conventional marriage itself. During the supper, Boris, who likes to cast himself as an actor upon the stage of life, begins to understand Athena, now seeing the two of them as participants in a drama. He realizes that she is probably afraid for the first time in her life:

"Of what is she afraid?" he thought. "Of being made happy by my aunt and me? This is this tragic maiden's prayer: From being a success at court, a happy, congratulated bride, a mother of a promising family, good Lord, deliver me." As a tragic actor of a high standard himself, he applauded her.

(p. 142)

Boris sympathizes with Athena, for he, too, Langbaum suggests, is something of an innocent despite his surface worldliness and would like to hang onto that innocence he equates with freedom. Still, he has more to gain from this marriage and agrees, however reluctantly, with the Prioress' plans. Even though Dinesen validates the necessity of experience, she is opposed to the effects of conventional marriage upon both sexes. Gothic villainy here becomes not so much the province of males as the province of the conventionally minded. However, the consequences are much worse for women, and there is the implication that Dinesen's women, especially her young warrior girls, are aware of this.

Athena holds up well during the supper until the Prioress tells a story about a wild elephant that was caged. The symbolism is clear to Athena: she will be caged in marriage to Boris. She rather abruptly excuses herself from the scene and goes to bed. As a final resort the Prioress gives Boris an aphrodisiac and sends him off to Athena's chamber to seduce—or rather—rape her. The ensuing scene, when compared with Count Morano's sudden appearance in Emily's chamber, shows just how much Dinesen has tampered with the Gothic. In doing so she has added a marvelous element of humor. Whereas Emily's bedroom is enveloped in thick gloomy shadows, Athena's assigned chamber is a *tour de force* of eroticism with only the barest hint of Gothic terrors:

The whole room was hung with rose silks, and in the depths of it the crimson draperies of the four-poster bed glowed in the shade. There were two pink-globed lamps, solicitously lighted by the Prioress's maid. The floor had a wine-colored carpet with roses in it, which, near the lamps, seemed to be drinking in the light, and farther from them looked like pools of dark crimson into which one would not like to walk. The room was filled with the scent of incense and flowers.

(p. 151)

Just as this rose and crimson chamber is a world away from that of Radcliffe's Emily, so is Athena's response to the would-be seducer. Instead of battling the villain with strength of character and virtuous argument, teetering all the while on the edge of a terrified faint, Athena strikes Boris, knocking out two of his teeth. They engage in a physical battle with erotic overtones, rather like those Moers suggests in the nursery battles between brother and sister. Indeed, there has been an earlier hint of incest, though it appears that Boris and Athena are not physically brother and sister. Instead they share something of that relation in a spiritual sense—one fairly typical in Dinesen and which seems to appeal to her on the grounds of her belief in the different but equal status of women and men, a concept underlying the comradely nature of the brother/sister relation. Athena holds her own against Boris until he manages to force a kiss upon her. This is simply too much for her to take. "She, surely, had never been kissed in her life, she had not even heard or read of a kiss. The force used against her made her whole being rise in mortal disgust." Athena collapses as if she were dead. This is hardly the kiss that awakens the innocent sleeping beauty, and Athena's collapse is no weak-kneed faint. Her response comments both humorously and effectively on the more traditional outcomes of such female-male encounters. Boris, all interest in and capacity for seduction gone, lifts her on the bed and leaves her unconscious and untouched.

Dinesen's changes in the heroines, in the nature of the villain, and in what the heroines fear point up an important difference from the early Female Gothic. In Dinesen it is obvious that the fear is not related to the supernatural or even to a loss of virginity, itself not always particularly important to Dinesen's women. In clearing away the ostensible fears made so much of in early Gothic—the fear for the loss of one's physical virginity and, by extension, one's honor—Dinesen's presentation reveals a much more serious underlying meaning, the knowledge that this loss can bring a far greater one, and an enslavement. The heroine battles against this loss; if she, like Emily and Athena in their different ways, can retain her self-possession, in both senses of the term, then she defeats the villains.

> "[Emily] opposed his turbulence and indignation," writes Mrs. Radcliffe in a sentence that is my choice for Emily's epitaph, "only by the mild dignity of a superior mind, but the gentle firmness of her conduct served to exasperate still more his resentment, since it compelled him to feel his own inferiority."
>
> (p. 210)

Athena also withstands the villains by her supreme innocence. Boris felt she was like the old martyrs who drew everything, even their tortures, into themselves in a harmonious beauty but left the torturer outside: "No matter what efforts he made to possess them, they stood in no relation to him, and in fact deprived him of existence." The Prioress endeavors to convince Athena that

she has indeed been seduced, counting on trapping the young woman with the ignorance of her innocence and a feeling of guilt and concern for the supposedly lost honor of herself and her family. In so doing the Prioress plays on some of those very real fears and "grim realities" that Moers notes in women writers generally: ". . . the terrible need always to appear, as well as always to be, virtuous; and, over all, the terrible danger of slippage from the respectable to the unrespectable class of womanhood."[26] Athena does not seem to care what the world or the Prioress think of her, so the Prioress plays her last card, suggesting that Athena might be pregnant. Although Athena finds this hard to believe, she rises to the occasion in her own unque way: "'If I have a child,' said Athena, from her quaking earth thrusting at the heavens, 'my father will teach him astronomy.'"

The conflict seems never to be satisfactorily resolved for either side until the Prioress' pet monkey bursts suddenly into the room and in the ensuing scramble what we thought was the Prioress turns into the monkey and the invading monkey materializes as the true Prioress. Early in the tale we had been told of the Prioress' close relation to her monkey and her restlessness whenever it disappeared on extended sojourns into the woods. Later, clues had been dropped about certain of the Prioress' behaviors linking her with the monkey. All of this seemed explicable in the rational psychological terms of Radcliffe. But now we must understand the incident in purely symbolic terms and through these make an imaginative grasp of the wisdom of experience that Athena, Boris, and we ourselves are set to learn in the tale's end. Here is the answe to that question about the old Wendish idol of love—properly understood it is not a question of front and back, but of duality. Love and life contain dual forces, the civilized and the animal, the Apolonian, says Langbaum, of young virgins and the Dionysian of the monkey: "Isak Dinesen said in regard to this story: 'When men by way of their conventions have got themselves into difficulties, then let the monkey in, he will find the unattainable solution.'"[27] Dinesen's statement associates the monkey with that imaginative response which jars us out of our limited perspective and lets us see the intersection of life's dualities.

Neither the young warrior woman nor the young man must be forced into a sham experience by the iron hand of convention. Instead, they must enter it through an understanding of the complex nature of existence which takes them out of their innocent egoism into an awareness of their relation to others and to the world with all its dualities. Athena gives Boris a look with which she recognizes both him as a being outside herself and the bond that ties them together against the rest of the world. Whether or not they will actually marry becomes irrelevant. They move into experience linked by a spiritual understanding because of what they have witnessed together. The young warrior woman can be won over by nothing less than the imagination and powers of life itself.

The monkey and the monkey-as-Prioress (or Prioress-as-monkey) relate to the use of monsters in Gothic fiction: "creatures who scare because they look different, wrong, non-human." Moers notes that Gothic monsters were originally created through some distortion of scale, particularly gigantism, and later by a crossing of species resulting in animaloid people like the goblins in Christina Rossetti's *Goblin Market*. Women writers in the twentieth century make monsters that are "not so often giants or animaloid humans as aberrant creatures with hideous deformities or double sex: hermaphrodites."[28] In the modern usage the physical aspect of the monster is often translated into characters who are in some way psychological or sociological misfits and outcasts. These are the sort of characters we find in Carson McCullers' "haunting monsters of ambivalence" or in Djuna Barnes with her cast of "lesbians, lunatics, Jews, spoiled priests, artists, nobleman, transvestites, and other masqueraders"—many of whom also appear in Dinesen's work. In **"The Monkey"** the monstrosity lies not in the animaloid human *per se* but in qualities carried to the extreme, in this case an Apollonian attention to duty that is too strict and conventional versus an overly chaotic and animalistic Dionysian mode.

These extremes, both of which are out of control throughout most of the tale, create the negative "monster" aspect as opposed to the positive balance of such dualities already achieved by the true Prioress. Most specifically, that old monster—the conventionally proper—is outwitted by the imaginative response. The physical Gothic monster is here transformed into psychological and sociological terms and the wild animal which we might ordinarily have seen as a probable monster figure, and which is certainly scary to the "domestic animal" (the conventionally minded), becomes the very opposite of monster. It becomes the means by which we can break convention's limits and find the "unattainable solution."

Dinesen expressed her position in a slightly less symbolic fashion in her series of memoirs called *Shadows on the Grass*. She and her friend Berkeley Cole made a distinction between "respectability" and "decency" and divided human and animal acquaintances according to this doctrine:

> We put down domestic animals as respectable and wild animals as decent, and held that, while the existence and prestige of the first were decided by their relation to the community, the others stood in direct contact with God.[29]

Dinesen aligned herself with the wild animals.

Moers sees the monster phenomenon as taking on a special significance in women's hands and connects it with themes of self-hatred, self-disgust and the impetus to self-destruction. She notes that these are increasingly prominent themes in twentieth-century women writers and suggests that they partially account for the persistence of the Gothic mode:

> Despair is hardly the exclusive province of any one sex or class in our age, but to give *visual* form to the fear of self, to hold anxiety up to the Gothic mirror of the imagination, may well be more common in the writings of women than of men. While I cannot prove this statistically, I can offer a reason: that nothing separates female experience from male experience more sharply, and more early in life, than the compulsion to visualize the self.
>
> (p. 163)

The horrors in the visualization are created by the gaps (real or imagined) between the self a woman finds and the self she is told woman is supposed to be. In Dinesen's tales such self-loathing and the consequent tendency to view oneself in the character of a monster can sometimes result from the imposition of conventional attitudes; often it appears to be a male-imposed syndrome. In its gentler manifestations, it occurs because of some failure of appreciation or understanding by men. In the most direct and devastating examples—Calypso in **"The Deluge at Norderney"** and Lady Flora in **"The Cardinal's Third Tale"**—it results from a perversely egoistic and self-serving desire by some men to see all or certain women in degrading light and to persuade the women to see themselves accordingly. The women view their bodies, and by extension, their selves, negatively until they learn to see themselves and the world by other standards.

Calypso had begun to accept the assessment of her worth made by her uncle (who is a bad kind of homosexual in Dinesen's terms because he refuses even to acknowledge the existence of women and has foisted such devaluation and self-loathing on his niece). Calypso is about to cut off her long hair and her breasts in an effort to look masculine and achieve some right to existence. Then she notices in the mirror not only her reflection, but also that of an old picture depicting satyrs adoring the charms of nymphs who look, of course, as purely female as she. Once she discovers this and a wardrobe full of her great-grandmother's old clothes, she changes her plans as well as her evaluation of herself and her uncle. She spends the night trying on her great-grandmother's finery, turning back and forth between the approval of the mirror and that of her newly discovered "friends" in the old painting. Calypso decides to leave the castle but takes one last look at her sleeping uncle: "'Had she been afraid of this creature—she, who was the sister of the nymphs and had centaurs for playmates? She was a hundred times as strong as he.'"[30]

The Gothic writer's use of gigantism as equivalent to monstrosity is seen in Lady Flora who is, like her mother, something of a giant of a woman. The two of them are subject to all manner of insulting variations by the father/husband on the subject of Gulliver among the Brobdingnagians. Lady Flora learns to loathe the very mention of flesh or sexuality but by the tale's end she, too, achieves a new self-evaluation (although her path is a great deal longer and more circuitous than Calypso's). In Athena and her equally large Dinesenian counterpart, Ehrengard—in the tale of the same name—there is just the hint of this gigantic woman/monster possibility, but neither suffers from any kind of self-loathing, and their giantism is played upon more in terms of its implications of power than in terms of monstrousness.

In "The Monkey," Dinesen's dislike of forced obedience to one's conventional duty is also embodied in her variation upon the Gothic elements of the good and the tyrannical parent. In *Udolpho*, Moers notes that these roles are played primarily by Emily's father and her uncle Montoni. Athena's father is the good parent; the Prioress, at least in the character she plays through most of the tale, functions as tyrant. The tale posits a need for an imaginative resolution of these dualities. Athena's resistance links Dinesen's stance with that of the last lines of Jane Austen's Gothic parody, *Northanger Abbey*: "'I leave it to be settled . . . by whomsoever it may concern, whether the tendency of this work be altogether to recommend parental tyranny, or reward filial disobedience.'"[31]

The emphasis at the end of "The Monkey" falls not on marriage but on the mutual under-standing gained by Athena and Boris, on their "spiritual" marriage. In terms of plot at least, this marks another of Dinesen's shifts in the use of the Gothic, since no marriage actually takes place. However, Moers show us that, despite the actuality of the marriage, even in Radcliffe's *Udolpho*, the main concern is really an overwhelming interest in property, which is all bound up, of course, with a woman's independence.

Dinesen, however, is rarely interested in such practicalities and never interested in respectability. She is passionately interested in freedom. For her, freedom comes not through such tangible means as property, but through the kind of understanding gained at the end of "**The Monkey**," an understanding available to both sexes.

Dinesen is not alone in her reliance upon the imagination, especially with regard to her women characters, to achieve freedom from restrictions. She is, however, unique in her insistence upon it, and in the extremes to which she employs this "solution" in her tales. Her women characters rarely rebel directly. They employ an imaginative response in order, as her character Matteo remarks about women's dancing, to move "'with such perfect freedom in such severely regulated figures.'"[32]

Notes

1. Karen Petersen and J.J. Wilson, *Women Artists: Recognition and Reappraisal from the Early Middle Ages to the Twentieth Century* (New York: Harper Colophon—Harper & Row, 1976), pp. 106-07.

2. Howard Green, "Isak Dinesen," *The Hudson Review*, 17 (1964-65), 526-27.

3. Robert Langbaum, *Isak Dinesen's Art: The Gayety of Vision*, Phoenix Edition (Chicago: Univ. of Chicago Press, 1975), p. 74.

4. Andrew Wright, Introd., *The Castle of Otranto*, by Horace Walpole; *The Mysteries of Udolpho*, by Anne Radcliffe; *Northanger Abbey*, by Jane Austen (San Francisco: Rinehart Press, 1963), pp. viii-ix.

5. *Karen Blixen fortoeller* . . . (Louisiana Grammofonplader) as quoted in Donald Hannah, *Isak Dinesen and Karen Blixen: The Mask and the Reality* (New York: Random House, 1971), p. 60.

6. Parmenia Migel, *Titania: The Biography of Isak Dinesen* (New York: Random House, 1967), p. 11.

7. Dinesen's personal tragedies included her father's suicide; the death of her close friend, Denys Finch-Hatton; her short, unhappy marriage; and the syphilis, contracted from her husband, which was never fully cured and which occasioned much of the illness she experienced in later years. In particular, she also turned to writing in order to help herself deal with the troubles on her farm—drought and an invasion of grasshoppers—that eventually led to the loss of her beloved African coffee plantation.

8. Hannah, p. 102.

9. Wright, p. ix.

10. Langbaum, p. 89.

11. Glenway Wescott, "Isak Dinesen, The Storyteller," in *Images of Truth* (New York: Harper & Row, 1962), p. 156.

12. Ellen Moers, *Literary Women*, Anchor Books Edition (Garden City, N.Y.: Anchor Press-Doubleday, 1977), p. 138.

13. See Moers' discussion in *Literary Women*: "Female Gothic" and "Traveling Heroinism: Gothic for Heroines."

14. Lionel Stevenson, *English Novel: A Panorama*, as quoted in Wright, p. xiv.

15. Wright, p. xvi.

16. Langbaum, p. 89.

17. Ibid., p. 31.

18. Isak Dinesen, "The Monkey," in *Seven Gothic Tales*, Vintage Books Edition (1934; rpt. of 1939 ed., New York: Random House, 1972), p. 109. All further references to this work appear in the text.

19. Langbaum, p. 83.

20. Moers, p. 139.

21. Ibid., p. 198.

22. Ibid., p. 191.

23. Ann Radcliffe, *The Mysteries of Udolpho* (Great Britain: Billing & Sons, Ltd., n.d.), p. 7.

24. Wright, p. xv.

25. Isak Dinesen, "The Caryatids, an Unfinished Tale," in *Last Tales*, 2nd ed. (New York: Random House, 1957), p. 122.

26. Moers, pp. 206-07.

27. Langbaum, p. 88.

28. Moers, pp. 155, 164.

29. Isak Dinesen, *Shadows on the Grass*, First Vintage Books Edition (1961; rpt., New York: Random House, 1974), p. 17.

30. Isak Dinesen, "The Deluge at Norderney" in *Seven Gothic Tales*, Vintage Books Edition (1934; rpt. of 1939 ed., New York: Random House, 1972), p. 49.

31. Wright, p. xxi.

32. Isak Dinesen, "Tales of Two Old Gentlemen," in *Last Tales*, 2nd ed. (New York: Random House, 1957), p. 66.

SUSAN C. BRANTLY (ESSAY DATE 2002)

SOURCE: Brantly, Susan C. "*Seven Gothic Tales*." In *Understanding Isak Dinesen*, pp. 12-71. Columbia: University of South Carolina Press, 2002.

In the following excerpt, Brantly surveys the themes in and critical response to Dinesen's Seven Gothic Tales.

Isak Dinesen was forty-nine when *Seven Gothic Tales* appeared in 1934. She had a wealth of life experience behind her, and the sophistication and maturity of her English-language debut is striking. Dinesen often said that if she had not lost the farm in Africa, she would never have become a writer. She had published a few tales in Danish journals under the name Osceola, but for many, *Seven Gothic Tales* represents the beginning of Isak Dinesen's literary career. When Isak Dinesen left Africa in 1931, she had already completed "**The Roads Round Pisa**" and "**The Monkey**." The other five tales were finished in Denmark. Originally, Dinesen intended to publish nine tales under the title *Tales of Nozdref's Cook*. Nozdref's Cook is a character out of Gogol's *Dead Souls* (1842). In the Danish edition of *Seven Gothic Tales*, Baron von Brackel notes that the modern world appears to be created the way "Nozdref's Cook made soup—a little pepper, salt, and herbs, whatever was around—and 'some flavor or another will come out of it'" (*MU*, 1:99). Evidently, Dinesen decided against comparing her collection to a culinary hodgepodge. The original nine tales would have included "**The Caryatids, an Unfinished Tale**," and "**Carnival**," but Dinesen felt that the contemporary references in "**Carnival**" would disturb the tone of the volume. "**The Caryatids**" was saved for later publication. . . .

In part, Dinesen wrote *Seven Gothic Tales* in English for economic reasons, since the English-language book market is much larger than the Danish. Dinesen also said she chose to write in English because she felt comfortable expressing herself in that language after seventeen years in Kenya. In addition, Dinesen felt that the English public would be more sympathetic to her tales, since, in her view, the English-speaking countries possessed a stronger tradition of fantastic literature than Denmark. In 1923, Dinesen wrote to her mother about the American writer James Branch Cabell and his novels *Jurgen* (1919) and *The Cream of the Jest* (1917) which she characterized as "full of fantasy, and all this has made me wonder whether a new direction in literature is about to develop, making use of fantasy" (*LA*, 164). In England, she pointed to Lewis Carroll's *Alice's Adventures in Wonderland* (1865) and David Garnett's *Lady into Fox* (1923) as examples of fantastic literature.[1] As far as her Danish audience was concerned, Dinesen felt, "We have few or no fantastic books here at home. We have Ingemann's *The Sphinx* and Heiberg's *Christmas Jests and New Year's Fun*, but who remembers them? I was afraid that people, after reading my book, would ask: 'What

ABOUT THE AUTHOR

JOHN UPDIKE ON DINESEN'S "DIVINE SWANK" IN SEVEN GOTHIC TALES

Though Isak Dinesen's leisurely and ornate anecdotes, which she furnishes with just enough historical touches to make the stage firm, have something in them of the visionary and the artificial, they are not escapist. From the sweeping flood of the first story to the casual and savage murder of the last, they face pain and loss with the brisk familiarity of one who has amply known both, and force us to face them, too. Far from hollow and devoid of a moral, the tales insistently strive to inculcate a moral stance; in this her fiction especially suggests that of Hemingway, who thought well enough of her to interrupt his Nobel Prize acceptance speech with a regret that she had not received it. Both authors urge upon us a certain style of courage, courage whose stoic acceptances are plumed with what the old Cardinal, in the first Gothic Tale, calls "divine swank." Dinesen even called this quality "chic," ascribing it to the costumed Masai warriors who, "daring, and wildly fantastical as they seem, are unswervingly true to their own nature, and to an immanent ideal." She also admired, in Africa, the Moslems, whose "moral code consists of hygiene and ideas of honor—for instance they put discretion among their first commandments."

SOURCE: Updike, John. *"Seven Gothic Tales*: The Divine Swank of Isak Dinesen." *New York Times Book Review* (23 February 1986): 3, 37.

is the meaning of what you write?' There is no meaning, and there should not be a meaning. It is dream. Fantasy!"[2] . . .

Dinesen's reception in the United States was enthusiastic beyond all expectation. The United States was in the grip of the Great Depression, and one American reviewer began by quoting Dinesen's **"The Poet"**: "When one is tied down heavily enough to an existence of care, it becomes pleasant to think of careless times and people" (*SGT*, 359).[3] The American reviewers embraced the imaginative qualities of the book: "*Seven Gothic Tales* has burst upon us from a gray literary sky."[4] It may be worthy of note that 1934 was also the year *King Kong* was released in theaters. Other films released in the 1930s include *Frankenstein* (1931), *The Mummy* (1932), and *Lost Horizons* (1937). Exotic locations and strange happenings were welcome because they could remove the reader from the harsh realities of the everyday. British reviews were also warm, "This belongs to the company of the world's great books."[5] Even so, one English reviewer found the style "pompous."[6]

Dinesen's misgivings about how the Danish audience would receive her book proved to be well founded. The predominant literary mode in Denmark was social realism. The public debate of contemporary social issues had not raged as strongly since the days when Georg Brandes called the Modern Breakthrough into being in the 1870's. Dinesen's imaginative tales set in the previous century were quite different from what most Danes were reading. Svend Borberg described Dinesen as a flamingo-red orchid in a cabbage patch, and Swedish reviewer Mario Grut compared her to "a crane in a dance with sparrows."[7] The most notorious of the Danish reviews accused Dinesen of "snobbism, the fantastic, and perversity."[8] The negative Danish reviews upset Dinesen. Svend Borberg, with a good dose of irony, suggested one reason for Dinesen's being subjected to such a beating by the Danish critics: "It was naturally very cheeky, not to say brash, of Isak Dinesen—alias Baroness Karen Blixen—to conquer the world first with her book *Seven Gothic Tales* and then come to Denmark with it. As a Danish author she should have felt obligated to ask her at home first if she was worth anything."[9] This was simply the beginning of an uneasy relationship between Dinesen and her Danish public that would last throughout her career. Even so, in 1999, the readers of the large Danish daily newspaper *Politiken* voted *Seven Gothic Tales* to be the third most important Danish work of the twentieth century.

The choice of *Seven Gothic Tales* as the title for the English work and *Syv fantastiske Fortællinger* (*Seven fantastic tales*) as that of the Danish is the result of a canny assessment of her potential audiences and the literary traditions with which they might be familiar. "Gothic" appeals, of course, to the English Gothic and "fantastic" is a word that draws one's thoughts towards the German romantic, as in *Fantasiestücke in Callots Manier* (1814-15, Fantasy pieces in the manner of Callot) by E. T. A. Hoffmann. In a Danish interview, Dinesen called **Seven Gothic Tales** a nonsense book: "I don't know another word for books in which all sorts of fantastic things happen. You probably know Hoffmann's Tales? It is something of the same sort, but not really the same."[10] With some reason, Dinesen felt her Danish interviewer would be more familiar with a reference to German romanticism, rather than the English Gothic. When asked why she chose the phrase "Gothic Tales," Dinesen answered, "Because in England it places the stories in time and implies something that both has an elevated tone and can erupt into jests and mockery, into devilry and mystery."[11] Both English and German traditions left their mark on Dinesen's writing, as she explained to her friend Bent Mohn: "I know more about the English 'Gothic' than German romanticism, but there are also works in that [tradition] which have meant a lot to me" (**KBD**, 1:500).

In English, the term "Gothic" has several associations, and Dinesen's critics have found a use for a number of them from time to time. The Goths were Germanic barbarians who attacked the Roman Empire. With reference to the sometimes subversive qualities of Dinesen's texts, Susan Hardy Aiken playfully suggests that Dinesen might be considered "a 'barbarous' marginal force that continually imperils the [traditional] center."[12] The Gothic also refers to an elaborate type of medieval architecture, and some critics have found similarities between the architecture of a Gothic cathedral and the complex construction of Dinesen's narratives: "The architecture of the . . . stories permitted the author to stop, at any moment, and add on a flying buttress or a whole new wing."[13] Dinesen herself specified, however: "I didn't mean the real Gothic, but the imitation of the Gothic, the Romantic age of Byron, the age of that man—what was his name?—who built Strawberry Hill, the age of the Gothic revival."[14]

The period of the English Gothic, roughly located between 1790 and 1830, came close on the heels of the Age of Reason. Many of the notable contributors to the Gothic were women: Ann Radcliffe, Mary Shelley, and the Brontë sisters. Dangerous and irrational forces seem to be at large in the Gothic, no doubt as a protest against the rationality of the era that preceded it. The Gothic is characterized by an interest in the past and exotic locations. Eric Johannesson has speculated, along with others, that the motive behind such a change in scene is to "liberate the imagination from the fetters which too familiar an environment imposes upon it."[15] The typical Gothic hero is a man with a secret past who rejects the moral claims of society—a Byronic rebel. All of these features are familiar elements in Dinesen's writing.

Sibyl James has written an important essay on Dinesen's relationship to the Gothic, in which she notes some significant points upon which Dinesen differs from the traditional English Gothic.[16] Gothic narrators often resort to preachiness. Evil villains assault the innocent heroine's virtue, but society's conventional morality is ultimately affirmed. Dinesen, on the contrary, is anything but preachy, and her villains are likely to be the conventionally minded. The Gothic usually resolves the supernatural into the natural: there is not a ghost, but a madwoman in Rochester's attic; Frankenstein animates his monster with galvanic energy, a scientifically acceptable principle at the time. Dinesen does not worry about confining herself to the plausible: prioresses turn into monkeys and vice versa. Dinesen does not use her supernatural effects to scare her readers, which was one of the main projects of the Gothic. The supernatural for Dinesen simply represents freedom of the imagination.

The styles of the English Gothic and German romanticism overlap a great deal. Both relish the fantastic. The Gothic ruin that engages the spectator's imagination finds its counterpart in the romantic textual fragment. The English Gothic and German romanticism share a common source of inspiration in *The Arabian Nights* and Boccaccio's *Decameron* (1353). German romantic authors spent a good deal of time theorizing about a short-story art form they called the *Novelle* (novella), developed on the model of Boccaccio's tales. According to Goethe, the novella should describe an extraordinary event, and August Schlegel thought the story should contain a distinct turning point. In general, plot in the novella is more important than character. E. T. A. Hoffmann and Adelbert von Chamisso, two writers deeply admired by Dinesen, are among the foremost creators of German novellas. Dinesen has learned a few tricks from her favorites.

Peter Schlehmihl, a character from a famous tale by Chamisso, makes a brief appearance in Hoffmann's "A New Year's Eve Adventure." In much the same way, the fictional Augustus von Schimmelman would surface in Dinesen's **Out of Africa,** or Henrik Ibsen would make a cameo appearance in "The Pearls." "Real" and "imaginary" worlds become linked, and the dividing line is blurred.

German romantic writers were also fond of irony and literary masks. Hoffmann's "Don Juan" is allegedly written by a traveling music enthusiast. Adopting a literary mask enables the author to relinquish narrative authority and forces the reader to assess the bias of the narrative. The narrative says one thing but may imply another, and the reader must be attentive to catch the nuances. This effect, which engages the participation of the reader in deciphering the text, is known as romantic irony.

Few authors do romantic irony better than Dinesen's countryman, Søren Kierkegaard. In *Either/Or* (1843), Kierkegaard, writing under the pseudonym of Victor Eremita, claims to have found two manuscripts in a desk, and he deduces they are written by two different people, whom he calls "A" and "B." Among "A's" papers there is another text called "The Diary of a Seducer;" which may or may not be written by "A" under the name Johannes. Similarly, Karen Blixen, writing under her pseudonym Isak Dinesen, nestles tales within tales within tales. The reader is consistently thwarted in her or his attempt to locate an ultimate voice of authority. Dinesen took such great pains to distance herself from the events in her tales that she was annoyed by the prospect of readers asking, "Did you really mean it? . . . Have you experienced this yourself?"[17] These narrative connections between Kierkegaard and Dinesen have been examined at length in an essay by Eric Johannesson.[18]

. . . . .

"The Monkey"

In the case of **"The Monkey,"** some of the most ingenious readings of the text have been performed by scholars publishing in academic journals or other venues not easily accessible to the general public. Annelies van Hees and William Mishler have exposed a number of the tale's secrets, inspired by the analytical tools of psychoanalysis, and Dag Heede has thrown fresh light on some of the troubling gender issues the story evokes. The following treatment of the tale draws on the work of all three of these scholars as well as others, but is especially indebted to Annelies van Hees's sensitive literary detective work.

The ending of **"The Monkey"** contains a startling revelation. The Virgin Prioress, whom we think we have known throughout the tale, turns out to have a double nature. She is able to exchange shapes with her monkey. The majority of Dinesen's tales, although they suggest fantastic possibilities, remain within the realm of the

plausible and do not resort to such overtly supernatural devices. The scene is shocking, and we are forced to reevaluate everything we thought we knew about the events preceding the metamorphosis. This narrative twist is similar to, though even more spectacular than, the Cardinal revealing himself to be Kasparson at the end of **"The Deluge at Norderney."**

Eric Johannesson has pointed out that the theme of doubles is common to Gothic literature, listing the examples of "Menardus in *Die Elixire des Teufels,* or Ambrosio in Lewis's *The Monk,* or Stevenson's *Dr. Jekyll and Mr. Hyde,* or the jeweler in Hoffmann's *Mademoiselle de Scudery.*"[19] In each of these stories, the person with a double nature is male, and one side is most certainly bad, while the other is good. Conventional morality prevails when the evil side of the character is destroyed. In David Garnett's "Lady into Fox" (1922), a story Dinesen once mentioned in an interview as a good example of the fantastic, a Victorian woman is inexplicably transformed into a vixen.[20] Her husband tries to adjust but grows increasingly distressed as more and more of her animal nature takes over, and the ex-Victorian angel goes so far as to run away, mate, and have a litter. The transgressions of the wife are ultimately punished when she is torn apart by hounds. In typical fashion, Dinesen has reinscribed the traditions of the Gothic. The Prioress and her monkey are not destroyed at the end of tale; conventional morality has not been confirmed, and it is not at all certain that one side is better than the other.

The emblem of this doubleness is the Wendish idol described by the Count, "the goddess of love had the face and facade of a beautiful woman, while, if you turned her around, she presented at the back the image of a monkey" (*SGT,* 130-31). Athena raises the question, "But how . . . did they know, in the case of that goddess of love, which was the front and which was the back?" (*SGT,* 131). Athena's remark, which questions the hierarchy of such dualisms, is much in keeping with the theme of the harmony of contrasts so prevalent in Dinesen's tales in general.

As Hans Brix pointed out, Dinesen could have learned about this Wendish idol, called "Sieba" or "Siwa," from Bernhard Severin Ingemann's *Grundtræk til en Nord-Slavisk og Vendisk Gudelære* (1824, Fundamentals of a North-Slavic and Wendish mythology).[21] Ingemann was one of Dinesen's favorite authors, and the double aspect of "Siwa" is described in a footnote to his *Valdemar den Store og hans Mænd* (1824, Waldemar the great and his men), a copy of which, much used, is in Dinesen's library at Rungstedlund.[22] According to Ingemann, all Wendish gods possessed a double nature, one dark and one light. Siwa was traditionally depicted as a woman with long hair holding an apple in one hand and grapes in the other. (Note that the Prioress serves Boris pears and grapes when he first arrives at the convent.) The other side of the idol depicts "a brash triumphant monkey."[23] Whereas Ingemann sees the woman as a representative of innocence, he says of the monkey, "Just as the monkey on the whole is mankind's most disgusting distortion, so it is especially, as is known, the natural image of lust and unchaste indecency."[24] Like his other romantic/Gothic compatriots, Ingemann is certain that one side is good and one side is bad. Dinesen takes a different view. To Robert Langbaum, Dinesen said, "When men by way of their conventions have got themselves into difficulties, then let the monkey in, he will find the unattainable solution."[25]

Looking back over the tale, it is difficult to tell at any given time with whom one has been dealing. When Boris first arrives, it is stated that the monkey had been missing for a few weeks, usually a sign that the Prioress has transformed herself and left the convent in charge of her monkey familiar while she enjoys a freer life. The same Prioress who greets Boris with the pears and grapes of the "front" of the idol, speaks with passionate feeling of forests and trees. Athena has seen the monkey in the place where Cupid stood just a few days earlier, and the monkey crosses Boris's path on the way back from his proposal visit. Is this the "real" Prioress, or not? The Prioress's private dining room has "just lately" been redecorated in a style that would appeal to a creature from Zanzibar. A heavy incense is being burned, perhaps to mask the scent of the monkey. When Boris is refused by Athena, the Prioress goes "up to the window, as if she meant to throw herself out" (*SGT*, 138). When the Prioress turns around again, "She was all changed" (*SGT*, 138). Marianne Juhl and Bo Hakon Jørgensen construe this transformation as the moment when the monkey takes over, but this "change" is nothing like the metamorphosis that occurs in the final scene of the story.[26] The monkey certainly seems to have the upper hand during the seduction supper, as body language would indicate: "From time to time she made use of a little gesture peculiar to her, of daintily scratching herself here and there with her delicately pointed little finger" (*SGT*, 144). The Prioress also savors the cloves from Zanzibar, which is another hint at who is in control. In the final scene, after the metamorphosis, we are presented with "the true Prioress of Closter Seven" (*SGT*, 162). William Mishler has noted that when assessing an appropriate translation of this phrase into Danish, Dinesen rejected Valdemar Rørdam's suggestion "den rigtige" (the correct, rightful) and chose instead "den virkelige" (the real, true).[27] Rørdam's term would have implied a hierarchy, a moral judgment on which side of the Prioress was the right side. Even if presented with the "true" Prioress, some readers may still be in doubt as to what that means.

Dag Heede has made the amusing suggestion that in the light of the Prioress's metamorphosis, if we consider "the cornucopia of pets present in the enclosed building, the uncanny suspicion arises that perhaps all the women from time to time change into their pets and vice versa."[28] The menagerie includes parrots, cockatoos, dogs, cats, a deer, and "a white Angora goat, like that of Esmeralda" (*SGT*, 109). The reference is to Victor Hugo's *The Hunchback of Notre Dame* (1831), in which Esmeralda is suspected of being a witch and her goat, an animal familiar. The hint does point to strange powers that may dwell in these "superfluous" women who have been set aside in a cloister. Closter Seven is more coven than convent.

The event that instigates the intrigue of the tale is Boris von Schreckenstein's need to escape a scandal. Although not stated explicitly, it is clear that Boris has been accused of homosexuality and needs to get married in order to repair his social reputation. In this society such matters are not discussed unless in euphemisms. The old librarian, when pressed as to the nature of the scandal, begins to talk about Greece. The connection lies in such texts as Plato's *Symposium*, in which love between men is treated as natural and positive. The cloistered women, however, associate Greece with coiffures and fashions from their youth, creating some delightfully comic confusion. The point of the scandal does seem to sink in eventually and disrupts the entire worldview of the women of the convent. They have been raised to consider women objects of desire to all men, and their entire social existence has been based upon it. Dinesen includes the almost wistful line: "Had they known that it might ever be called into question, all these lives, which were now so nearly finished, might have come to look very different" (*SGT*, 112).

Dag Heede has suggested that Dinesen uses Boris's homosexuality as "a way of representing the normal, not as natural, but as a construction, one single, possible version of reality among a multitude of others. . . . Boris is not only the most 'normal' person in the text, but as the focus of the story, the person whose thoughts and views . . . the reader follows, and who is the most obvious person for the reader to identify with."[29] The very existence of the idea of homosexuality creates a disruption in the minds of the convent women, which could also be described as the realization that what they had taken for normal and natural may instead be a mere social construction. This realization opens up limitless possibilities for living. The text of **"The Monkey"** does not express much sympathy with Boris's accusers, described as being "sanctimonious" and acting "under the pretense of moral indignation" (**SGT,** 111). Heede goes so far as to state: "Homosexuality is used here more than anything else as a positive anti-bourgeois metaphor, a way of rejecting the dull, settled life of 'supporters, fathers-in-law, authorities on food and morals.'"[30]

The Prioress decides on a match between Boris and Athena upon the receipt of a mysterious letter. The message no doubt contains the news that the Count has won his lawsuit, making Athena a particularly wealthy young heiress. Moreover, the Count's lawyer also has a monkey from Zanzibar, so perhaps the jungle telegraph has been at work. The choice of Athena surprises Boris since from his childhood both his mother and his aunt "had been joining forces to keep him and Athena apart" (**SGT,** 118). Why? Mishler argues convincingly that the possibility exists that Athena and Boris are brother and sister. The Count was a special admirer of Boris's mother in days gone by. When he greets Boris it is with the words: "Boris, my child . . ." (**SGT,** 124). Dinesen specifically rejected Rørdam's translation of "Boris, min Dreng . . ." (Boris, my boy) in lieu of "Boris, mit Barn!" (Boris, my child), perhaps in order to underline the suggestion that the Count might be Boris's father.[31] When the Count writes that he had hoped to see Boris's features in the unborn generations to follow, the Count might at the same time be seeing his own genotype through Boris as well as Athena. Incest, along with homosexuality, is yet another socially disruptive force brought into play in this tale. No wonder Pastor Rosenquist, the spokesperson for conventional morality, seems completely at a loss.

According to van Hees's analysis, Boris's homosexuality is the result of his Oedipus complex.[32] He has become so bonded to his mother that sexual relations with another woman would constitute a betrayal. Boris has just come from his mother and "a row of wild scenes which his mother's love and jealousy had caused" (**SGT,** 114). The Count comes to represent the father in this Oedipal triangle. Upon first sight of the Count, Boris thinks, "This old man knows all, and is going to kill me" (**SGT,** 124). After proposing, Boris feels like Don Giovanni waiting for the Commendatore. Don Giovanni is the notorious seducer of Mozart's opera, who is punished at the end by the stone replica of one of his victims' fathers. This, then, is another image of paternal retribution. Boris is repeatedly afflicted with the sense that something is wrong. He prefers to think of Athena as a skeleton, a desexualized being, and not a threat to his relationship to his mother. On his way to seduce Athena, Boris recalls some lines from Aeschylus's *Eumenides* in which Orestes asks for Athena's help as he is being brought to trial for the murder of his mother. He is thus expressing his fear of what this encounter will mean for him. Sex with another woman is tantamount to the murder of his mother and betrayal. After the botched seduction, Boris again invokes lines from Aeschylus, which are erroneously attributed to Euripides in the English text, but correctly identified in the Danish. This time, Boris quotes Orestes' words thanking Athena for helping him be acquitted of the crime of matricide. Boris no longer needs to feel guilt about becoming involved with another woman.

If Boris is unnaturally bound to his mother, more than one interpreter has felt that Athena is unnaturally bound to her father.[33] This may be what the Prioress implies with her scandalous anecdote about the Holy Family visiting Paris. The Duchess of Berri is rumored to be pregnant by her father, and even though she expostulates to the Virgin, "You would never have done it," in some sense the Virgin has been impregnated by her Father in heaven (**SGT,** 144).

Athena takes her name from the virgin goddess of wisdom, but she is more specifically a Diana, and as the Prioress tells us, Boris would make a fine Actaeon. According to the legend, Diana had Actaeon torn apart by his own hounds for daring to spy upon her taking a bath. Athena is six feet tall, able to do a chin-up on a hunting horn—lifting both herself and her horse off the ground—and defiantly virginal. She is compared to carnivora: a lioness and an eagle. When she stands on one leg like a stork, she is emulating the Masai warriors Dinesen knew in Africa. Athena is the typical adolescent heroine identified by Robin Lyndenberg, one who perceives marriage and maturity as equivalent to a loss of freedom.[34] "From being a success at court, a happy, congratulated bride, a mother of a promising family, good Lord, deliver me" (*SGT*, 142). She is perfectly happy with her tomboy existence and does not want anyone to take it from her.

During the first chat Athena has with Boris, they look up and see the constellation of the Great Bear. The story of the Great Bear can be found in Ovid's *Metamorphoses*. Callisto, a nymph in Artemis's (Diana's) hunting party, is loved by Zeus, and so the jealous Hera transforms her into a bear. When Callisto's son, Arcas, is about to kill her, Zeus turns them into constellations. Being transformed into a constellation is a common means of escaping physical jeopardy in Greek mythology. The very name of Closter Seven, which alludes to the constellation of the Pleiades, invokes another such tale. Zeus turns the seven daughters of Atlas into the Pleiades in order to save them from the amorous pursuit of Orion. Sexual attention is another form of physical jeopardy, and the image is a suitable one for a cloister. Later, when Athena is told she will have a child, she stubbornly announces, "My father will teach him astronomy" (*SGT*, 158). For both Athena and Agnese in the "**Roads Round Pisa**," the study of the stars takes them away from earthly cares and becomes a metaphor for escaping amorous attention.

Athena is a partisan of the French Revolution and she recites for Boris some lines from a French song by Auguste Barbier. The text describes a horse that eludes its masters, originally a metaphor for the French Revolution. Annelies van Hees notes that Athena no doubt sees herself as the mare, "which no hand has touched and no one has managed to saddle."[35] She no doubt also identifies with the bear who kills five men before she is taken. Athena identifies with wild, powerful animals and is distressed to hear the story of the African elephant that dies in a cage. She is afraid, with reason, that the Prioress wants to subdue her and put her into a cage, which is why the tale is the main *faux pas* of the evening. Long before Boris appears on her doorstep Athena has made it abundantly clear she will not relinquish her virginity without a fight.

The scene in which Boris and Athena engage in combat is riddled with symbolic import. Boris approaches through a hall with a black and white tiled floor, and he emerges into a pink and crimson bower: "Of all the memories which afterward Boris carried with him from this night, the memory of the transition from the coloring and light of the corridor to that of the room was the longest lasting" (*SGT*, 151). This event will signal a transfor-

mation for Boris, a type of rebirth. He moves from a space where black is black and white is white to a very feminine space where such clear distinctions are absent. Dag Heede reads this space as a womb:

> The whole room was hung with rose silks, and in the depths of it the crimson draperies of the four-poster bed glowed in the shade. There were two pink-globed lamps, solicitously lighted by the Prioress' maid. The floor had a wine-colored carpet with roses in it, which, near the lamps, seemed to be drinking in the light, and farther from them looked like pools of dark crimson into which one would not like to walk.
>
> (*SGT*, 151)

The room is being viewed through Boris's eyes, and of course he is the "one" who does not feel comfortable walking into this space.

The only unfeminine object in the room is Athena, who looks like "a sturdy young sailor boy about to swab the deck" (*SGT*, 152). Athena defends her virtue with considerable vigor. Annelies van Hees, Bill Mishler, Anders Westenholz, and Grethe Rostbøll all agree that when Athena knocks out Boris's two teeth it is a symbol of castration.[36] Curiously, this seems to make Boris happy. According to van Hees, his castration obviates the necessity for Boris to be unfaithful to his mother. The struggle goes on and ends with a kiss that disgusts them both. There is something out of proportion in Athena's reaction to the kiss. It is "as if he had run a rapier straight through her" (*SGT*, 154). The kiss is a symbolic consummation that saps the virgin warrior of her strength in an almost magical way, not altogether unlike the way in which Samson is deprived of his strength by having his hair cut off. Athena is later compared to Samson, but a Samson who has regained his strength again (*SGT*, 159).

The discussion the morning after is quite comic. The Prioress takes it for granted that the rape has been committed, and Athena is too ignorant of the birds and the bees to know whether one can get pregnant from a kiss or not. Even though the Prioress extorts from Athena the promise to marry Boris, Athena still remains true to her Diana nature and promises to kill Boris at the first opportunity. At this juncture there is a tapping at the window, and shortly thereafter the remarkable metamorphosis of the Prioress and the monkey takes place. Boris, Athena, and the reader are all quite startled, and Dinesen has her little joke by having the monkey sit on the bust of Immanuel Kant, author of *The Critique of Pure Reason* (1781). What has just happened exists beyond the limits of reason, and Kant can't help us. Interpretations of what this scene means for the two young people vary widely.

Hans Brix seems to feel that the Prioress's subjugation of the monkey has instructed Athena that she must subject herself to Boris.[37] Langbaum feels the scene makes Boris and Athena "ready for human love," by which he must mean that they have in some sense been "cured."[38] Juhl and Jørgensen believe that the two have learned that the relationship between men and women must be sexual, and thus, these critics also endorse the notion of a cure, as does Vibeke Schröder.[39] Mishler also seems to subscribe to the couple's experiencing a psychological liberation from their respective complexes.[40] Van Hees feels that the scene has caused Boris and Athena to accept their sexuality as it is and also to realize that they can marry in any case.[41] Dag Heede sees a happy ending, "in an 18th century view, that the two combine in a reasonable, sensible union, where they probably will do little damage to another."[42]

Indeed, Boris's homosexuality and Athena's desire to remain chaste are not in conflict, as the Prioress has already noted: "She will have nothing . . . and you will give nothing. It seems to me, in all modesty, that you are well paired" (*SGT*, 137). Athena and Boris can keep up appearances and enjoy a certain sort of freedom within the circle of their marriage. Closter Seven is the namesake of Kloster-Zeven, which is famous in history as the site for the signing of a treaty between England and France in 1757, in which England capitulated to France and agreed to remain neutral in the European arena for the rest of the Seven Years War. Thus, Closter Seven seems a suitable spot for generating peaceful agreements. Athena does not need to kill Boris, and they can probably get along in the future.

A fan wrote to Dinesen requesting clarification of **"The Monkey,"** and Dinesen's response is worth quoting at length:

> With regard to the tale **"The Monkey,"** I am, as always when a reader asks me what a story means, quite uncomfortable, since I feel the only honest answer would be: "There is no meaning." I think it would be a shame if an author could explain a story better with outside information than it explains itself! I believe that when I wrote **"The Monkey,"** I thought of the situation as follows: The Prioress has a monkey that is very close to her and in whose company she needs to take refuge from her limited life in the cloister. Every now and then she feels such an attraction and need for a free life in nature that she changes shape with the monkey and for a while is absent from the cloister, where the monkey takes charge. As a young girl, I myself had a beloved dog about

> which I had a similar fantasy. If one is looking for a deeper meaning to the story, it would probably be this: When human relations become unusually complicated or completely mixed up, let the monkey come. It is monkey-advice and monkey-help that Boris gets in the cloister; only when, through these methods, a way out can be glimpsed and darkness begins to lighten, does the Prioress come back and resume her place. The monkey has plainly chosen a criminal path upon which the Prioress would not have set foot, but in its solution there is salvation for Boris and, it should be understood, also a promise of a more human happiness for Athena. This is not a good explanation, but you are free to come up with a better one.
>
> (*KBD*, 2:433)

Dinesen's words about salvation for Boris and a more human happiness for Athena are sufficiently vague, so that interpreters are free to continue to speculate.

At the beginning of the tale, Boris fantasized about how his aunt would take the news of the scandal, and he weighs possible reactions in the form of Latin phrases. *"Et tu Brute"* (You too, Brutus!), which is an exclamation that marks betrayal: "How could you!" *"Ad sanitatem gradus est novisse morbum"* (It is a step towards health to recognize sickness) anticipates the Prioress's perception of Boris as a deviant who needs to be healed. *"Discite justitiam moniti, et non temnere divos"* (Be warned, learn justice and learn not to despise the divine) is an important phrase since it appears again, without the warning note, as the last line of the story. Since at the beginning of the tale, Boris and the reader both think of the Prioress as a defender of moral rectitude, the admonition Boris anticipates would be something like "Follow the rules of Christian behavior." By the end of the story, our understanding of the Prioress has changed and we realize that the divine forces at play have been pagan. The original *"Discite . . ."* quote is from Virgil's *Aeneid*, not a Christian text at all. The divine in **"The Monkey"** embraces the two-sided, double nature of Siwa. The second time the phrase is invoked, it might be construed: "Learn justice and embrace both sides of the divine." The revelation at the end of the story forces us to reevaluate not only this phrase, but the entire story. Repeating a phrase whose significance has changed is a technique that Dinesen will use again in **"Alkmene."** It is a device that makes the reader reexamine her or his assumptions. The sentence has not changed, but after experiencing the story, the reader has. The reader's expectations and understanding of this fictional world have altered—another metamorphosis has taken place. Now everything must be reexamined and reinterpreted.

Notes

1. Valdemar Rørdam, interview, *Berlingske Tidende,* 16 May 1934.

2. Ibid.

3. Lewis Gannett, "Books and Things," *New York Herald Tribune,* 9 April 1934: 13.

4. Jenny Ballou, "These Magic Tales Have an Air of Genius," *New York Herald Tribune Books,* 8 April 1934, VII: 3.

5. Howard Spring, *Evening Standard,* 6 Sept. 1934.

6. Gerald Gould, *Observer,* 9 Sept. 1934.

7. Scap, "Hyldest til Isak Dinesen," *Politiken,* 3 Dec. 1935; and Mario Grut, "Trana i sparvedansen," *Aftonbladet,* 13 Oct. 1958.

8. Frederik Schyberg, "Isak Dinesens, alias, Baronesse Blixen-Fineckes *Syv fantastiske Fortællinger,*" *Berlingske Tidende,* 25 Nov. 1935.

9. Svend Borberg, "Isak Dinesen-Karen Blixen," *Politiken,* 9 March 1936.

10. Vidi, interview, *Politiken,* 1 May 1934.

11. Ibid.

12. Susan Hardy Aiken, *Isak Dinesen and the Engendering of Narrative* (Chicago: University of Chicago Press, 1990), 70.

13. William Maxwell, "Suffused with a Melancholy Light," *New York Times Book Review,* 9 May 1943: 2.

14. Curtis Cate, "Isak Dinesen," *Atlantic Monthly,* December 1959, 153.

15. Eric O. Johannesson, *The World of Isak Dinesen* (Seattle: University of Washington Press, 1961), 28.

16. Sibyl James, "Gothic Transformations: Isak Dinesen and the Gothic," in *The Female Gothic,* ed. Juliann E. Fleenor (Montreal: Eden Press, 1983), 138-52.

17. Vidi, interview, *Politiken,* 1 May 1934.

18. Eric O. Johannesson, "Isak Dinesen, Søren Kierkegaard, and the Present Age," *Books Abroad,* winter 1962, 20-24.

19. Johannesson, *The World of Isak Dinesen,* 29.

20. George C. Schoolfield pointed out to me that another text along similar lines is Aino Kallas's (1878-1956) *Sudenmorsian* (1928), which was translated into English as *The Wolf's Bride* (1930), and was widely reviewed. In that tale, a forester's wife turns into a wolf.

21. Hans Brix, *Karen Blixens Eventyr* (Copenhagen: Gyldendal, 1949), 65.

22. Pointed out to me by George C. Schoolfield.

23. Bernhard Severin Ingemann, *Samlede Skrifter,* vol. 12 (Copenhagen: C. A. Reitzels Forlag, 1872), 208.

24. Ibid.

25. Robert Langbaum, *Isak Dinesen's Art: The Gayety of Vision* (Chicago: University of Chicago Press, 1975), 88.

26. Marianne Juhl and Bo Hakon Jørgensen, *Dianas Hævn* (Odense: Odense Universitetsforlag, 1981), 49.

27. William Mishler, "Parents and Children, Brothers and Sisters in Isak Dinesen's 'The Monkey,'" *Scandinavian Studies* 57, no. 4 (autumn 1985): 425.

28. Dag Heede, "Gender Trouble in Isak Dinesen's 'The Monkey,'" in *Karen Blixen—Out of Denmark: Papers from a Colloquium at the Karen Blixen Museum, April 1997* (Copenhagen, 1998), 116.

29. Ibid., 110.

30. Ibid., 112.

31. Mishler, "Parents and Children," 426.

32. Annelies van Hees, "Hemmeligheder i Karen Blixens 'Aben,'" *Edda,* 1984, no. 1: 9-24.

33. Mishler, "Parents and Children," 433; Robert S. Phillips, "Dinesen's 'Monkey' and McCuller's 'Ballad': A Study in Literary Affinity," *Studies in Short Fiction* 1 (1963-64): 73.

34. Robin Lyndenberg, "Against the Law of Gravity: Female Adolescence in Isak Dinesen's *Seven Gothic Tales,*" *Modern Fiction Studies* 24, no. 4 (winter 1978-79): 523.

35. Van Hees, "Hemmeligheder," 16.

36. Grethe F. Rostbøll, *Længslens vingeslag* (Copenhagen: Gyldendal, 1996), 55; Anders Westenholz, *Den glemte abe* (Copenhagen: Gyldendal, 1985), 109.

37. Brix, *Eventyr,* 69.

38. Langbaum, *Gayety of Vision,* 88.

39. Juhl and Jørgensen, *Dianas Hævn,* 51; Vibeke Schröder, *Selvrealisation og selvfortolkning i Karen Blixens forfatterskab* (Copenhagen: Gyldendal, 1979), 82.

40. Mishler, "Parents and Children," 449.

41. Van Hees, "Hemmeligheder," 22.

42. Heede, "Parents and Children," 121.

Abbreviations for Editions Used

AD   *Anecdotes of Destiny* and *Ehrengard.* New York: Vintage Books, 1993.

CV   *Carnival: Entertainments and Posthumous Tales.* Chicago: University of Chicago Press, 1977.

DG   *Daguerreotypes and Other Essays.* Chicago: University of Chicago Press, 1979.

KBD   *Karen Blixen i Danmark: Breve, 1931-1962.* 2 vols. Edited by Frans Lasson and Tom Engelbrecht. Copenhagen: Gyldendal, 1996.

LA   *Letters from Africa, 1914-1931.* Translated by Anne Born; Edited by Frans Lasson. Chicago: University of Chicago Press, 1981.

LT   *Last Tales.* New York: Vintage Books, 1991.

MU   *Karen Blixen Mindeudgave.* 7 vols. Copenhagen: Gyldendal, 1964.

OA	*Out of Africa and Shadows on the Grass.* New York: Vintage Books, 1989.
OC	*Osceola.* Copenhagen: Gyldendal, 1962.
OMM	*On Modern Marriage and Other Observations.* New York: St. Martin's Press, 1986.
SGT	*Seven Gothic Tales.* New York: Vintage Books, 1991.
WT	*Winter's Tales.* New York: Vintage Books, 1993.

FURTHER READING

Biographies

Migel, Parmenia. *Titania: The Biography of Isak Dinesen.* New York: Random House, 1967, 325 p.

Offers a balanced view of Dinesen's life.

Thurman, Judith. *Isak Dinesen: The Life of a Storyteller.* New York: Picador USA, 1995, 512 p.

Provides a detailed study of Dinesen's life.

Criticism

Aiken, Susan Hardy. "Gothic Cryptographies." In *Isak Dinesen and the Engendering of Narrative,* pp. 67-83. Chicago: University of Chicago Press, 1990.

Examines the ways in which Dinesen uses Gothic conventions to explore "the notions of writing and sexual difference" in her works.

Palevsky, Joan. "Tales of the Past." *Books West* 1, no. 7 (1977): 20-36.

Discusses Dinesen's ease in depicting mysterious characters and distant worlds in her fiction, as evidenced in the collection Carnival: Entertainments and Posthumous Tales.

Stoddart, Helen. "Isak Dinesen and the Fiction of Gothic Gravity." In *Modern Gothic: A Reader,* edited and with an introduction by Victor Sage and Allan Lloyd Smith, pp. 81-8. Manchester: Manchester University Press, 1996.

Explores the themes of storytelling as well as weightlessness and gravity in Dinesen's Seven Gothic Tales.

OTHER SOURCES FROM GALE:

Additional coverage of Dinesen's life and career is contained in the following sources published by Thomson Gale: *Contemporary Authors,* Vols. 25-28; *Contemporary Authors New Revision Series,* Vols. 22, 50; *Contemporary Authors Permanent Series,* Vol. 2; *Contemporary Literary Criticism,* Vols. 10, 29, 95; *Dictionary of Literary Biography,* Vol. 214; *DISCovering Authors 3.0; Encyclopedia of World Literature in the 20th Century,* Ed. 3; *European Writers,* Vol. 10; *Exploring Short Stories; Feminist Writers; Literary Movements for Students,* Vol. 1; *Literature and Its Times,* Vol. 3; *Literature Resource Center; Major 20th-Century Writers,* Eds. 1, 2; *Nonfiction Classics for Students,* Vol. 2; *Novels for Students,* Vol. 9; *Reference Guide to Short Fiction,* Ed. 2; *Reference Guide to World Literature,* Eds. 2, 3; *St. James Guide to Horror, Ghost & Gothic Writers; Short Stories for Students,* Vols. 3, 6, 13, 20; *Short Story Criticism,* Vols. 7, 75; *Something about the Author,* Vol. 44; and *World Literature and Its Times,* Vol. 2.

DAPHNE DU MAURIER

(1907 - 1989)

English novelist, playwright, nonfiction writer, and editor.

Regarded by many critics as a natural storyteller who made effective use of melodrama, du Maurier is best known for her Gothic novels and short stories. Unaffected by the literary fashions of her day, she wrote simple narratives that appealed to the average reader's love of adventure, fantasy, sensuality, and mystery. Perhaps best known for the Gothic novel *Rebecca* (1938), her writings have been extremely popular, and many have been adapted for film and television.

BIOGRAPHICAL INFORMATION

Du Maurier was born in London to a family whose members had been successful in arts and entertainment. Her father was a matinee idol and theater manager, and her grandfather was an artist for *Punch* and the author of several novels. Du Maurier was privately educated, and her youth was a swirl of yachting and skiing parties and trips abroad with wealthy friends. Her career as a novelist began on a visit to Cornwall when she was twenty. According to Margaret Forster (see Further Reading), du Maurier "was one of those writers in whom the right place releases a certain sort of psychic energy. . . . Cornwall, with its wild seas

and rocky coastline, its mists and moors, answered some deep longing inside her." She eventually settled there, and it became the setting of some her best-known stories. Much of her time was spent in Menabilly, a manor house in Cornwall that was the inspiration for Manderley, the location of her most famous novel, *Rebecca.* Du Maurier's earliest published works, articles and short stories, appeared primarily in women's magazines. She published her first novel, *The Loving Spirit,* in 1931. That work was followed by a number of novels and several collections of short stories, the first of which, *The Apple Tree: A Short Novel and Some Stories,* appeared in 1952. She died in 1989 at the age of eighty-one.

MAJOR WORKS

In her long career as a writer du Maurier produced nineteen novels, five volumes of short stories, two plays, and other writings. According to critics, most of her fiction can be classified as either cloak-and-dagger romances or Gothic novels. Like her acknowledged master, Robert Louis Stevenson, du Maurier wrote fantasies involving pirates, smuggling, and ladies in distress. Yet du Maurier preferred to be thought of as an author of mystery and suspense. *Rebecca* is the story of a woman who feels a sense of competition with her husband's first wife, who died under mysterious circumstances. In the opinion of many reviewers, it is an interesting psychological study of a young woman married to an older man, as well as a gripping Gothic novel that includes murder, violence, and a mysterious, haunted mansion. In her short story "The Birds" (1959) du Maurier creates a nightmare world in which great flocks of birds inexplicably attack and kill humans. The work was made into a popular motion picture directed by Alfred Hitchcock. "Don't Look Now" (1971), a macabre tale about an English couple in Venice who receive visions of the future, has been described as compelling and suspenseful; it was adapted as a film that, in the words of Pauline Kael (see Further Reading), "is the fanciest, most carefully assembled Gothic enigma yet put on the screen."

CRITICAL RECEPTION

In spite of her popularity, du Maurier has never won the full approval of the literary establishment. Many critics find her prose clear but uninteresting and deplore what they perceive as a lack of symbolism or imagery in her books. According to some, du Maurier wrote mostly on the surface, only rarely probing the psychological depths of her characters, and her plots seem conventional or contrived. Other commentators, however, have praised her works as imaginative and evocative, lauding her ability to create suspense and atmosphere. Richard Kelly (see Further Reading) described *Rebecca* as "the first major Gothic romance in the twentieth century and perhaps the finest written to this day." He pointed out that *Rebecca* includes many key components of Gothic romances, including "a mysterious and haunting mansion, violence, murder, a sinister villain, sexual passion, a spectacular fire, brooding landscapes, and a version of the madwoman in the attic." Sylvia Berkman assessed du Maurier as a "specialist in horror," noting that "her creative intelligence is resourceful, her command of eerie atmosphere persuasive and precise, her sense of shock-timing exceptionally skilled." Even du Maurier's detractors acknowledge her ability to create fantasy worlds that transport readers out of their daily existence and into places of romance and adventure.

PRINCIPAL WORKS

The Loving Spirit (novel) 1931

I'll Never Be Young Again (novel) 1932

The Progress of Julius (novel) 1933

Gerald: A Portrait (biography) 1934

Jamaica Inn (novel) 1936

The du Mauriers (family history and biography) 1937

Rebecca (novel) 1938

Come Wind, Come Weather (short stories) 1940

Rebecca [adaptor; from her novel] (play) 1940

Frenchman's Creek (novel) 1941

Hungry Hill (novel) 1943

The Years Between (play) 1944

The King's General (novel) 1946

September Tide (play) 1948

The Parasites (novel) 1949

My Cousin Rachel (novel) 1951

The Apple Tree: A Short Novel, and Some Stories (novella and short stories) 1952; also published as *Kiss Me Again, Stranger: A Collection of Eight Stories, Long and Short*, 1953; and as *The Birds, and Other Stories*, 1977

Mary Anne (fictionalized biography) 1954

The Scapegoat (novel) 1957

The Breaking Point (short stories) 1959; also published as *The Blue Lenses, and Other Stories*, 1970

Early Stories (short stories) 1959

The Infernal World of Branwell Brontë (biography) 1960

Castle d'Or [with Arthur Quiller-Couch] (novel) 1962

The Glass-Blowers (novel) 1963

The Flight of the Falcon (novel) 1965

The House on the Strand (novel) 1969

Don't Look Now (short stories) 1971; also published as *Not after Midnight*, 1971

Rule Britannia (novel) 1972

Echoes from the Macabre: Selected Stories (short stories) 1976

Myself When Young: The Shaping of a Writer (autobiography) 1977; also published as *Growing Pains: The Shaping of a Writer*, 1977

The Rendezvous, and Other Stories (short stories) 1980

Letters from Menabilly: Portrait of a Friendship (letters) 1994

DAPHNE DU MAURIER (NOVEL DATE 1938)

SOURCE: du Maurier, Daphne. "Chapter 1." In *Rebecca*. 1938. Reissue edition, pp. 1-4. New York: Avon Books, 1994.

The following excerpt comprises the first chapter of Rebecca, *which was first published in 1938.*

Last night I dreamt I went to Manderley again. It seemed to me I stood by the iron gate leading to the drive, and for a while I could not enter, for the way was barred to me. There was a padlock and a chain upon the gate. I called in my dream to the lodge-keeper, and had no answer, and peering closer through the rusted spokes of the gate I saw that the lodge was uninhabited.

No smoke came from the chimney, and the little lattice windows gaped forlorn. Then, like all dreamers, I was possessed of a sudden with supernatural powers and passed like a spirit through the barrier before me. The drive wound away in front of me, twisting and turning as it had always done, but as I advanced I was aware that a change had come upon it; it was narrow and unkept, not the drive that we had known. At first I was puzzled and did not understand, and it was only when I bent my head to avoid the low swinging branch of a tree that I realised what had happened. Nature had come into her own again and, little by little, in her stealthy, insidious way had encroached upon the drive with long tenacious fingers. The woods, always a menace even in the past, had triumphed in the end. They crowded, dark and uncontrolled, to the borders of the drive. The beeches with white, naked limbs leant close to one another, their branches intermingled in a strange embrace, making a vault above my head like the archway of a church. And there were other trees as well, trees that I did not recognise, squat oaks and tortured elms that straggled cheek by jowl with the beeches, and had thrust themselves out of the quiet earth, along with monster shrubs and plants, none of which I remembered.

The drive was a ribbon now, a thread of its former self, with gravel surface gone, and choked with grass and moss. The trees had thrown out low branches, making an impediment to progress; the gnarled roots looked like skeleton claws. Scattered here and again amongst this jungle growth I would recognise shrubs that had been land-marks in our time, things of culture and of grace, hydrangeas whose blue heads had been famous. No hand had checked their progress, and they had gone native now, rearing to monster height without a bloom, black and ugly as the nameless parasites that grew beside them.

On and on, now east, now west, wound the poor thread that once had been our drive. Sometimes I thought it lost, but it appeared again, beneath a fallen tree perhaps or struggling on the other side of a muddied ditch created by the winter rains. I had not thought the way so long. Surely the miles had multiplied, even as the trees had done, and this path led but to a labyrinth, some choked wilderness, and not to the house at all. I came upon it suddenly; the approach masked by the unnatural growth of a vast shrub that spread in all directions, and I stood, my heart thumping in my breast, the strange prick of tears behind my eyes.

There was Manderley, our Manderley, secretive and silent as it had always been, the grey stone shining in the moonlight of my dream, the mullioned windows reflecting the green lawns and the terrace. Time could not wreck the perfect symmetry of those walls, not the site itself, a jewel in the hollow of a hand.

The terrace sloped to the lawns, and the lawns stretched to the sea, and turning I could see the sheet of silver, placid under the moon, like a lake undisturbed by wind or storm. No waves would come to ruffle this dream water, and no bulk of cloud, wind-driven from the west, obscure the clarity of this pale sky. I turned again to the house, and though it stood inviolate, untouched, as though we ourselves had left but yesterday, I saw that the garden had obeyed the jungle law, even as the woods had done. The rhododendrons stood fifty feet high, twisted and entwined with bracken, and they had entered into alien marriage with a host of nameless shrubs, poor, bastard things that clung about their roots as though conscious of their spurious origin. A lilac had mated with a copper beech, and to bind them yet more closely to one another the malevolent ivy, always an enemy to grace, had thrown her tendrils about the pair and made them prisoners. Ivy held prior place in this lost garden, the long strands crept across the lawns, and soon would encroach upon the house itself. There was another plant too, some halfbreed from the woods, whose seed had been scattered long ago beneath the trees and then forgotten, and now, marching in unison with the ivy, thrust its ugly form like a giant rhubarb towards the soft grass where the daffodils had blown.

Nettles were everywhere, the van-guard of the army. They choked the terrace, they sprawled about the paths, they leant, vulgar and lanky, against the very windows of the house. They made indifferent sentinels, for in many places their ranks had been broken by the rhubarb plant, and they lay with crumpled heads and listless stems, making a pathway for the rabbits. I left the drive and went on to the terrace, for the nettles were no barrier to me, a dreamer, I walked enchanted, and nothing held me back.

Moonlight can play odd tricks upon the fancy, even upon a dreamer's fancy. As I stood there, hushed and still, I could swear that the house was not an empty shell but lived and breathed as it had lived before.

Light came from the windows, the curtains blew softly in the night air, and there, in the library, the door would stand half open as we had left it, with my handkerchief on the table beside the bowl of autumn roses.

The room would bear witness to our presence. The little heap of library books marked ready to return, and the discarded copy of *The Times*. Ashtrays, with the stub of a cigarette; cushions, with the imprint of our heads upon them, lolling in the chairs; the charred embers of our log fire still smouldering against the morning. And Jasper, dear Jasper, with his soulful eyes and great, sagging jowl, would be stretched upon the floor, his tail a-thump when he heard his master's footsteps.

A cloud, hitherto unseen, came upon the moon, and hovered an instant like a dark hand before a face. The illusion went with it, and the lights in the windows were extinguished. I looked upon a desolate shell, soulless at last, unhaunted, with no whisper of the past about its staring walls.

The house was a sepulchre, our fear and suffering lay buried in the ruins. There would be no resurrection. When I thought of Manderley in my waking hours I would not be bitter. I should think of it as it might have been, could I have lived there without fear. I should remember the rose-garden in summer, and the birds that sang at dawn. Tea under the chestnut tree, and the murmur of the sea coming up to us from the lawns below.

I would think of the blown lilac, and the Happy Valley. These things were permanent, they could not be dissolved. They were memories that cannot hurt. All this I resolved in my dream, while the clouds lay across the face of the moon, for like most sleepers I knew that I dreamed. In reality I lay many hundred miles away in an alien land, and would wake, before many seconds had passed,

in the bare little hotel bedroom, comforting in its very lack of atmosphere. I would sigh a moment, stretch myself and turn, and opening my eyes, be bewildered at that glittering sun, that hard, clean sky, so different from the soft moonlight of my dream. The day would lie before us both, long no doubt, and uneventful, but fraught with a certain stillness, a dear tranquility we had not known before. We would not talk of Manderley, I would not tell my dream. For Manderley was ours no longer. Manderley was no more.

TITLE COMMENTARY

Kiss Me Again, Stranger

JOHN BARKHAM (REVIEW DATE 8 MARCH 1953)

SOURCE: Barkham, John. "The Macabre and the Unexpected." *New York Times Book Review* (8 March 1953): 5.

In the following review, Barkham praises du Maurier's storytelling ability in Kiss Me Again, Stranger.

In her short stories, as in her novels, Daphne du Maurier is a firm believer in keeping her readers on tenterhooks. She cannot dazzle them with her prose or excite them with her imagination, but at least she baffles them with her mysteries. And baffle them she does, over and over again in this book [*Kiss Me Again, Stranger*]. Guessing the identity of du Maurier murderers is still likely to remain a favorite indoor sport this spring.

These eight tales are the mixture as before. All lean to the macabre, the strange, the unexplained. None of them is bad, and several are very good indeed. No wraiths or clanking ghosts, you understand, but subtle emanations, like a dying tree that bursts ominously into bloom, or a wife who falls under the spell of the mountains. In every case Miss du Maurier painstakingly creates her atmosphere before she begins spinning her web. No fleeting moods or impressions here: the style is deliberate, the pace leisurely, and the stories hold up as stories.

One is a masterpiece of horror. Twenty years ago an Australian named Carl Stephenson wrote a superb short story, "Leningen and the Ants," in which he described a South American planter's epic struggle against a column of jungle ants. It was an adventure you could not forget. Miss du Maurier has matched it with a story in the same genre. "**The Birds**" is set on a peaceful English farm. Its theme? The birds of the world have suddenly and inexplicably turned predatory, and all over the earth have begun to peck, scratch and tear human beings to death. We watch the attack on the farm. Like Leningen, farmer Nat Hocken fights a hair-raising battle against the winged warriors that darken the sky.

Two of the tales are straight studies in crime. There is the elegant marquise who dallies with a young photographer and pushes him over a cliff, only to find herself trapped through a revealing portrait, a piece of very neat plotting. Better still is "**The Motive**," a skillful unraveling of a seemingly purposeless suicide. Here Miss du Maurier does what J. B. Priestley did so well in his "Dangerous Corner." She opens with a motiveless death, then gradually leads the reader deeper and deeper into the mystery, until at last all the jigsaw pieces fall into place. This kind of progressive revelation requires real craftsmanship.

Have you noticed how often the agent of mystery or evil in a du Maurier story is a woman? Du Maurier women have been bewitching and bewildering their simple-minded menfolk for years, and in these stories they are still at it. The girl who lures a youth into a cemetery, the marquise who kills her lover, the nagging wife who haunts by way of a tree—these are *femmes fatales* who toy with their men and then get them, one way or another. They also leave this reviewer with some interesting theories as to the author's artistic motivations.

In these days of shiny-knobbed science fiction, the old-fashioned story of the supernatural, which used to chill the kids and keep old men from the chimney corner, is becoming somthing of a rarity. More's the pity. Miss du Maurier can still write them in the grand tradition. Try these tales and see how they dwarf those rockets and bug-eyed monsters.

SYLVIA BERKMAN (REVIEW DATE 15 MARCH 1953)

SOURCE: Berkman, Sylvia. "A Skilled Hand Weaves a Net of Horror." *New York Herald Tribune Book Review* 29, no. 31 (15 March 1953): 4.

In the following review of Kiss Me Again, Stranger, *Berkman lauds du Maurier as a "seasoned" and "skilled" author of horror and suspense literature.*

Daphne du Maurier is a specialist in horror. Her creative intelligence is resourceful, her command of eerie atmosphere persuasive and precise,

her sense of shock-timing exceptionally skilled. In this collection of eight stories (of which all but two are very long) she explores horror in a variety of forms; in the macabre, in the psychologically deranged, in the supernatural, in the fantastic, most painfully of all, in the sheer cruelty of human beings in interrelationship. Yet on the whole the volume offers absorbing rather than oppressive reading because chiefly one's intellect is engaged; the emotional content remains subordinate. Broadly speaking, for the most part these are stories of detection as well, with the contributing elements of excitation, suspense, and climax manipulated with a seasoned hand.

Miss du Maurier is most successful. I believe (as most of us are) when her intentions are unmixed. *Kiss Me Again, Stranger,* the title story, adaptly marshals the ingredients best suited to her abilities. Here in a trim, fluently moving narrative she developed an incident in war-torn London, with no purpose beyond the immediate recounting of a sad and grisly tale. A young mechanic, a simple, sensitive, likable good chap, attracted by a pretty usherette at a cinema palace, joins her on her bus ride home, to be led, bewildered, into a cemetery, where her conduct baffles him, to say the least. The girl, so gentle, wisful, languorous, and sleepy, turns out to be psychopathically obsessed, with a vindicative animus against members of the R. A. F. The summary is unjust, for Miss du Maurier forcibly anchors her story in a strange lonely graveyard atmosphere, with night rain falling cold and dreary on the flat tombs, which both reflects and reinforces the mortal impairment of the young girl's nature and the destruction of the young man's hopes, in a charnel world dislocated by the larger horror of war.

In *Kiss Me Again, Stranger,* all separate aspects of the narrative fuse. "**The Birds**," however, essentially a far more powerful story, is marred by unresolved duality of intent. Slowly, with intensifying accurate detail, Miss du Maurier builds up her account of the massed attack of the starving winter birds on humankind, the familiar little land birds, the battalions of gulls bearing in rank upon rank from the sea, the murderous predatory birds of prey descending with ferocious beaks and talons to rip, rend, batter and kill. The struggle involved is the ancient struggle of man against the forces of nature, Robinson Crusoe's struggle to overcome an elemental adversary through cunning, logic, and wit. The turning of this material also into a political fable, with the overt references to control from Russia and aid from America, to my mind dissipates the full impact of a stark and terrifying tale.

"**Monte Verità**" also clothes parable in an outer aspect of realism, this time for the statement of philosophical axiom: that the residence of truth is harsh, lonely and austere, by an ascent granted only to few, but its attainment the attainment of richest beatitude, even though in the general community below the few spirits who achieve the lofty summit are persecuted through hatred and fear. Again Miss du Maurier is most successful in the establishment of other-worldly atmosphere, the creation of impressive scene, particularly of the clear symbolic peaks of Monte Verità rising pure and unadorned against the sky. Perhaps this kind of story requires a special attitude on the part of the author—E. M. Forster's confident assumption that the dryad *is* in the tree, if only one looks hard enough; too heavy a grounding in realistic detail can arouse realistic questioning. Here the factual narration of events, in which Anna, forsaking worldly attachments enters the citadel on the heights of Monte Verità, and the subsequent development of the two men who love her, again imposes disunity. Yet "**Monte Verità**" contains an abundance of integrated incident to sustain the interest; one surely wants to know the end.

Equally, each of the stories exerts that claim: one surely wants to know the end. "**The Split Second**," with its investigation of the intertemporal in the instant of death, represents the author at her most skillful, weaving a logical, firm, constantly tautening web of mystification and suspense. "**The Little Photographer**," recounting the divertissement of a bored, vain, beautiful marquise with a crippled shopkeeper, in part recalls Thomas Mann's "Little Herr Friedemann"; but Miss du Maurier has given the denouement a characteristic turn (M. Paul is not idly cast as a photographer; he had a way of snapping pictures of his lady after their dalliance in the bracken), and the story ends with a sinister good chill.

Miss du Maurier is not primarily concerned with character. Her figures are presented with swift unhesitating strokes; through them a fairly complicated history unfolds. Yet every account of human action contains its residue of human experience; and Miss du Maurier's main themes, if seriously regarded, are neither haphazard nor trivial: again and again she returns to the consideration of our human predicament, to frustration, destruction, loss, betrayal, and needless suffering, Joyce's themes of the "Dubliners," conveyed through the obverse method of a decided empha-

sis on plot. In general in this volume complexities of plot disinfect horror to a pungent and provocative spice.

Rebecca

AVRIL HORNER AND SUE ZLOSNIK (ESSAY DATE 2000)

SOURCE: Horner, Avril, and Sue Zlosnik. "Daphne du Maurier and Gothic Signatures: Rebecca as Vamp(ire)." In *Body Matters: Feminism, Textuality, Corporeality,* edited and with an introduction by Avril Horner and Angela Keane, pp. 209-22. Manchester: Manchester University Press, 2000.

In the following essay, Horner and Zlosnik examine the Gothic and symbolic significance of du Maurier's representation of the title character in Rebecca.

Gothic fiction over the last two hundred years has given us characters such as Dracula and Frankenstein's monster who have passed into popular culture and taken on an almost mythic dimension (Day 1985: 3). *Rebecca,* Daphne du Maurier's most famous novel, has given us one such character. This essay will attempt to retrieve Rebecca's textual Gothic ancestry and relate it to a discussion of the destabilising nature of her absent/present body and its status as ghostly yet corporeal trace. In particular, it will explore the significance of signature as bodily trace in relation to the writing identities of both Rebecca and her creator, Daphne du Maurier.

In what is still probably the most memorable representation of *Rebecca* (published in 1938), Hitchock's film (made in 1940) retains the novel's Gothic emphasis. However, Alison Light's influential reading of the novel has resulted in an argument centred on the class dynamics of the text; this sees the narrator's bourgeois feminine subjectivity as both inflected and threatened by that of a wayward, aristocratic Rebecca who enjoys a freedom of self-expression and lifestyle denied the timid second wife of Maxim de Winter (Light 1984). Whilst providing some invaluable insights, this reading has necessitated a fairly free, and sometimes inaccurate, portrayal of the social class of both Rebecca and her creator.[1] In fact, Rebecca's social class is not entirely clear from the novel. Indeed, Michelle A. Massé, in speculating that Rebecca was married for her money, opens up the possibility that her marriage to Maximilian de Winter combined his aristocratic status with her *nouveau riche* wealth and was thus a marriage of expediency for both parties (as she points out, 'Manderley's splendor is very recent' (Massé 1992:

181)). Nor is it accurate to describe du Maurier herself as 'aristocratic': her father's title came with a knighthood earned in 1922 and her own title of 'Lady Browning' derived from her marriage to Major 'Boy' Browning. Moreover, such an approach tends to shift du Maurier's novel out of the Gothic paradigm: for example, relating the writing of **Rebecca** to the rise of the love-story during the inter-war period, Light describes the novel as 'a thriller or murder story . . . as well as a love-story' (Light 1991: 163). A subsidiary effect of such categorisations has been to define Rebecca as a vamp or a *femme fatale*; indeed Light refers to du Maurier as finding 'her scarlet woman irresistible' (Light 1991: 157).

Yet the term '*femme fatale*' is not simply a sign of aristocratic femininity; there are racial and gendered positions embedded in the term which are brought to light when we examine the close but distinct etymological and cultural relationship between the words '*femme fatale*', 'vamp' and 'vampire'. The first phrase, imported from the French in 1912, according to the *Oxford English Dictionary*, linguistically 'otherises' a particular type of woman as a source of threat. The *femme fatale* has, of course, a long cultural history which goes back to Jezebel, Salome and Cleopatra, but she does not become prominent in art and literature until the late nineteenth century when she emerges, according to Mary Ann Doane, as a response to an industrialised and rapidly changing society in which women were resisting Victorian models of femininity (Doane 1991: 1-2). She is associated, according to Doane, with distinct characteristics. She is never really what she seems to be; her rather morbid sexuality connects her beauty with barrenness, lack of production, death and obliteration; because her power situates the *femme fatale* as evil, she is invariably punished or killed (often by a man); finally, she is often associated with a sexually ambiguous identity, in so far as she is frequently linked with androgyny, bisexuality and/or lesbianism. Rebecca manifests all of these characteristics. She is not what she seems to be: the outward conformity of the sophisticated chatelaine figure, adored by the Cornish community, hides a secret self who behaves differently in London and within the privacy of her boat house. Her beauty is certainly associated with barrenness and death. She is indeed perceived as evil by Maxim and is punished accordingly by him. Finally, her sexual identity is ambiguous; the text makes it clear that she has committed adultery but also hints that she and Mrs Danvers have been lesbian lovers. More broadly, she destabilises cur-

rent notions of gender: seen through Mrs Danvers's eyes, Rebecca signifies both femininity and masculinity. On the one hand, the housekeeper emphasises her beauty, sensuality and femininity by endowing her fine clothes with a metonymic significance. On the other hand, she stresses Rebecca's power and masculinity: what she loved in Rebecca, it seems, was her strength, her courage and her 'spirit', which she associates with masculinity: 'She ought to have been a boy, I often told her that' (du Maurier [1938] 1992: 253). At the level of plot, then, Rebecca is presented, it would seem, as a classic *femme fatale* figure.

The discourses of film and literature invariably use the phrase '*femme fatale*' interchangeably with the word 'vamp'.[2] Yet 'vamp' is defined by the OED as a Jezebel figure who is deliberately destructive, whereas the *femme fatale* is often perceived as having 'power *despite herself*' (Doane 1991: 2). A few critics, however, do perceive this distinction. Pierre Leprohon, for example, in his book *The Italian Cinema,* suggests that the *femme fatale* and the vamp are quite different, the latter being connected with a conscious desire to destroy: she is, he argues, 'deliberately devastating, the woman who lives off her victims' misfortunes, a kind of vampire'. In contrast, 'the fate of the *femme fatale* is often as dreadful as that of her lovers, and this makes her even more appealing' (cited in Doane 1991: 127). Interestingly, the *OED* suggests that the word 'vamp' (first used in this sense in 1918 and quite distinct from to 'vamp' on a piano, which has a different etymology) does indeed derive from the word 'vampire'. This slippage between the words 'vampire' and 'vamp' is attributed by several critics to a *fin-de-siècle* anxiety concerning the shifting status of women. For example, Bram Dijkstra has noted that '[b]y 1900 the vampire had come to represent woman as the personification of everything negative that linked sex, ownership, and money' (Dijkstra 1986: 351); according to Alexandra Warwick, the changing representation of the female vampire in late nineteenth-century texts reflected a growing anxiety about the 'masculinisation' of women in their transition from angels of the hearth to 'wandering' New Women (Warwick 1995: 202-20).[3] The actual threats embodied in real women, then, resulted in the female vampire being culturally transmuted into the vamp; by the early twentieth century the sinister polyvalency of the former had become translated into the sexual threat of the latter.

The corporeal code of the vamp is, of course, immediately recognisable: invariably her direct gaze emanates from a slender, nubile body; she usually has dark hair, either in abundance or cut very short, so that it sits like a cap on her head; above all, her presence is strongly erotic. Lulu, in G.W. Pabst's famous 1929 film *Pandora's Box,* played by Louise Brooks, was portrayed in just such a way. Du Maurier's Rebecca, when she *is* made visible in film or television adaptations, is often rendered as the classic vamp.[4] We are not claiming that this is a misrepresentation: du Maurier's famous novel, set in the mid-twenties according to its author (du Maurier [1981] 1993: 10), certainly draws on late nineteenth- and early twentieth-century constructions of the independent and sexually active woman as vamp. Yet the corporeal charisma so important in portrayals of the 'vamp' is communicated in the novel only through traces of Rebecca's body and the things connected with her: her scent, her clothes, the rhododendrons, her signature, her script. In du Maurier's text, it is, paradoxically, the very *absence*

of Rebecca that is used to denote so powerfully the *presence* of adult female sexuality. Rebecca, then, is *ghost* as well as vamp. Du Maurier's work is, after all, a Gothic novel, not a *film noir*; the threatening woman is 'otherised' not only through physical difference, but also through the supernatural. Not surprisingly, then, we find du Maurier subtly drawing on the vampiric tradition in her creation of Rebecca and this, we suggest, contributes much to the evocation of the uncanny in the novel. However, we shall argue that the cultural slippages between the terms 'vamp', 'vampire' and '*femme fatale*' are reflected not only in the unstable status of Rebecca's body but also by Maurier's construction of a writing persona which, in flight from the feminine and the corporeal, embraces the masculine and the disembodied.

Like those of the vampiric body, the status and whereabouts of Rebecca's corpse are problematic. When her boat is raised and a body is found in it, doubt is cast upon the identity of the body in the crypt. Rebecca's body—to use Tania Modleski's words—'becomes the site of a bizarre fort/da game'[5] (Modleski 1988: 49). What Anne Williams describes as 'that intensely Gothic phenomenon, the sight of a worm-eaten corpse' (Williams 1995: 73), is denied the reader: instead, various characters present us with vivid but different narratives of watery disintegration. So Rebecca's corpse is 'absent' for much of the novel yet remains insistently and disturbingly present in the imaginations of these characters—just as her absent body remains insistently 'alive' for the narrator, whose continual association of Rebecca with the blood-red rhododendrons and headily scented azaleas of the Manderley estate evokes a charismatic female sexual presence for both herself and the reader. Yet the narrator's final thoughts on Rebecca's body link it not with water, but with dust:

> Ashes to ashes. Dust to dust. It seemed to me that Rebecca had no reality any more. She had crumbled away when they had found her on the cabin floor. It was not Rebecca who was lying in the crypt, it was dust. Only dust.
> (du Maurier [1938] 1992: 334)

Thus Rebecca's 'second' burial (which seeks literally to encrypt her ungovernable force) is associated with the end of Dracula, whose body crumbles to dust at the moment of death: 'It was like a miracle, but before our very eyes, and almost in the drawing of a breath, the whole body crumbled into dust and passed from our sight' (Stoker [1897] 1993: 484). The apparent finality of Rebecca's burial, however, is undercut by an earlier incident in which the narrator thought she had 'finally' destroyed Rebecca's writing (the inscription in the book of poems), only to find it resurfacing again and again at Manderley. The 'dust' that is Rebecca's body is no more final than the 'feathers of dust' of the burned fly-leaf or the ash scattered by the 'salt wind' of the novel's final line. Like the vampire, Rebecca seems able to reconstitute herself endlessly and, like the vampire, her corporeal status is unstable: she is neither visibly a body nor visibly a corpse.

Rebecca is also associated throughout the novel with several characteristics which, according to Ernest Jones, traditionally denote the vampiric body: facial pallor, plentiful hair and voracious sexual appetite (Jones [1991] 1992: 409). And like the vampire, she has to be 'killed' more than once: the plot's excessive, triple killing of Rebecca (she was shot; she had cancer; she drowned) echoes the folk belief that vampires must be 'killed' three times. Although Rebecca lacks the requisite fangs and only metaphorically sucks men dry, she can none the less be placed within Christopher Frayling's second category of vampires, that of the Fatal Woman who, according to Frayling, 'altered the whole direction of the vampire tale' from the mid-nineteenth century onwards: 'sexually aware, and sexually dominant . . . attractive and repellent at the same time', she is clearly symptomatic of a cultural anxiety concerning adult female sexuality (Frayling [1991] 1992: 68, 71-2). Seen in this light, Rebecca's literary lineage includes Prosper Mérimée's Carmen, Poe's Berenice, Gauthier's Clarimonde and Le Fanu's Countess Carmilla—not forgetting, of course, Charlotte Brontë's Bertha Mason, described in Chapter 25 of *Jane Eyre* as 'the foul German spectre—the Vampyre'. Rebecca may, then, be read not only as vamp but also as vampire: she is a clear descendant of the female demon lover who transmuted into the female vampire in mid- to late Victorian Gothic texts and into the vamp in twentieth-century cinema.

Like all vampire figures, Rebecca is associated with a transgressive, polymorphous sexuality. She is also, like all vampire figures, a figure of abjection. Recent critics of the Gothic have used Julia Kristeva's *Powers of Horror: An Essay on Abjection* ([1980] 1982) to explore how representations of the abject in certain texts relate to certain discourses and cultural values at a particular historical moment.[6] Kristeva's concept of the abject thereby becomes a concept which enables them to define how shared constructions of 'otherness' are predicated upon shared cultural values at specific times: by this logic, you may know a culture by what it 'throws off' or 'abjects'. But the figure of abjection in a *Gothic* text may, of course, be presented as simultaneously repellent *and* charismatic, thus allowing the reader to indulge in a transgressive redefinition of 'self'. This 'other' is also invariably the focus of more than one cultural anxiety and may therefore act as a vehicle of abjection in several ways. It is not surprising, then, to find that the sexual threat represented by Rebecca as 'vamp' is further inflected by the text's association of her with vampirism and 'Jewishness'. Rebecca was supposedly based on Jan Ricardo who was engaged to Major 'Boy' Browning before his marriage to du Maurier; she was a 'dark-haired, rather exotic young woman, beautiful but highly-strung', according to Margaret Forster (Forster 1993: 91). However, du Maurier's presentation of Maxim's first wife as a dangerous and beautiful dark-haired woman with an Hebraic name might well have been unconsciously influenced by the air of anti-semitisim prevalent in Europe during the 1930s. In this context, it is perhaps worth nothing that David Selznick, the producer of Hitchcock's film version of **Rebecca,** is reputed to have had misgivings about the film's title, commenting that it would not do 'unless it was made for the Palestine market' (Shallcross [1991] 1993: 69-70). As both Ken Gelder and Judith Halberstam have noted, the nineteenth-century vampire was often portrayed as having Jewish characteristics—the physical appearance, the often perverse desires and the unrooted, wandering nature of 'the Jew' (as then constructed) all being projected onto the vampire (Gelder 1994: 13-17; Halberstam 1995a: 86-106). Indeed, Judith Halberstam argues that 'the nineteenth-century discourse of anti-Semitism and the myth of the vampire share a kind of Gothic economy in their ability to condense many monstrous traits into one body' (Halberstam 1995a: 88). Many anxieties are written on the body of Rebecca, including that of the woman author whose social identity is transgressively inflected by her writing identity.

For it is Rebecca's signature and handwriting which constitute the metonymic representation of her body throughout the text, indelibly inscribing her presence. Certainly the semiotic of her script complicates our perception of her function in the novel. On the one hand, her writing—as we see it, for example, in the loving dedication to 'Max' and in the contents of the morning-room desk—is proof of her ability, during her life, to play an allotted role within the realm of 'everyday legality' and to masquerade effectively as a country-house hostess. Rebecca's writing initially appears to tell the tale of an ideal wife, loving towards her husband and the perfect hostess for his elegant country mansion. However, the script itself, which continually irrupts into the text, tells a different story, since it is also associated with a masculine strength and an indelible authority; as such it indicates a wayward, wilful quality that runs counter to Maxim's idea of the good wife. Moreover, it is sharply differentiated from that of the narrator who describes her own handwriting as 'cramped and unformed' (du Maurier [1938] 1992: 93) with all the intimations of immaturity and social inhibition that this suggests. This narrator connects Rebecca's 'curious', 'sloping' or 'slanting' script with a vibrant vitality: 'How alive her writing though, how full of force' (62). Always Rebecca's handwriting suggests supreme confidence and knowledge. In particular, the capital letter 'R', embroidered on the handkerchief the narrator finds in Rebecca's mackintosh and on Rebecca's nightdress case, takes on a runic force which derives from its powerful visual impact and its refusal to be destroyed. In this novel Rebecca surfaces most clearly through her signature, which uncannily inscribes the body's presence despite its absence through death. Above all, it is her autonomous energy, implicit in Rebecca's handwriting, which impresses itself on both the narrator and the reader. Thus, there is a duality in Rebecca's script, which seems to tell one story but which gives the lie to it in the actual appearance of the writing itself. The activity of writing is thereby seen to be implicated in the production of sexual subjectivity.

Yet, despite her accentuated difference from Rebecca, it is the timid and nameless young second wife who has been transformed into the older, wiser narrator of Rebecca's story. She has become empowered to do this, however, only by modifying her perception of Rebecca as 'other' and assimilating her autonomy. Her initial attempts to exorcise Rebecca's presence, through, for example, burning the fly-leaf in Maxim's book which contains her signature, are doomed to failure. Instead, what we see in the novel is a gradual identification between the narrator and Rebecca, quite literally enacted in the Manderley Ball scene when the narrator's appearance as Maxim's ancestress, Caroline de Winter, seems to raise Rebecca from the dead (even Maxim's sister, sensible Beatrice, says 'You stood there on the stairs, and for one ghastly moment I thought . . .' (225). Indeed, we learn at the beginning of the

novel that the (now older) narrator *has* finally acquired the confidence for which she envied Rebecca as a young woman: 'and confidence is a quality I prize, although it has come to me a little late in the day' (13). The conclusion must be that only with Rebecca 'really' dead can she write Rebecca's story, although it is only *through* Rebecca that she can write. Significantly, then, in the final dream of a novel haunted by disturbing dreams the narrator finds herself writing *as* Rebecca:

> I was writing letters in the morning-room. I was sending out invitations. I wrote them all myself with a thick black pen. But when I looked down to see what I had written it was not my small square handwriting at all, it was long, and slanting, with curious pointed strokes. I pushed the cards away from the blotter and hid them. I got up and went to the looking-glass. A face stared back at me that was not my own. It was very pale, very lovely, framed in a cloud of dark hair. The eyes narrowed and smiled. The lips parted. The face in the glass stared back at me and laughed. And I saw then that she was sitting on a chair before the dressing-table in her bedroom and Maxim was brushing her hair. He held her hair in his hands, and as he brushed it he wound it slowly into a thick rope. It twisted like a snake, and he took hold of it with both hands and smiled at Rebecca and put it round his neck.
>
> 'No', I screamed. 'No. no . . .'.
>
> (395-6)

Whereas the firing of Manderley reminds us of the burning of Thornfield and of a work which finally eliminates the 'other' woman, this dream perpetuates the psychic disruption which Rebecca signifies. Although the narrator harbours a distrust and fear of Rebecca's sexuality, communicated by the snake image,[7] the dream also reveals her unconscious identification *with* it. For much of the novel she has consciously wished to be the model wife and hostess she believed Rebecca to have been; yet the mirror image of the dream signals a further desire for identification with Rebecca's sexual and *textual* charisma.

This is because Rebecca, despite—or because of—her corporeal absence, embodies a dynamic multivalent alterity for the nameless narrator: she is adulteress, lesbian, bisexual, vampire, Jew. The fact that Rebecca's body shows traces of both Jewishness and vampirism indicates the essentially Gothic quality of the novel; for in the Gothic text perverse sexuality, as Judith Halberstam (citing Sander Gilman) notes, is inevitably 'ascribed to the sexuality of the Other' (Halberstam 1995: 68). In assimilating both psychological and corporeal aspects of Rebecca, the narrator implicitly rejects the social categorisations which separate the 'bad' from the 'good' woman. Furthermore, in absorbing the 'disembodied spirit' of Maxim's first wife, the narrator comes to embody aspects of Rebecca's power and self-confidence. Above all, she writes, and with the maturity and adult sexual identity implied by Rebecca's 'bold, slanting hand' rather than with the childish ingenuousness of her former self. Her signature and her text are thus haunted by that of another.

However, that phrase we have just used, 'disembodied spirit', is taken not from the novel, but from letters written by du Maurier in the 1940s. Here we wish to link the issue of Rebecca's signature and corporeal identity *within* the text with that of du Maurier as author *of* the text. As Margaret Forster's biography has revealed, Daphne du Maurier seemed to follow the lifestyle expected of women of her class, yet such conformity hid several unconventional relationships and a complex and conflicted sense of identity (Forster 1993). Furthermore, in spite of living an apparently happy life as wife, mother and successful novelist, du Maurier experienced a great deal of anxiety and ambivalence concerning her identity as a woman writer. For much of the time she felt that part of herself was a 'disembodied spirit', a phrase she uses in two separate letters to Ellen Doubleday, wife of her American publisher, Nelson Doubleday. She uses it first in a letter dated December 1947, which is written in a parodic fairy-tale manner, to describe what we would now call a sense of split subjectivity:

> And then the boy realised he had to grow up and not be a boy any longer, so he turned into a girl, and not an unattractive one at that, and the boy was locked in a box forever. D. du M. wrote her books, and had young men, and later a husband, and children, and a lover, and life was sometimes lovely and sometimes rather sad, but when she found Menabilly and lived in it alone, she opened up the box sometimes and let the phantom, who was neither girl nor boy but disembodied spirit, dance in the evening when there was no one to see.
>
> (Forster 1993: 222)

In a letter written to Ellen almost a year later in September 1948, reflecting on her husband's reliance on her money-earning capacity as a best-selling novelist, she uses the phrase in a slightly different way:

> I mean, really, women should not have careers. It's people like me who have careers who really have bitched up the old relationship between men and women. Women ought to be soft and gentle and dependent. Disembodied spirits like myself are all *wrong*.
>
> (Forster 1993: 235)

In the first letter, she describes a masculine dimension of her being which, while 'locked' away, undergoes a metamorphosis into the 'disembodied spirit' which is androgynous and suggestive (to her) of a more authentic 'self'. Such a creative spirit, associated as it is in this letter with her life at Menabilly, is intrinsic to her life as a writer. However, the second letter suggests that while acknowledging her career as that of author, she felt ill at ease as a successful *woman* writer in the wider world; this is confirmed by another letter to Ellen Doubleday written in October 1948, in which she confesses to seeing her work as having given her a 'masculine approach to life' (Forster 1993: 232). Later, having become intrigued by the work of Jung and Adler during the winter of 1954, she explains her 'disembodied' self by reference to Jung's vocabulary of duality and identifies her writing persona as having sprung from a repressed 'No. 2' masculine side. In a letter to her seventeen-year-old daughter in the same year she explains, 'When I get madly boyish No. 2 is in charge, and then, after a bit, the situation is reversed . . . No. 2 can come to the surface and be helpful . . . he certainly has a lot to do with my writing' (Forster 1993: 276). Thus du Maurier came to perceive her *writing* identity as masculine. While such a 'disembodied spirit' was containable, while it could be put back in the box, it could do no harm; when, however, du Maurier perceived it as taking over—when she referred to *herself* as the 'disembodied spirit'—then she believed it to be socially destructive. Arguably, it was this anxiety concerning the 'Other' contained within the 'self' which gave Jung's work particular resonance for her. Du Maurier's creation of Rebecca as the narrator's transgressive double can also be seen, then, as a manifestation of an anxiety concerning writing, identity and gender.[8]

Interestingly, Forster's biography and Oriel Malet's *Letters from Menabilly* (1993) provide evidence that in letters to friends du Maurier identified, at different points in her life, with both Rebecca and the narrator. For example, in a letter to Maureen Baker-Munton, written in 1957, du Maurier comments: 'I wrote as the second Mrs. de W. twenty-one years ago, with Rebecca a symbol of Jan. It could also be that . . . I—in Moper's dark mind—can be the symbol of Rebecca. The cottage on the beach could be my hut. Rebecca's lovers could be my books' (Forster 1993: 424). In these letters quoted by Forster, the narrator tends to be linked with du Maurier's social, 'feminine' identity and Rebecca with her creative writing persona, that 'No. 2' masculine 'self'. As we have established, this sense of the writing self as masculine 'Other' can be seen in the inscription of Rebecca's 'masculine' energy through 'those curious, sloping letters' that continually surface in du Maurier's most famous novel, a text in which the transgressions of the 'Other' are both written on the body and embodied in the writing process itself. Du Maurier's letters suggest that, as she grew older, she moved towards seeing identity as something multiform and fissured, rather than unitary and coherent. Arguably, the writing process itself provided du Maurier with a way of manipulating such multiplicity and of harnessing the potentially destructive aspect of the 'Other'—as it does for the narrator of *Rebecca*. Rebecca's death within the plot suggests the containment of transgressive desire but her 'disembodied spirit', with all its divergent energies, continues to inform the writing process. We suggest, then, that Rebecca's power to haunt the modern imagination has much to do with her textual and culture lineage. In creating her, du Maurier drew both on the Gothic tradition and on a broad cultural anxiety concerning the changing status of women in the late nineteenth and early twentieth centuries. For du Maurier, that anxiety was further inflected by the association of the writing woman with a transgressive female identity and this, too, finds expression in her most famous novel. Such anxieties manifest themselves in the way Rebecca's character dissolves some important boundary lines. Neither visibly a body nor visibly a corpse, she upsets the line between life and death; between eros and thanatos; between absence and presence; and between the two stereotypes—that of the asexual virgin-mother and that of the prostitute-vamp—which Andreas Huyssen sees as sustaining 'the myth of the dualistic nature of woman' (Huyssen 1986: 73). Rebecca also disrupts the dividing lines which separate the *femme fatale* from the vamp and the vamp from the female vampire.

This instability of meaning is emphasised by the Gothic nature of Rebecca's body. In addition, the suspended 'R' of her name and the quasi-illegible 'M' in her engagement diary, by constituting a semiotic of fragmentation and incompleteness within the text, indicate metonymically the mysterious uncertainty of her absence/presence. The materiality of Rebecca's signature further signals an anxiety concerning the relation between writing, autonomy and sexual identity. This can be seen as a textual trace of du Maurier's own anxiety about the relation between the 'sexed'

body and the cultural construction of authorial identity as 'masculine'. There are, as Elizabeth Grosz has noted:

> ways in which the sexuality and corporeality of the subject leave their traces or marks on the texts produced . . . The signature not only signs the text by a mark of authorial propriety, but also signs the subject as the product of writing itself, of textuality.
>
> (Grosz 1995: 23)

Just as du Maurier's use of the phrase 'disembodied spirit' in her letters indicates a bodily unease in occupying the authorial position, so Rebecca's uneasy status as both too fleshly (vamp) and too uncanny (vampire) reflects a cultural ambivalence towards the sexually expressive and autonomous woman. Such anxieties are condensed in the way that Rebecca's signature haunts the text; in this sense, writing itself is Gothic.

Notes

1. Even more recent essays on *Rebecca* continue to be heavily infuenced by Light's approach. See, for example, Janet Harbord 1996.

2. See, for example, Linda Ruth Williams's use of the terms as interchangeable (Williams 1993: 53, 56).

3. In this connection, see also Rebecca Stott 1992, especially Chapter 3 on *Dracula*.

4. The Carleton Television adaptation of the novel, shown in January 1997, portrayed Rebecca in this way, for example.

5. Modleski uses this phrase to describe the manner in which representations are played out on the narrator's body, but it is just as appropriate to describe the absence/presence of Rebecca's (dead) body.

6. For example, Gelder 1994 and Halberstam 1995 relate Gothic presentations of the abject to cultural constructions of 'Jewishness' in the late nineteenth and early twentieth centuries, whilst Warwick 1995 explores it in relation to the changing status of women during that period. See also Jerrold E. Hogle (1996) for an example of how textual representations of the abject reflect anxiety concerning changing class structures in early twentieth-century France.

7. The snake image is often associated with female vampires as in, for instance, Tieck's *Wake Not the Dead*, Coleridge's *Christabel*, Baudelaire's *Les Métamorphoses du Vampire* and (obliquely) Keats's *Lamia*.

8. For a fuller exploration of the connection between writing, identity, gender and du Maurier's use of the Gothic genre, see Avril Horner and Sue Zlosnik 1998.

References

Day, W. P. (1985) *In the Circles of Fear and Desire: A Study of Gothic Fantasy*, Chicago and London, University of Chicago Press.

Dijkstra, B. (1986) *Idols of Perversity: Fantasies of Feminine Evil in Fin de Siècle Culture*, New York and Oxford, Oxford University Press.

Doane, M. A. (1991) *Femmes Fatales: Feminism, Film Theory, Psychoanalysis*, New York and London, Routledge.

du Maurier, D. ([1938] 1992) *Rebecca*, London, Arrow.

———. ([1981] 1993) *The Rebecca Notebook and Other Memories*, London, Arrow.

Forster, M. (1993) *Daphne du Maurier*, London, Chatto and Windus.

Frayling, C. ([1991] 1992) *Vampyres: Lord Byron to Count Dracula*, London, Faber and Faber.

Gelder, K. (1994) *Reading the Vampire*, London and New York, Routledge.

Grosz, E. (1995) *Space, Time and Perversion: Essays on the Politics of Bodies*, New York and London, Routledge.

Halberstam, J. (1995) *Skin Shows: Gothic Horror and the Technology of Monsters*, Durham and London, Durham University Press.

Harbord, J. (1996) 'Between Identification and Desire: Rereading *Rebecca*', *Feminist Review*, 53, 95-106.

Hogle, J. E. (1996) 'The Gothic and the "Otherings" of Ascendant Culture: The Original *Phantom of the Opera*', *South Atlantic Quarterly*, 95 (3), 821-46.

Horner, A. and S. Zlosnik (1998) *Daphne du Maurier: Writing, Identity and the Gothic Imagination*, London, Macmillan.

Huyssen, A. (1986) *After the Great Divide: Modernism, Mass Culture, Postmodernism*, Bloomington and Indianapolis, Indiana University Press.

Jones, E. ([1991] 1992) 'On the Vampire', in C. Frayling, *Vampyres: Lord Byron to Count Dracula*, London, Faber and Faber.

Kristeva, J. ([1980] 1982) *Powers of Horror: An Essay on Abjection*, trans. Leon Roudiez, New York, Columbia University Press.

Ledger, S. and S. McCracken, (eds) (1995) *Cultural Politics at the Fin de Siècle*, Cambridge, Cambridge University Press.

Light, A. (1984) '"Returning to Manderley": Romance Fiction, Female Sexuality and Class', *Feminist Review*, 16.

———(1991) *Forever England: Femininity, Literature and Conservatism Between the Wars*, London and New York, Routledge.

Malet, O. (ed.) (1993) *Daphne du Maurier: Letters from Menabilly*, London, Weidenfeld and Nicolson.

Massé, M. A. (1992) *In the Name of Love: Women, Masochism, and the Gothic*, Ithaca and London, Cornell University Press.

Modleski, T. (1988) *The Women Who Knew too Much: Hitchcock and Feminist Theory*, London and New York, Routledge.

Shallcross, M. ([1991] 1993) *The Private World of Daphne du Maurier*, London, Robson Books.

Stoker, B. ([1897] 1993) *Dracula*, Harmondsworth, Penguin.

Stott, R. (1992) *The Fabrication of the Late Victorian Femme Fatale: The Kiss of Death*, London, Macmillan.

Warwick, A. (1995) 'Vampires and the Empire: Fears and Fictions of the 1890s', in S. Ledger and S. McCracken (eds), *Cultural Politics at the Fin de Siècle*, Cambridge, Cambridge University Press.

Williams, A. (1995) *Art of Darkness: A Poetics of the Gothic*, Chicago and London, University of Chicago Press.

Williams, L. R. (1993) *Sex in the Head: Visions of Femininity and Film in D.H. Lawrence*, Hemel Hempstead, Harvester Wheatsheaf.

FURTHER READING

Biography

Auerbach, Nina. *Daphne du Maurier: Haunted Heiress.* Philadelphia: University of Pennsylvania Press, 2000, 180 p.

Biography of du Maurier that also focuses on her lesser-known writings, which Auerbach contends are du Maurier's most compelling.

Forster, Margaret. *Daphne du Maurier: The Secret Life of the Renowned Storyteller.* New York: Doubleday, 1993.

Detailed account of du Maurier's life and career, including critical analysis and biographical interpretation of her works.

Criticism

Bakerman, Jane S. "Daphne du Maurier." In *And Then There Were Nine . . . More Women of Mystery*, edited by Jane S. Bakerman, pp. 12-29. Bowling Green, Ohio: Bowling Green State University Popular Press, 1985.

Discusses six of du Maurier's novels, including Rebecca *and* Jamaica Inn, *as accomplished examples of romantic suspense fiction.*

Butterly Nigro, Kathleen. "Rebecca as Desdemona: 'A Maid that Paragons Description and Wild Fame.'" *College Literature* 27, no. 3 (fall 2000): 144-57.

Compares du Maurier's Rebecca *to William Shakespeare's play* Othello *as a means of reexamining the character of Rebecca.*

Horner, Avril, and Sue Zlosnik. "The Secrets of Manderley: *Rebecca.*" In *Daphne du Maurier: Writing, Identity, and the Gothic Imagination*, pp. 99-127. New York: Twayne, 1998.

Examines Rebecca *as a complex, layered study of female identity.*

———. "Deaths in Venice: Daphne du Maurier's 'Don't Look Now.'" In *Spectral Readings: Towards a Gothic Geography*, edited by Glennis Byron and David Punter, pp. 219-32. London and New York: Macmillan, 1999.

Asserts that in the story "Don't Look Now," du Maurier used Gothic conventions to explore issues of identity, particularly gender identity.

Kael, Pauline. "Labyrinths." *New Yorker* 49 (24 December 1973): 68, 71.

Favorable review of Don't Look Now, *the film based on du Maurier's short story.*

Kelly, Richard. *Daphne du Maurier.* New York: Twayne, 1987.

Book-length survey of du Maurier's works.

Shallcross, Martyn. "Sinister Stories." In *The Private World of Daphne du Maurier*, pp. 144-55. New York: St. Martin's Press, 1991.

Discusses the film adaptations of two of du Maurier's most famous short stories, "The Birds" and "Don't Look Now."

Smith, Harrison. "The Anatomy of Terror." *The Saturday Review* (14 March 1953): 29, 52.

Review of Kiss Me Again, Stranger, *in which Smith asserts that du Maurier "has the gift of making believable the unbelievable."*

Wisker, Gina. "Don't Look Now! The Compulsions and Revelations of Daphne du Maurier's Horror Writing." *Journal of Gender Studies* 8, no. 1 (March 1999): 19-33.

Focuses on du Maurier's horror writings, examining their relationship to traditional Gothic literature and their exploration of gender identity and power.

OTHER SOURCES FROM GALE:

Additional coverage of du Maurier's life and career is contained in the following sources published by Thomson Gale: *Authors and Artists for Young Adults,* Vol. 37; *Beacham's Encyclopedia of Popular Fiction: Biography and Resources,* Vol. 1; *British Writers Supplement,* Vol. 3; *Contemporary Authors,* Vols. 5-8R, 128; *Contemporary Authors New Revision Series,* Vols. 6, 55; *Contemporary Literary Criticism,* Vols. 6, 11, 59; *Contemporary Popular Writers; Dictionary of Literary Biography,* Vol. 191; *DISCovering Authors: British; DISCovering Authors: Canadian; DISCovering Authors Modules: Most-studied Authors* and *Popular Fiction and Genre Authors; DISCovering Authors 3.0; Literature and Its Times,* Vol. 3; *Literature Resource Center; Major 20th-Century Writers,* Eds. 1, 2; *Mystery and Suspense Writers; Novels for Students,* Vol. 12; *Reference Guide to English Literature,* Ed. 2; *Reference Guide to Short Fiction,* Ed. 2; *St. James Guide to Crime and Mystery Writers,* Vol. 4; *St. James Guide to Horror, Ghost & Gothic Writers; Short Stories for Students,* Vols. 14, 16; *Short Story Criticism,* Vol. 18; *Something about the Author,* Vols. 27, 60; *Twayne's English Authors;* and *Twentieth Century Romance and Historical Writers.*

WILLIAM FAULKNER

(1897 - 1962)

(Born William Cuthbert Falkner; changed surname to Faulkner) American novelist, short story writer, poet, screenwriter, and essayist.

A preeminent figure in twentieth-century American literature, Faulkner created a profound and complex body of work that examines exploitation and corruption in the American South. Many of Faulkner's novels and short stories are set in Yoknapatawpha County, a fictional area reflecting the geographical and cultural background of his native Mississippi. Faulkner's works frequently reflect the tumultuous history of the South while developing perceptive explorations of human character. His use of bizarre, grotesque, and violent imagery, melodrama, and sensationalism to depict the corruption and decay of the region make him one of the earliest practitioners of the subgenre known as Southern Gothic literature. Faulkner's works that are especially well known for their Gothic qualities include the novels *Sanctuary* (1931), *Light in August* (1932), and *Absalom, Absalom!* (1936); the novella *As I Lay Dying* (1930); and the short story "A Rose for Emily" (1930). They combine burlesque and dark humor with realism and elements of the horrific and macabre to caricature a society that is unable to break from its past and look to the future. Faulkner employs gothicism, then, as a searing social critique, using it to paint a picture of a culture in ruins, populated by grotesques and living ghosts who refuse to recognize their alienation and defeat.

BIOGRAPHICAL INFORMATION

Faulkner was born in New Albany, Mississippi, into a genteel Southern family. When Faulkner was five, the family moved to the town of Oxford. He showed considerable artistic talent as a boy, drawing and writing poetry, but was an indifferent student. He dropped out of high school in 1915 to work as a clerk in his grandfather's bank, began writing poetry, and submitted drawings to the University of Mississippi's yearbook. During World War I, Faulkner tried to enlist in the U.S. army, but was rejected because of his small stature. Instead, he manipulated his acceptance into the Royal Canadian Air Force by affecting a British accent and forging letters of recommendation. The war ended before Faulkner experienced combat duty, however, and he returned to his hometown, where he intermittently attended the University of Mississippi as a special student. In August, 1919, his first poem, "L'Apres-midi d'un faune," was published in *New Republic*, and later that year the *Mississippian* published one of his short stories, "Landing in Luck." After a brief period of employment as a bookstore clerk in New York, Faulkner returned to Oxford, where he was hired as a university postmaster. He resigned, however, when the postal inspector noticed that Faulkner often brought his writing to the post office and became so immersed in what he was doing that he ignored patrons.

In 1924, with the help of his friend Phil Stone, Faulkner published *The Marble Faun,* a volume of poetry. The following year he moved to New Orleans, where he associated with other writers, including Sherwood Anderson, and wrote his first novel, *Soldiers' Pay* (1926), which was accepted for publication. He traveled in Europe for a few months and then returned to New Orleans and continued to write. His first notable success came in 1929 with *Sartoris.* Later that year, a few months after he married his childhood sweetheart Estelle Oldham, Faulkner published what is regarded as his greatest work, *The Sound and the Fury* (1929). The following year his novella *As I Lay Dying* and "A Rose for Emily" were published, and in 1931 *Sanctuary,* which had been rejected by publishers two years earlier, appeared and became a bestseller. *Light in August* followed in 1932, the same year Faulkner began his career in Hollywood as a screenwriter. He traveled between Mississippi and Hollywood for several years, writing scripts when he was not working on his novels and short stories. Among his film credits were *To Have and Have Not* (1945), based on Ernest Hemingway's novel, and *The Big Sleep* (1946), an adaptation of Raymond Chandler's detective thriller. Works that appeared during these years include *Absalom, Absalom!, The Unvanquished* (1938), *The Wild Palms* (1939), *The Hamlet* (1940), and *Go Down, Moses and Other Stories* (1942).

By the mid-1940s, most Americans had largely ceased to read Faulkner's works, although they were popular in Europe. This changed in 1946 with the publication *The Portable Faulkner,* which renewed critical and popular interest in Faulkner's works in his native country. His election in 1948 to the American Academy of Arts and Letters was followed by his receipt of the 1949 Nobel Prize for Literature, making Faulkner one of the most respected living American writers. He continued to write novels and stories as well as essays and plays. Faulkner won the National Book Award for his *Collected Stories,* published in 1950, and was awarded Pulitzer Prizes for his novels *A Fable* (1954) and *The Reivers* (1962). In the 1950s Faulkner was a much-sought-after lecturer throughout the world. In 1957 he became writer-in-residence at the University of Virginia, dividing his time between Virginia and Mississippi. In 1959

he suffered serious injuries in horse-riding accidents. Faulkner died of a heart attack on July 6, 1962.

MAJOR WORKS

From the beginning of his career, Faulkner's writing showed the influence of the Gothic tradition. His first great work, *The Sound and the Fury,* contains elements typical of Southern Gothic literature: grotesque characters, violence, and a dilapidated, decaying setting. The novel chronicles the disintegration of members of the Compson family who are obsessed with and controlled by forces and events from their pasts. The siblings Quentin and Caddy fall from a state of innocence and succumb to the family pattern of incest, erotomania, and suicide. Faulkner called his next novel, *Sanctuary,* "the most horrific tale I could imagine." Containing graphic violence and extravagant depravity, the crime thriller about the coquettish Temple Drake is a study of human evil that includes a psychopathic bootlegger, corrupt local officials, the trial of an innocent man, and a public lynching. *As I Lay Dying* charts the journey of a poor family to bury their mother, Addie Bundren, in Jefferson. They make the coffin themselves and survive crossing the flooded Yoknapatawpha River, a fire, and other difficulties before reaching their destination. The novella, composed of fifty-nine interior monologues providing various perspectives through constantly shifting, contrasting points of view, including that of the dead mother, is humorous, tragic, and horrifying.

As I Lay Dying was followed by Faulkner's acclaimed horror story "A Rose for Emily," considered an exemplary work of Southern Gothic fiction. The tale begins with the announcement of the death of Miss Emily Grierson, an alienated spinster living in the South in the late nineteenth or early twentieth century. The narrator, who speaks in the "we" voice and appears to represent the people of the town, recounts the story of Emily's life as a lonely and impoverished woman left penniless by her father, who drove away suitors from his overprotected daughter. Emily was left when her father died with a large, dilapidated house, into which the townspeople have never been invited, and there is an almost lurid interest among them when they are finally able to enter the house upon Emily's death. At that point they discover the truth about the extent of Emily's problems: she has kept the body of her lover, a Northerner named Homer Barron, locked in a bedroom since she killed him years before, and she has continued to sleep with him. Some critics initially criticized Faulkner for writing what they saw as an exploitative horror story, but commentators since then have recognized the power of the work as a commentary on the South wrapped up in the past and unable to accept change.

Other notable works by Faulkner with Gothic-inspired settings and themes include *Light in August*, which examines the origins of personal identity and the roots of racial conflicts, and *Absalom, Absalom!*, about Thomas Sutpen, a poor white man from the Virginia hills who marries an aristocratic Mississippi woman, inadvertently launching a three-generation family cycle of violence, degeneracy, and mental retardation.

CRITICAL RECEPTION

Early criticism of Faulkner's fiction ranged from considering it hopelessly incoherent to the work of unparalleled genius. Since the mid-1940s, the latter opinion has prevailed, and critics have come to regard Faulkner as a singular talent and writer of extraordinary scope and power. Since Faulkner's death, his work has been extensively analyzed and critics have remarked that his writing, while distinctively American and Southern, reflects, on a grander scale, the universal values of human life. In his Nobel Prize acceptance speech, Faulkner declared that the fundamental theme of his fiction is "the human heart in conflict with itself." One of the most notable ways in which he depicts this struggle is in his portrayal of the corruption and decay of the South, and he uses Gothic imagery and atmosphere in particular to highlight this idea. Gothicism is also used in Faulkner's work to emphasize distorted religious views, the clash between those with power and those without, the isolation of the individual, humans' powerlessness in an indifferent universe, the moral decay of the community, the burden of history, the horrors of humans' treatment of each other, and the problem of evil. The vast body of Faulkner criticism that has been generated since the 1960s has included discussions of the Gothic elements in his writing, which have focused on his particular brand of American Southern Gothic; the use of gothicism to portray Southern dislocation and decadence; the Gothic influences on his writing, including English novelists and Nathaniel Hawthorne; and his influence on younger writers of Southern Gothic such as Truman Capote, Carson McCullers, and Flannery O'Connor.

PRINCIPAL WORKS

The Marble Faun (poetry) 1924

Soldiers' Pay (novel) 1926

Mosquitoes (novel) 1927

Sartoris (novel) 1929; also published as *Flags in the Dust*, 1973

The Sound and the Fury (novel) 1929

As I Lay Dying (novella) 1930

"A Rose for Emily" (short story) 1930; published in the journal *Forum*

Sanctuary (novel) 1931

*These Thirteen (short stories) 1931

Light in August (novel) 1932

A Green Bough (poetry) 1933

Pylon (novel) 1935

Absalom, Absalom! (novel) 1936

The Unvanquished (short stories) 1938

The Wild Palms (novellas) 1939

The Hamlet (novel) 1940

Go Down, Moses and Other Stories (short stories) 1942

To Have and Have Not [with Jules Furthman] (screenplay) 1945

The Big Sleep [with Furthman and Leigh Brackett] (screenplay) 1946

The Portable Faulkner (novellas and short stories) 1946; revised as *The Essential Faulkner*, 1967

Intruder in the Dust (novel) 1948

Knight's Gambit (short stories) 1949

Collected Stories of William Faulkner (short stories) 1950

Requiem for a Nun (play) 1951

A Fable (novel) 1954

The Town (novel) 1957

Faulkner in the University: Class Conferences at the University of Virginia 1957-1958 (lectures) 1959

The Mansion (novel) 1959

The Reivers (novel) 1962

Essays, Speeches and Public Letters (essays, speeches, and letters) 1966

Lion in the Garden: Interviews with William Faulkner, 1926-1962 (interviews) 1968

Selected Letters of William Faulkner (letters) 1976

Uncollected Stories of William Faulkner (short stories) 1979

* This collection includes the stories "A Rose for Emily," "All the Dead Pilots," "Victory," and "Divorce in Naples."

PRIMARY SOURCES

WILLIAM FAULKNER (STORY DATE 1930)

SOURCE: Faulkner, William. "A Rose for Emily." In *American Gothic Tales*, edited by Joyce Carol Oates, pp. 182-90. New York: Plume, 1996.

The following excerpt is from one of Faulkner's best-known stories, first published in Forum *in 1930.*

IV

So the next day we all said, "She will kill herself"; and we said it would be the best thing. When she had first begun to be seen with Homer Barron, we had said, "She will marry him." Then we said, "She will persuade him yet," because Homer himself had remarked—he liked men, and it was known that he drank with the younger men in the Elk's Club—that he was not a marrying man. Later we said, "Poor Emily," behind the jalousies as they passed on Sunday afternoon in the glittering buggy, Miss Emily with her head high and Homer Barron with his hat cocked and a cigar in his teeth, reins and whip in a yellow glove.

Then some of the ladies began to say that it was a disgrace to the town and a bad example to the young people. The men did not want to interfere, but at last the ladies forced the Baptist minister—Miss Emily's people were Episcopal—to call upon her. He would never divulge what happened during that interview, but he refused to go back again. The next Sunday they again drove about the streets, and the following day the minister's wife wrote to Miss Emily's relations in Alabama.

So she had blood-kin under her roof again and we sat back to watch developments. At first nothing happened. Then we were sure that they were to be married. We learned that Miss Emily had been to the jeweler's and ordered a man's toilet set in silver, with the letters H. B. on each piece. Two days later we learned that she had bought a complete outfit of men's clothing, including a nightshirt, and we said, "They are married." We

were really glad. We were glad because the two female cousins were even more Grierson than Miss Emily had ever been.

So we were not surprised when Homer Barron—the streets had been finished some time since—was gone. We were a little disappointed that there was not a public blowing-off, but we believed that he had gone on to prepare for Miss Emily's coming, or to give her a chance to get rid of the cousins. (By that time it was a cabal, and we were all Miss Emily's allies to help circumvent the cousins.) Sure enough, after another week they departed. And, as we had expected all along, within three days Homer Barron was back in town. A neighbor saw the Negro man admit him at the kitchen door at dusk one evening.

And that was the last we saw of Homer Barron. And of Miss Emily for some time. The Negro man went in and out with the market basket, but the front door remained closed. Now and then we would see her at a window for a moment as the men did that night when they sprinkled the lime, but for almost six months she did not appear on the streets. Then we knew that this was to be expected too; as if that quality of her father which had thwarted her woman's life so many times had been too virulent and too furious to die.

When we next saw Miss Emily, she had grown fat and her hair was turning gray. During the next few years it grew grayer and grayer until it attained an even pepper-and-salt iron-gray, when it ceased turning. Up to the day of her death at seventy-four it was still that vigorous iron-gray, like the hair of an active man.

From that time on her front door remained closed, save for a period of six or seven years, when she was about forty, during which she gave lessons in china-painting. She fitted up a studio in one of the downstairs rooms, where the daughters and granddaughters of Colonel Sartoris' contemporaries were sent to her with the same regularity and in the same spirit that they were sent on Sundays with a twenty-five-cent piece for the collection plate. Meanwhile her taxes had been remitted.

Then the newer generation became the backbone and the spirit of the town, and the painting pupils grew up and fell away and did not send their children to her with boxes of color and tedious brushes and pictures cut from the ladies' magazines. The front door closed upon the last one and remained closed for good. When the town got free postal delivery Miss Emily alone refused to let them fasten the metal numbers above her door and attach a mailbox to it. She would not listen to them.

Daily, monthly, yearly we watched the Negro grow grayer and more stooped, going in and out with the market basket. Each December we sent her a tax notice, which would be returned by the post office a week later, unclaimed. Now and then we would see her in one of the downstairs windows—she had evidently shut up the top floor of the house—like the carven torso of an idol in a niche, looking or not looking at us, we could never tell which. Thus she passed from generation to generation—dear, inescapable, impervious, tranquil, and perverse.

And so she died. Fell ill in the house filled with dust and shadows, with only a doddering Negro man to wait on her. We did not even know she was sick; we had long since given up trying to get any information from the Negro. He talked to no one, probably not even to her, for his voice had grown harsh and rusty, as if from disuse.

She died in one of the downstairs rooms, in a heavy walnut bed with a curtain, her gray head propped on a pillow yellow and moldy with age and lack of sunlight.

V

The Negro met the first of the ladies at the front door and let them in, with their hushed, sibilant voices and their quick, curious glances, and then he disappeared. He walked right through the house and out the back and was not seen again.

The two female cousins came at once. They held the funeral on the second day, with the town coming to look at Miss Emily beneath a mass of bought flowers, with the crayon face of her father musing profoundly above the bier and the ladies sibilant and macabre; and the very old men—some in their brushed Confederate uniforms—on the porch and the lawn, talking of Miss Emily as if she had been a contemporary of theirs, believing that they had danced with her and courted her perhaps, confusing time with its mathematical progression, as the old do, to whom all the past is not a diminishing road, but, instead, a huge meadow which no winter ever quite touches, divided from them now by the narrow bottleneck of the most recent decade of years.

Already we knew that there was one room in that region above stairs which no one had seen in forty years, and which would have to be forced. They waited until Miss Emily was decently in the ground before they opened it.

The violence of breaking down the door seemed to fill this room with pervading dust. A thin, acrid pall as of the tomb seemed to lie everywhere upon this room decked and furnished as for a bridal: upon the valance curtains of faded rose color, upon the rose-shaded lights, upon the dressing table, upon the delicate array of crystal and the man's toilet things backed with tarnished silver, silver so tarnished that the monogram was obscured. Among them lay a collar and tie, as if they had just been removed, which, lifted, left upon the surface a pale crescent in the dust. Upon a chair hung the suit, carefully folded; beneath it the two mute shoes and the discarded socks.

The man himself lay in the bed.

For a long while we just stood there, looking down at the profound and fleshless grin. The body had apparently once lain in the attitude of an embrace, but now the long sleep that outlasts love, that conquers even the grimace of love, had cuckolded him. What was left of him, rotted beneath what was left of the nightshirt, had become inextricable from the bed in which he lay; and upon him and upon the pillow beside him lay that even coating of the patient and biding dust.

Then we noticed that in the second pillow was the indentation of a head. One of us lifted something from it, and leaning forward, that faint and invisible dust dry and acrid in the nostrils, we saw a long strand of iron-gray hair.

GENERAL COMMENTARY

ELIZABETH M. KERR (ESSAY DATE 1979)

SOURCE: Kerr, Elizabeth M. "From Otranto to Yoknapatawpha: Faulkner's Gothic Heritage." In *William Faulkner's Gothic Domain*, pp. 3-28. Port Washington, N.Y.: Kennikat Press, 1979.

In the following excerpt, Kerr surveys the Gothic as it is exemplified in Faulkner's novels set in his fictional Yoknapatawpha.

The term "Gothic" unfortunately has pejorative connotations which we must recognize before giving it the comprehensive definition necessary to an examination of the pervasive Gothic elements in William Faulkner's Yoknapatawpha novels. In current literary criticism "Gothic" either refers in the historical sense to the Gothic novel as a subgenre, from Horace Walpole through his literary successors such as Ann Radcliffe, Matthew

Gregory Lewis, and Charles Maturin, or is loosely applied to various aspects of serious modern novelists such as Faulkner and Carson McCullers. The modern popular "Gothic romance," so labeled and advertised on the covers of paperback editions by a picture of an archetypal castle with a girl in flight in the foreground, is scorned by critics as subliterary, sentimental "formula" fiction, easily recognized because, as Northrop Frye pointed out in *The Secular Scripture,* "the more undisplaced the story, the more sharply the design stands out," being undisguised by representational realism. Like melodrama, with which it has much in common, the popular Gothic romance arouses sham terror and has a reassuring happy ending. Because such romances tend to be fabricated of ordinary or cheap stuff, with slick or sloppy workmanship, the critical eye may not perceive that they are often copied from such original and superior designs as those of Ann Radcliffe or the Brontës. This polluted stream of Gothicism is but a shallow branch of the deep and dark waters which, if one accepts Leslie Fiedler's thesis in *Love and Death in the American Novel,* might be called the Father of Waters of American novels, the Mississippi to which Faulkner's Yoknapatawpha River is tributary. Fully to appreciate that tributary, we must return to its deep Gothic source, for, in Harry Levin's words, "When we come to appreciate the strategic part that convention is able to play, we shall be better equipped to discern the originality of individual writers." . . .

From its beginning Gothicism had embraced medievalism, fantasy, realism, and burlesque, categories of the *roman noir* listed by Montague Summers. Burlesque, with its kinship to caricature and parody, is of special interest in a modern context. In *Love and Death* Leslie Fiedler explained the "gothic mode" as "essentially a form of parody, a way of assailing clichés by exaggerating them to the limit of grotesqueness": in *Absalom, Absalom!* Faulkner mocked "the banal harsh taunt "Would you want a nigger to sleep with your sister!'" In "The Dream of the New" Fiedler explained further that for the American writer the only "fruitful relationship" to the past "compatible with the tradition of the New" is parody, "which simultaneously connects and rejects." Fiedler identified "conscious parody" ("one of the chief modes of our books"); "unconscious parody"; and "parody of parody"—illustrated by Mark Twain "consciously parodying Sir Walter Scott" and then being "inadvertently parodied by Ernest Hemingway." Self-parody is the fourth kind. Without reference to Gothicism, Fiedler

cited Faulkner to exemplify all kinds of parody. Fiedler concluded that parody is "a kind of *necessary* final act of destroying the past, required of all who belong to the tradition of the New."

Exaggeration, one element in burlesque, is identified by Eric Bentley as a basic element in melodrama, which he defined as "the Naturalism of the dream life," akin to the exaggerated fantasies of childhood and adult dreams. Eric Newton credited "the romantic thirst for melodrama" with penetrating "so deeply into the common consciousness that excess had ceased to be ridiculous." Characteristics of melodrama given by James Smith sound much like white Gothic fiction: to provide what Michael Booth termed "'the fulfillment and satisfaction found only in dreams,'" melodrama presented stereotyped, unreal characters on a stage filled with "gigantic pictures" and "grandiose scenery," in which the hero is exposed to physical dangers. "Every act leads up to its 'tableau.'" The hero is finally rewarded by dream justice. Predictably, Smith cites among variations in melodrama the Gothic; in late Gothic the hero is sometimes "a poor man's Faust."

"Medievalism, fantasy, realism, and burlesque"—all but medievalism, in the literal sense, are found in modern American Gothic fiction. Ironic inversion, a strategy by which a kind of parody can be used seriously to convey values directly opposed to those ostensibly presented, may be used with any varieties of literary or black Gothic.

In *Love and Death* Leslie Fiedler stressed the absence in American fiction of eroticism based on adult, heterosexual love. The transformation of European Gothic themes to express the "obsessive concerns" of Americans identified by Fiedler (see p. 8 above) are all exemplified in William Faulkner's Yoknapatawpha novels, as are the general characteristics of Gothicism already dealt with. Romantic solitude sought by Old World characters was found in the New World in primeval forests or unbroken prairies, affording frontier freedom; as Fiedler said, "Scott's romantic North" became Cooper's "romantic West," and flight to escape oppressive society became flight from women and society to male companions in the wilderness. The bandits and outlaws of Europe—German freebooters and Italian banditti, according to Montague Summers—were replaced by Indians. The English gentleman-highwayman was brother under the skin to southern Civil War guerrillas. The iniquities of the Old World authoritarian church and state and corrupt social institutions were matched by New World exploitation of nature, by Negro slavery, and by frontier roughness and violence. Anti-Catholicism gave place to anti-Calvinism. The defiance of Faust, which Fiedler called "the diabolic bargain," became the center of the modern American Gothic novel, with the vast New World as the stage for the drama of superhuman ambition—a recurrent theme noted by Robert Hume in Dark Romantic writing. In a society founded by rebels, rebels and outcasts could be redeemed in the general Romantic revolt against the past and its values. Fiedler noted that the redeemed ones included Prometheus, Cain, Judas, the Wandering Jew, and even Lucifer. The use of superstition and the supernatural, made more plausible by a medieval setting, in the New World lost its power to produce Gothic mystery, awe, and shudders. Dream experience, Howard Lovecraft said, "helped to build up the notion of an unreal or spiritual world." In fiction the supernatural could be replaced by psychological phenomena which readers could accept with at least "a willing suspension of disbelief": common experiences such as dreams; rarer phenomena such as hallucination; special power such as telepathy, prescience, and clairvoyance; psychological abnormalities, including mental deficiency and paranoia. As Leslie Fiedler observed in *Love and Death*, rejection of superstition was succeeded by the realization that such belief, "far from being the fabrication of a Machiavellian priesthood, was a projection of a profound inner insecurity and guilt, a hidden world of nightmare not abolished by manifestos or restrained by barricades. The final horrors, as modern society has come to realize, are neither gods nor demons, but intimate aspects of our own minds."

With modifications and transformations noted above, the new American literary Gothic continues the Gothic tradition, chiefly the black Gothic, in character types and psychological concerns, in settings, and in thematic ideas and narrative patterns. The character types of the Gothic novel, described by Eino Railo, largely paralleled by those in poetry and drama of the Romantic decadence, discussed by Mario Praz, flourished in both European and American fiction. Parallels also to medieval romance are obvious in such characters as the chivalric hero and the persecuted maiden, the villain and the evil woman, and in the general polarity of good and evil. Here will be listed the chief types of characters from which Faulkner, in following the Gothic tradition, could make his choice. Prominent among leading male characters are the heroes or villain-heroes descended from Elizabethan drama

and from Milton's Lucifer, culminating in the Faustian or Byronic hero—handsome, melancholy, mysterious, and passionate, with exceptional capacity for both good and evil. Byron inherited this hero from Gothic romance and the poems of Sir Walter Scott. Lovecraft said that the Gothic villain and the Byronic hero are "essentially cognate types." Eric Bentley stated that villains in melodrama "stem from the archvillain Lucifer." "The dark, rebellious Byronic hero," as Byron developed the type, was described by John Ehrstine as "a composite and evolutionary figure," relentlessly pursuing in isolation "the demonic root of all evil." The Don Juan type, of which Lovelace is the prime example in the novel, is less typical of American Gothic than is the Byronic or Faustian hero. The Romantic hero is descended from the virtuous chivalric heroes but is less interesting than the knights errant. The leading female characters offer parallels to the males; the persecuted maiden, rescued from the villain by the hero, is contrasted with the evil, strong woman, often dark and sometimes a prostitute.

The relationship between the Romantic decadence and the Gothic tradition is reflected by Addison Bross's study of the influence of Aubrey Beardsley on Faulkner in **Soldiers' Pay.** Bross concluded that Beardsley contributed to "Faulkner's inherent sense of the grotesque and absurd element in man" and to the contrast between Margaret, the evil dark beauty, and the girl Cecily. In the South the Dark Lady, termed by Fiedler in *Love and Death* the "sinister embodiment of the sexuality denied the snow maiden," might be expected to have Negro blood. Faulkner did not use this contrast, not even when a woman with Negro blood was the rival to a white heroine. In **Absalom, Absalom!** Charles Bon's octoroon mistress is Judith Sutpen's rival. She is even described with explicit reference to Beardsley, as Bross and Timothy Conley noted. This passage exemplifies Conley's point that in Faulkner's mature works "his own pictorial genius" carried Beardsley's art "to its fictional heights." The octoroon is a victim, not an evil woman, and Judith provides no blonde contrast to the "magnolia-faced woman" as they stand together at the grave of Charles Bon. The octoroon suggests the Suffering Wife of the Gothic tradition, created in Horace Walpole's Hippolita and found, as Eino Railo observed, "in every later romance in which an unhappy mother and child is needed."

Development of servants as distinctive characters, whether loyal and amusing or treacherous and disgusting, was a feature of *The Castle of*

Otranto in which Walpole imitated Shakespeare's servants. Only in the southern Gothic is a servant likely to be a member of the family. Clytie, half-sister in *Absalom, Absalom!* to Judith and Henry Sutpen, combines the Dark Woman with the Loyal Servant.

Most typical of Gothic fiction and least common in other kinds of narrative are the grotesque characters which, in the Gothic tradition, reflected the acceptance in eighteenth- and nineteenth-century aesthetic theory of the grotesque as an aspect of the sublime. The grotesque was one means of achieving the terror which, as Samuel Monk said, was the foundation of Edmund Burke's theory of sublimity. Ugliness could be "associated with sublimity if it is 'united with such qualities as excite strong terror.'" Maurice Lévy considered Burke's evidence valuable because "Burke formulated strictly what his epoch felt vaguely." Lévy regarded the Gothic as the product of a fantastic or grotesque imagination.

John Ruskin, however, was more influential than Burke in forming the tastes of readers and writers in nineteenth-century Romanticism. Ruskin's "Grotesque Renaissance" (chapter 3 in *The Stones of Venice,* volume 2) differentiates true or noble grotesque from false grotesque by the qualities of the spirit revealed in art. (In "The Grotesque in the Fiction of William Faulkner" Robert Ferguson applies Ruskin's categories to characters.) Howard Lovecraft referred to "the grotesque gargoyles," "the daemonic gargoyles of Notre Dame and Mont St. Michel," as gauges of "the prevalence and depth of the medieval horror-spirit in Europe, intensified by the dark despair which waves of pestilence brought." The psychological justification for the grotesque in aesthetic theory and the arts is stated by Wolfgang Kayser in "a final interpretation of the grotesque: AN ATTEMPT TO INVOKE AND SUBDUE THE DEMONIC ASPECTS OF THE WORLD." In "The Victim" Ihab Hassan noted the ancient association between "evil and the ludicrous" and cited "the grotesque magnification of evil" by Dante as a religious act. Whether "grotesque" is limited to characters or is extended to imagery and to incongruities and distortions of all kinds, the grotesque is an integral part of the total pattern of Gothic fiction and usually combines the terrible and the ludicrous in some deformation of what is regarded as natural and pleasing, some nightmarish violation of the daylight world, some ominous disruption of order and harmony.

In substantial agreement with Leslie Fiedler's basic idea in *Love and Death in the American Novel,* Irving Malin said that the "New American Gothic is in the mainstream of American fiction." Malin found the source of the grotesque in Gothic fiction to be the breakdown of order into dream effects. Agreeing with William Van O'Connor that "the grotesque is produced by disintegration," Malin observed that this disintegration, evident in narcissism and the breakdown of the family, is reflected "by the technique of new American Gothic." In "Flannery O'Connor and the Grotesque," Irving Malin grouped her "grotesquerie" with that of "Capote, Hawkes, Carson McCullers, and Purdy," all new American Gothic novelists.

Although the grotesque extends beyond characters to structure and imagery, we are concerned here only with the kinds of grotesque characters, all being deviations from the normal in appearance, capacities, and actions. Defining the grotesque as "the unresolved clash of incompatibles in work and response; the ambivalently abnormal," Philip Thomson stated that "the grotesque has a strong affinity with the *physically abnormal,*" to which our uncivilized response is "unholy glee and barbaric delight." Such grotesques include: sexual deviants who are visibly so, such as hermaphrodites, epicene persons, and transvestites; the blind, or dumb; characters whose appearance or manner shows mechanical rigidity or some other nonhuman quality; cripples; mentally deficient or insane persons. From the dwarves of medieval romance to the dwarf in Carson McCullers's *The Ballad of the Sad Café,* grotesques have been prominent in romances and novels. In modern Gothic, popular or literary, grotesque characters may even predominate, a tendency illustrated in the works of Carson McCullers, Truman Capote, and Flannery O'Connor, all southern followers of Faulkner. In *The Mortgaged Heart,* a miscellany of works by Carson McCullers, Margarita Smith, the editor and the sister of McCullers, ventured an explanation of Gothic fiction: "I wonder sometimes if what they call the 'Gothic' school of Southern writing, in which the grotesque is paralleled with the sublime, is not due largely to the cheapness of human life in the South."

A Season of Dreams by Alfred Appel deals with Eudora Welty. In the chapter "The Grotesque and the Gothic" Appel explains the relationship between his book and chapter titles:

> The grotesque is characterized by a distortion of the external world, by the description of human beings in nonhuman terms, and by the displacement we associate with dreams. The infinite possibilities of the dream inform the grotesque at every turn, suspending the laws of proportion and symmetry: our deepest promptings are projected

into the details of the scene—inscape as landscape. Because the grotesque replaces supernaturalism with hallucination, it expresses the reality of the unconscious life—the formative source which the Gothic writer, in his romantic flights, may never tap. The grotesque is a heightened realism, reminiscent of caricature, but going beyond it to create a fantastic realism or realistic fantasy that evokes pathos and terror.

Although Appel erroneously equates "grotesque" with "gothic" in his chapter title, instead of subordinating the grotesque to the encompassing Gothic configuration, his analysis sheds light on all the southern Gothic novelists.

In *Radical Innocence,* without reference to Gothicism, Ihab Hassan noted the prevalence of the grotesque in southern writers and explained the functions of grotesque characters in serious fiction.

> The grotesque, as clown and scapegoat, is both comic and elegiac, revolting and pathetic. As hunchback or cripple, he is born an outsider, his very aspect an affront to appearances. His broken body testifies to the contradictions of the inner man, the impossible and infrangible dream, raging against his crooked frame and against the world in which flesh is housed.

The prominence of the grotesque in Faulkner's novels is a significant aspect of his Gothic world.

In this world "the obsessive images and recurring emblematic figures" constitute what G. R. Thompson termed "an 'iconography' of the Gothic": the recurring character types and edifices and landscapes serve as "some sort of objective correlative" of "the themes of physical terror, moral horror, and religious mystery." The most obvious single objective correlative is derived from *The Castle of Otranto* and is suggested by the term "Gothic": the medieval castle or ancient abbey, an image of somber ruin and mystery symbolizing the past. The haunted castle, one of the three images Irving Malin deals with in *New American Gothic,* is prevalent in popular Gothic romance which clings to the splendor that "falls on castle walls" remote in time and place; in literary Gothic, with an American setting, the "castle" must be less ancient and magnificent and may be merely a ruined mansion like Faulkner's Old Frenchman's place or the Sutpen mansion. The second of Malin's images, the voyage into the forest, also has characterized Gothic fiction since Horace Walpole and Ann Radcliffe: the unaxed forest, the prairie, a mighty river, and any other scene offering solitude, danger, and mystery represent aspects of the American experience in the New World and the American dream which dominate the transfor-

mation of the Gothic novel into an American genre. Jonathan Baumbach's title *The Landscape of Nightmare* might well suggest these two images, the castle and the forest, although Baumbach selected the novels he dealt with on the basis of their treatment of a typically Gothic theme, the "spiritual passage from innocence to guilt and redemption," without regard to other Gothic features. A third kind of setting adds another nightmare image: enclosed places representing retreat and asylum or imprisonment or both. Taking the phrase from the title of Truman Capote's most Gothic novel, *Other Voices, Other Rooms,* Irving Malin in *New American Gothic* refers to the "other room" in the haunted castle which is "'the final door' through which the ghost-like forces march." The other room is the transformation in new American Gothic of the haunted castle, "the metaphor of confining narcissism, the private world." Insane asylums like the one at Jackson where Benjy Compson and Darl Bundren were sent, the jail in Jefferson, Miss Reba's brothel in Memphis, the room in Sutpen's Hundred where Henry Sutpen ended his flight and exchanged freedom for safety and care—these are only a few of the many enclosed places where people of Yoknapatawpha were trapped or hid themselves.

In front of the castle on covers of popular Gothic paperbacks forever flees the girl who represents one of a small cluster of narrative patterns of dreamlike motion. In *Love and Death* Leslie Fiedler said that the Persecuted Maiden in flight, descended from Horace Walpole's Isabella or Richardson's Clarissa, may be fleeing "through a world of ancestral and infantile fears projected in dreams"; pursued by the villain and threatened with violation, she may be fleeing from her own darker impulses as well. But according to Fiedler the flight of "the typical male protagonist of our fiction" has been from "the confrontation of a man and woman which leads to the fall to sex, marriage, and responsibility." The hero may also be in flight from guilt, pursued by conscience and justice. The ultimate issue of any flight, if escape from a fate worse than death is impossible, is suicide.

In contrast to the flight-pursuit pattern but also involving recurrent or prolonged motion is the quest, the positive journey directed toward a goal, what Northrop Frye in *The Secular Scripture* called "the epic of the creature, man's vision of his own life as a quest." In *New American Gothic* Irving Malin viewed the journey or voyage as opposed to "the other room" but equally fraught with anxiety, the movement being usually "erratic, circular, violent, or distorted." The journey in the *nouveau roman* is envisioned by Enrico Garzilli "as an anonymous quest toward self-understanding," portrayed by "the metaphor of the labyrinth." The journey in a quest for self-understanding or self-realization may follow an initiation pattern. In *The Quest* Mircea Eliade linked the initiation with the quest, noting that most "scenarios in the Arthurian cycle have an initiatory structure" and that "the pattern of initiation persists in the imaginary universes of modern man—in literature, dreams, and day-dreams." Dealing in *Radical Innocence* with some of the writers that Malin discussed, Ihab Hassan saw their work as "a parody of man's quest for fulfillment," an ironic tragicomedy. A quest that resembles Hassan's parody quest was observed by Robert Phillips in the work of Carson McCullers: "the search for a sexless, dim ideal, a manifestation of the hero's avoidance and fear of reality." The quest may, however, be quite directly the equivalent of a common traditional theme, the search for identity which involves ascertaining the facts of one's parentage and finding one's father and family. In the old romances and in Gothic fiction, this search culminated in the recognition and acceptance of the hero and often in his claiming his rightful heritage. In new American Gothic the climax of the quest is more likely to be the rejection and destruction of the hero, as in *Absalom, Absalom!* The Faustian theme also usually involves a quest or purposeful journey in order to realize an ambition, such as Sutpen's design in *Absalom, Absalom!* The purpose of the quest may be evil, such as murderous revenge, or it may be a search for truth and justice involving the detective story pattern. But serious Gothic fiction is likely to have more than one pattern: the detection in *Intruder in the Dust,* for example, is subordinated to the story of Chick Mallison's successful initiation.

A third pattern of motion contrasts with both flight and quest: purposeless wandering. The stories of the Wandering Jew and of Cain have been absorbed into the Gothic tradition: wandering imposed as a doom casts a man out of human society into isolation, often literally into the wilderness. Geoffrey Hartman interprets the significance of this theme as one "which best expresses this perilous nature of consciousness":

> Those solitaries are separated from life in the midst of life, yet cannot die. They are doomed to live a middle or purgatorial existence which is neither life nor death, and as their knowledge increases, so does their solitude. It is consciousness, ultimately, which alienates them from life and im-

poses the burden of a self which religion or death or a return to the state of nature might dissolve.

The wandering of Joe Christmas in *Light in August* combined the racial doom of alienation with a flight from both racial identities. The purgatorial life of Henry Sutpen, Faulkner's Cain, is left to our imagination until death rid him of "the burden of self."

Scenes of violence are so characteristic of Gothic themes and patterns that they are too diverse to allow specification. The effect of horror which distinguishes Gothic fiction may be secured by any and all means, realistic or fantastic, objective or psychological, but underlying all scenes of horror are the dream images and nightmare sensations in the thematic patterns noted above. Modern Gothic fiction not only makes frequent use of dreams but lends such subjective distortion to physical events that it is sometimes difficult to distinguish the inner from the outer nightmare, as in the riot scenes in West's *The Day of the Locust* and in Ellison's *Invisible Man.*

The frequency with which the landscape of nightmare in recent Gothic fiction takes on distinctly southern features is due only in part to the pervasive influence of William Faulkner upon younger southern writers. The southern background and tradition which Faulkner shared with his successors accounts in large measure for their Gothic tendencies. In explaining the prevalence of Gothic fiction in the South, Leslie Fiedler, in *The Return of the Vanishing American,* contrasted the South with "the real West," which "contains no horrors which correspond to the Southerner's deep nightmare terrors." Robert Phillips noted the frequency of violent themes in southern fiction and the shift at times to the minds of tormented souls caught in a labyrinthine life. To Jacques Cabau, the South and the North join "in nostalgia for the West, the lost prairie." Phillips observed that the southern obsession with the problem of evil sprang from a sense of guilt. Referring specifically to Flannery O'Connor, William Faulkner, Robert Penn Warren, and Eudora Welty, Carter W. Martin's view confirms that of Phillips: "The themes that arise from their use of the Gothic mode are essentially spiritual ones, for they speak of matters of the soul and not matters of the glands or the nervous system."

Adaptation of Gothic patterns to existing social scenes has proved easier in the South than in most other regions of the United States. Indeed, some Gothic features which attract readers can be plausibly approximated in very few other American settings. Of genuine medieval ruins, of course, there is a complete lack in the United States; popular Gothic romances cherish the phony Gothic castles along the Palisades of the Hudson River. But the plantation world of antebellum days provided an analogy to feudal society and fostered chivalric ideals. The plantation aristocrat might see himself as like the lord of a manor, ruling over his serfs in a little world over which he held sovereign sway. This inclination toward medievalism accounted in part for the popularity in the South of Sir Walter Scott's novels and, in turn, strengthened by the influence of Scott, provided the foundation of the southern myth of the past, with its ideal of noblesse oblige and its devotion to a lost cause. Although, according to Fiedler, in *Love and Death*, Scott had retained Gothic devices without penetrating to the meanings of Gothic, his novels preserved and transmitted the Gothic tradition in the South. The plantation house which, in its prosperity, had stood for the orderly life of a semi-feudal society, in its ruin and decay resembled the ruined castle in Gothic novels, symbolizing the collapse of the old order. As Jacques Cabau said: "Only the South was material rich enough to express in artistic terms all the aspects—religious, social, political, psychological—of the reaction." The reaction was against liberalism and faith in human perfectibility: the most characteristic of the "artistic terms" chosen was Gothicism.

The influence of Scott strengthened also the southern white Protestant version of medieval courtly love, the cult of the White Goddess. In *Love and Death*, Fiedler cited Mark Twain's hatred of Scott as based on a conviction that Scott had "utterly corrupted the Southern imagination by dreams of chivalry and romance, which made it quite impossible for any Southern writer to face reality or describe an actual woman." In *The Mind of the South* W. J. Cash showed how southern gyneolatry developed as a consequence of cultural and literary influences and social circumstances. The sexless three decades described by Fiedler, the 1860s to the 1890s, contributed to the cult of the white virgin, which could evoke such fervid devotion only in a racially mixed society with aristocratic white leaders. Furthermore, Calvinistic repression of sex moved from New England to the South during the religious awakening of the early 1800s, with the consequent equating of sin and sex; the image of woman as temptress became the obverse of the image of woman as savior. Fiedler in *Love and Death* sums up this duality by saying that the underside of adoration was "fear and contempt": women were goddesses or bitches. The effect of the cult of the white virgin was to inhibit healthy sexuality in upper class white women and to make them frigid physically or psychologically. Mr. Compson in *Absalom, Absalom!* well described the white gentleman's attitude toward women and his solution of his sexual problems. There were "three sharp divisions" of women: "ladies, women, females—the virgins whom gentlemen someday married, the courtesans to whom they went while on sabbaticals to the cities, the slave girls and women upon whom that first caste rested and to whom in certain cases it doubtless owed the very fact of its virginity . . ." (p. 109). Mr. Compson continued to explain how a young man on a plantation, with the first two classes inaccessible psychologically and financially, would turn to the accessible slave girls, among whom he could freely choose. Hence, the most prevalent sexual offense was miscegenation, but it was also in principle the most abhorred; miscegenation between a white woman and a Negro man was regarded as sodomy, punishable by summary death.

The remoteness and exclusiveness of the plantation contributed to other sexual aberrations than miscegenation. In the absence of eligible companions of the opposite sex, narcissism, incest, or homosexuality might result from the aristocratic self-esteem and pride that sought the image of self in the loved one. The Gothic tradition had transmitted the theme of incest which Northrop Frye, in *The Secular Scripture*, showed to be recurrent in romance and which, according to J. M. S. Tompkins, pervaded the popular eighteenth-century novel. But the plantation society after the Civil War provided a scene in which "incest was a constant," according to Andrew Lytle, not merely a literary convention which by that time had come to be regarded with horror.

This was a defeated society, cherishing the myth of the past and fostering in the southern psyche elements characteristic of romance and the Gothic tradition, with their conservative and nostalgic attitude toward the past, to which Maurice Lévy's observation that "man dreams to the right" perfectly applies. The southern myth was more aristocratic and conservative, especially in the later-settled states like Mississippi, than the past had actually been. The Gothic delight in landscape was gratified by the picturesque landscape of the South, with its moss-and-vine-draped trees and flamboyant flowers and mysterious forests and swamps. This natural setting was conducive to the paranoid "melodramatic vision"

ABOUT THE AUTHOR

MAX PUTZEL ON FAULKNER'S GOTHIC

One effect of all the several Gothic revivals was to domesticate the past and make it uniquely our own—whatever ownership might claim it. In England and then in Germany that past was felt to be distinct from the mysterious lost perfection of Greece or Rome. Its crumbling, ivied ruins betokened authority overcome and mouldering decay, lost greatness and failing powers. I think that Faulkner's impression of his American past is an accelerated panorama of similar decay and decline. He sees Southern chivalry as a belated but genuine survival of medieval values and faith. It arose as the product of a noble dream and perished in the nightmare of civil war, victim of mercenary force and sterile philistinism. There is a dreamlike quality to the sequence of disclosure in *Absalom*. We perceive through the medium of Quentin's meandering, helpless search—the dreamer's agony in bondage to that with which he has no strength to cope.

SOURCE: Putzel, Max. "What Is Gothic About *Absalom, Absalom!*?" *Southern Literary Journal* 4, no. 1 (1971): 3-19.

described by Eric Bentley: "We are being persecuted, and we hold that all things, living and dead, are combining to persecute us." "The landscape in *Light in August,*" Francois Pitavy said, "is never immutable or dead: motion still inhabits it and is potentially present, as in the stilled characters. Indeed, as in a dream or nightmare, the shadows tremble and bulge monstrously, and the landscape slowly alters. . . ." The landscape is "a projection or a reflection" of the characters. One is not surprised when Pitavy concludes: "The Faulknerian landscape in *Light in August* is above all the image of a state of mind." The reality, as seen by Doc Peabody, conditioned its inhabitants: rivers and land were "opaque, slow, violent; shaping and creating the life of man in its implacable and brooding image" (*As I Lay Dying*, p. 44).

The South was an agrarian society, hostile to the urban North and to evil cities, the scenes of southerners' own premeditated sins—an attitude shared with southerners by Romanticism and the Romantic decadence. London, the sum of felicity to Dr. Samuel Johnson in the age of reason, was the City of Dreadful Night to James Thomson in the next century.

Most obviously and perhaps most significantly, only the South could provide writers with an emotionally satisfying parallel for the ruined castle which was virtually the protagonist of early Gothic fiction. But the mood of tender melancholy inspired by the southern ruin had a personal, family, and community significance lacking in most haunted castles in which Gothic heroines were immured. The paintless and dilapidated mansion, vacant or inhabited, is still a familiar sight in the South, a reminder of glory and suffering only a century past, rather than a bit of stage scenery in a tale about distant times. The ghosts which haunt these southern ruins may be the living, like Faulkner's Quentin Compson, who dwell in a past more real to them than the present and who have rejected the modern world which offers them no gratifications commensurate with those of the myth of the past. The cult of the past in the South, as symbolized in its ruins, its preserved glories displayed in spring pilgrimages, its monuments and graveyards, owes less to cultural climate and imagination than to remembered history. In the South new intensity reanimates the original Gothic feeling for ruins as described by Montague Summers: "The ruin was a sacred relic, a memorial, a symbol of infinite sadness, of tenderest sensibility and regret." The southern ruin also is a symbol of a legendary Golden Age little more than a century past.

In *The Return of the Vanishing American* Leslie Fiedler's summing up of the significance of the southern plantation setting, with references to southern writers from Poe through William Faulkner to Flannery O'Connor and Truman Capote, suggests why the Gothic mode was naturalized particularly and uniquely in the South and why Yoknapatawpha was conceived in the Gothic tradition:

> . . . the Southern, as opposed to the Northern, does not avoid but seeks melodrama, a series of bloody events, sexual by implication at least, played out in the blood-heat of a "long hot summer" against a background of miasmal swamps, live oak, Spanish moss, and the decaying plantation house so dear to the hearts of moviemakers. . . . The mode of the Southern is Gothic, American Gothic, and the Gothic requires a haunted house at its center. It demands also a symbolic darkness to cloak its action. . . .

Thus, the South provided William Faulkner and other southern writers with a reality which could be depicted with the strong contrasts of the Gothic genre to reveal social and psychological truths less accessible to purely objective and realistic treatment. Seldom, however, does modern southern Gothic play it straight and depict society and characters in terms of the myth and the tradition, as in the old-fashioned historical novel about the South or the modern popular Gothic romance. With a foundation of realistic displacement which conceals Gothic structure beneath the representation of modern society, all the strategies of point of view, discontinuity, ironic inversion, exaggeration, and parody are employed to give new meaning to old formulas, to "penetrate the instinctual reservoirs out of which terror arises," as Dr. Kubie said, or in Fiedler's words in *The Vanishing American,* to evoke "the nightmare terror," the "blackness of darkness."

To discern the new meaning in the old formulas, the reader must recognize what the writer could choose from in the Gothic tradition, what he did choose, and how he transformed a type of fiction originally distanced in time and space to deal with recent or present realities, often of universal urgency, the nightmares that do not vanish with the dawn. William Faulkner's Yoknapatawpha novels cover the whole range of American Gothic; his original modifications and modulations of Gothic elements are uniquely combined with non-Gothic, daylight views of the same society, within individual works or in the extended scope of the Yoknapatawpha chronicles.

Bibliography

The following works of fiction and nonfiction by William Faulkner are published in New York by Random House.

Yoknapatawpha novels and stories:

Flags in the Dust, ed. Douglas Day. 1973.

Sartoris. © 1929, 1956.

The Sound and the Fury. Modern Library College ed., photographic reproduction of 1st printing, 7 October 1929.

Sanctuary. © 1931, 1958.

Light in August. Vintage ed., photographic reproduction of 1st printing, 6 October 1932.

Absalom, Absalom! Modern Library ed., facsimile of 1st ed., 1936.

The Unvanquished. Photographic reproduction of 1st printing, 15 February 1938.

Go Down, Moses. Modern Library ed., © 1942.

Intruder in the Dust. 12th printing, © 1948.

Knight's Gambit. 4th printing, © 1949.

Collected Stories of William Faulkner. N.d.

Requiem for a Nun. N.d.; © 1950, 1951.

Works Cited

KEY: Italicized numbers indicate pages of [*William Faulkner's Gothic Domain*] on which reference to cited work appears. Numbers following colon indicate the specific page reference in the *cited* work.

Appel, Alfred. "The Grotesque and the Gothic." *A Season of Dreams: The Fiction of Eudora Welty.* Baton Rouge: Louisiana State University Press, 1969, pp. 73-103. [*21:* 74]

Baumbach, Jonathan. *The Landscape of Nightmare: Studies in the Contemporary American Novel.* New York: New York University Press, 1965. [*22:* 15]

Bentley, Eric. "Melodrama." *Tragedy: Vision and Form.* Ed. Robert W. Corrigan. San Francisco: Chandler, 1965, pp. 217-31. [*17:* 223, 222; *18:* 221; *26:* 221;]

Bross, Addison C. "*Soldiers' Pay* and the Art of Aubrey Beardsley." *American Quarterly* 19 (Spring 1967): 3-23. [*19:* 23, 6]

Cabau, Jacques. *La Prairie perdue: histoire du roman américain.* Paris: Éditions du Seuil, 1966. [*24:* 228; *25:* 57]

Conley, Timothy K. "Beardsley and Faulkner." *Journal of Modern Literature* 5 (September 1976): 339-56. [*19:* 348]

Ehrstine, John. "Byron and the Metaphysic of Self-Destruction." *The Gothic Imagination.* Ed. G. R. Thompson. Pullman: Washington State University Press, 1974, pp. 94-108. [*18:* 94, 95]

Eliade Mircea. *The Quest: History and Meaning in Religion.* Chicago: University of Chicago Press, 1969. [*23:* 121, 66]

Ferguson, Robert C. "The Grotesque in the Fiction of William Faulkner." Ph.D. dissertation, Case Western Reserve University, 1971. [*20*]

Fiedler, Leslie A. "The Dream of the New." *American Dreams, American Nightmares.* Ed. David Madden. Carbondale: Southern Illinois University Press, 1970, pp. 19-28. [*16:* 24, 26, 27]

——. *Love and Death in the American Novel.* Rev. ed., New York: Dell, Delta Books, 1967. *16:* 205, 369, 421 *17:* 179, 181 *17:* 134, 34 *18:* 38 *19:* 296 *23:* 128, 26 *25:* 172, 194 *26:* 259, 312

——. *The Return of the Vanishing American.* New York: Stein and Day, 1969. [*24:* 134; *28:* 18]

Frye, Northrop. *The Secular Scripture: A Study of the Structure of Romance.* Cambridge: Harvard University Press, 1976. *23:* 15 *26:* 5

Hartman, Geoffrey H. "Romanticism and 'Anti-Self-Consciousness,'" *Romanticism and Consciousness.* Ed. Harold Bloom. New York: Norton, 1970, pp. 46-56. [*24:* 51]

Hassan, Ihab. *The Dismemberment of Orpheus: Toward a Postmodern Literature.* New York: Oxford University Press, 1971. [*16:* 24, 27]

————. "The Novel of Outrage: A Minority Voice in Postwar American Fiction." *American Scholar* 34 (Spring 1965): 239-53. [*16*: 252]

————. *Radical Innocence: Studies in the Contemporary American Novel.* Princeton: Princeton University Press, 1961. [*21*: 78; *23*: 118]

————. "The Victim: Images of Evil in Recent American Fiction." *College English* 21 (December 1959): 140-46. [*20*: 145]

Hume, Robert D. "Exuberant Gloom, Existential Agony, and Heroic Despair: Three Varieties of Negative Romanticism." *The Gothic Imagination.* Ed. G. R. Thompson. Pullman: Washington State University Press, 1974, pp. 109-27. [*17*: 112]

Kayser, Wolfgang. *The Grotesque in Art and Literature.* Trans. Ulrich Weisstein. Bloomington: Indiana University Press, 1963. [*20*: 188]

Kubie, Lawrence S., M.D. "William Faulkner's *Sanctuary.*" *Saturday Review of Literature* (20 October 1934). Rpt. in *Faulkner: A Collection of Critical Essays.* Ed. Robert Penn Warren. Englewood Cliffs, N.J.: Prentice-Hall, 1966, pp. 137-46. [*28*: 139]

Lévy, Maurice. *Le Roman "Gothique" anglais, 1764-1824.* Toulouse: Association des publications de la faculté des lettres et sciences humaines de Toulouse, 1968. [*19*: 71, 53; *26*: 612]

Lovecraft, Howard Phillips. *Supernatural Horror in Literature,* with a new introduction by E. F. Bleiler. Republication of 1945 ed., New York: Dover, 1973. [*18*: 13; *18*: 37; *20*: 19]

Lytle, Andrew. "The Working Novelist and the Mythmaking Process." *Daedalus* (Spring 1959), pp. 326—38. [*26*: 331]

Malin, Irvng. "Flannery O'Connor and the Grotesque." *The Added Dimension: The Art and Mind of Flannery O'Connor.* Eds. Melvin J. Friedman and Lewis A. Lawson. New York: Fordham University Press, 1966, pp. 108-22. [*20*: 108]

————. *New American Gothic.* Crosscurrents: Modern Critiques. Carbondale: Southern Illinois University Press, 1962. [*20*: 4, 9; *22*: 11, 80; *23*: 106]

Martin, Carter W. *The True Country: Themes in the Fiction of Flannery O'Connor.* Nashville: Vanderbilt University Press, 1969. [*24*: 160]

Monk, Samuel. "The Sublime: Burke's Inquiry." *Romanticism and Consciousness.* Ed. Harold Bloom. New York: Norton, 1970, pp. 24-41. [*19*: 27, 39]

Newton, Eric. *The Romantic Rebellion.* New York: Schocken, 1964. [*17*: 130]

O'Connor, William Van. *The Grotesque: An American Genre and Other Essays.* Crosscurrents: Modern Critiques. Carbondale: Southern Illinois University Press, 1962. [*23*: 19]

Phillips, Robert S. "The Gothic Architecture of *The Member of the Wedding.*" *Renascence* 16 (Winter 1964): 59-72. [*23*: 60; *24*: 63]

Praz, Mario. *The Romantic Agony.* Trans. Angus Davidson. 1933; rpt. New York: Meridian, 1951. [*17*]

Railo, Eino. *The Haunted Castle: A Study of the Elements of English Romanticism.* 1927; rpt. New York: Humanities Press, 1964. [*18*; *19*: 49]

Smith, James L. *Melodrama. The Critical Idiom,* no. 28. London: Methuen, 1973. [*17*: 17, 26-27, 34, 39]

Summers, Montague. *The Gothic Quest: A History of the Gothic Novel.* 1938; rpt. New York: Russell, 1964. [*17*: 397]

Thompson, G. R., ed. *The Gothic Imagination: Essays in Dark Romanticism.* Pullman: Washington State University Press, 1975. [*22*: 6]

Thomson, Philip. *The Grotesque. The Critical Idiom,* no. 24. London: Methuen, 1972. [*20*: 27]

Tompkins, J. M. S. *The Popular Novel in England, 1770-1800.* 1932; rpt. Lincoln: University of Nebraska Press, 1961. [*26*: 62]

Walpole, Horace. *The Castle of Otranto.* New York: Collier Books, 1963. [*22*: 20]

TITLE COMMENTARY

"A Rose for Emily"

JAMES M. MELLARD (ESSAY DATE FALL 1986)

SOURCE: Mellard, James M. "Faulkner's Miss Emily and Blake's 'Sick Rose': 'Invisible Worm,' Nachträglichkeit, and Retrospective Gothic." *Faulkner Journal* 2, no. 1 (fall 1986): 37-45.

In the following essay, Mellard argues that in "A Rose for Emily" Faulkner utilizes William Blake's "The Sick Rose" as a source and inspiration for his Gothic narrative.

Men have died from time to time, and worms have eaten them, but not for love.

—Shakespeare

Perhaps the last thing the world needs just now is another study of Faulkner's macabre masterpiece, **"A Rose for Emily."** Least of all, perhaps, do we need another suggestion regarding the story's plot sources, titular allusions, or literary analogues. By now the most frequently anthologized and, therefore, the most frequently written about story in the Faulkner canon, Faulkner's **"Rose"** has been rooted in everything from the author's own verse to Browning's "Porphyria's Lover," from John Crowe Ransom's "Emily Hardcastle, Spinster," to Edgar Allan Poe's "Helen," from Hawthorne's "White Old Maid" to Dickens' Miss Havisham, to say nothing of Oxford's Captain Jack Hume and Miss Mary Louise Neilson.[1] The only question in the story as vexed as where Faulkner got it is that of chronology,[2] which also hinges on Miss Emily's origins, at least as far as her year of birth is concerned. But we live in a world of the superfluous, the gratuitous—whether of the word or of violence; so it will come as no surprise that I shall propose yet one more possible source, analogue, allusion—this one in William Blake's "The Sick Rose." I want to do so, however, in the context of a reading of the story as an innovative version of the Gothic. I believe that Faulkner's apparent allusion to Blake is a direct reflection of the *retrospective* Gothic form of the story, but the necessary retrospection, which causes readers to have missed the "sick rose" and the "invisible worm" lurking there, also reflects a psychoanalytic phenomenon called *Nachtraglichkeit* or "deferred action" that helps to account for the story's unsettling appeal.

I

Many different figures from literature have been suggested by scholars as Faulkner's "source" for the story's title. Moreover, Faulkner himself has contributed to the probable misunderstanding regarding the nature of the titular rose. He has either been rather vague about its significance— "It was just '**A Rose for Emily**'—that's all" (Inge 22)—or has suggested that the idea for the story came from an entirely different image—"from a picture of the strand of hair on the pillow" (Inge 22). Thus, readers have tended to look for some salutary image of the rose, and have consequently thought in terms of Gertrude Stein's a "Rose is a rose is a rose is a rose," Robert Burns's "Oh, my luve is like a red, red rose," or Shakespeare's "That which we call a rose by an other name would smell as sweet" (Inge ix). Indeed, Faulkner did contribute to the notion that the titular gesture was an acknowledgement of triumph; he told a Japanese audience at Nagano that the title "was . . . allegorical; the meaning was, here was a woman who had had a tragedy, an irrevocable tragedy and nothing could be done about it, and I pitied her and this was a salute . . . To a woman you would hand a rose" (Inge 81). With Faulkner causing interference, it is no wonder that readers have not looked to the lines in Blake that virtually delineate the tale.

> O rose, thou art sick!
> The invisible worm
> That flies in the night,
> In the howling storm,
>
> Has found out thy bed
> Of crimson joy,
> And his dark secret love
> Does thy life destroy.[3]

Anyone who knows Faulkner's story will see the Blakean parallels immediately. The "rose" that is *taken by* Miss Emily in tribute can be none other than Homer Barron, the lover she murdered, ap-

parently by arsenic poisoning, and stashed in her bedroom for some forty years of nocturnal ministrations. In this context, we can say that Miss Emily has to be the "invisible worm" whose "dark secret love / Does thy life destroy"—that is, destroys the life of the Homeric rose, the romantic lover, or, shall we say, the Barronic hero. Or, on a more abstract level, we might say that the worm is merely Miss Emily's murderous love, for it is love that serves as the worm of destruction, finding Homer's bed and turning it into one "Of crimson joy." A reading of the story could turn on either interpretation, perhaps, but in fact Faulkner's text makes it rather dificult to deny that the conquering worm is in there somewhere. And, indeed, that worm, after years of battening upon the now blind Homer, would look a lot like Miss Emily herself.

Faulkner includes clear evidence in the story that Miss Emily has been transformed into the deadly, invisible worm. His precise pictures of her show the change. As a young woman, before Homer appears, she is seen as "a slender figure in white," cast into the background behind her father, "a spraddled silhouette in the foreground" (*CS* [*Collected Stories of William Faulkner*] 123). Still young, but following the much-mourned death of that spraddled-legged parent, she is seen with her hair "cut short, making her look like a girl, with a vague resemblance to those angels in colored church windows—sort of tragic and serene" (*CS* 124). Pictured twice before Homer's demise, Miss Emily is pictured twice afterwards, too. Six months after Homer had last been seen in Jefferson, Miss Emily is seen again for the first time: "she had grown fat and her hair was turning gray." Here, Faulkner makes much of her graying locks: "During the next few years it grew grayer and grayer until it attained an even pepper-and-salt irongray, when it ceased turning." Moreover, Faulkner makes of the hair a metonym of Emily's now somewhat masculine vitality: "Up to the day of her death at seventy-four it was still that vigorous iron-gray, like the hair of an active man" (*CS* 127-28). Later in her life, though the account comes earlier in the narration, Miss Emily is seen again. She is "a small, fat woman in black, with a thin gold chain descending to her waist and vanishing into her belt, leaning on an ebony cane with a tarnished gold head. Her skeleton was small and spare; perhaps that was why what would have been merely plumpness in another was obesity in her. She looked bloated, like a body long submerged in motionless water, and of that pallid hue. Her eyes, lost in the fatty ridges of her face, looked like two small pieces of coal pressed into a lump of dough" (*CS* 121). Not a pretty sight, is she?

But would a nice Southern Belle like Miss Emily stoop to conquer a man like Homer—a Northerner and a day laborer, to boot—and in that ghoulish way? Faulkner's text suggests rather strongly that, indeed, she had done so. The townsfolk in Jefferson think that she is a bit crazy, perhaps inheriting insanity from her aunt on the Alabama side of her kin—from "old lady Wyatt, the crazy woman" (*CS* 125), over whose estate Emily's father had had a falling out with those relatives. Miss Emily does try, we know, to hold on to a body longer than the ordinary. When her father had died, Faulkner writes, she had put off the town's delegation of mourners, meeting "them at the door, dressed as usual and with no trace of grief on her face. She told them that her father was not dead. She did that for three days, with the ministers calling on her, and the doctors, trying to persuade her to let them dispose of the body. Just as they were about to resort to law and force, she broke down, and they buried her father quickly" (*CS* 123-24). The story, thus, establishes that—given the opportunity—she would keep a body around just for moral support, if not an immoral rapport. "We did not say she was crazy then," says our narrator; "We believed she had to do that. We remembered all the young men her father had driven away, and we knew that with nothing left, she would have to cling to that which had robbed her, as people will" (*CS* 124).

But would she lie with the body? Again, the text makes it pretty clear that she had, though it does not make clear for just how many nights or for how many years after Homer's death. As all who know the story can say, the telltale bit of evidence is Miss Emily's hair. We have seen already the emphasis Faulkner places on its color—its graying over the years, becoming "that vigorous iron-gray" (*CS* 128). Thus, when, upon the opening up of the above stairs bedroom that had become Homer's mausoleum, "a long strand of iron-gray hair" (*CS* 130) was noticed on the second pillow, next to Homer's, it is as if Miss Emily has left her personal signature. Not only had she killed Homer and lain next to the corpse, she also had grown fat as a result. Faulkner makes that plain. In this case the sign lies in a difference: she is thin before Homer, and even "thinner than usual" (*CS* 125) when she buys the arsenic for doing him in. Within six months of his demise, she is the fat, pallid, bloated body one expects to turn

out from under a log, or pull out of stagnant water, or find beneath the fleshless shell of a decomposed cadaver.

II

By now almost every detail of "**A Rose for Emily**" is familiar to most readers before they ever actually read the story. At least, readers now almost invariably know in advance what the townspeople will find when they break into that dusty bridal suite. From the beginning, readers have found the story's ending so shocking that very soon a sort of mythology arose around it as it took on a life of its own, particularly in the critical reactions to Faulkner's work. This reaction has meant that new readers of the story are seldom "innocent" any more. If they are truly innocent, they may well miss the point. Robert Crosman, in a recent article called "How Readers Make Meaning," recounts an experience he had teaching the story. He and the students were expected to keep journals of their reading responses. Crosman's own journal entry records the response one is more likely to find among sophisticated readers who nonetheless have not read it before: "This is a story I had never actually read," he says, "though I had heard of it, read something about it, and in particular knew its ending, which kept me from feeling the pure shock that the reader must feel who knows nothing of what is coming. Even so I felt a shock, and reacted with an audible cry of mingled loathing and pleasure at the final and most shocking discovery: that Emily has slept with this cadaver for forty years" (Crosman 207). His student named "Stacy," however, read entirely around the presumably crucial Gothic elements: "On questioning, she said that Emily's poisoning of Homer remained shadowy and hypothetical in her mind, and she had completely missed the implication of the strand of Emily's hair found on the pillow next to the corpse. Instead, Stacy had written a rather poetic reverie about her *grand-mother*, of whom she was strongly reminded by Emily" (Crosman 209).

These rather different responses may simply represent different "styles of reading," as Norman Holland or George L. Dillon might suggest. Stacy would represent, for instance, what Dillon calls the "Character-Action Moral" (CAM) reader, Crosman the "Digger-for-Secrets."[4] But to attribute readings of the story to personal *styles* of reading is to denigrate—if not deny—the role played by the form of the story itself in shaping readerly and, perhaps, informed critical responses. The same denial, perforce, would pertain to the role of the generic shape or tradition of the story. Do readers *not* respond to familiar genres? Once a story has been classified, most critics believe, generic classification not only will have a bearing on what we read and how we read, but also on when we read the generic signals into it. The instant mythologization of the ending of **"A Rose for Emily,"** where its *genre* is concerned, has caused most readers to overlook one of Faulkner's innovations. As most critics, if not the more naive student-readers, recognize, the story belongs to the tradition of the literary Gothic. But not even the critics have recognized its innovation within the form of the Gothic: its being what can only be called *retrospective* Gothic. Unlike the Gothic stories and novels most of us know, **"A Rose for Emily"** is Gothic after the fact, not before. That is, we recognize the story's details as part of a total Gothic form only after we read through to the ending. Then, we look back over the story or our experience of the story and say, "Oh, that's what was going on." Our response, thus, is likely to be that of the person who has learned that the strange landscape she was just passing by is a graveyard, or it might be that of the person who has just realized he's missed being in a terrible accident, say, on a plane that later crashes. The chill of terror comes, yes, but it comes later, deferred, after the fact. That is the effect, I think, of the retrospective form of Gothic Faulkner has created in **"A Rose for Emily."**

The most extensive reading of the story as conventional Gothic is by Edward Stone.[5] But Stone simply misses the way in which Faulkner modifies the genre. He notes the presence of the aging recluse in the "majestic stronghold" of a decaying mansion (Stone 86) in his comparison of Faulkner's to George Washington Cable's story, "Jeanah Poquelin" (1879). But the innovation he recognizes in both Cable and Faulkner is their emphasis on a particular "time and place" (Stone 86); of Faulkner, he says, "With 'A Rose for Emily' morbidity is domesticated in the American small town" (Stone 86). Stone, of course, is correct in these judgments, but he is quite wrong in most of his other claims because he does not pay attention to the effect of the retrospective form Faulkner creates. Stone calls Miss Emily a "pathetic yet sinister relic" (Stone 88), but in fact she is not *sinister* (as Crosman's "Stacy" illustrates) until one looks back over the story-as-narrated (its *récit* as opposed to its *histoire*). Stone is correct in claiming that the story does not maintain suspense, but he is wrong in his reason for making the claim. There is little or no suspense as such because the story does not engender in the reading process an anticipation of some particular type of event or climax.

The question that readers will have is much more primitive, almost like that of the auditor of a shaggy-dog story: what *is* the point of the tale or, even, *is* there a point to it? Stone claims, however, that "not only do we early anticipate the final outcome with a fair degree of accuracy: for this very reason we are imbued with the horror of the heroine's personality at every step throughout the story, and thus in her case the basic mystery outlives the working out of the plot" (Stone 95). In this respect, the story, says Stone, is comparable to Poe's "A Cask of Amontillado": "both stories have a total horror, rather than a climax of horror, for in both we are given at the start a distinct impression of the moral depravity of the central figure, and the following pages deliberately heighten that impression rather than merely solve for us a mystery that the opening pages have set forth" (Stone 95). But Stone is simply wrong inasmuch as he is speaking of the *process* of interpretation that goes on during the reading. Crosman's naive readers demonstrate that such claims about the story's "total horror" or Miss Emily's sinister depravity can only be made retrospectively; only from the end can the "precise prodigality" (Stone 95) of clues Faulkner indeed scatters throughout be put together to form a horrifying Gothic heroine of Miss Emily, "a necrophile or a veritable saprophytic organism" (Stone rightly notes) that grows fat from her ghoulish marriage (Stone 96-7). Faulkner's story *is* Gothic, but it is not common so much as retrospective Gothic.

III

In his own journal entries on **"A Rose for Emily,"** Crosman points to another dimension of this story and the Gothic form generally. Crosman notes that "the whole feeling of the story is of a mystery, something to do with male-female relationships, as well as time, perhaps, but a mystery one doesn't entirely want solved" (Crosman 208). He goes on to say that his response is governed largely by a "considerable *fear* of the discovery I know is waiting, the sex-and-death thing, though there is a *fascination*, too" (Crosman 208). Crosman recognizes this combination of fear and fascination as Oedipal, likely to "give comfort to literary Freudians" (Crosman 208).

> For what I saw in **"A Rose for Emily"** was pretty certainly a "primal scene." Both my fear and my interest, my loathing and pleasure, derived, at

least in part, from remembered childish speculation as to what went on in the parental bedroom. The structure of the story's plot is to set up a dark and impenetrable mystery—what is troubling Emily?—and to penetrate deeper and deeper into her past in hopes of getting an answer. Formally the pleasure is derived from solving the mystery, but the solution is a shocking one.

(Crosman 208)

What Crosman suggests here about the specific tale seems very accurate, but his perception also points to a dimension implicit in the genre of the Gothic. This dimension is certainly Freudian and Oedipal, but it also relates to the psychoanalytic concept of *Nachträglichkeit* or "deferred action."

The concept of *Nachträglichkeit* is persistent in Freud's theories of repression, primal fantasies, and psychical cause and effect. According to Laplanche and Pontalis, the authors of the authoritative *The Language of Psycho-Analysis,* "The credit for drawing attention to the importance of this term must go to Jacques Lacan" (LP-A 111). The notion has become important today because it modifies somewhat the usual understanding that for Freud every neurosis was to be attributed to an actual event, one usually occurring in the early life of the subject. The concept of "deferred action" suggests, instead, that it is the reinterpretation of an earlier event or scene in light of a later one and within certain structures emanating from culture or language or the register that Lacan (not Freud) calls the Symbolic. Laplanche, for example, in *Life and Death in Psychoanalysis* shows how Freud's analysis of "Emma" in that famous case-history illustrates the way in which the subject's "primal" experience of seduction or sexual assault by an adult is neither remembered nor pathogenic until a second scene triggers the memory at a time when Emma is then sexually mature enough to attribute sexual motives to the original molestor. Emma's phobia is a fear of entering stores by herself. The onset of the fear at age twelve occurred upon her observing two store clerks laughing—she thinks at her clothes. Freud's analysis shows, however, that this scene is associated with another one that had occurred when Emma was about eight years old and her clothes were twice grabbed in her genital area by a shopkeeper. Laplanche's commentary on Freud's analysis points out that "the first scene does not penetrate into consciousness with its full meaning of assault but does so through an entirely extraneous [metonymic] element: the clothes" (*LDP* 41). Moreover—and this is particularly important to Lacan's rereading of Freud—"we try to track down the

trauma, but the traumatic memory was only secondarily traumatic: we never manage to fix the traumatic event historically" (*LDP* 41), a situation Laplanche compares to Heisenberg's principle of indeterminacy in physics: "in situating the trauma, one cannot appreciate its traumatic impact, and *vice versa*" (*LDP* 41).

I would argue that the normal or ordinary first reading of "**A Rose for Emily**" would illustrate this concept of "deferred action," which might better be called *deferred interpretation.* In effect, there are two crucial scenes represented in the tale. In temporal order, the first is the scene in which Miss Emily "seduces" Homer Barron in her upstairs bedroom: this is the scene of the "parental bedroom," as Crosman puts it, but it is also associated at the same time with other evidences of mysterious and potentially dangerous activity—the purchase of the arsenic and, later, the unexplained odor emanating from the mystified scene (the old house). The second scene in the temporal order is that of the discovery of the skeleton on the bed in the upstairs bedroom and the strand of gray hair on the pillow with the indentation of a person's head. The "deferred action" here is defined in the way in which the details of the second scene suddenly cause a reinterpretation of the details of the other, earlier scene. Now, Homer Barron's disappearance is explained as a function of the explanation of the purchase of the arsenic and the subsequent emanation of the foul odor from the old Grierson house. All at once, then, the earlier details of the story become Gothic—in the way that, within the boundaries of *Nachträglichkeit,* earlier scenes become "Oedipal" or scenes of seduction or sexual assault. In the reading of "**A Rose for Emily**," I suggest, one's sudden chill or thrill at the recognition of the sexual *and* thanatic significance of the earlier scene (or scenes, for the number is not so important as the deferred interpretation) is indeed—as Crosman suggests—related to the significance of sexuality and the vital order.

It is the combination of the sexual and the thanatic that makes Faulkner's story so effective as a Gothic tale, retrospective or otherwise. For the core of the Gothic is the fusion of the two elements of sex and death, especially forbidden or incestuous sex and the most heinous of mortal crimes—parricide and other versions of family murder such as matricide, fratricide, or infanticide. Incest and family murder underlie Poe's Gothic tales, for example, as they have underlain other classic Gothics since the first—Walpole's *The Castle of Otranto* (1764). In Walpole, for instance,

Manfred (the Gothic villain) intends to marry off his son to a young woman (Isabella), but when the son is killed beneath a mysterious gigantic helmet, Manfred decides he will marry Isabella himself. But when she comes under the protection of her father—so Freudianly named the Knight of the Gigantic Sabre—Manfred decides to trade his own daughter (Matilda) to the Knight, thus creating the possibility of two unnatural weddings. But the good Knight (upon dire warnings from the spirit world) chooses to give up Matilda, whom Manfred by mistake later murders, thinking to stab his betrothed Isabella instead. His crime leaves the true heir of the Castle—Theodore, son of good Father Jerome—to marry Isabella, daughter of the Knight who appears in the image of Alfonso the Good, original owner of the Castle whose ownership Manfred had usurped. Poe's "The Fall of the House of Usher" is a stripped down, highly condensed version of such Gothic goings on. In place of all the doubling of parents and children found in Walpole, Poe collapses all—parents and children—into just the two remaining Ushers—Roderick and Madeline. They have to stand for the paternal and the maternal forces and for the son and the daughter, but also for the groom and the bride, as well as for the murderer and his victim. Thus, Poe gives us the inevitable incest and the family murder, in addition to the thrill of the double discovery of *eros* and *thanatos,* in one dense, Narcissistic, mirror-laden tale. It is no wonder—from a psychoanalytic viewpoint—that "The Fall of the House of Usher" has been so persistent a reader's favorite over the years.

From a Freudian-*cum*-Lacanian perspective, the classic Gothic and, especially, its rather transparent symbols interpret some of the motivations underlying "A Rose for Emily." The classic question is simply, "What does Miss Emily want?" Walpole's answer (filtered through Freud) would be, she wants a night with a giant saber; a Lacanian answer would be that she wants the plenitude of power and knowledge associated with the place of the Father (in the structure of the unconscious) and symbolized in the Phallus. In the simplest psychoanalytic terms, she wants to hang on to the father himself, for he is of course the symbol of that Phallus. If she cannot have him in life, then she will keep the body as an object that stands for him, a desire expressed in her effort to keep his corpse from proper burial (a feat she does manage, Faulkner tells us, for three days, after which, were this a tale of the Christian scapegoat, instead of a phallic surrogate, she might have expected it to rise again). But if she cannot

have the father, who loomed over her in life and then loomed over her in death, then she will have a substitute.

Enter Homer Barron. This time she will hang on to her symbol of phallic power in life and in death. But her behavior, finally, does make of Homer a ritually slain "god" whose powers can be claimed through contiguity—the transfer achieved by physical proximity or even ingestion. What makes the thought of Emily's sexual acts with Homer's corpse so repulsive to any reader is the evidence Faulkner gives us that it is oral, not genital; not merely necrophiliac, but also—as Stone astutely observes—saprophitic or, perhaps more accurately, saprophagous. The two signs that Faulkner gives us that link Emily, bodily, to Homer's cadaver are the gray strand of hair and the odious obesity that overtakes her after she has murdered the man. Faulkner's strategic emphasis on her repulsive shape—"bloated, like a body long submerged in motionless water, and of that pallid hue" (*CS* 121)—really makes absurd the interpretation of John V. Hagopian et al.—that the hair was placed beside Homer "as a gesture of grief and farewell" (Inge 79). Emily's gesture certainly has to do *with* grief and farewell, for it has indubitably to do with death. But the significance of the gesture, finally, is more properly associated not with some noble chivalric token, but with Blake's song of experience celebrating the penetration of the sick rose by the invisible worm of mortality. Thus, **"A Rose for Emily"** suggests the principle that Laplanche outlines in *Life and Death in Psychoanalysis*—that human sexuality, the sex *drive*, is less associated with life than, finally, with death. Such may be the reason Faulkner's story has aroused very intense reader-response and critical debate.

Notes

1. These different suggestions have been made, respectively, by Going (Faulkner), Edwards and Winchell (Browning), Barber and Levitt (Ransom), Stevens and Stronks (Poe), Barnes (Hawthorne), and Stewart (Dickens). I should add that Inge (ed.), *William Faulkner: A Rose for Emily* includes many of the most interesting essays written on the story, and I am very grateful to him for providing me with a copy of the out-of-print book.

2. See the essays by Going, McGlynn, Nebeker, Sullivan, Wilson, and Woodward.

3. See Bidney (278), who suggests an allusion to Blake's image of the "worm" in Faulkner's *Light in August,* but he does not refer to "A Rose for Emily." I am not aware that any other critic has made this suggestion about Blake and Faulkner. I have not been able to find

evidence in *Blotner* or in Blotner's *William Faulkner's Library: A Catalogue* that Faulkner is likely to have read "The Sick Rose" in any volumes he *owned* by 1929 when he wrote the story.

4. A third readerly style, not illustrated here, is that of the "Anthropologist," who looks for cultural norms and values, and who would be represented by, say, Feminist or Marxist or other "ideological" critics (see Allen's essay as a recent example).

5. See Benton for a discussion of the central issues in the Gothic; see Carothers for discussions of Faulkner's habits of style, composition, and genre in his short fiction.

Works Cited

Allen, Dennis W. "Horror and Perverse Delight: Faulkner's 'A Rose for Emily.'" *Modern Fiction Studies* 30.4 (Winter 1984): 685-96.

Barber, Marion. "The Two Emilys: A Ransom Suggestion to Faulkner?" *Notes on Mississippi Writers* 6 (Winter 1973): 103-05.

Barnes, Daniel R. "Faulkner's Miss Emily and Hawthorne's Old Maid." *Studies in Short Fiction* 9 (Fall 1972): 373-77.

Benton, Richard P. "The Problem of Literary Gothicism." *ESQ* 18 (1972): 1-5.

Bidney, Martin. "Faulkner's Variations on Romantic Themes: Blake, Wordsworth, Byron, and Shelley in *Light in August*." *Mississippi Quarterly* 38.3 (Summer 1985): 277-86.

Blotner, Joseph. *William Faulkner's Library: A Catalogue.* Charlottesville: U. of Virginia Press, 1964.

Carothers, James B. *William Faulkner's Short Stories.* Ann Arbor, MI: UMI Research Press, 1985.

Crosman, Robert. "How Readers Make Meaning." *College Literature* 9.3 (1982): 207-15.

Cullen, John B., with Floyd C. Watkins. *Old Times in the Faulkner Country.* Chapel Hill: U of North Carolina P, 1961.

Dillon, George L. "Styles of Reading." *Poetics Today* 3.2 (1982): 77-88.

Edwards, C.H., Jr. "Three Literary Parallels to Faulkner's 'A Rose for Emily.'" *Notes on Mississippi Writers* 7 (Spring 1984): 21-5.

Faulkner, William. "A Rose for Emily." In *Collected Stories of William Faulkner.* New York: Random, 1950: 119-30.

Going, William T. "Chronology in Teaching 'A Rose for Emily.'" *Exercise Exchange* 5 (February 1958): 8-11.

——. "Faulkner's 'A Rose for Emily.'" *Explicator* 16 (February 1958): Item 27.

Hagopian, John V., and Martin Dolch. "A Rose for Emily." *Insight I: Analyses of American Literature.* Frankfurt am Main: Hirschgraben-Verlag, 1964: 43-50.

Holland, Norman N. "Fantasy and Defense in Faulkner's 'A Rose for Emily.'" *Hartford Studies in Literature* 4 (1972): 1-35.

——. *5 Readers Reading.* New Haven, CT: Yale U. P., 1975.

Inge, M. Thomas, ed. *William Faulkner: A Rose for Emily.* Columbus, OH: Merrill, 1970.

Laplanche, Jean. *Life and Death in Psychoanalysis.* Trans. Jeffrey Mehlman. Baltimore, MD: Johns Hopkins, 1976.

——, and J.-B. Pontalis. *The Language of Psycho-Analysis.* Trans. Donald Nicholson-Smith; Intro. Daniel Lagache. New York: Norton, 1973.

Levitt, Paul. "An Analogue for Faulkner's 'A Rose for Emily.'" *Papers on Language and Literature* 9 (Winter 1973): 91-4.

McGlynn, Paul D. "The Chronology of 'A Rose for Emily.'" *Studies in Short Fiction* 6 (Summer 1969): 461-62.

Nebeker, Helen E. "Chronology Revised." *Studies in Short Fiction* 8 (Summer 1971): 471-73.

Stevens, Aretta J. "Faulkner and 'Helen': A Further Note." *Poe Newsletter* 1 (October 1968): 31.

Stewart, James Tate. "Miss Havisham and Miss Grierson" *Furman Studies* 6 (Fall 1958): 21-3.

Stone, Edward. *A Certain Morbidness: A View of American Literature.* Carbondale, IL: Southern Illinois U. P., 1969: 85-100.

Stronks, James. "A Poe Source for Faulkner? 'To Helen' and 'A Rose for Emily.'" *Poe Newsletter* 1 (April 1968): 11.

Sullivan, Ruth. "The Narrator in 'A Rose for Emily.'" *Journal of Narrative Technique* 1 (September 1971): 159-78.

Wilson, G. R., Jr. "The Chronology of Faulkner's 'A Rose for Emily' Again." *Notes on Mississippi Writers* 5 (Fall 1972): 44, 56, 58-62.

Winchell, Mark Royden. "'For All the Heart's Endeavor': Romantic Pathology in Browning and Faulkner." *Notes on Mississippi Writers* 15.2 (1983): 57-63.

Woodward, Robert H. "The Chronology of 'A Rose for Emily.'" *Exercise Exchange* 13 (March 1966): 17-19.

Sanctuary

TERRY HELLER (ESSAY DATE SUMMER 1989)

SOURCE: Heller, Terry. "Mirrored Worlds and the Gothic in Faulkner's *Sanctuary*." *Mississippi Quarterly* 42, no. 3 (summer 1989): 247-59.

In the following essay, Heller focuses on Faulkner's use of mirrors in Sanctuary *as it relates to the convention of mirroring in Gothic fiction.*

In *Sanctuary* Faulkner presents a mirror structure, the underworld of bootlegging and prostitution mirroring the respectable world of law and order. This mirroring is extended from the world to characters and to language. William Patrick Day's study of the Gothic tradition, *In the Circles of Fear and Desire,*[1] suggests a fruitful way of interpreting the meanings of this mirroring in relation to romantic definitions of sexual identity.

Interpreters of *Sanctuary* have noted the multiple appearances of mirrors, the first being Horace's discovery of Popeye mirrored in the spring from which Horace drinks. For each of the main characters in the respectable world, there is at least one mirrored opposite in the disreputable world. Opposed to Horace as a protector of innocence is Popeye, a violator of innocents. Opposed to Narcissa and her son are Ruby and her son. Also opposed to the ruthlessly respectable Narcissa and the Baptist ladies she manipulates are the ruthlessly respectable, but disreputable Reba and her retired prostitute friends. Opposed to Gowan, the Virginia gentleman, are Lee, Van, Tommy, and Red, who become or attempt to become Temple's "dates" in the underworld. Opposed to the respectable Temple, daughter of Judge Drake, is the sexually active Temple at the Grotto who calls Popeye "Daddy."

There is enough symmetry here to establish a mirror relationship between the two worlds, but not so much and so exact a symmetry as to suggest that the underworld is merely a fantasy projection of the respectable world. This rough and limited symmetry distinguishes *Sanctuary* from the central works of the Gothic tradition where it appears that "the Gothic world," as Day argues, is not a representation of the real world, but rather, a fantasy projection of the unconscious side of a romantic imagination (Day, pp. 27-42). *Sanctuary*'s underworld is pointedly *not* fantastic, though it is presented with techniques that make it seem alien and "unreal" to those respectable characters who come into contact with it.

Even though this underworld is not merely a fantastic projection of the unconscious of particular characters, it is a projection. The underworld of *Sanctuary* exists in part because respectable society needs it; it is a *real* projection of the respectable world. The underworld exists to provide alcohol to respectable Virginia gentlemen, to provide the services of prostitution to the "biggest" lawyers, politicians, and other civic leaders in the area, as Reba repeatedly reminds her visitors, and to cooperate with political powers such as Eustace Graham, to maintain the *status quo*. Reba's comments on the protection she enjoys in Memphis emphasize the degree to which her institution, illegal and disreputable, is nevertheless essential and valued.

The underworld mirrors the respectable world in a particular way; it reveals those parts of society that belong to its "unconscious," which are placed out of sight, repressed but not eliminated. The mirroring underworld points to the fictionality of respectable society, to its pretense that its ideology is comprehensive. Even though the underworld has a real existence and real functions in relation to the respectable world, there is a sense in which

it is also a fantasy. For example, respectable characters often make use of the underworld to maintain fantasies of self and social relations.

The usefulness of the split worlds is obvious, for example, in the cases of Narcissa and Reba. Narcissa is a respectable widow with no apparent desire to marry. She has found a socially acceptable feminine identity in which she is completely independent of male domination. She has no desire to change, and she ruthlessly, even viciously, maintains her position. Reba occupies a similar position in the underworld, though she appears less ruthless, perhaps because her position depends less on appearances than Narcissa's does. Reba, too, will do whatever is necessary to protect her position from real threats, and she has no compunctions about helping Popeye to hold Temple prisoner. Narcissa's independence from male domination depends, at least in part, upon the services Reba's business provides, satisfying the sexual drives of respectable men so that they may do without the services of respectable women. Likewise, Reba's business depends to some extent upon the various reasons respectable women have for avoiding sex, one of which is to avoid submission to men. This convenient arrangement is one symptom of the social sickness of which the split in the world is a major sign. The arrangement suggests that unjust gender relations are somehow at the center of social illness. The extent and seriousness of the disease are indicated by a more sinister connection between Narcissa and Reba.

Narcissa maintains her social position by making indirect use of the underworld. To separate Horace from the Goodwin case, she goes to Eustace Graham with the information that Clarence Snopes has talked with Horace. Eustace, then, is able to muscle information from Snopes, to reach through Reba, presumably, and a Memphis "Jew lawyer," to Popeye in hiding with Temple after the murder of Red, and to bring Temple to the Jefferson courtroom where she cooperates in asserting Narcissa's view of the case. Narcissa's view is that Goodwin is a bootlegger and murderer, who lives with a whore and, therefore, deserves violent destruction; by threatening her social position, Goodwin is violating a lady, so it is appropriate that he also be a perverted rapist. Her view of the situation coincides almost perfectly with the view most advantageous to Popeye. Narcissa's portrayal of Horace and of the ideals of justice that he believes should underpin society is justified by the event, an event in which the underworld is preserved at the expense of a bootlegger who has become inconvenient to the respectable world, an "embarrassment" to the underworld, and a useful sacrifice for both worlds. Narcissa's identity is affirmed, the *status quo* is preserved, and Popeye evades charges of murder and rape.

Respectable society gives up the genuine truth, justice, and virtue that law, order, and morality should serve. The respectable world maintains the social order by using the underworld to help sustain false but desirable definitions of people and events. Such cooperation between the two worlds reveals that the split between them is a form of disease. This disease is manifested in virtually every choice and activity in the two worlds. For example, Faulkner introduces parodies of respectable activities that illustrate the disease. Red's funeral and the gathering afterwards at Reba's house parody grief and moral outrage by showing underworld characters acting out the external behavior of grief and outrage without the feeling that would make the actions sincere. Though some people at each event may have genuine feelings, the groups cannot sustain the behavior without sharing the feelings. In both cases the result is grotesque black humor: the corpse spilled from the casket in a riot about beer, the beer-stealing child punctuating with vomit the retired prostitutes' detailed condemnation of Popeye's voyeurism. Clarence's initiation of Virgil and Fonzo into bargain-basement sex parodies the processes of moral education that lead to the arrogance and mendacity of the college students Horace observes on the train to Oxford and that lead to Gowan's learning how to drink like a gentleman at Virginia. These people mask utterly self-indulgent and amoral behavior with grossly insufficient pieties. The grief of Red's drunken mourners and the outrage of the madames may seem more sincere and moral than the petty economies of Clarence, the wit and polish of the students, or Gowan's ridiculous idea that a gentleman is defined by the quantity of liquor he can consume while remaining conscious, but all are missing the necessary core of a deeply held belief about what is good for individuals and society. The self-indulgent amorality of the respectable world rests upon an almost universally shared fantasy that evil impulses remain confined to the underworld. Sustained by this belief, respectable people depend daily upon the existence of an underworld, yet manage through false pieties, both large and small, to remain blind to their dependence and to the horrors they commit in preserving it.

The split between these two worlds extends into language and character: words fragment into double meanings that reflect the two worlds; the main characters reveal internal divisions that also parallel their divided world.

Words repeatedly double their meanings in the novel, from Horace's and Popeye's transformations of *bird* in the opening chapters, through Horace's and Little Belle's unravelling of *shrimp*, the chaos unleashed at Red's funeral by *blue* and the confusion of *bier* with *beer*, to Popeye's and his associates' problems with *jack*, to Popeye's finally getting entangled in the meanings of *fix*. Horace needles Popeye about his ignorance of birds, except those he eats; then Popeye tells Ruby that there is a "bird" outside (meaning a man from the respectable world). Horace carries shrimp home, his life is measured in drops of shrimp juice on the sidewalk, his wife *eats* shrimp, and Little Belle, in calling him a shrimp, taunts him with his role as Belle's servant and suggests that Belle consumes him body and soul. Popeye calls all males "Jack" and spends his life dragging down jack until he is tired of it. When he asks the hangman (also Jack) to fix his disarranged hair, the hangman agrees and springs the trap. These are only a few examples of transforming puns in which significant words shift meanings between one situation and another in arbitrary and often highly dangerous ways. These point again to the way in which this culture is diseased, for they emphasize the degree to which people remain blind to the forces that manipulate them. These characters assume their control over language, only to find that it turns back upon them in surprising, usually violent ways, especially when the characters move outside their familiar social worlds. They remain unable to see the eddies and currents of the culture within which they are submerged, but this flow is revealed to us readers. We see how all are trapped in diseased cultural assumptions, the main sign of which is society's very split into two antithetical worlds.

One of the most terrifying of these revelations of blindness centering on a shifting word occurs when Temple stands before a mirror at the Grotto looking for marks on her face of Popeye's recent violence that she might use to incite Red to kill Popeye: "'Shucks,' she said, 'it didn't leave a mark even;' drawing the flesh this way and that. 'Little runt,' she said, peering at her reflection. She added a phrase, glibly obscene, with a detached parrot-like effect."[2] Though for the reader *shucks* is a heavily laden word by this point in the novel, associated with the corn cob, the mocking sounds of her bed at the Old Frenchman place, the laughing in the coffin in her death fantasy, and with Horace's nightmare rape vision after he interviews her, she is blind to these associations, just as she fails to see that she is utterly changed at this moment compared to her moral state when she pitied Ruby's baby. Even though he has left no visible mark, Popeye has helped transform her from a somewhat rebellious co-ed into a sexually active "moll" contemplating murder. Her failure to appreciate this transformation is a symptom of her society's failure to provide Temple with an inner, "spiritual" identity, a perspective like the reader's from which the transformation would be visible.

The split in Temple, which this unconscious pun emphasizes, is visible as well in Popeye and Horace. In Popeye, the split appears as a lack, indicated by his impotence. He reaches out blindly for self-realization by imitating others, having no inner understanding of the spiritual qualities beneath the surfaces he can observe. As a result, his behavior seems arbitrary and self-contradictory. In Horace, as in Temple, the split is between two selves. The Old Frenchman place and Reba's present a surface where it becomes possible for people from the respectable world to view their mirrored images in the disreputable world. Horace meets his opposite, Popeye, at the Old Frenchman place, and he encounters another much more complex mirroring when he talks with Temple at Reba's. Temple comes from the respectable world to the Old Frenchman place, where she "passes through the looking-glass" to be seen on the other side of it when Horace talks with her.

Why Popeye approaches "the surface of the mirror" by spending time at the Old Frenchman place is essentially mysterious, but his behavior suggests at least one interesting possibility. Popeye talks more intimately with Ruby than with anyone else, trying to persuade her to come to Memphis with him. Ruby implies to Horace that she and Lee are living and working at the Old Frenchman place, despite its isolation and inconvenience, for the sake of their child. When Horace persists in asking why Ruby and Lee remain in such an out-of-the-way place, she shows him her child (pp. 17-20); and both Lee and Ruby see Popeye as an unwelcome intruder. That Popeye has joined them there, that he tries to obtain Ruby, and that he appropriates Temple, when she proves more attractive to the other men than Ruby, may indicate that he, like the Goodwins, is reaching toward a meaningful, fulfilling identity. Such an identity proves incomprehensible to him. Unable to love or to understand love, he can never escape the underworld to another world as Ruby and Lee have attempted, with limited success, to do. Instead, he grasps at the physical symbol of desire. Of course, Lee and Ruby have not attempted to enter the respectable world, but to separate themselves from the trap or disease of the entire mirroring structure of two worlds. Popeye's attempt is futile, then, not only because he cannot love, but also because passing through the mirror, as he might do by appropriating a woman and imitating a marriage, is not really a solution. Temple's fate makes this clear.

Temple's split is perhaps the clearest, for she tries life in both worlds. As a college freshman, Temple is a child moving into respectable womanhood. Before her arrival at the Old Frenchman place she has mastered respectable courtship in which a woman depends upon the man to restrain his and her sexual desire by not forcing sex upon her. Therefore, she is always "safe," especially in the groups of men where she is usually found. At the Old Frenchman place she is forced into a new group of men, among whom this rule does not apply. Her split appears when she is simultaneously attracted to and repelled by the possibilities of this world. Temple at the Old Frenchman place looks and behaves as Day describes the typical Gothic heroine in her fantastic Gothic world. When Popeye rapes her with a corn cob and kidnaps her, he takes her through the mirror. At Reba's, Temple puts away her respectable self and enters fully into her dark, sexually aggressive side.

She finds that this life does not provide the gratification it promised, in part because it is based on a false opposition in which female sexual desire is evil. She expects to be free when she passes through to the dark side, but she finds that the underworld controls female sexuality as rigidly as does the respectable world. Popeye does not allow her to have sex except when he is present. When he sees that she is enjoying sex with Red, Popeye separates them. Because Popeye does not experience "normal" sexual desire, she cannot use her attractiveness to gain satisfaction by manipulating him. Her attempt to have Red kill Popeye fails. She is as powerless in the underworld as in the respectable world, and she is as ungratified, though she has experienced sexual desire and pleasure. She relives a version of Ruby's experience when Ruby's father killed her first lover. Wrested back through the mirror, Temple appears at Goodwin's trial, dressed in black, like Popeye, beneath her white coat, as Popeye's and Eustace's puppet. When her father and brothers take her away from court, she responds to the completion of her return to respectability with gestures reminiscent of her violation and abduction at the Old Frenchman place.[3] Shifting from one group of men to another, from one "daddy" to another, changes nothing important for her. Her last gestures, a look into her mirror and, then, out at a Parisian "waste land," underline a discontent that borders upon despair.

Like Narcissa in her preservation of respectability, Temple, in her movement through the underworld, seems unconsciously concerned with a problem of feminine identity. While Narcissa ruthlessly preserves an identity she has achieved, Temple tries out and finds wanting two versions of feminine identity. Horace's split also concerns feminine identity. Indeed, an examination of Horace's divided self helps to open another perspective on these mirroring worlds.

Several critics, but most notably John T. Matthews (pp. 247-255), have noticed Horace's attraction to his step-daughter, Little Belle. This attraction takes the form of a concern for her respectability. When he becomes drunk at the Old Frenchman place, he expresses frustration at his inability to influence Little Belle's moral development. Her budding sexuality appears to him as a natural force that will bloom as it may; because she sees him as a sort of employee rather than as a fatherly moral guide, he cannot successfully direct her sexual life. Horace wants to exercise the traditional authority of the father who superintends his daughter's sexual behavior in order to guarantee her respectability and her entrance into the moral order he wishes to affirm. His narration of recent events shows that he has sublimated his response to her sexual attractiveness by recourse to the father's role. He leaves home in part because nothing there confirms him in that role. Indeed, when he sees in the double mirrors Little Belle's dissimulation of her affirmation of his role as father, he sees quite literally the split that troubles him. The mirrors show the lack of restraint beneath her pretense. If he accepts this lack of restraint, then his sublimation will be defeated; he will have to recognize the natural as fundamental. In his case, sexual attraction to this step-daughter is "natural." In the absence of social agreement that sublimation is valuable and necessary, Horace will have to know himself as split. He will be forced to acknowledge his desire for Little Belle, a fate that could be liberating, since it would tend to dissolve Horace's rigid separation of the split worlds.

Horace, like Narcissa, depends upon the existence of the two mirroring worlds. His desire to bring Popeye to justice is justified by the literal truth of Popeye's guilt, but it is also necessary to Horace's concept of himself. As Horace is forced to recognize when he interviews Temple (though he seems to repress it afterwards), Popeye has apparently had intercourse with Temple, thereby enacting the desire Horace tries so hard to repress, to have intercourse with Temple's double, Little Belle. When Horace vomits the coffee he drank in Memphis, he envisions that violation of Temple as his own desire to violate Little Belle, and he views the composite act as utter self-destruction, as his own rape by "the world."

Horace needs Popeye to stand for his repressed self. This need accounts for Horace's great mistake in attempting to save Lee by accusing Popeye. However, he cannot eliminate the "Popeye" in himself. Horace's attempt to create a scapegoat by accusing Popeye is no more successful than Temple's to eliminate Popeye as forbidding "father." Furthermore, Horace's attempt contributes to Lee's destruction just as surely as do Narcissa's betrayal and Temple's perjury.

Horace's split between a conscious desire to control his women for their own good and the good of society and his unconscious desire to possess them sexually is mirrored in his entire culture. This is especially apparent in the novel's many misogynist jokes. For example, the jokes of the college boys on the train to Oxford reduce sexual intercourse to the violent, mechanical punching of tickets, and their women to pieces of meat:

"I'm going to punch mine Friday night."
"Eeeeyow."
"Do you like liver?"
"I cant reach that far."
"Eeeeeyow."

(pp. 178-179)

When the salesmen discuss Temple after the trial, one says, "She was some baby. Jeez. I wouldn't have used no cob" (p. 309). While condemning Lee as a pervert, they also identify with his desire to possess the violated woman. The Kinston cab driver who returns Horace home says, "We got to protect our girls. Might need them ourselves" (p. 313). These and several other similar jokes reveal the doubleness of all men's attitudes toward women. Protecting their violated respectability is a matter for "a bonfire of gasoline" because genitals are the *most* sacred parts of "that most sacred thing in life: womanhood" (p. 298). But every man secretly desires to do what these prohibitions and punishments are to prevent.

Therefore, all such desires are projected onto the underworld, where one can go to indulge them, but of which one makes an example whenever the opportunity arises, thus reaffirming the repression.

The mirroring worlds of *Sanctuary* form a recognizable representation of Faulkner's contemporary, social world. The doubling of that split in Horace and in the general misogyny of his culture points toward one important aspect of the origin and meaning of this split. William Patrick Day provides a way of coming at the origin of the split that will help to explain its meaning.

Day argues that the Gothic tradition in fiction in the eighteenth and nineteenth centuries is concerned with the psychological adjustments of the new middle class to an industrial capitalist society. Of primary concern to the consumers of Gothic novels were adjustments of family structure and gender role. Hence popular Gothic novels repeatedly deal with themes of the relationships between parents and children, between brothers and sisters, and between lovers. One of the functions of the Gothic novels was to parody the romantic conceptions of gender roles illustrated in Richardson's *Pamela*. In such novels, good females exhibit a will to virtue that tends to render them passive before male authority. Good males are characterized by a will to power consistent with their duty to dominate and to order life. Gothic novels parody these conceptions of gender roles by revealing their dark sides: the feminine desire to submit in order to partake of power and the masculine desire to ravish in order to possess the feminine without restraint. Day contends that human identity is artificially split by these conventional archetypes, that males find themselves cut off from aspects of themselves culturally defined as feminine and that females are cut off from aspects of themselves culturally defined as masculine. Gothic fiction shows such characters attempting to establish wholeness of identity in perverse ways, by projecting the forbidden self onto another, then attempting to appropriate the other. The other is often a family member, making the relationship incestuous. Incest conveys the tension between the two parts of the self that desire unity in identity, but which are forbidden it by a strongly internalized cultural ideology. The results of attempting to unify are usually terror and destruction (Day, Chapter 2).

Faulkner produces a more self-conscious and sophisticated text than is usual in the Gothic tradition. He brings the acts of fantasy and projection into the fiction, making them visible to rather than merely available to the reader. *Sanctuary* is not a reader's fantasy as are *The Mysteries of Udolpho* or *Dracula*. Instead, the reader observes the fantasy-making of characters and culture. Nevertheless, the characters of *Sanctuary* seem to be dealing with the same Gothic problems Day discusses, though at a later historical stage. Horace is closest to the tradition as described by Day, but the women and the male culture apart from Horace reveal changes in attitudes. At this historical stage, women show a strong discontent with their culturally defined roles, and male misogyny bubbles near the surface of the whole culture.

Horace really wants to fulfill the traditional father's role, seeing it as necessary to familial, social, and moral order. Beneath that desire is a repressed desire to claim "feminine" aspects of his self. This desire takes the form of sexual attraction to Little Belle. When he encounters an enactment of that desire in Popeye's violation of Temple, Horace contemplates the loss of his world and his self. Unable to bear this loss, he represses his vision of an androgynous, self-destroying monster and attempts a return to his mission of destroying Popeye. Seeing only the horror of Temple's violation, he is confirmed in his inability to see that in desiring Little Belle he is really trying to unify his self. Furthermore, Horace cannot repress his own desires by repressing their projections in the external world as do the protagonists of Charles Brockden Brown's *Wieland* and Stoker's *Dracula*. Like those Gothic protagonists who attempt to achieve wholeness through the exercise of power, Horace destroys or, at least, maims himself; he is unable to achieve unity by asserting separation.

The women of *Sanctuary* are discontented with their socially defined roles, unlike the Gothic heroine Day describes, who wants most of all to live a conventional life (Day, p. 17). When Horace recounts his argument with Little Belle over how she should regulate her sex life, he reveals that Little Belle is asserting her right to choose her male friends without the intervention of fathers and brothers. When Ruby tells the story of how her father and brother killed her first lover, branding her a whore for loving in defiance of their choices, she asserts her freedom, a freedom she has subsequently exercised despite that early defeat. However, though Ruby's attempts come closest to success, she does not break away from the sickness of the split worlds. Neither do Narcissa and Temple.

Narcissa's role as virtuous widow makes her independent of the masculine; she need not submit. Of course, Narcissa's rebellion against male domination is self-defeating. In order to insulate herself from particular males and to assert power over them, she surrenders utterly to the cultural ideology that confines her to a narrow and grossly immoral life, which deprives her of spiritual being as the price of her independence. She becomes cold, soulless, and loveless. Temple's perpetual discontent, though it is terrifyingly childish in comparison with Ruby's pursuit of love, is yet another indicator of the failure of traditional female roles, whether respectable or disreputable, to provide fulfillment for women in *Sanctuary*'s world. She, too, surrenders her soul in order to experience freedom and power. Though the women of *Sanctuary*, unlike most women in earlier Gothic novels, actively, if not always consciously, oppose the roles imposed upon them by their culture, their opposition remains partial and unsuccessful, leading to stunning defeats and wrenching horrors. Only Ruby approaches a vision of her situation as inclusive as that granted the reader.

Males' protests against evisceration by their culture take the form of a violence that almost constantly boils near the surface of social behavior. They seem required to place respectable women on the pedestal of purity, and then to hate them for their unattainability. Their anger shows not only in their misogynous humor but also in the fury and perversity of their repression. While destroying Goodwin, Jefferson duplicates the crime of which it accuses him: "Do to the lawyer what we did to him. What he did to her. Only we never used a cob. We made him wish we had used a cob" (p. 311). They threaten Horace with his own nightmare vision of multiple, mutual, self-destructive rape, revealing how fully they violate themselves to preserve what their diseased ideology tells them are virtue and justice. In a terrifying reflection of Red's funeral that perverts the ritual it attempts, the town repeats and extends the crime it punishes. In earlier Gothic novels, aggression against women is usually confined to the male protagonists and their particular victims. In *Sanctuary*, the will to aggression against all females is general among the males, for all the men seem to sense that their cultural ideology, in effect, castrates them by forbidding them the unity with the other sex that they naturally desire, the unity of pleasure in the procreative act. This unity is only possible if, as Day argues, men and women can affirm and "identify with" the other sex in themselves (Day, p. 132), and the culture of this novel places such an ideal beyond anyone's reach.

In *Sanctuary*, the old moribund definitions of gender roles have become so restrictive that they inevitably lead to real, rather than fantasized, perversity and destruction in whatever direction one attempts to extend them. The only sane alternative suggested in the novel is to leave society behind, to found a family on mutual love and commitment as far away from contemporary social values as one can get. There, perhaps, conventional gender roles may be abandoned, and the "androgyny" of pleasure in reproduction may be realized (Day, pp. 146-149). Ruby and Lee seek sanctuary from the dangers of Memphis, Ruby sacrificing the comforts that Horace and Popeye believe she could easily have, were she willing to abandon Lee or let her child grow up the way Popeye did. Like many an escapee before them in American fiction—Ishmael, Huckleberry Finn, and Jake Barnes spring to mind—Ruby and Lee are drawn back into the corrupt and powerful social structure by their needs and desires, their weaknesses and errors, and the arbitrary disasters brought on by others such as Popeye, Temple, and Horace.

In *Sanctuary*, then, Faulkner continues the exploration of concerns that were central to the Gothic tradition as described by Day. By placing these concerns more explicitly in a social context than was often the case in earlier Gothic classics and by representing the characters and culture as fantasy-makers, Faulkner exposes the fictionality as well as the terrifying destructiveness of a decadent social ideology that has descended from the conventions of gender role parodied in the earlier Gothic tradition. Faulkner shows women making futile and destructive attempts to escape the conventional definitions of feminine and masculine identities, and he shows men in violent, unconscious protest against the psychologically castrating power of those same definitions.

Notes

1. (Chicago: University of Chicago Press, 1985).

2. William Faulkner, *Sanctuary: The Corrected Text* (New York: Vintage, 1987), p. 245.

3. John T. Matthews, "The Elliptical Nature of *Sanctuary,*" *Novel*, 17 (1984), 257-258.

A Selection of Other Sources Consulted

Adamowski, T. H. "Faulkner's Popeye: The 'Other' as Self." *Canadian Review of American Studies*, 8 (1977), 36-51.

Brooks, Cleanth. *William Faulkner. The Yoknapatawpha Country.* New Haven: Yale University Press, 1963.

Broughton, Panthea R. *William Faulkner: The Abstract and the Actual.* Baton Rouge: Louisiana State University Press, 1974.

Canfield, J. C., ed. *Twentieth Century Interpretations of "Sanctuary."* Englewood Cliffs, New Jersey: Prentice-Hall, 1982. Reprints several authors on this list as well as other useful selections.

Cox, Dianne Luce. "A Measure of Innocence: *Sanctuary*'s Temple Drake." *Mississippi Quarterly*, 39 (1986), 301-324.

Frazier, D. L."Gothicism in *Sanctuary*: The Black Pall and the Crap Table." *Modern Fiction Studies*, 2 (1956), 109-113.

Heller, Terry. "Terror and Empathy in Faulkner's *Sanctuary*." *Arizona Quarterly*, 40 (1984), 344-364.

———. *The Delights of Terror.* Urbana: University of Illinois Press, 1987.

Kerr, Elizabeth. *William Faulkner's Gothic Domain.* Port Washington, New York: Kennikat Press, 1979.

Mellard, James M. "Lacan and Faulkner: A Post-Freudian Analysis of Humor in the Fiction," in *Faulkner and Humor: Faulkner and Yoknapatawpha, 1984,* ed. Doreen Fowler and Ann J. Abadie. Jackson: University Press of Mississippi, 1986.

Muhlenfeld, Elisabeth. "Bewildered Witness: Temple Drake in *Sanctuary*." *Faulkner Journal*, 1 (1986), 43-55.

Page, Sally R. *Faulkner's Women.* Deland, Florida: Everett/Edwards, 1972.

Polk, Noel. "'The Dungeon was Mother Herself': William Faulkner: 1927-1931," in *New Directions in Faulkner Studies: Faulkner and Yoknapatawpha, 1983,* ed. Doreen Fowler and Ann J. Abadie. Jackson: University Press of Mississippi, 1984.

Rossky, William. "The Pattern of Nightmare in *Sanctuary;* or Miss Reba's Dogs." *Modern Fiction Studies*, 15 (1969-70), 503-515.

Seidel, Kathryn Lee. "From Narcissist to Masochist: A New Look at Temple Drake." *Journal of Evolutionary Psychology*, 5 (1984), 27-35.

Vickery, Olga. *The Novels of William Faulkner.* Baton Rouge: Louisiana State University Press, 1964.

Zink, Karl E. "Flux and Frozen Moment: The Imagery of Stasis in Faulkner's Prose." *PMLA*, 71 (1956), 285-301.

FURTHER READING

Biographies

Blotner, Joseph. *Faulkner: A Biography.* Jackson, Miss.: University Press of Mississippi, 2005, 778 p.

Originally published in 1974, this is an updated version of what is considered by many to be the definitive Faulkner biography.

Parini, Jay. *One Matchless Time: A Life of William Faulkner.* New York: Harper Collins, 2004, 512 p.

Biography that includes interviews with Faulkner's friends and family, and an examination of each of Faulkner's works.

Criticism

Burns, Margie. "A Good Rose Is Hard to Find: Southern Gothic as Signs of Social Dislocation in Faulkner and O'Connor." In *Image and Ideology in Modern/Postmodern Discourse*, pp. 105-23. Albany: State University of New York Press, 1991.

Contends that Southern Gothic is a literary technique that both represents and hides the dehumanization of the South into perceived stereotypes; analyzes works by Flannery O'Connor and Faulkner as examples of this technique.

Donaldson, Susan V. "Making a Spectacle: Welty, Faulkner, and Southern Gothic." *Mississippi Quarterly* 50, no. 4 (fall 1997): 567-83.

Compares the portraits of women created by Faulkner and Eudora Welty, noting that while Faulkner's narratives reverberate with the effort to impose cultural ideas of femininity on his Southern characters, Welty's narratives present Gothic heroines that break out of the narrow confines of their worlds.

Jarraway, David R. "The Gothic Import of Faulkner's 'Black Son' in *Light in August*." In *American Gothic: New Inventions in a National Narrative*, edited and with an introduction by Robert K. Martin, pp. 57-74. Iowa City: University of Iowa Press, 1998.

Uses the critical theory of Julia Kristeva to explore Gothic identity in Light In August, *focusing on the tragic career of Joe Christmas.*

Machinek, Anna. "William Faulkner and the Gothic Tradition." *Kwartalnik Neofilologiczny* 36, no. 2 (1989): 105-14.

Traces the Gothic elements in Faulkner's fiction.

Martin, Robert K. "Haunted Jim Crow: Gothic Fictions by Hawthorne and Faulkner." In *American Gothic: New Inventions in a National Narrative*, edited and with an introduction by Robert K. Martin, pp. 129-42. Iowa City: University of Iowa Press, 1998.

Compares Nathaniel Hawthorne's The House of the Seven Gables *with* Absalom, Absalom! *and argues that Faulkner's novel presents a more complicated picture of the world, as it replaces Hawthorne's happy ending with a vision that is ultimately nightmarish.*

Perry, J. Douglas. "Gothic as Vortex: The Form of Horror in Capote, Faulkner, and Styron." *Modern Fiction Studies* 19 (1973): 153-67.

Proposes that in addition to the commonality of theme and images, American Gothic fiction also uses traditional structures and techniques to create a concentric series of events, drawing the reader into an intense interaction between human communities that exist inside and outside the novel.

Stone, Edward. "Usher, Poquelin, and Miss Emily: The Progress of Southern Gothic." *Georgia Review* 14 (winter 1960): 433-43.

Considers "A Rose for Emily" in the tradition of Southern Gothic fiction.

OTHER SOURCES FROM GALE:

Additional coverage of Faulkner's life and career is contained in the following sources published by Thomson Gale: *American Writers; American Writers Retrospective Supplement*, Vol. 1; *Authors and Artists for Young Adults*, Vol. 7; *Beacham's Encyclopedia of Popular Fiction: Biography and Resources*, Vol. 1; *Beacham's Guide to Literature for Young Adults*, Vols. 5, 15; *Concise Dictionary of American Literary Biography, 1929-1941; Contemporary Authors*, Vols. 81-84; *Contemporary Authors New Revision Series*, Vol. 33; *Contemporary Literary Criticism*, Vols. 1, 3, 6, 8, 9, 11, 14, 18, 28, 52, 68; *Dictionary of Literary Biography*, Vols. 9, 11, 44, 102; *Dictionary of Literary Biography*

Documentary Series, Vol. 2; Dictionary of Literary Biography Yearbook, 1986, 1997; DISCovering Authors; DISCovering Authors: British; DISCovering Authors: Canadian; DISCovering Authors Modules: Most-studied Authors and Novelists; DISCovering Authors 3.0; Encyclopedia of World Literature in the 20th Century, Ed. 3; Exploring Novels; Exploring Short Stories; Literary Movements for Students, Vol. 2; Literature and Its Times, Vol. 2; Literature and Its Times Supplement, Vol. 1; Literature Resource Center; Major 20th-Century Writers, Eds. 1, 2; Novels for Students, Vols. 4, 8, 13; Reference Guide to American Literature, Ed. 4; Reference Guide to Short Fiction, Ed. 2; Short Stories for Students, Vols. 2, 5, 6, 12; Short Story Criticism, Vols. 1, 35, 42; Twayne's United States Authors; Twentieth-Century Literary Criticism, Vol. 141; and World Literature Criticism.

WILLIAM GODWIN

(1756 - 1836)

English philosopher, novelist, essayist, historian, playwright, and biographer.

Although known primarily for his philosophical works and his influence on English Romantic writers, Godwin is also remembered for his contributions to the Gothic literary tradition. His best-known novel, *Things As They Are; or, The Adventures of Caleb Williams* (1794), is a didactic tale about the evils of government that borrows heavily from the popular Gothic fiction of the day. *Caleb Williams* dramatizes many of the anarchistic and rationalistic beliefs that Godwin put forward in his philosophical masterpiece, *An Enquiry Concerning Political Justice and Its Influence on General Virtue and Happiness* (1793), which argues that humankind is innately good and capable of living harmoniously without laws or institutions. Godwin's only other work in the Gothic tradition is the occult tale *St. Leon* (1799), which also has philosophical overtones. Critics point out that this novel, as well as his numerous other works, lack the emotional power and intellectual appeal of *Caleb Williams* and *Political Justice*. The influence of Godwin's writings on his younger contemporaries, including novelists, poets, economists, and philosophers, was considerable. However, Godwin's philosophical and literary reputation has declined, and he is chiefly known today as a figure of historical importance—as the husband of philosopher Mary Wollstonecraft, as the father of novelist Mary Wollstonecraft Shelley, and as the author of two minor Gothic novels.

BIOGRAPHICAL INFORMATION

The seventh of thirteen children, Godwin was born in Wisbeach, England, to a Presbyterian minister and his wife. Raised in a strict, puritanical environment, Godwin trained for the ministry at an early age and became a Sandemanian clergyman in 1777. However, after studying the French revolutionary philosophers, he grew disenchanted with religion and eventually became an atheist. Leaving the church in 1783, Godwin moved to London, intending to make his living as an author. He began writing pamphlets and literary parodies, most of them published anonymously. Against the backdrop of revolution in France and the repression of seditious writings and speech in Britain, he produced *Political Justice*, which met with immediate success. Although its primary appeal was to intellectuals, it also found its way into the hands of the working class. A year later Godwin addressed that audience more directly with the publication of *Caleb Williams*, which he claimed to have written for people who would never read books of science or philosophy.

Godwin was already an established and influential writer and radical when in 1796 he met

Wollstonecraft, the author of *A Vindication of the Rights of Woman* (1792), an attack on society's treatment of women. Their rapport was immediate, and soon the two began living together. When Wollstonecraft became pregnant a few months later, the two wed despite their mutual distaste for the institution of marriage because they wanted to ensure the legal rights of their child. By all accounts, both found great joy in wedlock, but their happiness was short-lived. Several days after the birth of their daughter in 1797, Wollstonecraft died of complications from the delivery. A desolate Godwin recorded his memories of their brief life together in *Memoirs of the Author of "A Vindication of the Rights of Woman"* (1798), in which he wrote of his wife, "I honoured her intellectual powers and the nobleness and generosity of her propensities; mere tenderness would not have been adequate to produce the happiness we experienced." Left with his infant daughter as well as a stepdaughter to care for, Godwin set out to find a mother for his children. He was turned down by one woman after another before marrying Mary Jane Clairmont, by all accounts a harsh, cruel woman who treated his children poorly.

Although he continued to write and publish works of philosophy and fiction, Godwin was struggling financially, and around 1805 he and his wife began publishing children's books, histories, and biographies in a desperate attempt to support their growing family. Godwin also relied heavily on the financial assistance of the young followers who sought his philosophical guidance; most notable among these was the Romantic poet Percy Bysshe Shelley. In 1814, Shelley, who was already married, eloped with Godwin's sixteen-year-old daughter, Mary. Though a furious Godwin disowned them both, he continued to demand Shelley's monetary support. Godwin's wrath diminished when the two married several years later, and he became once again extremely close to his daughter. Shelley too remained a devoted disciple of his father-in-law, supporting his writing even as his popularity was declining and his ideas were falling out of favor. Godwin continued to write until his death due to complications of a cold in 1836.

MAJOR WORKS

Political Justice contains the theoretical essence of all Godwin's later writings. In this work, Godwin denounced contemporary governments as corrupt and ineffective, arguing that reason rather than law should provide the ruling force of society. Through the development of reason, he declared, humanity could become perfect. Godwin maintained too that criminals should be reformed, not merely punished. Of all the arguments advanced in *Political Justice*, perhaps the best known is Godwin's disdain for the institution of marriage: he advocated that men and women should be united solely by a bond of mutual respect rather than a social and legal contract. Godwin was nearly prosecuted for these unconventional beliefs. However, among those who sympathized with its unorthodox tenets, *Political Justice* met with immediate acclaim, and its author was widely hailed as an influential philosopher.

Following the success of *Political Justice*, Godwin produced *Caleb Williams*, a novel inspired by his desire to disseminate the ideas of *Political Justice* through a more popular form. A tale of good triumphing over evil and an individual conquering a corrupt system, the novel tells the story of Caleb Williams, a man persecuted by his employer, Ferdinando Falkland, and jailed for a crime he did not commit. Williams's troubles begin when he learns that Falkland once committed murder. When he confesses his discovery, he gets swept up in a series of events over which he has no control, as Falkland frames him for a capital crime. Falkland is an important prototype of the seemingly benevolent but cruel and morally bankrupt Gothic villain, a dual personality that foreshadows Robert Louis Stevenson's Dr. Jekyll and Mr. Hyde. The account of Caleb's imprisonment and exile is a calculated indictment of the horrors of the British criminal justice. Godwin's plot combines historical events with psychological realism and Gothic and detective elements. Though undeniably propagandistic, the novel won critical praise for its synthesis of content and style. It established the sub-genre of "political Gothics" and was a precedent for the popular Victorian crime-fiction genre. It was a great success, to the extent that the publishers reinstated in the later editions of 1795 the controversial preface they had not dared to print in 1794 because it had been considered politically subversive.

Godwin's other Gothic-inspired tale, *St. Leon*, is a historical novel that reflects his interest in heroic drama and his desire to modify some of his earlier radical beliefs, which were considered harsh and insensitive. A sentimental depiction of the joys of domesticity, *St. Leon* is also a tribute to his late wife. In the apologetic preface to an 1831 edition of *St. Leon*, Godwin observed that he had been urgently solicited to follow up the success of his first, but had long remained in a state of "diffidence and irresolution" for lack of a new idea. What he eventually produced was a longer and far more orthodox Gothic tale following the adventures of a dissolute French nobleman who takes to farming after gambling away his inheritance but loses everything to a caprice of nature. Response to the novel was mixed, and critics termed *St. Leon* more ambitious in design than Godwin's range would permit. *St. Leon* is, however, regarded as significant in several respects. In its flirtation with Rosicrucian mysticism it anticipates Edward Bulwer-Lytton's *Zanoni* and further compounded the influence of Godwin on that writer. It also provided inspiration for Mary Shelley's *Frankenstein*.

Two years before he died at the age of seventy-eight, Godwin published another work that delves into the occult. *Lives of the Necromancers* (1834), despite its title, is less a series of biographies than a study of the way the mind is readily deceived by the overwrought imagination and the desire for immortality. The work has been described as a series of tales of sorcery culled from the Bible, the Ancient World, and the Far East, as well as from medieval Europe. One of the admirers of the book was Edgar Allan Poe.

CRITICAL RECEPTION

At the time of his death, Godwin's contemporaries considered him a figure of historical and literary importance whose beliefs had inspired such individuals as Samuel Taylor Coleridge, Robert Southey, Percy Bysshe Shelley, and William Wordsworth. However, Godwin's works soon fell into relative obscurity, receiving attention only from critics who censured his verbosity and excessive didacticism. It was not until the turn of the century that critics began to demonstrate a renewed interest in Godwin as a philosopher and author. Early twentieth-century studies stressed the literary merits of *Political Justice,* and its value as one of the main documents of English Romantic philosophy is now firmly established. *Caleb Williams,* too, has enjoyed a revival. Since the 1940s, critics have analyzed various aspects of the work, including its elements of tragedy and mystery, its status as a work of Gothic fiction, its two endings, and its prose style. Scholars regard the work as an important contribution to the evolution of the English novel and one of the first novels to successfully combine fiction and philosophy. Critics who have focused on the work's gothicism have argued that the author used Gothic devices to make the work less of a simple

adventure narrative and to focus on the psychological and emotional excesses of the characters. They have pointed out too that the use of Gothic elements highlights the defenselessness of the protagonist against a cruel and often faceless power.

Critical commentary on Godwin's other Gothic novel, *St. Leon,* is more scant today, but shortly after it was published in 1799 there appeared a parody entitled *St. Godwin: A Tale of the Sixteenth, Seventeenth and Eighteenth Century* (1800), which is a testament, if nothing else, to the work's popularity—or notoriety. Criticism of the novel today has focused on its exploration of life-extension and immortality, its influence on *Frankenstein,* as well as its debt to the philosophy of Jean Jacques Rousseau. Despite Poe's appreciation of *Lives of the Necromancers,* it is of little more than historical interest. Godwin's more important legacy, at least for readers of Gothic literature, is the influence he had on later practitioners of the genre and the synthesis of philosophy, social criticism, and horror in his novels.

PRINCIPAL WORKS

An Account of the Seminary That Will Be Opened at Epsom (essay) 1783

The History of the Life of William Pitt (biography) 1783

An Enquiry Concerning Political Justice and Its Influence on General Virtue and Happiness (essay) 1793

Cursory Strictures on the Charge delivered by Lord Chief Justice Eyre to the Grand Jury, October 2, 1794. First Published in the Morning Chronicle, October 21 (essay) 1794

Things as They Are; or, The Adventures of Caleb Williams (novel) 1794

Considerations on Lord Grenville's and Mr. Pitt's Bill Concerning Treasonable and Seditious Practices, and Unlawful Assemblies (essay) 1795

The Enquirer: Reflections on Education, Manners, and Literature (essays) 1797

Memoirs of the Author of "A Vindication of the Rights of Woman" (memoirs) 1798

St. Leon: A Tale of the Sixteenth Century (novel) 1799

Life of Geoffrey Chaucer (biography) 1803

Fleetwood; or, The New Man of Feeling (novel) 1805

Faulkener (play) 1807

Mandeville: A Tale of the Seventeenth Century in England (novel) 1817

Of Population: An Enquiry Concerning the Power of Increase in the Numbers of Mankind, Being an Answer to Mr. Malthus' Essay on That Subject (essay) 1820

Cloudesly: A Tale (novel) 1830

Thoughts on Man: His Nature, Productions, and Discoveries (essay) 1831

Deloraine: A Tale (novel) 1833

Lives of the Necromancers; or, An Account of the Most Eminent Persons Who Have Claimed or to Whom Has Been Imputed by Others, the Exercise of Magical Power (biographical sketches) 1834

Essays Never before Published (essays) 1873

PRIMARY SOURCES

WILLIAM GODWIN (ESSAY DATE 1794)

SOURCE: Godwin, William. Preface to *The Adventures of Caleb Williams; or, Things as They Are.* 1794. Revised edition, pp. xix-xx. London: Richard Bentley, 1849.

In the following preface to Caleb Williams, *written in 1794, Godwin explains the philosophical underpinnings of the novel. In a note appended to the original preface for the 1796 edition of the novel, Godwin explains why the preface was deleted from the first edition of the novel in 1794.*

The following narrative is intended to answer a purpose more general and important than immediately appears upon the face of it. The question now afloat in the world respecting *Things as they are,* is the most interesting that can be presented to the human mind. While one party pleads for reformation and change, the other extols in the warmest terms the existing constitution of society. It seemed as if something would be gained for the decision of this question, if that constitution were faithfully developed in its practical effects. What is now presented to the public is no refined and abstract speculation; it is a study and delineation of things passing in the moral world. It is but of late that the inestimable importance of political principles has been adequately apprehended. It is now known to philosophers that the spirit and character of the government intrudes itself into every rank of society. But this is a truth highly worthy to be communicated to persons whom books of philoso-

phy and science are never likely to reach. Accordingly it was proposed in the invention of the following work, to comprehend, as far as the progressive nature of a single story would allow, a general review of the modes of domestic and unrecorded despotism, by which man becomes the destroyer of man. If the author shall have taught a valuable lesson, without subtracting from the interest and passion by which a performance of this sort ought to be characterised, he will have reason to congratulate himself upon the vehicle he has chosen.

MAY 12, 1794

This preface was withdrawn in the original edition, in compliance with the alarms of booksellers. Caleb Williams made his first appearance in the world, in the same month in which the sanguinary plot broke out against the liberties of Englishmen, which was happily terminated by the acquittal of its first intended victims, in the close of that year. Terror was the order of the day; and it was feared that even the humble novelist might be shown to be constructively a traitor.

OCTOBER 29, 1795

WILLIAM GODWIN (ESSAY DATE 1834)

SOURCE: Godwin, William. "Ambitious Nature of Man." In *Lives of the Necromancers; or, An Account of the Most Eminent Persons in Successive Ages, Who Have Claimed for Themselves, or to Whom Has Been Imputed by Others, the Exercise of Magical Power.* 1834. Reprint edition, pp. 13-18. Whitefish, Mont.: Kessinger Publishing, 2004.

In the following excerpt from a book originally published in 1834, Godwin discusses certain pursuits and practices of persons skilled in magic and the supernatural.

The Desire to Command and Control Future Events.

Next to the consideration of those measures by which men have sought to dive into the secrets of future time, the question presents itself of those more daring undertakings, the object of which has been by some supernatural power to control the future, and place it in subjection to the will of the unlicensed adventurer. Men have always, especially in races of ignorance, and when they most felt their individual weakness, figured to themselves an invisible strength greater than their own; and, in proportion to their impatience, and the fervour of their desires, have sought to enter into a league with those beings whose mightier force might supply that in which their weakness failed.

Commerce with the Invisible World.

It is an essential feature of different ages and countries to vary exceedingly in the good or ill construction, the fame or dishonour, which shall attend upon the same conduct or mode of behaviour. In Egypt and throughout the East, especially in the early periods of history, the supposed commerce with invisible powers was openly professed, which, under other circumstances, and during the reign of different prejudices, was afterwards carefully concealed, and barbarously hunted out of the pale of allowed and authorised practice. The Magi of old, who claimed a power of producing miraculous appearances, and boasted a familiar intercourse with the world of spirits, were regarded by their countrymen with peculiar reverence, and considered as the first and chiefest men in the state. For this mitigated view of such dark and mysterious proceedings the ancients were in a great degree indebted to their polytheism. The Romans are computed to have acknowledged thirty thousand divinities, to all of whom was rendered a legitimate homage; and other countries in a similar proportion.

Sorcery and Enchantment.

In Asia, however, the gods were divided into two parties, under Oromasdes, the principle of good, and Arimanius, the principle of evil. These powers were in perpetual contention with each other, sometimes the one, and sometimes the other gaining the superiority. Arimanius and his legions were therefore scarcely considered as entitled to the homage of mankind. Those who were actuated by benevolence, and who desired to draw down blessings upon their fellow-creatures, addressed themselves to the principle of good: while such unhappy beings, with whom spite and ill-will had the predominance, may be supposed often to have invoked in preference the principle of evil. Hence seems to have originated the idea of sorcery, or an appeal by incantations and wicked arts to the demons who delighted in mischief.

These beings rejoiced in the opportunity of inflicting calamity and misery on mankind. But by what we read of them we might be induced to suppose that they were in some way restrained from gratifying their malignant intentions, and waited in eager hope, till some mortal reprobate should call out their dormant activity, and demand their aid.

Various enchantments were therefore employed by those unhappy mortals whose special desire was to bring down calamity and plagues upon the individuals or tribes of men against whom their animosity was directed. Unlawful and detested words and mysteries were called into action to conjure up demons who should yield their powerful and tremendous assistance. Songs of a wild and maniacal character were chaunted. Noisome scents and the burning of all unhallowed and odious things were resorted to. In later times books and formulas of a terrific character were commonly employed, upon the reading or recital of which the prodigies resorted to began to display themselves. The heavens were darkened; the thunder rolled; and fierce and blinding lightnings flashed from one corner of the heavens to the other. The earth quaked and rocked from side to side. All monstrous and deformed things showed themselves, "Gorgons, and Hydras, and Chimeras dire," enough to cause the stoutest heart to quail. Lastly, devils, whose name was legion, and to whose forms and distorted and menacing countenances superstition had annexed the most frightful ideas, crowded in countless multitudes upon the spectator, whose breath was flame, whose dances were full of terror, and whose strength infinitely exceeded everything human. Such were the appalling conceptions which ages of bigotry and ignorance annexed to the notion of sorcery, and with these they scared the unhappy beings over whom this notion had usurped an ascendency into lunacy, and prepared them for the perpetrating flagitious and unheard-of deeds.

The result of these horrible incantations was not less tremendous, than the preparations might have led us to expect. The demons possessed all the powers of the air, and produced tempests and shipwrecks at their pleasure. "Castles toppled on their warder's heads, and palaces and pyramids sloped their summits to their foundations;" forests and mountains were torn from their roots, and cast into the sea. They inflamed the passions of men, and caused them to commit the most unheard-of excesses. They laid their ban on those who enjoyed the most prosperous health, condemned them to peak and pine, wasted them into a melancholy atrophy, and finally consigned them to a premature grave. They breathed a new and unblest life into beings in whom existence had long been extinct, and by their hateful and resistless power caused the sepulchres to give up their dead.

Witchcraft.

Next to sorcery we may recollect the case of witchcraft, which occurs oftener, particularly in modern times, than any other alleged mode of changing by supernatural means the future course of events. The sorcerer, as we shall see hereafter, was frequently a man of learning and intellectual abilities, sometimes of comparative opulence and respectable situation in society. But the witch or wizard was almost uniformly old, decrepid, and nearly or altogether in a state of penury. The functions, however, of the witch and the sorcerer were in a great degree the same. The earliest account of a witch, attended with any degree of detail, is that of the witch of Endor in the Bible, who among other things, professed the power of calling up the dead upon occasion from the peace of the sepulchre. Witches also claimed the faculty of raising storms, and in various ways disturbing the course of nature. They appear in most cases to have been brought into action by the impulse of private malice. They occasioned mortality of greater or less extent in man and beast. They blighted the opening prospect of a plentiful harvest. They covered the heavens with clouds, and sent abroad withering and malignant blasts. They undermined the health of those who were so fortunate as to incur their animosity, and caused them to waste away gradually with incurable disease. They were notorious two or three centuries ago for the power of the "evil eye." The vulgar, both great and small, dreaded their displeasure, and sought, by small gifts, and fair speeches, but insincere, and the offspring of terror only, to avert the pernicious consequences of their malice. They were famed for fabricating small images of wax, to represent the object of their persecution; and, as these by gradual and often studiously protracted degrees wasted before the fire, so the unfortunate butts of their resentment perished with a lingering, but inevitable death.

Compacts with the Devil.

The power of these witches as we find in their earliest records, originated in their intercourse with "familiar spirits," invisible beings who must be supposed to be enlisted in the armies of the prince of darkness. We do not read in these ancient memorials of any league of mutual benefit entered into between the merely human party, and his or her supernatural assistant. But modern times have amply supplied this defect. The witch or sorcerer could not secure the assistance of the demon but by a sure and faithful compact, by which the human party obtained the industrious and vigilant service of his familiar for a certain term of years, only on condition that, when the term was expired, the demon of undoubted right was to obtain possession of the indentured party, and to convey him irremissibly and for ever to the regions of the damned. The contract was drawn out in authentic form, signed by the sorcerer, and attested with his blood, and was then carried away by the demon, to be produced again at the appointed time.

Imps.

These familiar spirits often assumed the form of animals, and a black dog or cat was considered as a figure in which the attendant devil was secretly hidden. These subordinate devils were called Imps. Impure and carnal ideas were mingled with these theories. The witches were said to have preternatural teats from which their familiars sucked their blood. The devil also engaged in sexual intercourse with the witch or wizard, being denominated *incubus,* if his favourite were a woman, and *succubus,* if a man. In short, every frightful and loathsome idea was carefully heaped up together, to render the unfortunate beings to whom the crime of witchcraft was imputed the horror and execration of their species.

Talismans and Amulets.

As according to the doctrine of witchcraft, there were certain compounds and matters prepared by rules of art, that proved baleful and deadly to the persons against whom their activity was directed, so there were also preservatives, talismans, amulets, and charms, for the most part to be worn about the person, which rendered him superior to injury, not only from the operations of witchcraft, but in some cases from the sword or any other mortal weapon. As the poet says, he that had this,

> Might trace huge forests and unhallowed
>   heaths,—
> Yea there, where very desolation dwells,
> By grots and caverns shagged with horrid shades,

nay, in the midst of every tremendous assailant, "might pass on with unblenched majesty," uninjured and invulnerable.

Necromancy.

Last of all we may speak of necromancy, which has something in it that so strongly takes hold of the imagination, that though it is one only of the various modes which have been enumerated for the exercise of magical power, we have selected it to give a title to the present volume.

There is something sacred to common apprehension in the repose of the dead. They seem placed beyond our power to disturb. "There is no work, nor device, nor knowledge, nor wisdom in the grave."

After life's fitful fever they sleep well:
Nor steel, nor poison,
Malice domestic, foreign levy, nothing,
Can touch them further.

Their remains moulder in the earth. Neither form nor feature is long continued to them. We shrink from their touch, and their sight. To violate the sepulchre therefore for the purpose of unholy spells and operations, as we read of in the annals of witchcraft, cannot fail to be exceedingly shocking. To call up the spirits of the departed, after they have fulfilled the task of life, and are consigned to their final sleep, is sacrilegious. Well may they exclaim, like the ghost of Samuel in the sacred story, "Why hast thou disquieted me?"

There is a further circumstance in the case, which causes us additionally to revolt from the very idea of necromancy, strictly so called. Man is a mortal, or an immortal being. His frame either wholly "returns to the earth as it was, or his spirit," the thinking principle within him, "to God who gave it." The latter is the prevailing sentiment of mankind in modern times. Man is placed upon earth in a state of probation, to be dealt with hereafter according to the deeds done in the flesh. "Some shall go away into everlasting punishment; and others into life eternal." In this case there is something blasphemous in the idea of intermeddling with the state of the dead. We must leave them in the hands of God. Even on the idea of an interval, the "sleep of the soul" from death to the general resurrection, which is the creed of no contemptible sect of Christians, it is surely a terrific notion that we should disturb the pause, which upon that hypothesis, the laws of nature have assigned to the departed soul, and come to awake, or to "torment him before the time."

TITLE COMMENTARY

Things as They Are; or, The Adventures of Caleb Williams

THE BRITISH CRITIC (REVIEW DATE JULY 1794)

SOURCE: A review of *Things as They Are; or, The Adventures of Caleb Williams*, by William Godwin. *The British Critic* 4 (July 1794): 70-1.

In the following excerpt, the critic condemns Caleb Williams *as an "evil use" of Godwin's talents.*

[*Things as They Are; or, The Adventures of Caleb Williams*] is a striking example of the evil use which may be made of considerable talents, connected with such a degree of intrepidity as can inspire the author with resolution to attack religion, virtue, government, laws, and above all, the desire (hitherto accounted laudable) of leaving a good name to posterity.

In this extraordinary performance, every gentleman is a hard hearted assassin, or a prejudiced tyrant; every Judge is unjust, every Justice corrupt and blind. Sentiments of respect to Christianity are given only to the vilest wretch in the book; while the most respectable person in the drama abhors the idea of "shackling his expiring friend with the fetters of superstition."

In order to render the laws of his country odious, the author places an innocent prisoner, whose story he (avowedly) takes from the Newgate Calendar of the first George's reign, in a dungeon; the wretched, unhealthy state of which he steals (as avowedly) from one of the benevolent Howard's painful descriptions of a worse gaol than common. We will only add, that the character, on which the author seems to dwell with most pleasure, is that of a leader of robbers, one who dwells in a ruinous retreat, and dispatches felons and murderers, in parties, around the country.

When a work is so directly pointed at every band which connects society, and at every principle which renders it amiable, its very merits become noxious as they tend to cause its being known in a wider circle.

THE MONTHLY REVIEW (REVIEW DATE OCTOBER 1794)

SOURCE: "Godwin's *Things as They Are.*" *The Monthly Review* 15 (October 1794): 145-49.

In the following review, the critic terms the plot of Caleb Williams *"a whining love tale," but praises the novel as an outstanding example of philosophical fiction.*

Between fiction and philosophy there seems to be no natural alliance:—yet philosophers, in order to obtain for their dogmata a more ready reception, have often judged it expedient to introduce them to the world in the captivating dress of fable. It was not to be supposed that the energetic mind of Mr. Godwin, long inured as it must have been to abstract speculation and sublime inquiry, would condescend to employ itself in framing a whining love tale; which, after having drawn a few tears from the eyes of a number of tender virgins, would have reposed in eternal peace on the loaded shelves of some circulating libraries. In writing the *Adventures of Caleb Williams*, this philosopher had doubtless

ABOUT THE AUTHOR

EDGAR ALLAN POE REVIEWS GODWIN'S *LIVES OF THE NECROMANCERS*

The name of the author of *Caleb Williams*, and of *St. Leon*, is, with us, a word of weight, and one which we consider a guarantee for the excellence of any composition to which it may be affixed. There is about all the writings of Godwin, one peculiarity which we are not sure that we have ever seen pointed out for observation, but which, nevertheless, is his chief idiosyncrasy—setting him peculiarly apart from all other *literati* of the day. We allude to an air of mature thought—of deliberate premeditation pervading, in a remarkable degree, even his most common-place observations. He never uses a hurried expression, or hazards either an ambiguous phrase, or a premature opinion. His style therefore is highly artificial; but the extreme finish and proportion always observable about it, render this artificiality, which in less able hands would be wearisome, in him a grace inestimable. We are never tired of his terse, nervous, and sonorous periods—for their terseness, their energy, and even their melody, are made, in all cases, subservient to the sense with which they are invariably fraught. No English writer, with whom we have any acquaintance, with the single exception of Coleridge, has a fuller appreciation of the value of *words*; and none is more nicely discriminative between closely-approximating meanings.

SOURCE: Poe, Edgar Allan. "Godwin's Necromancy." *Southern Literary Messenger* 2, no. 1 (December 1835): 65.

some higher object in view; and it is not difficult to perceive that this object has been to give an easy passport, and general circulation, to some of his favourite opinions. Having laid it down as a first principle that virtue consists in justice, or the wise and equal pursuit of general good, he thinks it necessary, in order to carry his system into effect, to investigate many sentiments which, though hitherto considered as the legitimate offspring of nature, and even as possessing some degree of moral value, are in his judgment only the creatures of error and prejudice. In this class he appears to rank that sense of honour which seeks its ultimate reward in the good opinion of mankind. Accordingly, this fictitious narrative seems to have been written chiefly for the purpose of representing, in strong colours, the fatal consequence of suffering the love of fame to become predominant.

Mr. Falkand, who ought, perhaps, rather than Caleb Williams, to be considered as the principal actor in this drama, exhibits a character wholly formed on the visionary principles of honour. Early tinctured with extravagant notions on this subject, by the heroic poets of Italy, he cherishes a romantic pride; which, notwithstanding his natural propensity toward benevolence, displayed in occasional acts of generosity, soon forms his ruling passion, and at length overwhelms him with accumulated wretchedness. He is the fool of honour; a man whom, in the pursuit of reputation, nothing could divert; who would purchase the character of a true, gallant, and undaunted hero, at the expence of worlds; and who thinks every calamity nominal except a stain on his honour. His virtue, his life, his everlasting peace of mind, are cheap sacrifices to be made at the shrine of same; and there is no crime too horrible for him to commit in pursuit of this object.—In the early part of his history, his pride suffers extreme irritation from the insulting provocations of a neighbour, Tyrrel; a man who has no other title to distinction than a large estate, and great bodily strength; whose ferocious temper, brutal manners, and shocking cruelties, render him to Falkland an object of profound contempt and abhorrence: but who, nevertheless, continually finds means to harass and torment him, and, while he is bringing on himself universal disgust by his enormities, and even at the very moment when he is suffering the extreme mortification of being driven from a public room, offers Falkland personal insult of the most disgraceful kind. Falkland, to whom disgrace is worse than death, wholly incapable of supporting this load of humiliating and public ignominy, yields to the irresistible impulse of detestation and revenge, and secretly assassinates his rival. The reproach and the penalty of the murder, however, fall on two innocent persons, Hawkins and his son, formerly tenants of Tyrrel; they are convicted on circumstantial evidence; and Falkland suffers them to die, rather than disclose the secret which would load his name with eternal infamy. This fatal secret becomes the burden of his soul, and the torment of his life.

The fear of the infamy of detection drives him to a thousand acts of phrenzy and cruelty, and, after having tortured him with perpetually increasing anguish, at last destroys his existence.

This visionary character is drawn with uncommon strength of conception and energy of language. The reader, while he respects and adores the virtues of Falkland, feels infinite regret that his mad passion for reputation should suppress every feeling of humanity, and become the source of unspeakable misery to himself, and of the most tragical calamity to others. The character, though original, will perhaps be admitted to be consistent; unless it should be thought difficult to reconcile the benevolence every where ascribed to Falkland, with the *deliberate* injustice and cruelty which were shewn in suffering the innocent Hawkins and his son to be executed, in preference to confessing his own guilt.—It will perhaps be said that the ruling passion of Falkland was not benevolence, but the love of fame; yet it may be questioned whether such benevolence, as is ascribed to Falkland, be not utterly incompatible with the tyrannical sway which is given in his character to the *selfish* passion of the love of fame.

A farther object in this story appears to have been to exhibit an example of the danger of indulging an idle curiosity, merely for its own gratification; and the fatal consequences of this folly were perhaps never so impressively exemplified as in the story of Caleb Williams, the confidential servant of Falkland. Williams, having been made acquainted with many particulars of his master's history by his steward, begins to suspect that the murder of Tyrrel had been committed by Falkland: he is therefore determined, at all hazards, to detect the secret; he becomes a perpetual spy on his master's actions, and practises a thousand artifices to accomplish his purpose, till at length he extorts the truth from Falkland, on a solemn oath of secrecy. Having gained his wish, he finds the secret a most painful burden, which, through his master's jealous apprehension for his reputation, brings on him a long series of persecution and perils; and the relation of them forms a large and interesting part of the narrative. Nothing can exceed the skilful management with which that part of the story is conducted, in which the reader remains unacquainted with the real occasion of Tyrrel's death, till the suspicion against Falkland is gradually excited, and at length confirmed by the persevering ingenuity of Williams. The sufferings of Williams in prison, on a fictitious charge of having robbed his master,—the contrivances by which he repeatedly regains his liberty,—and the

adventures through which he passes, while he is wantonly persecuted as the perpetrator of a heinous felony, and flies in disguise from place to place for safety; till, in the last extremity of danger, he discloses the fatal secret, and becomes miserable under a load of self-reproach: all are related with an interesting particularity that evidently shews the hand of a master. The general result is a forcible conviction of the hazard of suffering any foolish desire, or curiosity, (that restless propensity,) to creep into the mind. 'Error, (as Caleb well remarks,) once committed, has a fascinating power, like the eyes of the rattlesnake, to draw us into a second error. It deprives us of that proud confidence in our own strength, to which we are indebted for so much of our virtue.'

This narrative seems, moreover, intended to give the author an opportunity of making an indirect attack on what he deems vulgar prejudices respecting religion, morals, and policy. On these subjects, he expresses himself with that kind of latitude which those, who are acquainted with his treatise on Political Justice, will be prepared to expect. Striking pictures are drawn, in various parts of the work, of the oppression which is often practised under the form of law, and of the hardships which are inflicted in our prisons even on those whom the law has not convicted of any crime. Artful apologies are put into mouths of professional robbers, without any adequate refutation. Law is said to be better adapted for a weapon of tyranny in the hands of the rich, than for a shield to protect the humble part of the community against their usurpation. Caleb Williams thinks with unspeakable loathing of those errors, in consequence of which every man is fated to be, more or less, the tyrant or the slave; and he is astonished at the folly of his species, that they do not rise up as one man, and shake off chains so ignominious, and misery so insupportable. Mind, to his untutored reflections, is vague, airy, and unfettered; the susceptible perceiver of reasons, but never intended by nature to be the slave of force. He thinks it strange that men should, from age to age, consent to hold their lives at the breath of another, merely in order that each in his turn may have a power of acting the tyrant according to law; and he *prays* that he may hold life at the mercy of the elements, of the hunger of beasts, or of the revenge of barbarians, but not at that of the cold-blooded prudence of monopolists and kings!—What all this means we cannot precisely say: but, before the old fences of law be broken down, we hold it prudent that some effectual provision should be made for taming the ferocious

FROM THE AUTHOR

AN EXCERPT FROM THE PREFACE TO
FLEETWOOD

Yet another novel from the same pen, which has twice before claimed the patience of the public in this form. The unequivocal indulgence which has been extended to my two former attempts, renders me doubly solicitous not to forfeit the kindness I have experienced.

One caution I have particularly sought to exercise: "not to repeat myself." *Caleb Williams* was a story of very surprising and uncommon events, but which were supposed to be entirely within the laws and established course of nature, as she operates in the planet we inhabit. The story of *St. Leon* is of the miraculous class; and its design, to "mix human feelings and passions with incredible situations, and thus render them impressive and interesting."

Some of those fastidious readers—they may be classed among the best friends an author has, if their admonitions are judiciously considered—who are willing to discover those faults which do not offer themselves to every eye, have remarked, that both these tales are in a vicious style of writing; that Horace has long ago decided, that the story we cannot believe, we are by all the laws of criticism called upon to hate; and that even the adventures of the honest secretary, who was first heard of ten years ago, are so much out of the usual road, that not one reader in a million can ever fear they will happen to himself.

Gentlemen critics, I thank you. In the present volumes I have served you with a dish agreeable to your own receipt, though I cannot say with any sanguine hope of obtaining your approbation.

SOURCE: Godwin, William. "Preface." In *Fleetwood; or, The New Man of Feeling.* Vol. 1, 1805. Reprint edition, pp. v-xii. New York: Garland, 1979.

passions of those animals, who have never yet been turned loose into the wilds of nature without biting and devouring one another.

With due allowance for systematical eccentricity, (the reader will pardon the paradoxical expression,) this performance, interesting but not gratifying to the feelings and the passions, and written in a style of laboured dignity rather than of easy familiarity, is singularly entitled to be characterized as a work in which the powers of genius and philosophy are strongly united.

KENNETH GRAHAM (ESSAY DATE WINTER 1984)

SOURCE: Graham, Kenneth. "The Gothic Unity of Godwin's *Caleb Williams.*" *Papers on Language and Literature* 20, no. 1 (winter 1984): 47-59.

In the following essay, Graham examines how Godwin utilized the Gothic narrative to unify disparate themes and plot lines in Caleb Williams.

In *Caleb Williams* a conflict between Godwin the novelist and Godwin the philosopher seems to have resulted in a work that is woefully bifurcated. A divided attitude to the prose narrative is reflected in the two titles, two prefaces, and two conclusions he conferred on the work. All reveal opposed assessments of the novel's nature. This binary pattern is continued in a fourth opposition—in the form of two beginnings—that signals a source of unity amidst all this discrepancy and suggests that Godwin found in a young but flourishing Gothic tradition the way to reconcile apparent divisions.

At times it appears that Godwin intended *Caleb Williams* to be a fictionalization of *Political Justice* directed toward an audience not accustomed to the dizzy atmospheres of philosophical speculation but content to take their radical philosophy coated in engaging fictions. It was a practice favored by Holcroft, Wollstonecraft, Inchbald, and others of the coterie published by Joseph Johnson in the 1780s and 90s. Didactic intent is apparent in what was the work's main title in its early editions, *Things as They Are,* and is apparent as well in radical reflections on specific social and political conditions. These include the pernicious effects of the class system in Britain, the debilitating and dangerous dependence of women, the foul conditions in prisons (with a reference to John Howard's studies), and the injustice of the legal system. The preface to the first edition, withdrawn amidst the threats and repressions of May 1794 but published in the following year, informs the reader that "the spirit and character of government intrudes itself into every rank of society" encouraging the kinds of "domestic . . . despotism" that the novel illustrates.[1] Thus, in the early editions, title and preface prepared the reader for a *Tendenz-roman* very much in the spirit of its radical author and its revolutionary times.

In a preface published thirty-eight years after the first edition, Godwin presents his novel in quite a different light. Discussing **Caleb Williams** in an 1832 edition of **Fleetwood,** he places his emphasis on the spirit of the work's sub-title, **The Adventures of Caleb Williams,** and describes his work as "a series of adventures of flight and pursuit." Underlining this emphasis on plot rather than on theme is Godwin's account of the process of composition. He wrote it backwards, he tells us, presenting Falkland's protracted harrying of Caleb before establishing the motivation for the pursuit. According to this later preface, then, the political message that centers on the tyrannies of Tyrrel and Falkland was an afterthought; the Tendenzroman was subordinate to the adventure story. Godwin does not mention in his preface that he rewrote the ending, but Gilbert Dumas discovered in the holograph manuscript of **Caleb Williams** an original ending in which Falkland triumphs and grows strong while Caleb, imprisoned and harassed, declines into mental and physical debility and death. Caleb leaves behind only his manuscript to proclaim a final condemnation of *Things as They Are.*[2] In the published version a debilitated Falkland reveals his crimes but Caleb expresses no triumph in the victory of truth and justice but, rather, expresses guilt and revulsion at his own complicity in the destruction of Falkland.

Thus with titles, prefaces, and conclusions, Godwin offers us a systematic contradiction that reveals diverging conceptions of two quite different works. On one hand, one finds the Tendenzroman bearing the title **Things as They Are,** illustrating the teaching of **Political Justice** and ending (given the power of the prejudices that **Political Justice** was seeking to undermine) on the victory of tyranny. This is the novel that Godwin, in one of his moods, appears to have thought he had written. The novel he published lacks this "thematic logic."[3] It focuses on Caleb Williams, offers "a series of adventures of flight and pursuit," but concludes on a paradox that probes the psychological implications of dominance and submission. That terrible peripety in which tyrant becomes victim and victim tyrant permits neither the simple triumph of an adventure story nor the healing catharsis that the death of a victim of tyranny might arouse. That Godwin's novel leaves Caleb in a condition of self-contempt and disillusionment represents a victory of art over politics and adventure.

Whether the victory came about consciously or unconsciously we shall never know, but there may be a wry self-awareness in an assertion that Godwin makes in *The Enquirer* of 1797. On the subject of moral and immoral tendencies in writing, Godwin remarks: "authors themselves are continually falling into the grossest mistakes in this respect, and show themselves superlatively ignorant of the tendency of their own writings."[4] The 1832 preface may reveal how Godwin came *not* to write a politically appropriate and logically coherent Tendenzroman, for in it one finds a brief account of another (and fourth) binary opposition. He reports that he began the narrative in the third person but soon changed to first person point of view as "best adapted . . . to my vein of delineation," remarking at the same time that "the thing in which my imagination revelled the most freely was the analysis of the private and internal operations of the mind" (339). That second start makes the second ending comprehensible. Despite suggestions to the contrary, the peripety that leaves Caleb not vindicated and triumphant but guilty and depressed is not to be explained by the politics of the time but by narrative demands exerted by the change in point of view.[5] That change reflects the true emphasis of the narrative which is on character and not on theme or plot.

Caleb's subjective narrative introduces into the world of the novel a solipsism that integrates the novel of politics with the novel of adventure and, yet, owing to imperatives inherent in the point of view and the subject, responds to purposes separate from those of politics and adventure. Godwin imposed on his novel a rigorous empiricism that creates fictional reality from Caleb's conscious adversions to the swarm of impressions, ideas, and thoughts flowing through his mind.

The wavering, nervous account of passion and compulsion, temptation and harassment, despite the two titles, is neither a Tendenzroman nor an adventure story. It is a Gothic romance of modern times that embraces the other two narrative purposes in fascinating and ambivalent ways. Broadly speaking, because of the inclination of Gothic narrative to operate at the furthest verges of fictional reality where the natural confronts the supernatural, all Gothic conflict tends to represent or enact psychomachia. Thus, to exemplify the universal conflict between tyranny and liberty, Godwin chose a narrator who perceives the world in Gothic polarities. It is owing to Caleb's perspective that Falkland takes his place among a class of

Gothic tyrants that includes Walpole's Manfred, Beckford's Vathek, and Radcliffe's Montoni.

The Gothic mode is appropriate also to the presentation of an adventure of flight and pursuit since such action is stimulated by irrational hatreds and terrors. Ultimately the Gothic emphasis carries **Caleb Williams** away from the narrative simplicities of either an adventure story or a Tendenzroman and into the complexities natural to the portrayal of abnormal psychologies.

While Caleb's is the dominant solipsism, the major characters are similarly confined by their own extreme views of reality. Their perspectives combine to engender a narrative full of characteristics we associate with the Gothic novel but with subtle and significant transformations appropriate to its contemporary setting. Intense psychological energies unleashed by the interaction of characters take the place of conventional ghosts and demons. As expressed through Caleb's guilt- and fear-ridden consciousness, those energies give rise to a chain of hauntings, of obsession and compulsion, of guilt and anxiety, that lead Tyrrel to attack Falkland, Falkland to murder Tyrrel, and Caleb to uncover Falkland's secret. The searing conjunction of the sensibilities of the three characters impels them to confer upon one another the roles of malignant supernatural agency. To Falkland, Caleb is "devil"; Falkland haunts Tyrrel "like a demon"; Caleb describes Falkland's energy and rage as "more than mortal." Each acts, voluntarily or involuntarily, to threaten the tranquility or self-esteem of another.

To portray a world solipsistically projected by the emotional intensities of his characters, Godwin draws upon a Gothic vocabulary that invokes and evokes ideas of infernal supernatural agency, of physical torture and murder, and of psychological and emotional excess. I have already mentioned some instances of the use of terms like *ghost* and *demon* as characters project the powers of supernatural evil upon one another. One can multiply examples of such usage as actions are portrayed to represent "supernatural barbarity," "demoniac malice," or suffering as the "torment of demons." The very recurrence of terms evoking the demonic supernatural such as *spectre, devil, chimera, basilisk, demon* expresses the nature of the world the characters experience.

A vocabulary of physical and psychological excess reflects the terrible violence of this world. Characters "writhe with agony," "poison . . . pleasures," endure "insufferable tortures . . . upon the rack." Their emotional frenzies are often presented in the language of psychological aberration as they are "stung . . . to madness," "drunk with choler," foaming "with anguish and fury," or in a "paroxysm of insanity." Coral Ann Howells has called attention to the use of theatrical convention in the Gothic novel, and Peter Brooks reminds us of the similarities in source and subject of the Gothic novel and late eighteenth-century melodrama.[6] While often awkward and artificial, Godwin's theatrical rhetoric does succeed in evoking the vibrant emotional intensities of his characters and the reality they experience. Tyrrel, tormented with a jealousy of Falkland that grows in him like Ambrosio's lust, "writh[es] with intolerable anguish, his rage . . . unbounded and raving" (93). This violent vocabulary reaches an extreme in the robber-woman who, in her hatred of Caleb, with "fevrous blood of savage ferocity" threatens to "tear" his flesh "piecemeal," to thrust her fingers through his ribs and drink his blood (231). A rational vocabulary is not appropriate to the rages and frenzies of the "divine intoxication" that Georges Bataille asserts is the traditional definition of evil.[7] The images of cannibalism and vampirism help portray the physical and psychological violence of his novel's world that is forever forcing Godwin to challenge the expressive limits of language.

Thus, the reality that the passionate and violent minds of the characters project is a characteristically Gothic one. The elemental conflicts of pleasure/pain, reason/unreason, good/evil are enacted, and actions succeed one another with a terrible inevitability. When Horace Walpole replaced the drawing room of eighteenth-century fiction with the Gothic labyrinth, he introduced a Manichean dimension to the novel and offered glimpses of evil as a vital, independent force as he set a series of dark heroes on the path to inevitable damnation. The Gothic reality projected by Caleb's consciousness is marked by emotional extremes. His pleasures are ecstasies that are describable only in near-sexual terms. Here is his reaction to the discovery of Falkland's guilt:

> My mind was full almost to bursting. . . . I was conscious to a kind of rapture for which I could not account. I was solemn, yet full of rapid emotion, burning with indignation and energy. In the very tempest and hurricane of the passions, I seemed to enjoy the most soul-ravishing calm. . . . I was never so perfectly alive as at that moment.
>
> [129-30]

More familiar than such euphoria in the worlds of the major characters is the experience of pain. Theirs is a manic world of stark polarities.

From Caleb's viewpoint the major characters he encounters are angelic or demonic: Clare, Collins, Emily, and Laura are in seraphic contrast to Tyrrel, Grimes, and Gines. Falkland passes through Caleb's vacillating percipience from one extreme to the other. The world of the characters' experiences, colored by their intermittent episodes of mania and melancholia, is subject to a demonic destiny. Entrapped in their intense emotional states, the three major characters—Caleb, Falkland, and Tyrrel—create the world they experience, a world bereft of Providence and presided over by a demonic fatality that draws each character ever deeper into suffering.

The malignant destiny of *Caleb Williams* is, in fact, an adaptation of Godwin's concept of necessity. Although Godwin keeps his philosophical beliefs subordinate to the demands of his narrative, in this instance he has employed his philosophy to enrich his fiction. Godwin was a determinist. He saw life as "a vast system of interrelated events, an eternal chain of causes and effects"[8] in which particular outcomes can be foreseen if one's knowledge of causes is full enough. The world of *Caleb Williams* is subject to necessity, but it is a Gothic necessity characterized as mysterious, inexorable, and malignant. Caleb confers a sense of dark foreboding on the work through his continual references to "painful presentiments," "mysterious fatality," and "ill destiny." The characters frequently express a sense of being compelled or acted upon by merciless forces, both within and outside themselves. Caleb characterizes Falkland's life as "the uninterrupted persecution of a malignant destiny." Emily's infatuation with Falkland "appeared to [Tyrrel] as the last persecution of a malicious destiny" (46).

All three major characters seem driven also from within by passions they cannot control: Tyrrel to persecute Emily, Falkland to kill Tyrrel, and Caleb to discover Falkland's secret. Caleb talks about his curiosity as a "fatal impulse . . . destined to hurry me to my destruction" and terms like "uncontrollable passion" and "unconquerable impulse" recur in the narrative to characterize the irrational compulsions of all three characters. Often involuntarily, they inflict terrible sufferings on each other. Caleb excoriates Falkland's tender conscience; Falkland's very presence in the district assaults Tyrrel's self-worth; and Falkland, fearing the effects of Caleb's knowledge, harasses him for ten long years, denying him any peace and security. In accordance with Godwin's determinism, the characters are subtly directed by their interaction with the world around them. But through

their own intense irrationalities and imaginative energies, they create Gothic monsters of each other and impose a perspective that transforms a morally neutral necessity into a Gothic fatality and their world into a region of sorrow presided over by a malignant demon.

Two motifs very much associated with the politics of the time undergo fascinating transformation as a result of this Gothic perspective. Modern audiences may be baffled by the vehemence the novel directs against, of all unlikely subjects, chivalry and its corrupting influence. Caleb's penultimate paragraph, in overwrought rhetoric, establishes and attacks the source of Falkland's degeneration: "But thou imbibedst the poison of chivalry with thy earliest youth,"—a potion, Godwin suggests, though not in these anachronistic terms, that transformed Falkland from a Dr. Jekyll into a Mr. Hyde. David Mc-Cracken explains the attack as a reaction to the praise of chivalry[9] in Burke's *Reflections on the Revolution in France* that soars to this ringing *ubi sunt* lament:

> I thought ten thousand swords must have leaped from their scabbards to avenge even a look that threatened [the Queen of France] with insult. But the age of chivalry is gone. That of sophisters, economists, and calculators has succeeded, and the glory of Europe is extinguished forever.[10]

Godwin's response to Burke resulted in the creation of a unique character type. With his passion for chivalry, his sensitivity to personal honour that, when threatened, drives him to paroxysms of anger, tyranny, and guilt, Falkland is a Gothic quixote, and as such must take his place with the female quixote, the spiritual quixote, and the other quixotic types that adorn the fiction of the eighteenth century.

Another political motif that undergoes a Gothic distortion is the social contract. The novel's demonstration of the distortions of solipsism that must be corrected through sympathetic social intercourse is a more convincing moral for *Caleb Williams* than the dangers of a socially inculcated corruption based on myths of chivalry. A perverse relationship between Caleb and Falkland is established through the operation of Caleb's passionate curiosity upon Falkland's overwhelming sense of guilt and shame. Together they enact a kind of courtship ritual as Caleb assaults Falkland's guilty sensitivities with probing questions and remarks, and Falkland, tempted to share the burden of guilt and allured by self-destruction, alternately encourages and rejects Caleb's overtures. Waxing in intensity through an intimacy of guilt, Falkland for his secret and Caleb for his curiosity, their relationship reaches a consummation as Falkland swears Caleb to secrecy and confesses his guilt. Their covenant, sworn by "every sacrament, divine and human" (135), is a kind of marriage distorted into a satanic bargain. It confirms Godwin's demonstration in *Political Justice* of the immorality of oaths and promises as forms of compulsion that restrict unnaturally the mutable individual.[11] "You have sold yourself," declares Falkland, and for the rest of their lives the two are joined by guilt, secrecy, and forbidden knowledge in a Gothic social contract that precludes development or change in their relationship and entraps both in bonds of suspicion and fear.

When Godwin decided on a first person point of view he changed, consciously or not, the purpose of his novel from an illustration of *Political Justice* to a study of solipsism.[12] The decision reflects a willingness to sacrifice objectivity to subjectivity and political to aesthetic purpose. His chosen point of view is fraught with distortion: Caleb moves in and out of dream states; his sense of time is frequently awry—indeed he acknowledges the subjective distortions of time in his prison experiences. In the subsequent nightmare of prolonged harassment Caleb is so immersed in his own misery that he has little sense of objective time, and it is with shock that we discover with the return of Collins from the West Indies that ten years have elapsed since Caleb's discovery of Falkland's secret.

The years of flight, disguise, and anxiety also affect his sense of identity. Seeking laboriously to evade Falkland's omniscient eye (305) and vainly to establish creative and normal relationships with ordinary societies, Caleb is in turn a beggar, an Irish vagabond, a farmer's son, a Jew, a deformed young man, twisted and lisping, and a rural watchmaker. The adoption and maintenance of alterations in behavior and appearance impose strains on his sense of self that are exacerbated by the assessments of his character expressed by others. In the story he is thrilled to overhear in a public house he is "the notorious housebreaker, Kit Williams" (235). In the broadsheet printed by Gines he is "the most accomplished swindler in plausibleness, duplicity and disguise" (269). He is devastated when Laura Denison gives credence to such stories and dismisses him as "a monster, and not a man" (300). Characterizations that disagree so markedly with his sense of self contribute to Caleb's disorientation.

The last few paragraphs of Godwin's rewritten conclusion demonstrate how far his conception of his narrative had developed beyond political polemic. Falkland's degeneration and death have acted so strongly on Caleb's wavering sense of self-approbation that the logic of Falkland's decline and his own survival has forced him to redefine himself not as persecuted but as persecutor. "I began these memoirs with the idea of vindicating my character. I have now no character that I wish to vindicate" (326). Caleb ends his narrative enveloped by an uncertainty that extends even to his own identity.

The assaults on his sense of identity are accompanied by other distortions in perspective that demonstrate the limitations of *Caleb Williams* as a political document. One hears reverberations of paranoia in his confession: "I could almost have imagined . . . that the whole world was in arms to exterminate me" (238). Caleb acknowledges the effects of his nightmare life in two revealing statements: "My sensations at certain periods amounted to insanity" (306) and "I sometimes fear that I shall be wholly deserted of my reason" (314). Godwin, having made reason central to his conception of human nature in *Political Justice,* entrusts his narrative of "Things As They Are" to a narrator who doubts his own reason. Such acknowledgments of uncertainty with regard to time, identity, and sanity make Caleb's narrative dubious testimony.

The problem of credibility is complicated by inconstancies of narrative purpose. Caleb is writing his story in three stages and each stage is subject to different moods and purposes. He begins the process of composition on being driven out of Wales. His deep longings to be a respected and useful member of a community have been frustrated by false reports of a criminal past. His opening paragraph establishes for his narration the two aims of therapy and self-vindication. By writing he will divert his mind from his calamitous situation and rescue his reputation from wrongful accusation. The first and most extensive narrative stage extends to the fourteenth chapter of the third volume. Demonstrating a kind of modal unity, it ends with a repetition of its double purpose:

> For some time I had a melancholy satisfaction in writing. . . . I conceived that my story faithfully digested would carry in it an impression of truth that few men would be able to resist; or at worst that . . . posterity might be induced to do me justice.
>
> [303-4]

The second main stage of the narrative is marked by impatience and depression. Caleb has just encountered Collins' reluctance to be of assistance in his struggles with Falkland. His earlier aims, he writes, "have diminished in their influence. . . . Writing . . . is changed into a burthen. I shall compress . . . what remains to be told" (303-4). Caleb here asserts a narrative freedom that heretofore he has scrupulously avoided admitting: he will take a liberty with truth by compressing his story. In this narrative stage he declares also a new aim, revenge on Falkland for years of torment. "I will tell a tale . . . justice . . . shall hear me. . . . His fame shall not be immortal" (314-15). With this declaration, his tone has modulated from impatience to indignation and for the passive aim of therapy he has substituted the active one of revenge. This last purpose has the potential to carry the story even further away from truth.

Caleb's postscript, written after Falkland's death, represents the third and final narrative stage. In a tone of desperate remorse, the chastened and disillusioned Caleb regrets his aim of revenge and seeks to repair Falkland's reputation, tarnished by public trial and confession. For Caleb, now, the truth is that "a nobler spirit lived not among the sons of men"; Caleb stands self-condemned for "the baseness of my cruelty" (325). Ten years of persecution have shrunk in the face of his perceived responsibility for Falkland's death. The limitations of a solipsistic perspective had blinded Caleb to the effects of a prosecution on Falkland. The narrative that begins in self-assertive protest ends on the psychological vacuity of that final paragraph with its repudiation of the former aim of self-vindication. The narrative that begins as apologia ends as confession. Opening with vehement appeals to Truth and Justice, the narrative closes on fundamental doubts about the nature of guilt and innocence.

Such neat reversals in narrative purpose are part of a series of ironic patterns in the structure of *Caleb Williams* that demonstrate Godwin's willingness to reject conventional realisms. It is the nature of realistic fiction to enact a tension between the demands of verisimilitude for empirical randomness and the demands of aesthetics for attractive resolutions and surprising reversals. Godwin was able to satisfy his aesthetic impulses as an artist and his disciplined investigations as a philosopher by substituting for empirical reality the realm of necessity. In this realm of necessity the hidden forces behind appearances reside, and seemingly casual events are seen to spring from

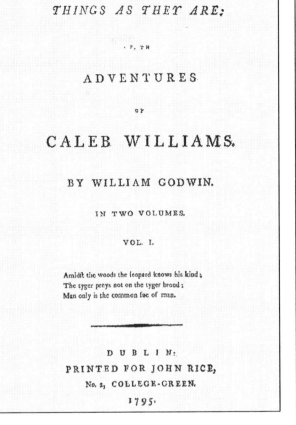

THINGS AS THEY ARE:

. ,. ,H

ADVENTURES

OF

CALEB WILLIAMS.

BY WILLIAM GODWIN.

IN TWO VOLUMES.

VOL. I.

Amidst the woods the leopard knows his kind;
The tyger preys not on the tyger brood;
Man only is the common foe of man.

D U B L I N:
PRINTED FOR JOHN RICE,
No. 2, COLLEGE-GREEN.
1795.

Title page from the 1795 edition of *Things as They Are; or, The Adventures of Caleb Williams.*

basic drives to form strange patterns of irony, reversal, and inevitability.

The hidden laws of Gothic necessity shape the action of the novel. The story of Falkland's long harassment of Caleb is punctuated by coincidences in which Caleb's escapes are prevented and his sanctuaries discovered. When the violation of Falkland's sense of honour drives him to a frenzied murder of Tyrrel, the instrument, "a sharp-pointed knife," Falkland tells us, by unexplained coincidence "fell in my way." That mysterious fate behind the unlikely events of the plot is in harmony with a world of surprising peripeties in which victim becomes oppressor, accuser becomes accused, freedom means imprisonment and imprisonment freedom, the peripeties that carry the work so far beyond the novel of adventure.

While Godwin's consciousness of the demands of philosophical consistency confers significance on his anti-realism, we should not be too blinded by his philosophy to overlook his use of the conventional anti-realism of the Gothic romance. Indeed, a fictional world that can contain a secret chamber, a locked truck bearing a dreadful secret, banditti and their violent consort reminds us that even at its most philosophical, the Gothic novel is still a thriller.

The importance of Godwin's employment of a solipsism that transforms his narrative from a political to a Gothic novel can be assessed by viewing *Caleb Williams* in its context in the young but developing Gothic tradition. It is a tradition that begins with Horace Walpole's impatience with Richardson specifically and the novel of bourgeois realism generally. "I thought . . . that a god, at least a ghost, was absolutely necessary to frighten us out of too much senses."[13] The natural-supernatural tension takes a particular direction with Clara Reeve's strictures against the over-use of the marvelous and her complaint that *Otranto* should have been kept "within the utmost *verge* of probability."[14] That movement comes to a significant focus with Ann Radcliffe who, by the example of excellence that she set, established a particular school of the Gothic in which the verge of probability is firmly located on the natural side of the boundary, and the focus of narrative is on the frightened apprehensions of her heroines.

Godwin appears to have learned from Ann Radcliffe's example that the Gothic romance need not rely on supernatural events; it does not need even a pseudo-medieval setting. What is essential is terror, a frightened uncertainty enwrapped in a threat of violence. Radcliffe demonstrates that terror need not be supernaturally generated. Godwin represents a further significant stage in the internalization of the sources of Gothic apprehensiveness by demonstrating that a response of terror is not dependent upon such physical properties of a Radcliffian scenario as mirrors, gloom, creaking stairs, wax works, and servant girls sleepwalking.

In *Caleb Williams*, Godwin's fearful Gothic reality is almost entirely generated internally. He demonstrates his creative grasp of the psychological Gothic by founding a series of Gothic motifs and images on the swarming thoughts and impressions of his characters. We find the hauntings, the demonic villains, the fearful threatenings, the passion and the violence that we expect in a Gothic novel, but all are psychologically generated. There is little physical description in *Caleb Williams* and none of the sublime word-painting characteristic of Ann Radcliffe's novels. Godwin's fictional setting is a projection of the experiences and expectations of his characters. Owing to their intense psychological agitation, Godwin's Gothic world is a charged reality, a subtle complex of strange tensions arising from the irrational willful-ness of the characters and the uncanny destiny to which they believe themselves subject.

Ann Radcliffe's narrative technique that impels and enthralls the reader in engulfing excitement and suspense is subject to a serious liability, as Coleridge noted in his 1794 review of *Udolpho* in the *Critical Review*:

> Curiosity is raised oftener than it is gratified; or rather, it is raised so high that no adequate gratification can be given it; the interest is completely dissolved when once the adventure is finished, and the reader, when he is got to the end of the work, looks about in vain for the spell which had bound him so strongly to it.[15]

Like the structures created by Swift's spider, Ann Radcliffe's novel has ingenious form but lacks substance. Such criticism is not applicable to *Caleb Williams* because its characters and its world are emanations from a thoroughly conceived philosophical system. They may not always illustrate *Political Justice* (which Godwin intended as an inquiry and not as fixed doctrine) but they derive substance and significance from a theoretical foundation.

True to Godwin's political beliefs, *Caleb Williams* undermines the notions of sacred hierarchy and Burkean chivalry, and it replaces Providence with Necessity. It satisfies the demands of doctrine and adventure without being merely doctrinaire or merely sensational. Consequently, it does not leave the reader with curiosity gratified but unsatisfied. Rather it encourages reflection on the human need for social interaction and the distortions of solipsism. Godwin recognized with Hume that there may be no resemblance between a sensation and its cause and that reality must remain a mystery to a human experience limited by sensation. But, as F. E. L. Priestley points out in his edition of *Political Justice*, in the development of Godwin's thought, human isolation is mitigated by the resemblance between the contents of one mind and another.[16] Perhaps it was a reflection on the plights of Falkland, Caleb, and Tyrrel, isolated and imprisoned in their own consciousness, or perhaps it is a normal development in his philosophy that had Godwin write in *Thoughts on Man* (1831): "The belief in the reality of matter explains nothing. . . . But the belief in the existence of our fellow-men explains much." And "sympathy is the only reality of which we are susceptible; it is our heart of hearts."[17]

For different reasons, Falkland, Caleb and Tyrrel resist communication with their fellow men and thus create conditions for the distortions of a

Gothic perspective to operate. Godwin's narrative builds to a climactic anagnorisis at Falkland's trial as Falkland's terrible physical degeneration acts upon Caleb, and Caleb's forthright testimony upon Falkland, to dissipate the demonic illusions that they had projected upon each other. Simplified, the underlying meaning of *Caleb Williams* is that solipsism distorts perspective and sympathy counteracts solipsism. That is the real focus of the narrative and the real basis for the title, *Things As They Are*.

Notes

1. William Godwin, *Caleb Williams*, ed. David Mc-Cracken (1970; rpt. London, 1977), p. 1. Subsequent citations from this edition will appear parenthetically in the text. This edition includes the prefaces of 1794, 1795, and 1832 as well as the extant fragments of the original ending.

2. For a discussion of the political events surrounding the revised ending see D. Gilbert Dumas, "Things As They Were: The Original Ending of *Caleb Williams*," *Studies in English Literature, 1500-1900* 6 (1966): 575-97.

3. The term is used by Dumas who prefers the original ending. I incline to Gary Kelly's opinion that the second ending "raises the novel above the doctrinaire." *The English Jacobin Novel 1780-1805* (Oxford, 1976), p. 197.

4. *The Enquirer* (1797; rpt. New York, 1965), p. 132.

5. By linking his discussion of Godwin's revision of the conclusion to *Caleb Williams* to the political arrests of radicals in May 1794, D. Gilbert Dumas encourages the conclusion that the revisions were politically motivated.

6. Howells, *Love, Mystery and Misery: Feeling in Gothic Fiction* (London, 1978), pp. 20-23; Brooks, *The Melodramatic Imagination* (New Haven, 1976), pp. 16-21.

7. *Literature and Evil*, trans. Alastair Hamilton (London, 1973), p. 9.

8. F. E. L. Priestley, "Critical Introduction" in William Godwin, *Enquiry Concerning Political Justice* (Toronto, 1946), 3:6.

9. "Godwin's *Caleb Williams*: A Fictional Rebuttal of Burke," *Studies in Burke and His Times* 11 (1970):1442-52.

10. Ed. Thomas H. D. Mahoney (New York, 1955), p. 86.

11. William Godwin, *Enquiry Concerning Political Justice*, ed. K. Codell Carter (Oxford, 1971), pp. 98-112.

12. Gay Clifford makes the solipsistic limitations of first-person narratives the basis for a fruitful comparison between *Caleb Williams* and *Frankenstein*. See "*Caleb Williams* and *Frankenstein*: First-Person Narratives and 'Things as They Are,'" *Genre* 10 (1977): 601-17.

13. *The Letters of Horace Walpole*, ed. Mrs. Paget Toynbee (Oxford, 1904), 6:201.

14. *The Old English Baron*, ed. James Trainer (London, 1967), p. 4.

15. Included in *A Wiltshire Parson and His Friends: The Correspondence of William Lisle Bowles*, ed. Garland Greever (Boston, 1926), pp. 169-70.

16. "Critical Introduction," 3:98.

17. Ibid.

BETTY RIZZO (ESSAY DATE 1992)

SOURCE: Rizzo, Betty. "The Gothic *Caleb Williams*." *Studies on Voltaire and the Eighteenth Century* 305 (1992): 1387-89.

In the following essay, Rizzo addresses the disagreement over the classification of Caleb Williams *as a Gothic novel, and argues that "Godwin's novel is squarely in the tradition."*

William Godwin's 1794 novel *Caleb Williams* has long been placed firmly but uneasily in the Gothic tradition. If one defines the Gothic as that form that describes a mortal combat between one or more virtuous but comparatively powerless protagonists and others far more unscrupulous and powerful, as well as that form which deals obliquely with subjects which cannot be directly addressed, then Godwin's novel is squarely in the tradition.

In his preface to the book Godwin states his intention: to provide 'a general review of the modes of domestic and unrecorded despotism, by which man becomes the destroyer of man'. A recent editor of the book has noted that this preface has 'by no means an obvious conection with the novel itself'. On the contrary, the preface points squarely to the purport of the book, which is to expose the malignancy of the patriarchal establishment of the England of his day.

In exposing the corruptions and terrible injustices inflicted for the perpetuation of their own power on the dependents it was their avowed responsibility to protect, by both the seeming worst and the seeming best of the English aristocracy, Godwin adopts the devices of the Gothic: the hidden past crime of the patriarch, his willingness to take any course to avoid exposure, his sacrifice of every human relationship, every human right, to preserve the reputation necessary to preserve his prerogative.

Much Gothic material lies on the surface of the plot. Godwin himself began with the compelling image of flight and pursuit of his third and final book. But the political import of the persecution of the less privileged must soon have attached itself to this pursuit theme, as Godwin worked out the circumstances which were to lead to the chase. Caleb Williams in the course of the persecution he endures, is isolated, terrorised, imprisoned, and denied the opportunity for personal development. He cannot settle down and work, cannot have human relationships, cannot win respect or love. These are the conditions of the Gothic; they are also the conditions of the victims of the patriarchy.

More hidden Gothic material has to do with the nature of the administration of the English social system—its true pernicious nature. The corruption of the law as a tool in the hands of the law's administrators is obviously highlighted. The defenceless Hawkinses, who think they can stand up for their own rights, are ruined and gaoled. The defenceless Emily who believes she can refuse to marry a brutish suitor chosen by her cousin Tyrrel is sued for her maintenance as a minor and thrown ill with a fever into gaol, where she dies. The law co-operates with the persecution of Caleb Williams at every turn.

Less obvious is the lesson that the swinish Tyrrel and his opponent the courtly gentleman Falkland are not opposites at all, but are doubles. And in both cases their corruption derives from their proud determination to be preeminent. Tyrrel is crude, abusive, and obviously an enemy of the rights of all other humans. Falkland opposes with abhorrence his destruction of the Hawkinses and Emily. But in fact he is simply a far more clever and subtle version of Tyrrel. The corruption of both men has been caused by their having been given control of others. Corrupted by their power, Tyrrel demands the incense of perpetual adulation; Falkland demands only the public acknowledgement of his impeccable honour. To protect that 'honour', Falkland murders Tyrrel, allows the Hawkinses to go to the gallows for the crime—now he is clearly branded as Tyrrel's double—and takes control of the life of Caleb Williams, who has learned his secret.

On the level of the Gothic plot this secret is the motive for the patriarchal concern to hide the truth in order to retain control. Caleb's function in the plot therefore is not to provide a clinical example of a curiosity wildly out of bounds, but to represent the rational just man who pursues truth from a love of truth and justice and from a sense that something is 'wrong'. Caleb Williams represents the new emerging man, not privileged, not tenderly educated, but a reader, and a man who, even while young and inexperienced, sees the criminality of Alexander the Great, whom Falkland defends. Furthermore Williams, who does not have an empire to protect, is compassionate and kind. Knowing Falkland's guilt, he still reveres and respects him, and would never have turned him in. His is the proper love and respect of the son for the father.

The patriarchy, however, has perverted every system including that of the proper relationship of fathers and sons. Though the Hawkinses were a model in this regard Caleb is denied the paternal care he needs and longs for. The fatherly Collins is sent away on Falkland's concerns, on his return is turned against Caleb, and finally is too old and frail to be burdened with the truth about Falkland's plots. The watchmaker who adopts Caleb as a surrogate son is seduced into betraying him by Falkland's proffered reward. Humbler characters are more likely to sense the truth. Old Tom, Caleb's fellow servant, even against his own reason, smuggles him tools with which to escape from prison, and in London Mrs Marney protects him even though she herself is followed—and characteristically is rewarded by being arrested herself.

The novel therefore *is* Gothic, dealing with the persecution of a humble, defenceless protagonist by others who wield the power. And it confirms the idea that the Gothic in fact exposes the vicious excesses of the patriarchal establishment seeking to perpetuate and confirm its ascendancy.

FURTHER READING

Bibliography

Pollin, Burton R. *Godwin Criticism: A Synoptic Bibliography.* Toronto, Ontario: University of Toronto Press, 1967, 659 p.

Bibliography of works by and about Godwin published between 1783 and 1966.

Criticism

Chandler, Anne. "Romanticizing Adolescence: Godwin's *St. Leon* and the Matter of Rousseau." *Studies in Romanticism* 41, no. 3 (fall 2002): 399-416.

Discusses the influence of Jean Jacques Rousseau's Emile *on* St. Leon.

Clemit, Pamela. *The Godwinian Novel: The Rational Fictions of Godwin, Brockden Brown, Mary Shelley.* Oxford: Clarendon Press, 1993, 254 p.

Analysis of the school of fiction inaugurated by Godwin and developed in the works of his principal followers, Charles Brockden Brown and Mary Wollstonecraft Shelley.

Ellis, Kate Ferguson. "Men as They Are: William Godwin." In *The Contested Castle: Gothic Novels and the Subversion of Domestic Ideology,* pp. 151-65. Urbana: University of Illinois Press, 1989.

Examines the reconceptualization of manhood and the presentation of opposing ideals of masculinity in Caleb Williams.

Flanders, Wallace. "Godwin and Gothicism: *St. Leon.*" *Texas Studies in Literature and Language* 8 (1967): 533-45.

Interprets St. Leon *as an elaboration of the literary techniques Godwin used in* Caleb Williams *and of his philosophical theories in* Political Justice; *asserts that the novel uses the trappings of Gothic fiction for didactic purposes.*

Fludernik, Monika. "Spectacle, Theatre, and Sympathy in *Caleb Williams.*" *Eighteenth-Century Fiction* 14, no. 1 (October 2001): 1-30.

Traces the theatrical metaphors in Caleb Williams *and explores the idea of sympathy in the novel.*

———. "William Godwin's *Caleb Williams*: The Tarnishing of the Sublime." *ELH* 68, no. 4 (winter 2001): 857-96.

Examines Godwin's deployment of the Burkean notion of the sublime.

Handwerk, Gary. "Of Caleb's Guilt and Godwin's Truth: Ideology and Ethics in *Caleb Williams.*" *ELH* 60, no. 4 (winter 1993): 939-60.

Argues that the tendency of Godwin's fiction runs contrary to the political assumptions and expectations of Political Justice.

Leaver, Kristen. "Pursuing Conversations: *Caleb Williams* and the Romantic Construction of the Reader." *Studies in Romanticism* 33, no. 4 (winter 1994): 589-610.

Discusses the relationship of author and reader in Caleb Williams.

Meyers, Mitzi. "Godwin's Changing Conception of *Caleb Williams.*" *SEL: Studies in English Literature* 12, no. 4 (autumn 1972): 591-628.

Asserts that Godwin's views about morality and psychology evolved as he was writing Caleb Williams.

Morse, David. "The Social Novel and the Gothic." In *Romanticism: A Structural Analysis*, pp. 13-49. New York: Barnes and Noble Books, 1972.

Suggests that Godwin's use of the Gothic form in Caleb Williams *enabled him to combine psychological exploration with social criticism.*

Roberts, Marie. "William Godwin's Darkness of Enlightenment." In *Gothic Immortals: The Fiction of the Brotherhood of the Rosy Cross*, pp. 25-52. London and New York: Routledge, 1990.

Charts Godwin's role in the development of the Rosicrucian novel, showing why it was that this reformer and anarchist philosopher became the founder of a branch of Gothic fiction inspired by the Brothers of the Holy Cross.

OTHER SOURCES FROM GALE:

Additional coverage of Godwin's life and career is contained in the following sources published by Thomson Gale: *Concise Dictionary of British Literary Biography, 1789-1832; Dictionary of Literary Biography*, Vols. 39, 104, 142, 158, 163, 262; *Literature Resource Center; Nineteenth-Century Literature Criticism*, Vols. 14, 130; *Reference Guide to English Literature*, Ed. 2; *St. James Guide to Crime and Mystery Writers*, Vol. 4; and *St. James Guide to Horror, Ghost & Gothic Writers.*

JOHANN WOLFGANG VON GOETHE

(1749 - 1832)

German poet, novelist, playwright, short story writer, essayist, critic, biographer, memoirist, and librettist.

Goethe is considered Germany's greatest writer and a genius of the highest order. He distinguished himself as a scientist, artist, musician, philosopher, theater director, and court administrator. Excelling in various genres and literary styles, Goethe was a shaping force in the major German literary movements of the late eighteenth and early nineteenth centuries. His first novel, *Die Leiden des jungen Werthers* (1774; *The Sorrows of Young Werther*), epitomizes the *Sturm und Drang,* or storm and stress, movement, and his dramas *Iphigenie auf Tauris* (1787; *Iphigenia in Tauris*) and *Torquato Tasso* (1790), as well as the poetry collection *Römische Elegien* (1795; *Goethe's Roman Elegies*), exemplify the neoclassical approach to literature. His drama *Faust* is considered one of the greatest works of nineteenth-century Romanticism. *Faust* is ranked beside the masterpieces of Dante and Shakespeare, thus embodying Goethe's humanistic ideal of a world literature transcending the boundaries of nations and historical periods.

BIOGRAPHICAL INFORMATION

The son of an Imperial Councilor, Goethe was born in Frankfurt am Main into an established bourgeois family. By the age of eight, he had composed an epistolary novel in which the characters correspond in five languages. Against his wishes, Goethe was sent to study law at the University of Leipzig, but he devoted most of his time to art, music, science, and literature. His university studies were interrupted by illness, and Goethe spent his convalescence learning about alchemy, astrology, and occult philosophy, subjects that would inform the symbolism of *Faust*. His earliest literary works, including the rococo-styled love poetry of *Buch Annette* (1767), are considered accomplished but not outstanding. A decisive influence on Goethe's early literary work was Johann Gottfried von Herder, whom the poet met in Strasbourg, where he continued his legal studies. Herder taught Goethe to appreciate the elemental emotional power of poetry, directing his attention to Shakespeare, Homer, Ossian, and German folk songs. *Goetz von Berlichingen mit der eisernen Hand* (1773; *Goetz of Berlichingen with the Iron Hand*) exemplifies Goethe's work of this period. Somewhat Shakespearean in its emphasis on action and high emotion, the drama was popular in its time, but modern critics generally consider it superficial.

MAJOR WORKS

While critics have debated whether certain of Goethe's works might be classified as Gothic, most agree that elements of the genre can be found in his work. Chief among Goethe's works noted for containing Gothic elements is his two-part retelling of the classic legend of Faust, the scholar who gives Mephistopheles, or the devil, a chance to claim his soul in exchange for unlimited knowledge and eternal life. Goethe began working on the drama during his student days in Strasbourg. In 1790 he published an incomplete version, known as *Faust: Ein Fragment*. In 1808, the complete version of the first part appeared. Goethe continued to work on the play, and *Faust II* was published posthumously in 1832. For its poetic power, formal variety and complexity, as well as its philosophical universality, the first part of *Faust* was immediately recognized as a masterpiece of mythic proportions. *Faust II*, however, was not fully analyzed or appreciated until the twentieth century. Goethe addressed the Gothic in his nonfiction writing as well. In his essay "Von deutscher Baukunst" (1773) and in book nine of his autobiography, *Aus meinen Leben* (1811-22; *Memoirs of Goethe*), he discusses at length his initial distaste for Gothic architecture, recalling that the wholeness and harmony he found in the cathedral at Strasbourg changed his views.

CRITICAL RECEPTION

Following his death, Goethe's literary reputation diminished outside of the German-speaking world. Twentieth-century British and American critics have generally acknowledged Goethe's greatness. Generally more favorable to Goethe than their American and European colleagues, German critics have viewed their national poet as one of the central figures of world literature. Criticism of the Gothic in Goethe's work centers on *Faust*. Noting that the play "lacks almost totally the sadistic terror that was the visible hallmark of the gothic," critics Jane K. Brown and Marshall Brown identify several Gothic tendencies in the work, including the title character's pact with Mephistopheles, the appearance of supernatural figures (and human characters' reaction to them), and depictions of transcendental consciousness. The legend of Faust, and Goethe's telling in particular, has been credited with influencing such classic works of Gothic fiction as Charles Robert Maturin's *Melmoth the Wanderer*, Mary Shelley's *Frankenstein*, and Matthew Gregory Lewis's *The Monk*. In the twenty-first century *Faust* continues to be regarded as Germany's great contribution to world letters and one of the most important works of Western civilization.

PRINCIPAL WORKS

Buch Annette (poetry) 1767

Die Laune des Verliebten (play) 1767

Neue Lieder (poetry) 1769

Rede Zum Schäkespears Tag (criticism) 1771

Götz von Berlichingen mit der eisernen Hand [*Goetz of Berlichingen with the Iron Hand*] (play) 1773

Von deutscher Baukunst (criticism) 1773

Clavigo (play) 1774

Die Leiden des jungen Werthers [*The Sorrows of Werter*; also published as *Werter and Charlotte*, *The Sorrows of Young Werther*, and *The Sufferings of Young Werther*] (novel) 1774

Stella (play) 1776

Die Geschwister [*The Sister*] (play) 1787

Iphigenie auf Tauris [*Iphigenia in Tauris*] (play) 1787

Der Triumph der Empfindsamkeit (play) 1787

Egmont (play) 1788

Faust: Ein Fragment (play) 1790

Torquato Tasso [*Torquato Tasso: A Dramatic Poem from the German with Other German Poetry*] (play) 1790

Versuch die Metamorphose der Pflanzen zu erklären [*Goethe's Botany: The Metamorphosis of Plants*; also published as *Tobler's Ode to Nature*] (essay) 1790

Beiträge zur Optik (essay) 1791-92

Der Gross-Kophta (play) 1792

Der Bürgergeneral (play) 1793

Reineke Fuchs [*History of Renard the Fox*; also published as *Reynard the Fox*] (poetry) 1794

Römische Elegien [*Goethe's Roman Elegies*] (poetry) 1795

Wilhelm Meisters Lehrjahre [*Wilhelm Meister's Apprenticeship*] (novel) 1795-96

Venezianische Epigramme (poetry) 1796

Xenien [with Friedrich Schiller; *Goethe and Schiller's Xenions*] (poetry) 1797

Hermann und Dorothea [*Herman and Dorothea*] (poetry) 1798

Die natürliche Tochter (play) 1804

Winckelmann und sein Jahrhundert (biography) 1805

Faust—Der Tragödie erster Teil [*Faust. Part I.*; published in *Faust: A Drama by Goethe and Schiller's "Song of the Bell"*] (play) 1808

Die Wahlverwandtschaften [*Elective Affinities*] (novel) 1809

Pandora (unfinished play) 1810

Wanderers Sturmlied (poetry) 1810

Zur Farbenlehre [*Theory of Colours*; also published as *Goethe's Colour Theory*] (essay) 1810

Aus meinen Leben: Dichtung und Wahrheit [*Memoirs of Goethe: Written by Himself*; also published as *The Autobiography of Goethe: Truth and Poetry from My Own Life*] (autobiography) 1811-22

Des Epimenides Erwachen (play) 1815

Sonnette (poetry) 1815

Italienische Reise [*Travels in Italy*; also published as *Italian Journey*] (travel essay) 1816

Ueber Kunst und Altertum von Goethe. 6 vols. (criticism) 1816-32

Zur Morphologie (essay) 1817-23

West-öestlicher Divan [*Goethe's West-Easterly Divan*; also published as *West-Eastern Divan*] (poetry) 1819

Wilhelm Meisters Wanderjahre; oder, Die Entsagenden [*Wilhelm Meister's Travels; or, The Renunciants*] (novel) 1821

Die Campagne in Frankreich: 1792 [*Campaign in France in the Year 1792*] (history) 1822

Trilogie der Leidenschaft (poetry) 1823

Marienbader Elegie (poetry) 1827

Briefwechsel zwischen Schiller und Goethe [*Correspondence between Schiller and Goethe from 1794 to 1805*] (letters) 1828

Novelle [*Goethe's Novel*; also published as *Novella*] (novella) 1828

*Wilhelm Meisters Wanderjahre; oder, Die Entsagenden [*Wilhelm Meister's Travels: Translated from the Enlarged Edition*] (novel) 1828

Annalen: Tag-und Jahreshefte [*Annals; or, Day and Year Papers*] (journal) 1830

Faust II [*Goethe's Faust: Part II*] (play) 1832

Gespräche mit Goethe in den letzten Jahren seines Lebens: 1823-1832 [with J. P. Eckermann; *Conversations with Goethe in the Last Years of His Life*] (conversations) 1837-48

The Poems of Goethe (poetry) 1846

Goethes sämmtliche Werke. 30 vols. (poetry, plays, essays, novels, novellas, short stories, criticism, history, biography, autobiography, letters, and librettos) 1848

Goethes sämmtliche Gedichte (poetry) 1869

Goethe's Works. 9 vols. (autobiography, plays, poetry, novels, essays, travel essays) 1885

†*Goethes Faust in urspünglicher Gestalt nach der Göch hausenschen Abschrift herausgegeben* (play) 1888

Wilhelm Meisters theatricalische Sendung [*Wilhelm Meister's Theatrical Mission*] (unfinished novel) 1911

Werke. 14 vols. (poetry, plays, novels, novellas, short stories, autobiography, biography, criticism, essays, history) 1961-64

---

*   This work is a revision of the earlier *Wilhelm Meisters Wanderjahre; oder, Die Enstagenden.*

†   This work is generally referred to as *Urfaust.*

PRIMARY SOURCES

JOHANN WOLFGANG VON GOETHE (POEM DATE 1808)

SOURCE: Goethe, Johann Wolfgang von. "Dedication." In *Faust: Part One*, translated by David Luke, p. 3. Oxford: Oxford University Press, 1987.

The following poem serves as Goethe's dedication to his Faust I, *first published in 1808.*

Uncertain shapes, visitors from the past
At whom I darkly gazed so long ago,
My heart's mad fleeting visions—now at last
Shall I embrace you, must I let you go?
Again you haunt me: come then, hold me fast!
Out of the mist and murk you rise, who so
Besiege me, and with magic breath restore,
Stirring my soul, lost youth to me once more.

You bring back memories of happier days
And many a well-loved ghost again I greet;
As when some old half-faded legend plays
About our ears, lamenting strains repeat
My journey through life's labyrinthine maze,
Old griefs revive, old friends, old loves I meet,
Those dear companions, by their fate's unkind
Decree cut short, who left me here behind.

They cannot hear my present music, those
Few souls who listened to my early song;
They are far from me now who were so close,
And their first answering echo has so long
Been silent. Now my voice is heard, who knows
By whom? I shudder as the nameless throng
Applauds it. Are they living still, those friends
Whom once it moved, scattered to the world's
    ends?

And I am seized by long unwonted yearning
For that still, solemn spirit-realm which then
Was mine; these hovering lisping tones returning
Sigh as from some Aeolian harp, as when

I sang them first; I tremble, and my burning
Tears flow, my stern heart melts to love again.
All that I now possess seems far away
And vanished worlds are real to me today.

GENERAL COMMENTARY

KENNETH S. CALHOON (ESSAY DATE MARCH 2001)

SOURCE: Calhoon, Kenneth S. "The Gothic Imaginary: Goethe in Strasbourg." *Deutsche Vierteljahrsschrift für Literaturwissenschaft und Geistesgeschichte* 75, no. 1 (March 2001): 5-14.

In the following essay, Calhoon studies how Goethe's recorded early encounters with Gothic architecture informed his representations of fear and horror in his later works.

In the spring of 1771 Goethe, on the mend after a long illness, and aching to escape the sphere of his father's influence, rode the mail to Strasbourg, where he would convalesce further and read the law. Immediately upon alighting—so he reports in *Dichtung und Wahrheit*—he rushed to view at close range what had been visible for miles, namely the great thirteenth-century cathedral at the heart of town. His encounter with this medieval colossus is described dithyrambically in the essay *Von Deutscher Baukunst,* which Herder included in his *Von Deutscher Art und Kunst* (1772). A hymn to master-builder Erwin von Steinbach, the essay mounts a diatribe against a prevailing Neo-Classicism whose tenets had left Goethe disinclined to appreciate anything Gothic. He admits to sharing the common prejudice that made the term "Gothic" interchangeable with every conceivable aesthetic flaw—the absence of proportion and definition, ornamental excess, a jumbled mess of naturally incompatible forms. It is thus with apprehension that he approaches, braced to confront an unsettling amalgam of ill-matched components, in a word, a "monster": "so graute mir's im Gehen vorm Anblick eines mißgeformten krausborstigen Ungeheuers."[1] To his surprise, Goethe discovers not a monster, but a structure suffused with a wholeness and harmony commensurate with the natural world. The building's formal integrity, moreover, seems an outgrowth of its creator's soul, in which the whole is one with its parts: "Er [der Genius] ist der erste, aus dessen Seele die Teile, in ein ewiges Ganze zusammengewachsen, hervortreten" (*HA* XII, 9). The facade, then, functions as a medium through which a wholeness, proper to the creator, is installed in the spectator: "Ein ganzer, großer Ein-druck füllte meine Seele, den, weil er aus tausend harmonierenden Einzelheiten bestand, ich wohl schmecken und genießen, keineswegs aber erkennen und erklären konnte" (*HA* XII, 11).

This opposition of intuitive and cognitive faculties favors an immediacy of perception, which here smacks of oral pleasure and a concomitant unity of self and world. The physical connotation of the verb "schmecken" undoes the distance from necessity that conditions "good taste". To be sure, the canons of taste are present as Goethe, recalling his wary approach, enumerates the frightful attributes that supposedly awaited him: "Unter die Rubrik *Gotisch* . . . häufte ich alle synonymische Mißverständnisse, die mir von Unbestimmtem, Ungeordnetem, Unnatürlichem, Zusammengestoppeltem, Aufgeflicktem, Überladenem jemals durch den Kopf gezogen waren" (*HA* XII, 10). Goethe identifies the confused synonymy by which the eighteenth-century champions of Classical restraint invoked the monstrous as something common to a range of distinct styles and representational practices. When Batty Langley observed in 1742 that "every ancient building, which is not in the Grecian mode, is called a Gothic building", he echoed a Palladian Classicism, later embraced by Goethe himself, that had long defined itself in pointed opposition to the grotesque.[2] With its inorganic aggregates of human, animal and plant forms, the grotesque lent expression to forces of instability—of "disruptive or insurgent vitality"—embodied catastrophically by Dr. Frankenstein's "gothic" monster, who is stitched together out of disparate and aesthetically incompatible parts, both human and animal.[3]

Finding in the great Gothic structure a dynamic, organic integrity, Goethe absolves the cathedral of the "grotesque" promiscuity that an ascendant bourgeois order was prone to project onto the styles of the old régime. Indeed, the excessive and imbalanced ornamentation that Goethe anticipated is suggestive of the Baroque and Rococo. The latter was at hand when Quatremère de Quincy, writing in 1798, warned of an enduring taste for the bizarre, which he ascribed to a "satiety that comes from abundance". *Bizarrerie* he condemned as an "incurably immoral use of form"—one that "makes the simple beauties of nature seem insipid". De Quincy laments the wide-ranging influence that this predilection for the bizarre exercised over architecture: "[S]traight lines were replaced by convolutions; severe outlines by undulations; regular plans by over-elaborate, mixtilinear designs; the symmetrical by the picturesque; and order by the confusion of chaos."[4]

Straight, severe, regular, symmetrical, ordered—these normative values convey the moralism behind a new, ideal architecture governed by the language of geometry and the law of function. The doctrine that would subordinate the edifice to the principle of uniform visibility stood opposite an old régime whose revelry in the play of appearances was now understood as spiritual dissipation—as *Zerstreuung.* The anodyne of distraction, namely concentration (*Sammlung*), is aligned with *Anschauung,* which in its full anthropological import denotes a simultaneous, undivided seeing. Something of this kind is evoked by de Quincy when he extols an architecture that refuses to divide itself into a variety of dissociated effects: "To produce an effect of grandeur, the object in which it is to inhere must be simple enough to strike us *at a glance,* that is to say, in its entirety, and at the same time to strike us in relation to its parts."[5] Commenting on these lines, Jean Starobinski cites "a *nouveau régime* of sensibility" that "set aside multiplicity of sensation in favor of the unity of one great spiritual intuition"[6].

One great spiritual intuition: so closely does this echo Goethe's evocation of the informing principle of the Gothic that it seems possible to situate his essay within a discourse whose other is that same "multiplicity of sensation". Subverting the logic that made the Gothic synonymous with the dispersive energies of the grotesque, Goethe enlists this architecture as an amalgam by which to conflate otherwise dissimilar Baroque and Neo-Classical traditions. The Baroque and Rococo make more or less explicit appearances in the *Baukunst*-essay, Baroque in the form of Bernini's much-maligned colonnade in front of St. Peter's, Rococo in the guise of those whom Goethe decries as "geschminkte Puppenmaler". One thinks of the brightly painted figurines from Meissen and elsewhere, so popular at the time, which perfectly epitomize the minute elaborations of a waning aristocratic society built on delicacy, intimation, politesse, not to mention the studied effeminacy of the *honnéte homme*: "Sie [unsre geschminkten Puppenmaler] haben durch theatralische Stellungen, erlogne Teints, und bunte Kleider die Augen der Weiber gefangen" (*HA* XII, 14). Rejecting the precepts of *trompe-l'oeil,* Goethe removes himself from a specularity that would implicate him in so blatantly narcissistic a self-presentation. His own image fragmented, he proceeds from a lack that stands opposite the aforementioned "satiety that

comes from abundance". He describes himself early on as a "patched up vessel" poised between death and prosperity but drifting toward the former: "eh' ich mein geflicktes Schiffchen wieder auf den Ozean wage, wahrscheinlicher dem Tod als dem Gewinst entgegen . . ." (*HA* XII, 7), etc. He goes on to recount his attempt to improvise a monument to Erwin, whose grave-marker he has failed to locate. The missing crypt marks an emphatic absence, which is offset by the vision of the cathedral, itself the product of an ostensibly undivided genius. In this context, David Wellbery notes the "semantics of verticality" that pervades Goethe's essay and specifies the symbolic position as *phallic.*[7] The observation is doubly applicable to the cathedral in question, given that only one of its twin towers was finished, leaving the lone spire forever shadowed by a symmetrical lack.

Goethe's vision of the massive church as a natural, harmonious and eternal whole does not neutralize his anxiety but confirms it—in the way that, in a certain psychoanalytic regimen, the tension between belief and disavowal is sustained through hallucinations that represent both. The cathedral acquires a strangely hallucinatory quality, as when Goethe comments on how the huge building seems suspended aloft: "wie das festgegründete, ungeheure Gebäude sich leicht in die Luft hebt" (*HA* XII, 12). In *Dichtung und Wahrheit,* Goethe remembers how the church, at first sight, struck him as something monstrous—*ein Ungeheures*—which would have terrified him were it not so finely conceived and carefully wrought (*HA* IX, 357-58). In the same account, he describes his repeated climbs to the top of the tower. In one instance, he forces himself out onto the narrow platform, from which the vertiginous spectacle, which he likens to the view from a hot-air balloon, is not framed or foregrounded by any part of the church: "Es ist völlig, als wenn man sich auf einer Montgolfiere in die Luft erhoben sähe. Dergleichen Angst und Qual wiederholte ich so oft, bis der Eindruck mir ganz gleichgültig ward . . ." (*HA* IX, 374). He adds that this strategy of exposing himself to unpleasant or disturbing experiences for the purpose of mastering them served him well in other endeavors, in particular his anatomical studies, where he learned to bear even the most repulsive sight, i.e., "den widerwärtigsten Anblick [zu] ertragen".

A certain "compulsion to repeat" (*Wiederholungszwang*) defines a sequence of exclamatory gestures that build on Goethe's first close encounter with the Gothic giant: "Mit welcher unerwarteten Empfindung überraschte mich der Anblick, als ich davor trat!" (*HA* XII, 11). The experience is represented not only in terms of an unalloyed sensation but also as the resolution of the tension, indeed the *suspense,* that informs Goethe's approach. We have noted how Goethe, winding his way through town, virtually trembles at the prospect of confronting "a misshapen, curly-bristled monster" ("eines mißgeformten krausborstigen Ungeheuers"). And while the actual encounter does not initially appear fear-inducing, the long paragraph describing Goethe's reaction—in which the spirit of the architect whispers ("lispelt") his secrets to the visitor—builds to a point of equilibrium that supersedes fear: "Deinem Unterricht dank' ich's, Genius, daß mir's nicht mehr schwindelt an deinen Tiefen" (*HA* XII, 12). The intervening one-and-one-half pages take their structure from Goethe's repeated trips to the church—return journeys that here seem apocryphally condensed between evening and morning. The following sentences are not consecutive, but they convey the *Steigerung* that this passage achieves: "wie oft bin ich zurückgekehrt, diese himmlisch-irdische Freude zu genießen. . . . Wie oft hat die Abenddämmerung mein durch forschendes Schauen ermattetes Aug' mit freundlicher Ruhe geletzt, wenn durch sie die unzähligen Teile zu ganzen Massen schmolzen, und nun diese, einfach und groß, vor meiner Seele standen . . ." (*HA,* XII, 11). Not only is this repetitiveness made explicit, but the repetition also coincides with a refreshment of vision, which in turn corresponds to a melting of divisions that establishes the plenitude of presence. This presencing culminates in the image of the awakening Goethe, childlike, his arms outstretched toward the shimmering church, which is suddenly animated by the birds that inhabit its pierced and porous facade: "Bis die Vögel des Morgens, die in seinen tausend Öffnungen wohnen, der Sonne entgegenjauchzten und mich aus dem Schlummer weckten. Wie frisch leuchtet' er im Morgenduftglanz mir entgegen, wie froh konnt' ich ihm meine Arme entgegenstrecken, schauen die großen harmonischen Massen . . ." (*HA* XII, 12). These figures of fluidity, of masses melting into each other, and of organic wholeness, are juxtaposed to the spectacle of a church perceived to be incomplete, fragmented, discordant, constructed mathematically and piece by piece. This sense of incompleteness, like the anxiety it provokes, is not invalidated by the experience of wholeness, but is part of the dynamism that structures the suspense. Incidentally, Richard Sennett, in his study of visibility and urban design, takes issue

with the common idea that the physical immensity of Gothic cathedrals served to make conspicuous the predominance of the Church over secular life: "God's power was in no need of advertisement; the problem was how humankind . . . can approach Him, a problem of how to bring the congregation to an apprehension of His presence rather than an affirmation of His existence."[8]

With rather less confidence in "His existence", the Baroque orchestrates apprehension on a grand scale. Secrecy and obscurity are used to engage subjects in processes of decipherment, as wonder and astonishment ensure contemplation by bringing it temporarily to a halt. In his defining study of Baroque culture, José Antonio Maravall identifies a technique of *suspension* (not unrelated to *suspense*)—a means of "[arresting] one's attention in a state of anxious instability so as to reinforce the consequences of emotional effects"[9]. Hence a taste for difficulty, one manifestation of which was anamorphosis, where geometrical virtuosity was used to predict and project—or correct—visual distortion. This is part of a more general technique of incompleteness that Maravall finds in the later works of Shakespeare, sometimes thought to be loosely constructed, or the paintings of Velásquez, which typically have an unfinished quality: "It is a process of suspension wherein one expects the contemplating eye to end up supplying what is missing. . . . All painting of 'splotches' or 'smears' . . . is to a certain extent an *anamorphosis* that calls for spectator intervention to recompose the image."[10] Goethe supplies what is missing, his eye reassembling the image, finding completeness in place of "zerstreute Elemente" and "unzählig kleine Teile". The cathedral at Strasbourg, as it functions in his essay, is anamorphic, wavering between a wholeness, which Goethe hallucinates, and the monstrosity lurking behind it, whereby "monster" carries the connotation of something ill-born.[11] We may add that adjectives like "sinuous" and "flaccid", commonly applied to architecture at the time, superimpose onto the structure an image of the body. To the extent that Goethe finds in the church a counterpart to his own "geflicktes Schiffchen"—*Schiff* ("nave") being itself an architectural term—the stone edifice constitutes an imaginary reflection built around an internal sense of disunity. There is something here of Lacan's mirror-stage—of the child's jubilant recognition of his reflected image, which offers a semblance of wholeness that contrasts markedly with what the child experiences in himself. (The "disruptive or insurgent vitality" of the grotesque may here be thought of in analogy to the emerging *I*'s sense of inner turbulence, which in dreams, as in the works of Bosch, takes the form of anatomical monstrosities.)[12] And there is Goethe—again childlike—roused from sleep to the sight of the church, redolent with the dawn, and shining back at him, i.e., *entgegenleuchtend*. The earlier feeling of fragmentation, now expiated, reappears through a doubling expressed as elective affinity: "Aber zu dir, teuerer Jüngling, gesell' ich mich, der du bewegt dastehst und die Widersprüche nicht vereinigen kannst, die sich in deiner Seele kreuzen . . ." (*HA* XII, 13).

Lacan is concerned with the manner in which living beings adapt to an internal bi-partitioning. This division is evident in the natural world in the phenomenon of mimicry, whereby the organism splits itself between its being and its semblance, the latter taking the form of masks, camouflage, alluring and threatening gestures. Lacan observes that the mechanism by which organisms assume the mottled coloration of the surrounding world is "the equivalent of the function which, in man, is exercised by painting"[13]. He suggests provocatively that if a bird were to paint it would do so by "letting fall its feathers"[14]. It is intriguing that Goethe, as an example of the "bildende Natur" that inheres in man and engenders artistic creation, refers to the self-decoration—the "body art"—of primitive peoples: "Und so modelt der Wilde mit abenteuerlichen Zügen, gräßlichen Gestalten, hohen Farben, seine Kokos, seine Federn und seinen Körper" (*HA* XII, 13). Art is atavistically derived. Lacan asserts that the stroke of the painter's brush is a gesture, meant to intimidate, calculated to make an impression. Maravall has said with respect to the gestural excess of mannerism that painters like Michelangelo and Vasari "understood that what was unrestrained, taken to the extreme, possesses an ability to *impress*"[15]. Likewise, Lacan affirms that "the [painted] picture is first felt by us, as the terms *impression* and *impressionism* imply, as having more affinity with the gesture than any other type of movement"[16].

By ascribing an *evasive* function to the painting of "splotches" and "smears" (typical of but not limited to Velásquez), Maravall echoes the suggestion that "those touches that fall like rain from the painter's brush" are analogous to natural mimicry and thus constitute a screen.[17] Ortega y Gasset, who locates Velásquez at the beginning of a series of "successive impressionisms", identifies a revolution in painting that "denied the pretensions of solidity", replacing tactile, corporeal shapes with "a mere surface that intercepts vi-

sion". Impressionism proper (Ortega's account has the tone of complaint) represents a more complete withdrawal from the visible world and into the subject. This gradual distancing from things favors the genre of landscape, which formalizes the separation between subject and object: "The point of view has been retracted, has placed itself farther from the object, and we have passed from proximate to distant vision. . . . Between the eye and the bodies is interposed the most immediate object: hollow space, air."[18]

As if to confirm Ortega's claim that distant vision issues from the increasing self-absorption of the modern subject, Goethe produces, literally in place of the cathedral, a landscape. Having just arrived in Strasbourg, and anxious to take advantage of remaining daylight, he climbs the lone spire to partake of the view. The rustic panorama that greets him unfolds in accordance with the movements of the eye as it traces the courses of rivers and contours of the land:

> Und so sah ich denn von der Plattform die schöne Gegend vor mir, in welcher ich eine Zeitlang wohnen und hausen durfte: die ansehnliche Stadt, die weitumherliegenden, mit herrlichen dichten Bäumen besetzten und durchflochtenen Auen, diesen auffallenden Reichtum der Vegetation, der, dem Laufe des Rheins folgend, die Ufer, Inseln und Werder bezeichnet. Nicht weniger mit mannigfaltigem Grün geschmückt ist der von Süden herab sich ziehende flache Grund, welchen die Iller bewässert; selbst westwärts, nach dem Gebirge zu, finden sich manche Niederungen, die einen ebenso reizenden Anblick von Wald und Wiesenwuchs gewähren, so wie der nördliche mehr hügelige Teil von unendlichen kleinen Bächen durchschnitten ist, die überall ein schnelles Wachstum begünstigen. Denkt man sich nun zwischen diesen üppig ausgestreckten Matten, zwischen fröhlich ausgesäeten Hainen alles zum Fruchtbau schickliche Land trefflich bearbeitet, grünend und reifend, und die besten und reichsten Stellen desselben durch Dörfer und Meierhöfe bezeichnet, und eine solche große und unübersehliche, wie ein neues Paradies für den Menschen recht vorbereitete Fläche näher und ferner von teils angebauten, teils waldbewachsenen Bergen begrenzt; so wird man das Entzücken begreifen, mit dem ich mein Schicksal segnete, das mir für einige Zeit einen so schönen Wohnplatz bestimmt hatte.
>
> (*HA* IX, 356-357)

Heroic in its own right, the Gothic structure is less something seen than the source of a point of view. We might even venture that Goethe's first act in Strasbourg was to rush to the one spot from which the cathedral is not visible. The above landscape, which carefully adheres to eighteenth-century formulas, constitutes a screen—a holistic counterpart to the Gothic "monster", whose potentially grotesque features disappear behind a pleasing surface.

If Impressionism represents a culmination of the pleasing surface, it also manifests the triumphal gaze of the modern subject which, following Ortega, organizes visual phenomena into a certain *mise-en-scène*: "The eye of the artist is established as the center of the plastic Cosmos, around which revolve the form of objects."[19] Hence Goethe's synoptic view from the mighty spire, which fixes a monumental vantage point.[20] While not impressionist as such, the landscape Goethe describes resembles those painted by John Constable, whose often rough application of color is consistent with the "technique of incompleteness" described by Maravall, and whose "Claudian" renderings of the English countryside depict not objects, but "objects transformed by atmosphere"[21]. Between 1892 and -95, a good hundred-twenty years after Goethe's arrival in Strasbourg, Claude Monet produced some thirty canvases depicting the cathedral at Rouen, each painted from the same point of view. Accommodations of ambient light, many of these paintings bear supplementary titles such as "Morning Effect", "Gray Day", or "Sunset"—appellations that identify the object as an effect of its surroundings. Camouflaged as it were, the great facade appears always on the verge of dissolving into flecks of color, which fade or deepen in accordance with the hour, season, indeed atmosphere. While not tethered to a single point of view, Goethe likewise celebrates the variety supplied by changing light: "Wie oft bin ich zurückgekehrt, von allen Seiten, aus allen Entfernungen, in jedem Lichte des Tags zu schauen seine Würde und Herrlichkeit!" (**HA** XII, 11). This exclamation illustrates what is apparent throughout, namely that Goethe describes little while saying much about his affective response to what he sees. His repeated returns to the building, and his repeated affirmation of its wholeness, has the effect of a compulsive disavowal, for that structural integrity does not reveal itself to the eye. Rather, it is fantasmatic, conveyed in darkness by the whispering spirit of the architect. Goethe's *Baukunst*-essay begins with an affirmation of a lack, his failure to locate Erwin's grave-marker inducing melancholy ("da ward ich tief in die Seele betrübt" [**HA** XII, 7]). The cathedral, rising into the air, seems little more than a substitute—an anamorphic ghost whose apparition oscillates between *Abenddämmerung* and *Morgenduftglanz*, hovering at the threshold of the visible.

Notes

1. Johann Wolfgang von Goethe, *Werke. Hamburger Ausgabe,* ed. Erich Trunz and Hans Joachim Schrimpf, 8th edition, Munich 1978, XII, 11. All subsequent references to the *Hamburger Ausgabe* are abbreviated as *HA.*

2. Ronald Paulson, *Representations of Revolution (1789-1920),* New Haven 1983, 176. See William J. Lillyman, "Andrea Palladio and Goethe's Classicism", *Goethe Yearbook* V (1985), 85-102.

3. See Paulson (note 2), 178, 239-247.

4. Cited in Jean Starobinski, *1789: Emblems of Reason,* trans. Barbara Bray, Cambridge/Mass. 1988, 74.

5. Starobinski (note 4), 75. Emphasis added.

6. Starobinski (note 4), 75.

7. David Wellbery, *The Specular Moment. Goethe's Early Lyric and the Beginnings of Romanticism,* Stanford 1996, 128.

8. Richard Sennett, *The Conscience of the Eye. The Design and Social Life of Cities,* New York 1990, 13.

9. José Antonio Maravall, *Culture of the Baroque. Analysis of a Historical Structure,* trans. Terry Cochran, Minneapolis 1986, 216.

10. Maravall (note 9), 218.

11. In an essay from 1823 also entitled *Von Deutscher Baukunst* Goethe characterizes the cathedral at Cologne, which at the time was still substantially incomplete, as something monstrous ("so tritt uns hier ein Unvollendetes, Ungeheures entgegen"), the sight of which arroused apprehension ("eine gewisse Apprehension in mir erregte") (HA XII, 180).

12. Jacques Lacan: "This fragmented body . . . usually manifests itself in dreams . . . in the form of disjointed limbs, or of those organs represented in exoscopy, growing wings and taking up arms for intestinal persecutions—the very same that the visionary Hieronymus Bosch fixed, for all time, in painting, in their ascent from the fifteenth century to the imaginary zenith of modern man" (*Écrits. A Selection,* trans. Alan Sheridan, New York 1977, 4-5).

13. Jacques Lacan, *The Four Fundamental Concepts of Psychoanalysis,* ed. Jacques-Alain Miller, trans. Alan Sheridan, New York 1981, 109.

14. Lacan, *The Four Fundamental Concepts* (note 13), 114.

15. Maravall (note 9), 211.

16. Lacan, *The Four Fundamental Concepts* (note 13), 115.

17. Maravall (note 9), 219; Lacan, *The Four Fundamental Concepts* (note 13), 110.

18. José Ortega y Gasset, "On Point of View in the Arts", trans. Paul Snodgrass and Joseph Frank," in: *The Dehumanization of Art and Other Writings on Art and Culture,* Garden City, New York 1956, 111-112. See Albert Schug, "Über den Gegenstand der impressionistischen Landschaftsmalerei," in: Götz Czymmek (ed.), *Landschaft im Licht. Impressionistische Malerei in Europa und Nordamerika,* Cologne, Zurich 1990, 67 f.

19. Ortega y Gasset (note 18), 112.

20. That Goethe's view from the tower is paradigmatic is suggested by a comparison to Lynkeus, the tower-watch in *Faust II.* See Helmut J. Schneider: "Lynkeus

. . . betreibt jene von [Joachim] Ritter analysierte Kosmos-Schau, die *speculatio*, die wörtlich nichts anderes als Turm-Schau bedeutet" ("Utopie und Landschaft im 18. Jahrhundert", in: Wilhelm Voßkamp [ed.], *Utopieforschung. Interdisziplinäre Studien zur neuzeitlichen Utopie*, Stuttgart 1982, III, 187).

21. Ronald Paulson, *Literary Landscape. Turner and Constable*, New Haven 1982, 112.

TITLE COMMENTARY

Faust

SYNDY M. CONGER (ESSAY DATE 1977)

SOURCE: Conger, Syndy M. "An Analysis of *The Monk* and Its German Sources." In *Matthew G. Lewis, Charles Robert Maturin and the Germans: An Interpretive Study of the Influence of German Literature on Two Gothic Novels*, pp. 12-42. Salzburg: Institut fur Englische Sprache unde Literatur, Universitat Salzburg, 1977.

In the following excerpt, Conger studies the influence of Goethe's Faust *on Matthew Gregory Lewis's* The Monk.

The Monk *and Goethe's* Faust

Various critics have noticed the Faust-like characteristics of Lewis's Ambrosio, but no one has gone beyond jotting down basic similarities between the two, nor has anyone even tried to establish whether *The Monk* stands more indebted to Christopher Marlowe's *The Tragical History of Dr. Faustus* or Johann Goethe's *Faust*.[1] To students interested in determining the extent of German influence on English gothic fiction, this issue is crucial, even more so because the marriage of gothic fiction and the Faust legend, first performed by Lewis in *The Monk*, was one of the important events in the history of gothicism, producing some of the world's best-known gothic novels: *Melmoth the Wanderer, Frankenstein,* and *Moby Dick*.[2] . . .

While it cannot be said that Lewis's *The Monk* is a carbon copy of Goethe's Storm and Stress *Faust* either, there are nevertheless many more points of resemblance between these two works, making Goethe's influence on Lewis decidedly more pervasive than Marlowe's. At crucial points in his novel Lewis draws upon those scenes from Goethe's *Faust* which constitute the kernel of the Gretchen tragedy. Some of these parallel scenes have been noted by one critic, but none has analyzed them carefully.[3] At first the parallels between characters are casual and fleeting, as if

Lewis was unable to decide who should play the role of Faust to his "Gretchen," Antonia. For example, in the first scene of the novel, while Lorenzo is the obvious admirer of Antonia, Don Christoval speaks the lines that Faust speaks to Gretchen on first meeting her. Once Antonia meets Ambrosio, however, Lewis's indecision is over. Ambrosio becomes his Faust, and then parallel scenes follow one another in quick succession. But before we analyze these scenes, a closer look at the fragmentary version of Goethe's *Faust* available to Lewis is necessary.

What has not been widely recognized is that the *Faust* that Lewis had to draw upon was not the completed version we have today; it was *Faust: Ein Fragment*, published first in 1790, but despite the late date essentially a product of the Storm and Stress.[4] Goethe had begun working on a Faust drama in 1771 or 1772 at the height of his own Storm and Stress period; and around the time he made his permanent move to the Weimar court in 1776, he was able to take with him a Faust manuscript of at least twenty-one scenes.[5] For the next ten years, however, his new courtly duties and a gradual change in literary taste prevented him from working on the play, and not until he took his first extended vacation to Italy in 1786 was he able to return to it. Because "the material would not yield to Goethe," as one critic has put it,[6] he decided to publish a version to which he had added two scenes, "Hexenküche" and "Wald und Höhle," but which as yet had neither the crucial pact scene nor a resolution. Important final scenes known to have been written at the time, among them Gretchen's mad scene in prison, Goethe omitted.[7] A more complete version of the early play in manuscript form existed at Weimar; but whether Lewis saw it during his half-year in Weimar in 1792 is not known, though is there some evidence in *The Monk* to support such a hypothesis.[8]

This early *Faust* is hardly a scholar's tragedy at all, but a tragedy of love[9] which was one of Goethe's unique additions to the Faust material.[10] Responsive to Storm and Stress sympathy for unwed mothers or dishonored women,[11] he wrote the story of a simple middle-class maiden Margarethe (or Gretchen, as she is called by Faust) whose seduction and subsequent abandonment by Faust leads her to child murder, imprisonment, madness and death.[12] The central subject of Goethe's early *Faust* is, then, quite different from Marlowe's *Dr. Faustus*.

Even the initial discontent Faust feels and the solution he seeks are quite different from those of

FROM THE AUTHOR

SIR WALTER SCOTT'S TRANSLATION OF GOETHE'S "DER ERLKONIG" ("THE ERL-KING")

O! who rides by night thro' the woodlands so
    wild?
It is the fond Father embracing his Child;
And close the Boy nestles within his lov'd arm,
From the blast of the tempest to keep himself
    warm.

"O Father! see yonder, see yonder!" he says.
"My Boy, upon what dost thou fearfully gaze?"
"O! 'tis the Erl-King, with his staff and his shroud!"
"No, my Love! it is but a dark wreath of the
    cloud."

[THE PHANTOM SPEAKS.]

"O! wilt thou go with me, thou loveliest Child!
"By many gay sports shall thy hours be beguil'd;
"My Mother keeps for thee full many a fair toy,
"And many a fine flow'r shall she pluck for my
    Boy."

"O Father! my Father! and did you not hear,
"The Erl-King whisper so close in my ear?"
"Be still my lov'd Darling, my Child be at ease!
"It was but the wild blast as it howl'd thro' the
    trees."

[THE PHANTOM.]

"O wilt thou go with me, thou loveliest Boy!
"My Daughter shall tend thee with care and with
    joy;
"She shall bear thee so lightly thro' wet and thro'
    wild,
"And hug thee, and kiss thee, and sing to my
    Child."

"O Father! my Father! and saw you not plain
"The Erl-King's pale daughter glide past thro' the
    rain?"
"O no, my heart's treasure! I knew it full soon,
"It was the Grey Willow that danc'd to the Moon.

[THE PHANTOM.]

"Come with me, come with me, no longer delay!
"Or else, silly Child, I will drag thee away."
"O Father! O Father! now, now, keep your hold!
The Erl-King has seiz'd me—his grasp is so cold."

Sore trembled the Father; he spurr'd thro' the
    wild,
Clasping close to his bosom his shuddering Child;
He reaches his dwelling in doubt and in dread;
But, clasp'd to his bosom, the Infant was dead!

Scott, Sir Walter. "The Erl-King. From the German of Goethe. Author of the *Sorrows of Werter*." In *An Apology for Tales of Terror*. Kelso: printed at the Mail office, 1799.

Marlowe's Faustus. Both plays do open with the scholars sitting in their studies, fulminating about how little they know, but for Faustus discontent springs from pride and a lust for near-divine power, while Goethe's Faust despairs because he has failed to learn nature's best kept secret, the Truth. Faustus rejects analytics because it will afford him "no miracle" (l.9), medicine because it cannot teach him Christ's gift for raising the dead (l.24-26), law because it's not worthy of his intellect (l.35), and divinity because it would teach him humility and penitence (l.40-45). On the other hand, Goethe's Faust has wearied of his studies because they have only taught him that he knows nothing ("Nacht," l.11), nor have they enabled him to teach or help others (ll.19-20). Even though he has cut himself off from the joys of living for years, ultimate knowledge is still beyond his grasp: he still has not seen "was die Welt / Im Innersten zusammen hält" (l.29-30).[13] Faustus' solution to his discontent is to barter with the devil for the power he longs for. Faust's solution is to clap shut his books and barter with the devil to give him wisdom through experience:

> Und was der ganzen Menschheit zugetheilt ist,
> Will ich in meinem innern Selbst geniessen,
> Mit meinem Geist das Höchst' und Tiefste greifen,
> Und so mein eigen Selbst zu Ihrem Selbst erweitern
>
>   ("Nacht," ll.247-52)[14]

Faust is not to blame that Mephistopheles interprets this reductively as a wish for wine, women and song.

As Goethe's *Fragment* springs over any conjuration or pact scene between Faust and Mephistopheles, the next important scene for the purposes of this comparison is "Hexenküche," added at the revision. Part of Mephistopheles' scheme for winning Faust's soul is to restore his youth and with it his youthful longings. While the witch brews the right potion, Mephistopheles makes sure Faust catches a glimpse of a beautiful woman in the witch's mirror. The potion and the mirror have done their job well, for the first girl he sees, as it happens Gretchen, he desires. "Hör," he barks at Mephistopheles the moment she has passed on the street, "du musst mir die Dirne schaffen!" ("Strasse," l.1080).[15] When Mephistopheles balks, claiming he has "no power" over such a virtuous girl (l.1087), Faust responds with a threat to call off their deal and the boast that he could arrange it in seven hours without the devil's help (ll.1103-05). Even Mephistopheles' mockery ("Ihr sprecht schon fast wie ein Franzos," l.1106) doesn't budge

Faust's resolve ("Hab' Appetit . . . ," l.1114).[16] The disillusioned professor is hungry for sensual experience.

The rest of the drama is the Gretchen tragedy. Mephistopheles arranges a rendezvous for Faust and Gretchen at a neighbor's house ("Marthens Garten"), Faust easily overwhelms the naive Gretchen with costly jewels and a display of affection and erudition, they arrange to meet at night at Gretchen's house by giving the mother a sleeping potion, the mother dies as a result, and the now pregnant Gretchen is separated from Faust. The *Fragment* stops abruptly at a very unhappy moment for both lovers. Faust is last seen in a forest ("Wald und Höhle"), deciding under Mephistopheles' pressure that he cannot resist seducing Gretchen even if it means her perdition. Gretchen is then seen in three moments of panic which follow her discovery that she is pregnant. We see her guilt-stricken at the village well ("Am Brunnen") when a neighbor slanders another girl in similar straits; then praying to Mary ("Zwinger"); and finally fainting in church ("Dom"), terrified by both the mass being sung for the dead and an evil spirit plaguing her for her crimes. Because the *Fragment* breaks off where it does, it is painfully pessimistic;[17] the forces of evil appear to have total control at the end.

Much more than conjuration, pact, and ending are missing in the *Fragment.* Faust is also less sympathetic in this version, for Goethe has not yet included those scenes which will depict him as God's devoted "Knecht," the good man who "in seinem dunklen Drange, / Ist sich des rechten Weges wohl bewusst,"[18] and the man who makes the clever wager he's bound to win with the devil. The *Fragment* also skips over the pathos of scholar Faust:[19] his despair, his near suicide when he believes he will never know nature's secret, his self-revealing talks with his student Wagner, and with Mephistopheles, the adulation of the townspeople for their doctor. At the earliest possible moment in the *Fragment,* the reader sees Faust, raw and hungry, wooing Gretchen. Clearly, Lewis would not have had much difficulty seeing a likeness between this Faust, who abandons the recluse's life of contemplation for the pleasures of the flesh, and his Ambrosio.

Despite the fragmentary nature of the 1790 version, its ties to the Storm and Stress movement are unmistakable. Even though Goethe cast some of his earlier rhapsodic prose into verse during the revisions in the 90's, for the most part the form is typical of dramatic form of the movement. It is essentially non-neoclassical: the action is a series of loosely allied scenes with huge gaps in time and leaps in space.[20] The content even more markedly reflects the preoccupations of the Storm and Stress.

First of all, the fact that **Faust** is a drama drawn from German folklore identifies it as a response to Herder's plea for German authors to revive their own national heritage in literature.[21] Secondly, the values which receive emphasis in the play are Storm and Stress values. Faust demonstrates an appreciation for both nature and the natural. The forest is where he retreats to regain some peace and control over his life; and for a few moments nature heals him and restores his virtue until Mephistopheles intervenes. Faust treasures Gretchen, too, for her unspoiled, spontaneous response to life, and she gives him the same peaceful feeling the forest does ("Abend," 11.1147-55). Faust is also an enthusiastic exponent of experience.[22] It is this which first causes him to turn to Mephistopheles, and he admits in "Wald und Höhle" that the devil is now indispensible to him in gratifying what has become his quenchless yearning for one experience after another: "So tauml' ich von Begierde zu Genuss, / Und im Genuss verschmacht' ich nach Begierde" (11.1919-20).[23] It was not just physical experience that Faust initially longed for, but emotional or subjective experience. His conviction that "Gefühl ist alles" ("Feeling is all," from "Marthens Garten," 1.1756) is behind the special nature of his first request to Mephistopheles to "feel within" everything the human being has ever felt ("Nacht," 11.247-49).

Finally, the central conflict of the drama links it with the Storm and Stress: the conflict between unorthodox inner values and constricting social forms. Both Faust and Gretchen are caught up in this conflict, though not in the same way. Faust openly disregards the codes of church and society. He would rather bask in his own sensibility than contemplate God ("Marthens Garten," 11.1731-58), and he would rather seduce Gretchen than marry her. Gretchen is no conscious rebel, yet she too unwittingly violates the moral code, thinking Faust will eventually marry her.[24] When she realizes her love has made her criminal, something she imagined to be impossible, this tragic truth snaps her mind.[25] Both characters' attempts to assert their own private values are viewed sympathetically by Goethe, though it must be added that he does not paint their society as black as some of his fellow *Stürmer und Dränger.*[26] He leaves the impression instead that the conflict at the center of life is not one easily resolved by changing laws. The persistent assertion of private values, the repeated search for gratification of self, always eventually lead to a tragic clash with society. If Lewis's *The Monk* is Storm and Stress, then it should at least share some of these characteristics.

What Lewis clearly shares with Goethe is an interest in the Gretchen tragedy; and this fact alone makes Goethe's influence on *The Monk* certain, since the Gretchen tragedy had been his own original contribution to the Faust legend. The first three scenes from *Faust* Lewis draws upon to create his opening episode are lighthearted, buoyed up by Mephistopheles' devilish wit: "Strasse," the initial meeting of Faust and Gretchen outside a cathedral; "Der Nachbarinn Haus," Mephistopheles' successful attempt to convince neighbor Marthe she's a widow, so that he and Faust can return to come courting (ostensibly to bring her the death certificate of her long-absent husband); and "Garten," the subsequent rendezvous at Marthe's house. Whenever possible, Lewis tries to approximate that tone in his forest scene. Faust is immediately fascinated by Gretchen when he sees her for the first time leaving a church, and he accosts her on the spot, asking if he may walk her home: ". . . darf ich wagen / Meinen Arm und Geleit Ihr anzutragen" (11.1066-67). Don Christoval and Lorenzo are just as taken with Antonia when they first see her in church, and Don Christoval asks her a very similar question: "Will you permit us to attend you home?" (p. 10). Gretchen and Antonia react similarly also. Gretchen has little to say, though what she does say is said with spirit: "Bin weder Fräulein, weder schön, / Kann ungeleitet nach Hause gehen" (11.1068-69).[27] Antonia is shy and taciturn: ". . . the Lady did not open her lips. . . . At last, in so low a voice as to be scarcely intelligible, she made shift to answer,—'No segnor'" (p. 10). Both also avert their eyes and when pressured to do something they think improper, plead they cannot because it is not "the custom." Gretchen rejects the suggestion from Mephistopheles that she take a lover; Antonia tries to keep on her veil:

Margarethe:	Antonia:
"Das ist des Landes nicht der Brauch." ("Der Nachbarinn Haus," l.1410)	"Dear Aunt; it is not the custom in Murcia." (p. 11)

In order to help Faust in his pursuit of Gretchen, Goethe's Mephistopheles makes friends with Gretchen's neighbor Marthe and arranges a rendezvous in her garden for the four of them. His task is to make sure Marthe's attention will be diverted so that Faust can woo Gretchen, a task which comically turns out to be much more painful than Mephistopheles expected. The aging Marthe, a woman whose husband left her long ago, is aggressively interested in men, money (Mephistopheles seems to be a nobleman), and marriage, and immediately begins an attack. Understandable in the light of his profession, Mephistopheles prefers the witch's bacchanals of *Walpurgisnacht* to holy wedlock, and deliberately misinterprets all her blatant advances. He does avoid committing himself, but is only too anxious to leave, muttering to himself as he goes: "Die hielte wohl den Teufel selbst bey'm Wort!" (l.1466).[28]

In the first scene of *The Monk* Don Christoval functions in an analogous way. He is to divert Leonella's attention so that Lorenzo may make Antonia's acquaintance, and he also finds himself trapped. Leonella is as aggressive and man hungry as Marthe, and makes the clever rhetorical assumption that Don Christoval wishes to marry her (p. 23). In Lewis's description of Don Christoval's reaction to Leonella, an echo from *Faust* is audible: ". . . at the end of an hour I find myself upon the brink of matrimony! . . . Diavolo!" (pp. 23-24). Since Don Christoval's aversion to the old woman is so similar to Mephistopheles' to Marthe, Lewis's use of the word "devil" was probably not accidental.

. . . . .

Besides the death of the mother, two other potentially sensationalistic scenes in *Faust* are never dramatized by Goethe: the seduction and eventual execution-death of Gretchen. No doubt he recognized that, since Faust was responsible for both to some extent, they would blacken his hero's character irreparably. Again, Lewis spells out what Goethe left out. In what are usually acknowledged to be the least palatable scenes in *The Monk*, Lewis depicts Ambrosio raping and murdering Antonia in the church vaults surrounded by moldering corpses.

No comparatists have yet noticed that these scenes yield something positive. They offer textual evidence that Lewis may have been familiar with the *Faust* manuscript at Weimar[29] which included Gretchen's prison scene. In this scene in the *Urfaust*, Mephistopheles has managed to get Faust into Gretchen's prison the night before her execution, and Faust has been trying in vain to convince the deranged girl to flee with him. At dawn Mephistopheles reappears and presses Faust to hurry or he is lost: "Auf! oder *ihr seyd verlohren*! Meine Pferde schaudern!" (italics mine, "Kercker," p. 65).

Margrete (alternate spelling in *Urfaust*) reacts hysterically, sensing she is in the presence of God's enemy: "Der! Der! Lass ihn, schick ihn fort! der will mich! Nein! Nein! *Gericht Gottes, komm über mich . . .*" (p. 65).[30] In Antonia's dungeon scene, Ambrosio is thinking of granting her liberty, when, like Mephistopheles, Matilda rushes into the vault to urge Ambrosio to take quick action: "*We are lost,* unless some speedy means is found of dispelling the Rioters" (p. 389). Antonia's response is a cry of joy followed by increased terror as she realizes that Matilda is no friend: "'Help! *for God*'s sake.'" (italics mine, p. 391).

. . . . .

Goethe's *Faust* helped Lewis move beyond a stereotyped villain to this more ethically complex one, a character one step closer to a Victor Frankenstein or a Melmoth. Melmoth and Frankenstein are admittedly closer to Faust than is Ambrosio, for they have Faust's insatiable, self-destructive desire to know. But the gothic novel with a villain-hero whose goal is to know the unknowable is a novel markedly different in plot and theme from pre-Lewis gothic novels, and it was Lewis, under Goethe's influence, who pointed later gothic novelists in this new direction.

Another innovation in the cast of characters which was inspired by Lewis's interest in Goethe's Faust is the addition of the devil. Bredvold heralds *The Monk* as the first gothic novel to exploit the "Satanic as a thrill,"[31] and it may very well be true that Lewis did add the devil for the thrill of it.[32] It is not true, however, that the devil's presence adds thrills only. It makes evil more absolute, more unmanageable, especially since Lewis's devil controls not only human actions, but also even the thoughts and dreams of the virtuous. Such ubiquitous and all-powerful demons encourage just as many unsettling questions as the villain-hero Ambrosio does. Is life something we can never fully understand or control? Are we at the mercy of inexplicably demonic forces outside ourselves? Within ourselves?[33] These questions had not been raised so effectively in gothic fiction before *The Monk*.

Goethe's influence can be traced also in the plot of *The Monk*, where enough episodes of the Gretchen tragedy are reenacted to necessitate a basic tragic structure: the meeting at the church, the conversations about religion, the vision in the mirror, the visit to the bedroom, seduction for the girl, and death for the mother and the girl. Lewis does for the gothic romance, then, what Richardson did for the epistolary romance and Goethe did for the Faust legend: he introduces to it the pattern of a lovers' tragedy.[34] Such an innovation was an important one, again, bound to invite later gothic romancers to choose more serious themes. One needs only to look at the increasing thoughtfulness of such tragic gothic novelists as Mary Shelley, Maturin, Brontë, and Melville to realize that Lewis's tragic ending, however absurd or grotesque it is, freed future gothic romancers from the intellectually shackling concept of poetical justice and its conventional happy ending.

Notes

1. Of the four critics who discuss the subject, neither Railo nor Dédéyan specifies any particular Faust. Carré and Guthke deal exclusively with the relationship between Goethe's *Faust* and *The Monk*.

2. Robert D. Hume, "Exuberant Gloom, Existential Agony, and Heroic Despair: Three Varieties of Negative Romanticism," in *The Gothic Imagination: Essays in Dark Romanticism*, ed. G. R. Thompson (Pullman: Washington State Univ. Press, 1974), pp. 109-27, devotes considerable time to the discussion of Faust as an apt archetypal figure for the Dark Romantics, and mentions these three novels in the process (p. 112).

3. Carré, pp. 35-36, lists the following scenes in *The Monk* as partially derived from Goethe's *Faust*: the first in the church, Ambrosio's mirror vision, Matilda's getting him into Antonia's chamber, and the sacrifice of mother and daughter. Guthke, *Englische Vorromantik*, pp. 38-39, 133, concurs with just three: the mirror vision and the double sacrifice.

4. For an excellent discussion of the history of the composition and publication of Goethe's Faust, see "Introduction," *Goethe's Faust* ed. R-M. S. Heffner, Helmut Rehder, W. F. Twaddell (Boston: D. C. Heath, 1954), pp. 31-46. See also Pascal, p. 306. Only the German critics have noted that Lewis probably only knew Goethe's 1790 *Fragment*: Guthke, *Englische Vorromantik*, p. 34, and Otto Ritter, "Studien zu M. G. Lewis' Roman 'Ambrosio, or The Monk,'" *Archiv für das Studium der neueren Sprachen und Literaturen*, 111, NS, 11 (1903), 117.

5. A copy of Goethe's 1774 manuscript, made by a lady of the Weimar court by the name of Luise von Göchhausen, was discovered in 1887 and published with the designation of *Urfaust*. See Heffner, et al, pp. 32-34, and J. G. Robertson, *A History of German Literature*, 5th ed., rev. Edna Purdie (Edinburgh: Wm. Blackwood & Sons, 1966), p. 271. It would have been available and certainly known when Lewis was in Weimar, as it was made sometime before 1786.

6. Frenzel and Frenzel, Vol. 1, 218.

7. To compare the three available versions of *Faust* (*Urfaust*; *Faust: Ein Fragment*; and *Faust: Eine Tragödie*) see *Die Faustdichtungen*. Referred to in notes as Artemis.

8. Lewis was well acquainted with *Faust* according to Byron's biographer Moore. See *The Life and Correspondence of M. G. Lewis, author of "The Monk," "Castle Spectre," & c., with many Pieces in Prose never before*

Published (London: Henry Colburn, 1839), I, 73. Since Göchhausen's transcription was done sometime between 1775 and 1786, it would have been available.

9. Heffner, p. 33; Robertson, p. 271.

10. Heffner, p. 33.

11. Frenzel and Frenzel, p. 172; Garland, p. 144; Pascal, pp. 66-68.

12. Much of this is not shown in the fragment, however, which breaks off with Gretchen in church, the child not yet born.

13. "What secret force / Hides in the world and rules its course." I have used Walter Kaufmann's translation of Goethe's *Faust* (Garden City, New York: Doubleday and Company, 1963), p. 95. Page numbers after translations are Kaufmann's.

14.   And what is portioned out to all mankind,
        I shall enjoy deep in my self, contain
        Within my spirit summit and abyss,
        Pile on my breast their agony and bliss
        And thus let my own self grow into theirs,
        unfettered. . . .

                                    (p. 189)

15. "Get me that girl, and don't ask why?" (p. 257).

16. Mephistopheles: "You speak just like a Frenchman"; Faust: "I've appetite . . ." (pp. 257, 259).

17. "Infinitely more pessimistic" than the *Urfaust* is Heffner's assessment of tone, p. 38.

18. "A good man in his darkling aspiration / Remembers the right road throughout his quest" (p. 89).

19. The *Fragment* contains only fifteen pages concerning the scholar's tragedy as compared to roughly fifty in the 1808 version.

20. See Frenzel and Frenzel, pp. 172-73.

21. Pascal, p. 266.

22. Heffner, p. 37.

23. "Thus I reel from desire to enjoyment, / And in enjoyment languish for desire" (p. 313).

24. When Faust tells Gretchen his love for her is "eternal" and will have "no end" (11.1648-49), he means the feeling will always endure; she thinks he means he will marry her. Lecture, Albrecht Schöne, 30 October 1973, Univ. of Göttingen.

25. Pascal, pp. 64-65.

26. Pascal, p. 145.

27. "I'm neither a lady nor am I fair, / And can go home without your care" (p. 257).

28. "She'd keep the Devil to his word, I fear" (p. 289).

29. See n. 5 above.

30.

MEPHISTOPHELES:

    Up! Or you are lost.
    Prating and waiting and pointless wavering.
    My horses are quavering
                        . . . . .

MARGARET:

    He! He! Send him away!
                        . . . . .

    He wants me!
                        . . . . .

    Judgment of God! I give
    Myself to you.

                                    (p. 421)

31. Bredvold, *The Natural History of Sensibility* (Detroit: Wayne State Univ. Press, 1962), p. 95.

32. I base this on Lewis's own admission that he strove for "strong colours" in writing *The Monk*, see above, n. 23.

33. An excellent discussion of the internalization of the demonic is Francis Russell Hart's "The Experience of Character in the English Gothic Novel," in *Experience in the Novel*, Selected Papers from the English Institute, ed. Roy Harvey Pearce (New York: Columbia Univ. Press, 1968), pp. 83-105; Lowry Nelson, Jr., "Night Thoughts on the Gothic Novel," *Yale Review*, 52 (1963), 242, also remarks that gothic novelists become ever more interested in the "presentation of the subconscious drama of the mind."

34. Sheldon Sacks suggests in "*Clarissa* and the Tragic Traditions," in *Irrationalism in the Eighteenth Century*, Vol. 2 of *Studies in Eighteenth Century Culture*, ed. Harold E. Pagliaro (Cleveland: Case Western Reserve Univ. Press, 1972), that all new literary forms may feel the "subtle influence" of poetical justice, p. 197.

JANE K. BROWN AND MARSHALL BROWN (ESSAY DATE 1994)

SOURCE: Brown, Jane K. and Marshall Brown. "*Faust* and the Gothic Novel." In *Interpreting Goethe's* Faust *Today*, edited by Jane K. Brown, Meredith Lee, and Thomas P. Saine, in collaboration with Paul Hernadi and Cyrus Hamlin, pp. 68-80. Columbia, S.C.: Camden House, 1994.

In the following essay, the Browns trace various common elements in Gothic fiction and Faust.

. . . un vampire, une goule, un homme artificiel, une espèce de Faust . . .

                        (H. de Balzac, *Sarrasine*)

Our aim in the present paper is to conjure up an unfamiliar vision of **Faust.** So far as we know, our topic is nearly virgin, though Faust's vision of Gretchen appears for a moment at the start of Mario Praz's classic *La Morte, la carne e la diavola*.[1] Since, after all, **Faust** isn't a gothic novel, we are not inclined to call this neglect startling. Goethe's play lacks almost totally the sadistic terror that was the visible hallmark of the gothic, and what motifs it shares with the gothic novel are also Shakespearean or general romantic features. Yet while Goethe was cool toward the fashionable gothic, he was not ignorant about it.[2] Surely, for instance, he knew the work of the Jena professor of philosophy, Justus Christian Hennings, since he attacks Hennings in the "Walpurgisnacht-straum," both by name and as the "*Ci-devant Genius der Zeit.*" Writing in the spirit of the Enlightenment about supernatural beliefs in his book of 1780, *Von Geistern und Geistersehern,* Hennings asks derisively, "Vielleicht denkst du, der böse Feind spucke zum Wohl des Menschen?"[3]—a possibility that the more imaginative *Faust* plays with. As Faust says in the last speech before his blinding, "Dämonen, weiß ich, wird man schwerlich los" (11491). Perhaps it isn't so foolish to wonder what the old men—Faust and his creator—thought about ghosts and those who see them.

Early readers of the play clearly perceived its gothic tendencies or potential. Despite their differences, Faust's devilish wager is readily assimilated to demonic pacts in works like Maturin's *Melmoth the Wanderer.*[4] When Balzac's Raphaël starts hallucinating in the old curiosity shop of *La Peau de chagrin,* it was, the narrator says, "un mystérieux sabbat digne des fantaisies entrevues par le docteur Faust sur le *Brocken.*"[5] In opera, too, there is no doubt that the Faustian witches' sabbath provided a stimulus for gothic creators. *Der Freischütz, La Damnation de Faust,* and *Mefistofele* are likely to leave spectators feeling they have missed something in Goethe's more pedestrian world. Or there is that quintessentially gothic concert piece, the *Symphonie fantastique,* where the hallucinatory witches' sabbath is accompanied by so many other representative features: the dream of an ideal beloved (with its ungrounded or immaterial consciousness evoked by unsupported treble melodies), primitive pastoralism, the dissolution of aristocratic society in a mad waltz that serves as a kind of "Walpurgisnachtstraum," and the concluding march to the scaffold.

A review like this calls to mind how many elements *Faust* really does share with gothic novels dating from before, during, and after its composition. Supernatural figures: devils, angels, witches, hags. Excessively natural figures: the innocent maiden, fatherless and ultimately orphaned, the warrior, the tormented natural scientist and philosopher. Figures of exceptional authority in church and state: rulers and holy men. Plot motifs: dangerous and illicit sexuality (though infanticide replaces the more common gothic incest), disguises and Doppelgänger figures, spying on actions near and far, religious rites and mysteries, political despotism and usurpation, a last-minute deathbed struggle of good and evil. Elements of setting: prison-like enclosures, gothic chambers, churches, and fortresses, vast, moonlit natural expanses through which the characters voyage in space and time. Psychodynamics: a feminine focus, regression to infantile states, haunted reverie, impending doom, with the clock either stopped or moving with unnatural swiftness, helpless unconsciousness. Formal characteristics: most obviously the inserted songs and ballads, but also the multitude of fictional frames, together with the combination of epic sweep and dramatic concentration that makes the gothic novel into its own peculiar kind of *Gesamtkunstwerk.* And, in addition to all these familiar gothic features, an important, but less well recognized one—a certain ambivalence of tone and a self-conscious playfulness that the gothic often reinforced with themes of playing or gambling. Unfamiliar as a Faustian device, wagers and contests are almost inescapable as a gothic one, whether centrally, or else—what is even more revealing—as an almost gratuitous kind of generic tag.[6] In gothic play, it's often not even a step from the sublime to the ridiculous. If critics argue endlessly about how we are supposed to feel at different moments in Goethe's play, perhaps the moral is not the futility of critical analysis, but rather the affinity of the play with a mode in which such things are generically, uncannily undecidable.[7] "Ihr naht euch wieder, schwankende Gestalten."

The wavering visions of the notorious "Proktophantasmist," for example, lead directly to the gothic milieu. Although commentaries correctly identify him as Friedrich Nicolai, Germany's leading rationalist, they do not mention that the story was originally reported (without the name, as in *Faust*) in 1797 by Christoph Wilhelm Hufeland, who at the time was court physician in Weimar and Goethe's family doctor.[8] A delightfully prosaic vitalist, Hufeland was widely known for his lifelong preoccupation with the premature burial of the dead, a topic on which he wrote a book and numerous essays. Faust, like his epigones in the various sections of *Melmoth,* is prone to falling asleep at moments of crisis, in order to revive refreshed. And at the end, when Mephisto is in too much of a hurry to inter him, Faust rises like one of Hufeland's none-too-dead souls to complete the proof that you can't keep a good self down.[9] Flea-bitten rationalism proves to be the nightmare from which even Goethe's gothic is always trying to awaken.

* * *

Mostly, when *Faust* approaches the characteristic gothic mood of terror, it veers off into satire— "Hexenküche," "Walpurgisnacht" with its dissolve into "Walpurgisnachtstraum," the scene with—or, better, without—the Mothers, "Grablegung." But then, the Burkean terror that is often identified as the defining characteristic of the gothic is, in our view, the least of the genre. Rather, the romantic gothic naturally interrogates or ironizes its worst imaginings. It presupposes Olympian detachment, whether in Goethe's apparent serenity[10] or in the triumph of a demon confronting a shipwreck (*Melmoth*, ch. 4). Hence Radcliffe is full of reverie and reflection, Lewis and Maturin are full of exotic pageantry and meticulous exposition, Hoffmann of witty outrage. Whether underdone or over-done—or, typically, some of each—romantic gothic novels achieve their effects by testing, tantalizing, and teasing their characters and their readers alike. Like *Faust* they offer sophisticated pleasures of crafty, knowing superiority. The true focus is not on the supernatural, but on the human response and resistance to the supernatural. The conclusions, as in *Faust,* are characteristically rapid, and whether the victims *ultimately* triumph or fail, the issue is not so much suffering as survivability.

In their own way, then, romantic gothic novels are as much a critique of gothic terror as *Faust* is.[11] If works like *Dracula* bare the inhuman desires that gnaw at all of us, romantic gothic novels display the human face within their extraordinary events. Poe's "The Pit and the Pendulum" shows how much punishment the human spirit can take; Tieck's "Der blonde Eckbert" or Byron's "Prisoner of Chillon" show how much punishment it takes to overwhelm the human spirit. And though the back cover of our edition of Walpole's *Castle of Otranto* proclaims in red, "A Bleeding Statue, A Praying Skeleton, A Castle of Horror!," the author's preface has this to say:

> The author of the following pages . . . wished to conduct the mortal agents in his drama according to the rules of probability; in short, to make them think, speak, and act, as it might be supposed mere men and women would do in extraordinary positions. He had observed, that, in all inspired writings, the personages under the dispensation of miracles, and witnesses to the most stupendous phenomena, never lose sight of their human character.[12]

What Walpole wished in his book never to lose sight of is also what our approach to the gothic aims to keep in view. It is the humanity that matters, not the inhumanity. Consequently, in admitting that *Faust* is opposed to the gothic in its vulgar sense, we are also in a position to claim that it is allied with the deeper tendencies

of the mode. Were we given to paradox, we might say that *Faust* is gothic precisely because it is anti-gothic.

Where the supernatural character of events lies in melodramatic externals, the human character of agents might naturally be expected to lie in their inward reserves. The mysterious physical powers of an overwhelming world are encountered by a mysterious spiritual integrity. The best language that we have discovered for analyzing this configuration is that of Kantian philosophy, and it turns out indeed that a direct line leads from Kant's own works to the abnormal psychiatry of high romantic medicine and into the tradition of the gothic itself. As the post-Kantian analysis develops, it relates the supernatural mysteries beyond our knowledge or control to the impenetrable world of things in themselves, and it locates the power confronting that world in what Kant calls the transcendental consciousness. Again, we cannot fully argue this thesis here, which will eventually be developed in a book on the gothic novel. But the terms that generate the analysis—and specifically the notion of a transcendental inwardness as defense against a supernatural outwardness—will provide the framework for our consideration of *Faust,* both in its partial affiliation with and in its distinctive response to the gothic mode.

Here, still as a series of largely undeveloped theses, are the basic features of the transcendental consciousness as they emerge in romantic philosophical and medical discourse, as well as in gothic representations. The first is the unity of the individual, or, as Kant terms it, the transcendental unity of apperception. In contrast to the heterogeneity of experience as envisioned by Enlightenment empiricism, romanticism envisions an integral self whose fundamental character is immutably generated from within. For Kant himself, the unity of the self is a universal phenomenon defined by the laws of experience that all humans share; for those who come after, it often appears as a psychological rather than a logical unity and may differ in character or mood from one individual to another. Second, as the unity of the self is removed from and precedes any possible experience, it cannot be manifested to ordinary consciousness. But those who followed Kant and tried to apply his conceptions to real life looked for the essence of the person in manifestations that lie beyond the conditioning of empirical existence. Specifically, it is in the dream state that we come into contact with our most inward and most fundamental self. Third, however, there also exist waking states in which the core of humanity surfaces. These are the states in which we are least responsive to the world around. Daydreaming and mesmeric states—such as, for instance, Charles Brockden Brown's *Wieland; or, The Transformation* (1798) explores—are borderline conditions where the inward self enters into a kind of contact with the outside world. But most commonly in the romantic period the inner self is brought into view by madness. Those driven beyond the bounds of normal experience are also not vulnerable to the pressures of experience, and they reveal instead the inviolable, transcendental basis of humanity. Hence, in Maturin, the more successful the devil's persecutions are in corporeal terms, the more he frustrates his endeavour to win over the minds of his victims. Fourth, then, there is a fundamental continuity to the self that cannot be broken by any force short of complete annihilation. The inward self reposes on a real, if indeterminate, inner sense of self, in its continuous and unbroken integrity. Kant's name for the inner sense is likewise that of those who come after him—namely, time. Our outer, spatial existence may be broken, fragmented, cut off—may be infringed in countless ways. But our true life is our life in time. So long as our mental existence continues—even in dreams, even in madness—so long do we continue to feel the pulse of existence. Fifth and finally, that pulse then beats through and despite all the forces that would destroy it. In the gothic, life often seems to hang by a thread. Yet the thread persists with a remarkable obstinacy that transcends the mere necessity to keep the narrative going. It becomes hard to keep even the dead down, starting with the ancestral ruler of *The Castle of Otranto*, who rises up after generations to restore his rightful heir to the throne. The gothic, in this period, is one of the most striking manifestations of the pervasive vitalism of the romantic period. There may be nothing else—not wealth, not health, not even sanity—but there is still life. "Des Lebens Pulse," these books keep insisting, "schlagen frisch lebendig."

* * *

In order to outline Goethe's complex stance toward this complex mode, we propose to scrutinize his use of the typically gothic terms *schaudern* and *Grauen*.[13] "O schaudre nicht!" (3188) Faust tells Gretchen after she has plucked the last petal from the daisy and discovered that Faust loves her. Both recognize in this shudder the doom allegorically executed upon the flower that bears her name. Gretchen had already had a similar moment of premonitory terror in "Abend" (2757),

right after Mephistopheles left the first casket of jewels in her cupboard; in "Dom" the evil spirit transforms her into an object of terror for others (3831). Faust also has his moments of terror—when the Erdgeist appears (473) and when he enters the dungeon at the end of Part I (4405), where the phrase "längst entwöhnt" connects his *Schauer* to his response to his study and to the Erdgeist. The conventional gothic sensationalism manifested in such moments is at its height in the prison scene at the end of Part I. "Kerker" predates the gothic fad, which began in the 1780s, yet the early text of the **Urfaust** contains the most explicit mention of terror, "Inneres Grauen der Menschheit," altered in the final version to the more sentimental, "Der Menschheit ganzer Jammer" (4406). And the **Urfaust**'s gothic stage direction, "Er hört die Ketten klirren und das Stroh rauschen," turns into self-conscious discourse: "Sie ahnet nicht, daß der Geliebte lauscht, / Die Ketten klirren hört, das Stroh, das rauscht" (4421-22). Thus, quite apart from the addition of Gretchen's abrupt salvation, Goethe distances himself from the gothic even as its popularity was spreading. And then, just a few lines before Faust terrifies Gretchen for the last time ("Mir graut's vor dir," 4610), Mephistopheles' horses shudder because dawn arrives (4599). Suddenly the supernatural is subject to nature, reversing the gothic norm. Indeed, natural and supernatural complement one another: for the archangels in the "Prolog im Himmel" night is "schauervoll" (254); for the devil day is. The process of terror is reversible; it can be part of building up a consciousness as well as of reducing one to its core.

As Part II unfolds, it becomes increasingly gothic on a cosmic scale. Despite its moments of uncanny terror such as the arrival of Faust's antimasque or Mephistopheles's reference to the Mothers, Act I hardly evokes a full-scale gothic response. Indeed the gothic Mothers—regressive, awakening shudders—prompt Faust to say, "Das Schaudern ist der Menschheit bestes Teil" (6272), just as he had earlier told Mephistopheles "In deinem Nichts hoff' ich das All zu finden" (6255). Terror evokes the answering assertion of creation from the self. This is more explicit in Act II, where *Schauer* and its compounds occur nine times (of the total of twenty-two occurrences in all of **Faust II**). First, terror is trivialized in a series of elaborate compounds from the beginning of the act ("Schauderfest" 7005, "Schaudergrauen" 7041, "schauderhaft" 7518 and 7788, "schauern" 7798, 7968—notice the progression away from absurd compounds once the point is made). The most specific moment of terror is the eruption of Seismos, who makes the earth itself shake. He unleashes human greed and violence, supernatural forces of destruction (the meteor that destroys the mountain), and dream (we finally learn that the entire affair was an illusion). Other gothic elements around this scene include descent, night, uncertainty, disorientation, and the demonic encounters of Mephistopheles, the Lamien, and the Phorcyads, where sexuality is a constant threat to identity. But the great oddity of these gothic elements is that terror is felt by the supernatural figures who themselves ought to evoke terror—the witch Erichtho, the sirens, Mephistopheles, the dryads, and Homunculus all experience *Schauer*. Whose consciousness is actually being narrated in Act II? Whose dream is it? Stuart Atkins (note 7, 142) has long since asserted that Act II is Faust's dream, but we might go even further. Somehow this is a dream Goethe dreams for the spectator, calling the very boundaries of the individual into question.

Act V is more traditionally gothic. The three mighty men terrorize the world about, especially Baucis and Philemon, who are also terrorized by the mysterious nighttime goings-on at Faust's castle. Here are the evil and violence we conventionally expect from the gothic. Faust himself has become part of this terrorizing mentality, so that the alien shadow of Baucis's and Philemon's trees makes him shudder. A "Schauerwindchen" (11380) brings the four ghosts Death, Care, Want, Need. In a gesture of stripping down to core consciousness Care blinds Faust; as Faust dies, Mephistopheles calls for the clock to stop. Faust's last moments in "Mitternacht" are perhaps the only moments of full gothic horror in *Faust*. Yet they too are soon ironized as angels descend to the rescue. Even here terror is rapidly commuted into play.

Crucial to Faust's death is the experience of time. Gothic time fluctuates between the extremes of frenzied disorientation and empty, rudderless waiting. The most revealing period terms come from Kant's student and close friend, the physician Markus Herz, who in the 1780s wrote a treatise on vertigo. Herz's term for proper time, like Goethe's, is *Weile*; *Schwindel* is the insane pace associated with supernatural action and *Langerweile* the aimlessness found in the demon's lost victims.[14] Clearly Faust suffers at the beginning of the play from boredom; he is desperate to speed time up, to experience *Schwindel* ("das Rauschen der Zeit," "[das] Rollen der Begebenheit," 1754-55.). But the wager as formulated challenges Me-

phisto to instill in him a healthy, purified temporal *Weilen*. Similarly, though Care claims the power to stop time just before she blinds Faust (11455ff.), the night of his soul approaches apace, without terrifying suddenness (11499: "Die Nacht scheint tiefer tief hereinzudringen"). And though early in the play Care was associated with the shipwreck of hopes in the maelstrom of time (643-44), that is, with arrested time, even earlier yet the Erdgeist had awakened in Faust the courage to overcome shipwrecks (467). It follows, then, that Care now only provokes a counterspirit (11510: "*ein* Geist") into activity. Faust resists Care with his famous speech about slowing down to the pace of nature (11450: "Wenn Geister spuken, geh' er seinen Gang"): his absolute striving yields to a relation to transcendence mediated by his own imaginative consciousness. Thus **Faust** confronts the gothic challenge differently from the gothic novels: in place of a reduction to pure consciousness and internal selfhood, Faust outlines a healthy relationship to time extending beyond the self dynamically into the future.

Such reversals are characteristic of **Faust**'s response to the gothic. In the first line of "Zueignung" wavering forms approach us with their madness (4) and "Zauberhauch" (8), bringing in their train the temporal disorientation of the second and third stanzas. The moment of terror, however, comes only in the second half of the last stanza, "Ein Schauer faßt mich" (29), in the same language as the terror of the Erdgeist (472-74: "Es weht / Ein Schauer vom Gewölb' herab / Und faßt mich an!"). Yet in "Zueignung" the terror brings peace:

> Ein Schauer faßt mich, Träne folgt den Tränen,
> Das strenge Herz, es fühlt sich mild und weich;
> Was ich besitze, seh' ich wie im Weiten,
> Und was verschwand, wird mir zu Wirklich-
>   keiten.
>
> (29-32)

The heart softens, consciousness releases its hold, yet what follows is the return of the whole world that had been lost. Gothic nothingness is nowhere to be found, let alone feared.

But if there is no nothingness, there is then no pressing need for the unconditional selfhood explored so intensely by the gothic. Gothic novels usually reach their climax in a prison, but Faust begins in one, feeling imprisoned in his "hochgewölbten, engen *gotischen* Zimmer." We know what the first word of the play proper is not: instead of "ich," Faust has only a depressive and paranoid "ach" to offer. Friedrich Kittler, who has called our attention to these words, sees in this opening a condition of "pure soul" preceding Faust's fall into writing, a change in mode vital to the action of the play.[15] Yet Faust's initial condition of "pure soul" is as much an unhappy limbo as the successor condition is: whatever "pure" means here, it does not include healthy or effective. Suspended in such gothic chambers, "Wandering between two worlds, one dead, / The other powerless to be born" (Arnold, "Stanzas from the Grande Chartreuse"), the continuity of the self is tested and, very often, assured. The gothic novel is, generically, a thought experiment with premature burial, and Faust in his dark and narrow chamber, almost like a figure from Poe, starts off already dead and waiting to be reborn.

What normally symbolizes a late stage in the reduction to pure consciousness is here a starting point Faust rejects with vigor. Consciousness of self is not Faust's defense in the prison; on the contrary, it is itself the very prison to be escaped.[16] Time and again the play unmasks self-consciousness as empty solipsism. Imprisoned Gretchen in her madness is a paradigm of gothic reduction to the essential core of the self: her continuing love for an infant and family and her unstained innocence are unchanged from her earlier, sane moments, and she desires only to return to the past. But in *Faust* this essential self represents the temptation to stasis articulated in the bet—"verweile doch." It must be rejected, and indeed, "Anmutige Gegend" brings growth and change through positive erasure of the past; as Emrich says, "Schlaf und spontan organisches 'Vergessen' sind Funktionen einer Natur, die nur darum 'mildert', versöhnt und 'heilt', weil sie ihren 'Liebling' bis zu den Grenzen des Daseins geführt hat, über die hinaus es nur Entsetzen oder—Vergessen geben kann."[17] Faust's monologue once again contains all the themes of the post-Kantian gothic self. "Des Lebens Pulse schlagen frisch lebendig": the life force is the first thing to impinge on the consciousness of the waking Faust. Next comes continuity in time: "Du, Erde, warst auch diese Nacht beständig." But as Faust's awakening consciousness gathers force, it focuses less and less on a unified self, and more and more on a world that comes into being through the words he utters ("Ein Paradies wird um mich her die Runde"). By the end of the monologue his consciousness extends beyond the earth to the rainbow, a sign that is anchored both in scientific objectivity and in a tradition that evokes not gothic shudders but rather pastoral showers (as "Schauer" must clearly be translated in line 4726).

In such manner *Faust* adds layer after layer until consciousness of self disappears in consciousness of the world. The first three acts of Part II abandon self-absorption for a phantasmagoria of the history of our culture and bring Faust and Helena onto the stage only as literary figures in elaborate costumes, conscious at every moment of themselves as constructs from a long tradition (hence Helena: "Ich schwinde hin und werde selbst mir ein Idol," 8881). And what then of the apparent return to an authentic self when Faust resists Care? Faust grounds his satisfaction with time and his supposed identity in the labors of others who will do what he has done all through Part II—be conscious not of themselves but of the need to recreate the world each day through their own labor (11575-76).

Faust's death provokes a mock-epic battle in which each side looks gothic to its opponents. "Grablegung" gives us, of course, the devil's perspective.[18] To Mephisto all the wavering rescuers (11723: "Schon schwebts heran"; 11740 s.d.: "Sich mit den schwebenden Rosen herumschlagend"; 11787: "Ihr schwanket hin und her") appear as demons; he calls them "ein überteuflisch Element," "Liebesspuk," and the like (11754, 11814). But the final scene revives the perspective of "Zueignung," in which wavering and swaying are associated with the uncertain, preconscious reawakening to life. The "Chor und Echo" that open "Bergsschluchten" begin the last revival of the song whose "erster Widerklang" resonated behind "Zueignung" (20). Answering to the gothic interior of Faust's monologue, the stage now presents a gothic exterior, a mountainous region reminiscent of the landscapes of *The Mysteries of Udolpho*. Yet the setting sheds the contamination by individualized conflict that polarizes the gothic self. Release proceeds in stages, without the cathartic shudder that would memorialize what is to be left behind. Hence, responding to Mephisto's mistaken boast, "Gerettet sind die edlen Teufelsteile" (11813), Goethe produces the following sequence. First angels "schwebend in der höheren Atmosphäre," emit a counterboast, "Gerettet ist das edle Glied / Der Geisterwelt vom Bösen" (11934-35). Next the more perfect angels correct them, complaining, "Uns bleibt ein Erdenrest / Zu tragen peinlich, / Und wär er von Asbest, / Er ist nicht reinlich" (11954-57). And then the purifying Doctor Marianus, "in der höchsten, reinlichsten Zelle," mediates the ultimate release, "Hier ist die Aussicht frei, / Der Geist erhoben" (11989-90), once more evoking "Zueignung," which ends, "Was ich besitze, seh ich wie im Weiten, / Und was verschwand [Faust's body, in the final instance], wird mir zu Wirklichkeiten" (31-32). Redeeming the blinded, haunted Faust, the clarified vision into the distance lifts spirituality to a new and higher level.

At the end gothic conflict gives up the ghost. The younger angels, who were there, appear to speak of victory: "Böse wichen, als wir streuten, / Teufel flohen, als wir trafen" (11947-48). But in truth their attack transformed the nature of the encounter: "Statt gewohnter Höllenstrafen / Fühlten Liebesqual die Geister" (11949-50). War has become passionate love, and the necessary lessons of human violence have forged bonds between individuals. "Und aus ätherischem Gewande / Hervortritt erste Jugendkraft!" (12090-91). Finally Faust is truly born—but not into a merely personal condition of separated consciousness: "Er ahnet kaum das frische Leben [not self-conscious], / So gleicht er schon der heiligen Schar [not personal]" (12086-87). A powerfully active response replaces the spiritual essentialism typical of the gothic, as the blessed youths say, with a circling motion, "Er überwächst uns schon / An mächtigen Gliedern" (12076-77). The professor has become a good learner, and hence a good teacher at last: "Doch dieser hat gelernt, / Er wird uns lehren" (12082-83). But he becomes a good teacher by virtue of confronting his *Unmündigkeit*. A powerful child rather than an independent adult, Goethe's counter-gothic personality does not free himself by force of will, for "Wer zerreißt aus eigner Kraft / Der Gelüste Ketten?" (12026-27). Rather, the gothic manacles lose their terror and become an ecstatic living union transcending any possible individualism. In the penultimate strophe of the play the Doctor Marianus describes the process thus: "Euch zu seligem Geschick / Dankend umzuarten" (12098-99), in a pair of lines whose collective plural is as essential as its perhaps unprecedented verb of communal response, "umzuarten."[19]

Faust, then, preserves the legacy of the gothic in the very process of transmuting it. There is, to be sure, no novelty in contending that *Faust* in some sense transvalues evil and that in some sense it honors collectivities. But it does make a difference if we stress the gothic tonalities that persist into the final scene, even as the play abandons a conventionally gothic vision. The gothic is the realm of the sublime, of the unspeakable and unperformable that the final "Chorus Mysticus" invokes. Consequently, the gothic bequeaths to the play's ideological convictions a sense of urgency and a restless energy beyond conceptual

grasp.[20] Because it has passed through the gothic crucible, the world of *Faust* must always view love as passion—a better form of war and not a negation of it. It must always view maturity under the sign of power, breaking the bonds of earth, and not as settled conviction. And it must always view teaching as a stab in the dark: even through the desperate straits of Sorge and her companions men must risk the *Hinanziehen* and *Hinangezogensein* of and by the Eternal Feminine, formerly the spinning Gretchen whose rest is always and forever gone because she does not and cannot hold her beloved firmly on the spot. She knows, as the blessed youths in their blissful ignorance do not, that Faust has not really learned and cannot really teach: she answers them with a reminder that their new teacher is blind, with a blindness carried over from his prior, gothic existence into a new day that can never fully dawn for humans, since humanity lies in acceptance, not rejection, of their gothic fetters: "Vergönne mir, ihn zu belehren! / Noch blendet ihn der neue Tag" (12092-93). That is the sublime condition we transcend exactly to the extent that we learn to submit to it.[21]

What *Faust* rejects, then, is not the gothic as such—not human limitation, not the confrontation with evil, not fatality—so much as the rebelliousness that the gothic novels inscribe into their portrayal of the gothic condition. Gothic rebellion is contaminated by the forces it opposes; as Act V shows, if you command the devil, it is only to become a stronger devil yourself. Resistance is always tainted, whether by the perpetual melancholy of *The Castle of Otranto,* Radcliffe's undercurrents of sexual indulgence, or the recalcitrant monstrousness of Mary Shelley's pure-hearted monster. Like his creators in the "Vorspiel auf dem Theater," Faust begins angry. Unlike his fellows in confrontation with forces of evil—and most unlike the increasingly angry Mephisto—Faust wins by losing, swallowing his pride, and submitting. The gothic mode is divided against itself, and Goethe rectifies it by refusing to bring its dialectic to a standstill.

Amid all the differences, then, *Faust* shares with the gothic a radical dialectic.[22] Indeed, insofar as the gothic novels bring their dialectic to a terminus, *Faust* outdoes their radicalism. It is a dialectic because its values insistently come in competing pairs: good and evil, heaven and earth, man and woman. Its two-souledness is radical in the political sense that human structures will not satisfy its demands; radical in the moral sense that erring, sin, and care, hopeless blindness and the struggle against it remain inevitable; radical in the epistemological sense that mediations are relentlessly excluded or satirized in a series of ever more astonishing dramatic confrontations; and radical in the aesthetic sense that this is all a wondrous spectacle, of value precisely to the extent that it does not touch real—ordinary, petty—life. *Faust* consummates the gothic self-critique not by turning against the gothic but rather by pursuing the gothic impulse to its logical, bittersweet end.

Notes

1. Mario Praz, *The Romantic Agony*, trans. Angus Davidson (London and New York: Oxford University Press, 1970) 26, following only a long Shelley quote. Other bits of Part I figure very occasionally through the rest of the book as analogies to Maturin's *Melmoth the Wanderer* and to victimized females.

2. Cf. WA I, 42.2:86-88 (Scott, Hoffmann); he made repeated references to Walpole's *Castle of Otranto* (WA III, 2:224; WA IV, 13:91, 343, 361; 14:54; and 15:50), also to Walpole's "Das Geheimnis der Mutter" (WA I, 35:86). He even translated a bit of Maturin's *Bertram* (WA I, 11:353-58) and was aware of Monk Lewis. Closer to home he knew both Tieck's "romantic" writings, as he refers to them (WA III, 2:259), and Schiller's "Geisterseher" (WA III, 3:124). On Kant as an ironist, WA II, 11:54-55 and 13:448.

3. [Justus Christian Hennings], *Von Geistern und Geisterse-hern* (Leipzig: Weygand, 1780) 368.

4. The most detailed comparison of *Faust* and *Melmoth* can be found in Syndy M. Conger, *Matthew G. Lewis, Charles Robert Maturin and the Germans: An Interpretative Study of the Influence of German Literature on Two Gothic Novels*, Salzburg Studies in English Literature 67 (Salzburg: Institut für englische Sprache und Literatur, Universität Salzburg, 1977) 12-42.

5. Honoré de Balzac, *La Peau de chagrin*, in *La Comédie humaine*, ed. Marcel Bouteron, 10 vols. (Paris: Gallimard, 1950) 9:30.

6. On gothic play see Marshall Brown, "Kant e i demoni della notte," *Studi sull'estetica* 12 (1984): 155-65.

7. See for instance the "quite astonishing" claim by Jane K. Brown that the final moments of Part I derive from the comic-opera tradition (quoted words on p. 111). The more conventional reading can be illustrated with Stuart Atkins's emphasis on the "tragic defeat," "horror," and "tragic dignity" of Gretchen's "secular-sentimental apotheosis": *Goethe's "Faust": A Literary Analysis* (Cambridge, Mass.: Harvard University Press, 1964) 99-100.

8. We quote a sentence to illustrate the tone of Hufeland's narrative: "Es fängt wirklich diesem äußerst aufgeklärten und vorurtheilsfreyen Manne endlich an darüber zu schwindeln; nie allein zu seyn, sich ewig von sonderbaren und immer wechselnden Gestalten umgeben, ja angesprochen zu sehen, dieß raubt ihm endlich alle Gemüthsruhe, ja alle Gedanken, und es versetzt ihn in die peinlichste Agitation." C.W. Hufeland, "Sonderbare Geistererscheinung," in *Kleine medizinische Schriften* 2 (Berlin: G. Reimer, 1823): 378 (originally in Hufeland's *Journal der praktischen Heilkunde*).

9. Emil Staiger mentions Hufeland in connection with Faust's resurrection, 3:451.

10. Matthew Arnold's lines on Goethe in "Memorial Verses: April, 1850," note the gothic ground of his detachment: "And he was happy, if to know / Causes of things, and far below / His feet to see the lurid flow / Of terror, and insane distress, / And headlong fate, be happiness." Wilhelm Emrich (73-74) builds his passing mention of madness on a line from *Egmont*, "eingehüllt in gefälligen Wahnsinn versinken wir und hören auf zu sein"; his Hegelian bias toward redemptive *Gefälligkeit* leads him to slight the significance of *Wahnsinn*, a word that is absent from his index of concepts.

11. See Marshall Brown, "A Philosophical View of the Gothic Novel," *Studies in Romanticism* 26 (1987): 275-301, for a fuller presentation of the way that gothic novels test the limits of terror.

12. Horace Walpole, *The Castle of Otranto*, ed. Marvin Mudrick (New York: Collier, 1963) 19.

13. As part of his demonstration of the thematic unity of *Faust*, Joachim Müller surveys representative occurrences of *schauern* and *schaudern* in the play, without discussing their significance: "Zur Motivstruktur von Goethes 'Faust,'" in: *Sitzungsberichte der sächsischen Akademie der Wissenschaften zu Leipzig: Philologisch-historische Klasse* 116:3 (Berlin: Akademie-Verlag, 1972) 9-11.

14. Herz defines *Langerweile* [sic] as "ein einförmiger Spatziergang oder Reiseweg, auf welchem sich keine abwechselnde Mannichfaltigkeit darbietet," leading to despair; *Schwindel* is "der widernatürlich schnelle Fortgang der Ideen." Markus Herz, *Versuch über den Schwindel*, 2nd ed. (Berlin: Vossische Buchhandlung, 1791) 158-59.

15. Friedrich Kittler, *Discourse Networks 1800/1900*, trans. Michael Metteer (Stanford: Stanford University Press, 1990) 3.

16. See the groundbreaking general discussion of this phenomenon by Geoffrey H. Hartman, "Romanticism and Anti-Self-Consciousness," *Beyond Formalism* (New Haven: Yale University Press, 1970) 298-310.

17. Emrich 71. See further Peter Michelsen's nice analysis of "Anmutige Gegend" in relation to Faust's opening monologue, "Fausts Schlaf und Erwachen," *Jahrbuch des freien deutschen Hochstifts* (1983) 21-61. Michelsen identifies cathartic forgetting as the new motif at this point in the play, and he compares the action here to the procedures "des Experiments in der Naturwissenschaft" (38). For his theory of sleep Michelsen draws on the *Aphorismen aus der Physiologie der Pflanzen* (1808) by Goethe's friend and admirer Dietrich Georg Kieser. The passages he quotes (40-41) were, however, commonplace both among mystics and, in variants, among rationalists like Heinrich Nudow, whose *Versuch einer Theorie des Schlafs* was published by Kant's (and Fichte's) publisher Nicolovius in Königsberg in 1795. For a stronger account of the power of forgetting in the play, see Theodor Adorno, "Zur Schlußszene des Faust," *Noten zur Literatur* (Frankfurt/Main: Suhrkamp, 1981) 129-38. Helmut Schanze presents the final scene as a *theatrum memoriae* in "Szenen, Schema, Schwammfamilie: Goethes Arbeitsweise und die Frage der Struktureinheit von *Faust I* und *II*," *Euphorion* 78 (1984) 383-400; however, Schan-

ze's thesis differs less from ours than might appear, since he emphasizes collective memory and a transcendence of the individual perspective.

18. On the importance of perspective and point of view in *Faust* see Jane K. Brown, *Faust: Theater of the World* (New York: Twayne, 1992) 26-34.

19. Grimm's *Deutsches Wörterbuch* cites only this passage to illustrate a transitive use of "umarten." Its two prior instances of intransitive "umarten" do not appear to constitute a precedent. In a subsection (145-52) of his essay "Theatrum Mundi: Anfang und Schluß von Goethes 'Faust'" called "Umartung," Hermann Kunisch transmutes the reflexive into a passive, "ein Umgeartetwerden in dem gnadevollen Sichmitteilen der Liebe": *Goethe-Studien,* ed. Franz Link (Berlin: Duncker & Humblot, 1991) 131-58 (quotation is on p. 146).

20. We argue here against the type of idealizing reading canonized by Max Kommerell in "Faust II: Letzte Szene," *Geist und Buchstabe der Dichtung* (Frankfurt/Main: Klostermann, 1956) 112-31. "In Prosa aufgelöst" (116)—which is to say, substituting doctrinal pieties for human feeling—the conclusion seems to Kommerell a "Mysterium" that preaches "eine seraphische Geselligkeit und Kollegialität" (121) and that portrays "die Genialität des Liebeszustands in jener Allgemeinheit, wie sie der Stil des zweiten Teils mit sich bringt" (129). "D'un coup," writes one pygmy working the vein of this generalissimo and oblivious of the Ibycean cranes on the horizon, "les scènes de magie noire, les interminables promenades de la seconde partie à travers les diableries anciennes et modernes, pâlissent devant cette fin d'un centenaire aveugle et visionnaire," Pierre Grapin, "Faust aveugle," *Etudes germaniques* 38 (1983): 146.

21. Jean-François Lyotard has provided the most apposite analyses of the sublime as a darkness that wrings morality out of disintegration. See in particular "L'Intérêt du sublime," *Du sublime* (a collective volume with preface by Jean-Luc Nancy) (n.p.: Belin, 1988) 149-77. In the more concise formulation of another essay, "the sublime is the affective paradox, the paradox of feeling (of feeling publicly) in common a formlessness for which there is no image or sensory intuition," "The Sign of History," trans. Geoff Bennington, *Post-Structuralism and the Question of History,* ed. Derek Attridge et al. (Cambridge: Cambridge University Press, 1987) 176.

22. There are valuable comments about *Faust* as a dialectic in extremis in Jochen Schmidt, "Die 'katholische Mythologie' und ihre mystische Entmythologisierung in der Schlußszene des *Faust II,*" *Jahrbuch der deutschen Schillergesellschaft* 34 (1990) 230-56. See particularly the essay's last sentence: "So weitet sich das Spektrum der Entmythologisierung ins Totale, indem nicht bloß eine alte Welt von gestalthaft ausgeprägten Glaubens-

vorstellungen und Sinn-Figuren, sondern überhaupt die Vorstellung einer allumfassenden Sinn-Figur: die Vorstellung des ganzheitlich geordneten Kosmos als mythologische Vorstellungsform aufgehoben wird in einem Jenseits, das als Sphäre des irreal Gewordenen schon umschlägt ins Nichts" (256). Having let the genie out of the bottle, however, Schmidt simultaneously tries to nail it to the wall, claiming that Dionysius the Areopagite is the secret source that explains all. "Erst damit wird der Sinn der bisher unerschlossenen berühmten Verse [of the final chorus] exakt faßbar" (245)—a claim that would be more persuasive if the "exact" meaning that he finds were more than a conventionally hermetic approximation: "Daher ist Gott nicht in seiner Eigentlichkeit, sondern nur uneigentlich zu erkennen" (246).

FURTHER READING

Criticism

Hildebrand, Janet. "An Ecology of Elemental Spirits and Mortals in Goethe's Ballads." *History of European Ideas* 12, no. 4 (1990): 503-21.

Explores supernatural and folkloric elements in Goethe's ballads.

Wicksteed, Philip H. "'Magic'—A Contribution to the Study of Goethe's *Faust.*" *Hibbert Journal* 10, no. 4 (1911): 754-64.

Contends that the magic practiced by Mephistopheles and Faust impedes Faust's search for intellectual and spiritual contentment.

Wood, Robin. "'Der Erlkönig': The Ambiguities of Horror." In *American Nightmare: Essays on the Horror Film,* edited by Robin Wood and Richard Lippe, pp. 29-32. Toronto, Ontario: Festival of Festivals, 1979.

Analysis of the Goethe's handling of horror in his poem "Der Erlkönig" ("The Erl-King").

OTHER SOURCES FROM GALE:

Additional coverage of Goethe's life and career is contained in the following sources published by Thomson Gale: *Concise Dictionary of World Literary Biography,* Vol. 2; *Dictionary of Literary Biography,* Vol. 94; *DISCovering Authors; DISCovering Authors: British Edition; DISCovering Authors: Canadian Edition; DISCovering Authors Modules: Dramatists, Most-Studied Authors,* and *Poets; DISCovering Authors 3.0; Drama Criticism,* Vol. 20; *European Writers,* Vol. 5; *Literary Movements for Students,* Vol. 1; *Literature and Its Times Supplement; Literature Resource Center; Nineteenth-Century Literature Criticism,* Vols. 4, 34, 90, 154; *Poetry Criticism,* Vol. 5; *Reference Guide to World Literature,* Eds. 2, 3, *Short Story Criticism,* Vol. 38; *Twayne's World Authors;* and *World Literature Criticism.*

NATHANIEL HAWTHORNE

(1804 - 1864)

American novelist, short story writer, and essayist.

Hawthorne is an acknowledged master of American fiction. His novel *The Scarlet Letter* (1850) is one of the most-read classics of American literature, and several of his short stories are ranked as masterpieces of the genre. Hawthorne's works reflect his dark vision of human nature, as he frequently portrays Puritanism as an expression of humanity's potential for cruelty, obsession, and intolerance. His strange, haunting tales of guilt, isolation, and death betray his fascination with the macabre even as they plumb the depths of human psychology and moral responsibility. With Edgar Allan Poe, Hawthorne was instrumental in the evolution of American Gothic fiction, moving away from sensationalism to focus on the aesthetic and emotional response to horror and dissecting the mental processes of his characters. His highly allegorical works use Gothic conventions to explore questions about human actions and their consequences and the effects of sin on the human psyche. Gothic elements are seen in his most important works, from the short story "Young Goodman Brown" (1835) to *The Scarlet Letter* to his last completed novel, *The Marble Faun* (1860). All these works are highly symbolic, challenging moral fantasies that are chilling in their dark assessment of the human character. The Gothic world Hawthorne created in his fiction—with its his gloomy settings, concern with death, and explorations of the demonic—is central to his moral and thematic purposes as it allowed him a wider fictive realm through which he could tell the dark truths about the world as he perceived it.

BIOGRAPHICAL INFORMATION

Born in Salem, Massachusetts, in 1804, Hawthorne was descended from a line of staunch Puritans that included William Hathorne (Hawthorne himself added the "w" to the family name), an ardent defender of the faith who participated in the persecution of Quakers during the seventeenth century, and his son John Hathorne, a presiding judge at the infamous Salem witch trials. This melancholy heritage was augmented by the premature death of Hawthorne's father, which left the four-year-old Nathaniel in the care of his grief-stricken and reclusive mother. Spending much time alone during his childhood, Hawthorne developed an intensely introspective nature and eventually came to believe that the misfortunes of his immediate family were the result of divine retribution for the sins of his ancestors.

An avid reader with an affinity for the works of John Bunyan and Edmund Spenser, Hawthorne began to write while attending Bowdoin College, where he met Franklin Pierce and Henry Wadsworth Longfellow. After graduation, Hawthorne returned to his mother's home in Salem where he passed a twelve-year literary apprenticeship, occasionally publishing unsigned tales in journals but more often than not destroying his work. He published a novel, *Fanshawe: A Tale* (1828), but later withdrew it from circulation and burned every available copy. Many of Hawthorne's early pieces appeared in *The Token*, an annual anthology published by Samuel Goodrich, during the early 1830s. Goodrich played a major role in the development of the young author's career, naming him editor of the *American Magazine of Useful and Entertaining Knowledge* in 1836 and arranging for the publication of his first collection of short stories, *Twice-Told Tales* (1837), one year later. *Twice-Told Tales* contains historical sketches and stories displaying the dark themes and skillful technique that would characterize his later work. Although lavishly praised by critics, the volume sold poorly, and an enlarged edition issued in 1842 fared no better. This pattern of critical appreciation and public neglect continued throughout Hawthorne's literary career, and he was forced to occupy a series of minor governmental posts in order to supplement the meager income from his writings.

Soon after the publication of *Twice-Told Tales*, Hawthorne became engaged to Sophia Peabody, a neighbor who had admired his work. Hoping to find a permanent home for himself and Sophia, Hawthorne joined Brook Farm in 1841. An experimental utopian community outside of Boston, Brook Farm was intended to be an agricultural cooperative that would provide its members—through the principle of shared labor—with a living while allowing them leisure for artistic and literary pursuits. The community was founded by the literary critic and social reformer George Ripley, and various prominent authors expressed interest in the scheme, including Margaret Fuller, Ralph Waldo Emerson, Theodore Parker, and Orestes Brownson. Hawthorne's enthusiasm for the venture quickly wore off, however. He left after six months, convinced that intellectual endeavor was incompatible with hard physical exertion. Although his literary efforts at Brook Farm proved a failure, Hawthorne kept careful records of his time there in his journals and letters; these later informed the plot, physical settings, and characters of *The Blithedale Romance* (1852).

In July of 1842, Hawthorne married Peabody, and the couple moved into a large house in Concord, Massachusetts, known locally as the "Old Manse." There Hawthorne wrote many of the pieces included in his next collection of stories and sketches, *Mosses from an Old Manse* (1846). He worked in the Salem customhouse from 1846 to 1849, when he was fired because of a change in political administrations. After his dismissal, in an intense outpouring of creative effort, he wrote *The Scarlet Letter* in just four months. The book was an immediate success, and Hawthorne soon followed with a number of others, including two important novels, *The House of the Seven Gables* (1851) and *The Blithedale Romance*, as well as a volume of short pieces, *The Snow-Image, and Other Tales* (1851). The years 1850-1852 were Hawthorne's most intensely productive period. After this time, he had great difficulty writing any more fiction. His position as United States consul at Liverpool from 1853 to 1857 left him with enough free time to write, but during that period he could only fill up his notebooks with jottings from his travels in Europe. In 1860 he did manage to finish one last novel, *The Marble Faun*, which was drawn from his tour of Italy, but the remaining years of his life were marked by a frustrating series of false starts. His unfinished manuscripts were periodically interrupted by marginal notes asking, "What meaning?" Hawthorne died on May 19, 1864 in Plymouth, New Hampshire, at the age of fifty-nine.

MAJOR WORKS

Hawthorne's stories written shortly after he graduated from college indicate his early interest in the occult and the supernatural. "The Hollow of the Three Hills" (1830) and "An Old Woman's Tale" (1830), for example, use Gothic devices and contain witches and burial grounds. They display as well Hawthorne's concern with questions of religion and morality, sin and guilt. Stories written just a few years later and published in the 1837 volume *Twice-Told Tales*, such as "Roger Malvin's Burial," "The Minister's Black Veil," and "The May-Pole of Merry Mount," illustrate Hawthorne's mastery of the technique of the symbolic tale, as they present deeply felt moral and psychological concerns in a highly evocative fictional form. Other important fabular tales in *Twice-Told Tales* include "The Prophetic Pictures," in which a painter captures the fates as well as the faces of his subjects; "Dr. Heidegger's Experiment," about an elixir of life; and "Legends of the Province-House," which features three rationalized ghost stories.

Mosses from an Old Manse is often regarded as Hawthorne's best collection of short stories. It features "Young Goodman Brown," regarded as perhaps Hawthorne's greatest work of Gothic fiction, which expresses the darkest and most universal truths about human nature with particular simplicity and intensity. In the story, Young Goodman Brown goes into the forest one night for an admittedly evil purpose, leaving behind his young wife, Faith. There he meets the devil and, in a gradual series of revelations, learns that everyone in his world—including his minister, the pious old woman who taught him his catechism, all the elders of his church, even his father and mother—has gone into the forest before him, and has met with the devil. He returns to the village a changed man: stern, sad, darkly meditative, and distrustful; he has lost all faith in the human race and he spends a gloomy life cut off from the chain of humanity. Other tales of psychological horror in *Mosses from an Old Manse* include "The Birthmark," about a scientist who tries to erase a slight flaw in his wife's complexion and obliterates her entirely; "Rappaccini's Daughter," in which a young student falls in love with a girl raised in a garden of poisons; and "Ethan Brand," about the unpardonable sin which a laborer-turned-showman claims to have discovered after a long search.

Gothic elements and devices abound in Hawthorne's longer fiction as well. *The Scarlet Letter*, which treats the cruel and unusual punishment of an adulteress, begins with the discovery of a dusty manuscript found in a garret from which the narrator learns the story he recounts. *The House of the Seven Gables* is a Gothic romance in which a monstrous house infects and corrupts all who live in it. Hawthorne's last completed novel, *The Marble Faun*, is a symbolic romance as well as a story of a murder and a parable of the Fall of Man. In these works, as in his shorter fiction, Hawthorne uses gothicism to create a sense of mood and place in which to explore the somber truths about human nature, morality, and the struggles of the human soul.

CRITICAL RECEPTION

Critics have long acknowledged Hawthorne to be among the United States' most important writers. He projected profound moral concerns on a distinctly American background and sought to interpret the spiritual history of a nation. He is regarded as one of the architects of the modern short story and an important figure in the development of Gothic American fiction. His portrayal of the protagonists in *The Scarlet Letter* set the standard for psychological realism for generations of writers. Through his depiction of the consequences of Hester Prynne and Arthur Dimmesdale's adulterous union, Hawthorne explored the historical, social, theological, and emotional ramifications of sin, concealment, and guilt. In this novel as in his other fiction, he used gothicism as a vehicle to investigate the dark side of the human soul, not terrifying readers but horrifying them with clinical depictions of the inner workings of his characters' minds. Critics who have investigated Hawthorne's Gothic vision have focused on the Gothic influences on his work, his use of particular Gothic devices for symbolic purposes, the thematic importance of horror in his fiction, and his concern with sin and evil. They have also paid particular attention to the relationship between religion and the fantastic in Hawthorne's work and to his use of the supernatural to explore the psychological and social effects of guilty knowledge.

PRINCIPAL WORKS

Fanshawe: A Tale (novel) 1828

Twice-Told Tales (sketches and short stories) 1837

Twice-Told Tales [second series] (sketches and short stories) 1842

Mosses from an Old Manse (sketches and short stories) 1846

The Scarlet Letter: A Romance (novel) 1850

The House of the Seven Gables, a Romance (novel) 1851

The Snow Image, and Other Tales (short stories) 1851

The Blithedale Romance (novel) 1852

Life of Franklin Pierce (biography) 1852

A Wonder-Book for Girls and Boys (short stories) 1852

Tanglewood Tales for Girls and Boys; Being a Second Wonder-Book (short stories) 1853

The Marble Faun; or, The Romance of Monte Beni (novel) 1860; published in England as *Transformation; or, The Romance of Monte Beni*, 1860

Our Old Home (essays) 1863

Passages from the American Notebooks of Nathaniel Hawthorne (journal) 1868

PRIMARY SOURCES

NATHANIEL HAWTHORNE (STORY DATE 1830)

SOURCE: Hawthorne, Nathaniel. "The Hollow of the Three Hills." In *Great Ghost Stories: 34 Classic Tales of the Supernatural,* compiled by Robin Brockman, pp. 305-09. New York: Gramercy Books, 2002.

The following short story was originally published in 1830 in the Salem Gazette.

In those strange old times, when fantastic dreams and madmen's reveries were realized among the actual circumstances of life, two persons met together at an appointed hour and place. One was a lady graceful in form and fair of feature, though pale and troubled and smitten with an untimely blight in what should have been the fullest bloom of her years; the other was an ancient and meanly-dressed woman, of ill-favored aspect, and so withered, shrunken, and decrepit, that even the space since she began to decay must have exceeded the ordinary term of human existence. In the spot where they encountered, no mortal could observe them. Three little hills stood near each other, and down in the midst of them sunk a hollow basin, almost mathematically circular, two or three hundred feet in breadth, and of such depth that a stately cedar might but just be visible above the sides. Dwarf pines were numerous upon the hills, and partly fringed the outer verge of the intermediate hollow, within which there was nothing but the brown grass of October, and here and there a tree trunk that had fallen long ago, and lay mouldering with no green successor from its roots. One of these masses of decaying wood, formerly a majestic oak, rested close beside a pool of green and sluggish water at the bottom of the basin. Such scenes as this (so gray tradition tells) were once the resort of the Power of Evil and his plighted subjects; and here, at midnight or on the dim verge of evening, they

were said to stand round the mantling pool, disturbing its putrid waters in the performance of an impious baptismal rite. The chill beauty of an autumnal sunset was now gilding the three hill-tops, whence a paler tint stole down their sides into the hollow.

"Here is our pleasant meeting come to pass," said the aged crone, "according as thou hast desired. Say quickly what thou wouldst have of me, for there is but a short hour that we may tarry here."

As the old withered woman spoke, a smile glimmered on her countenance, like lamplight on the wall of a sepulchre. The lady trembled, and cast her eyes upward to the verge of the basin, as if meditating to return with her purpose unaccomplished. But it was not so ordained.

"I am a stranger in this land, as you know," said she at length. "Whence I come it matters not; but I have left those behind me with whom my fate was intimately bound, and from whom I am cut off forever. There is a weight in my bosom that I cannot away with, and I have come hither to inquire of their welfare."

"And who is there by this green pool that can bring thee news from the ends of the earth?" cried the old woman, peering into the lady's face. "Not from my lips mayst thou hear these tidings; yet, be thou bold, and the daylight shall not pass away from yonder hill-top before thy wish be granted."

"I will do your bidding though I die," replied the lady desperately.

The old woman seated herself on the trunk of the fallen tree, threw aside the hood that shrouded her gray locks, and beckoned her companion to draw near.

"Kneel down," she said, "and lay your forehead on my knees." She hesitated a moment, but the anxiety that had long been kindling burned fiercely up within her. As she knelt down, the border of her garment was dipped into the pool; she laid her forehead on the old woman's knees, and the latter drew a cloak about the lady's face, so that she was in darkness. Then she heard the muttered words of prayer, in the midst of which she started, and would have arisen.

"Let me flee—let me flee and hide myself, that they may not look upon me!" she cried. But, with returning recollection, she hushed herself, and was still as death.

For it seemed as if other voices—familiar in infancy, and unforgotten through many wanderings, and in all the vicissitudes of her heart and fortune—were mingling with the accents of the prayer. At first the words were faint and indistinct, not rendered so by distance, but rather resembling the dim pages of a book which we strive to read by an imperfect and gradually brightening light. In such a manner, as the prayer proceeded, did those voices strengthen upon the ear; till at length the petition ended, and the conversation of an aged man, and of a woman broken and decayed like himself, became distinctly audible to the lady as she knelt. But those strangers appeared not to stand in the hollow depth between the three hills. Their voices were encompassed and re-echoed by the walls of a chamber, the windows of which were rattling in the breeze; the regular vibration of a clock, the crackling of a fire, and the tinkling of the embers as they fell among the ashes, rendered the scene almost as vivid as if painted to the eye. By a melancholy hearth sat these two old people, the man calmly despondent, the woman querulous and tearful, and their words were all of sorrow. They spoke of a daughter, a wanderer they knew not where, bearing dishonour along with her, and leaving shame and affliction to bring their gray heads to the grave. They alluded also to other and more recent wo, but in the midst of their talk their voices seemed to melt into the sound of the wind sweeping mournfully among the autumn leaves; and when the lady lifted her eyes, there was she kneeling in the hollow between three hills.

"A weary and lonesome time yonder old couple have of it," remarked the old woman, smiling in the lady's face.

"And did you also hear them?" exclaimed she, a sense of intolerable humiliation triumphing over her agony and fear.

"Yea; and we have yet more to hear," replied the old woman. "Wherefore, cover thy face quickly."

Again the withered hag poured forth the monotonous words of a prayer that was not meant to be acceptable in heaven; and soon, in the pauses of her breath, strange murmurings began to thicken, gradually increasing so as to drown and overpower the charm by which they grew. Shrieks pierced through the obscurity of sound, and were succeeded by the singing of sweet female voices, which, in their turn, gave way to a wild roar of laughter, broken suddenly by groaning and sobs, forming altogether a ghastly confusion of terror and mourning and mirth. Chains were rattling, fierce and stern voices uttered threats, and the scourge resounded at their command. All these noises deepened and became substantial to the listener's ear, till she could distinguish every soft and dreamy accent of the love songs that died causelessly into funeral hymns. She shuddered at the unprovoked wrath which blazed up like the spontaneous kindling of flame, and she grew faint at the fearful merriment raging miserably around her. In the midst of this wild scene, where unbound passions jostled each other in a drunken career, there was one solemn voice of a man, and a manly and melodious voice it might once have been. He went to and fro continually, and his feet sounded upon the floor. In each member of that frenzied company, whose own burning thoughts had become their exclusive world, he sought an auditor for the story of his individual wrong, and interpreted their laughter and tears as his reward of scorn or pity. He spoke of woman's perfidy, of a wife who had broken her holiest vows, of a home and heart made desolate. Even as he went on, the shout, the laugh, the shriek, the sob, rose up in unison, till they changed into the hollow, fitful, and uneven sound of the wind, as it fought among the pine-trees on those three lonely hills. The lady looked up, and there was the withered woman smiling in her face.

"Couldst thou have thought there were such merry times in a madhouse?" inquired the latter.

"True, true," said the lady to herself; "there is mirth within its walls, but misery, misery without."

"Wouldst thou hear more?" demanded the old woman.

"There is one other voice I would fain listen to again," replied the lady faintly.

"Then, lay down thy head speedily upon my knees, that thou mayst get thee hence before the hour be past."

The golden skirts of day were yet lingering upon the hills, but deep shades obscured the hollow and the pool, as if sombre night were rising thence to overspread the world. Again that evil woman began to weave her spell. Long did it proceed unanswered, till the knelling of a bell stole in among the intervals of her words, like a clang that had travelled far over valley and rising ground, and was just ready to die in the air. The lady shook upon her companion's knees as she heard that boding sound. Stronger it grew and sadder, and deepened into the tone of a death bell, knelling dolefully from some ivy-mantled tower, and bearing tidings of mortality and wo to the cottage, to the hall, and to the solitary wayfarer, that all might weep for the doom appointed in turn to them. Then came a measured tread, passing slowly, slowly on, as of mourners with a coffin, their garments trailing on the ground, so that the ear could measure the length of their melancholy array. Before them went the priest, reading the burial service, while the leaves of his book were rustling in the breeze. And though no voice but his was heard to speak aloud, still there were revilings and anathemas, whispered but distinct, from women and from men, breathed against the daughter who had wrung the aged hearts of her parents—the wife who had betrayed the trusting fondness of her husband—the mother who had sinned against natural affection, and left her child to die. The sweeping sound of the funeral train faded away like a thin vapor, and the wind, that just before had seemed to shake the coffin pall, moaned sadly round the verge of the Hollow between three Hills. But when the old woman stirred the kneeling lady, she lifted not her head.

"Here has been a sweet hour's sport!" said the withered crone, chuckling to herself.

GENERAL COMMENTARY

NEAL FRANK DOUBLEDAY (ESSAY DATE FEBRUARY 1946)

SOURCE: Doubleday, Neal Frank. "Hawthorne's Use of Three Gothic Patterns." *College English* 7, no. 5 (February 1946): 250-62.

In the following essay, Doubleday illustrates Hawthorne's view of the Gothic tradition and how he adapted it to treat moral and psychological themes.

Hawthorne's critics have generally considered Hawthorne's literary methods as manifestations of his temperament and, in particular, his use of the Gothic convention as evidence of limited imaginative resources or of morbidity. There is a tempting picturesqueness in a disproportionate emphasis upon the "spectral" qualities of Hawthorne's art; but the interpreters of Hawthorne have often lost sight of important contemporary influences upon his literary practice and important motives for it. Hawthorne's use of the Gothic is a particularly good illustration of his way of adapting conventional materials to allegorical and psychological uses.[1]

In Hawthorne's work the familiar resources of the Gothic romancer are not used primarily to awaken terror or wonder but to embody a moral—not to induce an intense psychological state in the reader but to make imaginatively concrete a truth of general and permanent significance or to symbolize a condition of mind or soul. A romance, Hawthorne tells us, whatever its liberties, "sins unpardonably so far as it may swerve aside from the truth of the human heart." He has been, he avers, "burrowing, to his utmost ability, into the depths of our common nature"; he has "appealed to no sentiment or sensibilities save such as are diffused among us all"; he has been "merely telling what is common to human nature." "Everything," he makes Sybil Dacy say, "has its spiritual meaning, which to the literal meaning is what the soul is to the body."[2] Hawthorne's use of Gothic materials for his special artistic purpose sets us interesting questions in the problem of his relation to his time and in the problem of literary convention.

Certainly, Hawthorne had read a sufficient number of Gothic romances.[3] Wilbur Cross has written:

> Nearly all the Gothic machinery of Walpole, Mrs. Radcliffe, and Godwin is to be found in this Puritan: high winds, slamming doors, moonlight and starlight, magic and witchcraft, mysterious portraits, transformations, malignant beings, the elixir of life, the skeleton, the funeral, and the corpse in its shroud. To these were added, as time went on, mesmerism and clairvoyance.[4]

But Hawthorne is never more in accord with the general fictional practice of his time than he is in the use of these Gothic materials. It is entirely natural—almost inevitable—that a young writer in America looking for material should work a vein that had been present in English literature since the mid-eighteenth century; that was an important part of the German literature which was becoming so influential in New England; and that had been apparent in, almost characteristic of, American literature since its very beginnings.[5] The appeal of the Gothic is strikingly illustrated by Poe's deliberate choice of the tale of terror as the form calculated to win immediate acceptance.[6] Hawthorne, no less than Poe, was under the necessity of writing salable material, and he paid attention to his market, adapting his work to the conventions of that market and, at the same time, adapting the conventions to his peculiar purposes. As time went on, the Gothic became part of his literary habit—perhaps too persistently.

The use of the Gothic convention was a recognized method of making romance from American materials, which were considered too new to be entirely available for fiction. Hawthorne was very much influenced by the demand for the use of American materials in fiction;[7] and the Gothic convention and literary nationalism had already been combined by Charles Brockden Brown, by John Neal, and, to some extent, by Cooper. A passage from an 1826 review of Cooper by W. H. Gardiner makes explicit a motive for the use of the Gothic which the modern interpreter may easily overlook:

> The same sort of magical authority over the spirit of romance, which belongs in common to Scott, Radcliffe, Walpole, and our countryman Brown, is, for us at least, possessed by this writer in an eminent degree. Places, for example, familiar to us from our boyhood, and which are now daily before our eyes, thronged with the vulgar associations of real life, are boldly seized upon for scenes of the wildest romance; and yet our imaginations do not revolt at the incongruity. . . . A military conclave at the Province House possesses something of the same interest as if it were holden before the walls of Tillietudlem; and we attend a midnight marriage at the altar of King's Chapel, and feel our blood curdle at the overshadowing arm upon the wall, with the same superstitious terror as when the gigantic armor rattles in the purely imaginative Castle of Otranto. . . . It is the creation and adaptation of a kind of machinery, which may be original in its character, and yet within the narrowed limits of modern probability, that stretch to the utmost the inventive faculties of the novelist. . . .[8]

Acknowledging this motive as his own, Hawthorne remarks at the end of "Howe's Masquerade": "In truth, it is desperately hard work, when we attempt to throw the spell of hoar antiquity over localities with which the living world, and the day that is passing over us, have aught to do." And he frequently uses the Gothic for atmospheric effect, as well as for allegorical or psychological purposes.

Hawthorne's debt to his Gothic sources is more general than specific; and although specific derivation, when it can be found, is important, discussion of Hawthorne's Gothic is not therewith complete. And we can hardly assume that the influences upon him came exclusively from the well-known writers we know him to have read; we must at least assume his familiarity with the publications to which he contributed. Nor need we suppose that everything in his work that has a Gothic flavor has an immediate literary source: mesmerism and clairvoyance, for instance, although they may be considered Gothic, did not come into Hawthorne's work from literary tradition, for they were present in his New England.[9]

The three Gothic patterns which appear in Hawthorne's tales (each one at least twice) and recur in his romances best illustrate his attitude

ABOUT THE AUTHOR

EDGAR ALLAN POE REVIEW'S HAWTHORNE'S TWICE-TOLD TALES

[The Essays in *Twice-Told Tales*] are each and all beautiful, without being characterised by the polish and adaptation so visible in the tales proper. A painter would at once note their leading or predominant feature, and style it *repose*. There is no attempt at effect. All is quiet, thoughtful, subdued. Yet this repose may exist simultaneously with high originality of thought; and Mr. Hawthorne has demonstrated the fact. At every turn we meet with novel combinations; yet these combinations never surpass the limits of the quiet. We are soothed as we read; and withal is a calm astonishment that ideas so apparently obvious have never occurred or been presented to us before. Herein our author differs materially from Lamb or Hunt or Hazlitt—who, with vivid originality of manner and expression, have less of the true novelty of thought than is generally supposed. . . . The essays of Hawthorne have much of the character of Irving with more of originality, and less of finish. . . . [In the case of Mr. Irving,] repose is attained rather by the absence of novel combination, or of originality, than otherwise, and consists chiefly in the calm, quiet, unostentatious expression of commonplace thoughts, in an unambitious unadulterated Saxon. In them, by strong effort, we are made to conceive the absence of all. In the essays before us the absence of effort is too obvious to be mistaken, and a strong undercurrent of *suggestion* runs continuously beneath the upper stream of the tranquil thesis. In short, these effusions of Mr. Hawthorne are the product of a truly imaginative intellect, restrained, and in some measure repressed, by fastidiousness of taste, by constitutional melancholy and by indolence.

SOURCE: Poe, Edgar Allan. "Review of New Books: Twice-Told Tales." *Graham's Magazine* (1842): 298-300.

toward the convention and his special uses of it. They are (1) mysterious portraits, (2) witchcraft, and (3) the esoteric arts or researches which would break through the limitations of mortality.

I

From *The Castle of Otranto* down, the mysterious portrait is an important item in the list of Gothic paraphernalia and sometimes, as in Maturin's *Melmoth the Wanderer,* a most effective one. Hawthorne's use of it is a particularly good example of his way of taking a wholly conventional property and making it a symbol for a moral truth. Two stories—**"The Prophetic Pictures"** (1837) and **"Edward Randolph's Portrait"** (1838)—are built around mysterious portraits, and the portrait of Colonel Pyncheon is an important element in **The House of the Seven Gables.** Old portraits interested Hawthorne, as they do any sensitive person—indeed, the mysterious portrait is one of the most imaginatively convincing of Gothic properties. He records in his notebooks for 1837 his impressions of some old portraits in the Essex Historical Society—a portrait of John Endicott (**"Endicott and the Red Cross"** was published in the same year); a portrait of Sir William Pepperell, a sketch of whom he had published in 1833; a portrait of Governor William Pyncheon; and others. His comment in summary of his impressions suggests the use he was to make of a portrait in **The House of the Seven Gables,** some thirteen years later: "Nothing gives a stronger idea of old worm-eaten aristocracy—of a family being crazy with age, and of its being time that it was extinct—than these black, dusty, faded, antique-dressed portraits. . . ."[10]

"The Prophetic Pictures" is characteristic of Hawthorne's attitude toward Gothic materials. The suggestion for the story, Hawthorne's footnote tells us, came from Dunlap's *History of the Arts of Design in the United States* (1834). Hawthorne works out the suggestion in a Gothic manner, but he does not exploit the elements of terror and wonder and, indeed, refuses obvious opportunities to play upon his reader's nerves. He is usually careful and here particularly careful, not to allow the interest of the Gothic element to obscure the theme—in this story the theme that individual destiny is the result of what the individual is and does. What is Gothic is merely a vehicle for the theme—a theme that Professor Leach does not hesitate to compare with that of *Oedipus Rex:* "The portentous knowledge of the oracle does not save the man; as with Oedipus, the impulsive nature flashing out in wrath brings upon him the very doom he sought to escape. Does not the Greek drama, in its treatment of oracles, express something similar to the profound truth here uttered by the American novelist?"[11]

The Gothic element in **"Edward Randolph's Portrait"** has a comparable use. The suggestion for the story, it has been pointed out, may have come from *The Bride of Lammermoor,* though the mysterious portrait with glaring eyes is too common a device to be positively identified with a specific source. The story concerns an awful warning against trampling on a people's rights, a warning that comes to Colonel Hutchinson in the "peculiar glare" in the eyes, and in the tortured countenance, of the temporarily restored portrait of Edward Randolph. The story may be considered as a sort of companion piece to **"The Grey Champion,"** which concerns Randolph's contemporary, Sir Edmund Andros. In **"Edward Randolph's Portrait"** the Gothic is used as atmosphere, but it is primarily, as in **"The Prophetic Pictures,"** a vehicle for the theme, this time a nationalistic one. Hawthorne is never closer to the main stream of the American fiction of his time than he is when, in this story, he uses materials from the Gothic convention to fulfil the demand for "patriotism and native incident."

When, in **The House of the Seven Gables,** Hawthorne returns to the use of the mysterious portrait, he makes clear at the outset how we are to take the portrait of old Colonel Pyncheon. And, frequently reminding us in the course of the book that the portrait is a symbol, he depreciates the notion that there may be any real terror connected with it: he "is tempted to make a little sport with the idea"—as if he were afraid that his readers might become interested in the portrait as a thing in itself and that, therefore, the delicate balance of atmosphere and meaning might be destroyed.[12]

Hawthorne, then, in his use of mysterious portraits, finds a way of adapting a common device to his peculiar purposes. Yet he is also careful to give the Gothic property a local habitation: it was supposed that the painter of the prophetic pictures was "the famous Black Man, of old witch times"; one of the speculations about Edward Randolph's portrait, before its restoration, was that it was "an original and authentic portrait of the evil one, taken at a witch meeting, near Salem"; the Colonel's portrait gets its significance from "the affair of the old Puritan Pyncheon and the wizard Maule." The Gothic device is made part of New England legend.

II

In witchcraft, indeed, Hawthorne found a special opportunity. "We know not the country or age," wrote J. G. Palfrey in 1821, "which has such capacities" for the purposes of fiction "as N. England in its early day."[13] But American writers, deeply influenced by the Gothic tradition, complained for a long time about the lack of ruins and castles; even Cooper felt American materials unsatisfactory. Charles Brockden Brown attempted in *Edgar Huntly* to find an American Gothic in Indian material instead of in "Gothic castles and chimeras," and Freneau was once reduced to writing some stanzas about the ruins of a country inn. Hawthorne echoes the complaint in the Prefaces to the **The Blithedale Romance** and **The Marble Faun**; and the ancestral home of the Pyncheons is probably the best substitute for a Gothic castle any American romancer ever devised. Witchcraft, however, was part of American history and legend, and Hawthorne's treatment of New England witchcraft is an American Gothic that deserves separate consideration, an answer to the demand for the use of distinctively American materials.

If it is true that **"Alice Doane's Appeal"** was written in its original form before Hawthorne's graduation from college in 1825, the first version was one of the earliest fictional treatments of New England witchcraft.[14] The tale as published in the *Token* (1835) suggests the influence of John Neal or "Monk" Lewis and has a macabre quality; but it is not, certainly, in Hawthorne's best vein. The original seems to have escaped[15] the holocaust of tales which Hawthorne describes in **"The Devil in Manuscript"**; but it is just such tales that Hawthorne has in mind when he makes Oberon say to his friend:

> You have read them, and know what I mean,—
> that conception in which I endeavored to embody
> the character of a fiend, as represented in our
> traditions and the written records of witchcraft.
> Oh, I have a horror of what was created in my
> own brain, and shudder at the manuscripts in
> which I gave that dark idea a sort of material existence!"[16]

The version published in the *Token* is a description and summary of a tale, not the tale itself, and has for a frame an account of the narrator's afternoon walk on Gallows Hill with two young women. I think we may take it that Hawthorne is really giving us a condensed account of a tale he once wrote and that we are fortunate not to have the original. Although he speaks of "good authority in our ancient superstitions," the tale obviously does not come out of New England legend but out of the Gothic tradition, in which the motif of potential incest is not infrequent.[17] But if Hawthorne was unable to make use, in **"Alice Doane's Appeal,"** of the possibilities for fiction in New England witchcraft, he nevertheless had shown himself aware of them, probably before he was twenty-one.

In **"The Hollow of the Three Hills"** (1830), which may also have been written before 1825,[18] Hawthorne's treatment of the Gothic is somewhat more restrained, and his use of it has a moral purpose. But Hawthorne here makes no use of New England witchcraft materials, and the setting is not localized. Poe, who speaks as an expert in the Gothic, finds the tale original in that it makes the ear instead of the eye the medium by which the witch's revelations are received, a substitution for the conventional pictures in a mirror or a cloud of smoke.[19] And the use made of the Gothic device is probably more original than the change made in the device. Nevertheless, the tale has the marks of Hawthorne's immaturity, for it is overwritten and without the imaginative substantiation of tradition and locale.

Hawthorne's later treatments of witchcraft are governed by carefully worked-out principles. "Almost all forms of popular superstition," he says, "do clothe the ethereal with earthly attributes, and so make it grossly perceptible."[20] And witchcraft in particular has a serious import. Randall Stewart quotes an interesting passage from a letter of 1845 in which Hawthorne replies to Evert A. Duyckinck's suggestion that he write a history of witchcraft:

> I had often thought of such a work, but I should
> not like to throw it off hastily, or to write it for
> the sole and specific purpose of getting $500. A
> mere narrative, to be sure, might be prepared easily enough; but such a work, if worthily written,
> would demand research and study, and as deep
> thought as any man could bring to it. The more I
> look at it, the more difficulties do I see—yet difficulties such as I should like to overcome. Perhaps
> it may be the work of an after time.[21]

Moreover, traditional material is particularly valuable to the artist. Hawthorne puts the principle into the mouth of Septimius Felton: genuine legends

> adopted into the popular belief . . . incrusted over
> with humanity, by passing from one homely mind
> to another . . . get to be true, in a certain sense,
> and indeed in that sense may be called true
> throughout, for the very nucleus, the fiction in
> them, seems to have come out of the heart of man
> in a way that cannot be imitated of malice aforethought.[22]

And this quality of traditional material must be preserved in its literary treatment. In a review of Whittier's *The Supernaturalism of New England*, Hawthorne writes:

> The proper tone for these legends is, of course, that of the fireside narrative, refined and clarified to whatever degree the writer pleases. . . . Above all, the narrator should have faith, for the time being. If he cannot believe his ghost-story while he is telling it, he had better leave the task to somebody else.[23]

The principles of simplicity and imaginative assent are exemplified in **"Young Goodman Brown"** (1835), although balanced against the imaginative assent there is an alternative explanation, characteristic of Hawthorne and used (I think) to point up for the reader the symbolic value of the action. If the reason would conclude that Goodman Brown had a dream, "be it so if you will"; the reason thus satisfied need not interfere with the imagination's assent to the fable and to its spiritual implications. Even when Hawthorne is writing, in **"Main Street,"** as a historical essayist, he implies that, though the witch judges were horribly wrong in their interpretation, witchcraft was a psychological state and often a manifestation of a wilful devotion to evil. His remarks about Martha Carrier and George Burroughs serve as a commentary on **"Young Goodman Brown."** If such persons *were* wilfully devoted to evil, witchcraft would be only the sign of their spiritual pride. The symbolic value of witchcraft is inherent in the thing itself. Martha Carrier "the Devil found in a humble cottage, and looked into her discontented heart, and saw pride there, and tempted her with his promise that she should be Queen of Hell"; as for George Burroughs, "it may have been in the very strength of his high and searching intellect that the Tempter found the weakness which betrayed him."[24]

Certainly, the witchcraft material of **"Young Goodman Brown"** functions as imaginative substantiation for a parable of the soul. The tale holds in solution much witch-lore and some historical incident, most of which is from Cotton Mather's *Wonders of the Invisible World*.[25] But this material is not precisely the source of the tale, though it gives the tale substance. **"Young Goodman Brown"** may be read on at least three levels: as a witch story; as an analysis of a state of mind in which, through the contact of the individual with evil, all virtue seems hypocrisy; and as a theological allegory, the allegorical interpretation being pointed up by the double meaning of the title character's name and by the name of his wife, Faith, whom he left for one night. Yet the discrimi-

nation of those three levels is the result of analysis and not the experience of the tale itself, in which the three fuse and in which meaning does not separate itself from symbol.

We, as readers, view the action through Hawthorne, who consistently maintains the air of one who tries to interpret an action that has come to his knowledge, not an action created by him—an air which gives the tale the effect of legend. That effect may be illustrated: the staff of Goodman Brown's guide looked like a snake, but perhaps that was "an ocular deception assisted by the uncertain light"; "some affirm that the lady of the governor was there," but we cannot be sure; Goodman Brown did not actually see the minister and Deacon Gookin, but "he could have sworn" he heard their voices. But illustration is insufficient; the effect must be realized in its totality.

The allegory is very delicately pointed. Faith is not an allegorical type; she does not represent Goodman Brown's creed. Her name and his duty to her are enough to give her husband's simple statement, "Faith kept me back a while," or his question, "But where is Faith?" sufficient meaning. That Goodman Brown's guide was his own evil nature is never explicit, but the guide was like Goodman Brown in expression, and even, but for a worldly air, in manner. The guide's discourse, moreover, was so apt "that his arguments seemed rather to spring up in the bosom of his auditor than to be suggested by himself." When he left Goodman Brown, "as if he had vanished into the deepening gloom," it is a sign to us that no longer were a good and an evil nature contending in Goodman Brown; he was, for the time being, governed completely by "the instinct that guides mortal man to evil."

"Young Goodman Brown" has been called morbid. That judgment arises (I think) from not taking the tale on Hawthorne's terms. Goodman Brown comes from his experience, not disillusioned, but under a terrible illusion. Goodman Brown put himself in peril; of his own will he went into the wood of evil, "and there is this peculiarity in such a solitude, that the traveller knows not who may be concealed by the innumerable trunks and thick boughs overhead." The tale may appear morbid to one who assumes that men do not will evil. Hawthorne uses witchcraft as a symbol of the will to evil.

And so it is, too, in the twentieth chapter of ***The Scarlet Letter.*** Just after Dimmesdale "had yielded himself, with deliberate choice, as he had never done before, to what he knew was deadly sin," he met the governor's sister and reputed witch, old Mistress Hibbens; and this encounter, "if it were a real incident, did but show his sympathy and fellowship with wicked mortals, and the world of perverted spirits." "If it were a real incident"—just as in **"Young Goodman Brown,"** the doubt of actuality is the sign of symbolic value, and witchcraft becomes the symbol for the will to evil. When Dimmesdale returned from the forest and the interview with Hester in which he had chosen to flee with her, he had put aside the possibility of atonement and confession; like Goodman Brown in his home-coming, "another man had returned out of the forest; a wiser one; with a knowledge of hidden mysteries which the simplicity of the former never could have reached." "A bitter kind of knowledge that!" Hawthorne exclaims and shows that from his new knowledge came temptations—temptations the minister had never known before—and the ability to lie with fluency and grace. "Am I mad?" the minister asked just before he saw Mistress Hibbens, "or am I given over utterly to the fiend? Did I make a contract with him in the forest, and sign it with my blood? And does he now summon me to its fulfilment by suggesting the performance of every wickedness which his most foul imagination can conceive?"

Despite the nineteenth-century setting of the book, witchcraft is an important element in **The House of the Seven Gables.** The prophecy of the wizard Matthew Maule was used, Professor Orians shows, in John Neal's *Rachel Dyer* (1828) and has a source in actual records.[26] But in Hawthorne's romance the fulfilment of the prophecy is the symbol of retribution: "The act of the passing generation is the germ which may and must produce good or evil fruit in a far-distant time." So far Hawthorne's use of witchcraft serves to unify his "legend prolonging itself from an epoch now grey in the distance, down into our own broad daylight." Nevertheless, the reader is likely to feel that Hawthorne's use of witchcraft in **The House of the Seven Gables** does not always make for unity of impression. One difficulty is that Hol-grave, a type who "in his culture and want of culture . . . might fitly enough stand forth as the representative of many compeers in his native land," is made the descendant of the legendary Matthew Maule. Now, although that descent may be taken to signify, perhaps, the new importance of the economic class to which the Maules belong, the hereditary connection between the Gothic wizard and a type disciple of the "newness" is hard to realize. Then, too, Holgrave's experiments in

mesmerism and the interpolated story of Alice Pyncheon and Matthew Maule offer a disappointing explanation for the power of the Maules. Of course, the "explained supernatural" is a part of the Gothic convention[27] and so characteristic of Gothic fiction in America that Professor Coad finds Mrs. Radcliffe the dominant influence on it before 1835.[28] But mesmerism and apoplexy as the cause of the sudden deaths of the Pyncheons remind us of the kind of explanation in Brown's *Wieland;* and Hawthorne himself suggests, in **The Marble Faun,** that he thought the "explained supernatural" tedious.[29] His near-approach to it in **The House of the Seven Gables** is less subtle than his way, in earlier work, of suggesting a doubt of the literal witchcraft even while asking imaginative assent, and seems less characteristic.

The success of any portion of an artist's work is to a great extent imponderable. But Hawthorne's success with witchcraft material admits of some definition. He discovers an inherent symbolism in the material itself, and he pays careful attention to historical appropriateness and to the congruity of his treatment of witchcraft in a particular work with the other elements in that work.[30] In **"Young Goodman Brown"** and in **The Scarlet Letter** the imaginative strength of his treatment of witchcraft is fully displayed.

III

A considerable body of Gothic literature concerns itself with the transcendence of the limits of mortality. The legend of the Wandering Jew, the compact with the devil for extended existence, and elixir of life had been, by Hawthorne's time, often used and often combined,[31] and they are the elements of the Gothic tradition which most influence Hawthorne. He was attracted to these materials because they were capable of carrying much meaning; indeed, Gothic work with serious implications had already been written around them. In Hawthorne's work the attempt to transcend the limits of mortality is a symbol for intellectual pride, a symbol that has for him, I believe, immediate contemporary reference.[32] As in his treatments of witchcraft, there is an inherent symbolism in the material itself. And his specialized use of his materials takes him far enough beyond his literary sources so that those sources are never entirely apparent.

Hawthorne wrote no story around the Wandering Jew, but that significant and credible figure turns up sometimes in his work. He is a guest of the Man of Fancy in **"A Select Party"** (1844), and Hawthorne remarks that he "had grown so common by mingling in all sorts of society and appearing at the beck of every entertainer that he could hardly be deemed a proper guest in a very exclusive circle." Yet Hawthorne had made him curator of **"A Virtuoso's Collection"** (1842); and the aged Seeker in **"The Great Carbuncle"** (1837), though not the Wandering Jew, has much in common with him. In his notebooks for 1845 Hawthorne records a plan for a treatment of the Wandering Jew, a plan which would give him a career remarkably like that of Goethe's Faust and which suggests the career Septimius Felton hopes for when he shall have found the elixir of life:

> A disquisition—or a discussion between two or more persons—on the manner in which the Wandering Jew has spent his life. One period, perhaps, in wild carnal debauchery; then trying, over and over again, to grasp domestic happiness; then a soldier; then a statesman & c—at last, realizing some truth.[33]

And in **"Ethan Brand"** (1851) the showman who operates the diorama is, I take it, the Wandering Jew. The showman and his diorama Hawthorne took from his notebook account of a visit to North Adams in 1838, but there the showman is merely "the old Dutchman."[34] This transformation, not essential to Hawthorne's fable, suggests the persistence of the Wandering Jew in his imagination and something of the literary background of his tale.

Bliss Perry has shown us how interesting an example of Hawthorne's literary methods **"Ethan Brand"** is;[35] and its combination of the Gothic with the materials of Hawthorne's own observation makes it important to the present purpose. The person, character, career, and death of Ethan are all in the Gothic tradition; one may find almost every aspect of them paralleled in Maturin's *Melmoth the Wanderer*. Particularly, **"Ethan Brand"** resembles the last two chapters of the romance, and Hawthorne's subtitle, "A Chapter from an Abortive Romance," points up that resemblance; for, if **"Ethan Brand"** be considered a chapter from a romance, it must surely be the last.[36]

This likeness suggests that Hawthorne was influenced by Maturin; but, because Maturin's book combines many elements of the Gothic tradition,[37] it may only indicate Hawthorne's general indebtedness to Gothic literature. Both Ethan and Melmoth are distinguished by their wild laughter and their unearthly gleaming eyes.[38] They are alike, too, in essential character: Ethan's sin was the "sin of an intellect that triumphed over the sense of brotherhood with man and reverence for God, and sacrificed everything to its own mighty claims"; Melmoth's sin, he says, "was the great angelic sin—pride and intellectual glorying. It was the first mortal sin—a boundless aspiration after forbidden knowledge."[39] The careers of the two are said to have had the same sort of inception: the legend was that Ethan invoked a fiend to aid him in his search for the Unpardonable Sin; "it has been reported of me," says Melmoth, "that I obtained from the enemy of souls a range of existence beyond the period allotted to mortality" and other preternatural powers.[40] Yet neither has the direct aid of the devil; Ethan's remark, "I have left him behind me," is true of both. Both are wanderers, driven by their own unrest to and fro upon the earth, though Ethan's time of wandering is shorter. Both, having worn out their fate, come home to die. Ethan casts himself into the lime kiln, and in their sleep the lime burners hear a fearful peal of laughter; Melmoth casts himself (or is cast, the matter is left unclear) over a cliff, and there are horrible sounds in his room and then at the cliff. The night before his death the Wanderer dreams of a sea of flame into which he must go—Ethan's lime kiln seems to be that sea in little. But the most important parallel is that both suffer in the same kind of awful isolation. Maturin's best critic says: "The character of Melmoth the Wanderer becomes . . . distinct from all common men . . . what causes him his keenest sufferings is not that he is shut out of paradise but that he is shut out of the community of the good among human beings."[41] Yet nothing in Maturin's book approaches the power of Hawthorne's irony. Ethan's success in his quest is his punishment for it: "My task," he says, "is done and well done."

Neither of the two suggestions for **"Ethan Brand"** which Hawthorne wrote in his notebook in 1844 does more than outline the bare allegory of the tale.[42] When he wrote it more than four years later, he used material from his notebook account of a visit to North Adams in 1838. Perhaps the story came about in this manner: No way of embodying the allegorical outline of 1844 occurred to Hawthorne until 1848, when a reminiscence of *Melmoth the Wanderer* suggested a Gothic treatment, which he found a way to substantiate and to localize with material from the account of his North Adams visit.

"Rappaccini's Daughter" (1844) may be considered a companion piece to **"Ethan Brand."** Both concern the efforts of an individual to transcend the limits of mortality, and both are treatments of the sin of pride. "**Rappaccini's Daughter,**" however, is concerned primarily with the effect of the sin on persons innocent in intent, not with the effect of the sin on the sinner himself; Beatrice is united in "fearful sympathy" with Giovanni, isolated from all the world beside. Though the tale is connected in theme with other tales in which Gothic symbols represent the sin of pride, in treatment it stands apart. The Gothic atmosphere is intense, unrelieved, and used for an effect different from any in Hawthorne's other work. The suggestion for a tale that Hawthorne found in Sir Thomas Browne and recorded in his notebook[43] is developed in that half-real, half-imaginary Italy that has been, since Elizabethan times, traditional in English fiction for romantic terror. There, experienced readers will easily believe, such a toxicologist as Dr. Rappaccini might have lived. And Hawthorne is careful to recall the associations which his readers will have with the locale by references to Dante's *Inferno*, the University of Padua, Benvenuto Cellini, and the Borgias. The persons in the tale are less allegorical types than the persons in his tales with similar themes, and the symbolism less explicit. He develops the hectic and unwholesome atmosphere of terror and wonder to enforce the truth and the horror "of the fatality that attends . . . perverted wisdom."

From "**Dr. Heidegger's Experiment**" (1837) to the unfinished romances of the last years of his life, Hawthorne frequently used in his fiction, or referred to, the search for the elixir of life and kindred attempts to transcend the limits of mortality. Randall Stewart has pointed out that Hawthorne's interest in the subject may have come from his early reading of William Godwin's *St. Leon,* and one can see that the moral isolation of the hero is like that of several of Hawthorne's characters.[44] Yet when Hawthorne writes of practitioners of the esoteric arts in old New England, he is in historical keeping. Lowell, in "New England Two Centuries Ago," notes the presence of students of the esoteric in Colonial New England and, implying that Hawthorne could not have known historical instances, remarks: "And yet how perfectly did his genius divine that ideal element in our early New England life, conceiving what must have been without asking proof of what actually was!"[45] Hawthorne could not have seen the work Lowell was reviewing, but the appearance of students of the esoteric in his work is not all based on divination. In "**Sir William Pepperell**" (1833), he refers to an alchemist and

seeker for the elixir of life as a historical person of Colonial times; in his notebooks for 1838 he speaks of a Salem house where an alchemist had resided and of "other alchemists of old in this town,—one who kept his fire burning seven weeks, and then lost the elixir by letting it go out"; and again in "**Main Street**" (1849) he speaks of the house of an alchemist.[46]

Of all the tales, "**Dr. Heidegger's Experiment,**" in its apparent simplicity, reveals most clearly Hawthorne's attitude toward his Gothic materials. Those materials are entirely conventional; the attitude toward them is peculiarly fresh. In a single paragraph, just after the doctor has welcomed his friends to his study, Hawthorne crowds in and heaps together a welter of Gothic properties and devices—this one room, indeed, has enough Gothic paraphernalia for all the romances Jane Austen's Catherine Morland ever read. There is, in this catalogue of the Gothic romancer's stock in trade, a delicate satire on the very convention Hawthorne is using. Yet "**Dr. Heidegger's Experiment**" is not primarily satire; it has an intent as a parable. The touch of satire is a sign to the reader to accept the tale as allegory—a way of restraining one kind of interest in the action so that another kind may emerge. We have noted in the treatment of the portrait in *The House of the Seven Gables* somewhat the same kind of whimsical depreciation of Gothic materials.

In "**The Birthmark**" (1843), Hawthorne depends upon his reader's familiarity with the materials he is using to insure their acceptance on the lowest level of approach. But the Gothic figures, by their very familiarity, are available for symbolism; and Hawthorne, having the existing type, simply makes it a symbol. Aylmer's assistant, the earthly Aminadab, "seemed to represent man's physical nature." Aylmer himself represents the intellectual and spiritual and (as the theme develops) the intellectual gone wrong, or at least defeated in an attempt to break through the limits of mortal power. Aylmer will not accept the fact that imperfection is a necessary part of mortality, that perfection and existence are incompatible. Too wise to attempt the unnatural extension of life—though that seems to be within his power—he is not wise enough to know the limits to which human aspiration ought to keep. For Georgiana, Hawthorne has taken the Gothic lady of remarkable and perfect beauty and added a tiny hand, the color of blood, to her cheek—added the symbol of the imperfection in everything mortal.

Hawthorne's most interesting use of the esoteric arts is in the development of the character of Roger Chillingworth. Nothing in the action of **The Scarlet Letter** requires that he be an adept, and the frequent suggestion that he is has value primarily as psychological symbolism. Chillingworth speaks of his "old studies in alchemy" and of teaching the Indians "some lessons . . . as old as Paracelsus"; his medical knowledge seems to be a by-product of his unholy researches; it is reported that he has been an associate of Dr. Simon Forman and that his dark knowledge has been extended by instruction by Indian priests; the popular opinion is that he is "Satan himself, or Satan's emissary."[47] In Chillingworth—as in Ethan Brand, Dr. Rappaccini, and Aylmer—the Gothic furnished Hawthorne a means of representing the sin of pride. But Chillingworth's skill in unholy arts means something more, for the suggestion that Chillingworth is the servant of Satan prepares us for his greatly enlarged significance in the final scene. The people of Boston (who, like the chorus in Greek tragedy, comment on the action without full knowledge of it) see Chillingworth as a diabolical agent pitted against Dimmesdale, but look "with an unshaken hope, to see the minister come forth out of the conflict transfigured with the glory he would unquestionably win." Their hope is ironically fulfilled; and in the moment of Dimmesdale's victory, Chillingworth has a representative character beyond his significance as a vengeful individual. If this were not so, his words to Dimmesdale in this final scene would be mere fustian, but I think few readers take them so. He has "thrust himself, through the crowd,—or, perhaps, so dark, disturbed, and evil, was his look, he rose out of some nether region." And he says: "Hadst thou sought the whole earth over, there was no place so secret,—no high place nor lowly place, where thou couldst have escaped me,—save on this very scaffold!"

Hawthorne's last attempts at romance—**Dr. Grimshawe's Secret, The Dolliver Romance,** and **Septimius Felton**—throw into relief his successful practice in the Gothic, for in them the Gothic materials get out of hand, assume too great an importance in and for themselves, and get in the way, therefore, of the meaning. And this is not just another way of saying that the romances are unfinished; Hawthorne's own term for this work— "abortive"[48]—is precise, for it had never come to full birth. The intention itself cannot be understood, for the relationship between symbol and theme is never fully established. Of course, it is true that Hawthorne sometimes had been embarrassed by the plot material of his long fictions, but his meaning had never been frustrated. He seems to have been aware of the trouble without being able to correct it; for example, in **Septimius Felton** we can observe him endeavoring to balance and offset the Gothic interest of Septimius' quest for the elixir by long reflective expositions, often in his best manner. But the delicate balance of interest that distinguishes Hawthorne's best work is gone.

Taken all together, the tales and romances which have characters who refuse to recognize the conditions in which humanity subsists are an important part of Hawthorne's work and of his thought. A recent critic complains that Hawthorne did not know the meaning of his own symbols.[49] But he was at least in positive opposition to the spiritual attitudes of his own time; he was, indeed, preoccupied throughout most of his career with allegorical warning against the sin of pride. That is why Gothic symbols for the effort to be more than mortal, more than man, recur so often in his work.

Hawthorne's use of the Gothic extends much beyond the three patterns here discussed; there is, for example, evidence of Radcliffean influence in **The Marble Faun** and in **Dr. Grimshawe's Secret,** the two romances with settings in which Mrs. Radcliffe's materials might be appropriate. But because the three patterns considered in this paper recur most often, they are the best means of illustrating his intent in the use of the Gothic. The illustrations must substantiate, as best they may, the paper's initial generalizations; for a summary would inevitably reduce Hawthorne's practice to a formula, and no formula will represent the flexibility and the convolution of his use of Gothic materials or his way of making them the means to individual and often significant ends. "There are some works in literature," Hawthorne once wrote, "that bear an analogy to his [Bernini's] works in sculpture, where great power is lavished a little outside of nature, and therefore proves to be only a fashion, and not permanently adapted to the tastes of mankind."[50] The impulse of Gothic literature has evidently often been abnormal, and it is one of the distinctions of Hawthorne's work in the Gothic that in it he has kept to a humane purpose. His control of the Gothic is a double control—a control of his materials and a control of his reader's reaction. The reader's response to a tale or romance by Hawthorne is, on its final level, intellectual, and toward such response he carefully directs his work.

Notes

1. I am indebted to Professor Austin Warren for his generous help and for a copy of his unpublished "Hawthorne and the Craft of Fiction," a paper read at the 1941 meeting of the Modern Language Association.

2. *Works* ("Riverside" ed.), III, 13, 386; II, 44; IX, 336; XI, 330.

3. Hawthorne read Mrs. Radcliffe, Godwin, Scott, and John Neal in his youth (see Julian Hawthorne, *Hawthorne and His Wife* [Boston, 1885], I, 105 and 145; G. P. Lathrop, *A Study of Hawthorne* [Boston, 1876], p. 108; *Works*, II, 426). It is likely that his first reading of Charles Brockden Brown and Walpole was also early (see Lathrop, *op. cit.*, p. 343; *Works*, II, 198 and 428, and VIII, 528).

4. *Development of the English Novel* (New York, 1926), pp. 163-64.

5. See Oral Coad, "The Gothic Element in American Literature before 1835," *JEGP*, XXIV (January, 1925), 72-93.

6. See Napier Wilt, "Poe's Attitude toward His Tales," *Modern Philology*, XXV (August, 1927), 101-5.

7. See my "Hawthorne and Literary Nationalism," *American Literature*, XII (January, 1941), 447-53.

8. *North American Review*, XXIII (July, 1826), 152-53.

9. See *Works*, III, 312; V, 544-45; IX, 244-45.

10. *Works*, IX, 88-89.

11. Abby Leach, "Free Will in Greek Literature," in Lane Cooper (ed.), *The Greek Genius and Its Influence* (New Haven, 1928), p. 137.

12. See, e.g., *Works*, III, 50, 116-17, 236, 329-31.

13. *North American Review*, XII (April, 1821), 480.

14. Julian Hawthorne, *op. cit.*, I, 124; G. H. Orians, "New England Witchcraft in Fiction," *American Literature*, II (March, 1930), 54-71.

15. *Works*, XII, 282.

16. *Ibid.*, III, 575.

17. See Eino Railo, *The Haunted Castle* (London, 1927), pp. 269-72.

18. See Elizabeth Chandler's study of Hawthorne's sources in *Smith College Studies in Modern Languages*, VII, No. 4 (July, 1926), 8-9.

19. *Works* ("Virginia" ed.), XI, 112.

20. *Works*, VIII, 271.

21. Randall Stewart, "Two Uncollected Reviews by Hawthorne," *New England Quarterly*, IX (September, 1936), 505.

22. *Works*, XI, 326.

23. Stewart, *op. cit.*, p. 507.

24. See *Works*, III, 467-71.

25. Austin Warren cites the most important passages in a note on the tale (*Nathaniel Hawthorne* [New York, 1934], pp. 361-62).

26. *Op. cit.*, p. 67.

27. See Montague Summers, *The Gothic Quest* (London, n.d.), pp. 135-40.

28. *Op. cit.*, pp. 91-92.

29. *Works*, VI, 514.

30. Two witches, Mother Rigby, of "Feathertop" (1852), and Septimius Felton's Aunt Keziah, Hawthorne makes humorous, not strictly Gothic, figures. Yet in his treatment of them he in no way violates his general principles.

31. Eino Railo's discussion of these materials, though disappointing, is perhaps the best (see *op. cit.*, pp. 191-217).

32. See my "Hawthorne's Inferno," *College English*, I (May, 1940), 658-70.

33. *American Notebooks*, ed. Stewart, p. 117; cf. *Works*, XI, 404-10.

34. *American Notebooks*, pp. 58-59.

35. "Hawthorne at North Adams," *The Amateur Spirit* (Boston, 1904).

36. The reader will remember that *Melmoth* is a series of six tales, connected only by the appearance of Melmoth in each, set in a frame consisting of five chapters of introductory narrative and two concluding chapters. Melmoth, in return for his preternatural powers, must endure an existence prolonged by one hundred and fifty years unless he can persuade someone to take his place. But no one will lose his soul to gain the whole world (which is Maturin's theme), and the Wanderer cannot leave the existence he comes to hate until his time comes. Only in the last two chapters does the nature of his curious destiny become clear.

37. See Niilo Idman, *Charles Robert Maturin* (London, 1923), pp. 197 ff.; Edith Birkhead, *The Tale of Terror* (New York, n.d.), pp. 84-85. H. Arlin Turner has noted the likeness of Ethan's laugh to Melmoth's (see his "Hawthorne's Literary Borrowings," *PMLA*, LI [June, 1936], 556).

38. See *Melmoth the Wanderer* (3 vols.; London, 1892), I, 44 and 50.

39. *Ibid.*, III, 358.

40. *Ibid.*, pp. 326-27.

41. Idman, *op. cit.*, p. 265.

42. *American Notebooks*, ed. Stewart, p. 106.

43. *Works*, IX, 209.

44. *American Notebooks*, pp. lxxxii-lxxxviii; and see *St. Leon: A Tale of the Sixteenth Century* (4 vols.; London, 1816), II, 110-11.

45. See *Writings* ("Riverside" ed.), II, 46-57.

46. *Works*, XII, 239; IX, 206; III, 456.

47. *Works*, V, 94-95, 146-47, 155-56.

48. *Works*, VII, 16; VIII, 10.

49. Yvor Winters, *Maule's Curse* (Norfolk, Conn., 1938), p. 20.

50. *Works*, X, 143.

JANE LUNDBLAD (ESSAY DATE 1946)

SOURCE: Lundblad, Jane. "Hawthorne and the Gothic Romance." In *Nathaniel Hawthorne and the Tradition of The Gothic Romance*. 1946. Reprint edition, pp. 24-94. New York: Haskell House, 1964.

In the following excerpt from an essay originally published in 1946, Lundblad surveys the impact of Gothic works on Hawthorne's writing.

The student of Hawthorne's life and writings is usually regarded as a privileged person because of the fact that Hawthorne's posthumous note-books, manuscripts, and letters have been so scrupulously kept and published. It is true that his widow, out of misguided zeal and exaggerated modesty, made a great many deletions and alterations in his manuscripts before she authorized their publication, in order to weed out items and remarks concerning the family or herself that she deemed improper. But on the whole, all this extensive material remains intact. Day by day, the reader may follow Hawthorne's life, step by step the composition of his romances and stories. As has already been remarked, Hawthorne applied the method of the later naturalistic school: he made notes of every spectacle, every acquaintance, idea or memory that might be turned to literary use. But there are nearly no notes on his reading. The scholar who is looking for literary influences on Hawthorne must therefore avail himself largely of the method of indirect induction. During my work on this essay, I have had direct access only to printed editions of Hawthorne's note-books and his unfinished manuscripts. The letters have not been available to me otherwise than as quotations in the works of various other authors.

It has been pointed out that the chief Gothic novels written in English may be presumed to have been well known in America during the first decades of the nineteenth century, while the works of the German writers were only partly translated or reviewed in the periodical press. Hawthorne's own disposition, and the environment in which he grew up, made him receptive, from the beginning, towards tales concerning the supernatural world. In the above-mentioned review of Morris's biography,[1] we find an excellent characterization of Hawthorne's attitude: ". . . he was no mystic, and was, if anything, repelled by mysticism. But he was absorbed in something which is often confused with mysticism—in mystery and mysteriousness. And this fact is really the clue to his character, if we can arrive at an understanding of it." In the introduction to his edition of Hawthorne's first diary, Samuel T. Pickard mentions a letter from one of the young Nathaniel's friends, W. Symmes, who wrote in later years:[2] "One of your correspondents . . . describes the mother of Nathaniel as being somewhat superstitious, and from what I recollect of her, he is correct. Not a gross and ignorant, but a polished and pious superstition. Perhaps this proclivity in the parent may account for his filling his journal with so many of the local stories of the supernatural." The stories referred to treat of Pulpit Rock Hill, from which the devil was said to have preached to the Indians, thereafter to make them sink down into a swamp, so that great masses of skeletons were still lying under the surface of the field—or of an enchanted apple-tree, whose fruit was guarded by spirits, so that the reapers were in constant danger of being hit by stones thrown from nowhere—or of a bewitched house, the windows of which perpetually sprang open, etc., etc. Certainly Nathaniel also heard in childhood many of the stories from the early immigration days when witchery was rampant among the pious settlers—stories which have left so many traces in his later works.

Like any other American schoolboy, Hawthorne was, from his early youth, acquainted with the English classics. Spenser and Bunyan are generally indicated as the most important sources of inspiration derived from his early reading. Randall Stewart[3] also mentions Shakespeare and Milton. A. Turner, in his treatise on Hawthorne's literary borrowings,[4] points to the important influence wrought on Hawthorne by the historical writings of Increase and Cotton Mather on the legends and customs of 17th century Massachusetts, especially stressing "the Mather witch tradition" with its accounts of witch meetings, ridings through the air on broomsticks, etc., which we shall meet in some of Hawthorne's stories, e. g. **"Young Goodman Brown."**[5] As to the literature of terror and wonder, we have direct evidence of his having read some of the best-known novels in a couple of letters written to his sister Elizabeth. On September 28th, 1819, he writes:[6] "I have read *Waverley, Roderick Random* and the first volume of *The Arabian Nights.*" And on October 31st, 1820:[7] "I have read Hogg's *Tales, Caleb Williams, St. Leon* and *Mandeville*. I admire Godwin's Novels, and intend to read them all." The deep impression which Mathurin's

Melmoth had made on him is apparent in the evident traces that its reading has left on his first novel, *Fanshawe,* as also in the fact that the motto of one of its chapters is directly drawn from *Melmoth.* An item in his English note-book of 1857 shows that Walpole's *The Castle of Otranto* was once familiar to him. Hawthorne is wandering about in a picture-gallery, and remarks:[8] "Of all the older pictures, the only one that I took pleasure in looking at, was a portrait of Lord Deputy Falkland, by Vansomer, in James I's time—a very stately, full-length figure in white, looking out of the picture as if he saw you. The catalogue says that this portrait suggested an incident in Horace Walpole's Castle of Otranto; but I do not remember it."

That the contemporaries of Hawthorne, or at least his European critics, were fully aware of the fact that a considerable part of his literary background was of the traditional Gothic kind, is clearly shown by an article in the *Revue des deux mondes,* of 1852,[9] by E. D. Forgues. The writer is speaking of the rôle assigned to the portrait of Colonel Pyncheon in *The House of the Seven Gables*: "Ce portrait se trouve mêlé à l'action, où il joue le rôle réservé aux fantômes avant l'invention de la peinture à l'huile: c'est lui qui cache le document perdu; c'est lui qui suspend et dénoue la chaîne des revenants, comme Walter Scott, Lewis, Mme Radcliffe et Washington Irving, sans parler de Maturin, de Hoffmann et de bien d'autres encore, en ont tous écrit."

Hoffmann is here mentioned in the same breath as the English and American authors of novels of terror and wonder. We have already discussed the question of Hawthorne's acquaintance with the German Romanticists, and only a few facts shall here be added. Contemporary criticism sometimes accused Hawthorne of being influenced by the Germans. As an example may be cited an article in the *National Magazine* of 1853[10] where it is cursorily remarked: "Saving certain shadowy resemblances to some of the Germans . . ." and above all Poe's criticism of *Mosses from an Old Manse,* where he deliberately accuses Hawthorne of having imitated Tieck. The critical discussion of this problem has attracted many participants (Cp. p. 13, note 3) but may be regarded as settled. H. M. Belden[11] has succeeded in proving beyond doubt that Hawthorne may have read in translation some of Tieck's better-known tales before 1833, but that the imitation with which Poe tried to charge him is exceedingly unlikely. Another scholar who has thoroughly examined the possibilities of European influence on Hawthorne's writings, A. Schönbach, arrives at a similar result:[12] "Am ehesten räume ich noch Balzac etwas Einfluss auf Hawthorne ein, ferner mag sein Liebling Walter Scott ihn ermutigt haben, die Geschichten aus der Colonialzeit zu schreiben, später hat er noch von Dickens ein weniges gewonnen. Aber, wie Poe glaubte, und seither mit Ausdauer nachgeschrieben wird, dass Tieck Hawthornes Muster gewesen und von ihm nachgebildet worden sei, das ist mir schon aus diesen inneren Gründen höchst unwahrscheinlich. In Tiecks Erzählungen sind Dargestelltes und Darsteller von derselben Stimmung erfüllt: wird das Reale an einer Stelle verlassen, dann aber sofort auch an allen und im Ganzen." To Hawthorne's attitude towards the unreal and supernatural we will revert later on. First, we shall for a moment occupy ourselves with the possibilities of an influence from the earlier American versions of the Gothic novel.

The most prominent representative of the Gothic school in America was, as has already been said, Charles Brockden Brown. It is to be assumed that Hawthorne was well versed in his tales. An American scholar, Professor Quinn, who has devoted a study[13] to the rôle of the supernatural in the literature of his country, is of opinion that no impressions of real import derive from this source: "Brown, however, has little direct influence upon Poe or Hawthorne." We have greater reason to assume an influence from Washington Irving. From the point of view of literary form, it is likely that Hawthorne acquired something of his early predilection for the short story by reading the works of his countryman. There are also stylistic similarities. Woodberry remarks:[14] "From the former (the eighteenth century) he had that pellucid style, whose American flow began with Washington Irving and ceased with his own pen." But neither in respect of actual plots, nor when it comes to the general trend of ideas, need we believe Hawthorne to be indebted to the author of the *Tales of a Traveller*—so perfect in their kind, where common sense pervades the atmosphere far too thoroughly to permit any kind of transcendental extravagance.

There is a close affinity between Hawthorne's taste for magic and supernatural stories and his interest for Swedenborg, for spiritualism and mesmerism, which we find expressed in different ways in his writings and is surreptitiously mentioned in his notebooks. During his stay in England, in 1857, he discusses spiritualism thoroughly with some friends, and sums up his own position in a passage in his note-book, which gives a fair

ABOUT THE AUTHOR

HERMAN MELVILLE REVIEWS *MOSSES FROM AN OLD MANSE*

"The Christmas Banquet," and "The Bosom Serpent," would be fine subjects for a curious and elaborate analysis, touching the conjectural parts of the mind that produced them. For [in] spite of all the Indian-summer sunlight on the hither side of Hawthorne's soul, the other side—like the dark half of the physical sphere—is shrouded in a blackness, ten times black. But this darkness but gives more effect to the ever-moving dawn, that forever advances through it, and circumnavigates his world. Whether Hawthorne has simply availed himself of this mystical blackness as a means to the wondrous effects he makes it to produce in his lights and shades; or whether there really lurks in him, perhaps unknown to himself, a touch of Puritanic gloom,—this, I cannot altogether tell. Certain it is, however, that this great power of blackness in him derives its force from its appeals to that Calvinistic sense of Innate Depravity and Original Sin, from whose visitations, in some shape or other, no deeply thinking mind is always and wholly free. . . . [Perhaps] no writer has ever wielded this terrific thought with greater terror than this same harmless Hawthorne. Still more: this black conceit pervades him through and through. You may be witched by his sunlight,—transported by the bright gildings in the skies he builds over you; but there is the blackness of darkness beyond; and even his bright gildings but fringe and play upon the edges of thunderclouds.

SOURCE: Melville, Herman. "Hawthorne and His Mosses." *Literary World* 7, no. 7 (17-24 August 1850): 53-86.

together like the white and yolk of an egg, merely out of respect to Dr———'s sanity or integrity. I would not believe my own sight, nor touch of the spiritual hands; and it would take deeper and higher strains than those of Mr. Harris to convince me. I think I might yield to higher poetry or heavenlier wisdom than mortals in the flesh have ever sung or uttered. Meanwhile, this matter of spiritualism is surely the strangest that ever was heard of, and yet I feel unaccountably little interest in it—a sluggish disgust, and repugnance to meddle with it—insomuch that I hardly feel as if it were worth this page or two in my not very eventful journal." But regarded as literary themes, these things possessed for him an interest as great as all other problems concerning the human soul.

The scenery and the whole machinery of Gothic Romance became, just like Puritanism or Spiritualism, one of Hawthorne's media of artistic expression. He called all his whole-length stories romances,[16] and has given reason for this in the introduction to *The House of the Seven Gables*: "When a writer calls his work a Romance, it need hardly be observed that he wishes to claim a certain latitude, both as to its fashion and material, which he would not have felt himself entitled to assume had he professed to be writing a Novel. The latter form of composition is presumed to aim at a very minute fidelity, not merely to the possible, but to the probable and ordinary course of man's experience. The former—while, as a work of art, it must rigidly subject itself to laws, and while it sins unpardonably so far as it may swerve aside from the truth of the human heart—has fairly a right to present that truth under circumstances, to a great extent, of the writer's own choosing or creation. If he think fit, also, he may so manage his atmospherical medium as to bring out or mellow the lights and deepen and enrich the shadows of the picture. He will be wise, no doubt, to make a very moderate use of the privileges here stated, and especially to mingle the Marvellous rather as a slight, delicate, and evanescent flavour, than as any portion of the actual substance of the dish offered to the public. He can hardly be said, however, to commit a literary crime, even if he disregard this caution."

Hawthorne's literary ideal has been in a certain measure foreshadowed by Leigh Hunt who once wrote:[17] "A ghost story, to be a good one, should unite as much as possible objects such as they are in life with a preternatural spirit. And to be a perfect one—at least to add to the other utility of excitement a moral utility." Moral utility is, however, not the accurate term for the aim of

idea of his view on these matters:[15] "Do I believe in these wonders? Of course; for how is it possible to doubt either the solemn word or the sober observation of a learned and sensible man like Dr———? But again do I really believe it? Of course not; for I cannot consent to have heaven and earth, this world and the next, beaten up

Hawthorne's writings. Utility of any kind was hardly sought by this **"Artist of the Beautiful."**[18] And moralist is certainly not the right word to denote this indefatigable seeker, incessantly hunting for the innermost motives of human actions. Henry James, whose Life of Hawthorne[19] is of a masterly composition but stamped by too much cool insensibility wholly to convince the reader, has, however, in this respect found a good formula: "He was not a moralist," says James, "and he was not simply a poet. The moralists are weightier, denser, richer in a sense; the poets are more purely inconclusive and irresponsible. He combined in a singular degree the spontaneity of the imagination with a haunting care for moral problems." It is difficult to find a label to fix on to this methodical and intense, not to say frantic plumber of the depths of sin in the human soul. Childhood remembrances, religious and philosophical conceptions, literary reminiscences, and the creations of his own fantasy are to him only artistic means for throwing a penetrating light over the truths of the human soul, which he believes to have found out during years of never-ceasing, devoted study. His work is of a deeply individual stamp. We cite P. Kaufman who writes:[20] ". . . into traditional form he infused profound brooding and achieved the distinction of making romance profoundly subjective. Hitherto this genre both in prose and verse had been, in the psychological phrase of our day, of extrovert nature. He created an original introvert form true to his own character, thus introducing the recent romantic preoccupation with individual feeling and imagination into the traditional type." But at the same time, Hawthorne always remained the "detached observer" of which Erskine[21] speaks in his biographical study. His oversensibility and his scepticism alike prevented him from giving way to any kind of self-reflection. He consciously sought to avoid any form of it, as he expressly declares in the introduction to **Mosses from an Old Manse**: "Has the reader gone wandering hand in hand with me, through the inner passages of my being, and have we groped together into all its chambers and examined their treasures or their rubbish? Not so. We have been standing in the greensward, but just within the cavern's mouth, where the common sunshine is free to penetrate and where every footstep is therefore free to come. I have appealed to no sentiment or sensibilities, save such as are diffused among us all. So far as I am a man of really individual attributes, I veil my face; nor am I nor have I ever been, one of those supremely hospitable people, who serve up their

own hearts delicately fried, with brain-sauce, as a tit-bit for their beloved public." Hawthorne is no psychologist in the proper meaning of the word. Hardly any of his figures possesses a life of its own. They are all embodiments of ideas that have been made to borrow features from his Puritan forefathers, from honest citizens of Salem or Concord, from the intellectuals of Brook Farm or from artists and tourists he had chanced to meet in his work or during his travels. Not one of them finds his own path, being driven by that inner necessity which may compel a figure of fiction to develop in a way contrary to the original intentions of its creator. They all move more or less like puppets in skilfully constructed tracks which go to prove the author's ethical theories. Of this art, Hawthorne attained an ever-growing mastery.

Notes

1. *The Times Literary Supplement,* May 3rd, 1928.

2. *Hawthorne's First Diary.* With an Account of its Discovery and Loss, by Samuel T. Pickard. London 1897.

3. Randall Stewart, *The American Note-books.* New York 1932.—The author classifies Hawthorne's villains into three types, of which one, the type of Chillingworth, "old men stooped and gray," traces his ancestry to Spenser's Archimago (*Faerie Queene* I. 1.29. 1-7). He also refers to Milton's *Paradise Lost* IV, 127-130.

4. A. Turner, *Hawthorne's Literary Borrowings. Publications of the Modern Language Association of America,* 1936.

5. Cp. pages 35, 36, 37 of the present essay.

6. Cited from J. Hawthorne, *Nathaniel Hawthorne and his Wife.*

7. Cited from Randall Stewart, *Hawthorne's American Note-books.*

8. *Hawthorne's English Note-book,* July 30th, 1857.

9. E. D. Forgues, *Nathaniel Hawthorne. La revue des deux mondes.* 15.4. 1852.

10. Cited from Bertha Faust, *Hawthorne's Contemporaneous Reputation.* Philadelphia, 1939.

11. *Anglia,* 1900.

12. *Anglia,* 1886.

13. Quinn, *Some Phases of the Supernatural in American Literature. Modern Language Association of America,* XVIII, Baltimore, 1910.

14. Woodberry, *Hawthorne, How to Know Him.*

15. *Hawthorne's English Note-book.* December 20th, 1857.

16. Cp. p. 14.

17. Cited from Cross, *The Development of the English Novel.* London, 1905.

18. The title of a story included in *Mosses from an Old Manse.*

19. Henry James Jr, *Hawthorne*. London, 1902.

20. Paul Kaufman, *The Romantic Movement*. In the *Reinterpretation of American Literature*.

21. In the *Cambridge History of American Literature*.

TITLE COMMENTARY

The Marble Faun

MARJORIE ELDER (ESSAY DATE 1972)

SOURCE: Elder, Marjorie. "Hawthorne's *The Marble Faun*: A Gothic Structure." *Costerus*, no. 1 (1972): 81-8.

In the following essay, Elder studies Hawthorne's Gothic narrative structure in The Marble Faun.

Hawthorne has frequently been referred to as, to some extent and in some ways, a "Gothic" novelist. Whether mentioned in general revaluation of the Gothic,[1] looked at within the tradition of the Gothic Romance for his use of devices like castles, ghosts, crime and blood, or works of art with signs of life,[2] or cited for his appreciation of Gothic architecture,[3] Hawthorne is variously labeled "Gothic." It is the purpose of this study to interrelate Hawthorne's use of what may be called Gothic structure in a work of art with his use of specific Gothic devices and techniques in **The Marble Faun.**

It is, in part, the uniqueness in the Hawthorne canon of his last finished romance that prompts the critic to try to account for the different "art of style of narrative"[4] characterizing this work. One of the most obvious differences is in the extent and kind of mystery and its effect on the reader. No other Hawthorne work has a "Postscript" to deal with "the mysteries of the story."[5] Since mystery characterizes the Gothic novel, and reader involvement within a particular atmosphere is of central significance in both Gothic and romantic writings, it may be asked whether it is the Gothic element that accounts in some ways for the uniqueness of this work.

In his *French and Italian Notebooks,* where he entered the idea for and extensive details used in **The Marble Faun,** Hawthorne admires a Gothic structure for its delightful intricacies comprehended into one idea: "that solemn whole, mightily combined out of all these minute particulars."[6] Such a view is quite consistent with his aesthetics as expressed in earlier statements and works.[7] But

a new emphasis may well be suggested when he writes: "the *multitudinous richness* . . . the thousand forms of Gothic fancy . . . A *majesty* and a *minuteness,* neither interfering with the other; each assisting the other; this is what I love in Gothic architecture."[8] This implies (1) an increased majesty and (2) a more extensive minuteness which could be artistically combined to produce a Gothic structure of "multitudinous richness" surpassing any of Hawthorne's other work.

The majesty of **The Marble Faun** is evident first in Hawthorne's idea. Hawthorne himself felt that "a high truth" could "add an artistic glory" to a work though "never any truer, and seldom any more evident, at the last page than at the first."[9] While for Hawthorne any work of art was a reflection by the imagination of the artist acting upon life to produce an image of "the truth of the human heart,"[10] his usual method in both stories and romances is to speak what might be called a side of the truth to reflect the whole; whereas in **The Marble Faun,** he begins with the whole truth, noting a symbol for the scope of his thought in the first paragraph of his work: "the Human Soul, with its choice of Innocence or Evil close at hand, in the pretty figure of a child, clasping a dove to her bosom, but assaulted by a snake" (5). Or as he phrases his thought midway in the book: "Every human life, if it ascends to truth or delves down to reality, must undergo a similar change" (262). Hawthorne undertakes, then, to delineate "the mystery of human life," "as Gothic structures do."[11] One can ask of **The Marble Faun** the large questions of life, though for answers he may well get "mysteries."

As Hawthorne shapes his idea in **The Marble Faun,** he introduces symbolically some of the mysteries. Miriam, with her "ambiguity" (Hawthorne's word in the chapter, "Subterranean Reminiscences," 20), is representative of a human life with which most readers can identify. What human life has not its own past of guilt or sorrow, however deeply buried within? Hawthorne emphasizes the mystery of Miriam, centering it in her relation to the spectre of the catacombs, who comes out of "that immenser mystery which envelopes our little life" (26-27). She is shadowed by that "mysterious, dusky, death-scented apparition" (36) through some "sadly mysterious fascination" (93). Where does the guilt, the sorrow, come from? Why is it related to us as it is? Why are we tormented and fascinated, shadowed, perhaps destroyed? The reader may fill in Miriam's ambiguous past with Gothic details brought to mind by the suggestions in the work: perhaps incestuous love? perhaps a bloody crime? Perhaps something even more horrible than the imagination can suggest. The mystery of the spectre's demonic relation to Miriam is the "mystery of human life" with all its horror. Hawthorne's "Postscript" shows that he knew that readers who asked questions about Miriam's past asked questions whose answers are mystery: "the mystery of evil."

While the central mystery in *The Marble Faun* lies in the source and nature of evil, a related mystery is symbolically pictured through another question left mysterious: Where was Hilda when the light went out? Literally, the saintly Hilda is imagined pursued by all the corruptions of Rome, but to Kenyon she is hope and truth personified. Hawthorne's "Postscript" leaves the reader with the question: What happens to hope and truth in times of great evil? Without attempting to answer that unanswerable question, Hawthorne pictured them as somewhere in the midst of all the corruption and believed they could be found again. This is the transcendent majesty of hope, the hope of redemption, that (in the last words of the romance) sees "sunlight on the mountain-tops" (462).

Not only does Hawthorne's idea reach into the unfathomable darkness and toward the infinite heavens, but his development to show every human life has the majesty of four interrelated parallel plots. Each of his four major characters moves through human life toward truth or reality. Donatello finds a soul in the depths and struggles with it toward the light of heaven. Miriam in her relation to Donatello exemplifies a second search. Hilda comes down from her high and isolated tower to know reality through Miriam's crime. Kenyon symbolically seeks truth in seeking Hilda.

The Marble Faun has a majesty not only in idea but also in the keynote of the work: resemblance: the resemblance of an actual young Italian to a marble statue, *The Faun of Praxiteles*. Hawthorne points this up both within the work (22) and by the double title, ***The Marble Faun: or, The Romance of Monte Beni.*** This is the sublimity of a double removal of the artist from his work with a centering at the heart of the creative: resemblance. Hawthorne creates artists who create, and those artists picture the inner selves. Miriam's inner torments, her haunted mind with its grotesqueness and sadness, her thoughts of bloodshed—she recognizes in her sketches as "ugly phantoms that stole out of my mind" (45). Hilda's "Beatrice," a copy of Guido's, which she let sink into her heart, "makes us shiver as at a spectre," with its "mysterious force" (64-65). Beatrice Cenci, whose look is a

mystery of innocence, guilt, and oppressive sorrow indescribable, at first reflects Miriam and, later in the story, Hilda herself. Kenyon models the bust of Donatello and the Cleopatra that Miriam resembles.

Often the Gothic novel used works of art in more or less magical ways as they "came to life," and modern critics may read Gothic actions as revealing an inner grotesqueness. But in *The Marble Faun,* Hawthorne chose to use works of art as better than magical devices by having his artists reveal the inner selves through their created art works.

Since a picture kindles the imagination more than the reality would, the keynote of *The Marble Faun* places the reader in a doubly-removed position which will involve his imagination to a greater degree than would otherwise be possible. If the atmosphere of any good romance or Gothic novel is unique to itself, expecting the reader to adopt a somewhat different set of values, it may at least be said that here Hawthorne not only chooses his usual romantic atmosphere, his "poetic or fairy precinct" (3) but gives the reader more room yet for imagination in reading the mystery. In one instance he indicates that the reader should not depend too heavily on suspense (28), an important factor in Gothic stories of flight and pursuit, but more than once he talks of the importance of the imagination of the reader. He says, "A picture, however admirable the painter's art, and wonderful his power, requires of the spectator a surrender of himself, in due proportion with the miracle which has been wrought . . . There is always the necessity of helping out the painter's art with your own resources of sensibility and imagination" (335).

Hawthorne may be termed Gothic in that he builds on terror and horror, but the building is from the inside out and moves from physical terror to psychological horror. Between Miriam and the model the feeling has at some time in the ambiguous past developed into horror; Miriam's heart trembles with horror and the model finds "an equal horrour" in his own heart as her presence makes a "tremour and horrour" seize her persecutor until he shakes and turns "ashy pale" (95). But Donatello, though capable of terror, is psychologically and spiritually incapable of horror in his early state. When he first sees Miriam's inner self reflected in her self-portrait, her dark mood produces terror for him. But through Miriam's influence and his active response he comes to know horror. First, he witnesses "a spectacle that had its own kind of horrour," when Miriam, fancying herself unseen, "began to gesticulate extravagantly, gnashing her teeth, flinging her arms wildly abroad, stamping with her foot" (157). Then, on the edge of the precipice with Miriam, he seems "to feel that perilous fascination which haunts the brow of precipices, tempting the unwary one to fling himself over, for the very horrour of the thing" (169-70). But the understanding of horror comes with his own personal crime; with "the dead thump" of the murdered model upon the stones beneath the precipice comes to him "an unutterable horrour" (173).

Then Hawthorne shadows both the terror and the horror: after the crime they are afraid of the "terrour and deadly chill" of solitude (174), but a more fearful day comes when Donatello is "horrour-stricken" (188) at Miriam. When Miriam sees a "little stream of blood" oozing "from the dead monk's nostrils" (189), it is not the obvious "vulgar horrour" (191) that makes her quail; her horror comes from within herself. After viewing the crime, Hilda sees, "nor was it without horrour" (205), that her own face resembles the face of Beatrice. The horror follows the young count to his ancestral home and leaves the observant Kenyon "aghast at the passionate horrour," "wild gestures, and ghastly look" (261). Then Donatello recognizes the "distorted and violent look" which Kenyon accidentally catches in the countenance of Donatello's bust, a look "more horrible" than "the dead skull" his forefathers had handed down to him (272). His horror is in and of himself and is a horror from which only divine hope can save him.

Kenyon studies "the group of the Laocoon, which, in its immortal agony," impressed him "as a type of the long, fierce struggle of Man, involved in the knotted entanglements of Errour and Evil, those two snakes, which (if no Divine help intervene) will be sure to strangle him and his children, in the end . . . Thus, in the Laocoon, the horrour of a moment grew to be the Fate of interminable ages" (391).

The second major component of Hawthorne's "multitudinous richness" of the Gothic is the minuteness. He notes in his preface to **The Marble Faun** that he was surprised in rewriting the novel "to see the extent to which he had introduced descriptions of various Italian objects, antique, pictorial, and statuesque" (3), and any serious reader of Hawthorne senses a proliferation of such details beyond the usual Hawthorne technique. The specific details of atmosphere and setting, of character and plot, in a typical Hawthorne story can usually be shown to be effective in terms of

what Hawthorne called an "iron rod" of truth running through the tale.[12] This view of the use of all details in a work of art is essentially the romantic view which sees "every natural fact" as "symbol of some spiritual fact."[13] Typically, in Hawthorne, this minuteness is evident, and one senses the specificity of meaning suggested by a "transcendental" image of that meaning. However, in **The Marble Faun,** it appears that the minuteness of detail expands beyond this. Whether one argues that Hawthorne included more realistic details because of the highly imaginative nature of the "tissue of absurdities" he wished "to impose . . . upon the public"[14] or because of the larger scope of his thought, the fact remains that while the minuteness of individual detail never interferes with the majesty of single idea, neither can each minute detail be taken as quite so individually meaningful to the central idea. It is as though the reader passes through the ruins and through the galleries with Hawthorne and his artists, catching glimpses of many details among which he chooses some on which to focus his imagination, often helped along by one of the artists or by Hawthorne himself in authorial comment. This proliferation of detail is of itself meaningful in the Gothic structure of **The Marble Faun.** Obviously, somewhere beneath the great idea of "the mystery of human life" there must be room for all details, but as Hawthorne suggests a great many, creating an atmosphere of "multitudinous richness," he chooses to center his attention and the reader's minutely on those details that speak most meaningfully to the imagination. These details are often significantly Gothic.

Hawthorne's Italian setting, a romantic, even a Gothic setting of desolation and decay, provides its ruins, artistic and religious—its catacombs, its old castles and palaces. Of all the castles and palaces Hawthorne chooses several for particular picturing, among them, for a sketch of his total picture, the ancestral home of Monte Beni. It is here where all sorts of mystical suggestions hover over the pedigree of Donatello, and it is Donatello's tower which Hawthorne uses to make a symbolic sketch of the pathway of the soul's struggle toward heaven when he pictures Donatello showing Kenyon the slow movement up the long staircase toward the summit, with the details of each successive room suggesting the inner progress of that soul. Donatello shows Kenyon up the first flight of stairs to a forlorn chamber with brick-paved floor, bare iron-grated holes in the massive walls, and one old stool—the prisoner's cell; up the narrow staircase to another room, with the pair of owls; up the third flight, as the windows and narrow loop-holes give more extensive eyeshots over the hills and valleys, to the topmost chamber with its crucifix, its holy emblems, and its gray alabaster skull; and after one more flight of stairs, out upon the summit whence can be seen all the surrounding area, where the sculptor gets such a view of God's dealings with mankind that he says: "It is a great mistake to try to put our best thoughts into human language. When we ascend into the higher regions of emotion and spiritual enjoyment, they are only expressible by such grand hieroglyphics as these around us" (258).

Of the number of palaces in Rome, perhaps the most Gothic for its suggestion through name alone is the Palazzo Cenci, to which Hilda was to deliver the secret packet from Miriam as Hawthorne lets the very secrecy of the packet represent an inward giving of Miriam's secret that made her look a Beatrice Cenci to Hilda, who came to appear so after she saw Miriam's and Donatello's crime.

Not only are Hawthorne's minutely detailed settings particularly Gothic, but the plot itself is a "succession of sinister events" that "followed one spectral figure" (426) out of the catacombs. That "death-scented apparition" (36) produces the grotesqueness often characteristic of the Gothic novel—an insidious and horror-filled grotesqueness that through Miriam's influence reaches Donatello and Kenyon, each in a different way.

The overt crime and scenes of blood, often a large part of "Gothic horrour" (156), are suggested in *The Marble Faun* through the single murder committed near "one of the especial blood-spots of the earth" (154), overshadowed by the crimes of ages, and effected by the influence of the vile spectre from the surrounding darkness. Then that "individual wrong-doing melts into the great mass of human crime, and makes us—who dreamed only of our own little separate sin—makes us guilty of the whole" (177). There is "an odour of guilt, and a scent of blood," "a stain of ensanguined crime" (97), no doubt flowing from some "fatal gulf," some "mighty subterranean lake of gore, right beneath our feet" (163). In one sense all mankind becomes "cemented with blood" (175).

So Hawthorne creates the "multitudinous richness" of *The Marble Faun,* to speak the majestic mystery of human life, a majesty of horror and hope, with its majestic keynote in resemblance, doubly involving the reader's imagination to see the inner soul revealed outwardly and so to be caught up in a deeper, truer horror and a higher, more eternal hope. Assisting the majesty by the thousand forms of Gothic fancy, Hawthorne enriches the work by unusually extensive minuteness. He selects and elaborates such Gothic devices of setting as the catacombs and the castle tower while he chooses for the protagonist a spectre who prompts the mysterious Miriam to a crime of blood. In its "multitudinous richness," with "a majesty and minuteness, neither interfering with the other, each assisting the other,"[15] *The Marble Faun* is Hawthorne Gothic at its best.

Notes

1. Robert D. Hume, "Gothic Versus Romantic: A Revaluation of the Gothic Novel," PMLA, 84 (1969), 282-90.

2. Jane Lundblad, *Nathaniel Hawthorne and the Tradition of Gothic Romance,* Essays and Studies on American Language and Literature, 4 (Upsala: A.-B Lundequistska Bokhandeln, 1946).

3. Maurice Charney, "Hawthorne and the Gothic Style," NEQ, 34 (1961), 36-49.

4. Hawthorne letter quoted in James T. Fields, *Hawthorne,* Modern Classics (Boston: Houghton, Mifflin and Co., 1879), p. 79.

5. Nathaniel Hawthorne, *The Marble Faun: or, The Romance of Monte Beni,* Centenary Edition (Ohio State Univ. Press, 1968), IV,463. All subsequent page citations in the text are to this edition.

6. Quoted by Charney from Norman Holmes Pearson, ed. (Unpublished Yale doctoral diss., 1941), p. 555.

7. See my study of Hawthorne's art, *Nathaniel Hawthorne: Transcendental Symbolist* (Ohio Univ. Press, 1969), for detailed analysis of Hawthorne's aesthetic theory and practice.

8. *French and Italian Notebooks,* p. 555. Italics mine.

9. "Preface," *The House of the Seven Gables,* Centenary Edition, 1965, II, 2-3.

10. *House of the Seven Gables,* II, 1.

11. Randall Stewart, ed., *The English Notebooks by Nathaniel Hawthorne* (New York: Modern Language Association of America, 1941), p. 413.

12. Letter to Charles A. Putnam, *The Critic,* N. S. 3 (Jan. 17, 1885), p. 30.

13. Ralph Waldo Emerson, *Nature,* Centenary Edition (Boston: Houghton Mifflin and Co., 1903), I, 26.

14. Fields, pp. 78-79.

15. *French and Italian Notebooks,* p. 555.

FURTHER READING

Bibliography

Scharnhorst, Gary. *Nathaniel Hawthorne.* Metuchen, N. J.: Scarecrow Press, 1990, 416 p.

Provides a list of nineteenth-century reviews and book-length studies of Hawthorne.

Biography

Stewart, Randall. *Nathaniel Hawthorne: A Biography.* New Haven, Conn.: Yale University Press, 1948, 279 p.

Full-length biography that contains commentary on Hawthorne's interest in the works of Radcliffe, Godwin, Maturin, and Scott.

Criticism

Allen, M. L. "The Black Veil: Three Versions of a Symbol." *English Studies* 47 (1966): 286-89.

Discusses the significance of the veil in Hawthorne's fiction.

Baym, Nina. "Hawthorne's Gothic Discards: *Fanshawe* and 'Alice Doane.'" *Nathaniel Hawthorne Journal* (1974): 105-15.

Studies Hawthorne's attempts to Americanize the English Gothic tradition.

Berthold, Dennis. "Hawthorne, Ruskin, and the Gothic Revival: Transcendent Gothic in *The Marble Faun.*" *ESQ: A Journal of the American Renaissance* 74 (1974): 15-32.

Delineates the influence of the Gothic on The Marble Faun *and relates this to the novel's theme.*

Calhoun, Thomas O. "Hawthorne's Gothic: An Approach to the Four Last Fragments: 'The Ancestral Footstep,' 'Dr. Grimshawe's Secret,' 'The Dolliver Romance,' 'Septimus Felton.'" *Genre,* no. 3 (1970): 229-41.

Examines the Gothic elements in Hawthorne's unfinished works.

Charney, Maurice. "Hawthorne and the Gothic Style." *The New England Quarterly* 34, no. 1 (March 1961): 36-49.

Discusses Hawthorne's affinity for Gothic art and architecture.

DeLamotte, Eugenia C. "'Deadly Iteration': Hawthorne's Gothic Vision." In *Perils of the Night: A Feminist Study of Nineteenth-Century Gothic,* pp. 93-117. New York: Oxford University Press, 1990.

Analyzes Hawthorne's use of the Gothic narrative pattern of repetition in his works, and in The Marble Faun *in particular.*

Elbert, Monika M. "Bourgeois Sexuality and the Gothic Plot in Wharton and Hawthorne." In *Hawthorne and Women: Engendering and Expanding the Hawthorne Tradition,* edited by John L. Idol Jr. and Melinda M. Ponder, pp. 258-70. Amherst: University of Massachusetts Press, 1999.

Maintains that in Hawthorne's opinion, the judgment of others is itself the profoundest evil.

Graham, Wendy. *Gothic Elements and Religion in Nathaniel Hawthorne's Fiction.* Marburg: Tectum Verlag, 1999, 101 p.

Explores the parallels and differences between English Gothic fiction and its religious critique and the fiction of Hawthorne.

Levin, David. "Shadows of Doubt: Specter Evidence in Hawthorne's 'Young Goodman Brown.'" *American Literature* 34, no. 3 (November 1962): 344-52.

Examines Hawthorne's short story from a seventeenth-century perspective and notes that Goodman Brown succumbs to despair on only spectral evidence of evil.

Lewis, Paul. "Mournful Mysteries: Gothic Speculation in *The Scarlet Letter.*" *American Transcendental Quarterly* 44 (fall 1979): 279-93.

Examines the use and function of mystery, particularly as a challenge to orthodoxy, in The Scarlet Letter.

Lloyd-Smith, Allan. "Hawthorne's Gothic Tales." In *Critical Essays on Hawthorne's Short Stories,* edited by Albert J. Von Frank, pp. 232-43. Boston, Mass.: G. K. Hall, 1991.

Overview of Hawthorne's gothicism.

Ringe, Donald A. "Nathaniel Hawthorne." In *American Gothic: Imagination and Reason in Nineteenth-Century Fiction,* pp. 152-76. Lexington: University Press of Kentucky, 1982.

Discusses the Gothic influences on Hawthorne's work and analyzes the Gothic elements and devices in various novels and stories.

Voller, Jack G. "Allegory and Fantasy: The Short Fiction of Hawthorne and Poe." In *The Supernatural Sublime: The Metaphysics of Terror in Anglo-American Romanticism,* pp. 209-39. DeKalb: Northern Illinois University Press, 1994.

Discusses the use of symbolism and allegory in Hawthorne's fantastic tales.

OTHER SOURCES FROM GALE:

Additional coverage of Hawthorne's life and career is contained in the following sources published by Thomson Gale: *American Writers; American Writers: The Classics,* Vol. 1; *American Writers Retrospective Supplement,* Vol. 1; *Authors and Artists for Young Adults,* Vol. 18; *Beacham's Encyclopedia of Popular Fiction: Biography and Resources,* Vol. 2; *Beacham's Guide to Literature for Young Adults,* Vol. 3; *Children's Literature Review,* Vol. 103; *Concise Dictionary of American Literary Biography, 1640-1865; Dictionary of Literary Biography,* Vols. 1, 74, 183, 223, 269; *DISCovering Authors; DISCovering Authors: British; DISCovering Authors: Canadian; DISCovering Authors Modules: Most-studied Authors* and *Novelists; DISCovering Authors 3.0; Exploring Novels; Exploring Short Stories; Literature and Its Times,* Vol. 1; *Literature Resource Center; Nineteenth-Century Literature Criticism,* Vols. 2, 10, 17, 23, 39, 79, 95, 158; *Novels for Students,* Vols. 1, 20; *Reference Guide to American Literature,* Ed. 4; *Reference Guide to Short Fiction,* Ed. 2; *St. James Guide to Horror, Ghost & Gothic Writers; Short Stories for Students,* Vols. 1, 7, 11, 15; *Short Story Criticism,* Vols. 3, 29, 39; *Supernatural Fiction Writers,* Vol. 1; *Twayne's United States Authors; World Literature Criticism; Writers for Children;* and *Yesterday's Authors of Books for Children,* Vol. 2.

E. T. A. HOFFMANN

(1776 - 1822)

(Born Ernst Theodor Wilhelm Hoffmann, changed third name to Amadeus) German short story writer, novella writer, novelist, and music critic.

Composer, musician, and artist E. T. A. Hoffmann is best known as a writer of bizarre and fantastic fiction. Drawing from English Gothic romance, eighteenth-century Italian comedy, the psychology of the abnormal, and the occult, he created a world in which everyday life is infused with the supernatural. Hoffmann's tales were influential in the nineteenth century throughout Europe and America. Edgar Allan Poe, Charles Baudelaire, Fyodor Dostoevsky, Heinrich Heine, and George Meredith are among the authors who derived plots, characters, and motifs from Hoffmann.

BIOGRAPHICAL INFORMATION

The child of estranged parents, Hoffmann lived with his uncle, a pragmatic civil servant who did not encourage his nephew's prodigious talents. Hoffmann studied law and accepted a government appointment, but cared for music above all and devoted himself to composing theatrical scores, opera, and ecclesiastical pieces. A public official by day and a composer of romantic music by night, Hoffmann experienced the conflict that became a recurring theme in his fiction: the opposition between artistic endeavors and mundane concerns and the struggle of the artist to create in an unsympathetic, philistine society. In 1806 Hoffmann lost his bureaucratic post and joined the Bamberg theater as musical conductor and stage director. His theatrical experience provided Hoffmann with an understanding of character, dialogue, and dramatic structure that enriched his fiction. Also significant was Hoffmann's passionate attachment to Julia Marc, a gifted voice student whom he idealized in his writings as a representation of music incarnate. In Hoffmann's life, however, as in his fiction, the ideal is inviolable, and his love for Julia remained platonic.

MAJOR WORKS

Hoffmann's first published works were reviews of the works of composers such as Ludwig von Beethoven, Johann Sebastian Bach, Christoph Willibald Gluck, and Wolfgang Amadeus Mozart, the last of whom Hoffmann honored by changing his own third name from Wilhelm to Amadeus. Believing that music was the supreme mode of expression, Hoffmann tried to replicate in his fiction what he viewed as music's superior traits, such as its immediacy, emotional power, and supernatural qualities. Hoffmann hoped to transport readers beyond the physical realm by thrusting them into an environment palpably real, yet strangely unfamiliar. Hoffmann's stories range from fairy tales to traditional narratives, but his most characteristic works feature *doppelgängers,* automata, and mad artists and each has a dark, hallucinatory tone. His most famous story is "Der Sandmann" (1817; "The Sandman"). The tale begins in epistolary form and centers on a young man, Nathanael, who believes a salesman he encounters is a gruesome childhood fairy tale character come to life. As with many of Hoffmann's stories, the line between fantasy and reality is blurred. Nathanael links the Sandman to an associate of his late father's, by whom he was once attacked. The eerie similarities between the Sandman, the father's friend and the salesman inspired Sigmund Freud's celebrated essay "The Uncanny," in which Freud uses Hoffman's story to illustrate his ideas, which eventually led to his theory of the Oedipal castration complex.

Hoffmann himself considered "Der goldene Topf" (1814; "The Golden Pot"), in which the supernatural enters a poet's everyday life, as his best piece of writing. Additional stories in the Gothic tradition include "Die Automate" (1814; "Automata") a two-part tale containing a ghost story and a mystery centering on an automaton or robot, and "Die Abenteuer der Silvester-Nacht" (1814; "A New Year's Eve Adventure") in which two characters in two different settings represent polarities of the same personality. In both stories, Hoffmann underscores his belief that real-life activities can open doors to the supernatural. In "The Golden Pot" the impetus is creative expression while in "A New Year's Eve Adventure" it is alcohol. One of Hoffmann's recurring themes was the descent of the artist into a madness caused by being forced to live in a mundane world. While "The Golden Pot" centers on a poet, "Rat Krespel" (1819; "The Cremona Violin," also translated as "Councillor Krespel") portrays a musician's fall into what E. F. Bleiler describes as "sane insanity," a result of his hypersensitivity to daily occurrences. "Die Bergwerke zu Falun" (1819; "The Mines of Falun") was inspired by the real-life discovery of a preserved body in archaic clothing in a Swedish mining tunnel. Hoffman's miner became a supernatural being with intimate knowledge of nature and creation. Hoffmann also produced one Gothic novel, *Die Elixiere des Teufels* (1815-16; *The Devil's Elixir*), a *doppelgänger* tale in which two characters' identities are so intermeshed that neither can tell where one begins and the other ends.

CRITICAL RECEPTION

Hoffmann's potent language and images sometimes shocked and offended his contemporaries. Sir Walter Scott wrote that Hoffmann required "the assistance of medicine rather than of criticism," and an anonymous reviewer in *The Literary World* insisted his plots and characters stemmed from "a diseased imagination." Many critics, however, still appreciate the grotesque humor, social satire, and extravagant artistry beneath the horrific surface. Commentators have noted Hoffmann's adept placement of the supernatural against the backdrop of the everyday. An anonymous writer for *Blackwood's Edinburgh Magazine* in 1824 called Hoffmann "a man of rare and singular genius" and noted his ability to "mix up the horrible notion of the double-goer, with ordinary human feelings of all kinds." Hoffmann is credited with influencing the work of numerous literary descendants, from Poe and the symbolists to the surrealists and modernists.

PRINCIPAL WORKS

Fantasiestücke in Callot's Manier: Blätter aus dem Tagebuche eines reisenden Enthusiasten. 4 vols. [published anonymously] (short stories) 1814-15

Die Elixiere des Teufels. 2 vols. [published anonymously; *The Devil's Elixir*] (novel) 1815-16

†*Nachtstücke, herausgegeben von dem Verfasser der Fantasiestücke in Callots Manier.* 2 vols. [published anonymously] (short stories) 1817

Klein Zaches genannt Zinnober: Ein Mährchen herausgegeben von E. T. A. Hoffmann [*Little Zack*] (novella) 1819

Seltsame Leiden eines Theater-Direktors: Aus mündlicher Tradition mitgeteilt vom Verfasser der Fantasiestücke in Callots Manier [published anonymously] (novella) 1819

‡*Die Serapions-Brüder: Gesammelte Erzälungen und Mährchen. Herausgegeben von E. T. A. Hoffmann.* 4 vols. [*The Serapion Brethren*] (short stories) 1819-21

Lebens-Ansichten des Katers Murr nebst fragmentarischer Biographie des Kapellmeisters Johannes Kreisler in zufälligen Makulaturblättern (unfinished novel) 1820-22

Prinzessin Brambilla: Ein Capriccio nach Jacob Callot [*Princess Brambilla*] (novella) 1821

Meister Floh: Ein Märchen in seiben Abenteuern zweier Freunde [*Master Flea*] (novella) 1822

Die letzten Erzählungen von E. T. A. Hoffmann. 2 vols. (short stories) 1825

Hoffmann's Strange Stories (short stories) 1855

Hoffmann's Fairy Tales (short stories and novellas) 1857

Weird Tales. [translated by J. T. Bealby] 2 vols. (short stories) 1885

Tales of Hoffmann [edited and translated by Christopher Lazare] (short stories) 1946

Selected Writings of E. T. A. Hoffmann. 2 vols. [translated by Leonard J. Kent and Elizabeth C. Knight] (short stories, novellas, and novel) 1969

---

* Volume 3 contains the short story "Der goldene Topf: Ein Märchen aus der neuen Zeit" ("The Golden Pot" or "The Golden Flower Pot"), and Volume 4 contains the short story "Die Abenteuer der Silvester-Nacht" ("A New Year's Eve Adventure").

† Volume 1 contains the short story "Der Sandmann" ("The Sandman").

‡ Volume 1 contains the short stories "Rat Krespel" ("The Cremona Violin" or "Councillor Krespel") and "Die Bergwerke zu Falun" ("The Mines of Falun"), and Volume 2 contains "Die Automate" ("Automata").

PRIMARY SOURCES

E. T. A. HOFFMANN (STORY DATE 1817)

SOURCE: Hoffmann, E. T. A. "The Sand-Man." In *The Best Tales of Hoffmann*, edited by E. F. Bleiler, pp. 184-214. New York: Dover, 1967.

The following excerpt was originally published in German as "Der Sandmann," in the first volume of Nachtstücke, herausgegeben von dem Verfasser der Fantasiestücke in Callots Manier *in 1817.*

Nathanael rushed in, impelled by some nameless dread. The Professor was grasping a female figure by the shoulders, the Italian Coppola held her by the feet; and they were pulling and dragging each other backwards and forwards, fighting furiously to get possession of her.

Nathanael recoiled with horror on recognizing that the figure was Olimpia. Boiling with rage, he was about to tear his beloved from the grasp of the madmen, when Coppola by an extraordinary exertion of strength twisted the figure out of the Professor's hands and gave him such a terrible blow with her, that Spalanzani reeled backwards and fell over the table among the phials and retorts, the bottles and glass cylinders, which covered it: all these things were smashed into a thousand pieces. But Coppola threw the figure across his shoulder, and, laughing shrilly and horribly, ran hastily down the stairs, the figure's ugly feet hanging down and banging and rattling like wood against the steps.

Nathanael was stupefied—he had seen only too distinctly that in Olimpia's pallid waxed face there were no eyes, merely black holes in their stead; she was an inanimate puppet. Spalanzani was rolling on the floor; the pieces of glass had cut his head and breast and arm; the blood was escaping from him in streams. But he gathered his strength together by an effort.

"After him—after him! What do you stand staring there for? Coppelius—Coppelius—he's stolen my best automaton—at which I've worked for twenty years—my life work—the clockwork—speech—movement—mine—your eyes—stolen your eyes—damn him—curse him—after him—fetch me back Olimpia—there are the eyes." And now Nathanael saw a pair of bloody eyes lying on the floor staring at him; Spalanzani seized them with his uninjured hand and threw them at him, so that they hit his breast.

Then madness dug her burning talons into Nathanael and swept down into his heart, rending his mind and thoughts to shreds. "Aha! aha! aha! Fire-wheel—fire-wheel! Spin round, fire-wheel! merrily, merrily! Aha! wooden doll! spin round, pretty wooden doll!" and he threw himself upon the Professor, clutching him fast by the throat.

He would certainly have strangled him had not several people, attracted by the noise, rushed in and torn away the madman; and so they saved the Professor, whose wounds were immediately dressed. Siegmund, with all his strength, was not able to subdue the frantic lunatic, who continued to scream in a dreadful way, "Spin round, wooden doll!" and to strike out right and left with his doubled fists. At length the united strength of several succeeded in overpowering him by throwing him on the floor and binding him. His cries passed into a brutish bellow that was awful to hear; and thus raging with the harrowing violence of madness, he was taken away to the madhouse.

Before continuing my narration of what happened further to the unfortunate Nathanael, I will tell you, indulgent reader, in case you take any interest in that skillful mechanician and fabricator of automata, Spalanzani, that he recovered completely from his wounds. He had, however, to leave the university, for Nathanael's fate had created a great sensation; and the opinion was pretty generally expressed that it was an imposture altogether unpardonable to have smuggled a wooden puppet instead of a living person into intelligent tea-circles—for Olimpia had been present at several with success. Lawyers called it a cunning piece of knavery, and all the harder to punish since it was directed against the public; and it had been so craftily contrived that it had escaped unobserved by all except a few preternaturally acute students, although everybody was very wise now and remembered to have thought of several facts which occurred to them as suspicious. But these latter could not succeed in making out any sort of a consistent tale. For was it, for instance, a thing likely to occur to anyone as suspicious that, according to the declaration of an elegant beau of these tea-parties, Olimpia had, contrary to all good manners, sneezed oftener than she had yawned? The former must have been, in the opinion of this elegant gentleman, the winding up of the concealed clockwork; it had always been accompanied by an observable creaking, and so on.

The Professor of Poetry and Eloquence took a pinch of snuff, and, slapping the lid to and clearing his throat, said solemnly, "My most honourable ladies and gentlemen, don't you see then where the rub is? The whole thing is an allegory, a continuous metaphor. You understand me? *Sapienti sat.*"

But several most honourable gentlemen did not rest satisfied with this explanation; the history of this automaton had sunk deeply into their souls, and an absurd mistrust of human figures began to prevail. Several lovers, in order to be fully convinced that they were not paying court to a wooden puppet, required that their mistress should sing and dance a little out of time, should embroider or knit or play with her little pug, & c., when being read to, but above all things else that she should do something more than merely listen—that she should frequently speak in such a way as to really show that her words presupposed as a condition some thinking and feeling. The bonds of love were in many cases drawn closer in consequence, and so of course became more engaging; in other instances they gradually relaxed and fell away. "I cannot really be made responsible for it," was the remark of more than one young gallant.

At the tea-gatherings everybody, in order to ward off suspicion, yawned to an incredible extent and never sneezed. Spalanzani was obliged, as has been said, to leave the place in order to escape a criminal charge of having fraudulently imposed an automaton upon human society. Coppola, too, had also disappeared.

When Nathanael awoke he felt as if he had been oppressed by a terrible nightmare; he opened his eyes and experienced an indescribable sensation of mental comfort, while a soft and most beautiful sensation of warmth pervaded his body. He lay on his own bed in his own room at home; Clara was bending over him, and at a little distance stood his mother and Lothair. "At last, at last, O my darling Nathanael; now we have you again; now you are cured of your grievous illness, now you are mine again." And Clara's words came from the depths of her heart; and she clasped him in her arms. The bright scalding tears streamed from his eyes, he was so overcome with mingled feelings of sorrow and delight; and he gasped forth, "My Clara, my Clara!"

Siegmund, who had staunchly stood by his friend in his hour of need, now came into the room. Nathanael gave him his hand—"My faithful brother, you have not deserted me." Every trace of insanity had left him, and in the tender hands of his mother and his beloved, and his friends, he quickly recovered his strength again. Good fortune had in the meantime visited the house; a niggardly old uncle, from whom they had never expected to get anything, had died, and left Nathanael's mother not only a considerable fortune, but also a small estate, pleasantly situated not far from the town. There they resolved to go and live, Nathanael and his mother, and Clara, to whom he was now to be married, and Lothair. Nathanael had become gentler and more childlike than he had ever been before, and now began really to understand Clara's supremely pure and noble character. None of them ever reminded him, even in the remotest degree, of the past. But when Siegmund took leave of him, Nathanael said, "By heaven, brother! I was in a bad way, but an angel came just at the right moment and led me back upon the path of light. Yes, it was Clara." Siegmund would not let him speak further, fearing lest the painful recollections of the past might arise too vividly and too intensely in his mind.

The time came for the four happy people to move to their little property. At noon they were going through the streets. After making several purchases they found that the lofty tower of the town hall was throwing its giant shadows across the market place. "Come," said Clara, "let us go up to the top once more and have a look at the distant hills." No sooner said than done. Both of them, Nathanael and Clara, went up the tower; their mother, however, went on with the servant-girl to her new home, and Lothair, not feeling inclined to climb up all the many steps, waited below. There the two lovers stood arm in arm on the topmost gallery of the tower, and gazed out into the sweet-scented wooded landscape, beyond which the blue hills rose up like a giant's city.

"Oh! do look at that strange little gray bush, it looks as if it were actually walking towards us," said Clara. Mechanically he put his hand into his side pocket; he found Coppola's perspective and looked for the bush; Clara stood in front of the glass.

Then a convulsive thrill shot through his pulse and veins; pale as a corpse, he fixed his staring eyes upon her; but soon they began to roll, and a fiery current flashed and sparkled in them, and he yelled fearfully, like a hunted animal. Leaping up high in the air and laughing horribly at the same time, he began to shout in a piercing voice, "Spin round, wooden doll! Spin round, wooden doll!" With the strength of a giant he laid hold upon Clara and tried to hurl her over, but in an agony of despair she clutched fast hold of the railing that went round the gallery.

Lothair heard the madman raging and Clara's scream of terror: a fearful presentiment flashed across his mind. He ran up the steps; the door of the second flight was locked. Clara's scream for help rang out more loudly. Mad with rage and fear, he threw himself against the door, which at length gave way. Clara's cries were growing fainter and fainter—"Help! save me! save me!" and her voice died away in the air. "She is killed—murdered by that madman," shouted Lothair. The door to the gallery was also locked.

Despair gave him the strength of a giant; he burst the door off its hinges. Good God! there was Clara in the grasp of the madman Nathanael, hanging over the gallery in the air, holding on to the iron bar with only one hand. Quick as lightning, Lothair seized his sister and pulled her back, at the same time dealing the madman a blow in the face with his doubled fist, which sent him reeling backwards, forcing him to let go his victim.

Lothair ran down with his insensible sister in his arms. She was saved. But Nathanael ran round and round the gallery, leaping up in the air and shouting, "Spin round, fire-wheel! Spin round, fire-wheel!" The people heard the wild shouting, and a crowd began to gather. In the midst of them towered the lawyer Coppelius, like a giant; he had only just arrived in the town, and had gone straight to the market place.

Some were for going up to overpower and take the madman, but Coppelius laughed and said, "Ha! ha! wait a bit; he'll come down of his own accord;" and he stood gazing up along with the rest.

All at once Nathanael stopped as if spellbound; he bent down over the railing and perceived Coppelius. With a piercing scream, "Eh! Fine eyes-a, fine eyes-a!" he leaped over the railing.

When Nathanael lay on the stone pavement with a shattered head, Coppelius had disappeared in the crush and confusion.

Several years afterwards it was reported that, outside the door of a pretty country house in a remote district, Clara had been seen sitting hand in hand with a pleasant gentleman, while two bright boys were playing at her feet. From this it may be concluded that she eventually found that quiet domestic happiness which her cheerful, blithesome character required, and which Nathanael, with his tempest-tossed soul, could never have been able to give her.

GENERAL COMMENTARY

BLACKWOOD'S EDINBURGH MAGAZINE (REVIEW DATE JULY 1824)

SOURCE: A review of *The Devil's Elixir*, by E. T. A. Hoffmann. *Blackwood's Edinburgh Magazine* 16, no. 90 (July 1824): 55-67.

In the following excerpt, the critic provides a laudatory assessment of The Devil's Elixir, *noting especially Hoffmann's skillful handling of the device of the* doppelgänger, *or double.*

The Devil's Elixir is, we think, upon the whole, our chief favourite among the numerous works of [E. T. A. Hoffman,] a man of rare and singular genius. It contains in itself the germ of many of his other performances; and one particular idea, in which, more than any other, he, as a romancer, delighted, has been repeated by him in many various shapes, but never with half the power and effect in which it has been elaborated here. . . .

[This idea is] what he calls, in his own language, a *doppelgänger*. . . . [In some works using

ABOUT THE AUTHOR

SIR WALTER SCOTT ON HOFFMANN'S TALENT AND MENTAL STATE

The author who led the way in [the Fantastic style] of literature was Ernest Theodore William Hoffmann; the peculiarity of whose genius, temper, and habits, fitted him to distinguish himself where imagination was to be strained to the pitch of oddity and bizarrerie. He appears to have been a man of rare talent,—a poet, an artist, and a musician, but unhappily of a hypochondriac and whimsical disposition, which carried him to extremes in all his undertakings; so his music became capricious,—his drawings caricatures,—and his tales, as he himself termed them, fantastic extravagances. . . .

It is no wonder that to a mind so vividly accessible to the influence of the imagination, so little under the dominion of sober reason, such a numerous train of ideas should occur in which fancy had a large share and reason none at all. In fact, the grotesque in his compositions partly resembles the arabesque in painting, in which is introduced the most strange and complicated monsters, resembling centaurs, griffins, sphinxes, chimeras, rocs, and all other creatures of romantic imagination, dazzling the beholder as it were by the unbounded fertility of the author's imagination, and sating it by the rich contrast of all the varieties of shape and colouring, while there is in reality nothing to satisfy the understanding or inform the judgment. Hoffmann spent his life, which could not be a happy one, in weaving webs of this wild and imaginative character, for which after all he obtained much less credit with the public, than his talents must have gained if exercised under the restraint of a better taste or a more solid judgment. . . .

[T]he inspirations of Hoffmann so often resemble the ideas produced by the immoderate use of opium, that we cannot help considering his case as one requiring the assistance of medicine rather than of criticism.

SOURCE: Scott, Sir Walter. "On the Supernatural in Fictitious Composition." *The Foreign Quarterly Review* 1, no. 1 (July 1827): 61-98.

the *doppelgänger,*] the idea is turned to a half-ludicrous use—and very successfully too—but by far the best are those romances in which it has been handled quite seriously—and of all these, the best is [*The Devil's Elixir*]. . . .

The superior excellence of the *Devil's Elixir* lies in the skill with which its author has contrived to mix up the horrible notion of the double-goer, with ordinary human feelings of all kinds. He has linked it with scenes of great and simple pathos—with delineations of the human mind under the influences of not one, but many of its passions—ambition—love—revenge—remorse. He has even dared to mix scenes and characters exquisitely ludicrous with those in which his haunted hero appears and acts; and all this he has been able to do without in the smallest degree weakening the horrors which are throughout his *corps de reserve.* On the contrary, we attribute the unrivalled effect which this work, as a whole, produces on the imagination, to nothing so much as the admirable art with which the author has married dreams to realities, the air of truth which his wildest fantasies draw from the neighbourhood of things which we all feel to be simply and intensely human and true. Banquo's ghost is tenfold horrible, because it appears at a regal banquet—and the horrors of the Monk Medardus affect our sympathies in a similar ratio, because this victim of everything that is fearful in the caprices of an insane imagination, is depicted to us as living and moving among men, women, and scenes, in all of which we cannot help recognizing a certain aspect of life and nature, and occasionally even of homeliness.

LITERARY WORLD (REVIEW DATE 4 APRIL 1885)

SOURCE: "Hoffmann's Weird Tales." *Literary World* 16, no. 7 (4 April 1885): 111-12.

In the following excerpt from a review of Serapions-brüder (The Serapion Brethren), *the critic maintains that Hoffmann's collection is without literary merit and is worthwhile only as an object of morbid curiosity.*

Hoffmann is one of the idols of literature whose powers are spoken of with traditional reverence, but whose works few take the trouble to read. How much we heard in our younger days of the fearful joys to be snatched from the pages of this uncanny romancer, and how little did the result appear in the full measure of breathless expectation! And now, after an interlude of Trollope, and Daudet, and Howells, we find it more difficult than ever to awaken a sympathetic thrill over the antiquated psychological horrors of the

Serapionsbrüder [*The Serapion Brethren*]. Clever the tales undoubtedly are, but their fantastic episodes and characters are the fruit of a diseased imagination, rather than of poetical genius. Hoffmann's mental traits were akin to those of Poe (the comparison is general) but the German lacked Poe's marvelous faculty of concentration. His representations of character, as such, have no value, for they are devoid of coherency, they are marionettes, and are wholly at the mercy of the grotesque whims of their creator.

Where, then, lies the secret of Hoffmann's fascination? It is in the consummate art with which he conveys passing impressions, and the unflagging fertility of invention which is constantly bringing forth new and startling episodes.

> Master Martin, as was his wont, threw his head back into his neck, played with his fingers upon his capacious belly, and, opening his eyes wide and thrusting forward his under-lip with an air of superior astuteness, let his eyes sweep round the assembly.

Later on, you may get a wholly different portrait, but here, for the time being, is Master Martin, as if reflected from the author's mind into a mirror. This wonderful gift of expression lends a seemingly vivid realism to the most improbable of Hoffman's productions. . . . And yet, a careful perusal of Hoffmann's tales brings no feeling of gratification. The mind is perturbed with all this fantastic imagery; the satire is acrid and leaves unpleasant traces; the passion is too much like brute instinct; the magic wand of the enchanter is thrust too often or our notice; the grim, unyielding doctrine of fatalism, which the author takes occasion to profess so often, stimulates an instinct of revolt. Hoffmann's tales are to be read, if read at all, as one would take hasheesh or opium—to note the effects upon the mind and cull therefrom an interesting experience. Of no other series of romances can it be said so absolutely that the effects vary with the temperament of the reader. Only an abnormal intellect could find in them genuine and habitual enjoyment.

E. F. BLEILER (ESSAY DATE 1967)

SOURCE: Bleiler, E. F. Introduction to *The Best Tales of Hoffmann*, pp. v-xxxiii. New York: Dover, 1967.

In the following excerpt, Bleiler surveys some of Hoffmann's works of short fiction.

III

Most critics agree that "**The Golden Flower Pot**" ("**Der goldne Topf**") is Hoffmann's best story. Hoffmann himself considered it such, and while working on it, he wrote, "God grant me to finish the story as I have begun it. I have never done anything better; everything else is still and lifeless compared to it." Nowhere else has Hoffmann been so successful in blending the real and the fantastic as in this story, in which the powers of the supernatural world run rampant through Dresden.

"**The Golden Flower Pot**" first appeared in 1814 in *Fantasiestücke in Callots Manier*, Hoffmann's first collection of stories, and was revised slightly in 1819 for the second edition of the book. It is his first major literary work, and it marks his unheralded emergence as an author of world stature after he had written only a few critical essays and semifictional musical critiques.

It is a many-leveled story, and as might be expected, a great amount of time has been spent in trying to interpret Hoffmann's intentions. Two opposing general interpretations have been the most favored: (1) that it is an optimistic story about the emergence of a poet, and (2) that it is a basically pessimistic story in which the sad problems of the poet are treated with irony. The proponents of optimism claim that this story mirrors Hoffmann's excitement and joy at his decision to turn to literature instead of to music for his livelihood. According to the pessimists, however, Hoffmann states that a poet must abandon the life of this world, marry a dream girl of his own projection, neglect all worldly advantages—and where shall he go? To Atlantis, the mythical kingdom that does not exist and never did exist. At present the pessimistic interpretation seems the stronger, especially since the text incorporates a letter which Hoffmann first wrote to accompany the story. In this letter he stated his discouragement at the turn that events had taken.

A modern reader, perhaps more than Hoffmann's contemporaries, is likely to find difficulty in isolating and evaluating the various levels of interpretation that lie within "**The Golden Flower Pot**." On the most superficial level, it can be read simply as a fantastic thriller, in which the supernatural emerges and invades the world of everyday life, just as supernaturalism within a pseudohistorical setting did in the Gothic novels that Hoffmann delighted in reading. Some of Hoffmann's minor fiction, indeed, is written on this level, but it is very unlikely that "**The Golden Flower Pot**" is to be taken this way.

Beyond the external events of magic in Dresden and the emergence of the elemental world of the Renaissance Rosicrucians, for example, there lie several themes that appear in much of Hoffmann's other work: that loss of faith or denial of revelation can be destructive; that there is a connection between madness and the suffering world; and that art and life do not mingle, but must be separated.

Individuation, in the modern psychological sense, offers one of the most plausible symbolic interpretations of "The Golden Flower Pot." This amounts to a statement (in fantastic terms) of character growth. It is thus the story of the awakening of poetic sensibility in Anselmus, and of the upheaval which the new developments cause in Anselmus's personality. According to this interpretation the incidents in the story are simply fictionalized metaphors. The old apple woman, Liese, is simply fear, and Anselmus's hesitation before the doorknocker which assumes her shape is simply a metaphoric way of saying that Anselmus became frightened and did not enter. Serpentina would stand for Poesy; the strange experiences in the boat and around the punchbowl are simply ironic ways of stating that all parties had had too much to drink and that alcohol evoked the demonic forces within each. The enclosure of Anselmus in a glass bottle simply describes the paralysis which occurs when faith and hope have been lost. According to this interpretation the entire story of "The Golden Flower Pot" is the projection of Anselmus's mind. His emergent sense of ecstasy colors and transforms everything he beholds, and the daily life of a staid, bourgeois early 19th-century city is seen as a mad scramble of occult powers, half-insane super-humans, strange perils and remarkable benisons as Anselmus becomes a poet.

Yet beyond this there are other possible levels of interpretation. It has been noticed that the characters and ideas of "The Golden Flower Pot" are arranged in two series, each with one pole in the world of reality and another in the world of fantasy. Indeed, there is even a sort of identity between the two forms: Serpentina with Veronica, Anselmus with the Registrator Heerbrand, Archivarius Lindhorst with Conrector Paulmann, and so on. According to this interpretation, Anselmus is simply a projection of the Registrator which disappears in the world of fantasy, while the Registrator, giving up his dreams, marries Veronica. She, in turn, recognizes that she cannot possess the Anselmus complex but must be content with the Registrator-turned-Geheimrat.

Both of these interpretations may seem to be far-fetched interpretation for its own sake, but the fact remains that some justification exists for them or comparable unriddlings. Hoffmann's work is permeated with the concept of personality fragments coming to separate identity and acting as characters. To quote one example which is beyond dispute, in Hoffmann's remarkable novel *The Devil's Elixir* (*Die Elixiere des Teufels*) the identities of two of the characters, the Monk Medardus and the Graf Viktorin, are so merged and interchanged that the characters themselves do not know where one begins and the other ends.

The heart of "The Golden Flower Pot" is the märchen, or literary myth, that the Archivarius begins in the tavern; it is concluded by a strange glossologia from an Oriental manuscript that Anselmus is copying. The archphilistine of the story calls this märchen "Oriental bombast," but as the Archivarius replies, it is not only true but important. It recapitulates the central thought of "The Golden Flower Pot" sub specie aeternitatis, stripped of the accidentals of time, space, and personality.

The central idea of this märchen is the birth of poetry, expressed in terms of cosmic symbols drawn from the Naturphilosophie. It tells of the divine spark (phosphorus was the chemical symbol for the nervous fluid or intelligence in some of the systems of the day) which awakens and fertilizes a vegetative life. This in terms of mounting triads (a concept borrowed from the philosophical systems of the day) must die to give birth to a higher principle.

Lindhorst's märchen is thus a combination of several elements: a pseudobiblical creation statement; an allegory in which details have special meaning, although it is not always clear now what each point means; a fanciful statement of the human situation; and perhaps an ironic spoofing of some of the philosophical systems of the day. Hoffmann, although he was greatly interested in the outgrowths of Schelling's philosophy and accepted much of it, could be expected to retain a pawky incredulity at certain aspects of it. But perhaps analysis should not be pushed too far; it may be enough to say that this is a numinous statement of life, in which both profound and trivial concepts are fused.

German literature at the end of the 18th century frequently made use of märchen, or literary myths. These often appeared as symbolic kernels or germs within the larger context of a story, offering in a frankly poetic and mythical form the point offered more or less realistically in the full story. The märchen was thus a microcosm within a macrocosm.

This form and its use were not Hoffmann's invention. Goethe had written an independent allegorical story called "Das Märchen," which aroused a great deal of criticism among the Romantics, and Wackenroder had incorporated the fairytale of the Naked Saint in his *Her zensergiessungen eines kunstliebenden Klosterbruders*. Novalis, who represents the high point of the Early Romantic School in Germany, had incorporated two such märchen in his unfinished novel *Heinrich von Ofterdingen*. Novalis characterized the märchen as being "like a dream vision . . . beyond logic . . . an assembly of wonderful things and happenings . . . a [pregnant] chaos." This description fits his own work and Hoffmann's when it is remembered that chaos to the Romantics did not mean an empty waste as it usually does for us, but an infinitely rich, undifferentiated, undiversified "plasma," out of which universes could be formed.

All in all, it seems unlikely that there ever will be complete agreement about all the details of **"The Golden Flower Pot."** Perhaps Hoffmann himself was not entirely clear about his intentions. It would lie more within the realm of the Romantic movement to leave things in a tantalizing mist than to strip them of illusion. The symbol should be permitted to unroll and expand as it will. In any case, the modern reader can exercise his own judgment in deciding what really happened to Anselmus.

"Automata" (**"Die Automate"**) first appeared as a whole in the *Zeitung für die elegante Welt* in 1814, although it was written between parts of **"The Golden Flower Pot."** It falls into two parts: the untitled Ghost Story in the foreword, and secondly, the experiences of Ferdinand with an automaton called the Talking Turk. There are also other elements in the story, notably an essay on the mechanical creation of music, new musical instruments and man's relation to music; Hoffmann is said to have included this material so that he could sell the story to a music journal.

The Ghost Story is built on two supernatural motives, one of which has had considerable importance in the history of the supernatural story. This is the motive of the White Lady, in which someone impersonates a ghost and receives supernatural punishment for his rashness. M. G. Lewis based his narrative of the Bleeding Nun in *The Monk* on this idea; it is the subject of one of the *Ingoldsby Legends*; and in more recent times Ambrose Bierce, E. F. Benson, W. W. Jacobs, H. Russell Wakefield and others have made effective use of it. In most instances, however, the story has been developed beyond Hoffmann's narrative, which remains at best sketchy. The second element in the Ghost Story is an attempt to defeat fate by distorting the time sense. It is related to an important literary form of the day, the so-called Fate Novel, the central idea of which was an attempt (usually unsuccessful) to dodge an inevitable fate.

In the second part of **"Automata"** much space is devoted to one of Hoffmann's idées fixes, the automaton or robot. The story reveals Hoffmann's own strong feelings when he describes the horror he feels at the possibility of mistaking an automaton for a human being. (This concept later became even more important in the episode of the dancing doll in **"The Sand-Man."**) For us much of the emotional power of Hoffmann's story may be lost since the late 18th-century and early 19th-century automata are now mostly destroyed or inoperative. We can have no real idea of their remarkable performances nor can we regain their emotional impact, since robots and mechanized intelligence have become part of our daily life. During Hoffmann's lifetime, however, Maelzel's chess player (which was a fraud) aroused a sensation in Europe, while Vaucanson's mechanical duck (a remarkable mechanism that would grace any era) and his speaking head and similar marvels of mechanics were held to be almost miraculous. The historical works of Chapuis and Droz can hint to the modern reader something of the wonder which these figures inspired. In Hoffmann they aroused a multiple reaction: admiration for their skill, horror at their inhumanness, and perhaps fear.

"Automata" remains a mystery story in the narrower acceptance of the form, for no convincing explanation can be given for the mysterious events that befall Ferdinand. Hoffmann's "explanation" of the functioning of the Turk involves clairvoyance, which is awakened through the mechanical medium of the Turk. This strange theory, which Hoffmann does not propound in the clearest way, is not his own, but was advanced by several early 19th-century psychologists to account for paranormal phenomena. It is connected with theories of animal magnetism derived ultimately from F. A. Mesmer on one side and from philosophical mysticism on the other. Even beyond the phenomena of the Talking Turk, however, are Ferdinand's adventures in Poland, which simply cannot be explained rationally.

"A New Year's Eve Adventure" (**"Die Abenteuer der Silvester-Nacht"**) was written late in 1814 and was published in 1816 in Hoffmann's first collection of stories, ***Fantasiestücke in Callots Manier.*** It demonstrates a literary device that is very common in Hoffmann's work: the narration of two or more stories, which at first seem different, but upon closer examination prove to be the same story told on different levels. The two levels usually consist of the level of daily life and the level of fantasy, which are so intermingled that the reader sometimes is not sure of boundaries.

Just as the student Anselmus in **"The Golden Flower Pot"** lives two lives (one in the realm of poetry and the other around the Biedermeier establishment of Conrector Paulmann), the Travelling Enthusiast or Roving Romanticist of **"A New Year's Eve Adventure"** and Erasmus Spikher are polarities of the same personality and situation. One is set in humdrum Berlin, the other in the counter-pole of Italy, which often appears in Hoffmann's work as a synonym for luxury and decadence. Whether Hoffmann was completely successful in telling his story in this way is open to dispute; at worst he tells two repetitive stories, at best his method offers a strange parallelism and fusion of experience. The mundane narrator confines the fantasy of Spikher and is in turn enriched by it.

Personal elements from Hoffmann's life are evident in this story. It was not too long after his unhappy association with Julia Marc in Bamberg that Hoffmann wrote **"A New Year's Eve Adventure,"** and when he read it to his circle of friends in Berlin, as was his custom with new work, they must have recognized the reflection of Hoffmann's personal affairs in the story. Hoffmann pictures Julia in two facets, on the one hand a cold opportunist who did not even have vision enough to recognize the quality of her admirer and on the other hand as a witch of Satan.

Another element of Hoffmann's personal life appears here in the presence of the famous Peter Schlemihl, the character created by his close friend Adelbert von Chamisso. The story of Peter Schlemihl, who sold his shadow to the Devil, was one of the most famous and most popular stories of the day, and Hoffmann obviously admired it greatly. Many of the details of the episode in the Bierkeller acquire new depth if the reader is acquainted with Chamisso's story. Just what Peter Schlemihl lost, however, is no clearer in Hoffmann's story than it was in Chamisso's. For Chamisso, interpretations of Schlemihl's plight have ranged from poverty to statelessness, from loss of virility to the inability to form human associations. What Hoffmann considered the "shadow" is also mysterious; indeed, he evaded the question. Erasmus Spikher's lost reflection, on the other hand, is rather clearly identified with an alter ego, a dream-self, the ability to dream, a personality focus that is associated with dreams and passions. This story would then be another statement about the separateness of art and life.

The mechanisms that evoke the world of fantasy in **"A New Year's Eve Adventure"** are quite different from those in **"The Golden Flower Pot."** While it was the poetic impulse that awakened the ecstatic experience in Anselmus, in the Travelling Enthusiast/Spikher the impulse was alcohol. For Hoffmann there were several such doors to the supramundane world, and the type of door could condition the transcendent experience which was attained. In this theory Hoffmann simply stated in fictional terms what several of the psychologists and natural philosophers of the day said in more or less technical terminology. For such theorists the human autonomous nervous system, to which they assigned a center in the solar plexus, was an organ of experience which far transcended the sense organs of the conscious mind. This nervous system was the seat of a secondary, unconscious personality, which by its very essence was in intimate contact with all Nature. Normally, this Dream Self was silent, submerged by the clatter of the conscious mind, but in sleep, in religious ecstasy, in drug states, and in insanity it sent its energy up to the cortex, where it could be perceived. If this energy were controlled by the higher spiritual faculties of man, the result could be a great aesthetic impulse, or prophecy; if it were uncontrolled, it could be the distorted mumblings of the clairvoyant, or the unhappy visions of the addict. It is the lesser voice which inspires Spikher.

In the fall of 1816 Hoffmann finished **"Nutcracker and the King of Mice"** (**"Nussknacker und Mausekönig"**), which first appeared in a Christmas collection of children's stories entitled *Kindermärchen von C.W. Contessa, Friedrich Baron de la Motte Fouqué und E. T. A. Hoffmann.* The story was based in part on his own life situation: the family among whom the adventure takes place were modelled after the Hitzigs, friends of Hoffmann's Polish and early Berlin days. The two children in the story, Fritz and Marie, represent Hitzig's children. Hoffmann himself served as a prototype for Grandfather Drosselmeier, for he had built a cardboard castle for the Hitzig children the previous year, just as Drosselmeier does in the story. It might be noted that the same combinations of whimsy, aberration, ineffectuality, insight and ecstasy enter the character of Drosselmeier as enter the other masks of Hoffmann.

In **"Nutcracker and the King of Mice"** a märchen or literary fairytale serves as the "unconscious focus" of the story. It indicates the inner relationships in the ideal world that created the present story situation, together with possibilities for future resolution. In this case, however, the märchen is not a literary myth, as in **"The Golden Flower Pot"** or *The Master Flea*. It is basically a children's story, in which medieval Nuremberg receives one of its first glorifications. The concept linking this myth with the relationships Drosselmeier-Hoffmann and Stahlbaum-Hitzig is that a child is closer to the primal innocence (as in Wordsworth's "trailing clouds of glory") than an adult, and can enter and savor realms of experience or beyond-experience that even an adult with insight cannot enter. Dreams can become real only for children.

Hoffmann himself did not regard **"Nutcracker and the King of Mice"** as an entirely successful story, and apparently his friends agreed with this opinion. In the critical parts of *Die Serapionsbrüder* two of Hoffmann's characters, Lothar (a sceptic, modelled in part on Fouqué) and Ottmar (perhaps modelled on Hitzig), discuss the story. They conclude that the mixture of children's elements with elements that only an adult would appreciate is not completely acceptable. Hoffmann would have been better advised, it is stated, to have written either a children's story or a symbolic narrative for adults, not both. In a later story, **"The Stranger Child"** (**"Das fremde Kind"**), which was written for the Christmas annual of the following year, Hoffmann adhered more closely to a children's level. Despite this formal improvement the story itself lacks the vitality of **"Nutcracker and the King of Mice,"** which has long been a favorite, both in itself and in its various musical and dramatic adaptations.

"The Sand-Man" (**"Der Sandmann"**), which appeared in *Nachtstücke*, Volume 1 (1816-1817), is one of Hoffmann's most bewildering stories. His contemporaries were inclined to read many personal references into it, and Hoffmann's friend Fouqué considered himself reflected in the personality of Nathanael.

There are many problems involved in **"The Sand-Man."** The first and greatest, of course, is the meaning of the story. Are Nathanael's adventures to be taken literally or symbolically? Is Hoffmann again using his old device of treating mental projections as personalities? Do the characters in the story exist, or are they fragments of personalities, or are both conditions true?

Psychiatrically oriented readers have considered Nathanael to be mad, and have dismissed the story of Coppelius/Coppola as a projection, as the influence of a traumatic childhood experience on an unstable young man. The story is thus interpreted as a figurative statement of growing mental illness, in other words, the emergence of insanity. Everything that Nathanael sees is distorted by this peculiar defect of his "vision," and his life is a succession of wild misinterpretations.

Other readers, however, have taken the position that Hoffmann intended the story to be primarily a fate drama, in which the central idea is that man is powerless against an external fate that moves in on him. According to this interpretation Nathanael was saved from death once by his father, once by Clara and her brother, but must succumb on the third occasion. Nathanael may go mad at the end, but his previous experiences are objective. Coppelius/Coppola really exists; he is the Enemy.

It would be pointless to select one of these interpretations and reject the other, since Hoffmann offered clues to support both. In all probability he had both interpretations in mind when he wrote the story, and was deliberately creating a mystery. A unifying factor can possibly be found in the saying, "Things are as we see them."

Many strange threads run through this story. One is the motive of the eye. Over and over Hoffmann brings the physical organ and its function (or malfunction) into the story: the eyes that appear during the experiment that Nathanael watches, Coppelius's threat to destroy Nathanael's eyes, the distorted vision of Nathanael when he assigns life to Olimpia, the destruction of the dancing doll's eyes, and the manifestations at the end of the story when Nathanael goes mad. Indeed, even the names Coppola and Clara are important: "coppola" means eye-socket in Italian, while the significance of Clara is obvious. Allied to the motive of eyes is the nature of the "experiments" performed by Coppelius and Nathanael's father. They are usually interpreted as alchemy or perhaps magic, but we cannot be sure of this. To Hoffmann's contemporaries this incident may simply have been a fanciful way of suggesting coining. Certainly the furnaces and cauldrons are all to be connected with casting.

"Rath Krespel" first appeared as an untitled story in the *Frauentaschenbuch für das Jahr 1818*, where it was prefaced by a long letter of dedication to Fouqué. It was revised a little when it was included in *Die Serapionsbrüder*.

One source of the story was Johann Bernhard Crespel (1747-1815), an eccentric German official who was a friend of the Goethe family and is mentioned in a letter from Goethe's mother to the poet. Crespel apparently designed his own clothing to fit his moods, and at one time designed and built a house in the same way as Hoffmann's Rath Krespel. How Hoffmann learned about Crespel is not known, although it has been speculated by H. W. Hewett-Thayer in his excellent *Hoffmann, Author of the Tales* that Hoffmann may have heard of him through Brentano. This, however, is only part of the personality of Krespel. It is generally conceded that an element of Hoffmann's own personality has been added to that of the historical Crespel. Hoffmann's Krespel is not really mad, but is very much like Hoffmann himself. He is really a man without a skin—as, indeed, Hoffmann describes him. Krespel's sensitivity is so great that daily life would be impossible for him if he could not take refuge in semi-madness to abreact his unconscious processes. Ultimately, he is really horribly sane.

Hoffmann's musical life is also reflected in this story, particularly in the clash of the Italian and German musical cultures of the day. Such a clash of musics is often described in Hoffmann's work. **"The Interrupted Cadence"** (**"Die Fermate"**), for example, describes a tempestuous affair between an Italian soprano and a German composer, who discover that there is no real possibility of understanding between them. Hoffmann himself shared such a tension between his admiration for the German tradition of Bach and Mozart on one hand, and his delight in Italian opera. It may be significant to Hoffmann's point of view that in **"Rath Krespel"** the ideal combination of power and beauty, Antonia, cannot survive; she bears within herself germs of destruction.

"Rath Krespel" is one of the most tragic of Hoffmann's stories, since it involves not only death, but the destruction of an art and the misery of sane insanity. Equally sinister is the equation of Antonia and the strange violin, and the life-bond between them. It would be curious to know if the name Antonia had any special significance for Hoffmann, what with Antonio Stradivari.

"Tobias Martin, Master Cooper and His Men" (**"Meister Martin der Küfner und seine Gesellen"**) first appeared in the *Taschenbuch zum geselligen Vergnügen auf das Jahr 1819,* and was reprinted with some alterations in the second volume of **Die Serapionsbrüder** (1819). Like another of Hoffmann's stories, **"Doge und Dogaressa,"** it is essentially a program piece written to explain a painting by a now nearly forgotten Romantic artist, Karl Wilhelm Kolbe. **"Tobias Martin"** was suggested by a very large oil entitled "Die Böttcherwerkstatt," which shows a group of coopers in antique costume working in an open shed. Hoffmann's story creates the background against which this picture situation arose, and also carries the situation through to a resolution. Hoffmann thereby transmuted an academic painting into one of the most entertaining stories in early 19th-century German literature.

The source for Hoffmann's information about medieval Nuremberg and the meistersingers and early guilds was Johann Christoph Wagenseil's *De sacri romani imperii libera civitate Noribergensi Commentatio,* or *Chronicle of Nuremberg,* which later became more famous as the source for Wagner's *Die Meistersinger.* This same book also served as the source for Hoffmann's well-known story about a homicidal maniac motivated by aesthetic impulses, **"Das Fräulein von Scuderi,"** which has been variously translated under the titles **"Mademoiselle de Scuderi," "Cardillac the Jeweller," "Cardillac,"** and so forth.

In **"Tobias Martin, Master Cooper,"** as in most of his historical nouvelles, Hoffmann used a straight-line mode of narration which contrasts greatly with the involved avant-garde development of his fantasies, what with their double narratives, symbolic cores and fragmentations of personality. Yet even here there are unusual features. Another author might have told the story more strongly from the point of view of Friedrich, and might have pushed Meister Martin, the title figure, more into the background. Another artist might have treated Martin's "growth" and his interpretation of the mysterious prophecy a little less ambiguously. At times it almost seems as if the story cannot be permitted to end until all of the major characters have learned that they must be honest with themselves.

"Meister Martin" has long been a favorite, and around the turn of the present century it was usually regarded as Hoffmann's best story. It has since fallen in esteem, while the fantasies have risen. To me it seems unfortunate that Hoffmann confined himself to writing "program fiction" simply to elucidate a mediocre painting. If the story had been independently written, it might be stronger in central situation and less sentimental. Nevertheless, the basic personalities of the story emerge with charm and clarity, and Hoffmann evokes the personality of Nuremberg so attractively that the story has served as the suggestion for much other work, chief of which is Richard Wagner's *Die Meistersinger.*

"The Mines of Falun" ("Die Bergwerke zu Falun") first appeared in 1819 in *Die Serapions-brüder.* In a critical afterword to the story one of Hoffmann's spokesmen tells where the idea came from: an anecdote in G. H. Schubert's *Ansichten von der Nachtseite der Naturwissenschaften,* one of the most influential books of the day. According to Schubert, when miners opened a new tunnel in the great Swedish mine complex at Falun, they found the perfectly preserved body of a man dressed in archaic garments. Hoffmann was one of many writers who seized upon this incident as the kernel for a story, and the basic idea became as important for the early 19th century as the mo-tive of the Frozen Pirate was at the turn of the 19th and 20th centuries.

Hoffmann's story is written against a back-ground that is strikingly romantic in its concepts and associations. Starting with Novalis (Count Friedrich von Hardenberg), prophet of German Romanticism, the miner as such took on a peculiar significance in German literature. He was not considered to be an exploited toiler or a laborer in a particularly dirty and dangerous mode of work. He became a quasisupernatural being who knew the intimate secrets of nature, of creation, and of the fructifying force that was believed to create the minerals. His knowledge passed beyond that of ordinary men, and he had a touch of the divine or demonic about him. Novalis in his *Heinrich von Ofterdingen* says of miners and mining, "Possessors of a much-envied happiness in learning nature's hidden mysteries, and communing in solitude with the rocks, her mighty sons. . . . It is enough for the miner to know the hiding places of the metallic powers and to bring them forth to light; but their brilliance does not raise thoughts of covetousness in his pure heart. Untouched by this dangerous madness, he delights more in their marvellous formations, the strangeness of their origin, and the nooks in which they are hid-den. . . . His business cuts him off from the usual life of man, and prevents his sinking into dull indifference as to the deep supernatural tie which binds man to heaven. He keeps his native simplic-ity, and sees in all around its inherent beauty and marvel. . . . In these obscure depths there grows the deepest faith in his heavenly Father, whose hand guides and preserves him in countless dangers. . . . He must have been a godlike man who first taught the noble craft of mining, and traced in the rocks so striking an image of life." Novelis's comments are not simply a literary

device; there are also elements here of the ancient magic associated with metals and minerals (as Mir-cea Eliade has discussed them in his *Forge and the Crucible*) which persisted strongly up through the Renaissance.

For Hoffmann, the miner owes allegiance to a supernatural power personified as the Metal Queen. The heart of the story is Elis's rejection of the metal revelation. Once again the artist (as in many other stories by Hoffmann) must choose between loss of his supernatural aims and the death of the domestic man. The agent of Elis's death, the demonic Torbern, is really a creature out of Germanic literary folklore. Many of the Numbernip (Rübezahl) stories by Fouqué, for example, discuss folkloristic demons as erratically malevolent beings who are associated with the chthonic powers and serve both to lead and mislead man.

"Signor Formica," or **"Salvator Rosa,"** first appeared in late 1819 in the *Taschenbuch zum ge-selligen Vergnügen auf das Jahr* 1820, and was reprinted with minor changes in the fourth volume of *Die Serapionsbrüder.* It was subtitled a "novella," and probably was written with the work of the Italian Renaissance novelists in mind. One of the critics in *Die Serapionsbrüder,* however, criticized it as resembling Boccaccio more in the beatings its characters received than in much else. Another facet of Hoffmann defended the story mildly by pointing out that both Cervantes and Boccaccio did not hesitate to propel their stories by physical violence.

For **"Signor Formica,"** which in many ways is one of Hoffmann's most interesting stories, Hoff-mann drew upon the life of the great 17th-century Italian painter Salvator Rosa. At the time that Hoffmann wrote, Rosa stood high critically. The early Romantic revival of the late 18th century found him congenial. His well-known *terribilità*; his devastating energy; his highly felt painting technique and subject matter, in which the forces of nature seemed to be the real subjects, with but a few scattered humans as symbolic punctuation; and his general evocation of untamable, dynamic violence—all aroused enthusiasm. Rosa's life was reasonably well known in Hoffmann's day, and Hoffmann made a thorough study of French, Ital-ian, and German sources. To get local color and to create the atmosphere of Italy, Hoffmann read extensively in travel accounts, particularly the reminiscences of Karl Philipp Moritz, an 18th-century German traveller. Hoffmann also collected Italian prints and maps, which he hung on the walls of his rooms, for inspiration, just as his character Peregrinus Tyss in *Meister Floh* does for China. Hoffmann, of course, was saturated in Italian musical life, and for this needed no special sources.

Basically **"Signor Formica"** is accurate—with occasional liberties—although the personality of Antonio Scacciati and the incidents of his courtship are fictitious. Salvator Rosa did leave Naples a few steps ahead of the police because of his share in Masaniello's insurrection; he did act as a member of a commedia dell' arte group in Rome; and he did later found an accademia in Florence. Like Hoffmann himself the historical Rosa was a virtuoso in many media: painting, literature, music, and the stage. Today, however, he is a nearly forgotten member of a branch of Baroque painting.

One of the most curious aspects of **"Signor Formica"** lies in its use of the double or doppelgänger. Originally, the doppelgänger was an element of Germanic folklore. It amounted to seeing one's own ghost, an exact double of oneself: this meeting was usually an omen of death. (In origin this idea would seem to go back to the primitive idea of multiple souls and soul-loss as a cause of death.) Around the end of the 18th century the doppelgänger became an important element in German fiction. The sinister elements were often suppressed and in their place came an intellectual interest in seeing oneself. The most curious incident involving a doppelgänger came from the life of Goethe: the great poet believed that on several occasions he had seen his own doppelgänger.

For Hoffmann the doppelgänger had a special significance. It was not simply a mysterious, supernatural double; instead it was associated with the strange phenomena of the mind, with personality fragments, with multiple personalities (a phenomenon which interested early 19th-century psychologists) and with emergence of an unconscious mind. In story technique this meant that a personality complex could assume spontaneous, autonomous life and become a character itself. From a converse point of view, two persons who were physically nearly identical might fuse, to form a single personality, or to create an impermanent, rotating personality which shifts from pole to pole of identity. This is the case in *The Devil's Elixir* where two persons in a doppelgänger relationship to one another contaminate each other. At times this concept of the doppelgänger (as in Jean Paul's *Doppelgänger* and Goethe's *Wahlverwandschaft*) can become attenuated enough to drop the idea of likeness or identity,

and to indicate inner relationships, like "elective affinities" in the chemistry of the day. This results in a horizontal concept of kinship as opposed to a vertical one. The strongest bonds of relationship are between persons who are similar rather than those of vertical blood descent. Persons in a doppelgänger relationship are *sympathetic* (in the derivational sense of the word) to one another's experiences. A later stage of this idea, familiar to us from Dumas' novel, is the motive of the "Corsican brothers"—identical twins, perhaps separated Siamese twins, who both feel pain if one is injured, no matter how far apart they may be.

In **"Salvator Rosa"** Hoffmann makes use of the doppelgänger motive in a novel way. The idea is now completely secularized and stripped of its supernatural associations, and as stage imposture it serves to resolve the story. The confrontation of a lecherous old miser with his double twice dissolves the frame of difficulties that beset Antonio and Salvator Rosa.

All in all, Hoffmann's story is successful in evoking the atmosphere of baroque Italy, with its violence, egotism, saturation in the pictorial arts, and devotion to music. It is probably not an exaggeration to say that in this respect **"Salvator Rosa"** is the most successful historical novel that had yet appeared in Europe. Where Hoffmann may have lagged somewhat in literary technique (as compared with, say, Goethe), he was ahead in the intuitive apprehension of alien times and places which was so characteristic of the German Romantics from Herder on. As a result, his picture of 17th-century Italy carries conviction. In other respects, however, the novel suffers a little from Gothic survivals. The concept of the hero as one "der nie als Held des Stückes, sondern nur als Vermittler" forces Antonio Scacciati to have a passive role, while Salvator Rosa, the demonic activist, initiates and creates. The point would seem to be that the artist can succeed in his work and his love-life only with the assistance of a daimon. To a modern reader, this peculiar plot device may make the story seem less a true nouvelle than a narrative, but the fact that **"Salvator Rosa"** is written to an unfamiliar aesthetic need not impair our pleasure in reading it.

"The King's Betrothed" ("Die Königsbraut") was written especially for the last volume of *Die Serapionsbrüder* (1821). Each volume of the collection ends with a fantastic story, and **"The King's Betrothed"** concludes Volume IV and the set on a note of fantasy. It is very heavily ironic in tone, and it satirizes several contemporary phenomena: bad poets, particularly the sickly sentimental poets of a school parallel to the English Della Cruscans; ineffectual, ivory-tower mystical philosophers and philosophy; and stories describing erotic relationships between mortals and supernatural beings. Of such stories Fouqué's *Undine* is the most famous.

The subject matter of **"The King's Betrothed"** has been taken from Renaissance and Enlightenment books on occultism and magic, an area in which Hoffmann was well-read. The doctrine of Paracelsus and others in this tradition was that the natural forces were the product of ideal substances, which were personified as supernatural beings, usually called elementals because of their relationship to the Aristotelian elements: salamanders as the spirits or essence of fire; undines for water; sylphs for the air; and gnomes for the earth. Slightly variant classifications may be found in the several sources. Hoffmann found the precise origins of his system and many of the ludicrous historical details about human-elemental relationships in one of the early books associated with the Renaissance Rosicrucian movement, *Le Comte de Gabalis,* an eccentric novel by the Abbé Montfaucon de Villars. Yet beyond this occult background is Hoffmann's probable intention of showing a personality (Aennchen) who has submerged herself in the vegetative life so deeply that it emerges separately and tries to swallow her.

TITLE COMMENTARY

"Der Sandmann" ("The Sandman")

S. S. PRAWER (ESSAY DATE 1965)

SOURCE: Prawer, S. S. "Hoffmann's Uncanny Guest: A Reading of 'Der Sandmann.'" *German Life and Letters* 18 (1965): 297-308.

In the following essay, Prawer analyzes the psychological issues addressed through Hoffmann's use of various narrative patterns in "Der Sandmann" ("The Sandman").

Why should we interest ourselves in such grossly improbable tales as E. T. A. Hoffmann's **"Der Sandmann"**? That is the question raised forcibly—and justly—by Sir Walter Scott, in a critique which Goethe endorsed but which is far too often dismissed, nowadays, as an explosion of jealousy at Hoffmann's success with a foreign as well as a German public. 'It is impossible', Scott maintains in his essay *On the Supernatural in Fictitious Compositions,*

to subject tales of this nature to criticism. They are not the visions of a poetical mind, they have scarcely even the seeming authenticity which the hallucinations of lunacy convey to the patient; they are the feverish dreams of a lightheaded patient, to which, though they may sometimes excite by their peculiarity, or surprise by their oddity, we never seem disposed to yield more than momentary attention. In fact, the inspirations of Hoffmann so often resemble the ideas produced by the immoderate use of opium, that we cannot help considering his case as one requiring the assistance of medicine rather than of criticism.

And Scott breaks off his attempt to retell the plot of **"Der Sandmann"** with the words: 'But we should be mad ourselves were we to trace these ravings any farther.'[1]

What Sir Walter seems to have missed is that the questions he quite properly raised were very much in Hoffmann's own mind, and that his indictment is in fact anticipated in **"Der Sandmann"** itself. Nathanael, the hero of the tale, reads a horrific poem to Clara in order to excite her, 'wiewohl er nicht deutlich dachte, wozu denn Clara entzündet und wozu es denn nun eigentlich führen solle, sie mit grauenvollen Bildern zu ängstigen.' Clara's reactions to this poem are clear enough, and should have won Scott's approval: 'Wirf das tolle—unsinnige—wahnsinnige Märchen ins Feuer.'[2] When Hoffmann's narrator, however, comes to speak of his own motives in setting down Nathanael's history, he suggests another line of approach. No-one, he declares, had asked him for his story:

> Du weisst ja aber wohl, dass ich zu dem wunderlichen Geschlechte der Autoren gehöre, denen, tragen sie etwas so in sich, wie ich es vorhin beschrieben, so zumute wird, als frage jeder, der in ihre Nähe kommt, und nebenher auch wohl noch die ganze Welt: 'Was ist es denn? Erzählen Sie, Liebster!'—So trieb es mich denn gar gewaltig, von Nathanaels verhängnisvollem Leben zu dir zu sprechen.

He then discusses the difficulty he had in giving his tale a suitable literary form (affording Hoffmann an opportunity to indulge in some delightful self-parody) and continues:

> Vielleicht wirst du, o mein Leser! dann glauben, dass nichts wunderlicher und toller sei als das wirkliche Leben und dass dieses der Dichter doch nur wie in eines mattgeschliffnen Spiegels dunklem Widerschein auffassen könne.[3]

That is one possible answer to Scott's objections: a story like **"Der Sandmann"** is *true*, it gives literary shape to insights which cannot be conveyed in any way that is less grotesque, absurd and uncanny. The narrator sees himself as an

Ancient Mariner driven to speak of what he has seen, driven to compel the attention of his auditors through every possible rhetorical device. One remembers that Cyprian, in *Die Serapionsbrüder,* rejects 'Grauen ohne Not, ohne Beziehung' as forcibly as Scott himself.[4]

In the opening paragraph of **"Der Sandmann"** two worlds confront each other; and this confrontation determines the structure of the whole story that is to follow. We need only list the adjectives of this paragraph: 'Hold', 'süss', 'hold' again, 'freundlich', 'hell'—all attributes of Clara who represents (as her very name tells us) a realm of light, clarity and simplicity that stands in dialectical relationship to another realm of which the following adjectives speak: 'zerrissen', 'dunkel', 'grässlich', 'drohend', 'schwarz' and—a little further on—'feindlich', 'tödlich'.[5] These two realms belong together, and it is only because we are given so plain a vision of the first that the second has such power to terrify. This is what Dostoevsky hinted at when he contrasted the 'poetic' fantasy of Hoffmann with the 'materialistic' fantasy of Edgar Allan Poe.

> Hoffmann is immeasurably greater than Poe as a poet. With Hoffmann there is an ideal, not always explicit perhaps, but in this ideal there is purity, real beauty. . . . If there is fantasy in Poe, it is a kind of materialistic fantasy, if one may speak of such a thing. It is obvious that he is wholly American even in his most fantastic tales.[6]

The 'ideal' of which Dostoevsky speaks in this passage is quite different from that presented in **"Der goldne Topf,"** for Clara belongs firmly to the world we all know—she is Veronica raised to the status of a 'holdes Engelsbild';[7] but it is an ideal nevertheless, and it says much for Hoffmann's psychological penetration that he makes his Nathanael send to Clara (by what we would now call a Freudian error) the letter addressed to Lothar in which he speaks of his encounter with Coppola. The world of the 'Sandmann' and that of Clara belong together—the tension between them constitutes the ultimate theme of this as of so many other of Hoffmann's tales.

That is one important pattern of which the opening of the story makes us aware; but there are others that are no less important. The first paragraph rises to a climax of apprehension ('Dunkle Ahnungen eines grässlichen . . . Geschicks') and seems suddenly to swoop down, bathetically, into the banal everyday. 'Kurz und gut, das Entsetzliche, was mir geschah, dessen tödlichen Eindruck zu vermeiden ich mich vergeblich bemühe' (now it comes, we think, now we

are to be given a good look at the object of terror that has been so consistently hinted at) 'besteht in nichts anderm, als dass vor einigen Tagen, nämlich am 30. Oktober mittags um 12 Uhr, ein Wetterglashändler in meine Stube trat und mir seine Ware anbot. Ich kaufte nichts und drohte, ihn die Treppe herabzuwerfen, worauf er aber von selbst fortging.'[8] But this is not really an anticlimax at all, for Hoffmann's subject is precisely the terror that lurks in the most apparently ordinary and everyday. Almost immediately he repeats the pattern just described, in Nathanael's childhood reminiscence of lying in wait for the dreadful, the fascinating Sandman. 'Der Sandmann, der fürchterliche Sandmann'—again tension is built up with the characteristic, often over-insistent Hoffmann rhetoric—'ist der alte Advokat Coppelius, der manchmal bei uns zu Mittage isst!' 'Aber', Nathaniel continues, in terms that make the intention crystal-clear, 'die grässlichste Gestalt hätte mir nicht tieferes Entsetzen erregen können, als eben dieser Coppelius.'[9] Here we have an exact reversal of the structural pattern of, say, Mrs Radcliffe's novels, in which 'supernatural' events are given a 'natural' explanation at the end. Hoffmann's explanations explain nothing at all: they point, instead, to the real mystery, to the connexion between the familiar and the uncanny; they suggest the working of unknown powers in a world in which we feel at home.

Yet a third important pattern may be observed in the opening paragraphs of **"Der Sandmann."** We are taken into a comfortable family circle—all the members of the family are disposed about a round table at which the father smokes his pipe, drinks his glass of beer and tells the children fantastic stories. Into this circle breaks the terrifying figure of the Sandman, at first in the nurse's tale, then in the shape of the lawyer Coppelius; there is a climax of terror, until, it seems, the Sandman is cast out and the family circle closes again protectively about the child. 'Ein sanfter warmer Hauch glitt über mein Gesicht, ich erwachte wie aus dem Todesschlaf, die Mutter hatte sich über mich hingebeugt. "Ist der Sandmann noch da?" stammelte ich. "Nein, mein liebes Kind, der ist lange, lange fort, der tut dir keinen Schaden!"—So sprach die Mutter und küsste und herzte den wiedergewonnenen Liebling.'[10] But this is nothing but a *reculer pour mieux sauter,* for soon afterwards all 'Gemütlichkeit' is dispelled and the family group shattered by the father's death.—The pattern of Nathanael's childhood reminiscence is repeated exactly in the second part of the story, where we find the idyllic love of Nathanael and

Clara disturbed by the appearance of Coppola and Olimpia; instead of the swoon of the earlier episode we now have a fit of madness, until the protective circle closes, or seems to close, again. Nathanael 'erwachte wie aus schwerem, fürchterlichem Traum, er schlug die Augen auf und fühlte wie ein unbeschreibliches Wonnegefühl mit sanfter himmlischer Wärme ihn durchströmte . . .'[11] But this too proves to be nothing but the calm before the real storm, before the last appearance of Coppelius and Nathanael's incurable madness and death.

What appears in **"Der Sandmann"** as a structural principle is made explicit when Cyprian, in *Die Serapionsbrüder,* comments on a story significantly entitled **"Der unheimliche Gast."**

> In einen stillen gemütlichen Familienkreis trat, als eben allerlei Gespenstergeschichten aufgetischt wurden, plötzlich ein Fremder, der allen unheimlich und grauenhaft erschien, seiner scheinbaren Flachheit und Alltäglichkeit unerachtet. Dieser Fremde verstörte aber durch sein Erscheinen nicht nur den frohen Abend, sondern das Glück, die Ruhe der ganzen Familie auf lange Zeit.[12]

A stranger, an 'uncanny guest', who appears at first banal and undistinguished, destroys the family idyll. The very form of the sentence which introduces him, however, shows that he really belongs to this family idyll—that he is witness to a realm with which the family was seeking contact at the very moment of his irruption: '. . . trat, als eben allerlei Gespenstergeschichten aufgetischt wurden, plötzlich ein Fremder . . .' The stranger is 'unheimlich' not only in the sense that after his appearance men no longer feel 'at home' in their world, but also in that deeper sense of which Schelling spoke when he defined the word 'unheimlich' as 'Alles, was im Geheimnis, im Verborgnen, in der Latenz bleiben sollte und hervorgetreten ist';[13] or Freud, when he endorsed Schelling's definition and added: 'Das Unheimliche ist . . . das ehemals Heimische, Altvertraute. Die Vorsilbe *un* an diesem Worte ist aber die Marke der Verdrängung.'[14]

In the essay from which the sentence just quoted comes, Freud discusses **"Der Sandmann"** as a notable example of the Uncanny in literature. He lays particular stress, not so much on the motif of the mechanical doll (which had attracted Offenbach, Délibes and many others) as that of 'fear for the loss of one's eyes'. The Sandman threatens the boy's eyes in the nurse's tale and in the scene in which Coppelius and Nathanael's father are observed at their alchemistic experiments; and he later comes between Nathanael and the consummation of his love. Freud sees in Coppelius-Coppola, Spalanzani and Nathanael's father parts of a single image, a 'split type figure' like the two fathers of Hamlet; fear for the loss of one's eyes is a disguise assumed by fear of castration; and Olimpia, the mechanical doll, is an objectified complex of Nathanael's, a sign that his father-fixation has made him incapable of normal love. Freud concludes:

> Wir haben das Recht, diese Liebe [zu Olimpia] eine narzissistische zu heissen, und verstehen, dass der ihr Verfallene sich dem realen Liebesobjekt entfremdet. Wie psychologisch richtig es aber ist, dass der durch den Kastrationskomplex an den Vater fixierte Jüngling der Liebe zum Weibe unfähig wird, zeigen zahlreiche Krankenanalysen, deren Inhalt zwar weniger phantastisch, aber kaum minder traurig ist als die Geschchte des Studenten Nathaniel [*sic*].[15]

But as with Scott so with Freud—we find once again that Hoffmann has himself anticipated his interpreter's point of view. 'Gerade heraus', writes Clara in the letter whose rationalizing Nathanael finds so distasteful, 'will ich es Dir nur gestehen, dass, wie ich meine, alles Entsetzliche und Schreckliche, wovon Du sprichst, nur in Deinem Innern vorging, die wahre, wirkliche Aussenwelt aber daran wohl wenig Teil hatte.'[16] The possibility that everything in the story which transcends ordinary experience may be taken as Nathanael's delusion is an important part of the effect of **"Der Sandmann."**[17] This does not mean, however, that the story has only private significance. In *Die Serapionsbrüder,* Lothar defends the fascination that insanity has for him by speculating 'dass die Natur gerade beim Abnormen Blicke vergönne in ihre schauerliche Tiefe';[18] and Kreisler is shown, in *Kater Murr* and elsewhere, to see more deeply into the heart of things than his more obviously 'sane' contemporaries. In **"Der Sandmann"** Clara puts it as follows:

> Gibt es eine dunkle Macht, die so recht feindlich und verräterisch einen Faden in unser Inneres legt, woran sie uns dann festpackt und fortzieht auf einem gefahrvollen, verderblichen Wege, den wir sonst nicht betreten haben würden—gibt es eine solche Macht, so muss sie in uns sich wie wir selbst gestalten, ja unser Selbst werden. . . .[19]

The 'dark powers', 'uncanny powers', 'inimical principles' of which Hoffmann likes to speak work through men's minds, but are not necessarily identical with men's minds, are not necessarily merely signs of our personal unconscious. There is something devilish, something motivelessly malign in Coppelius-Coppola, something which connects him with that more than natural realm of evil which is hinted at in the nurse's story.

Freud is undeniably right when he maintains that a story like **"Der Sandmann"** taps deeper regions than that of our normal waking consciousness; and it is interesting to find Hoffmann himself, through the mouth of Belcampo-Schönfeld in *Die Elixiere des Teufels*, anticipating Freud's image of a 'censor' of the mind whose activities must be circumvented. Hoffmann's image is that of a customs-official:

> Ei, ehrwürdiger Herr! . . . Was haben Sie denn nun davon! Ich meine von der besonderen Geistesfunktion, die man Bewusstsein nennt, und die nichts anders ist, als die verfluchte Tätigkeit eines verdammten Toreinnehmers—Acciseofficianten—Oberkontrollassistenten, der sein heilloses Comptoir im Oberstübchen aufgeschlagen hat und zu aller Ware, die hinauswill, sagt: 'Hei . . . hei . . . die Ausfuhr ist verboten . . . im Lande, im Lande bleibt's.' Die schönsten Juwelen werden wie schnöde Saatkörner in die Erde gesteckt und was emporschiesst, sind höchstens Runkelrüben . . . Und doch sollte jene Ausfuhr einen Handelsverkehr begründen mit der herrlichen Gottesstadt da droben, wo alles stolz und herrlich ist.[20]

The last sentence of Belcampo's speech, like the extract from Clara's letter quoted above, suggests that Hoffmann's sympathies would have been with Jung rather than Freud—as is indeed only natural when we consider that there is a direct line between Jung's mode of thinking and that of writers like Schelling, Baader, Reil and G. H. Schubert, whom Hoffmann read with great avidity. For Hoffmann the personal unconscious is a means of gaining contact with something larger and deeper, something to which Belcampo gives the Augustinian name 'die herrliche Gottesstadt' but which we may equate, without serious distortion, with Jung's 'Collective Unconscious'. We already have an illuminating exegesis of **"Der goldne Topf"** by Jung's closest associate;[21] but **"Der Sandmann"** too—which may be regarded as the reversal or 'Zurücknahme' of **"Der goldne Topf"**—has many elements that would seem to demand a Jungian analysis. Coppelius-Coppola may be seen as the hero's 'Shadow'; Lothar and Siegmund give us (rather colourlessly, it must be admitted) the archetype of the 'Seelenfreund'; Clara and Olimpia clearly represent two opposing aspects of the Anima; and the 'circle of fire', which plays so prominent a part in Nathanael's visions and poems, may be seen as a perverted Mandala.[22]

The important point, here and elsewhere, is that **"Der Sandmann"** must not be regarded—as Scott clearly tried to do—as a mere capriccio or arabesque; that it reproduces through its figures, incidents and structure, the logic of the unconscious. And this leads us back to a motif which we have already seen to be of central importance: the irruption of an 'uncanny guest' into a cosy family-circle to which he seems, somehow, to belong. We may now interpret this as the irruption of dark images from below the threshold of consciousness, images that push past the 'censor' or 'Acciseofficiant' of the conscious mind. This may lead to disaster, as in **"Der Sandmann"**; but it may also lead to healing and salvation as in **"Der goldne Topf."** No wonder that we owe a close analysis of the former story to Freud, while an analysis of the latter has been inspired by Jung.

There is great danger, however, in Freud's approach to **"Der Sandmann"**—the danger of treating literary figures and episodes as mere disguises, as mere analogies to psychic processes. This does violence to the complexity and concreteness of the work. Take the 'eye'-motif, for instance, whose importance in **"Der Sandmann"** Freud quite properly stressed. It is undeniable that 'eyes' often seem to suggest something else in this story: when we see Spalanzani take up Olimpia's bleeding eyeballs and throw them at Nathanael, exclaiming that they had been stolen from the very Nathanael who is *watching* all this—then we may be forgiven for believing, with Freud, that organs of generation rather than organs of sight are here in question. But elsewhere in the story, 'eyes' are clearly something with which one sees, something whose loss is particularly dreadful to an artist who must view the world he uses as material for his art. In **"Der Sandmann,"** eyes are mirrors at once of the soul and of the universe; painters compare Clara's eyes with Ruisdael's lakes that mirror a whole landscape, while musicians exclaim: 'Was See—was Spiegel!—Können wir denn das Mädchen anschauen, ohne dass uns aus ihrem Blick wunderbare himmlische Gesänge und Klänge entgegenstrahlen, die in unser Innerstes dringen, dass da alles wach und rege wird?'[23] Then there are the eyes of the hypnotist, the 'stechende Augen' of Coppelius and Spalanzani, means of subduing the will, of imposing one man's dominance on another: this too is a motif that does not fit easily into the scheme Freud suggested. In the same way, one may agree with Freud in seeing the doll Olimpia as a sign of Nathanael's narcissism—especially since Hoffmann makes Nathanael call Clara a 'lebloses, verdammtes Automat' when she fails to admire his literary compositions. But Olimpia is surely more than this. She embodies the fascination—half terror, half delight—that Hoffmann felt, ever since his early studies of Wiegleb's 'Natural Magic', in the face of magical tricks.

She is also, quite consciously, made into a symbol of all that is soulless in art and in society: a certain kind of *bel canto* singing, in which the human voice is reduced to the level of a mechanical instrument; a purely passive and receptive attitude to art, which enervates the artist and harms him more than the most destructive criticism; the state of mind of those who attended the 'aesthetic tea-parties' which were so prominent a feature of German social life in the early nineteenth century. Fouqué once maintained that Hoffmann conceived Olimpia after meeting a lady who provoked comment because of 'das streng Gemessene in ihrem Benehmen . . . wie auch das allzu Taktmässige ihres Gesanges.'[24] Moreover: we may see Spalanzani as part of a split father-image, as Freud would have us do—but he is also Cagliostro, the swindler whose tricks are an earnest of real wonders and miracles; he is also the scientist and mechanician, who was already beginning, in Hoffmann's time, to usurp the functions of God and the Devil and whom Hoffmann was to pillory again in **Klein Zaches.**

Last but not least, there is the grotesque figure of Coppelius, the 'Sandmann' of the title. On his delineation Hoffmann has expended more care than on anything else in the story—almost all the alterations he made between the first draft and the final printing have to do with Coppelius. He strikes out, for instance, a passage in which the lawyer, dressed all in white, is seen as a walking snowman whose face has been painted red; he removes the episode in which Coppelius lays his hands on the eyes of Nathanael's little sister, who thereupon falls into a sickness that first blinds and then kills her; he remodels the end of the story, in which Coppelius was originally made to challenge Nathanael to throw himself down from the tower he has climbed with Clara; and he cancels sentences which make Coppelius appear, even before the death of Nathanael's father, as a social outcast:

> Mit wüthendem Blick fuhr er auf mich loss ich schrie Hülfe—Hülfe, des Nachbars Brauers Knecht sprang in die Thür, Hey hey—hey—der tolle Advokat—der tolle Coppelius—macht euch über ihn her—macht euch über ihn her—so rief es und stürmte von allen Seiten auf ihn ein—er floh gehetzt über die Strasse. . . .[25]

Coppelius remains eccentric and sinister—but in the later version he is more integrated into the small-town world in which he and Nathanael live. He is not only a childhood bogey-man, not only part of a threatening father-image; as lawyer and secret alchemist he is also an embodiment of greedy Philistinism as Hoffmann saw it (in **Die Serapionsbrüder**, it will be remembered, Lothar

talks at one point of 'tiefer, gespenstischer Philistrismus'[26]). The small provincial town, and the university-town too, with its professors who live only for their science and who see in man (like the doctor in *Woyzeck*) no more than a guinea-pig for their psychological or physiological or mechanical experiments—these places have become uncanny, they are no longer a home for a sensitive child or an artistic adult. Coppelius and Spalanzani objectify feelings of alienation that we meet again and again in the literature of the last century and a half: the alienation of man from the world he has created; the alienation of man from parts of his own personality that have been repressed only to return as spectral 'doubles' to hound and torment him. Here Hoffmann must be seen together with Poe, with Dickens, with Dostoevsky; with all those writers who have depicted the city as the home of uncanny presences that haunted, in earlier times, the castles of the Gothic novel and of de Sade, or the mountains and woods of Tieck's first 'Märchen'. Once again we are confronted by the image of the 'uncanny guest'. Coppola *seems* an outsider, an itinerant Italian in the world of the small German town: but is he not identical with the lawyer Coppelius, who belonged to that world and whom Nathanael's father venerated above all his fellow-citizens? The neurotic constitution that makes Nathanael appear predestined to madness, gives him at the same time a clear insight into social realities; and his 'Zerrissenheit' makes him into a drastic paradigm for the fate of a sensitive, artistically gifted man in the world of cities.

In a letter to Nathanael from which I have quoted several times already, Clara speaks of a 'dunkle, psychische Macht'[27] that draws the strange shapes of the outer world into ourselves. 'Es ist das Phantom unseres eigenen Ichs', she concludes, 'dessen innige Verwandtschaft und dessen tiefe Einwirkung auf unser Gemüt uns in die Hölle wirft oder in den Himmel verzückt.'[28] Once again we have that opposition of two worlds, one of darkness and one of light, which we noted at the beginning; but this time they are termed 'Hölle' and 'Himmel', and on other pages we meet again and again words like 'Engel' and 'Teufel', or 'ewiges Verderben', which seem to take us into familiar theological regions. In **Die Elixiere des Teufels** Hoffmann tried his hand at integrating such elements into a traditional, Christian scheme; but in works like **"Der Sandmann"** they seem to be floating loose, torn from their moorings by secularization. This contributes to the uncanny effect of such stories: transcendence breaks, literally as an 'Ammenmärchen', into a world that has no generally accepted theological scheme to accommodate it; the demonic breaks into a world in which thoughts of the devil tempt to laughter as well as atavistic terror.

> Mag der ehrliche alte Hafftitz [Lothar tells his fellow-'Serapionsbrüder' at one point] Anlass gehabt haben, jenes seltsame Ereignis, wie der Teufel in Berlin ein bürgerliches Leben geführt, anzumerken, welchen er will, genug, die Sache bleibt für uns rein fantastisch, und selbst das unheimlich Spukhafte, das sonst dem 'furchtbar verneinenden Prinzip der Schöpfung' beiwohnt, kann, durch den komischen Kontrast in dem es erscheint, nur jenes seltsame Gefühl hervorbringen, das, eine eigentümliche Mischung des Grauenhaften und Ironischen, uns auf gar nicht unangenehme Weise spannt.[29]

Once again the image of the 'uncanny guest' obtrudes itself. Once again something dark breaks into a circle of light—the 'Diesseitigkeit' of Hoffmann's world (attested by the strong realistic elements of his art) is invaded by mysterious and threatening messengers from beyond.

In reading **"Der Sandmann"** and other, similar, stories one has the impression that the wondrous, the transcendent, the demonic are playing a game of hide-and-seek—or, more accurately, of cat-and-mouse—with the characters; and this game seems to have materially determined the structure of such stories too. Everywhere in **"Der Sandmann"** we meet on the one hand motifs of dressing up and disguising, of keeping secret and mystifying; and on the other motifs of peeping from a hiding-place, peering out from cupboards and curtains, peering across into strange houses with the aid of telescopes. (This 'Peeping Tom' motif is of course connected with the 'eye' images whose prominence has already been noted). The cat-and-mouse game, however, determines not only *what* Hoffmann tells but also his manner of telling it. The author retreats behind a fictitious narrator, an imagined friend of Nathanael's engaged in piecing his story together. This narrator, in his turn, sometimes identifies himself with his readers' tastes, sometimes ironically distances himself from them, ascribing Philistine imperceptiveness to his 'dear reader'; sometimes he seeks to draw the reader into his spell by every possible rhetorical device, then again he retreats in a cloud of witticisms à la Jean Paul. The somewhat bizarre construction of the tale—hovering between epistolary and third person narrative, between flashback and straightforward time-sequence interrupted, again and again, by an ironic excursus—this too is part of the pervading cat-and-mouse game. Zigzagging narrative hides an action that is

logical and symmetrical: twice Nathanael's life moves from idyll to a crescendo of terror; this is followed, on each occasion, by a fit of swooning or of madness, after which the idyll is re-established; and only after this false reassurance does fate show its hand completely, bringing death at first to Nathanael's father and then to Nathanael himself.[30]

The shifts in tone imposed by the 'game' that has just been noticed affect the structure of Hoffmann's sentences, too; paratactic, breathless sentences alternate startlingly with hypotactic, long-winded, encapsulated ones:

> Siegmund, so stark er war, vermochte nicht den Rasenden zu bändigen; der schrie mit fürchterlicher Stimme immerfort: 'Holzpüppchen, dreh' dich'' und schlug um sich mit geballten Fäusten. Endlich gelang es der vereinten Kraft mehrerer, ihn zu überwältigen, indem sie ihn zu Boden warfen und banden. Seine Worte gingen unter in entsetzlichem tierischen Gebrüll. So in grässlicher Raserei tobend wurde er nach dem Tollhause gebracht.

> Ehe ich, günstiger Leser! dir zu erzählen fortfahre, was sich weiter mit dem unglücklichen Nathanael zugetragen, kann ich dir, solltest du einigen Anteil an dem geschickten Mechanikus und Automat-Fabrikanten Spalanzani nehmen, versichern, dass er von seinen Wunden völlig geheilt wurde. . . .[31]

These are Hoffmann's two voices, which stand in the same relationship to one another as the worlds of Clara and Coppelius, or the fantastic and realistic elements of the tale: the voice of the visionary who wants to draw the reader into his spell by fair means or foul, and the voice of the ironic artist who knows how to distance himself from his creation. It is the co-presence in him of visionary and coolly weighing craftsman which makes Hoffmann find such exact expression for the physiology as well as the psychology of fear; makes him experiment so successfully with grotesquely distorted language and gradations of sound; enables him to blend so perfectly exactly observed vignettes of German small-town life with terrifying fantasy. Only occasionally he writes too quickly and takes the easy way out—then he produces passages (like his description of the abortive duel between Nathanael and Lothar) that read like parodies of Spiess, Benedicte Neubert or even Clauren.

For all their occasional lapses of taste, Hoffmann's tales of terror have not lost their fascination for us today. It is not their plot that draws us (for that is often melodramatic) nor is it the characters Hoffmann presents (for these are often either colourless or grotesquely incredible). We read them for the complicated and tortured personality that shows itself behind and within plot and characters, revealing itself in rhetoric of terror, in play of irony, in complex narrative structures. We read them for the strange and haunting visions that are evoked as precisely as the familiar setting into which they break. We read them because they exemplify perfectly what Hoffmann called the 'Serapiontic principle': the ability to mould the materials of the outer world (men, landscapes, events, literary reminiscences) into images for an exactly apprehended inner world. In one sense such visions are private—they are clearly connected with Hoffmann's experiences in the broken home of his youth, his life with the 'Oh-Weh-Onkel', his affairs with Julia Marc and Cora Hatt, and all those sufferings and annoyances which he depicted so faithfully in his books about Kreisler. But they also have representative force: they constitute powerful symbols of the experience of artists in a world of cities, of Germans in the early nineteenth century, of men in a world which they have themselves made but which now confronts them in strange, hostile, terrifying shapes. Sir Walter Scott preferred **"Das Majorat"** to **"Der Sandmann,"** because the old 'Justitiarius' in the former story corresponded more exactly than any figure in the latter with Sir Walter's image of a German (that 'upright honesty and firm integrity which is to be met with in all classes which come from the ancient Teutonic stock'); and also because the 'Justitiarius' showed himself able 'as well to overcome the malevolent attacks of evil beings from the other world as to stop and control the course of moral evil in that we inhabit'.[32] Twentieth-century readers may well feel more sceptical, not only about the innate virtuousness of the 'ancient Teutonic stock', but also about man's ability to control moral and metaphysical evil; they have learnt to see the grotesque and absurd in art as more than just 'feverish dreams of a light-headed patient'; they are able to sense the experienced truth behind Hoffmann's luminous fantasies; they feel a shudder of intimate recognition when they are shown, again and again and in ever new ways, the irruption of an 'uncanny guest' into a homely, familiar and interpreted world.[33] Sir Walter Scott, we may feel, asked the right question—but most modern readers will give an answer that differs fundamentally from his.

Notes

1. *Essays on Chivalry, Romance and the Drama*, London n.d. (*The Chandos Classics*), pp. 467-8.

2. *E. T. A. Hoffmanns Sämtliche Werke. Historisch-kritische Ausgabe*, ed. C. G. v. Maassen, München und Leipzig 1908-1928, III, 24, 25. This edition is henceforward cited as S.W.

3. S.W., III, 18-19.

4. *E. T. A. Hoffmann's Sämtliche Werke*, ed. E. Grisebach, Leipzig n.d., VI, 102. This edition is henceforward cited as Grisebach.

5. S.W., III, 3.

6. Quoted in C. E. Passage, *Dostoevski the Adapter. A Study of Dostoevski's Use of the Tales of Hoffmann*, Chapel Hill, 1954, pp. 191-2.

7. S.W., III, 3.

8. S.W., III, 3-4.

9. S.W., III, 7.

10. S.W., III, 10.

11. S.W., III, 40.

12. S.W., VII, 158.

13. F. W. J. v. Schelling, *Sämtliche Werke*, Stuttgart and Augsburg 1857, 2. Abt., II, 649.

14. Sigmund Freud, *Das Unheimliche. Aufsätze zur Literatur*, Frankfurt 1963, p. 75.

15. Ibid., pp. 60-1.

16. S.W., III, 13.

17. Cf. E. F. Hoffmann, 'Zu E. T. A. Hoffmanns 'Sandmann'', *Monatshefte für deutschen Unterricht, deutsche Sprache und Literatur*, Wisconsin, LIV (1962), pp. 244 ff.

18. Grisebach, VI, 28.

19. S.W., III, 14-15.

20. S.W., II, 263.

21. A. Jaffé, *Bilder und Symbole aus E. T. A. Hoffmanns Märchen 'Der goldne Topf'*, in: C. G. Jung, *Gestaltungen des Unbewussten*, Zürich 1950, pp. 240 ff.

22. An interesting account of the connexion between Jung and the 'natural philosophers' of German Romanticism will be found in K. Ochsner, *E. T. A. Hoffmann als Dichter des Unbewussten*, Frauenfeld und Leipzig 1936, pp. 133 ff.

23. S.W., III, 20.

24. S.W., III, ix-x.

25. S.W., III, 359.

26. Grisebach, VI, 16.

27. 'Physisch' (in all editions) is probably a misprint for 'psychisch'. cf. Hoffmann's MS version, S.W., III, 363: 'die unheimliche *psychische* Gewalt'.

28. S.W., III, 15.

29. S.W., VII, 17.

30. Cf. M. Kuttner, *Die Gestaltung des Individualitätsproblems bei E. T. A. Hoffmann*, Düsseldorf 1936, p. 40.

31. S.W., III, 38.

32. Scott, op. cit., pp. 452, 462.

33. Hoffmann does not dismiss his readers without another glimpse of that world of light which he had opposed, from the beginning, to that of Coppelius. "Der Sandmann" ends with a vision—a dim one, hedged around by suggestions of hear-say and inference—of the kind of idyllic contentment from which Nathanael is excluded but which Peregrinus Tyss is allowed to achieve in the 'Märchen' world of *Meister Floh*.

SHELLEY L. FRISCH (ESSAY DATE 1985)

SOURCE: Frisch, Shelley L. "Poetics of the Uncanny: E. T. A. Hoffmann's 'Sandman.'" In *The Scope of the Fantastic: Theory, Technique, Major Authors*, edited by Robert A. Collins and Howard D. Pearce, pp. 49-55. Westport, Conn.: Greenwood, 1985.

In the following essay, Frisch asserts that the reader provides a crucial component in the creation of the uncanny elements in "The Sandman."

The tale's narrators continually force an identification of their narratees with the unnerving events of Nathanael's life, so that the narratees adopt their own anxieties and fear of the uncanny.

Sigmund Freud defined the "uncanny" as "that class of the frightening which leads back to what is known of old and long familiar."[1] He illustrated this conception of the uncanny by analyzing E. T. A. Hoffmann's **"Sandman,"** which comprises the first of Hoffmann's "Night Pieces," written in 1816.[2] Hoffmann's **"Sandman"** explores the increasingly schizophrenic world of a young man, Nathanael, who cannot shake his obsession with a childhood fairy tale, and who reacts hysterically to a salesman who seems to be the Sandman come to life. Readers share Nathanael's mounting distress and find themselves, like Nathanael, ultimately incapable of distinguishing between the fantasy of fairy tales and the reality stressed by other characters in the story.

The story begins in epistolary format. In a letter from Nathanael to his friend Lothar, Nathanael reflects on his recent encounter with a barometer salesman/optician, whom he identifies with the Sandman. From a flashback we learn that when Nathanael was a boy, his father had associated with a dreadful alchemist named Coppelius, and during the experiments the two conducted together, Nathanael's father died. On the evenings that Coppelius came to visit, Nathanael was always sent to bed early, with the warning that the Sandman was coming. Upon questioning his nurse Nathanael discovered that the Sandman plucks out the eyes of children who do not obey their parents' orders to go to bed; he then trans-

ports the eyes to the "half-moon" to feed his children. Curious to see the dreaded Sandman for himself, Nathanael hides in the closet of his father's study one night and is discovered by Coppelius, who attempts to harm the boy: but Nathanael is saved by the intervention of his father.

We then return to the present and to Nathanael's encounter with an Italian optician named Giuseppe Coppola, who exclaims in faulty German that he has eyes to sell. Nathanael draws back in terror, both at the similarity of the optician's name to the alchemist Coppelius's and to the mention of eyes as the product for sale. Memories of the Sandman come flooding back, and Nathanael reels in panic until he realizes that Coppola is selling spectacles and telescopes, not eyes. Still, he is struck by these uncanny similarities and remains haunted by the possibility of their identity.

Nathanael buys a telescope from Coppola and with its aid discovers a neighbor of whom he was hitherto unaware, a beautiful but strangely immobile woman named Olimpia. He pursues her, only to discover that she is an automaton, whose eyes have been implanted in her by Coppola. At this discovery Nathanael goes mad and falls into a long illness, during which he produces eerie, fantastic poetry. Upon recovering he returns to the "rational" world of his correspondent Lothar and his girlfriend Klara, who, he now believes, are right in dismissing the extraordinary events he has experienced. Nathanael is disappointed that they reject his poetic ventures but agrees that they are irrational. Finally, though, he spies Coppola/Coppelius once again, through his telescope, and jumps to his death from a tower.

This short summary provides the essentials of the material from which Freud drew in his essay to explain how events become uncanny. Freud noted that Nathanael's fear of losing his eyes represents a castration complex, akin to Oedipus' self-blinding when he discovers that he has killed his father and slept with his mother. Nathanael may harbor a secret wish to kill his father, Freud explained, and finds his wish fulfilled in the figure of the Sandman/Coppelius, the instrument of his father's death. Because he then wishes to repress that fulfilled wish, Nathanael buries the memory of the Sandman. When he encounters the optician Coppola and notices in him two uncanny resemblances (similarity of name and business of selling "eyes"), Nathanael succumbs to a temporary madness. The "un-" prefix of *uncanny*, Freud explained, denotes a confrontation with that which is familiar but until that moment successfully repressed. Repeated encounters with Coppola/Coppelius, in which the motif of eyes continues to play an important role, reinforce the feeling of the uncanny, in which repetition constitutes an important factor.

Freud isolated the Sandman as the focal point of interest in the story, thereby countering the view of other critics who attributed the presence of the uncanny to the mechanical doll Olimpia. Freud considered it irrelevant to debate the humanity of Olimpia, because establishing whether she is in fact living or a mere automaton does not address the *effect* of the uncanny on Nathanael. It is through his perceptions of the uncanny, maintained Freud, that we can best understand the meaning of the story. Freud concentrated in part on the biographical background of E. T. A. Hoffmann himself, whose father abandoned the family when Hoffmann was young, and on Freud's own case studies; both of these factors are said to bear out the verisimilitude of Nathanael's experiences.

Freud's dissection of Nathanael's psychoses illuminates the character of Nathanael and the relationship of Hoffmann to his main character. Freud followed Nathanael's increasing madness with a shrewd explication of how Nathanael's feelings of the uncanny escalate. He accurately noted the central role of the Sandman and the subsidiary role of Olimpia in unleashing long-repressed anxieties, which may be connected to an ambivalent feeling of Nathanael (and perhaps of Hoffmann) toward an inattentive father. Most important, Freud stressed that the uncanny involves something long familiar and yet unfamiliar, which by its reappearance at unexpected moments disconcerts an unwary victim.

Overall, however, Freud's interpretation of **"The Sandman"** fails as a literary interpretation of the fantastic. Freud admitted that the uncanny in literature differs from the uncanny in life; yet he treated the confusion of Nathanael, in which fantasy and reality intermingle, more as a case study of schizophrenia than as a work of literature. Freud even underscored the psychological "truth" of Nathanael's visions by describing similar personality disorders among his own patients. Freud once remarked to a friend that he was not fond of reading and commented: "I invented psychoanalysis because it had no literature."[3] He viewed the story through the perspective of the protagonist's neuroses and constantly judged its truth value. Freud thereby committed the error that Jonathan Culler called "premature foreclosure—the unseemly rush from word to world."[4]

It is within the German Romantic circle itself that we discover a more pertinent analysis of the literary creation of the uncanny. Ludwig Tieck's "Shakespeares Behandlung des Wunderbaren" of 1796 lays a theoretical foundation for the manner in which the illusion of the supernatural is created in the comedies and tragedies of Shakespeare.[5] Tieck's discussion of comedies treats the *Wunderbare* ("marvelous") in much the same manner as Tzvetan Todorov's recent *Fantastic: A Structural Approach to a Literary Genre:* the supernatural events described provoke no definitive reaction of anxiety in either the characters or in the implicit reader.[6] According to Tieck the supernatural world is moved so close to the reader (or viewer) that it becomes accepted as part of the fictional premise.[7] His examination of tragedies demonstrates how fear and anxiety can be induced in the reading or viewing audience by the use of particular fictional techniques.

The characteristics of the tragedies that compel the viewer both to accept and to be repelled by the supernatural are three, according to Tieck. First, the world of the supernatural is presented as distant and incomprehensible and is always subordinated to the "real" world; consequently, the passions and events concerning the major characters attract the attention of the viewer and are of more interest than the ghosts themselves. Thus we yearn to understand Hamlet's dilemma but care little for his father's apparition. Second, the supernatural must be prepared in some way. If the appearance of Hamlet's father's ghost were to open the play, Tieck explained, we would not have developed a necessary fear of him; instead, we would simply accept the ghost as part of the fictional frame work. We must be convinced that it is both possible and frightening for him to appear, so as to share the characters' dismay when we must formally face him. Therefore, *Hamlet* opens not with the ghost himself but with the frightened sentries who ponder his reality. Third, a natural explanation of the supernatural increases our intellectual uncertainty and thus augments our suspense. In the case of Hamlet we can attribute his vision of the ghost in part to Hamlet's proclivity to melancholy and superstition.

All three of these characteristics accurately describe the evocation of the supernatural in Hoffmann's **"Sandman."** First, the "real" character Nathanael commands our attention far more than the Sandman Coppelius or the automaton Olimpia. The fantastic characters remain abstractions for us, but Nathanael's raptures and fears seem close and comprehensible. Second, the Sandman does not appear in the story until the reader has heard of the evil he can perpetrate and how great Nathanael's fear of him is, and so we are prepared to experience with the sympathetic character Nathanael the uncanny similarity he draws to the optician Coppola who sells "eyes." Finally, although we identify with Nathanael we have just enough reason to doubt the reliability of his perceptions that we cannot shake a nagging doubt about the actuality of the Sandman throughout much of the story.

Recent "reader-response" criticism has called for a renewed interest in this type of poetics. Like Tieck reader-response critics examine the means by which readers' reactions are encoded into texts. However, their analyses go further than those of Tieck by showing that the reader is *addressed* directly and indirectly within the text. Walker Gibson spoke of the "mock reader" in texts, Stanley Fish of the "informed reader," Gerald Prince of the "narratee," Walter J. Ong of the "fictionalized audience," Wolfgang Iser of the "implied reader," and Christine Brooke-Rose of the "encoded reader."[8] None of these "readers" is identical to the "real" reader who peruses a book in his living room. These *narratees* (to use Prince's apt term) are the fictional counterparts of "narrators": they exist within the fictional framework itself. Although the critical literature on Hoffmann has nowhere recognized the role that the narratee plays in his works, I will demonstrate that this role is crucial in creating the uncanny effects of **"The Sandman."**[9]

The story opens with a letter from Nathanael to his friend Lothar, which he begins by exclaiming: "*You* certainly must be disturbed" (Hoffmann, **"The Sandman,"** p. 93). The exclamation sets the narrative tone for the tale as a whole. Second-person narration, addressed to a sympathetic narratee, appears not only in the introductory letters but in the subsequent interpretation of them by an additional narrator whose reliability is even more questionable than Nathanael's. The second narratee is told by this narrator that he has experienced similar encounters with the fantastic: "Have you, gentle reader, ever experienced anything that possessed your heart, your thoughts, and your senses to the exclusion of all else? Everything seethed and roiled within you; heated blood surged through your veins and inflamed your cheeks. Your gaze was peculiar, as if seeking forms in empty space invisible to other eyes, and speech dissolved into gloomy sighs" (p. 104). We, the "real" readers, are thus allied with the anxieties of Nathanael, with an equally nervous narrator

who continually apologizes to us for needing to set down Nathanael's experiences in a story, and with two narratees in whom Nathanael and the narrator explicitly attempt to instill feelings of the uncanny. Our uncomfortable intimacy with all of these figures forces us to confront the fantastic along with them and heightens our personal horror of each appearance of the dreaded Sandman.

The narrator overtly states his intention to make his narratee, whom he calls the "gentle reader" and the "sympathetic reader," receptive to the supernatural occurrences of the story (pp. 104-5): "my dear reader, it was essential at the beginning to dispose you favorably towards the fantastic—which is no mean matter" (p. 105). He expresses the hope that his narratee will picture the characters as vividly as if he had seen them with his own eyes. Nathanael pleads for understanding and acceptance of the supernatural from his narratee Lothar.

The "real" reader is left with the question of whether he ought to accept the role assigned to both of these narratees and thereby declare its events uncanny. Christine Brooke-Rose's article "The Readerhood of Man" suggests that a text with an apparent overencoding of the reader gives rise to the truly ambiguous text:

> The clearest type is the truly ambiguous text. . . . [It] *seems* to overdetermine one code, usually the hermeneutic, and even to overencode the reader, but in fact the overdetermination consists of repetitions and variations that give us little or no further information. The overdetermination functions, paradoxically, as underdetermination.[10]

Hoffmann's **"Sandman"** provides us with two narratees after whom we may model our own interpretation of events. The "real" reader thus becomes an overencoded reader, who is told repeatedly that he ought to accept the uncanny. That this text remains nonetheless fundamentally underdetermined is attested to in the ample critical literature on **"The Sandman,"** which debates and redebates the question of the relative reliability of the narratees and the story's other characters.

In the end the "real" reader must dismiss as inconsequential any attempt to distinguish between "actual" supernatural events and "mere" products of Nathanael's and the narrator's imaginations. The production of uncanny effects in literary texts rests precisely on the intellectual uncertainty built into the text. Freud's study of the uncanny concentrates on removing stories from the literary sphere and ascertaining their degree of psychological truth. Tieck directed his attention to the manner in which responses to the supernatural events are incorporated structurally into a text and thereby addressed the specifically literary conventions that separate fact from fiction. In applying reader-response critical theory to Hoffmann's "**Sandman**," I hope to have demonstrated that the tale's narrators continually force an identification of their narratees with the unnerving events of Nathanael's life, so that the narratees adopt their own anxieties and fear of the uncanny. Remarks addressed in the second person to these narratees necessarily draw in the "real" reader as well. We become the "gentle" and "sympathetic" reader about whom the narrator exclaims: "Everything seethed and roiled within *you*" (Hoffmann, "**The Sandman**," p. 104).

Notes

1. Sigmund Freud, "The Uncanny," in *The Standard Edition of the Complete Works of Sigmund Freud*, trans. and ed. James Strachey et al. (London: The Hogarth Press, 1955), 17: 220.

2. E. T. A. Hoffmann, "The Sandman," in *Tales of E. T. A. Hoffmann*, trans. and ed. Leonard J. Kent and Elizabeth C. Knight (Chicago and London: University of Chicago Press, 1969), 93-125. Further references appear in parentheses in the text.

3. Quoted in Neil Hertz, "Freud and the Sandman," in *Textual Strategies: Perspectives in Post-Structuralist Criticism*, ed. Josue Harari (Ithaca, N.Y.: Cornell University Press, 1979), 318.

4. Jonathan Culler, *Structuralist Poetics* (Ithaca, N.Y.: Cornell University Press, 1975), 130.

5. Ludwig Tieck, "Shakespeares Behandlung des Wunderbaren," in *German Essays*, ed. Max Dufner and Valentine C. Hubbs (New York: Macmillan, 1964), 4: 61-101.

6. Tzvetan Todorov, *The Fantastic: A Structural Approach to a Literary Genre* (Cleveland: Case Western Reserve Press, 1973), 53-57.

7. Tieck, "Shakespeares Behandlung des Wunderbaren," 65. Recent research on the fairy tale has led to similar conclusions about the presentation and reception of the supernatural in that genre. See especially Max Luthi, *Es War einmal*, 4th ed. (Gottingen and Zurich: Vandenhoeck & Ruprecht, 1973).

8. Walker Gibson, "Authors, Speakers, Readers, and Mock Readers," *College English* 11 (1950): 265-69; Stanley Fish, "Literature in the Reader: Affective Stylistics," *New Literary History* 2 (1970): 123-62; Gerald Prince, "Introduction to the Study of the Narratee," in *Reader-Response Criticism*, ed. Jane P. Tompkins (Baltimore: The Johns Hopkins University Press, 1980), 7-25; Walter J. Ong, "The Writer's Audience Is Always a Fiction," *PMLA* 90 (1975): 9-21; Wolfgang Iser, *The Implied Reader: Patterns of Communication in Prose Fiction from Bunyan to Beckett* (Baltimore: Johns Hopkins University Press, 1974); idem, *The Act of Reading: A Theory of Aesthetic Response* (Baltimore: Johns Hopkins University Press, 1978); Christine Brooke-Rose, "The Readerhood of Man," in *The Reader in the Text*, ed.

Susan R. Suleiman and Inge Crosman (Princeton, N.J.: Princeton University Press, 1980), 120-48.

9. Most of the recent literature on the "Sandman" can be grouped according to the following six goals. 1. Analyzing the psyche of the main character Nathanael, generally with reference to Freud's "Uncanny" essay: Ilse Aichinger, "E. T. A. Hoffmann's Novelle 'Der Sandmann' und die Interpretation Sigmund Freuds," *Zeitschrift für deutsche Philologie* 95 (1976): 113-32; Hélène Cixous, "Fiction and Its Phantoms: A Reading of Freud's *Das Unheimliche*," *New Literary History* 7 (1976): 525-48; and Hertz, "Freud and the Sandman." 2. Describing the roles of peripheral characters in evoking the suspense of the tale: S. S. Prawer, "Hoffmann's Uncanny Guest: A Reading of *Der Sandman*," *German Life and Letters* 18 (1965): 297-308; Allan J. McIntyre, "Romantic Transcendence and the Robot in Heinrich von Kleist and E. T. A. Hoffmann," *German Review* 54 (1979): 29-34. 3. Uncovering implicit and explicit social criticism: Lienhard Wawrzyn, *Der Automaten-Mensch: E. T. A. Hoffmanns Erzahlung von Sandmann* (Berlin: Klaus Wagenback, 1977); Herbert Kraft, "E. T. A. Hoffmann: Geschichtlichkeit und Illusion," *Romantik: Ein literaturwissenschaftliches Studienbuch*, ed. Ernst Ribbat (Konigstein: Athenaum, 1979), 138-62. 4. Fixing the role of the narrator: Maria Tatar, "E. T. A. Hoffmann's 'Der Sandmann': Reflection and Romantic Irony," *MLN* 95 (1980): 585-608. 5. Ascertaining Hoffmann's attitudes toward the writing process as reenacted by the story's characters: Raimund Belgardt, "Der Kunstler und die Puppe: Zur Interpretation von Hoffmanns *Der Sandmann*," *German Quarterly* 42 (1969): 686-700; Ursula Mahlendorf, "E. T. A. Hoffmann's *The Sandman*: The Fictional Psycho-Biography of a Romantic Poet," *American Imago* 32 (1975): 217-39; Jean Delabroy, "L'Ombre de la theorie (A propos de *L'Homme au sable* de Hoffmann)," *Romantisme* 24 (1979): 29-41. 6. Exploring the natural or supernatural basis of the events related: Ernst Fedor Hoffmann, "Zu E. T. A. Hoffmanns 'Sandmann,'" *Monatshefte* 54 (1962): 244-52.

10. Brooke-Rose, "Readerhood of Man," 135.

JOSEPH ANDRIANO (ESSAY DATE 1993)

SOURCE: Andriano, Joseph. "'Uncanny Drives': The Depth Psychology of E. T. A. Hoffmann." In *Our Ladies of Darkness: Feminine Daemonology in Male Gothic Fiction*, pp. 47-67. University Park: Pennsylvania State University Press, 1993.

In the following excerpt, Andriano views "The Sandman" as an example of "The Ambiguous Gothic" tradition, and illustrates how Hoffmann treats issues of identity crisis in the story.

The first glimmerings of a sophisticated "literary psychology" in the Gothic were in *The Monk*, for Lewis seemed intuitively aware of mental entities to which Freud and Jung would later give a habitation and a name. But it was, appropriately, the German Romantics who first fully realized the psychological implications of the supernatural, not only in the fairy tale, which they raised to high art (*Kunstmärchen*), but also in the lowly genre of the *Schauerroman*. The masters of psycho-

ABOUT THE AUTHOR

PALMER COBB ON HOFFMANN'S GENIUS

It has been the fashion among certain of Hoffmann's critics to give him no higher rating than that of a skillful spinner of ghost yarns. He is more than that. . . . Hoffmann conjures up before our eyes figures and events which the greatest skill of other virtuosos of the ghost story could not invest with a semblance of probability. We see most fearful transformations. Divided personalities in a double physical embodiment confront us. One student falls in love with a doll with glass eyes, another with a "gentle green serpent." Cats and dogs philosophize over and satirize the life of their human associates. Diseased states of mind are portrayed with startling distinctness, while uncanny noises, stupefying odors of marvelous flowers, magic organ music, etc., all play their part in Hoffmann's machinery of the narrative. How is it possible that he is able to rescue such material from the realm of the ridiculous and childish, pass it through the mill of his genius, and turn out a product which is food for intelligent minds? . . . The explanation is to be sought in the fact that Hoffmann's figures are, to him at least, absolutely real. He believed with all his heart in the most improbable figure of his fevered fancy. It was as real and tangible to him as the most prosaic fact or object in his daily existence. For him the trivial, commonplace, work-a-day world about him was filled with the marvelous and supernatural. In his stories he hovers always on the boundary between the real and the supernatural, crossing and recrossing at will. And one realm was as real to him as the other. Given his faith in his productions, add to that his remarkable power of description, and the secret of the peculiar character of his art is revealed.

SOURCE: Cobb, Palmer. "Poe and Hoffmann." *South Atlantic Quarterly* 8 (1909): 68-81.

Hoffmann was profoundly interested in the philosophers who were forebears of Jungian thought—Kant, Schelling, and G. H. von Schubert, to name the most important.[2] He was, for example, intrigued by Schelling's conception of the world soul (*Weltseele*), and Schubert's idea that the Unconscious provided a bridge between the world soul and the individual (Taylor, 78; Ellenberger, 729). Like Schelling and Schubert, Hoffmann believed that the unconscious was a person's link to cosmic forces, if only he or she could understand its language.[3]

Unlike Cazotte and Lewis, who had much less control over their material, Hoffmann deliberately makes his supernatural beings into numinous symbols of the *Weltseele* or the *Geisterreich*. The green snake Serpentina in "**The Golden Pot,**" for example, is clearly both a Nature figure and an image of feminine forces within Anselmus.[4] A Jungian reading of Hoffmann, then, should reveal how thoroughly and how profoundly this "literary psychologist" anticipated Jungian ideas about the archetypal feminine and its relation to men.[5] A post-Jungian reading should avoid the Platonism of *Geisterreich* and *Weltseele* as forerunners of the Collective Unconscious. Instead, I will examine specific texts for signs of archetypes.

Whether Hoffmann was psychoanalyzing himself in these works I will not conjecture;[6] my focus remains on the universal, on what the texts reveal—albeit parabolically—about the problems of growing up a male human being. The Ambiguous Gothic, which Hoffmann learned from Cazotte, Tieck, and Schiller,[7] is an excellent vehicle for psychological parables, especially fables of identity crisis, since (as has been seen) the genre tends to break down boundaries between self and other, male and female.[8]

Hoffmann's two stories "**The Sandman**" (1815) and "**The Mines of Falun**" (1818) are perfect examples of this Ambiguous Gothic. They mingle the moral with the macabre, the humorous with the grotesque, the horrific with the absurd. Both may be read as cautionary stories of sensitive young men who go mad. Though merely absurd and anomalous to some early critics,[9] these tales have more recently found readers and rereaders (e.g., Hertz and Fass) who have created brilliantly coherent texts out of Hoffmann's ambiguities. Below are two post-Jungian attempts to create coherence out of the seemingly anomalous numinous figures haunting Hoffmann's protagonists.

logical horror in Germany were Schiller, Tieck, and especially E. T. A. Hoffmann.[1]

"The Sandman": The Failure of Vision

Dramatized in Offenbach's opera *Tales of Hoffmann* and analyzed by Freud in his famous essay "The Uncanny," the much anthologized **"Der Sandmann"** is perhaps the most familiar of Hoffmann's tales. The close reading offered below, to some extent an elaboration on Freud's, involves a study of the language of archetypes; that is, how they attempt to communicate to the protagonist, who misinterprets their message.

The tale opens with a letter from the student protagonist, Nathanael, to his friend Lothar, the brother of his fiancée, Klara. Worried that his friend, fiancée, and mother are disturbed and angry with him, Nathanael is writing to convince them that he is not "a crazy visionary" ("einen aberwitzigen Geisterseher") (**K**, 137; **W**, 7).[10] As the story will ironically reveal, however, Nathanael's problem is that he is *not* a visionary and that he *is* a ghost-seer.

Archetypal implications begin with Nathanael's description of Klara, his "pretty angel-image, so deeply imprinted in heart and mind" ("holdes Engelsbild, so tief mir in Herz und Sinn eingeprägt") (**K**, 137; **W**, 7). Immediately, Hoffmann reveals that the young man perceives the beloved as a divine figure within him. She seems his guardian angel. She even accepts the role (**K**, 146), but for her it is only a figure of speech, while for Nathanael it is a literal reality. Unfortunately for him, however, she cannot live up to the role he has projected onto her from his own Idea of Woman. Klara is a fairly complex character in her own right, refusing to be inflated to the archetypal or reduced to the stereotypical angel.

In his letter to Lothar, Nathanael attempts to explain his apparent paranoia by going back to his early childhood, when he formed an obsession with that goblin of the nursery, the Sandman, whom he identifies with a friend of his father, Coppelius. Freud has shown that Coppelius is really the boy's image of his father (*Vater Imago*), who seems to have made a diabolic alliance with this ominous figure of horror.[11] But why does Nathanael come to view his father as the ally of the evil one? At first, before he knows about Coppelius, Nathanael describes the father in nostalgic terms. When he was little (he writes to Lothar) he enjoyed the "marvelous stories" his father told the children while he smoked his pipe, which Nathanael loved to light for him (**K**, 138; **W**, 8). But *"mother was very sad on such evenings, and hardly had the clock struck nine when she would say: 'Now children, off to bed with you! The Sandman is coming, I can already hear him'"*

(**K**, 138; emphasis added). And Nathanael would hear someone clumping up the stairs. The child perceives a conflict here between the parents. His mother does not seem to share his enthusiasm for the father's marvelous tales. She is sad and nervous. At such a young age (he is still in the nursery), he remains very attached to his mother (**K**, 142), whom he perceives as angelic. Unconsciously, then, the father's smoke is seen as issuing not from a genial pipe but from hellfire.

Nathanael does not yet realize the reason for his mother's sadness: the lawyer Coppelius is coming over to continue on some mysterious alchemical work with Nathanael's father. She tells her son that in fact there is no Sandman—"it only means that you are sleepy, that your eyes feel *as though someone had sprinkled sand in them*" (**K**, 139; emphasis added). But he does not believe her; he is already frightened, traumatized by the first rift he has ever seen between his parents. He knows that it has something to do with the Sandman. Asking the nurse, he discovers that the Sandman is "a wicked man who comes to children when they refuse to go to bed and *throws handfuls of sand in their eyes* till they bleed and pop out of their heads." (**K**, 139; emphasis added).

Here the possibility arises that Nathanael is an unreliable narrator—anticipating Poe's insane narrators. There may actually be no nurse; she could be a hag projection of the mother—an image of Nathanael's *interpretation* of his mother's words, which were supposed to comfort him. A figure of speech, a simile, becomes a literal horror, magnified in the lens of the child's soul, which is troubled by a disharmony between his parents. The simile "feeling as though" sand is in the eyes transforms into literal sand thrown in the eyes by an ogre, who is really a father: "Then he throws the eyes into a sack and takes them to the half-moon as food for his children" (**K**, 139). The half-moon ("Halbmond"—**W**, 9) could also be a sign of partition, the splitting of the parental image. The boy's fantasy, in any case, attempts to assert that the father is an Other father, one who may steal his eyes. Freud considered this anxiety to be that of castration, an idea that remains controversial among critics.[12] Eyes are complex symbols; as "windows of the soul," they are more than mere sexual symbols. They are metonymies for vision. **"The Sandman"** is about the failure of vision, what Hoffmann calls "faulty vision" (**K**, 142; "Augen Blödigkeit"—**W**, 13). Nathanael fails to see the real Coppelius, who is indeed a wicked man, but a man only. The youth has magnified the lack of harmony between his parents into an archetypal conflict between the maternal feminine—which he knows to be angelic—and the paternal masculine, which must therefore be diabolic. When Nathanael realizes that the clumping footfalls belong to Coppelius, and that Coppelius is the source of the parental rift, he jumps to the only conclusion that makes sense—Coppelius, not father, is the diabolical sandman.

But "his intimacy with my father occupied my imagination more and more" (*K*, 139). Try as he might, he cannot separate the father from the Sandman. The boy consciously likes his father, however. The tales he tells stimulate Nathanael's imagination and probably help develop his later aspiration to be a writer. But the conflicts struggling just below consciousness create ambivalence; "I liked nothing better than to hear or read horrible tales about goblins, witches, dwarfs [*Kobolten, Hexen, Daumlingen*] and such; but at the head of them all was the Sandman, of whom I was always drawing hideous pictures" (*K*, 141-42; W, 9). He likes what he fears; he is compelled to draw pictures of his nightmare, and the pictures give him pleasure. When he concludes, however, that the Sandman is not just a "hobgoblin of the nurse's tale," but is actually a creature of flesh and blood named Coppelius, fear dominates, and all of the lawyer's grotesque features are magnified (*K*, 140-41). In his presence, the father magically changes—all of his good qualities vanish: "As my old father now bent over the fire, he looked completely different. His mild and honest features seemed to have been distorted into a repulsive and diabolical mask. . . . He looked like Coppelius" (*K*, 141-42).

As the boy observes the diabolic alliance between his father and Coppelius, he begins hallucinating. His father is some sort of demon now, servant to the satanic Sandman. This delusion precipitates a nightmare in which Coppelius treats Nathanael like a doll, twisting his hands and feet, saying, "There's something wrong here! It's better the way they were. The Old Man knew his business" (*K*, 142). The Old Man, the reader does not realize until later, is the scientist Spalanzani. The nightmare has revealed, before Nathanael has even met the scientist, that he too is a father image; but why Nathanael sees himself in the dream as the mechanical creation of the old man is not yet clear. The nightmare ends when "a gentle warm breath passed across my face" (*K*, 142) and his nurturing mother revivifies him, kisses and cuddles her reclaimed darling. In a revealing synecdoche, the mother is represented by her breath—as the child's inspiring soul image, she is his first incarnation of anima.

So far the tale has been narrated by Nathanael, and there is no way of telling which events are objectively true and which are psychic realities. The conflict between the parents has something to do with the mysterious experiments Coppelius and the father are conducting. When they result in an explosion that kills the father, Nathanael blames Coppelius, the "vile Satan" (*K*, 143). But if this is a tale told by a madman, the father may not literally be dead. In a story in which figures of speech become uncannily literal, it is also possible that apparently literal events are really figurative. The father does not die; only the good in him does. He leaves, and in so doing undergoes another transformation—into Spalanzani. When Nathanael swears to avenge his father's death, he may really be saying that he will get revenge on his father's real or imagined desertion of his mother. The original father/mother unity is completely severed now.

The second part of the story is a letter from Klara to Nathanael, who in his distraction has accidentally addressed the letter meant for Lothar to Klara. This young woman, somewhat reminiscent of Lewis's Agnes, is a bright levelheaded girl whom Hoffmann presents as a kind of Enlightenment heroine, toward whom he is therefore somewhat ambivalent.[13] She is perceptive enough to realize that "all the fears and terrors of which you speak took place only in your mind," and that "dark powers within" Nathanael seem "bent upon his destruction" (*K*, 145-46). She goes on to give a psychological analysis of doppelgängers:

> If there is a dark power . . . it must form inside us, from part of us, must be identical with ourselves; only in this way can we believe in it and give it the opportunity it needs if it is to accomplish its secret work. If our mind is firm enough and adequately fortified by the joys of life to be able to recognize alien and hostile influences as such . . . then this mysterious power will perish in its futile attempt to assume a shape that is supposed to be a reflection of ourselves.
>
> (*K*, 146)

She goes on to reveal that she and Lothar have come to grasp the mechanism of what psychoanalysts would later call projection; the "dark power" within frequently introduces in us "the strange shapes the external world throws in our way, so that we ourselves engender the spirit which in our strange delusion we believe speaks to us from that shape" (*K*, 146). But Klara's sanity goes too far in the other direction; this Enlightenment heroine dismisses Nathanael's Sandman as a "phantom of the ego"—mere figment of an imagination over-powered by uncanny drives ("unheimliche Treiben"—*W*, 16). Hoffmann's tale reveals, on the contrary, that the phantoms have their own psychic reality, even if it is not an external reality.

Nathanael, however, sees them as literal monsters. He has been unable to outgrow his childish fears because he still takes them literally, in a failure of vision that originates in a miscon-struction of his parents as diametrically opposed entities (mother/angel/moonlight; father/devil/hellfire). Another important—and related—split in the story is the dissociation of sensibility that also originates in Nathanael's bifurcation of the parental image: feminine/heart versus masculine/head. He is therefore, in his next letter to Lothar, outraged by Klara's letter, which he finds too "logi-cal" and "analytical" for a girl. He can only believe that Lothar has poisoned her feminine sensibility with lessons in masculine *Logos* (*K*, 147). And no sooner is his disenchantment with Klara spoken than he sees (through peeking, as usual) the "divinely beautiful face" of Olimpia, Spalanzani's supposed daughter (actually a mechanical doll). He does not realize that what he sees in her is a reflection of himself: "Her eyes seemed fixed, I might almost say *without vision*. It seemed as if she were sleeping with her eyes open" (*K*, 148—emphasis added; cf. Freud, 385 n. 1). But it is Nathanael (whose eyes have been "stolen" by the Sandman) who has no vision, who is the automa-ton. He has automatically withdrawn anima (*Engelsbild*) from Klara, no longer worthy of it, and projected it into Olimpia, his feminine ideal.

Hoffmann then switches to an omniscient narrative (*K*, 148),[14] prefacing it with a reminder that Nathanael's case is not an anomaly: he should be recognizable to the reader, "and you may feel as if you had seen him with your own eyes on very many occasions. Possibly also, you will come to believe that real life is more singular and more fantastic than anything else and that all a writer can do is present it as 'in a glass darkly'" (*K*, 149). Nor is Nathanael's anima projection of Klara unusual (though his withdrawal of it cer-tainly is). The authorial narrator himself has a tendency, he admits, to apotheosize Klara, liken-ing himself to poets and musicians who cannot "look at the girl without sensing heavenly music which flows into us from her glance and pen-etrates to the very soul until everything within us stirs awake and pulsates with emotion" (*K*, 150). But in reality, Klara is not a muse. "Dreamers and visionaries" have bad luck with her because she is practical; her "clear glance and rare ironical smile"

seem to dissipate their "shadowy images." Yet she is tenderhearted and intelligent (K, 151); in short, she is not a mere reflection ("'That is nonsense about a lake and a mirror!'"), magnified in the convex lens of the dreamer. She has her own substance. But Nathanael can only see the reflec-tion of his own projected image—the guardian angel inherited from his sense of the Feminine, formed from his perception of his mother. Unable to "dissolve the projection" (Jung, *CW* 9.1: 84) and recognize Klara as a woman rather than an *Englesbild*, he simply withdraws it and reprojects it onto Olimpia, who fits the mold.

Much has been made by critics of Nathanael's aspirations as a poet.[15] A common misreading of the tale, in my opinion, is to see Klara as a domestic philistine and Olimpia as the Romantic artist's true muse (cf. Veronika vs. Serpentina in **"The Golden Pot"**). But Nathanael is not a poet; he is at best a poetaster. Rather than a visionary, he is a literalist. Believing in the objective, external reality of those "dark powers" Klara wrote to him about (*K*, 151), he imagines himself their "play-thing." He also believes that poetic inspiration comes from external powers, rather than from an inner light. Consequently, his tales and poems are "really very boring" (*K*, 152), for he has reified the archetypes, mistaken them for external beings, for Others.

He writes a poem about his presentiment that Coppelius will destroy him:

> He portrayed himself and Klara as united in true love but plagued by some dark hand which oc-casionally intruded into their lives. . . . Finally, as they stood at the altar, the sinister Coppelius ap-peared and touched Klara's lovely eyes, which sprang onto Nathanael's breast, burning and scorching like bleeding sparks. Then Coppelius grabbed him and flung him into a blazing circle of fire.
>
> (*K*, 152)

The poem turns out to be prophetic, but not in a visionary sense; it is a self-fulfilling prophecy. Nathanael refuses to see that he himself is the impediment to their marriage, not only because of sexual cowardice, as McGlathery points out, but because of a fragmentation of his personal-ity.[16] Klara implores him to realize that what burned into his breast were not her eyes but the drops of his own heart's blood—a heart torn apart by the hands of his own inner daemon, an animus run amok, dissociated from anima.[17] The two must be in harmony for a man truly to love a woman. But all Nathanael can see in Klara's eyes now is death, which "looked upon him kindly" (*K*, 153). And as he gets more enrapt in his poem, more self-possessed, she cries out for him to throw the "mad, stupid tale into the fire." This is not philistinism; she knows rather that his poem is mentally dangerous, a blind rehearsing of his inner turmoil in occultist terms. But Nathanael is indignant: He "thrust Klara away, and cried, 'You damned lifeless automaton!'" (*K,* 154).

He is the automaton, of course, and though there are a few remissions from his mental disease when he manages momentarily to restore "Klara in his heart" (*K,* 153-55, 166), he keeps relapsing into a more and more psychotic paranoia. As long as he refuses to accept the "dark powers" as his own, he is doomed. During one of his remissions, he recognizes that he has been the victim of a "gruesome illusion . . . the product of his own mind," and that the optician Coppola cannot possibly be "the ghostly double [*verfluchter Doppelt-gänger*] and revenant of the accursed Coppelius" (*K,* 156; *W,* 28). But then, picking up one of Coppola's spyglasses, he "involuntarily" peeps at Olimpia. At first she looks lifeless and rigid (for he has momentarily withdrawn anima from the doll and reinvested Klara with it), but as he peeps she is transformed; "moist moonbeams were beginning to shine in Olimpia's eyes." Hoffmann again uses anima signs—water and the moon.[18] But what is more remarkable in this passage is his insight into the unconscious process of projection. Nathanael animates Olimpia with "everincreasing life," imposing on her his feminine ideal. Thus she becomes an angel that "hovered before him in the air," glowing with "divine beauty" (*K,* 156-57).

When Hoffmann has Nathanael acquire a new set of eyes, the author creates a symbol of what Nathanael has been doing all along—magnifying. Through apotheosis he turns people into archetypes, and through reification he turns archetypes into people. Olimpia, through projection, becomes a real girl, in character the opposite of Klara. Nathanael is the only man at her concert and coming-out party who does not see that she is dull, empty-headed, and inarticulate—a mere machine. When he dances with her, he animates her further, as his "warm life-blood surges through her veins" (*K,* 159). She merely takes life from him; she has none of her own. She cannot say anything intelligent, and yet he considers her a "magnificent and heavenly woman! You ray shining from the promised land of love! You deep soul, in which my whole being is reflected" ("du tiefes Gemut, in dem sich mein ganzes Sein spiegelt") (*K,* 159; *W,* 31).

Although Olimpia reminds him of "the legend of the dead bride" (*K,* 160), he continues to give life to her.[19] She is the ultimate in feminine passivity and receptivity, infinitely preferable to the more masculine Klara:

> Never before had he had such a splendid listener. . . . She sat for hours on end without moving, staring directly into his eyes, and her gaze grew ever more ardent and animated. . . . It seemed to him as if she expressed thoughts about his work and about all of his poetic gifts from the very depths of his own soul, as though she spoke from within him.
>
> (*K,* 162)

Perceiving her "utter passivity" as a fascination for him and his poetic genius, Nathanael is unable to see the significance of her identity as the "daughter" of the diabolical Spalanzani, even after he sees Spalanzani and Coppola/Coppelius fighting over her. They twist and tug her "this way and that, contending furiously for possession of her" (*K,* 163). For the first time, Nathanael sees that she is a lifeless doll; and worse, her eyes are missing. What he fails to see is the similarity between this scene and the dream that he had (*K,* 142) in which it was *his* hands and feet that were being twisted. Spalanzani now tells him that the eyes used in the doll had been stolen from Nathanael, at whom he now hurls the bloody things, which hit his breast. The poem comes true; Spalanzani is revealed as yet another doppelgänger of Coppelius, and Nathanael's mind, overwhelmed by this appearance of yet another goblin, is completely shattered by madness.

The dream, the poem, and now this hallucination are all messages from his unconscious that he is unable to decipher, because he takes the symbols literally. Convinced that the male phantoms are gone, he once again "recovers" by reprojecting anima onto Klara: "An angel guided me to the path of light" (*K,* 166). They prepare to marry, but one day after they have climbed a tower to look at the mountains, Nathanael "automatically" takes Coppola's spyglasses out of his pocket, and looks at Klara through them. Babbling incoherently about a whirling wooden doll and a circle of fire, he tries to hurl Klara from the tower. Lothar saves her, but Nathanael, seeing "the gigantic figure of the lawyer Coppelius" (*K,* 167) in the crowd below, throws himself to his death. The narrative ends with the assurance that Klara found a husband many years later, along with the "quiet domestic happiness" that "Nathanael, with his lacerated soul [*Innern zerrissene*], could never have provided her" (*K,* 167; *W,* 40). Klara here seems like Veronika in "**The Golden Pot**"—symbol of domesticity, inappropriate mate for an artist, who must be married to his muse. But since no woman can be a muse except in the imagination of the artist, he is better off not imposing upon mortal woman the awesome responsibility of "inspira-trice." At least, he should recognize, as Nathanael never does, that inspiration ultimately comes from within.

Nathanael is but the travesty of an artist. Instead of creating powerful poetic symbols out of the "dark powers" of his mind (as Hoffmann himself is able to do), he creates reifications, pathetic fallacies that take figures too literally— that make out of the archetypes of the soul mere bogeymen and dolls.

Hoffmann shows us that we all have our inner phantoms. We must recognize them as such without merely dismissing them (like Klara) as unreal figments. Nathanael never realizes that Coppelius, Coppola, Spalanzani, and the Sandman are all identical—all go back to his father imago, the child's unconscious image of the father. He is perceived as sinister only after the child notices a conflict with the mother. This split causes a dissociation of sensibility that makes it impossible for him to love Klara as a woman. He can only perceive her in the holy light of the angelic feminine, utterly dissociated from the analytical, scientific, logical masculine. When she fails to live up to this ideal, he withdraws the anima projection and apparently reprojects it onto a more feminine girl. But Olimpia is nothing more than a vacuous and passive receptacle for Nathanael's projections, a symbol of his own femininity. She is an Echo to his Narcissus.[20]

What dooms Nathanael, then, is his unconscious fission of the androgynous archetype— what Jung called "the divine syzygy"[21]—which is split when the child perceives an unresolvable conflict between his parents. Masculine and feminine become polar opposites; then each gets magnified as Nathanael is unable to outgrow his childish deification of the parents.[22] This polarization in turn causes him to reify the dark powers, mistaking inner daemons for external occult influences.[23] He is trapped in a vicious circle of deification and reification—the "circle of fire" through which he finally throws himself.

Notes

1. Schiller's "Der Geisterscher" (1789) was especially influential on later, more psychological horror (Frank, 145-46). Ludwig Tieck was the more innovative, blending Gothic and märchen elements in "Der Blonde Eckbert" (1797) and "Der Runenberg" (1812).

2. Hewett-Thayer (113-21) provides a concise summary of Hoffmann's reading of these and other philosophers. See also McGlathery's exhaustive source study *Mysticism and Sexuality: E. T. A. Hoffman. Part One: Hoffmann and His Sources*, 136-50.

3. Cf. Tymms, 60: "To Hoffmann, the apparent absurdities of dreams, visions, and other figments of the irrational mind imply deep mysteries of cosmic proportions, which might be revealed to man if he were but able to . . . decipher,the symbolism." Other readers draw direct links between Hoffmann and Jung. Prawer asserts: "For Hoffmann, the personal unconscious is a means of gaining contact with something larger and deeper . . . which we may equate . . . with Jung's collective unconscious" (302); Peters (62) agrees: "the Other Realm exists at a deep subconscious level . . . common to all human beings, not unlike C. G. Jung's concept of the Collective Unconscious."

4. Hoffmann's masterful "märchen for modern times" therefore inspired one of the best Jungian interpretations of literature: Aniela Jaffé's monograph. Prawer (302) and other non-Jungians have praised her study. Another Jungian interpretation more relevant to this essay is Elardo's dissertation, "The Chthonic Woman." But his study, heavily dependent on Neumann, overemphasizes the negative aspects of the feminine, forgetting the bipolarity of the archetype. She cannot be "always the vixen, never the virgin" (2704A), she is often imagined as both.

5. In a sense, Jungian analytical psychology is a "formulation . . . of the confluence of traditions that shaped . . . Romanticism" (Bickman, 5), but it must be remembered that Jung did not derive his theories from the Romantic philosophers. He made inferences, often in agreement with theirs, based on observations of dreams and fantasies of patients. Hoffmann seems to have made similar inferences based on his own observations.

6. Kiernan (310) thinks "The Sandman" is "an autobiographical sketch of Hoffmann's childhood." McGlathery (*Part One*, 35-37) sums up the psychobiographical interpretations. See also Mahlendorf's article, which reveals "the thin line between creativity and pathology" (232) in Hoffmann. Nathanael in "The Sandman" is that part of Hoffmann he wishes to exorcize. McGlathery (*passim*) sees Hoffmann's protagonists as "self-ironic" portraits.

7. *Le Diable amoureux* was one of Hoffmann's favorite books (McGlathery, *Part One*, 122; cf. Winkler), but it was probably mostly from Tieck that Hoffmann learned the techniques of Ambiguous Gothic—e.g., of refusing to explain away the supernatural, seeing in the uncanny a psychic reality that is not mere delusion.

8. Cf. Daemmrich, 23: The unconscious alter-ego projections appearing in the Romantic fiction of the Germans are "the first indication of the modern crisis in man's identity." This identity crisis involves doppelgängers of both sexes—it is a crisis also of gender identity, as Nathanael's identity in "The Sandman" dissolves into Olimpia.

9. Sir Walter Scott (467) missed their moral significance completely, seeing Hoffmann's tales as mere raving, the "feverish dreams of a lightheaded patient . . .

requiring the assistance of medicine rather than of criticism." Goethe agreed that they seemed meaningless. Their ambiguity has resulted in conflicting interpretations, from Neoplatonic Idealism (Negus) to Romantic Irony (Tatar) to the Absurd (Daemmrich, 75, and Prawer, 307).

10. All references in English to "The Sandman" and "The Mines at Falun" are to Knight and Kent's edition, *Selected Writings of E. T. A. Hoffmann, Volume One,* hereinafter abbreviated as *K*. References to the original German, given for key words and phrases, are to *E. T. A. Hoffmanns Werke,* vol. 2, hereinafter abbreviated *W*.

11. Freud, 384: "The figure of his father and Coppelius represent the two opposites into which the father-imago is split by the ambivalence of the child's feeling."

12. McGlathery (*Part One,* 36) considers Freud's equation of the fear of eye-loss with castration anxiety "unacceptable," since Freud was more interested here in supporting his theories than in understanding Hoffmann. Cf. Prawer, 303. For Prawer, the intrusion of the *unheimlich* into the cozy *heimlich* domestic circle is a matter of much more than sexual consequence.

13. That Klara may be an Enlightenment figure is further supported by the German word for Enlightenment: *Aufklärung.* Hoffmann's distrust of Enlightenment science is apparent in his sinister portrayal of Spalanzani, a prototype for Frankenstein and Rappaccini (see Cohen's article).

14. Thus complicating his tale even further. As several readers have noticed, the narrator who comes in after the epistolary first half seems yet another reflection—another "alter-ego projection" either of Nathanael (his sane self perhaps) or of Hoffmann himself. See Tatar's article for an explanation of these multiple reflections in terms of Romantic Irony. I see this narrator as an authorial voice of sanity.

15. Mahlendorf, for example, sees Nathanael as a Romantic poet. Although she recognizes in the tale "the thin line between genius and madness," she does not see that Nathanael, as a reifying literalist, is no poet. Nor does Kamla, for whom Olimpia is "the mirror image of the [Romantic] solipsistic poet" (95).

16. McGlathery reduces the tale to a comic *conte licencieux* involving sexual panic or "cold feet" (*Part Two,* 58). I do not deny the sexual element in the tale, but I think it is part of a larger whole. Sexuality is only part of Eros.

17. Here I am following the post-Jungian idea (supporting Freud's notion that humans are innately bisexual) that men must have an animus as well as an anima (Hillman, "Anima II," 141-43). Cf. Samuels, *Jung and the Post-Jungians,* 210; Logos and Eros exist within a person of either sex: "The balance and relation between the two separate principles regulate the individual's sense of himself as a sexed and gendered being." One might argue that Coppelius is better seen as a "shadow" than an animus (as Prawer [302] suggests), but as Hillman and Samuels imply, Jung's notion of the shadow developed in the absence of an animus theory in the male. Once dissociated from anima, the animus *becomes* the "shadow."

18. Emma Jung (65-70) reveals how frequently the anima is associated with water. The moon is traditionally viewed as feminine by men, while the sun is supposedly masculine. Icons of the androgynous archetype have often been presented as fusions of sun and moon (see *Man and His Symbols,* 69, woodcut illustration).

19. The corpse bride (discussed more fully in Chapter 5 below), as Knight and Kent point out in a footnote (*K*, 160), is an allusion to Goethe's ballad "The Bride of Korinth." In Hoffmann, the necrophilia made explicit in the poem is only hinted at; Goethe's bride is not ambiguous like Olimpia, whose corpselike features are an ironic metaphor for what Nathanael really wants in a woman and for the dead state of Nathanael's soul.

20. Cf. Irving Massey's chapter 6. He comes to a similar conclusion (that Nathanael is narcissistic) by a different route. When Klara refuses to become a projection of Nathanael, "she throws him back upon his . . . nothingness" (118). Cf. also G. R. Thompson, *Romantic Gothic Tales,* 50, and Kamla's article.

21. Jung, *CW* 9.1. 67: "It therefore seems probable that the archetypal form of the divine syzygy first covers up and assimilates the image of the real parents until, with increasing consciousness, the real figures of the parents are perceived—often to the child's disappointment. Nobody knows better than the psychotherapist that the mythologizing of the parents is often pursued far into adulthood and is given up only with the greatest resistance." Nathanael's parents at first fit the archetypal mold, which presents them as a unity.

22. Cf. Schneidermann, 285, who cites Heinz Hartmann's idea that "there is a tendency in the pre-phallic stage to identify the parents as idealized, powerful, magical protectors"—a tendency Jung explains as archetypal.

23. That Hoffmann was somewhat skeptical of occultism seems clear from McGlathery, *Part One,* chapter 9: "Hoffmann's tales are . . . ironic jests about the widespread occultism and spiritualism of his own day" (155).

Works Cited

Bickman, Martin. *The Unsounded Centre: Jungian Studies in American Romanticism.* Chapel Hill: University of North Carolina Press, 1980.

Cohen, Hubert I. "Hoffmann's 'The Sandman': A Possible Source for 'Rappaccini's Daughter.'" *ESQ* 68 (1972): 148-55.

Daemmrich, Horst S. *The Shattered Self: E. T. A. Hoffmann's Tragic Vision.* Detroit: Wayne State University Press, 1973.

Elardo, Ronald Joseph. "The Chthonic Woman in the Novellas and Fairy Tales of E. T. A. Hoffmann." *DAI* 40 (1979): 2704A.

Ellenberger, Henri F. *The Discovery of the Unconscious.* New York: Basic Books, 1970.

Frank, Frederick S. "The Gothic Romance—1762-1820." *Horror Literature: A Core Collection and Reference Guide,* ed. Marshall Tymn, 3-175. New York: Bowker, 1981.

Freud, Sigmund. "The Uncanny." 1919. Rpt. in *Collected Papers,* vol. 4, trans. Joan Riviere, 368-407. New York: Basic Books, 1959.

Hewett-Thayer, Harvey W. *Hoffmann: Author of the Tales.* Princeton: Princeton University Press, 1948.

Hillman, James. "Anima II." *Spring* (1974): 113-46.

Hoffmann, Ernst Theodor Amadeus. *Selected Writings of E. T. A. Hoffmann. Volume One: The Tales.* Ed. and trans. Elizabeth C. Knight and Leonard J. Kent. Chicago: University of Chicago Press, 1969.

———. *Werke.* Vol. 2. Ed. Herbert Kraft and Mandred Wacker. Frankfurt: Insel Verlag, 1967.

Jaffé, Aniela. *Bilder und Symbole aus E. T. A. Hoffmanns Märchen "Der goldne Topf." Gestaltungen des Unbewussten.* Ed. C. G. Jung. Vol. 7. Zurich: 1950.

Jung, Carl Gustav. *The Collected Works of C. G. Jung.* [CW] Trans. R. F. C. Hull, 20 vols. Princeton: Princeton University Press, 1953-79.

———. "Psychology and Literature." *Modern Man in Search of a Soul,* trans. W. S. Dell and Cary F. Baynes, 152-72. New York: Harcourt Brace Jovanovich, 1933.

———, ed. *Man and His Symbols.* Garden City, N.Y.: Doubleday, 1964. Jung, Emma. *Animus and Anima.* Dallas: Spring Publ., 1981.

Kiernan, James G. "An Ataxic Paranoia of Genius: A Study of E. T. A. Hoffmann." *The Alienist and Neurologist* 17 (1896): 295-310.

Knight, Elizabeth C., and Leonard J. Kent. "Introduction." *Selected Writings of E. T. A. Hoffmann. Volume One: The Tales,* 9-45. Chicago: University of Chicago Press, 1969.

McGlathery, James M. *Mysticism and Sexuality: E. T. A. Hoffmann. Part One: Hoffmann and His Sources.* Las Vegas: Peter Lang, 1981.

———. *Mysticism and Sexuality: E. T. A. Hoffmann. Part Two: Interpretation of the Tales.* Las Vegas: Peter Lang, 1985.

Mahlendorf, Ursula R. "E. T. A. Hoffmann's 'The Sandman': The Fictional Psycho-Biography of a Romantic Poet." *American Imago* 32 (1975): 217-39.

Massey, Irving. *The Gaping Pig: Literature and Metamorphosis.* Berkley and Los Angeles: University of California Press, 1976.

Negus, Kenneth. *E. T. A. Hoffmann's Other World: The Romantic Author and His New Mythology.* Philadelphia: University of Pennsylvania Press, 1965.

Neumann, Erich. *The Great Mother.* Trans. Ralph Manheim. 2d ed. Princeton: Princeton University Press, 1963.

Peters, Diana S. "The Dream as Bridge in the Works of E. T. A. Hoffmann." *Oxford German Studies* 8 (1973): 60-85.

Prawer, S. J. "Hoffmann's Uncanny Guest: A Reading of 'Der Sandmann.'" *German Life and Letters* 18 (1965): 297-308.

Samuels, Andrew. *Jung and the Post-Jungians.* London: Routledge & Kegan Paul, 1985.

Schneidermann, Leo. "E. T. A. Hoffmann's Tales: Ego Ideal and Parental Loss." *American Imago* 40.3 (Fall 1983): 285-310.

Tatar, Maria M. "E. T. A. Hoffmann's 'Der Sandmann': Reflection and Romantic Irony." *Modern Language Notes* 95 (1980): 585-608.

Taylor, Ronald. *Hoffmann.* London: Bowes & Bowes, 1963.

Thompson, G. Richard. ed. *Romantic Gothic Tales, 1790-1840.* New York: Harper & Row, 1979.

Tymms, Ralph. *Doubles in Literary Psychology.* Cambridge: Bowes & Bowes, 1949.

Winkler, Marcus. "Cazotte lu par E. T. A. Hoffmann: Du *Diable amoureux* à 'Der Elementargeist.'" *Arcadia* 23.2 (1988): 113-32.

FURTHER READING

Criticism

Bresnick, Adam. "Prosopoetic Compulsion: Reading the Uncanny in Freud and Hoffmann." *Germanic Review* 71, no. 2 (spring 1996): 114-32.

Builds on Sigmund Freud's theories by analyzing his essay "The Uncanny" and Hoffmann's short story "The Sandman."

Freud, Sigmund. "The Uncanny." In *The Uncanny,* by Sigmund Freud, translated by David McLintock, pp. 123-62. New York: Penguin, 2003.

An essay originally published in Imago *in 1919 as "Das Unheimliche" and considered the quintessential work on the subject of the uncanny. Defines the uncanny, provides examples of how it is exemplified in "The Sandman," and explains how the uncanny functions within the context of human psychology.*

Ireland, Kenneth R. "Urban Perspectives: Fantasy and Reality in Hoffmann and Dickens." *Comparative Literature* 30, no. 2 (spring 1978): 133-56.

Discusses the parallels between the works of Hoffmann and Dickens, with particular emphasis on doubling.

Jones, Malcolm V. "'Der Sandmann' and 'the Uncanny': A Sketch for an Alternative Approach." *Paragraph: A Journal of Modern Critical Theory* 7 (March 1986): 77-101.

Counters Sigmund Freud's reading of "The Sandman."

Kamla, Thomas A. "E. T. A. Hoffmann's Vampirism: Instinctual Perversion." *American Imago* 42 (1985): 235-53.

Examines the pathological behavior of the characters in the untitled vampire tale published in The Serapion Brethren.

Labriola, Patrick. "Edgar Allan Poe and E. T. A. Hoffman: The Double in 'William Wilson' and *The Devil's Elixirs.*" *International Fiction Review* 29 (2002): 69-77.

Using Sigmund Freud's "The Uncanny" as a guide, outlines the developmental stages of the double in Edgar Allan Poe's short story "William Wilson" and Hoffman's The Devil's Elixirs *and analyzes both authors' treatment of the divided self.*

McGlathery, James. *E. T. A. Hoffmann.* New York: Twayne Publishers, 1997, 195 p.

Full-length analysis of Hoffmann's life and works.

Negus, Kenneth. "The Allusions to Schiller's *Der Geisterseher* in E. T. A. Hoffmann's *Das Majorat*." *German Quarterly* 32, no. 4 (November 1959): 341-55.

Explores the influence of Johann Christoph Friedrich von Schiller's Der Geisterseher *on Hoffmann's* Das Majorat.

———. "The Family Tree in E. T. A. Hoffmann's *Die Elixiere des Teufels*." *PMLA: Publications of the Modern Language Association of America* 73, no. 5, Part 1 (December 1958): 516-20.

Assesses the significance of ancestry in The Devil's Elixier.

Romero, Christiane Zehl. "M. G. Lewis' *The Monk* and E. T. A. Hoffmann's *Die Elixiere des Teufels*: Two Versions of the Gothic." *Neophilologus* 63 (1979): 574-82.

Compares the gothicism in The Monk *and in* Die Elixiere des Teufels *(*The Devil's Elixir*).*

Willson, A. Leslie. "Hoffmann's Horrors." In *Literature and the Occult: Essays in Comparative Literature*, edited by Luanne Frank, pp. 264-71. Arlington, Tex.: University of Texas at Arlington, 1977.

Explores elements of magic and the supernatural in Hoffmann's tales.

OTHER SOURCES FROM GALE:

Additional coverage of Hoffmann's life and career is contained in the following sources published by Thomson Gale: *Concise Dictionary of World Literary Biography*, Vol. 2; *Dictionary of Literary Biography*, Vol. 90; *European Writers*, Vol. 5; *Literature Resource Center*; *Nineteenth-Century Literature Criticism*, Vol. 2; *Reference Guide to Short Fiction*, Ed. 2; *Reference Guide to World Literature*, Eds. 2, 3; *Short Story Criticism*, Vol. 13; *Something about the Author*, Vol. 27; *Supernatural Fiction Writers*, Vol. 1; and *Writers for Children*.

JAMES HOGG

(1770 - 1835)

Scottish poet, novelist, short story and song writer, journalist, editor, playwright, and essayist.

A nearly illiterate shepherd until the age of eighteen, Hogg became a prolific writer of poetry, ballads, songs, short stories, and historical narratives who was ranked among Scottish writers only below Robert Burns and Sir Walter Scott. He established a persona as the "Ettrick Shepherd," a rustic and provincial poet, and gained fame through his association with the influential *Blackwood's Edinburgh Magazine*. Yet that reputation declined after his death, and a century later he was remembered, if at all, only for an unconventional novel, *The Private Memoirs and Confessions of a Justified Sinner* (1824), which during his life had been dismissed as an obtuse satire on Christian fanaticism. Featuring Gothic and supernatural elements, including a schizophrenic narrator and a psychological double/devil figure, as well as proto-modern narrative complexity, the work has been rediscovered by modern critics who have come to view it as a masterpiece of prose fiction. In recent years, the revival of Scottish nationalism has led to new interest in Hogg and the reprinting of his other works as well. Despite his many imitations of Burns and Scott, the pieces that utilize the supernatural folk traditions represent Hogg's best achievements and also provide the most interest for modern readers. Ghosts, both real and explained, appear regularly in Hogg's works, as do less familiar creatures: brownies, fairies, kelpies, and wraiths. Critics continue to reevaluate Hogg's work and find much to recommend in it, showing how the author uses the occult for purposes other than mere shock and integrates his own humor and folk wisdom with strange and lively narratives to produce highly moral, extremely entertaining tales.

BIOGRAPHICAL INFORMATION

Born to a pious tenant farmer in 1770, Hogg spent his early life as a shepherd in the Ettrick hills of Scotland following his family's bankruptcy in 1777. With minimal formal schooling, he taught himself to read using the only book available, a Bible, while his early interest in literature was founded on the Scottish oral tradition of ballads, songs, and fairy tales that were recited to him by his mother. As his self-education continued in his late teens, Hogg began to read the great works of English and Scottish literature and composed his first pieces of poetry, including verses imitative of John Milton, Alexander Pope, and others. By 1802 he had met Sir Walter Scott as the famous writer was collecting folk ballads for his *Minstrelsy of the Scottish Border*. Hogg later read the work and, largely unimpressed with its quality, determined to compose superior verse on the same subject. He subsequently sent several poems to Scott, both his own original ballads and adaptations of those his mother had taught him. Hogg's poetic abilities and his knowledge of Scottish lore impressed Scott, and in the following years a friendship grew between the two men that had an important influence on Hogg's career. Hogg's writings of this period appeared in his 1807 collection, *The Mountain Bard: Consisting of Ballads and Songs, Founded on Facts and Legendary Tales.*

In February of 1810, after Hogg had lost two farms due to lack of funds, he departed the pastoral tranquility of Ettrick for several years and moved to Edinburgh. His weekly periodical, *The Spy*, containing articles, poems, and tales mostly written by Hogg himself, was published between 1810 and 1811, but collapsed following the printing of a particularly scandalous story. Meanwhile, Hogg began crafting his literary persona as the "Ettrick Shepherd," a self-taught poet of provincial Scotland. He contributed poetry and prose to Scottish literary magazines and established himself as a national literary figure with his collection *The Queen's Wake* in 1813. The parodies of *The Poetic Mirror; or, The Living Bards of Britain* (1816) delighted audiences and maintained Hogg's popularity, though many of his other works of this period were ignored or denigrated by contemporary critics. In 1817 Hogg began a successful relationship with the newly founded *Blackwood's Edinburgh Magazine*, which published the collaborative "Translation from an Ancient Chaldee MS." in October of that year. Coauthored with John Wilson and John Gibson Lockhart, the anonymous satire written in biblical form lampooned prominent Edinburgh Whigs and created a stir in the city. By 1820 Hogg had married and returned to rural life, retreating to his Altrive farm near Yarrow. The sales of his 1824 novel *The Private Memoirs and Confessions of a Justified Sinner* proved discouraging, and Hogg's writings of the subsequent period were frequently ignored or panned by his contemporaries, though he remained a recognizable figure in Scottish literary circles. His reminiscences of a lifelong friendship, *Familiar Anecdotes of Sir Walter Scott*, appeared in 1834 and capitalized on interest in Scotland's most popular writer, but his later collection of short stories, *Tales of the Wars of Montrose* (1835), was a failure. Hogg died in November of 1835 after a prolonged illness and was buried in Ettrick.

MAJOR WORKS

With few exceptions, Hogg's writings about the occult and paranormal are acknowledged to be his best. His attitude toward the supernatural is ambivalent: his ancestors believed fully in the existence of creatures from another level of reality, and Hogg constantly shifts between providing rational explanations of strange events and presenting them without comment—a technique that effectively increases the suspense. He recognized that religious faith, like superstition, demands the acceptance of things unseen, and although he was a devout Presbyterian, he saw no inconsistency in maintaining beliefs in both fairy lore and Christianity.

In the poem "Superstition" (1815), Hogg laments that "gone is [Superstition's] mysterious dignity, / And true Devotion wanes away with her." Supernatural creatures, he says, not only teach the necessity of accepting the unseen but also fill guilty hearts with dread and make known their dark deeds. Hogg's fiction features various supernatural beings, from conventional ghosts to fairies. "The Barber of Duncow" (1831), one of his best ghost stories, tells how a spirit reveals to a new bride her husband's profligate past. After the wife disappears, her ghost—with throat nearly severed—leads villagers to her corpse, and when the husband touches the body, it begins to bleed profusely. Other tales depict more unusual supernatural creatures, those found in the folklore with which Hogg was familiar such as wraiths, fairies, and brownies. In "Adam Bell" (1811), some servants, having seen the apparition of their missing master, learn that a wraith appearing in daylight prognosticated very long life. In "The Wool-Gatherer" (1811), a young shepherd, Barnaby, whiles away a journey by telling the heroine some fine ghost stories. His seriousness provokes her to ask if he truly believes in such events. He believes in them, he says, a much as he believes in the gospels; he believes in the apparitions that warn of death, that save life, and discover guilt. Brownies figure in two of Hogg's best works, the historical novel *The Brownie of Bodsbeck* (1818), which mixes legends of a preternatural creature with the efforts of several defeated revolutionaries to hide from political and religious persecution in the hills and farmlands of Scotland, and the story "The Brownie of the Black Haggs" (1828). Witches appear in the entertaining novel *The Three Perils of Man* (1822) and the story "The Hunt of Eildon" (1818).

In his poems, too, Hogg writes extensively of otherworldly creatures. In "Lyttil Pynkie" (1831), a beautiful elf-girl begins a wild dance that causes the death of the evil Baron and his profligate retainers; at the end, she enables the good priest who has come to exorcise her to see clearly the invisible evil at work throughout the world. *The*

Pilgrims of the Sun (1815), Hogg's most ambitious poem, combines an allegorical and philosophical journey through the universe with an effective ghost story, while "Kilmeny" (1813), often praised as Hogg's best lyric, deals with the visit of the purest maiden on earth to Fairyland—a conjunction of the fairy and Christian paradises—from which she returns to recount what she has seen. Hogg's comic poem "The Witch of Fife" (1813) presents a pleasure-loving old man who finds himself married to a witch, who later saves him as he is about to be burned at the stake.

Hogg's acknowledged masterpiece, *The Private Memoirs and Confessions of a Justified Sinner,* is more overtly religious than his other works and rather than using supernatural creatures presents supernatural events that emphasize terror and evil. The figure alluded to in the title is Robert Wringhim Colwan, the illegitimate son of a reverend, who is brought up as an Antinomian Calvinist and thus believes himself a member of God's elect—and therefore assured of divine salvation regardless of his sins in life. After the strange disappearance of his elder brother, Robert meets a mysterious individual, Gil-Martin, who encourages him to commit acts of violence against the "ungodly," culminating in several murders and Robert's own suicide. The novel features a dual narrative, first that of the deluded and possibly schizophrenic "sinner," followed by the apparently objective account of the work's fictional editor who had purportedly discovered Robert's memoirs after his body was exhumed some one hundred years later. The work, which explores questions about morality, religion, psychology, and the demonic, works up to a terrifying climax, and some critics have claimed that the character of Gil-Martin is one of the most convincing representations of the power of evil in literature.

CRITICAL RECEPTION

Hogg was a prolific writer who had enjoyed renown in his day, yet after his death and until the mid-twentieth century most of his work was ignored by commentators. Many of Hogg's short poems and tales were written purely to turn a profit, and these hastily composed works are generally regarded as deeply flawed and of little merit. But even his best writings, much appreciated by his contemporaries who enjoyed his celebrations of Scottish rural scenes and superstitions as well as his imitations of ancient Scottish ballads, generated little critical interest after his death. Those who read his work generally found

his plots inadequate, his endings haphazard, and his poetry poorly crafted. A turning point in Hogg's critical reputation occurred in the 1920s when André Gide (see Further Reading) "rediscovered" Hogg's novel *The Private Memoirs and Confessions of a Justified Sinner,* recognizing it as a significant work of world literature and as Hogg's masterpiece. Gide praised Hogg's depiction of the supernatural side of faith and the work's moral and religious effects. Since Gide's comments, numerous scholars have studied the novel and praised its sophisticated narrative technique, psychological complexity, and deeply ironic and ambivalent elements. Critics have begun to investigate the author's other neglected writings as well, and some have shown how the supernatural informs nearly all of the writer's best work. They have pointed out how it achieves its effects through the tension of belief and unbelief rather than through gratuitous horror and shows that supernatural events should not be ignored because the wonders of the invisible world reveal the moral universe. Critics acknowledge that much of Hogg's writing is ordinary and uninteresting, but his best work is enjoying renewed attention and gaining stature as some of the most original writing from the nineteenth century in its depiction of the tension between things of this world and those of other realms.

PRINCIPAL WORKS

Scottish Pastorals, Poems, Songs, etc., Mostly Written in the Dialect of the South (poetry) 1801

Memoir of the Author's Life (memoirs) 1806

The Mountain Bard: Consisting of Ballads and Songs, Founded on Facts and Legendary Tales (poetry, songs, and autobiographical sketch) 1807

The Forest Minstrel; A Selection of Songs, Adapted to the Most Favourite Scottish Airs [with Thomas M. Cunningham and others] (poetry and songs) 1810

The Spy [editor and main contributor] (journalism, poetry, and sketches) 1810-11

The Queen's Wake (poetry) 1813

The Pilgrims of the Sun (poetry) 1815

Mador of the Moor (poetry) 1816

The Poetic Mirror; or, The Living Bards of Britain [with Thomas Pringle] (poetry) 1816

Dramatic Tales. 2 vols. (short stories) 1817

"Translation from an Ancient Chaldee MS." [with John Gibson Lockhart, John Wilson, and others] (satire) 1817

The Brownie of Bodsbeck, and Other Tales (novel and short stories) 1818

A Border Garland (songs) 1819

The Jacobite Relics of Scotland: Being the Songs, Airs, and Legends of the Adherents of the House of Stuart. 2 vols. [editor and contributor] (songs) 1819-21

Winter Evening Tales, Collected among the Cottagers in the South of Scotland. 2 vols. (short stories) 1820

The Poetical Works of James Hogg. 4 vols. (poetry and songs) 1822

The Three Perils of Man; or, War, Women, and Witchcraft. 3 vols. (novel) 1822

The Three Perils of Woman; or, Love, Leasing, and Jealousy. 3 vols. (short stories) 1823

The Private Memoirs and Confessions of a Justified Sinner (novel) 1824; republished as *The Suicide's Grave,* 1828

Queen Hynde (poetry) 1825

The Shepherd's Calendar. 2 vols. (poetry) 1829

Songs, by the Ettrick Shepherd (songs) 1831

Altrive Tales: Collected from among the Peasantry of Scotland, and from Foreign Adventurers (short stories) 1832

A Queer Book (poetry) 1832

Familiar Anecdotes of Sir Walter Scott (reminiscences) 1834; also published as *The Domestic Manners and Private Life of Sir Walter Scott*

Tales of the Wars of Montrose. 3 vols. (short stories) 1835

Tales and Sketches. 6 vols. (novels and short stories) 1837

The Works of the Ettrick Shepherd. 2 vols. (ballads, poetry, and sketches) 1865

PRIMARY SOURCES

JAMES HOGG (STORY DATE 1836)

SOURCE: Hogg, James. "Expedition to Hell." In *Gothic Tales of Terror, Volume One: Classic Horror Stories from Great Britain,* edited by Peter Haining. 1972. Reprint edition, pp. 496-506. Baltimore, Md.: Penguin Books, 1973.

In the following excerpt from a story first published in 1836, the narrator addresses the reader on the significance of dreams.

There is no phenomenon in nature less understood, and about which greater nonsense is written than dreaming. It is a strange thing. For my part I do not understand it, nor have I any desire to do so; and I firmly believe that no philosopher that ever wrote knows a particle more about it than I do, however elaborate and subtle the theories he may advance concerning it. He knows not even what sleep is, nor can he define its nature, so as to enable any common mind to comprehend him; and how, then, can he define that ethereal part of it, wherein the soul holds intercourse with the external world?—how, in that state of abstraction, some ideas force themselves upon us, in spite of all our efforts to get rid of them; while others, which we have resolved to bear about with us by night as well as by day, refuse us their fellowship, even at periods when we most require their aid?

No, no; the philosopher knows nothing about either; and if he says he does; I entreat you not to believe him. He does not know what mind is; even his own mind, to which one would think he has the most direct access: far less can he estimate the operations and powers of that of any other intelligent being. He does not even know, with all his subtlety, whether it be a power distinct from his body, or essentially the same, and only incidentally and temporarily endowed with different qualities. He sets himself to discover at what period of his existence the union was established. He is baffled; for Consciousness refuses the intelligence, declaring, that she cannot carry him far enough back to ascertain it. He tries to discover the precise moment when it is dissolved, but on this Consciousness is altogether silent; and all is darkness and mystery; for the origin, the manner of continuance, and the time and mode of breaking up of the union between soul and body, are in reality undiscoverable by our natural faculties—are not patent, beyond the possibility of mistake: but whosoever can read his Bible, and solve a dream, can do either, without being subjected to any material error.

It is on this ground that I like to contemplate, not the theory of dreams, but the dreams themselves; because they prove to the unlettered man, in a very forcible manner, a distinct existence of the soul, and its lively and rapid intelligence with external nature, as well as with a world of spirits with which it has no acquaintance, when the body is lying dormant, and the same to the soul as if sleeping in death.

I account nothing of any dream that relates to the actions of the day; the person is not sound asleep who dreams about these things; there is no division between matter and mind, but they are mingled together in a sort of chaos—what a farmer would call compost—fermenting and disturbing one another. I find that in all dreams of that kind, men of every profession have dreams peculiar to their own occupations; and, in the country, at least, their import is generally understood. Every man's body is a barometer. A thing made up of the elements must be affected by their various changes and convulsions; and so the body assuredly is. When I was a shepherd, and all the comforts of my life depended so much on good or bad weather, the first thing I did every morning was strictly to overhaul the dreams of the night; and I found that I could calculate better from them than from the appearance and changes of the sky. I know a keen sportsman who pretends that his dreams never deceive him. If the dream is of angling, or pursuing salmon in deep waters, he is sure of rain; but if fishing on dry ground, or in waters so low that the fish cannot get from him, it forebodes drought; hunting or shooting hares is snow, and moorfowl wind, & c. But the most extraordinary professional dream on record is, without all doubt, that well-known one of George Dobson, coach-driver in Edinburgh, which I shall here relate; for though it did not happen in the shepherd's cot, it has often been recited there.

GENERAL COMMENTARY

DOUGLAS S. MACK (ESSAY DATE 1995)

SOURCE: Mack, Douglas S. "Aspects of the Supernatural in the Shorter Fiction of James Hogg." In *Exhibited by Candlelight: Sources and Developments in the Gothic Tradition,* edited by Valeria Tinkler-Villani, Peter Davidson, and Jane Stevenson, pp. 129-35. Atlanta, Ga. and Amsterdam: Rodopi, 1995.

In the following essay, Mack explores the sources that inform Hogg's use of the supernatural in his works.

This essay focuses on some of the roots of the use of the supernatural in the works of James Hogg; this subject will be approached through an examination of specific examples provided by *The Shepherd's Calendar,* a series of articles contributed by Hogg to *Blackwood's Edinburgh Magazine* between 1819 and 1828.

The Shepherd's Calendar is a title with a long history in the literature of the English language. Hogg, however, had a particular and unusual right to use it: in his youth he had spent many years as a professional shepherd in the remote and mountainous Ettrick district of southern Scotland. Indeed, in parts of his *Shepherd's Calendar* he draws upon the experiences of his own pastoral life in the 1790s; and elsewhere in the series he sets out to re-create on paper something of the manner and the content of the traditional oral story-telling of Ettrick. To describe *The Shepherd's Calendar* in this way seems to suggest that it is a project of a somewhat antiquarian nature, involving an attempt to record and preserve old customs and manners before they finally pass away. That is no doubt part of what Hogg is seeking to achieve; but his "Shepherd's Calendar" articles go far beyond a mere antiquarian interest. Indeed, these contributions to *Blackwood's* make up a sequence of sophisticated and complex narratives in which the supernatural plays a particularly striking role.

Let us begin by looking at **"Storms"**, a largely autobiographical article in which Hogg writes about the trials and dangers encountered by shepherds as a result of severe snow-falls. Much of the article is devoted to an account of Hogg's own experiences during the winter of 1794-95. At this time he was working as a shepherd at Blackhouse in the Yarrow valley, part of the Ettrick district, and he was a member of a local literary society formed by "a few young shepherds". At the society's meetings each of the members "read an essay on a subject previously given out; and after that every essay was minutely investigated, and criticised".[1] In *The Rise of the Historical Novel,* John MacQueen has convincingly argued that the society's agenda probably "included the forbidden subject of radical politics and the need for reform, if not revolution".[2] This was, after all, the 1790s: revolution was in the air.

Be that as it may, Hogg was on his way to a meeting of this society when signs of an approaching storm forced him to turn back. The meeting of the society went ahead in his absence; and as events turned out the shieling at which it was held "was situated in the very vortex of the storm; the devastations made by it extended all around that, to a certain extent; and no farther on any one quarter than another" (16). The storm was universally viewed in the Ettrick community "as a judgement sent by God for the punishment of some heineous offence" (15). Hogg goes on to record a conversation, during which he learned that the blame for the heinous offence was being laid at the door of his literary society:

"Weel chap" said he to me "we hae fund out what has been the cause of a' this mischief now."

"What do you mean John?"

"What do I mean? It seems that a great squad o' birkies that ye are conneckit wi', had met that night at the herds house o' Ever Phaup, an had raised the deil amang them."

Every countenance in the kitchen changed; the women gazed at John and then at me, and their lips grew white. These kind of feelings are infectious, people may say what they will; fear begets fear as naturally as light springs from reflection. I reasoned stoutly at first against the veracity of the report, observing that it was utter absurdity, and a shame and disgrace for the country to cherish such a rediculous lie.

"Lie!" said John "It's nae lie; they had him up amang them like a great rough dog at the very time that the tempest began, and were glad to draw cuts, an' gie him ane o' their number to get quit o' him again."

Lord how every hair of my head, and inch of my frame crept at hearing this sentence; for I had a dearly loved brother who was one of the number, several full cousins, and intimate acquaintances; indeed I looked on the whole fraternity as my brethern, and considered myself involved in all their transactions. I could say no more in defence of the society's proceedings, for to tell the truth, though I am ashamed to acknowledge it, I suspected that the allegation might be too true.

(16-17)

"For to tell the truth, though I am ashamed to acknowledge it, I suspected that the allegation might be too true." These are highly significant words. They show the young Hogg wholly at home with a system of assumptions in which a blizzard can be explained as the judgement of God, and in which it can seem natural to encounter the physical and active presence of the Devil, here and now, among one's relations and intimate acquaintances. On the other hand, he says "I am ashamed to acknowledge it". The mature Hogg is by no means contained by a naive acceptance of the old beliefs: he is fully aware that times have changed, and that in a post-Enlightenment world the old ideas have come to be seen as childishly absurd. All this points to a crucial feature of Hogg's intellectual and cultural position: he is situated between two worlds—or rather, he is fully part of two very different worlds. One of these worlds is the Ettrick of his pastoral youth, a district where he continued to spend much of his time throughout his life, and where he died. His other world is Edinburgh, which he graced for more than a quarter of a century as a professional author.

It would not be extravagant to say that in Hogg's lifetime each of these two worlds was in its own way a key site in the intellectual life of Europe. From Edinburgh, Walter Scott was enthralling an international audience with his poetry and his novels; and the Scottish capital was still basking in the afterglow of the great days of David Hume and Adam Smith, of Hutton the geologist and Black the chemist, and of all the other major figures of the Scottish Enlightenment. Ettrick also had its importance, at any rate for those sensitive to the living significance of the great traditional ballads. It was from Ettrick that Scott (with Hogg's help) obtained some of the material for *Minstrelsy of the Scottish Border*; and it was Yarrow (in Ettrick) that Wordsworth famously left Unvisited in 1803—and later Visited in the autumn of 1814, with Hogg as his guide. The mature Hogg was the heir of the Edinburgh of the Enlightenment, and he was also the heir, and even the embodiment, of Wordsworth's unvisited Yarrow, with its "treasured dreams of times long past".

Hogg's place within these two worlds is important for his fiction; indeed much of his writing can be seen as an assertion, aimed at a sceptical Edinburgh audience, of the validity of traditional Ettrick beliefs and values. An excellent example of this process is provided by "**Mr Adamson of Laverhope**", a story from *The Shepherd's Calendar* in which a narrator, who clearly shares the assumptions of Enlightenment Edinburgh, offers for our contemplation an account of what peasant superstition has made of a natural calamity—a man being killed by lightning during a thunderstorm.

How does the story of Mr Adamson appear if we accept the supernatural interpretation of the superstitious inhabitants of Ettrick? In this view, we are not dealing with a natural event in which a man is struck by lightning; we are dealing rather with a divine judgment. God's lightning strikes down an evildoer; and the Devil, who has been present in disguise, carries Mr Adamson's soul off to Hell in the last thunderclap of the storm. What has Adamson done to deserve this condign punishment? His first offence is that, while seeking to collect debts, he has evicted a poor family and caused their goods to be sold by public auction. Thereafter, the community comes together to shear Mr Adamson's sheep, "it being customary for the farmers to assist one another reciprocally on these occasions"; but Adamson, dissatisfied with himself over the eviction, sours the usual hilarity of the communal shearing by irritably and violently attacking first a sheep-dog, and then a boy who comes to the dog's defence. Finally, Adamson refuses the customary alms to a beggar who visits the shearing. It is made clear that all these actions are contrary to Adamson's duty as a professing Christian; and we are also made to see that his actions outrage the shared values of an agricultural community which must depend upon mutual support for survival in a harsh environment.

The values of Ettrick are celebrated within the story by means of a detailed and affectionate account of the shared pleasures of the communal sheep-shearing, and these values are given explicit expression through the words and actions of the shepherd Rob Johnson. The Good Shepherd is always a resonant figure in Hogg. Behind fictional characters like Rob Johnson and Daniel Bell of *The Three Perils of Woman* there lies, of course, the figure of James Hogg the Ettrick Shepherd; but we are also reminded of the biblical King David, once a shepherd boy—and of Jesus, the supreme Good Shepherd.

In the supernatural interpretation of "**Mr Adamson of Laverhope**", then, evil deeds provoke divine vengeance. This view is powerfully backed up by Hogg's detailed rendering of the convulsion of the thunderstorm, a notable feature of which is a description of a flood which sweeps down on Adamson's sheepfolds "with a cataract front more than twenty feet deep" (33). This is an apt image in a story of divine anger; but surprisingly enough it is also true to weather conditions in southern Scotland, where flash floods of this kind are by no means unknown. For example, a report on the front page of *The Scotsman* newspaper for 27 July 1983 describes "a wall of water 20ft high and 200yds wide in places" which earlier in the week had surged across a four-mile area in the valley of the Hermitage Water, causing widespread damage to property and considerable danger to life and limb.

The flood, then, however extraordinary, nevertheless remains firmly within the boundaries of the possible; and this may serve as a reminder that Hogg's Enlightenment narrator does not share the Ettrick community's supernatural interpretation of Mr Adamson's death. For the narrator, Adamson is simply the unfortunate victim of a natural event, and this interpretation is reinforced by the narrator's concluding anecdote concerning the death by lightning of Mr Adam Copland of Minnigess. In this anecdote there is not a hint of the supernatural; instead we have cool, detached and rational comments on the operation of "the electric matter that slew Mr Copland". The story of the death of Mr Copland is, as it were, an Enlightenment version of the story erected by peasant superstition around the death of Mr Adamson; but Hogg so manages matters that the peasant superstition becomes much more coher-ent, impressive and convincing than the views of his Enlightened narrator. Hogg, that is to say, subverts his own narrator—just as the Editor is subverted in *The Private Memoirs and Confessions of a Justified Sinner.*

It seems, then, that in "**Mr Adamson of Laverhope**" Hogg employs a devious narrative strategy in order to question the Enlightened assumptions of his readers; indeed, the thrust of the story is that the traditional Christian world-view, dismissed by the narrator as peasant superstition, is in fact the source of an enlightenment which is genuine and real. Such a view sits comfortably with opinions expressed by Hogg in other contexts, for example in the sermon on Deism in the *Lay Sermons* of 1834, and in the poem "**Superstition**", which dates from 1815. "**Superstition**" looks back with regret to the old Ettrick belief in the supernatural, which has faded under the advance of modern rationalism.

> Those were the times for holiness of frame;
>   Those were the days when fancy wandered free;
> That kindled in the soul the mystic flame,
>   And the rapt breathings of high poesy;
>   Sole empress of the twilight—Woe is me!
> That thou and all thy spectres are outworn;
>   For true devotion wanes away with thee.
> All thy delirious dreams are laughed to scorn,
> While o'er our hills has dawned a cold saturnine morn.[3]

The Ettrick tradition was a Christian one, but it contained elements surviving from pre-Christian times. This is reflected in a number of Hogg's works, in which a young woman is taken from Scotland to a heavenly land, from which she returns transformed in one way or another. Most of Hogg's variations on this theme have certain things in common: the story is usually set in pre-Reformation Scotland; the young woman is usually linked in some way to the Blessed Virgin Mary—indeed, she is usually called Mary; the question of whether she does, or does not, remain a virgin is always an issue of some importance; and the heaven to which she is taken always has strong hints of pre-Christian or non-Christian traditions about Fairyland. This group of Hogg texts includes such works as "**Kilmeny**", *The Pilgrims of the Sun*, "**A Genuine Border Story**", and "**Mary Burnet**".

The last-named, from *The Shepherd's Calendar*, is a story quite different in tone from "**Mr Adamson of Laverhope**". The central character, Mary Burnet, is subjected by her lover John Allanson to something between a seduction and a rape. Supernatural forces, both good and evil, are brought into play by this outrage; and Mary, apparently under the protection of the Blessed Virgin, disappears from earth to become a part-heavenly, part-fairy creature. In her fairy guise, Mary returns to earth to lure her seducer to his destruction, and seven years after her disappearance she returns again, in heavenly and fairy glory, to give comfort to her grieving parents. The word "glamour" came into use in the Scots language before becoming established in English usage; and this word, in its traditional Scots sense of "magic, enchantment, witchcraft", exactly captures the spirit of **"Mary Burnet"**.

Another aspect of Hogg's use of the supernatural in *The Shepherd's Calendar* comes to the fore in the story **"The Brownie of the Black Haggs"**, a work which explores deep and disturbing recesses of the human mind. Lady Wheelhope becomes obsessed by Merodach, a servant thought by the country people to be a brownie sent to haunt her as a punishment for her wickedness. Her obsession deepens and becomes more complex as, again and again, she tries unsuccessfully to harm him only to suffer herself from the results of her own actions. We are told that the lady "fixed her eyes on Merodach. But such a look! . . . It was not a look of love nor of hatred exclusively; neither was it of desire or disgust, but it was a combination of them all. It was such a look as one fiend would cast on another, in whose everlasting destruction he rejoiced" (105). The author of *The Private Memoirs and Confessions of a Justified Sinner* is very much on his home ground here.

I have been attempting to suggest that Hogg's short stories are richly complex works which draw on deep wells of tradition in their resonant use of the supernatural; and it would be fair to say that his shorter fiction is beginning to achieve a high reputation, especially in Scotland and North America. If this emerging reputation is deserved, why has it taken so long for the worth of these stories to be recognized? A clue is provided by **"Tibby Hyslop's Dream"**, another of the *Shepherd's Calendar* pieces. This is in effect a story of sexual harassment and attempted seduction; but in the numerous nineteenth-century collected editions of Hogg's works the text is so heavily bowdlerized as to be almost entirely innocent of sexual implication. The story is thus emptied of its significant content.

The posthumous nineteenth-century collected editions of Hogg are all deplorably inadequate; and, as was to be expected in the circumstances, his reputation—high in his lifetime—declined rapidly thereafter. There has been a substantial revival over the past forty years or so, as good modern editions of some of his works have become available. A complete and accurate edition of *The Shepherd's Calendar* has still to appear, however: and the same could be said of many other major Hogg texts and collections. It is therefore pleasant to be able to record that a new and complete edition of Hogg is at present in active preparation, under the auspices of the University of Stirling's Centre for Scottish Literature and Culture.

Notes

1. James Hogg, *Selected Stories and Sketches,* ed. Douglas S. Mack, Edinburgh, 1982, 5.

2. John MacQueen, *The Rise of the Historical Novel,* Edinburgh, 1989, 208.

3. James Hogg, *Selected Poems,* ed. Douglas S. Mack, Oxford, 1970, 75; ll. 91-99.

TITLE COMMENTARY

The Private Memoirs and Confessions of a Justified Sinner

THE NEW MONTHLY MAGAZINE (REVIEW DATE 1 NOVEMBER 1824)

SOURCE: "New Publications, with Critical Remarks: *The Private Memoirs and Confessions of a Justified Sinner.*" *The New Monthly Magazine* 11 (1 November 1824): 506.

In the following excerpt, the critic offers a strongly negative assessment of The Private Memoirs and Confessions of a Justified Sinner, *objecting especially to Hogg's "bad grammar."*

[*The Private Memoirs and Confessions of a Justified Sinner* is,] we presume, intended to bring that exaggerated and extravagant style of writing which has lately become too prevalent, into the contempt which it so richly merits. All former horrors are nothing to the ineffable enormities of this justified Sinner, who is a parricide, fratricide, and *clericide*—for we must coin new words to comprehend all his multifarious offences. Nothing more completely ridiculous can well be imagined than the whole of the story. . . . We do not altogether approve of the mode which the author has chosen of attacking the religious prejudices of numbers, who, notwithstanding their speculative opinions, are in no danger of becoming either parricides or fratricides. We must also remark, that in spite of the high seasoning given to these Confessions, they are still singularly dull and revolting, and that it is altogether unfair to treat the reader with two versions of such extraordinary trash as the writer has given us in "the Editor's narrative," and the Confessions themselves. Moreover, though we may be compelled to read as much bad Scotch, as any gentleman on the other side of the Tweed may choose to pour out upon us, yet we do protest most solemnly against the iniquity of bad English, of which the present work furnishes most abundant instances. We account his bad grammar amongst the most crying sins of the miscreant with whose history we are here regaled.

WILLISTON R. BENEDICT (ESSAY DATE SPRING 1983)

SOURCE: Benedict, Williston R. "A Story Replete with Horror." *Princeton University Library Chronicle* 44, no. 3 (spring 1983): 246-51.

In the following essay, Benedict studies the original, 1824 edition of The Private Memoirs and Confessions of a Justified Sinner *and interprets the novel within the context of the literature of the early nineteenth century and within Hogg's oeuvre.*

Among the books in the private collection of Mr. Robert H. Taylor, which is now housed in the Firestone Library, is a fine and uncut copy in the original boards of James Hogg's only novel, *The Private Memoirs and Confessions of a Justified Sinner.* Hogg (1770-1835) was born into a humble farming family of the Lowlands of Scotland. He taught himself to read and write at an early age, and had the good fortune, at about the age of 30, to be drawn from rural obscurity into Edinburgh's literary society through the aid and encouragement of Sir Walter Scott. Like his mentor, Hogg proved successful at publishing some volumes of poetry before turning to the composition of works of fiction about 1818. By 1824, the date of his novel's publication, he had demonstrated to the Edinburgh "literati" his interest in and vast knowledge of the traditional tales of rural Scotland, which constitute one of the principal sources of his novel.

Hogg's few references, in his other works and in his chiefly unpublished correspondence, to the *Justified Sinner* provide little information as to his intention in writing it. William Blackwood, Edinburgh's most important publisher of the age, had evidently declined to publish the novel, and it appeared instead under the London imprint of T. N. Longman and his associates in the summer of 1824. Departing from his previous practice, Hogg authorized publication of the book without the inclusion of his name on the title page. In a letter to Blackwood dated 28 June 1824 Hogg wrote, with considerable urgency in his usual hurried manner: "There is one hint I beseech you to remember to give. . . . It is that as some one of our friends are likely to be the first efficient noticers of *The Confessions* they will not notice them at all *as mine* but as written by a *Glasgow man* by all means. . . . This will give excellent and delightful scope and freedom."[1] In the preface to another volume published in 1832, Hogg explained his desire for anonymous authorship: "The next year, 1824, I published *The Confessions of a Sinner*; but it being a story replete with horror, after I had written it I durst not venture to put my name to it: so it was published anonymously, and of course did not sell very well."

Other comments on the book in Hogg's correspondence are rare. In a letter to Blackwood, probably dated 6 August 1828, he wrote that a certain Mrs. Hughes "insists on the *Confessions of a Sinner* being republished with my name, as she says it is positively the best story of that frightful kind that ever was written. I think you must buy up the remaining copies [of the 1824 edition] and make an edition of them for a trial."[2] This suggestion resulted in the reprinting in 1828 of the novel under Hogg's name, but with the title altered to *The Suicide's Grave.* A substantially revised version, expunged of its more sensational passages, was issued in 1837 as *The Confessions of a Fanatic.* Subsequent editions of the novel utilized the text of 1837 until 1895, when it was at last reprinted with the text of the original 1824 edition fully restored. Another edition containing Hogg's initial version appeared in 1924, with a short but perceptive introduction by T. Earle Welby. But not until an edition was printed in 1947, containing a cogent and more extended analysis of the novel by André Gide, did the *Confessions* begin to receive the serious attention of scholars of 19th-century Scottish literature. The "bowdlerization" of Hogg's novel throughout the 19th century gives a special importance to its initially published text under Hogg's own supervision.

For the setting of his "story replete with horror" Hogg chose Edinburgh and its environs in the early years of the 18th century. The memory of the terrible period of civil and religious conflict in Scotland during the second half of the 17th century remained vivid in the minds of men and women ca. 1710, as did the powerful influence of Calvinist doctrine. The most inveterate Calvinists were the children of those Cameronians who were

ABOUT THE AUTHOR

GEORGE SAINTSBURY ON *THE PRIVATE MEMOIRS AND CONFESSIONS OF A JUSTIFIED SINNER*

[In the midst of all of Hogg's] chaotic work, there is still to be found, though misnamed, one of the most remarkable stories of its kind ever written—a story which . . . is not only extraordinarily good of itself, but insists peremptorily that the reader shall wonder how the devil it got where it is. . . .

[In] truth, *The Confessions of a Justified Sinner*, while it has all Hogg's merits and more, is quite astoundingly free from his defects. His tales are generally innocent of the most rudimentary notions of construction: this goes closely ordered, with a few pardonable enough digressions, from beginning to end. He has usually little concentrated grasp of character: the few personages of the *Confessions* are consistent throughout. His dialogue is, as a rule, extraordinarily slipshod and unequal: here there is no fault to find with it. His greatest lack, in short, is the lack of form: and here, though the story might perhaps have been curtailed, or rather "cut" in the middle, with advantage, the form is excellent. . . .

In no book known to me is the grave treatment of the topsy-turvy and improbable better managed. . . . The story of the pretended Gil Martin, preposterous as it is, is told by the unlucky maniac exactly in the manner in which a man deluded, but with occasional suspicions of his delusion, would tell it. The gradual change from intended and successful rascality and crime into the incurring or the supposed incurring of the most hideous guilt without any actual consciousness of guilty action may seem an almost hopeless thing to treat probably. Yet it is so treated here.

SOURCE: Saintsbury, George. "Hogg." *Macmillan's Magazine* 60, no. 359 (September 1889). Reprinted in *The Collected Essays and Papers of George Saintsbury, 1875-1920.* Vol. I, pp. 26-52. London: J. M. Dent & Sons Ltd., 1923.

the determined opponents of episcopacy and of the doctrine of salvation through the efficacy of good works. The anonymous reviewer of Hogg's novel in London's *Literary Gazette* (July 1824) shrewdly judged that "the main object of his book . . . seems to be to satirize the excess of that Calvinical or Cameronian doctrine, which rests the salvation of mankind entirely on faith without good works." The novel functions principally as a severe indictment of the self-righteousness of the "just Pharisee," and as a fearful warning of the perils of religious mania, which can, as here, lead to a career of homicide. Hogg's presentation of this thesis in the *Confessions* constitutes the subtlest development of it in his works of fiction, and may well comprise its most powerful and original realization in British fiction.

To personify the homicidal "righteous Pharisee" Hogg created as his protagonist Robert Wringhim Colwan. Educated exclusively in the Calvinist tenets of the predestined salvation of a few souls and the damnation of the majority of mankind, Colwan espouses the unique efficacy of faith in one's personal salvation to justify the commission of crimes against those imagined to be personal and ideological enemies. These crimes culminate in a succession of homicides that envelop most of the members of Colwan's immediate family. He is impelled to perpetrate these acts by a mysterious being who, while giving his name as Gil-Martin, embodies most of the attributes traditionally associated by Scottish Calvinists with the Devil. The Cameronians, obsessed by the power and omnipresence of the forces of darkness, ascribed to these invisible entities an almost palpable reality. The Devil was to them the most fascinating and terrifying of imagined supernatural powers, possessing among other gifts the ability to appear and disappear at will and the possibility of assuming the physiognomy and shape of any mortal. Combining the talents of Calvinist minister and Scottish lawyer, Satan is described by one of Hogg's characters as often posing as "a strick believer in a' the truths of Christianity." It is while pretending to be a strict coreligionist of Colwan that Gil-Martin incites him to commit the succession of homicides and to kill himself after his insane acts have been revealed to the authorities. One of Gil-Martin's chief devices of persuasion was the assumption of Colwan's precise appearance, so that the former seemed to constitute Colwan's "second self." In the *Confessions* this delusion of the "second self" is linked in Colwan's mind with the possibility that his intrinsic self has been possessed by the Devil. In fact it represents a projection into visible form of Colwan's own spiritual pride, worldly ambition, and unresolvable inner conflicts.

While composing his novel during the early 1820s, Hogg was evidently relying upon the current vogue of the "Gothic novel" to assure it a readership readily excited by the terrifying and the improbable in fiction. A powerful revival of interest in German literature, especially of the sensational variety, had followed the publication in London in 1813 of Madame de Staël's *De l'Allemagne*. There ensued numerous translations of and reviews concerning German works of this genre from 1817 through 1828, chiefly by Hogg's fellow Scotsmen Thomas Carlyle and Robert Pearse Gillies. Preoccupation with the supernatural was an inherent theme in this proliferation of publications, some of the most interesting of which employ the idea of the "second self" (or "Doppelgänger") to create an atmosphere of suspense and terror. Hogg's novel appears to be the only extended work of fiction published in the British Isles during the early 19th century to utilize the motif of the "second self" in a manner comparable to such contemporary German authors as E. T. A. Hoffmann and Jean-Paul Richter. The works most resembling Hogg's novel to be translated at this period were Adalbert von Chamisso's *Peter Schlemihl* and Hoffmann's sole completed novel, *Die Elixiere des Teufels*. (The latter is unique in contemporary German fiction in linking the "Doppelgänger" theme to a criminally insane protagonist, resembling Hogg's Colwan.)

Can the appearance in 1824 in English translations of *Peter Schlemihl* and *Die Elixiere des Teufels* have materially influenced Hogg's treatment of the "second self" in the **Confessions**? A notice in the *Edinburgh Magazine and Literary Miscellany* for April indicates that Hogg's book was already in the press. It remained unpublished, however, until mid-July, when both the *Literary Gazette* and the magazine *John Bull* carried advertisements (on 17 and 18 July respectively) that it had just been published. However, the appearance of Hogg's important anecdote "A Scots Mummy," later incorporated almost verbatim into the novel, in the issue of *Blackwood's Magazine* for August 1823 indicates that Hogg had for many months pondered the composition of his book, and was already preparing readers of that periodical for its subsequent publication. It seems probable, therefore, that Hogg concentrated his efforts on composing the novel during the period from autumn 1822 to spring 1824, and that it was largely completed by April 1824. Information in *John Bull*

indicates the prior publication of both of the German novels; the periodical advertised *Peter Schlemihl* as available to the public on 14 March, while the first announcement of Gillies's translation of *Die Elixiere des Teufels* appeared there on 27 June. While the friendship of Hogg and Gillies complicates the problem of the influence of the latter's translation on Hogg's novel, one must conclude that it has so far proved impossible to establish any documented influence upon Hogg's employment of the "second self" in his novel by any contemporary German author.

Although he relied for the success of the **Confessions** upon the popularity of English and German fiction of the supernatural, Hogg introduced important elements into his novel which set it— and his numerous works of shorter fiction—apart from such authors as Ann Radcliffe, "Monk" Lewis, and Charles Robert Maturin. Hogg's works have as their settings predominantly rural environments, with characters drawn from the Scottish peasantry or lesser landed gentry rather than from the aristocracy or wealthy middle class. Also notable are the frequent use by Hogg's characters of Scots dialect, in contrast to the more genteel language of "Gothic" romances; a reliance upon prosaic and homely details to enhance the sense of horror; a less inhibited employment of explicit details of physically hideous and morally shocking occurrences; and, above all, a firm and frequently demonstrated conviction that ordinary men and women constantly experience the intervention of the supernatural in their everyday lives. The traditional elements of superstition, communicated orally from generation to generation among the Scottish peasantry, and the long legacy of Scottish Calvinism influenced Hogg's **Confessions** and his shorter works of fiction to a considerably greater degree than did the conventions of the "Gothic novel." These traditional themes included retribution for real or imagined grievances, with supernatural intervention being often employed to reveal past crimes and impose a vengeance (like that directed against Colwan) that human justice could not provide. Linked to this idea is Calvinism's emphasis upon the punishment of the "unrighteous," rather than upon their redemption, an emphasis that contributed to the fearful and mysterious ethos of Hogg's novel. Another element is Hogg's frequent use of dreams or hallucinations to prove (in Hogg's words) "in a very forcible manner, a distinct existence of the soul, and its lively and rapid intelligence with . . . a world of spirits with which it has no acquaintance, when the body is lying dormant, and the same to the soul as if sleeping in death."

Despite the modest but unflagging success of his previous published volumes of prose, the **Confessions** proved a complete failure with the reading public of 1824. The enigmatic nature of the book also baffled the four anonymous London reviewers who took the trouble to write about it after its publication. The critic for the *Westminster Review* (October 1824) dismissed Colwan as an insane fanatic, and Gil-Martin as a "mongrel devil." The reviewer in the *New Monthly Magazine and Literary Journal* (November 1824) attacked Hogg's style as "exaggerated and extravagant," ridiculed the narrative as totally implausible, and denounced the author for his adverse view of Calvinism. On 17 July there appeared in the *Literary Gazette and Journal of Belles Lettres* a much more searching analysis of the novel. The critic found it, although "mystical and extravagant," nonetheless "curious and interesting, such as we might have expected from Mr. Hogg, the Ettrick Shepherd, whose [creation] it is." The reviewer in the *British Critic* (July 1824) was also perspicacious enough to recognize Hogg as the author. While judging the novel a "most uncouth and unpleasant volume," he described and even reproduced verbatim many of its incidents in the review, and perceptively linked Hogg's work—in "machinery" and themes (including that of the "second self")—to Gillies's translation of the *Elixiere des Teufels*. After four reviews, generally adverse in tenor, the commercial failure of Hogg's novel was assured. As a result of this contemporary neglect, the book enjoys a reputation for scarcity among modern collectors of Scottish and English literature, copies in the original condition of publication (such as the Taylor copy) being exceedingly uncommon.

With the possible exception of one or two of his short tales, nothing in Hogg's copious body of prose fiction prepares the reader for a book of such psychological subtlety and tension as **The Private Memoirs and Confessions of a Justified Sinner.** It was, in fact, much closer in conception and spirit to certain celebrated works of German Romanticism than to the fiction of Hogg's own compatriots, including of course the vastly more popular Sir Walter Scott. Hogg's combination of traditional, theological, supernatural, and psychological motifs in a manner alien to the readers of his own day delayed critical recognition of the literary importance and originality of his work for more than a century.

Notes

1. Unpublished holograph letter, National Library of Scotland.

2. Ibid.

IAIN CRICHTON SMITH (ESSAY DATE 1993)

SOURCE: Smith, Iain Crichton. "A Work of Genius: James Hogg's *Justified Sinner*." *Studies in Scottish Literature* 28 (1993): 1-11.

In the following essay, Smith offers high praise for The Private Memoirs and Confessions of a Justified Sinner, *arguing that its sophisticated and advanced (by nineteenth-century standards) psychological and philosophical aspects, among others, distinguish the novel as "one of the very greatest of all Scottish books."*

It is a strange thing that in a biography of James Hogg written by Sir George Douglas and dated September 1899, there are only three references to the **Memoirs of Justified Sinner,** the most substantial of these occurring in a footnote rebutting an opinion apparently held by Andrew Lang that John Gibson Lockhart had a hand in the novel.[1] There is no attempt at an analysis of the book.

Yet this is a towering Scottish novel, one of the very greatest of all Scottish books. We know that Scott and Hogg were acquaintances and that their relationship was sometimes uneasy. Douglas writes:

His [i.e., Hogg's] principal grounds of irritation against Scott were the consistent abstinence of the latter from recognizing him in any of his published writing: his sometimes gratuitous and unhelpful criticism of the prose pieces. . . . and his rather inconsiderate recommendation of Hogg to the post of head shepherd to Lord Porchester, the condition of that appointment being that he should put his 'poetical talent under lock and key for ever.'[2]

Yet I believe that Scott wrote nothing as artistically satisfying, as brilliant in conception and execution and continuous logical power as Hogg's novel. When we set beside it the Walpoles and the Radcliffes one can see that Hogg moves in an altogether different dimension.

The story is easily told.

A life-loving laird called Colwan marries a religious zealot whose implacable spiritual adviser, a minister called Wringhim, believes utterly in the Calvinist Law of Election by Grace. Two sons are born of her, one called George whom her husband acknowledges as his and who is an amiable average normal boy, the other Robert (whom the laird does not acknowledge on the grounds that he has been separated from his wife who now lives with Wringhim). Robert is educated into the strict Calvinist religion and is persuaded of the truth of the Law of Election. Robert one day meets a young man who speaks to him about religious things but is really the Devil. On the latter's instructions he kills a minister, his brother George and possibly his mother. At the end of the book—his psyche tortured beyond endurance—he kills himself.

Now it is no use comparing Hogg with Scott or, as far as I can see, with anyone in his century (born in 1770, Hogg died in 1835).

This novel seems to me to be psychologically far in advance of Hogg's time and can only be properly understood in the twentieth century. (I believe this also to be true of Dostoevski with whom Hogg can without chauvinism be compared) I have often thought that there is a resemblance between Scottish and Russian writers in their primary concerns. The Scot is a metaphysical philosophical being, and, in general, refuses to rest content with the description of manners. It is no accident that Macdiarmid, for example, writes often of the Russians. In *A Drunk Man Looks at the Thistle* he asks for a share of Dostoevski's "appalling genius." I believe that Hogg had more than his share, especially (and probably exclusively) in this book.

Time and time again we are reminded of Dostoevski and of no one else. (If one compares the book with, say, Gogol's *Diary of a Madman* we are, I think, in a different world.)

One is reminded of Dostoevski first of all in the fact that both writers are capable of inducing a sense of vertigo in the reader. It is difficult to explain this clearly but I mean that one seems to be caught up in a curiously dizzy mechanism so that the normal appears strange and foggy and inverted. One thinks for instance of the Vision at Arthur's Seat which is metaphysical in its implications and much more sophisticated than the grotesque visions, say, in *The Castle of Otranto*.

Again, one gets, now and again, a scene in Hogg which reminds one directly of Dostoevski, that is, the proud glorying in abasement and injury as in the following. Robert is trying to spoil George's tennis game and has been hit:

In the meantime, young Wringhim [i.e., Robert] was an object to all of the uttermost disgust. The blood flowing from his mouth and nose he took no pains to stem, neither did he so much as wipe it away; so that it spread over all his cheeks, and breast, even off at his toes. In that state did he

take up his station in the middle of the competitors; and he did not now keep his place, but ran about, impeding everyone who attempted to make at the ball. They loaded him with execrations, but it availed nothing; he seemed courting persecution and buffetings, keeping steadfastly to his old joke of damnation, and marring the game so completely that, in spite of every effort on the part of the players, he forced them to stop their game and give it up. He was such a rueful-looking object, covered with blood, that none of them had the heart to kick him, although it appeared the only thing he wanted; and, as for George, he said not another word to him, either in anger or reproof.[3]

In another passage we get another Dostoevski theme, the contempt of the absolute man for the liberal. The passage begins:

He [i.e., Robert] then raised himself on his knees and hams, and raising up his ghastly face, while the blood streamed over both ears, he besought his life of his brother, in the most abject whining manner, gaping and blubbering most piteously.

(p. 41)

The passage continues, later on:

"Well, Robert, I will believe it. I am disposed to be hasty and passionate: it is a fault in my nature; but I never meant, or wished you evil; and God is my witness that I would as soon stretch out my hand to my own life, or my father's, as to yours." At these words, Wringhim uttered a hollow exulting laugh, put his hands in his pockets, and withdrew a space to his accustomed distance.

(p. 42)

There is a curious effeminacy (combined with absolutism) in Robert who, one senses, would have admired George more if he had been totally ruthless and not liberal.

Another Dostoevskian characteristic is the humor of the book. The opening section where the laird's wife sits up with a prayer book in her hand on her wedding night and refuses to come to bed is brilliantly funny, especially when the laird himself drops off to sleep in the middle of her prayers and begins to snore:

He began, in truth, to sound a nasal bugle of no ordinary calibre—the notes being little inferior to those of a military trumpet. The lady tried to proceed, but every returning note from the bed burst on her ear with a louder twang, and a longer peal, till the concord of sweet sounds became so truly pathetic that the meek spirit of the dame was quite overcome; and, after shedding a flood of tears, she arose from her knees, and retired to the chimney-corner with her Bible in her lap, there to spend the hours in holy meditation till such time as the inebriated trumpeter should awaken to a sense of propriety.

(p. 7)

True, this might appear to be pawky humor but a careful analysis will show that it is very purposeful. Hogg is asserting human values against absolute ones gone mad. He has learnt (what Walpole and Mrs. Radcliffe haven't) that there is a place for humor in the he kind of book he is writing, as Dostoevski also knew. Much of his other humor is on a more purely metaphysical level as for instance at the end of the book where the Devil gets into the printer's shop—a printer's devil. This is a nice metaphysical pun.

But there are many other instances of this nature, for the story belongs to the kingdom of the absurd. A number of names are bandied about in connection with Hogg, for example, Defoe, Poe, and Henry James in a book such as *The Turn of the Screw*. The latter, I think, is closer to him in conscious art: as for Defoe and Poe I cannot see that they are very like him. Poe is far more morbid than Hogg, and Defoe doesn't have his sense of ideology. It seems to me that the chosen theme suggests more the milieu of a Dostoevski in its ambiguous explorations of the spirit. And to find a writer treating a Dostoevskian theme in the eighteenth century—what a miracle!

I can in fact think of no other Scottish book which is a miracle of this kind. How did Hogg—a minor poet and minor prose writer in his other work—make this transcendental leap? It seems to be inexplicable except that in some strange fashion—perhaps in a hallucinatory logical vision—he was given the sight of this particular extreme form of religion carried to its ultimate conclusion, and worked out the implications with the instantaneous grasp of genius.

The crucial discovery he made is overwhelmingly simple. It is this. What if the Doctrine of Divine Election is actually a doctrine not of God but of the Devil? What if the Devil should find himself able to acquiesce quite sincerely in the implications of the doctrine? What if the Devil should on these terms admit that he is a Christian and really mean it?

It is worth thinking about this before we discuss it in more detail. There are plays by Marlowe and Goethe about a man who sells his soul to the Devil. In these plays the man is intellectually brilliant but he knows that he is dealing with the Devil—he is selling his soul to him. It is the ultimate capitalist transaction. The Devil offers, in return, knowledge, luxury and women. But the Devil in this particular book doesn't offer luxury or women. He offers in fact what God appears to offer—Divine Election—and this in itself is the damnable thing because the theory is in its axioms devilish for it states that a certain number are elected to be saved. God does the selection. The inexorable logic of the theory arises from the attempt to deny that good works are enough—for a man could do all sorts of good works and still be a heathen. There is a logic to the theory but it is the logic of madness since it leads unequivocally to the conclusion that ideology is more important than humanity, and it is therefore in essence a peculiarly twentieth-century preoccupation. It is a special instance of a general theory which has perverted our own civilization. It implies the creation of a spiritual elite implacable against all those who do not belong to it. It is a Mensa society of theology. It leads to the kind of thinking that enticed Leopold and Loeb to carry out their murder on the grounds of their own superiority. It is not so unlike the ideas of Nietzsche as commonly understood and put into practice, say, by the student in *Crime and Punishment*.

Members of the elite elect each other. Robert Wringhim's father elects Robert as he elected himself previously. One of the victims is not a heathen but a minister. Here we are in the presence of something very modern. The Communist, for instance, hates the Socialist more than he hates the Tory.

Now this theory can also be compared with Dostoevski's work. In *The Brothers Karamazov* Dostoevski begins with the proposition, "If there is no immortality all things are permissible." Hogg begins essentially with the proposition: "If a man knows that he is saved no matter what he does—saved to all eternity—and all good works are irrelevant—then all things are permissible."

Such ideas lead to a totalitarian philosophy. That is why I said that Hogg and Dostoevski can only be fully understood in the twentieth century.

Now Robert does not recognize the Devil for the simple reason that the Devil agrees with all his ideas and does so sincerely since the ideas themselves are devilish. Again and again we find this idea:

> "Tell me this, boy:" [says Wringhim to Robert after he has seen and spoken to the Devil] "did this stranger, with whom you met, adhere to the religious principles in which I have educated you?"
>
> "Yes, to every one of them in their fullest latitude," said I.
>
> "Then he was no agent of the Wicked One with whom you held converse," said he.
>
> (pp. 110-11)

"For a man who is not only dedicated to the King of Heaven in the most solemn manner, soul, body, and spirit, but also chosen of him from the beginning, justified, sanctified, and received into a communion that never shall be broken, and from which no act of his shall ever remove him—the possession of such a man, I tell you, is worth kingdoms . . ."

(p. 131)

The Devil quotes the Old Testament in order to justify murder:

"If the acts of Jehu, in rooting out the whole house of his master, were ordered and approved of by the Lord," said he, "would it not have been more praiseworthy if one of Ahab's own sons had stood up for the cause of the God of Israel, and rooted the sinners and their idols out of the land?"

(p. 134)

The most astounding passage of all is this:

"We are all subjected to two distinct natures in the same person" [says the Devil]. "I myself have suffered grievously in that way. The spirit that now directs my energies is not that with which I was endowed at my creation. It is changed within me, and so is my whole nature. My former days were those of grandeur and felicity. But, would you believe it? *I was not then a Christian.* Now I am. I have been converted to its truths by passing through the fire, and, since my final conversion, my misery has been extreme."

(p. 174)

The methods Hogg uses for involving the reader in this whirlpool are various in operation but similar in essence. They all depend on ambiguity. The quotation just given shows ambiguity operating linguistically and in ideology. We find ambiguity at the very beginning of the book. Robert tries to enter the inn into which George and his companions have gone after their tennis game. They won't let him, and eventually he attracts a crowd to attack the inn saying that it is occupied by Jacobites. However there happens to be a number of Whigs in the inn and the landlord tells them that the crowd is composed of Jacobites whereupon the Whigs sally out and attack their own people, not finding out till the end of the fray what has happened.

The Devil, too, often transforms himself into all kinds of shapes. Sometimes he looks like George, sometimes like Robert, sometimes like a minister. One of the interesting bits in the novel is when the Devil disguises himself as an actual preacher just after he and Robert have murdered Blanchard, the minister, and causes that preacher to be arrested for the crime though he wasn't in the area at all. This does not seem to me to be akin to the horseplay in Marlowe's *Dr. Faustus.* It

is much more seriously intended and more metaphysical in its implications.

There is also a continuous confusion of identities. At times Robert doesn't know who he is. He is supposed to have killed his mother and seduced a neighboring girl but he has no recollection of such things. There are typical schizophrenic manifestations: indeed Hogg's book can be partly discussed in modern psychological terms.

At the end of the book Hogg, or rather the narrator, writes as follows:

Were the relation at all consistent with reason, it corresponds so minutely with traditionary facts that it could scarcely have missed to have been received as authentic; but in this day, and with the present generation, it will not go down that a man should be daily tempted by the Devil, in the semblance of a fellow-creature; and at length lured to self-destruction, in the hopes that this same fiend and tormentor was to suffer and fall along with him. It was a bold theme for an allegory, and would have suited that age well had it been taken up by one fully qualified for the task, which this writer was not. In short, we must either conceive him not only the greatest fool, but the greatest wretch, on whom was ever stamped the form of humanity; or, that he was a religious maniac, who wrote and wrote about a deluded creature, till he arrived at that height of madness that he believed himself the very object whom he had been all along describing.

(pp. 229-30)

Now clearly the latter part cannot be true. The woman called Calvert (and her male accomplice) did see Robert Wringhim and a companion kill George. There are other phenomena that can only be explained on the basis that there was a real physical person, Devil or otherwise.

Nevertheless, parts of the narrative reveal perfectly explicable psychological phenomena of a modern kind.

There is no reason for doubting that Robert might, without consciously knowing it, have killed his own mother. By the time that she was killed he was beginning to repent of his association with a person whom he believed to be the Devil and, recognizing perhaps that his mother by her religious bigotry was partly the cause of his own spiritual destruction, he might indeed have killed her. Similarly he might have seduced the neighboring girl. The suffocated Id might have taken its revenge on the Superego. The novel does give a continuous impression of psychological insight as when Robert sees himself divided into two persons, none of them his own, one George and the other his new friend, the Devil.

It would, in fact, have been of the greatest interest to have had a Freudian analysis of this novel which has come out of that country where for long periods the Superego has been rampant. It is clear for instance that the suicide at the end is psychologically right. If all is predestined, the mind can only prove that it is not a machine by asserting at least its right to suicide—if that too is not predestined.

In the second half of the *Memoirs* we feel a certain pity for this tortured being, Robert Wringhim, who has gone irretrievably to the good which at a certain point turns into the bad. It reminds one of the pity one feels for the Frankenstein's monster of Mary Shelley. The righteousness of the parents is visited upon Robert with a vengeance.

Trying to escape, he is at the end enmeshed in a weaver's web and is relentlessly pursued by the Devil with a friendship which is really hatred. One can quite clearly imagine a mind so imprisoned by the Superego of a Calvinism carried to extremes that it would in fact follow the logic contained in this book. The Id would presumably emerge in aggression and pride. Burns's "Holy Willie" occasionally lifted a leg on various girls. Robert doesn't even do this and consequently he might later have seduced the neighboring girl (losing the memory of it in the process).

The possibility of schizophrenia is always present but Hogg didn't as yet have the knowledge to be consistently accurate. One feels, however, that his imagination had seized the essentials of it. If one, for instance, compares this book with *Dr. Jekyll and Mr Hyde*, one recognizes that the latter emerges from a cardboard world manufactured in a metaphysical void.

A very interesting and specially Scottish paragraph is this:

There was only one boy at Mr Wilson's class who kept always the upper hand of me in every part of education. I strove against him from year to year . . . and I was convinced he had dealings with the Devil . . . and I was at length convinced that it was no human ingenuity that beat me with so much ease in the Latin, after I had often sat up a whole night with my reverend father, studying my lesson in all its bearings.

(p. 99)

Altogether, in his use of shifting identity, ambiguity as a deliberate device, the cult of the superior mind, a possibly traumatic loss of memory and other methods, Hogg's novel impresses one as being a manifestation of hallucinatory genius which has resulted from intense concentration on a specifically Scottish theme projected itself into the future. It might be worth reminding ourselves once again of the work of Mrs. Radcliffe and Walpole to realize how essentially different Hogg's book is. What he has in fact done is to pursue a logic to its conclusion and then uncover what he finds. The device of describing the events externally in the third person and then shifting to the first person works extremely well especially for this kind of book. He has instinctively realized that a standard of external reality must be given before the Memoir itself is quoted. Otherwise, it would be difficult for the reader to establish himself.

There is however one other point which might be profitably discussed and that is the use to which Scots has been put in this novel.

Clearly an important thing that Hogg has to do is to establish a mean by which the inhumanity of Robert can be judged. I believe that he has done this by using the Scottish language.

If English is alien to the Scottish consciousness (especially in the eighteenth century) then why not let the alienation of a particular consciousness be expressed in it? Similarly if the Scottish language is the natural language of the Scottish consciousness why not let the normal, the average, the human, be expressed in it?

Consider this passage:

"Ineffectual Calling? There is no such thing, Robert," said she. [i.e. his mother]

"But there is, madam," said I, "and that answer proves how much you say these fundamental precepts by rote, and without any consideration. Ineffectual Calling is *the outward call of the gospel* without any effect on the hearts of unregenerated and impenitent sinners. Have not all these the same calls, warnings, doctrines, and reproofs, that we have? And is not this Ineffectual Calling? Has not Ardinferry the same? Has not Patrick M'Lure the same? *Has not the Laird of Dalcastle and his reprobate heir* the same? And will any tell me that *this is not In*effectual Calling?"

"What a wonderful boy he is!" said my mother.

"I'm feared he turn out to be a conceited gowk," said old Barnet, the minister's man.

(p. 90)

Now I believe that this last sentence establishes by the use of the Scottish language the reaction of ordinary humanity when confronted by what it senses to be abstract ideological nonsense. And I believe farther that only the Scottish language at this point could have had the power to be so curt and precise and yet at the same time so intimate. The very words recall even in their contempt a human intimacy which Robert has lost. Even more, their gestures, while to be considered as an impatient demolition, invite him into a world which he has abandoned, imprisoned as he is in a language—representative of a world—that will destroy him. Consider another passage: Robert has told Wringhim that Barnet has been insulting him (that is Wringhim). The latter cross-examines Barnet; and concludes as follows in what I consider to be a crucial linguistic confrontation:

> "Hear then my determination, John. If you do not promise to me, in faith and honour, that you never will say, or insinuate such a thing again in your life, as that that boy is my natural son, I will take the keys of the church from you, and dismiss you from my service."

> John pulled out the keys, and dashed them on the gravel at the reverend minister's feet. "There are the keys o' your kirk, sir! I hae never had muckle mense o' them sin' ye entered the door o't. I hae carried them this three and thretty year, but they hae aye been like to burn a hole i' my pouch sin' ever they were turned for your admittance. Tak them again, an' gie them to wha you will, and muckle gude may he get o' them. Auld John may dee a beggar in a hay barn, or at the back of a dike, but he sall aye be master o' his ain thoughts an' gie them vent or no, as he likes."

> (pp. 97-8)

This last sentence I consider of particular importance. It represents the assertion of human freedom against abstract repression true for all ages and all times. It is life rebelling against the ideological.

One further instance should be enough to show this use of the Scots language. Mrs. Logan has lost some valuables and a woman called Calvert has been accused of stealing them. Mrs. Logan's maid refuses to identify certain of the stolen objects in court as belonging to her mistress so that Calvert may not be hanged. Here the values of ordinary humanity—unpredictable and comic—are established again and again in the maid's intimate Scots language. In this passage she talks about herself and Mrs. Logan.

> "What passed, say ye? O, there wasna muckle: I was in a great passion, but she was dung doitrified a wee. When she gaed to put the key i' the door, up it flew to the fer wa'. 'Bless ye, jaud, what's the meaning o' this?' quo she. 'Ye hae left the door open, ye tawpie!' quo she. 'The ne'er o' that I did,' quo I, 'or may my shakel bane never turn another key.' When we got the candle lightit, a' the house was in a hoad-road. 'Bessy, my woman,' quo she, 'we are baith ruined and undone creatures.' 'The deil a bit,' quo I; 'that I deny positively. H'mh! to speak o' a lass o' my age being ruined and undone!

I never had muckle except what was within a good jerkin, an' let the thief ruin me there wha can.'"

> (p. 61)

Later there is the passage:

> "Perhaps you are not aware, girl, that this scrupulousness of yours is likely to thwart the purposes of justice, and bereave your mistress of property to the amount of a thousand merks." (*From the Judge.*)

> "I canna help that, my lord: that's her look-out. For my part, I am resolved to keep a clear conscience, till I be married, at any rate."

> "Look over these things and see if there is any one article among them which you can fix on as the property of your mistress."

> "No ane o' them, sir, no ane o' them. An oath is an awfu' thing, especially when it is for life or death. Gie the poor woman her things again, an' let my mistress pick up the next she finds: that's my advice."

> (pp. 62-3)

It is unnecessary to indicate the relevance of this scene (apparently discursive) to the rest of the book. The maid has a sense of proportion: she realizes that a human life is worth more than a thousand marks.

What in effect the Scots language does is to keep things in proportion. It is, as in *The House with the Green Shutters*, a marvellous instrument for deflation, though it can also be cruel.

What then does this book teach us? It teaches us that to go beyond the bounds of humanity is to lose oneself so utterly that one cannot tell God from the Devil.

In a long section about the Cameronian sect this ambiguity is discussed. Apparent irrelevancies in this book turn out not to be irrelevant at all as the book is beautifully made. This is not true of many of Hogg's other stories.

A careful reading of Hogg's other prose shows nothing comparable to the *Memoirs.* The stories, though always readable, are often rambling. One at least, "**Welldean Hall,**" which depends on a ghost who has left a will among the classics in a library, reminds one of Mrs. Radcliffe. However, Hogg tends to be more humorous than she is and less portentous. "**The Bridal of Polmood**" has a very funny multiple bedroom scene and an interesting detective-story denouement dependent on two bodies both of whose heads have disappeared.

Many of the stories are about devils or wraiths but none shows the metaphysical treatment found in the *Memoirs. The Brownie of Bodsbeck,* though apparently about the supernatural, is not: the events are cleared up in a perfectly rational manner at the end. It is interesting too that this story is about the Covenanters, a harried sect almost as fanatical as Robert himself. Though the story tends to ramble a bit I think that, outside of the **Memoirs,** it is his best. The Covenanters are saved by the daughter of a man who is himself on the other side and when praising his daughter for saving them in spite of his own ideological hostility he expresses the humanity which transcends ideas: "Deil care what side they war on, Kate!" cried Walter, in the same vehement voice; "ye hae taen the side o' human nature; the suffering and the humble side, an' the side o' feeling, my woman . . ."[4] The story is notable too for the portrait of Claverhouse but above all for the marvellous Highland soldier, Daniel Roy MacPherson, who says: "Any man will stand py me when I am in te right, put wit a phrother I must always pe in te right."[5]

"The Wool Gatherer" is a nice romantic story with the inevitable happy ending. The stories show interesting though conventional invention. In them Hogg is always strongest on his home ground around the Borders and in Scots of which he has a remarkable command.

However, there is nothing in them to prepare us for the **Memoirs,** though they contain, scattered here and there, many of the themes treated on in that book—including stories about the Devil and the supernatural, stories about religious extremists and ambiguities of motive.

Only, however, in the **Memoirs** do all these themes take on a logical rigor and undeviating development. Only in the **Memoirs** do we sense the continuous shadow of metaphysical meaning running below the external one.

All that this proves is that the productions of genius are ultimately inexplicable.

Notes

1. George Douglas, *James Hogg* (Edinburgh & London, 1899), p. 104.

2. *Ibid.,* p. 109. The quotation is from Hogg's *Domestic Manners of Sir Walter Scott.*

3. James Hogg, *The Private Memoirs and Confessions of a Justified Sinner* (New York, 1959), pp. 23-4. Further references will be to this edition and will appear in the text.

4. James Hogg, *The Brownie of Bodsbeck,* ed. Douglas S. Mack (Edinburgh and London, 1976), p. 163.

5. *Ibid.,* p. 144.

FURTHER READING

Criticism

Bligh, John. "The Doctrinal Premises of Hogg's *Confessions of a Justified Sinner.*" Studies in Scottish Literature 19 (1984): 148-64.

Interprets The Private Memoirs and Confessions of a Justified Sinner *as a didactic but finally ambivalent attack on Antinomian Calvinism and the associated theological doctrine of Predestination.*

Campbell, Ian. "James Hogg and the Bible." *Scottish Literary Journal* 10, no. 1 (May 1983): 14-29.

Considers Hogg's understanding of the Bible and his use of this knowledge for artistic and satirical ends in The Private Memoirs and Confessions of a Justified Sinner.

Gide, André. Introduction to *The Private Memoirs and Confessions of a Justified Sinner,* by James Hogg, pp. ix-xvi. London: The Cresset Press, 1947.

Influential introduction, in which Gide pioneered the concept of the psychological nature of Hogg's personal demon. Gide's comments triggered a resurgence of interest in The Private Memoirs and Confessions of a Justified Sinner, *and provided a foundation for later critics' interpretations of the work.*

Gosse, Edmund. "*The Confessions of a Justified Sinner.*" In *Silhouettes,* pp. 121-30. London: William Heinemann Ltd., 1925.

Grudging appraisal of Hogg's novel that finds fault with its ambiguity and reckless introduction of the supernatural.

Groves, David. "Allusions to *Dr. Faustus* in James Hogg's *A Justified Sinner.*" Studies in Scottish Literature 18 (1983): 157-65.

Explores the ways in which Christopher Marlowe's Dr. Faustus *is reflected in the imagery, theme, and structure of* The Private Memoirs and Confessions of a Justified Sinner.

———. "Other Prose Writings of James Hogg in Relation to *A Justified Sinner.*" Studies in Scottish Literature 20 (1985): 262-66.

Emphasizes the theme of Christian moderation in Hogg's writing, concluding that neither of the narrators in The Private Memoirs and Confessions of a Justified Sinner *entirely represent the author's own beliefs.*

———. *James Hogg: The Growth of a Writer.* Edinburgh: Scottish Academic Press, 1988. 160 p.

Study of Hogg's self-education and development as a writer.

Heinritz, Reinhard Silvia Mergenthal. "Hogg, Hoffmann, and Their Diabolical Elixirs." *Studies in Hogg and his World,* no. 7 (1996): 47-58.

Considers Hogg's relationship to the Gothic tradition and compares his work to that of E. T. A. Hoffmann.

Hutton, Clark. "Kierkegaard, Antinomianism, and James Hogg's *Private Memoirs and Confessions of a Justified Sinner.*" Scottish Literary Journal 20, no. 1 (May 1993): 37-48.

Compares Hogg's treatment of antinomianism in The Private Memoirs and Confessions of a Justified Sinner *with that of the Danish philosopher Søren Kierkegaard.*

Jackson, Richard D. "James Hogg and the Unfathomable Hell." *Romanticism on the Net*, no. 28 (November 2002): <http://www.erudit.org/revue/ron/2002/v/n28/007206ar.html>.

Examines Hogg's depiction of opium use in the nightmarish experiences of Robert Wringhim in The Private Memoirs and Confessions of a Justified Sinner.

Jones, Douglas. "Double Jeopardy and the Chameleon Art in James Hogg's *Justified Sinner*." *Studies in Scottish Literature* 23 (1988): 164-85.

Argues against psychoanalytic interpretations of The Private Memoirs and Confessions of a Justified Sinner, *concentrating instead on the narrative's concern with subjectivity, ambiguity, circularity, and disguise*

Mack, Douglas S. "James Hogg in 2000 and Beyond." *Romanticism on the Net*, no. 19 (August 2000): <http://users.ox.ac.uk/~scat0385/19mack.html>.

Maintains that despite Hogg's status as a disenfranchised marginal writer, his texts have a part to play at the heart of current discussion of British literature of the Romantic era because they give voice to the insights, culture, and concerns of non-elite, subaltern Scotland.

Mackenzie, Scott. "Confessions of a Gentrified Sinner: Secrets in Scott and Hogg." *Studies in Romanticism* 41, no. 1 (spring 2002): 3-32.

Discusses the allusions in The Private Memoirs and Confessions of a Justified Sinner *to Walter Scott's authorship of the* Waverley *novels.*

Oost, Regina B. "'False Friends, Squeamish Readers, and Foolish Critics': The Subtext of Authorship in Hogg's *Justified Sinner*." *Studies in Scottish Literature* 31 (1999): 86-106.

Contends that in The Private Memoirs and Confessions of a Justified Sinner *Hogg comments on the writing profession and the act of authorship.*

Pope, Rebecca A. "Hogg, Wordsworth, and Gothic Autobiography." *Studies in Scottish Literature* 27 (1992): 218-40.

Argues that The Private Memoirs and Confessions of a Justified Sinner *parodies William Wordsworth, undermines conventional realism, and utilizes a Gothic logic of ironic reversal.*

Sedgwick, Eve Kosofsky. "Murder Incorporated: *Confessions of a Justified Sinner*." In *Between Men: English Literature and Male Homosocial Desire*, pp. 97-117. New York: Columbia University Press, 1985.

Examines the articulations of male paranoia in The Private Memoirs and Confessions of a Justified Sinner.

Simpson, Louis. *James Hogg: A Critical Study.* Edinburgh: Oliver & Boyd, 1962, 222 p.

Detailed analysis of Hogg's life and works.

Smith, Nelson C. *James Hogg.* Boston: Twayne Publishers, 1980, 183 p.

Critical study of Hogg's life and works.

OTHER SOURCES FROM GALE:

Additional coverage of Hogg's life and career is contained in the following sources published by Thomson Gale: *British Writers Supplement*, Vol. 10; *Dictionary of Literary Biography*, Vols. 93, 116, 159; *Literature Resource Center*; *Nineteenth-Century Literature Criticism*, Vols. 4, 109; *Reference Guide to English Literature*, Ed. 2; *St. James Guide to Horror, Ghost & Gothic Writers*; and *Supernatural Fiction Writers*, Vol. 1.

WASHINGTON IRVING

(1783 - 1859)

(Also wrote under the pseudonyms Fray Antonio Agapida, Geoffrey Crayon, Diedrich Knickerbocker, Launcelot Langstaff, and Jonathan Oldstyle) American short story writer, essayist, historian, journalist, and biographer.

Irving is considered both the first American man of letters and the creator of the American short story. Although best known for such tales of rural Americana as "Rip Van Winkle" and "The Legend of Sleepy Hollow" (both published in *The Sketch Book of Geoffrey Crayon, Gent.*, 1819-20), Irving later became a prolific and accomplished biographer as well as a distinguished statesman. He explored a number of literary styles and genres in his writings, with many of his best-known stories incorporating elements of Gothic literature. Such works, many of which were written in a humorous, lighthearted tone, reveal the author's interest in mystery, horror, and the supernatural.

BIOGRAPHICAL INFORMATION

Born in New York in 1783, Irving was the youngest of eleven children. Although he studied the law and eventually worked at a law office, his legal studies were halfhearted; he much preferred writing for his brother Peter's journal, *The Morning Chronicle*. In 1802 Irving wrote a series of letters to the *Chronicle* under the pseudonym of Jonathan Oldstyle. These letters gently mocked New York society and brought Irving his first recognition as a writer. Failing health forced him to seek a change of climate, and he traveled to Europe. In 1806 he returned home and was admitted to the bar. Irving, his brother William, and brother-in-law James Kirke Paulding, along with some other friends, were known as the "Nine Worthies of Cockloft Hall," named after their favorite place for "conscientious drinking and good fun." They collaborated on the satirical journal *Salmagundi; or, The Whim-whams and Opinions of Launcelot Langstaff, Esq., and Others* (1807-8), which included many essays by Irving that reflected his Federalist political attitudes and social stance. The venture proved unprofitable, however, and the young men were forced to abandon the publication. In 1809 Irving enjoyed literary success with the publication and favorable reception of the satirical *A History of New York, from the Beginning of the World to the End of the Dutch Dynasty*. His success, however, was overshadowed by the death of his fiancee, Matilda Hoffman, in 1809. Grief consumed Irving, and from that time on his works reflected a more serious tone. In an effort to ease his sorrow, Irving entered a period of fervid activity. He acted as his brother's law partner, helped in the family hardware business, and edited a magazine, the *Analectic*.

Irving eventually returned to England and worked in the Liverpool branch of his family's import-export firm for three years until it went bankrupt. After years of wavering indecisively between a legal, editorial, and mercantile career, he finally decided to make writing his livelihood. He began recording impressions, thoughts, and descriptions in a small notebook. These, polished and revised in Irving's meticulous manner, eventually became *The Sketch Book of Geoffrey Crayon, Gent.* Irving's most enduring work, the collection—which includes the stories "Rip Van Winkle" and "The Legend of Sleepy Hollow"—ensured his reputation as a man of letters. Its timing proved opportune, as no one had yet produced a universally appealing piece of American literature. In 1826 he traveled as a member of the American diplomatic corps to Spain, where he wrote *A History of the Life and Voyages of Christopher Columbus* (1828). A subsequent tour of Spain produced *A Chronicle of the Conquest of Granada* (1829) and *The Alhambra* (1832). During the 1830s, Irving returned to America, taking part in a tour of the Oklahoma territory. His travels in the West were fodder for several of his subsequent books, including *The Crayon Miscellany* (1835), *A Tour on the Prairies* (1835), *Astoria; or, Anecdotes of an Enterprise beyond the Rocky Mountains* (1836), and *The Rocky Mountains; or, Scenes, Incidents, and Adventures in the Far West* (1837). In 1842 Irving became minister to Spain. Although he enjoyed his role as a diplomat, he returned to the United States to further his career as a biographical writer. His biography of Oliver Goldsmith is considered a particularly fine example of Irving's concise, balanced style. His last years were spent at work on a biography of George Washington; though assessed as overly elaborate and lacking his former naturalness of tone, the work expresses Irving's belief in a glorious American past. Irving's funeral was attended by thousands of admirers who mourned the death of a beloved author.

MAJOR WORKS

Irving's initial forays into writing were essays that satirized the political, social, and cultural life of his native New York City. A number of these were published in the short-lived journal *Salmagundi*. Irving continued in this satirical vein with his first book, *A History of New York*. Narrated by the fictional Diedrich Knickerbocker, a fusty, colorful Dutch American, the work provided a comical, deliberately inaccurate account of New York's past. *A History of New York* has been considered Irving's most consistently optimistic work, in which he expounds on native themes with affection and candor; indeed, the name "Knickerbocker" has become synonymous with a period of early American culture. The *Sketch Book of Geoffrey Crayon, Gent.*, Irving's subsequent effort, is considered a landmark work in American fiction. The book not only introduced the modern short story form in the United States but was also the first work by an American author to gain recognition abroad. The collection was widely popular in both England and the United States. Purportedly the work of Geoffrey Crayon, a genteel, good-natured American wandering through Britain on his first trip abroad, *The Sketch Book* consists largely of his travel impressions. These sketches are picturesque, elegant, and lightly humorous in the tradition of the eighteenth-century essayists Richard Addison and Oliver Goldsmith, Irving's literary models. The most enduring pieces, however, are those in which Irving wove elements of legend, folklore, and drama into narratives of the New World. "Rip Van Winkle," the story of a lackadaisical Dutch American who slumbers for twenty years, and "The Legend of Sleepy Hollow," which recounts Ichabod Crane's meeting with a headless horseman, have long been considered classics. Critics generally agree that these were the models for the modern American short story and that both tales introduced imagery and archetypes that enriched the national literature.

After the appearance of *The Sketch Book*, Irving wrote steadily, capitalizing on his international success with two subsequent collections of tales and sketches that also appeared under the name Geoffrey Crayon. *Bracebridge Hall; or, The Humorists: A Medley* (1822) centers loosely on a fictitious English clan that Irving had introduced in several of the *Sketch Book* pieces. *Bracebridge Hall* further describes their manners, customs, and habits, and interjects several unrelated short stories, including "The Student from Salamanca" and "The Stout Gentleman." *Tales of a Traveller* (1824) consists entirely of short stories arranged in four categories: European stories, tales of London literary life, accounts of Italian bandits, and narrations by Irving's alter-ego, Diedrich Knickerbocker. The most enduring of these, according to many critics, are "The Adventure of the German Student," which some consider a significant early example of American Gothic and supernatural fiction, and "The Devil and Tom Walker," a Yankee tale that like "Rip Van Winkle" draws upon myth and legend for characters and incident.

Irving's later career is marked by his shift toward biography writing. While traveling through Europe in the 1820s, Irving was asked to translate some documents relating to Christopher Columbus. Instead, Irving decided to write a biography on the man central to the American identity. Critics praised *A History of the Life and Voyages of Christopher Columbus* as one of the greatest biographies ever written; the book earned Irving distinction both as a scholar and as a biographer. Irving employed his skills as a researcher again in his biographies on Oliver Goldsmith and George Washington. In addition, Irving's keen interest in the American character and identity led him to write several books about the American West. In his works *A Tour on the Prairies, Astoria,* and *Captain Bonneville,* Irving recounted the adventurous and sometimes brutal life of the frontiersman. He is credited with realistically portraying the pioneers' cruel treatment of Native Americans. However, he championed American enterprise and the courage of American men forging a future for the country.

CRITICAL RECEPTION

Contemporaneous reviews illustrate the level of approval Irving won in the nineteenth century. While many of these reviewers were aware of deficiencies in Irving's work, their praise is generally overwhelming. Not all subsequent critics have been so enthusiastic; critical reception of the author's work has been mixed over the past two centuries. However, most modern critics classify Irving as one of the greatest American writers, responsible for establishing an American style of writing, especially in the short story genre. He is well respected as a biographer and as a chronicler of American culture. His short stories "The Legend of Sleepy Hollow" and "Rip Van Winkle" are considered American masterpieces, their legacy so great that they have become part of popular culture.

Many of Irving's stories, particularly "The Adventure of the German Student," have received attention for their unique handling of the supernatural and the Gothic. At the time Irving began working on his earliest—and best known—tales, the popularity of Gothic literature had begun to wane. In recognition of the genre's declining appeal, Irving opted for a fresh approach, employing Gothic conventions in nontraditional ways. For example, a number of his stories feature supernatural or macabre happenings, but such events are presented in a comical, lighthearted way—a technique described by some critics as "sportive" Gothic. Michael Davitt Bell has suggested that Irving's influence on the American Gothic tradition is undervalued in part because of his humorous and sometimes satiric tone. While some critics may dismiss his impact as minimal, John Clendenning has asserted that Irving's works "anticipated the advanced gothic fiction of [Edgar Allan] Poe and [Nathaniel] Hawthorne."

PRINCIPAL WORKS

Salmagundi; or, The Whim-whams and Opinions of Launcelot Langstaff, Esq., and Others [with William Irving and James Kirke Paulding] (journal) 1807-8

A History of New York, from the Beginning of the World to the End of the Dutch Dynasty [as Diedrich Knickerbocker] (parody) 1809

The Sketch Book of Geoffrey Crayon, Gent. [as Geoffrey Crayon] (short stories) 1819-20

Bracebridge Hall; or, The Humorists: A Medley [as Geoffrey Crayon] (short stories) 1822

Tales of a Traveller [as Geoffrey Crayon] (short stories) 1824

A History of the Life and Voyages of Christopher Columbus (biography) 1828

A Chronicle of the Conquest of Granada (history) 1829

The Alhambra [as Geoffrey Crayon] (sketches and short stories) 1832

The Crayon Miscellany [as Geoffrey Crayon] (sketches and short stories) 1835

A Tour on the Prairies (travel sketches) 1835

Astoria; or, Anecdotes of an Enterprise beyond the Rocky Mountains (history) 1836

The Rocky Mountains; or, Scenes, Incidents, and Adventures in the Far West: Digested from the Journal of Captain B. L. E. Bonneville, of the Army of the United States, and Illustrated from Various Other Sources (biography and history) 1837; also published as *The Adventures of Captain Bonneville,* 1898

Oliver Goldsmith (biography) 1849

The Life of George Washington (biography) 1855-59

WASHINGTON IRVING (STORY DATE 1824)

SOURCE: Irving, Washington. "Adventure of the German Student." In *Great Tales of Terror from Europe and America: Gothic Stories of Horror and Romance, 1765-1840,* edited by Peter Haining. 1972. Reprint edition, pp. 424-30. Harmondsworth, Middlesex, England: Penguin Books Ltd., 1973.

The following short story was originally published in 1824 in Tales of a Traveller.

On a stormy night, in the tempestuous times of the French revolution, a young German was returning to his lodgings, at a late hour, across the old part of Paris. The lightning gleamed, and the loud claps of thunder rattled through the lofty, narrow streets—but I should first tell you something about this young German.

Gottfried Wolfgang was a young man of good family. He had studied for some time at Göttingen, but being of a visionary and enthusiastic character, he had wandered into those wild and speculative doctrines which have so often bewildered German students. His secluded life, his intense application, and the singular nature of his studies, had an effect on both mind and body. His health was impaired; his imagination diseased. He had been indulging in fanciful speculations on spiritual essences until, like Swedenborg, he had an ideal world of his own around him. He took up a notion, I do not know from what cause, that there was an evil influence hanging over him; an evil genius or spirit seeking to ensnare him and ensure his perdition. Such an idea working on his melancholy temperament produced the most gloomy effects. He became haggard and desponding. His friends discovered the mental malady that was preying upon him, and determined that the best cure was a change of scene; he was sent, therefore, to finish his studies amidst the splendours and gaieties of Paris.

Wolfgang arrived at Paris at the breaking out of the revolution. The popular delirium at first caught his enthusiastic mind, and he was captivated by the political and philosophical theories of the day: but the scenes of blood which followed shocked his sensitive nature; disgusted him with society and the world, and made him more than ever a recluse. He shut himself up in a solitary apartment in the *Pays Latin,* the quarter of students. There in a gloomy street not far from the monastic walls of the Sorbonne, he pursued his favourite speculations. Sometimes he spent hours together in the great libraries of Paris, those catacombs of departed authors, rummaging among their hoards of dusty and obsolete works in quest of food for his unhealthy appetite. He was, in a manner, a literary ghoul, feeding in the charnel-house of decayed literature.

Wolfgang, though solitary and recluse, was of an ardent temperament, but for a time it operated merely upon his imagination. He was too shy and ignorant of the world to make any advances to the fair, but he was a passionate admirer of female beauty, and in his lonely chamber would often lose himself in reveries on forms and faces which he had seen, and his fancy would deck out images of loveliness far surpassing the reality.

While his mind was in this excited and sublimated state, he had a dream which produced an extraordinary effect upon him. It was of a female face of transcendent beauty. So strong was the impression it made, that he dreamt of it again and again. It haunted his thoughts by day, his slumbers by night; in fine he became passionately enamoured of this shadow of a dream. This lasted so long, that it became one of those fixed ideas which haunt the minds of melancholy men, and are at times mistaken for madness.

Such was Gottfried Wolfgang, and such his situation at the time I mentioned. He was returning home late one stormy night, through some of the old and gloomy streets of the *Marais,* the ancient part of Paris. The loud claps of thunder rattled among the high houses of the narrow streets. He came to the Place de Grève, the square where public executions are performed. The lightning quivered about the pinnacles of the ancient Hôtel de Ville, and shed flickering gleams over the open space in front. As Wolfgang was crossing the square, he shrunk back with horror at finding himself close by the guillotine. It was the height of the reign of terror, when this dreadful instrument of death stood ever ready, and its scaffold was continually running with blood of the virtuous and the brave. It had that very day been actively employed in the work of carnage, and there it stood in grim array amidst a silent and sleeping city, waiting for fresh victims.

Wolfgang's heart sickened within him, and he was turning shuddering from the horrible engine, when he beheld a shadowy form cowering as it were at the foot of the steps which led up to the scaffold. A succession of vivid flashes of lightning revealed it more distinctly. It was a female figure, dressed in black. She was seated on one of the lower steps of the scaffold, leaning forward, her face hid in her lap, and her long dishevelled tresses hanging to the ground, streaming with the rain which fell in torrents. Wolfgang paused. There was something awful in this solitary monument of woe. The female had the appearance of being above the common order. He knew the times to be full of vicissitude, and that many a fair head, which had once been pillowed on down, now wandered houseless. Perhaps this was some poor mourner whom the dreadful axe had rendered desolate, and who sat here heartbroken on the strand of existence, from which all that was dear to her had been launched into eternity.

He approached, and addressed her in the accents of sympathy. She raised her head and gazed wildly at him. What was his astonishment at beholding, by the bright glare of the lightning, the very face which had haunted him in his dreams. It was pale and disconsolate, but ravishingly beautiful.

Trembling with violent and conflicting emotions, Wolfgang again accosted her. He spoke something of her being exposed at such an hour of the night, and to the fury of such a storm, and offered to conduct her to her friends. She pointed to the guillotine with a gesture of dreadful signification.

'I have no friend on earth!' said she.

'But you have a home,' said Wolfgang.

'Yes—in the grave!'

The heart of the student melted at the words.

'If a stranger dare make an offer,' said he, 'without danger of being misunderstood, I would offer my humble dwelling as a shelter; myself as a devoted friend. I am friendless myself in Paris, and a stranger in the land; but if my life could be of service, it is at your disposal, and should be sacrificed before harm or indignity should come to you.'

There was an honest earnestness in the young man's manner that had its effect. His foreign accent, too, was in his favour; it showed him not to be a hackneyed inhabitant of Paris. Indeed there is an eloquence in true enthusiasm that is not to be doubted. The homeless stranger confided herself implicitly to the protection of the student.

He supported her faltering steps across the Pont Neuf, and by the place where the statue of Henry the Fourth had been overthrown by the populace. The storm had abated, and the thunder rumbled at a distance. All Paris was quiet; that great volcano of human passion slumbered for a while, to gather fresh strength for the next day's

eruption. The student conducted his charge through the ancient streets of the *Pays Latin,* and by the dusky walls of the Sorbonne to the great, dingy hotel which he inhabited. The old portress who admitted them stared with surprise at the unusual sight of the melancholy Wolfgang with a female companion.

On entering his apartment, the student, for the first time, blushed at the scantiness and indifference of his dwelling. He had but one chamber—an old fashioned saloon—heavily carved and fantastically furnished with the remains of former magnificence, for it was one of those hotels in the quarter of Luxembourg palace which had once belonged to nobility. It was lumbered with books and papers, and all the usual apparatus of a student, and his bed stood in a recess at one end.

When lights were brought, and Wolfgang had a better opportunity of contemplating the stranger, he was more than ever intoxicated by her beauty. Her face was pale, but of a dazzling fairness, set off by a profusion of raven hair that hung clustering about it. Her eyes were large and brilliant, with a singular expression that approached almost to wildness. As far as her black dress permitted her shape to be seen, it was of perfect symmetry. Her whole appearance was highly striking, though she was dressed in the simplest style. The only thing approaching to an ornament which she wore was a broad, black band round her neck, clasped by diamonds.

The perplexity now commenced with the student how to dispose of the helpless being thus thrown upon his protection. He thought of abandoning his chamber to her, and seeking shelter for himself elsewhere. Still he was so fascinated by her charms, there seemed to be such a spell upon his thoughts and senses, that he could not tear himself from her presence. Her manner, too, was singular and unaccountable. She spoke no more of the guillotine. Her grief had abated. The attentions of the student had first won her confidence, and then, apparently, her heart. She was evidently an enthusiast like himself, and enthusiasts soon understand each other.

In the infatuation of the moment Wolfgang avowed his passion for her. He told her the story of his mysterious dream, and how she had possessed his heart before he had even seen her. She was strangely affected by his recital, and acknowledged to have felt an impulse towards him equally unaccountable. It was the time for wild theory and wild actions. Old prejudices and superstitions were done away; everything was under the sway of the 'Goddess of reason'. Among other rubbish of the old times, the forms and ceremonies of marriage began to be considered superfluous bonds for honourable minds. Social compacts were the vogue. Wolfgang was too much of a theorist not to be tainted by the liberal doctrines of the day.

'Why should we separate?' said he: 'our hearts are united; in the eye of reason and honour we are as one. What need is there of sordid forms to bind high souls together?'

The stranger listened with emotion: she had evidently received illumination at the same school.

'You have no home nor family,' continued he; 'let me be everything to you, or rather let us be everything to one another. If form is necessary, form shall be observed—there is my hand. I pledge myself to you for ever.'

'For ever?' said the stranger, solemnly.

'For ever!' repeated Wolfgang.

The stranger clasped the hand extended to her: 'Then I am yours,' murmured she, and sunk upon his bosom.

The next morning the student left his bride sleeping, and sallied forth at an early hour to seek more spacious apartments, suitable to the change in his situation. When he returned, he found the stranger lying with her head hanging over the bed, and one arm thrown over it. He spoke to her, but received no reply. He advanced to awaken her from her uneasy posture. On taking her hand, it was cold—there was no pulsation—her face was pallid and ghastly.—In a word—she was a corpse.

Horrified and frantic, he alarmed the house. A scene of confusion ensued. The police were summoned. As the officer of police entered the room, he started back on beholding the corpse.

'Great heaven!' cried he, 'how did this woman come here?'

'Do you know anything about her?' said Wolfgang eagerly.

'Do I?' exclaimed the police officer: 'she was guillotined yesterday!'

He stepped forward; undid the black collar round the neck of the corpse, and the head rolled on the floor!

The student burst into a frenzy. 'The fiend! the fiend has gained possession of me!' shrieked he: 'I am lost for ever!'

They tried to soothe him, but in vain. He was possessed with the frightful belief that an evil spirit had reanimated the dead body to ensnare him. He went distracted, and died in a madhouse.

Here the old gentleman with the haunted head finished his narrative.

'And is this really a fact?' said the inquisitive gentleman.

'A fact not to be doubted,' replied the other. 'I had it from the best authority. The student told it me himself. I saw him in a madhouse at Paris.'[1]

Note

1. The latter part of the above story is founded on an anecdote related to me, and said to exist in print in French. I have not met with it in print.

GENERAL COMMENTARY

JOHN CLENDENNING (ESSAY DATE 1964)

SOURCE: Clendenning, John. "Irving and the Gothic Tradition." *Bucknell Review* 12, no. 2 (1964): 90-8.

In the following essay, Clendenning assesses Irving's works within the context of a developing American Gothic tradition.

Although we may scoff at the thrills, tricks, and flights of gothic fiction, its durable influence cannot be ignored. How this popular genre, despite its medieval twaddle and its supernatural bombast, was appropriated by our most serious writers remains an enigma, though some critics have argued convincingly that the genre was, in some ways, serious from the outset. Whatever the case, everyone will agree that the gothic element which survived in the novels of Henry James was distinctly different from the heavy machinery of *The Monk*. To identify this difference, let me risk a generalization: James learned to subjectify all that Lewis had to objectify; in James unvarnished horror may occur in full sunlight, whereas the grimness of *The Monk* exists only behind the abbey's closed door. The gothicists' traditional "machinery" was necessarily tangible, because it produced a terror which always fascinated them. But when Isabel Archer Osmond sits before her fireplace, her anguish produces the images which are identifiably gothic in origin. She sees herself in "a dark, narrow alley with a dead wall at the end"; she is locked behind a closed door; she is "draped . . . in pictured tapestries . . . shut up with an odor of mould and decay." Lewis was admittedly an interesting psychologist, having accurately described phenomena which today we call suppression, sublimation, projection, and so forth, and yet he could not treat human motivation without a chiller-thriller cause. On the other hand, we admire James because he preserved the gothicists' imagery but treated it as a psychic result, not the factual cause of terror. It was a major accomplishment of the modern novelist to have seen the images of the gothic world as distorted perceptions of reality.

Washington Irving was about half-way between modern fiction and the cult of Mrs. Radcliffe. When he began producing his major works—*The Sketch Book* (1819-20), *Bracebridge Hall* (1822), and *Tales of a Traveller* (1824)—the popularity of gothic novels was falling apart, and a period of reaction, represented chiefly by Jane Austen's *Northanger Abbey* (1818), was under way. That Irving probably sensed this decline of gothicism and the dangers of aping its style is indicated by these remarks to his brother in 1823:

> There are such quantities of the legendary and romantic tales now littering from the presses, both in England and in Germany, that one must take care not to fall into the commonplace of the day. Scott's manner must likewise be avoided. In short, I must strike out some way of my own, suited to my own way of thinking and writing.[1]

Instead, therefore, of continuing an exhausted tradition, Irving hoped to find some original use for gothic material. To be sure, he did not always succeed, but at his best he became a skillful parodist and a highly suggestive psychologist.

When Irving failed, and his failures were frequent, he merely imitated the "littering" sensationalism at its worst. **"The Story of the Young Robber,"** a sentimental bandit tale commonly associated with gothic fiction, will serve as an example. Here we have the inane plot of a young Italian who falls madly in love with a girl, appropriately named Rosetta, but has his hopes spoiled when he learns that the girl's father has arranged a more lucrative marriage. Unable to control his rage, the young man murders his rival and joins a band of robbers, who eventually kidnap Rosetta and attempt to sell her back for ransom. Unfortunately, the father rather curiously decides that, since the robbers have probably raped his daughter, she may as well be left to die. And die she must. But hoping to make her death painless, the young bandit volunteers to murder her himself, an act which is described with the cheap sentiment typical of the whole tale: "So perished this unfortunate." Everything is false— the bizarre actions, the feigned passions, the histrionic prose. The story exists on the most

Illustration from "The Legend of Sleepy Hollow."

superficial of surfaces. Never do we enter the world of motives; never is the description a sign of the unwilling killer's agony.

But as innovator of the so-called "sportive" gothic, Irving was a master. Although the term "sportive" is too vague, it is generally assumed to describe a tale which employs an abundance of "machinery" assembled in a light-hearted tone, as is characteristic of **"The Legend of Sleepy Hollow."** So pervasive is this tone that the mystery and terror common to most gothic tales are permitted to flourish only in the ironic sense that melodrama is used to promote humor and satire. How Irving managed to employ the machinery without its usual tone is not easy to determine. Certainly his zestful narrator, whom he had used earlier in his *Knickerbocker History* and who was conspicuously missing in **"The Story of the Young Robber,"** provides the basic ingredient for the humorous tone. The structure of **"Sleepy Hollow"** also guards against gothic terror, for though the headless Hessian dominates the last pages of the story, he is preceded by amusing details that never lose their influence on the narrative. Finally, the central characters themselves resist a melodramatic treatment. The original gothic hero (a fair representative being Irving's Italian robber) claimed only an ideal existence, whereas Ichabod Crane, the prototypic Yankee schoolmaster who wants only food, comfort, and a plump Dutch wife, brings to the story such a weight of actuality that a world of haunted forests seems, by contrast, absurd.

This local-color element is, on the simplest level, what Irving made the story's central interest: the Connecticut Yankee meets the New York Dutch. The same element, however, by itself so superficial, gives way to an exploration of the role of imagination and the artistic process. Ichabod, we are told, was "an odd mixture of small shrewdness and simple credulity." Having the wit of a Yankee peddler, he is careful to win the affection and confidence of the village. But having also the superstitions of a Puritan, he trembles in fear. One quality enables him to deal with the world as he wishes; the other eventually causes him to leave town at midnight, fearful for his life, never to return. But the "odd mixture" is really two applications of the same thing; for what chiefly characterizes Ichabod's mind is his rich imagination, a mind which dreamingly arranges the pieces of his experience—sometimes giving vivid impressions of himself luxuriating in food, wealth, and women, and giving also clues for realizing them. Thus the New England pedagogue manages, until the end of the story to stay a few steps ahead of the intellectually lethargic Dutch. And when Ichabod is defeated, Brom Bones is not the real victor; he merely stimulated the Yankee's self-destructive imagination. Thus the capacity that enables Ichabod to see the world as it may be—a "sumptuous promise of luxurious winter fare"—is the same irresistible curse which makes ghosts and goblins as palpable as pigeon pies. The story can, then, be understood as an allegory of the artistic process itself, for the literary artist must imaginatively create legends for the world's sleepy hollows. But the limits on the imagination—limits that Irving failed utterly to observe in his **"Italian Robber"**—demand that the artistically created world coexist with actuality. Permit the imagination to be wholly separated from human experience—as gothic fiction constantly separates them—and the art is destroyed. This problem is, of course, familiar to every student of American literature; our writers, particularly the New Englanders, have repeatedly felt a tension, whether as identified by Emerson between experience and reality, or as seen by Henry James between art and life. Thoreau, Hawthorne, Dickinson, Robinson, Frost, Cummings, Stevens—all of these Yankee artists felt the tension. Frost wanted to climb his birch tree of imagination *toward* the ideal, but he feared it, prayed that the tree would set him down again to

earth, the right place for love. Ichabod's fate was not so kind; he is indeed snatched away not to return, for he rambled too exclusively in the world of pure imagination, and was lost. Thus, the gothic material in **"Sleepy Hollow"** serves a vital function. Constantly juxtaposed with the actual world, it represents the extreme form in literary art of the imagination disassociated from life. Hence, if Irving has given us a "sportive" gothic, he has not done so uncritically.

But "sportive" gothicism is not parody, though Irving's critics have tended to confuse them. **"Sleepy Hollow"** is only allegorically an attack on gothicism; parody reveals the excesses of a genre by imitating it. This distinction should be clear enough if we examine a genuine parody of gothic fiction, **"The Spectre Bridegroom."**

Unlike the other *Sketch Book* tales, this story has the stereotypic setting of medieval Germany, complete with the satiric names, Baron Von Landshort, Herman Von Starkenfaust, and Katzenellenbogen. For his plot, Irving chose the impossibly obvious formula of the supernatural *expliqué*, popularized by Mrs. Radcliffe and imitated extensively in America: the hero pretends to be the ghost of the murdered bridegroom in order to win the affections of the heroine and the confidence of her family. The major element, however, which makes **"The Spectre Bridegroom"** a travesty is not the artificial structure, the grotesque setting, or the ridiculous names, but rather the minds of the characters. Irving presents a society which, craving the supernatural, is ideally prepared to find it. The daughter's literary fare consists exclusively in "church legends" and "the chivalric wonders of the Heldenbuch." Her morbid imagination is clearly indicated by the agonized expressions of the saints she embroiders, who "looked like so many souls in purgatory." Other members of the family seem equally drawn to gothic themes. The baron's greatness seems to consist chiefly in his ability to tell ghost stories. "He was much given to the marvellous and a firm believer in all those supernatural tales with which every mountain and valley in Germany abounds." Indeed, young Starkenfaust got his idea of posing as a spectre from one of the baron's stories, and the family's commitment to the supernatural explanation was their own idea. Like Catherine Morland in *Northanger Abbey*, the Katzenellenbogens attempt to interpret their experience in terms of German legends. In fact, the poor relation who suggests the truth—that the spectre may be some evasive young cavalier—draws upon himself the "indignation of the whole company." And when the hoax is finally revealed, one of the aunts is "particularly mortified at having her marvellous story marred. . . ." The most important facet of this parody, therefore, is Irving's interest in the psychology of gothicism. Turning the external gothic theme inward, he treated the supernatural world as an expression of an excessively morbid imagination.

If **"The Spectre Bridegroom"** is a delightful though serious parody of the gothic tale—particularly of the Radcliffian supernatural *expliqué*—Irving designed other stories to render it quite as ridiculous, but in an exactly opposite manner. Instead of resolving the supernatural in natural terms, his heroes sometimes—as in **"The Bold Dragoon,"** for example—disguise their very embarrassing natural activities under a gothic mask. Here is our saucy-eyed dragoon, a bold fellow indeed, weaseling his way into an already-filled inn by blarneying the landlord and charming the women, notably "the hostess's daughter, a plump Flanders lass." Then after rousing the entire house by crashing to the floor in the middle of the night, he tells a perfectly incredible story about a "weazen-faced" ghost of a bagpiper, dancing furniture, and a midnight caper with a clothes-press. Though doubts are suggested, these are easily silenced by the dragoon's ever-threatening sword and shillelah and by the even more preposterous corroboration of the daughter, who, we are told, was already with the dragoon when the rest of the house appeared. Apparently, therefore, we have an inverted form of the explained supernatural tale; Irving has given us what we may, in fact, call the *inverted* gothic story—not unlike Chaucer's "Miller's Tale"—in which the lusty dragoon escapes recrimination for his midnight peccadillo with the landlord's daughter by throwing up an absurd haze of supernaturalism.

Although this form has failed to survive in modern fiction, it was one of Irving's favorites. In **"Dolph Heyliger,"** for instance, we have a similarly inverted gothic tale, in which the picaresque hero returns with his life's fortune and a ghost story to explain how he got it. Doubts of Dolph's honesty are never uttered, not of course because his character is spotless but because it is noted that he is "the ablest drawer of a long-bow in the whole province."

If we consider **"Rip Van Winkle"** in the context of **"Dolph Heyliger"** and **"The Bold Dragoon,"** it appears that this most famous of Irving's stories also employs the techniques of inverted gothicism. Like Dolph, Rip disappears, only to return later with a supernatural account of his

absence. And like the dragoon's story, Rip's tale is "authenticated" in a fashion which is as irrational as the story itself; crucial testimony is given by Peter, "the most ancient inhabitant of the village, and well versed in all the wonderful events and traditions of the neighborhood." The gullible narrator, old Diedrich Knickerbocker, who relates the story without a flicker of doubt, believes Rip's account because (1) stranger stories have been told, (2) Rip was "venerable," "rational," and "consistent," and (3) the story had been recorded by an illiterate country justice. Indeed, the whole community refused even to consider what they should have suspected from the first: that Rip had finally become exasperated with his "termagant wife," took his dog and gun, and deserted. He was, long before his disappearance, a great teller of ghost stories and a notorious malingerer—exactly the sort of man who would ramble for twenty years, then return with a bit of gothic nonsense designed to amuse the town and avoid its scorn. The final paragraph of the story seems to point directly toward this conclusion. Old Knickerbocker admits that Rip had several versions of his account: "He was observed, at first, to vary on some points every time he told it. . . ." Only later did Rip settle down to the story as we have it related. Those few who doubt it suspect that Rip has lost his faculties. The others—men, women, children—have the story memorized. Some even literally believe that thunder is the sound of "Hendrick Hudson and his crew . . . at their game of ninepins. . . ." We have, then, a society willingly trying to turn life into a gothic legend; as such, **"Rip Van Winkle"** is a brilliant satire on the gothic mind.

But what should we make of Rip? Only he escapes Irving's satire, for he unites both Starkenfaust and Ichabod: the poseur in one sense, the artist in another. Like Irving himself, and like countless writers in America, Rip's problem is that of a vocation. What is a creature of the imagination to do in a world whose values are represented by Dame Van Winkle? Art in such a world is, as Hawthorne complained in his sketch "The Custom-House," driven to become a mere escape. Thus, the youthful Rip spends his days "telling endless sleepy stories about nothing." Finally, "reduced almost to despair," he is driven to an actual escape: he rambles off, a sad counterpart to Odysseus, not to return for twenty years, a ragged old man, greeted by his dog with a snarl. Yet one quality in him has not been destroyed by age; his imagination is even richer than before, and he had "arrived at that happy age when a man can be idle with impunity. . . ." Perhaps that was

ABOUT THE AUTHOR

DONALD A. RINGE ON IRVING'S GOTHIC

All of Irving's Gothic tales, sportive though most of them may be, are fundamentally concerned with a problem of human perception, the reasons why people sometimes fail to perceive the world as it is, but see instead a world of Gothic terror. Most of those who fall prey to these self-engendered delusions are men whose minds are filled with superstition, much like the common folk whom Geoffrey Crayon describes in *The Sketch Book* and *Bracebridge Hall*. Others, however, are hardly men of this type. The guests at the hunting dinner in the Nervous Gentleman's tales are by no means credulous men like Ichabod Crane or Wolfert Webber. Rather, the very stories they tell clearly reveal their disbelief in ghosts and goblins, and their initial response to the Nervous Gentleman's experience with the mysterious picture is to laugh uproariously at his discomfort.

As Crayon observes in *Bracebridge Hall*, however, men like these are not immune from feeling Gothic effects, especially if they submit themselves, however lightheartedly, to the influence of supernatural tales. This is, of course, the point of the Nervous Gentleman's stories. All the guests eventually feel the effect of even the sportive stories that have been told, and the comic conclusion makes it especially plain that what happens to them when they view what they think is the mysterious picture bears no relation to reality. . . . Their imaginations have led them to perceive what their reason would deny. But the comic conclusion serves yet another purpose. In revealing the purely mental basis of the Gothic experience, it returns the series of stories to the world of actuality from which it began. In effect, it affirms the reality of the world perceived through reason—the world of common sense and prosaic daylight, which, though less attractive perhaps than the world of fantasy, is nonetheless the one in which Irving's Gothic tales are always firmly anchored.

SOURCE: Ringe, Donald A. "Irving's Use of the Gothic Mode." *Studies in the Literary Imagination* 7, no. 1 (1974): 51-65.

what brought him home, the hope that his world could finally accommodate him. It does: Rip becomes an honored village patriarch and chronicler. Unlike Ichabod, therefore, Rip is not defeated by his gothic imagination, because, for him, it was never dissociated from life. Even if the village skeptics are right, and they may be, in believing that old Van Winkle is edging toward senility, he is granted "an old man's frenzy," which Yeats hoped for and which he recognized in King Lear and William Blake. Imagination alone, whether inspired by frenzy or plain cunning, makes Rip's life significant. Thus, in **"Rip Van Winkle,"** Irving accomplished a judgment of the extremes of the gothic mind and a frail reconciliation between it and the role of the artist.

In most of these modifications of the gothic tradition, Irving's "psychology" played an important part. The too richly imaginative Ichabod Crane, with Puritan superstitions whirling in his brain, was able to manufacture his own midnight goblin, whether or not the external world of fact could give evidence of it. An imitation spectre bridegroom captured the credulity of nearly all the Katzenellenbogens, nourished as they were on the gothic thrills of German legends. This emphasis on the subjective rather than the objective, which was, as I have indicated, the really significant use of gothic motifs in the nineteenth and twentieth centuries, was brought to an intriguing climax in **"The Adventure of the German Student."** At the outset of the story we learn that young Gottfried Wolfgang, a student of German philosophy who literally believes that he is dwelling among "spiritual essences," had been sent by his family to Paris to regain his mental stability. Unfortunately, his monastic life at the Sorbonne, together with the sobering effect of the reign of terror, cancels "the splendors and gayeties of Paris." In the extremity of his isolation. Gottfried has a recurring dream of a woman, "a female face of transcendent beauty." Occupied constantly with thoughts of this dream-woman, he comes one evening upon the guillotine at the Place de Grève, where he meets her, exactly the woman of his dreams. They talk; he brings her home; they make love. The next morning, on rising to greet his bride, he finds her dead. A closer examination reveals that she has been decapitated; in fact, she is the very woman who had been guillotined the day before. This knowledge is too much for Gottfried who screams, "I am lost forever," just before he suffers a mental breakdown. We are left, as we are often left in Irving's stories with two possible explanations: either Gottfried met the transcendent lady truly incarnated, a ghost who became a corpse in the morning, or the woman was a corpse from the beginning. If the psychic condition of Gottfried who, we are told, related the story to the narrator in a madhouse, is significant, then the second version has the greater validity. Viewed in this way, the tale is a story of a madman having sexual intercourse with a decapitated cadaver, thinking she is the transcendent lover of his wildest dreams. No doubt the whole plan is too fantastically sensational. But this is not the sensationalism of "The Young Robber" or indeed of the usual gothic novel. For the factual events are not those that create the terror of the story, nor can the avowal of supernaturalism account for its effectiveness; the acute terror of "The German Student" results from the derangement and the delusions that give a horribly false view of the world. Irving has, therefore, given us one of the first examples of psychological gothicism, in which the crude supernatural motif is dismissed and the gothic tale becomes genuinely a study of grim terror and anguish.

I do not pretend that Irving was a great artist; he was not. But as a parodist, he mirthfully helped to destroy all that was crude in gothic fiction. More importantly, one cannot deny that he anticipated the advanced gothic fiction of Poe and Hawthorne. Then following admittedly in their wakes, we have French symbolism and Henry James—two fundamental forces behind twentieth-century fiction. We should not be surprised, therefore, to find traces of Irving's "sportive" gothic in the works of William Faulkner or his subjectified "machinery" in the midnight novels.

Notes

This paper was presented in an earlier and somewhat different form at the annual meeting of the Modern Language Association at Chicago in December, 1963.

1. Pierre M. Irving, *The Life and Letters of Washington Irving*, II (New York, 1864), 166.

MICHAEL DAVITT BELL (ESSAY DATE 1980)

SOURCE: Bell, Michael Davitt. "Strange Stories: Irving's Gothic." In *The Development of American Romance: The Sacrifice of Relation*, pp. 77-85. Chicago, Ill.: University of Chicago Press, 1980.

In the following excerpt, Bell discusses Irving's humor and treatment of ambiguity as part of the American Gothic tradition.

It has long been a critical truism that the tradition of gothic romance played an essential role in the development of American fiction—far more so than in England, where the tradition originated. It is curious, then, that Irving, although the bulk of his fiction falls clearly within the gothic mode, has been accorded little recognition in this connection. Scholars concerned specifically with his work acknowledge and sometimes analyze his gothicism, but they do not generally concern themselves with his place in the larger American tradition. Leslie Fiedler and Richard Chase, in their major studies of the development of American fiction, virtually ignore him.[1] Yet Irving was clearly the most important American practitioner of gothic fiction in the 1820s, when Poe and Hawthorne were beginning to write. In view of his contemporary stature, so total a lack of recognition would seem to constitute a serious oversight on the part of modern literary historians.[2]

The reasons for this oversight are not mysterious. Recent critical interest in American gothic has called attention to what Melville called "the power of blackness" in our classic writers: the terrors of unconscious motives and forbidden fantasies, the horrors of the soul and the wilderness. Such matters have more importance in Irving than is generally supposed, but, as we have seen, he is more interested in covering them up than in probing them. Furthermore, readers have had trouble in reconciling what Henry A. Pochman called Irving's "sportive Gothic" with the intensity of the major American gothicists. As Stanley T. Williams has complained: "The strength and weakness in Irving's treatment of the supernatural is that he is partly satiric; he loves to end a wild tale with a good-humored chuckle."[3] Had Irving determined the later course of American gothic, it would seem, Ligeia might simply have been a substitute lover in disguise, like the Spectre Bridegroom. Fedallah, no doubt, would have but masked a fun-loving Brom Bones figure (perhaps Bulkington), permitting Ahab to retire into cabbage patches of spermacetti prosperity, while Ishmael regaled a small-town circle in upstate New York with yarns of his twenty-year sleep on a whaling ship. Even Young Goodman Brown might have escaped to New York, following his encounter with a Satanic Pumpkin, to become a justice of the Ten Pound Court.

Yet Irving's humor is worth taking seriously. He may avoid the intensity of later writers (though they were not themselves uniformly serious, particularly Poe and Melville), but behind his humor lies a penetrating inquiry into the very mode the later writers would develop more soberly. Irving's sportive satire is directed, first of all, at gothic fiction itself, at the conventions and attitudes with which such fiction was associated.[4] Thus, for instance, the "Strange Stories by a Nervous Gentleman," which open *Tales of a Traveller*, repeatedly burlesque the central situation of Ann Radcliffe's gothic romances: the anxiety of a quivering, sensitive heroine in a haunted chamber. Only, in Irving's tales we do not have sensitive heroines; instead, there is the far from terrified and "very manly" (46) widow of "**The Adventure of My Aunt**," who apprehends the intruder in her chamber without a superstitious tremor, or there is the boisterous Irish soldier in "**The Bold Dragoon**," who grossly burlesques the Radcliffean stereotype and whose "supernatural" story is probably, in any case, an ingenious cover for alcoholic or sexual excesses.

Irving especially delights in lampooning the attention Mrs. Radcliffe's characters—like Cooper's Natty Bumppo—always manage to devote to refined aesthetic response in the midst of terrifying scenes and circumstances. Hence the Misses Popkins, in "**The Adventure of the Popkins Family**," who "were very romantic, and had learnt to draw in watercolors, [and] were enchanted with the scenery around; it was so like what they had read in Mrs. Radcliffe's romances" (370). Even after being robbed, we are told, "they declared the captain of the band to be a most romantic-looking man, they dared to say some unfortunate lover or exiled nobleman; and several of the band to be very handsome young men—'quite picturesque!'" (373).[5] It is small wonder that Irving's easy humor irritates those who admire the working-up of similar effects in Cooper (one thinks particularly of *The Deerslayer*, in which Natty is always registering the Claude- or Salvator-esque lighting of scenes fraught with imminent danger).

Irving's burlesque of the Radcliffean sublime does not, however, stop with the "good-humored chuckle." Mrs. Radcliffe allows her virtuous characters to thrill to the sublimity of evil without making them see the connection between their opposed aesthetic and moral responses. Irving forces this connection. In "**The Painter's Adventure**," the artist-narrator is captured by bandits, to whom he responds very much in the idiotic manner of the Misses Popkins. Imprisoned in a mountain hideout, with execution possible at any moment, he yet can muse: "I forgot in an instant all my perils and fatigues at this magnificent view of the sunrise in the midst of the mountains of the Abruzzi" (385). He imagines himself a Salvator among *banditti* and spends most of his time sketching his "picturesque" captors.

The tone of light comedy is dropped, however, in the interpolated "**Story of the Young Robber**." Here a member of the band tells the painter of his own complicity in the capture of his beloved, who was then gang-raped by his comrades and murdered by himself. This tale was universally condemned by Irving's contemporaries and is hardly more favorably regarded today, but it makes its point, and it reveals something deeper than "good humor" in *Tales of a Traveller*; for it is the purpose of the tale to affront the reader's complacency by shattering the aesthetic bounds of its genre. "I was sick at heart," the painter confesses at the close, "with the dismal story I had heard. I was harrassed and fatigued, and the sight of the banditti began to grow insupportable to me" (418).

One reason modern readers fail to appreciate the anti-Radcliffean humor of the *Tales* is that we no longer care very much about Ann Radcliffe. Even in 1824 Irving's concern with her was rather old-fashioned. In the popular mind she had been rendered obsolete by the more diabolical gothicism of Lewis, Maturin, and Byron, but Irving, unlike these writers—and unlike Hawthorne and Melville later[6]—was not often willing to break through the protective shield of sublimity to confront outright moral diabolism. Nevertheless, he was fully aware, as his Radcliffean parodies make clear, that to do so was implicit in the appeal of gothic. *True* terror had to have genuine horror as its basis. Otherwise it was a sham, a hoax.

It is this latter perception that informs Irving's most profound sportiveness. His tales—refusing the plunge into satanism, the true "power of blackness"—come to burlesque not only the gothic tradition but themselves as well. "**The Adventure of My Uncle**" prepares us for the explanation of a midnight apparition and then brusquely denies it when the Marquis, apparently out of family delicacy, refuses to disclose the "secret" of the portrait of his ancestress. In "**The Little Antiquary**" we share the title character's fear for his ring, but at the last moment the bandit declines to take it. "You think it," he explains, "an antique, but it's a counterfeit—a mere sham" (338), and so, of course, is the story, which, having built up our expectations only to deflate them, reveals to us our own complicity in the duplicitous pursuit of fictional titillation.[7] Following the incredible "**Adventure of the German Student**" an incredulous auditor asks: "And is this really a fact?" "A fact not to be doubted," replies the narrator. "I had it from the best authority. The student told it me himself. I saw him in a mad-house in Paris" (74). Which information also—it should be observed—incriminates the narrator.

Sir Walter Scott, in 1824, noted the gothic ambiguity of "some modern authors" who

> have exhibited phantoms, and narrated prophe-cies strangely accomplished, without giving a defined or absolute opinion, whether these are to be referred to supernatural agency, or whether the apparitions were produced (no uncommon case) by an overheated imagination, and the presages apparently verified by a casual, though singular, coincidence of circumstances.[8]

Such ambiguity informs the characteristic procedure of later American writers. Ishmael, for instance, never establishes the authority of Eli-jah's or Fedallah's prophecies. Melville was at his most mawkish in the realm of rational, Radcliffean gothic, as in the unintentionally ludicrous "expla-nation" of the legends surrounding Yillah's origin in *Mardi*; but he took gothic ambiguity to extraor-dinarily effective lengths, leaving open, for ex-ample, the question of the Confidence-Man's "supernatural" origin. Poe consistently moots the question of whether the occurrences in his tales are truly "supernal" or merely the products of the narrators' "overheated" imaginations, and Haw-thorne's reliance on the formula of "multiple choice," as with the apparitions in the heavens or on Dimmesdale's chest in *The Scarlet Letter*, has received considerable discussion.[9]

Irving, too, normally establishes the super-natural in this ambiguous manner, as did his friend Scott, from whom he may have learned the trick; but unlike Scott—and well before Poe, Haw-thorne, and Melville—Irving saw the crucial significance of gothic ambiguity. On the formal level it removed the narrator to the position of nonprivileged reporter, permitted only to infer motives and meanings from phenomenal appear-ances. It severed his relation with his material, and it severed as well what Hawthorne, in "The Custom-House," would call his "true relation" (4) with the reader. In such fiction *all* phenomena, in effect, become supernatural and ambiguous. The importance of such a stance to Hawthorne and Melville should be clear; one thinks, for example, of "The Minister's Black Veil" and of much of *Billy Budd*. Toward the end of the latter work the Surgeon defines "phenomenal," in trying to ac-count for the strange manner of Billy's death, as "an appearance the cause of which is not im-mediately to be assigned" (498). Irving's experi-ments with gothic ambiguity might be said, in this sense, to have given currency to the "phenom-enal" stance and style in American fiction.

This ambiguity is not for him, as it was for Scott, primarily a technique for compounding "betwixt ancient faith and modern incredulity." Rather, it provides a formal strategy for dealing with what Irving saw as the central problem presented by fiction itself, in any imaginative mode. Irving's parodies of Radcliffe, and his phenomenal style, force the reader from the supernatural to the psychological—to the consid-eration of the irrational or duplicitous motives of characters and narrators. Irving is an important transitional figure in the increasing subjectifica-tion of gothic terror.[10] But he is more than that, for in the gothic quandary over the nature and status of the supernatural he found a metaphor, and an established form, for investigating the larger question of the nature and status of fictional imagination and its appeal—a question of direct relevance to the predicament he shared with his fellow romancers. What Irving perceived in the 1820s was that the crisis of the gothic tradition— how was one plausibly to pass off the supernatural in modern times?—precisely corresponded to the crisis of romance in nineteenth-century America— how was one to pass off the literary imagination and its products in a hostile culture?

This is not to say that questions about the nature and status of imagination were not already important in the gothic tradition as it came down to Irving. In fact, Mrs. Radcliffe's great accomplish-ment was the conversion of the pseudo-supernatural thriller into a forum for enacting the great psychological-moral contest between fancy and judgment. In her romances the passionate terrors of the seduction novel become explicitly linked with imagination and subjectivity. The alternation between illusory terror and rational reassurance becomes the essential action of her tales. Mrs. Radcliffe may appeal to the imagina-tion, but the virtue of her virtuous characters always consists in their ultimate adherence to "solid" reason and virtue, if only after long and interesting struggles.

Radcliffean gothic, considered in terms of its overt moral appeal, is really antigothic, since it subjects the supernatural and imaginary, in the end, to firm, rational control. Its strength and its weakness lie in Mrs. Radcliffe's ability to ignore the stark contradiction between her fiction's ir-rational appeal and its rational message. She refuses to see the obvious analogy between the terrors besetting her heroes and heroines and the power of romance itself as it besets the reader.

There are times when she seems on the verge of such a recognition. Emily St. Aubert's adventures at Udolpho appear to her "like the dream of a distempered imagination, or like one of those frightful fictions in which the wild genius of the poets sometimes delighted"; and in *The Italian,* Ellena Rosalba reflects, after successfully surviving her various ordeals, that "contrasted with the sober truth of her present life, the past appeared like romance."[11] But Mrs. Radcliffe never becomes self-conscious about her own role as romancer. The most incredible events are reported with the earnest seriousness of the domestic novelist. Thus in her fiction the contest between imagination and judgment remains entirely a matter of theme. There is nothing in her procedure, in her handling of narrative stance and voice, to suggest that she has made the connection between her great subject and the hazards or duplicity of her own practice.

This is precisely the connection that Irving does make. Which is to say that in his best fiction—as later in Poe's, Hawthorne's, and Melville's—gothic romance becomes aesthetically self-aware. Irving's skepticism about gothic fiction is as thorough as Jane Austen's in *Northanger Abbey,* but he does not follow her when, in rejecting romantic imagination, she allies fiction instead with judgment and "novelistic" realism.[12] Rather, he continues to indulge in romance but does so in full awareness of its duplicity. What distinguishes his best gothic tales is the self-consciousness with which they simultaneously exploit and burlesque the basis of their own narrative appeal.

"The Adventure of the German Student" is a case in point. After listening to the first three of the "Strange Stories by a Nervous Gentleman," the old gentleman with the haunted head observes, so we are told, "that the stories hitherto related had rather a burlesque tendency. 'I recollect an adventure, however,' added he, 'which I heard of during a residence at Paris, for the truth of which I can undertake to vouch, and which is of a very grave and singular nature'" (65). There follows the grisly tale of Gottfried Wolfgang's copulation with an animated corpse, guillotined the day before, and of his ensuing insanity when, the black collar removed from her neck, her head rolls to the floor. The story is gruesome and compelling. Even the final revelation that it may all have been a delusion of Gottfried's "diseased" imagination hardly lessens the horror, and perhaps it increases it—like the hideous "explanation" at the end of Alfred Hitchcock's gothic

masterpiece, *Psycho.* To such delusions, who would not prefer "real" specters?

But the tale is ludicrous all the same, and a "burlesque tendency," despite the narrator's disavowal, is seldom far from its verbal surface. It is indeed "grave," this tale of a reanimated corpse whom Gottfried meets in the "Place de Grève."[13] The reader, already in on the secret, is charmed to learn, of the "vicissitude" afflicting this decapitated darling, that "many a fair head, which had once been pillowed on down, now wandered houseless." She is truly one "whom the dreadful axe had rendered desolate." By the time the narrator informs us that "she raised her head" (69)—which may also be a joking reference to **"The Legend of Sleepy Hollow"**—we recognize that there is a consistent employment of *double-entendre* here and, behind it, a consistent duplicity of narrative motive. We have been trapped by a tale whose verbal surface advertises it as a trap. This is not to say that we have been duped—although that is also true—but that our appreciation of the story derives from its form, its texture, rather than from the thrills it offers. Our real engagement is not with Gottfried, the Radcliffean victim, but with the narrator, with enjoying the interplay between his "heated brain" and what Canby calls his "rhetorical display." This display exists all on the surface; calling into doubt both the authority of the tale and the sanity of the teller, it provides no solid clues for a final judgment of either. The style, that is, becomes as ambiguously "phenomenal" as the world—possibly real, possibly illusory—about which it pretends to report.

Much of Irving's fiction is perfunctory, flat, even lazy, but in his best tales the Radcliffean tension between extremes of illusion and judgment is fully integrated into the act of narration. As the protective terminology of rational, associationist aesthetics breaks down, the predicament of Mrs. Radcliffe's characters becomes the predicament of Irving's narrators and auditors, including the reader. At the close of his "Strange Stories," the Nervous Gentleman is even put through the archetypal ordeal of the Radcliffean heroine. Following the evening's tale-telling, he retires to a chamber remarkably similar to "those eventful apartments described in the tales of the supper-table" (76). Here he is terrified by the "Mysterious Picture" painted by the Young Italian, which awakens in him a "horror of the mind"[14]—just as Clithero Edny's irrational tale upset the rational equipoise of Edgar Huntly. "I tried to persuade myself," he writes in true Radcliffean fashion, "that this was chimerical, that my brain was confused by the fumes of mine host's good cheer, and in some measure by the odd stories about paintings which had been told at supper" (78). "It is my own diseased imagination," he insists, "that torments me" (80). In spite of this rational reassurance, however, he spends the night on a couch downstairs.

The next morning, the Baronet "explains" the odd effect of the Italian's painting by reading "**The Story of the Young Italian**"—a nice way to rationalize the effects of a work of art! Then each guest is taken to see the picture. All agree that "there was a certain something about the painting that had a very odd effect upon the feelings." The displaced, aesthetic vocabulary for rationalizing imagination is apparently vindicated in the end. The nearly hysterical fantasies of the Nervous Gentleman are "fixed" to a "real" object with "real" associations. "After all," moralizes the now less nervous Nervous Gentleman, willing to probe the unconscious once it has been rationalized and generalized, "there are certain mysteries in our nature, certain inscrutable impulses and influences, which warrant one in being superstitious. Who can account for so many persons of different characters being thus strangely affected by a mere painting?" "And especially," replies the Baronet, "when not one of them has seen it! . . . I gave the housekeeper a hint to show them all to a different chamber!" (139).

This final, wonderful hoax calls attention, once again, to the fragile complicity between artist and audience, narrator and reader, in the imaginary indulgence of romance, and it traces this imaginative complicity, finally, to those unconscious "mysteries in our nature," those "inscrutable impulses and influences," behind the serene mask of rational aesthetic discourse. One thinks of the importance of such "mysteries" and "impulses" to Brown, Poe, Hawthorne, and Melville. Yet Irving holds back—and this is, perhaps, his limitation—from any full exploration of these "mysteries" and "impulses." He does not wish, or perhaps dare, to probe the unconscious sources and implications of the imagination—to probe the "energy" (in Brown's terms) behind rational literary and psychic "order." His is a fictional world of sophisticated duplicity, of shimmering surfaces that only imply the depths their author himself refuses to enter. That he was aware of what went on in these depths is suggested by the nervousness of his Nervous Gentlemen and by the clear patterns—clear to us, anyway—of

alienation, guilt, and frustrated rage that animate his artist fables and such stories as "**Annette Delarbre.**" Perhaps he understood these patterns too well and too personally to confront them directly. His way, in any case, was not the way of sincerity.

But we can exaggerate the significance of his evasion of sincerity. Even Brown, for all his sincerity of intention, found himself trapped by the duplicitous order of rhetoric, by the tyranny of "words" over "sentiments." Poe, Hawthorne, and Melville would discover the same trap. And the Baronet's hoax, while it may undercut the authority of the Italian's painting and story, does not deny the "mysteries" and "impulses" implicit in the Nervous Gentleman's uncontrollable fantasies. In fact, it comments in a rather sinister fashion on these fantasies; for in denying them a last associational link with the "real" painting, in undercutting the last possibility of Radcliffean "explanation," it testifies that in romance the Jamesian cable of relation—psychological, social, and aesthetic—has indeed been cut. In such romance, "at large and unrelated," motive could only be ambiguous, and style "phenomenal."

Notes

1. Richard Chase, *The American Novel and Its Tradition* (Garden City, N.Y.: Doubleday, 1957); Leslie Fiedler, *Love and Death in the American Novel* (Cleveland: Meridian, 1960). Chase's omission of Irving is understandable; dealing only with long fictions, he also excludes Poe. Fiedler, however, who devotes forty-four pages to Poe (and the "Development of the Gothic") and forty-two pages to Brown (and the "Invention of American Gothic"), mentions Irving only once—in a reference to "such popular histories as Irving's *Astoria* or *Adventures of Captain Bonneville*" (*Love and Death,* p. 371). Similarly, Joel Porte, who discusses Poe at length in *The Romance in America* (Middletown, Conn.: Wesleyan University Press, 1969), virtually ignores Irving.

2. Chase, Fiedler, and Porte all stress the importance of Cooper, and quite rightly. He had his own debts and contributions to the gothic tradition; moreover, his writings were certainly as influential as Irving's, and (together with the influence of Scott) they spawned a host of imitations. Yet to exclude Irving seems perversely myopic. Poe and Hawthorne, for instance, in turning to the short gothic tale rather than the long historical romance, began their careers by following Irving's example, not Cooper's.

3. Henry A. Pochman, "Irving's German Sources and *The Sketch-Book,*" *Studies in Philology* 27 (1930): 506; Williams, *Life,* vol. 1, p. 274.

4. Lady Lillycraft, in *Bracebridge Hall,* "places the Castle of Otranto at the head of all romances" (22). But Irving was not quite so old-fashioned. The principal target of the *Tales* is the rational English gothic of

Ann Radcliffe, whom Irving placed "at the head of her line" (Williams, *Life*, vol. 2, p. 288). He also undoubtedly read Lewis and Maturin and, as well, a good deal of the German literature that influenced them. The effect of such reading can be detected in such tales as "The Story of the Young Italian" and "The Story of the Young Robber." Also, the opening pages of Maturin's *Melmoth the Wanderer* seem very much in force in the description of Buckthorne's miserly uncle. On these matters, see Henry A. Pochman, "Irving's German Tour and Its Influence on His Tales," *PMLA* 45 (1930): 1150-87, and Williams, *Life*, vol. 2, pp. 286-96 (esp. pp. 288-89).

5. This "exiled nobleman" suggests that Schiller's *Die Räuber*, or at least its immense and abiding popularity, lies behind the Misses Popkins' sensationalism. Schiller's play, which gave birth to the literary vogue of *banditti*, clearly influences the "Italian Banditti" section generally and "The Story of the Young Robber" in particular. For an argument that it also lies behind "The Story of the Young Italian," see Pochman, "Irving's German Tour," pp. 1172-73; for a rejoinder, see Williams, *Life*, vol. 2, pp. 288-89.

6. Poe is often included in lists of American gothic diabolists. In fact, however, he consistently expressed his scorn for diabolism. In 1831 he dismissed "the devil in Melmoth" as one who "labors indefatigably through three octavo volumes, to accomplish the destruction of one or two souls, while any common devil would have demolished one or two thousand" (*Works*, 7:xxviii; cf. 11:13). "Pure Diabolism," he wrote in 1849, "is but Absolute Insanity. Lucifer was merely unfortunate in having been created without brains" (16:160). "Absolute Insanity" was not, of course, without interest for Poe, and there may be some defensive special pleading in his dismissal of "Pure Diabolism." But his interest was more in self-torture or passive victimization than in external, proselytizing evil. In "The Pit and the Pendulum," for instance, the Inquisition, that great subject of gothic fiction, is simply a convenience. As an active presence it is not "treated" at all. What matters are its effects, not its motives.

7. It must be admitted that some of the deflations in Irving's tales seem to result more from indolence than from calculation. For instance, following the spectral shenanigans in "Wolfert Webber," we are simply told: "In fact, the secret of all this story has never to this day been discovered" (*Tales*, 540). Irony may be intended here, but one's impression is that Irving, having written himself into a corner, wishes to extricate himself as rapidly as possible.

8. Sir Walter Scott, "Ann Radcliffe," in Ioan Williams, ed., *Sir Walter Scott on Novelists and Fiction* (London: Routledge & Kegan Paul, 1968), p. 116.

9. On this aspect of Hawthorne, see, for instance, Yvor Winters, *In Defense of Reason* (Denver: Alan Swallow, 1947), p. 170, and F. O. Matthiessen, *American Renaissance* (New York: Oxford University Press, 1941), pp. 276-77.

10. This aspect of Irving's achievement is discussed in John Clendinning, "Irving and the Gothic Tradition," *Bucknell Review* 12 (1964): 90-98.

11. Ann Radcliffe, *The Mysteries of Udolpho* (1794) (New York: Dutton, 1931), vol. 1, p. 301, and *The Italian: or,*

the Confessional of the Black Penitents (1797) (New York: Oxford University Press, 1968), p. 302.

12. Jane Austen's attack on gothicism also includes her most sustained defense of her own chosen mode (which she carefully distinguishes from romance): the "realistic" novel of manners, "in which the most thorough knowledge of human nature, the happiest delineation of its varieties, the liveliest effusions of wit and humour, are conveyed to the world in the best-chosen language" (*Northanger Abbey* [1818] [New York: New American Library, 1965], p. 30). What distinguishes Irving is his refusal to make this kind of distinction. In these contrasting responses to Mrs. Radcliffe—burlesque rejection as opposed to burlesque indulgence—one comes perhaps as close as one can to the point of divergence between the "realistic" "Great Tradition" of nineteenth-century British fiction and the tradition of American romance.

13. Gottfried's first encounter with the female victim of the Terror is strikingly similar to Tobias Pearson's first encounter with Ilbrahim, victim of the Puritan persecution of the Quakers, in Hawthorne's "The Gentle Boy" (first published in 1832, in *The Token*). Gottfried, wandering alone at night, sees the spectral woman at the foot of the guillotine. Pearson, wandering alone at evening, sees Ilbrahim at the foot of the gallows. "What is your name," Pearson asks the strange boy, "and where is your home?" "They call me Ilbrahim," replies the boy, "and my home is here" (*Twice-Told Tales*, 72). "But you have a home," Gottfried suggests to the stranger, to which she replies: "Yes—in the grave!" (70). Gottfried, in compassion, takes her to his home; Pearson, in compassion, takes Ilbrahim to his. One scarcely wishes to argue, here, deliberate allusion by Hawthorne to Irving's story or even conscious imitation. One feels, nevertheless, that Hawthorne read his Irving carefully.

14. The terrifying, mysterious portrait was a standard, even hackneyed, device in gothic fiction; but given Poe's special admiration for "The Young Italian," it is interesting to note how close Irving's uses of the device, here, is to Poe's use of it in the narrative frame of "The Oval Portrait."

TITLE COMMENTARY

"Adventure of the German Student"

JAMES E. DEVLIN (ESSAY DATE SPRING 1979)

SOURCE: Devlin, James E. "Irving's 'Adventure of the German Student.'" *Studies in American Fiction* 7, no. 1 (spring 1979): 92-5.

In the following essay, Devlin analyzes "Adventure of the German Student" as a "cautionary tale warning against sexual fantasy and masturbation."

Although it remains one of Washington Irving's more popular pieces, "**Adventure of the Ger-**

man Student" has escaped the critical attention accorded his best known tales. Regarded usually as an eerie hoax on the basis of a trick narration that seems to dismiss any more serious meaning, or seen simply as a Gothic fancy, "Adventure of the German Student" has failed to profit from the sort of scrutiny that has proved so successful in the study of other of Irving's tales.

One need be no dyed-in-the-wool Freudian to recognize the host of disguised sexual allusions that haunt the work of the "genteel" Irving and provide considerable insight into his mind. William L. Hedges wrote accurately some years ago that "an interplay of desire, fear and guilt . . . characterizes his treatment of love, sexuality, and marriage."[1] Indeed, his two best-loved tales, "Rip Van Winkle" and "The Legend of Sleepy Hollow," are now read as replete with sexual innuendo.

The first of these, as Leslie Fiedler,[2] Philip Young,[3] and others have convincingly shown, expresses a desire to escape adult male sexual responsibility and the duties of marriage for a second childhood of advanced old age; of the second, it is enough to note that the devastatingly seductive Eula Varner owes both her being and her mentality to Faulkner's vivid recollection of Katrina Van Tassel.[4] In short, Dame Van Winkle's depiction represents a disavowal of the mature woman while Katrina Van Tassel's offers an unflattering picture of a nubile maiden. In the latter tale Irving's careful diction, ostensibly used to describe a fertile farm, serves in its plosive bounty to characterize a blouse-bursting Dutch coquette whose chief delight is the torment of young men. It is hardly surprising, then, that the "Adventure of the German Student," one of the *Tales of a Traveler* (1824), yields considerably more meaning when viewed from a similar perspective.

This brief tale, which the reader ultimately discovers is narrated at several removes, recounts, in terms anticipating Poe, the progressive psychic disintegration of young Gottfried Wolfgang, who leaves the University of Goettingen for Paris in hope of escaping "the mental malady preying upon him." The Paris of the Reign of Terror proves even less accommodating than his German habitat, however. Crossing a dark, stormy Parisian square late at night in a state of perturbation, he encounters a "female figure" languishing at the foot of the guillotine whom he leads back to his rooms in the Latin Quarter near the Sorbonne. There, agreeing to be his "forever," she "sank upon his bosom." On his return home the next morn-

ing from a quest to find "more spacious apartments suitable to the change in his situation," he discovers the woman still lying on his bed and apparently dead. When the police are summoned, an officer immediately recognizes her as a victim of yesterday's guillotine. Stepping forward he undoes the black ribbon around her neck as her head falls rolling to the floor. The distracted student is shortly thereafter committed to an asylum whence his story is ultimately spread.

The tale, the plot of which Irving had at second hand from Thomas Moore,[5] is clearly more than a ghost story. It turns out to be, in fact, a cautionary tale warning against sexual fantasy and masturbation, with overtones and situations that will remind German readers of Frank Wedekind's pointed assault on sexual repression in the daring *Fruehlings Erwachen* written some fifty years later. Evidence to support such a "Freudian" reading, one might almost say "orthodox reading" in the light of recent Irving scholarship, appears at every turn.

A young man, whose morbid habits of seclusion are constantly reiterated in the story, has "impaired his health" by "indulging in fanciful speculations" of an uncertain nature, but which are later revealed to involve fantasies of "female beauty." Convinced that there is "an evil influence hanging over him," he agrees to exchange his "secluded life" for a less morbid environment lest he "ensure his perdition." His "imagination" is already "diseased" and he himself "haggard and desponding" in need of a "cure." While neither Gottfried Wolfgang's condition nor its cause is in any wise identified, apart from a vague reference to the intensity of his studies, Irving's diction consistently draws on the oblique terminology regularly employed in the last century (and much of this) to describe the milieu and effects of "self-abuse" or the "solitary sin." In Gottfried's seclusive behavior, indulgence in erotic fantasies, frantic effort to change his habits, and his concomitant guilt and fear for both his health and soul, Irving offers a contemporary profile of the solitary sinner.

In Paris Gottfried is unable to change his ways. He continues to keep to his room and to indulge his "ardent temperament." While he is "too shy" to "make any advances to the fair," or to seek the companionship and love of a real woman, he remains "a passionate admirer of female beauty, and in his lonely chamber would often lose himself on forms and faces which he had seen, and his fancy would deck out images of loveliness far surpassing the reality." No words here are quite so revealing as the phrase "lose himself" which suggests that the student's lonely erotic reveries frequently culminated in the dread loss of virility solitary sexual indulgence was feared to cause. But Gottfried Wolfgang's final commitment to unwholesome fantasy comes only after a series of dreams of a particular woman of whom he grows "passionately enamoured." This fantasy woman, who appears to him only in an "excited and sublimated state," represents his acceptance of a life governed by sensual satisfaction and an allegiance to his indulgence even at the cost of growing madness.

On a stormy night some time later, how long is uncertain, he finds her, crouching at the foot of the guillotine, prototypical symbol of castration. Thus is the sin (masturbation) emblematically linked to its punishment (the loss of manhood). The spectral creature, "ravishingly beautiful," of course, and "clad in black" accompanies the gaunt student home where Gottfried enjoys a final night, not of necrophilial passion, as the story would suggest, but rather of final surrender to sexual satisfacion *in solo*. The otherwise ascetic young German's pleasure with a French lamia in the decadent environment of an ancient *hôtel* in the Latin Quarter, an image that would certainly have appealed to Thomas Mann, is undoubtedly tempered by dreadful anxieties. But it is only on the next day when the lady's head falls from her body that Gottfried's emasculation is complete. If the looming silhouette of the guillotine has not established what is transpiring, the decapitation must, for as William Hedges has seen, Irving's "images of maiming and cutting down seem to carry an unconscious implication of fear of castration."[6] The story is over. Wolfgang is indeed "lost forever" as he shrieks. Mad and impotent, at least psychically, he is led off to the madhouse since the penalty for masturbation is insanity.

Notes

1. William L. Hedges, *Washington Irving: An American Study* (Baltimore: Johns Hopkins Press, 1965), p. 11.

2. Leslie A. Fiedler, *Love and Death in the American Novel* (New York: Stein and Day, 1966), pp. 339-43.

3. Philip Young, "Fallen from Time: The Mythic Rip Van Winkle," *KR*, 22 (1960), 547-73.

4. Cecil D. Eby, Jr., "Ichabod Crane in Yoknapatawpha," *GaR*, 16 (1962), 465-69.

5. Hedges, pp. 148-49.

6. Hedges, p. 201n.

BARBARA TEPA LUPACK (ESSAY DATE FALL 1984)

SOURCE: Lupack, Barbara Tepa. "Irving's German Student." *Studies in Short Fiction* 21, no. 4 (fall 1984): 398-400.

In the following essay, Lupack examines aspects of delusion, fantasy, parody, and the Gothic in "Adventure of the German Student."

Sensing the decline of gothicism and the dangers of aping its style, Washington Irving rejected an exhausted tradition.[1] Not wanting to abandon "the legendary and romantic tales" entirely, however, he sought an original use for gothic material and turned to a manner more "suited to [his] own way of thinking and writing."[2] Suggestive psychology through parody, a technique which reveals the excesses of a genre by imitating it, allowed Irving simultaneously to employ and to burlesque the conventional treatment of the elements of "German" romanticism: angst, weltschmerz, sentimentality, supernatural intervention, horror, sexual aberration, and psychological disorders.

"**Adventure of the German Student,**" one of Irving's most delightful and enduring tales, is indeed a successful parody of the "exhausted" gothic form. Gottfried Wolfgang, a young and impressionable student of German philosophy living in Paris during the bloody reign of terror, believes that he is possessed by an evil spirit. His imagination, fired by his loneliness and melancholy, creates a "shadow," the recurrent dream of a woman of "transcendent beauty." One evening, Gottfried, preoccupied with the vision of this female face, encounters a young woman dressed in black at the Place de Greve. He offers her lodging, brings her back to his home, and there he recognizes her as the woman of his dreams; that same evening, they pledge eternal affection for each other and consummate their compact. The next morning, Gottfried is shocked to find his "wife" dead—indeed the corpse of a woman guillotined the previous day. Realizing that "the fiend" had reanimated her body to ensnare him and to ensure his perdition, he goes mad.

John Clendenning has argued that the reader is left with two possible explanations: either Gottfried met the transcendent lady truly incarnated, a ghost who becomes a corpse in the morning, or the woman was a corpse from the beginning. If the reader concedes the imbalance of the protagonist, as suggested by the fact that he related his adventure to the narrator of the tale while in a madhouse, then, according to Clendenning, the second version has the greater validity. Viewed in this way, a madman has sexual intercourse with a decapitated cadaver, thinking she is the transcendent lover of his wildest dreams.[3]

While Clendenning's arguments are convincing—as far as he pursues them—he overlooks a third alternative, another viable and plausible reading of the sketch's ending. Admitting Irving's suggestion that Gottfried is insane—which most critics of the tale, including Clendenning, do—it follows that the entire adventure may have been no more than the mere psychological projection of a deranged and repressed young man. That Gottfried is deranged can be assumed from his peculiarly melancholic disposition which leads to his breakdown and subsequent incarceration in a Paris asylum; that he is repressed is clear from his lack of involvement with real women and his commitment to the pursuit of his fantasy female. "His imagination [was] diseased," writes Irving early in the story; it is probable, therefore, that the woman by the guillotine was nonexistent, a manifestation of this madman's imagination, the perfect sado-masochistic relationship, as in Browning's "Porphyria's Lover."

Regardless of which interpretation the reader chooses, neither the "facts" of the sensational plot nor the intimations of supernaturalism constitute the terror of the tale; the ultimate terror results, rather, from the psychological gothicism Irving achieves, based upon the derangements and delusions which create a horribly false view of the world. As a parody, "German Student" destroys the crudeness which exists in nineteenth-century romance, playfully dispels the excesses of gothic fiction, and anticipates the advanced gothicism of Poe, Hawthorne, Faulkner, and such diverse forces behind twentieth-century literature as Henry James and the French symbolists.[4]

Nowhere in the tale, however, is Irving's parody more skillful than in the description and treatment of the character, Wolfgang. A tremendous irony is implicit in his very name: Gottfried literally means "God's peace," yet peace—particularly God's peace—is one virtue the young student glaringly lacks. He is a rebellious and restless romantic whose "visionary and enthusiastic character" has caused him to wander "into those wild and speculative doctrines which have so often bewildered German students." He indulges in fanciful speculations on spiritual essences and rejects conventional Christian beliefs to create his own "ideal world." Like Faust—and the archetypal ramifications of Wolfgang's perverse quest for knowledge are deliberate and pervasive—he, in ef-

fect, sells his soul to an evil and forbidden agent. Then he consummates his bargain, somewhat unknowingly, by engaging in intercourse with a demon, a succubus not unlike the beautiful Helen in the Faust legend. His damnation is inevitable and he dies, despairingly, in a madhouse. Ironically, he becomes the victim of his own rapacious appetite for arcane knowledge. Yet it is precisely this rapaciousness, as integral to the typical gothic hero as his despondent Germanic nature and brooding melancholy, which, when deliberately exaggerated in "**Adventure of the German Student**," makes Irving's protagonist a parody of the very type he epitomizes.

Notes

1. John Clendenning, "Irving and the Gothic Tradition," *Bucknell Review*, 12 (May 1964), 91. Mr. Clendenning provides a perceptive study of Irving's "inverted gothic" form and a fine analysis of "Adventure of the German Student."

2. Pierre M. Irving, *The Life and Letters of Washington Irving* (New York: G. P. Putnam, 1864), II, 166.

3. Clendenning, pp. 97-98.

4. Clendenning, p. 98.

FURTHER READING

Biography

Reichart, Walter A. *Washington Irving and Germany*. Ann Arbor: University of Michigan Press, 1957, 212 p.

Biographical discussion of Irving's experiences in Germany. The author points out the similarity between Irving's short stories and German folktales.

Criticism

Aderman, Ralph M. "Washington Irving As a Purveyor of Old and New World Romanticism." In *The Old and New World Romanticism of Washington Irving*, edited by Stanley Brodwin, pp. 13-25. New York: Greenwood Press, 1986.

Considers the influence of European Romanticism on Irving's writings, particularly his later works.

Bowden, Mary Weatherspoon. *Washington Irving*. Boston: Twayne Publishers, 1981, 201 p.

Book-length study of Irving's life and works.

Christensen, Peter. "Washington Irving and the Denial of the Fantastic." In *The Old and New World Romanticism of Washington Irving*, edited by Stanley Brodwin, pp. 51-60. New York: Greenwood Press, 1986.

Provides an overview of Irving's treatment of the supernatural in his writings from 1819 to 1832.

Coad, Oral Sumner. "The Gothic Element in American Literature before 1835." *The Journal of English and Germanic Philology* 24, no. 1 (January 1925): 72-93.

An historical overview of gothicism in American literature that includes a survey of Gothic elements in The Sketch Book.

Critical Essays on Washington Irving, edited by Ralph M. Aderman. Boston: Hall, 1990, 276 p.

*A collection of essays exploring varied aspects of Irving's
works.*

Dawson, Hugh J. "Recovering 'Rip Van Winkle': A Corrective Reading." *ESQ: A Journal of the American Renaissance* 40, No. 3 (1994): 251-73.

*Contends that the forest scene in "Rip Van Winkle" is
Gothic rather than comic and that the story is not anti-
feminist.*

Griffith, Kelley, Jr. "Ambiguity and Gloom in Irving's
'Adventure of the German Student.'" *CEA Critic* 38
(1975): 10-13.

*Asserts that the ambiguity in Irving's "Adventure of the
German Student" accounts for the story's "shocking and
depressing psychological realism."*

Ringe, Donald A. "Washington Irving." In *American Gothic:
Imagination and Reason in Nineteenth-Century Fiction*,
pp. 80-101. Lexington: University Press of Kentucky,
1982.

*Examines Irving's Gothic writings, asserting that they are
"fundamentally concerned with a problem of human
perception."*

Rodes, Sara Puryear. "Washington Irving's Use of Traditional
Folklore." *Southern Folklore Quarterly* 19, no. 3
(September 1956): 143-53.

*Describes Irving's effective use of folklore in "Rip Van
Winkle" and "The Legend of Sleepy Hollow" and recounts
the original folktales from which Irving drew his stories.*

Roth, Martin. "Irving and the Old Style." *Early American
Literature* 12, no. 3 (winter 1977-78): 256-70.

*Focuses on Irving's "Letters of Jonathan Oldstyle," sug-
gesting that these early essays shed light on the author's
later works.*

Turner, Deanna C. "Shattering the Fountain: Irving's Re-
Vision of 'Kubla Khan' in 'Rip Van Winkle.'" *Symbiosis:
A Journal of Anglo-American Literary Relations* 4, no. 1
(April 2000): 1-17.

*Compares "Rip Van Winkle" to Samuel Taylor Coleridge's
poem "Kubla Khan," suggesting similarities in theme,
symbolism, and form.*

Veeder, William. "Form, Psychoanalysis, and Gender in
Gothic Fiction: The Instance of 'Rip Van Winkle.'" In
Gothick Origins and Innovations, edited by Allan Lloyd
Smith and Victor Sage, pp. 79-94. Atlanta, Ga. and Am-
sterdam: Rodopi, 1994.

*Analyzes "Rip Van Winkle" to demonstrate that "form
and psychology are . . . intricately related to questions of
gender in the Gothic."*

OTHER SOURCES FROM GALE:

Additional coverage of Irving's life and career is contained
in the following sources published by Thomson Gale: *American Writers*; *Authors and Artists for Young Adults*, Vol. 56;
Children's Literature Review, Vol. 97; *Concise Dictionary of
American Literary Biography, 1640-1865*; *Dictionary of Literary
Biography*, Vols. 3, 11, 30, 59, 73, 74, 183, 186, 250, 254;
DISCovering Authors; *DISCovering Authors: British*; *DISCover-
ing Authors: Canadian*; *DISCovering Authors Modules: Most-
studied Authors*; *DISCovering Authors 3.0*; *Exploring Short Sto-
ries*; *Literature and Its Times*, Vol. 1; *Literature Resource Center*;
Nineteenth-Century Literature Criticism, Vols. 2, 19, 95; *Refer-
ence Guide to American Literature*, Ed. 4; *Reference Guide to
Short Fiction*, Ed. 2; *Short Stories for Students*, Vols. 1, 8, 16;
Short Story Criticism, Vols. 2, 37; *Supernatural Fiction Writers*,
Vol. 1; *Twayne's United States Authors*; *World Literature Criti-
cism*; *Writers for Children*; and *Yesterday's Authors of Books for
Children*, Vol. 2.

HENRY JAMES

(1843 - 1916)

American novelist, short story and novella writer, essayist, critic, biographer, autobiographer, and playwright.

James is considered one of the great novelists in the English language and the writer at the forefront of the movement toward more realism in literature. By enlarging the scope of the novel, introducing dramatic elements to the narrative tale, using highly self-conscious narrators, and refining the point-of-view technique to a new level of sophistication, he advanced the art of fiction. He also probed a number of social and psychological concerns, such as the artist's role in society, the need for both the aesthetic and moral life, and the benefits of a developed consciousness receptive to the thoughts and feelings of others. Psychological and social questions pervade James's small body of supernatural fiction as well, which uses hauntedness and horror to offer insights into the conscious self and the truth that lies within the human soul. James's best-known Gothic works are the novella *The Turn of the Screw* (1898) and the ghost stories that he wrote over the course of his long career, notably "The Ghostly Rental" (1876) and "The Jolly Corner" (1908). Absent from these works are the typical Gothic conventions found in other works of the genre, as James concentrates on the internal rather than the external conditions of his fictional subjects. The psychological ghost story is taken to new heights as it focuses not on external specters but on the perceiving consciousness. In James's fiction, Gothic elements are used in the service of realism and psychology to emphasize the impenetrable depths of human emotion and to highlight the strange and often frightening nature of the human mind.

BIOGRAPHICAL INFORMATION

James was born in New York City, the second son of well-to-do, liberal parents. Because of his grandfather's enormous wealth, a fortune he divided equally among his children, James's father never had to work for his income. Henry James, Sr. was an intellectual man of his day: a devotee of the philosopher Emanuel Swedenborg and an occasional theorist on religion and philosophy. He sometimes had hallucinations that he regarded as religious experiences, and as he was growing up James witnessed his father's strange behavior during such episodes. James's mother had a more practical bent, a quality she was forced to develop in order to compensate for her husband's erratic conduct. James himself was a shy, bookish boy who assumed the role of a quiet observer beside his active elder brother William, who later became the founder of psychological study in America and the prominent philosopher of pragmatism. Both Henry and William spent much of their youth traveling between the United States and Europe. They were schooled by tutors and governesses in such diverse environments as Manhattan, Geneva, Paris, and London. Both developed a skill in foreign languages and an awareness of Europe rare among Americans in their time.

At the age of nineteen James enrolled at Harvard Law School, briefly entertaining thoughts of a professional career. However, this ambition soon changed and he began devoting his study time to reading literature, particularly the works of Honoré de Balzac and Nathaniel Hawthorne. Inspired by the literary atmosphere of Cambridge and Boston, James wrote his first fiction and criticism, his earliest works appearing in the *Continental Monthly, The Atlantic Monthly,* and *The North American Review.* From the beginning of his career James wrote supernatural stories, inspired by his love for the work of Hawthorne; his first two unearthly stories, "The Romance of Certain Old Clothes" (1868) and "De Grey: A Romance" (1868) clearly show Hawthorne's influence.

In the 1860s James met and formed lifelong friendships with William Dean Howells—then assistant editor at *The Atlantic*—Charles Eliot Norton, and James Russell Lowell. Howells was to become James's editor and literary agent, and together the two could be said to have inaugurated the era of realism in American literature. In 1869 James went abroad for his first adult encounter with Europe. While in London he was taken by the Nortons to meet some of England's greatest writers, including George Eliot, John Ruskin, Dante Gabriel Rossetti, and Alfred Lord Tennyson. The year 1869 also marked the death of James's beloved cousin Minny Temple, for whom he had formed a deep emotional attachment. This shock, and the intensity of his experiences in Europe, provided much of the material that would figure in such later works as *The Portrait of a Lady* (1881) and *The Wings of the Dove* (1902).

James returned to the United States in 1870 determined to discover whether he could live and write in his native country. He continued to write stories and began work on his first novel, *Watch and Ward* (unpublished until 1878). However, after a winter of unremitting hackwork in New York, James became convinced that he could write better and live more cheaply abroad. In 1875 he moved permanently to Europe, settling first in Rome, then in Paris, and eventually in London, where he found the people and conditions best suited to his imagination. He wrote stories and wasted no time in producing the early novels which would establish his reputation—*Roderick Hudson* (1876), *The American* (1877), and *The Europeans* (1878). While in Paris, James was admitted into the renowned circle of Gustave Flaubert, Emile Zola, Guy de Maupassant, Alphonse Daudet, and Ivan Turgenev. He greatly admired the French writers, but felt closest to Turgenev, who confirmed his own view that a novelist need not worry about "story," but should focus exclusively on character. Though James earned recognition with his first European novels, it was not until the publications of *Daisy Miller* (1879) and *The Portrait of a Lady* that he gained popular success. The latter marked the end of what critics consider the first period in his career. Throughout the following decades and into the twentieth century he progressed toward more complex effects in his novels and stories. Because of his experiments he eventually lost the popularity that he had achieved with *Daisy Miller* and *The Portrait of a Lady.* Many critics suggest that it was this growing neglect by the public which induced him to try his hand as a playwright. However, after several attempts at drama—most notably his dramatization of *The American* (1891) and his new productions, *Guy Domville* (1895) and *The High Bid* (1908), all of which failed at the box office—James gave up the theater.

The years 1898 to 1904 were the most productive of James's literary career. During this period he published several volumes of stories, his ghostly novella *The Turn of the Screw,* and the consummate novels of his late maturity—*The Wings of the Dove, The Ambassadors* (1903), and *The Golden Bowl* (1904). After 1904 James's health and creativity began to decline. Though he still produced a sizeable amount of work, consisting mainly of his autobiographies, essays, and criticism, he finished only one novel, *The Outcry* (1911). With the outbreak of World War I, James became particularly distressed. He devoted much of his remaining energy to serving the Allied cause, and when the United States did not immediately back the Allies he assumed British citizenship in protest against his native land. On his deathbed the following year he received the British Order of Merit.

MAJOR WORKS

James's reputation rests primarily on his novels, the best of which are acknowledged to be the "international" novels and those depicting the American character, including *Portrait of a Lady, The Bostonians* (1886), *Washington Square* (1881) and *The Golden Bowl.* James's ghost stories are less well known, but they continue to be read and admired. Written over the course of his career, they reveal how the author's interests and craftsmanship developed. The early stories "The Romance of Certain Old Clothes" and "De Grey: A Romance," for example, explore the Hawthornian themes of pride, envy, and guilt as well as the "presentness of the past," but without the psychological complexity of Hawthorne's short fiction. But then in the lurid 1876 tale "The Ghostly Rental," centered around a haunted house, James leaves the reader to judge the authenticity of ghosts, supplying just enough psychological detail to make the characters' supernatural experiences genuinely convincing but the reality of the ghosts equally problematic.

The "reality" of the ghostly experience is further complicated in "Sir Edmund Orme" (1891). The story is framed by an unidentified speaker who claims that he came into "possession" of this manuscript—narrated in the first person—after the death of the narrator's wife, "whom I take," the speaker conjectures, "to have been one of the persons referred to. There is nothing in the strange story to establish this point." The uncertainty as to how the reader should take the story is further emphasized when the speaker cautions that the manuscript may not be a "report of a real occurrence." The reader's incredulity is matched by the speaker's skepticism. In less than a paragraph, James establishes a sense of verisimilitude and gently leads the reader into a willing suspension of disbelief. In "The Private Life" (1892) there is no question as to the reality of the supernatural—at least as far as the main characters are concerned—but the story is more amusing than terrifying, both for the characters who experience the strange phenomena and for the reader who is privy to their adventure. James based his story and the character of Clare Vawdrey on the great Victorian poet Robert Browning. Observing him socially, James found Browning "loud" and aggressive but mundane, even banal. Yet James acknowledged his greatness as a poet. This story playfully explores the contradiction. "Owen Wingrave" (1892) is a more somber effort. Trained as a soldier, young Owen Wingrave challenges the family military tradition and leaves school. Shocked, his tutor, his friends, and his family accuse him of selfishness and cowardice, and put enormous pressure on him to continue in the military. All of the characters—including Owen's teacher—meet for a weekend in one of the family's homes, one room of which is supposedly haunted by the ghost of Owen's ancestor Colonel Wingrave, who had killed one of his sons. To prove that he is not a coward, Owen accepts a dare to spend the night in the room, and the next day is found dead. The circumstances of both his ancestor's and Owen's death suggest a supernatural explanation, but the horror is not in the account of Owen's death but in the portrait of the family that pressures Owen and leads him to this desperate act.

The Turn of the Screw is by common consent James's best tale of supernatural horror. It is framed with a speaker, Douglas, who produces a manuscript by a governess who had been infatuated with her employer. Her manuscript describes how she is confronted by a pair of ghosts that she suspects is corrupting the two young children in her charge. The apparitions are those of Peter Quint, a man formerly employed in the household, and Miss Jessel, the previous governess. As her suspicions deepen, the new governess confronts each of the children concerning their collusion with the ghosts; during each confrontation, one of the specters appears to the governess, bringing the action to a crisis. The girl, Flora, denies having seen the wraiths and, apparently hysterical, is sent to her uncle in London. The boy, Miles, dies in the governess's arms during the culmination of a psychic battle between the governess and the ghost of Peter Quint. In this story James once again leaves the nature and "reality" of the supernatural a mystery, and the story has been read variously as a horrifying ghost story and a penetrating psychological study of an emotionally unstable woman whose visions of ghosts are mere hallucinations.

"The Jolly Corner" is James's last and one of his best stories involving the supernatural. Its hero, Spencer Brydon, returns to New York after a thirty-year absence to visit his boyhood home (the house on the jolly corner). Obsessed by a desire to know what he might have become had he remained in New York, Brydon visits the house several times and senses "presences," which he interprets to be members of his family, now dead, and their history. Brydon is so frightened that he faints. When he awakens, his head is in the lap of a woman friend, who has also seen this ghost. While not as ambiguous as *The Turn of the Screw*— Brydon's friend confirms the existence of the ghost—the story is similarly powerful as a study of one's search for personal identity, as the protagonist gains insight into himself by his comparison with his "other self." Moreover, the core idea, the consequences of his choices, is the basis of art itself. It is the exploration through the imagination of the possibilities of human action, a theme that has universal appeal.

CRITICAL RECEPTION

James achieved commercial and critical success during his lifetime. However, because of the subject matter of his works—their lack of social and political concerns and emphasis on high society—his reputation suffered after World War I, only to be revived again in the 1940s. By the 1960s most critics realized the depth of James's fiction, and since then he has been acknowledged as a master of the novel. Although James is not thought of primarily as a Gothic writer, some critics regard *The Turn of the Screw* as perhaps the world's finest ghost story, and the most satisfyingly ambivalent and provocative piece of fiction James ever wrote. Because of the work's relative accessibility and popularity compared to much of James's other work, the novella is often read as an introduction to James. A critical debate has raged since the 1930s as to the exact nature of the piece. Is it a ghost story or a psychological study of an unstable woman? Like James's ghost stories, the novella is admired not only for its ability to horrify but because it presents so realistically the ambiguity inherent in questions of the occult and supernatural. Critics writing about the Gothic elements in James's fiction have discussed his ghost stories as aesthetic experiments in which the author tries to come to terms with questions about consciousness that he explores more fully in other works; the use of the supernatural to investigate complex questions about human psychology; and the ghosts in the works as representations or manifestations of the human psyche.

PRINCIPAL WORKS

A Passionate Pilgrim, and Other Tales (short stories) 1875

Roderick Hudson (novel) 1876

The American (novel) 1877

The Europeans (novel) 1878

French Poets and Novelists (criticism) 1878

Watch and Ward (novel) 1878

Daisy Miller (novel) 1879

Hawthorne (criticism) 1879

The Madonna of the Future, and Other Tales (short stories) 1879

Confidence (novel) 1880

The Portrait of a Lady (novel) 1881

Washington Square (novel) 1881

Daisy Miller [first publication; adaptation of the novel] (play) 1883

The Siege of London. Madame de Mauves (novellas) 1883

A Little Tour in France (travel essays) 1885

The Bostonians (novel) 1886

The Princess Casamassima (novel) 1886

The Aspern Papers. Louisa Pallant. The Modern Warning (novellas) 1888

"The Lesson of the Master" (short story) 1888; published in the journal *Universal Review*

Partial Portraits (criticism) 1888

A London Life (short stories) 1889

The Tragic Muse (novel) 1890

The American [adaptation of the novel] (play) 1891

"The Real Thing" (short story) 1892; published in the journal *Black and White*

The Real Thing, and Other Tales (short stories) 1893

Theatricals. Two Comedies: Tenants, Disengaged [first publication] (plays) 1894

Guy Domville (play) 1895

Theatricals, Second Series: The Album, The Reprobate [first publication] (plays) 1895

The Other House (novel) 1896

The Spoils of Poynton (novel) 1897

What Maisie Knew (novel) 1897

The Two Magics: The Turn of the Screw, Covering End (novellas) 1898

The Awkward Age (novel) 1899

The Sacred Fount (novel) 1901

The Wings of the Dove (novel) 1902

The Ambassadors (novel) 1903

"The Beast in the Jungle" (short story) 1903; published in the journal *The Better Sort*

The Golden Bowl (novel) 1904

English Hours (travel essays) 1905

The American Scene (travel essays) 1907

The Novels and Tales of Henry James. 24 vols. (novels, novellas, and short stories) 1907-09

The High Bid (play) 1908

"The Jolly Corner" (short story) 1908; first published in the journal *The English Review*

PRIMARY SOURCES

HENRY JAMES (STORY DATE FEBRUARY 1868)

SOURCE: James, Henry. "The Romance of Some Old Cloths." In *Great Ghost Stories: 34 Classic Tales of the Supernatural,* compiled by Robin Brockman, pp. 167-85. New York: Gramercy Books, 2002.

The following excerpt is from a short story originally published February 1868 as "The Romance of Certain Old Clothes" in the Atlantic Monthly.

The marriage was to all appearance a happy one, and each party obtained what each had desired—Lloyd 'a devilish fine woman', and Rosalind—but Rosalind's desires, as the reader will have observed, had remained a good deal of a mystery. There were, indeed, two blots upon their felicity, but time would perhaps efface them. During the first three years of her marriage Mrs Lloyd failed to become a mother, and her husband on his side suffered heavy losses of money. This latter circumstance compelled a material retrenchment in his expenditure, and Rosalind was perforce less of a fine lady than her sister had been. She contrived, however, to carry it like a woman of considerable fashion. She had long since ascertained that her sister's copious wardrobe had been sequestrated for the benefit of her daughter, and that it lay languishing in thankless gloom in the dusty attic. It was a revolting thought that these exquisite fabrics should await the good pleasure of a little girl who sat in a high chair and ate bread-and-milk with a wooden spoon. Rosalind had the good taste, however, to say nothing about the matter until several months had expired. Then, at last, she timidly broached it to her husband. Was it not a pity that so much finery should be lost?— for lost it would be, what with colours fading, and moths eating it up, and the change of fashions. But Lloyd gave her so abrupt and peremptory a refusal, that she saw, for the present, her attempt was vain. Six months went by, however, and brought with them new needs and new visions. Rosalind's thoughts hovered lovingly about her sister's relics. She went up and looked at the chest in which they lay imprisoned. There was a sullen defiance in its three great padlocks and its iron bands which only quickened her cupidity. There was something exasperating in its incorruptible immobility. It was like a grim and grizzled old household servant, who locks his jaws over a family secret. And then there was a look of capacity in its vast extent, and a sound as of dense fullness, when Rosalind knocked its side with the toe of her little shoe, which caused her to flush with baffled longing. 'It's absurd,' she cried; 'it's improper, it's wicked'; and she forthwith resolved upon another attack upon her husband. On the following day, after dinner, when he had had his wine, she boldly began it. But he cut her short with great sternness.

'Once for all, Rosalind,' said he, 'it's out of the question. I shall be gravely displeased if you return to the matter.'

'Very good,' said Rosalind. 'I am glad to learn the esteem in which I am held. Gracious heaven,' she cried, 'I am a very happy woman! It's an agreeable thing to feel one's self sacrificed to a caprice!' And her eyes filled with tears of anger and disappointment.

Lloyd had a good-natured man's horror of a woman's sobs, and he attempted—I may say he condescended—to explain. 'It's not a caprice, dear, it's a promise,' he said—'an oath.'

'An oath? It's a pretty matter for oaths! and to whom, pray?'

'To Perdita,' said the young man, raising his eyes for an instant, and immediately dropping them.

'Perdita—ah, Perdita!' and Rosalind's tears broke forth. Her bosom heaved with stormy sobs—sobs which were the long-deferred sequel of the violent fit of weeping in which she had indulged herself on the night when she discovered her sister's betrothal. She had hoped, in her better moments, that she had done with her jealousy;

but her temper, on that occasion, had taken an ineffaceable hold. 'And pray, what right had Perdita to dispose of my future?' she cried. 'What right had she to bind you to meanness and cruelty? Ah, I occupy a dignified place, and I make a very fine figure! I am welcome to what Perdita has left! And what has she left? I never knew till now how little! Nothing, nothing, nothing.'

This was a very poor logic, but it was very good as a 'scene'. Lloyd put his arm round his wife's waist and tried to kiss her, but she shook him off with magnificent scorn. Poor fellow! he had coveted a 'devilish fine woman', and he had got one. Her scorn was intolerable. He walked away with his ears tingling—irresolute, distracted. Before him was his secretary, and in it the sacred key which with his own hand he had turned in the triple lock. He marched up and opened it, and took the key from a secret drawer, wrapped in a little packet which he had sealed with his own honest bit of glazonry. *Je garde,* said the motto—'I keep.' But he was ashamed to put it back. He flung it upon the table beside his wife.

'Put it back!' she cried. 'I want it not. I hate it!'

'I wash my hands of it,' cried her husband. 'God forgive me!'

Mrs Lloyd gave an indignant shrug of her shoulders, and swept out of the room, while the young man retreated by another door. Ten minutes later Mrs Lloyd returned, and found the room occupied by her little step-daughter and the nursery-maid. The key was not on the table. She glanced at the child. Her little niece was perched on a chair, with the packet in her hands. She had broken the seal with her own small fingers. Mrs Lloyd hastily took possession of the key.

At the habitual supper-hour Arthur Lloyd came back from his counting-room. It was the month of June, and supper was served by daylight. The meal was placed on the table, but Mrs Lloyd failed to make her appearance. The servant whom his master sent to call her came back with the assurance that her room was empty, and that the women informed him that she had not been seen since dinner. They had, in truth, observed her to have been in tears, and, supposing her to be shut up in her chamber, had not disturbed her. Her husband called her name in various parts of the house, but without response. At last it occurred to him that he might find her by taking the way to the attic. The thought gave him a strange feeling of discomfort, and he bade his servants remain behind, wishing no witness in his quest. He reached the foot of the staircase leading to the

topmost flat, and stood with his hands on the banisters, pronouncing his wife's name. His voice trembled. He called again louder and more firmly. The only sound which disturbed the absolute silence was a faint echo of his own tones, repeating his question under the great eaves. He nevertheless felt irresistibly moved to ascend the staircase. It opened upon a wide hall, lined with wooden closets, and terminating in a window which looked westward, and admitted the last rays of the sun. Before the window stood the great chest. Before the chest, on her knees, the young man saw with amazement and horror the figure of his wife. In an instant he crossed the interval between them, bereft of utterance. The lid of the chest stood open, exposing, amid their perfumed napkins, its treasure of stuffs and jewels. Rosalind had fallen backward from a kneeling posture, with one hand supporting her on the floor and the other pressed to her heart. On her limbs was the stiffness of death, and on her face, in the fading light of the sun, the terror of something more than death. Her lips were parted in entreaty, in dismay, in agony; and on her blanched brow and cheeks there glowed the marks of ten hideous wounds from two vengeful ghostly hands.

GENERAL COMMENTARY

RAYMOND THORBERG (ESSAY DATE SUMMER 1967)

SOURCE: Thorberg, Raymond. "Terror Made Relevant: James's Ghost Stories." *Dalhousie Review* 47, no. 2 (summer 1967): 185-91.

In the following essay, Thorberg considers James's approach to writing ghost stories as an aesthetic, artistic experiment.

Henry James experimented with what he called the "ghost-story", though with the apology of quotation marks, early in his career; and then after a hiatus of a decade and a half returned to active contribution to the genre through the 1890s and into the new century. This later phase or period divides also, with a number of stories of lesser merit like those of his earlier career dating from 1891-92 and followed now by a briefer pause; then **"The Altar of the Dead"** in 1895 initiated a list which includes besides itself such accomplishments as *The Turn of the Screw,* **"The Beast in the Jungle"**, and **"The Jolly Corner"**.

In what may seem coincidence, the first half of the decade of the 1890s marks James's all-out effort to conquer the theatre, ending with the *Guy*

Domville disaster of 1895. But the lessons learned from the conditions of dramatic presentation stayed with him to show their influence in his fiction, in the emphasis on scene and also in the control of viewpoint and degree of awareness in his characters. In the early **"The Art of Fiction"**, the concept of point of view as chiefly a means of selection and interpretation of the material of one's experience is considerably transcended, along with the relatively facile separation between subject and technique assumed in that essay. Of course, had it not been for his conservative views in regard to all kinds of art except his own, James might have seen that what he was doing had its parallel in painting from the Impressionists onward. But he was required to pay part of the price of his individual genius by the necessity of discovering many things very largely by himself, so that the habit sometimes persisted without the need. There might also be noted the increasing isolation that he felt from the rejection of his work by the general public, the loss of his sister and old friends, the awareness of aging; and the nature of the concern itself in the kind of ghost stories that interested him now, with their emphasis upon obsessions and upon internal rather than external terrors.

The ghost story as a type lends itself especially to exercises in the metering of comprehension, in the adjustment of shutters to let in exactly the desired amount of light. The genuine ghost must be made believably existent, yet not so familiar that he becomes accepted as simply part of the scheme of things. The terror that takes place in the mind must be treated in such fashion that it seems not wholly enclosed within this precinct and therefore the concern merely of abnormal psychology, but capable of objectifying itself, actually doing so under the force of the reader's apprehension. Given the predilection that always remained with him, it is hardly to be accounted for by mere chance that James's most significant period in the writing of ghost stories should have coincided with the great advance in his development of the dramatic method as applied to fiction. More clearly now, he saw the possibilities of the mind as a principal source of terror. The suggestion had of course always been present in an incident in the family history, the "vastation" experienced by his father when James was still a child. Also available in "Father's ideas" was the notion of selfhood, with its imputation of guilt deriving from the individual's separation and isolation. Reading of Hawthorne provided additional source and support for this—but in fact

James could hardly have escaped it, growing up as he did in the intellectual and moral climate of an America of Calvinist background and contemporary commitment to the democratic ideal.

With some qualification to permit inclusion of *The Turn of the Screw,* James's greatest ghost stories are those concerned with the isolating effects of obsession. James fully exploits the relation between guilt and terror to achieve the greater terror of the depths of the consciousness—a terror greater than any deriving from the offered external example, the specifically cited act. His attitude toward obsession is the opposite of that of Emerson, who with inadequate sanction from any realistic standpoint still approved of it as the guide for one's life. James, as has frequently been pointed out, takes his place on the side of those writers of darker vision who could create an Ethan Brand or an Ahab.

The Turn of the Screw is something of a special case among these stories, its terror meaningful in a different way, except in so far as all terror breaks through our defences to give insight into our nakedest selves. **"The Altar of the Dead"** shares with **"The Beast in the Jungle"** and **"The Jolly Corner"** in having a central character under the control of an intense obsession. It is a powerful story. No one at all susceptible to James can deny the force of the brooding image of George Stransom at his altar. Yet a limitation exists because of the nature of his concerns, with the dead and with a perverse revenge; intermingled with the incense from the candles is the atmosphere of morbidity. By contrast the concerns of John Marcher and Spencer Brydon seem our own, however magnified in these stories by obsession. **"The Beast in the Jungle"** and **"The Jolly Corner,"** among the ghost stories, perhaps reach us most nearly in the way the great novels do.

It is John Marcher's lot to be possessed by an idea of selfhood too strong to serve beneficially as it otherwise might. The experience which seems available to him seems also inadequate, and he will not settle for less, in his evaluation of his worth, than he deserves. He is an idealist, living for and in service to an abstract ideal of himself, his life, and his fate. The terms in which the ideal might be achieved are expressed no further, until the end of the story, than in the metaphor of the title. The lack of a definition eliminates any relatively easy solution, comparable, say, to that achieved in the assimilation of the culture of Europe by the American protagonists of the international stories. The result is the refusal by Marcher to settle for, in his estimate, a half-loaf;

Ingrid Bergman and Heyward Morse in the 1959 television production of *The Turn of the Screw.*

and not until too late does he realize that the specific instance of May Bartram's love has proved his estimate wrong, and that he has been wondrous only to himself. The development is that of the initiation into knowledge without the undergoing of experience; Marcher comes at last to a full knowledge of life without having in this sense lived it. It is an instance of consciousness grasping, not experience—because this has been excluded by his obsession—but only the void. The effect is to increase and sharpen but never to satisfy that consciousness.

The story presents, of course, one of the most notable examples in fiction of the missed life. The external fact is simply that Marcher failed to marry the woman who was in love with him. Quite frequently this is treated both in actual life and in fiction as nothing more than comic. In other respects, Marcher seems in possession of all those perquisites which make for the comfortable existence. Numerous characters out of Zola, or Dickens, would of a certainty regard him with envy. Therefore it is not what happens, or does not happen, to him which is the basic concern of the story. The concern is rather Marcher's own turn-

ing away from outward experience and inward toward the mind. The horror which develops for him is self-created. And for the reader it exists in part from being taken along in Marcher's realization, but in another and perhaps greater part in a growing awareness of the capabilities James established for the human consciousness. It is the limitlessness of these capabilities that causes one to shrink back from what he seems about to discover of possibility within himself.

The absence of any concrete specification of what Marcher feels is to happen to him is necessary and appropriate; it does not owe to the Jamesian reluctance, irritating at times, as in the question of the object manufactured at Woollett, Massachusetts; nor does it owe to the intentional obscuring of what could be visible and concrete and clear, if artistic purpose allowed, as the evil in **The Turn of the Screw.** In "**The Beast in the Jungle**" the reader is not under the urge to try to see a little more specifically than the author permits—the non-specification exists for itself, is in no sense merely a concealment. The concreteness of the image evoked by the title of course arouses fear by itself; but also, by deriving from the area of the actively and physically violent, it emphasizes further the quality of the undefinable that awaits Marcher, to increase the effect of terror.

In "The Jolly Corner" the house is for Spencer Brydon the symbol of his consciousness; the action in the house is an adumbration of his explorations during a third of a century into that consciousness. Here James, like Hawthorne in "Young Goodman Brown", externalizes, establishes in concrete form the product of the mind's workings, and consequently a tight relationship between the two. In *The American Henry James* (New Brunswick, N. J., 1957), Quentin Anderson makes the point that it is a mistake to read the story as being about a man "who discovers what he *would have been*. What Spencer Brydon discovers is what he *has been*" (pp. 177-8). For the horror must remain superficial if "The Jolly Corner" is read as presenting alternate lives, one that Brydon did live and another that he did not. Thus the life that he did not live should become now merely an object of Brydon's curiosity, to be satisfied by the co-operation of the apparitional world, as in *Macbeth,* which is willing to answer questions put to it if the proper formulae are employed, as Brydon might be credited with having done by his psychological preparations and physical probing of the house. Such inadequate reading of the story takes no account of the intensity of Brydon's consciousness, of his great hunger for experience. This force proves that the life he actually lived in the external sense, in Europe, which for another person might have been sufficient, was not sufficient—the consequence being that he had engaged himself through all his years there in the construction of another life, in the mind, in the subconscious mind if you will. The Spencer Brydon of this existence is as real, indeed more real—for the reason that it is his inner and profounder self—than the one of his visible external career.

The autobiographical relevance of the story has frequently been noted; the point might be emphasized that "The Jolly Corner" owes to James's return to America in 1904-05 chiefly as the prepared and waiting fire owes to the match. It is testimony to the importance that James placed upon the life contained within the consciousness, especially in his later years, and which he manifests in so many ways in his writing. Specifically one might note the choice of themes and subjects, the movement towards the language of concepts rather than of images except in the creation of figures, and perhaps most important the greatly increased use of dramatization of point of view as a basic means of fictional development. Brydon discovers in the apparition in the house what can be called his "other" self only by reason of James's choice of point of view from which to tell the story. In a way the formula of presentation is the reverse of that of "The Beast in the Jungle", while Marcher and Brydon are alike in that each is obsessively aware of his life as a sort of double existence, with the external and visible being by such virtue by no means the more real.

One of the notable qualities of James is that, especially considering the age and society in which he lived and the kinds of periodicals in which so much of his work appeared, he is so seldom softheaded or sentimental or even to the slightest degree merciful. Unlike Emerson, he matches the possibilities open to man in his inner life by an insistence upon a responsibility, so to speak, with teeth in it. Man is free to choose his experience—James sees to it that economic and other similar conditions do not impair this freedom—but all experience is hazardous, and the encounter with evil is always possible, even probable. James is virtually as rigid on this as the most legalistic seventeenth-century New England Calvinist. Yet he offers an alternative which can lead to salvation—in of course a secularized version—while by no whit mitigating the encounter. His "American" heroes and heroines are made possible to be what they are by their right choice of alternatives, by their immersing themselves to the fullest in the kind of experience which James, with his values set upon culture, tradition, social relationships on a high level of sophistication, saw as best, as most completely identifying and expressing the human. Isabel Archer is at the head of a distinguished roster. James, to repeat, is seldom merciful—yet to these, in a sense, he is. He permits them the acceptance of their fates, in various kinds of renunciation, bringing a measure of peace. To the incomprehension of Henrietta Stackpole and Caspar Goodwood, Isabel goes back to Gilbert Osmond; Newman burns the letter; Milly Theale in all good intent and forgiveness provides the means for Merton Densher and Kate Croy to have their future. That her act destroys the possibility is the irony of their lives, not of hers. Implicit is a final achieved immunity as a consequence of having undergone all, given the terms of the story, that could have happened to them.

The basic circumstance is otherwise with the obsessed protagonists of the ghost stories. While a Christopher Newman may stand in a position of openness to the hazards of life, the obsessed protagonist of one of James's ghost stories presents the extreme among his characters whose reaction to life is to redefine it in their own terms. Illustration may again be drawn from American characters in his fiction in general—those Americans whose smallness of soul manifests itself in ways owing to the American experience rather than to that of Europe. In James's terminology they are "Unitarian"; or they are representative of the "New England conscience". In an early sense of the word, revived in our own time with chief credit due perhaps to John Crowe Ransom, they are "puritans", simplifying experience into preconceived, inadequate abstractions. They are invulnerable to life, having developed a hardened outer shell which saves them from knowing what is going on outside in any detail, remaining satisfied rather in their assurance that it is very probably immoral. Like them the obsessed figures of the ghost stories have set their lives in terms of abstraction and simplification; but unlike them they possess the greatest possible capacity for moral consciousness, for awareness of the opportunities and significance of the human situation.

Thus James achieves the paradox of capacity for experience being negated by the specific means—the obsession itself—by which the obsessed protagonist seeks to live a fuller, more significant life than he might otherwise. The obsessions are themselves powerful, and in further contrast to the abstractions of the New England conscience, active. The direction that they lead, however, is inward, with greater penetration into and control of the consciousness as the distractions of noise and light from the outer world lose their relevance to the life that the obsessed protagonist is creating for himself. Yet it is not simply that nothing happens to these figures, even John Marcher; rather, what happens is the action of the mind turning inward upon itself. To describe the product of this, one might perhaps use the term anti-experience, as the physicists are beginning to speak more confidently of something they call anti-matter. But if it is escape from experience, at least from external experience, it is by no means escape without penalty. For one thing, the intensity of the protagonist's awareness develops inevitably its dark and perverse aspects; and in several instances James corroborates Hawthorne's belief that this can lead to the guilt involved in the violation by one person of the life of another. Chiefly, however, there is the guilt deriving from the knowledge that one has failed in the responsibility toward his own life, such

responsibility being a secularized version of man's duty, and met in the Jamesian system of values by the full acceptance of experience and complete immersion in it. The strength of the feeling of guilt is in measure to the capacity for consciousness—thus it is no accident that James's most powerfully obsessed characters are also those most capable of the fullness of experience which their obsessions have deprived them of. If evil is linked with experience, equally guilt is linked with and measured by knowledge. Somehow Marcher's flinging himself in agony on May Bartram's grave at the end of **"The Beast in the Jungle"** is closer to us than the acceptant renunciations of Newman and Isabel Archer and Milly Theale; to us, in our time, as we reject the tragic solution no less than the sentimental, it strikes closer to the actualities of the human condition. For us the ultimate terror is that which is based on some distortion of the human, of which the sense of guilt is the indicator and proof. The terror invoked in these stories of James is, more truly than in Poe's, the terror not so much of the world of external circumstance as of that consciousness which may be called the soul.

TITLE COMMENTARY

"The Jolly Corner"

PAMELA JACOBS SHELDEN (ESSAY DATE SPRING 1974)

SOURCE: Shelden, Pamela Jacobs. "Jamesian Gothicism: The Haunted Castle of the Mind." *Studies in the Literary Imagination* 7, no. 1 (spring 1974): 121-34.

In the following essay, Shelden considers James's use of Gothic conventions, centering on his use of the doppelgänger, *or double, and other Gothic devices in "The Jolly Corner."*

I

Many critics consider [Charles] Brockden Brown, [Edgar Allan] Poe, and [Nathaniel] Hawthorne the American heirs of the Gothic tradition in literature, born when Horace Walpole published *The Castle of Otranto* in 1764. Few, however, treat the supernatural tales of Henry James within this context. Typical Gothic conventions such as haunted castles, flickering candles, time-yellowed manuscripts, and dimly-lighted midnight scenes may, at first, appear rather remote from James's world where the drama of consciousness, the internal rather than the external condition, is the central concern. Indeed, William James, after reading Henry's first ghostly tale, **"The Romance of Certain Old Clothes"** (1868), in the *Atlantic Monthly,* wired his brother that the tale was different in "tone" from Henry's earlier efforts. According to William, the story, written "with the mind unbent and careless," was "trifling," especially for an author of Henry's ability.[1] This criticism notwithstanding, James continued to work in the genre through the nineties and into the new century.

Like his novels, the supernatural tales divide conveniently, if somewhat artificially, into three groups: the early, rather contrived, tales of the sixties and seventies; the middle group, including *The Turn of the Screw* (1898); and the late ones, when James adds to the surprising number and quality of his accomplishments such tales as **"The Beast in the Jungle"** (1903) and **"The Jolly Corner"** (1908).[2] In general, the richness of the individual tales keeps pace with James's development in the novel form. In the early **"The Romance of Certain Old Clothes"** (1868), for example, a dead woman's strangling hands reach beyond the grave to resolve a jealous rivalry with her sister. As James continues to explore the possibilities of the terror tale, however, he places the emphasis upon the life contained within the consciousness, as opposed to the external circumstance. Although the narrator of **"The Ghostly Rental"** (1876) is not well integrated into the story (one thinks, by comparison, of the narrator of **"The Friends of the Friends"** or *The Turn of the Screw*), it is superior to **"The Romance of Certain Old Clothes"** in its use of the point of view of a person who comes to appreciate the "vivid meaning" of a house that is "spiritually blighted" (p. 108). However, in James's late supernatural tales, especially, the mind is seen as the principal source of terror. In **"The Beast in the Jungle"** and **"The Jolly Corner,"** the horror is self-created as Marcher and Brydon become conscious of the dreadful potential within themselves.

Of interest, also, are the Gothic echoes heard in several of James's non-ghostly novels.[3] In **"The Friends of the Friends"** (1896), a supernatural tale in which James makes use of the Gothic manuscript convention, a device which he later turns to advantage in *The Turn of the Screw* (1898), a deluded, jealous narrator charges that her fiancé has fallen in love with the memory of her dead friend and, indeed, that he is having an affair with her ghost. In *The Wings of the Dove* (1902), a similar charge reverberates with rich

potential since it carries profound moral implications in the novel. In speaking to Merton Densher, who is haunted by Milly Theale's presence, Kate Croy accuses her lover of wanting no other love than Milly's memory (XX, 405). Eventually, Densher's consciousness of Milly's goodness and own duplicity drives him to repudiate his relationship with Kate.

Another example of the non-ghostly novel that makes use of Gothic conventions is *The*

Portrait of a Lady (1881). Like Mrs. Radcliffe's beautiful heroine in *The Mysteries of Udolpho*, the lovely, innocent Isabel Archer finds herself in the midst of intrigue and deceit as she struggles to assess the meaning of her experiences. In James's novel, moreover, houses figure importantly. One recalls Gardencourt, the manor house which is haunted by a ghost that Isabel will see only after she has had "some miserable knowledge" (III, 64). The English dwelling, with its open, expansive gardens may be contrasted with the Palazzo Roccanera, the elaborate, convoluted home of the evil Gilbert Osmond—this ominous structure, with its weird eye-like windows, the emblem of Osmond's terribly narrow consciousness, "the mansion of his own habitation" (II, 194). Later in the novel, Pansy Osmond, a passive victim of her father's machinations, is committed to a Catholic convent, a confinement not unlike Claire de Cintre's imprisonment in a Carmelite nunnery in *The American* (1877). The point, of course, is that James places his heroines in conventional Gothic settings—the secluded palace and the cloistered monastery—as he portrays innocents who are menaced by psychological, spiritual, and moral evils.

Early in his career, indeed, James had demonstrated an attraction to the house metaphor, the American counterpart of the medieval castle, perhaps the Gothicist's most promising and important symbol.[4] In the supernatural tale "**The Ghostly Rental**" (1876), for example, the house is a "container" of the life within, a tangible symbol of the intangible psychological and spiritual evil that a father and daughter inflict on one another. Later, James's interest in the metaphor is reflected in such works as *The Other House* (1896), *The Spoils of Poynton* (1897), *The Turn of the Screw* (1898), and the unfinished *The Sense of the Past* (1907). In *Within the Rim and Other Essays, 1914-15,* in fact, when James describes his outburst of activity in World War I and his aspirations for the future, he pictures himself in terms of the Gothic castle with its ascending turrets. "I found myself," James writes, "before long building on additions and upper stories, throwing out extensions and protrusions, indulging even, all recklessly, in gables and pinnacles and battlements."[5]

II

That James should have been attracted to an exploration of the supernatural experience in his fiction comes as no surprise when one remembers that his family history is a veritable storehouse of such adventures. Although James never personally experienced a supernatural visitation, Henry Sr., his father, and William, his brother, offer accounts of such encounters.[6] Conversely, while Alice, Henry's sister, never underwent a "vastation" like her father, she suffered a nervous breakdown between 1867 and 1868, a period when she was plagued by horrifying fantasies. In her journal accounts of this time, Alice bears a striking resemblance to the Gothic victim who is also in terror of what he can neither understand nor control.[7]

But James himself was conscious of the occult experience. When his mother died, for example, he wrote that "Her death has given me a passionate belief in certain transcendent things. . . . One can hear her voice in . . . [the stillness]."[8] We are further told that James was deeply affected by his brother's promise to make contact with him six months after his death. As the appointed time approached, Henry was driven into a state of acute anxiety.[9] Also relevant is James's account of a nightmare in *A Small Boy and Others* in which James, struggling to defend himself from an invader who menaces him from behind a closed door, finally finds himself alone racing down the Galerie d'Apollon in the Louvre. The situation reverses itself when the haunted becomes the haunter. As James remarks, ". . . I, in my appalled state, was probably still more appalling than the awful agent. . . ."[10]

It is no coincidence then, that in "**The Jolly Corner**," Spencer Brydon is also terrorized by an agent behind a closed door. However, unlike the figure in James's dream-nightmare or Ralph Pendrel in James's sketch of the unfinished novel, *The Sense of the Past*, Brydon is eventually overwhelmed by his pursuer. But "**The Jolly Corner**" offers yet another illustration of James's use of fantasy to express his inner disturbance. In *The American Scene* (1907), when James describes his revisit to the United States after an absence of twenty years, he writes of his distress that his "birthplace"—specifically, Number Two, Washington Place—has vanished.[11] In a sense, the house on the "jolly corner," another birthplace located in New York, functions as the *"commemorative tablet"* whose loss James had lamented in *The American Scene* since for Brydon—an expatriot like James—it serves as an embodiment of the past and a commemorative for the future. In short, the supernatural tale provided a release for James as he eased himself of anxieties, much as terror literature had afforded a similar outlet for the eighteenth-century Gothicist. The dream itself, we are told, is the vehicle by which repressions are liberated. One has only to recall then that, like James's **"The Jolly Corner,"** Walpole's *The Castle of Otranto* and Mary Shelley's *Frankenstein* were "born" following their authors' dream-nightmares. As James indicates in *The Art of the Novel,* "The extraordinary is most extraordinary in that it happens to you and me, and it's of value (of value for others) but so far as visibly brought home to us."[12]

That James found the Gothic tradition a means of quelling personal fears and tensions is further borne out by his activities after the shock of his theatrical venture in 1895. About this period of failure, James remarks, ". . . I have the imagination of disaster—and see life indeed as ferocious and sinister."[13] Not coincidentally, thus, the powerful middle group of supernatural tales—among them, **"The Friends of the Friends"** (1896), *The Turn of the Screw* (1898), and **"The Real Right Thing"** (1899)—appear in the nineties after the failure of *Guy Domville.* In fact, the first entry in James's *Notebooks,* one week after the opening of the play, contains the germ of *The Turn of the Screw.*[14] To this extent, at least, James routs and exorcises his own "ghosts" in his tales of terror.

Indeed, in the last few years, especially, it is generally acknowledged that the ambiguities, the unknowables, and the uncertainties which derive in large measure from man's sense of his incalculable inner world are deeply woven into the Gothic fabric.[15] In James's case, when one adds to the *données* of the familial psychic disturbances, his own personal tensions, his attempts to follow William's work in psychology,[16] and his interest in the Society for Psychical Research,[17] it is not surprising to discover that he employed the Gothic vocabulary to describe the enigmatic self. To further explore James's use of Gothicism, I shall pay special attention to **"The Jolly Corner"** (1908), James's last supernatural tale. In this work, certainly, the central Gothic metaphor—the house on the "jolly corner"—serves as the objective correlative of the psyche, while it also images the internal *Doppelgänger.* As the hero confronts the "other," his mind is seen as haunted by itself—the Gothic devices, in turn, are merely emblematic of his psychological and spiritual condition.

III

"The Jolly Corner" is the story of Spencer Brydon, an expatriate, who at the age of fifty-six returns to New York after an absence of thirty-three years in Europe to explore the "other" he might have become had he remained in America. He arrives ostensibly to supervise his "property":

two houses, one which is being renovated into an apartment-house, and the other, his "birthplace, . . . his house on the jolly corner" (p. 727), which he wishes to preserve in its original form. Alice Staverton, an old-time, ever-faithful friend, who has foregone marriage to await patiently his return, acts as a buffer between the past and the present, neutralizing the complex discomfort of modern life. In fact, since Alice and Brydon supposedly share "communities of knowledge . . . of the other age," they communicate splendidly—or so, at least, the hero trusts (p. 729). By the end of the first section, Alice, who had always wondered how Brydon might have been had he remained in America, tells him that she has seen his alter-ego in a dream "twice over." Although he presses her to know what "the wretch" is like, she will tell him "some other time" (p. 738).

As time passes, the impulse to know the "so differently other person," crystallized by Alice's remark and by Brydon's newly-discovered "capacity" for business and his sense of construction, becomes so much an obsession that he habitually returns late at night to his "birthplace," the "jolly corner" of his youth, to haunt the empty house with flickering candle in hand in search of the other self. He steals through the house "very much as he might have been met by . . . some unexpected occupant, at a turn of one of the dim passages of an empty house" (p. 730). He tells no one, not even Alice, of the expeditions which he pursues with great concentration as the need to confront the "other" intensifies into a "morbid obsession": "He knew what he meant and what he wanted . . . His alter-ego 'walked'" and Brydon is determined to "waylay him and meet him" (p. 741).

Interestingly, this impulse to provoke a confrontation is an extension of the chase motif—the villain's pursuit of the fleeing victim—that figures importantly in Gothic literature. As in the Gothic tale, the chase occurs in the labyrinthine building. In Jame's tale, in fact, the pattern is reinforced by jungle imagery, with the self as hunter and the alter-ego as hunted: Brydon, who had been a big game hunter on the Continent, "roamed, slowly, warily"; he stalked the alter-ego much as he would any "beast of the forest" since the "terms, the comparisons, the very practices of the chase . . . came . . . into play"; Brydon steps "back into shelter or shade" of the recesses of the house, "effacing himself behind a door or in an embrasure, as he had sought of old the vantage of rock and tree"; he holds his breath "living in the joy of the instant, the supreme suspense created by big game alone"; he gains "to an extraordinary degree the power to penetrate the dusk of distances and the darkness of corners," the instinctive response of the tracking man or beast; indeed, he wonders if he would have glared at these moments with "large shining yellow eyes," having now gained the sense of "some monstrous stealthy cat" (pp. 741-42). In brief, although tradition has it that one is usually frightened by apparitions, he had "turned the tables and become himself, in the apparitional world, an incalculable terror" (p. 742).

Quite unexpectedly, however, the situation reverses itself. On the occasion of the last, climactic visit to the house, Brydon feels himself "being definitely followed" (pp. 743-44). In the upper rooms of the house, he senses that the alter-ego has "'turned': that, up there, is what has happened—he's the fanged or the antlered animal brought at last to bay" (p. 744). The "other" who had "been dodging, retreating, hiding" will fight, now that it is "worked up to anger." Upon this discovery, "Brydon . . . tasted probably of a sensation more complex than had ever before found itself consistent with sanity." Like the narrator of **"The Ghostly Rental"** and the figure in James's dream-nightmare, Brydon, in the shadow of the grotesque, oscillates between joy and fear, "so rejoicing that he could . . . actively inspire that fear, and simultaneously quaking for the form in which he might passively know it" (p. 745). Yet, though this is a terrifying moment, Brydon does not confront the shape in evening dress until the end of the second section.

IV

The universal implications of the first experience, as well as the second more horrifying situation, emerge only when the house is seen as an emblem of the victim's interior landscape, the place where Brydon makes his way through the labyrinth, aided only by the flickering street light and the dim light of the candle which heighten the terror. In the semi-darkness—a fitting metaphor for internal confusion—Brydon tracks down, confronts, but fails to comprehend the meaning of the "ghost" which the victim, haunted by self, "scares up." Appropriately, since the house functions as an objective correlative of the psyche, the "presence" haunts the individual rather than the place. That the house is a "container" of life is clear from the first section in which as Mrs. Muldoon, the housekeeper, leads Alice and Brydon on a tour, she precedes "them from room to room . . . pushing back shutters and throwing up sashes—all to show them as she remarked, how

little there was to see." There was little indeed to see in the *"great gaunt shell,"* filled with *"great blank rooms"* (p. 731, my italics). Although Brydon fails to recognize the "other" as an aspect of self (not comprehending, he will indeed see "little"), he confronts and repudiates the alter-ego since, in its grotesque ugliness, it is "little" as opposed to that which is noble or significant.

But as Mrs. Muldoon reminds Alice, "The fact that there was nothing to see didn't militate . . . against what one *might* see" (p. 731). Whereas the good lady refers only to the terror of the supernatural, Brydon will shortly experience the real terror of the psychic adventure. Unlike the housekeeper, however, he finds great personal significance in the house, which is, after all, emblematic of self (one recalls, certainly, that the tale begins with Brydon's egotistical assertion, *"'Every one asks me what I 'think' of everything.'"* (p. 725, my italics): "He spoke of *the value of all he read into it,* into the mere sight of the walls, mere shape of the rooms, mere sound of the floors" (p. 733, my italics). In this fashion, James underscores Brydon's self-centeredness; he is like the "great gaunt shell," filled with "great blank rooms" in which the self is all that matters.

Alice, in fact, likens the empty house to "the death-mask of a handsome face" (p. 734)—her observation, an ironic anticipation of the figure Brydon finally confronts. Significantly, the woman's selflessness may be juxtaposed to the man's selfishness. Alice, who livingly "listened to everything," suppresses her impression, producing "instead a vague platitude": "Well, if it were only furnished and lived in—!" (pp. 733-34). She cherishes the hope that loving care will bring out its finer points, unlike Brydon who feels "it *is* lived in . . . [already] furnished" (p. 734). For Brydon, certainly, the structure houses only the self he might have been.[18] As he tells Alice, "It comes over me that I had then a strange *alter ego* deep down somewhere within me, as the full-blown flower is in the small tight bud." To this, his protective mother-figure responds reassuringly, "I believe in the flower" (p. 736). So much is at least clear: whatever he has been, might have been, is, or will be, Alice Staverton loves and accepts Spencer Brydon under all conditions.

Brydon, intrigued with self, pursues his "morbid obsession" to know himself. Assured of "calm proprietorship," his is an "ample house which he visits from attic to cellar" (pp. 738-39). The "shell" throbs with life; he feels "the pulse of the great vague place" (p. 739)—"vague" perhaps, because there are always unchartable, nebulous regions of the self. Yet, it is just these inner recesses that Brydon wishes to explore: "He preferred the lampless hour and only wished he might have prolonged each day the deep crepuscular spell"; he watches "with his glimmering light: moving slowly, holding it high, playing it far, rejoicing above all . . . in open vistas, reaches of communication between rooms and by passages" (p. 739). The house, in short, an expression of the spiritual and psychic spheres, is more real to Brydon than the physical self: "He projected himself all day, in thought, . . . into the other, the real, the waiting life . . . that . . . began for him, on the jolly corner" (p. 740). Equally significant, since Brydon pursues the self that might have been, he "scares up" images of the past within the house. Thus the house is the "container" of life itself, a womb which holds, since it has yet to give birth to, the "other." Brydon, in fact, likens the place to "some great glass bowl, all precious concave crystal, set delicately humming by the play of a moist finger round its edge. The concave crystal held . . . this mystical other world" (p. 740).

For all this, Brydon preferred "the open shutters. He opened everywhere those Mrs. Muldoon had closed" (p. 742). Similarly, "he liked—. . . above all in the upper rooms!—. . . the hard silver of the autumn stars through the window panes, and scarcely less the glare of the streetlamps below, the white electric lustre. . . . This was human actual social: *this was of the world he had lived in,* and he was *more at his ease* . . . for the countenance, coldly general and impersonal. . . ." (pp. 742-43, my italics). Thus is foreshadowed the fact that when the confrontation occurs, when he is forced to face that which he *is,* Brydon will be unable to bear it. He contents himself with the "white electric lustre," mere superficiality, though it is "coldly general and impersonal," blithely seeking "support . . . mostly in the rooms at the wide front and the prolonged side"—and, certainly, he encounters himself in the outer part of the house—since "it failed him considerably in the central shades and the parts of the back" (p. 743). Because he revels in the "social" Brydon, it is indeed ironic that he is unable to accept or at least to recognize this aspect of the self when the final confrontation occurs.

But the house, of course, is emblematic of the whole convoluted psyche. Its vast reaches are of especial interest, for here lives the alter ego Brydon seeks:

But if he sometimes, on his rounds, was glad of his optical reach, so none the less often the rear of the house affected him as the very jungle of his prey. The place was there more subdivided; a large "extension" in particular, where small rooms for servants had been multiplied, abounded in nooks and corners, in closets and passages, in the ramifications especially of an ample back staircase over which he leaned, many a time, . . . while aware that he might, for a spectator, have figured some solemn simpleton playing at hide-and-seek.

(p. 743)

While playing at hide-and-seek with the "other," the self that he might have been, he is at liberty, as he indicates, to think, feel, and act as he so blissfully and egotistically wills within the walls and frames of his own psyche. Most at home in the front of the house, he is equally proud that he does not retreat from the upper rooms as he moves forward like a medieval knight with sword, his light, in hand (p. 747).

Upstairs, however, in the inner recesses or, in Brydon's words, in "the more intricate upper rooms" (p. 746), the game finally becomes insupportable. Behind the closed door which he had left open lurks the "other": "Ah this time at last they *were,* the two, the opposed projections of him, in presence; and this time, as much as one would, the question of danger loomed" (p. 749). The haunter is now the haunted. In this new role, Brydon approaches the closed door, terrified, knowing that if he should open it, he would confront the "other." At this point, of course, Brydon reaches an impasse, resolving to abandon the chase, now that the seeker has become the sought. "I spare you and I give up," he tells the alter ego. "I retire, I renounce—never on my honour, to try again. So rest for ever—and let *me*!" (p. 750). Having made peace with the past, having concluded that the "closing had practically been for him an act of mercy" (p. 752), he is prepared to "sacrifice" his "property": "They might come in now, the builders, the destroyers—they might come as soon as they would" (p. 753).

But in descending from the upper recesses, "he had the whole house to deal with, this fact was still there" (p. 753). In his flight of terror, "he stole back from where he had checked himself [the closed door]—merely to do so was suddenly like safety—and, making blindly for the greater staircase, left gaping rooms and sounding passages behind." Here, Brydon retreats from the inner recesses of mind, the subconscious, those "sounding passages." Yet, the house, a womb which contains life, holds more than Brydon anticipates:

The house, withal, seemed immense, the scale of space again inordinate; the open rooms to no one of which his eyes deflected, gloomed in their shuttered state like mouths of caverns; only the high skylight that formed the drown of the deep well created for him a medium in which he could advance. . . .

(p. 753)

As the metaphor of the mind, the house is indeed "immense"—the container of many selves, some of which are suppressed consciously and some unconsciously. Nevertheless, for Brydon, the building houses only the potential self of the past.

By now, having descended two flights of stairs, Brydon is in the middle of the third, "with only one more left" (p. 753). Retreating from the subconscious to the external, outer self, he "recognized the influence of the lower windows of half-drawn blinds, of the occasional gleam of street-lamps, of the glazed spaces of the vestibule." Here, too, as he sinks "a long look over the banisters," he sights "the marble squares of his childhood." Those reminders of childhood, "the old black-and-white slabs," are comforting. More soothing still, "the closed door, blessedly remote now, was still closed—and he had only in short to reach that [the door] of the house" (pp. 753-54). At this juncture, however, the greatest shock awaits him. Ironically, the front of the house where he had found the most "support" is the scene of the keenest terror, since the "other" he might have been, the alter ego he had lost at the rear of the fourth floor, is not as terrifying as the self he finally confronts. At the bottom of the lowest staircase, the double doors of the vestibule stand wide open, though he had left these closed. Steeling himself to confront the shadowy figure of the past, the "other" he has been tracking, he sees instead a man dressed in evening clothes, "his planted stillness, his vivid truth, his grizzled bent head and white masking hands, his queer actuality of evening dress, of dangling double eye-glass, of gleaming silk lappet and white linen, of pearl button and gold watchguard and polished shoe" (p. 755). For Brydon, however, the figure represents neither the past he left upstairs nor the present: "A thousand times yes, as it came upon him nearer now—the face was the face of a stranger." In short, he has been "'sold' . . . the waste of his nights had been only grotesque and the success of his adventure an irony" (p. 756).

Although Brydon thinks it an irony that his adventure should end with the confrontation of one who is "evil, odious, blatant," instead of the noble "other" he had envisioned, the irony is compounded since the face, which "was too hideous as his" (admitting this, Brydon still will not concede the identity), is an aspect of the self that "is." So terrifying is this possibility that Bry-

don can deal with it only by losing himself, falling unconscious in an attempt to repudiate it entirely. Alice, who had already seen the apparition twice, saw it in the early dawn at the moment it appeared to Brydon: "*He* didn't come to me," said Brydon, referring to the "other" who might have been. To this, Alice responds knowingly, "'You came to yourself,' she beautifully smiled" (p. 761). Whereas Brydon remains oblivious to her nuances, Alice plays the role of the clever protector, totally aware: "And it was as if, while her face hovered, he might have made out in it . . . some particular meaning blurred by a 'smile'" (p. 760). That Brydon conjures up his vision, since he is haunted by his own mind, is suggested when he compares himself to a Pantaloon, "buffeted and tricked from behind by ubiquitous Harlequin" (p. 744). The Harlequin that eludes him—that remains, in a real sense, beyond his comprehension—is the repugnant self that he cannot acknowledge. Alice, for her part, immersed in Brydon's fantasies and fears, is also haunted, though not terrified, by his vision.

Like Poe's William Wilson, then, Brydon "comes to" himself at the end when he confronts an aspect of the personality that he neither accepts nor recognizes as his own. Although he does not attempt to kill it, nonetheless, he falls unconscious as he tries to lose it. Unlike William Wilson, of course, Brydon's vision is not of the moral self but of the self that is "unknown, inconceivable, awful, disconnected from any possibility." Yet the figure is dressed in evening wear like Brydon who hunts "on tiptoe, the points of his evening-shoes, from room to room" (p. 741). Moreover, the figure appears against the background of the open vestibule doors, the world without the house, since it represents the self that "is," rather than the "other" of the past which Brydon leaves behind in the convoluted upper recesses. Whereas Brydon uses his monocle for charm and sophistication, the figure sports "a great convex pince-nez . . . for his poor ruined sight" (p. 762). However, because we are told that Brydon is that individual who has always been "more at ease . . . for the countenance, coldly general and impersonal," clearly the double eyeglass only further serves to underscore the blindness to the selfish egoism. Conceding that "it had been the theory of many . . . persons . . . that he was wasting [his] life in a surrender to sensations" (p. 741), Brydon is that individual whose "'thought' would still be almost altogether about something that concerns only" himself (p. 725). In fact, the superficial self that he wishes to deny at the end is indicated quite early in the tale: at parties, Brydon "circulated, talked, renewed, loosely and pleasantly, old relations. . . . He was *a dim secondary social success*—and all *with people who had truly not an idea of him.* It was *all mere surface sound*: this murmur of their welcome . . . just as his gestures of response were *extravagant shadows*, emphatic in proportion as they meant little" (pp. 739-40, italics mine).

Blissfully unaware, hence, Brydon visits the house, seeking the unknown self, oblivious to the empty reality of the self that "is." Whereas Brydon speaks of his "selfish frivolous scandalous life" to Alice, her reply means little to him, "You don't care for anything but yourself" (p. 737). In short, Brydon, who seeks to disprove the identity, refuses to acknowledge, before or after his vision, that the repugnant, selfish figure is the self that "is." Instead, "the missing two fingers, which were reduced to stumps as if accidentally shot away," are "proof" that the figure is a "stranger," even though the reader is aware that Brydon had been an adventurer and big-game hunter (p. 756).[19]

So great is Alice's love that she tells Brydon she has come to terms with the ghost, welcoming him because she recognizes him. Appropriately, the womb-like images of the house as a container of life recur in the third section in which Alice, as the all-forgiving, all-accepting mother figure, pillows and cradles Brydon's head in her lap. The return to childhood is further suggested by the fact that Brydon is symbolically reborn as he regains consciousness on the "old black-and-white slabs" of his youth, his thoughts child-like in his desire for protection and security (p. 757). Alice comforts her child-love with the reassurance, "He isn't—no, he isn't—*you!*" (p. 762). Given the fact that Brydon does not understand what has taken place, that Alice's and Brydon's lines of communication rarely converge, the ending is at best ambiguous. Theirs is an ironic exchange. "He [the 'ghost'] has been unhappy; he has been ravaged," she explains. To this, Brydon responds, uncomprehendingly: "And haven't I been unhappy? Am not I—you've only to look at me!—ravaged?" (p. 762). Although Alice justly observes that Brydon had come to himself in the morning hours, Brydon interprets the remark to mean his return to consciousness (p. 761). After declaring her love for Brydon, finally, Alice asks reasonably, "'So why,' she strangely smiled, 'shouldn't I like him?'" Unable to understand his plight, however, this remark only "brought Spencer Brydon to his feet. 'You "like" that horrow—?'" (pp. 761-62). Their conversation is, in effect, typical of the pattern throughout: Brydon's sole concern for self juxta-

posed to Alice's generous offer of love. Unlike John Marcher in "The Beast in the Jungle" who has irrevocably forfeited his opportunity with May Bartram, Brydon is given another chance by Alice, but the reader has no assurance that Brydon will take advantage of her offer.

In James's *A Passionate Pilgrim,* the narrator advises the unhappy Clement Searle, "All that you have told me is but another way of saying that you have lived hitherto in yourself. The tenement's haunted! Live abroad—take an interest."[20] Certainly, Brydon is haunted by himself, his "ghost," a manifestation of the internal, rather than external, situation. The "turn of the screw," the peculiar twist, is that the source of terror lies within: the aspect of a personality so terrifying that Brydon must repudiate it. Granted that the Gothic mode has come a long way from Manfred's chase and pursuit of Isabel in the caves beneath the castle, the basic pattern is identifiable, although James, enjoying the advantage of another era, discovers new images and innuendoes in the Gothic vocabulary: the house as an emblem of the mind haunted by itself; its victim alienated from those around him, a lonely prisoner incapable of understanding or controlling his descent into his private maelstrom of terror; the chase as the self in pursuit of the "other" warring impulse; the victim's terror as a correlative of the mind beset with images and haunted by itself where the ambiguities of existence are preserved by James's dual realization of man's strength and weakness conjoined. "We want it [the supernatural] clear, goodness knows," James had said, "but we also want it thick, and we get the thickness in the human consciousness that entertains and records, that amplifies and interprets it."[21] As a result of his peregrination into self, Brydon discovers a horror which he fails to recognize as in any way related to himself. The apparition is but a projection of Brydon's haunted mind—the situation, an ironic one, since as a wish-fulfillment turned rancid, Brydon "scares up" his own nightmare figure within his own haunted house.

Notes

1. Ralph Barton Perry, *The Thought and Character of William James,* 2 vols. (Boston: Little, Brown, 1935), I, 264.

2. For a collection that gathers the supernatural tales together, see Henry James, *Stories of the Supernatural,* ed. Leon Edel (New York: Taplinger, 1970). All references to the tales are to this collection, with pagination cited parenthetically. References to the novels are from *The Novels and Tales of Henry James,* 26 vols., including 2 posthumous vols. (New York: Scribner's, 1907-17), pagination cited parenthetically.

3. See Martha Banta, "The House of the Seven Ushers and How They Grew: A Look at Jamesian Gothicism," *Yale Review,* 57:1 (1967), 56-65.

4. Relevant is J. M. S. Tompkins's observation that "the basis of *Otranto* is architectural and in this respect is the true starting point of the Gothic." *The Popular Novel in England, 1770-1800* (1932; rpt. Lincoln: Univ. of Nebraska Press, 1961), p. 226. Also see Montague Summers who, in making a similar point, observes that the castle often becomes the actual protagonist in Gothic tales, *The Gothic Quest: A History of the Gothic Novel* (London: The Fortune Press, 1938), pp. 189-91.

5. Henry James, *Within the Rim and Other Essays, 1914-15* (London: W. Collins, [c. 1918]), pp. 19ff.

6. See Henry James, Sr., *The Literary Remains,* ed. with intro. William James (Upper Saddle River, N. J.: Literature House, 1970), pp. 59ff., and William James, *The Varieties of Religious Experience* (New York: Longmans, Green, 1902), pp. 160ff.

7. See Alice James, *Alice James: Her Brothers—Her Journal,* ed. Anna Robeson Burr (1934; rpt. Boston: Milford House, 1972), pp. 181-82. Alice's remarks are filled with the jungle imagery which pervades "The Beast in the Jungle" and "The Jolly Corner."

8. Henry James, *The Notebooks of Henry James,* ed. F. O. Matthiessen and Kenneth B. Murdock (New York: Oxford Univ. Press, 1947), p. 41.

9. Somerset Maugham, ed., "Introduction," *Tellers of Tales; 100 Short Stories from the United States, England, France, Russia and Germany* (New York: Doubleday, 1939), pp. xxxv-xxxvi.

10. Henry James, *A Small Boy and Others* (New York: Scribner's, 1913), p. 348.

11. Henry James, *The American Scene* (Bloomington, Ind.: Indiana Univ. Press, 1968), pp. 88ff.

12. Henry James, *The Art of the Novel: Critical Prefaces,* ed. R. P. Blackmur (New York: Charles Scribner's, 1934), p. 257.

13. E. F. Benson, ed., *Henry James: Letters to A. C. Benson and Auguste Monod* (1930; rpt. New York: Haskell House Publishers, 1969), p. 35.

14. James, *The Notebooks,* p. 178.

15. See, for example, Robert D. Hume, "Gothic Versus Romantic: A Revaluation of the Gothic Novel," *PMLA,* 84 (1969), 282-90; Lowry Nelson, Jr., "Night Thoughts on the Gothic Novel," *Yale Review,* 52 (1962), 236-57; Francis Russell Hart, "The Experience of Character in the English Gothic Novel," *Experience in the Novel,* ed. Roy Harvey Pearce (New York: Columbia Univ. Press, 1968), pp. 83-105.

16. See, for example, *The Letters of Henry James,* ed. Percy Lubbock (London: Macmillan, 1920), I, 180-81; Perry, I, 427-28; James, *The Letters,* II, 83; Alice James, *Her Journal,* p. 112.

17. For more documentation of James's well-known interest in psychical phenomena, see Francis X. Roellinger, Jr., "Psychical Research and 'The Turn of the Screw,'" *AL,* 20 (1949), 401-12.

18. So, too, critics who find in the tale a reverberation of James's personal history suggest that the figure represents the self that might have been. See, for example, Christof Wegelin, *The Image of Europe in Henry James* (Dallas: Southern Methodist Univ. Press, 1958) or Marius Bewley, *The Complex Fate: Hawthorne, Henry James and Some Other American Writers* (London: Chatto and Windus, 1952). A somewhat different reading—which nonetheless also identifies the figure at the end as the self that might have been—is Saul Rosenzweig's well-known psychoanalytic study, "The Ghost of Henry James" in *Art and psychoanalysis,* ed. William Phillips (New York: Criterion Books, 1957), pp. 89-111. For Rosenzweig, the apparition is James's own ". . . ghost which [is] an apotheosis of his unlived life . . . ," p. 109. The specter, thus, is typical of James: "Unlike the ghosts of other writers, the creatures of James's imagination represent not the shadows of lives once lived, but the immortal impulses of the unlived life." p. 104.

19. For further discussion of the figure as an aspect of the Brydon that "is," see Floyd Stovall, "Henry James's 'The Jolly Corner,'" *NCF,* 12 (June 1957), 72-84, a reading which runs counter to many critical readings in which the figure at the end is seen as the Brydon who might have been, had not his absence in Europe saved him from becoming a man of business.

20. Henry James, *A Passionate Pilgrim* (Boston: Houghton Mifflin, 1892), p. 37.

21. Henry James, "Preface to *The Altar of the Dead,"* *The Art of the Novel,* p. 256.

FURTHER READING

Biography

Edel, Leon. *Henry James: A Life.* New York: Harper Collins, 1985, 740 p.

Abridged version of Edel's five volume comprehensive biography of James's life; revised with additional source material.

Criticism

Akiyama, Masayuki. "James and Nanboku: A Comparative Study of Supernatural Stories in the West and East." *Comparative Literature Studies* 22 (1985): 43-52.

Explores parallels between the Kabuki dramas of Nanboku and James's short fiction, especially East and West variations on the "revenge-beyond-the-grave" motif.

Banta, Martha. "The House of Seven Ushers and How They Grew: A Look at Jamesian Gothicism." *Yale Review* 57 (autumn 1967): 56-65.

Highlights James's Gothic consciousness in works such as The Portrait of a Lady *and* The Wings of a Dove.

———. *Henry James and the Occult: The Great Extension.* Bloomington: Indiana University Press, 1972, 273 p.

Investigates James's psychological modification of the Gothic tradition in his tales and novels.

Beidler, Peter. *Ghosts, Demons, and Henry James:* The Turn of the Screw *at the Turn of the Century.* Columbia: University of Missouri Press, 1989, 252 p.

Study of James's novella that includes discussions of James's use of the Gothic tradition and its motifs.

Burleson, Donald. "Identity and Alterity in Henry James' 'The Jolly Corner.'" *Studies in Weird Fiction* 8 (fall 1990): 1-11.

Explores the notions of "self" and "other" in "The Jolly Corner."

Craig, J. A. "James's *The Bostonians*." *Explicator* 49, no. 2 (winter 1991): 100-101.

Note on Gothic elements in James's novel.

Lustig, T. J. *Henry James and the Ghostly*. Cambridge: Cambridge University Press, 1994, 317 p.

Full-length study of the use of occultism and the supernatural in James's fiction, arguing that the ghostly is a far more inclusive rubric in James's work than the reader might expect.

Matheson, Neill. "Talking Horrors: James, Euphemism, and the Specter of Wilde." *American Literature* 71, no. 4 (December 1999): 709-50.

Analyzes the use of Gothic tropes and indirect erotic language in The Turn of the Screw and argues that the novella comments on the homosexual scandal and trial involving Oscar Wilde.

Merivale, Patricia. "The Esthetics of Perversion: Gothic Artifice in Henry James and Witold Gombrowicz." *PMLA: Publications of the Modern Language Association of America* 93, no. 5 (October 1978): 992-1002.

Compares James's The Turn of the Screw and The Sacred Fount to Witold Gombrowicz's "Gothic artist parables," arguing that both are metaphysical detective stories and self-reflexive texts.

Miall, David S. "Designed Horror: James's Vision of Evil in *The Turn of the Screw*." *Nineteenth-Century Fiction* 39, no. 3 (December 1984): 305-27.

Offers a reading of The Turn of the Screw based on Sigmund Freud's essay "The Uncanny."

Nettles, Elsa. "*The Portrait of a Lady* and the Gothic Romance." *South Atlantic Bulletin* 39, no. 4 (1974): 73-82.

Analyzes James's appropriation and transformation of stock Gothic types and tropes, including the heroine in distress, the villain-hero, and the imprisoning castle.

Punter, David. "The Ambivalence of Memory: Henry James and Walter de la Mare." In *The Literature of Terror: A History of Gothic Fictions from 1765 to the Present Day*. Vol. 2., pp. 47-66. Essex, England: Longman, 1996.

Compares The Turn of the Screw to Walter de la Mare's short stories, emphasizing the psychological sophistication, use of the unconscious, and the concern with the past in the works of both writers.

Rozenzweig, Saul. "The Ghosts of Henry James." *Partisan Review* 11, no. 4 (fall 1944): 436-55.

Psychological analysis of James's ghosts that maintains that the ghosts point to the irrepressible unlived life.

Salzberg, Joel. "The Gothic Hero in Transcendental Quest: Poe's 'Ligea' and James' 'The Beast in the Jungle.'" *ESQ: A Journal of the American Renaissance* 67 (1972): 108-14.

Compares the heroes in ghostly tales by James and Edgar Allan Poe.

Savoy, Eric. "Spectres of Abjection: The Queer Subject of James's 'The Jolly Corner.'" In *Spectral Readings: Towards a Gothic Geography*, edited by Glennis Byron and David Punter, pp. 161-74. New York: St. Martin's Press, 1999.

Evaluates James's treatment of repressed identity—in terms of sexual orientation and homosexual desire—as a "ghostly double" in "The Jolly Corner."

Schleifer, Ronald. "The Trap of the Imagination: The Gothic Tradition, Fiction and *The Turn of the Screw*." *Criticism* 22, no. 4 (fall 1980): 297-319.

Points out James's debt in The Turn of the Screw to Bram Stoker's Dracula and asserts that the novella anticipates the irony, laughter, and self-consciousness of the twentieth-century Gothic writings of Jorge Luis Borges, Franz Kafka, Isak Dinesen, and Thomas Mann.

Sklepowich, E. A. "Gossip and Gothicism in *The Sacred Fount*." *Henry James Review* 2 (1981): 112-15.

Shows how expertly James used Gothic properties and places in the urbane Gothicism of the novel and its dynamics of social stigmatization.

Sweeney, Gerard M. "Henry James's 'De Grey': The Gothic as Camouflage of the Medical." *Modern Language Studies* 21, no. 2 (1991): 36-44.

Offers a medical explanation for James's supernatural in "De Grey: A Romance," maintaining that the male line of the De Greys is infected with syphilis.

Thorberg, Raymond. "Terror Made Relevant: James's Ghost Stories." *Dalhousie Review* 47 (1967): 185-91.

Psychological reading of James's ghost stories.

Veeder, William. "The Nurturance of the Gothic: *The Turn of the Screw*." *Gothic Studies* 1 (1999): 47-85.

Asserts that the Gothic is a mechanism that was developed for society to heal their self-afflicted wounds.

Wiesenfarth, Joseph. "The Portrait of a Lady: Gothic Manners in Europe." In *Reading and Writing Women's Lives: A Study of the Novel of Manners*, edited by Bege K. Bowers and Barbara Brothers, pp. 119-40. Ann Arbor, Mich.: University Microfilms International Research Press, 1990.

Discusses James's debt to George Eliot and his use of Gothic manners and the horror of respectability in The Portrait of a Lady.

Willen, Gerald, ed. *A Casebook on Henry James's The Turn of the Screw*. New York: Crowell, 1969, 325 p.

Notes and critical essays on James's most popular ghostly tale.

Zablotny, Elaine. "Henry James and the Demonic Vampire and Madonna." *Psychocultural Review* 3 (1979): 203-24.

Focuses on James's exploration of psychic vampirism in several of his ghost stories.

OTHER SOURCES FROM GALE:

Additional coverage of James's life and career is contained in the following sources published by Thomson Gale: *American Writers; American Writers: The Classics*, Vol. 1; *American Writers Retrospective Supplement*, Vol. 1; *Beacham's Encyclopedia of Popular Fiction: Biography and Resources*, Vol. 2; *British Writers*, Vol. 6; *Concise Dictionary of American Literary Biography, 1865-1917; Contemporary Authors*, Vols. 104, 132; *Dictionary of Literary Biography*, Vols. 12, 71, 74, 189; *Dictionary of Literary Biography Documentary Series*, Vol. 13; *DIS-*

Covering Authors; *DISCovering Authors: British; DISCovering Authors: Canadian; DISCovering Authors Modules: Most-studied Authors* and *Novelists; DISCovering Authors 3.0; Encyclopedia of World Literature in the 20th Century,* Ed. 3; *Exploring Short Stories; Literature and Its Times,* Vol. 2; *Literature Resource Center; Major 20th-Century Writers,* Eds. 1, 2; *Major 21st-Century Writers; Novels for Students,* Vols. 12, 16, 19; *Reference Guide to American Literature,* Ed. 4; *Reference Guide to English Literature,* Ed. 2; *Reference Guide to Short Fiction,* Ed. 2; *St. James Guide to Horror, Ghost & Gothic Writers; Short Stories for Students,* Vol. 9; *Short Story Criticism,* Vols. 8, 32, 47; *Supernatural Fiction Writers,* Vol. 1; *Twayne's United States Authors; Twentieth-Century Literary Criticism,* Vols. 2, 11, 24, 40, 47, 64; and *World Literature Criticism.*

STEPHEN KING

(1947 -)

(Full name Stephen Edwin King; has written as Steve King, and under pseudonyms Richard Bachman, John Swithen, and Eleanor Druse) American novelist, short story writer, novella writer, scriptwriter, nonfiction writer, autobiographer, and author of children's books.

Stephen King is a prolific and immensely popular author of horror fiction. In his works, King blends elements of the traditional Gothic tale with those of the modern psychological thriller, detective, and science fiction genres. His fiction features colloquial language, clinical attention to physical detail and emotional states, realistic settings, and an emphasis on contemporary problems. His exploration of such issues as marital infidelity and peer group acceptance lend credibility to the supernatural elements in his fiction. King's wide popularity attests to his ability to tap into his reader's fear of and inability to come to terms with evil confronted in the everyday world.

BIOGRAPHICAL INFORMATION

King was born in Portland, Maine, on September 21, 1947, to Donald Edwin King, a U.S. merchant marine, and Nellie Ruth Pillsbury King. His father abandoned the family when King was two years old. King, his brother, and his mother went to live with relatives in Durham, Maine, and then to various other cities. They returned to Durham to stay in 1958. King was very close to his mother, who supported the family with a series of low-paying jobs and read to him often as a child. She later encouraged King to send his work to publishers. She died of cancer in 1973 without seeing the enormous success her son achieved as a writer. King published his first short story, "I Was a Teenage Grave Robber," in *Comics Review*, in 1965. He also wrote his first full-length manuscript while still in high school. King received a scholarship to the University of Maine at Orono, where he majored in English and minored in speech. King has a deep political awareness, and was active in student politics and the anti-war movement; with the exception of his short story "The Children of the Corn," he has avoided setting his stories in the 1960s and 1970s because of the painful and difficult issues associated with the time period. After his graduation in 1970, King was unable to secure a teaching position, and worked as a gas station attendant and in a laundry. On January 2, 1971, King married novelist Tabitha Jane Spruce; the couple has three children. King spent a short time teaching at the Hampden Academy in Hampden, Maine, until the success of his first novel *Carrie* (1974) enabled him to focus on writing full time. In 1978 he was writer in residence and instructor at the University of Maine at Orono; this experience informed his *Danse Macabre* (1981), a series of essays about the horror genre. King suffered a serious health challenge on June 19, 1999, when he was struck by a van while walking alongside a road near his home. He sustained injuries to his spine, hip, ribs, and right leg. One of his broken ribs punctured a lung, and he nearly died. He began a slow progress towards recovery, cheered by countless cards and letters from his fans. King had also begun work on a writer's manual before his accident, and the result, *On Writing: A Memoir of the Craft* (2000), sold more copies in its first printing than any previous book about writing. In addition to King's advice on crafting fiction, however, the book includes a great deal of autobiographical material. The author chronicles his childhood, his rise to fame, his struggles with addiction, and the 1999 accident that almost ended his life. While King has played with the idea of giving up publishing his writings, his legion of fans continues to be delighted that the idea has not yet become a reality. In 2004, under the pseudonym of Eleanor Druse, King published *The Journals of Eleanor Druse: My Investigation of the Kingdom Hospital Incident*. He has also continued with his "Dark Tower" series with the publication of *The Dark Tower V: Wolves of the Calla* in 2003. King completed the final two installments of the series—*The Dark Tower VI: The Songs of Susannah* and *The Dark Tower VII: The Dark Tower*—in 2004.

MAJOR WORKS

King's fiction has extended into a variety of categories within the horror genre, including vampire and zombie stories, tales of possession, and incidents involving a character's discovery of supernatural powers. He has also successfully branched out into science fiction, fantasy, and westerns. Most of his adult protagonists are ordinary, middle-class people who find themselves involved in some otherworldly nightmare from which they cannot escape. Many of his stories have elements of Gothic fiction. Most notable among these are *'Salem's Lot* (1975), *The Shining* (1977) and *Pet Sematary* (1983). *'Salem's Lot* centers on a series of mysterious deaths in a once-idyllic New England village. *The Shining* tells the tale of Jack Torrance, an alcoholic writer who brings his family to live in an empty mountain hotel for the winter. Demonized by the spirits that haunt the hotel, he tries to kill his wife and child but ultimately kills himself instead. In *Pet Sematary*, a college professor resurrects his young son, who is killed when he ventures onto a nearby highway, by burying him in his neighbor's pet cemetery.

The child, like the family's cat before him, returns, but with sinister results. Other King novels cited for containing elements of the Gothic include *The Dead Zone* (1979), *Christine* (1983), *Cycle of the Werewolf* (1983), *The Talisman* (1984), *Bag of Bones* (1997), and *Black House* (2001).

CRITICAL RECEPTION

Reviewers who have analyzed King's novels often praise the rhythm and pacing of his narratives. Others praise the author for his ability to make the unreal seem entirely plausible. Critics who dismiss King's work usually accuse him of being a formula writer, but his supporters assert that this is part of King's talent, and praise his ability to adapt the Gothic and melodrama in popular literature for contemporary audiences. Heidi Strengell recounts King's repeated use of the Gothic double in his oeuvre, and highlights the numerous forms that double assumes. Critics have also pointed to the influence of literary classics, especially Mary Shelley's *Frankenstein*, Bram Stoker's *Dracula*, and Herman Melville's *Moby Dick* on King's use of the Gothic. Jesse W. Nash, on the other hand, argues that King's Gothic is particularly rooted in popular culture and his own life experiences and therefore represents a singular, postmodern interpretation of the genre.

PRINCIPAL WORKS

Carrie: A Novel of a Girl with a Frightening Power (novel) 1974

'Salem's Lot (novel) 1975

The Dark Tower: The Gunslinger (novel) 1976

Rage [as Richard Bachman] (novel) 1977

The Shining (novel) 1977

Night Shift (short stories) 1978; also published as *Night Shift: Excursions into Horror*, 1979

The Stand (novel) 1978; revised edition, 1990

Another Quarter Mile: Poetry (poetry) 1979

The Dead Zone (novel) 1979

The Long Walk [as Richard Bachman] (novel) 1979

Firestarter (novel) 1980

Cujo (novel) 1981

Roadwork: A Novel of the First Energy Crisis [as Richard Bachman] (novel) 1981

Stephen King's Danse Macabre (nonfiction) 1981

Creepshow (short stories) 1982

The Dark Tower: The Gunslinger (novel) 1982

Different Seasons (short stories and novellas) 1982

The Running Man [as Richard Bachman] (novel) 1982

Stephen King's Creepshow: A George A. Romero Film [adapted from the stories in King's collection] (screenplay) 1982

Christine (novel) 1983

Cycle of the Werewolf (short stories) 1983; also published as *The Silver Bullet*, 1985

Pet Sematary (novel) 1983

Cat's Eye (screenplay) 1984

The Eyes of the Dragon (juvenile novel) 1984

The Talisman [with Peter Straub] (novel) 1984

Thinner [as Richard Bachman] (novel) 1984

Silver Bullet (screenplay) 1985

Stephen King's Skeleton Crew (short stories) 1985

It (novel) 1986; first published in limited edition in Germany as *Es*, 1986

Maximum Overdrive [writer and director] (screenplay) 1986

Misery (novel) 1987

The Tommyknockers (novel) 1987

The Dark Half (novel) 1989

The Dark Tower II: The Drawing of Three (novel) 1989

My Pretty Pony (children's novel) 1989

Pet Sematary (screenplay) 1989

Four Past Midnight (novellas) 1990

The Dark Tower III: The Waste Lands (novel) 1991

Needful Things (novel) 1991

Dolores Claiborne (novel) 1992

Gerald's Game (novel) 1992

Nightmares and Dreamscapes (short stories, poem, and essay) 1993

Rose Madder (novel) 1995

Desperation (novel) 1996

The Regulators [as Richard Bachman] (novel) 1996

Bag of Bones (novel) 1997

The Dark Tower IV: Wizard and Glass (novel) 1997

The Girl Who Loved Tom Gordon (juvenilia) 1999

Hearts in Atlantis (novel) 1999

Storm of the Century (screenplay) 1999

On Writing: A Memoir of the Craft (nonfiction) 2000

Black House [with Straub] (novel) 2001

Dreamcatcher (novel) 2001

Everything's Eventual: 14 Dark Tales (short stories) 2002

From a Buick 8 (novel) 2002

The Dark Tower V: Wolves of the Calla (novel) 2003

The Dark Tower VI: Song of Susannah (novel) 2004

The Dark Tower VII: The Dark Tower (novel) 2004

The Journals of Eleanor Druse: My Investigation of the Kingdom Hospital Incident [as Eleanor Druse] (novel) 2004

PRIMARY SOURCES

STEPHEN KING (ESSAY DATE 1982)

SOURCE: King, Stephen. "October 4, 1957, and an Invitation to Dance." In *Stephen King's Danse Macabre*, pp. 1-15. New York: Everest House, 1982.

In the following excerpt, King comments on the dual nature of horror in popular literature and film.

2

If there is any truth or worth to the danse macabre, it is simply that novels, movies, TV and radio programs—even the comic books—dealing with horror always do their work on two levels.

On top is the "gross-out" level—when Regan vomits in the priest's face or masturbates with a crucifix in *The Exorcist*, or when the raw-looking, terribly inside-out monster in John Frankenheimer's *Prophecy* crunches off the helicopter pilot's head like a Tootsie-Pop. The gross-out can be done with varying degrees of artistic finesse, but it's always there.

But on another, more potent level, the work of horror really is a dance—a moving, rhythmic search. And what it's looking for is the place where you, the viewer or the reader, live at your most primitive level. The work of horror is not interested in the civilized furniture of our lives. Such a work dances through these rooms which we have fitted out one piece at a time, each piece expressing—we hope!—our socially acceptable and pleasantly enlightened character. It is in search of another place, a room which may sometimes resemble the secret den of a Victorian gentleman, sometimes the torture chamber of the Spanish Inquisition . . . but perhaps most frequently and most successfully, the simple and brutally plain hole of a Stone Age cave-dweller.

Is horror art? On this second level, the work of horror can be nothing else; it achieves the level of art simply because it is looking for something beyond art, something that predates art: it is looking for what I would call phobic pressure points. The good horror tale will dance its way to the center of your life and find the secret door to the room you believed no one but you knew of—as both Albert Camus and Billy Joel have pointed out, The Stranger makes us nervous . . . but we love to try on his face in secret.

Do spiders give you the horrors? Fine. We'll have spiders, as in Tarantula, The Incredible Shrinking Man, and Kingdom of the Spiders. What about rats? In James Herbert's novel of the same name, you can feel them crawl all over you . . . and eat you alive. How about snakes? That shut-in feeling? Heights? Or . . . whatever there is.

Because books and movies are mass media, the field of horror has often been able to do better than even these personal fears over the last thirty years. During that period (and to a lesser degree, in the seventy or so years preceding), the horror genre has often been able to find national phobic pressure points, and those books and films which have been the most successful almost always seem to play upon and express fears which exist across a wide spectrum of people. Such fears, which are often political, economic, and psychological rather than supernatural, give the best work of horror a pleasing allegorical feel—and it's the one sort of allegory that most filmmakers seem at home with. Maybe because they know that if the shit starts getting too thick, they can always bring the monster shambling out of the darkness again.

We're going back to Stratford in 1957 before much longer, but before we do, let me suggest that one of the films of the last thirty years to find a pressure point with great accuracy was Don Siegel's Invasion of the Body Snatchers. Further along, we'll discuss the novel—and Jack Finney, the author, will also have a few things to say—but for now, let's look briefly at the film.

There is nothing really physically horrible in the Siegel version of Invasion of the Body Snatchers;[1] no gnarled and evil star travelers here, no twisted, mutated shape under the facade of normality. The pod people are just a little different, that's all. A little vague. A little messy. Although Finney never puts this fine a point on it in his book, he certainly suggests that the most horrible thing about "them" is that they lack even the

most common and easily attainable sense of aesthetics. Never mind, Finney suggests, that these usurping aliens from outer space can't appreciate La Traviata or Moby Dick or even a good Norman Rockwell cover on the Saturday Evening Post. That's bad enough, but—my God!—they don't mow their lawns or replace the pane of garage glass that got broken when the kid down the street batted a baseball through it. They don't repaint their houses when they get flaky. The roads leading into Santa Mira, we're told, are so full of potholes and washouts that pretty soon the salesmen who service the town—who aerate its municipal lungs with the life-giving atmosphere of capitalism, you might say—will no longer bother to come.

The gross-out level is one thing, but it is on that second level of horror that we often experience that low sense of anxiety which we call "the creeps." Over the years, Invasion of the Body Snatchers has given a lot of people the creeps, and all sorts of high-flown ideas have been imputed to Siegel's film version. It was seen as an anti-McCarthy film until someone pointed out the fact that Don Siegel's political views could hardly be called leftish. Then people began seeing it as a "better dead than Red" picture. Of the two ideas, I think that second one better fits the film that Siegel made, the picture that ends with Kevin McCarthy in the middle of a freeway, screaming "They're here already! You're next!" to cars which rush heedlessly by him. But in my heart, I don't really believe that Siegel was wearing a political hat at all when he made the movie (and you will see later that Jack Finney has never believed it, either); I believe he was simply having fun and that the undertones . . . just happened.

This doesn't invalidate the idea that there is an allegorical element in Invasion of the Body Snatchers; it is simply to suggest that sometimes these pressure points, these terminals of fear, are so deeply buried and yet so vital that we may tap them like artesian wells—saying one thing out loud while we express something else in a whisper. The Philip Kaufman version of Finney's novel is fun (although, to be fair, not quite as much fun as Siegel's), but that whisper has changed into something entirely different: the subtext of Kaufman's picture seems to satirize the whole I'm-okay-you're-okay-so-let's-get-in-the-hot-tub-and-massage-our-precious-consciousness movement of the egocentric seventies. Which is to suggest that, although the uneasy dreams of the mass subconscious may change from decade to decade, the pipeline into that well of dreams remains constant and vital.

This is the real danse macabre, I suspect: those remarkable moments when the creator of a horror story is able to unite the conscious and subconscious mind with one potent idea. I believe it happened to a greater degree with the Siegel version of *Invasion of the Body Snatchers,* but of course both Siegel and Kaufman were able to proceed courtesy of Jack Finney, who sank the original well.

Note

1. There is in the Philip Kaufman remake, though. There is a moment in that film which is repulsively horrible. It comes when Donald Sutherland uses a rake to smash in the face of a mostly formed pod. This "person's" face breaks in with sickening ease, like a rotted piece of fruit, and lets out an explosion of the most realistic stage blood that I have ever seen in a color film. When that moment came, I winced, clapped a hand over my mouth . . . and wondered how in the hell the movie had ever gotten its PG rating.

GENERAL COMMENTARY

HEIDI STRENGELL (ESSAY DATE SPRING 2003)

SOURCE: Strengell, Heidi. "'The Monster Never Dies': An Analysis of the Gothic Double in Stephen King's Oeuvre." *Americana: The Journal of American Popular Culture (1900-Present)* 2, no. 1 (spring 2003): <http://www.americanpopularculture.com/journal/articles/spring_2003/strengell.htm>.

In the following essay, Strengell maintains that the use of the Gothic literary mechanism of the double is central to King's works and serves as a symbol of the deep-seated fear of the average person's capacity for evil.

In *Danse Macabre* (1981), his non-fiction study of the horror genre, Stephen King distinguishes three Gothic archetypes that embody the central issues with which the Gothic era was concerned. To be more precise, Mary Shelley's *Frankenstein or, the Modern Prometheus* (1818) deals with "the refusal to take personal responsibility for one's actions because of pride" (62); Bram Stoker's *Dracula* (1897) portrays perverse or, in medical terms, abnormal and repressed sexuality as well as double standards of sexuality; and, finally, Robert Louis Stevenson's *The Strange Case of Dr. Jekyll and Mr. Hyde* (1886) exploits the possibilities provided by the discovery of the human psyche during the Gothic period, that is, the question of the double. Taking this third archetype as the subject for this paper, I will show that one of the central issues in the Gothic era, namely the paradoxical existence of both good and evil in a single person, remains an important issue in the

fiction of Stephen King. This perpetuation reveals our inability to evolve past our base instincts, to purge them completely from the human psyche. The appearance and reappearance of the Gothic double also shows us that popular fiction provides a useful repository for our deepest fear—specifically the fear that each of us is capable of great evil.

The Gothic Double

I will begin by distinguishing *the Gothic double* from the terms related to it. Alongside Frankenstein's monster, the Wandering Jew, and the Byronic vampire, David Punter sets a fourth Gothic character, the *Doppelganger* which, in his view, signifies "the mask of innocence" and which is found in, for instance, *Dr. Jekyll and Mr. Hyde* (21). On another occasion, he refers to the novel as a record of a *split personality* (2), and since the terms are far from being identical, they need to be defined at the outset. The term *Doppelganger* is defined in *The New International Webster's Comprehensive Dictionary of the English Language* (1999) as "1 A person exactly like another; a double. 2 A wraith, especially of a person not yet dead" (378). Since the German equivalent, too, primarily assumes that the word refers to two separate entities, the term Doppelganger is rejected in this context, although it is widely used in literary criticism. The term *split personality* is not included in *The New International Webster's Comprehensive Dictionary of the English Language,* rightly so, because such a diagnosis is no longer considered scientifically valid. After Eugen Bleuler in the late nineteenth century coined the term *schizophrenia* to replace the old one, *dementia procox,* the lay public mistakenly understood it as an equivalent to the term *split personality.* The confusion of the terms meant that the lay term *split personality* became replaced in scientific usage by *dissociative identity disorder* (Kaplan, Sadock and Grebb 457). The latter includes various states and signifies a personality disorder in which the person is unaware of what his "other half" is doing. Whether Dr. Jekyll/Mr. Hyde can be diagnosed as a dissociative disorder patient or possibly a borderline personality may occupy a few psychiatrists, but the term Gothic double will do for my purposes.

Like *Doppelganger,* the word *double* calls upon ambiguous interpretations and needs therefore to be defined. My definition takes as a starting point the concept of personality. According to *The New International Webster's Comprehensive Dictionary of the English Language,* personality is: "1. That which constitutes a person; also, that which distinguishes and characterizes a person; personal existence" (942). As the unity of the personality was endangered by Freudian notions, similarly, many Gothic narratives were consumed "by a paranoid terror of involution or the unraveling of the multiformed ego" (Halberstam 55). *Dr. Jekyll and Mr. Hyde* fittingly displays this juxtaposition of the smooth surface of Dr. Jekyll and that of the "dwarfish" (18), "ape-like" (27) Mr. Hyde. While Dr. Jekyll is pleasant and sophisticated, Mr. Hyde, stunted, crumpled, and ugly, is designed to shock. Indeed, the "Gothic effect depends upon the production of a monstrous double" (Halberstam 54). Thus, for my purposes, the term *Gothic double* refers to the essential duality within a single character on the further presumption that the duality centers on the polarity of good and evil.

Like many of King's works, Stevenson's novella examines the conflict between the free will to do good or to do evil as well as the theme of hypocrisy. King believes the conflict between good and evil is the conflict between, in Freudian terms, the id and the superego and refers also to Stevenson's terms: the conflict between mortification and gratification. In addition, King views the struggle both in Christian and mythical terms. The latter suggests the split between the Apollonian (the man of intellect, morality, and nobility) and the Dionysian (the man of physical gratification) (*Danse* 75). Influenced by James Hogg's *Confessions of a Justified Sinner* (1824) and Edgar Allan Poe's "William Wilson" (1839), Stevenson wrote his novella in three days in 1886 (Punter 1; *Danse* 69). King expresses his admiration for *Dr. Jekyll and Mr. Hyde*, regarding it as a "masterpiece of concision" (*Danse* 69, 80-81).

Dr. Jekyll and Mr. Hyde, the story of a Victorian gentleman who leads a secret life of vice, uses multiple narrators to relate the story of a man doomed by the chemical reproduction of his double. "Man is not truly one but two" says Dr. Jekyll, tormented by a sense of "the thorough and primitive duality of man" (Stevenson 70). Through chemical experimentation, he discovers a potion which dissociates the "polar twins" of the self, transforming his body into that of his other self (70). The other self, Mr. Hyde, allows Dr. Jekyll to satisfy his undignified desires untrammeled by moral scruples. Haunting the streets of London, this small and indescribably ugly character "springs headlong into the sea of liberty" which finally leads him to murder a respectable gentleman (75). Frightened, Dr. Jekyll determines never to use the potion again. However, the metamorphosis has become spontaneous, and, as King

aptly notes, Dr. Jekyll "has created Hyde to escape the strictures of propriety, but has discovered that evil has its own strictures" (*Danse* 73). In the end, Dr. Jekyll has become Mr. Hyde's prisoner, and Jekyll/Hyde's life ends in suicide.

Many of the themes of *Dr. Jekyll and Mr. Hyde* appear in King's work. Like Dr. Jekyll, Reverend Lester Lowe of *Cycle of the Werewolf* bases his influence on moral superiority, and his high views of himself produce morbidity in his relations with his own appetites. Arnie Cunningham of *Christine* illustrates another angle of the werewolf myth even more clearly, that is, the werewolf as an innocent victim, predestined to its destruction. While the Gage creature in King's *Pet Semetary* constructs part of its maker, the dialectic between monster and maker is resolved in, for instance, *Cycle of the Werewolf* as a conflict in a single body. Gage Creed's monstrosity in *Pet Semetary* depends upon the fragility of his father's humanity, whereas the repulsive nature of the werewolf can only be known through the failed respectability of Reverend Lester Lowe. King characterizes Lowe as genuinely evil, whereas Jekyll, although a hypocrite and a self-deceiver, only desires personal freedom and keeps certain pleasures repressed. Punter points out that while Hyde's behavior manifests an urban version of "going native," Jekyll struggles with various pressures (3). Similarly, Lester Lowe who embodies social virtue takes great pleasure in his bloody nocturnal adventures.

Thad Beaumont's alter ego in *The Dark Half* expresses the violent part of the protagonist's character, of which he himself is not constantly aware. Likewise, the degree to which Dr. Jekyll takes seriously his public responsibilities determines the "hidden-ness" of his desire for pleasure. Punter notes that since the public man must appear flawless, he must "hide" his private nature, to the extent of completely denying it (3). Defying all logic, Beaumont's "dark half," George Stark, has somehow come into existence, and Beaumont must literally face his dark half in a confrontation in which either Beaumont's Jekyll or Stark's Hyde has to die.

The Drawing of the Three introduces a dissociative patient, Odetta Holmes/Detta Walker, who through Roland the Gunslinger and Eddie Dean's intervention is able to merge her two personalities into the woman named Susannah Dean. Odetta developed a second personality as a young girl, when Jack Mort dropped a brick on her head. Her two personalities—the sophisticated and wealthy Odetta and the uneducated and vulgar Detta—lead separate lives, completely unaware of each other. Since both are aspects of her self, she cannot become a whole until those "polar twins" are united in Susannah Dean. When the compassion of Odetta and the strength of Detta merge into Susannah, she becomes a worthy gunslinger on Roland's team.

The dark halves of King's Gothic doubles express unrestrained sexuality. Reverend Lester Lowe "wolf-rapes" Stella Randolph, and the shy Arnie Cunningham transforms into a vulgar senior citizen in the form of the beast; the sexually insatiable Detta Walker uses both foul language and teases men, whereas George Stark commits a sexually charged murder of Miriam Cowley—not to mention the rape-murders of Frank Dodd and the child murders of Carl Bierstone/Charles Burnside. Gothic monsters underline the meaning of decadence and are thus concerned with the problem of degeneration. Punter maintains that they pose, from different angles, the same question appropriate to an age of imperial decline: how much can one lose—individually, socially, nationally—and still remain a man? (1). The question has remained a central issue in the modern Gothic and in King's fiction in particular.

Dr. Jekyll and Mr. Hyde was published at a time when the problem of prostitution was receiving considerable public attention in England. As in *Frankenstein* and *Dracula*, the protagonist's vice and decadence are once again sex-related, but also clearly sadistic—the serial killers, Frank Dodd (**Dead Zone**) and Charles Burnside (**Black House**), feature these sadistic traits in King. Stevenson had read W. T. Stead's series of articles on child prostitution and was aware that the demand for child prostitutes was being stimulated by the sadistic tastes of the Victorian gentlemen (Clemens 123). More importantly, the theme is evoked at the outset of the novella when Mr. Hyde tramples on a young girl. The violation of the girl's body is settled with a hundred pounds, which reinforces the prostitution motif. Also, the foggy night side of Mr. Hyde's London gives a glimpse of the Victorian gentlemen's subculture: "Once a woman spoke to him, offering, I think, a box of lights" (Stevenson 85)—clearly, she was offering something else. As in **Black House** where the Fisherman lusts for a young boy's buttocks, the hints of sexual exploitation also suggest male victims, as for instance, in the scene in which Mr. Utterson, "tossing to and fro" on his "great, dark bed," imagines Mr. Hyde blackmailing Dr. Jekyll. This dark "figure to whom power was given" would stand by Jekyll's bedside, "and even at that dead hour he must rise and do its bidding" (20). A disturbing novella, *Dr. Jekyll and Mr. Hyde* gave a detailed depiction of some upper-class gentlemen, but as Valdine Clemens notes, criticized moralistic middle-class sexual repression (for instance, the prevalent homosexual abuse in public schools and prostitution) and patriarchal power (124, 132).

Arnie Cunninham of **Christine** perishes because of his desperate loneliness. An unattractive teenager who finds little solace at home or at school, Arnie falls in love with a 1958 Plymouth Fury. Possessed by the evil spirit of Christine's earlier owner, Roland LeBay, Arnie is alienated from his family, best friend Dennis, and even his high school sweetheart Leigh Cabot. Like *Dr. Jekyll and Mr. Hyde*, **Christine** focuses on "humanity's vulnerability to dehumanization" which coexists with the fear of internal evil: "the upsurge of the animal, the repressed unconscious, the monster from id," or, as Douglas E. Winter points out, "the monster from the fifties" (137, 139; **Danse** 75). The novel also discusses the conflict between the will to do evil and the will to deny evil; the car becomes a symbol of the duality of human nature, as telling as the two sides of Henry Jekyll's town house which bordered both a graceful Victorian street and a slumlike alley (Winter 139-140; **Danse** 75): "It was as if I had seen a snake that was almost ready to shed its old skin, that some of the old skin had already flaked away, revealing the glistening newness underneath" (**Christine** 57-58). As Christine magically returns to street condition, Arnie also begins to change, at first for the better, but then he matures beyond his years: "a teenage Jekyll rendered into a middle-aged Hyde" (Winter 140).

In brief, although Stevenson's classic finds no single counterpart in King, its motifs occur in several of King's works.

The Werewolf

Cycle of the Werewolf and *The Talisman* introduce us to another Stephen King double: the werewolf. Perhaps nowhere else in King's fiction is the Gothic double more pronounced than in this figure.

Beginning as a calendar, displaying twelve colored drawings by Bernie Wrightson with brief accompanying text by King, *Cycle of the Werewolf* evolved into a twelve-chapter novella. Each successive segment takes place on a specific holiday of the year, from January to December, relating the story of the recurring appearance of a werewolf in isolated Tarker's Mills, Maine, and its

Scene from John Carpenter's 1983 film adaptation of *Christine*.

destruction at the hands of a crippled boy. King defines the predestined nature of the disaster: "It is the Werewolf, and there is no more reason for its coming now than there would be for the arrival of cancer, or a psychotic with murder on his mind, or a killer tornado" (**Werewolf** 14). Although the werewolf arouses fear and suspicions, only in October do the residents take systematic action to defend themselves. Like "Salem's Lot, Castle Rock, or Derry, Tarker's Mills keeps its secrets, and, similarly, the residents of Tarker's Mills embody all of the diversifying virtue and ugliness found in everyday people" (Larson 104).

What is more, each of the werewolf's victims expands the constant sense of isolation, due to the flaws in their physiques and in their characters (Collings, *The Many Facets of Stephen King* 80). As an illustration, the February victim, Stella Randolph, is isolated by her skewed romanticism and by her corpulence (80). However, this Valentine's day the lonely old maid receives a visitor: "a dark shape—amorphous but clearly masculine" (**Werewolf** 21). King depicts Stella's encounter with the werewolf in Gothic terms, combining dreams, sex, and death (21-24). He uses the com-

mon French metaphor "orgasm is a little death" to reinforce the Gothic effect of the February section. Indeed, what takes the place of the Valentine figure is a "beast" with "shaggy fur in a silvery streak" (22) its breath "hot, but somehow not unpleasant" (23). Despite Berni Wrightson's illustration of a lustful redhead embracing a werewolf, King never graphically describes the wolf-rape and killing of the fat old maid, but veils it in quasi-romantic images that might have derived from John Keats's classic poem, "The Eve of St. Agnes" (Reino 136).

Like the wheel-chair bound protagonist Marty Coslaw, the Reverend Lester Lowe did nothing to deserve his destiny. Until May, he remains as unaware of the werewolf's identity as anybody else in Tarker's Mills. On the night before Homecoming Sunday, he has, however, a most peculiar dream. In his dream, Lowe has been preaching with fire and force, but has to break off, because both he and his congregation are turning into werewolves. Lester Lowe's relief after the nightmare turns into knowledge when he opens the church doors next morning, finding the gutted body of Clyde Corliss.

King refers to the werewolf in biblical terms as "the Beast" and "the Great Satan," and in the Gothic manner the Beast can be anywhere or, even worse, anybody (**Werewolf** 45). Unlike a number of other monsters, werewolves, however, frequently arouse pity. Aptly, Collings states that the werewolf is more sinned against than sinning, and that the curse works in two ways: on the level of plot, it transforms an otherwise sensible man into a rapacious monster; on the level of theme and symbol, it divorces him from reality, isolating the person from society and from personal standards of morality (*Facets* 78).

Although Reverend Lester Lowe shares a fate similar to that of Arnie Cunningham of **Christine,** he does not evoke fear and pity to the same extent. In the same way as his hypocritical predecessor in *Dr. Jekyll and Mr. Hyde,* Lester Lowe makes excuses for his behavior without fighting against it. In November, having found out that hunters have been sent out after the werewolf, he deliberately takes the role of the beast and defends himself by comparing the hunters with irrational animals. Ignoring the threat of these adult men, Marty Coslaw's lined notepads, and his direct question—"*Why don't you kill yourself?*" (**Werewolf** 108, 111; italics original)—the Reverend Lester Lowe (that is, the werewolf) is forced to analyze his situation. With hubris like that of Victor Frankenstein, he turns to God: "*If I have been cursed from Outside, then God will bring me down in His time*" (**Werewolf** 111; italics original). In other words, against the advice of his own creator, Stephen King, Reverend Lester Lowe readily lays the guilt on "God the Father" (**Danse** 62) and refuses to take responsibility for his actions or to fight his werewolf instincts. Moreover, blinded by his own logical reasoning, Lester Lowe succumbs to even greater evil by deliberately contemplating the murder of Marty Coslaw—this time both premeditated and in full possession of his senses (**Werewolf** 111).

While many contemporary treatments tend to glamorize the virtues of evil, King's approach is more traditional (Larson 106-107). Larson regards Reverend Lowe as a man unable to free himself from the overwhelming influence of evil, and he is eventually only able to do so through the aid of an outside agency, through the sympathy and concern of Marty Coslaw (107). Despite his fear of the werewolf, Marty recognizes the human being beneath the beast. While aiming his pistol with silver bullets towards the attacking werewolf, he says: "Poor old Reverend Lowe. I'm gonna try to set you free" (**Werewolf** 125). In the same way,

Mina Harker pities the vampire in *Dracula:* "The poor soul who has wrought all this misery is the saddest case of all" (367). Clearly, King's allusion to this sentiment reinforces the moral tradition that has lain at the heart of the horror genre and has been much absent in contemporary horror fiction (Larson 108).

Undoubtedly, King takes a traditional stand by letting evil perish in the end of the novella, thus, unlike Larson or Anthony Magistrale in *The Moral Voyages of Stephen King* (57-67), I argue that evil can often be conquered in King's fiction. Although Jack Torrance of **The Shining** succumbs to evil and takes the mallet to attack his family, Dick Hallorann is able to resist the same evil influence of the hotel—similarly, Lowe could have acted otherwise. In **The Talisman,** we encounter Wolf, a slow-witted werewolf from the Territories. When he senses that the full moon is rising and that his instincts might lead him to hurt Jack Sawyer who has become his "herd" and whom he is thus expected to defend against all imaginable threats, this righteous creature takes measures to prevent possible accidents and locks up the herd, that is Jack Sawyer, in a shed for three days: "He Would Not Injure His Herd" (321). Unlike the godly Lowe who attempts to silence his crippled eye witness, the animal-like Wolf avoids killing people. Lowe considers his werewolf nature alien to his true self and allows this alien part to commit even grimmer crimes, which pushes him toward greater levels of moral corruption. Wolf, in contrast, lives by the laws of nature, takes into account the facts caused by his instincts, and respects himself. It is interesting to note, however, that while an evil impulse may be conquered the temptation toward evil is never entirely eliminated.

The Writer/His Pseudonym

Another variation of the Gothic double in Stephen King's work is Thad Beaumont/George Stark or the writer/his pseudonym. In the author's note of **The Dark Half,** King expresses his gratitude to his pseudonym, Richard Bachman, maintaining that the "novel could not have been written without him." In an interview with Walden Books (November/December 1989) and quoted in Magistrale, King acknowledged prior to the publication of **The Dark Half** that Richard Bachman is the darker, more violent side of Stephen King, just as Stark is the dark half of Thad Beaumont (*The Second Decade* 66). Remarkably, then, the Gothic double resides within the Gothic double, that is, the reality of the novel reflects reality. Undoubtedly, both pseudonyms function as a dark alter ego for the artist, a chance to realize his most violent and pessimistic visions. Tony Magistrale notes that the details surrounding the union between Beaumont and Stark underscore King's intimate relationship with Bachman. Furthermore, even information relevant to those trusted persons who knew, protected, and finally revealed King's pseudonym corresponds to the fictional events that the reader discovers in **The Dark Half** (*Decade* 63-64).

Like Dr. Jekyll/Mr. Hyde, whose transformation is occasioned by scientific explanation, King attempts to establish credibility by the means of medicine. Having suffered from constant headaches, the eleven-year-old Thad Beaumont is operated on, and, instead of a supposed brain tumor, a fetal twin is discovered in his brain. In addition to being Thad's physical twin, George Stark has his origin in the writer's imagination. Considering George "a very bad man," Thad knows that he has "built George Stark from the ground up" (**The Dark Half** 155). The symbolic funeral of George Stark becomes a moral stand for Thad's part, because he has both indulged his dark fantasies in Stark's fiction and profited financially from his success (Magistrale, *Decade* 64). Wendy and William, Beaumont's identical twins, underscore the symbiotic relationship of Stark and Beaumont. While responding with similar affection to these different looking men, Wendy and William sense their identical nature. Sharing identical fingerprints and a capacity for mental telepathy, it becomes more obvious that George has a right to feel insulted (**The Dark Half** 331). Not even Thad is able to make a clear distinction between himself and George: "*Who are you when you write, Thad? Who are you then?*" (**The Dark Half** 129; italics original).

Since George constitutes an integral part of Thad's psyche, he does not genuinely attempt to get rid of George. Elisabeth compares the relationship with alcohol or drug addiction, stating that Thad revealed George's identity only through the force of circumstances: "If Frederick Clawson hadn't come along and forced my husband's hand, I think Thad would still be talking about getting rid of him in the same way" (**The Dark Half** 202). Indeed, this contradiction has resulted in alcohol addiction, a suicide attempt, and life-like dreams. However, only as Stark threatens Beaumont's immediate circle, does he realize the intimacy of their relationship and its fatal consequences. Starting as a thriller, the final confrontation of the two brothers and its victory for Thad

receives a mythological explanation. Conducting human souls back and forth between the land of the living and the land of the dead, sparrows are able to distinguish the original brother from the dead one and to take the latter where he belongs. Nevertheless, Thad's victory may prove of short duration, and he is referred to in a less pleasant context later in King: in **Needful Things** (1991) we learn that Thad Beaumont has broken up with his wife and in **Bag of Bones** (1998) that he has committed suicide.

The Serial Killer

The serial killer also represents the modern counterpart of Dr. Jekyll/Mr. Hyde. **The Dead Zone**, for example, concerns the removal of masks, both political and psychological. The Gothic duality is displayed even in the novel's central symbol, the wheel of fortune, which, apart from representing blind chance, reveals a second disc. Winter explains that at its heart is the Presidential Seal, a symbol of a different game of chance—politics—and its paradoxes (76). Focusing on the masquerade of politics, Greg Stillson, a Congressional candidate whose name is an intentional conjunction of "still" and "Nixon" (263), takes the Vietnamese masquerade-game of the "Laughing Tiger" a step further: "inside the beast-skin, a man, yes. But inside the man-skin, a beast" (**The Dead Zone** 297). **The Dead Zone** also connects the fates—and masks—of Johnny Smith whose resemblance to Everyman is signaled in the prosaic simplicity of his name and Frank Dodd, the strangler-rapist whose identity is withheld until one of "Faithful John's" psychic revelations.

As a consequence of a car crash, Johnny lies in a coma for four and a half years. Awakening in May 1975 at the age of twenty-seven, he discovers that the world has changed: the war in Vietnam has ended, a Vice-President and President have resigned, Johnny's girlfriend is married and has borne a child, Stillson has made his political move, and an unidentified rapist is killing young women in Castle Rock. Apart from regaining consciousness, Johnny has acquired occult powers of precognition and telepathy which both cause his estrangement from his past life and force him to take a moral stand: whether or not to stop Stillson and Dodd. Although this Faithful John serves the purpose of good, his Jekyll-and-Hyde mask (**The Dead Zone** 14) haunts his girlfriend Sarah Bracknell (later Sarah Hazlett) throughout the novel.

While Johnny is comatose, the policeman Frank Dodd commits his brutal rapestranglings.

Joseph Reino maintains that the crimes seem to emerge from the blankness of the coma, as if they were merely the dark side of the otherwise sunny personality, and as if Frank was Johnny's evil "other"—this pair thus possessing something like Edgar Allan Poe's "bi-part soul" (67). Despite the grim verdict, King provides the character with a background which explains some of the hideous acts. While awaiting a young victim (Alma Frechette) to walk into his trap, Dodd's mind is momentarily obsessed with an embarrassing childhood memory: a lesson in sexual education given by his abusive mother. When Frank was innocently playing with his penis, his mother, a huge woman, caught him in the act and began to shake him back and forth. Here King emphasizes parental responsibility for aberrant personality development, arguing that Frank "was not the killer then, he was not slick then, he was a little boy blubbering with fear" (*The Dead Zone* 65). Albeit somewhat simplistically, King underscores the significance of the formative years.

When Alma Frechette appears, fate plays a decisive role in a genuinely Gothic manner, and, again, everybody must be suspected. Familiar with the killer, Alma does not suspect anything but wonders at his Little Red Riding Hood outfit (*The Dead Zone* 66). Before long, she is strangled at the moment of Dodd's ejaculation. "Surely no hometown boy could have done such a dreadful thing," states the pious narrator (*The Dead Zone* 68), and from then on almost two years pass without more killings.

Significantly, Johnny Smith's awakening from the coma coincides with the fourth murder. However, it takes deep self-exploration on the recovered Johnny's part before he accepts the sheriff George Bannerman's request to assist in the murder investigation. By acknowledging his psychic abilities and acting accordingly, Johnny humbles before fate. In King's world, nobody escapes his destiny, and, at any rate, a well-developed brain tumor would cause Johnny's death within a few months. However, by bearing responsibility for his next, Johnny prevents Greg Stillson's presidency and its likely consequence, a nuclear war, as well as Frank Dodd from continuing his murder series. After all, the investigation turns out to be of short duration, since the deputy Frank Dodd commits suicide the same evening the two men meet at the police department. Remarkably, the childish face hides the Gothic mark of the beast (*The Dead Zone* 233), evil actions having their root in childhood. After gathered enough evidence, Bannerman and Smith visit

Dodd's house and find him dead: "*Knew, Johnny thought incoherently. Knew somehow when he saw me. Knew it was all over. Came home. Did this*" (*The Dead Zone* 253). In other words, the two men are connected, and their interrelations are further reinforced by the nature of their mothers: the sexual neurotic, Henrietta Dodd, who "knew from the beginning" (*The Dead Zone* 252) and Vera Smith who marks her son with her religious frenzies: "God has put his mark on my Johnny and I rejoice" (*The Dead Zone* 61).

The opening page of *Cujo* repeats the story of Frank Dodd, stating that "he was no werewolf, vampire, ghoul, or unnameable creature from the enchanted forest or from the snowy wastes; he was only a cop named Frank Dodd with mental and sexual problems" (*Cujo* 3). Like Buffalo Bill in *The Silence of the Lambs* (1991), Frank Dodd personifies a victimized human being who does not "suit in his skin." Although regarded as a respected resident of Castle Rock, Frank Dodd lacks identity and is perhaps therefore a master of disguise.

A number of serial killers suffer from impotence except during their violent acts and are not considered genuinely males, but are despised as freaks and monsters. Charles Burnside a.k.a. Carl Bierstone and the Fisherman of *Black House* has all but one of these characteristics: born evil and without conscience, he justifies cruelty as an end in itself.

Black House is a kind of sequel to *The Talisman,* both works being jointly authored by Peter Straub and Stephen King. A Victorian novel with allusions to Charles Dickens's *Bleak House,* Dickensian characters, and references to Edgar Allan Poe and Mark Twain, *Black House* reads as a tale of horror or a detective story with a blend of thriller and fantasy (Gaiman 2). The narrative reintroduces the then twelve-year-old Jack Sawyer of *The Talisman.* Now this retired, burned out ex-LAPD homicide detective lives in the small Wisconsin town of French Landing—interestingly, in scenery resembling Tom Sawyer's and Huckleberry Finn's foggy riverside. Children are being abducted from French Landing by a cannibal named "The Fisherman" who has disguised himself as an Alzheimer's patient in the local old people's home and is aided in his dastardly misdeeds by a talking crow called "Gorg." The Fisherman is a pawn in the hand of the Crimson King, evil monarch of End World, who attempts to abduct a wunderkind in order to annihilate the universe with his powers. Jack and a gang of philosophically inclined

ABOUT THE AUTHOR

EDWIN F. CASEBEER ON THE INFLUENCE OF KING'S LIFE ON HIS WORKS

Overall, King's canon is a quest. But his battle cry is not "excelsior!" The direction is downwards and the path is a spiral. Many of King's characters experience life as a quest: Ben Mears of *'Salem's Lot* questing for self and conquering the vampire; *The Tommyknockers*' Gardener questing for death and finding self; the comrades of *The Stand* marching against the Dark One and founding the New Jerusalem; the boys of *It* killing fear; and the boys of *The Talisman* killing death. The gunslinger of *The Dark Tower* series is, however, probably most typical of King: he seeks to understand what the quest itself is. His enemies become his friends, his guides his traitors, his victims those he has saved, and his now a then. Paradox; transformation; balancing the dualities, an emergent, tenuous, ever-fading, and ever-appearing balance—these are the duplicitous landmarks in the terrain of King's work and his life. Both are open enough and fluent enough to mirror us and ours as we seek to make our own accommodations with modern monsters, personal meaninglessness, social chaos, physical decay, and death.

SOURCE: Casebeer, Edwin F. "Stephen King's Canon: The Art of Balance." In *A Dark Night's Dreaming: Contemporary American Horror Fiction,* edited by Tony Magistrale and Michael A. Morrison, pp. 42-54. Columbia: University of South Carolina Press, 1996.

motor bikers called the Hegelian Scum take action to save the wunderkind, Ty Marshall, and arrest the Fisherman.

Parodying the thriller formula, the narrator takes us to the murder scene of Irma Freneau:

We are not here to weep. . . . Humility is our best, most accurate first response. Without it, we would miss the point, the great mystery would escape us, and we would go on deaf and blind, ignorant as pigs. Let us not go on like pigs. We must honor the scene—the flies, the dog worrying the severed foot, the poor, pale body of Irma Freneau, the magnitude of what befell Irma Freneau—by acknowledging our littleness. In comparison, we are no more than vapors.

(*Black House* 35-36)

The Fisherman himself is named after Albert Fish, a real-life child-killer and cannibal, whose crimes he imitates in the novel's fictional world. In his study of the interrelationship between the reader and the novel, Edward Bullough states that a work of fiction has succeeded when the reader participates in the communication process so completely as to be nearly convinced that the art is reality (758). In *Black House,* the authors gap the bridge between the reader and the text by equating the reader with the narrator (a first-person plural narration), by using the present tense, and even by letting the reader choose the story ending that best serves his purpose. Perhaps the otherwise too fantastic occurrences of the story become more realistic by these means, combined with King's usual artillery: lifelike characters and initially realistic settings.

The serial killer turns out to be a tall, skinny, and senile old man (*Black House* 22). Although a soul brother to the other men who reside at the Maxton Elder Care Facility with his "sly, secretive, rude, caustic, stubborn, foul-tongued, meanspirited, and resentful" character (*Black House* 23), Charles Burnside hides his true self:

Carl Bierstone is Burny's great secret, for he cannot allow anyone to know that this former incarnation, this earlier self, still lives inside his skin. Carl Bierstone's awful pleasures, his foul toys, are also Burny's and he must keep them hidden in the darkness, where only he can find them.

(*Black House* 26)

The secrets with which Charles Burnside indulges himself turn him into a loner, forcing him to hide his misdeeds. As a tool in the hands of a greater evil, Burnside takes his pleasure feeding on children who are not worth sending to the End-World to the Crimson King, a creature who ultimately hides beneath the Fisherman mask.

Assisted by Gorg, the speaking crow, Charles Burnside addresses the End-World like a vassal or a stray dog fed with crumbs. While action is needed, the senior citizen undergoes a transformation. In Charles Burnside's place is Carl Bierstone and something inhuman (*Black House* 111). The inhuman inside Burny's head signifies Mr. Munshun, Crimson King's close disciple and servant, a vampire-like figure. Nearing the end of his usefulness, Burny is at Mr. Munshun's request forced to take Ty Marshall, a promising breaker to an appointed meeting place. The term breaker is used for those slaves of Crimson King who break the beams leading to the Tower, thus aiming at the total annihilation of the universe. Driven by contradictory urges, this odd serial killer is afraid of the consequences of his actions (**Black House** 541), but, despite a deadly wound, still lusts for Ty Marshall's "juicy buttocks." Like the witch of "Hansel and Gretel," he is reluctant to hand over his prey: "A good agent's entitled to ten percent" (**Black House** 550). Only seldom can a parallel be drawn between a serial killer and a wicked witch from a fairy tale, which perhaps bears further witness to King's genre blending.

Conclusion

The Gothic double of *Dr. Jekyll and Mr. Hyde* shares some traits with characters in King's work. First, flawed humanity moves between the two poles of good and evil, causing contradiction and anguish to the subject. Second, the Gothic gnome, that is, the "dwarfish" and "ape-like" half of the personality is hidden at the cost of hypocrisy and oft hideous crimes. Therefore, a disguise is needed, which causes further tension and the fear of getting caught. Tension also intensifies from the constant threat of transformation.

Monsters of the nineteenth century scare us from a distance while at the same time, as Halberstam notes, "We wear modern monsters like skin, they are us, they are on us and in us" (163). King, too, states that "the monsters are no longer due on Maple Street, but may pop up in our own mirrors—at any time" (**Danse** 252). Presumably, both convictions are based on two facts; good and evil can and do exist within a single person and, concomitantly, we are ultimately unable to evolve, to purge our baser selves from our psyche. King puts it straightforwardly: "Werewolf, vampire, ghoul, unnameable creature from the wastes. The monster never dies" (**Cujo** 4).

Works Cited

Briggs, Julia. *Night Visitors: The Rise and Fall of the English Ghost Story*. London: Faber & Faber, 1977.

Bullough, Edward, "'Psychical Distance' as a Factor in Art and an Aesthetic Principle." In Adams, Hazard (ed) *Critical Theory since Plato*. New York: Harcourt Brace Jovanovich, 1971: 758.

Clemens, Valdine. *The Return of the Repressed: Gothic Horror from The Castle of Otranto to Alien*. New York: State University of New York, 1999.

Collings, Michael R. *The Many Facets of Stephen King*. Mercer Island, Washington: Starmont House, 1985.

———. *Stephen King as Richard Bachman*. Mercer Island, Washington, Starmont House, 1985.

Halberstam, Judith. *Skin Shows: Gothic Horror and the Technology of Monsters*. Durham: Duke University Press, 2000 1995.

Kaplan, Harold I., Benjamin J. Sadock, Jack A. Grebb. *Kaplan and Sadock's Synopsis of Psychiatry: Behavioral Sciences, Clinical Psychiatry*. Baltimore, Maryland: Williams & Wilkins, 1994 (Seventh edition) 1972.

King, Stephen. *Black House*. London: HarperCollinsPublishers, 2001.

———. *Carrie*. New York: Pocket Books, 1999 1974.

———. *Christine*. London: Hodder and Stoughton, 1983 1983.

———. *Cujo*. New York: Signet, 1982 1981.

———. *Cycle of the Werewolf*. New York: Signet, 1985 1983.

———. *Danse Macabre*. New York: Berkley Books, 1983 1981.

———. *The Dark Half*. New York: Signet, 1990 1989.

———. *The Dead Zone*. New York: Signet, 1980 1979.

———. *The Gunslinger*. The Dark Tower I. New York: Plume, 1988 1982.

———. *On Writing*. New York: Scribner, 2000.

———. *Pet Semetary*. New York: Signet, 1984.

———. *The Talisman* (with Peter Straub). New York: Berkley, 1985, 1984.

Larson, Randall D. "*Cycle of the Werewolf* and the Moral Tradition of Horror." In Schweitzer, Darrell (ed), *Discovering Stephen King*. Mercer Island, Washington: Starmont House, Inc., 1985: 102-108.

Magistrale, Anthony, *The Moral Voyages of Stephen King*. Mercer Island, Washington: Starmont Studies, 1989.

———. *Stephen King: The Second Decade*, Danse Macabre *to* The Dark Half. New York: Twayne Publishers, 1992.

The New International Webster's Comprehensive Dictionary of the English Language. Florida: Trident Press International, 1999, 1958.

Punter, David. *The Literature of Terror. A History of Gothic Fictions from 1765 to the Present Day. Volume 2. The Modern Gothic*. Harlow, Essex: Pearson Education Limited, 1996.

Reino, Joseph. *Stephen King: The First Decade*, Carrie *to* Pet Semetary. Boston, Massachusetts: Twayne, 1988.

Stevenson, Robert Louis. *The Strange Case of Dr. Jekyll and Mr. Hyde*. London: Penguin Books, 1994, 1886.

Stoker, Bram. *Dracula*. London: Penguin, 1994, 1897.

Tropp, Michael. *Images of Fear: How Horror Stories Helped Shape Modern Culture (1818-1918)*. Jefferson, N. C.: McFarland and Co., 1990.

Winter, Douglas E. *Stephen King: The Art of Darkness*. New York: Signet, 1986, 1984.

TITLE COMMENTARY

The Shining

KENNETH GIBBS (ESSAY DATE 1986)

SOURCE: Gibbs, Kenneth. "Stephen King and the Tradition of American Gothic." *Gothic* New Series 1 (1986): 6-14.

In the following essay, Gibbs assesses the influence of Herman Melville's approach to the Gothic on King's work, particularly The Shining.

In the foreword to **Night Shift** Stephen King names many well-known literary forebearers from whom he derives the Gothic techniques central to his fiction—among those mentioned are Bram Stoker, the Beowulf poet, Henry James, Nathaniel Hawthorne, and, of course, Edgar Allan Poe; but he omits any reference to one major figure in American literature—Herman Melville. The omission seems justified, since, admittedly, Melville's use of the Gothic in his fiction often seems peripheral to his central thematic concerns. For Poe, Gothic techniques are definitely a necessary adjunct to his artistic vision, and Poe is therefore the recipient of far more recognition as a master of the Gothic than is Melville. Yet, when the overall spirit behind King's use of the Gothic in his major novels, especially **The Shining**, is compared with that of, for example, Melville's *Moby-Dick*, such close parallels appear that Poe's traditionally exclusive position at the fountainhead of American Gothic fiction may be profitably revalued.

King's affinity with Melville stems not only from their mutual dependence on standard Gothic techniques but from their employment of what Joseph Campbell refers to as the "monomyth" of "separation—initiation—return" (30) in relation to the achievement of transcendence in their fiction. Since Gothic literature has its roots in Romanticism, it shares the basic tenet of Romanticism that there is a division between the world we perceive with our senses and the intuitively apprehended world of the spirit. Whereas the mythic hero departs from his social world on his quest, the Romantic hero not only leaves society but also travels beyond the constraints of the physical world. If the Romantic artist has a strong penchant towards subjective idealism and feels that dreams may have greater reality than conscious, objective existence, the significance of the world of the senses can diminish until he, as does Poe, may plaintively wonder "Is *all* that we see or seem /

But a dream within a dream?" (482). If the common reality of sensuous, rational experience has no integral validity, then nothing exists for the questor to return to, the dreamer can never awake, and the mythic circle of separation and return is broken.

In accord with the optimistic tenor of Emerson's theories on transcendence, American writers have often been eager to commence the artistic quest beyond the phenomenal world. For example, Walt Whitman writes in "Passage to India": "For we are bound where mariner has not yet dared to go, / And we will risk the ship, ourselves and all" (347). In contrast to this trend, Melville's *Moby-Dick* cautions that when the artist's ship seeks to break through the containing masks of the phenomenal world, the voyage is captained by a madman who will sink the entire enterprise before a return from the outward journey is possible. But one character in *Moby-Dick*, Ishmael, does survive precisely because he balances Ahab's desire to transcend the phenomenal worlds, the empirical world of masks, with a deep appreciation of the beauty and necessity of the opposing world of the senses. Ishmael has seen the whale from both sides, both as symbol of transcendence and as a physical, living entity, and he has learned to respect each side of the transcendental dialectic: "Doubts of all things earthly, and intuitions of some things heavenly, this combination makes neither believer nor infidel, but makes a man who regards them both with equal eye" (480). Like the symbolic bifurcation of the whale's vision, Ishmael views existence from a dual perspective; he skeptically and rationally investigates the actual, material world, discounting authorities who have not immediately experienced the whale, and he does intuit that there is a level of reality that exists beyond. Ishmael's stance is somewhat akin to Whitman's period of more sensual mysticism in "Song of Myself," where he declares, "I am the poet of the Body and I am the poet of the Soul" (42). In this perspective both the material and the spiritual worlds coexist, allowing the protagonist to complete the mythic journey from this world to the beyond and back.

Poe, on the other hand, exemplifies in his art what David Halliburton identifies as "pure transcendence" (278). In "The Poetic Principle" Poe locates the source of the beautiful beyond the phenomenal world; "It [man's sense of the beautiful] is no mere appreciation of the Beauty before us—but a wild effort to reach the beauty above" (418). Once someone reaches such beauty above, he certainly would not willingly return to the far less desirable beauty before him. As illustrated in "The Fall of the House of Usher," the movement in Poe's fiction is completely, and irrevocably, away from any contact with the material world, for Roderick Usher, the only character possessing knowledge of higher, spiritual, aesthetic principles, disappears and will never return to illuminate the terrified, uncomprehending narrator. The two worlds—the spiritual intuitions of Usher and the rational, skeptical proclivities of the narrator—do not harmoniously cojoin as they do in Ishmael's character. Poe ends his tale with, as described by David Halliburton, a "fall from life as we know it to life as we know it not" (292).

It should be noted that Poe not ony disregards the aesthetic importance of the material world but also struggles to reach the Beauty above with a *wild* effort" [italics mine]. Contained in the drive toward pure transcendence is the potential for the wild monomanic fury found in the characters Ahab in *Moby-Dick* and Jack Torrence in **The Shining**. In both Melville and King, an attempt to break through the material world in order to reach the beyond carries with it the danger of an uncontrolled, unbalanced aggression toward elements of the physical world.

A very succinct analysis of Poe's approach to transcendence occurred during a lecture by Richard Wilbur, renowned poet and critic of Poe, when he responded to a question about the similarity between his poetry and Poe's with the remark:

> . . . his [Poe's] attitude toward poetry and toward the world is not mine at all. I'm not at all interested in writing a kind of poetry that annihilates the world so as to bring us closer to some sort of beyond. I'd rather proceed toward the beyond by way of a concrete world affectionately taken.

A key word in this quotation, "affectionately," indicates that for Wilbur art must lovingly retain the "concrete world," the world before us, while at the same time moving toward the beyond. In other words, both worlds must cohere in a mysterious unity of diversity; otherwise, the circle of separation and return is broken and all that is left is half an arc into the unknowable world beyond and an annihilation of the world as we know it.

Richard Wilbur's remarks do not specifically refer to Gothic art, and before proceeding further in this paper some understanding of what differentiates Gothic art from other forms of literary creativity is necessary. In the foreword to **Night Shift,** Stephen King defines the main constituent of Gothic art to be *fear*. And this fear occurs when the artist demonstrates that ". . . the good fabric of things has a way of unraveling with shocking suddenness" (xi). The sense that another reality underlies the good fabric of the conventional, rationally perceived world can as easily initiate fear as it does joy. Entrance into the world beyond can be joyful as it is for Emerson in "Nature" when he becomes a transparent eyeball and bathes in the circulation of "Universal Being" (189) or fearful as it is to Ishmael when on the masthead he learns that entrance into that universal, oceanic state may be personally destructive. In the Gothic fiction of Melville and King, this fear of what may be in the beyond becomes closely analogous to a descent into that other world of the mind, the subconscious, where the dream existence may as easily be nightmarish as idyllic. Hence, for Gothic fiction the journey of separation—initiation—return often assumes a parallel psychological movement of separation from the rational, conventional mind, an initiation into the demonic potential of the subconscious, and a return back to rationality tempered with a sense of the energies of the subconscious.

Since it is one of the functions of the Gothic artist to reveal the fears that arise once the threshold of the rational world is passed, his creative energy may itself be conceived as productive of fear. If the artist successfully completes the circular journey through fear back to the rational and conventional, his artistry may signify that both sides may be held in balance, a situation that accounts for Melville's remark after completing *Moby-Dick*: "I have written a wicked book, and feel spotless as the lamb" (142). Since both creative energy and demonic force are often symbolized by fire, the Gothic artist must, as Ishmael so clearly demonstrates in *Moby-Dick*, not be consumed and confused by fire, but must master it and integrate its power productively, not destructively, with the rational, concrete world. In both the try-works of the Pequod and the cellar of the Overlook resides a burning core which is the primal manifestation of creative power. When first encountered in the Gothic tale that utilizes elements of the psychological journey into the subconscious, this power may seem wicked and evil, but this fearful sense of evil can be assimilated into the artistic vision in order to produce that balance of the subconscious and the conscious that reflects the completed cycle of the psychological quest.

The images surrounding the advent of a positive outcome from the rending of the fabric of the material and rational world generally indicate that some sort of rebirth has occurred. As in the epilogue of *Moby-Dick* where Ishmael surfaces back into the conventional world charged with an understanding of the mysteries of the beyond, re-entrance into this world by the protagonist signals a successful completion of the mythic journey. In contrast to Ishmael, who surfaces from the vortex of the Pequod's descent, Roderick Usher disappears into the tarn at the end of "The Fall of the House of Usher." Nothing is reborn at the end of Poe's fiction. Even A. Gordon Pym, who survives the events recorded in his tale, did not live to conclude his artistic rendering of the end of those events. Gordon V. Boudreau presents an interesting highlight on this discussion when he quotes D. H. Lawrence in his article "Of Pale Ushers and Gothic Piles: Melville's Architectural Symbology": "While 'the rhythm of American art-activity is dual . . . a sloughing of the old consciousness' and 'the forming of a new consciousness underneath,' there is 'only the disintegrative vibration' in Poe" (80). Boudreau's study perceptively argues that in Melville the Gothic symbology ushers us into the presence of a new eschatology, in effect a rebirth of the new from the old. Poe, in contrast, presents us with a disharmony between the conventional attitudes of his narrator in "The Fall of the House of Usher" and the esoteric knowledge of Usher; at the end of the narrative the narrator, unlike Ishmael, understands little more than at the beginning. This disharmony occurs because of Poe's Gnostic-like tendency to annihilate the concrete world in order to reveal the beyond, tendency that violates the motif of rebirth as exemplified in Melville's art.

Other than as rebirth, the coupling of the beyond with the concrete world can be symbolically presented as an atonement between father and son. In *The Shining* and *Moby-Dick*, however, the father figures seek to violently rend the fabric of the material world and display little affection for the son. Both Ishmael, who rejects the one-sided nature of the father figure Ahab's quest, and Danny, who tricks his father into destruction, do not reach atonement with these father figures, but rather with a father surrogate whose black skin signifies the dark, sometimes terrifying mystery of the beyond. Both Ahab and Jack Torrence personify a state close to what Poe described as the "wild effort to reach the Beauty above," and the fury and single-mindedness of their efforts preclude atonement. It is the son who completes the circular journey and forms a harmonious relationship with the beyond by entering into a parallel relationship with a dark character—Queequeg in *Moby-Dick* and Halloran in *The Shining*.

A close inspection of the ending of *The Shining* reveals how close the symbolic parallels are between Melville and King. At the end of King's novel, Danny is fishing like a rejuvenated fisher king for a "pink whale." Then, "The tip of the fishing rod bent. Danny pulled it back and a long fish, rainbow-colored, flashed up in a sunny, winking parabola, and disappeared again" (447). The reference to whales obviously recalls Melville, but King's use of the rainbow more seriously indicates his sympathy with Melville's artistic concerns. Traditionally, the rainbow signifies the end of a destructive phase and the beginning of a new order. In *Moby-Dick* Melville expands the conventional use of the rainbow into a comprehensive symbol for artistic vision:

> For, d'ye see, rainbows do not visit the clean air; they only irradiate vapor. And so, through all the thick mists of the dim doubts in my mind, divine intuitions now and then shoot, enkindling my fog with a heavenly ray.
>
> (480)

King's *The Shining* ends with the rainbow, which, as in *Moby-Dick*, signifies a balance between the fogs, vapors, and doubts that well up from the subconscious, that area opened to view once the fabric of the rational and conventional parts, and the conscious mind, the instrument of the concrete world. When Danny's fishing pole brings the rainbow fish from the waters of the subconscious up in one, graceful parabolic arc, he performs an act as representative of artistic harmony as Melville's rainbow. And since the rainbow is an arc, the drawing of the rainbow fish up from the depths and down again illustrates the completion of the circular journey of myth and the artistic union of opposites.

A detailed exploration of *The Shining* reveals that the novel contains more parallels to *Moby-Dick* than just the ending. Each novel investigates the nature of the artist's creativity. Each envisions the artistic mind as split between two powers: on one side is a father figure, monomanic and destructive; on the other is a filial figure, receptive of ambiguity, interested in reconciliation, and harmoniously creative at the end of the narrative. Both Ishmael and Danny are protected by a dark man, whose function, so profoundly symbolized in the character of Queequeg, is to wed the youthful mind with the aphotic instinctual powers that roll like lava beneath the thin layer of rationality.

In the basement of the Overlook fumes the raging volcanic furnace, centrally located as is the try-works on the Pequod. This is the center of creative energy which must be controlled, for "she creeps." The furnace's "channeled destructive force" (15) is often equated with Jack Torrence's vicious temper which strikes out at both his son Danny and his former student George Hatfield. Also, in the crates beside the furnace lies the whole sordid history of the Overlook, which Jack views as the factual source for a future great novel. Thus, in conjunction with the furnace resides the substance of Jack's art.

While Jack becomes obsessed with the history of the Overlook that rests deep within the building, his son Danny is as deeply lost inside himself with Tony, his imaginary playmate, and the mysterious word "Redrum." Both father and son are obsessed with the horror of murder that lies deep under their consciousness. D. H. Lawrence states in *Studies in Classic American Literature* that "Murder is a lust to get at the very quick of life itself, and kill it . . ." (80); hence, a tenuous but valid connection exists between Ahab and his quest to slay Moby Dick and Jack and his crazed, homicidal assults upon his son and George Hatfield. Ahab seeks to strike through the mask of the White Whale, and Jack seeks to strike through his son into the supernatural level that inhabits the Overlook. Although the spiritual manifestations of the Overlook are surrounded with references to Poe's "The Masque of the Red Death," Jack Torrence is actually in Ahab's symbolic world on a quest for some way to break through the mask of the rationally perceived world into the supernatural realm beyond.

Danny, on the other hand, approaches the murderous areas within himself in a much more controlled way than his father's mad use of force. Rather than using a rocque mallet, a weapon like Ahab's harpoon that would smash into the other world, Danny observes the anagram "Redrum" in a mirror and deciphers its meaning by reflection. Reflection is a much more rational, balanced act than the method pursued by his father, for it unites the intellect, the mirror, with the object reflected, the subconscious impulses toward murder.

The rocque mallet wielded by Jack Torrence has two sides—one hard, the other soft; but Jack chooses only one side—the hard. Like Ahab, he forsakes balance and succumbs to monomania. In the process Jack becomes the very thing he has always desperately sought to avoid; he becomes his father, a despicable drunkard with little, pig-like eyes, who once beat Jack's mother with a cane in tempo with the phrase, "'I guess you'll take your medicine now'" (224). Despite Jack's pathetic protest that "'You're [his father] not in me at all'"

(227), the pulse beats in his forehead as it did when his father became mindlessly angry, the pig eyes set into Jack's head, and his hand thirsts for the rocque mallet, a phallic weapon similar to his father's cane, in order to give his son Danny "his medicine."

Jack's madness occurs because he cannot deal adequately with the forces that surge beneath his conscious mind. One of the most prominent images in the novel, the wasp image, focuses on Jack's inability to balance conscious control with subconscious impulses. Again recalling the foreword to *Night Shift*, the wasp nest that Jack uncovers beneath the roof of the Overlook is comparable to the frightening prospects revealed once the fabric of conventional reality is parted. Wasps, anti-creative insects whose nests hold venom, not honey, symbolize how radically Jack's own mind has fallen from its creative potential to destruction. The brain-shaped wasp nest, or wasps themselves, always appear in conjunction with Jack's mental disintegration; the image is there when Jack loses his temper with Danny and George Hatfield; it is present as Jack's dipsomania returns; and, significantly, the image coheres around Jack's attitudes toward his own father, who once exterminated a wasp nest while the youthful Jack watched in awe. And a strong connection between the wasp image and the maliciousness that begins to dominate Jack's creative self is evidenced in lines such as *The moving wasp, having stung, moves on . . ."* (189).

Jack cannot control the wasp impulse within himself because he does not know how to assimilate the positive elements of his father. His father was both cruel and loving, yet Jack hopelessly muddles these two sides so that his art which should be productive, loving one might say, becomes perverted into a need to destroy. As Jack's sanity deteriorates, he listens more intently to his father's illusionary voice which connects art with murder:

> You have to kill him [Danny], Jacky, and her, too. Because a real artist must suffer. Because each man kills the thing he loves. Because they'll always be conspiring against you, trying to hold you back and drag you down.
>
> (227)

According to Erich Neumann, an outstanding interpreter of Jungian psychology, the hero, the creative man, must battle against these negative aspects of the father and unite himself with the father's positive qualities. In other words, the father must be split so that his destructive side can be eliminated and his creative side salvaged

Jack Nicholson as Jack Torrance in Stanley Kubrick's 1980 film adaptation of *The Shining.*

and integrated into the personality. In contrast to Jack's failure to do this, Danny performs this necessary bifurcation of the father by acquiring as a surrogate father the nurturing and loving Dick Halloran, who, like Queequeg, fosters a productive association with the subconscious.

Dick Halloran performs the service of awakening Danny to the affirmative nature of his gift—the shining. Since it is Danny's shining that sets the supernatural forces of the Overlook into motion, his shining is associated with the artistic and creative talents of a writer of Gothic tales. Rightly employed, the shining would give insight into others (a necessary foundation for the novelist's ability to develop character) and it releases the supernatural sensibilities so vital to a Gothic writer. Although Halloran concludes that Jack does not possess the shining, Jack certainly sees the same supernatural occurrences that Danny's shining empowers him to see. But unlike Danny, he denies his gift. Just as his denial of his father only strengthens the father's evil dominance, his ignorance of the potential of his shining leads to the upsurgence of its negative, evil side. The more insane Jack becomes, the more the affirmative

creativity of the child turns into a diabolical threat to his artistry. Even his play *The Little School* is rewritten so that the young protagonist Gary Benson changes from a force for good against authority into a "monster masquerading as a boy" (259). Jack's authority toward his son Danny likewise changes into the obsession that Danny's greater imaginative powers impede his own. The supernatural occurrences at the hotel seem more dependent upon Danny than upon Jack; therefore, in order to convince himself that "It's not you [Danny] they want," Jack twistedly feels that he must insinuate himself into the service of the occult hierarchy of the hotel by sacrificing Danny.

Danny, however, proves more powerful than his father. Before his confrontation with his mallet-swinging, murderous father, Danny discovers the identity of Tony, the imaginary playmate who always announces the arrival of Danny's full shining powers. Again Danny looks into a mirror, that symbol of the rational mind, and sees that "the stamp on his features was that of his father" (420). This father figure is Tony, Danny's alter ego which arises from Danny's heretofore undisclosed middle name Anthony. At the moment of this discovery Danny understands that his is "a halfling caught between father and son, a ghost of both, a fusion" (421). This moment of revelation results in Danny's birth into a whole self: "He seemed to be bursting through some placental womb . . ." (426). Now Danny directly experiences what King describes in his foreward to **Night Shift** as "that connection point between the conscious and the subconscious" where "the horror tale lives" (xix). Danny defeats the destructive side of his father by harmonizing the adult, conscious life with the horror that lies underneath. In effect, his shining has illuminated the fogs and vapors of horror. Danny next remembers the all-important need for control and by reminding his own completely demonic father about the creeping temperature gauge on the hotel's furnace, sends this negative father figure to destruction.

Like Ishmael's, Danny's initiation into adulthood teaches him how to balance the positive features of the paternal nature with the imaginative energies that originate in the more subconsciously liberated area of childhood. Mark in **'Salem's Lot** follows essentially the same process when he discovers that Barlow, the vampire, speaks to him in "a friendly voice, amazingly like his father's" (292). After both discern the true nature of this bogeyman/father and cause the horrifying figure to be purified in fire, each is united at the end of the novel with a new father figure and a new balance has been struck thereby between the conscious and the subconscious.

Because Stephen King's novels, especially **The Shining,** do not end in annihilation of conventional reality, but in rebirth symbology that signals harmony between the spiritual, the beyond, and this world, they reflect the spirit of the Gothic in Melville's *Moby-Dick*. King's basic artistic sympathies do not lie as closely to Poe's aesthetic, where the Gothic vision necessitates the dropping of this world like a husk in order to reach the beyond, as they do in Melville's where the Gothic vision harmonizes the rational, concrete world with a profound sense of the interpenetration of the sometimes beatific, sometimes horrifying, mysteries of another world.

Works Cited

Boudreau, Gordon V. "Of Pale Ushers and Gothic Piles: Melville's Architectural Symbology." *Emerson Society Quarterly* 18 (1972).

Campbell, Joseph. *The Hero with a Thousand Faces.* Cleveland: Meridian, 1956.

Emerson, Ralph Waldo. *Selected Writings.* Ed. William H. Gilman. New York: New American Library, 1965.

Halliburton, David. *Edgar Allan Poe: A Phenomenological View.* Princeton: Princeton UP, 1973.

King, Stephen. Foreword. *Night Shift.* New York: New American Library, 1976 xiv-xv.

———. *'Salem's Lot.* New York: New American Library, 1975.

———. *The Shining.* Garden City, NY: Doubleday, 1977.

Lawrence, D. H. *Studies in Classic American Literature.* New York: Viking, 1961.

Melville, Herman. *Moby-Dick.* Indianapolis: Bobbs-Merrill, 1964.

Poe, Edgar Allan. *Selected Prose and Poetry.* Ed. W. H. Auden. New York: Holt, Rinehart, and Winston, 1967.

Wilbur, Richard. Lecture. Antiquarian Society. Worcester, MA, 21 Oct. 1980.

Pet Sematary

JESSE W. NASH (ESSAY DATE SPRING 1997)

SOURCE: Nash, Jesse W. "Postmodern Gothic: Stephen King's *Pet Sematary*." *Journal of Popular Culture* 30, no. 4 (spring 1997): 151-60.

In the following essay, Nash examines the influence of the popular culture representation of sensational literature and the Gothic tradition on King's works, arguing that these influences led King to create a "postmodern Gothic."

Although sympathetic critics have given it an impressive literary lineage, Stephen King's novel **Pet Sematary** has resisted easy categorization. Mary Ferguson Pharr detects the influence of Mary Shelley's *Frankenstein,* but she notes that King's work is the least self-conscious of many such variations (120). Tony Magistrale, in "Stephen King's **Pet Sematary**: Hawthorne's Woods Revisited" and in his book *Landscape of Fear: Stephen King's American Gothic,* finds a strong affinity in theme and purpose with Nathaniel Hawthorne, among other New England and/or transcendentalist writers. Slavoj Zizek relates **Pet Sematary** to the tragedies of Sophocles (25-26).

One need not, however, give King such a distinguished pedigree to appreciate **Pet Sematary**'s complexity or recognize its importance in contemporary popular culture. To do so, one might suggest, runs counter to the very spirit of King's works. As he himself informs us in Douglas Winter's *Stephen King: The Art of Darkness,* King's primary sources for his novel are his own life experiences and fantasies, popular culture, and his reading of archaic burial lore (145-146, 150). In other words, the key to understanding **Pet Sematary** does not lie in the "classical" literary tradition so much as in popular culture itself and how popular culture appropriates, reworks, and re-presents more classical literary artifacts.

Pet Sematary's connection to Shelley's *Frankenstein* in particular must be seen within the dynamics of a contemporary popular culture matrix. In *Danse Macabre,* King refers to *Frankenstein* as "caught in a kind of cultural echo chamber" (65). People are often less familiar with Shelley's actual text than they are re-presentations of the figure of Frankenstein in popular culture. It is helpful to think of the echoes *Frankenstein* sets in motion in terms of Clifford Geertz' notion of "webs of significance" (5). The webs in which King is enmeshed are not entirely those of Shelley; even when he shares webs of significance with Shelley, such as the problematic nature and popular fear of science and technology, his attitude in regard to those webs is entirely different. For example, in her introduction to the 1831 edition of *Frankenstein,* Shelley credits the ultimate origin of her novel to her husband's and Lord Byron's rather tabloid, sensationalistic discussions of "Dr. Darwin," but she distances herself from those discussions, confessing that she does not know if they are accurate depictions of what Darwin had actually written or done (xxiv).

In *Pet Sematary,* on the other hand, King revels in the tabloid and the sensational, using at one point in the novel the supposed authenticity of the Shroud of Turin as an argument against scientific rationalism and its debunking of the possibility of miracles (200). Along with "penis envy" and the "oedipal conflict," the Shroud is one of those strange truths that Arnie Cunningham in *Christine* recognizes and to which he subscribes (24). Similarly, to emphasize his preference of the sensational over the purely realistic, King tells his readers in the introduction to *Skeleton Crew* that in *The Thorn Birds* his "favorite part was when the wicked old lady rotted and sprouted maggots in about sixteen hours" (21).

In *Frankenstein,* Shelley's focus is not on what is scientifically or realistically possible but rather the moral dilemmas of modern human beings. *Pet Sematary,* however, does want us to reconsider what is possible precisely because King is a child of the tabloid, the medical oddity, and archaic lore. Therefore, if King is rewriting *Frankenstein,* he is rewriting it from a vastly different personal, cultural, and historical perspective, and so much so, I would like to suggest, that *Frankenstein* and *Pet Sematary* no longer share the same genre.

King's novel is an example of what we might fruitfully think of as "postmodern Gothic," which is a transformation or historical mutation of the traditional Gothic tale. Such a designation takes seriously King's ties to the traditional Gothic genre but also recognizes the influence of the prevailing postmodernism of much of late twentieth century popular culture (see Collins). Such a designation has the added benefit of allowing us to determine what is gained and what is lost in King's transformation of traditional literary forms. It will be suggested in this essay that King's postmodern Gothic is more amenable to popular or mass sentiment than the traditional Gothic work, and thus King is more willing to tackle explicitly cultural issues as opposed to the traditional Gothic preoccupation with personality and character. In the process, King is able to launch a full frontal attack on the modern American experience, developing a powerful and consistent cultural critique, using the voices of those he understands to be typically marginalized in contemporary American society, the child, the adolescent, the ordinary Joe and Josephine of lower, middle, and rural America, the wise non-academic, and at least in the case of *Carrie,* Verena Lovett forcefully argues, the tabooed, menstruating woman (175).

What is lost in King's mutation of the Gothic genre is more difficult to grasp, especially since his Gothic fiction is often more successful in portraying middle America than so-called "realistic" mainstream fiction (Nash 38), but the problematic nature of his postmodern mutation cannot be avoided. What is often lost in the gale of fright, supernatural menace, and cynical social commentary is a certain sense of textual logic, integrity, and purpose. *Pet Sematary* is a good instance of the dilemmas King's postmodern Gothic poses. In that novel, King gives us a cast of characters whose actions and eventual fate are truly horrifying, but they are placed in a logically inconsistent fictional universe, a universe so supernaturally oppressive that they have no choice in the matter. Horror is achieved at the expense of logic, but with the loss of logic, the novel's ability to address real problems in a real America is compromised. What we must eventually fear in King's fiction is not the real world of oppressive parents and governments but the imaginary, but if this is the case, King's work loses its critical edge, its power to engage American society. Thus, King's greatest problem is a side effect of his greatest asset, his postmodernism, his privileging of folk, archaic, and popular traditions over that of scientific rationalism.

This postmodern privileging of the popular and the archaic converges nicely in *Pet Sematary.*

If Rabelais is the master preserver of popular culture's history of unrestrained and subversive laughter, as Bakhtin argues (3-58), then Stephen King is the master of popular culture's history of unrestrained, subversive, and thus unsettling fear. In the case of *Pet Sematary,* the fear in question is the primordial fear of the dead and the archaic forces associated with death and dying. Zizek is at least partly correct when he notes that the "fundamental fantasy of contemporary mass culture" is that "of a person who does not want to stay dead but returns again and again to pose a threat to the living" (22).

Zizek's description is lacking in two regards. First, the fantasy, as it is rooted in the popular imagination and the archaic religious mind, is based on a fear of the dead, and that fantasy is not that someone will "want" to come back from the dead but that someone or something will bring that person back. In *Pet Sematary,* it is not little Gage who wants to come back; it is his father who will not let him go. A second and perhaps even more significant aspect of this common fantasy is that it expresses a pre-scientific or superstitious fear that death is not final, that death can somehow be overturned, that one can be both dead and alive at the same time. The importance of this fear is that it flies in the face of what we know from our own experience and from what we know medically and scientifically.

But it is precisely this superstitious fear that King privileges in his critique of the American family and society in *Pet Sematary.* The fear he evokes is not escapist; it is evoked in earnest. It is obvious from King's comments in Winter's work and his own *Danse Macabre* that he takes his novel, its social commentary, *and* its supernatural ambience seriously. Winter refers to King's use of the supernatural as "rational supernaturalism," in which the order and facade of everyday life is overturned (5-9). That is, King and his admirers tend to take his supernatural creations seriously, as more than literary creations, as in nineteenth century ghost stories. These supernatural beings represent a popular and archaic distrust of the scientific and the rational. In King's hands, the supernatural and the fear it generates do not offer an escape from the rigors of culture, as in more traditional Gothic novels, but they offer an avenue by which a direct confrontation with the problematic nature of the modern American experience can be launched.

More often than not, the object of the supernatural attack in King's fiction, especially in *Pet Sematary,* is the modern family and its hapless members. King's postmodernism is nowhere more in evidence than in his insistent deconstruction of the "magic circle" that is the modern American family. An essential element of this deconstruction is King's privileging of adolescent discourse over that of adults and rationalism. Adolescents must battle the supernatural because adults cannot or will not, as in *IT.* Even when the supernatural is not introduced, as in *Rage,* the adolescent is given a privileged place from which to speak, and to speak unchallenged. The enemy of such adolescents, of course, is that symbol of American modernism, the middle-class family. It is the family that makes of adolescence such a gruesome age. According to King, it is the sorry state of relationships within the family that makes the adolescent vulnerable to the enticements of the supernatural, especially in *Christine.* It is the fragile, illusory nature of the nuclear family that gets Louis Creed in trouble in *Pet Sematary.* But one could easily point out that King's own "rage" in this instance is misplaced. The American family is not designed to prepare its young for battles with the supernatural. Whether or not such families do a good job of preparing their members for the adult world is another question, but that is not the focus of *Pet Sematary* or his other postmodern Gothic novels. The irony is somewhat incredible. The American family is judged to be inadequate because it does not prepare its members to deal with the imaginary.

In King's works, it is as if troubled, hypocritical families attract the attention of the supernatural. There is a logical problem, however, with King's presentation in these novels, one that also plagues and eventually undermines the textual integrity of *Pet Sematary.* The supernatural in King's fiction is rather catholic in its choice of families. In *IT,* the children of both "healthy" families and obviously dysfunctional ones are targeted. In *Christine,* Arnie Cunningham is an easy mark for the supernatural because of his rebellion against an overbearing mother and a weak father, but so is his friend Dennis who comes from a more normal and loving family. In *Pet Sematary,* ancient supernatural forces toy with the Creeds, a young family riddled with problems, but also with an older more mature family, their neighbors, the Crandalls. Thus, whether or not one comes from a healthy or a dysfunctional family makes little difference in the battle with the supernatural.

So we have to wonder if, logically, the attack of the supernatural has anything to do with the health or structure of the American family. If this is the case, we have to wonder what role a critique of the American family actually plays in the postmodern Gothic novel. The American family is not the source of the evil that threatens people, and it is not ultimately the family itself that attracts evil. More often than not, it is the child, the adolescent, and the "adolescing" adult, to use Erikson's apt description (91), who attract evil because they are in rebellion against the adult world. King's privileging of the discourse of adolescents and the discourse of fear traps him. The ultimate complaint of adolescents is that they are misunderstood by adults, but King's monsters and supernatural beings seem to understand them well enough, that they are akin to monsters in their own right, giving awkward credence to what adults have feared all along, that their children are monsters, that they might want to eat their parents, as they do in both **Salem's Lot** and **Pet Sematary**. In short, what King says he is doing in his novels is not what his novels actually do. In fact, his novels work so well as artifacts of popular culture because that old subversive fear that popular culture has preserved since archaic times is rarely challenged. But if the supernatural, the object of archaic and popular fear, is so catholic in its choice of families and individuals, what difference does family structure make? One can only assume that because King's work is popular and postmodern, it must include an attack on adulthood and the family even if that attack has no logical place in the tale. One can go even further. In the battle with the supernatural, as we learn in **IT**, coming from a dysfunctional family may be to one's benefit.

Such contradictions especially complicate the narrative logic of **Pet Sematary** and Louis Creed's symbolic role in that narrative. A physician, Creed moves his wife, two children, and cat from Chicago and the tyranny of his wife's Jewish natal family to Ludlow, Maine, which is not as bucolic as it seems. Creed finds a father-figure in his older neighbor, Jud Crandall, but it is this father-figure who introduces him to the old Indian burial ground that lies just beyond the pet cemetery and who first suggests that he might use the burial ground to resurrect the cat Church. When he resurrects Church, Creed only learns what the town and Crandall have known for a long time: the dead do come back, but "changed," if not psychotic. But this does not stop Creed from eventually burying his son and then his wife in the burial ground, bringing them both back but with horrifying consequences.

It is clear from King's own comments that it would be a mistake to think of Creed as a hero (Winter 145-54). King is actually quite critical of his protagonist. According to King, Creed "never ceases to be the rational man" (Winter 151). It is not clear, though, how Creed is a rationalist, and on this point, the inherent weaknesses in King's postmodern Gothic resurface. More specifically, Creed is made to represent something he is not, rational. One does not have to be a clinical psychologist to realize early on in the novel that Creed is acting and behaving irrationally.

Inside his new house, Creed experiences a "premonition of horror" (35). One might accuse Creed of being rational for not taking seriously that premonition, but of far more importance is Creed's seemingly irrational avoidance of an everyday problem, the potentially dangerous location of his home near a road frequented by speeding trucks, and yet he takes no precautions to protect his two young children, Ellie and Gage, by erecting a fence. When the family cat Church is presumably killed by one of those trucks, Creed responds irrationally. He does not build a fence at that point, heeding a real warning; no, he considers resurrecting Church. So central is the cat to the health of his family—and thus the significance of the cat's name—that Creed takes the cat to the old Indian burial ground and resurrects him. When Gage is killed by still another of those trucks, he, too, is resurrected in spite of how badly Church turns out. Gage goes on a killing spree, committing the ultimate atrocity, killing and cannibalizing his own mother. Still, Creed does not learn from his mistake. He takes the corpse of his wife to the old Indian burial ground and resurrects her. No, Creed is not a rational man, but that is because King as author will not let him be rational.

As Natalie Schroeder cautions us, the causes of Creed's behavior are ultimately "ambiguous" (137). By the time we are near the end of the novel, it is not clear if Creed acts as he does to protect the "magic circle" of his family, or once he has been introduced to the magic circle of the Pet Sematary and what lies beyond it, the magic circle of Little God Swamp, if it is not the powers of that other, more primordial magic circle guiding and pulling him. By the end of the novel, we know that the powers at work in the Indian burial ground have the ability to put Jud to sleep and thus block his possible interference with Creed's plans to exhume and rebury Gage; they warn the older man to stay out of things (321). At roughly the same time, as Creed is exhuming his son's body, he feels the power of the "place" growing and calling out to him (323). Even earlier, Jud voices his fear that the "place" had arranged the death of little Gage (274-75), and he, too, can feel the power of the place growing (319). The driver of the truck which hits Gage cannot explain why he speeded up instead of slowing down. Something came over him, and he put the "pedal to the metal" (293). And Creed himself is put into a deep sleep while Gage returns to wreck havoc at the Crandall home (376). Because of the nature of the supernatural involvement in his world and its manifest power, Creed does not really have the freedom to be rational. What would it mean to be rational in the world of the Wendigo?

Because we are in the midst of a postmodern Gothic universe in *Pet Sematary,* wherein the premonition is privileged over reason, where the dream should be taken seriously, and where ghosts have more authority than scientists, we might expect King's portrayal of the ghost Victor Pascow to be less contradictory, but we would be wrong. Pascow dies in the infirmary while under Creed's care. Before he dies, he issues a warning. "In the *Pet Sematary,*" he begins but falters and then eventually says, "It's not the real cemetery" (73-74). Later that night, now as a ghost, Pascow visits Creed again. With dried blood on his ghostly face, Pascow seems to Creed to be an "Indian" (83). His appearance is noteworthy. We are tempted to think of him as the representative of a more archaic, more natural form of religion, but Pascow's warnings only seem to plant the seed of temptation in Creed's mind. Creed fails to heed Pascow's warnings, but Creed's daughter, Ellie, does heed those warnings and yet, because she does heed those warnings, she actually contributes to a deepening of the tragedy that is unfolding in Ludlow.

While in Chicago visiting her grandparents, and presumably under the influence of Pascow, Ellie dreams the truth about Church, that he has been killed (172). Back in Ludlow, after Gage's death, she dreams that Creed, too, will die (300). On the plane trip back to her grandparents after the funeral, she dreams of Gage coming back and retrieving a scalpel from his father's medicine bag (312). Pascow personally visits her dreams to warn her that her father is in danger (316). But Pascow's warnings have a tragic consequence. Because of Ellie's dreams, Rachel decides to make a return trip to Ludlow to check on her husband. Basically, Ellie and Pascow send Rachel to a rather gruesome death.

It is not clear if Pascow represents forces inimical to the Wendigo of the Indian burial ground or if he himself is an "Indian" spirit. In any case, the forces at work in Ludlow are so powerful that they can insure that Rachel and Ellie will be away when Creed exhumes and reburies Gage. And those forces can extend their power beyond the realm of Ludlow. There are sudden flight cancellations that make it possible for them to fly to Chicago with Rachel's parents immediately after Gage's funeral (295). When it becomes apparent that something is wrong in Ludlow, Rachel is able to get a ticket back to Ludlow, but it is in a roundabout, time-consuming fashion. She thanks "God" for saving her the last seats on the various legs of her flight back (326), but it is obvious that she is being kept out of the way until it is too late for either her or Creed. She, like her husband, has been carefully orchestrated from the very beginning and orchestrated in such a way that they cannot resist.

In this postmodern Gothic novel, King weaves together archaic lore and myth and the postmodern rebellion against rationalism. In fact, the key to understanding *Pet Sematary* and appreciating its rich complexity lies in noting the tension in that text between the supernatural and the modern American experience. The ultimate symbol King uses to denote the Mystery of death in *Pet Sematary* is a circle or spiral (286), and the ultimate symbol of the modern American family, referred to cynically as a "magic circle" (121), is Church the family cat. The modern American family's bonds are so fragile that it is held together by a pet, and when that pet is killed, those bonds are so threatened that a man of reason, Louis Creed, attempts the forbidden and what we normally think of as impossible.

The problem with King's postmodern Gothic universe is that in that universe Creed *can* resurrect his son. When King discusses Creed, he evaluates him as if he lived in our world and not in the Gothic world King has created for him. King's momentary lapses in this regard indicate a greater problem with many postmodern Gothic artifacts of popular culture. It is a problem King shares with such diverse authors as Frank Miller, Dean Koontz, John Saul, and Anne Rice, to mention but a few. The very real problems these authors wish to address, such as the nature of the American family, child abuse, crime, and gender, are addressed in such mythologically-exaggerated worlds that those worlds become the problem to be overcome, and not the issues that first inspired them. In *Pet Sematary,* King has transformed the Gothic tale in an exciting and truly horrifying fashion, but in doing so, he has made something so much more frightening that we forget to confront death.

One of the things that holds the American family together, King tells us in **Pet Sematary,** is its fear and avoidance of death. Unfortunately, in the "flash" of the novel, the true horror of death, its mundane character and its very ordinariness, is lost, and that defeats King's stated purpose in writing the novel. He tells Douglas Winter that he "had never had to deal with the consequences of death on a rational level" (147). The novel was to be such an exercise, but very quickly the novel ceased to be an investigation of death and funerals. As King tells Winter, when the ideas came for the novel, and they came very quickly, it was not the death of a cat or the possible death of his own son that triggered his emotional response. It was the possibility that they might come back from the dead (Winter 146). In this sense, King's novel does not deal with death. It deals with a fear that replaces the fear of death, and that fear is the fear of the return of the dead. Such a replacement is a defense mechanism no doubt, and that is probably why King's novel is so popular and why the ideas that form the basis for that novel are so persistent in folk and popular culture. Death may well be an issue the American family and society will not face, but then neither will Stephen King.

Works Cited

Bakhtin, Mikhail. *Rabelais and His World.* Trans. Helene Iswosky. Bloomington: Indiana UP, 1968.

Collins, Jim. *Uncommon Cultures: Popular Culture and Post-Modernism.* New York: Routledge, 1989.

Erikson, Erik H. *Insight and Responsibility.* New York: Norton, 1964.

Geertz, Clifford. *The Interpretation of Cultures.* New York: Basic, 1973.

King, Stephen. *Carrie.* New York: NAL, 1975.

———. *Christine.* New York: Viking, 1983.

———. *Danse Macabre.* New York: Everest House, 1981.

———. *IT.* New York: Viking, 1983.

———. *Pet Sematary.* New York: Doubleday, 1983.

———. *Rage.* The Bachman Books: Four Early Novels by Stephen King. New York: NAL, 1986.

———. *Salem's Lot.* New York: NAL, 1975.

———. *Skeleton Crew.* New York: NAL, 1985.

Lovett, Verena. "Bodily Symbolism and the Fiction of Stephen King." *Gender, Genre and Narrative Pleasure: Popular Fiction and Social Relations.* Ed. Derek Longhurst. London: Allen and Unwin, 1989.

Magistrale, Tony. *Landscape of Fear: Stephen King's Gothic American.* Bowling Green: Bowling Green State University Popular Press, 1988.

———. "Stephen King's *Pet Sematary*: Hawthorne's Woods Revisited." *The Gothic World of Stephen King: Landscape of Nightmares.* Ed. Gary Hoppenstand and Ray B. Browne. Bowling Green: Bowling Green State University Popular Press, 1987.

Nash, Jesse W. "Gerald's Game: The Art of Stephen King." *The New Orleans Art Review* 11 (1990).

Pharr, Mary Ferguson. "A Dream of New Life: Stephen King's *Pet Sematary* as a Variant of *Frankenstein.*" *The Gothic World of Stephen King: Landscape of Nightmares.* Ed. Gary Hoppenstand and Ray B. Browne. Bowling Green: Bowling Green State University Popular Press, 1987.

Schroeder, Natalie. "'Oz the Gweat and Tewwible' and 'The Other Side': The Theme of Death in *Pet Sematary* and *Jitterbug Perfume.*" *The Gothic World of Stephen King: Landscape of Nightmares.* Ed. Gary Hoppenstand and Ray B. Browne. Bowling Green: Bowling Green State University Popular Press, 1987.

Shelley, Mary. *Frankenstein.* New York: Bantam, 1981.

Winter, Douglas. *Stephen King: The Art of Darkness.* New York: NAL, 1986.

Zizek, Slavoj. *Looking Awry: An Introduction to Jacques Lacan through Popular Culture.* Cambridge, MIT P, 1991.

FURTHER READING

Criticism

Egan, James. "Antidetection Gothic and Detective Conventions in the Fiction of Stephen King." *Clues: A Journal of Detection* 5, no. 1 (summer 1983): 131-46.

Surveys King's use of Gothic elements throughout his oeuvre.

———. "'A Single Powerful Spectacle': Stephen King's Gothic Melodrama." *Extrapolation* 27, no. 1 (spring 1986): 62-75.

Analyzes King's use of the Gothic and melodrama.

Hicks, James E. "Stephen King's Creation of Horror in *'Salem's Lot*: A Prologomenon towards a New Hermeneutic of the Gothic Novel." In *Consumable Goods: Papers from the North East Popular Culture Association Meeting,* edited by David K. Vaughan, pp. 85-93. Orono, Maine: University of Maine National Poetry Foundation, 1987.

Delineates King's handling of the Gothic, horror, and the American pastoral in 'Salem's Lot.

Hoppenstand, Gary, and Ray B. Browne, eds. *The Gothic World of Stephen King: Landscape of Nightmares.* Bowling Green, Ohio: Bowling Green State University Popular Press, 1987, 143 p.

A collection of essays on such topics as King's use of allegory, his use of the grotesque as metaphor, and the symbolism of the automobile in his work.

Keesey, Douglas. "'Your Legs Must be Singing Grand Opera': Masculinity, Masochism and Stephen King's *Misery.*" *American Imago: Studies in Pyschoanalysis and Culture* 59, no. 1 (spring 2002): 53-71.

Recounts the numerous instances of male suffering in Misery, and asserts that these episodes ultimately result in a triumph of masculinity.

Magistrale, Anthony. "Art versus Madness in Stephen King's *Misery.*" In *The Celebration of the Fantastic: Selected Papers from the Tenth Anniversary International Conference on* the Fantastic in the Arts, edited by Donald E. Morse, Marshall B. Tymn, and Csilla Bertha, pp. 271-78. Westport, Conn.: Greenwood Press, 1992.

Examines the various roles art plays in the lives of the characters in Misery.

Magistrale, Tony. *Landscape of Fear: Stephen King's American Gothic.* Bowling Green, Ohio: Bowling Green University Popular Press, 1988, 132 p.

Collection of essays on such subjects as King's treatment of technology, his use of social criticism, and the role of children in his works.

Punter, David. "Problems of Recollection and Construction: Stephen King." In *Modern Gothic: A Reader,* edited and with an introduction by Victor Sage and Allan Lloyd Smith, pp. 121-40. Manchester: Manchester University Press, 1996.

Argues that in many of his works King sets up a universal "we" that in adulthood is able to overcome feelings of childhood inadequacy.

OTHER SOURCES FROM GALE:

Additional coverage of King's life and career is contained in the following sources published by Thomson Gale: *American Writers Supplement,* Vol. 5; *Authors and Artists for Young Adults,* Vols. 1, 17; *Beacham's Encyclopedia of Popular Fiction: Biography and Resources,* Vol. 2; *Bestsellers* 90:1; *Contemporary Authors,* Vols. 61-64; *Contemporary Authors New Revision Series,* Vols. 1, 30, 52, 76, 119, 134; *Contemporary Literary Criticism,* Vols. 12, 26, 37, 61, 113; *Contemporary Popular Writers; Dictionary of Literary Biography,* Vol. 143; *Dictionary of Literary Biography Yearbook,* 1980; *DISCovering Authors Modules: Novelists* and *Popular Fiction and Genre Authors; DISCovering Authors 3.0; Junior Discovering Authors; Literature and Its Times,* Vol. 5; *Literature Resource Center; Major 20th-Century Writers,* Eds. 1, 2; *Major 21st-Century Writers; Reference Guide to American Literature,* Ed. 4; *St. James Guide to Horror, Ghost & Gothic Writers; St. James Guide to Young Adult Writers; Short Story Criticism,* Vols. 17, 55; *Something about the Author,* Vols. 9, 55; *Supernatural Fiction Writers,* Vols. 1, 2; and *Writers for Young Adults Supplement.*

INDEXES

The main reference

Austen, Jane 1775-1817 **1:** 2, 7, 35, 37, 74-76, 80, 217, 220, 324, 333, 353, 354, 453, 466; **2: 25-47**

lists the featured author's entry in volumes 2 and 3 of Gothic Literature; *it also lists commentary on the featured author in other volumes of the set, which include topics associated with* Gothic Literature. *Page references to substantial discussions of the author appear in boldface.*

The cross-references

See also AAYA 19; BRW 4; BRWC 1; BRWR 2; BYA 3; CD-BLB 1789-1832; DA; DA3; DAB; DAC; DAM MST, NOV; DLB 116; EXPN; FL 1, 2; LAIT 2; LATS 1; LMFS 1; NCLC 1, 13, 19, 33, 51, 81, 95, 119, 150; NFS 1, 14, 18, 20, 21; TEA; WLC; WLIT 3; WYAS 1

list entries on the author in the following Gale biographical and literary sources:

AAL: Asian American Literature

AAYA: Authors & Artists for Young Adults

AFAW: African American Writers

AFW: African Writers

AITN: Authors in the News

AMW: American Writers

AMWR: American Writers Retrospective Supplement

AMWS: American Writers Supplement

ANW: American Nature Writers

AW: Ancient Writers

BEST: Bestsellers (quarterly, citations appear as Year: Issue number)

BG: The Beat Generation: A Gale Critical Companion

BLC: Black Literature Criticism

BLCS: Black Literature Criticism Supplement

BPFB: Beacham's Encyclopedia of Popular Fiction: Biography and Resources

BRW: British Writers

BRWS: British Writers Supplement

BW: Black Writers

BYA: Beacham's Guide to Literature for Young Adults

CA: Contemporary Authors

CAAS: Contemporary Authors Autobiography Series

CABS: Contemporary Authors Bibliographical Series

CAD: Contemporary American Dramatists

CANR: Contemporary Authors New Revision Series

CAP: Contemporary Authors Permanent Series

CBD: Contemporary British Dramatists

CCA: Contemporary Canadian Authors

CD: Contemporary Dramatists

CDALB: Concise Dictionary of American Literary Biography

CDALBS: Concise Dictionary of American Literary Biography Supplement

CDBLB: Concise Dictionary of British Literary Biography

CLC: Contemporary Literary Criticism

CLR: Children's Literature Review

CMLC: Classical and Medieval Literature Criticism

CMW: St. James Guide to Crime & Mystery Writers

CN: Contemporary Novelists

CP: Contemporary Poets

CPW: Contemporary Popular Writers

CSW: Contemporary Southern Writers

CWD: Contemporary Women Dramatists

CWP: Contemporary Women Poets

CWRI: St. James Guide to Children's Writers

CWW: Contemporary World Writers

DA: DISCovering Authors

DA3: DISCovering Authors 3.0

DAB: DISCovering Authors: British Edition

DAC: DISCovering Authors: Canadian Edition

DAM: DISCovering Authors: Modules

   DRAM: Dramatists Module; *MST:* Most-Studied Authors Module;

   MULT: Multicultural Authors Module; *NOV:* Novelists Module;

   POET: Poets Module; *POP:* Popular Fiction and Genre Authors Module

DC: Drama Criticism

DFS: Drama for Students

DLB: Dictionary of Literary Biography

DLBD: Dictionary of Literary Biography Documentary Series

DLBY: Dictionary of Literary Biography Yearbook

DNFS: Literature of Developing Nations for Students

EFS: Epics for Students

EXPN: Exploring Novels

EXPP: Exploring Poetry

EXPS: Exploring Short Stories

EW: European Writers

FANT: St. James Guide to Fantasy Writers

W

TITLE INDEX

The Subject Index includes the authors and titles that appear in the Author Index and the Title Index as well as the names of other authors and figures that are discussed in the Gothic Literature set. The Subject Index also lists literary terms and topics covered in the criticism. The index provides page numbers or page ranges where subjects are discussed and is fully cross referenced. Page references to significant discussions of authors, titles, or subjects appear in bold-face; page references to illustrations appear in italic.

"Edgar Allan Poe" (Lovecraft) (sidebar) 3: 219

Edgar Huntly or Memoir of a Sleep-Walker (Brown) 1: 250–51; 2: 154, 159–60

Edgeworth, Maria 1: 207, (sidebar) 3: 306

The Edible Woman (Atwood) 2: 1, 9

Edinburgh Journal of Science, 1: 334–35

Edinburgh (Scot's) Magazine, 1: 25

Edmundson, Mark 1: 520

"Edward Randolph's Portrait" (Hawthorne) 2: 370

Edwards, Jonathan 3: 277–78

The Effusions of Sensibility; or, Letters from Lady Honoria Harrowhart to Miss Sophonisba Simper (Lewis) 3: 37–38

Egan, James 3: 168–78

Ehrengard (Dinesen) 2: 258

"The Eighteenth-Century Psyche: *The Mysteries of Udolpho*" (Williams) 3: 252–60

Elbert, Monika 3: 466–75

Elder, Marjorie 2: 382–86

Elinor and Marianne (Austen) 2: 25, 33

Eliot, T. S. (sidebar) 2: 215

Die Elixiere des Teufels (Hoffmann) 2: 388, 394, 405
  compared to *The Private Memoirs and Confessions of a Justified Sinner* 2: 431
  doppelgänger 2: 391–92, 400
  influence of *The Monk* 3: 40–41
  uncanny 1: 304

Elizabethan literature 1: 17

Ellis, Bret Easton 1: 36–38

Ellis, S. M. (sidebar) 3: 6

Elwin, Malcolm 3: 368

Emden, Cecil S. 2: 31–35

Emerson, Ralph Waldo 3: 468, 470, 472, 474

"Emily's Demon-Lover: The Gothic Revolution and *The Mysteries of Udolpho*" (Graham) 3: 249–52

Emma (Austen) 2: 26–27, 32

Emmeline,or, the Orphan of the Castle (Smith) 1: 96

"Endicott and the Red Cross" (Hawthorne) 2: 370

Enfield, William 3: 246–49

The English Review, 2: 85

Enigmatic code 1: 319–20

Enlightenment 1: 48–57, 67

An Enquiry Concerning Political Justice and Its Influence on General Virtue and Happiness (Godwin) 1: 22; 2: 321–23, 330–31, 334; 3: 212

"Epistle to Thomas Ashton from Florence" (Walpole) 3: 446

The Epistolary Intrigue (Lewis) 3: 37–38

"The Erl-King" (Goethe). *See* "Der Erlkonig" (Goethe)

"The Erl-King. From the German of Goethe. Author of the *Sorrows of Werter*" (Scott) (sidebar) 2: 350

"The Erl-King's Daughter" (Scott) 3: 293–94

"Der Erlkonig" (Goethe) (sidebar) 2: 350

Eroticism
  in *Dracula* 1: 136–38
  homoeroticism 3: 274–75
  vampires 3: 274–76
  See also Sexuality

Essay on Sepulchres (Godwin) 1: 98, 101

An Essay on the Sublime (Baillie) 1: 56

"Ethan Brand" (Hawthorne) 2: 365, 374

Ethan Frome (Wharton) 3: 457–58

Ethics of the Sexual Difference (Irigaray). *See Ethique de la difference sexuelle*

Ethique de la difference sexuelle (Irigaray) 1: 90–91

Ethwald (Baillie) 2: 58

Europe, eighteenth century
  aestheticism in 1: 48–57
  attitude toward architecture 1: 486–87, 488; 3: 142–43
  copyright laws 1: 95
  function of literary criticism 1: 95–96
  as impetus for Gothic movement 1: 1, 30–31
  marriage laws 1: 224–26
  role of women 2: 63–65
  value of Gothic fiction 1: 221–27; 3: 23–24

"European Disruptions of the Idealized Woman: Matthew Lewis's *The Monk* and the Marquis de Sade's *La Nouvelle Justine*" (Wright) 3: 61–70

European Gothic tradition 1: 74–104, 3: 124–25
  vs. American Gothic tradition 1: 57–65; 2: 156–58
  Caleb Williams 2: 337–38
  development of Gothic fiction 1: 260–64
  Dinesen, Isak 2: 261–68, 271
  Faulkner, William 2: 298–305
  feminist literary theory of 1: 86–91
  French Revolution and 1: 74–85
  German Romanticism 2: 271–72

Hawthorne, Nathaniel 2: 378–79; 3: 125
  influence on Poe, Edgar Allan 3: 188, 194–95
  Melmoth the Wanderer 3: 84–91
  Melville, Herman 3: 118–22
  nationalism in 1: 93–102, 158–71; 2: 240
  Romanticism 1: 249–58
  See also Gothic movement

The Europeans (James) 2: 462

"The Eve of St. Agnes" (Keats) 1: 19, 24

Evil eye (superstition) 1: 307

Examples of the Interposition of Providence in the Detection and Punishment of Murder (Fielding) 3: 24–25

"Excerpt from a letter dated 3 March 1886" (Symonds) (sidebar) 3: 365

Excess (theme) 3: 352–55, 355

The Exorcist (Blatty) 1: 450

The Exorcist (film) 1: 450–51

"Expedition to Hell" (Hogg) 2: 424–25

Expensive People (Oates) 3: 164, 178

"Extract from a note appended to a letter on December 9, 1838" (Beckford) 2: 83–85

Eyes (motif) 3: 472–73

"The Eyes" (Wharton) 3: 457, 459, 472–73

F

A Fable (Faulkner) 2: 294

"The Face of the Tenant: A Theory of American Gothic" (Savoy) 1: 66–74

The Fair Maid of Perth (Scott) 3: 312–13

Fairy tales 2: 13, 185–86

"The Fall of the House of Clennam: Gothic Conventions in *Little Dorrit*" (Jarrett) 2: 251–55

"The Fall of the House of Usher" (Poe) 1: 71–72; 3: 188–89, *196*
  aristocracy 3: 221
  castle in 3: 194–97
  compared to "Bartleby the Scrivener" 3: 122–23
  family curse in 2: 221
  family murder 2: 311
  film adaptation 3: *224*
  haunted house in 3: 225–26
  madness in 3: 204
  miscegenation 3: 221–27
  slavery 3: 223

"I and My Chimney" (Melville) **3**:
114

SUBJECT INDEX

SUBJECT INDEX

SUBJECT INDEX

deleted